W9-BMQ-604

BOYLE

THE GUINNESS CONCISE ENCYCLOPEDIA

GUINNESS PUBLISHING

First published 1993

© Guinness Publishing Ltd., 1993

Published in Great Britain by Guinness Publishing Ltd.,
33 London Road, Enfield, Middlesex

No part of this book may be reproduced, stored in a retrieval
system or transmitted in any form or by any means, electronic,
chemical, mechanical, photocopying, recording or otherwise,
without a licence or other permission in writing from the
copyright owners.

Colour origination by Bright Arts (HK) Ltd., Hong Kong
Printed and bound in Italy by New Interlitho SpA, Milan

'Guinness' is a registered trademark of
Guinness Publishing Ltd.

British Library Cataloguing in Publication Data:
A catalogue record for this book is available from the
British Library.

ISBN 0-85112-566-2

Editor
Ian Crofton

Deputy Editors
Clive Carpenter
Ben Dupré
Richard Milbank
Tina Persaud

Editorial Systems
Alex Reid
Kathy Milligan
Sallie Collins

Design
David Roberts
Sarah Silvé
Amanda Ward
Amanda Sedge

Picture Consultants
Image Select

Picture Assistant
Muriel Ling

Illustrators
Peter Harper
Robert and Rhoda Burns
Edward Q. Botchway
Pat Gibbon
The Maltings Partnership
Matthew Hillier SWLA
Peter Bull
Chris Forsey
David McCarthy
Ray Hutchins
John Mitchell
Kathy Aldridge
Mike Long (Design Associates)
Ad Vantage
Kevin Williamson
Suzanne Alexander

Index
Kathie Gill

INTRODUCTION

The word *encyclopedia* is derived from the Greek for 'general education', and it is a general introduction to all the main fields of knowledge that *The Guinness Concise Encyclopedia* aims to provide. This aim is achieved by a thematic rather than an alphabetical arrangement: the world of knowledge is divided into twelve main sections – the physical sciences, animals and plants, history, the visual arts, and so on. Each section is then subdivided into a series of in-depth articles on key topics. In this way, the Encyclopedia does not just list facts – it explains them, and puts them in context.

The Sections of the Encyclopedia

The Guinness Concise Encyclopedia provides a network of knowledge, around which readers will soon find their way. To start with, a quick glance through the Contents on the following pages will show the main sections of the Encyclopedia and what subjects fall under which heading.

The first section, **The Nature of the Universe**, deals with the physical sciences – astronomy, physics and chemistry – together with mathematics. The earth sciences – geology and physical geography – are dealt with under **The Restless Earth**, while the life sciences are covered under **The Living Planet** and **The Human Organism**. The former section is concerned with broad biological topics such as evolution, genetics, behaviour and ecology, and also provides details of the main animal and plant groups. The latter section, focused on the human being, deals with anatomy and physiology, psychology, and medicine.

The way human beings organize themselves is reviewed under **The World Today**, which not only includes sociology, politics and economics, but also discusses a range of important contemporary issues, such as the women's movement, Third World development, and threats to the environment. **Technology and Industry** is concerned both with how things work – from nuclear power stations to jet aircraft – and with how they are made. Although the emphasis is on the latest developments, historical perspectives – including details of key inventors – are also given.

A History of the World gives a broad overview of world history, from prehistoric times to the present. The emphasis is on Europe and America, although coverage is also given of non-Western history and civilizations. Further details on the recent history of each of the world's countries will be found under **The Countries of the World** section (▷ below). The arts are divided into three sections – **The Visual Arts** (which mainly deals with painting and sculpture, but also includes articles on architecture and cinema), **Music and Dance**, and **Language and Literature**. **Religion and Philosophy** examines the main religious traditions of the world, as well as the principal fields, theories and thinkers of Western philosophy.

The last section of the Encyclopedia, **The Countries of the World**, differs from the other sections in that it is an alphabetical listing of all the world's sovereign states. The flag and a map of each state are included, together with basic statistics and details of government, geography, economy and recent history.

How to use the Encyclopedia

In the body of the Encyclopedia itself, the pages have colour-coded flashes at the top to indicate to which main section they belong. The reader will quickly become familiar with these colours and be able to flick from section to section with ease.

Within every main section each article includes a 'See Also' box to guide the reader to related articles in the same section or elsewhere. There are also cross-references within the text itself to guide the reader to other pages where further relevant details will be found. Each time a technical term is introduced, it is either *italicized* and defined on the spot, or a cross-reference is given to a page where a definition will be found.

In highly interrelated subjects such as physics, cross-referencing is particularly important, as the full understanding of one concept may well depend on the understanding of other concepts dealt with elsewhere. For example, a fuller understanding of light – which is principally dealt with under 'Optics' – will be gained if the reader also refers to the articles on 'Wave Theory' and 'Electromagnetism'; those articles are also important to the understanding of 'Quantum Theory' and 'Atoms and Subatomic Particles'.

In addition to consulting the Contents, using the colour codes and following up cross-references, a final invaluable tool in finding one's way around the Encyclopedia is the index, in which every key concept, idea, object, institution, person and place mentioned in the Encyclopedia is listed, together with a page reference. Where there are numerous page references, the index entry is subdivided to indicate which aspect of the entry is dealt with on which page.

Acknowledgements

A vast number of people were involved in the planning and building of the original *Guinness Encyclopedia*, and also in the preparation of this concise edition. They include writers, advisers, editors, designers, illustrators, picture researchers and many others, and they – together with all those who supplied pictures for use in the Encyclopedia – are listed on the following pages and on the page opposite. To all those who have contributed in whatever capacity, Guinness Publishing wish to extend their sincere thanks.

Ian Crofton
Editor

CONTENTS

1. THE NATURE OF THE UNIVERSE

The Universe and Cosmology 2
Stars and Galaxies 4
The Sun and the Solar System 6
The Planets 8
The History of Astronomy 10
Space Exploration 12
Motion and Force 14
Forces affecting Solids and Fluids 16
Heat and Energy 18
Wave Theory 20
Acoustics 22
Optics 24
Electromagnetism 26
Electricity in Action 28
Atoms and Subatomic Particles 30
Quantum Theory and Relativity 32
What is Chemistry? 34
Elements and the Periodic Table 36
Chemical Bonds 38
Chemical Reactions 40
Small Molecules 42
Metals 44
Organic Chemistry 46
The History of Science 48
Mathematics and its Applications 50
Geometry and Trigonometry 52
Number Systems and Algebra 54
Sets 56
Functions, Graphs and Change 58

2. THE RESTLESS EARTH

The Earth's Structure and
  Atmosphere 60
Plate Tectonics 62
Earthquakes and Volcanoes 64
The Formation of Rocks 66
Mountains 68
Ice 70
Deserts 72
Rivers and Lakes 74
The Oceans 76
Weather 78
Climate 80

3. THE LIVING PLANET

The Beginnings of Life 82
Evolution 84
Genetics 86
Plants 88
Non-Flowering Plants 90
Flowering Plants 92
Primitive Animals 94
Arthropods 96
Crabs and other Crustaceans 97
Insects 98
Fishes 100
Amphibians 102
Reptiles 103
Birds 106
Mammals 108
Marsupials 110
Anteaters, Sloths and Armadillos 111
Bats 112
Insectivores 113
Carnivores 114
Hoofed Mammals 116
Rodents 118
Marine Mammals 120
Primates 122
Animal Behaviour 124
The Biosphere 126
Terrestrial Ecosystems 128
Aquatic Ecosystems 130
Farming 132

4. THE HUMAN ORGANISM

Reproduction and Development 134
How People Move 136
Food, Diet and Digestion 138
Respiration and Circulation 140
The Immune System 142
Glands and Hormones 143
The Senses 144
The Brain and the Nervous
  System 146
Learning, Creativity and
  Intelligence 148
Mental Disorders 150
Non-Infectious Diseases 152
Infectious Diseases 154
The History of Medicine 156

5. THE WORLD TODAY

The Family 158
Social Stratification and Divisions 160
Education 162
Law and Crime 164
Government and the People 166
Political Ideologies 168
Economic Systems 170
Microeconomics 172
Macroeconomics 174
Trade 176
International Organizations 178
Nuclear Weapons 181
Human Rights 182
Women's Movement 183
The Third World 184
Threats to the Environment 186

6. TECHNOLOGY AND INDUSTRY

Energy 1: Coal, Oil and Nuclear 188
Energy 2: Other Sources 190
Engines 192
Oil and Gas 194
Mining, Minerals and Metals 196
Iron and Steel 198
Rubber and Plastics 199
Textiles 200
Chemicals and Biotechnology 201
Printing 202
Photography 204
Radio, TV and Hi-Fi 206
Telecommunications 208
Seeing the Invisible 210
Computers 211
Construction 214
Ships 216
Railways 218
Cars 219
Aircraft 222
Weaponry 224

CONTENTS

7. A HISTORY OF THE WORLD

Human Prehistory 226
The Ancient Near East 228
Ancient Greece 230
Ancient Rome 232
China to the Colonial Age 234
India and Southeast Asia to the 236
  Colonial Age
Africa, Australasia and Oceania 237
  to the Colonial Age
Pre-Columbian America 238
The Successors of Rome 240
The Rise of Islam 242
Vikings and Normans 243
The Crusades 244
Crisis in Europe 245
Medieval and Renaissance
  Economy and Society 246
Medieval and Renaissance
  Culture 248
The Reformation 250
The Spanish and Portuguese 252
  Empires
The Rise of Britain 254
Louis XIV 256
European Empires in the 17th 257
  and 18th Centuries
The Industrial Revolution 258
The Birth of the USA 260
The French Revolution 262
The Revolutionary and 263
  Napoleonic Wars
Nationalism in Europe 264
The Peak of Empire 266
World War I 268
The Russian Revolutions 270
The Growth of Totalitarianism 272
World War II 274
China in the 20th Century 276
Decolonization 278
The Cold War 280
The Middle East 282

8. RELIGION AND PHILOSOPHY

What is Religion? 284
Ancient Religions 286

The Religions of India 288
Buddhism 290
Religions of China and Japan 292
Judaism 294
Christianity: Belief and Practice 296
World Christianity 298
Islam 300
Philosophy 302

9. THE VISUAL ARTS

Greek and Roman Art 306
Non-Western Art 308
Medieval Art 310
Renaissance Art 312
Art in the 17th and 18th 315
  Centuries
Art in the 19th Century 318
Modern Art 322
Architecture 326
Cinema 328

10. MUSIC AND DANCE

What is Music? 330
Early Music 332
The Classical Period 334
Music of the Romantics 336
Modern Music 338
The Symphony Orchestra 340
Opera 342
Popular Music in the 20th 344
  Century
Ballet and Dance 346

11. LANGUAGE AND LITERATURE

The World's Languages 348
Writing Systems 350
The Story of English 352
How Language Works 354
Classical Literature 356
Medieval Literature 358

Renaissance Literature 360
Classicism in Literature 362
The Beginnings of the Novel 364
Romanticism 366
Realism in Literature 368
Modern Poetry 372
Modern Drama 374
The Modern Novel 376

12. THE COUNTRIES OF THE WORLD

An A-Z of all the world's 378
countries. Basic facts, plus details
on government, geography, economy
and recent history.

INDEX 425

PICTURE ACKNOWLEDGEMENTS

The publishers would like to thank the following for permission to reproduce the pictures in this book, which are individually credited by the abbreviations listed below:

AAAC	Ancient Art and Architecture Collection	Kobal	The Kobal Collection
AKG	Archiv für Kunst und Geschichte	LSO	London Symphony Orchestra
AL	Aquarius Library	ME	Mary Evans
AR	Ann Ronan	NASA	NASA
BAL	Bridgeman Art Library	Paysan	Klaus Paysan
BP	BP (British Petroleum)	Popperfoto	Popperfoto
CA	Catherine Ashmore	Redfern	Redfern
CD	Chemical Design Ltd., Oxford	RD	Ronald Draper
ET	E.T. Archive	Rex	Rex Features
Explorer	Explorer	Scala	Scala
Fox	Fox Photos	Spectrum	Spectrum Photo Library
Gamma	Gamma	SPL	Science Photo Library
Giraudon	Giraudon	UN	The United Nations
Images	Images Colour Library	WHO	World Health Organization
Image Select	Image Select	WWF	Worldwide Fund for Nature Photo Library
Jacana	Jacana	Zefa	Zefa

ADVISORS

Ronald Alley, formerly of The Tate Gallery, London

Professor Matthew Anderson, formerly of the London School of Economics

Dr Hugh Brigstocke, Sotheby's, London

Dr Noël Burton-Roberts, University of Newcastle-upon-Tyne

Dr Dominique Collon, The British Museum

Dr Tim Cornell, University College London

Dr J.T. Fitzsimons, University of Cambridge

Professor Brian Gardiner, King's College, University of London

John Gillingham, London School of Economics

Professor A.J.R. Groom, University of Kent

Albert Hourani, Emeritus Fellow, St Antony's College, Oxford

Professor G.W. Jones, London School of Economics

Bryan Loughrey, The Roehampton Institute, London

Dr John Marshall, The Radcliffe Infirmary, Oxford

Professor D.A. Martin, London School of Economics

Dr Colin McEvedy, author of *The Penguin Atlas of History*

Robin McKie, Science Correspondent, *The Observer*

Dr D.M.P. Mingos, Keble College, Oxford

Professor J.R.A. Mitchell, University of Nottingham

Dr Raymond Monelle, University of Edinburgh

Dr Patrick Moore

Professor Robert O'Neill, All Souls College, Oxford

Professor Adam Roberts, University of Oxford

Professor A.T.H. Smith, University of Reading

Dr Peter J. Smith, The Open University

Professor William Vaughan, Birkbeck College, London

Professor Andrew F. Walls, University of Edinburgh

Dr John Warren, Brunel University

Paul Williamson, The Victoria and Albert Museum

CONTRIBUTORS

Ronald Alley, formerly of The Tate Gallery, London

Dr Mike Anderson, University of Edinburgh

Dr Elaine Baldwin, University of Salford

Ben Barkow

Dr Philippa Baylis, University of Edinburgh

Dr Clio Bellenis

Matthew Bennett, The Royal Military Academy Sandhurst

Dr Piotr Bienkowski, Liverpool Museum

Professor Michael Black, King's College, University of London

Dr Brian Bocking, Bath College of Higher Education

E.J. Borowski, University of Glasgow

Antonia Boström

British Nutrition Foundation (Anne Halliday)

Professor Charles G.D. Brook, Middlesex Hospital, London

John A. Burton

Clive Carpenter

Stephen Chan, University of Kent

Professor Raymond Chapman, London School of Economics

Kim Chesher

Dr Sara Churchfield, King's College, University of London

Dr Margaret Collinson, Royal Holloway and Bedford New College, University of London

Dr Robert Cook, Fitzwilliam College, Cambridge

Dr Linda Cookson, Central School of Speech and Drama

Dr Tim Cornell, University College London

Dr Peter V. Coveney, University of Wales, Bangor

Dr John Cowan, formerly of King's College, University of London

Ian Crofton

John Cunningham

Dr Brian N. Davies, St Bartholomew's Hospital, London

Steve Dawes

Nicole Douek, The British Museum, London

Professor Ronald Draper, University of Aberdeen

Dr Stephen Edgell, University of Salford

Colin Egan, University of Bradford

P. Ellwood, University of Sheffield

Dr John Emsley, King's College, University of London

Dr Roland Emson, King's College, University of London

Geoff Endacott

Dr David G. Evans, University of Exeter

Dr Mark Evans, National Museum of Wales, Cardiff

Peta Evelyn, The Victoria and Albert Museum, London

Dr N.R.E. Fisher, University of Wales, Cardiff

Hamish Forbes, University of Liverpool

Dr Trevor Ford, formerly of the University of Leicester

Dr D.P. Fowler, Jesus College, Oxford

Lin Foxhall, University College London

Andrew Frankel, *Autocar & Motor Magazine*

Professor Peter Gahan, King's College, University of London

Dr Nigel Gauk-Roger

John Gillingham, London School of Economics

Professor Frank Glockling, University of Oxford

Dr Martin Godfrey, *GP Magazine*

Dr W.P. Grant, University of Warwick

The late Dr Beverly Halstead, University of Reading

Dr Graham Handley, University of London

Rosemary Harris, The Tate Gallery, London

Nigel Hawkes, Science Editor, *The Times*

Dr Peter Hobson, Brunel University

Graham Holderness, The Roehampton Institute, London

Nick Hooper

International Consultancy on Religion, Education and Culture, Manchester Metropolitan University

Robert Jameson

Ann Jones, The Tate Gallery, London

Dr Gareth Jones, University of Strathclyde

Richard Jones

Colin Juneman

Dr Randolph Kent

Sharon Kingman

Dr Kim Knott, University of Leeds

Meredith Lloyd-Evans, Biobridge, Cambridge

Dr Bryan Lowes, University of Bradford

Howard Loxton

Dr Paul Markham, King's College, University of London

J.P. Mathias, University of Sheffield

Angeli Mehta

James Michael, University College London

Carol Michaelson

Sian Mills

Dr D.M.P. Mingos, Keble College, Oxford

Dr Peter Moore, King's College, University of London

Trevor Mostyn, Editor of *The Cambridge Encyclopedia of the Middle East and North Africa*

Joanne O'Brien

Olwen Glynn Owen

Pat Owen

Dr R.V. Parish, University of Manchester Institute of Science and Technology

Dr Christopher Pass, University of Bradford

Mark Pegram

Dr J.L. Pimlott, The Royal Military Academy Sandhurst

Dr Gillian Pocock, Royal Free Hospital School of Medicine, London

Paulette Pratt, Clinical Communications

Antony Preston

Jonathon Ree, Middlesex University

Martin Redfern

Aileen Reid

Dr Kimberley Reynolds, Thames Valley University

Peter Reynolds, The Roehampton Institute, London

James Roberts

Samantha Roberts

Dr Gillian Sales, King's College, University of London

Andrew Scott, University College London

Ian Sinclair

Dr Elizabeth Sirriyeh, University College, Oxford

Dr Peter J. Smith, The Open University

Dr Sandra Smith, The Open University

Peter A. Smithson, University of Sheffield

Philip de Souza, University of Leicester

Andi Spicer

Lesley Stevenson

Dr J.F. Stoddart, University of Sheffield

Dr Christopher Storrs

Michael J.H. Taylor

Dr David Thomas, University of Sheffield

Dr T.J. Thomson, Selly Oak Colleges, Birmingham

Professor Anthony K. Thorlby, University of Sussex

Dr Francis Toase, The Royal Military Academy, Sandhurst

Dr Loreto Todd, University of Leeds

E.C. Tupper

Michael Vickers, The Ashmolean Museum, Oxford

Dr Linda Walker

Professor Andrew F. Walls, University of Edinburgh

Martin Wasik, University of Manchester

Peter Washington, Middlesex University

Dr Shearer West

Dr John Westwood

Paul Williamson, The Victoria and Albert Museum, London

Conrad Wilson, *The Scotsman*

Professor E.C. Wragg, University of Exeter

Dr Nicolas Wyatt, University of Edinburgh

Dr Robert M. Youngson

UNITS OF MEASUREMENT

SI units – Système Internationale d'Unités – are the most widely used units of measurement and are used universally for scientific and most technical purposes. SI is the modern form of the metric system, which is based on the metre as a unit of length and the kilogram as a unit of weight, and was first adopted in France in 1799. Other systems of units commonly employed include the British imperial system and the related US customary units.

In the SI system there are seven *base units*, which relate to fundamental standards of length, mass, time, etc. Additionally, there are two geometrical *supplementary units*. The base units may be combined to form *derived units*; for example, the SI units of length and time may be combined to form units of acceleration or velocity. Further details on the more commonly used units will be found in the sections on physics and chemistry (pp. 14–47).

SI Base Units

Quantity	SI unit	symbol
Length	metre	m
Mass	kilogram	kg
Time	second	s
Electric current	ampere	A
Thermodynamic temperature	kelvin	K
Luminous intensity	candela	cd
Amount of substance	mole	mol

SI Supplementary Units

Quantity	SI unit	symbol
Plane angle	radian	rad
Solid angle	steradian	sr

Named SI Derived Units

Quantity	SI unit	symbol
Frequency	hertz	Hz
Force	newton	N
Pressure	pascal	Pa
Energy	joule	J
Power	watt	W
Temperature	degree Celsius	°C
Electric charge	coulomb	C
Potential difference	volt	V
Electric resistance	ohm	Ω
Electric conductance	siemens	S
Electric capacitance	farad	F
Inductance	henry	H
Magnetic flux	weber	Wb
Magnetic flux density	tesla	T
Luminous flux	lumen	lm
Illumination	lux	lx
Radiation activity	becquerel	Bq
Radiation absorbed dose	gray	Gy

Additional SI Derived Units

Quantity	SI unit	symbol
Area	square metre	m^2
Volume	cubic metre	m^3
Velocity	metres per second	$m\,s^{-1}$
Acceleration	metres per second per second	$m\,s^{-2}$
Density	kilograms per cubic metre	$kg\,m^{-3}$
Mass rate of flow	kilograms per second	$kg\,s^{-1}$
Volume rate of flow	cubic metres per second	$m^3\,s^{-1}$

Multiples and Submultiples

SI units are used in decimal *multiples* and *submultiples* of both the base units and derived units, for example 1 kilogram is divided into 1000 milligrams.

Submultiple	prefix	symbol
$\times 10^{-18}$	atto-	a
$\times 10^{-15}$	femto-	f
$\times 10^{-12}$	pico-	p
$\times 10^{-9}$	nano-	n
$\times 10^{-6}$	micro-	μ
$\times 10^{-3}$	milli-	m
$\times 10^{-2}$	centi-	c
$\times 10^{-1}$	deci-	d

Multiple	prefix	symbol
$\times 10$	deca-	da
$\times 10^2$	hecto-	h
$\times 10^3$	kilo-	k
$\times 10^6$	mega-	M
$\times 10^9$	giga-	G
$\times 10^{12}$	tera-	T
$\times 10^{15}$	peta-	P
$\times 10^{18}$	exa-	E

Metric Conversions

Length

1 mm	= 0.039 37 in
1 cm (10 mm)	= 0.393 700 78 in
1 m (100 cm)	= 3.280 840 ft (1 foot = 12 inches)
1 m	= 1.093 61 yd (1 yard = 3 feet)
1 km (1000 m)	= 0.621 371 1 mi (1 mile = 1760 yards)

Area

1 cm²	= 0.155 sq in
1 m² (10 000 cm²)	= 10.763 9 sq ft (144 sq in = 1 sq ft)
	= 1.195 99 sq yd (9 sq ft = 1 sq yd)
1 hectare (10 000 m²)	= 2.471 05 acres (4840 sq yd = 1 acre)
1 km²	= 0.386 1 sq mi (640 acres = 1 sq mi)

Mass

1 gram	= 0.035 274 ounces (avoirdupois)
1 kilogram (1000 grams)	= 2.204 62 lb (16 oz = 1 pound)
1 tonne (1000 kg)	= 0.984 206 5 tons (imperial) (2240 lb = 1 ton)
	= 0.8786 tons (US) (2000 lb = 1 US ton)

Volume

1 cm³	= 0.061 02 cubic in
1 dm³ (1000 cm³/1 litre)	= 61.023 cubic in
1 m³ (1000 dm³)	= 35.314 cubic ft

THE
GUINNESS
CONCISE
ENCYCLOPEDIA

The Universe and Cosmology

The study of the universe, its overall structure and origin, is known as *cosmology*. In the 17th century, the universe was thought to be static, infinite and unchanging. Modern cosmology can be traced back to the 1920s when the American astronomer Edwin Hubble, using observations made by Vesto Slipher in 1912, showed that the space between galaxies is increasing and the universe is therefore expanding.

There are several theories describing the origin and future of the universe. One model, no longer generally accepted, is the *steady-state theory*, which supposes that the universe has always existed and will always exist. Today most scientists agree that the universe originated in a 'big bang'; opinions differ, however, as to the future of the universe.

The origin of the universe

The universe is thought to be some 14 000 million years old (although current estimates vary between 11 000 million and 17 000 million years). It is now generally accepted that the universe originated in a cataclysmic event known as the *big bang*. Theoretical models of the big bang suggest that events in the early history of the universe occurred very rapidly.

At the beginning of time, the universe comprised a mixture of different subatomic particles, including electrons, positrons, neutrinos and antineu-

SEE ALSO

● STARS AND GALAXIES p. 4
● THE HISTORY OF ASTRONOMY p. 10
● ATOMS AND SUBATOMIC PARTICLES p. 30
● QUANTUM THEORY AND RELATIVITY p. 32

trinos (▷ p. 30–1), together with photons of radiation. The temperature was 100 000 million °C (180 000 million °F) and its density 4000 million times that of water.

One second later, the temperature has dropped to 10 000 million °C (18 000 million °F). Matter is spreading out and the density of the universe has fallen to 400 000 times that of water. Heavier particles – protons and neutrons – begin to form.

Fourteen seconds later the temperature has dropped to 3000 million °C (5400 million °F). Oppositely charged positrons and electrons are annihilating each other and liberating energy. Stable nuclei of helium consisting of two protons and two neutrons begin to form.

Three minutes after the creation of the universe, the temperature has fallen to 900 million °C (1620 million °F). This is cool enough for deuterium nuclei consisting of one proton and one neutron to form.

Thirty minutes later, the temperature is 300 million °C (540 million °F). Very few of the original particles remain, most of the electrons and protons having been annihilated by their antiparticles – positrons and antiprotons. Many of the remaining protons and neutrons have combined to form hydrogen and helium nuclei and the density of the universe is about one tenth that of water. Expansion of the universe continues and the hydrogen and helium begins to form into stars and galaxies (▷ p. 4).

Evidence for the big bang

In 1868, the English amateur astronomer Sir William Huggins (1824–1910) noticed that lines in the spectra of certain stars were displaced towards the red end of the spectrum. Huggins realized that this was due to the Doppler effect, which had been discovered in 1842 (▷ pp. 22–3). Just as the noise from a moving vehicle will appear to change pitch as it passes, the colour of light from a star will change in wavelength as the star moves towards us, or away from us. Stars moving away from the Earth have their light moved towards the red end of the spectrum (*red shift*), while those moving towards us exhibit a shift towards the blue end.

In 1929, Edwin Hubble (1889–1953) – who also worked on the classification of galaxies (▷ p. 4) – analysed the red shifts of a number of galaxies. He found that the speed at which a galaxy is moving away from us is proportional to its distance – i.e. the more distant a galaxy, the faster it is receding. This principle was formulated as Hubble's law, which can be written in the form: speed = H × distance, where H is the *Hubble constant*. Various values for the Hubble constant have been proposed, but the generally accepted value is 70 km (44 mi) per second per megaparsec (a megaparsec is 3.26 million light years; ▷ box). Thus a galaxy that is receding from the Earth at 70 km/sec will be 326 000 light years distant.

Cosmic background radiation

Astronomers can detect an 'echo' from the big bang in the form of microwave radiation. The radiation has a maximum intensity at a wavelength of 2.5 mm (0.1 in) and represents a temperature of 3 K (−270 °C or −454 °F). In the vicinity of

---

ASTRONOMICAL DISTANCES

The *light year* is a unit used to measure great distances, and is equal to the distance travelled by light in one year. Light (in a vacuum) travels at 300 000 km/sec (186 000 mi/sec), and so a light year is approximately 9 461 000 million km (5 875 000 million mi).

Distances to nearby stars can be measured by the *parallax method*. Any object, when viewed from two different vantage points, will appear to move against a background of more distant objects. This apparent change in position is called the *parallax*, and is measured as an angle. Thus if a nearby star is viewed from the Earth at intervals of six months, the Earth will have moved from one side of its orbit to the other and the star will seem to move against the background of more distant stars. The diameter of the Earth's orbit is known, so the distance of the star can be calculated.

The parallax method leads to the definition of the *parsec*, which is the distance at which an object would exhibit a parallax of one second of arc (i.e. $^1/_{3600}$ of a degree). One parsec is 3.26 light years, so with the exception of the Sun, no stars are as close as one parsec.

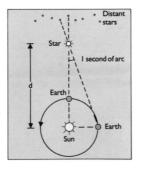

Definition of the parsec. If the change in angle between the two observations of the star is 1 second of arc, then d = 1 parsec (equivalent to 3.26 light years). In fact, no star is as close to the Solar System as 1 parsec. Note that the angle in the diagram has been exaggerated for the sake of clarity.

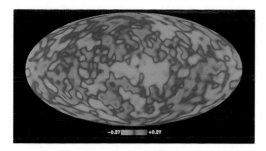

Echoes of the early universe. This microwave map of the whole sky was created using data from the Cosmic Background Explorer (COBE) satellite. It shows minute variations (between blue and pink) in the cosmic microwave radiation some 300 000 years after the big bang, and may explain the origin of the 'lumpiness' of the universe. (SPL)

the Solar System, the radiation appears to have equal intensity in all directions.

The apparent uniformity of the background radiation provided a problem for big-bang theorists, in that it posed the question of how the universe became as irregular ('lumpy') as it is, with clusters of galaxies in some areas, and empty space in others. A possible answer came in 1992, when data from the COBE satellite (⊳ photo) showed minute differences in temperature (+ and − 0.27 millikelvins) in the background radiation. These have been interpreted as evidence of infinitesimal density fluctuations, which in turn would have led to local gravitational effects in the expanding fireball. With the beginnings of gravitational instability in certain regions, matter would begin to coalesce, eventually giving rise to proto-galaxies.

The future of the universe

At present the universe is still expanding, but whether or not this will continue for ever depends upon the amount of matter it contains. One possible ending for the universe is the *big crunch*. The galaxies and other matter may be moving apart, but their motion is restrained by their mutual gravitational attraction. If there is sufficient matter in the universe, gravity will eventually win and begin pulling the galaxies together again, causing the universe to experience a reverse of the big bang – the big crunch.

What will follow the big crunch is hard to imagine. One possibility is that a new universe will come into being, perhaps containing completely different types of particles from our present universe. The *cyclic theory* suggests that the universe may continue alternately to expand and collapse.

However, it may be that there is not enough matter in the universe for the big crunch to happen. If this is the case, the universe will continue to expand for ever. Although this means there may never be an 'edge' to the universe, there is bound to be an end to the observable universe. Hubble's law states that the speed of recession of a galaxy is proportional to its distance. A galaxy which is far enough away to be travelling at the speed of light will no longer be visible and this will therefore mark the end of the universe we can see. The end of the observable universe lies at a distance of between 11 000 and 17 000 million light years.

—TIME SYSTEMS—

The Earth's orbit is not circular but elliptical, so the Sun does not appear to move against the stars at a constant speed. Most everyday time systems are therefore based on a hypothetical 'mean Sun', which is taken to travel at a constant speed equal to the average speed of the actual Sun.

A *day* is the time taken for the Earth to turn once on its axis. A *sidereal day* is reckoned with reference to the stars and is the time taken between successive passes of the observer's meridian by the same star. One sidereal day is 23 hours 56 minutes 4 seconds. A *solar day* is calculated with respect to the mean Sun. The mean solar day is 24 hours long.

A *year* is the time taken for the Earth to complete one orbit of the Sun. The Earth's true revolution period is 365 days 6 hours 9 minutes 10 seconds, and this is known as a *sidereal year*. However, the direction in which the Earth's axis points is changing due to an effect known as precession. A *tropical year* compensates for the effects of precession and is 365 days 5 hours 48 minutes 45 seconds long. It is the tropical year that is used as the basis for developing a calendar.

The SI unit of time is the *second*, which was originally defined as $1/86\,400$ of the mean solar day, but is now defined as the duration of 9 192 631 770 periods of the radiation corresponding to the transition between the two hyperfine levels of the ground state of a caesium-133 atom.

Greenwich Mean Time (GMT) **is the local time at Greenwich, England. The *Greenwich Meridian* is the line of 0° longitude which passes through Greenwich Observatory. The mean Sun crosses the Greenwich Meridian at midday GMT. Also known as *Universal Time* (UT), GMT is used as a standard reference time throughout the world. *Sidereal time* literally**

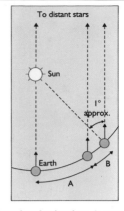

Sidereal and solar days. In travelling through distance A the Earth rotates once in relation to more distant stars, so completing one *sidereal day* (23 hours 56 minutes 4 seconds). To complete a *mean solar day*, with the Sun in the same position in the sky as it was 24 hours before, the Earth has to turn approximately 1° more, and in so doing travels the additional distance B. (Diagram not to scale.)

means 'star time'. It is reckoned with reference to the stars and not the Sun.

CALENDARS

The Earth takes 365.2422 days to complete one orbit of the Sun, which makes planning a calendar rather difficult, as the extra 0.2422 days per year have to be accounted for. The calendar system now used was first introduced in 1582 by Pope Gregory XIII, replacing the earlier Julian calendar (introduced by Julius Caesar in 46 BC). In the *Gregorian calendar*, to compensate for the extra 0.2422 days per year, there is a leap year every fourth year, although only those century years divisible by 400 (e.g. 2000, but not 1800 or 1900) are leap years. The Gregorian calendar allows an extra 0.2425 days per year and is in error by just 0.0003 days per year. It will therefore be many centuries before the calendar will need to be revised again.

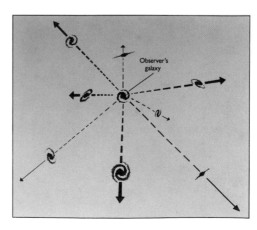

The expanding universe. The speed (indicated by the length of arrow) at which a galaxy is moving away from the observer becomes greater the further the galaxy is from the observer. Wherever the observer is in the universe, all other galaxies are seen to be receding.

Stars and Galaxies

A galaxy is a system of many thousands of millions of stars, together with interstellar gas and dust. Many galaxies are spiral in shape, while others can be spherical, elliptical or irregular. Telescopes have revealed the existence of about 1000 million galaxies, although apart from our own galaxy, only three can be clearly seen with the naked eye.

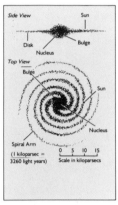

The position of our Sun in the Galaxy, shown schematically.

The Hertzsprung-Russell diagram for classifying stars.

Stars – of which our Sun is an example – are accretions of gas that radiate energy produced by nuclear-fusion reactions. They range in mass from about 0.06 to 100 solar masses, one solar mass being equivalent to the mass of the Sun. The properties of a star and the manner in which it evolves depend principally on its mass.

Stars are formed within clouds of dust and gas called *nebulae*. Patches of gas and dust inside a nebula collapse under gravity forming dark regions called *protostars*. As the protostars continue to collapse, they become denser and hotter. Eventually, they may become hot enough for nuclear-fusion reactions to start and thus turn into stars.

Galaxies

The American astronomer Edwin Hubble (▷ pp. 2–3) devised a system for classifying galaxies that is still in use. He grouped galaxies into three basic categories: elliptical, spiral and irregular. *Elliptical galaxies* range from the spherical EO type to the very flattened E7. *Spiral galaxies* are labelled Sa, Sb or Sc, depending upon how tightly wound the arms are. Some spirals appear to have their arms coming from the ends of a central bar

and these *barred spirals* are designated SBa, SBb or SBc. *Irregular galaxies* are those whose shape is neither spiral nor elliptical.

Sometimes known as the *Milky Way*, our own galaxy – 'the Galaxy' – contains about 10 000 million stars. It is an ordinary spiral galaxy and the Sun is situated in one of the spiral arms. The diameter of the Galaxy is about 100 000 light years and the Sun is some 30 000 light years from the centre. The nearest star to the Sun, Proxima Centauri, is 4.2 light years distant. The Galaxy is rotating and the Sun takes 225 million years to complete one revolution. This is sometimes called a *cosmic year*.

Some galaxies are extremely active and emit vast amounts of radiation. One such galaxy is the powerful radio source Centaurus A. *Quasars* (quasi-stellar radio sources) are very distant and immensely bright objects, which are thought to represent the nuclei of active galaxies. They may be powered by massive central black holes (▷ below). The most distant quasar yet detected, PKS 2000–330, is 13 000 million light years from the Earth.

Binary, multiple and variable stars

The majority of stars – over 75% – are members of binary or multiple star systems. *Binary stars* consist of two stars each orbiting around their common centre of gravity. An *eclipsing binary* can occur where one component of the system periodically obscures, and is obscured by, the other (as seen from Earth). This leads to a reduction in the light intensity seen from Earth – which is how binary stars were first discovered. Some stars are actually complex *multiple stars*. For example, the 'star' Castor in the constellation of Gemini has six individual components.

Most stars are of constant brightness, but some – *variable stars* – brighten and fade. The variability can be caused by a line-of-sight effect, as in eclipsing binaries (▷ above). In other cases, changes in the star itself cause periodic increases and reductions of energy output. Variable stars can have periods ranging from a few hours to several years.

Magnitude

Magnitude is a measure of a star's 'brightness'. *Apparent magnitude* indicates how bright a star appears to the naked eye. Paradoxically, the lower the magnitude the brighter the star. Magnitude is measured on a logarithmic scale, taking as its basis the fact that a difference of 5 in magnitude is equivalent to a factor of 100 in brightness. On this basis, a star of magnitude $+1$ is 2.512 times brighter than a star of $+2$, 2.512^2 ($= 6.310$) times brighter than a star of $+3$, and 2.512^5 ($= 100$) times brighter than a star of $+6$.

The limit of naked-eye visibility depends upon how clear the sky is, but the faintest stars that can be seen on a really clear night are about magnitude $+6$. The world's largest telescopes can detect objects as faint as magnitude $+27$. Very bright objects can have negative magnitudes: the planet Venus can reach -4.4, the full Moon -12.0 and the Sun -26.8.

The nearer a star is, the brighter it will appear. Different stars lie at different distances, so

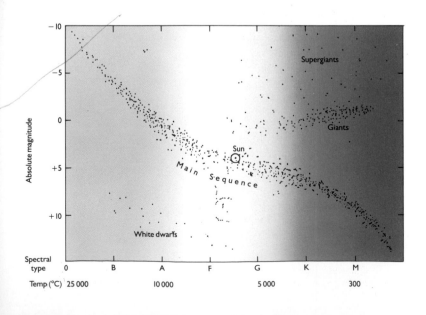

apparent magnitude does not measure the true brightness of a star. *Absolute magnitude* compensates for a star's distance by calculating its apparent magnitude if it were placed at a distance of 32.6 light years (= 10 parsecs; ▷ pp. 2–3). For example, Sirius is a nearby star and has an apparent magnitude of −1.5. However, its absolute magnitude is +1.3. The Sun has an absolute magnitude of +4.8.

Colour and temperature

The colour of a star gives an indication of its temperature. Hot stars are blue, while cool stars are red. Stars are grouped into *spectral types* according to their temperatures.

Type	Colour	Temperature	
		(°C)	(°F)
O	Blue	25 000–40 000	45 000–72 000
B	Blue	11 000–25 000	19 800–45 000
A	Blue-white	7500–11 000	13 500–19 800
F	White	6000–7500	10 800–13 500
G	Yellow	5000–6000	9000–10 800
K	Orange	3500–5000	6300–9000
M	Red	3000–3500	5400–6300

Each spectral type is further subdivided on a scale 0–9. The Sun is classified as G2.

The Hertzsprung-Russell diagram

Stars can be arranged on a diagram that plots their absolute magnitudes against their spectral types. This is known as a *Hertzsprung-Russell diagram*, after the Danish astronomer Ejnar Hertzsprung (1873–1967) and Henry Norris Russell (1877–1957), an American. Most stars fit into a diagonal band (called the *main sequence*) across the diagram.

Stellar evolution and black holes

The manner in which a star evolves depends upon its mass. Protostars with mass less then 0.06 of the Sun will never become hot enough for nuclear reactions to start. Those with mass between 0.06 and 1.4 solar masses quickly move on to the main sequence and can remain there for at least 10 000 million years. When the available hydrogen is used up, the core contracts, which increases its temperature to 100 million °C (180 million °F). This produces conditions in which helium can begin a fusion reaction and the star expands to become a *red giant*. Finally, the outer layers of the star are expelled, forming a *planetary nebula*. The core then shrinks to become a small *white dwarf* star.

Stars of between 1.4 and 4.2 solar masses evolve more quickly and die younger. They remain on the main sequence for about one million years before the red giant phase begins. The temperature continues to increase as even heavier elements are synthesized until iron is produced at the temperature of 700 million °C (1260 million °F). The star is then disrupted in a huge *supernova* explosion producing a vast expanding cloud of dust and gas. At the centre of the cloud a small *neutron star* will remain. This rotates very rapidly and is incredibly dense: 1 cm³ (0.061 cu in) of neutron-star material has a mass of about 250 million tonnes (tons).

The centre of the **Milky Way** (above), here shown in a false-colour image produced from data from the Infrared Astronomical Satellite. Black represents the dimmest regions of infrared emission, with blue the next dimmest and red and white the brightest. Streamers of dust around the galactic centre are clearly visible. (NASA)

The evolution of more massive stars is stranger still. They may end their lives by producing a *black hole* – an object so dense that not even light can escape. The only means of detecting a black hole is by observing its gravitational effects on other objects. The X-ray source Cygnus X-1 may comprise a giant star and a black hole. Material would be pulled away from the star by the black hole and heated – giving off X-rays as it is pulled in.

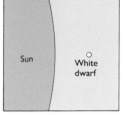

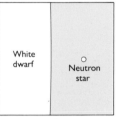

The relative sizes (above) of different types of stars. Typical red giants are 100 times the size of the Sun, which in turn is 100 times the size of a white dwarf. White dwarfs are 1000 times larger than neutron stars, which typically have a diameter of 10–20 km (6–12 mi). Red supergiants may be 5 times larger than a typical red giant.

SEE ALSO

- THE UNIVERSE AND COSMOLOGY p. 2
- THE SUN AND THE SOLAR SYSTEM p. 6
- THE HISTORY OF ASTRONOMY p. 10
- NUCLEAR FUSION pp. 30 and 189

The Sun and the Solar System

The Sun, the principal source of light and heat for planet Earth, is a very ordinary star, situated near the edge of a spiral arm about 30 000 light years from the centre of the Galaxy (▷ diagram, p. 4). The Sun is the centre of the Solar System, which includes at least nine major planets and their satellites, together with interplanetary material and thousands of minor planets, comets and meteoroids.

The surface of the Sun, seen here in a false-colour extreme ultraviolet image, taken by the Skylab space station in 1973. At the top a huge solar prominence – some 500 000 km (300 000 mi) in height – leaps up through the Sun's atmosphere. (Image Select)

The Sun mainly consists of the gases hydrogen and helium. At its centre is a vast nuclear reactor whose temperature is at least 14 million °C (25 million °F). The Sun produces energy by nuclear fusion (▷ pp. 30–1), a process in which hydrogen is converted into helium.

The Sun is losing mass at a rate of 4 million tonnes (tons) per second, but its total mass is 2 x 10^{27} tonnes (tons), which is 330 000 times that of the Earth and 745 times that of all the planets put together. The diameter of the Sun is 1 392 000 km (863 000 mi) – 109 times greater than that of the Earth – and its volume is 1 300 000 times that of the Earth.

The Sun's surface and atmosphere

When the image of the Sun is projected through a telescope, dark patches, called *sunspots*, can often be seen. Although they look black, sunspots are actually quite bright – they only appear dark by contrast with the surrounding brighter areas. Sunspots are about 2000 °C (3600 °F) cooler than other parts of the Sun's surface. The number of sunspots that can be seen on the Sun varies over an 11-year cycle. At the maximum of the cycle it is possible to see many sunspot groups, whereas at the minimum of the cycle no spots may be seen for several days.

The bright surface of the Sun is called the *photosphere*. A closer view of the photosphere shows that it consists of millions of granules, each of which is several hundred kilometres in diameter. The surface of the Sun is constantly changing its appearance, with individual granules persisting for about 10 minutes. Rising up from the photosphere are huge jets of gas called *spicules*. These can reach 15 000 km (9000 mi) in diameter, but last for just a few minutes.

The part of the Sun that lies above the photosphere is called the *chromosphere*. It is red in colour and consists mainly of hydrogen gas. It is normally impossible to see with the naked eye, owing to the proximity of the much brighter photosphere. However, during a total eclipse of the Sun, when the photosphere is obscured by the Moon, the chromosphere can be seen.

Masses of glowing hydrogen called *prominences* are sometimes ejected from the chromosphere.

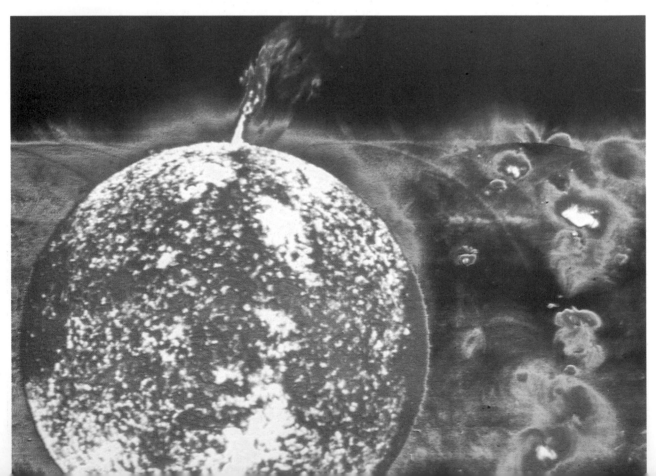

THE MINOR PLANETS

The minor planets, sometimes known as *asteroids*, comprise several thousand objects, most of which orbit between Mars and Jupiter (the *asteroid belt*). The largest of the minor planets is Ceres, which has a diameter of 940 km (584 mi). Once thought to be the residue of a planet broken up by the gravitational pull of Jupiter, most astronomers now think that the minor planets represent a class of primitive objects that were 'left over' during the formation of the Solar System, due to Jupiter's disruptive pull.

These penetrate the outermost part of the Sun's atmosphere. Prominences average 100 000 km (60 000 mi) in length. There are two types of prominences – active and quiescent. *Active prominences* are violent and short-lived phenomena, whereas *quiescent prominences* are much calmer and may persist for several weeks.

The outermost layer of the solar atmosphere is the *corona*, which consists of thin hydrogen gas at high temperature. *Solar flares* are another category of brilliant outbursts in the solar atmosphere. They are often associated with sunspot groups and can reach maximum brightness in just a few minutes. They are essentially magnetic phenomena and send out large amounts of charged particles and radiation.

The solar wind and aurorae

The Sun is constantly sending out a stream of charged particles into space. This is known as the *solar wind*. The strength of the solar wind is not constant, but changes with the activity of the Sun. Near the peak of the sunspot cycle, the solar wind is at its strongest.

The Earth has a strong magnetic field, which traps ionized particles from the solar wind in the upper atmosphere. These regions are the *Van Allen Zones*, two belts that extend from 1000 to 5000 km (620 to 3100 mi) and from 15 000 to 25 000 km (9300 to 15 500 mi) above the equator.

The solar wind also interacts with the Earth's magnetic field to produce brilliant displays of light called *aurorae* – the *aurora borealis* (or 'northern lights') in the northern hemisphere and the *aurora australis* in the southern. Aurorae are formed by the charged particles in the solar wind interacting with gases in the Earth's atmosphere at a height of about 100 km (60 mi), causing them to emit visible light. This can be seen from the ground as an ever-changing pattern of white or multicoloured lights. The charged particles are attracted towards the Earth's magnetic poles and aurorae are therefore best seen from high latitudes. The most spectacular displays occur about 24 hours after major solar-flare activity.

The Solar System

The Solar System consists of the Sun together with a large number of bodies and matter that is gravitationally bound to it. These include the planets, their satellites, minor planets, comets, meteoroids and interplanetary gas and dust.

There are nine known planets, all going round the Sun in elliptical orbits. In order of mean distance from the Sun, the planets are Mercury, Venus, Earth, Mars, Jupiter, Saturn, Uranus, Neptune and Pluto (⊳ pp. 8–9). Of these, Pluto

METEORS AND METEORITES

In addition to the planets, millions of minute particles called *meteoroids* also orbit the Sun. They are about the size of grains of sand and are therefore too small to be seen in space. When a meteoroid enters the Earth's atmosphere, it is heated by friction and destroyed. As this happens, the air glows, producing the effect we see as a *meteor* or 'shooting star'. Over 40 million meteoroids enter the atmosphere every day.

Larger bodies may survive and reach the Earth intact. These are called *meteorites*. Sometimes a meteorite may produce a crater – one of the best preserved of such craters is in Arizona and measures 1265 m (4150 ft) in diameter.

A meteorite found in Antarctica in 1979. Weighing 6.8 kg (15lb), it may have originated as debris from another meteorite impact on Mars. The rock is mainly basaltic (⊳ pp. 66–7), and is approximately 1300 million years old. (SPL)

has a rather eccentric orbit so that although its average distance from the Sun is greater than that of Neptune, part of its orbit brings it closer to the Sun than Neptune. Thus from 1979 to 1999 Neptune holds the title of the outermost planet. However, in 1992 the discovery was announced of a body even further from the Sun. This body, which has a diameter of 200 km (120 mi), is thought to be an asteroid or comet (⊳ boxes). It has been designated 1992 QB_1, and its mean distance from the Sun may be as much as 8800 million km (5400 million mi).

The Solar System is generally thought to have formed 4600 million years ago by accretion (cumulative coming together) from the *solar nebula* – a spinning cloud of gas and dust that also gave birth to the Sun. Gravity was the dominant force during the formation of the Solar System, and at some stage nuclei developed within the solar nebula that eventually accreted into the planets we now know. The fact that the planets all orbit the Sun in the same direction is thought to be a relic from the rotation of the original solar nebula.

SEE ALSO

● STARS AND GALAXIES p. 4
● THE PLANETS p. 8

COMETS

Comets are thought to consist of a small nucleus of ice and dust, and have been described as 'dirty snowballs'. When a comet approaches the Sun, part of the nucleus vaporizes to form a luminous cloud (the *coma*) and the tail, which always points away from the Sun. Although the nucleus may only be a few km in diameter, comas may have diameters up to 1 million km (620 000 mi).

Comets are thought to originate in a region known as the *Oort Cloud*, about one light year from the Sun. Sometimes comets are perturbed from the Oort Cloud and swing in towards the Sun. The gravitational attraction of a planet may trap a comet into a closed but highly elliptical orbit, which will periodically bring it close to the Sun. The best-known example is Halley's Comet, which has a period of 76 years. Halley's Comet is named in honour of the English astronomer Edmond Halley (1656–1742), who successfully predicted the comet's return in 1758.

Other comets may reach open parabolic or hyperbolic orbits. These will swing past the Sun just once and then be lost from the Solar System for ever.

Comets may have on occasion collided with the Earth. On 30 June 1908 a great explosion occurred in the sparsely populated Tunguska area of Siberia, flattening trees over a wide area. The object that caused this enormous devastation may have been the nucleus of a small comet, rather than a meteorite, which would have left a crater.

The Planets

The four inner planets – Mercury, Venus, Earth and Mars – are relatively small, rocky planets. In contrast, the outer planets – with the exception of Pluto – are giant 'gas' planets without solid surfaces.

SEE ALSO

● THE SUN AND THE SOLAR SYSTEM p. 6
● THE HISTORY OF ASTRONOMY p. 10
● SPACE EXPLORATION p. 12
● THE RESTLESS EARTH pp. 60–81

Much of our knowledge of the planets has been gained from American and Soviet space probes, which have landed on Venus and Mars, and visited all the other planets except Pluto. Some of the best data came from *Voyager 2*, which flew past Jupiter, Saturn, Uranus and Neptune in turn from 1979 to 1989.

Mercury

Diameter: 4880 km / 3032 mi (0.38 × Earth)
Mass: 0.555 × Earth

Average temperature: 420 °C / 790 °F (day) − 180 °C / − 290 °F (night)
Rotation period: 59 Earth days *
Tilt of axis: 2°
Average distance from Sun:
57 900 000 km / 36 000 000 mi (0.387 × Earth)
Length of year: 88 Earth days
* The length of a solar day (sunrise to sunrise) on Mercury is 176 Earth days.

Mercury's proximity to the Sun makes it a difficult planet to see, as it only appears low in the west after sunset, or low in the east before sunrise. The planet shows phases like the Moon, and has virtually no atmosphere. The pictures returned by *Mariner 10* show a barren, rocky world, covered in craters, some of which are over 200 km (120 mi) in diameter.

Venus

Diameter: 12 103 km / 7520 mi (0.95 × Earth)
Mass: 0.81 × Earth
Average temperature: 464 °C / 867 °F
Rotation period: 243 Earth days *
Tilt of axis: 178°
Average distance from Sun:
108 200 000 km / 67 200 000 mi (0.723 × Earth)
Length of year: 225 Earth days
* The length of a solar day on Venus is 116 Earth days.

Venus is often the brightest object in the night sky, apart from the Moon, and can be seen with the naked eye in the morning or evening. It also shows phases, and rotates in the opposite direction to the Sun and nearly all the other planets.

Venus is covered by a dense atmosphere – mainly composed of carbon dioxide with clouds of sulphuric acid floating in it – so telescopes cannot show any surface detail. The carbon dioxide causes a major 'greenhouse' effect (r> pp. 186–7), and the atmospheric pressure is 90 times that on Earth. Radar maps have shown Venus to have a complex surface with low-lying plains, upland areas, volcanoes and rift valleys.

The Earth

Diameter: 12 756 km / 7921 mi
Mass: 1.00 × Earth
Average temperature: 15 °C / 59 °F
Rotation period: 24 h
Tilt of axis: 23.5°
Average distance from Sun:
149 600 000 km / 92 900 000 mi
Length of year: 365 days

For details on the Earth's physical characteristics, r> pp. 60–81.

Mars

Diameter: 6780 km / 4213 mi (0.53 × Earth)
Mass: 0.11 × Earth
Average temperature: − 53 °C / − 63 °F
Rotation period: 24 h 37 m
Tilt of axis: 24°
Average distance from Sun:
227 900 000 km / 141 500 000 mi (1.523 × Earth)
Length of year: 687 Earth days

Mars is the most hospitable planet other than the Earth, having a thin carbon dioxide atmosphere. It has a distinct red colour, and can easily be seen with the naked eye. Early observers believed they saw canals and vegetation on Mars, but modern observations have shown that these do not exist.

THE MOON

The Moon, which maintains a mean distance from the Earth of 384 400 km (238 700 mi), is the Earth's largest satellite and has a mass 1/81 of that of the Earth. The Moon has a diameter of 3475 km (2159 mi), making it larger than the planet Pluto. The Moon orbits the Earth once every 27.3 days in *synchronous rotation* – i.e. it keeps the same face towards the Earth.

Surface features include craters formed by meteoritic bombardment, mountains and broad plains, which in the past were mistakenly named 'seas' or *maria* (Latin, singular *mare*). The temperature on the lunar surface ranges from − 163 °C (− 261 °F) to + 117 °C (+ 243 °F).

It was not until October 1959 that the Soviet probe *Luna 3* returned the first pictures from the far side of the Moon – which turned out to be much the same as the near side, except for the absence of maria. When men first landed on the Moon in 1969 (r> p. 12) they found rocks that were 3700 million years old – as old as some of the oldest rocks found on the Earth.

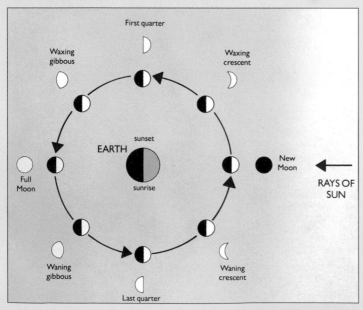

The phases of the Moon. The drawings in the outer circle show how the Moon is viewed from the Earth at its various phases. The Moon goes through the complete cycle of phases every 27.3 days.

Space probes show Mars to have a barren, cratered surface, massive extinct volcanoes and deep chasms, together with certain features that may have been caused by running water at some time in the past. Mars has two small satellites, Phobos and Deimos.

Jupiter

Diameter: 139 892 km / 86 925 mi (11.0 × Earth)
Mass: 318 × Earth
Average temperature: − 150 °C / − 238 °F
Rotation period: 9 h 55 m
Tilt of axis: 3°
Average distance from Sun:
778 300 000 km / 483 300 000 mi (5.202 × Earth)
Length of year: 11.9 Earth years

Jupiter is the largest planet in the Solar System, and appears very bright to the naked eye. Through a telescope, several belts or bands can be seen in Jupiter's atmosphere. The planet's rapid rotation rate throws the equator outwards, producing a distinct 'squashed' appearance. One of the most prominent features is the Great Red Spot (now turning a dull orange), which is a whirling storm in Jupiter's atmosphere.

At the centre of Jupiter is a rocky core. Above this are layers of metallic hydrogen (i.e. so cold that it is solid) and liquid hydrogen. Jupiter's upper atmosphere is mainly hydrogen and helium, but also contains small amounts of many other gases.

Jupiter is known to have at least 16 satellites. Four of these, Io, Europa, Ganymede and Callisto, were seen by Galileo (▷ p. 10) with his early telescope in 1610. The remaining satellites are small objects. There is also a very faint ring around Jupiter (▷ box).

Saturn

Diameter: 116 600 km / 72 452 mi (9.41 × Earth)
Mass: 95 × Earth
Average temperature: − 180 °C / − 292 °F
Rotation period: 10 h 39 m
Tilt of axis: 27°
Average distance from Sun:
1 427 000 000 km / 886 000 000 mi (9.538 × Earth)
Length of year: 29.5 Earth years

The next planet out from the Sun is Saturn, with its magnificent system of rings (▷ box). At the centre of Saturn there is a small rocky core, above which is a region of metallic hydrogen, followed by a deep ocean of liquid hydrogen. The outside layer of the planet is made of hydrogen gas, together with some helium, and tiny amounts of other gases. Saturn has at least 18 satellites, including Titan, which has a dense nitrogen atmosphere.

Uranus

Diameter: 50 724 km / 31 519 mi (4.11 × Earth)
Mass: 15 × Earth
Average temperature: − 210 °C / − 346 °F
Rotation period: 17 h 14 m
Tilt of axis: 98°
Average distance from Sun:
2 869 600 000 km / 1 782 000 000 mi (19.181 × Earth)
Length of year: 84.0 Earth years

When the sky is very dark and very clear, Uranus can just be seen with the naked eye. However, the planet is always extremely faint, and it was not until 1781 that its existence was discovered by Sir William Herschel (1738–1822).

Uranus has an atmosphere of hydrogen and helium, which surrounds a layer of water,

---

PLANETARY RINGS

The gas planets Jupiter, Saturn, Uranus and Neptune all possess systems of rings. Of these, Saturn's is by far the most spectacular.

Rings are made from millions of small particles of ice and dust. Rings can have diameters of thousands of kilometres, but they are typically less than one kilometre thick. The mechanics of ring systems are not fully understood, but, especially in the case of Saturn, the ring particles appear to be kept in place by tiny 'shepherd' satellites.

---

methane and ammonia ices. At the centre is a rocky core. Uranus has 15 moons and a system of 11 rings (▷ box).

Neptune

Diameter: 49 248 km / 30 601 mi (3.87 × Earth)
Mass: 17 × Earth
Average temperature: − 225 °C / − 373 °F
Rotation period: 16 h 7 m
Tilt of axis: 30°
Average distance from Sun:
4 496 700 000 km / 2 792 500 000 mi (30.058 × Earth)
Length of year: 164.8 Earth years

Neptune is so distant that it can never be seen with the naked eye. Observing irregularities in the orbit of Uranus, John Couch Adams (1819–92) and Urbain Le Verrier (1811–77) independently worked out that these must be caused by an unseen planet. They calculated its position, on the basis of which two German astronomers, Johann Galle (1812–1910) and Heinrich d'Arrest (1822–75), found it in 1846.

Larger telescopes show that Neptune is bluish-green in colour, but it was not until August 1989 that *Voyager 2* revealed Neptune's most prominent feature, the Great Dark Spot, a massive storm system.

The outside layer of Neptune is made of the gases hydrogen and helium. Beneath this comes a layer of ice. The ice is made of frozen methane and ammonia, as well as frozen water. At the centre of the planet is a rocky core.

Neptune is now known to have eight satellites and a system of four rings (▷ box). Triton is the largest of Neptune's satellites, with a diameter of 2705 km (1681 mi). It has an atmosphere and its surface is covered with a frozen mixture of nitrogen and methane.

Pluto

Diameter: 2302 km / 1430 mi (0.09 × Earth)
Mass: 0.002 × Earth
Average temperature: − 220 °C / − 364 °F
Rotation period: 6 d 9 h
Tilt of axis: 117°
Average distance from Sun:
5 900 000 000 km / 3 700 000 000 mi (39.44 × Earth)
Length of year: 248 Earth years

Pluto was not discovered until 1930, when the American Clyde Tombaugh (1906–) detected it using a systematic photographic search. For Pluto's eccentric orbit, ▷ p. 7.

Pluto is a very small, icy planet. Its satellite, Charon, is very large by comparison, having 10% of Pluto's mass – compared to the Moon, which has only 1.2% of the Earth's mass. Together, Pluto and Charon virtually form a twin-planet system. Little is known about the nature of Pluto, but evidence of a thin methane atmosphere has been detected.

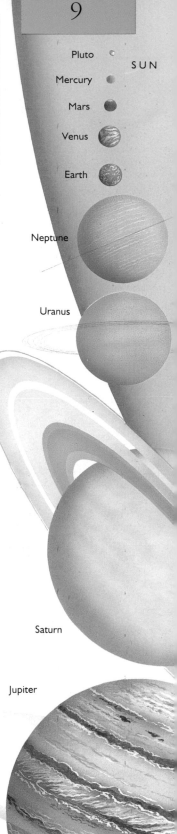

Pluto
Mercury
Mars
Venus
Earth
SUN
Neptune
Uranus
Saturn
Jupiter

The History of Astronomy

Mankind has always been fascinated by the stars. The history of astronomy stretches back in time to the beginnings of civilization. Prehistoric structures such as the stone circles at Stonehenge and Avebury in England are aligned on astronomical principles, so the civilizations that built them must have had some astronomical knowledge. The earliest recorded astronomical observations were made by the Chinese, the Egyptians and the Babylonians, who, however, made no real effort to interpret what they saw.

Many important astronomical observations were made by the Greeks during a period of roughly 800 years from 600 BC to AD 200. No major breakthroughs were then made until the 16th century.

The early astronomers

Thales of Miletus (640–560 BC) was the first of the great Greek philosophers. Though he believed the Earth to be flat, he initiated serious astronomical observation. Thales is accredited with predicting an eclipse in 585 BC. A *solar eclipse* occurs when the Moon passes between the Earth and the Sun, and a *lunar eclipse* is caused by the Moon passing into the Earth's shadow.

The Greek astronomer ***Aristarchus of Samos*** (c. 310–250 BC) was one of the first people to state that the Earth turns on its axis and orbits the Sun. He attempted to measure the relative distances of the Sun and Moon, arriving at a value of between 18 and 20. Modern measurements have shown that the true value is about 390.

Eratosthenes (276–196 BC) was a librarian in the Greek city of Alexandria in Egypt. He devised an experiment for measuring the circumference of the Earth, based on the observation that the Sun shone directly down a well in Aswan at midday on Midsummer's Day. Eratosthenes found that the angle of the Sun at the same time in Alexandria, 800 km (500 mi) north of Aswan, was about $\frac{1}{50}$ of a circle. He therefore deduced that the distance from Alexandria to Aswan was $\frac{1}{50}$ of the circumference of the Earth, which he calculated to be 40 000 km (25 000 mi). This is in close agreement with the modern value of 40 007 km (24 844 mi).

Claudius Ptolemaeus or ***Ptolemy*** (c. AD 120–180) was an Alexandrian scholar, whose *Almagest* was regarded as a standard text until the 16th century. In the *Ptolemaic system*, the Earth was stationary at the centre of the Universe, with the Sun, planets, Moon and stars revolving around it; their paths were small circles, whose centres moved along larger circles.

Nikolaus Copernicus (1473–1543) was a Polish astronomer who argued that the Sun, not the Earth, is at the centre of the Universe. His theories were published in 1543 in the book *Concerning the Movement of the Heavenly Bodies*, and mark the beginning of modern astronomy. Although Copernicus was correct in believing that the planets orbited the Sun and not the Earth, he mistakenly thought that the Sun marked the centre of the Universe and that the planets moved in perfect circles.

The Danish astronomer ***Tycho Brahe*** (1546–1601) had intended to become a lawyer, but changed his mind upon witnessing a solar eclipse in 1560. In 1572 he witnessed the supernova in Cassiopeia and wrote a book about it. From 1576 to 1596 he worked at Uraniborg on the Danish island of Hven, compiling an accurate star catalogue. Tycho was the last of the great astronomers to rely on the naked eye, and he improved every previous astronomical observation. Among other things he calculated the length of the year to an accuracy of less than one second.

The German mathematician ***Johannes Kepler*** (1571–1630) was the first person to show that the planets move around the Sun in elliptical orbits. He was originally an assistant to Tycho Brahe and his work was based on Tycho's observations. Kepler devised three important laws of planetary motion that are still in use today:

Kepler's frontispiece to his astronomical tables of 1627 pays homage to his predecessors. (AR)

1. The motion of a planet around the Sun describes an ellipse, with the Sun at one of the foci (i.e. centres).

2. A line joining the centre of the Sun with the centre of a planet sweeps out equal areas in equal times.

3. The square of a planet's orbital period is proportional to the cube of its mean distance from the Sun.

The Italian *Galileo Galilei* (1564–1642) developed the astronomical telescope and used it to discover the four main satellites of Jupiter. He also observed the stars of the Milky Way and craters on the Moon, and found that the planet Venus showed phases. Galileo's book, *Two Chief Systems of the World*, published in 1632, backed up the theory of a Sun-centred Solar System, but was banned by the Roman Catholic Church as this theory went against Church dogma, which stated that the Earth was the centre of the Universe. He was forced to retract his views by the Inquisition and placed under house arrest.

The laws of motion derived by the English scientist **Sir Isaac Newton** (1642–1727) are fundamental to our understanding of the physical world (▷ p. 14) and are also of enormous importance to astronomers. Newton's discovery of gravity is also essential to all subsequent astronomical theory.

Several later astronomers are mentioned on previous pages in relation to their particular discoveries.

Early instruments and observations

One of the first astronomical instruments was the *astrolabe*, a circular disc marked off in degrees along its rim, which was used to measure the altitudes of stars and planets.

The *quadrant* was another device for measuring the positions of celestial objects. As its name implies, the quadrant is a 90° arc, together with a pointer for sighting stars. Before the advent of the telescope, astronomers would use astrolabes and quadrants for measuring stellar positions.

One of the earliest good star charts was the *Uranometria*, published by the Bavarian Johann Bayer (1572–1625) in 1603. Bayer introduced the system of identifying individual stars within a constellation by letters of the Greek alphabet.

Optical telescopes

The optical telescope was invented by the Dutch spectacle maker Hans Lippershey (died c. 1619), but its first practical form was developed by Galileo. There are two principal types: *refracting telescopes*, which employ lenses, and *reflecting telescopes*, which use mirrors (▷ p. 25). Most large modern telescopes are of the latter type.

The two largest optical telescopes using single mirrors are at Mount Semirodriki in the Caucasus, Russia, with a 6 m (19 ft 8 in) diameter mirror, and the Hale Telescope at Mount Palomar, California, which has a 5 m (16 ft 5 in) diameter mirror. The Keck telescope on Mauna Kea, Hawaii, has a 10 m (32 ft 10 in) mirror made up of 36 segments, while the 'Very Large Telescope' being planned by the European Southern Observatory in Chile will have four 8 m (26 ft 3 in) telescopes working together, providing a light-

> ### — IS THERE LIFE ELSEWHERE? —
>
> The acronym SETI stands for Search for Extra-Terrestrial Intelligence. The search began in earnest with Project Ozma in 1960, when a 26 m (85 ft) diameter radio telescope at Green Bank, West Virginia, USA, was used to search for signals from the nearby stars Tau Ceti and Epsilon Eridani. Nothing was found. Since Project Ozma, several further attempts have been made to detect radio signals produced by other intelligent civilizations, but without success.
>
> It is possible to represent the probable number of advanced civilizations in the Galaxy by a mathematical equation. This was originally done by Frank Drake of Cornell University in the USA, and the equation thus bears his name.
>
> Drake's equation states that the number (N) of advanced technical civilizations in the Galaxy can be expressed as follows:
>
> $$N = N_* \times f_p \times n_e \times f_l \times f_i \times f_c \times f_L$$
>
> where:
>
> N_* is the number of stars in the Galaxy;
>
> f_p is the fraction of stars that have planetary systems;
>
> n_e is the number of Earth-like planets in every star system (again, this will be a fraction, in that it is thought that most stars do not have Earth-like planets);
>
> f_l is the fraction of suitable planets on which life actually arises;
>
> f_i is the fraction of inhabited planets on which intelligent life evolves;
>
> f_c is the fraction of planets inhabited by intelligent beings that attempt to communicate; and
>
> f_L is the fraction of the planet's life for which the civilization survives.
>
> A major problem with the Drake equation is that some of the terms are very difficult to estimate. Different estimates can yield wildly different results. These range from mankind being the only intelligent civilization in the Galaxy, to our being one among many millions of intelligent Galactic life forms.

grasp equal to a single 16 m (52 ft 6 in) mirror. Such telescopes will be able to detect far fainter objects than is possible with conventional optical telescopes.

The ideal place for telescopes is in space, where there is no atmosphere to distort the optical image. The Hubble Space Telescope, launched by space shuttle in 1990, should have outperformed any ground-based telescope, even though it has a relatively small reflector of 2.4 m (7 ft 10½ in). However, it has suffered from technical problems.

Radio astronomy

In 1931 the American radio engineer Karl Jansky (1905–1949) used an improvised aerial to detect radio emissions from the Milky Way. This marked the beginnings of *radio astronomy*, which has made possible such exciting developments as the discovery of quasars (▷ p. 4).

The most famous steerable radio telescope is the 75 m (250 ft) diameter Lovell Telescope at Jodrell Bank, England. The world's largest radio telescope, the 300 m (1000 ft) diameter dish at Arecibo in Puerto Rico, is built into a natural hollow in the ground.

Many astronomical bodies also emit gamma rays and X-rays, which can give us information about the physical properties of those bodies. However, these radiations are difficult to study, because they do not pass through the Earth's atmosphere. Most observations are therefore confined to spacecraft.

Modern astronomy now covers the whole of the electromagnetic spectrum (▷ p. 27), and observations are also being made at infrared, ultra-violet and microwave wavelengths.

SEE ALSO

● THE UNIVERSE AND COSMOLOGY p. 2
● THE PLANETS p. 8
● SPACE EXPLORATION p. 12
● THE HISTORY OF SCIENCE p. 48
● SEEING THE INVISIBLE p. 210

Space Exploration

The development of space technology has been remarkably rapid. Less than 10 years after Yuri Gagarin became the first person in space, Neil Armstrong set foot upon the Moon. During the 21st century, space travel is likely to become routine. Permanent space stations will operate in Earth orbit, bases will be built on the Moon, and man will begin to explore the planet Mars.

The theory of rocketry was developed at the beginning of the 20th century by the Russian physicist Konstantin Tsiolkovsky (1857–1935). He produced designs for multistage liquid-fuelled rockets decades before such vehicles were actually built. Tsiolkovsky also wrote about space suits, satellites and colonizing the Solar System.

The inscription on his tombstone reads: 'Mankind will not remain tied to Earth forever.'

The pioneers of rocketry

The first successful liquid-propellant rocket was launched by the American physicist Robert Goddard (1882–1945) in 1926. By the mid-1930s, Goddard had perfected rockets that could travel to an altitude of several kilometres.

Born in Germany, Wernher von Braun (1912–77) helped to develop the V-2 rocket during World War II. He surrendered to the Americans in 1945 and led the team that in 1958 launched *Explorer 1*, the first American artificial satellite. He then turned his attention to the Apollo programme, which landed a man on the Moon in 1969.

The first artificial satellites

The first object successfully launched into space was the Soviet *Sputnik 1*, which lifted off on 4 October 1957. The satellite measured temperatures and electron densities, before burning up as it re-entered the atmosphere on 4 January 1958.

The dog Laika became the first living creature in space following her launch aboard *Sputnik 2* on 3 November 1957. Laika spent 10 days in orbit, but died when her oxygen supply was exhausted.

Man in space

The era of manned spaceflight began on 12 April 1961, when the Soviet cosmonaut Yuri Gagarin (1934–68) was launched aboard *Vostok 1*. His spacecraft completed a single orbit of the Earth in a flight lasting 90 minutes. Gagarin landed by parachute, having been ejected from the capsule during its descent.

The USA became the second country to put a man into orbit when John Glenn (1921–) was launched aboard his *Friendship 7* capsule on 20 February 1962.

Following the success of Gagarin's flight, President Kennedy announced that the USA intended to place a man on the Moon by the end of the decade. Thus the Apollo programme was born, which used the massive Saturn V rockets. The project reached a successful climax on 20 July 1969 when Neil Armstrong (1930–) and Edwin 'Buzz' Aldrin (1930–) landed their *Apollo 11* lunar module *Eagle* at the Sea of Tranquillity. The Apollo Moon-landing programme ended in 1972, five more successful missions having landed 10 more men on the Moon.

Space stations

Space stations are primarily used for scientific research, but have also been used to test the ability of humans to endure long periods of weightlessness in preparation for interplanetary flight. The weightless conditions can also be used for manufacturing new materials such as perfect crystals. The first space station was the Soviet Union's *Salyut 1*, which was launched on 19 April 1971. This was followed by six further stations in the Salyut series, before the larger *Mir* space station was launched on 20 February 1986. Two

The first Moon landing took place on 20 July 1969. 'That's one small step for a man,' said Neil Armstrong as he stepped out of the spacecraft, 'one giant leap for mankind.'
(Image Select)

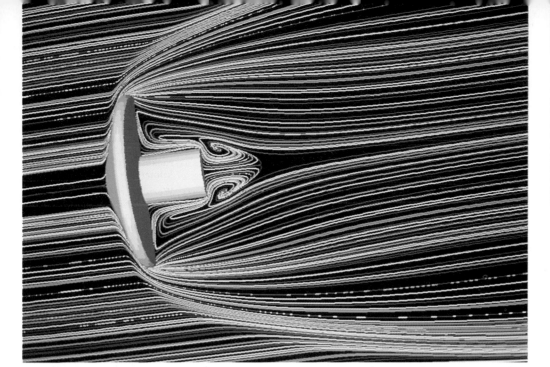

Mission Mars? A computer simulation of the type of spacecraft that may take humans to Mars in the 21st century. The simulation shows how the shape of the spacecraft may use the planet's atmosphere to slow it down, enabling it to be placed in a stable 'parking' orbit. (SPL)

cosmonauts spent a year aboard *Mir* from 21 December 1987 to 21 December 1988.

The American *Skylab* space station was launched on 14 May 1973 and was subsequently visited by three crews, the last of which stayed for 84 days.

Space shuttles

Unlike earlier spacecraft, space shuttles are reusable. The main vehicle is winged like an aeroplane, but is launched into orbit by booster rockets that are then discarded. The main vehicle can subsequently land like a conventional glider.

SATELLITES AND THEIR USES

Many artificial satellites are used for communications. *Comsats*, as they are sometimes known, are often placed in *geostationary orbit*, 36 900 km (22 900 mi) above the equator. Satellites in this orbit travel at the same speed as the Earth rotates and thus appear to remain fixed in the sky.

Weather satellites operate either in geostationary orbit or *polar orbit*. A polar orbit carries a satellite over the North and South Poles, passing over a different strip of the Earth on every orbit. Such satellites can survey the entire planet every 24 hours.

Earth-resources satellites, such as those in the US Landsat series, can be used to prospect for new mineral resources, check the spread of diseases in crops and monitor pollution.

Satellites are also used as platforms for astronomical instruments (▷ p. 11), and by the military, both for surveillance and for weapons. Spy satellites can detect objects as small as individual vehicles and people. The US Strategic Defence Initiative ('Star Wars') programme aims to provide a space-based laser defence system against nuclear weapons (▷ p. 181). However, many scientists doubt whether an effective system can ever be built and others doubt the wisdom of even trying to do so.

The American space shuttle made its debut on 12 April 1981, with the launch of the orbiter *Columbia*. The programme came to an abrupt halt on 28 January 1986, 73 seconds after the 25th shuttle launch. A leak from a rocket booster caused an explosion that destroyed the *Challenger* orbiter and killed its crew of seven. Shuttle operations resumed on 29 September 1988, when *Discovery* was launched on the 26th shuttle mission.

The USSR developed a reusable spacecraft – the VKK (*Vosdushno Kosmicheski Korabl*, 'airborne spacecraft'). The first VKK to be launched was *Buran* ('snowstorm'), which completed two orbits of the Earth on 15 November 1988. Although designed to carry a crew, *Buran*'s first flight was unmanned.

Unmanned probes

Much of our knowledge of the Solar System has come from unmanned probes (▷ pp. 8–9). These have now returned data from every known planet except Pluto. Spacecraft have landed on Venus and Mars and probes are either planned, or on course, to enter orbit around Jupiter and Saturn.

The future

The rocket is the space launcher of the 20th century, but the spaceplane will be the launcher of the 21st century. Spaceplanes will be fully reusable and able to take off as well as land from runways like conventional aeroplanes. One such spaceplane was the British Hotol project, abandoned in 1992 owing to lack of funding. Other designs for spaceplanes are being studied by the USA (the X–30 project), Japan and Germany.

The early years of the 21st century are likely to see a return to the Moon. However, unlike the Apollo missions, the next time human beings venture to the Moon they will be equipped to stay and establish a permanent base. Following the return to the Moon, a manned flight to Mars is likely to be undertaken. The collapse of the Soviet economy and the break-up of the USSR (1991) raised doubts concerning future Russian missions.

SEE ALSO

- THE PLANETS p. 8
- NUCLEAR ARMAMENT AND DISARMAMENT p. 181
- ENGINES p. 192
- SEEING THE INVISIBLE p. 210
- AIRCRAFT p. 222

COMPARATIVE SIZES OF VARIOUS LAUNCH VEHICLES

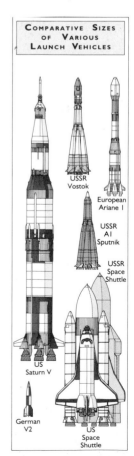

USSR Vostok

European Ariane I

USSR AI Sputnik

USSR Space Shuttle

US Saturn V

German V2

US Space Shuttle

Motion and Force

THE KINEMATIC EQUATIONS

For a body moving in a straight line with uniformly accelerated motion:

1. $v = u + at$
2. $s = ut + \frac{1}{2}at^2$
3. $v^2 = u^2 + 2as$
4. $s = \frac{1}{2}t(u + v)$

where s = displacement
t = time
u = initial or starting velocity
v = velocity after time t
a = acceleration

Physics is the study of the basic laws that govern matter. Mechanics is the branch of physics that describes the movement or motion of objects, ranging in scale from a planet to the smallest particle within an atom. Sir Isaac Newton (1642–1727) developed a theory of mechanics that has proved highly successful in describing most types of motion, and his work has been acclaimed as one of the greatest advances in the history of science.

SEE ALSO

- THE HISTORY OF ASTRONOMY p. 10
- FORCES AFFECTING SOLIDS AND FLUIDS p. 16
- HEAT AND ENERGY p. 18
- QUANTUM THEORY AND RELATIVITY p. 32
- THE HISTORY OF SCIENCE p. 48

The Newtonian approach, although valid for velocities and dimensions within normal experience, has been shown to fail for velocities approaching the speed of light and for dimensions on a subatomic scale. Newton's discoveries are therefore considered to be a special case within a more general theory (▷ pp. 32–3).

Motion

When a body is in *motion* it can be thought of as moving in space and time. If the body moves from one position to another, the straight line joining its starting point to its finishing point is its *displacement* (▷ diagram 1). This has both magnitude and direction, and is therefore said to be a *vector quantity*. The motion is *linear*.

The rate at which a body moves, in a straight line or *rectilinearly*, is its *velocity*. Again, this has magnitude and direction and is a vector quantity. In contrast, the *speed*, which has magnitude, but is not considered to be in any particular direction, is a *scalar quantity*. The *average velocity* of the body during this rectilinear motion is defined as the change in displacement divided by the total time taken. Its dimensions are therefore length divided by time, and are given in metres per second (m s⁻¹).

If the body moves with a changing velocity, then the rate of change of the velocity is the *acceleration*. This is defined as the change in velocity in a given time interval. Its dimensions are velocity divided by time, and are given in metres per second per second (m s⁻²). When a body moves with uniform acceleration (uniformly accelerated motion), the displacement, velocity and acceleration are related. These relationships are described in the *kinematic equations* (▷ box), sometimes called the *laws of uniformly accelerated motion*. *Kinematics* is the study of bodies in motion, ignoring masses and forces.

Galileo (▷ p. 10) investigated the motion of objects falling freely in air. He believed that all objects falling freely towards the Earth have the same downward acceleration. This is called the *acceleration due to gravity* or the *gravitational acceleration*. Near the surface of the Earth it is 9.80 m s⁻², but there are small variations in its value depending upon latitude and elevation. In the idealized situation, air resistance is neglected, although in a practical experiment it would have to be considered. In a demonstration on the Moon in August 1971, an American astronaut showed that, under conditions where air resistance was negligible, a feather and a hammer, released at the same time from the same height, would fall side by side.

When real motion is considered, both the magnitude and the direction of the velocity have to be investigated. A golf ball, hit upwards, will return to the ground. During flight its velocity will change in both magnitude and direction. In this case, instead of average velocity, the *instantaneous velocities* have to be evaluated. The velocity can, at any instant, be considered to be acting in two directions, vertical and horizontal. Then the velocity at that instant can be separated into a vertical and a horizontal component (▷ diagram 2). Each component can be considered as being uniformly accelerated rectilinear motion, so the kinematic equations can be applied in each direction. Then the instantaneous velocity and position at any point of the flight can be calculated.

Circular motion

If a body moves in a circular path at constant speed its direction of motion (and therefore its velocity) will be changing continuously. Since the velocity is changing, the body must have

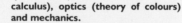

SIR ISAAC NEWTON

Sir Isaac Newton was born in a small village in Lincolnshire in 1642. In 1661 he was sent to Trinity College, Cambridge. By 1666, at the age of 24, he had made important discoveries in mathematics (the binomial theorem, differential calculus), optics (theory of colours) and mechanics.

Newton became Professor of Mathematics at Cambridge, and in 1687 he published his *Philosophiae Naturalis Principia Mathematica*, known as the *Principia*. Through careful analysis of the available experimental data and the application of his theory he was able to explain many previously inexplicable phenomena, such as the tides and the precession of the equinoxes. In 1689 and 1701 he represented Cambridge University in Parliament. From 1703 until his death in 1727 he was President of the Royal Society. He was buried in Westminster Abbey. (Image Select)

acceleration, which is also changing continuously. Thus the laws of uniformly accelerated motion do not apply. The acceleration of a body moving in a circular path is called the *centripetal* ('centre-seeking') *acceleration*. This is directed inward, towards the centre of the circle (▷ diagram 3).

Newton's laws of motion

Newton's laws of motion state relationships between the acceleration of a body and the forces acting on it. A *force* is something that causes a change in the rate of change of velocity of an object.

Newton's first law states that a body will remain at rest or travelling in a straight line at constant speed unless it is acted upon by an external force. Notice that the force has to be an external one. In general, a body does not exert a force upon itself.

The tendency of a body to remain at rest or moving with constant velocity is called the *inertia* of the body. The inertia is related to the *mass*, which is the amount of substance in the body. The unit of mass is the *kilogram* (kg).

Newton's second law states that the resultant force exerted on a body is directly proportional to the acceleration produced by the force:

$$F = ma$$

where F is the force exerted,
m is the mass of the body
a is the acceleration.

The unit of force is the *newton* (N), which is defined as the force that, acting on a body of mass 1 kg, produces an acceleration of 1 m s^{-2}.

The mass of a body is often confused with its weight. The mass is the amount of matter in the body, whereas the *weight* is the gravitational force acting on the body, and varies with location. The unit of weight is the newton (▷ above). Thus a body has the same mass on the Moon as on Earth, but its weight on the Moon will be less than on Earth since the gravitational force on the Moon is approximately one sixth of that on Earth.

Newton expressed his second law by stating that the force acting on a body is equal to the rate of change in its 'quantity of motion', which is now called *momentum*. The momentum of a body is defined as the product of its mass and velocity.

Newton's third law states that a single isolated force cannot exist on its own: there is always a resulting 'mirror-image' force. In Newton's words, 'To every action there is always opposed an equal reaction.' This means that, because any two masses exert on each other a mutual gravitational attraction, the Earth is always attracted towards a ball as much as the ball is attracted towards the Earth. Because of the huge difference in their sizes, however, the observable result is the downward acceleration of the ball.

The *principle of the conservation of momentum* follows from this third law. This states that, when two bodies interact, the total momentum before impact is the same as the total momentum after impact:

$$m_1 u_1 + m_2 u_2 = m_1 v_1 + m_2 v_2$$

where m_1, m_2 are the masses
u_1, u_2 are the initial velocities
v_1, v_2 are the resultant velocities of the bodies.

Thus the total of the components of momentum in any direction before and after the interaction are equal.

In an *accelerating* or *non-inertial* frame of reference, Newton's second law will not work unless some fictitious force is introduced. For example, passengers on a circus merry-go-round feel as if they are being forced outward when the machine is operating. This is ascribed to a 'centre-fleeing' or 'centrifugal force'. The passengers experience this because they are moving within the system; they are within an accelerating frame of reference (▷ circular motion, above). To an observer on the ground it appears that the passengers on the ride should fly off at a tangent to the circular motion unless there were a force keeping them aboard. This is the centripetal force and is experienced as the friction between each passenger and the seat. If a passenger were to fall off, it would be because the centripetal force was not strong enough, not because the 'centrifugal force' was too great.

Gravitation

Gravitational force is one of the four fundamental forces that occur in nature. The others are electromagnetic force (▷ p. 26), and the strong and the weak nuclear forces (▷ p. 30).

Gravitational force is the mutual force of attraction between masses. The gravitational force is much weaker than the other forces mentioned above. However, this long-range force should not be thought of as a weak force. An object resting on a table is acted on by the gravitational force of the whole Earth – a significant force. The almost equal force exerted by the table is the result of short-range forces exerted by molecules on its surface.

Newton first described his *law of gravitation* in 1687. Newton used the notion of a *particle*, by which he meant a body so small that its dimensions are negligible compared to other distances. He stated that every particle in the universe attracts every other particle with a force that is directly proportional to the product of their masses and inversely proportional to the square of the distance between them:

$$F = G \frac{m_1 m_2}{x^2}$$

where F is the force
m_1, m_2 are the masses
x is the distance between the particles.

The constant of proportionality is represented by G and is known as the *gravitational constant*.

Newtonian mechanics were so successful that a mechanistic belief developed in which it was thought that with the knowledge of Newton's laws (and later those of electromagnetism) it would be possible to predict the future of the Universe if the positions, velocities and accelerations of all particles at any one instant were known. Later the quantum theory and the Heisenberg Uncertainty Principle (▷ p. 32) confounded this belief by predicting the fundamental impossibility of making simultaneous measurements of the position and velocity of a particle with infinite accuracy.

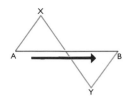

1. Displacement. Anna walks from A to X, then to Y, then to B. AB is her displacement, and the arrow shows the direction of the displacement.

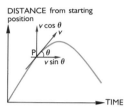

2. Instantaneous velocity v can be expressed as a horizontal component and a vertical component. The velocity at point P is v. It has a horizontal component $v \cos \theta$ and a vertical component $v \sin \theta$ (for explanations of sine, cosine and θ, ▷ p. 53).

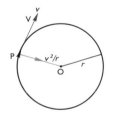

3. Centripetal acceleration. At point P the body is moving with instantaneous velocity v. The centripetal acceleration along PO is v^2/r (where r is the radius of the circle), and the centripetal force along PO is mv^2/r, where m is the mass of the body. This force prevents the body from moving in a straight line along PV.

Forces affecting Solids and Fluids

In addition to the fundamental forces (▷ pp. 15, 26 and 30), other forces such as frictional, elastic and viscous forces may be encountered. Because of their different natures, solids and fluids appear in some ways to react differently to similar applied forces.

When forces are applied to solids they tend to resist. Friction inhibits displacement, but is overcome after a certain limit. Bodies may be deformed by tensions. Fluids, although lacking definite shape, are held together by internal forces. They exert pressure on the walls of the containing vessel (▷ pp. 18–19). Fluids – by definition – have a tendency to flow; this may be greater in some substances than in others and is governed by the viscosity of the fluid.

Statics

Newton's first law (▷ pp. 14–15), stated for a single particle, can also apply to real bodies that have definite sizes and shapes and consist of many particles. Such a body may be in *equilibrium*, which means it is at rest or moving with constant velocity in a straight line. This means that it is acted on by *zero net force*, and that it has no tendency to rotate.

A body is acted on by zero net force if the total or resultant of all the forces acting on it is zero – i.e. all the forces cancel each other out (▷ diagram 1). If the body is at rest it is in *static equilibrium*. Studies of such conditions are important in the design of bridges, dams and buildings.

Forces involved in rotation

Torque (or *moment of a force*) measures the tendency of a force to cause the body to rotate. In this case the force causes *angular acceleration*, which is the *rate of change of angular momentum* of the body. Torque is defined as the product of the force acting on a body and the perpendicular distance from the axis of the rotation of the body to the line of action of the force (▷ diagram 2). Torque has units of force × distance, usually expressed as *newton metres* (N m). Torque is increased if either the force or the perpendicular distance is increased. If a wedge is used to keep a door open, it has maximum effect if it is placed on the floor as far from the hinge as possible.

When a body is acted on by two equal and opposite forces, not in the same line, then the result is a *couple*, which has a constant turning moment about any axis perpendicular to the plane in which the forces act (▷ diagram 3). When the total or net torque on a body is zero

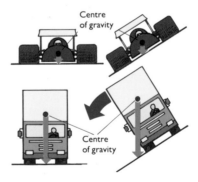

1. Equilibrium. The net force on the body is zero. The mass is balanced by the reaction force: $R = mg$ (mg is the gravitational force acting on the mass). The men are pulling with equal force: $F = F$. The body will not move.

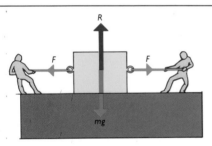

2. Torque. Torque or moment of a force = force × perpendicular distance = Fd.

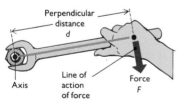

3. A couple. The total turning force acting on the wing nut is $2Fd$.

4. Centre of gravity. A racing car has a very low centre of gravity and will remain stable even on a slope. A loaded truck will have a high centre of gravity and will topple over if driven on too steep a slope.

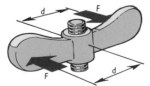

5. Hydraulic brakes: a simple hydraulic system.

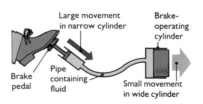

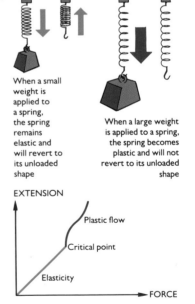

When a small weight is applied to a spring, the spring remains elastic and will revert to its unloaded shape

When a large weight is applied to a spring, the spring becomes plastic and will not revert to its unloaded shape

EXTENSION

Plastic flow

Critical point

Elasticity

FORCE

6. Elasticity and plastic flow. Some bodies behave elastically when small forces are applied, but above a critical point they experience plastic flow, i.e. they are irreversibly extended.

about any axis, the body is in *equilibrium*. A body is in stable equilibrium if a small linear displacement causes a force to act on the body to return it to its previous position, or an angular displacement causes a couple to act to bring it back to its previous position, called the *equilibrium position*.

The *centre of mass* of a body is a point, normally within the body, such that the net resultant force produces an acceleration at this point, as though all the mass of the body were concentrated there. For bodies of certain shapes this point may lie outside the object.

If a uniform gravitational field is present, the *centre of gravity* coincides with the centre of mass. Thus all the weight can be considered to act at this single point. The stability of an object is helped by keeping the centre of gravity as low as possible (▷ diagram 4).

Friction

Sliding friction occurs when a solid body slides on a rough surface. Its progress is hindered by an interaction of the surface of the solid with the surface it is moving on. This is called a *kinetic frictional force*.

Another type of friction is called *static friction*. Before the object moves, the resultant force acting on it must be zero. The frictional force acting between the object and the surface on which it rests cannot exceed its limiting value. Thus, when the other forces acting on the object, against friction, exceed this value the object is caused to accelerate. The limiting or maximum value of the frictional force occurs when the stationary object acted on by the resultant force is just about to slip.

Both these types of friction involve interaction with a solid surface. The frictional forces depend on the two contacting surfaces and in particular on the presence of any surface contaminants. The friction between metal surfaces is largely due to adhesion, shearing and deformation within and around the regions of real contact. Energy is dissipated in friction and appears as internal energy, which can be observed as heat. Thus car brakes heat up when used to slow a vehicle. The results of friction may be reduced by the use of lubricants between the surfaces in contact. This is one function of the oil used in car engines. A further type of friction is *rolling friction*, which occurs when a wheel rolls. Energy is dissipated through the system, because of imperfect elasticity (▷ below). This effect does not depend upon surfaces and is unaffected by lubrication.

Elasticity

Elasticity deals with deformations that disappear when the external applied forces are removed. Most bodies may be deformed by the action of external forces and behave elastically for small deformations.

Strain is a measure of the amount of deformation. *Stress* is a quantity proportional to the force causing the deformation. Its value at any point is given by the magnitude of the force acting at that point divided by the area over which it acts. For small stresses the stress is proportional to the strain. The constant of proportionality is called the *elastic modulus* and it varies according to the material and the type of deformation.

── VISCOSITY AND TURBULENCE ──

Viscosity relates to the internal friction in the flow of a fluid – how adjacent layers in the fluid exert retarding forces on each other. This arises from cohesion of the molecules in the fluid. In a solid the deformation of adjacent layers is usually elastic. In a fluid, however, there is no permanent resistance to change of shape; the layers can slide past each other, with continuous displacement of these layers. Fluids are described as *newtonian* if they obey Newton's law that the ratio of the applied stress to the rate of shearing has a constant value. This is not true for many substances. Some paints, for example, do not have constant values for the coefficient of viscosity; as the paint is stirred it flows more easily and the coefficient is diminished. Molten lava is another non-newtonian fluid.

If adjacent layers flow smoothly past each other the steady flow is described as *laminar flow*. If the flow velocity is increased the flow may become disordered with irregular and random motions called *turbulence*. Smoke rising from a cigarette starts with smooth laminar flow but soon breaks into turbulent flow with the formation of eddies. If the speed, density, dimension and viscosity of a system are known, then the onset of turbulence can be predicted. The study of viscosity and turbulence is important in understanding problems such as the flow of arterial blood around the body (▷ pp. 140–1). For larger arteries, turbulence will be a major consideration.

A special example of deformation is the extension or elongation of a spring by an applied force. *Hooke's law*, formulated by the English scientist Robert Hooke (1635–1703), states that, for small forces, the extension is proportional to the applied force. Thus a spring balance can have a uniform scale for the measurement of various weights, because spring steel – which returns to its initial state readily – is almost *perfectly elastic*. In contrast, a soft rubber ball dropped on hard ground bounces to only about half its initial height, demonstrating *imperfect elasticity*.

Some bodies behave elastically for low values of stress, but above a critical level they behave in a perfectly viscous manner and 'flow' like thick treacle (▷ box), with irreversible deformation. This is called *plastic flow* (▷ diagram 6).

Fluids at rest – hydrostatics

Pressure is defined as the perpendicular or normal force per unit area of a plane surface in the fluid, and its unit is the *pascal* (Pa), equivalent to 1 newton per square metre ($N\,m^2$). At all points in the fluid at the same depth the pressure is the same. The pressure depends only on depth in an enclosed fluid, and is independent of cross-sectional area. In the hydraulic brakes of a car (▷ diagram 5), a force is applied by the foot pedal to a small piston. The pressure is transmitted via the hydraulic fluid to a larger piston connected to the brake. In this way the force applied to the brake is magnified by comparison with the force applied to the pedal.

Atmospheric pressure may be measured using a barometer. At sea level, it is equivalent to the weight of a column of mercury about 0.76 m high, which is about 1.01×105 Pa. It varies by up to about 5%, depending on the weather systems passing overhead (▷ p. 78).

The *buoyancy force* was described by the Greek mathematician and physicist Archimedes (287–212 BC). *Archimedes' principle* states that an object placed in a fluid is buoyed up by a force equal to the weight of fluid displaced by the body. A body with density greater than that of the fluid will sink, because the fluid it displaces weighs less than it does itself. A body with density less than that of the fluid will float.

SEE ALSO

- MOTION AND FORCE p. 14
- HEAT AND ENERGY p. 18
- CARS p. 219

Heat and Energy

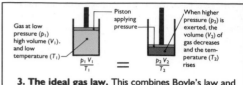

3. The ideal gas law. This combines Boyle's law and Charles' law.

Heat is a form of energy and the *temperature* of a substance is a measure of its internal energy. The study of heat and temperature is called *thermodynamics*. One fundamental principle in the study of thermodynamics is the *law of the conservation of energy*, which states that in any interaction, energy is neither created nor destroyed.

Much of the energy that seems to be lost in typical interactions – such as a box sliding across a floor – is converted into internal energy; in the case of the sliding box, this is the kinetic energy (⇨ below) gained by the atoms and molecules within the box and the floor as they interact and are pulled from their equilibrium positions. The name given to the energy in the form of hidden motion of atoms and molecules is *thermal energy*. Strictly speaking, heat is transferred between two bodies as a result of a change in temperature, although the term 'heat' is commonly used for the thermal energy as well. Processes that turn kinetic energy, which is the organized energy of a moving body, into thermal energy, which is the disorganized energy due to the motion of atoms, include friction and viscosity (⇨ pp. 16–17). In a steam engine, heat is turned into work (⇨ p. 192).

Work and energy

When a force (⇨ p. 14) acts on a body, causing acceleration in the direction of the force, *work* is done. The work done on a body by a constant force is defined as the product of the magnitude of the force and the consequent displacement of the body in the direction of the force (⇨ diagram 1).

The unit of work is the *joule* (sometimes referred to as the *newton metre*) – named after the English scientist James Joule (1818–89). A joule (J) is defined as the work done on a body when it is displaced 1 metre as the result of the action of a force of 1 newton (⇨ p. 14) acting in the direction of motion: $1\,J = 1\,N\,m$. The result may be expressed more generally (⇨ diagram 2).

Energy is the capacity of a body to do work. The total energy stored in a *closed system* – one in which no external forces are experienced – remains constant, however it may be transformed. This is the principle of *conservation of energy*. It may take the form of mechanical energy (kinetic or potential; ⇨ below), electrical energy, chemical energy, or heat energy. There are also other forms of energy, including gravitational, magnetic, the energy of electromagnetic radiation, and the energy of matter.

The *kinetic energy* (E_k) of a body is the energy it has because it is moving. It is equal to half the product of the mass (m) and the square of the velocity (v): $E_k = \frac{1}{2}\,mv^2$.

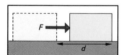

1. Work. Work done on a body by a constant force is the product of the magnitude of the force and the displacement of the body as a result of the action of the force: $W = Fd$.

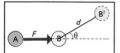

2. Work done. A exerts a force F on B and as a result B moves to position B' with displacement d at angle θ to the line of F. Work $W = Fd\cos\theta$. (For explanations of cosine and θ, ⇨ p. 53.)

Alternatively, a body may have *potential energy*, which is dependent upon position. The gravitational potential energy (E_p) of a body of mass m at a height h above the ground is mgh, where g is the acceleration due to gravity. This gravitational potential energy is equal to the work that the Earth's gravitational field will do on the body as it moves to ground level.

Potential energy can be converted into kinetic energy or it can be used to do work. It acts as a store of energy. If a body moves upward against the gravitational force, work is done on it and there is an increase in gravitational potential energy.

Temperature

Temperature is a measure of the internal energy or 'hotness' of a body, not the heat of the body. The temperature scale used by physicists is based on a unit called the *kelvin* (K), named after the Scottish physicist William Thomson, later Lord Kelvin (1824–1907). On the kelvin scale the freezing point of water is 273.15 K (0 °C or 32 °F) and its boiling point is 373.15 K (100 °C or 212 °F): one kelvin is equal in magnitude to one degree on the Celsius scale. The temperature of 0 (zero) K (-273.15 °C) is known as *absolute zero*. At this temperature, for an ideal gas (⇨ below and diagram 3), the volume would be infinitely large and the pressure zero.

Heat and internal energy

The molecular energy (kinetic and potential) within a body is called *internal energy*. When this energy is transferred from a place of high energy to one of lower energy, it is described as a flow of heat.

——— HEAT TRANSFER ———

CONDUCTION
Heat conduction occurs when kinetic and molecular energy is passed from one molecule to another. Metals are good conductors of heat because of electrons that transport energy through the material (⇨ p. 45). Air is a poor conductor in comparison. Thus a string vest keeps its wearer warm by trapping air and so preventing the conduction of heat outwards from the body.

CONVECTION
Heat convection results from the motion of the heated substance. Warm air is less dense than cold air and so, according to Archimedes' principle (⇨ p. 17), it rises. Convection is the main mechanism for mixing the atmosphere and diluting pollutants emitted into the air.

RADIATION
Radiation is the third process for heat transfer. All bodies radiate energy in the form of electromagnetic waves (⇨ p. 26). This radiation may pass across a vacuum, and thus the Earth receives energy radiated from the Sun. A body remains at a constant temperature when it both radiates and receives energy at the same rate.

If two bodies of different temperatures are placed in thermal contact with each other, after a time they are found both to be at the same temperature. Energy is transferred from the warmer to the colder body, until both are at a new *equilibrium temperature*. The unit of internal energy and heat is the *joule*, as defined above.

The kinetic theory of gases

The kinetic theory of gases takes Newton's laws (➤ pp. 14–15) and applies them statistically to a group of molecules. It treats a gas as if it were made up of extremely small – dimensionless – particles, all in constant random motion. It is based on an *ideal gas*, i.e. a gas that would obey the ideal gas law perfectly (➤ below and diagram 3). In fact no gas is ideal, but most behave sufficiently closely that the ideal gas law can be used in calculations.

One conclusion is that the pressure and volume of such a gas are related to the average kinetic energy for each molecule. The kinetic theory explains that pressure in a gas is due to the impact of the molecules on the containing walls around the gas. There is an equation that relates the pressure, temperature and volume of an ideal gas – the *ideal gas law* (➤ diagram 3).

The temperature of an ideal gas is a measure of the average molecular kinetic energies. At a higher temperature the mean speed of the molecules is increased. The internal energy of a gas is associated with the motion of its molecules and their potential energy.

Laws of thermodynamics

A *thermally isolated system* is one that neither receives nor transmits transfer of heat, although the temperature within the system may vary. If mechanical or electrical work is performed on a thermally isolated system, its internal energy increases. James Joule discovered an equivalence relation between the amount of work done (*W*) on a thermally isolated system and the heat gained (*Q*): $W = JQ$. The constant J was described by Joule as the *mechanical equivalent of heat*.

The *first law of thermodynamics* is a development of the law of conservation of energy (➤ above). It states that it is possible to convert work totally into heat. Another statement of this law is that the change in internal energy of a body depends only on its initial and final states. The change may be the result of an increase in energy in any form – thermal, mechanical, gravitational, etc.

The *second law of thermodynamics* states that the converse is not true. In essence, the second law means that heat cannot itself flow from a cold object to a hot object. Thus the law shows that certain processes may only operate in one direction.

The second law was established after work by a French engineer, Sadi Carnot (1796–1832), who was trying to build the most efficient engine. His ideal engine established an upper limit for the efficiency with which thermal energy could be converted into mechanical energy. Real engines fall short of this ideal efficiency because of losses due to friction and heat conduction (➤ box).

Entropy

Entropy describes the *disorder* or *chaos* of a system. A highly disordered state is one in which

molecules move haphazardly in all directions, with many different velocities. An alternative form of the second law of thermodynamics is that the entropy of the universe never decreases. It follows that the universe is moving through increasing disorder towards thermal equilibrium. Therefore the universe cannot have existed for ever, otherwise it would have reached this equilibrium state already.

In a nuclear explosion a small mass is converted into a large amount of energy. Mass and energy are linked by Einstein's famous equation $E = mc^2$, where c is the speed of light (➤ p. 33). (SPL)

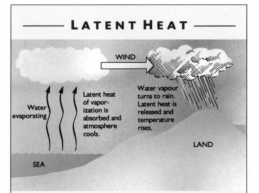

LATENT HEAT

WIND

Water evaporating

Latent heat of vaporization is absorbed and atmosphere cools.

Water vapour turns to rain. Latent heat is released and temperature rises.

SEA

LAND

4. Latent heat. The effect of latent heat on climate.

When heat flows between a body and its surroundings there is usually a change in the temperature of the body, as well as changes in internal energies. This is not so when a change of form occurs, as from solid to liquid or from liquid to gas. This is called a *phase change* and involves a change in the internal energy of the body only.

The amount of heat needed to make the change of phase is called the *hidden* or *latent heat*. To change water at 100 °C (212 °F) to water vapour requires nearly seven times as much heat (*latent heat of vaporization*) as to change ice to water (*latent heat of fusion*). This varies for water at different temperatures – more heat is required to change it to water vapour at 80 °C (176 °F), less at 110 °C (230 °F). In each case the attractive forces binding the water molecules together must be loosened or broken.

Latent heat has an important effect on climate (➤ diagram 4). A similar cycle takes place in a heat pump or refrigerator (➤ p. 193).

SEE ALSO

- MOTION AND FORCE p. 14
- FORCES AFFECTING SOLIDS AND FLUIDS p. 16
- THE HISTORY OF SCIENCE p. 48
- ENERGY pp. 188–91
- ENGINES p. 192

Wave Theory

Water waves are a phenomenon that can be seen, and the effects of sound waves are sensed directly by the ear. Some of the waves in the electromagnetic spectrum (▷ p. 27) can also be sensed by the body: light waves by the eye, and the heating effect of infrared by the skin. There are other electromagnetic waves, however, that cannot be experienced directly through any of the human senses, and even infrared can generally only be observed using specialized detectors (▷ p. 210).

SEE ALSO

● QUANTUM THEORY AND RELATIVITY p. 26
● ACOUSTICS p. 30
● OPTICS p. 32
● ELECTROMAGNETISM p. 34
● COASTS p. 96
● THE OCEANS p. 100
● MEDICAL TECHNOLOGY p. 242
● RADIO, TELEVISION AND VIDEO p. 326
● SEEING THE INVISIBLE p. 332

Wave phenomena are found in all areas of physics, and similar mathematical equations may be used in each application. Some of the general principles of wave motions are explored here. Special types of wave motion – relating to acoustics and optics – are examined on pp. 22–5, and electromagnetic waves in general are examined on pp. 26–7 and 32–3.

Wave types and characteristics

A *travelling wave* is a disturbance that moves or *propagates* from one point to another. *Mechanical waves* are travelling waves that propagate

Water waves (▷ also p. 76) may be produced by the wind or some other disturbance. The particles move in vertical circles so there are both transverse and longitudinal displacements. The motion causes the familiar wave profile with narrow peaks and broad troughs. (Spectrum)

through a material – as happens, for example, when a metal rod is tapped at one end with a hammer. An initial disturbance at a particular place in a material will cause a force to be exerted on adjacent parts of the material. An *elastic force* (▷ p. 17) then acts to restore the material to its equilibrium position. In so doing, it compresses the adjacent particles and so the disturbance moves outward from the source. In attempting to return to their original positions, the particles overshoot, so that at a particular point a *rarefaction* (or stretching) follows a *compression* (or squeezing). The passage of the wave is observed as variations in the pressure about the equilibrium position or by the speed of oscillations. This change is described as *oscillatory* (like a pendulum) or *periodic*.

There are two main types of periodic oscillation – *transverse* and *longitudinal* (▷ diagrams 1 and 2). In transverse waves the vibrations are perpendicular to the direction of travel. In longitudinal waves the vibrations are parallel to the direction of travel. *Sound waves* are alternate compressions and rarefactions of whatever material through which they are travelling, and the waves are longitudinal.

Wave motions transfer energy – for example, sound waves (▷ p. 22), seismic waves (▷ p. 64) and water waves (▷ p. 76) transfer mechanical energy. However, energy is lost as the wave passes through a medium. The amplitude (▷ below) diminishes and the wave is said to be attenuated. There are two distinct processes – *spreading* and *absorption*. In many cases there is little or no absorption – electromagnetic radiation from the Sun travels through space without any absorption at all, but planets that are more distant than the Earth receive less radiation because it is spreading over a larger area and so the *intensity* (the ratio of power to area) decreases according to an inverse-square law. The same applies to sound in the atmosphere. In some cases, however, energy is absorbed in a medium, as, for example, when light enters and exposes a photographic film, or when X-rays enter flesh. For homogeneous radiation, absorption is *exponential*, for example if half the radiation goes through 1 mm of absorber, a quarter would go through 2 mm and an eighth through 3 mm.

The *frequency* (f) of the wave motion is defined as the number of complete oscillations or cycles per second (▷ diagram 3). The unit of frequency is the *hertz* (Hz), named after the German physicist Heinrich Rudolf Hertz (▷ p. 27): 1 hertz = 1 cycle per second. The *amplitude* is the maximum displacement from the equilibrium position (▷ diagram 4). The *wavelength* (λ) is the distance between two successive peaks (or troughs) in the wave (▷ diagram 5). The *speed of propagation* (v) of the compressions, or *phase speed* of the wave, is equal to the product of the frequency and the wavelength: $v = f(\lambda)$.

Reflection and refraction

Reflection of plane waves (▷ diagram 6) at a plane surface are as shown in diagram 7. The behaviour of waves reflected at curved surfaces is shown in diagram 8.

If a wave travels from one medium to another, the direction of propagation is changed or 'bent'; the wave is said to be *refracted*. The wave will travel in medium 1 with velocity v_1, and come upon the

---

——STANDING OR STATIONARY WAVES——

These are the result of confining waves in a specific region. When a travelling wave, such as a wave propagating along a guitar string towards a bridge, reaches the support, the string must be almost at rest. A force is exerted on the support that then reacts by setting up a reflected wave travelling back along the string. This wave has the same frequency and wavelength as the source wave. At certain frequencies the two waves, travelling in opposite directions, interfere to produce a stationary- or standing-wave pattern. Each pattern or mode of vibration corresponds to a particular frequency.

The standing wave may be transverse, as on a plucked violin string, or longitudinal, as in the air in an organ pipe. The positions of maximum and minimum amplitude are called *antinodes* and *nodes* respectively (▷ p. 23). At antinodes the interference is constructive. At nodes it is destructive.

If a periodic force is applied to a system with frequency at or near to the *natural frequency* of the system, then the resulting amplitude of vibration is much greater than for other frequencies. These natural frequencies are called *resonant frequencies*. When a driving frequency equals the resonant frequency then maximum amplitude is obtained.

The natural frequency of objects can be used destructively. High winds can cause suspension bridges to reach their natural frequency and vibrate, sometimes resulting in the destruction of the bridge. Soldiers marching in formation need to break step when crossing bridges in case they achieve the natural frequency of the structure and cause it to disintegrate.

surface of medium 2 with angle of incidence i. Then the wave will be refracted, as in diagram 9, and r is the angle of refraction. The new velocity will be v_2, which will be less than v_1 if medium 2 is more dense than medium 1, but greater than v_1 if medium 2 is less dense. The velocities are related by:

$$\frac{v_1}{v_2} = \frac{\sin i}{\sin r}$$

and the ratio of $\sin i / \sin r$ is a constant ($\triangleright$ p. 53 for an explanation of sine). This constant is the refractive index ($\triangleright$ below) of medium 2 with respect to medium 1. This relationship was formulated by the Dutch astronomer Willebrord Snell (1591–1626) and is known as *Snell's law*.

Basically, *the refractive index* of a material determines how much it will refract light, and it is often expressed relative to another material. If no other material is quoted, the refractive index is assumed to be relative to air. The refractive index of a medium can also be derived as the ratio of the speed of light in a vacuum to the speed of light in the medium.

Interference

If several waves are travelling through a medium, the resultant at any point and time is the vector sum of the amplitudes of the individual waves. This is known as the *superposition principle*. Two or more waves combining together in this way exhibit the phenomenon of *interference*. If the resultant wave amplitude is greater than those of the individual waves then *constructive interference* is taking place ($\triangleright$ diagram 10); if it is less, *destructive interference* occurs ($\triangleright$ diagram 11). If two sound waves of slightly different frequencies and equal amplitudes are played together (for example two tuning forks), then the resulting sound has what is called *varying amplitude*. These varying amplitudes are called *beats* and their frequency is the *beat frequency*. This frequency is equal to the difference between the frequencies of the two original notes. Listening for beats is an aid to tuning musical instruments: the closer the beats, the more nearly in tune is the instrument.

Diffraction

Waves will usually proceed in a straight line through a uniform medium. However, when they pass through a slit with width comparable to their wavelength, they spread out, i.e. they are diffracted ($\triangleright$ diagram 12). Thus waves are able to bend round corners. For a sound wave of 256 Hz the wavelength is about 1.3 m (4¼ ft), comparable with the dimensions of open doors or windows.

If a beam of light is shone through a wide single slit onto a screen that is close to the slit, then a bright and clear image of the slit is seen. As the slit is narrowed there comes a point where the image does not continue getting thinner. Instead, a diffraction pattern of light and dark fringes is seen.

Huygens' principle was proposed in 1676 by the Dutch physicist Christiaan Huygens (1629–95) to explain the laws of reflection and refraction. He postulated that light was a wave motion. Each point on a wavefront becomes a new or secondary source. The new wavefront is the surface that touches all the wavefronts from the secondary sources. Diffraction describes the interference effects observed between light derived from a continuous portion of a wavefront, such as that at a narrow slit. The work of the British physician and physicist Thomas Young (1773–1829) and others eventually supported Huygens' theory.

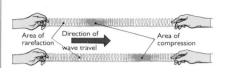

1. A longitudinal wave in a 'slinky' spring.

2. A transverse wave in a 'slinky' spring.

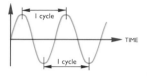

3. Frequency. Frequency = cycles per second. 1 cycle per second = 1 hertz (Hz).

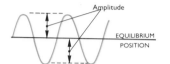

4. Amplitude is the maximum displacement from the equilibrium position.

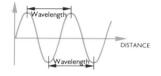

5. Wavelength. Wavelength is the distance between two successive points along a wave with similar amplitudes.

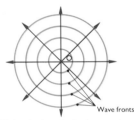

6. Spherical and plane wavefronts. Wavefronts propagating outwards from point source O will be spherical in a three-dimensional context (such as light waves propagating from the Sun) or circular in a two-dimensional context (such as water waves propagating from a dropped pebble). Once far enough from the source, such wavefronts can for most practical purposes be considered as straight lines – *plane wavefronts* – much in the same way that the curvature of the Earth is not noticeable to someone standing on it.

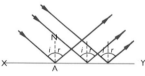

7. Reflection of plane waves at a plane surface. The waves are parallel as they approach XY and after they are reflected. The *normal* (AN) is a line perpendicular to the plane surface (XY) at A. i is the *angle of incidence* of the wave as it meets XY. The *angle of reflection* is r, and $i = r$.

8. Waves reflected at a curved surface. Waves behave in the same way as light reflected in a concave mirror. S is the principal focus of the surface A.

9. Refraction of a plane wavefront. MAN is the normal to XY; i is the angle of incidence; r is the angle of refraction. The waves are parallel after refraction.

results in

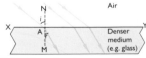

10. Constructive interference results in the effect of the waves being combined.

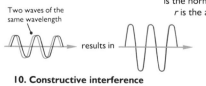

results in

11. Destructive interference results in the waves cancelling each other out.

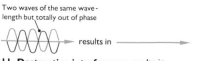

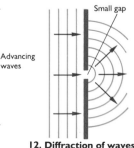

12. Diffraction of waves passing through a small gap.

Acoustics

Sound shares the general characteristics of other wave forms (▷ pp. 20–1). Sound waves are longitudinal compressions (squeezings) and rarefactions (stretchings) of the medium through which they are travelling, and are produced by a vibrating object.

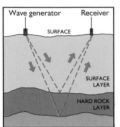

I. Seismic surveying relies on the variation of seismic velocities in different rocks; this causes some layers to reflect the waves more strongly than others.

If a sound wave is travelling in any medium then the pressure variations formed along its path cause strains as a result of the applied stresses. The velocity of the sound is given by the square root of the appropriate elastic modulus (▷ pp. 16–17) divided by the density.

The velocity of sound

The velocity of sound – as with the velocity of other types of wave – differs in different media. In still air at 0 °C, the velocity of sound is about 331 m s^{-1} (1191.6 km/h, or 740 mph). If the air temperature rises by 1° C, then the velocity of sound increases by about 0.6 m s^{-1}. The velocity of sound in a metal such as steel is about 5060 m s^{-1}. Sometimes, in a Western film, someone will put an ear to a railway line to listen for an oncoming train. This works because the sound wave travels much faster through the steel track than through the air.

In the ocean depths the combined effect of salinity, temperature and pressure results in a minimum velocity for sound. The channel that is centred around this minimum velocity at a depth of about 1000–1300 m (3300–4250 ft) allows sound waves, travelling at the minimum velocity, to propagate within it with relatively little loss over large horizontal distances. Signals have been transmitted in this way from Australia to Bermuda.

The fact that the velocity of sound varies in different media is one reason why seismic techniques can be used to probe layers of rock or minerals underground (▷ diagram 1). Similarly ultrasonic scanning can be used in medicine – for example, in the imaging of a baby in its mother's womb (▷ p. 210). In each case variations in materials are shown up through variations in the time it takes sound waves to travel to the detector.

Refraction of sound

At night the air near the ground is often colder than the air higher up, as the Earth cools after sunset. Thus a sound wave moving upward will be slowly bent back towards the horizontal as it meets warmer layers of air. Eventually it will be reflected back downwards. Under these circumstances sound can be heard over long distances. This phenomenon is explained by Snell's law of refraction (▷ pp. 20–1); layers of air at different temperatures act as different media through which sound travels at different velocities (▷ diagram 2).

During World War I the guns at the front in northern France could sometimes be heard in southern England, although not in the intervening area. This was a significant piece of evidence for the existence of the stratosphere, that part of the atmosphere above the troposphere (the lowest layer); in the middle and upper stratosphere the temperature increases with altitude (▷ p. 61).

The human ear

The ear is an extremely sensitive detector. Its threshold of hearing corresponds to an intensity of sound of 10^{-12} watts per square metre (W m^2): this is a measure of the energy impinging on the ear, and is known as the *threshold intensity*. The loudest tolerable sound is about 1 W m^2. This range is enormous, and so a logarithmic scale, to the base 10, is used. The original unit was the *bel*, named after Alexander Graham Bell (1847–1922), the Scottish inventor of the telephone.

The bel is graduated using a logarithmic scale, but as the bel is rather a large unit, the *decibel* (db) is more normally used (1 bel = 10 db). If threshold intensity is at 0 db, then a sound at ten times threshold intensity is 10 db, one at a hundred times threshold intensity is 20 db, one at a thousand times threshold intensity is 30 db, and so on. This means that the value of 1 W m^2 is at 120 db above threshold.

The ear canal resonates slightly to sounds with frequencies of about 3200 Hz. The human ear is

SEE ALSO

● WAVE THEORY p. 20
● OPTICS p. 24
● EARTHQUAKES p. 64
● THE SENSES p. 144
● SEEING THE INVISIBLE p. 210
● WHAT IS MUSIC? p. 330

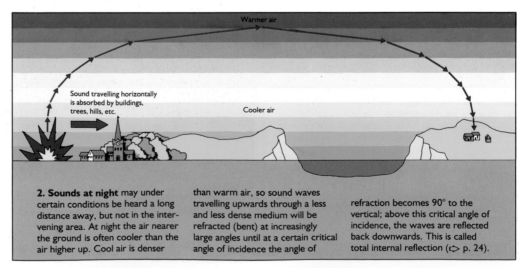

2. Sounds at night may under certain conditions be heard a long distance away, but not in the intervening area. At night the air nearer the ground is often cooler than the air higher up. Cool air is denser than warm air, so sound waves travelling upwards through a less and less dense medium will be refracted (bent) at increasingly large angles until at a certain critical angle of incidence the angle of refraction becomes 90° to the vertical; above this critical angle of incidence, the waves are reflected back downwards. This is called total internal reflection (▷ p. 24).

SONIC BOOMS

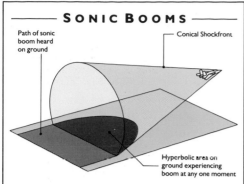

Path of sonic boom heard on ground

Conical Shockfront

Hyperbolic area on ground experiencing boom at any one moment

If the velocity of the source of the sound wave is greater than the velocity of sound – 300 m s⁻¹ (1080 km/h, or 670 mph) in the upper troposphere (up to 10 km / 6 mi above the Earth's surface) – then the wavefront produced is not spherical but conical. Different wave crests bunch together, forming a shock wave. A supersonic plane (travelling faster than the speed of sound) produces such a shockfront, causing a loud bang (a *sonic boom*) and large pressure variations.

most sensitive in the range 2500–4000 Hz. Even then, only about 10% of the population can hear a 0 db sound and then only in the 2500–4000 Hz region. The response of the ear is not linear, i.e. there is no direct relationship with the intensity of the sound it detects. Sensitivity is related to frequency: it decreases strongly at the lowest audible frequencies, but less so at the highest.

The audible range of the normal human ear varies with age. It is usually about 20–20 000 Hz in the mid-teens. For someone 40 years old, the upper limit is more likely to be 12 000–14 000 Hz. At the lower hearing threshold, the pressure fluctuations from the sound wave are about 3×10^{-10} of atmospheric pressure. The eardrum (called the *tympanic membrane*) vibrates at very low velocities – about 10 cm (4 in) per year. This may seem strange, given that it can vibrate at frequencies of up to 20 000 Hz (cycles per second); however, the low velocity is explained by the fact that the detected displacement of the air molecules adjacent to the eardrum each time it moves is less than the typical atomic radius (about 10^{-10} m). The human ear is an astonishingly sensitive detector and so it is not surprising that constant overload will bring deterioration in its performance.

Frequencies that are lower than the human audible range are referred to as *infrasonic*, and those above as *ultrasonic*. Some mammals such as dolphins and bats have sensitive hearing in the ultrasonic range, and they use high-pitched squeaks for echolocation (⊳ pp. 112 and 120–1). Large animals such as whales and elephants use frequencies in the infrasonic range to communicate over long distances. It is thought that migrating birds can detect infrasonic sounds produced by various natural features, and that they use the distinctive sounds produced by particular features as aids to navigation.

Characteristics of notes

There are three main characteristics of the notes played by musical instruments. *Loudness* would seem to be the most simple, but it is complicated by the non-linear response of the ear (⊳ above). At 100 Hz and 10 000 Hz the hearing threshold is about 40 db compared to the 0 db at 2500–4000 Hz. Thus the concept of loudness is not dependent

just on the energy reaching the ear, but also on frequency.

Pitch is closely related to frequency. If the frequency of vibration is doubled the pitch rises by one octave (⊳ pp. 330–1). In general, the higher the frequency the higher the pitch.

Sounds created by musical instruments are not simple waveforms, but are the result of several waves combining. This complexity results in the *tone quality* or *timbre* of a note played by a particular musical instrument. Even a 'pure' note may contain many waves of different frequencies. These frequencies are *harmonics* or *multiples* of the fundamental or lowest frequency, which has 2 nodes and 1 antinode, and is called the *first harmonic* (⊳ diagram 3, and p. 21). The *second harmonic* has 3 nodes and 2 antinodes. The wavelength is halved and the frequency is doubled. The *third harmonic* has 4 nodes and 3 antinodes. The wavelength is one third of the original wavelength, and the frequency has tripled. Different instruments emphasize different harmonics. Musical synthesizers are able to mimic instruments by mixing the appropriate harmonics electronically at various amplitudes.

3. Harmonics

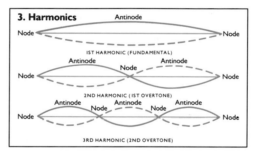

Antinode

Node — Node

1ST HARMONIC (FUNDAMENTAL)

Antinode — Antinode
Node — Node
Node — Node

2ND HARMONIC (1ST OVERTONE)

Antinode — Antinode — Antinode
Node — Node
Node — Node

3RD HARMONIC (2ND OVERTONE)

THE DOPPLER EFFECT

The Doppler effect (or Doppler shift) – first described by the Austrian physicist C.J. Doppler (1803–53) – is valid for all waves. It is more often noticed in acoustics and is particularly noticeable in the sirens used for emergency-service vehicles. The intensity and pitch of the siren seems to rise as the vehicle is approaching, then diminishes as it moves away.

This is explained by the fact that, as an observer moves towards a sound source, the pressure oscillations are encountered more frequently than if the observer were stationary. Thus the source seems to be emitting at a higher frequency. Conversely, if the observer is moving away from the source, the frequency seems to decrease. It also applies if the source is moving and the observer is stationary.

Horseshoe bats emit beams of sound at constant frequency; the frequency from different species of horseshoe bat varies in the range of about 40–120 kilohertz (kHz: 1 kHz = 1000 Hz). Applying the Doppler effect, the frequency of the echo returning to their ears after reflection from an

object depends on whether the bat and object are getting closer together or moving apart. The bats seem able to observe Doppler shifts of less than 1%. The nostrils are spaced a quarter of a wavelength apart so that along the *normal* – or perpendicular – to a line between the nostrils the waves are in phase and thus of maximum total amplitude. Thus the emitted sound is beamed straight in front.

The Doppler effect is also observed in optics, and has proved to be of profound significance in our understanding of the universe. If a stellar spectrum is compared with an arc or spark spectrum of an element present in the star, then its spectral lines may be displaced. A shift to the red end of the spectrum – to the longer wavelengths – means that the star is moving away from the Earth. The US astronomer Edwin Hubble (1889–1953) studied the red shift in various galaxies, and determined that their velocity of recession was proportional to their distance from the Earth. He thus confirmed that the universe appears to be expanding (⊳ pp. 2–3).

Optics

Optics is the branch of physics that deals with light, which is that small part of the electromagnetic spectrum (▷ pp. 26–7) that can be detected by the human eye. The wavelength of visible light extends from 700 nanometres (nm; 1 nm = 10^{-9} m) in the red region to 400 nm in the violet (▷ the prism, below). For many purposes light can be treated as a classical wave phenomenon (▷ pp. 20–1), but some effects can only be described by using the full quantum theory (▷ pp. 30–3).

A *beam* of light may be considered to be made up of many *rays*, all travelling outwards from the source. In geometric simplifications, as in the diagrams used here, rays of light are drawn as straight lines. The basic concept is very simple: light travels in straight lines unless it is reflected by a mirror or refracted (bent) by a lens or prism.

A point source of light emits rays in all directions. For an isolated point source in a vacuum the geometric wavefront will be a sphere (▷ p. 21). The variation of the speed of light in different materials must be taken into account – the speed of light (as of other electromagnetic waves) in a vacuum is 3×10^8 m s^{-1} (300 000 km or 186 000 miles per second), but it travels more slowly through other media. Light waves have transverse magnetic and electric fields (▷ p. 32).

Total internal reflection

Light is reflected and refracted in the same way as other waves (▷ pp. 20–1). When light travels from one medium to another less dense medium it is *deviated* or turned away from the *normal* – perpendicular to the interface at the point of incidence. This means the angle of refraction (*r*) is greater than the angle of incidence (*i*). When the angle of refraction is less than 90°, some of the incident light will be refracted and some will be reflected. If the angle of incidence increases, the angle of refraction will increase more. It is possible to increase the angle of incidence to such a value that eventually the refracted ray disappears and all the light is reflected. This is known as *total internal reflection* (▷ diagram 1).

The prism

White light (e.g. sunlight) is actually a mixture of monochromatic coloured lights – from red to violet – each with its own frequency and wavelength. This is demonstrated by shining a beam of white light through a *prism*, a block of glass with a triangular cross-section. Because the refractive index (▷ pp. 20–1) of optical glass is not the same for light of all frequencies, the light leaves the prism with the different frequencies bent (refracted) by different amounts – forming the familiar rainbow effect. The display of separated colours is called the *spectrum* of the original beam, and the effect of prisms on light is called *dispersion*.

The lens

A lens is a piece of transparent material made in a simple geometric shape. Usually at least one

surface is spherical, and often both are. In diagram 2 the features of lenses are described. A lens can produce an image of an object by refracting rays of light from the object.

Some rays are refracted more than others, depending on how they arrive at the surface of the lens. The lens affects the velocity of the rays, since light travels more slowly in a dense medium such as the lens than in a less dense medium such as air. In this way, the expanding geometric wavefront that is generated by the object is changed into a wavefront which, for a *convex* or *converging lens*, converges to a point behind the lens. If the object is located a long way from the lens (strictly an *infinite* distance, but a star is an excellent approximation for practical purposes) this point is known as the *rear focal point* or *principal focus* of the lens (▷ diagram 2). Notice that a lens has two principal foci – one on each side. The distance between the optical centre of the lens and the principal focus is the *focal length (f)*. If a point source of light is placed at the principal focus of the convex lens, the rays of light will be refracted to form a parallel beam.

Because of the effects of dispersion (▷ above), the distance from the lens at which red light and blue light from an object will be focused will be different. This can be demonstrated in the colour fringes that can be seen in simple hand magnifiers (small magnifying glasses). Such fringes are unacceptable in, for example, camera lenses. A lens made from two different types of glass can be made to bring two colours to exactly the same focus with only a very small variation for other frequencies. Such a lens is called *achromatic*. Single-element lenses are, therefore, only used for simple applications. Lenses for cameras, binoculars, telescopes and microscopes are made with many elements, with different curvatures. These lenses are made from glasses with different refractive indices and dispersions. The additional elements allow the lens designer greatly to reduce the faults or *aberrations* of the lens.

Mirrors

Mirrors are reflecting optical elements. Plane mirrors are used to deviate light beams without dispersion or to reverse or invert images. Curved mirrors, which usually have spherical or parabolic surfaces, can form images, and are often

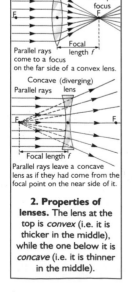

1. Total internal reflection. In the lower diagram, the angle of incidence (*i*) has become so large that the ray is not refracted but is reflected back into medium 1.

2. Properties of lenses. The lens at the top is *convex* (i.e. it is thicker in the middle), while the one below it is *concave* (i.e. it is thinner in the middle).

A rainbow is produced when white light shining from behind the observer is dispersed by spherical raindrops into its component colours – red, orange, yellow, green, blue, indigo and violet. In a double rainbow, the colours of the outer bow are reversed. (Spectrum)

─── **H O L O G R A M S** ───

A hologram is a 'three-dimensional' or stereoscopic image formed by two beams of light. Holography differs from conventional photography in that both the amplitude of the light and its phase (a measure of the relative distance the light has travelled from the object) are recorded on the film. It has many scientific uses as well as the more familiar display holograms now being used, for example, on credit cards.

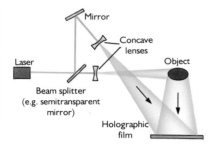

Recording a hologram. When light beams from sources such as lasers overlap they produce interference fringes due to the wave nature of light. A hologram is produced by recording the fringes from the interference of two beams of laser light. The reference beam (RB) falls directly onto the film, while the object beam (OB) is reflected from the object.

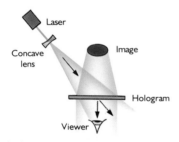

Replaying a hologram. When the hologram is replayed by shining a beam of laser light onto it, the light is diffracted in such a way that it appears to come from the position of the original object. The image can be viewed from a range of angles and is a true three-dimensional reconstruction of the object.

─── **L A S E R S** ───

The term 'laser' is derived from the technical name for the process – Light Amplification by Stimulated Emission of Radiation. *Stimulated emission* is the emission of a photon – a particle of light (▷ pp. 30–3).

When an amplifying material, such as a gas, crystal or liquid, is placed between appropriate mirrors, photons from a light beam repeatedly pass through it, stimulating more photons and thus increasing their number with each pass. The additional photons all have the same frequency, phase and direction. One of the mirrors is made so that a small amount of light passes through it; this is the external laser beam, which can be continuous or pulsed. This beam can be focused onto very small areas and the intensity – the ratio of power to area – can be very great, enabling some lasers to burn through thick metal plates. Lasers have a wide variety of uses, for example in surveying, communications and eye surgery.

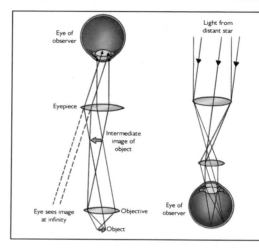

3. A rudimentary microscope. A small object placed close to the front focal point of the objective is greatly magnified. The eye views the intermediate image at infinity through the eyepiece.

4. The astronomical telescope magnifies the angular deviation of light rays from an infinitely distant object, such as a star. To the viewer this makes the star appear much closer.

with short focal length – is used to form a highly magnified image of a small object placed close to its focal point (▷ diagram 3). This can be viewed directly, by means of another lens called the *eyepiece*. It can also be recorded directly on film or viewed via a video camera.

The *telescope* is used to form an enlarged image of an infinitely distant object, and the enlarged image is viewed by the observer by means of an eyepiece (▷ diagram 4). The term 'infinite' is used relatively in this context: compared with the length of the telescope, the distance of the object can be considered as infinite. Telescopes are often made with reflecting mirrors instead of glass lenses, as large lenses sag under their own weight, thereby introducing distortions into the image. The primary mirror is often a large concave paraboloid.

Fibre optics

Light can be transmitted over great distances by the use of flexible glass fibres. These fibres are usually each less than 1 mm (1/25 in) in diameter, and can be used singly or in bunches. Each fibre consists of a small core surrounded by a layer of 'cladding' glass with a slightly lower refractive index. Certain rays experience total internal reflection (▷ above), and this, coupled with the very low absorption of modern silica glasses, allows light to travel very long distances with little reduction in intensity. Fibre optics provide the basis of endoscopy, a medical diagnostic technique in which fine fibres can be introduced into the body, enabling the physician to see what is going on. Fibre optics are also used extensively in telecommunications, as light in a fibre optic cable can carry more digital (on or off) signals with less loss of intensity than a copper wire carrying electrical digital signals (▷ pp. 208–9).

used in illumination systems such as car headlamps.

Mirrors can be coated with metals such as aluminium or silver, which have high reflectance for visible light (or gold for the infrared). Alternatively, they may be coated with many thin layers of non-metallic materials for very high reflectances over a more restricted range of frequencies. A freshly coated aluminium mirror will reflect about 90% of visible light. Special mirrors, such as those used in lasers (▷ box), can reflect over 99.7% of the light at one frequency.

Mirrors do not introduce any chromatic aberrations into optical systems. Those with large diameters are also lighter than glass lenses of equivalent size. For these reasons they are always used as the primary reflectors of large astronomical telescopes.

The microscope and the telescope

The *microscope* is a device for making very small objects visible. It was probably invented by a Dutch spectacle-maker, Zacharias Janssen (1580–1638), in 1609. Essentially, it is an elaboration of the simple magnifying glass. The *objective* – a lens

SEE ALSO

- THE HISTORY OF ASTRONOMY p. 10
- WAVE THEORY p. 20
- ELECTROMAGNETISM p. 26
- ATOMS AND SUBATOMIC PARTICLES p. 30
- QUANTUM THEORY AND RELATIVITY p. 32
- PHOTOGRAPHY p. 204
- RADIO AND TV p. 206
- TELECOMMUNICATIONS p. 208
- SEEING THE INVISIBLE p. 210

Electromagnetism

Electricity and magnetism were originally observed separately, but in the 19th century, scientists began to investigate their interaction. This work resulted in a theory that electricity and magnetism were both manifestations of a single force, the electromagnetic force.

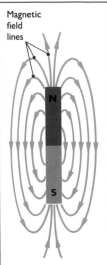

1. The magnetic field around a bar magnet can be plotted using a small compass, or by scattering iron filings on a sheet of paper placed above it.

The electromagnetic force is one of the fundamental forces of nature, the others being gravitational force (▷ pp. 14–15) and the strong and weak nuclear forces (▷ pp. 30–1). Recently the electromagnetic and weak forces have been shown to be manifestations of an electro-weak force. Magnetism has been known about since ancient times, but it was not until the late 18th century that the electric force was identified – by the French physicist Charles Augustin de Coulomb (1736–1806).

Magnetism

Metallic ores with magnetic properties were being used around 500 BC as compasses. It is now known that the Earth itself has magnetic properties (▷ pp. 60–1). Investigation of the properties of magnetic materials gave birth to the concept of *magnetic fields*, showing the force one magnet exerts on another (▷ diagram 1). An important feature of a magnet is that it has two poles, one of which is attracted to the Earth's magnetic north pole, while the other is attracted to the south pole. Conventionally, the north-seeking end of a magnet is called its *north pole*, and the other is the *south pole*. Magnets are identified by the fact that unlike or opposite poles (i.e. north and south) attract each other, while like poles (north and north, or south and south) repel each other. Magnetic effects are now known to be caused by

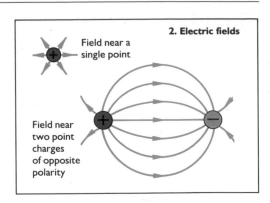

2. Electric fields

Field near a single point

Field near two point charges of opposite polarity

moving electric charges. Atomic electrons (▷ pp. 30–1) are in motion, and thus all atoms exhibit magnetic fields.

Static electric charges

In dry weather, a woollen sweater being pulled off over the hair of the wearer may crackle; sparks may even be seen. This is caused by an *electric charge*, which is the result of electrons being pulled from one surface to the other. Objects can gain an electric charge by being rubbed against another material.

There are two types of charge, associated with the negative and positive charges on electrons and protons respectively (▷ pp. 30–1). Similar electric charges (i.e. two positives, or two negatives) repel each other and unlike charges (i.e. a positive and a negative) attract.

The force of repulsion or attraction is known as the *electric force*. It is described by *Coulomb's law*, which states that the attractive (or repulsive) force (F) between two point (or spherically symmetrical) charges is given by:

$$F = k\frac{Q_1 Q_2}{r_2}$$

where k is a constant, Q_1 and Q_2 are the magnitudes of the charges, and r is the distance between them. The force acts along the direction of r. The unit of charge is called a *coulomb* (C) and is the quantity of electric charge carried past a given point in 1 second by a current of 1 ampere (▷ below).

Electric field

Arrows can be plotted to show the magnitude and direction of the magnetic force that acts at points around a magnet (▷ diagram 1), or the electric force that acts on a unit charge at each point. In the latter case, such a map (▷ diagram 2) would show the distribution of the electric field intensity. It is measured in terms of a force per unit charge, or newtons (▷ pp. 14–15) per coulomb.

In the same way that a mass may have gravitational potential energy because of its position (▷ p. 18), so a charge can have *electrical potential energy*. This potential per unit charge is measured in *volts* (V), named after the Italian physicist Alessandro Volta (1745–1827). The volt may be defined as follows: if one joule (▷ p. 18) is required to move 1 coulomb of electric charge between two points, then the *potential difference* between the points is 1 joule per coulomb = 1 volt. The electrical potential may vary with distance. This change may be measured in volts per metre (V m^{-1}).

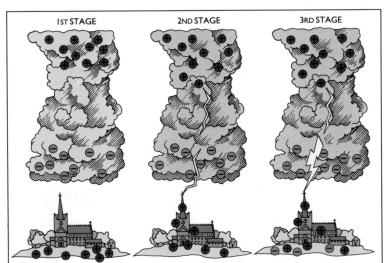

| 1ST STAGE | 2ND STAGE | 3RD STAGE |

3. How lightning is caused. In the *1st stage*, a net charge collects on top of the cloud, equal in polarity to the charge collecting on the surface of the Earth. A net charge of opposite polarity collects at the base of the cloud. In the *2nd stage*, if the cloud has become very large, discharges start to take place. A 'leader' (invisible to the naked eye) opens an ionized channel through the air – which will allow electricity to follow. In the *3rd stage*, the lightning strikes, following along the path made by the leader.

Electric current

Electric current consists of a flow of electrons (⊳ pp. 30–1), usually through a material but also through a vacuum, as in a cathode-ray tube in a TV set (⊳ pp. 206–7). Current flows when there is a potential difference or voltage (⊳ above) between two ends of a conductor (⊳ p. 29). Conventional current flows from the positive terminal to the negative terminal. However, electron flow is in fact from negative to positive.

For measurement purposes, an electric current is defined as the rate of flow of charge. The unit of electric current is the *ampere* (A), often abbreviated to amp:

1 ampere = 1 coulomb per second.

The ampere is named after the French physicist André Marie Ampère (1775–1836; ⊳ below). (More information on current, conductors, semiconductors and insulators will be found on p. 29.)

Electromagnetic fields

In 1820 the Danish physicist Hans Christiaan Oersted (1777–1851) discovered a connection between the electrical and magnetic forces (⊳ diagram 4). Shortly afterwards Ampère found a more fundamental relationship between the current in a wire and the magnetic field about it. This relationship has been applied to the Earth's magnetic field (⊳ pp. 60–1), which is thought to be generated by the motion of charged particles in the liquid iron part of the core.

Just as a moving charge generates a magnetic field, so a magnetic field can exert a force on a moving charge. For example, a magnet can be used to deflect a beam of electrons in a cathode-ray tube.

Electromagnetic induction

The next advance came in 1831, when the English physicist Michael Faraday (1791–1867) found that an electric current could be induced in a wire by another, changing current in a second wire. Faraday published his findings before the US physicist Joseph Henry (1797–1878), who had first made the same discovery. Faraday showed that the magnetic field at the wire had to be changing for an electric current to be produced. This may be done by changing the current in a

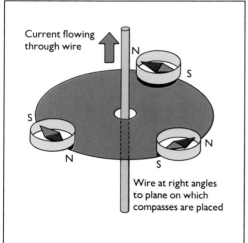

4. Oersted's discovery. When a current flows through a wire, magnetic compasses on a plane at right angles to the wire will be deflected until they are tangential to a circle drawn round the wire.

Current flowing through wire

Wire at right angles to plane on which compasses are placed

THE ELECTROMAGNETIC SPECTRUM

Prior to Maxwell's discoveries it had been known that light was a wave motion, although the type of wave motion had not been identified. Maxwell was able to show that the oscillations were of the electric and magnetic field. Hertz's waves had a wavelength of about 60 cm; thus they were of much longer wavelength than light waves.

Nowadays we recognize a spectrum of electromagnetic radiation that extends from about 10^{-15} m to 10^9 m. It is subdivided into smaller, sometimes overlapping, ranges. The extension of astronomical observations from visible to other electromagnetic wavelengths has revolutionized our knowledge of the universe (⊳ pp. 11 and 210).

Radio waves have a large range of wavelengths – from a few millimetres up to several kilometres (⊳ p. 206).

Microwaves are radio waves with shorter wavelengths, between 1 mm and 30 cm. They are used in radar and microwave ovens.

Infrared waves of different wavelengths are radiated by bodies at different temperatures. (Bodies at higher temperatures radiate either visible or ultraviolet waves.) The Earth and its atmosphere, at a mean temperature of 250 K ($-23\,°C$ or $-9.4\,°F$) radiates infrared waves with wavelengths centred at about 10 micrometres (μm) or 10^{-5} m ($1\,\mu$m $= 10^{-6}$ m).

Visible waves have wavelengths of 400–700 nanometres (nm; 1 nm $= 10^{-9}$ m). The peak of the solar radiation (temperature of about 6000 K / 6270 °C / 11 323 °F) is at a wavelength of about 550 nm, where the human eye is at its most sensitive.

Ultraviolet waves have wavelengths from about 380 nm down to 60 nm. The radiation from hotter stars (above 25 000 K / 25 000 °C / 45 000 °F is shifted towards the violet and ultraviolet parts of the spectrum.

X-rays have wavelengths from about 10 nm down to 10^{-4} nm.

Gamma rays have wavelengths less than 10^{-11} m. They are emitted by certain radioactive nuclei and in the course of some nuclear reactions.

Note that the *cosmic rays* continually bombarding the Earth from outer space are not electromagnetic waves, but high-speed protons and x-particles (i.e. nuclei of hydrogen and helium atoms; ⊳ pp. 30–1), together with some heavier nuclei.

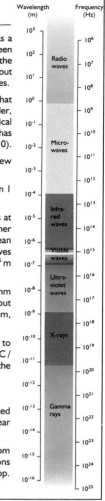

Wavelength (m)		Frequency (Hz)
10^3		10^6
10^2	Radio waves	10^7
10^1		10^8
10^0		10^9
10^{-1}	Micro-waves	10^{10}
10^{-2}		10^{11}
10^{-3}		10^{12}
10^{-4}		10^{13}
10^{-5}	Infra-red waves	10^{14}
10^{-6}		10^{15}
10^{-7}	Visible waves	10^{16}
10^{-8}	Ultra-violet waves	10^{17}
10^{-9}		10^{18}
10^{-10}	X-rays	10^{19}
10^{-11}		10^{20}
10^{-12}		10^{21}
10^{-13}	Gamma rays	10^{22}
10^{-14}		10^{23}
10^{-15}		10^{24}
10^{-16}		10^{25}

---

second wire, by moving a magnet relative to the wire, or by moving the wire relative to a magnet. This last technique is that employed in a dynamo generator, while an electric motor uses the reverse process (⊳ pp. 28–9).

Maxwell's theory

The work of the Scottish physicist James Clerk Maxwell (1831–79) on electromagnetism is of immense importance for physics. It united the separate concepts of electricity and magnetism in terms of a new *electromagnetic force*. In 1864 Maxwell proposed that a magnetic field could also be caused by a changing electric field. Thus, when either an electric or magnetic field is changing, a field of the other type is induced. Maxwell predicted that electrical oscillations (as when an electric current in a wire changes) would generate *electromagnetic waves* – waves in which the electric and magnetic field components are perpendicular to each other and to the direction of propagation. When he calculated the speed of these waves he found that it was equal to the speed of light in a vacuum (⊳ p. 24). This suggested that light might be electromagnetic in nature – a theory that was later confirmed in various ways.

The existence of electromagnetic waves was demonstrated experimentally in 1887 by the German physicist Heinrich Rudolf Hertz (1857–94) – who also gave his name to the unit of frequency (⊳ p. 20).

SEE ALSO

- THE UNIVERSE AND COSMO-LOGY p. 2
- STARS AND GALAXIES p. 4
- WAVE THEORY p. 20
- OPTICS p. 24
- ELECTRICITY IN ACTION p. 28
- ATOMS AND SUBATOMIC PARTICLES p. 30
- QUANTUM THEORY AND RELATIVITY p. 32
- RADIO AND TV p. 206
- SEEING THE INVISIBLE p. 210

Electricity in Action

Electric current is the flow of electrons through a conductor. The first source of a steady electric current was demonstrated by the Italian physicist Alessandro Volta (1745–1827) in 1800. His original *voltaic pile* used chemical energy to produce an electric current. The pile consisted of a series of pairs of metal plates (one of silver and one of zinc) piled on top of each other, each pair sandwiching a piece of cloth soaked in a dilute acid solution (▷ also box, pp. 44–5).

The same principle is still used in the modern electric *cell* (▷ diagram 1). The plates are called *electrodes* and must be made of dissimilar metals. Alternatively, one may be made of carbon. The positive electrode – the one from which electrons flow inside the cell – is called the *anode*. The negative electrode is the *cathode*. The acid solution is called the *electrolyte* and in a dry cell is absorbed into a paste (▷ diagram 2). A number of cells connected in a series (positive to negative) is called a *battery* and will give a higher voltage than a single cell. Some batteries, known as *accumulators*, are designed so that they can be 'recharged' by the passage of an electric current back through them. Similar principles as those used in cells are used in electrolysis and electroplating (▷ pp. 40–1).

Circuitry

A circuit is a complete conductive path between positive and negative terminals; conventionally current flows from positive to negative, although the direction of electron flow (▷ pp. 26–7) is actually from negative to positive. When electrical components such as bulbs and switches are joined end to end the arrangement is a *series* connection. When they are connected side by side, this is called *parallel* connection (▷ diagram 3).

Power

Power is the rate at which a body or system does work (work and its unit, the joule, are defined on p. 18). The power in an electric conductor is measured in *watts* (W), named after the British engineer James Watt (1736–1819). One watt is one joule per second, or the energy used per second by a current of one amp flowing between two points with a potential difference of one volt (volts and amps are defined on pp. 26–7). In an electric conductor the power (W) is the product of the current (I) and the voltage (V): $W = IV$.

Resistance

When an electric current passes through a conductor there is a force that acts to reduce or *resist* the flow. This is called the *resistance* and is dependent upon the nature of the conductor and its dimensions. The unit of resistance is the ohm (Ω), named after the German physicist Georg Simon Ohm (1787–1854). He discovered a relationship between the current (I), voltage (V) and resistance (R) in a conductor: $V = IR$. This is known as *Ohm's law*.

Resistance has various useful applications. When electrons pass through a wire they cause the atoms in it to vibrate and generate heat – the greater the resistance, the greater the heat generated. This effect is used in electric heating devices, in which special tough resistance wire glows red hot when a suitable current is passed through it. Similarly, in light bulbs, the filament is a fine coiled tungsten wire of high resistance that glows white hot. The same principle is used in a fuse, in which low-resistance wire with a low melting point is used to prevent a circuit from being overloaded. If too much current flows the fuse wire will overheat and melt, breaking the circuit.

However, in many cases it is desirable to reduce resistance – and hence energy loss – to a minimum. In 1911 it was discovered that below a certain critical temperature, various metals show zero resistance to current flow. This phenomenon is called *superconductivity*. Once current is started in a closed circuit, it keeps flowing as long as the circuit is kept cold. For most metals the critical temperature is impractically low – around 1.19 K (−272 °C/−457 °F). But recently various new kinds of man-made materials have been developed that show superconductivity at significantly higher temperatures. These developments promise enormous savings in energy.

AC, DC, generators and motors

There are two types of current electricity. The type produced by a battery is *direct current* (DC), in which there is a constant flow of electrons in one direction. The type used in most electrical appliances is *alternating current* (AC), in which

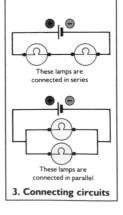

1. A simple cell. The lamp lights but soon goes out because bubbles of hydrogen cling to the copper electrode, thus decreasing the output of the cell. This is known as polarizing. The zinc electrode is eventually eaten away.

Electrolyte of dilute sulphuric acid

Lamp

Copper electrode

Zinc electrode

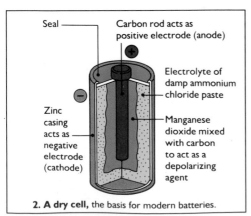

Seal

Carbon rod acts as positive electrode (anode)

Electrolyte of damp ammonium chloride paste

Zinc casing acts as negative electrode (cathode)

Manganese dioxide mixed with carbon to act as a depolarizing agent

2. A dry cell, the basis for modern batteries.

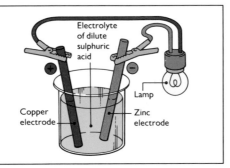

These lamps are connected in series

These lamps are connected in parallel

3. Connecting circuits

the direction of flow of electrons alternates. The frequency of alternating current can vary over an enormous range. The electric mains operate at 50 Hz (cycles per second) in the UK and Europe, and at 60 Hz in the USA. Most of today's electricity is produced by AC generators.

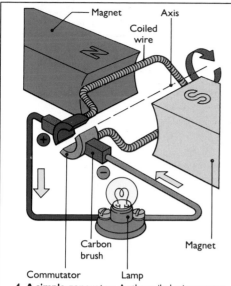

4. A simple generator. As the coiled wire rotates within the magnetic field, an electrical current is induced within the circuit, illuminating the lamp. This simple device shows the basic principle by which all electricity is generated.

Labels: Magnet, Axis, Coiled wire, Carbon brush, Magnet, Commutator, Lamp

A *dynamo* (⊳ diagram 4) is an electrical current generator, consisting of a coil that is rotated in a magnetic field by some external means. This is based on Faraday's discovery of electrical induction (⊳ pp. 26–7). In most generators, the source of rotation is a turbine, powered by a variety of sources of energy (⊳ pp. 188–91). Different types of generator produce either AC or DC current, while *alternators* (used to charge car batteries) produce AC current that is then rectified to DC current using semiconductor diodes (⊳ below).

An *electric motor* is a similar device to a generator, but works in reverse. An electric current is applied to the coil windings, causing rotation of the *armature*, which consists of a shaft on which are mounted electromagnet windings.

Electron emission

If the filament of a light bulb is heated, the energy of some of the electrons in the filament is greatly increased by thermal motion, although the average increase for all the electrons is very small. If their energy reaches an adequate level, many are able to escape; this process is called *thermionic emission*. If another electrode is put in the evacuated bulb and placed at a higher potential than the filament, this will act as an anode and will attract electrons towards it. A current will then flow in an external circuit; the device thus formed is called a *diode*. If a third electrode in the shape of a grid is placed in the tube between the filament and the anode, then the anode current is so sensitive to changes in the grid voltage that the whole device, called a *triode*, can act as an amplifier (⊳ also transistors below). Electrons are also emitted from the surface of a metal if light of a sufficiently high frequency is shone onto it. This is the *photoelectric effect* (⊳ pp. 32–3).

Conductors and semiconductors

A metal consists of an array of positive ions in a 'sea' of free electrons. The electrons move randomly, but when a potential difference is applied across a metal the electrons migrate freely through the material. Metals are good *conductors* of electricity because there are always many unoccupied quantum states into which electrons can move (⊳ pp. 32–3). Non-metallic solids and liquids have nearly all their quantum states occupied by electrons, so it is difficult to produce large currents. If the numbers of unoccupied states and of electrons free to move into them are small the material is an *insulator*. If there are more free electrons and unoccupied states than in an insulator, but fewer than in a conductor, the substance is called a *semiconductor*.

The metal-like elements silicon and germanium are the two semiconductors used most frequently. These may be 'doped' with an impurity to modify their conduction behaviour – n-type doping increases the number of free electrons, p-type increases the number of unoccupied states. Most semiconductor devices are made from materials that are partly p-type and partly n-type. The boundary between them is known as a *p–n junction*. Such a device, called a *semiconductor diode*, will act as a *rectifier*, a device used to convert alternating current to direct current. A *transistor* consists of semiconductor material in n–p–n or p–n–p form. Transistors (first introduced in 1948) can act both as switches and as amplifiers, and have replaced the much more cumbersome valves. An *amplifier* is a device that boosts electrical signals using energy from a separate source. An *integrated circuit* consists of many transistors and other components embedded in a chip of silicon.

In some materials, such as gallium arsenide, a p–n junction will emit light whenever an electric current passes through it. This device is called a *light-emitting diode*. These are used in digital displays in clocks and radios. The light is emitted when an electron and hole meet at the junction and annihilate each other.

Solar cells

The *photovoltaic effect* occurs when light is absorbed by a p–n or n–p junction. Electrons are liberated at the junction by an incident photon and diffuse through the n-type region. The hole drifts through the p-type layer until it recombines with an electron flowing round the external circuit. The first practical photovoltaic device – called a *solar cell* – was made in 1954. In essence a solar cell is a light-emitting diode acting in reverse – it converts light into electric current, which is the basis of solar power (⊳ pp. 190–1).

SEE ALSO

- ELECTROMAGNETISM p. 26
- ATOMS AND SUBATOMIC PARTICLES p. 30
- QUANTUM THEORY AND RELATIVITY p. 32
- CHEMICAL REACTIONS p. 40
- METALS p. 44
- ENERGY pp. 188–91
- RADIO AND TV p. 206
- TELECOMMUNICATIONS p. 208
- COMPUTERS p. 210

TRANSFORMERS

If two insulated coils of wire are wound on the same soft iron core and an alternating current is passed through one of the coils, a current will be induced in the other coil. The ratio of the numbers of turns on the input coil (N_1) and the output coil (N_2) will determine the ratio of the output voltage (V_2) to the input voltage (V_1). The relationship is:

$$\frac{V_2}{V_1} = \frac{N_2}{N_1}$$

In this way transformers can either step voltage up or step it down. Note that they have the reverse effect on current. This principle is used for efficient long-distance power transmission (⊳ p. 188).

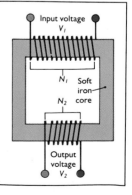

Labels: Input voltage V_1, N_1, Soft iron core, N_2, Output voltage V_2

Atoms
and Subatomic Particles

Of the fundamental forces that are important in the natural world, the gravitational force (▷ pp. 14–15) is the dominant long-range force when the motion of planets and other celestial bodies is considered. When the smallest entities are investigated, the other fundamental forces – the electromagnetic force (▷ pp. 26–7), the *strong force* (which holds together the atomic nucleus) and the *weak force* (which is involved in nuclear decay) – become important.

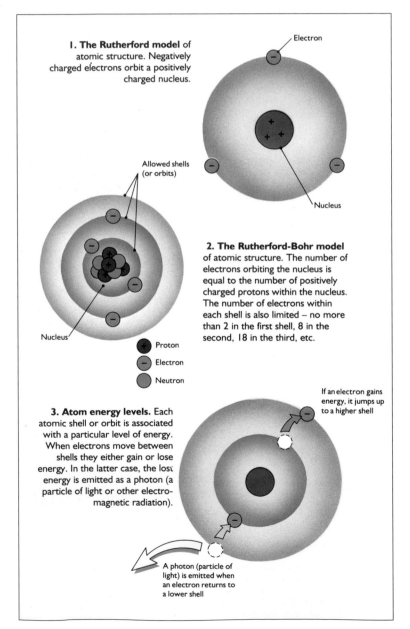

I. The Rutherford model of atomic structure. Negatively charged electrons orbit a positively charged nucleus.

Electron

Allowed shells (or orbits)

Nucleus

Nucleus

Proton

Electron

Neutron

2. The Rutherford-Bohr model of atomic structure. The number of electrons orbiting the nucleus is equal to the number of positively charged protons within the nucleus. The number of electrons within each shell is also limited – no more than 2 in the first shell, 8 in the second, 18 in the third, etc.

3. Atom energy levels. Each atomic shell or orbit is associated with a particular level of energy. When electrons move between shells they either gain or lose energy. In the latter case, the lost energy is emitted as a photon (a particle of light or other electromagnetic radiation).

If an electron gains energy, it jumps up to a higher shell

A photon (particle of light) is emitted when an electron returns to a lower shell

The word *atom* is derived from an ancient Greek word for a particle of matter so small it cannot be split up. In his atomic theory of 1803, the British chemist John Dalton (1766–1844) defined the atom as the smallest particle of an element (▷ p. 36) that retained its chemical properties. Various phenomena could be explained using this hypothesis – which still holds good today.

Atomic structure

However, no physical description of the atom was available until after the discovery of the *electron* in 1897 by the British physicist J.J. Thompson (1856–1940). The nuclear atom was proposed by the English physicist Ernest Rutherford (1871–1937) in 1911 (▷ diagram 1). His model consists of a small but dense central *nucleus*, which is positively charged, surrounded by negatively charged electrons. Rutherford suggested that the electrons orbited the nucleus, and that the force of their angular velocity in their orbits was sufficient to counteract the attractive force of the oppositely charged nucleus. The nucleus contains over 99.9% of the mass of the atom, but its diameter is of the order of 10^{-15} m – compared to the much larger size (about 10^{-10} m) of the atom.

A fundamental objection to Rutherford's model was raised by the Danish physicist Niels Bohr (1885–1962). Bohr pointed out that an electron moving in a circular orbit is continuously accelerating (▷ pp. 14–15), and that an accelerating charge must radiate energy in the form of electromagnetic waves (▷ p. 27). If the electron were to radiate energy continuously, it would lose energy and collide into the nucleus, so no permanent orbit could exist.

To overcome this problem Bohr proposed that the electrons only moved round the nucleus in certain allowable orbits or shells (▷ diagram 2), each with its own energy level, and that while in these orbits they do not emit radiation. Radiation such as light would only be emitted when an electron jumps from one allowed level to another of lower energy (▷ diagram 3). Thus electrons would not lose energy continuously, but only in *photons* or *quanta* (discrete amounts; ▷ p. 32) equivalent to the difference in energies between allowed orbits. Drawing on the theory of wave-particle duality (▷ p. 32), the Austrian physicist Erwin Schrödinger (1887–1961) refined Bohr's model further. He suggested that the allowable orbits had to have a circumference that was a multiple of the electron's wavelength.

Nuclear structure

With the exception of the hydrogen atom, which only contains one proton, atomic nuclei contain a mixture of protons and neutrons, collectively known as *nucleons*. The *proton* carries a positive charge, equal in magnitude to that of the negatively charged electron. The *neutron* is of similar size but is electrically neutral. Each has a mass about 1836 times that of the electron (which has a rest mass of 9.11×10^{-31} kg). The protons and neutrons in the atomic nucleus are held tightly together by the *strong nuclear force*, which overcomes the much weaker electromagnetic force of repulsion between positively charged protons.

It is possible for atoms of the same element to contain equal numbers of protons but different numbers of neutrons in their nuclei – these different atoms are called *isotopes*. Isotopes of an element contain the same nuclear charge, and their chemical properties are identical, but they display different physical properties. An isotope may be represented in various ways, such as uranium-235, U-235 or ^{235}U.

Radioactivity

Radiation – either as a spontaneous emission of particles or as an electromagnetic wave – may occur from certain substances. This is *radioactivity*. The three types of radiation are from alpha decay, beta decay and gamma decay.

In *alpha (α) decay* nuclei of helium are produced that each contain two neutrons and two protons. These are called *alpha-particles* and are formed in spontaneous decay of the parent nucleus. Thus uranium-238 decays to thorium-234 with emission of an alpha-particle.

In *beta (β) decay* the emitted particles are either electrons or *positrons* (identical to the electron but with a positive charge). The parent nucleus retains the same number of nucleons but its charge varies by plus or minus 1. In these processes another kind of particle – either a *neutrino* or an *antineutrino* – is produced. The neutrino has no charge and a mass that – if it could be measured at rest – would probably be zero.

In *gamma (γ) decay* high-energy photons (⯈ p. 32) may be produced in a process of radioactive decay if the resultant nucleus jumps from an excited energy state to a lower energy state.

The rate at which radioactive decay takes place depends only on the number of radioactive nuclei that are present. Thus the *half-life*, or the time taken for half a given number of radioactive nuclei to decay, is characteristic for that type of nucleus. The isotope carbon-14 has a half-life of 5730 years, and measurement of its decay is used in carbon-dating of organic material. Decay can result in a series of new elements being produced, each of which may in its turn decay until a stable state is achieved.

Nuclear particles

Over 200 elementary particles are now known. They may be divided into two types: hadrons and leptons. *Hadrons* are heavy particles that are affected by the strong force. *Leptons* are generally light particles, such as electrons and neutrinos (⯈ above), that are not subject to the strong force. A further very important distinction is that between fermions and bosons. *Fermions* have a permanent existence, whereas *bosons* can be produced and destroyed freely. Leptons are fermions.

Every type of particle is thought to have a companion *antiparticle*, that is, a particle with the same mass but opposite in some other characteristic such as charge. Thus the positron with positive charge is the antiparticle of the negatively charged electron. Some particles such as the photon may be their own antiparticles.

Whilst the leptons are thought to be fundamental particles, the hadrons are thought to be made up of *quarks*. Quarks may have fractional electrical charge. It is probable that free quarks do not exist. If three quarks combine, the resulting hadron is called a *baryon*; if a quark and antiquark combine the result is called a *meson*. A meson is a boson; it is a short-lived particle that jumps between protons and neutrons, thus holding them together. A pattern of hadrons may be drawn up based on combinations of different types of quark. This pattern is called the *eight-*

FISSION AND FUSION

Nuclear power comes from either of two processes – fission and fusion, which are both forms of *nuclear reaction*. In the *fission* process (⯈ diagram 4) a large nucleus, such as uranium-235 (^{235}U), splits to form two smaller nuclei that have greater binding energies than the original uranium. Thus energy is given out in the process. Fission is used in nuclear reactors (⯈ pp. 188–9) and in atomic weapons (⯈ p. 181). There are other isotopes in addition to uranium-235, such as plutonium-239, that give rise to fission.

In the *fusion* process (⯈ diagram 5), two light nuclei fuse together to form two particles, one larger and one smaller than the original nuclei. Usually one of them is sufficiently strongly bound to give a great release of energy. The fusion of hydrogen to form helium is a power source in stars such as the Sun (⯈ p. 6), although the solar fusion process differs in detail from the simpler process described. Nuclear fusion is the basis of the hydrogen bomb (⯈ p. 181), and research is continuing into the possible use of fusion in power generation (⯈ p. 189).

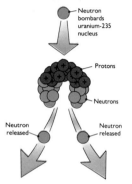

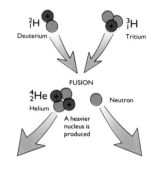

4. Nuclear fission. A neutron bombards the uranium-235 nucleus, causing it to split and release energy when the strong nuclear force is broken. Two lighter nuclei are formed and these are also radioactive. The neutrons released may bombard and split other nuclei – further fission can take place. A *chain reaction* will be set up if the mass of uranium-235 is above a certain level – the *critical mass*.

5. Nuclear fusion occurs when two small nuclei collide and combine, breaking the weak nuclear force and releasing energy. The reaction shown involves nuclei of deuterium and tritium (isotopes of hydrogen) combining to produce helium (a waste product), a neutron, and released energy. This type of reaction releases considerably more energy than a fission process for a given mass of material. However, the neutrons released have to be contained or controlled in some way.

NUCLEAR ACCELERATORS

Accelerators are large machines that accelerate particle beams to very high speeds, so enabling research into particle physics. Electric fields are used to accelerate the particles, either in a straight line (*linear accelerator*) or in a circle (*cyclotron, synchrotron* or *synchrocyclotron*). Powerful magnetic fields are used to guide the beams. Energy levels of the particles may be as high as several hundred giga electronvolts. An electronvolt (eV) is the increase in energy of an electron when it undergoes a rise in potential of 1 volt: $1 \text{ eV} = 1.6 \times 10^{-19}$ joules (J). Nuclear accelerators have provided experimental evidence for the existence of numerous subatomic particles predicted in theory.

fold way, and has successfully predicted the existence of particles subsequently discovered. There are believed to be six types or *flavours* of quark – up, down, charmed, strange, top and bottom.

Quarks carry electrical charge and another type of charge called *colour*. The force associated with the colour charge binds the quarks together and is thought to be the source of the strong force binding the hadrons together. Thus the colour force is the more fundamental force. The weak force is associated with the radioactive beta-decay of some nuclei. It has been shown – in the theory of the *electroweak* force – that the electromagnetic and weak forces are linked. This theory predicted the existence of the W and Z° particles, which have since been discovered.

SEE ALSO

- ELECTROMAGNETISM p. 26
- ELECTRICITY IN ACTION p. 28
- QUANTUM THEORY AND RELATIVITY p. 32
- ELEMENTS AND THE PERIODIC TABLE p. 36
- CHEMICAL BONDS p. 38
- NUCLEAR WEAPONS p. 181
- ENERGY 1 p. 188

Quantum Theory and Relativity

Three of the most important theories of the 20th century are the quantum theory and the theories of special and general relativity. When special relativity is combined with the full quantum theory and with electromagnetism (▷ p. 26), almost all of the physical world is described by it. The most important application is in the theory of subatomic particles (▷ also pp. 30–1). General relativity is as yet not fully combined with quantum theory and is a theory of gravity and cosmology.

The physical world is not as simple as the theories of Newton supposed (▷ pp. 14–15), although such views are appropriate simplifications for large objects moving relatively slowly with respect to the observer. Quantum mechanics is the only correct description of effects on an atomic scale, and special relativity must be used when speeds approaching the speed of light, with respect to the observer, are involved.

The development of quantum theory

At the very beginning of the 20th century scientists such as the German physicist Max Planck (1858–1947) discovered that the theories of classical physics were not sufficient to explain certain phenomena on the subatomic scale, particularly in the field of electromagnetic radiation (▷ p. 27) and the study of light waves. Their work resulted in the development of the quantum theory, which states that nothing can be measured or observed without disturbing it: the observer can affect the outcome of the effect being measured.

If light is directed onto a piece of metal in a vacuum, electrons (▷ p. 30) are knocked from the surface of the metal. This is the *photoelectric effect*. For light of a given wavelength, the number of electrons emitted per second increases with the intensity of the light, although the energies of the electrons are independent of the wavelength.

This discovery led Einstein (▷ below) to deduce that the energy in a light beam exists in small, discrete (i.e. indivisible) 'packets' called *photons* or *quanta*. These can be detected in experiments in which light is allowed to fall on a detector, usually photographic film. This has led to the theory of the *dual nature of light*, which behaves as a wave during interference experiments (▷ diagram 1 and pp. 20–1) but as a stream of particles during the photoelectric effect. Further work on this phenomenon has led to the acceptance of *wave-particle duality*, which is a fundamental principle in quantum physics. The way a system is described depends upon the apparatus with which it is interacting: light behaves as a wave when it passes through slits in an interference experiment, but as a stream of particles when it hits a detector (▷ diagram 2).

Just as light waves can behave like particles, so subatomic particles such as electrons can in certain circumstances behave like waves. This idea, first suggested by the French physicist Louis Victor de Broglie (1892–1987), was subsequently confirmed by experiments, and applied in Schrödinger's model of atomic structure (▷ p. 30).

Uncertainty

The German physicist Werner Karl Heisenberg (1901–76) proposed that when a beam of light is directed at a screen with two slits, the interference pattern formed exists only if we do not know which slit the photon passed through. If we make an additional measurement and determine which slit was traversed, we destroy the interference pattern. Heisenberg showed that it was impossible to measure position and momentum simultaneously with infinite accuracy; he expressed his findings in the *uncertainty principle* named after him. This changed the thinking about the precision with which simultaneous measurements of two physical quantities can be made.

Quantum mechanics

Quantum mechanics is the study of the observable behaviour of particles. This includes electromagnetic radiation in all its details (▷ p. 27). In particular, it is the only appropriate theory for describing the effects that occur on an atomic scale.

Quantum mechanics deals exclusively with what can be observed, and does not attempt to describe what is happening between measurements. This is not true of classical theories, which are essentially complete descriptions of what is occurring whether or not attempts are made to measure it. In quantum mechanics the experimenter is directly included in the theory. Quantum mechanics predicts all the possible results of making a measurement, but it does not say which one will occur when an experiment is actually carried out. All that can be known is the probability of something being seen. In some experiments one

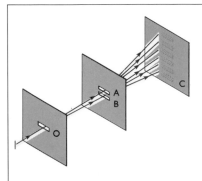

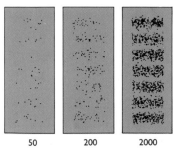

1. Interference. The waves passing through slits A and B and reaching the screen C will be either in phase or out of phase and will either reinforce or cancel each other (▷ diagrams 10 and 11, pp. 20–1). The result is a series of light and dark bands on the screen. Reinforcement occurs when the path difference is a whole number of wavelengths.

2. The photon nature of light. The results of two-slit interference after the passage of 50, 200 and 2000 photons have passed through. The characteristic pattern is only observed after many photons have passed. The initial results appear random.

event is very much more likely than any other, therefore most of the time this is what will be found, but sometimes one of the less probable events will occur. It is impossible to predict which will occur; the only way to find out is by making the appropriate measurement. For example, in an isotope of the element americium, 19% of the nuclei decay purely by alpha-particle emission (▷ p. 31) and 81% decay by alpha emission followed by photon emission. For any individual americium nucleus it is not possible to say which decay will occur, only what will be observed on average. In some experiments the same event can occur in different ways. What is measured depends on whether it is known which of the possible paths was taken. Thus any additional knowledge, which can only be gained by making an additional measurement, changes the outcome of the first experiment.

Special relativity

Relativity is based on the idea that all motion is relative to the observer. For example, a person who raises a flag on a ship moving with a constant velocity only observes the upward movement of the flag, whereas to a stationary observer on the shore the flag will also be seen to be moving forward. This is why physical laws such as Newton's laws of mechanics (▷ pp. 14–15) are stated with respect to some *frame of reference* that allows physical quantities such as velocity and acceleration to be defined. This frame of reference has to be non-accelerating and without a gravitational field; this is called an *inertial frame*.

Given that the universe offers no fixed point of reference, the German physicist Albert Einstein (1879–1955) proposed that all inertial frames are equivalent – the laws of physics are the same in all such frames. He also stated, on the basis of experimental evidence, that the velocity of light (and of all other electromagnetic radiation) in a vacuum (▷ p. 22) is a constant, independent of the velocity of the observer. For example, if a car coming towards you flashes its headlights at the same time and at the same distance from you as a stationary car, both light beams will travel at the same velocity and arrive at the same time. This would not be the case if two bullets were fired simultaneously from a moving and stationary car; the bullet from the moving car would travel faster.

The equivalence of inertial frames and the finite nature of the velocity of light led Einstein to develop the theory of special relativity in 1905. Special relativity forces us to modify the classical concepts of mass, energy, space and time.

If a spaceship were able to travel relative to the Earth at a velocity approaching that of light, an Earth-bound observer would detect that the spaceship had increased its mass and decreased its length (in the direction of travel) compared to when it was stationary. However, if the pilot in the spaceship were to measure these quantities, he would find that they had not changed. Time aboard the fast-moving spaceship would also appear to the Earth-bound observer to be moving more slowly, although again this would not be apparent to the pilot. These predictions have been supported by experiment. When sub-atomic particles approach the velocity of light in a nuclear accelerator (▷ p. 31), their increase in

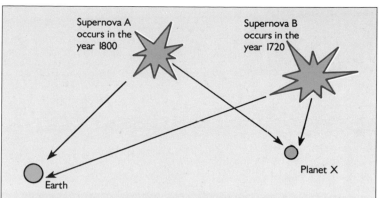

Relative time. Supernova A occurs 120 light years from Earth (i.e. light takes 120 years to travel from Supernova A to Earth), and Supernova B is 200 light years from Earth. From Earth the two events are observed simultaneously in 1920, even though Supernova B occurred 80 years before Supernova A. From Planet X, in contrast, the two events are not observed simultaneously. Planet X is only 40 light years from Supernova B, but 150 light years from Supernova A. Therefore, on Planet X, Supernova B is observed in 1760, while Supernova A is not seen until 1950.

mass has been measured; and highly accurate atomic clocks have detected a minuscule 'slowing down' of time in aircraft flying at supersonic speeds.

Taken to its ultimate, if the spaceship were to reach the velocity of light, to the Earth-bound observer its mass would appear infinite, its length zero, and time on the spaceship would seem to come to a standstill. This is why it is theoretically impossible for anything to travel faster than light. The fact that time is related to the frame of reference in which it is being measured means that time and space have to be considered as unified – as *space-time* – and not as two separate things.

General relativity

General relativity is an extension of the theory of special relativity to include gravitational fields and accelerating reference frames. Gravitational fields arise because of the distortions of space-time in the vicinity of large masses, and space-time is no longer thought of as having an existence independent of the mass in the universe. Rather, space-time, mass and gravity are interdependent. The concept of 'curved space-time' was put forward by Einstein in his general theory of relativity (1915). The motion of astronomical bodies is controlled by this deformation or curvature of space and time close to large masses. Light is also bent by the gravitational fields of large masses. Light rays have been observed to bend as they pass close to the Sun, so providing experimental verification of Einstein's theories.

SEE ALSO

- MOTION AND FORCE p. 14
- WAVE THEORY p. 20
- ELECTROMAGNETISM p. 26
- ATOMS AND SUBATOMIC PARTICLES p. 30

$E = mc^2$

The gain in mass that occurs in a body moving at high speed led Einstein to conclude that the energy (E) and mass (m) of a body are equivalent. He derived a formula to relate them – the well-known $E = mc^2$, where c is the speed of light. Given the magnitude of c, it is apparent that a small amount of mass is equivalent to a large amount of energy. This is the basis of nuclear power (▷ fission and fusion, p. 31). Perhaps the most elegant verification of the theory of equivalence is shown by the annihilation at rest of an electron and a positron into two gamma rays (▷ pp. 30–1), each with an energy equal to the particle rest mass.

What is Chemistry?

In modern chemistry, the philosopher's stone of the alchemists (▷ box) has been replaced by a fundamental belief in the importance of understanding the physical laws that govern the behaviour of atoms and molecules. Such an understanding has resulted in the development of methods for converting cheaply available and naturally occurring minerals, gases and oils into substances that have high commercial or social value.

During the last 150 years this approach has completely transformed our world. The discovery that iron could be made into steel (▷ p. 198) by chemical means played a major part in the Industrial Revolution. In the 20th century, spectacular increases in the yields of cereals from an acre of farmland can be traced to the discovery in Germany in 1908 that nitrogen from air could be converted into ammonia fertilizers. Similarly, the greater understanding of the structures and reactions of carbon-based (organic) compounds has resulted in products such as medicines and synthetic fibres (▷ pp. 199–200) that affect all our lives.

The evolution of chemistry from small laboratories making new substances in tiny quantities to modern industrial processes producing millions of tonnes of chemicals brings its own problems. The rotten-egg smell of hydrogen sulphide in a school chemistry laboratory may be relatively harmless, but a leakage of a noxious gas, on a proportionate scale, from a chemical plant can represent a major health hazard. There is therefore a twofold responsibility in modern industrial chemistry – not only to produce the chemical products that an affluent society needs in ever-increasing quantities, but to do so in a way that does not lead to major local or global environmental effects.

Elements and molecules

The structure of atoms (▷ p. 30) serves as a convenient starting point for discussing chemical phenomena. In chemical processes, the nuclei of atoms remain unchanged – shattering at once the alchemist's dream of transmuting elements. The great variety of known chemical compounds results from the different ways in which the electrons of atoms are able to interact either with atoms of the same kind or with atoms of a different kind. In an *element*, all the atoms are of the same kind, but the varying strengths of the interactions between the electrons in different types of atom means that elements have very different properties. For example, helium melts at $-272\,°C$ ($-458\,°F$), whereas carbon in the form of diamond has a melting point of $3500\,°C$ ($6332\,°F$). This ability of electrons to interact between atoms is known as *chemical bonding* (for more details, ▷ p. 38).

The elements nitrogen, oxygen, fluorine and chlorine form strong bonds, with two identical atoms linked together. They therefore exist at room temperature as gases, with pairs of linked atoms moving chaotically in space. Two or more atoms linked in this fashion are described as *molecules*, and a shorthand notation is used to describe their chemical identity. The atomic symbol for the element (▷ p. 37) is used in conjunction with the number of atoms present to define the *chemical formula* of the molecule. The elements described above are therefore designated, respectively, by the formulae N_2, O_2, F_2 and Cl_2.

Other familiar elements, such as sulphur and phosphorus, form additional bonds to like atoms, and their formulae reflect this fact. Thus sulphur forms a ring of eight atoms and is described by the formula S_8 (▷ pp. 38–9). As the number of atoms in the fundamental unit increases, the element is no longer a gas but becomes a solid with a low melting point; thus sulphur can be extracted from the Earth as a molten fluid (▷ pp. 196–7).

Most elements do not form discrete molecular entities such as those described above, but have structures that are held together by chemical bonds in all directions. Most of the 109 known elements are metals, such as iron and copper, and have *infinite structures* of this kind. Such elements can no longer be given distinct molecular formulae and are therefore represented by the element symbol alone; thus iron, for example, is represented simply as Fe. (For a more detailed discussion of the properties of metals, ▷ p. 44.)

Chemical compounds

In *chemical compounds*, the atoms of more than one element come together to form either molecules or infinite structures. They are described by formulae similar to those given above for elements. For example, water has a finite structure based on one oxygen atom chemically bonded to two hydrogen atoms and is denoted by the formula H_2O (▷ p. 42). Common salt (sodium chloride; NaCl) has sodium (Na) and chlorine (Cl) atoms linked together in an infinite

---

ALCHEMY

Alchemy, from which modern chemistry derives its name, probably had its origins in the region of Khimi, 'the land of black earth', in the Nile Delta. It was here, more than 4000 years ago, that it was first discovered that the action of heat on minerals could result in the isolation of metals and glasses with useful properties – and which could therefore be sold at a profit. The practice of alchemy spread throughout the Arab world and into Asia, gaining from the Chinese the secret of making gunpowder in the process.

One of the aims of alchemy was the transmutation of metals: alchemists strove for a 'philosopher's stone' that could be used to convert easily corrupted 'base' metals such as iron, copper and lead into the 'noble' metal gold, which retained its lustre and its commercial value. They thought that the philosopher's stone would also be the 'elixir' of immortality – that it would confer eternal health on those who possessed it. Much experimentation followed, which – although not leading to the desired ends – led to the development of techniques that formed the basis of modern chemistry.

Alchemy became associated with mystical practices and ideas, but from the 12th century the availability of Arab writings on alchemy gradually led to the study of chemical processes using more rational techniques and ideas – although many of the original aims were retained. Indeed, even Sir Isaac Newton (▷ p. 14) experimented with the transmutation of base metals into gold – relevant research, given that he was Master of the Royal Mint!

— STINKS AND SCENTS —

Ethanethiol (CH_3CH_2SH) is an evil-smelling chemical that is added in small amounts to natural gas, which is otherwise odourless. The ethanethiol thus aids detection of gas leaks and escapes. (CD)

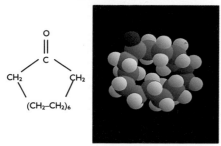

Exaltone was the first synthetic chemical to be used in the manufacture of perfumes. Now a major industry is based on the production and use of chemicals with a wide range of smells. These chemicals obviate the need to extract tiny amounts of chemicals from animals, such as musk from deer and civettone from civets. (CD)

─── HANGOVERS AND HEADACHES ───

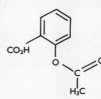

The alcohol present in beers, wines and spirits is ethanol (CH_3CH_2OH). The discovery of alcoholic fermentation is lost in the mists of time. Noah's first task after the Flood was to plant a vineyard (Genesis 9:20). The art of distilling alcohol from fermented juices represents an important early example of a chemical separation technique. (CD)

Aspirin, or acetylsalicylic acid. In 1763 a clergyman in Chipping Norton, England, described the effect of willow bark for the cure of 'agues' (fevers). In Naples in 1838 the first chemical synthesis of salicylic acid (from Latin *salix*, a willow) was achieved – the precursor of aspirin. Large-scale production of aspirin has continued since 1900; it is still the most widely used analgesic (pain-killer). (CD)

─── LAUGHTER AND TEARS ───

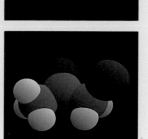

Laughing gas is nitrous oxide (N_2O), a sweet-smelling, colourless, non-flammable gas, which has been used as an anaesthetic (⊳ pp. 43 and 157). Its popular name is derived from the euphoric initial effects on inhalation; in the early 1800s, the English chemist Sir Humphrey Davy (1778–1829) used to invite his poet friends – Coleridge, Southey and Wordsworth – to experience its effects. (CD)

Tear gas is a variant of bromoacetone, which reacts with water on the surface of the eye to produce acids that irritate the eye and cause tears to flow. (CD)

three-dimensional lattice (similar to that formed by potassium chloride; ⊳ p. 38).

In a pure chemical compound, all the molecules have the same ratio of different atoms and behave in an identical chemical fashion. Thus a pure sample of water, for example, behaves identically to any other pure sample, however different their origins may be. Furthermore, the same ratios of atoms are retained irrespective of whether the compound is a solid, a liquid or a gas. For example, ice, water and water vapour all have molecules with the constitution H_2O. The transformation of ice into water and then into water vapour by heating is not a chemical reaction, because the identities of the molecules do not change (⊳ latent heat, p. 19).

From the 109 chemical elements now known, more than 2 million chemical compounds have been made during the last 100 years. The chemist views chemistry as a set of molecular building blocks, constructing more and more complex and diverse molecular structures, the variety of which is limited only by his or her imagination. It is important to emphasize that the properties of a chemical compound are unique and not a sum of the properties of the individual elements from which it is made. For example, common salt does not have any properties remotely like those of metallic sodium, which catches fire on contact with water, or chlorine, which is a harmful yellow-green gas.

Although all compounds are unique, they can be classified into broad families based on common chemical properties. Acids, bases, salts, and oxidizing and reducing agents are examples of such families (⊳ pp. 40–1). Classifications reflecting the atoms present are also useful for cataloguing

purposes: for example, hydrides, chlorides and oxides indicate compounds containing hydrogen, chlorine and oxygen respectively. Another particularly important classification is that of organic compounds (⊳ p. 46), which contain carbon and are not only important for life processes but make up many modern industrial chemicals such as plastics, paints and artificial fibres (⊳ pp. 47, 199 and 200).

Mixtures

When elements or compounds are mixed together but not chemically bonded, they form a *chemical mixture*. A mixture can be of two solids (e.g. salt and sand), two liquids, two gases or permutations of these. A mixture can be separated into its pure chemical constituents by either chemical or physical means. For example, adding water to the sand–salt mixture dissolves the salt, leaving the sand in a pure state. The salt and water is itself a mixture described as a *solution*, from which the pure salt can be obtained by boiling off the water.

The modern-day chemist has many other techniques for separating mixtures, such as distillation, chromatography, crystallization and electrolysis. The petrochemical industry is a prime example of how this technology can be used to convert natural gas and crude oil into a range of useful commercial and domestic products (⊳ pp. 194–5).

KEY

- ⬤ Carbon (C)
- ⚪ Hydrogen (H)
- ⬤ Oxygen (O)
- ⬤ Nitrogen (N)
- ⬤ Bromine (Br)
- ⚪ Sulphur (S)

SEE ALSO

- ● ATOMS pp. 30–1
- ● CHEMISTRY pp. 36–47
- ● OIL AND GAS p. 194
- ● IRON AND STEEL p. 198
- ● RUBBER AND PLASTICS p. 199
- ● TEXTILES p. 200
- ● CHEMICALS AND BIO-TECHNOLOGY p. 201

Elements
and the Periodic Table

The world we see around us is made up of a limited number of chemical elements (⊳ p. 34). In the Earth's crust, there are 82 stable elements and a few unstable (radioactive) ones. A few are very abundant, while others are extremely rare. Indeed, 98% of the Earth's crust is made up of just eight elements (⊳ pie chart).

Each element is associated with a unique number, called its *atomic number*. This figure represents the number of protons (positively charged particles; ⊳ p. 30) in the nucleus of each atom of the element. Hydrogen has one proton, so it is the first and lightest of the elements and is placed first in the Periodic Table; helium has two protons, and thus is the second lightest element and is placed second in the Table; and so we continue through each of the elements, establishing their order in the Table according to their atomic numbers.

The atomic number of bismuth is 83, and this number of protons represents the upper limit for a stable nucleus. Beyond 83, all elements are unstable, although their radioactive decay (⊳ p. 31) may be so slow that some of them, such as thorium and uranium, are found in large natural deposits. The largest atomic number so far observed is 109, but only a few atoms of this element have been made artificially, so little is known about it. Its provisional name is unnilennium, meaning 'one-zero-nine'.

Groups and blocks

When an atom is electrically neutral, the number of electrons (negatively charged particles; ⊳ p. 30) circling the nucleus is the same as the number of (positive) protons in the nucleus. Thus, for example, an electrically neutral atom of calcium contains 20 protons and 20 electrons. While the atomic number identifies an atom and determines its order in the Periodic Table, it is these electrons surrounding the nucleus that determine how it behaves chemically. Electrons can be thought of as moving around the nucleus in certain fixed orbits or 'shells', the electrons in a particular shell being associated with a particular energy level (⊳ p. 30). With regard to an atom's chemical behaviour, it is the electrons in the outer shell that are most important, and it is these that fix the *group position* of the atom in the Table.

The major energy levels are numbered 1, 2, 3, etc., counting outwards from the nucleus. This number is called the *principal quantum number*, and is given the symbol n. Each energy level can hold only a certain number of electrons; the further out it is, the more it can accommodate. This capacity is related to the value of n: the maximum number of electrons each shell can hold

is $2n^2$. Thus the nearest shell to the nucleus can hold only 2 electrons (2×1^2), the next 8 (2×2^2), then 16, then 32, and so on.

Each principal energy level is divided into smaller sub-levels, called s, p, d and f, which hold a maximum of 2, 6, 10 and 14 electrons respectively. The first principal energy level thus contains only the s sub-level; the second contains the s and p sub-levels; and so on. It is these sub-levels that identify the main blocks of the Periodic Table: thus the s-block is made up of 2 columns or groups, the p-block of 6, the d-block of 10, and the f-block of 14.

Group position and reactivity

Hydrogen (⊳ also p. 42) has one electron in the first principal energy level, while helium has two – the maximum capacity for this level. The possession of one extra electron may seem a trivial difference, but a world of difference separates hydrogen and helium: hydrogen is very reactive and forms compounds with many other elements; helium combines with nothing. These two elements are rather exceptional in all their chemical behaviour and are given a small section of their own in the Table, above groups 17 and 18 of the p-block.

Hydrogen and helium are placed on the far right of the Table so that the latter falls in the same group (group 18) as other elements – the so-called *noble gases* – that have full outer shells. Thus below helium we find neon, another chemically unreactive gas, which has the second principal energy level filled and is said to have an *electron configuration* of 2.8. Just as we find hydrogen, a highly reactive element, immediately to the left of helium, so we find another reactive element – fluorine (configuration 2.7) – to the left of neon. Fluorine (like the other elements in group 17 – the *halogens*) is one electron short of a full outer shell. Fluorine's tendency to combine with other elements in order to achieve a full (and so stable) outer shell (⊳ p. 38) makes it one of the most reactive of all the elements.

The noble gases, with their stable electron arrangement, make a natural break in the arrangement of the Periodic Table. After the p sub-shell has been filled, the next electron starts another shell further out from the nucleus. This lone electron makes the elements of group 1 – the *alkali metals* (⊳ p. 44) – highly reactive, because they tend to lose the extra electron in order to form a full outer shell (⊳ p. 38).

The groups of the Periodic Table are numbered 1 to 18, with the f-block not included. Members of the same group have the same number of electrons in the outer shell of the atom and consequently behave in a similar manner chemically. This fact is reflected in the composition of their chemical compounds (which can in turn be explained in terms of their oxidation states; (⊳ box, p. 45). Thus, for example, the formulae of the chlorides of sodium and potassium in group 1 are $NaCl$ and KCl, while their oxides are Na_2O and K_2O.

As we go from left to right across the Table, we can see particular properties change in a regular fashion. It was this periodic rise and fall in such properties as density and atomic volume that led to the term 'Periodic Table'.

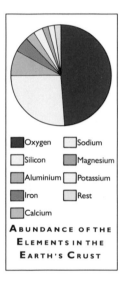

- Oxygen
- Silicon
- Aluminium
- Iron
- Calcium
- Sodium
- Magnesium
- Potassium
- Rest

ABUNDANCE OF THE ELEMENTS IN THE EARTH'S CRUST

SEE ALSO

- ATOMS AND SUBATOMIC PARTICLES p. 30
- QUANTUM THEORY AND RELATIVITY p. 32
- CHEMICAL BONDS p. 38
- CHEMICAL REACTIONS p. 40
- METALS p. 44

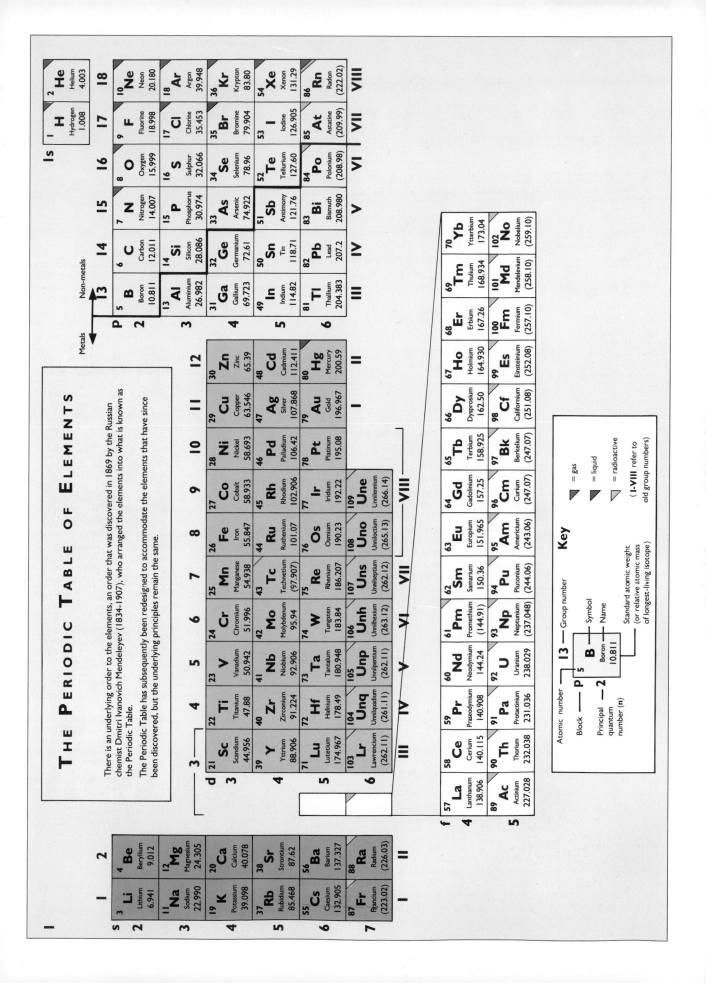

THE PERIODIC TABLE OF ELEMENTS

There is an underlying order to the elements, an order that was discovered in 1869 by the Russian chemist Dmitri Ivanovich Mendeleyev (1834-1907), who arranged the elements into what is known as the Periodic Table.

The Periodic Table has subsequently been redesigned to accommodate the elements that have since been discovered, but the underlying principles remain the same.

Key

= gas
= liquid
= radioactive

(I-VIII refer to old group numbers)

Atomic number
Block
Principal quantum number (n)

Group number
Symbol
Name

Standard atomic weight (or relative atomic mass of longest-living isotope)

Chemical Bonds

Although there are only 109 known elements, there are millions of chemical substances found in nature or made artificially. These substances are not simply mixtures of two or more elements: they are specifically determined chemical compounds, formed by combining two or more elements together in a chemical reaction. The chemical 'glue' that holds these compounds together is known as *chemical bonding*.

SEE ALSO

- ATOMS p. 30
- WHAT IS CHEMISTRY? p. 34
- ELEMENTS AND THE PERIODIC TABLE p. 36
- CHEMICAL REACTIONS p. 40
- SMALL MOLECULES p. 42
- THE REACTIVITY SERIES p. 45

The properties of compounds vary very widely. Some are highly reactive, others inert; some are solids with high melting points, others are gases. Furthermore, the properties of a compound are generally very different from those of its constituent elements. To understand how and why these differences arise, we need to understand the different types of chemical bond.

Ionic bonding

The atoms of the element neon have a full outer shell of electrons, with the electron configuration 2.8 ($\Rightarrow$ p. 36). This arrangement is very stable and neon is not known to form chemical bonds with any other element. An atom of the element sodium (Na) has one more electron than neon (configuration 2.8.1), while an atom of the element fluorine (F) has one electron less (configuration 2.7). If an electron is transferred from a sodium atom to a fluorine atom, two species are produced with the same stable electron configuration as neon. Unlike neon, however, the species are charged and are known as *ions*. The sodium atom, having lost a (negative) electron, has a net positive charge and is known as a *cation* (written Na^+), while the fluorine atom, having gained an electron, has a net negative charge and is called a fluoride *anion* (written F^-).

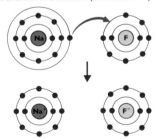

IONIC COMPOUNDS

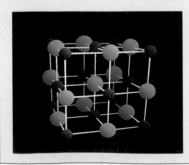

In a crystal of potassium chloride (KCl), each K^+ ion (represented here as a purple sphere) surrounds itself with as many Cl^- ions (green spheres) as there is space for – which turns out to be six; in the same way, each Cl^- ion is surrounded by six K^+ ions. The ions are packed in a regular repeating manner, so that – even though the smallest crystal of KCl contains many millions of ions – it has the same cubic shape as a simple model cube containing just 27 ions.

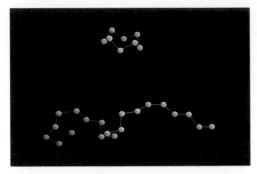

The allotropes of sulphur. One type of sulphur crystal, known as *rhombic sulphur*, contains rings of eight atoms (top). When this is melted and poured into water, *plastic sulphur* is formed, containing long tangled zigzag chains of covalently bonded sulphur atoms (bottom). (CD)

When oppositely charged ions such as Na^+ and F^- are brought together, there is a strong attraction between them; a large amount of energy is released – the same amount of energy as would have to be supplied in order to separate the ions again. This force of attraction is called an *ionic* (or *electrovalent*) *bond*. The energy released more than compensates for the energy input required to transfer the electron from the sodium atom to the fluorine atom. Overall there is a net release of energy and a solid crystalline compound – sodium fluoride (NaF) – is formed. The structure of a similar ionic compound – potassium chloride (KCl) – is illustrated in the box.

Atoms that have two more electrons than the nearest noble gas (such as magnesium, configuration 2.8.2) or two less (such as oxygen, 2.6) also form ions having the noble-gas configuration by transfer of electrons – in this case Mg^{2+} and O^{2-}. The ionic compound magnesium oxide (MgO) has the same arrangement of ions as NaF, but since the ions in MgO have a greater charge, there is a stronger force between them. Thus more energy must be supplied to overcome this force of attraction, and the melting point of MgO is higher than that of NaF. Although the ions are fixed in position in the solid crystal, they become free to move when the solid is melted. As a liquid, therefore, the compound becomes electrolytic ($\Rightarrow$ pp. 40–1) and is able to conduct electricity.

Many other more complex ionic structures are known. The formula of any ionic compound can be worked out by balancing the charges of its ions. For example, Mg^{2+} and F^- form MgF_2, while Na^+ and O^{2-} form Na_2O.

Covalent bonding

If we bring together two fluorine atoms, each with seven outer electrons (one less than neon), the formation of two ions with the noble-gas configuration is not possible by transfer of electrons. If, however, they share a pair of electrons – one from each atom – then both effectively achieve the noble-gas configuration and a stable molecule results:

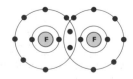

There is a force of attraction between the shared pair of electrons and both positive nuclei, and this is what is known as a *covalent bond*. The stronger the attraction of the nuclei for the shared pair, the stronger the bond.

An atom of oxygen, having two electrons less than neon, must form two covalent bonds to attain a share in eight electrons. For example, a molecule of water (H_2O), consisting of two hydrogen atoms (H) and one oxygen atom (O), has two covalent O–H bonds (⊳ also p. 42). Another way for oxygen to achieve the stable noble-gas configuration is to form two bonds to the same atom. Thus two oxygen atoms bond covalently to one another by sharing two pairs of electrons (⊳ p. 42). This is known as a *double bond*.

Like oxygen, sulphur (S) has six outer electrons and again needs to form two bonds to attain a share in eight electrons. There are two ways in which sulphur atoms join together – either in rings of eight atoms (S_8) or in long chains of many atoms bonded together (⊳ photo). The different forms in which elemental sulphur exist are known as *allotropes*; other elements found in allotropic forms include carbon (graphite, diamond and newly discovered buckminsterfullerene) and oxygen (oxygen and ozone; ⊳ p. 42).

Atoms of nitrogen (N), containing five outer electrons, need to form three covalent bonds to attain a share in eight electrons. This may be done, for example, by forming one bond to each of three hydrogen atoms, to give ammonia (NH_3; ⊳ pp. 42–3). Another possibility is to form all three bonds to a second nitrogen atom, which produces a nitrogen molecule (N_2; ⊳ pp. 42–3), containing a *triple covalent bond*.

The carbon atom (C), which has four outer electrons, needs to form four bonds to attain the noble-gas configuration. Thus a carbon atom forms one bond to each of four hydrogen atoms to give methane (CH_4; ⊳ table, pp. 42–3). Although carbon is not known to form a quadruple bond to another carbon atom, some other elements, such as the heavy metal rhenium, do form such quadruple bonds. (For more on carbon bonding, ⊳ p. 46.)

Giant molecules

Although two carbon atoms do not form a quadruple bond to one another, carbon atoms can combine to form a giant crystal lattice in which each atom is bonded to four others by single covalent bonds. This is the structure of diamond, one of the allotropes of elemental carbon. Many other elements and compounds exist as giant covalent crystal lattices, including quartz, which is a form of silicon dioxide (SiO_2). Crystals of these substances contain many millions of atoms held together by strong covalent bonds, so that a large amount of energy is needed to break them. Thus these substances all have high melting points and are hard solids.

Intermolecular forces

As we have seen, two neon atoms do not form covalent bonds with one another because of their full outer shells of electrons. There are, however, weak forces of attraction between two neon atoms. We know this because, when neon gas is compressed or cooled, it eventually turns into a liquid in which the atoms are weakly attracted to one another. These weak forces are called *van der Waals forces* and their strength depends on the size of the molecule.

Bromine (Br_2) is made up of large covalently bonded molecules that have much stronger van der Waals forces between them than exist between atoms of neon. Thus at room temperature bromine exists as a mixture of liquid and vapour. However, the forces *between* the bromine molecules are much weaker than covalent bonds, so that – while it is easy to separate the bromine molecules from one another and vaporize the liquid – it requires much more energy to separate the bromine atoms by breaking the covalent bond between them.

Hydrogen bonds

Some small molecules have much higher melting and boiling points than would be expected on the basis of their size. One such example is water (H_2O), which has about the same mass as a neon atom but has a much higher melting point (⊳ also p. 42). There must therefore be unusually strong intermolecular forces between the water molecules. Although the oxygen and hydrogen atoms share a pair of electrons in a covalent bond, the oxygen atom exerts a stronger 'pull' on these electrons and so becomes electron-rich, leaving the hydrogen atom electron-poor. As a result, there is a force of attraction between hydrogen and oxygen atoms on neighbouring molecules. This is known as *hydrogen bonding*.

As well as accounting for the surprisingly high melting point of water, hydrogen bonding is responsible for the rigid open structure of ice crystals, and is very important in influencing the structures and properties of biological molecules (⊳ pp. 46–7). Although hydrogen bonds are stronger than van der Waals forces, they are still much weaker than covalent bonds.

Crystals of menthol, seen through a polarizing optical microscope. The components (atoms or molecules) of crystals are held together by strong covalent bonds. (SPL)

Chemical Reactions

Chemical reactions are the means by which new substances are formed from old ones. Among the chemical reactions occurring everywhere around us are the changes that take place when fuels are burnt, the industrial methods by which metals are extracted from their ores, and the processes controlling life itself.

During a chemical reaction, the atomic constituents of the substances that react together (the *reactants*) are rearranged to produce different substances (the *products*). Thus, for example, in the reaction of potassium (K) with water (H_2O), potassium hydroxide (KOH) and hydrogen gas (H_2) are formed. This information can be represented as a chemical equation. By convention the reactants appear on the left-hand side and the products on the right; letters may also be added after each chemical species to indicate its physical state – s means 'solid', l 'liquid', aq 'aqueous' (solution) and g 'gas':

$$2K(s) + 2H_2O(l) \rightarrow 2KOH(aq) + H_2(g)$$

An essential characteristic of chemical reactions is that there is an exchange of energy between the reacting system and the surroundings. So much heat is liberated during the reaction of potassium and water that the highly inflammable hydrogen gas frequently ignites above the molten metal.

Reactions of acids and bases

Acids are substances that tend to donate protons (ionized hydrogen atoms, H^+) to other molecules.

For example, gaseous hydrogen chloride (HCl) readily dissolves in water to form hydrochloric acid, by donating a proton to a water molecule:

$$HCl(g) + H_2O(l) \rightarrow H_3O^+(aq) + Cl^-(aq)$$

The products of the reaction are ions (electrically charged species; ⊳ p. 38): H_3O^+ (the hydronium ion) and Cl^- (the chloride ion). Many non-metal oxides form acids when dissolved in water; for example, sulphur trioxide gas (SO_3) dissolves in water to form sulphuric acid (H_2SO_4) – the reaction that occurs in the formation of acid rain (⊳ pp. 43 and 186).

By contrast, *bases* are defined as proton acceptors, capable of accepting protons from hydronium ions present in solution. A good example of a base is the hydroxide ion, $OH^-(aq)$, which reacts with the hydronium ion to produce two molecules of water:

$$H_3O^+(aq) + OH^-(aq) \rightarrow 2H_2O(l)$$

Examples of bases include sodium and potassium hydroxides (NaOH and KOH), which generate aqueous hydroxide ions in solution. Many metal oxides are also basic, such as calcium oxide (CaO; 'lime'), which reacts violently with water to form calcium hydroxide ($Ca(OH)_2$; 'slaked lime'). Aqueous solutions of bases are known as *alkalis*.

Acids and bases can be detected by their effects on a class of natural dyes called *indicators*. The best-known indicator is *litmus*, a dye derived from lichen, which is turned red by acids and blue by bases.

Acids and bases react together to form compounds known as *salts*, which are neither acidic nor basic. For example, sodium hydroxide reacts with hydrochloric acid to form sodium chloride (common salt):

$$NaOH(aq) + HCl(aq) \rightarrow NaCl(aq) + H_2O(l)$$

This is an example of a *neutralization reaction*.

Precipitation reactions

Ionic compounds (⊳ p. 38) that dissolve in water produce *electrolyte* solutions. These consist of ions moving randomly throughout the solution; for example, sodium chloride in aqueous solution contains sodium (Na^+) and chloride (Cl^-) ions. These ions are responsible for the electrical conductivity of electrolytes (⊳ also below).

Silver nitrate ($AgNO_3$) is another ionic solid that dissolves readily in water, producing a colourless solution of aqueous silver (Ag^+) and nitrate (NO_3^-) ions. If solutions of silver nitrate and sodium chloride are mixed, a white turbidity (cloudiness) instantly forms; this is due to the *precipitation* of fine particles of highly insoluble silver chloride. The precipitate gradually accumulates at the bottom of the vessel, leaving colourless sodium nitrate in solution:

$$NaCl(aq) + AgNO_3(aq) \rightarrow AgCl(s) + NaNO_3(aq)$$

The overall reaction is one in which ions are exchanged between partners.

Electron-transfer reactions: oxidation and reduction

Magnesium metal (Mg) burns with an incandescent white flame in air because of a vigorous

Firework displays involve violent oxidation reactions in which light and heat are released. (Spectrum)

SEE ALSO

- ELEMENTS AND THE PERIODIC TABLE p. 36
- CHEMICAL BONDS p. 38
- SMALL MOLECULES p. 42
- METALS p. 44
- ORGANIC CHEMISTRY p. 46

reaction with oxygen, forming magnesium oxide:

$$Mg(s) + O_2(g) \rightarrow 2MgO(s)$$

This is an example of the class of reactions known as *oxidations*, which include all combustion processes such as those occurring when fuels burn in air, as well as the reactions that cause metals to corrode in air ($\rhd$ p. 45). The product in this case is an ionic solid, which we could write more specifically as $Mg^{2+}O^{2-}$. During the reaction, magnesium loses two electrons to form the cation Mg^{2+}; the electrons are accepted by oxygen, which becomes the oxide anion O^{2-} ($\rhd$ also p. 38).

The transfer of electrons between chemical species is a common process in many chemical reactions, so the term oxidation has come to possess a wider meaning than that implying solely the addition of oxygen atoms to an element or compound. As in the case of the formation of magnesium oxide, oxidation means the loss of electrons by a compound; the opposite process, *reduction*, implies a gain of electrons. Thus magnesium is said to be oxidized to Mg^{2+}, while oxygen is reduced to O^{2-}; the overall reaction is described as a *redox* process. Many metals are extracted from their ores by reduction reactions ($\rhd$ p. 44).

If an electric current is passed through an electrolyte such as an aqueous solution of copper(II) chloride ($CuCl_2$), a redox process known as *electrolysis* occurs. Positively charged Cu^{2+} ions are attracted to the negative electrode (the cathode; $\rhd$ p. 28), where they take up two electrons each and are thereby reduced to copper metal, which is deposited on the cathode. At the same time, the negatively charged Cl^- ions are attracted to the positive electrode (the anode), where they give up their extra electrons (i.e. are oxidized) to form chlorine gas. Electrolysis is the basis of *electroplating*, in which a thin layer of metal, such as copper, tin, chromium or silver, is applied as a protective or decorative finish on cheaper or less durable materials. It is also used to purify metals and to extract reactive metals such as aluminium from their ores ($\rhd$ p. 44).

Reaction equilibria

All the reactions described so far have gone to completion, i.e. a fixed quantity of reactants is converted into a fixed quantity of products. However, in general such a state of affairs is more the exception than the rule. The end of a reaction occurs when there is no further change in the amount of products formed or reactants destroyed: this is the point at which a reaction is said to reach *equilibrium*. At equilibrium, there may be appreciable amounts of reactants still present. For example, when acetic acid is dissolved in water, it forms a *weak acid*, because at equilibrium there is only a low concentration of hydronium ions:

$$CH_3COOH(l) + H_2O(l) \rightleftharpoons$$
$$CH_3CO_2^-(aq) + H_3O^+(aq)$$

The equilibrium, indicated by the two half-headed arrows, lies in favour of the reactants (in contrast to *strong acids*, such as hydrochloric acid, which are totally dissociated into ions). For the same reason, aqueous ammonia is a *weak base*, because at equilibrium there is a low concentration of hydroxide ions in the solution. Most of the solution consists of unreacted ammonia and water, in contrast to *strong bases*, which consist solely of ions.

Some complex reactions involve a remarkable degree of underlying organization, in which vast numbers of molecules 'beat' in unison. This computer simulation shows three-dimensional waves of chemical change moving through an excitable medium. Such complex reactions are now recognized to be of crucial importance in the regulation of many processes in living systems. (Dr Arthur Winfree/SPL)

Rates of chemical reactions

Very often it is important to know not only where the position of a chemical equilibrium lies but how fast it is reached. A graphic illustration is provided by a mixture of hydrogen gas and oxygen gas at room temperature. If undisturbed, the mixture does not react, but if a spark is passed through the gases, there is a violent explosion leading to the formation of water ($\rhd$ also p. 42). Thus temperature is seen to exert a strong influence on the rate at which a reaction proceeds – the higher the temperature, the faster the reaction.

On the other hand, the same reaction can be made to proceed smoothly at room temperature by the addition of finely divided platinum metal, which acts as a catalyst. A *catalyst* is a substance that is not chemically transformed during a reaction but whose presence serves to accelerate its rate.

Another factor influencing the rate of reaction is the intrinsic reactivity – i.e. willingness to undergo chemical reaction – of the chemical species involved. An example is provided by the reactions of the halogens – fluorine, chlorine, bromine and iodine ($\rhd$ p. 36) – with hydrogen gas. The form of the reaction is identical for all the halogens, in each case producing the hydrogen halide (halogen-containing compound). However, the rate of the reaction decreases progressively down the series, fluorine reacting violently and iodine sluggishly at room temperature.

STOICHIOMETRY AND MOLES

According to the *law of constant composition*, matter cannot be created or destroyed during a chemical reaction. Thus in the reaction of potassium with water ($\rhd$ main text), the number of atoms of potassium, hydrogen and oxygen (calculated by multiplying each element in the equation by the numbers placed before the chemical formula) is the same before and after the reaction, and the equation is said to be balanced. The numerical proportions in which substances combine to form the products of a chemical reaction is described as the reaction *stoichiometry*.

A balanced equation is thus a quantitative statement about the chemical reaction concerned. Such an equation (in conjunction with the mole concept; $\rhd$ below) enables us to predict how much product will be formed from a given mass of reactants. This provides valuable information that can be put to use, for example, in industrial production processes and in the analysis of chemical samples of unknown composition.

A *mole* is a measure of the amount of substance, based on the atomic theory of matter ($\rhd$ p. 30). A mole is defined as the number of carbon atoms in 12 grams of the isotope carbon-12 and has the colossal value of 6.022×10^{23}. Every chemical compound has a fixed *relative molecular mass* or RMM (determined by the relative atomic masses of its constituent elements), so that molar quantities (the number of moles) of any substance can be found using simple arithmetic.

Small Molecules

Although the Earth's atmosphere consists almost entirely of two gases – nitrogen and oxygen – a number of other gases are present at low concentration, together with varying amounts of water vapour (▷ p. 61). With the exception of the noble gases (▷ p. 36), most other components of air form part of natural cycles, each remaining in the atmosphere only for a limited time. Not only are these gases of major importance in relation to industrial processes that dominate economies throughout the world, but cyclical processes involving water, oxygen, carbon dioxide and nitrogen – together with solar radiation – are essential to plant and animal life.

Current interest in various atmospheric gases centres on the possible global effects of changes in their atmospheric concentration due to human activities (▷ also p. 186). Increase in carbon dioxide may upset the heat balance at the Earth's surface, while the use of chlorofluorocarbons (CFCs) might result in depletion of the ozone layer, thereby allowing destructive high-energy solar radiation to reach the Earth's surface.

Although these small molecules are simple in the sense that they are composed of few atoms, their structures and – for those with three or more atoms – their shapes vary (▷ table). In most cases, their atoms are held together in the molecule by two, four or six electrons, resulting in single, double or triple covalent bonds (▷ pp. 38–9). Three of these molecules (nitric oxide, nitrogen dioxide and oxygen) are paramagnetic – i.e. attracted to a magnet, like iron – because of the number or arrangement of their electrons.

Hydrogen

Hydrogen (H_2) is the simplest of all stable molecules, consisting of two protons and two electrons. It is a colourless, odourless gas and is lighter than air. The last of these properties led to its use in lifting airships, but this use was discontinued because of its explosiveness when ignited. Most hydrogen is used on the site where it is produced, but it is also transported as compressed gas in steel cylinders and in liquid form at very low temperature.

Water

The total amount of water (H_2O) on Earth is fixed, and most is recycled and re-used (▷ pp. 75 and 78). The largest reservoirs are the oceans and open seas, followed by glaciers, ice caps and ground water (▷ pp. 70, 74 and 76). Very little is actually contained within living organisms, although water is a major constituent of most life forms.

Water is one of the most remarkable of all small molecules. On the basis of its molecular weight (18), it should be a gas; its high boiling point (100 °C / 212 °F) is due to the interaction of water molecules with each other (hydrogen bonding; ▷ p. 39), which effectively increases its molecular weight. Water is also unusual in that – as ice – it is less dense than the liquid at the same temperature.

Carbon dioxide

Carbon dioxide (CO_2) is a colourless gas with a slight odour and an acid taste. It is available as gas, as liquid and as the white solid known as 'dry ice'. Its cycle in nature is tied to that of oxygen, the relative levels of the two gases in the atmosphere (apart from human activity) being regulated by the photosynthetic activity of plants (▷ p. 88). It is produced on a vast scale, mostly as a by-product of other processes. Some scientists believe that the ever-increasing input of carbon dioxide to the atmosphere from human activities will lead to a greenhouse effect (▷ p. 186).

Oxygen and ozone

Oxygen (O_2) is a highly reactive colourless, odourless and tasteless gas. At low temperature, it condenses to a pale blue liquid, slightly denser than water. Oxygen supports burning, causes

Molecule	Hydrogen	Water	Oxygen	Ozone	Carbon dioxide	Carbon monoxide
Formula	H_2	H_2O	O_2	O_3	CO_2	CO
Structure — Single bond ═ Intermediate between single and double bond ═ Double bond ≡ Triple bond ≡ Intermediate between double and triple bond						
Concentration in unpolluted air (parts per million)	0.5	Variable	209 400	c. 0.01	c. 315	0.1
Industrial production	Reaction of coal or petroleum with steam in the presence of a catalyst; electrolysis of water	–	Liquefying and distilling	Ultraviolet irradiation of air; electric discharge through air	By-product of other processes, e.g. burning of fossil fuels, fermentation and calcining limestone	Action of steam on carbonaceous material
Major uses	Synthesis of ammonia and methanol (CH_3OH, the simplest alcohol); removal of impurities such as sulphur-containing compounds from natural gas, oil and coal	Solvent	Steel manufacture; all combustion processes; extensively used in chemical industry, e.g. in conversion of ethylene (ethene, $CH_2:CH_2$) to ethylene oxide	Treatment of drinking water; bleach for clay materials	Fire extinguishers; coolant	Fuel; reducing agent in metallurgy; chemical production of e.g. methanol (CH_3OH), acetic acid (CH_3CO_2H) and phosgene ($COCl_2$)

rusting ($\triangleright$ p. 45) and is vital to both plant and animal respiration ($\triangleright$ pp. 88 and 140).

Ozone (O_3) is a highly toxic, unstable, colourless gas. Its primary importance stems from its formation in the stratosphere ($\triangleright$ p. 61), where it functions as a very effective filter for high-energy ultraviolet solar radiation. Radiation in this energy range is sufficiently high to break bonds between carbon and other atoms, making it lethal to all forms of life. It is currently thought that the introduction of CFCs (used in sprays and refrigerants) and the related 'halons' (used in fire extinguishers) may contribute to the partial or even total destruction of the ozone layer ($\triangleright$ pp. 186–7).

Carbon monoxide

Carbon monoxide (CO) is a colourless, odourless, toxic gas. The input to the atmosphere due to human activity is about 360 million tonnes (tons) per year, mostly from the incomplete combustion of fossil fuels. The natural input is some 10 times this figure and results from the partial oxidation of biologically produced methane ($\triangleright$ table). The background level of 0.1 parts per million (ppm) can rise to 20 ppm at a busy road intersection, and a five-minute cigarette gives an intake of 400 ppm.

Since the atmospheric level of carbon monoxide is not rising significantly, there must be effective sink processes, one being its oxidation in air to carbon dioxide. In addition, there are soil micro-organisms that utilize carbon monoxide in photosynthesis.

Nitrogen

Nitrogen (N_2) is a colourless, odourless gas. Although very stable and chemically unreactive, it cycles both naturally and as a result of its use in the chemical industry. The natural cycle ($\triangleright$ pp. 126–7) results from the ability of some types of bacteria and blue-green algae (in the presence of sunlight) to 'fix' nitrogen – i.e. to convert it into inorganic nitrogen compounds (ammonium and nitrate salts) that can be assimilated by plants. Since 1913 human activity has increasingly contributed to the cycling of nitrogen, because of the catalytic conversion of nitrogen into ammonia (used mainly in nitrate fertilizers; $\triangleright$ below), which ultimately reverts to nitrogen gas.

Oxides of nitrogen

The presence of nitric oxide (NO) and nitrogen dioxide (NO_2) at high levels in the atmosphere is closely connected with the internal-combustion engine ($\triangleright$ pp. 192–3 and 219–21). At the high temperature reached when petroleum and air ignite, nitrogen and oxygen combine to form nitric oxide, which slowly reacts with more oxygen to form nitrogen dioxide. Most internal-combustion engines also produce some unburnt or partially burnt fuel; in the presence of sunlight, this reacts with nitrogen dioxide by a sequence of fast reactions, forming organic peroxides, which are the harmful constituents of photochemical smog (smoke plus fog).

Ammonia

Ammonia (NH_3) is a colourless gas with a penetrating odour, and is less dense than air. It is highly soluble in water, giving an alkaline solution ($\triangleright$ p. 41). World production is of the order of 100 million tonnes (tons) a year, most of which is converted into fertilizers (80%), plastics (9%) and explosives (4%).

Oxides of sulphur

Both sulphur dioxide (SO_2) and sulphur trioxide (SO_3) are pungent-smelling acidic gases, which are produced by volcanic action and – to the extent of some 150 million tonnes (tons) a year – by the burning of fossil fuels and smelting operations.

The level of sulphur dioxide in unpolluted air is 0.002 parts per million (ppm), but in the 1952 London smog the levels rose to 1.54 ppm, accompanied by a dramatic increase in the death rate. In the atmosphere sulphur dioxide is slowly oxidized to sulphur trioxide, reactions that are catalysed by sunlight, water droplets and particulate matter in the air. Ultimately the latter is deposited as dilute sulphuric acid – *acid rain* ($\triangleright$ pp. 40 and 186).

SEE ALSO

- WHAT IS CHEMISTRY? p. 34
- CHEMICAL BONDS p. 38
- THE EARTH'S ATMOSPHERE p. 61
- THE HYDROLOGICAL CYCLE p. 75
- WEATHER p. 78
- PLANTS p. 88
- THE BIOSPHERE p. 126
- THREATS TO THE ENVIRONMENT p. 186

Methane CH_4	Nitrogen N_2	Nitric oxide NO	Nitrous oxide N_2O	Nitrogen dioxide NO_2	Ammonia NH_3	Sulphur dioxide SO_2	Sulphur trioxide SO_3
1–1.6	780 900	Variable	0.5	c. 0.02	Variable	Variable (c. 0.002)	Variable
–	Liquefying and distilling air	Catalytic oxidation of ammonia	Heating ammonium nitrate (NH_4NO_3)	Oxidation of nitric oxide	Catalytic reaction of nitrogen and hydrogen	Oxidation of sulphur	Oxidation of sulphur dioxide
The main constituent of natural gas ($\triangleright$ p. 195); major feedstock for the chemical industry	Synthesis of ammonia; uses due to its inertness, e.g. in metallurgy and in the chemical and food industries	Vital in the chemical industry, as an intermediate in the production of nitric acid (HNO_3)	Anaesthetic (laughing gas; $\triangleright$ pp. 35 and 157); propellant in the food industry, e.g. in whipped ice cream	As nitric oxide	Fertilizers; plastics; explosives	Vital in the chemical industry, as an intermediate in the production of sulphuric acid (H_2SO_4)	As sulphur dioxide

Metals

Metals are usually defined by their physical properties, such as strength, hardness, lustre, conduction of heat and electricity, malleability and high melting point. They can also be characterized chemically as elements that dissolve (or whose oxides dissolve) in acids, usually to form positively charged ions (cations; ▷ p. 38). By either definition, more than three quarters of the known elements can be classified as metals. They occupy all but the top right-hand corner of the Periodic Table (▷ figure), the remainder being non-metals. A few elements on the borderline, such as germanium, arsenic and antimony, have some of the properties of both metals and non-metals, and are often classed as *metalloids*.

Given such a large number of metals, it is not surprising that some of them have rather untypical properties. For instance, mercury is a liquid at room temperature, and – with the exception of lithium – all the alkali metals (▷ Periodic Table) melt below 100 °C (212 °F). The alkali metals are also quite soft – they can easily be cut with a knife – and extremely reactive: rubidium and caesium cannot be handled in air and may react explosively with water.

Occurrence

Most metals occur naturally as oxides, while some – mostly the heavier ones, such as mercury and lead – occur as sulphides. Only a few – the noble and coinage metals (▷ Periodic Table) – are found in the metallic state, being chemically the most inert metals. It is their chemical unreactiveness that makes them useful in coinage and jewellery, since they do not corrode (▷ below).

A few metals do not occur naturally at all, because they are radioactive and have decayed away (▷ p. 31). Technetium and all the elements with higher atomic numbers than plutonium (Pu, 94; ▷ Periodic Table) are made by the 'modern alchemy' of nuclear reactors or accelerators (▷ pp. 30–1 and 188–9), while promethium is found only in minute amounts as a product of the spontaneous fission of uranium. The very heaviest elements have been obtained only a few atoms at a time, and are intensely radioactive.

The discovery and extraction of metals

Artificial elements have of course been known only in modern times, since the 1940s or later. The discovery of most other metals was also comparatively recent: with the exception of zinc, platinum and the handful of metals known to the Ancients, all metals have been discovered since 1735. The only metals known in antiquity were copper, silver, gold, iron, tin, mercury and lead. Of these, it was not the most abundant – iron – that was discovered first: the Bronze Age came before the Iron Age (▷ pp. 226–7). The reason for this is that it is easier to extract the metals used in bronze – copper and tin – from their minerals than it is to extract iron from its ores. The discovery of copper is thought to have been accidental: pieces of the metal ore used in fireplaces came into contact with the hot charcoal, so releasing the metal. Essentially the same process under controlled conditions (*smelting*) is used in modern blast furnaces (▷ p. 198). Any of the metals from manganese (Mn) to zinc (Zn) in the Periodic Table (▷ figure) can be obtained by roasting their oxides with coke at temperatures of up to about 1600° C (2912° F).

The ores of the lighter, more reactive metals cannot be reduced by carbon at practical temperatures, because their atoms are more strongly bonded in the ore (▷ box on reactivity). These metals are usually obtained by electrolysis (▷ pp. 40–1) or by the reaction of their compounds with an even more reactive metal. For instance, the reduction of aluminium oxide with carbon requires a temperature in excess of 2000 °C (3632 °F); so electrolysis of a melt of aluminium oxide in a mixture of cryolite (a double fluoride of aluminium and sodium) and calcium fluoride at about 950 °C (1742 °F) is used. On the other hand, titanium is obtained by converting its oxide into the chloride, which is then reduced with elemental sodium or magnesium. These methods are rather expensive, but are justified by the useful-

---

THE REACTIVITY SERIES

The widely varying reactivity of metals can be related to their positions in the Periodic Table (▷ figure). The s-block metals are highly reactive, while the transition metals typically become less reactive from left to right across the table, with the noble and coinage metals least reactive of all.

When metals react, they usually lose electrons to form positively charged ions (cations, ▷ p. 38). This charge (also known as the *oxidation state*) is again related to the position of a metal in the Periodic Table. In the s-block, the charge equals the group number, $+1$ or $+2$ (e.g. K^+, Mg^{2+}). In the transition metals, variability of oxidation state is the rule: for instance, iron may lose 2 or 3 electrons (Fe^{2+}, Fe^{3+}), and this fact is indicated in the names and formulae of its compounds – iron(II) chloride ($FeCl_2$) and iron(III) chloride ($FeCl_3$).

The reactivity of a metal can thus be explained in terms of its readiness to lose electrons to form cations: potassium (K) readily loses an electron to form a K^+ ion, while gold (Au) is highly unreactive and dissolves only in aqua regia, a fiercely oxidizing mixture of hydrochloric and nitric acids. Metals can be placed in order of reactivity, in a sequence known as the *reactivity series*; for some of the more important metals, the series runs as follows (in order of decreasing reactivity):

K Na Ca Mg Al Zn Fe Pb Cu Hg Ag Au Pt

A metal can be displaced from a solution of one of its salts simply by addition of a metal higher (earlier) in the series. For instance, if zinc metal (Zn) is added to a solution of copper(II) sulphate ($CuSO_4$), the zinc becomes coated by copper metal and the blue colour of the solution fades, as the coloured copper ions in solution are displaced by zinc ions:

$$Zn(s) + Cu^{2+}(aq) + SO_4^{2-}(aq) \rightarrow Zn^{2+}(aq) + SO_4^{2-}(aq) + Cu(s)$$

The reactivity series also indicates the affinity of a metal for oxygen. As such, it explains the differing susceptibility of metals to corrosion (surface oxidation) and underlies the extraction of metals from their oxides. The more reactive a metal is, the higher the temperature required to reduce its oxide by carbon. In practice, the most reactive metals cannot be economically reduced by carbon, and are therefore obtained by electrolysis or by displacement by an even more reactive metal.

The reactivity series can also be seen as an *electrochemical series*. When two different metals are dipped into an electrolyte solution (▷ pp. 40–1), a voltage forms between them and the metal higher in the series becomes the anode (positive electrode). The distance between the two metals in the series reflects the size of the voltage produced. Electrochemical reactions of this kind underlie electroplating and the operation of electrolytic cells and batteries (▷ pp. 28–9). Frequently some hydrogen is also produced: such a reaction often occurs in domestic central heating systems, where copper pipes and iron radiators are both in contact with hot water; the 'air' that accumulates in the system is actually hydrogen.

ness of the metals obtained, which are both strong and light.

Conductivity

The conduction of heat and electricity (⊳ pp. 19 and 26–9) that characterizes metals is due to their unique type of bonding. The solid metals behave as if they were composed of arrays of positively charged ions, with electrons free to move throughout the crystalline structure of the metal (⊳ below). This results in high electrical conductivity. The conduction of heat can also be seen in terms of the motion of electrons, which becomes faster as temperature rises. Since the electrons are mobile, the heat can be conducted readily through the solid.

The majority of metals are good conductors of electricity, but germanium and tin (in the form stable below 19 °C / 64 °F) are semiconductors (⊳ p. 29).

Mechanical strength

Many metals are used because of their strength. However, most pure metals are actually quite soft. In order to obtain a tough hard metal, something else has to be added. For instance, the earliest useful metal was not copper but bronze, which is copper alloyed with tin. Similarly, iron is never used in the pure state but as some form of steel (⊳ p. 198).

The softness of a pure metal results from a lack of perfection in the crystal framework formed by its atoms (⊳ deformation diagram). Even when the most rigorous conditions are employed, it is impossible to grow any material in perfect crystalline form. There will always be some atoms in the wrong place or missing from their proper place. When solidification occurs fairly rapidly, as when a molten metal is cooled in a mould, even more defects occur. Under bending or shearing stresses, such defects can move and allow the metal to change shape easily. When the foreign atoms of an alloying element are present, they usually have a different size from those of the host and cannot easily fit into the crystal lattice. They therefore tend to site themselves where the lattice is irregular, i.e. where the defects are. The effect of this is to prevent the defects from moving, and so to increase the rigidity of the metal (⊳ alloying diagram).

Tarnishing and corrosion

Nearly all metals are prone to surface oxidation, i.e. the surface of the metal reacts with oxygen or other components of the atmosphere (⊳ box on reactivity). The major exceptions are the coinage

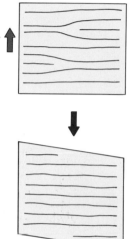

A steelworks. Steel is an iron-based alloy containing varying proportions of carbon, and often small amounts of other elements, including chromium, nickel, manganese, phosphorus and sulphur. (Spectrum)

Metal deformation (below) occurs as defects in the crystalline structure move under a shearing stress (red arrows).

metals and those of the platinum group (⊳ Periodic Table), and even these react with sulphur compounds (⊳ p. 43) in industrially polluted atmospheres and turn black. All other metals should, in principle, react with moisture and the oxygen in air, yet some corrode badly and others appear to be inert. In fact, they all oxidize, but in many cases a thin layer of oxide adheres firmly to the metal surface and prevents further reaction. This is the case with aluminium and titanium. On the other hand, iron forms porous oxides that readily break away, allowing corrosion to continue. Stainless steels are produced by alloying iron with chromium and sometimes also with nickel, which form a protective oxide on the surface; the thickness of this layer is so small that the surface still appears shiny and metallic.

An alternative way of preventing corrosion is essentially electrochemical. Corrosion can be prevented by connecting a metal object to a piece of more reactive metal and completing the circuit through the earth. The more reactive metal becomes the anode (⊳ box on reactivity) and gradually 'dissolves' or degrades. This method is sometimes used for metal tanks that have to stand outdoors: a block of magnesium buried and connected by a wire to the tank slowly oxidizes – it acts as a 'sacrificial' anode. This is also the reason why galvanization works. Contrary to what would be expected, the layer of zinc on the iron needs to be somewhat porous so that water can bring the two metals into electrochemical contact. It is then the zinc that reacts instead of the iron.

Alloying (below). Impurity atoms (blue) are the wrong size to fit into the metal's crystal lattice. They therefore tend to site themselves at defective points in the lattice, where they become immobile and thus 'pin' the defects in place.

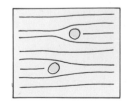

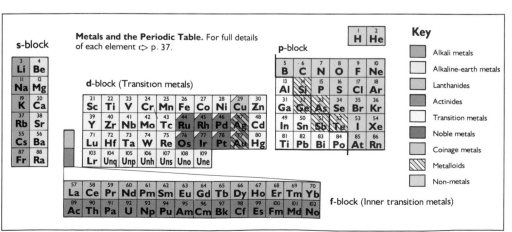

Metals and the Periodic Table. For full details of each element ⊳ p. 37.

SEE ALSO

- ELECTROMAGNETISM p. 26
- ELECTRICITY IN ACTION p. 28
- ATOMS p. 30
- ELEMENTS AND THE PERIODIC TABLE p. 36
- CHEMICAL BONDS p. 38
- CHEMICAL REACTIONS p. 40
- MINING, MINERALS AND METALS p. 196
- IRON AND STEEL p. 198

Organic Chemistry

The molecular basis for life processes, which have evolved with such remarkable elegance around carbon as the key element, is beginning to be understood, thanks to the combined triumphs of biological, chemical and physical scientists during the last hundred years.

Although the chemist can now make synthetically almost any chemical compound that nature produces, the challenge remains to achieve this objective routinely with the efficiency and precision that characterizes the chemistry of living systems.

There is something very special about the chemistry of carbon that has singled it out as the atomic building block from which all naturally occurring compounds in living systems are constructed. The subject that deals with this important area of science, nestling between biology and physics, has become so vast and significant that it has earned recognition as a separate field of scientific investigation. As it was originally thought that such carbon-based compounds could be obtained only from natural sources, this field of study became known as *organic chemistry*.

The unique carbon atom

Carbon's unique feature is the readiness with which it forms bonds both with other carbon atoms and with the atoms of other elements. Having four electrons in its outer shell, a carbon atom requires four more electrons to attain a stable noble-gas configuration ($\rhd$ p. 38). It therefore forms four covalent bonds with other atoms, each of which donates a single electron to each bond. In this way the electronic requirements are

SEE ALSO

● THE BEGINNINGS OF LIFE
   p. 82
● GENETICS p. 86
● OIL AND GAS p. 194
● RUBBER AND PLASTICS p. 199
● TEXTILES p. 200
● CHEMICALS AND BIO-
   TECHNOLOGY p. 201

satisfied, and a three-dimensional 'tetracovalent' environment is built up around the carbon atom.

Carbon bonds are found both in pure forms of carbon (graphite, diamond and the newly discovered buckminsterfullerene) and in association with other atoms in a vast array of compounds. Compounds consisting of just carbon and hydrogen – *hydrocarbons* – are extremely important, notably as the principal constituents of fossil fuels. In addition, carbon readily bonds with many other atoms, including oxygen, nitrogen, sulphur, phosphorus and the halogens, such as chlorine and bromine. Often the covalent bonds between carbon and other atoms are stable enough for us to handle the resulting compounds at room temperature; yet these compounds are not so strongly bonded that they cannot be manipulated by means of well-known chemical reactions.

Functional groups and reactivity

Carbon combines with itself and other atoms to produce open-chain (*acyclic*) and ring (*cyclic*) skeletons, into which are built highly characteristic arrangements of atoms, known as *functional groups* ($\rhd$ table). The diverse but predictable chemical behaviour of the different functional groups is a consequence of their ability either to attract or to repel electrons compared with the rest of the carbon skeleton. The overall effect of the resulting charge distribution is to create a molecule in which some regions are slightly negatively charged (*nucleophilic*), and others slightly positively charged (*electrophilic*).

Most organic reactions involve the electrophilic and nucleophilic centres of different molecules coming together as a prelude to the formation of new covalent bonds. An appreciation of how particular compounds behave towards others and of the various mechanisms by which such reactions occur forms the basis of classical organic synthesis. This allows chemists to build up large molecules, containing many different functional groups and with a great diversity of chemical properties, in a controlled and predictable manner.

Chirality and the tetrahedral carbon atom

Alanine ($\rhd$ photo) is one of the 20 naturally occurring amino acids from which proteins are synthesized in living organisms ($\rhd$ below and p. 86). Amino acids are characterized by their possession of two functional groups – a carboxylic-acid group (CO_2H) and an amine group (NH_2). Different amino acids, often with very different properties, are distinguished by the identity of a third group – a methyl group (CH_3) in the case of alanine.

A more detailed examination of alanine reveals another feature of paramount importance to the modern chemist. The four groups bonded to the central carbon atom are arranged in such a way as to define a tetrahedron in three dimensions. This spatial arrangement (or *configuration*) can exist in two different forms, one the non-superimposable mirror image of the other. They differ as our right hand does to our left, so the central carbon atom is said to be *chiral* (from the Greek for 'hand'), or *asymmetric*. The two different forms are known as *enantiomers*.

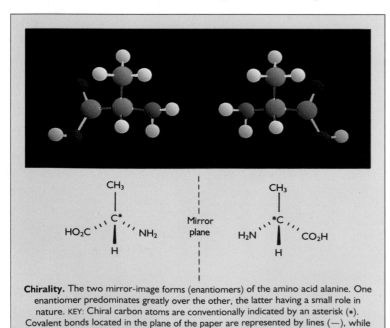

Chirality. The two mirror-image forms (enantiomers) of the amino acid alanine. One enantiomer predominates greatly over the other, the latter having a small role in nature. KEY: Chiral carbon atoms are conventionally indicated by an asterisk (∗). Covalent bonds located in the plane of the paper are represented by lines (—), while bonds orientated (tetrahedrally) above and below this plane are displayed as wedges (▶) and dashes (|||) respectively. (CD)

The physical consequences of this apparently minor difference can be quite startling. Limonene is a liquid hydrocarbon with one chiral carbon atom, and occurs as two enantiomers. While one enantiomer smells strongly of lemons, the other smells strongly of oranges. The different spatial arrangements of the groups and consequently the different overall shapes of the two molecules cause them to interact differently with molecular sensors in our nose, so each initiates a different message that is then sent to our brain.

Molecular recognition of this kind, based upon chirality, is prevalent in the chemistry of the molecules of life. Nucleic acids (DNA, RNA; ▷ p. 86), polysaccharides (large natural sugar molecules) and proteins (▷ p. 86), especially enzymes, all discriminate between enantiomers in their respective modes of action. The *enzymes* are nature's catalysts, providing a very efficient environment in which molecules can come together and react. Like other proteins, they are built up from chains of amino acids, joined together in numerous different combinations. The chains twist and coil, so causing the functional groups of different amino acids to come together or 'converge', thereby creating specific regions known as *active sites*. It is at the active site that particular molecules may be held briefly while reactions are performed on them, before being released as new molecules. However, an enzyme is generally very selective about which molecules it will accept; often, only one of a pair of enantiomers will be accepted, the other being the wrong shape to fit comfortably into the active site. In this way, life itself depends vitally upon chirality.

Designing organic molecules

If a desired compound does not occur naturally, it must be made, or synthesized, by modifying a molecule that already exists. Such a chemical synthesis may involve a number of different steps, and even relatively simple molecules could, in principle, be synthesized in many different ways from many different starting materials. Using their knowledge of chemical reactions, chemists examine several possible routes to a molecule before setting out upon its synthesis. *Retrosynthetic analysis* is a design method in which the desired product is broken down theoretically, or 'disconnected', into smaller and smaller fragments until a convenient starting material is reached. It relies upon a knowledge of how different functional groups can be manipulated to build up the desired molecule gradually.

The art of synthetic design has progressed rapidly over the last 30 years. Chemists have learnt to handle and manipulate new families of compounds, and discovered new synthetic transformations that may operate under milder conditions than existing ones or at a much faster rate. This has been coupled with great advances in the methods used to purify and analyse molecules; such methods have allowed the structures of molecules to be probed more deeply, thereby revealing how they react together and how a particular molecule may interact with its surroundings. In principle, the expertise already exists to synthesize any molecule, however complex; the only constraint is time. As we learn more and more about the chemicals that exist all around us – and within us – we put ourselves in an increasingly strong position to tackle the many intricate scientific and environmental issues facing humanity.

SYNTHETIC POLYMERS

One of the most far-reaching influences chemistry has had on our lives in the 20th century has been the introduction of increasingly advanced materials based on *synthetic polymers* (which include the plastics; ▷ also p. 199). These are materials composed of repeating small molecules, or *monomers*, joined together to make long chains. The way in which these chains interact with one another depends on the monomers from which they are composed, and can differ greatly. This accounts for the wide range of properties that polymers can possess, including flexibility, strength and heat resistance. Demand for improved materials, both for technological and household application, is still increasing, and – although already widespread – there is still a lot more polymer-based technology to come into our lives.

Along with the emergence of excellent new dyes and paints, the fashion and display industries have been revolutionized by the advent of polyester fibres such as Dacron, and polyamide fibres such as Nylon 6 and Nylon 66 (▷ p. 199). These early synthetic polymers were all composed of moderately flexible chains. More recently, stiff-chain polymers – often incorporating aromatic rings (▷ table) – have found many applications. Because of their low flammability, high thermal stability and great tensile strength, compounds such as Kevlar and Victrex PEEK are becoming very widespread; they may be found in an enormous range of products, from electrically heated hair-styling brushes to bullet-proof vests.

Not only has Kevlar a tensile strength higher than that of steel but it also has a strength-to-weight ratio that is six times better. Composite materials containing Kevlar have been used to build the tail sections of jumbo jets; it is transparent to radar (and is thus used in stealth technology; ▷ pp. 222–3), it eliminates corrosion, and its lightness lowers fuel costs. The outstanding mechanical and electrical properties of Victrex PEEK, particularly when employed in fibre-reinforced composites with glass, carbon or Kevlar, are such that it can be used to replace metal alloys to great advantage in many engineering situations. The day of the all-plastic motor car is just around the corner.

FUNCTIONAL GROUPS

A selection of important functional groups. An 'R' indicates a site where another functional group or an atom may be attached.

Alkenes are hydrocarbons that contain one or more carbon double bonds. Alkenes with just one double bond form a series including ethene (ethylene; C_2H_4), propene and butene.

Alcohols. Examples include methanol (CH_3OH) and ethanol (C_2H_5OH; ▷ p. 34).

Ketones. Examples include propanone (acetone; CH_3COCH_3).

Aldehydes. An important example is methanal (formaldehyde; HCOH), used in the production of formalin (a disinfectant) and synthetic resins.

Carboxylic acids. As well as occurring in organic acids, such as acetic (ethanoic) acid (CH_3CO_2H; vinegar), this group occurs in all amino acids, including alanine (▷ photo).

Amines, together with the carboxylic-acid group, occur in all amino acids.

Amides. The most important type of amide bond is that formed in protein synthesis, when the carboxylic-acid group of one amino acid condenses with the amine group of another to give a *peptide bond*.

Thiols. This group is characterized by a strong, disagreeable odour. An example is ethanethiol (▷ p. 35).

Aromatic compounds. The six-membered ring containing three double bonds is highly stable and is thus a very common characteristic of organic compounds.

The History of Science

If we consider science as the systematic investigation of reality by observation, experimentation and induction (the derivation of general laws from particular observations), then among early civilizations science did not exist. Certainly discoveries were made, but they were piecemeal. Myth and religion dominated as modes for explaining the world.

This began to change with the speculations of the early Greek philosophers, who excluded supernatural causes from their accounts of reality. By the 3rd century BC Greek science was highly sophisticated and producing theoretical models that have shaped the development of science ever since.

With the fall of Greece to the Roman Empire, science fell from grace. Few important advances were made outside medicine (▷ p. 156), and the work done was firmly within the Greek traditions and conceptual frameworks.

For several centuries from the fall of Rome in the 5th century AD, science was practically unknown in Western Europe. Islamic culture alone preserved Greek knowledge (▷ p. 240), and later transmitted it back to the West (▷ p. 248). Between the 13th and 15th centuries some advances were made in the fields of mechanics and optics, while men like Roger Bacon insisted on the importance of personal experience and observation.

The 16th century marked the coming of the so-called 'Scientific Revolution', a period of scientific progress beginning with Copernicus (▷ p. 10) and culminating with Newton (▷ p. 14). Not only did science break new conceptual ground but it gained enormously in prestige as a result. Science and its trappings became highly fashionable from the later 17th century, and also attracted a great deal of royal and state patronage.

MAJOR DEVELOPMENTS IN SCIENCE

3500–3000 BC
The Sumerians develop metallurgy and the use of a lunar calendar.

3000–2500 BC
Multiplication tables are invented and mathematics used for calculating areas. In Egypt a solar calendar is used.

2500–2000 BC
A superior lunar calendar is used in Babylon. Units of time such as the minute and hour are introduced.

2000–1500 BC
Babylonians use maths to plot planetary positions. The stellar constellations are identified. Simple taxonomies for classifying animals are used.

1500–1000 BC
Mathematics continues to develop. Chemicals are used to make paints and cosmetics.

1000–500 BC
Early Greek philosophers conceive rational theories of the universe. Those of **Thales of Miletus** (640–560 BC; ▷ p. 10) and **Anaximander** (611–547 BC) are notable. Anaximander introduced the concept of infinity into cosmology and believed that life had evolved from the sea. The notion that the world is a sphere is attributed to **Pythagoras** (c. 580–c. 500 BC), who also formulated basic laws of geometry (▷ pp. 50 and 51–3).

500–400 BC
The concept of elementary matter was introduced by **Empedocles of Agrigentum** (c. 490–430 BC), who believed that there are four elements, namely earth, water, fire and air. **Democritus** (c. 460–c. 370 BC) and **Leucippus** (c. 500–450 BC) conceived of matter as consisting of minute invisible particles called atoms (▷ p. 30).

400–300 BC
The first fully comprehensive cosmology to give a rational account of all physical phenomena was devised by **Aristotle** (384–322 BC; ▷ also pp. 302–5). Aristotle's cosmology and physics ruled until the time of Galileo and Newton. He did the first systematic work on comparative biology.

300–200 BC
Archimedes of Syracuse (287–212 BC) pioneered the sciences of mechanics and hydrostatics (▷ pp. 16–17), invented the lever and the Archimedian screw for raising water, and made many contributions to mathematics. **Aristarchus of Samos** (c. 310–250 BC) realized that the Earth rotates on its own axis and orbits the Sun (▷ p. 10). **Eratosthenes of Cyrene** (276–196 BC) calculated the circumference of the Earth (▷ p. 10).

200–100 BC
The most accurate ancient star catalogue was constructed by **Hipparchus of Nicaea** (c. 190–120 BC), who also discovered the precession of the equinoxes.

100 BC–AD 100
Little original science was done in these centuries, although Greek astronomy was perfected by **Ptolemy** (Claudius Ptolemaeus, AD 100–170), in whose system the Earth was the centre of the universe (▷ p. 10). Greek knowledge was codified by encyclopedists such as **Pliny the Elder** (Gaius Plinius Secundus, AD 23–79). The earliest known alchemical text appeared (▷ alchemy, p. 34).

AD 200–1200
Much of classical learning disappeared from Europe during the so-called 'Dark Ages', but was preserved by Islamic scholars such as **Avicenna** (Ibn Sinna, AD 980–1037) and **Averroës** (ibn-Rushd, 1126–98). From c. 1100 it was transmitted back when Christian scholars translated Arabic texts into Latin.

1200–1300
Albertus Magnus (Count von Böllstadt, c. 1193–1280), a German scholastic philosopher, worked to reconcile Aristotelian science and philosophy with Christian doctrine. The English friar **Roger Bacon** (c. 1214–92) became a great advocate of experimentation. He did important work in optics and was the first European to describe the manufacture of gunpowder.

1300–1400
The English philosopher **William of Ockham** (c. 1285–1349) propounded the principle (known as *Ockham's razor*) that 'entities are not to be multiplied beyond necessity'. This principle, that the simplest explanation is the best, was adopted by many later scientists, including the French bishop **Nicole d'Oresme** (c. 1325–82), who worked on cosmology and motion. In the latter field, Oresme confirmed the theories of the Merton School at Oxford, and both Oresme and the Mertonians worked on the mathematization of science.

1400–1500
There was little of scientific note in this century, although at the end of the century **Leonardo da Vinci** (1452–1519; ▷ p. 312) began his studies of all kinds of natural phenomena. The discovery of the New World in 1492 contradicted the geographical teachings of Ptolemy, so helping to free science from its psychological dependence on ancient authorities.

1500–1550
Nicholas Copernicus (1473–1543), the Polish astronomer, revived the heliocentric theory, placing the Sun at the centre of the universe (▷ p. 10). Because this theory threatened the Church's cosmology, Copernicus only circulated it among a few friends. Chemistry was to some extent freed from its alchemical bonds by **Paracelsus** (Theophrastus Bombastus von Hohenheim, 1493–1541).

1550–1600
The study of terrestrial magnetism was developed by English physician **William Gilbert** (1540–1603), who introduced the concept of magnetic

The Alchemist (detail) by the 17th-century Dutch painter David Ryckaert. Although the theoretical basis of alchemy was an extraordinary mixture of occult and esoteric ideas, the alchemists of the Middle Ages made many practical chemical discoveries, including alcohol and the mineral acids.
(Kunsthistorisches Museum, Vienna/ AKG)

SEE ALSO

- ASTRONOMY pp. 2–9
- THE HISTORY OF ASTRONOMY p. 10
- PHYSICS pp. 14–33
- CHEMISTRY pp. 34–47
- EMINENT MATHEMATICIANS p. 50
- EVOLUTION p. 84
- GENETICS p. 86
- THE HISTORY OF MEDICINE p. 156
- TECHNOLOGY pp. 188–225

In the course of the 19th century science became professionalized, with clearcut career structures and hierarchies emerging, centred on universities, government departments and commercial organizations. This trend continued into the 20th century, when science became highly dependent on technological advances. These have not been lacking.

Modern science is immense and extremely complex. It is virtually impossible to have an informed overview of what science as a whole is up to. This has made many people regard it with some suspicion. Nevertheless Western civilization is fully committed to a belief in the value of scientific progress as a force for the good of humanity. While some of the world's greatest dangers and horrors have their roots in scientific endeavour, there is some hope that science will also eventually provide viable solutions to them.

---

poles (⊳ p. 26). **Tycho Brahe** (1546–1601; ⊳ p. 10) produced a very accurate star catalogue, and his assistant **Johann Kepler** (1571–1630; ⊳ p. 10) demonstrated that planetary orbits round the Sun are elliptical. The English statesman and philosopher **Sir Francis Bacon** (1561–1626) revived the use of induction in scientific method.

1600–1650

The modern science of mechanics (⊳ p. 14) was founded by **Galileo Galilei** (1564–1642). Galileo formulated laws of motion that conflicted with ancient physics, and tended to support the heliocentric hypothesis (⊳ p. 10). The French philosopher and mathematician **René Descartes** (1596–1650; ⊳ also pp. 50 and 302–5) proposed a radically mechanistic model of the universe that rendered God virtually redundant. He also invented coordinate geometry.

1650–1700

The controversy between ancient and modern cosmologies and physics was resolved in the work of Englishman **Sir Isaac Newton** (1643–1727). He formulated the law of universal gravitation and three laws of motion (⊳ pp. 14–15) and made important contributions to optics and calculus. Chemistry continued to be separated from its alchemical roots by the work of men such as the English scientists **Robert Boyle** (1627–1716) and **Robert Hooke** (1635–1703), who studied the chemistry of gases and the nature of respiration and combustion.

1700–1750

This problem was also tackled by the German chemist **Georg Stahl** (1660–1743), who suggested a hypothetical substance called *phlogiston* as the causal agent of combustion.

1750–1800

The Swedish botanist **Carl Linnaeus** (1707–78) introduced the modern system of biological classification (⊳ p. 83). The phlogiston theory was rendered obsolete with the discovery of oxygen by the English chemist **Joseph Priestley** (1733–

1804). However, it was left to the Frenchman **Antoine Lavoisier** (1743–94) to name oxygen and demonstrate its role in combustion. Lavoisier also formulated the important law of conservation of matter and recognized that air and water are chemical compounds. In geology the Scotsman **James Hutton** (1726–97) introduced the notion that the Earth is millions of years old, denying catastrophes such as Noah's Flood. In France **Charles Augustin Coulomb** (1736–1806) first identified the electric force (⊳ p. 26). In Italy **Count Alessandro Volta** (1745–1827) made important experiments with electricity (⊳ p. 28), while the Frenchman **André Ampère** (1775–1836) did pioneering work on electricity and magnetism (⊳ pp. 26–7). The Frenchman **Jean-Baptiste Lamarck** (1744–1829) proposed a theory of evolution (⊳ p. 84).

1800–1850

The conceptual groundwork of modern chemistry was laid by the Englishman **John Dalton** (1766–1844) when he revived atomic theory (⊳ p. 30) and applied it to gases. The Englishman **Michael Faraday** (1791–1867) and the American **Joseph Henry** (1797–1878) separately discovered electromagnetic induction (⊳ p. 26–7), the basis of electricity generation. Study of the nature of heat was furthered by American-born physicist **Benjamin Thompson** (**Count Rumford**, 1753–1814), who suggested that it was a form of motion rather than a substance. The English amateur scientist **James Joule** (1818–89) did important work on thermodynamics (⊳ pp. 18–19).

1850–1900

Thermodynamics was furthered by the Scottish physicist **William Thomson** (**Lord Kelvin**, 1824–1907). The Russian chemist **Dmitri Mendeleyev** (1834–1907) compiled the first periodic table of chemical elements (⊳ p. 36). The English naturalist **Charles Darwin** (1809–92) revolutionized biology with his theory of evolution (⊳ p. 84) and the study of genetics was furthered by the Austrian monk **Gregor Mendel** (1822–84;

⊳ p. 86). The Scottish physicist **James Clerk Maxwell** (1831–79) established the concept of the electromagnetic force (⊳ p. 27), and in 1887 the existence of electromagnetic waves was demonstrated experimentally by the German physicist **Heinrich Rudolf Hertz** (1857–94). At the end of the century another German physicist, **Wilhelm Röntgen** (1845–1923), discovered X-rays (⊳ pp. 27, 156 and 210). **Ernest Rutherford** (1871–1937), an English physicist, used X-rays to investigate gases, and discovered alpha, beta and gamma rays (⊳ pp. 30–1 and below).

1900–PRESENT

The American geneticist **Thomas Hunt Morgan** (1866–1945) discovered chromosomes (⊳ pp. 88–9). After the Canadian bacteriologist **Oswald Avery** (1877–1955) had demonstrated that DNA is responsible for inheritance, the Anglo-American team of **Francis Crick** (1916–), **James Watson** (1928–) and **Maurice Wilkins** (1916–) were able in 1953 to unravel its structure (⊳ p. 86).

The structure of atoms was investigated by Ernest Rutherford (⊳ above), who discovered the atomic nucleus (⊳ p. 30). The German physicist **Albert Einstein** (1879–1955) radically revised classical physics with his theories of special and general relativity (⊳ p. 33). The German **Max Planck** (1858–1947) formulated quantum theory (⊳ p. 32), which was applied to Rutherford's atom by the Dane **Niels Bohr** (1885–1962), thereby effecting another major revision of classical physics (⊳ p. 30). These ideas led to the development of nuclear power and nuclear weapons.

Modern science is dominated by expensive technology and extreme specialization. In physics subatomic particles (⊳ p. 31) continue to be investigated, and are thought to hold the key to understanding the origin and ultimate nature of the universe. In biology, genetic engineering (⊳ pp. 87, 132 and 201) has become feasible and may produce untold benefits – or otherwise.

Mathematics and its Applications

Many people think of mathematics in terms of rules to be learned in order to manipulate symbols or study numbers or shapes in the abstract for their own sake. Mathematical theory does develop in the abstract; it need have no dependence on anything outside itself. The truth of the theory is measured by logic rather than experiment. However, one of its most valuable uses is in describing or modelling processes in the real world, and thus there is constant interaction between pure mathematics and applied mathematics.

George Boole. Despite being largely self-taught, Boole became Professor of Mathematics at Cork University. He laid the foundations of Boolean algebra, which was fundamental to the development of the digital electronic computer (▷ box, p. 51).
(SPL)

Mathematics may be considered as the very general study of the structure of systems. Since the study is unrelated to the physical world, rigorous formal proofs are sought, rather than experimental verifications. Theory is presented in terms of a small number of given truths (known as *axioms*) from which the entire theory can be inferred. Thus, the aims are for generality in approach and rigour in proof, aims that explain the traditional concern of mathematicians for the unification of seemingly different branches of mathematics. As an example, Descartes showed that geometrical figures could be described in terms of algebra, enabling geometric proofs to be established in terms of arithmetic, so that both generality and rigour were advanced.

There is no sharp boundary between the study of mathematical systems in the abstract (*pure mathematics*) and the study of such systems to make inferences about certain physical systems that are described by the mathematical theory (*applied mathematics*). In principle, any branch of mathematics may turn out to describe some physical, economic, biological, medical, or other system. *Modelling* a physical system consists of seeking a formal mathematical theory that conforms with the properties of the physical system. Often, as for example in computer simulations of space travel, the mathematical theories are very large and complex, but sometimes the model can be simple. Sometimes, known mathematics can describe and predict the behaviour of the system; at other times, the modelling can give rise to new branches of mathematics. Although applied mathematics can include the application of statistical theory to such areas as sociology, the term is usually restricted to the application of the methods of advanced calculus, linear algebra and other branches of advanced mathematics to physical and technological processes.

SOME EMINENT MATHEMATICIANS

Pythagoras (c. 582–500 BC), Greek philosopher. His Pythagorean brotherhood – a religious community – saw mystical significance in the idea of number. Popularly remembered for Pythagoras' theorem (▷ p. 52).

Euclid (c. 3rd century BC), Greek mathematician. Euclid devised the first axiomatic treatment of geometry and studied irrational numbers. Until recent times, most elementary geometry textbooks were little more than versions of Euclid's great book.

Archimedes (c. 287–212 BC), Greek mathematician, philosopher and engineer, born in Sicily. His extensions of the work of Euclid especially concerned the surface and volume of the sphere and the study of other solid shapes. His methods anticipated the fundamentals of integral calculus.

Descartes, René (1596–1650), French philosopher, mathematician and military scientist. He is known for his doctrine that all knowledge can be derived from the certainty: *Cogito ergo sum* ('I think therefore I am'). He developed analytical geometry, whereby geometrical figures can be described in algebraic terms (▷ p. 58).

Newton, Sir Isaac (1643–1727), English mathematician, astronomer and physicist. Newton came to be recognized as the most influential scientist of all time. He developed differential calculus (▷ p. 59) and his treatments of gravity and motion (▷ p. 14) form the basis of much applied mathematics.

Euler, Leonhard (1707–83), Swiss-born mathematician, who was famed for being able to perform complex calculations in his head, and so was able to go on working after he went blind. He worked in almost all branches of mathematics and made particular contributions to analytical geometry, trigonometry and calculus, and thus to the unification of mathematics. Euler was responsible for much of modern mathematical notation.

Gauss, Carl Friedrich (1777–1855), German mathematician. He developed the theory of complex numbers (▷ p. 54). Director of an astronomical observatory, he conducted a survey, based on trigonometric techniques, of the kingdom of Hanover. He published works on the application of mathematics to electrostatics and electrodynamics.

Cauchy, Baron Augustin-Louis (1789–1857), French mathematician and physicist. He developed the modern treatment of calculus and the theory of functions, and introduced rigour to much of mathematics.

Boole, George (1815–64), English mathematician (▷ box, p. 51).

Cantor, Georg (1845–1918), Russian-born mathematician who worked in Germany. His most important work was on finite and infinite sets. He was greatly interested in theology and philosophy.

Klein, Christian Felix (1849–1925), German mathematician. Klein introduced a programme for the classification of geometry in terms of group theory. His interest in *topology* (the study of geometric figures that are subjected to deformations) produced the first description of a *Klein bottle* – which has a continuous one-sided surface.

Hilbert, David (1862–1943), German mathematician. In 1901, Hilbert listed 23 major unsolved problems in mathematics, many of which still remain unsolved. His work contributed to the rigour and unity of modern mathematics and to the development of the theory of *computability*.

Russell, Lord Bertrand (1872–1970), English philosopher, mathematician, pacifist and winner of the Nobel Prize for Literature. Russell did much of the basic work on mathematical logic and the foundations of mathematics. He found the paradox now named after him (▷ p. 56) in the theory of sets proposed by the German logician Gottlob Frege (1848–1925), and went on to develop the whole of arithmetic in terms of pure logic.

CHAOS THEORY

From its beginnings, science has been a quest for orderly laws that govern nature. And with each advance it has seemed that some element of disorder has been conquered. Complex dynamical systems, in particular, could be understood and quantified when the calculus was invented (▷ pp. 58–9). But scientists have long recognized that many natural phenomena – the movement of clouds, turbulence in streams or in the rising smoke from a cigarette (▷ box, p. 17), the movement of a leaf in the wind, the patterns of brain waves, disease epidemics or traffic jams – are so inherently disordered and chaotic as to seem to defy any attempt to find governing laws.

As early as 1903, however, the French mathematician Jules Henri Poincaré (1854–1912) – famous for his work on topology – recognized that there are circumstances in which tiny inaccuracies in initial conditions can be multiplied so as to lead to huge differences in the outcome. Poincaré's work was largely forgotten until in 1961 the American meteorologist and mathematician Edward N. Lorenz, working with a crude early computer, set out to produce a mathematical model of how the atmosphere behaves. In the course of this work Lorenz accidentally hit upon the first mathematical system in which small changes in the initial conditions led to overwhelming differences in the outcome. Lorenz showed that this phenomenon made long-range weather prediction almost impossible. His work and the analogies that developed from it attracted the attention of scientists in other fields and led to the development of a new branch of mathematics – chaos theory. One of the most striking of these analogies is known as the 'butterfly effect' – the idea that the air perturbation caused by the movement of a butterfly wing in China can cause a storm a month later in New York.

By the 1970s some scientists and mathematicians, and even some economists, were beginning to investigate disorder and instability. Physiologists were considering patterns of chaos in the action of the heart-patterns that could lead to sudden cardiac arrest; electronic engineers were investigating the sometimes chaotic behaviour of oscillators; ecologists were examining the seemingly random way in which wildlife populations changed; chemists were studying unexpected fluctuations in chemical reactions; and economists were wondering whether some order might be found in random stock-market price fluctuations.

The first indication for an underlying pattern in chaos was found by the American physicist Mitchell Feigenbaum. In 1976 Feigenbaum noticed that when an ordered system starts to break down into chaos, it often does so in accordance with a consistent pattern in which the rate of occurrence of some event suddenly doubles over and over again. This is exactly what happens in *fractal geometry* – in which any part of a figure is a reduced copy of a larger part. Feigenbaum also discovered that at a certain constant number of doublings, the structure acquires a kind of stability. This numerical constant, called Feigenbaum's number, can be applied to a wide range of chaotic systems.

To understand what mathematicians mean by chaos it is best to consider a simple example. Iteration is the mathematical process in which the result of a calculation is applied as the starting point for a repeat of the same process and so on. One might, for instance, take a number and halve it, then take the result and halve that, and so on repeatedly. The set of numbers that result is called the *orbit* of the number. Starting with, say, 16, the orbit would be 8, 4, 2, 1, 1/2, 1/4, 1/8, 1/16... Again, one might perform an iterative process on any number (x) between 0 and 1, the process being 'multiply the product of x and $1 - x$ by 3'. This gives a readily predictable orbit. Surprisingly, iteration for numbers between 0 and 1 using the process 'multiply the product of x and $1 - x$ by 4' produces a chaotic orbit for some numbers and a predictable one for others. Closely related starting values give orbital numbers that are widely different. In other words, the system is sometimes highly sensitive to its starting values, sometimes not. This is characteristic of what mathematicians mean by chaos. Chaos theory attempts to describe how such systems change from predictable to wholly disordered.

Today there is much debate as to whether chaos theory, so far as it goes at present, actually does adequately describe seemingly disordered dynamical systems in nature – whether it really is, as some have claimed, a new mathematical tool of the same order of importance as calculus, or even that it is a discipline to rank in importance with relativity and quantum mechanics. The controversy rages on but the level of interest and the volume of research continue to rise. Major developments, one way or the other, are to be expected soon.

BOOLEAN ALGEBRA

The English mathematician George Boole (1815–64) developed a system of symbolic logic, which he described fully in the book *An Investigation of the Laws of Thought* (1854). In this system Boole reduced logic to a simple algebra. This had two important effects – logical processes could now be treated mathematically, and logic, formerly a somewhat moribund discipline, was given a new lease of life and interest. Boole's symbolic logic was later used to put mathematics on a strictly logical basis by such men as Gottlob Frege and Bertrand Russell (▷ pp. 56–7).

Among other things, Boole envisaged a two-value (binary) algebra – a simple subset of his more general Boolean algebra. This has since become of enormous importance as the basis of the operation of digital computers in which any number (or, by coding, any letter or symbol) can be represented in terms of a series of 1s or 0s (▷ pp. 55 and 211). Boolean logic, in which all values are reduced to 'true' or 'false', fits well with the binary system in computers, in which a 1 can also be used to represent 'true' and a 0 also used to represent 'false'. Boolean *operators* are used to manipulate 'true' or 'false' values.

The laws of Boolean algebra are easily implemented by simple electronic computer 'gates'. In the operation of these, the Boolean AND operator gives a 1 (true) output if *both* inputs are 1 (true); otherwise the operator gives a 0 (false) output. The OR operator gives a 1 (true) output if *either or both* of the two inputs is 1 (true); otherwise it gives a 0 (false) output. The XOR (exclusive OR) operator gives a 1 (true) output if only one of the inputs is 1 (true); otherwise it gives a 0 (false) output. Finally, the NOT operator gives a 1 (true) output if the single input is 0 (false), or a 0 (false) output if the input is 1 (true). AND, OR, XOR and NOT gates, arranged in various ways, can perform any logical operation. (In fact the functions of all these gates can be carried out by various combinations of NAND gates, which are AND gates with a simple addition of a NOT gate to convert 1s into 0s or vice versa.) Countless millions of these Boolean devices are in constant use all over the world, carrying out Boolean algebra at speeds of millions of operations per second.

SEE ALSO

● PHYSICAL SCIENCES pp. 4–49
● MATHEMATICS pp. 52–9
● ECONOMICS pp. 170–7
● COMPUTERS pp. 211–13

Geometry and Trigonometry

Geometry is the branch of mathematics that studies space and shape. The classical ideas of geometry – generally known as Euclidean geometry after the mathematician Euclid (▷ p. 50) – were developed by the Ancient Greeks, who created a rigorous system of theorems and proofs built from a minimal basic axiomatic structure. The later development of coordinate systems – most notably through the studies of Descartes (▷ p. 58) in the 17th century – resulted in a more algebraic, descriptive approach to geometry. While in no way superseding Euclid, algebraic geometry provided a much more natural link with the theory of calculus which was also being developed at that time (▷ pp. 58–9).

The 20th century has seen a variety of new ideas in this field, such as *transformation geometry*, with its emphasis on symmetries, and *spherical geometry*, which studies shapes and measurement on the surface of a sphere.

Trigonometry was born from the need to find ways of evaluating angles and lengths, initially to compliment the use of Pythagoras' triangle (▷ below) in right-angled triangles, but rapidly expanding into all fields of geometry. The periodic nature of trigonometrical functions means they are also fundamental to the consideration of wave motion in many areas of physics and applied mathematics.

Triangulation

Geometry establishes that two triangles each have angles of the same sizes if, and only if, corresponding pairs of sides are in the same proportions.

In diagram 1 D, E and F are the centre-points of sides AB, BC and CA respectively. So, DE is half the length of AC, EF is half the length of AB, and FD is half the length of BC. Thus, the shaded triangle, DEF, is *similar* to the large triangle, and the angles at D, E and F are, respectively, equal to those at C, A and B. Furthermore, the triangles ADF, FEC, DBE and EFD are all *congruent*, i.e. identical in shape and size, and are thus all similar to triangle ABC.

A right-angled triangle is a triangle where one of the angles is 90°. *Pythagoras' theorem* states that, in a right-angled triangle, the square of the length of the *hypotenuse* (the side opposite the right angle) equals the sum of the squares of the lengths of the other two sides. So, in the triangle shown in diagram 2, $AC^2 = AB^2 + BC^2$. Trigonometry relies on the recognition that in a right-angled triangle the ratio of the lengths of pairs of sides depends only on the sizes of the two acute angles (i.e. angles less than 90°) of the triangle.

These ratios are given names. For example, the *sine* of an angle is the ratio of the side opposite the given angle to the hypotenuse. The Greek letters θ (*theta*) and ϕ (*phi*) are usually used to denote the angles; thus in the triangle shown we say that the sine of θ, usually written sin θ, is BC/AC. Similarly, since the *cosine* (cos) of the angle is the ratio of the side adjacent to the given angle to the hypotenuse, cos θ is AB/AC. The third basic ratio is the *tangent* (tan), which is the ratio of the opposite to the adjacent side, BC/AB in the example; it is easy to see that tan θ must always equal sin θ / cos θ. Pythagoras' theorem can be used to establish some very useful values for sin, cos and tan.

In triangle DEF (diagram 3), $DE = EF = 1$, so the angles at D and F are equal, that is they are each 45° (the internal angles of a triangle add up to 180°). Using Pythagoras' theorem, $DF^2 = 1^2 + 1^2 = 2$, so $DF = \sqrt{2}$. We can therefore conclude:

$$\sin 45° = 1/\sqrt{2}$$
$$\cos 45° = 1/\sqrt{2}$$
$$\tan 45° = 1.$$

In triangle GHK (diagram 4), $GH = HK = KG = 2$, so the angles at G, H and K are equal, that is they are each 60°. Using Pythagoras' theorem, $KL^2 + 1^2 = 2^2$, so $KL = \sqrt{3}$. We therefore have:

$$\sin 60° = \tfrac{1}{2}\sqrt{3} = \cos 30°$$
$$\cos 60° = 1/2 = \sin 30°$$
$$\tan 60° = \sqrt{3}$$
$$\tan 30° = 1/\sqrt{3}.$$

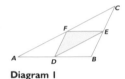

Diagram 1

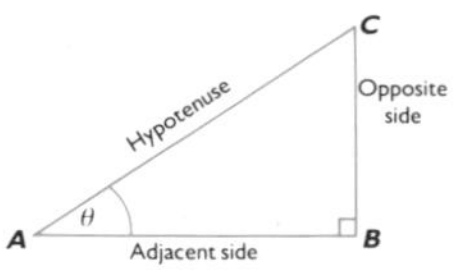

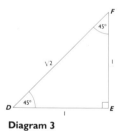

Diagram 2

Diagram 3

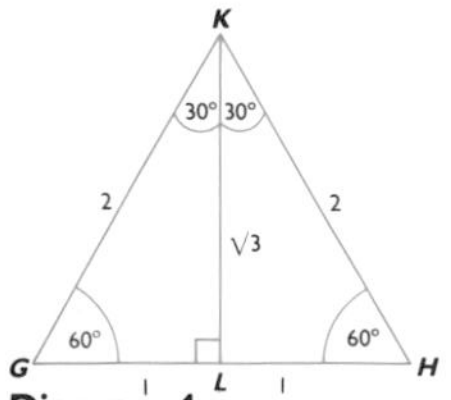

Diagram 4

SEE ALSO

● MATHEMATICS AND ITS APPLICATIONS p. 50
● FUNCTIONS, GRAPHS AND CHANGE p. 58

CONIC SECTIONS

Conic sections are curves that are formed by the intersection of a plane (▷ p. 53) and a cone.

An *ellipse* is a closed conic section with the appearance of a flattened circle. The orbital path of each of the planets around the Sun is approximately an ellipse.

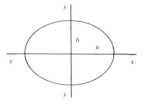

Area = πab

A *parabola* is a conic section that is formed by the intersection of a cone by a plane parallel to its side. If you throw a ball in the air, then the path of the ball will be approximately a parabola with its axis vertical.

A *hyperbola* is a conic section that is formed by a plane that cuts a cone making a larger angle with the base than the angle made by the side of the cone.

PLANE FIGURES

Plane figures lie entirely on one plane, i.e. they are two-dimensional.

Polygons

A polygon is a closed plane figure with three or more straight sides that meet at the same number of vertices and do not intersect other than at those vertices. (A *vertex* is a point at which two sides of a polygon meet.) Important polygons include triangles (3 sides), quadrilaterals (4), pentagons (5), hexagons (6), octagons (8), decagons (10) and dodecagons (12).

Triangles

A triangle is a three-sided polygon. A *scalene* triangle has sides of three different lengths, and has no axes of symmetry. If two sides of a triangle are equal in length, the triangle is *isosceles*, and has one axis of symmetry and a pair of equal angles.

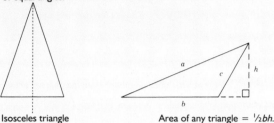

Isosceles triangle   Area of any triangle $= \frac{1}{2}bh$.

An *equilateral* triangle has all its sides equal and all its angles are equal to 60°. The area of a triangle is one half of the area of a parallelogram with the same base and the same height.

Quadrilaterals

A quadrilateral is any plane figure with four sides. A *rectangle* is a quadrilateral in which all the angles are right angles, thus the opposite sides are parallel in pairs. A rectangle may be a square (⇨ below). A rectangle that is not a square has two lines of symmetry.

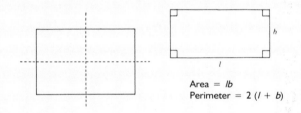

Area $= lb$
Perimeter $= 2 (l + b)$

A *square* is a rectangle whose sides are all equal. It has four lines of symmetry – both diagonals and the two lines joining the middle points of pairs of opposite sides.

Area $= l^2$
Perimeter $= 4 l$

A *parallelogram* is a quadrilateral whose opposite sides are equal in length and parallel. It has no lines of symmetry, unless it is also a rectangle, but it does have rotational symmetry about its centre, the point where the diagonals meet. A *rhombus* is a parallelogram whose sides are all equal in length. Its diagonals are both lines of symmetry, and therefore bisect each other at right angles.

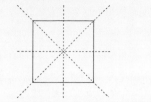

Parallelogram:
Area $= bh$
Perimeter $= 2(a + b)$

Rhombus:
Area $= \frac{1}{2}(2a)(2b)$
Perimeter $= 4 l$

A *trapezium* (or *trapezoid*) is a quadrilateral with two parallel sides of unequal length. The area of a trapezium is half the sum of the two parallel sides.

Circles

A circle is the path of a point that moves at a constant distance – the *radius* – from a fixed point (the centre of the circle).

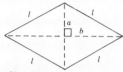

Circumference $= 2\pi r$ or πd
Area $= \pi r^2$
where r = radius, d = diameter and π = pi, the ratio of the circumference of a circle to its diameter (approximately 3.141592).

SOLIDS

Solids are three-dimensional figures, i.e. they have length, breadth and depth.

Polyhedra

A polyhedron is a solid shape with all plane faces. The faces of a regular polyhedron, or regular solid, are all identical regular polygons. There are just five regular polyhedra – the regular tetrahedron (which has 4 faces), the cube (6 faces), the regular octahedron (8 faces), the regular dodecahedron (12 faces) and the regular icosahedron (20 faces).

Prism

A prism is a solid with uniform cross section equal to either end. A rectangular block (or *cuboid*) is the commonest and simplest example.

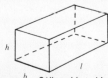

Surface area $= 2(lb + bh + hl)$
Volume $= lbh$ (i.e. the area of the base multiplied by the height).

Pyramid

A pyramid is a solid figure whose base is a polygon and whose special vertex – the *apex* – is joined to each vertex of the base. Therefore, all its faces – except the base – are triangles.

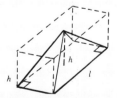

The volume of a pyramid on a rectangular base $= \frac{1}{3}(lbh)$.

A *Tetrahedron* is a pyramid whose base is a triangle. The volume of a tetrahedron $= \frac{1}{3}$ (area of the triangular base multiplied by the height).

Cylinder and Cone

A cylinder may be thought of as a circular prism. It is a solid figure with straight sides and a circular section.

Similarly a cone may be visualized as a circular pyramid. It is a solid figure with a circular base, narrowing to a point or apex.

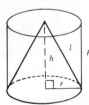

The area of the curved surfaces of a cylinder $= 2\pi rh$.

If the circles at both ends are included, the total area of a cylinder $= 2\pi rh + 2\pi r^2$.
The volume of a cylinder $= \pi r^2 h$.
The volume of a cone $= \frac{1}{3}\pi r^2 h$.

Sphere

A sphere is a solid figure every point of whose surface is equidistant from its centre.

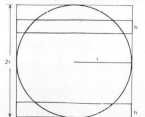

Surface area $= 4\pi r^2$

Volume $= \frac{4}{3}\pi r^3$

Number Systems and Algebra

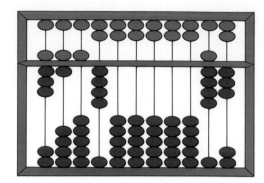

The Chinese abacus usually has two beads representing 5s on each wire above the cross bar, and five beads representing 1s on each wire below the bar. The beads are moved towards the bar. Two numbers are shown here, 8654 on the left and 93 on the right.

The *natural numbers* or *whole numbers* are those we use in counting. We learn these at an early age, perhaps pairing them with our fingers or else learning to chant their names in order: 'one, two, three, four, . . . '. These are both important features of our number system – that these numbers can be used to count sets of objects (▷ p. 56), and that they form a naturally ordered progression that has a first member, the number 1, but no last member: no matter how big a number you come up with, I can always reply with a bigger one – simply by adding 1.

However, even quite simple arithmetic, as we shall see, cannot be carried out wholly within the natural numbers. Ordinarily we take the principles that govern such systems for granted, yet merely to be able to subtract and divide, for example, requires other, more complex, number systems, such as fractions and negative numbers.

Natural numbers and arithmetic

If I have 3 sheep and you give me 4 more, I can count that I now have 7 sheep, or I can use the operation of *addition* to get the same answer: $3 + 4 = 7$. If I promise to give 5 children 4 sweets each, again I can count out 20 sweets altogether, or I can use the operation of *multiplication*: $5 \times 4 = 20$. Here, we have examples of another principle of natural numbers: any addition or multiplication of natural numbers gives another natural number. Such a system is said to be *closed* under these operations. (A closed system is one where an operation on two of its elements produces another element of that system.)

If I had 3 sheep and when you gave me your sheep I had 7, I can use the operation of *subtraction* to find how many sheep you gave to me: $7 - 3 = 4$. If I distribute 20 sweets equally to 5 children, I can use the operation of *division* to find how many I gave to each: $20 \div 5 = 4$. Subtraction is the *inverse operation* of addition; division is the inverse operation of multiplication. However, the natural numbers are not closed under the operations of subtraction and division, as we shall see later.

In simple algebra, we generalize arithmetic by using letters to stand for unknown numbers whose value is to be discovered, or to stand for numbers in general. Usually letters from the beginning of the alphabet are used in the latter way – for example, to express a general truth about numbers, such as $a + b = b + a$. The letters at the end of the alphabet are generally used to represent unknown numbers. For example, the information about the sheep can be expressed by the *equation*, $3 + x = 7$, where x represents the unknown number of sheep you gave to me. Since the two sides of this equation are equal, they remain equal if we treat them both the same way. If we then subtract 3 from each side we get $x = 7 - 3$, that is $x = 4$. We have *solved the equation*.

Subtraction and the integers

The set of natural numbers is not closed under the operation of subtraction; for example, $3 - 7$ does not give a natural number as an answer. We need a system of numbers that is closed under subtraction. The smallest set of numbers that is closed under subtraction is the set of *integers*, i.e. the set $\{..., -3, -2, -1, 0, 1, 2, 3, ...\}$. Here, the positive integers can be identified with the natural numbers; zero (0) is defined as the result of subtracting any integer from itself; and the negative integers are the result of subtracting the corresponding positive integers from zero (e.g. $-3 = 0 - 3$).

Now, every subtraction has an answer within the number system of integers, that is, the integers are closed under subtraction.

Division and the rational numbers

The integers, however, are still not closed under the operation of division. We can construct a system by defining the result of any division, $a \div b$, to be the pair of integers, a and b, written in a notation that clearly distinguishes which divides which. Thus, we write $a \div b$ as the *ratio* or *fraction*, a/b, and we have the system of *rational numbers*.

Leonhard Euler was fascinated by problems concerning number theory. He formulated the law of quadratic reciprocity, defining the properties of and relationship between integers. (AKG)

LAWS OF ARITHMETIC		
Commutative law		
for addition:	$a + b = b + a$	
for multiplication:	$a \times b = b \times a$	
Associative law		
for addition:	$(a + b) + c = a + (b + c)$	
for multiplication:	$(a \times b) \times c = a \times (b \times c)$	
Distributive law		
for multiplication over addition:	$a \times (b + c) = (a \times b) + (a \times c)$	

It is important to note that rational numbers are not identical with their symbols. The same rational number may be represented by many different fractions (in fact, an infinite number of them). For example, 24/8 is the same rational number as 12/4 or 6/2. We adopt the convention of representing them, where possible, by the unique fraction in which there is no *common factor* that can be cancelled out (thus, 14/21 becomes 2/3, where the factor, 7, has been cancelled out). It should also be noted that decimals are rational numbers, since, for example, 0.5 = 5/10 = 1/2, and 1.61 = 161/100.

We do have a problem, however: the rationals cannot be closed under division, because of the integer 0. We cannot give value to $a/0$ for any rational number a. This problem, however, cannot be avoided: we have to be content with the fact that the rationals, excluding the integer 0, are closed under division.

Roots and irrational numbers

6^9, which we read as, '6 to the *power* 9' means 6 multiplied by itself 9 times ($6 \times 6 \times 6 \times 6 \times 6 \times 6 \times 6 \times 6 \times 6$). Generally, a^b, which we read as, 'a to the power b', means a multiplied by itself b times. These are closed operations for the systems of numbers we have so far considered. However, none of these systems guarantees the possibility of the inverse operation, the *extraction of roots*. If $b = a^n$ (where n represents an integer), then a is the nth root of b, written $a = {}^n\sqrt{b}$. For example, since $3 \times 3 = 9$, the second or *square root* of 9 (written ${}^2\sqrt{9}$ or more usually $\sqrt{9}$) equals 3. To give another example, since $2 \times 2 \times 2 = 8$, the third or *cube root* of 8 (written ${}^3\sqrt{8}$) is 2. But none of the systems we have considered is closed under this operation. For example, $\sqrt{2}$, $\sqrt{3}$, and $\sqrt{5}$ cannot be expressed as fractions or as terminating decimals; they are examples of what are called *irrational numbers*. They have exact meaning – for example, by Pythagoras' theorem ($\triangleright$ p. 52), $\sqrt{2}$ is the length of the hypotenuse of a right-angled triangle whose other sides are each length 1; $\sqrt{5}$ is the length of the hypotenuse of a right-angled triangle whose other sides have lengths 1 and 2, etc. Obviously, we need to add the irrationals to our number systems to ensure closure under these calculations.

All the systems we have discussed, the natural numbers, the integers, the rational numbers and the irrationals form together the system of *real numbers*.

Imaginary and complex numbers

However, now we have admitted the extraction of roots, we have opened up a new gap in our number system: we have not, as yet, defined the square root of a negative number. At first sight, we may wonder why this omission should be of any great importance, but without the development of a system to include such numbers, many valuable applications to engineering and physics would not be possible. Surprisingly, we need only extend the number system by one new number. Since all negative numbers are positive multiples of -1 (for example, -6 is 6×-1, so that $\sqrt{-6} = \sqrt{6} \times \sqrt{-1}$) we are concerned only with the square root of -1. The square root of -1 is denoted by the letter i, so we have $i^2 = -1$.

Real multiples of i, such as $3i$, $2.7i$, $2i/3$, $i\sqrt{2}$, etc., are called *imaginary numbers*. The sum of a real number and an imaginary number, such as $5 + 3i$, is a *complex number*. It can be shown that every complex number can be expressed uniquely as the sum of its real and imaginary parts.

LOGARITHMS

Since $a^3 = a \times a \times a$, and $a^2 = a \times a$, then $a^2 \times a^3 = a \times a \times a \times a \times a = a^5$. This is an instance of the general rule for the multiplication of powers of the same base:

$$a^x \times a^y = a^{x+y}.$$

From this it is easy to see that $a^0 = 1$, whence also $a^{-x} = 1/a^x$, and the corresponding rule for division is

$$a^x / a^y = a^{x-y}$$

Similar considerations enable us to give a meaning to a^x even where x is not an integer; for example, since $\sqrt{x} \times \sqrt{x} = x = x^1$, $\sqrt{x}$ must be $x^{1/2}$.

The *logarithm* of a number to a given base is simply the power of that base that is equal to the given number. Tables of *common logarithms*, which use base 10, were used in the days before pocket calculators to assist with complicated multiplications and divisions. For example, it is obviously quite difficult to multiply 135.763 by 4386.734, but it is much easier to add their logarithms, which can be found in a table. Since 135.763 is 10 to the power 2.1327 we find that the logarithm of 135.763 is 2.1327; similarly, since 4386.734 is 10 to the power 3.6421, we find that the logarithm of 4386.734 is 3.6421. We then add these logarithms to find the logarithm of the product of the given numbers. Thus the logarithm of the product is 5.7748, which we can look up in a table of *antilogarithms* to find the answer 595400 (since 10 to the power 5.7748 is 595400). (NB: This is only approximate because the tables are only made up to four figures; the precise answer is 595556.168042.)

OTHER NUMBER NOTATIONS

The usual notation for numbers is a *decimal place-value system*. This means that there are ten distinct digits (0, 1, 2, 3, 4, 5, 6, 7, 8, 9) and that the position of each digit determines what it contributes to the value of the number. Each position gives a value 10 times as great as the position to its right, so, for example, 7234 can be written as 4 units (4×10^0) on the right, plus 3 tens (3×10^1) plus 2 hundreds (2×10^2) plus 7 thousands (7×10^3). We say that 10 is the *base* of the decimal place-value system.

We can easily construct systems with other bases to suit particular needs. The *binary system* uses only the digits 0 and 1; so it has base 2. This is used in the representation of numbers within computers, since the two numerals correspond to the on and off positions of an electronic switch. In the binary system we count as follows: $1, 10(=2+0), 11(=2+1), 100(=4+0+0), 101(=4+0+1), 110(4+2+0), 111(4+2+1), 1000(=8+0+0+0), 1001(=8+0+0+1)$, etc.

Sometimes, especially in computing, it is convenient to use *octal arithmetic* (with base 8) or *hexadecimal arithmetic* (base 16). In base 16, the letters A to F are used as well as the numerals 0 to 9. Obviously it is necessary to know which base is being used, so the base is indicated by a subscript, for example, $31_{10} = 1F_{16} = 37_8 = 11111_2$.

There are many other ways in which numbers systems can vary. Sometimes one can see vestiges of other systems in the numerical terms of a language: in French one counts up to 100 in a mixture of base 10 and base 20; for example, *quatre-vingt-dix* (four times twenty plus ten) equals 90. Even English retains vestiges of base 12, with the words 'eleven' and 'twelve'. The traditional Chinese abacus uses a mixture of base 5 and base 10.

The system of Roman numerals is not a place-value system: the letters have fixed values and are ordered from the largest to the smallest. For example, MDCLXVI = 1000 + 500 + 100 + 50 + 10 + 5 + 1 = 1666. When, however, a letter representing a smaller value precedes a larger, it is subtracted; thus CM = 900, and IX = 9. This makes calculations very difficult, and it has been suggested that the superiority of Eastern mathematics over that of early medieval Europe was a result of the system of Roman numerals.

The rules for using complex numbers are the same as those for real numbers. It can be shown, for example, that

$$(a + ib)(a - ib) = a^2 + b^2.$$

The terms in brackets are thus the factors of $a^2 + b^2$. In fact it turns out that in the complex number system any algebraic expression with integer powers has exactly the same number of factors as the highest power in the expression. This result is so important that it is called the *fundamental theorem of algebra*.

SEE ALSO
● SETS p. 56
● COMPUTERS p. 211

Sets

Sets can be considered simply as any collections of objects. However, in the early 20th century, when attempts were made to formalize the properties of sets, contradictions were discovered that have affected mathematical thinking ever since.

A *set* can be specified either by stipulating some property for an object as a condition of *membership* of the set, or by listing the *members* of the set in any order.

Sets are usually indicated by the use of curly brackets {}, known as *braces*. Thus, suppose we are considering a family that has a cat, a rabbit, a horse, a dog, a mouse and a piranha: we could represent the pets fed and looked after by Sue as {cat, rabbit, horse}. In that case {cat, rabbit, horse} = {x: x is a family pet looked after by Sue}. Sets are often pictured by drawing a circle around representations of their members, thus:

Union and intersection

We can use circles to show the relationship between two (or more) sets. Let us suppose that

Sue has a brother, Tim, who feeds and looks after the dog and the mouse; he also helps Sue look after the horse. If *S* is the set of pets looked after by Sue and *T* is the set of pets looked after by Tim, we can show their responsibilities like this:

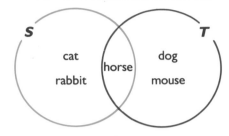

It is easy to see that the set of all the family pets looked after by the children is {cat, rabbit, horse, dog, mouse}. This is called the *union* of the two sets, and is written $S \cup T$ (we say, '*S* union *T*').

The two sets have a member in common, the horse. The set of members that belong to both of two given sets is known as their *intersection*; here, it is the set whose only member is the horse. This is written $S \cap T = \{horse\}$. This is a set, even though it has only one member (as far as the family's pets are concerned) and we write 'horse $\in \{$ horse$\}$', where the symbol '$\in$' means 'is a member of'.

Subsets

Formally, a set is a *subset* of another set if all the members of the first set are members of the other set, that is, one set is contained within another. Thus, among the family's pets, {horse} is a subset of {cat, rabbit, horse, dog, mouse}. If the bigger set is *A* and the subset is *H*, then we write $H \subset A$, to mean that *H* is a *subset* of *A*, or $A \supset H$, to mean that set *A contains* set *H*. These could be shown:

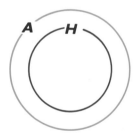

The universal set and complements

Often, we need to know which objects are *not members* of a given set. For example, we might wish to know which pets are not looked after by Sue. If we think of this as the set of all pets not looked after by Sue, this would then include any other pets in the world – which is obviously not what we intended. We are concerned only with the pets looked after by Sue and Tim and their family. A *universal set* contains all the objects being discussed – in this case, all the pets looked after by the whole family. Those pets not looked after by Sue, within the universal set, form what is known as the *relative complement* of the set of her pets. Where *S* is the set of pets looked after by Sue, the complement set is written $C(S)$ or S'. Let us suppose that Sue and Tim's parents look after the only other family pet, a piranha, and that the

---

RUSSELL'S PARADOX

Obviously, sets in general can be members of other sets; for example, {1,2} is a member of

$$\{\{0,1\}, \{1,2\}, \{2,3\}\},$$

and that set is a member of the set of three-membered sets, which in turn is a member of the set of large sets (since there are many three-membered sets). More particularly, some sets are members of themselves, like the set of large sets, while others are not members of themselves, like the set of small sets (since there are many small sets).

Let us then consider the set W of all sets that are not members of themselves: is it a member of itself or not? An element of a set must have the property that defines the set, so if W is a member of the set of sets that are not members of themselves, then it can't be a member of itself – but that just means that it can't be a member of W. On the other hand, if W is not a member of itself that just is the property that defines W, so that W must be a member of W – that is, it is a member of itself.

There are only two possibilities: if you think of any entity you like and any set you like, either the thing is in the set or it is not; there is no third possibility. Thus in particular, either W is a member of itself or it is not; yet whichever supposition we make leads straight to the contradiction. This is a deeper problem than the paradox in the text; there we said that although the description of the doctor's contract looks inoffensive, analysis shows it is really self-contradictory. Here there is no such description to reject; W was constructed out of pure logic. So the contradiction can only lie in one place – at the heart of logic itself.

children are banned from the piranha. The circle for Sue's pets is as before. The rectangle, identified U, is the universal set of the family's pets. We can see that the complement of S is $S' = \{$dog, mouse, piranha$\}$.

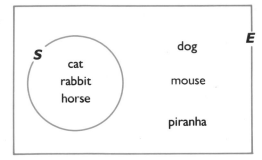

Empty and disjoint sets

The *empty set* (sometimes called the *null set*) has *no members*. It is written $\{\}$ or ø. If we consider the family's pets, we could write, for example,

$$\{\text{parents' pets}\} \cap \{\text{Sue's pets}\} = \text{ø},$$

meaning the set of pets looked after by both Sue and her parents is the empty set – it has no members.

Disjoint sets have *no members in common*. As the diagram below shows, the set of pets looked after by Sue does not intersect with the set of pets looked after by her parents, P; S and P have no members in common and their intersection is the empty set. That is, $S \cap P = \text{ø}$.

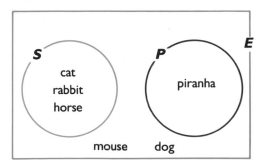

Sets and logic

There is a direct link with *logic* that becomes apparent if we write the formal definitions of union, intersection and complement in set notation:

$S \cup T \quad = \{x\colon x \text{ is a member of } S \text{ or} \\ \qquad\qquad\quad \text{a member of T }\}$

$S \cap T \quad = \{x\colon x \text{ is a member of } S \\ \qquad\qquad\quad and \text{ a member of } T \}$

$S' \qquad = \{x\colon x \text{ is } not \text{ a member of} \\ \qquad\qquad\quad S \}$

These words, 'and', 'or' and 'not', represent what logicians call *truth-functions*. That means that when they are attached to sentences to form more complex sentences, the truth or falsehood of the latter depends only on that of the former. For example, 'John is in London and Mary is in Paris' can only be true if both 'John is in London' and 'Mary is in Paris' are separately true; and in that case, 'John is not in London' must be false. These relations can be shown by the following tables:

P	– P		P	Q	P & Q	P v Q
T	F		T	T	T	T
F	T		T	F	F	T
			F	T	F	T
			F	F	F	F

Here, P and Q stand for any sentences whatever, ' – P' is 'not-P', 'P & Q' is read 'P and Q', and 'P v Q' represents 'P or Q'. The tables show every possible combination of values, and can be used to work out tables for more complex formulae. When 'T' represents a positive signal and 'F' the absence of one (sometimes written '1' or '0' respectively), these tables show the outputs from the electronic logic gates of the same names out of which computers are built.

Paradoxes

Although developments from the simple concept of sets – such as have been outlined – seem to work well enough for practical purposes, various paradoxes were discovered when *axioms* for the theory of sets were sought. The German Gottlob Frege (1848–1925) and the Englishman Bertrand Russell (1872–1970) were independently interested in showing that all of mathematics could be reduced to pure logic, and looked to set theory as a link. In 1908, just as Frege was publishing a major work on the subject, Russell discovered, and communicated to Frege, that his axioms generated an important contradiction; this has become known as *Russell's paradox*.

The simplest way of explaining Russell's paradox is by a particular example (a more general account is given in the box). Let us consider a doctor who serves a community. This doctor treats only those in the community who do not treat themselves. Now, if the doctor treats himself, he cannot be included in the set of those who do not treat themselves. If he does not treat himself, then he is included in the set of those he does treat. Either way, there is a contradiction; but there are only two possibilities and we cannot make sense of either of them. There has to be something wrong with the definition itself from which we were able to derive the contradiction. This, and other paradoxes, proved a great blow to mathematical logicians and new philosophies such as intuitionism grew up partly as a result.

SEE ALSO

● MATHEMATICS AND ITS APPLICATIONS p. 50
● COMPUTERS p. 211

Gottlob Frege was – with Bertrand Russell – the founder of mathematical logic (⊳ main text). Frege produced many publications on mathematics that were philosophical in character. He maintained that 'Every good mathematician is at least half a philosopher, and every good philosopher is at least half a mathematician'. (AKG)

Functions, Graphs and Change

In studying events in real life, we are often concerned with continuous change: a boulder rolling downhill picks up speed; a balloon expands as air is blown into it; our reaction-time slows as we grow older. Processes like these can be represented by a *function*. A function can be represented by a *curve*, so allowing us to picture how a process changes and develops.

Calculus is the branch of mathematics that studies continuous change in terms of the mathematical properties of the functions that represent it, and these results can also be interpreted in geometric terms relating to the graph of the function. Calculus was developed independently by Newton (⊳ pp. 14 and 50) and Leibniz (⊳ pp. 302 and 304) in the late 17th century.

Functions

Suppose we go out for a cycle run, and keep up a speed of 15 km/h. Then our distance from home is determined by how long we have been travelling. For example, after half an hour we will have travelled 7.5 km; after an hour 15 km; after 2 hours 30 km, and so on. We can express this relationship by saying that the distance we travelled is a *function* of the time we have been travelling. Here the two quantities, time and distance, might be represented by the *variables t* and *d*, and the mathematical relationship between them would then be written $d = 15t$.

In general, the notation for a function is $y = f(x)$, which indicates that the value of y depends upon the value of x; in that case, y is called the *dependent variable*, and x is called the *independent variable*.

Cartesian coordinates

The real numbers can be represented geometrically by a line (an *axis*) marked off from the origin (0) using some numerical scale. Any point in a *plane*, a two-dimensional area, can similarly be represented by the pair of numbers that correspond to its respective distances from two such axes, as shown in diagram 1; these numbers are the *coordinates* of the point. Thus the coordinates of the point P in diagram 1 are (1,2).

Here the independent and the dependent variables of a function are represented by two lines at right angles (the x-axis and the y-axis) that cross at the origin. The curve representing the function is then the line that passes through the points whose coordinates satisfy the function. For example, the curve of the function $y = x^2$ is the set of pairs, (x, y), of real numbers for which y is the square of x; thus, for example, (2,4), (−1,1), (−2,4), ($\sqrt{2}$,2), etc., are all in the graph of the function. The curve corresponding to this function is shown in diagram 2. This system of coordinates is named after the French philosopher and mathematician René Descartes (⊳ pp. 50, 303 and 304).

Average rates of change

If a ball is thrown straight up in the air, it is slowed down by gravity until it stops and falls back to the ground, falling faster all the time. This is an example of a functional relationship between time (t) and height (h). If this relationship is described, say, by the equation $h = 20t - 5t^2$ then it can be depicted as in diagram 3.

In diagram 3, the average velocity between A and B is the change of height, CB, divided by the change of time, AC. Where the dependent variable (in this case height) is represented by the vertical axis, and the independent variable (time) by the horizontal axis, this average is equivalent to the *gradient* or *slope* of the line joining the points on the curve that correspond to the ends of the interval, as indicated by the bold line linking A and B. However, in this case the average clearly conceals more than it reveals, since we

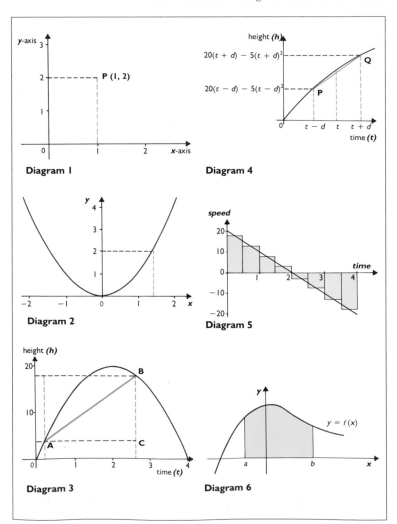

Diagram 1

Diagram 2

Diagram 3

Diagram 4

Diagram 5

Diagram 6

know that between $t = A$ and $t = C$, the ball actually changed direction, so that its upward velocity changed from positive to negative.

Instantaneous rates of change

Similarly if you want to know how fast the Orient Express was travelling as it flashed through the Simplon Tunnel, you obviously get a very poor answer if you divide the whole distance from London to Venice by the total time taken to cover it. You get a better approximation if you measure the distance and time between Paris and Milan, and a better approximation still if you time the train between the stations at either end of the tunnel. This suggests that if we had accurate enough clocks and measuring tapes we would be able to get closer and closer to a precise answer by timing the train over increasingly shorter distances. Although this still never tells us the speed at any one instant, it suggests that the instantaneous speed is the limit that this sequence of averages tends to as the length of the interval gets smaller.

Let us now return to the example of the ball, and apply this reasoning formally: here the vertical height could be expressed in terms of elapsed time as $h = 20t - 5t^2$; for example, the height after 0.5 second is 8.75 m, and after 1 second it is 15 m. Now consider an arbitrary time t after the ball is thrown and take an interval of duration d on either side of it ($\triangleright$ diagram 4). We can see that the average velocity over this distance is the difference between the values of the distance function at the arguments $t + d$ and at $t - d$, divided by the difference between these arguments. This is the slope of the chord PQ, that is

$$\frac{[20(t + d) - 5(t + d)^2] - [20(t - d) - 5(t - d)^2]}{(t + d) - (t - d)}$$

which simplifies to: $(40d - 20td)/2d = 20 - 10t$. Since this value is independent of d, this remains the average velocity round t no matter how small the interval d becomes, so that we can infer that the instantaneous velocity at time t from the starting point is actually equal to $20 - 10t$.

Derivatives and differentiation

The instantaneous velocity $20 - 10t$ is, of course, another function of t, so that the rate of change of a function is another function of the same independent variable. Where the original function was $y = f(x)$, the new function, known as its *derivative*, is written $f'(x)$ or dy/dx (read as 'dy by dx'), where dy and dx represent small *increments* in y and x respectively; here, for example, the derivative of $f(t) = 20t - 5t^2$ is $f'(t) = 20 - 10t$. Similarly, in the expression $y = x^2$, $f(x) = x^2$, and the derivative of $f(x) = x^2$ is

$$\frac{(x + d)^2 - (x - d)^2}{(x + d) - (x - d)} = \frac{4xd}{2d} = 2x$$

The process of finding the derivative of a function is called *differentiation*, and this branch of mathematics is known as the *differential calculus*. This process can also be interpreted geometrically: as d becomes smaller, the points P and Q come closer together until finally they coincide, at which point the slope has the value we have calculated, and represents the tangent to the curve.

However, it is not necessary always to work out a derivative either as we have done, or by drawing the graph. Instead, certain general principles apply; for example, as we have seen, the derivative of x^2 with respect to x is $2x$, and we can generalize this to state that the derivative of ax^n with respect to x is anx^{n-1} ($\triangleright$ also table).

Totals and integrals

So far we have been considering how much we can find out about speed if we are given functional information about distance in terms of time. Now consider the converse problem: if we know a train's velocity as a function of time, how can we calculate the total distance it has travelled? Clearly if we knew the average speed, the total distance would be the result of multiplying the overall average speed by the total duration of the journey; and if the journey was undertaken in stages for which we knew separate average speeds and durations, the total distance travelled would be the sum of the distances calculated by this method for each separate stage. However, this formula requires the journey to be broken down into separable stages whose average speeds are known; where we only know the instantaneous speed at any moment expressed as a function of time, it is of no help at all. On the other hand, we can conjecture that we can approximate to the right answer by breaking the whole journey down into more and more, shorter and shorter stages.

Let us now go back to the previous example: diagram 5 shows the function derived for the velocity of the ball. The complete duration is divided into equal intervals, and in each we take the speed at the midpoint as an approximation to the average. But this really represents the stepped graph (shaded), rather than the true continuous function. However, if we double the number of intervals and halve the duration of each, we get a better approximation, and carrying on in the same way gives a sequence of better and better approximations whose limit can be thought of as the sum of the areas of infinitely many infinitely thin slices of the area under the graph. The *integral calculus* is the study of such processes, and it enables us to calculate infinite sums that can be expressed in terms of continuous functions.

The sum of the value of the function $y = f(x)$ between arbitrary $x = a$ and $x = b$ (the shaded area on diagram 6) is written $\int_a^b f(x)\, dx$, and is equal to $F(b) - F(a)$, where $F(x)$ is the *indefinite integral* of $f(x)$; this is another continuous function of x, written $\int f(x)\, dx$. For example, in the ball example, the indefinite integral, $\int (20 - 10t)\, dt$, of $y = 20 - 10t$, is $20t - (10/2)t^2 + c$ (where c can be any constant). If we denote this new function $Int(x)$, then the definite integral between a and b is $Int(b) - Int(a)$, that is

$$(20b - 5b^2 + c) - (20a - 5a^2 + c)$$
$$= 5(a^2 - b^2) + 20(b - a).$$

In fact it turns out that this process of *integration* is the inverse of differentiation. This means that the indefinite integral of the derivative of a given function, and the derivative of its indefinite integral, are both equal to the given function.

Function	Derivative
x	1
x^2	$2x$
x^n	nx^{n-1}
$\sin x$	$\cos x$
$\cos x$	$-\sin x$

Function	Integral
x	$x^2/2$
x^2	$x^3/3$
x^n	$x^{n+1}/(n+1)$
$\sin x$	$-\cos x$
$\cos x$	$\sin x$

SEE ALSO

● MOTION AND FORCE p. 14
● MATHEMATICS AND ITS APPLICATIONS p. 50

The Earth's Structure and Atmosphere

Seismic wave paths through the Earth's interior. Two of the four kinds of seismic waves, P and S waves, travel through the interior of the Earth (see p.80). By measuring the time it takes these waves to reach seismograph stations around the world, scientists can trace the paths the waves take, observe how their velocities vary, and hence determine the Earth's structure.

Man has sent space probes to the outermost reaches of the Solar System. But in the opposite direction the story is very different. Direct access to the Earth's interior is limited to the depth of the deepest mine, which is less than 4 km (2.5 mi). In the 1980s the Russians drilled a hole in the crust to a target depth of 15 km (9.3 mi), but in doing so they penetrated only the upper 0.24% of the Earth, the average radius of which is 6371 km (3956 mi).

Unable to visit the Earth's deep interior or place instruments within it, scientists must explore in other ways. One method is to measure natural phenomena – the magnetic and gravitational fields are the chief examples – at the Earth's surface and interpret the observations in terms of the planet's internal properties. A second approach is to study the Earth with non-material probes, the most important of which are the seismic waves emitted by earthquakes (▷ diagram). As seismic waves pass through the Earth, they undergo sudden changes in direction and velocity at certain depths. These depths mark the major boundaries, or *discontinuities*, that divide the Earth into crust, mantle and core.

The crust

The outermost layer of the Earth, the crust, accounts for only about 0.6% of the planet's volume. The average thickness of the *oceanic crust* is 5–9 km (3–5½ mi) and varies comparatively little throughout the world. By contrast, the *continental crust* has the much higher average thickness of 30–40 km (18½–25 mi) and varies much more. Beneath the central valley of California, for example, the crust is only about 20 km (12½ mi) thick, but beneath parts of major mountain ranges it can exceed 80 km (50 mi).

The rocks that form the continental crust are highly varied, including volcanic lava flows, huge granite blocks, and sediments laid down in shallow water when parts of the continents were under the sea. Despite the diversity of materials, the average composition is roughly that of granite, and the most common elements (in addition to oxygen) are silicon and aluminium. The oceanic crust is much more uniform in composition and, apart from a thin covering of sediment, consists largely of basalt, possibly underlain by gabbro (which has the same composition as basalt but is coarser grained). Oxygen apart, the most common elements in the oceanic crust are again silicon and aluminium, but there is markedly more magnesium than in the upper continental crust.

The composition of the lower crust, which cannot be sampled directly, is uncertain, but the predominant rock is probably gabbro. The lower crust is certainly different from the upper crust because seismic waves pass through it at a higher velocity.

The mantle

The mantle extends from the base of the crust to a depth of about 2900 km (1800 mi) and accounts for about 82% of the Earth's volume. The sharp boundary between the crust and the mantle is called the *Mohorovičić discontinuity* (or *Moho* for short).

The mantle is thought to consist largely of peridotite, a rock that contains high proportions of the elements iron, silicon and magnesium, in addition to oxygen. The mantle is inaccessible, but evidence of its composition comes from surface rocks thought to have originated there. Although mostly solid, the mantle contains a partially molten layer (▷ below).

The core

The core extends from the base of the mantle to the Earth's centre and accounts for about 17% of the Earth's volume. The discontinuity between the mantle and core is called the *core-mantle boundary* or, sometimes, the *Gutenberg discontinuity*. The core actually comprises two distinct parts. The liquid *outer core* extends down to a depth of about 5155 km (3200 mi). The solid *inner core* mainly comprises iron, although measurements of the Earth's rate of rotation show that the density must be slightly lower than that of pure iron. The core must therefore contain a small proportion (5–20%) of some lighter element – possibly sulphur, silicon, carbon, hydrogen or oxygen.

An alternative view

The division of the Earth into crust, mantle and core is based on the fact that the three zones have different chemical compositions. However, there is another way of looking at the Earth, in terms of its physical state. In the upper mantle, at depths

SEE ALSO

● THE SUN AND THE SOLAR SYSTEM p. 6
● THE PLANETS p. 8
● PLATE TECTONICS p. 62
● THE FORMATION OF ROCKS p. 66
● THE WEATHER p. 78

of 75–250 km (46½–155 mi), the velocity of seismic waves is slightly lower than in the zones just above and below. Scientists believe that this layer of the upper mantle is partially molten, and they have named it the *asthenosphere*. It is this layer that is the source of volcanic *magma* (molten rock; ▷ p. 65). The rigid layer above the asthenosphere, the *lithosphere*, comprises the crust and uppermost mantle. The solid region of the mantle below the asthenosphere is called the *mesosphere*.

The magnetic field

The Earth has a magnetic field, which is why a compass needle points approximately north at most places on the Earth's surface. But where, and how, is the field generated?

The magnetic field has two parts. Most of it is that of a simple dipole (▷ p. 26); it is as if a giant bar magnet were placed at the centre of the Earth (although the magnet slopes at 11° to the Earth's axis of rotation). But a small proportion of it is much more complicated and changes very rapidly. This is why a compass needle points in a slightly different direction each year. The rapid changing indicates that the magnetic field must be produced in a part of the Earth that is fluid, for no solid region could reorganize itself rapidly enough without shaking the planet to pieces. The only liquid zone inside the Earth is the outer core.

This fits in with something else. The only conceivable way in which a magnetic field could be generated within the Earth is by the flow of very large electric currents, and electric currents need a conductor. The Earth's core is the most conductive zone in the whole Earth, because it consists largely of iron. The silicates of the mantle would simply not conduct well enough.

The atmosphere

The atmosphere is easier to investigate than the Earth's interior because it is directly accessible to instruments carried by kites, balloons, aeroplanes, rockets and satellites. These instruments have shown that traces of the atmosphere extend for thousands of kilometres above the Earth's surface. There is no sharp boundary between the atmosphere and 'interplanetary space'.

The atmosphere may be divided into four layers on the basis of temperature. In the layer nearest the Earth, the *troposphere*, temperature decreases with altitude to the top of the layer, which on average is at a height of 10–12 km (6–7½ mi), although the thickness of the layer varies from more than 16 km (10 mi) in the tropics to less than 9 km (5½ mi) in polar regions. Most weather phenomena occur in the troposphere (▷ p. 78).

Above the troposphere lies the *stratosphere*, in which the temperature remains virtually constant up to 20 km (12½ mi) and thereafter increases to the top of the layer at 45–50 km (28–31 mi). The reason for the temperature rise is that the stratosphere is the home of the atmosphere's ozone, which absorbs dangerous ultraviolet radiation from the Sun, protecting life on Earth in the process (▷ p. 186). In the next layer, the *mesosphere*, temperature also decreases to the top of the layer at 80–85 km (50–53 mi). Above this lies the *thermosphere*, throughout most of which the

temperature again rises. The thermosphere fades out over thousands of kilometres, gradually merging with 'space'. The region above about 500 km (310 mi) is sometimes called the *exosphere*. In the altitude range 80–400 km (50–250 mi) – but the upper limit is very poorly defined – the atoms of oxygen and molecules of nitrogen are electrically charged (ionized). This layer, part of the thermosphere, is known as the *ionosphere*. The ionosphere reflects radio waves and hence makes long-range communications possible.

The principal constituent of dry air is nitrogen, which accounts for 78.084% (by volume). The other principal constituents (by percentage volume) are oxygen (20.946), argon (0.934), carbon dioxide (0.034), neon (0.00182), helium (0.000524), methane (0.00015), krypton (0.000114) and hydrogen (0.00005).

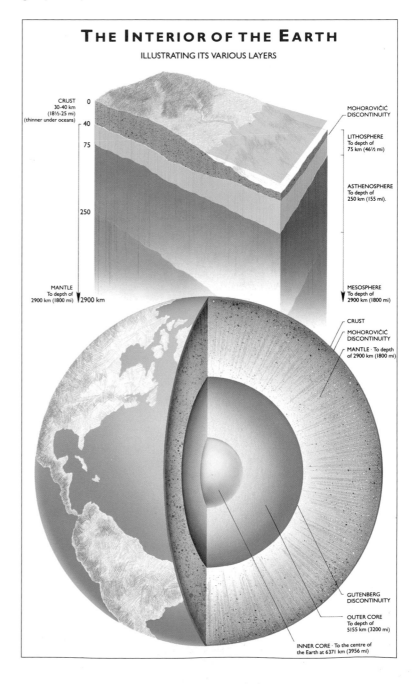

THE INTERIOR OF THE EARTH

ILLUSTRATING ITS VARIOUS LAYERS

CRUST 30-40 km (18½-25 mi) (thinner under oceans)

0
40
75
250

MANTLE To depth of 2900 km (1800 mi)   2900 km

MOHOROVIČIĆ DISCONTINUITY

LITHOSPHERE To depth of 75 km (46½ mi)

ASTHENOSPHERE To depth of 250 km (155 mi).

MESOSPHERE To depth of 2900 km (1800 mi)

CRUST

MOHOROVIČIĆ DISCONTINUITY

MANTLE · To depth of 2900 km (1800 mi)

GUTENBERG DISCONTINUITY

OUTER CORE To depth of 5155 km (3200 mi)

INNER CORE · To the centre of the Earth at 6371 km (3956 mi)

Plate Tectonics

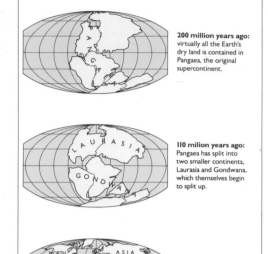

200 million years ago: virtually all the Earth's dry land is contained in Pangaea, the original supercontinent.

110 million years ago: Pangaea has split into two smaller continents, Laurasia and Gondwana, which themselves begin to split up.

0 million years ago: the continents have assumed their present positions, but are continuing to move (see arrows on main map).

Until the early 1960s, most people imagined the continents to be fixed in their present positions and the ocean floors to be the oldest and most primitive parts of the Earth. However, both of these assumptions were overthrown when it suddenly became possible to prove that the continents are drifting across the Earth's surface, that the ocean floors are spreading, and that none of the oceanic crust is more than about 200 million years old – less than 5% of the age of the Earth (4600 million years).

Continental drift was not a new idea in the 1960s – it had been proposed by Antonio Snider of Paris in 1858. But it was not taken seriously until, in 1915, the German meteorologist Alfred Wegener (1890–1930) wrote a book drawing together all the scientific evidence for drift then available. Many of Wegener's arguments are still valid today. He pointed out, for example, that the rocks along the west coast of Africa are very similar to those along the east coast of South America, suggesting that the two continents were once one. He also noted that certain identical fossils are found on continents now separated by thousands of kilometres of ocean. The animals concerned could never have swum so far; so the continents involved must once have been joined.

Wegener proposed that about 200 million years ago there was just one supercontinent, which he named Pangaea. Subsequently, Pangaea split into smaller landmasses, which then drifted to their present positions (and are still drifting, at rates of a few centimetres a year). But for over 40 years Wegener's arguments were rejected by most geologists, who could not envisage how solid continents could possibly plough their way through equally solid ocean floor.

The revolution

In the early 1960s scientists managed to prove continental drift by making use of the weak magnetism that many rocks contain (▷ box). Once this had been done, it was no longer possible to use the problem of *how* drift occurs as a reason

SEE ALSO

- THE EARTH'S STRUCTURE AND ATMOSPHERE p. 60
- EARTHQUAKES AND VOL-CANOES p. 64
- THE FORMATION OF ROCKS p. 66
- MOUNTAINS p. 68
- THE OCEANS p. 76

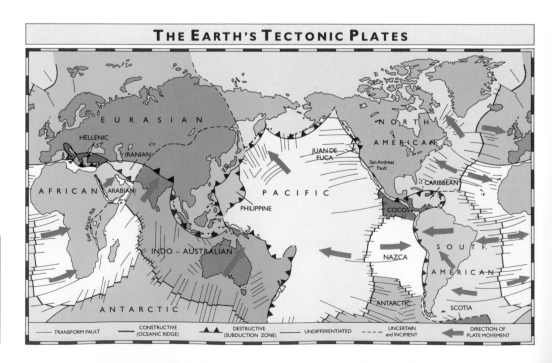

THE EARTH'S TECTONIC PLATES

EURASIAN · HELLENIC · IRANIAN · AFRICAN · ARABIAN · JUAN DE FUCA · San Andreas Fault · NORTH AMERICAN · CARIBBEAN · COCOS · PACIFIC · PHILIPPINE · East African Rift · INDO – AUSTRALIAN · NAZCA · SOUTH AMERICAN · ANTARCTIC · SCOTIA

TRANSFORM FAULT — CONSTRUCTIVE (OCEANIC RIDGE) — ▲▲ DESTRUCTIVE (SUBDUCTION ZONE) — UNDIFFERENTIATED — ---- UNCERTAIN and INCIPIENT — DIRECTION OF PLATE MOVEMENT

for rejecting it. A solution must exist and had to be found. It was not long in coming. Scientists soon realized that continents did not have to plough through ocean floors, because the ocean floors are moving too. Indeed, it is the spreading oceanic lithosphere (▷ pp. 60–1) that pushes the continents along.

The secret lay in the huge ocean-floor mountain ranges, known as oceanic ridges, discovered by oceanographers during the 1950s. These are now known to be the sites at which magma rises from the asthenosphere below (▷ pp. 60–1), cools, and solidifies to form new oceanic lithosphere. Once solid, the lava moves away on each side of the ridge, and more magma rises into the gap to take its place. Oceanic lithosphere is thus being created continuously at oceanic ridges.

But unless the Earth is expanding, lithosphere must also be destroyed at the same rate as it is created. This happens at *subduction zones*, most – but not all – of which lie around the margins of the Pacific. As the spreading oceanic lithosphere reaches the edges of the Pacific continents, it is forced down into the Earth's interior where it gradually melts and loses its identity. All the ocean floor is recycled in this way in less than about 200 million years.

Plate tectonics

By the late 1960s, continental drift and ocean-floor spreading had come to be seen as two aspects of a wider phenomenon – plate tectonics. The Earth's lithosphere (not just the crust) is divided into 15 major *plates* of various sizes. The plates 'float' on the partially molten asthenosphere below, and it is because they are floating that they have the freedom to move horizontally. A few of the plates (for example, the Pacific) are almost completely oceanic, but most include both oceanic and continental lithosphere. There are no completely continental plates.

CONTINENTAL DRIFT PROVED

Many rocks contain minute magnetic particles, usually oxides of iron and titanium. When a rock forms, these particles become magnetized in the direction of the Earth's magnetic field at the particular site. Using highly sensitive instruments, it is possible to measure this weak magnetism and from it determine the position of the north pole at the time the rock was formed. Scientists were surprised to discover that for rocks older than a few million years the north poles determined in this way did not lie at the present north pole, and that the older the rocks the greater was the discrepancy. They were even more surprised to find that rocks of the same age from different continents gave ancient north poles in quite different positions. There can only be one north pole at any given time, however, and that must lie close to the north end of the Earth's rotational axis. The only way of explaining the rock magnetic data, therefore, was to assume that the continents have drifted with respect to both the present north pole and each other.

PLATE BOUNDARIES

The boundaries between the plates are of three types (▷ diagram). The oceanic ridges are known as *constructive plate boundaries*, because they are where new lithosphere is being created. The subduction zones are known as *destructive plate boundaries*, because they are where lithosphere is being consumed by the Earth's interior. Finally, there are *conservative plate boundaries*, also known as *transform faults*, along which lithosphere is neither being created nor destroyed, but where the plate edges are simply sliding past each other. Most transform faults are on the ocean floor, where they offset sections of oceanic ridge, enabling the ridges to adjust to the curvature of the Earth. Occasionally, however, they impinge on land. The notorious San Andreas fault of California is a transform fault.

The plate boundaries are the most tectonically active parts of the Earth – they are where most mountain building, earthquakes and volcanoes occur (▷ pp. 64–5). The plates floating on the asthenosphere may be regarded as jostling against each other, generating tectonic activity at their margins. However, because plates have destructive and constructive plate boundaries, they are also continuously changing their sizes and shapes.

Not even the continents themselves are immune from change. Running for more than 6400 km (3975 mi) up eastern Africa, from the Zambezi to Syria, is a giant *rift valley*, where a long strip of crust has sunk between more or less parallel faults. Many scientists believe that this, the East African Rift, represents an early stage in the break-up of Africa, leading to the creation of a new spreading ocean.

PLATE BOUNDARIES

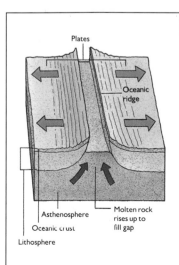

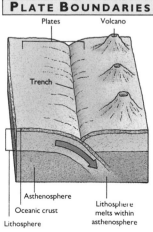

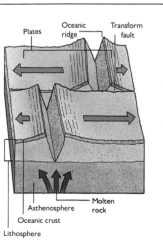

Constructive plate boundary: new lithosphere is formed at oceanic ridges by molten rock rising from the asthenosphere.

Destructive plate boundary: at subduction zones oceanic lithosphere is forced beneath continental lithosphere, descending into the asthenosphere at approximately 45° angle.

Conservative plate boundary: at transform faults, plates slide past each other, with lithosphere being neither created nor destroyed.

Earthquakes and Volcanoes

An earthquake is a sudden release of energy in the Earth's crust or upper mantle. As the planet's tectonic plates (⊳ p. 62) jostle against each other and become distorted, tremendous strain builds up – and from time to time the strain energy is discharged in zones where the rocks are weakest. Volcanism occurs where magma from the Earth's interior is able to force its way through a weak zone in the lithosphere. Because such weaknesses are most likely to occur where the Earth's tectonic plates interact and become distorted, most volcanism occurs in the vicinity of plate boundaries.

The damaging effects of an earthquake are due to the vibrations (*seismic waves*) emitted by the shock. For a brief moment the waves shake the ground close to the earthquake. Few people are ever killed or injured directly by an earthquake; death and injury are more likely to result from the collapse of buildings caused by the earthquake. Earthquakes may cause fissures to appear in the ground, produce changes in the level and tilt of the ground surface, divert rivers and streams, and trigger landslides and avalanches. Undersea earthquakes may also give rise to *tsunami* – huge sea waves that can travel across the oceans for thousands of kilometres, causing devastation when they hit land.

Where earthquakes occur

Most earthquakes take place along the boundaries of the tectonic plates (⊳ p. 62) – along oceanic ridges, transform faults and subduction zones – because this is where the plates interact most intensely, and hence where distortion and strain build-up are greatest. However, not all earthquakes occur along plate margins. In North America, for example, the most damaging earthquakes of historic times have taken place in South Carolina and Missouri, both of which are far from plate margins, and not in California, through which runs the San Andreas fault – a transform fault along which earthquakes are frequent.

The point at which an earthquake occurs is called the *focus*, or *hypocentre*. The point on the Earth's surface directly above the focus is called the *epicentre*. The world map of epicentres is largely a map of the Earth's plate boundaries. All earthquake foci lie within about the upper 700 km (435 mi) of the Earth. Within this range, earthquakes are classified as *shallow* (focal depths of 0–70 km / 0–43 mi), *intermediate* (70–300 km / 43–186 mi), or *deep* (below 300 km / 186 mi). There are about ten times as many shallow earthquakes as there are deep ones. Shallow shocks release the most energy and produce most of the damage at the Earth's surface, for the obvious reason that they are closer to it. The majority of earthquake foci occur along the subduction zones around the Pacific Ocean.

Measuring earthquakes

The size of an earthquake is specified by its *magnitude*, sometimes called the *Richter magnitude* after the American seismologist Charles Richter, who devised the magnitude scale in the 1930s. Magnitude is actually a measure of the size (*amplitude*) of the waves emitted by the earthquake. However, the magnitude scale is logarithmic. This means that each step up the scale represents a ten-fold increase in the amplitude of the emitted waves. Magnitude can also be regarded as a measure of the energy released by an earthquake, because energy is related to wave size. The relationship is such that each division on the magnitude scale represents an approximately thirty-fold difference in energy. Most of the energy released by earthquakes comes from the very few big shocks that occur each year rather than from the million or so smaller earthquakes. On the basis of magnitude, earthquakes are classified as *great* (magnitude above 7.5), *major* (6.5–7.5), *large* (5.5–6.5), *moderate* (4.5–5.5) or *small* (below 4.5).

Volcanism

More than 80% of molten rock, or magma, reaching the Earth's surface does so through long fissures in the Earth's outer shell, the lithosphere (⊳ p. 60); this is called *fissure volcanism*. As the most important of such fissures lie along the axes of the oceanic ridges, the bulk of the Earth's volcanism occurs, unseen, on the floors of the oceans. Volcanoes that have long ceased to erupt are said to be *extinct*. Other volcanoes that have been quiet for a very long time but that may erupt again are described as *dormant*. Those that have erupted in historic times are said to be *active*.

Volcanic products

Beneath the majority of volcanoes there appears to be a reservoir or *magma chamber*. The material in this chamber is liquid, but by the time it reaches the Earth's surface it can be liquid, solid or gaseous. Magma contains dissolved volatiles such as water and carbon dioxide. As the magma rises to the surface it experiences a reduction in pressure, and the volatiles are released, often

SEE ALSO

- THE EARTH'S STRUCTURE AND ATMOSPHERE p. 60
- PLATE TECTONICS p. 62
- THE FORMATION OF ROCKS p. 66
- MOUNTAINS p. 68
- OCEANS p. 76

EARTHQUAKE ZONES AND ACTIVE VOLCANOES

with explosive force. The explosion then shatters the magma and shoots the pieces into the air. By the time they reach the ground they are often solid, albeit still very hot. Such solid fragments are known as *pyroclasts* or, as a group, *tephra*. In particularly violent explosions, bombs weighing over 100 tonnes (tons) are known to have been thrown several kilometres. The finer particles can travel much further, however, carried by the wind. In some explosive eruptions there is no sudden blast but rather a continuous stream of hot gases and rock fragments – thrown up to a considerable height – issuing from the volcanic vent at high velocity for up to several hours. In some less violent cases, however, the volcanic fragments may stay close to the ground, where, in deadly association with hot gases, they roll along destroying everything in their path. This is known as a *nuée ardente*.

In many continental volcanic eruptions there is simply a quiet extrusion of magma. Magma erupted onto the Earth's surface is usually called *lava*, both in its molten state and when it has cooled and solidified into a *lava flow*. Although flow rates of molten lava are generally quite low, speeds of up to 100 km/h (62 mph) have been observed on occasions. Most lava solidifies close to the volcano, although some is known to have travelled up to 50 km (31 mi) from the vent.

Lava is usually extruded at temperatures of 800–1200 °C (1450–2200 °F), but as it flows it loses heat, solidifying from the outside inwards. As it solidifies, its surface takes on a variety of textures, depending largely on the viscosity of the lava in its molten form. When lava is extruded under water, it often acquires an altogether different form. As a result of very rapid cooling by the water, it splits and solidifies into sack-shaped segments, called *pillow lava*.

Volcanic forms

There are three main types of continental volcano. The simplest is the steep cone (a *cinder-cone volcano*) built from layers of tephra ejected from a succession of explosive eruptions. A well-known example is Paricutín, in Mexico, which began erupting in 1943 and in 10 years produced a cone over 460 m (1500 ft) high.

Many volcanoes eject tephra on some occasions and extrude lavas on others. The result is a cone with alternating layers of tephra and lava (a *composite volcano*). Well-known examples are Vesuvius and Stromboli (Italy), Etna (Sicily) and Fujiyama (Japan).

Where lava is plentiful and eruptions frequent – through several vents – the result is likely to be a *shield volcano*, a large structure up to tens of kilometres across and with gentle slopes constructed from hundreds to thousands of successive lava flows. Shield volcanoes are often found in mountain ranges adjacent to subduction zones (for example, the Andes), although Mauna Loa, Hawaii, is also a shield volcano.

Most volcanoes have a *crater* at, or near, the top, resulting from the sinking of solid lava back into the volcanic vent. However, if there has been a particularly violent explosion, or if the top of the volcano has collapsed because the lava has

retreated a long way down the vent, a very large basin-shaped depression known as a *caldera* may be formed.

About 6% of the Earth's volcanism takes place on the ocean floor away from plate margins. Such volcanoes are called *sea-mounts* if their tops fail to reach the surface, although some build up above sea level. More than 10 000 seamounts have been mapped on the Pacific Ocean floor alone, although most of them are now extinct.

EARTHQUAKE DAMAGE

Although magnitude is a fairly accurate scientific measure of the strength of an earthquake, it does not necessarily relate directly to the amount of death and damage that the earthquake causes, because the destructive power of a seismic disturbance depends on more than the quantity of energy released. For example, a magnitude-7 earthquake can, and often does, produce more devastation than a magnitude-8 shock, even though the latter releases about 30 times more energy than the former. This is because as important as the energy are the characteristics of the ground in the epicentral region, the population density there, and the nature of the buildings in the area.

Two earthquakes of the same magnitude may have quite different effects on two more or less identical cities if one of the cities is built on soft sediment (making it very vulnerable to vibrations) and the other does, on hard rock (less susceptible). The effects of the earthquakes will also depend on such factors as whether the shocks happen during the day (people at work, possibly in high-rise offices) or at night (people asleep in low-rise houses) and whether or not the cities concerned have made any attempt to construct earthquake-resistant buildings.

To specify the size of an earthquake in terms of its effects, an intensity scale is used. In the West (but not in Japan or the former Soviet republics, which use slightly different systems) this is usually the *Modified Mercalli Scale*, which ranges from *I* (least damage) to *XII* (most damage).

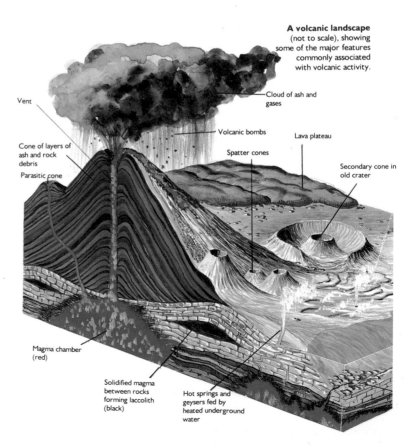

A volcanic landscape (not to scale), showing some of the major features commonly associated with volcanic activity.

Vent

Cloud of ash and gases

Volcanic bombs

Lava plateau

Cone of layers of ash and rock debris

Spatter cones

Parasitic cone

Secondary cone in old crater

Magma chamber (red)

Solidified magma between rocks forming laccolith (black)

Hot springs and geysers fed by heated underground water

The Formation of Rocks

Rock can be one of three types – igneous, sedimentary or metamorphic. Igneous rock starts deep in the Earth as molten magma, which then forces its way up through the crust to cool and solidify. Sedimentary rock is mostly formed when rock of any type is weathered down into fine particles that are then re-deposited under water and later compacted. Metamorphic rock is igneous or sedimentary rock that has been subjected to high pressure and/or temperature, thereby changing its nature.

The Earth is perpetually recycling its rocks. Material brought to the surface is eroded, transported and ultimately returned to the Earth's interior, where it becomes available to begin the cycle all over again. This series of processes is known as the *rock cycle*, or *geological cycle* (⯈ diagram). The energy to maintain it comes partly from the Sun (to fuel the erosion processes) and partly from the Earth's interior (to generate volcanic activity and uplift).

Igneous rock

Magma – which comes from the Earth's surface via volcanic activity (⯈ p. 64) – comprises a

SEE ALSO

● THE EARTH'S STRUCTURE p. 60
● PLATE TECTONICS p. 62
● EARTHQUAKES AND VOLCANOES p. 64
● MOUNTAINS p. 68

mixture of oxides (compounds with oxygen) and silicates (compounds with silicon and oxygen). When it cools and solidifies, the oxides and silicates produce a complex mixture of mineral crystals. The nature and properties of the crystals in any particular igneous rock depend partly on the composition of the original magma and partly upon the physical conditions under which the magma crystallized. As compositions and conditions vary greatly, there are thousands of different igneous rock types.

Igneous rocks that form on the Earth's surface are known as *extrusive*. Those that form within the crust from magma that never reached the surface are known as *intrusive*. Intrusive rocks cool more slowly because, being surrounded by other rock rather than being open to the air, the heat cannot escape so readily. As a result, the crystals have longer to grow, and the mineral grains are larger (coarser).

Despite the many varieties of igneous rock, just six account for most of the igneous components of the crust. These are *granite*, *diorite* and *gabbro*, which are coarse-grained intrusive rocks, and *rhyolite*, *andesite* and *basalt*, which are fine-grained extrusive rocks.

Most of the lava produced at constructive plate boundaries (⯈ p. 62) is basalt. Both basalt and andesite are generated at destructive plate boundaries (⯈ p. 62), and rhyolite is sometimes also produced. Granite is common in the upper continental crust, and gabbro probably dominates in the lower continental crust (⯈ p. 60).

Sedimentary rock

At least 75% of all sedimentary rock is known as *clastic sedimentary rock*, which means that it is derived from the erosion products of other rocks. All rocks, even those in the most massive of mountain ranges, are ultimately broken down into smaller and smaller fragments. When the particles become small enough they are then transported by water, wind or ice, usually ending up in the ocean. There they fall as sediment to the ocean floor where, under the pressure of subsequent deposits, they are compacted into hard rock. The most common sedimentary rock is *sandstone*.

The remaining 25% of sediment is either *chemical* or *organic*. Rivers dissolve minerals out of the rocks through which they pass, and the mineral solutions end up in the oceans. When the oceans reach their saturation limit for the particular mineral concerned, the excess mineral is precipitated out chemically as solid particles, which fall to the ocean floor. The most common chemical sedimentary rock is *limestone* (calcium carbonate – $CaCO_3$).

Not all limestone is precipitated chemically, however. Many ocean organisms extract calcium carbonate from the water to build their shells, and when they die the shells sink to the ocean floor to form sediment in their own right. The most common organic sedimentary rock is again limestone, but there are other organisms that in a similar way generate silica (SiO_2) sediments.

Most sedimentary rocks are a mixture of clastic, chemical and organic, although one type usually predominates.

Metamorphic rock

When igneous or sedimentary rocks are subjected

THE GEOLOGICAL TIME CHART			
ERA	**PERIOD**	**EPOCH**	**BEGAN** (Millions of years ago)
CENOZOIC	QUATERNARY	Holocene	0.01
CENOZOIC	QUATERNARY	Pleistocene	1.6
CENOZOIC	TERTIARY	Pliocene	5.3
CENOZOIC	TERTIARY	Miocene	23
CENOZOIC	TERTIARY	Oligocene	34
CENOZOIC	TERTIARY	Eocene	53
CENOZOIC	TERTIARY	Palaeocene	65
MESOZOIC	CRETACEOUS		135
MESOZOIC	JURASSIC		205
MESOZOIC	TRIASSIC		250
PALAEOZOIC	PERMIAN		300
PALAEOZOIC	CARBONIFEROUS (divided into lower Mississippian and upper Pennsylvanian in USA)		355
PALAEOZOIC	DEVONIAN		410
PALAEOZOIC	SILURIAN		438
PALAEOZOIC	ORDOVICIAN		510
PALAEOZOIC	CAMBRIAN		570
PRECAMBRIAN ERA			4600

THE ROCK CYCLE

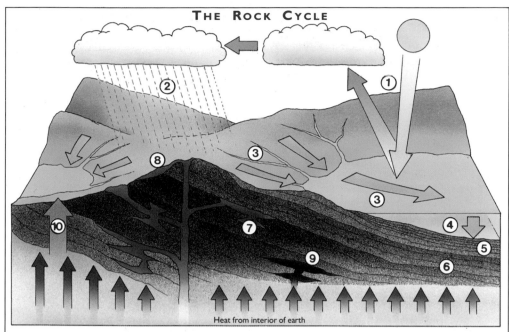

1. Heat from the Sun causes evaporation. Water vapour rises and condenses into clouds.

2. Water in cloud precipitates as rain or snow.

3. Water erodes rock, and rivers carry away sediment.

4. Rivers deposit sediment as alluvium on flat ground, or transport it to lakes and seas where it settles on the bottom as clay or sand.

5. As sediment builds up, increasing pressure changes lower layers into sedimentary rock.

6. Deeper sedimentary rock is turned into metamorphic rock by pressure from above and heat from below.

7. Magma – molten rock from deep inside the Earth – rises towards the surface. Some is trapped underground and hardens into intrusive igneous rock.

8. Some magma reaches the Earth's surface via volcanoes and fissures as lava and is classified as extrusive igneous rock.

9. Some intrusive igneous rock is forced deeper by the pressure of sedimentation, and is changed into metamorphic rock. This metamorphosis may be assisted by thermal energy from below.

10. Pressure from colliding continental plates pushes all kinds of rock to the surface, and forces them upwards, where they are eroded. The rock cycle begins again.

to high temperatures and pressures, especially in the presence of percolating fluids, their internal structures, and sometimes even their mineralogical compositions, may be changed. The processes involved are known collectively as *metamorphism*. The sort of temperatures and pressures required are, respectively, 300 °C (572 °F) and 100 megapascals (equivalent to 100 atmospheres).

The most extreme conditions in the Earth's crust occur at plate boundaries where continents collide (▷ p. 62). Most metamorphic rocks are thus generated in the roots of mountains. Depending upon temperature and pressure, there are various grades of metamorphism; but in the most intense (high-grade) metamorphism, rock structures, holes and even fossils are so completely obliterated that the original rock type can no longer be identified.

As a result of the realignment of minerals under pressure, many metamorphic rocks are layered, or banded. Sometimes the layering is visible; but even when it is not, it can often be detected by the way that the rock breaks. A common example is *slate*, which easily breaks into thin sheets along the layering.

Not all metamorphic rock is layered, however. Common examples of non-layered metamorphics are *marble*, formed by the metamorphism of limestone, and *quartzite*, derived from sandstone.

Faults and folds

As soon as rocks form they not only begin to erode, they are also subject to faulting and folding. The most intense faulting and the most intense folding both occur at plate boundaries, but these pressures are also very common within plates, on scales ranging from centimetres to thousands of kilometres.

Faults are fractures along which opposing blocks of rock are moving or have moved in the past. The surface over which the slippage occurs is called the *fault plane*, and the line along which the fault plane cuts the Earth's surface (if it does; not all faults reach the surface) is known as the *fault trace*.

Faults are classified according to the direction in which the blocks of rock slip. If the movement is basically vertical (up or down the fault plane) the result is a *dip-slip fault*, of which there are two basic types – *normal* and *reverse*. Horizontal movement gives rise to a *strike-slip fault*. Where there are two parallel faults, the result can be either a *horst* or a *graben* (rift valley).

Folding is the bending of rock without fracturing. The two sides of a fold are called *limbs*, and the surface that bisects the angle between the limbs is known as the *axial plane*. Folds are classified according to the severity of the folding, the shape of the resulting folds, and the angle of the axial plane. There are a few basic types of fold and a great number of variations.

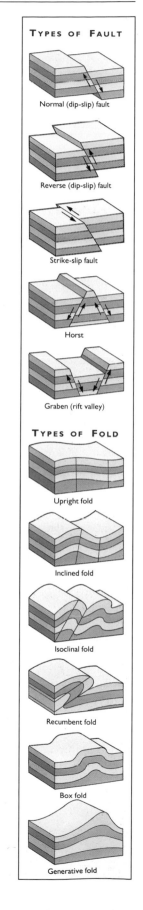

TYPES OF FAULT

Normal (dip-slip) fault

Reverse (dip-slip) fault

Strike-slip fault

Horst

Graben (rift valley)

TYPES OF FOLD

Upright fold

Inclined fold

Isoclinal fold

Recumbent fold

Box fold

Generative fold

Mountains

Mountains and mountain ranges are largely formed by the interaction of mountain-building processes (*orogeny*) and the subsequent erosional processes that tend to destroy them. The distribution of the world's major mountain ranges generally follows those belts of the Earth's landmasses where earthquakes and volcanoes are common. These phenomena are in turn caused by the collision of the moving plates that make up the Earth's lithosphere (▷ pp. 60–1). Such collisions often result in the margin of one plate being forced upwards, and this process has resulted in the formation of many mountain ranges – although other processes may also play a part in mountain building.

The Earth's largest mountain ranges today – the Alps, Himalaya, Rockies and Andes – are all relatively young, resulting from plate collisions in the last 25 million years or so. Much older ranges include the Scottish Highlands, the Scandinavian mountains and the Appalachians in the USA, which are all around 300–400 million years old. The deeply eroded remnants of even older ranges – up to 3000 million years old – occur in many parts of Africa and Australia.

Fold mountains

The world's largest and most complex continental mountain ranges are the result of the collision of tectonic plates. Mountains formed directly by plate collisions are known as *fold mountains*, because they are conspicuously folded, faulted and otherwise deformed by the huge collision pressures. In some cases the collision is between landmasses. Thus India is pressing into the rest of Asia to form the Himalaya, and Africa is being forced into Europe, producing the Alps. In other cases the collision is between an oceanic plate and a continent. Thus the Pacific plate is spreading towards South America, forcing up the Andes. The Himalaya, the Alps and the Andes are still being formed, but some mountain ranges – for example, the Urals and the Appalachians – are the products of older, long-ceased plate collisions.

Fault-block and upwarped mountains

Other types of mountain exist where plate collisions are at best only marginally involved. In *fault-block mountains* a central block of the Earth's crust has sunk and the adjacent blocks have been forced upwards. Mountains of this type define the Basin and Range Province of the western USA (Nevada and parts of Utah, New Mexico, Arizona and California) and form the Sierra Nevada of California and the Teton Range of Wyoming.

In *upwarped mountains*, on the other hand, a central block has been forced upwards. Examples are the Black Hills of Dakota and the Adirondacks of New York State.

Volcanic mountains

Spectacular mountains may also be built by volcanic action (▷ also p. 65). For example, Mauna Loa in Hawaii, is, at 10 203 m (33 476 ft), the world's highest mountain if measured from the Pacific Ocean floor, although less than half is above sea level. Much more important than such isolated volcanoes, however, are the oceanic ridges (▷ pp. 65 and 76), the undersea mountain ranges along which the bulk of the Earth's volcanism takes place. Intense volcanism also occurs where oceanic and continental plates collide. The Andes, for example, owe not a little of their mass to volcanic activity.

The erosion and destruction of isolated continental volcanoes can be a rapid process. Some volcanoes are partially self-destructive – for example, Mount St Helens in the northwest USA, which blasted part of its side out in 1980, or Vesuvius, whose crater top disintegrated in AD 79. Others are completely self-destructive – for example, Krakatau (sometimes incorrectly called Krakatoa), Indonesia, which in 1883 blasted itself entirely out of existence.

Apart from these spectacular episodes, the erosion of volcanoes can be fast, the loose ash of which they are partly built being easily transported by runoff of rainwater. In the case of some Andean volcanoes, earth tremors set off avalanches, which tear down into nearby valleys. Such an event occurred in 1970, when an estimated 40 million m^3 (52 million cu yd) of rock and ice avalanched off Huascarán in Peru, completely obliterating several towns and villages and killing many thousands of their inhabitants up to 20 km (12 mi) away.

Machapuchare, a frost-shattered peak in the Himalaya, Nepal. The uplift of the Himalaya began in the Cretaceous period (205 to 135 million years ago) when the massif of peninsular India moved north towards the Plateau of Tibet, causing the folding and lifting of deposits between them. The continued raising of river terraces indicates that Himalayan uplift continues. (Spectrum)

Volcanoes built up in the sea are sometimes easily eroded by wave action, as in the case of Surtsey, which grew out of the sea off Iceland in the 1960s and has largely been worn away now.

On the other hand, volcanoes built of harder rock can persist indefinitely. On the Pacific Ocean floor alone there are tens of thousands of extinct volcanic cones (*seamounts*), and in various parts of the world there are the remains of volcanoes up to hundreds of millions of years old.

Wind and water erosion

As soon as a mountain range starts to rise, the forces of erosion commence operation. Water, wind, ice and vegetation are all agents of erosion, often acting in unison. Mountains are the intermediate result of erosive processes that will ultimately wear everything away to sea level. Young mountain ranges are those which have only been uplifted to somewhere near their present height in the last 25 million years or so, and they tend to be high and jagged. Old mountain ranges are those that have suffered the processes of erosion for hundreds if not thousands of millions of years, and they tend to be lower and more rounded.

The processes of erosion start with weathering of exposed rocks. Rainfall provides water, which reacts chemically with many rocks and minerals. The loose rock fragments are then transported by water down streams into rivers and eventually to the sea, with the more resistant rock masses left upstanding as individual mountains. Mountains that have been worn away by water action alone are generally rounded, with shallow gullies radiating outwards.

Wind sculpture of whole mountain ranges is unusual on its own, but bare and polished surfaces on jagged rocks in desert regions may result from the wind hurling sand grains at rock faces at high speed as, for example, in Death Valley in California and the Hoggar mountains of the central Sahara. Wind sculpture in combination with storm-water runoff (flash floods) can cut canyons into the mountains. At the point where the canyon opens out, the water deposits its sediments in *alluvial fans*, whilst the wind-blown material covers adjacent lowlands with sand dunes.

The action of ice

When water freezes in cracks in rocks, it expands and forces the rocks apart, thus causing erosion of mountain peaks. (In a similar way, vegetation may also contribute to erosion – for example, roots may force open cracks.) As it accumulates, ice, in the form of *glaciers* (⊳ p. 70), sculpts most high mountain ranges – for example, the Alps, Himalaya, Rockies (particularly in Canada), and the Scandinavian mountains. Many other ranges were sculpted to their present shapes by glaciers during the last Ice Age (some 100 000 to 10 000 years ago), for example the Scottish Highlands, the US Rockies, much of the Andes, the Caucasus and the Ural Mountains.

Headward erosion by glaciers (i.e. erosion of the slope on which the glacier originates) etches out *corries* (also known as *cirques* or *cwms*) and, when two or three corries impinge, the result may be a pyramidal peak such as the Swiss Matterhorn. The high passes between corries cutting into a range are called *cols*, and gullies leading from them are called *couloirs*. Steep slopes on such mountains often yield avalanches, in which rock and soil, as well as snow and ice, may be swept away.

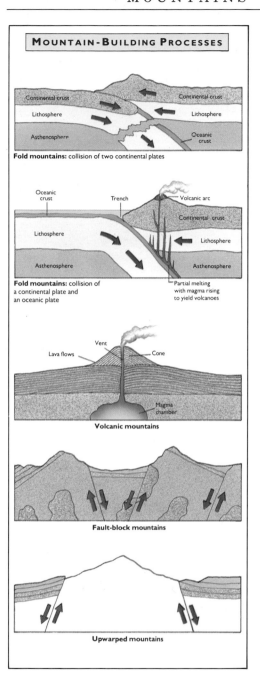

MOUNTAIN-BUILDING PROCESSES

Continental crust — Continental crust
Lithosphere — Lithosphere
Asthenosphere — Oceanic crust
Fold mountains: collision of two continental plates

Oceanic crust — Trench — Volcanic arc
Continental crust
Lithosphere — Lithosphere
Asthenosphere — Asthenosphere
Fold mountains: collision of a continental plate and an oceanic plate — Partial melting with magma rising to yield volcanoes

Vent
Lava flows — Cone
Magma chamber
Volcanic mountains

Fault-block mountains

Upwarped mountains

The lower parts of mountains that either have or have had glaciers tend to be characterized by *terminal moraines*, mounds of ice-borne debris across a valley at the melting limit of the glacier. Moraines may hold back lakes, but the meltwater streams eventually breach these and *outwash plains* spread out from the valley mouths.

Thus, as mountain ranges are gradually worn down, it is the more resistant parts that linger longest, giving their present shapes. A peculiarity is that mountains may continue to grow higher as their sides are worn away. The Alps and Himalaya, for example, are still being raised by plate-tectonic processes – Everest is getting higher in spite of the glaciers carving away its sides.

SEE ALSO

● PLATE TECTONICS p. 62
● EARTHQUAKES AND VOLCANOES p. 64
● THE FORMATION OF ROCKS p. 66
● ICE p. 70
● THE OCEANS p. 76

Ice

It has been estimated that over a tenth of the Earth's land surface – some 15 600 000 km² (6 021 000 sq mi) – is permanently covered with ice. Ice is in fact the world's biggest reservoir of fresh water, with over three-quarters of the global total contained in ice sheets, ice caps and glaciers. These range in size from the huge Antarctic and Greenland ice sheets to the small glaciers found in high-latitude and high-altitude mountain ranges.

Ice bodies develop where winter snowfall is able to accumulate and persist through the summer. Over time this snow is compressed into an ice body, and such ice bodies may grow to blanket the landscape as an *ice sheet* or *ice cap*. Alternatively, the ice body may grow to form a mass that flows down a slope – a *glacier* – often cutting a valley and eroding rock material that is eventually deposited at a lower altitude as the ice melts.

The formation of ice bodies

Ice bodies develop mainly through the accumulation of snow, or sometimes by the freezing of rain as it hits an ice surface. Obviously, not all the snow that falls is turned into ice – during the northern-hemisphere winter over half the world's land surface and up to one-third of the surfaces of the oceans may be blanketed by snow and ice. Most of this snow and ice is only temporary, as the Sun's warmth and energy are able to melt the cover during warm winter days or as winter passes into spring and summer.

In some places, however, the summer warmth is unable to melt all the snowfall of the previous winter. This may be because summer temperatures are rather low, or summer is very short, or because winter snowfall is very high. Where this occurs, snow lies all year round (this snow is sometimes called *firn* or *névé*) and becomes covered by the snow of the next winter. As this process continues from year to year, the snow that is buried becomes compressed and transformed into *glacier ice*.

Latitude and altitude both affect where permanent snow can accumulate. The level that separates permanent snow cover from places

The east coast of Greenland. The sea ice (right and centre foreground) includes floes, together with newer ice in the process of formation. Icebergs break off from the snouts of glaciers that are fed by a vast ice sheet that covers central Greenland.
(Explorer)

THE ICE AGES

During colder periods of the Earth's history, ice sheets, ice caps and glaciers have covered much larger areas of the land surface than they do today. There have been several *ice ages* or *glacial periods* in the past: scientists now believe that there have been between 15 and 22 glacial periods during the last 2 million years.

The last Ice Age ended about 10 000 years ago and, at its height, great ice sheets covered most of Canada and Scandinavia, ice caps covered Highland Scotland, Snowdonia and the English Lake District, and large glaciers extended into southern England. Throughout Europe, the ice extended roughly to the latitude of the English Midlands, the Netherlands and northern Germany, although in North America it extended even further south, into the northern USA. There are no ice bodies (apart from high-mountain glaciers) so far south today, but the landscape still records the presence of ice in the past, in the form of erosion valleys and large volumes of transported sediment.

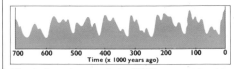

700   600   500   400   300   200   100   0
Time (x 1000 years ago)

Climatic fluctuations over the last 700 000 years are indicated by fluctuations in the relative proportions of oxygen isotopes derived from ocean sediments, as plotted on this graph. The high points indicate warm (interglacial) periods, while the lower points indicate glaciations.

where the snow melts in the summer is called the *snowline* or *firnline*. The snowline increases in altitude towards the equator: in polar regions it lies at sea level, in Norway at 1200–1500 m (4000–5000 ft) above sea level, and in the Alps at about 2700 m (9000 ft). Permanent snow and ice can even occur in the tropics close to the equator: in East Africa, for example, the snowline lies at about 4900 m (16 000 ft), so that glaciers are found on Mount Kenya, Kilimanjaro, and the Ruwenzori Mountains.

Ice sheets and ice caps

Ice sheets and ice caps are ice bodies that have grown into domes that blanket an area of land, submerging valleys, hills and mountains. Occasionally, 'islands' of land, called *nunataks*, protrude through the 'sea' of ice. Ice sheets are defined as having an area over 50 000 km² (19 000 sq mi); ice caps are smaller.

The continent of Antarctica is covered by an ice sheet, that rises to about 4200 m (13 800 ft) above sea level and spreads over an area of 12.5 million km² (4.8 million sq mi). Much of Greenland is covered by an ice sheet (1.7 million km² / 660 000 sq mi in area), while ice caps occur in Norway, Canada and Iceland. Together, the Antarctic and Greenland ice sheets account for 94% of the Earth's land area covered by ice bodies.

Sea ice

There is no ice sheet over the North Pole because there is no land there – however, the Arctic Ocean is always frozen and, during the winter, Arctic *sea ice* covers about 12 million km² (4.6 million sq mi).

An area of sea ice that is joined to a coast is called an *ice shelf*. Ice shelves occur in the Arctic, joined to the coasts of northern Canada and Greenland, and in the Antarctic – notably the Ross Ice Shelf, which has an area greater than France. Ocean currents and seasonal melting can cause ice sheets to break up, creating areas of *pack ice* or smaller *ice floes*.

Types of glacier

In comparison to ice sheets and ice caps, glaciers are small, relatively narrow bodies of ice, which flow down slopes. Some Arctic and Antarctic glaciers reach several hundred kilometres in length, but the longest glacier in the European Alps, for example, is only 35 km (22 mi) long.

There are several types of glacier: *outlet glaciers* extend from the edges of ice sheets and ice caps; *valley* or *alpine glaciers* are confined within valleys for much of their length; and *cirque* (sometimes called *corrie* or *cwm*) *glaciers* are totally confined to a small rock basin and may cover an area of less than 1 km² (⅓ sq mi).

Most glaciers terminate on land, but some – especially those that are outlets of extensive ice sheets or ice caps – may reach the sea. Where this occurs, large blocks of ice may break off the end of the glacier (the *snout*) to form *icebergs*, which are carried away by the tide and ocean currents (▷ p. 100).

Ice movements

Ice bodies move and flow under the influence of gravity. The movement of frozen water is obviously much slower than when it is in its liquid form. Most glaciers flow at a velocity between 3 and 300 m (10 and 1000 ft) per year. Glaciers on steep slopes may move much faster, and the Quarayaq Glacier, which is supplied with ice from the Greenland Ice Sheet, averages 20–24 m (65–80 ft) per day. Many glaciers experience *surges* – which may last a few days or several years – when flow is extremely rapid, often equivalent to rates of up to 10 km (6 mi) a year.

Glaciers move in two ways. The first, called *glacial sliding*, occurs when the base of a glacier slides over the rock beneath it. The other, called *internal deformation*, involves movements within the glacier, caused by the stresses resulting from the weight of the ice body itself. Many glaciers flow through the combination of both mechanisms, but in very cold environments, where a glacier may be frozen to its rock bed, internal deformation may account for all the movement that occurs.

At the steeper points in a glacier, deep cracks called *crevasses* will form, usually at right angles

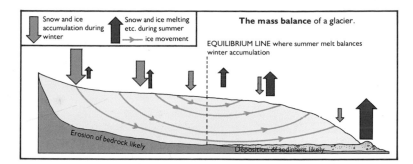

The mass balance of a glacier.

Snow and ice accumulation during winter

Snow and ice melting etc. during summer

→ ice movement

EQUILIBRIUM LINE where summer melt balances winter accumulation

Erosion of bedrock likely

Deposition of sediment likely

to the direction of flow. Where the glacier tumbles over an underlying cliff, an *icefall* will form, characterized by many crevasses and unstable towers of ice called *seracs*. Sometimes a glacier will flow round either side of an area of harder rock known as a *rognon*.

As a glacier flows downhill it will extend the snowline. The area below the snowline will be subject to greater melting than that above it, so the glacier is kept in equilibrium and prevented from growing indefinitely in size (▷ diagram).

Glaciers and landscape

Glacier ice is a very powerful erosional agent, smoothing rock surfaces and cutting deep valleys. *Fjords* (for example, along the coasts of Norway and Alaska) are U-shaped glacial valleys that become submerged by the sea after the melting of the ice that produced them. U-shaped valleys are classically regarded as glacial features, but they can be formed by other processes – for example, by rivers in their middle and lower reaches.

A sliding glacier erodes by *plucking* blocks of rock from its bed and by *abrading* rock surfaces, i.e. breaking off small particles and rock fragments. The rock that is eroded is transported by the ice and deposited as the glacier travels down slope and melts. Glacial deposits can form distinct landforms such as *moraines* and *drumlins* (▷ illustration), or they may simply be deposited as *glacial till*, a blanket of sediment covering the landscape. As glacial ice melts, especially during the summer months, the *meltwater* that emerges from beneath a glacier can carry large quantities of sediment away from the glacier system.

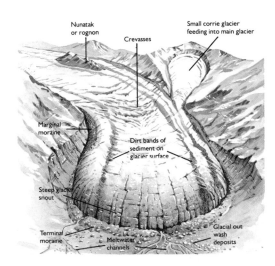

Nunatak or rognon

Crevasses

Small corrie glacier feeding into main glacier

Marginal moraine

Dirt bands of sediment on glacier surface

Steep glacier snout

Terminal moraine

Meltwater channels

Glacial out wash deposits

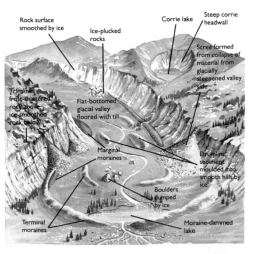

Rock surface smoothed by ice

Ice-plucked rocks

Corrie lake

Steep corrie headwall

Scree formed from collapse of material from glacially steepened valley side

Trimlines: frost-shattered rock above ice-smoothed rock below

Flat-bottomed glacial valley floored with till

Marginal moraines

Drumlins: sediment moulded into smooth hills by ice

Boulders dumped by ice

Terminal moraines

Moraine-dammed lake

SEE ALSO

- MOUNTAINS p. 68
- RIVERS AND LAKES p. 74
- THE OCEANS p. 76
- WEATHER p. 78
- CLIMATE p. 80
- TERRESTRIAL ECOSYSTEMS p. 128

Deserts

Deserts are areas of the world where there is a considerable deficiency of water. The major cause of this aridity is low precipitation, particularly rainfall, but desert areas also frequently experience a great variation in rainfall amounts from year to year. Although deserts are not necessarily hot, many are found in hot climates, which increases the shortage of water because of high rates of evaporation. The lack of water in deserts makes conditions difficult for human, animal and plant life. As a result, living organisms are less common than in wetter areas, with special adaptations necessary in order to allow survival.

Because water deficiency is the main characteristic of deserts, Arctic and Antarctic areas are sometimes called *polar deserts* because water is not generally available in its liquid form (⊳ p. 70).

What causes deserts?

Many of the world's deserts coincide with areas characterized by stable atmospheric high pressure (⊳ p. 80), conditions that not do not favour rainfall. These subtropical high-pressure belts are responsible for deserts such as the Sahara and Kalahari in Africa and the deserts of Australia and Arabia.

Other deserts – for example, the Gobi Desert in Asia – exist because of their *continentality*, that is, their distance from the sea. This prevents them being reached by moisture-bearing winds from the oceans. This effect may be enhanced by the shape of the landscape: for example, moist air coming in from the sea will precipitate on mountains as rain or snow, and by the time the air has reached the far side of the mountains it will be dry, so forming a *rain-shadow* desert. Such deserts occur, for example, to the north of the Himalaya.

The deserts of the west coasts of southern Africa and South America – the Namib and Atacama Deserts – are affected by the presence of cold ocean currents running along the coast. These cool the air that they come into contact with, so preventing evaporation of moisture from the ocean surface and the formation of rain. At some places in the Atacama Desert, no rain was recorded in the 400 years prior to 1971. The cold ocean water does, however, cause a high frequency of fog, which is the major source of moisture in these extremely dry or *hyper-arid* deserts.

Human activity may also contribute to the creation of new desert areas – a process known as *desertification* (⊳ p. 128).

Desert climates

Some deserts are drier than others. Because of this it is usual for a distinction to be made between *semi-arid* areas, which receive on average 200–500 mm (8–20 in) of rainfall per year; *arid* areas, with an average annual rainfall of 25–200 mm (1–8 in); and *hyper-arid* areas, which are so dry that rainfall may not occur for several years on end. Together, arid and hyper-arid areas form the world's true deserts. Semi-arid areas, which are often on the margins of deserts, cover about 15% of the world's land area, while arid and hyper-arid desert areas respectively cover about 16% and 4%.

Most deserts tend to experience warm or hot summer months, with mean temperatures greater than 20 °C (68 °F), and maximum temperatures sometimes reaching over 50 °C (122 °F) in the hotter deserts. However, temperatures in the winter months can vary widely, because of the range of latitudes in which deserts are found. The deserts formed by the subtropical high-pressure belts generally have the warmest winters; indeed parts of the Arabian Desert do not experience anything that really deserves to be called winter, with the mean temperatures of the coldest month being over 20 °C (68 °F). Some deserts do, however, experience cold winters. Parts of the central Sahara are extremely mountainous, so that high altitudes contribute to low winter temperatures, while the mean temperature of the coldest month in the Gobi Desert falls below –20 °C (–4 °F) owing both to its great distance from the sea and to its high altitude.

Many deserts also experience very high daily temperature ranges, with hot days and cold nights. This is due to clear, cloudless skies allowing heat to escape, combined with the lower ability of ground without vegetation to absorb heat. A daily temperature range of 55 °C (99 °F) has been recorded in the central Sahara: from 52 °C to –3.3 °C (126 °F to 26 °F).

Sand dunes at Kerzaz in the Sahara, Algeria. Despite the popular image, only a relatively small proportion of the world's deserts are sandy – for example, only 28% of the Sahara is composed of sand dunes and sand plains. (WWF)

Desert landscapes

Popular images of deserts paint a picture of vast plains of *sand dunes* without a plant or rock in sight. Although some deserts are composed of huge dunes shaped by the wind, it is by no means the case that all deserts are, or that this type of feature is typical of deserts as a whole.

Nevertheless, the wind can be an important landscaping agent in deserts because of the limited presence of vegetation to protect the ground surface. The wind can erode by *sandblasting* bare rock faces, creating smooth rock faces and upstanding features such as *yardangs* (▷ illustration). If a sufficient supply of sediment is available, the wind can also transport and deposit sand to form dunes. The sand making up desert dunes often comes from dry river courses and lake beds, or the coast. Rock weathering – which is encouraged by high daily temperature ranges – can also be effective on the bare rock surfaces, adding to the supply of sand-sized material.

Although rainfall is limited in deserts, the lack of vegetation and the high intensity of desert rainstorms does mean that water plays an important part in shaping desert landscapes. Desert river courses, often called *wadis*, can carry large volumes of water and sediment during storms. This can lead to the formation of canyons and heavily gullied areas, called *badlands*, in areas where soft and highly erodable sediments are found. Where mountains are present, highly erosive *flash floods* may occur. The large loads of sediments carried by these floods may be deposited where a river leaves the mountains and passes on to gentler, flatter ground, forming an *alluvial fan*. Over time, the work of wind and water can cause a desert landscape to become dissected. In areas where the bedrock consists of horizontally bedded strata – for example, in the desert areas of Arizona and New Mexico in the southwestern USA – this can lead to the develop-

THE LANDSCAPES OF FOUR DESERT AREAS
(percentages of total areas)

	Southwest USA	Sahara	Arabia	Australia
Mountains	38.1	43	47	16
Gentle rock slopes	0.7	10	1	14
Alluvial fans	31.4	1	4	} 13
Ephemeral rivers and floodplains	4.8	2	2	
Dry lakes	1.1	1	1	1
Gullied areas	2.6	2	1	0
Sand dunes and sand plains	0.6	28	26	38
Other miscellaneous	20.7	13	18	18

ment of isolated, flat-topped hills called *mesas* and *buttes* (▷ illustration). Where the rocks are not stratified in this way, more rounded 'island hills' (sometimes called *inselbergs*) may develop. A famous example is Ayers Rock in Australia.

Plants, animals and people

Plants and animals can survive in deserts if they become specially adapted to the harsh conditions that occur (▷ p. 128). People, too, have adapted to desert conditions by finding ways of using the water that is available – for example, by living at an *oasis* (a constant spring) or digging wells in the beds of dry rivers to tap water supplies. Today, technology has enabled more people than ever to exist and travel comfortably in deserts, as the cities in the North American deserts testify. However, desert life can remain precarious, and is always prone to the dangers of drought, as the human tragedies in recent years on the southern margins of the Sahara have so clearly demonstrated.

SEE ALSO

- MOUNTAINS p. 68
- ICE p. 70
- WEATHER p. 78
- CLIMATE p. 80

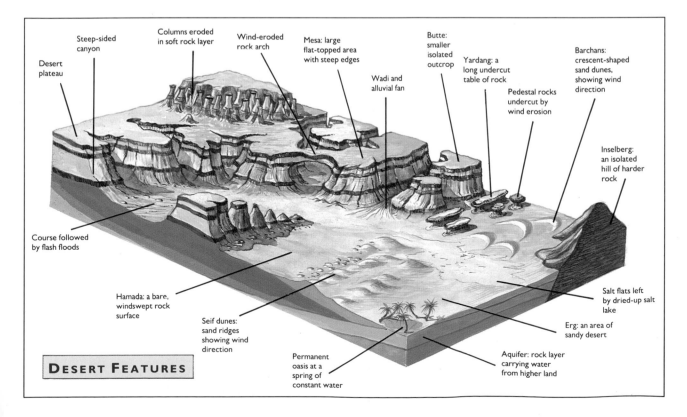

DESERT FEATURES

Desert plateau

Steep-sided canyon

Columns eroded in soft rock layer

Wind-eroded rock arch

Mesa: large flat-topped area with steep edges

Wadi and alluvial fan

Butte: smaller isolated outcrop

Yardang: a long undercut table of rock

Pedestal rocks undercut by wind erosion

Barchans: crescent-shaped sand dunes, showing wind direction

Inselberg: an isolated hill of harder rock

Course followed by flash floods

Hamada: a bare, windswept rock surface

Seif dunes: sand ridges showing wind direction

Permanent oasis at a spring of constant water

Aquifer: rock layer carrying water from higher land

Erg: an area of sandy desert

Salt flats left by dried-up salt lake

Rivers and Lakes

Rivers and lakes are the most important bodies of surface water on land masses. A river is a freshwater body confined in a channel that flows down a slope into another river, a lake or the sea, or sometimes into an inland desert. Small, narrow rivers may be called brooks, streams or creeks.

SEE ALSO

● THE FORMATION OF ROCKS
  p. 66
● ICE p. 70
● OCEANS p. 76
● AQUATIC ECOSYSTEMS p. 130

A lake is an inland body of water occupying a depression in the Earth's surface. Usually, lakes receive water from rivers, but sometimes only directly from springs. Lakes normally lose water into an outlet or river, but some, called *closed lakes*, have no outlet and lose water only by evaporation – for example, Lake Eyre in Australia and Great Salt Lake in Utah, USA.

Where do rivers get their water from?

Rivers may receive their water from several sources, but all of these are indirectly or directly related to *precipitation* – a collective term for the fall of moisture onto the Earth's surface from the atmosphere. Rain falling on the ground may immediately run down slopes as *overland flow*, becoming concentrated and eventually forming a stream. This occurs where the ground surface is *impermeable* (i.e. water cannot pass through it, as is the case with some kinds of rock). It may also occur where the ground is already saturated with water, or when rainfall is very heavy.

Often, however, rivers receive their water from *springs*. This is because rainfall will commonly soak into the ground, to accumulate in the soil or to pass into permeable and porous rocks as *groundwater*. In *permeable* rock, water can pass right through the rock itself, whereas in *porous* rock there are holes and fissures through which water can pass. A deposit of rock containing ground-

water is known as an *aquifer*. Springs occur where the top of the aquifer intersects with the ground surface. Groundwater is important as a source for rivers in that it can supply water even when precipitation is not occurring, thereby constantly maintaining river flow. A third source of water for rivers is the melting of solid precipitation (snow) or snow that has been turned to ice to form a glacier or ice sheet (▷ p. 70).

Perennial, seasonal and ephemeral rivers

Rivers occur in all the world's major environments, even in polar areas and deserts. In temperate areas, such as Western Europe, and in the wet tropics, enough precipitation tends to fall throughout the year to replenish groundwater constantly, and therefore to allow rivers to flow all year. These *perennial rivers* do, however, experience seasonal and day-to-day variations in the volume of water they carry (the *flow regime*), due to seasonal fluctuations in precipitation and additional inputs from individual storms.

Some rivers may only flow seasonally, particularly in environments with Mediterranean-type climates, which have a very distinct wet, winter season and a dry summer. Rivers in glaciated areas may also have very seasonal flow regimes. *Glacial meltwater streams*, which receive their water directly from glaciers, usually only flow during the few months in the summer when the ice melts. In dry desert climates, rivers may not flow for years on end, because of the infrequency of desert storms, and then only for a few days, or even hours. However, when storms do occur these *ephemeral* rivers may flow at great rates, because desert rainfall is often heavy. This gives them considerable power and the ability to erode and transport large quantities of sediment (▷ p. 72).

Some deserts do possess perennial rivers. The Nile, for example, despite experiencing a distinctly seasonal flow regime, flows all year round through the Egyptian Desert; likewise, the Colorado River passes through desert areas of the southwestern USA. The reason that these and other rivers can successfully exist in deserts is that their *catchments* (source areas) lie in areas with wetter climates.

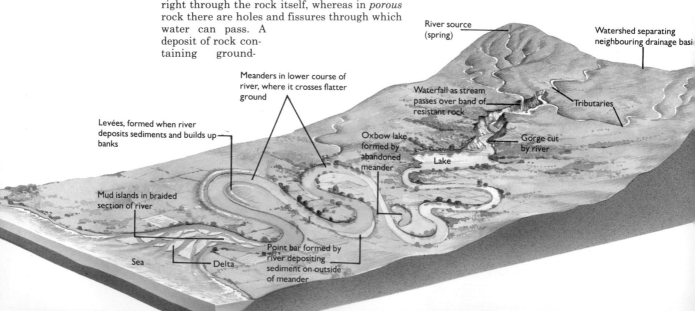

River source (spring)

Watershed separating neighbouring drainage basi

Meanders in lower course of river, where it crosses flatter ground

Waterfall as stream passes over band of resistant rock

Tributaries

Levées, formed when river deposits sediments and builds up banks

Oxbow lake formed by abandoned meander

Gorge cut by river

Lake

Mud islands in braided section of river

Sea

Delta

Point bar formed by river depositing sediment on outside of meander

THE HYDROLOGICAL CYCLE

Water exists in three states: liquid, gaseous (water vapour or steam) and solid (snow and ice). It can also pass from one state to another by freezing, melting, condensing and evaporating. New water is not created on the Earth's surface or in its atmosphere; nor is 'old' water lost. Rather, there is a finite amount, and this circulates in what is known as the *hydrological cycle*. Water moves around the cycle both by physically moving and by changing its state, as the diagram shows.

Today, 97% of the water in the hydrological cycle is contained in the world's seas, oceans and saline lakes. The remaining 3% is fresh water. About 75% of all fresh water is contained in glaciers and ice sheets, and just over 24% is groundwater (i.e. underground). The rivers, lakes, soil and atmosphere therefore contain a very small amount (less than 0.5%) of the world's fresh water at any one time.

During glacial periods of the Earth's history (▷ p. 91), the amount of water contained in ice sheets and glaciers has been greater, and the amount in oceans smaller.

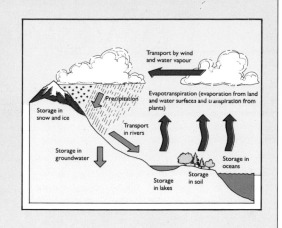

Only some very short rivers are able to flow from a source to the sea without either being joined by others or becoming a *tributary* of a larger river. Most rivers therefore form part of a *drainage network*, occupying a *drainage basin*. In fact, the whole of the Earth's land surface can be divided up into drainage basins, and these basins are separated by areas of relatively high ground called *watersheds*. Some drainage basins occupy only a few square kilometres, but others are enormous – the largest, the Amazon basin, covers over 7 million km² (2.7 million sq mi).

Rivers and landscapes

Rivers are a major force in shaping landscapes. They erode rock and sediment, thereby cutting channels and even valleys and shaping the landscape of upland areas. Such channels may be very shallow, but they may be as deep as the Grand Canyon, which the Colorado River has cut to a depth of up to 1500 m (5000 ft) in places. River valleys are commonly regarded as V-shaped, but in fact their shape can vary according to the position along the river's course, the size of the river, and the rock types in the landscape through which the river passes.

Rivers also transport vast quantities of material that has been eroded by other agencies – for example, rock-weathering processes, glaciers (▷ p. 70) and the wind. This sediment may in turn be deposited by the rivers themselves, within river channels or as *flood plains*, or carried into lakes or the sea. The deposition of sediment in a valley to form a flood plain tends to result in a lessening of the gradient of a river channel. A gentler gradient means that a river may cut *meanders* (wandering channels) in the soft flood-plain deposits. Over time, erosion of the river bank of the outside bend of a meander (where flow is fastest) may cause the channel to straighten and the meander to be 'cut off' to form an *oxbow lake*.

Mud islands may form within the channel of a river carrying a particularly large load of sediment, and a pattern of *braided channels* may develop. Where a river with a large load of sediment meets the sea, the loss of river energy can cause sediment to be deposited at the coast, forming a *delta*, as in the cases of the Mississippi and Nile. Over the centuries, deltas can build up large areas of land where once there was sea.

CAVES

Caves are among the most spectacular natural features formed by running water. The majority of caves of any significant size occur in limestone areas. This is because limestone – which consists almost entirely of calcium carbonate – is soluble in rainwater containing carbon dioxide. This solution is carbonic acid, which undergoes a reversible reaction with calcium carbonate to form calcium bicarbonate, which is soluble in water.

Massive, low-porosity, well-jointed limestones, such as Carboniferous limestone, are the most favourable rock types for caves. Bedding planes and joints, together with faults, are weaknesses through which rainwater can percolate, and where its acid can attack the limestone. Prolonged attack may lead to the formation of a cave. Free stream flow through caves leads to gradual drainage of the higher parts of the system, with the streams eventually rising at springs near the base of the limestone. Uplift of the limestone may lead to the underground streams finding still lower routes through the rock, and thus the old routes are abandoned. Undermining of cave walls by free-flowing streams may lead to the collapse of parts of the roof and the gradual enlargement of caverns, possibly resulting in openings to the surface known as *potholes*.

Stalactites and stalagmites (collectively known as *speleothems*) are caused by the precipitation of calcium carbonate from water rich in calcium bicarbonate percolating through the cave roof. Stalactites on the ceiling start as straw-like tubes with drops running down the inside, but as crystals grow inside the tubes they become blocked, and the stalactites thicken. Stalagmites grow where drops fall to the floor.

Lakes

Lakes can occur along the course of a river, where it flows into a depression. In some circumstances, a lake can mark the end point of a river course. Such depressions can be *erosional*, formed by the action of glaciers or wind. They may also be *depositional*, formed, for example, by a landslide blocking the course of a river. Finally, they may be *structural*, formed by Earth movements, for example in rift valleys (▷ p. 67). Lakes may also be formed behind the terminal moraines of retreating glaciers (▷ p. 70). A *volcanic lake*, formed by the accumulation of rainfall in a volcanic crater (▷ p. 65), may even have no inflowing or outflowing river.

In hot, relatively dry climates, lakes will lose a lot of water through evaporation. This results in the concentration of salts and the lake water becoming saline. The Caspian Sea, Aral Sea and Dead Sea are all saline lakes. These three lakes do have outlets, but lakes that lose as much water through evaporation as they gain from inputs will in fact be *closed*, that is, without an outflow.

The Oceans

The oceans cover a greater area of the Earth than does the land – 71% or almost three-quarters of the Earth's surface. The three major oceans are the Pacific, Atlantic and Indian Oceans. The Pacific is the largest ocean, and covers more than one-third of the surface of the Earth. The Arctic Ocean is smaller than the other three and is covered almost entirely by ice (⊳ p. 70).

Most of the water on the Earth, about 94% of it, is in the oceans. More pure water is evaporated from the oceans than is returned as precipitation (rain, snow, etc.), but the volume of water in the oceans remains the same because water is also returned to the oceans from the land by rivers.

Sea water has solid substances dissolved in it. Sodium and chlorine are the most abundant of these, and together with magnesium, calcium and potassium they make up over 90% of the elements

dissolved in sea water. The saltiness, or *salinity*, of sea water depends upon the amount of these substances dissolved in it.

Tides

Tides are caused by the gravitational pull of the Moon and the Sun on the Earth, causing the level of the oceans to change. The pull is greatest on the side of the Earth facing the Moon, and this produces a high tide. The pull is weakest on the side away from the Moon, where the sea water rises away from the Moon, and this also gives a high tide. There are two high tides and two low tides every day in most parts of the Earth, but a few areas have only one high tide and one low tide, or a mixture, with one high tide being much higher than the other.

The Sun is much further away than the Moon, so although it is much larger it has less effect on tides. When both the Moon and the Sun are on the same or opposite sides of the Earth, the pull is greatest, producing very high tides called *spring tides*. Weaker tides, known as *neap tides*, occur when the Moon and the Sun form a right angle with the Earth, because the pulls of the two are in different directions. Spring tides occur every 14 days and neap tides half-way between each spring tide.

The *tidal range* (the difference between the high and the low water levels) varies from place to

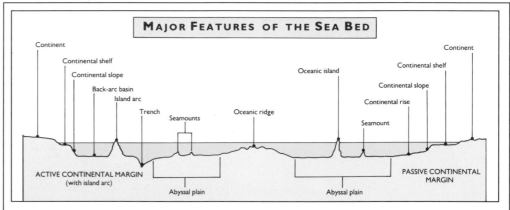

MAJOR FEATURES OF THE SEA BED

The major features are as described in the text. An *active continental margin* is one at which spreading ocean floor is being subducted (beneath the trench) into the mantle below. A *passive continental margin* is one where no subduction takes place; hence there is no trench (⊳ p. 62). Not all active margins have an island arc with a basin (a *back-arc* basin) between the arc and the adjacent continent; in some cases the trench lies at the foot of the continental slope, and the island arc and the back-arc are missing.

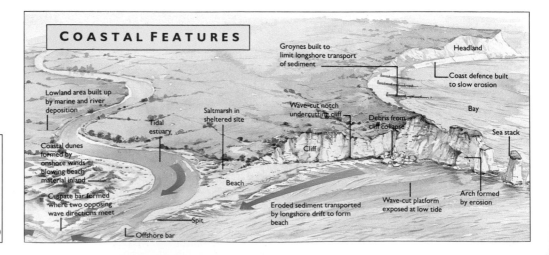

COASTAL FEATURES

SEE ALSO

● WAVE THEORY p. 20
● PLATE TECTONICS p. 62
● RIVERS AND LAKES p. 74
● PRIMITIVE ANIMALS p. 94
● CRUSTACEANS p. 97
● FISHES p. 100
● MARINE MAMMALS p. 120
● AQUATIC ECOSYSTEMS p. 130

place, from less than 1 m (3¼ ft) in the Mediterranean Sea and Gulf of Mexico to 14.5 m (47½ ft) in the Bay of Fundy on the east coast of Canada.

Currents

The currents near the surface of the oceans, like waves (▷ box), are driven by the winds. The wind drags the water along with it. Currents move much more slowly than the wind, with speeds of less than 8 km/h (5 mph). They do not flow exactly in the same direction as the wind, but are deflected to one side by the Earth's spin.

There are two main wind systems in each hemisphere. The *trade winds*, between latitudes 0° and 30°, blow from the northeast in the northern hemisphere, and the southeast in the southern. The *westerlies*, between latitudes 30° and 60°, blow from the southwest in the northern hemisphere, and the northwest in the southern. These two wind systems produce a circulating system of currents that flow from equatorial regions to latitudes of about 50° and return to the equator (▷ map on p. 80).

Currents may have a significant effect on climate. For example, the North Atlantic Drift, flowing from the Caribbean, gives northwest Europe much milder winters than other parts of the world at the same latitude. Conversely, cold currents, such as the Humboldt Current on the Pacific coast of South America, have a cooling effect on the climate.

Features of the sea bed

The region of the sea bed closest to land is the *continental margin*, which is divided into the *continental shelf*, the *continental slope* and (sometimes) the *continental rise*. The continental shelf is the shallowest – around 130 m (430 ft) deep – and is relatively flat. It is about 100 km (60 mi) wide.

Oceanic ridges are vast, rugged, undersea mountain chains often at the centre of oceans. On average they are some 1000 km (620 mi) wide and stand up to 3000 m (10 000 ft) above the adjacent ocean basins. They form a more-or-less linked system – about 80 000 km (50 000 mi) long – that enters all the major oceans. Different parts of it have different names: in the centre and South Atlantic, for example, it is called the Mid-Atlantic Ridge, and in the Pacific it is known as the East Pacific Rise. On average, ridge crests lie some 2500 m (8200 ft) below the ocean surface, but there are a few places, such as Iceland, where the rocks have risen above the water surface. Oceanic ridges are sites at which new oceanic lithosphere is being created (▷ p. 60).

Between the ocean ridges and the continental margins there are *abyssal plains*. These are very flat and featureless parts of the sea floor, around 4000 m (13 000 ft) deep. Abyssal plains are broken in some places by *seamounts*, underwater volcanoes that have erupted from the sea floor. Seamounts may rise above the sea surface to form islands, such as Hawaii.

The deepest parts of the oceans are the *ocean trenches*. Trenches are on average about 100 km (62 mi) wide and 7000–8000 m (23 000–26 000 ft) deep, and may be thousands of kilometres long. They occur in two different kinds of location: parallel to the edge of a continent, at the bottom of the continental slope; or in the open ocean, where they are arc-shaped, and are parallel to an island arc.

WAVES AND COASTS

Waves are the most important factor in shaping the coastline. Also important, where winds and waves from one direction dominate, is the sea's ability to transport material along the coast in a preferred direction, by *longshore drift*. Waves are generated by the wind blowing across the surface of the ocean. Water does not move along with waves but changes shape as a wave passes, moving in a roughly circular motion, rising towards a wave crest as it arrives and falling as it passes (▷ p. 20).

The height of waves and the distance between them (the *wavelength*), together with wave energy, are largely determined by wind strength and the distance (called the *fetch*) over which they have been transported. Waves with a long fetch tend to possess considerable energy with which to shape the coast. The effect that waves have on the coast is determined by whether they are *destructive* or *constructive*. Destructive waves are relatively high compared to their wavelength, and break with a force that generates a strong backwash that can remove material from a beach. Constructive waves break more gently, pushing material up the beach, building it up.

Longshore drift can result in the growth of a beach along the coast. Where this occurs, and the coastline changes direction, for example at an estuary (river mouth) or bay, the growth of the beach can continue to form a *spit*, a depositional landform that extends out into the sea. A spit can even rejoin the land again, forming a *sand bar* or *barrier beach*. Some bays are so sheltered from wave action that beaches do not form, although if fine sediment such as mud is supplied by a river, these sheltered places may develop *tidal salt marshes*.

Erosion occurs where coasts are exposed to waves that have a long fetch, or where strong onshore winds generate high-energy waves over relatively short distances. Erosional coastlines are commonly dominated by cliffs, at the foot of which a *wavecut platform* – the seaward remnant of eroded cliffs – may be exposed at low tide. Where the cliffs are formed of rocks that are well jointed and susceptible to erosion, *sea stacks* (free-standing pinnacles), arches and caves may be formed by the sea's erosive action.

ISLANDS

Islands, especially those in seas and oceans, have a range of origins. Islands can develop through *constructional* processes, involving the deposition (laying down) of sediment or the building up of volcanic or organic material. They may also be formed by *erosional* processes that cause an area of land to become separated from the mainland. Changes in sea level can cause new islands to appear or existing ones to disappear. During the last Ice Age (▷ p. 70) eastern Britain was joined to mainland Europe, because sea levels were lower as much of the world's water was frozen in the ice caps and glaciers.

When volcanic activity occurs beneath the oceans, it can lead to the growth of islands. This is often closely linked to the movement of the Earth's crustal plates, with island-building occurring both at constructive plate margins (e.g. Iceland) and at destructive margins (▷ p. 62). Volcanic islands (e.g. Hawaii) can also form far from any plate boundary (▷ below). When the collision zone of crustal plates at destructive margins (▷ p. 62) lies beneath an ocean, island development can result. Islands that are born in this way do not occur singly, but in chains or *archipelagos* ('arcs') that parallel the plate boundary (▷ p. 62).

The Hawaiian–Emperor island chain and some other mid-Pacific islands owe their existence to volcanic *hot-spot activity*. Volcanic activity has erupted through the Pacific plate as it has passed over areas of the Earth's mantle that are particularly active. As the plate has moved, so has the location of volcanic activity and island construction. The Hawaiian–Emperor chain includes more than 100 islands and *seamounts* (volcanoes that have not reached the ocean surface) and its youngest island, which is the furthest east, is Hawaii itself, where volcanic activity is still occurring.

Coral islands and reefs are an important component of warm tropical and subtropical oceans and seas. They are formed from the skeletons of the group of primitive marine organisms known as corals (▷ p. 94). Coral islands develop where coral grows up towards the ocean surface from shallow submarine platforms – often volcanic cones. If the cone is totally submerged, then a *coral atoll* will develop – a circular or horseshoe-shaped coral ring that encloses a body of sea water called a *lagoon*. Upward growth of the coral ceases once sea level has been reached. Coral islands are therefore flat and low, unless a change in sea level has caused their elevation to change.

Weather

The weather is the atmospheric conditions we experience at any one time. These can vary rapidly as rain gives way to sunshine or snow starts to melt. Such sudden changes of weather are more common in temperate latitudes than in the tropics.

Weather is the result of air movements in the atmosphere (➪ p. 60). The atmosphere responds to the differences in heat received from the Sun between the warm tropics and the cold poles. The Earth's rotation and the nature of the ground surface – land or sea, mountain or lowland – will all affect the way the atmosphere moves.

Pressure and temperature

In temperate parts of the world, the most important feature of the weather is atmospheric pressure. Atmospheric pressure represents the force exerted by a column of the atmosphere on the Earth's surface. If pressure is measured using a barometer and compared with readings taken elsewhere at the same time, patterns appear showing areas of higher and lower surface pressure.

From a pressure map (➪ illustration) it is possible to find wind direction. As a rough guide, winds blow parallel to the *isobars* – the lines that link points experiencing the same pressure. In the northern hemisphere, the low pressure lies to the left of the wind direction, while in the southern hemisphere it is to the right. The strength of the wind depends upon the *pressure gradient*. If the pressure gradient is steep, that means that the isobars are close together and winds will be strong.

A pressure map can also inform us about other aspects of weather. Temperature is affected by the origin of air. Air blowing from polar latitudes will be cold, while air from the tropics will be warm. Winds blowing from the Atlantic Ocean on to northwest Europe are relatively cool in summer but relatively mild in winter, while winds from the east are very cold in winter but warm in

PRESSURE CHARTS

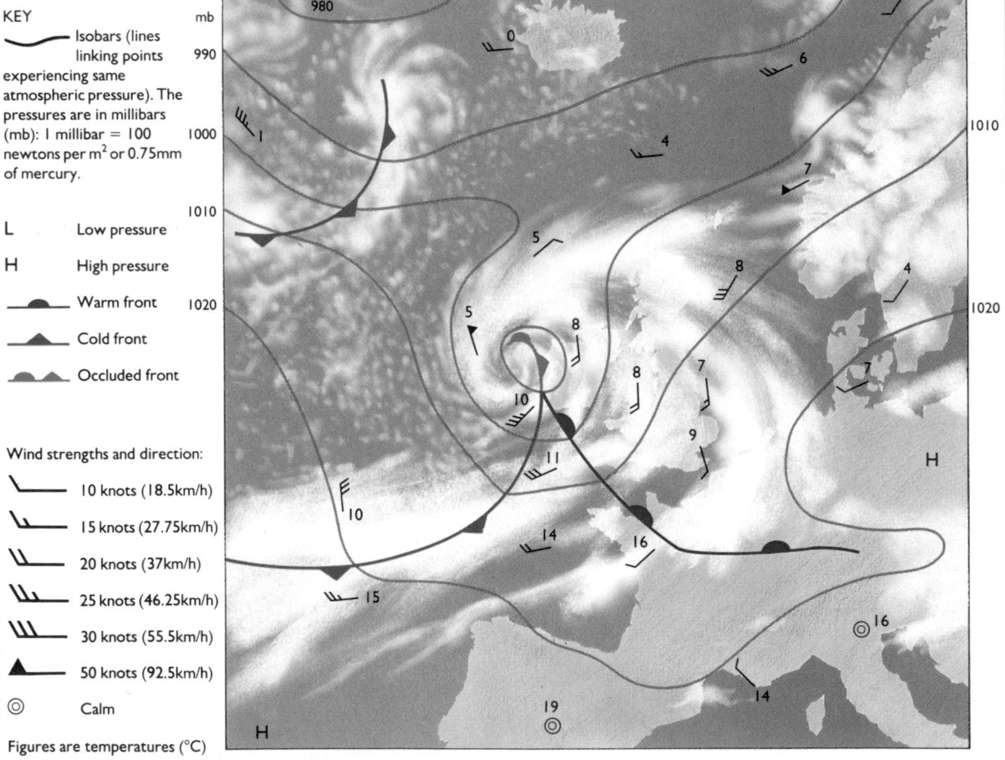
KEY
mb
Isobars (lines linking points experiencing same atmospheric pressure). The pressures are in millibars (mb): 1 millibar = 100 newtons per m² or 0.75mm of mercury.
990
1000
1010
1020
L Low pressure
H High pressure
Warm front
Cold front
Occluded front
Wind strengths and direction:
10 knots (18.5km/h)
15 knots (27.75km/h)
20 knots (37km/h)
25 knots (46.25km/h)
30 knots (55.5km/h)
50 knots (92.5km/h)
Calm
Figures are temperatures (°C)
980
L
H
mb
1000
1010
1020

Weather forecasters use pressure charts to help them decide what the weather is going to do. The satellite image and superimposed pressure chart show the way in which cloud systems and pressure systems are related. The main areas of thicker cloud are associated with the rising air near the low-pressure centre to the west of Ireland. The centre of the low marks the start of the typical spiral cloud pattern, with the cold front being a distinctive feature sweeping in from the west.

Ahead of the low pressure, high-level ice-crystal clouds cover much of Britain. They are often an indication of approaching rain – which duly fell later in the day. Behind the depression (to its west), the cellular cloud pattern produced by air rising from the relatively warm sea is typical. Occasional showers will fall. Further to the west a band of thicker cloud shows a weak cold front sweeping eastwards giving more frequent showers south of Iceland. Over the Mediterranean, high pressure keeps the skies clear.

SEE ALSO
- THE EARTH'S STRUCTURE AND ATMOSPHERE p. 60
- RIVERS AND LAKES p. 74
- CLIMATE p. 80

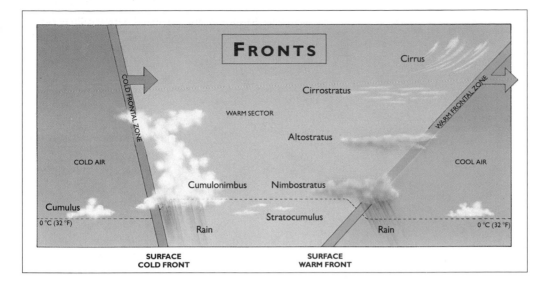

FRONTS

Cirrus

Cirrostratus

COLD FRONTAL ZONE

WARM FRONTAL ZONE

WARM SECTOR

Altostratus

COLD AIR

COOL AIR

Cumulonimbus

Nimbostratus

Cumulus

Stratocumulus

0 °C (32 °F)

0 °C (32 °F)

Rain

Rain

SURFACE
COLD FRONT

SURFACE
WARM FRONT

summer. Temperatures will also depend upon how much the Sun is obscured by clouds. However, nocturnal cloud cover helps to retain daytime warmth.

Weather systems

In temperate latitudes, one of the main areas of uplift and cloud formation – and so of rainfall – is the *low-pressure area* or *depression* (also called a *cyclone*). Seen from space, depressions often possess a distinctive swirl of clouds showing where the air is rising. In depressions the wind blows anticlockwise in the northern hemisphere and clockwise in the southern. Most cloud occurs near fronts, where temperatures change rapidly. In a typical low-pressure system, a warm front, a cold front, an occluded front and a warm sector are found (⊳ weather map and illustration). Away from the cloud bands of the depression, showers still occur but are less frequent as pressure rises away from the low-pressure centre. *High-pressure areas* or *anticyclones* contain generally sinking and warming air. As a result air does not rise enough for deep cloud to form, so rain is rare. In all temperate land areas, anticyclones can bring hot, sunny weather in summer or cold weather in winter, but they are always dry. Within anticyclones the wind blows clockwise in the northern hemisphere and anticlockwise in the southern.

In the tropics, distinctive pressure patterns are less common. Pressure gradients are usually much weaker than in temperate latitudes, so winds are generally light. One major low-pressure system that is found is the *tropical storm*. It has a number of names, including *hurricane*, *typhoon* and *cyclone*. Tropical storms normally occur in summer or autumn when tropical seas are warmest. At their centre is an area of very low pressure surrounded by strong winds, which can exceed 240 km/h (150 mph) in the worst storms. At the centre or *eye* of the storm, winds are light. Away from the eye sweep vast bands of cloud from which heavy rain falls. A less dramatic feature of the tropics is the seasonal change of winds known as the *monsoon*. Over parts of Africa, India, Southeast Asia and northern Australia, the monsoons bring rain during the summer season. The rest of the year is dry with winds blowing in the opposite direction.

CLOUDS

Clouds form when air rises or is forced to rise causing it to cool so much that it can no longer hold all its water as a vapour. Water droplets then appear, which we see as clouds. When the ground warms, *thermals* of warm, moist air may rise sufficiently to produce clouds. Clouds often develop over high ground where air is forced to rise. Some clouds, though by no means all, produce *precipitation* (rain, snow, sleet, etc.). To do this, the right sort of conditions have to exist in the cloud. One method of precipitation formation is through the collision and coalescence of water droplets of different size within the cloud.

The other method of precipitation takes place in clouds that consist of a mixture of water droplets and ice crystals. Not all droplets freeze at 0 °C (32 °F) – some remain as droplets down to –38 °C (–36 °F) because they are so small. Under these conditions, water tends to transfer from the droplets on to the larger, already frozen droplets. These ice crystals may eventually reach the ground as snow; more frequently, however, they melt as they fall to produce rain. Occasionally, some raindrops get swept to the upper parts of a *cumulonimbus* cloud, where they freeze. Repeated rising and sinking can produce a hailstone consisting of layers of ice.

Thunder and lightning may also occur in cumulonimbus clouds. A separation of electrical charge (positive from negative) develops during hail formation. The flash of lightning is a spark of electricity between cloud and Earth or from cloud to cloud resulting from the build-up of charges and potential differences of up to 1000 million volts. The air is heated by the lightning, and the sudden expansion of the air produces thunder.

Clouds are identified on the basis of their appearance and height. *Cirrus* clouds, the highest, form at heights between 6 and 10 km (3½ and 6 mi), where the temperatures are well below freezing point. They consist of ice crystals, which often tend to be spread out by the strong winds at those levels. Hooked cirrus ('mare's-tails') are usually found ahead of a depression and so indicate imminent rain. When the sheets of ice crystals thicken and cover more of the sky, they are called *cirrostratus* clouds.

Middle-level clouds of uniform greyness that totally obscure the Sun are known as *altostratus*. They often follow cirrostratus clouds. As rain approaches, the cloud base lowers to give a sheet of thick cloud called *nimbostratus*, which can give much rain. Where clouds are not able to develop upwards, as in anticyclones, *stratocumulus* clouds may form. These clouds indicate that air has only been able to rise to a certain level before sinking in the clear zones between the clouds. This gives a fish-scale effect ('mackerel sky') if the clouds are relatively high.

Cumulus clouds are associated with rapidly rising air. They have sharp outlines – often resembling cauliflowers – and can build up to enter the ice-crystal zone or even reach the base of the stratosphere. When this happens they cannot rise further but spread out to produce an anvil-like cloud that is known as *cumulonimbus*. Most give showers, and hail and thunder are possible.

Climate

The average weather condition found in a region is known as its *climate*, and this is based on long-term records, usually 30 years. In contrast, *weather* is the day-to-day variation in atmospheric conditions. Climate is the weather we might expect in a given area at a particular time, while the weather is the actual condition that prevails.

Climate has a crucial effect on the kinds of vegetation found in a particular region, although as the maps show, climate and vegetation zones do not always coincide.

Classification of climate

Climate can be classified in many complex ways. The most general method is to divide each hemisphere into broad belts or *climatic zones*. The ancient Greeks made the earliest attempts at classifying climate. They recognized a *winterless tropical region* located in the low latitudes, a *summerless polar region* where temperatures are usually very low, and an *intermediate* or *middle-latitude region*, now called the *temperate latitudes*, with cool summers and mild winters.

A simple classification can be based on two climatic elements, namely temperature and precipitation (rain, snow, dew, etc.). When both average temperature and precipitation are known it is possible to classify a particular location into a *climatic type*.

The seasons

Apart from those locations at or very near to the equator, all climatic regions show seasonal variation. Generally, the further away from the equator, the greater the seasonal variation becomes. Seasons are caused by the annual revolution of the Earth in a slightly elliptical orbit around the Sun, and by the daily rotation of the Earth on its axis. The axis of rotation is inclined at 23.5° from the vertical. The effect of the Earth's rotation and revolution around the Sun is to produce changing day length and varying angles at which the Sun's rays strike the surface of the Earth. Together these two factors cause a seasonal variation in climate (▷ diagram which shows the order of seasons in the northern hemisphere).

Twice during each year, on 21 March and 23 September, the Sun's rays are directly overhead at the equator. These two days are the *spring* and *autumnal equinoxes*. On 21 June the Earth is midway between the equinoxes and the North Pole is inclined at 23.5° towards the Sun; the Sun's rays are overhead at the Tropic of Cancer (latitude 23.5° N) and the *summer solstice* occurs in the northern hemisphere (and the *winter solstice* in the southern hemisphere). By 21 December the position is reversed. The Sun is overhead at the Tropic of Capricorn (23.5° S) and the winter solstice occurs in the northern hemisphere (summer solstice in the southern hemisphere).

Controls on climate

Climatic controls include the proximity of land to water, and the effects of elevation, mountain barriers and ocean currents. *Climatic effects* include the seasonal or daily ranges of temperature and precipitation, and humidity, winds, etc.

Even though two places may have similar average yearly temperature and precipitation values, or share the same latitude, they can experience different climates. If the climatic controls of the two places are not alike, then neither will be the resulting climatic effects.

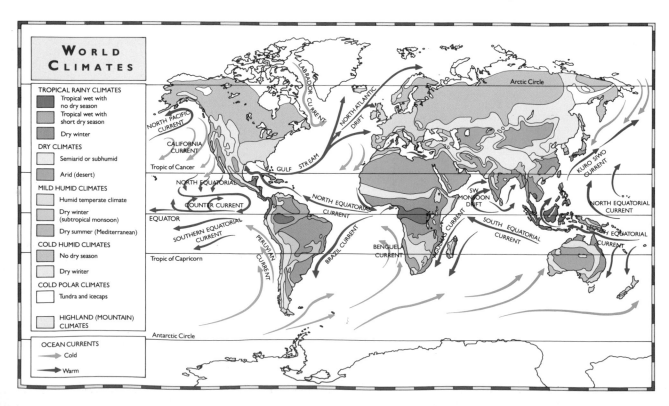

WORLD CLIMATES

TROPICAL RAINY CLIMATES
- Tropical wet with no dry season
- Tropical wet with short dry season
- Dry winter

DRY CLIMATES
- Semiarid or subhumid
- Arid (desert)

MILD HUMID CLIMATES
- Humid temperate climate
- Dry winter (subtropical monsoon)
- Dry summer (Mediterranean)

COLD HUMID CLIMATES
- No dry season
- Dry winter

COLD POLAR CLIMATES
- Tundra and icecaps

- HIGHLAND (MOUNTAIN) CLIMATES

OCEAN CURRENTS
- Cold
- Warm

As water is slower to heat up than land and slower to cool down, places in the mid-latitudes near the sea will have cooler summers and milder winters than those far from the sea. The former are said to have *maritime climates* while the latter have *continental climates*. Ocean currents can either give a place a milder climate than would be expected at that latitude (for example, the effect of the warm North Atlantic Drift on northwest Europe), or a cooler climate (such as the effect of the cold Labrador Current on Newfoundland).

Temperature decreases with altitude. High ground may also be wetter, because warm moist air will condense as it rises over a cool land mass, so producing rain or snow. If the rain-bearing winds mostly come from one direction, the land on that side will be wetter than the land on the opposite side, which will be in a *rain shadow*. On the South Island of New Zealand, for example, there is heavy precipitation to the west side of the New Zealand Alps, but on the east side precipitation in places is as low as 330 mm (13 in).

Climate and vegetation

The map showing the world's vegetation regions is complicated by the fact that it attempts to show the original distribution of *natural* vegetation, that is, the vegetation as it was before being greatly altered by human interference such as deforestation and agriculture. Elevation, slope, drainage, soil type, soil depth and climate all influence the vegetation distribution.

Climate is a major factor in determining the type and number of plants (and to a lesser extent animals) that can live in an area. Three main terrestrial ecosystems can be recognized: deserts, grasslands and forests (⯈ p. 128). Precipitation determines which vegetation type will occur in an area. If the annual precipitation is less than 250 mm (10 in) then deserts usually occur. Grasslands can be found when precipitation is between 250 and 750 mm (10 and 30 in) per annum, while areas that receive more than 750 mm (30 in)

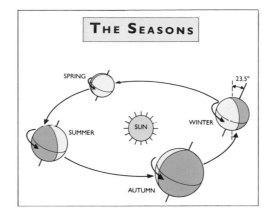

rainfall a year are usually covered by forests. The average temperature and the nature of the seasons in a region are important in that they can determine the type of desert, grassland or forest. Wherever the monthly average temperature exceeds 21 °C (70 °F) then hot deserts, savannah grasslands or tropical forests occur.

In the middle latitudes, the winter temperatures are low enough (one month or more below 5 °C / 41 °F) to cause vegetation to become dormant. In autumn, growth stops, leaves are often shed and the plant survives the unfavourable winter months in a resting or dormant phase. In spring, when temperatures rise, new growth begins. In high latitudes, the winter conditions are such that between four and six months are dark and average temperature falls well below 0 °C (32 °F). The evergreen conifers can survive these conditions, but growth is very slow and confined to the short, cool summers. In the highest latitudes, trees disappear and only small, low-growing plants can survive.

SEE ALSO

● THE OCEANS p. 78
● WEATHER p. 90
● THE BIOSPHERE p. 126
● TERRESTRIAL ECOSYSTEMS p. 128

WORLD VEGETATION

- Tundra
- Boreal and montane coniferous forest
- Temperate forest
- Temperate grassland
- Chaparral/Mediterranean
- Desert
- Tropical evergreen and tropical moist forest
- Tropical deciduous forest
- Tropical and semitropical scrub
- Tropical savannah, thorn forest
- Semidesert, arid grassland
- Mountains (complex zonation)

→ Distribution of tropical cyclones
→ Monsoon paths

Ice
Arctic Circle
Tropic of Cancer
HURRICANES
EQUATOR
Tropic of Capricorn
Antarctic Circle
Ice
TYPHOONS
WILLY – WILLIES

The Beginnings of Life

When the earth formed some 4.6 billion years ago, its atmosphere was very different from that of today, consisting of various gases such as water vapour (H_2O), hydrogen (H_2), nitrogen (N_2), carbon dioxide (CO_2) and carbon monoxide (CO). As the early atmosphere cooled, the hydrogen reacted with the oxides of carbon to form methane (CH_4) and with nitrogen to form ammonia (NH_3).

Ammonia and methane are able to combine with water and carbon dioxide if they are subjected to ultraviolet light (as emitted by the sun) and if an electrical spark (such as lightning) is passed through them. From reactions such as these, occurring many millions of years ago, simple *amino acids* may have formed: these are the building blocks of *proteins* – the essential components of living things ($\triangleright$ p. 86).

Stirrings in the primeval soup

Of all the planets in our solar system only the earth could have supported the subsequent development of life as we know it, for only here can water – the prime prerequisite for life – exist in its liquid form. The oceans were formed by the condensation of water vapour in the atmosphere, and in these a wide range of dissolved minerals and gases soon accumulated. In this way a 'primeval broth' developed in which the evolution of the organic molecules of life could take place.

The first crucial step towards life-like forms, perhaps occurring some 4 billion years ago, is

---

SIMPLE LIFE FORMS

Viruses

Viruses are extremely simple life forms, very much in a grey area between living and non-living things. All are tiny, ranging in size from 0.000018 to 0.0006 of a millimetre. A large range of viruses are now known to exist, many of which cause diseases, ranging from AIDS to the common cold.

Viruses consist simply of a single nucleic acid – either DNA or RNA ($\triangleright$ p. 86) – surrounded by a protein layer. On infecting a host cell, a virus may use the mechanisms of the host cell in order to make viral nucleic acids and proteins from which new virus particles can be constructed; the new particles then leave the cell, sometimes destroying the cell in the process. Alternatively a virus may enter a cell and remain silent for a period of time; it then replicates and leaves the host cell.

Bacteria

The first evidence of life on earth comes from minute globules preserved in rocks 3800 million years old. These are believed to be the fossils of primitive bacteria. Together with some other simple organisms, these form the kingdom Monera, the most primitive of the five kingdoms of living things. An individual bacterium consists of a single primitive form of cell, called a *prokaryote cell*. Unlike the cells of higher organisms, such cells do not have a nucleus in which their genetic material is held ($\triangleright$ below). Bacteria vary in shape from almost spherical (*coccus*) to rod-like (*bacillus*) or corkscrew-shaped (*spirochaete*). Some, such as *Salmonella*, are capable of independent movement, while others are immobile.

Bacteria vary considerably in size: the smallest are no more than 0.0003 mm, while the largest can be more than 0.02 mm. Under favourable conditions they reproduce by simple fission (division) and have a very high reproductive rate, a single bacterium being able to divide once every 20 minutes. Bacteria cause a wide range of diseases, including cholera, food poisoning, leprosy, plague, syphilis, tetanus, tuberculosis and typhoid.

Although we think of bacteria as disease-causing parasites, they are very diverse in both their habitat and biology. Many feed on dead matter, for instance, while others live in symbiotic relationships with plants and animals, in many of which they aid digestion. Some bacteria can make their own organic molecules from inorganic sources by means of photosynthesis ($\triangleright$ p. 88). One group of bacteria – the nitrogen-fixing bacteria – are able to convert nitrogen compounds derived from decomposing organic matter, especially in the soil, into the more stable form of nitrates. These are then exploited by higher plants to form organic amino compounds, which in turn become available to animals. Thus bacteria play a vital role in the maintenance of virtually all life on earth.

Protists

The kingdom Protista includes the single-celled algae and protozoans. Unlike the simpler bacteria, each protist consists of a single *eukaryote cell* (the type of cell found in all higher organisms): the genetic material is contained in chromosomes within the nucleus, which is surrounded by a membrane, and there are several miniature organs (*organelles*), each with a special function within the operation of the cell.

Although remaining single-celled, protists have developed incredible degrees of complexity and sophistication, and some of them form the first

approach to multicellular organisms through the construction of colonies. Most of the protists are very small organisms, ranging from 0.00001 to not more than 1 mm in length. Protists may reproduce asexually (by cell fission) or by sexual reproduction. Although it is not possible to distinguish separate sexes, it is clear that in many cases fusion occurs between cells from different individuals.

The protists are ubiquitous on land and in water, as well as inside other organisms as parasites or symbionts. Free-living forms of algae and protozoans can be found in the soil at a density of up to 200 000 per gram. Some parasitic forms cause well-known diseases in humans and animals, including malaria, sleeping sickness and dysentery.

Only a few of the protists (the primitive algal forms) are able to convert simple inorganic molecules into complex organic molecules by photosynthesis. The majority are dependent on the consumption of other organic matter. Many protists are mobile. They move either by 'amoeboid movement' (which involves a complex series of changes to the cell's shape) or by swimming with the aid of *cilia* or *flagella* (hair- and whip-like structures respectively).

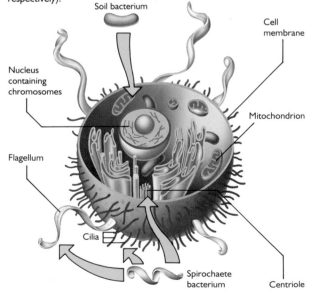

Soil bacterium
Cell membrane
Nucleus containing chromosomes
Mitochondrion
Flagellum
Cilia
Spirochaete bacterium
Centriole

From prokaryote to eukaryote? There is a striking resemblance between certain bacteria – which are simple prokaryotic organisms – and the organelles (miniature 'organs') found in the more complex eukaryotic cells of higher organisms. This has led some scientists to suggest that the first eukaryotic cells were the result of a cooperative coming together of various prokaryotic organisms.

THE CLASSIFICATION
OF LIFE

The study of biological classification, or *taxonomy*, aims to provide a rational framework in which to organize our knowledge of the great diversity of living and extinct organisms. The first well-authenticated system of classification goes back to Aristotle (384–322 BC), but it was not until the 17th century that the Englishman John Ray (1628–1705) proposed the first *natural classification* – an arrangement based on presumed relationships, rather than an artificial scheme aiming merely to facilitate correct identification of species. In the 18th century the Swedish naturalist Carl Linnaeus (1707–78) produced a rational system of classification based on patterns of similarity between different organisms.

The essential feature of Linnaeus's scheme is that it is *binomial*. He gave every distinct type or *species* of organism (e.g. the lion) a two-part (binomial) name (e.g. *Felis leo*) in which the second element identified the individual species, while the first element placed the species in a particular *genus* – a group comprising all those species that showed obvious similarities with one another. For instance, he grouped together all cat-like animals in the genus *Felis*: *Felis leo* – the lion; *Felis tigris* – the tiger; *Felis pardus* – the leopard; and so on. Having thus subordinated each species to a particular genus, he went on to place groups of genera in a higher rank or category called a *family*, then families in *orders*, and so on through *classes*, *phyla* (or *divisions*, for plants) and finally *kingdoms*.

Linnaeus used his highest taxonomic rank (kingdom) to separate plants and animals, but it is now clear that this simple subdivision is untenable, because certain groups such as bacteria, protists and fungi fit into neither category – and are now each assigned their own kingdom. Nevertheless, the binomial system has remained unchanged to this day and every newly discovered organism is given a Latin or Latinized binomial name.

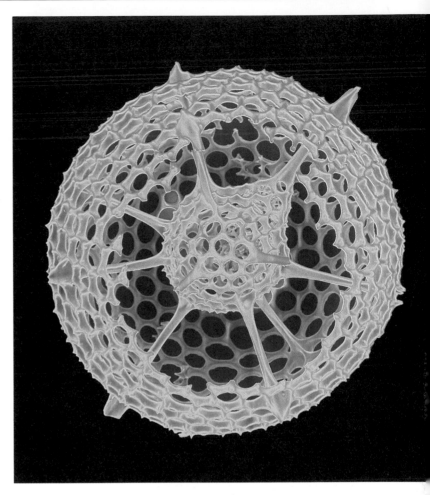

An amoeboid protozoan (*Radiolaria*), shown in false colour and magnified some 250 times. Part of the silica-based skeleton has been broken away to show the inner structure. In the living organism, numerous 'false feet' (pseudopodia) radiate from the skeleton, which are used in movement and feeding. (SPL)

thought to have been the appearance in the oceans of molecules – such as DNA (⊳ p. 86) – capable of self-replication. At this point it is probable that something like natural selection might have begun to operate (⊳ p. 84), with molecules able to replicate frequently and accurately faring better than others.

Bacteria and protists

The first forms of what we would unequivocally recognize as life were single-celled prokaryotic organisms such as *bacteria* (⊳ box), which fed on the abundant organic molecules available in the early oceans. Around 3.4 billion years ago, as supplies of these organic molecules began to be used up, new forms of bacteria started to emerge – *cyanobacteria* or *blue-green algae*. Being able to photosynthesize (⊳ p. 88), these could manufacture their own food, rather than depending on ready-made sources. At this point the by-product of photosynthesis – oxygen – began to accumulate in the atmosphere in large quantites. Previously oxygen had been poisonous to all living things, but now bacteria began to evolve that depended on oxygen for respiration.

About 1.5 billion years ago new kinds of single-celled organisms began to appear – the *protists*. Although still microscopic, these were many times larger than the bacteria. Some of these were animal-like consumers (*protozoans*), others plant-like photosynthesizers. Protists were the first organisms to possess eukaryote cells, which have a central nucleus containing the genetic material (⊳ box). It seems likely that sex-cell division (meoisis; ⊳ p. 86) must have quickly followed. The development of sex – the exchange of genetic material between two individual organisms – provided a level of variation that speeded up the process of natural selection, and thus of evolution.

Beyond the single cell

The next important development was the emergence of multicellular organisms, which occurred around 600 million years ago. The first multicellular animals may have been like sponges (⊳ p. 94), within which there are several types of cell, each of which is capable of functioning independently as well as in concert with other cells in the 'colony'. Within a few million years of the appearance of the first multicellular animals, most of the main groups of invertebrates had appeared. The first vertebrates – in the form of the jawless fishes – appeared around 500 million years ago, and it was from them that all the other fishes, together with the amphibians, reptiles, birds and mammals, eventually evolved.

SEE ALSO

● EVOLUTION p. 84
● GENETICS p. 86
● PLANTS pp. 88–93
● ANIMALS pp. 94–123

Evolution

Until the late 18th century it was generally accepted that the living world was the result of a single more-or-less instantaneous creation as outlined in the Bible. However, the discovery of giant bones in Ohio and also in Europe led a Frenchman, Baron Georges Cuvier (1779–1832), to demonstrate that many species preserved as fossils no longer existed – they had become extinct. By the beginning of the 19th century it was acknowledged by many thinkers that there had been worlds before man.

Furthermore, it was recognized that the history of life, as recorded by the geological sequence of fossils, portrayed a pattern of change through time. The idea of the evolution or transformation of species was born. The main issue of contention for many scientists was not whether change had taken place but rather concerned the nature of the change itself.

Lamarck and Darwin

There were two contrasting views on the nature of change. The view held by the Frenchman Jean-Baptiste Lamarck (1744–1829) was that change was gradual. The opposing view was held by Cuvier himself, who believed he detected a pattern of successive catastrophes and sudden replacements. The mechanism of change that Lamarck suggested in 1809 was that organisms during their lifetime develop structures that better enable them to adapt to their environment, and that they pass on these characteristics to their offspring. According to his scheme, the giraffe developed its long neck from its habit of browsing on tall trees.

At odds with Lamarck's ideas on the inheritance of acquired characteristics was the theory of evolutionary change proposed by the British naturalist Charles Darwin (1809–82). Darwin first developed his ideas on a voyage round the world as ship's naturalist on HMS *Beagle* in 1831–6, but he did not outline his theory until 1858, when he presented a paper jointly with Alfred Russel Wallace (1823–1913). He then expanded his theory the following year in his book *On the Origin of Species by Means of Natural Selection*. Predictably, Darwin's theory gave rise to bitter controversy, contradicting as it did the Bible's account of creation. Eventually, however, with the support of such eminent biologists as T.H. Huxley (1825–95), Darwin's theories became widely accepted.

Natural selection

When Darwin embarked on his voyage round the world, like most of his contemporaries he believed in the fixity of species. It was his obser-

---

THE EVIDENCE FOR EVOLUTION

Homologous structures: the pentadactyl limb (left)
The structure of the fore limbs of these five different animals shows that the pentadactyl (five-digit) limb is common to them all. Such basically similar structures are described as *homologous*, and the existence of such structures suggests that the animals concerned have all evolved from a common ancestor.

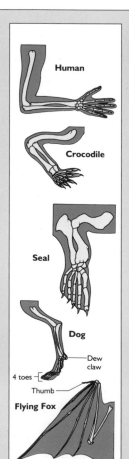

Human

Crocodile

Seal

Dog

— Dew claw

4 toes —

Thumb —

Flying Fox

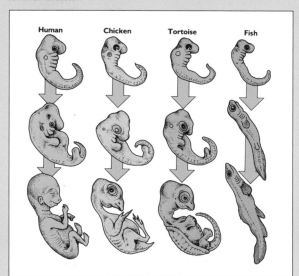

Human   Chicken   Tortoise   Fish

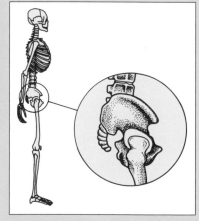

Vestigial structures: the coccyx (above)
One piece of evidence that humans and monkeys had a common ancestor is the existence in humans of the coccyx – the bone at the base of the spine. The coccyx is the remains of a tail, and is an example of a vestigial structure, i.e. one that no longer functions. In very rare cases humans are actually born with a stump of a tail.

Comparison of embryos (above)
The similarities between the embryos of vertebrates at comparable stages of development have provided considerable support to the theory of evolution. Thus fishes, amphibians (not shown), reptiles, birds and mammals all start with a similar number of gill arches (the folds below the head) and a similar vertebral column; even the early human embryo has a 'tail'. However, as the embryos develop, the similarities decrease and the individual species become more and more differentiated.

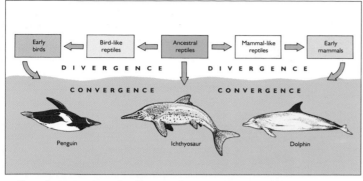

Aquatic convergence. In adapting to the marine habitat, such diverse animals as penguins, dolphins and the long-extinct ichthyosaurs have independently developed body forms similar to each other and to those of their remote fish ancestors: all have streamlined, cigar-shaped bodies and fin-like limbs.

Nature provides many variations on the theme of evolution by adaptation to a changing environment.

Convergent evolution is seen in cases where different organisms have evolved similar solutions to similar problems, even though they may have evolved from very different ancestors. Such solutions usually involve anatomical modifications, which are known as *analogous structures* – for example, the wings of insects, birds and bats, all of which arose independently. Other examples of convergent evolution include swallows and swifts (both of which look and behave very similarly, but which in fact belong to entirely different orders), and the adaptations that various reptiles, birds and mammals have made in returning to the seas (▷ illustration).

Similar in some respects to convergent evolution is **parallel evolution**, whereby unrelated plants and animals adapt in similar ways to fill ecological niches in similar but geographically separated ecosystems. Thus the marsupial mammals of Australia have evolved very similar forms to the placental mammals elsewhere (▷ p. 110).

Adaptive radiation is a speeding up of the normal process of evolutionary divergence of species, and may arise in two kinds of situation. The first is where a highly successful mutation or series of mutations occurs, bringing about new forms that outcompete existing forms, and which rapidly take over a range of ecological niches. A good example of this is the success of the flowering plants in ousting the conifers and their allies (▷ pp. 90–3): first

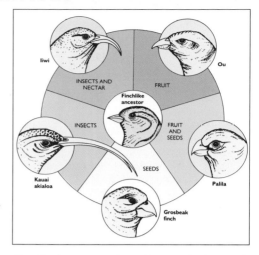

Hawaiian honeycreepers are thought to be descended from a finchlike bird that arrived on the newly formed volcanic islands several million years ago. With a wide range of vacant ecological niches available, the ancestral bird rapidly evolved into a large number of species, each with a distinctive shape of beak suited to its favoured food.

appearing about 118 million years ago, the flowering plants rapidly came to dominate the world's flora, and now show an incredible diversity of forms. The second kind of situation is where a new habitat arises with an array of vacant ecological niches. Famous examples of this include the colonization of relatively recent volcanic island groups such as the Galápagos and Hawaii, where birds such as Darwin's finches and the honeycreepers (▷ illustration) have evolved a wide array of types from a single ancestral species.

Coevolution is seen in a wide variety of relationships where two or more species evolve in continuous adaptation to each other. For example, a parasite may become highly specialized to feed on a particular host, and the host itself evolves increasingly more effective means of lessening the damage done by the parasite. Other striking examples of coevolution include the perennial 'arms race' that is waged between predators and their prey, and the astonishing mutual adaptations seen in flowers and their animal pollinators (▷ p. 92).

vations on the pampas of Patagonia that gave rise to his first doubts. Darwin noted that the extinct mammals whose fossilized remains he discovered were clearly directly related to forms still living. When he visited the Galápagos Islands, the British governor pointed out that he could identify the islands to which the giant tortoises belonged from the different patterns on their shells. This was the critical clue that led Darwin to realize that a number of distinct species could diverge from a common stock.

Like many of his colleagues Darwin was well aware that the fossil record revealed a history of change – albeit on a broad canvas. Darwin's genius was to suggest a mechanism by means of which such observed changes could have come about. It was a common observation of natural history that more eggs were laid and more offspring produced than ever reached breeding age. Darwin was also familiar with the weeding out of unfavourable strains by animal and plant breeders. However, what Darwin concluded was that in the natural world such weeding out was accomplished without direct intervention by man – the selection was natural. Individual organisms fortuitously better adapted to their environment than others of their species stood a better chance of surviving, and so of passing on their 'desirable' characteristics to the next generation. This process has been called 'the survival of the fittest'. In

this way, in the course of numerous generations, new species may arise.

One of the great problems of the theory of natural selection is that it does not explain how new changes arise in the first place. However, once the function of the DNA molecule in inheritance was established (▷ p. 86), it was discovered that it was very common for an accidental change to occur when DNA replicates itself. Such changes (known as *mutations*) usually have little effect, but in some instances the modified DNA gives rise to protein whose functioning is greatly altered. Although mutations may be harmful to the individual (▷ p. 152), they can also lead to desirable characteristics that enable the individual to survive more effectively than others of its species.

A classic example of natural selection is seen in the peppered moth. Usually about 2% of these normally pale moths are black, but, as they are conspicuous, the birds easily see them and eat them. During the 19th century, industrial towns became heavily polluted with soot, so that all the trees and buildings were blackened. In these conditions the black variety of moth was effectively camouflaged and the proportion of black moths rose to 98% of the population. With the introduction of legislation against air pollution the proportion of black moths began to decline.

SEE ALSO

● THE BEGINNINGS OF LIFE p. 82
● GENETICS p. 86

Genetics

Although theories of inheritance were put forward at least as early as the 5th and 4th centuries BC, genetics – the scientific study of inheritance – only truly began in the 18th and 19th centuries. Observations were made of how specific characteristics of plants and animals were passed from one generation to the next, to provide a rational basis for the improvement of crop plants and livestock.

The most significant breakthrough in genetics was made by the Austrian monk Gregor Mendel (1822–84). He observed specific features of the pea plant and counted the number of individuals in which each characteristic appeared through several generations. By concentrating on just a few features, he was able to demonstrate specific patterns of inheritance (▷ box, right).

DNA

By the start of the 20th century it was clear that organisms inherited characteristics by the reassortment and redistribution of many apparently independent factors, but the identity of the material that carried this information was unknown. In 1944, however, the American microbiologist Oswald T. Avery (1877–1955) demonstrated that the inheritable characteristics of a certain bacterium could be altered by *deoxyribonucleic acid* (DNA) taken up from outside the cell. To understand how genetic information was encoded required the structure of DNA to be determined. In 1953 the American James Watson (1928–   ) and the Englishman Francis Crick (1916–   ) reported that DNA is a large molecule in the shape of a double helix (▷ box).

Genes and chromosomes

Mendel discovered that characteristics are passed from generation to generation in the form of discrete units. Once the structure of DNA was established, these units, called *genes*, could be understood at the molecular level. A gene is a linear section of a DNA molecule that includes all the information for the structure of a particular protein or *ribonucleic acid* (RNA) molecule. Every sequence of nucleotide bases that makes up a single gene is called an *allele*. There are usually several different alleles available for each gene. The sum of all an organism's genetic information is called its *genome*.

A *mutation* occurs when there is a change in the sequence of nucleotide bases in a piece of DNA. The rate at which this process (*mutagenesis*) takes place may be accelerated by exposure to chemicals or radiation, and mutations may disrupt the functioning of the organism as a whole. However, natural mutations may also confer benefits and are essential to the process of evolution (▷ p. 84).

A *chromosome* consists of several different types of protein tightly associated with a single DNA molecule, and each chromosome carries a large number of genes. All the cells of a particular organism have the same number of different chromosomes, but numbers vary widely between different species. Humans have 23 different chromosomes per cell, but there are two copies of each (called *homologous* chromosomes), making 46 altogether.

Protein synthesis

The first stage in the process by which cells use genetic information stored in DNA is to make an RNA copy of a gene. This is called *gene transcription*. Most of the RNA copies (known as messenger RNA or mRNA) travel from the nucleus of the cell (where the genes are located) to special particles called *ribosomes*, where proteins are manufactured or *synthesized*. Ribosomes make proteins by joining together amino acids in the sequence dictated by the order of triplet groups in the mRNA. A living organism contains more than 10 000 different kinds of protein. Many are involved in the structure of cells, while others act as *enzymes* – catalysts that help to drive chemical reactions in cells without themselves being changed.

DNA replication and cell division

As organisms grow, their body cells divide and multiply. By the time a cell divides, its DNA will have doubled by a process called *replication*. The hydrogen bonds linking the two strands of a DNA molecule break apart, and each strand uses nucleotides present in the nucleus to synthesize a new strand complementary to itself; the result is that two daughter molecules are produced, each identical to the parent molecule. This process is completed just before cells divide, so that each chromosome contains two DNA molecules

---

THE STRUCTURE OF DNA

Deoxyribonucleic acid (DNA) is the basic genetic material of most living organisms. Although a large and apparently complex molecule, the structure of DNA is in fact astonishingly simple.

A single DNA molecule consists of two separate strands wound around each other to form a double-helical (spiral) structure. Each strand is made up of a combination of just four chemical components known as *nucleotides*, all of which have the same basic composition: each nucleotide consists of a sugar molecule (deoxyribose) linked to a phosphate group to form the helical backbone; different nucleotides are distinguished only by the identity of the nitrogen-based unit (called a *nucleotide base*) bonded to the sugar molecule. The four bases – adenine (A), cytosine (C), guanine (G) and thymine (T) – lie in the central region of the double helix, with each base linked by hydrogen bonds to a specific complementary base on the partner strand: A pairs only with T, and G only with C.

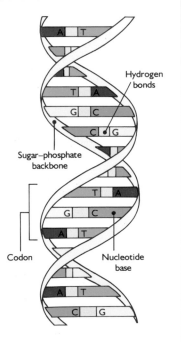

Hydrogen bonds

Sugar–phosphate backbone

Codon

Nucleotide base

This simple structure explains the two key properties of DNA – how it codes for the manufacture of amino acids (from which proteins are formed) and its capacity to replicate itself. Each combination of three bases (known as a *triplet* or a *codon*) within a DNA molecule codes for a particular amino acid, while the specific pairing of bases explains how two identical DNA molecules can be produced by the separation of the two strands of the parent molecule.

instead of the usual one. A mechanism called *mitosis* operates during cell division to ensure that each of the daughter cells receives one of the DNA molecules from every chromosome.

Most organisms are *diploid* – like humans, they have two copies of each different chromosome in normal body cells. However, sex cells or *gametes* (sperm and egg cells in most organisms) are *haploid* – they contain only one of each chromosome. Sex cells are produced from body cells by a process called *meiosis*. DNA replication takes place as before mitosis, but an extra stage of chromosome separation results in four sex cells being produced from a single body cell. As sex cells fuse at fertilization, a single diploid cell (called a *zygote*) is created, with the full complement of chromosomes.

Sex chromosomes

In humans, one of the pairs of chromosomes – the sex chromosomes – is responsible for determining the sex of an individual, and can have two different forms, X and Y. Females have a pair made up of two X chromosomes, while a male has an X and a Y. Thus the sex cells of a female always carry an X chromosome, while a male's sex cells may contain either an X or a Y. The sex of a child is therefore determined by the type of chromosome passed on by the father.

In organisms with several different chromosomes, the offspring receive some chromosomes from each parent and so a combination of genes different from either. Genetic diversity is further increased by a process known as *crossing-over*: during meiosis, homologous chromosomes can exchange bits of DNA between themselves, and so move genes into new combinations. Sexual interaction therefore greatly accelerates the rate at which genes are moved into new and potentially beneficial combinations; as such it is crucial to the evolutionary development of species (⊳ p. 83).

Dominant and recessive genes

In diploid organisms there are two copies of every gene, one in each member of every chromosome pair (the only exception being the sex chromosomes of the male). When both copies of a particular gene have identical alleles, the individual is said to be *homozygous* for that gene. However, many genes will have different alleles in each copy and the individual is said to be *heterozygous* for such genes. One allele may be *dominant* in that the gene product it codes for is used by the cell in preference to that of the other allele, which is called *recessive*. The outcome of such interactions between the alleles of all the different genes produces the characteristics of an individual, known collectively as the *phenotype*. The entire set of alleles in the genome of an individual is known as its *genotype*.

Molecular genetics and the future

The basis of *genetic engineering* is the use of certain bacterial enzymes that can cut DNA into small fragments. These fragments can be joined together in almost any combination, using a range of other enzymes. This can be done with DNA from any source – for example, human genes can be put into bacterial DNA. Bacteria are easy to grow in large quantities and can make useful products if they contain suitable genes. So human insulin, for example – the hormone that is deficient in diabetics (⊳ p. 153) – can be produced from genetically engineered bacteria.

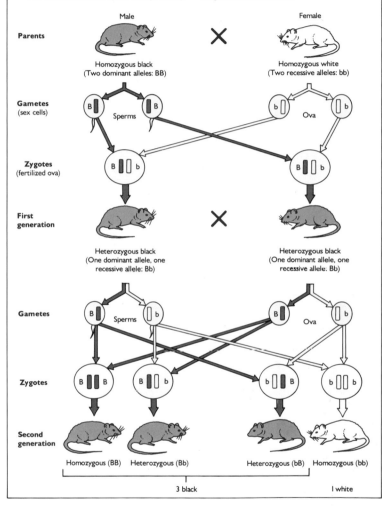

A SINGLE-FACTOR INHERITANCE

The simplicity of Mendel's laws is illustrated by a single-factor inheritance, in which an inheritable characteristic is determined by the action of a pair of dominant and recessive alleles of a single gene.

The coloration of rats is an example of such a characteristic, with the allele for black being dominant over the allele for white. If a homozygous black rat (i.e. with two identical alleles) mates with a homozygous white rat, all the offspring will be heterozygous black – each similar in appearance to the black parent, but with a recessive (and unexpressed)

white allele. However, mating between these offspring will result (potentially) in a mixture of black and white rats. The ratio of black rats to white will be on average 3 to 1, any white rat having inherited one recessive white allele from each of its parents.

The same pattern is found in the inheritance of certain human characteristics, including recessive genetic diseases such as cystic fibrosis. The inheritance of characteristics dependent on a number of different genes is more complex, but the underlying principle is the same in all genetic interactions.

Male   Female

Parents

Homozygous black (Two dominant alleles: BB)   Homozygous white (Two recessive alleles: bb)

Gametes (sex cells)

Sperms   Ova

Zygotes (fertilized ova)

First generation

Heterozygous black (One dominant allele, one recessive allele: Bb)   Heterozygous black (One dominant allele, one recessive allele: Bb)

Gametes

Sperms   Ova

Zygotes

Second generation

Homozygous (BB) Heterozygous (Bb) Heterozygous (bB) Homozygous (bb)

3 black   1 white

Genetic-engineering techniques can also be used to determine the exact sequence of nucleotide bases in short stretches of DNA. Many genes from different organisms have been sequenced. For some organisms with small genomes (such as viruses), the entire genome sequence has been determined: the HIV I virus that causes AIDS is one example. A worldwide project to sequence the human genome has begun and will take about 30 years to complete. It will reveal the location of many genes and probably unexpected information about human genetic organization. This type of information is likely to allow *gene-replacement therapy* – the replacement of defective genes with normal copies, to be used in the 21st century to cure many inherited diseases.

SEE ALSO

● ORGANIC CHEMISTRY p. 46
● THE BEGINNINGS OF LIFE p. 82
● EVOLUTION p. 84
● NON-INFECTIOUS DISEASES p. 152

Plants

The hundreds of thousands of species of plants comprise the kingdom Plantae, one of the five kingdoms of living things. Plants have colonized virtually every habitat on the planet, from the northern tundra to the equatorial forests, and from the driest desert to the oceans.

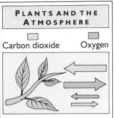

PLANTS AND THE ATMOSPHERE

Carbon dioxide   Oxygen

Day: plants absorb more carbon dioxide from the atmosphere by photosynthesis than they give out by respiration. They also give out more oxygen by photosynthesis than they absorb from the atmosphere for respiration.

Dawn and dusk: with less light available for photosynthesis, plants give out similar amounts of oxygen and carbon dioxide as they take in.

Night: with no light available, photosynthesis ceases. However, respiration continues, with oxygen being absorbed and carbon dioxide being given out.

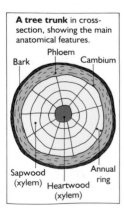

A tree trunk in cross-section, showing the main anatomical features.

Bark — Phloem — Cambium

Sapwood (xylem) — Heartwood (xylem) — Annual ring

The ability of virtually all plants to photosynthesize (⇨ below) distinguishes them from all other life forms apart from certain bacteria (⇨ p. 82). This ability to synthesize the complex organic molecules necessary for life from simple inorganic molecules – using the energy of the Sun – means that nearly all other living organisms are directly or ultimately dependent on plants as a source of organic molecules (⇨ pp. 126–7).

Plants are distinguished from animals by various characteristics. Plant cells are different from those of animals in one fundamental respect, in that they possess cell walls (made of cellulose). Many kinds of plant cell are also capable of giving rise to a whole new plant (the basis of vegetative reproduction; ⇨ below). Perhaps the most fundamental difference is the lack in plants of a nervous system – although plants do have various means of responding actively to their environment (growing towards the light, for example; ⇨ box). Another obvious difference is the inability of plants to move in a purposeful fashion, although plants can alter their growth direction in response to environmental stimuli, are capable of spreading over large areas by vegetative means, and can colonize new sites by passive dispersal of spores or seeds.

Photosynthesis and nutrition

Life is based on the chemical element carbon. Green plants obtain this from the air in the form of carbon dioxide, which they change (synthesize) into more elaborate chemicals – various carbohydrates such as sugars (glucose and sucrose) and starch. The energy required to drive this transformation is obtained from sunlight (although artificial lamps will work as well), and is absorbed by green plant pigments called *chlorophylls*, which are particularly abundant in leaves. This process is called *photosynthesis*. Water is also essential to photosynthesis as a source of the hydrogen atoms in the sugars, and, as a by-product, molecules of oxygen are given off. Because in photosynthesis carbon dioxide is used up and oxygen given out – the reverse of plant and animal respiration – the overall effect of plants and animals living together is to keep the atmospheric levels of these gases more or less constant.

The carbohydrates from photosynthesis provide the carbon from which nearly all the constituents of the plant body are made. Especially important among these is protein (⇨ p. 86). Protein contains nitrogen, an element that is taken up by plants from the soil or water, generally in the form of nitrates (⇨ the nitrogen cycle, p. 127). In the majority of higher plants nitrates are converted to ammonium, which is then combined with the carbon coming from the photosynthetic products to produce amino acids, the molecules from which proteins are constructed. This is another example of how plants are able to convert relatively simple substances from the environment into more complex organic forms. All animal life depends on this property, as all animals ultimately derive their protein from plants (⇨ pp. 126–7). Certain plants, prominently the legumes (e.g. peas, beans, clover), get most of their nitrogen from a beneficial association with bacteria that live in their roots; these bacteria convert gaseous nitrogen from the air into a form that is used by the host plant. This process, called fixation, plays a very important part in agriculture through its ability to enrich the soil.

Other elements required by plants are taken up from the soil by the roots and transported to regions where they are utilized (⇨ below).

Relatively massive production of carbohydrate (e.g. starch), proteins and vegetable oils occurs in plant reproductive structures – in seeds or other storage organs such as tubers (e.g. the potato). These materials are laid down as food reserves that are later digested to support the growth of the seedling or sprout until photosynthesis and other synthetic processes become well established. Animals and humans exploit these reserves as extremely valuable parts of the diet (cereal grains, pulses, etc.).

Uptake and transport

In higher land plants the roots take up water, mineral elements, nitrates and sulphates, sometimes using energy to do so. Water enters partly by osmosis, but more importantly by a process that is ultimately driven by *transpiration*, the evaporation of water through the *stomata*, microscopic pores on the surface of the leaves. Water exists in plants as an integral column in the conducting cells, the *xylem*. The xylem, one of the principal components of the vascular system, is continuous from the root, through the stem, the leaves and other parts of the plant. (In trees, the xylem, strengthened by a material called lignin, is the major component of the wood.) At the ends of the column, in the leaves, water is lost by transpiration and more water moves up to take its place. This effect is transmitted all the way down the stem, into the root, and eventually it is responsible for 'sucking' water in from the soil.

The substances taken up from the soil are also transported in the xylem, so the liquid in the xylem – the *sap* – is actually a very dilute solution of mineral elements, nitrates, etc. But the substances made within the plant, the carbohydrates (e.g. sugars) and amino acids, are carried in another vascular tissue, the *phloem* (part of the bark in woody plants). This process is called *translocation*. The driving force for this movement is set up by the relatively high concentration of sugars in the leaf cells. All these substances are carried around the plant to furnish material for growth and energy.

Energy and respiration

Although the energy that plants (and ultimately animals, too) need to maintain themselves is derived originally from sunlight, it is first transformed into the chemical energy residing in sucrose and other compounds, such as reserve

SEE ALSO

- WORLD VEGETATION (MAP) p. 81
- GENETICS p. 86
- NON-FLOWERING PLANTS p. 90
- FLOWERING PLANTS p. 92
- THE BIOSPHERE p. 126
- ECOSYSTEMS pp. 128–31
- FARMING p. 132

ENVIRONMENTAL STIMULI

Plant growth and development are greatly influenced by environmental factors – light, temperature, and gravity. Plant stems respond to the direction of light, growing towards it – an ability called *phototropism*. Stem extension is regulated by the brightness and quality of light, which are perceived by light-absorbing molecules (pigments). One of these pigments, phytochrome, is sensitive to the different parts of the red region of the spectrum and can tell the plant if it is shaded by the green leaves of its neighbours; if it is, the plant increases its stem growth to carry it out of the shade. This same property of phytochrome enables seeds (which also contain the pigment) to detect how deeply they are buried in the soil, or if they are in vegetational shade, and they can modify their germination behaviour accordingly.

Sensitivity to light also enables plants to judge seasonal changes in daylight hours, and this regulates the time of year when plants flower – an ability called *photoperiodism*. Temperature is effective in many ways, including the regulation of reproduction. *Vernalization* is the process by which a period of cold induces many plant species – such as winter wheat and barley – to form flowers. The direction of plant growth is influenced by gravity (*gravitropism*), roots reacting positively and stems negatively.

starch, protein and oil. The energy is later released by the process of respiration – the use of oxygen to 'burn' (oxidize) various compounds. This oxidation occurs in all living cells of the plant. Respiration is used to support the synthesis of various chemical compounds (e.g. new proteins, nucleic acids, cellulose), growth, and the uptake and accumulation of various mineral elements. We can therefore picture a flow of energy around the plant from the leaves or storage organs: sunlight (energy source) → photosynthesis (energy conversion) → intermediate compounds (energy storage) → respiration (energy conversion) → energy utilization.

Plant growth and development

Plants grow by increasing the number and size of their cells. New cells are produced by cell division in specialized areas, the *meristems*. The *primary meristems* are found at the tips (apexes) of shoots and roots, and in newly formed leaves and other organs. When cells in already established tissues start dividing they form the *secondary meristems*: these form the *cambium*, a layer between the xylem and the phloem, and are responsible, for example, for the growth in girth of a stem or root.

The new cells formed at the root apex gradually push back those produced previously. Some time after their formation cells begin to enlarge, mostly by an increase in their water content. Enlargement occurs when the cells are just a few millimetres behind the very tip itself: this is therefore the zone where the greatest elongation is taking place. A similar process occurs in the shoot, but here it is complicated by the production of new organs – the leaves or the flower parts. These organs are themselves meristematic at first, and in the case of the leaves, grow out of the

stem at the *nodes*. As the leaves grow, the lengths of stem between the nodes – the *internodes* – elongate, and this internode extension contributes a far higher proportion of lengthwise growth than the growth at the tip.

Reproduction

Reproduction operates in different ways in different groups of plants. A useful broad distinction can be made between the primitive and more advanced plants.

Many primitive plants – including mosses, liverworts, ferns and some algae – exhibit an obvious *alternation of generations*, a sexually reproducing (*gametophyte*) generation being followed by an asexual (*sporophyte*) generation; in most cases both generations are free-living, and again in most cases the sporophyte generation is the obvious plant, the gametophyte being very small. The gametophyte generation (in genetic terms, a haploid generation; ▷ p. 87) develops male and female organs, which in turn produce male and female sex cells (the *gametes*). Moisture is always needed to carry male sperm to female egg, and when these fuse they produce the sporophyte generation (in genetic terms, a diploid generation; ▷ p. 87), which in turn produces asexual spores that develop into the next gametophyte generation.

In contrast, the seed-bearing plants – comprising the gymnosperms (conifers, etc.) and the angiosperms (the flowering plants) – have no obvious alternation of generations, but there are nevertheless gametophyte and sporophyte stages: the gametophytes (the female ovule and the male pollen grain) are much reduced, and are nutritionally dependent on the adult sporophyte plant. Crucially, water is not necessary for fertilization to take place, and the sporophyte embryo so formed is contained within a resistant seed that is dispersed from the plant, and that can (if conditions are unfavourable) remain dormant for many years before finally germinating and growing into an adult sporophyte plant.

Many of the flowering plants are also able to reproduce asexually, by a process called vegetative reproduction (▷ p. 92).

UPTAKE AND TRANSPORT

Uptake: Water and minerals 'sucked up' from soil via roots and transported in xylem to all parts of plant.

Translocation: Amino acids (the components of proteins) and sugars transported in phloem from leaves to all parts of plant. In some cases (e.g. some trees in springtime) sugars from the roots are transported upwards.

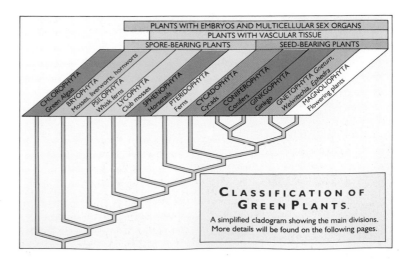

CLASSIFICATION OF GREEN PLANTS.
A simplified cladogram showing the main divisions. More details will be found on the following pages.

Non-Flowering Plants

Horsetails. Most modern horsetails are small, although one tropical species reaches 8 m (26 ft) in height. (Jacana)

The earliest plant-like organisms were the algae, which first evolved in the oceans 1·5 billion years ago. However, the first land plants did not evolve until the later part of the Ordovician period (510–438 million years ago). By the end of the Silurian period (438–410 million years ago) the first undoubted vascular plants (▷ below), such as club mosses, had established themselves on land, with the ferns following shortly afterwards, around 400 million years ago.

These primitive plants reproduce by means of spores, rather than seeds, and moisture is necessary for sexual reproduction to take place (▷ p. 89). With the evolution of the first seed-bearing plants – the conifers and their allies – between 400 and 300 million years ago, moist conditions were no longer necessary for reproduction to take place, and plants were able to colonize drier areas.

Algae

The term 'algae' is a broad one, generally applied to lower plants that do not possess any special modifications for life outside water. Although the larger algae – the seaweeds – are always considered as plants, the single-celled algae are often grouped with other unicellular eukaryotic organisms in the kingdom Protista (▷ p. 82), even though many of them possess, like plants, the ability to photosynthesize. The so-called blue-green algae – the cyanobacteria – are usually grouped with the bacteria and other unicellular prokaryotic organisms in the kingdom Monera (▷ pp. 82–3).

The majority of algae – including all the seaweeds – live in sea water, but others live in lakes, rivers, soils, damp tree trunks, hot springs, and snow and ice. Some unicellular forms are symbiotic with animals such as corals, while lichens (▷ box) are a symbiotic association of an alga and a fungus.

The seaweeds belong to three divisions of algae, each named after its most obvious pigmentation: red algae (Rhodophyta), brown algae, including wracks and kelps (Phaeophyta), and green algae (Chlorophyta); the green algae also include many single-celled algae. In seaweeds the plant body is not differentiated into root, stem and leaves. The seaweeds exhibit a complex variety of life cycles, with various types of alternation of generations (▷ p. 89).

Spore-bearing plants

There are five divisions of spore-bearing plants: mosses, liverworts and hornworts (Bryophyta); whisk ferns (Psilophyta); club mosses and quillworts (Lycophyta); horsetails (Sphenophyta); and ferns (Pteridophyta). Today, the most important groups are the mosses and ferns, although during the Carboniferous period (355–300 million years ago) giant tree-like horsetails and lycopods (relatives of club mosses) dominated the swamps that formed today's coal measures.

The bryophytes (mosses, etc.) generally lack vascular tissue, and water transport is mostly external, relying on capillary action – for example, in spaces between the leaves and stem. The other spore-bearing plants – together with the seed-bearing plants – all have vascular tissue (comprising xylem and phloem; ▷ pp. 88–9) that conducts water and nutrients around the plant. All these higher land plants are thus known as the *vascular plants* or *tracheophytes*.

Spore-bearing plants exhibit an obvious alternation of generations, with both gametophyte and sporophyte generations being for the most part free-living (▷ p. 89). In all groups except the bryophytes it is the sporophyte stage that is the obvious plant. The gametophyte plant has egg-producing organs and sperm-producing organs.

THE FERNS

The ferns are distinguished from other spore-bearing plants by their large leaves, known as fronds. These leaves have an extensive network of conducting strands and are often intricately subdivided; the spore-producing organs are found on the underside. Ferns include over 9000 species, making up about 90% of the diversity of the vascular spore-bearing plants.

TREE FERNS can reach up to 25 m (82 ft) in height. They have a crown of leaves topping an unbranched trunk. The trunks have no wood but rely on fibres strengthened by lignin, persistent leaf bases and a mantle of roots growing from the trunk for their structural strength and support. Tree ferns may form a major part of the leafy canopy along rivers in wet tropical and sub-tropical forests.

EPIPHYTIC FERNS grow on other plants, often trees, without damaging them. The bird's-nest fern (*Asplenium nidus*) has large shiny leaves arranged in a rosette. Water and leaf debris falling from the canopy above accumulates inside the base of the rosette where it can be utilized by the plant. The stag's-horn fern (*Platycerium*) utilizes some of its own dead leaves to accumulate moisture.

CLIMBING FERNS such as *Polypodium* use creeping rhizomes to climb trunks, while *Lygodium* climbs by means of evergrowing leaves that twine around objects they touch. This ability is very rare outside the flowering plants.

WATER FERNS such as *Azolla* grow free-floating on the water surface. The reduced leaves have a special waxy coating to prevent water swamping the plant. *Azolla* has a symbiotic association with a nitrogen-fixing cyanobacterium, and is used as a green fertilizer.

FILMY FERNS have delicate leaves only one cell thick. For those growing as epiphytes in wet forest even short exposure to the sun's rays penetrating the canopy can be fatal.

MARATTIA has one of the largest leaves in the plant world, reaching up to 7 m (23 ft) in length. There are massive leaf stalks (the thickness of an adult's lower arm) to support this enormous structure.

The egg is retained on the gametophyte plant, and the sperms need free water to enable them to swim to the egg for fertilization to take place. The *zygote* (fertilized egg) is retained on the gameto-phyte plant, where it develops into an *embryo* (a diminutive young sporophyte plant). This embryo cannot be dispersed and must grow wherever the gametophyte grows, however unsuitable the site. Furthermore, it has only the limited resources of a small gametophyte on which to rely for develop-ment. When the sporophyte plant matures it produces spores. The spores are dispersed in air currents, and if they land on a suitable site they germinate to form gametophyte plants.

Conifers and their allies

Conifers and their allies, together with the flowering plants, are distinguished from the spore-bearing plants by the production of seeds rather than spores as the units of dispersal. Seed-bearing has a number of advantages over spore-bearing in successfully spreading and in-creasing the species, and in ensuring survival if the parents are short-lived or suffer some catas-trophe.

Crucially, in seed-bearing plants, the female eggs are retained on the parent plant, while the male sperm (pollen grains) are carried to it by wind or (predominantly in the case of flowering plants) by pollinating animals – principally insects (▷ pp. 92–3). The vital difference here is that in seed-bearing plants, unlike spore-bearing plants, the egg and developing young plant are provided with food, water and protection by the parent plant. Equally important is the fact that free water is no longer required for fertilization to take place. In seed-bearing plants, the developing embryo and young plant is protected by a seed coat. Seeds are able to stay dormant for con-siderable periods if conditions are unfavourable, only germinating into a new young plant when favourable conditions return.

Seed plants (sometimes called spermatophytes) are usually subdivided into five divisions: Cycadophyta (cycads), Ginkgophyta (ginkgo or maidenhair tree), Coniferophyta (conifers), Gnetophyta (*Gnetum*, *Welwitschia* and *Ephedra*), and Magnoliophyta or Anthophyta (flowering plants; ▷ p. 92). The first four of these divisions are often grouped together as the *gymnosperms*, the common characteristic being that they bear naked seeds, i.e. the seeds are not enclosed by an ovary. In contrast, the flowering plants – the *angiosperms* – have their seeds enclosed in an ovary, which has a special extension (the stigma) for receiving pollen (▷ p. 92). However, the different gymnosperm groups are highly varied, and it is thought that only the ginkgo and the conifers share a common ancestor, while the other two groups evolved independently. Of the gymnosperm divisions, only the conifers are of importance today.

There are 6–9 families of conifer, with about 500 species, most of which are resinous softwood trees. Their leaves are typically needle-like and evergreen, and the reproductive structures are grouped in male and female cones. Most conifers have a very long life cycle, with several static periods, and this partially explains why they have been out-competed by the flowering plants in many parts of the world.

FUNGI AND LICHENS

The fungi are not in fact plants, but constitute an entirely separate kingdom, the Fungi or Myceteae, which first evolved around 1·5 billion years ago. Unlike the plants, the fungi lack chlorophyll and hence cannot photosynthesize. They therefore have to obtain the carbon and energy necessary for life from other sources.

In most fungal groups there are examples of parasites, which grow on living animals, plants or other fungi, and also of *saprotrophs*, which grow on their dead remains. The function of the latter as decomposers is a very important one, assisting in the recycling of materials needed for life (▷ p. 127). Other fungi have developed symbiotic relationships with other organisms: for example, some associate with algae to form lichens (▷ box).

Although some fungi, such as yeasts, are unicellular, most fungi consist of a mass of filaments. Aggregates of these filaments may give rise to quite large fruiting bodies – the obvious visible parts of fungi such as toadstools. An individual filament is called a *hypha*, and a mass of hyphae is called a *mycelium*. Although in some fungi the cell walls – like those of plants – contain cellulose, in most fungi the cell walls contain chitin (also the principal material in the exoskeletons of insects and other arthropods). Reproduction is by spores, which may be produced sexually or asexually. The spores are usually dispersed by wind, but sometimes by water or insects.

Lichens are composite organisms formed by the symbiotic relationship of a fungus and an alga or a cyanobacterium (▷ p. 83). The fungus provides a protective environment for the growth of the green partner, which provides the fungus with the products of photosynthesis. The metabolism of lichens is suspended while they are dry or exposed to the heat of the sun, but soon active again when conditions are moist. This intermittent activity gives rise to a very slow growth rate, but enables lichens to colonize inhospitable habitats such as rock surfaces, even at extreme altitudes and latitudes.

Many lichens are highly sensitive to pollution, particularly to sulphur dioxide, and can therefore be used as pollution monitors. (Jacana)

In the northern hemisphere coniferous trees are the main constituents of the high-latitude boreal forests of North America and Eurasia (▷ p. 129). The boreal forests are dominated by members of the Pinaceae family, including larch, pines, spruces, firs, Douglas fir and western hemlock. This family also often dominates high-altitude forests at lower latitudes. Conifers are much less diverse and abundant in the colder regions of the southern hemisphere, where only two families are found: the Araucariaceae (kauris and monkey puzzles) and the Podocarpaceae (podocarps). Many species of conifer are important commer-cially as sources of timber.

SEE ALSO

● WORLD VEGETATION (MAP) p. 81
● THE BEGINNINGS OF LIFE p. 82
● PLANTS p. 88
● FLOWERING PLANTS p. 92
● THE BIOSPHERE p. 126
● ECOSYSTEMS pp. 128–31

Flowering Plants

The flowering plants or *angiosperms* (division Magnoliophyta) are the most advanced and dominant plant forms on the Earth. Some 250 000 different species have been identified. The first true flowering plants appeared in the fossil record during the early Cretaceous period, some 118 million years ago.

POLLINATION

In primitive plants, reproduction is a haphazard event, reliant upon water and wind to propagate the species. In contrast, the flowering plants use the flight of insects (or occasionally birds and bats) to improve the efficiency of their reproduction.

The coloured, scented petals of flowers attract insects. Once inside the bowl-shaped flower, the insect crawls around eating pollen and brushing it off the stamens and onto its body. The insect then visits the flower of another plant, where the pollen from the first plant is brushed onto the stigma, so fertilizing the second flower (▷ main text).

This achieves the all-important process of *cross-fertilization*, the process whereby genetic material from different plants is exchanged. This ensures the maintenance of vigour within the species, and allows it to produce variants that can colonize new localities. If the male and female organs in the flower reach maturity at different times, cross-fertilization – rather than self-fertilization – is assured.

Many amazing examples of special relationships between flowers and insects have developed. Many flowers produce a sugary fluid called *nectar*, which serves no other purpose than to attract the insects that feed on it. It is a 'reward' to the insects for helping in pollination, and it also appears to stop insects from eating the all-important pollen.

Many flowers, such as foxgloves, violets and rhododendrons, provide 'signposts' to lead the insect into the flower. Some members of the orchid family have flowers that look like wasps or flies, and this deceives the appropriate insect into attempting to mate with the flower, so pollinating it.

A bee pollinating a flower while collecting nectar for honey. (Jacana)

The angiosperms differ from the gymnosperms (conifers, etc.; ▷ p. 91) in a number of major ways. The main difference is the presence of the flower, a specialized reproductive structure that develops into a fruit and within which is held one or more well-protected seeds. Other differences include broader leaves that are sometimes highly ornate, stems that do not contain resin ducts, and (in woody species) wood that is generally harder than that of conifers.

Flowering plants occupy every possible habitat apart from snow and ice, hot springs, and the oceans. Apart from these extreme locations, the flowering plants can grow in the driest, wettest, hottest, coldest, most exposed and most sheltered sites on this planet. They show an amazing variety of size and shape, ranging from just 1 mm ($^1/_{25}$ in) for the smallest to about 100 m (328 ft) for the tallest (a eucalyptus tree), while members of the baobab family have attained girths of almost 55 m (180 ft).

The structure of flowering plants

At the base of a flowering plant is a finely branched root system. The roots provide anchorage in the soil, and also collect moisture in which are dissolved the nutrients needed for growth (▷ pp. 88–9).

From the roots arise either a single, vertical cylindrical stem, or multiple, branched stems. The stem is held erect either by the presence of the fluid within it or by cells that have become strengthened by deposits of lignin (as in woody plants). The stem is strong yet very light and supple. Its purpose is to hold the leaves towards the Sun, thus maximizing the opportunity for photosynthesis (▷ p. 88). Growing from the junctions between leaves and stem are the flowers.

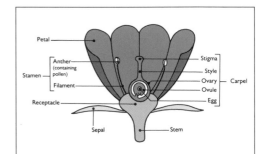

Cross-section of a typical flower showing the stamen containing the pollen (male sperm) and the carpel containing the female egg.

The flower consists of a series of circular structures. On the outside are the leaf-like *sepals*, which protect the flower at its bud stage. Inside are the *petals*, usually brightly coloured to attract pollinating insects (▷ box). At the centre of the flower are one or more *carpels*; these consist of the sticky stalk-like *stigma* and, below it, a slightly swollen area (the *ovary*), within which is the *ovule* containing the female egg. Immediately surrounding the stigma are the *stamens*, which consist of a thin stalk (*filament*) with pollen sacs (*anthers*) at the end. Each pollen sac ripens to produce millions of tiny pollen grains (containing the male sperm).

Reproduction

Fertilization occurs when a pollen grain (originating either from the stamens within the plant or transported by wind or an insect from an adjacent flower of the same type) is deposited on the stigma and cuts a channel (the *pollen tube*) down to the ovary. The ovary swells to form a *fruit*, within which is the *seed*, containing an embryo of a new individual.

In addition to sexual reproduction, many kinds of plants can also perform *vegetative reproduction*. Special shoots extend from the parent plant, either underground or overground, and from these shoots daughter plants (genetically identical to the parent) bud and send down their own roots. There is a variety of different kinds of shoot that perform this function, including underground rhizomes (as in irises), tubers (as in potatoes), bulbs (as in daffodils), and overground runners (as in strawberries). In some plants (such as begonias), daughter plants may grow from a broken leaf that becomes embedded in the soil.

Classifying the flowering plants

Despite such an amazing variety of species the flowering plants can be divided into just two main botanical groups based upon the structure of the embryo.

The first group (70 000 species) are the *monocotyledons* (abbreviated to monocots), which produce just one seed leaf from the germinating embryo. Examples of monocots include grasses, maize, wheat, orchids, daffodils, irises and palms. The leaves of monocots are generally long and narrow with parallel veins.

Monocots are considered to be more primitive than the larger, second group (180 000 species), the *dicotyledons* (or dicots). These produce new plants with two seed leaves. Examples include oak trees, roses, beans, tomatoes and dandelions.

SPECIAL ADAPTATIONS

The Venus flytrap has a 'snap trap', a two-lobed leaf that can snap closed when triggered by long, touch-sensitive hairs on the leaf surface. (Jacana)

A number of very specialized adaptations have taken place that allow certain plants to live upon other plants. Some, such as mistletoe growing on trees, are parasites. Others, such as some orchids, use other plants merely for support, and are known as *epiphytes*. Others again have become carnivorous and trap insects on their leaves: the insects are then digested and their fluids absorbed. Carnivorous plants (which include sundew, butterwort, Venus flytrap and pitcher plants) tend to have evolved in areas where the soil is poor in nutrients.

SOME COMMON TYPES OF FLOWERING PLANTS

Annual – a plant that completes its life cycle from germination to death in less than one year (e.g. marigold, zinnia).

Biennial – a plant that completes its life cycle from germination to death in more than one year but less than two. Flowering usually occurs in year two (e.g. foxglove, cabbage, carrot).

Herb or **herbaceous perennial** – a plant lacking woody cells that dies back to the roots at the onset of frost or drought, but that produces new growth on the return of spring or rain (e.g. dock, daisies, dandelion).

Woody perennial – a plant that takes longer than two years to complete its life cycle, and does not die back to its roots (e.g. trees, shrubs, roses).

Bulb – an underground fleshy stem that functions as a food-storage organ. Many spring-flowering plants grow rapidly from bulbs (e.g. daffodil, tulip).

Corm – a swollen underground stem-base with a similar shape and function as a bulb (e.g. crocus).

Rhizome – a horizontally creeping stem (sometimes swollen) that allows the plant to spread over a very wide area (e.g. mint, iris, couch grass).

Tuber – an underground swollen stem tip (e.g. potato) or root (e.g. dahlia) containing large reserves of food.

The leaves of dicots are generally more rounded, with branching veins.

The importance of flowering plants

The development of the flowering plants was one of the most significant events in the biological history of this planet. The existence of an advanced plant population that could survive unfavourable climatic events and that produced large quantities of leafy growth provided a super-abundance of food for grazing and browsing animals. The dead and decaying vegetation also aided the formation of a thick layer of humus on the soil surface, and this in turn helped retain the nutrients within the soil.

The great variety of vegetation types (▷ pp. 81 and 128) supports an equally varied animal population. Humans are totally dependent on the flowering plants for food (cereals, root crops, pulses, beans, nuts, fruit) or for feeding to domesticated animals. The flowering plants also provide industrial crops (cotton, jute, sisal) and timber, and are increasingly yielding vital medicinal extracts. Some 25% of medicines already contain extracts from the tropical rainforest, a figure thought likely to increase greatly in the future.

Not only are the flowering plants of immense economic value, but, with the non-flowering plants, they are also responsible – via photosynthesis – for stabilizing the carbon dioxide content of the atmosphere. As such they help to maintain the heat balance of the planet (▷ p. 186).

SEE ALSO

● WORLD VEGETATION (MAP) p. 81
● PLANTS p. 88
● NON-FLOWERING PLANTS p. 90
● THE BIOSPHERE p. 126
● TERRESTRIAL ECOSYSTEMS p. 128
● FARMING p. 132

Primitive Animals

One of the most important events in the evolution of life on earth was the development of multicellular organisms from unicellular animal-like protists (⊳ pp. 82–3). Enormously diverse in form, these range from simple sponges, to complex insects and squids, to sophisticated vertebrates such as ourselves.

Most groups of primitive multicellular invertebrates are found in very old fossil-bearing rocks, so it is clear that this major breakthrough occurred at least 600 million years ago.

Sponges

Sponges (phylum Porifera), the simplest of multicellular animals, are widespread and abundant in aquatic (mainly marine) habitats. Spending their adult lives attached to rocks or other hard surfaces, they feed by extracting small particles from the surrounding water. A typical sponge has a honeycomb-like structure of canals separated by cells and a hard skeleton. Some species form flat, brightly coloured incrustations, others a variety of single or multiple structures in the shape of vases, chimneys or purses.

Coelenterates

Although simple in structure, coelenterates (phylum Coelenterata) form the largest living structures on earth – the coral barrier reefs of Australia and Belize. All coelenterates have a simple two-layered body wall surrounding a central gut with a single opening. Tentacles bearing stinging cells surround the mouth in corals and sea anemones, and form a fringe to the bell of jellyfishes. The bodies of jellyfishes are given strength by the jelly between the two cell layers, while corals lay down a rigid basal skeleton.

Coelenterates are mostly predatory, capturing prey by means of their tentacles and the batteries of gripping and stinging cells these carry. The stinging cells touch prey and turn inside out, penetrating the tissues and injecting a neurotoxin – lethal even to humans in the case of some jellyfishes. Corals obtain nutrients in a symbiotic association with an alga, making use of the surplus products of photosynthesis (⊳ p. 88) and providing the algal cells with waste nitrogen.

The life cycles of many coelenterates involve an *alternation of generations*. A jellyfish stage (called a *medusa*), at which the animal is free-swimming and reproduces sexually, leads to a sedentary stage (a *polyp*) from which medusae are produced asexually. Sea anemones, corals and hydroids spend most of their lives as polyps, singly or in colonies, whereas jellyfishes spend almost all their lives as medusae.

Echinoderms

Echinoderms (phylum Echinodermata) are characterized as a group by their five-part symmetry, internal skeleton and tube feet, but are otherwise very diverse (⊳ box). Representatives are found in all marine habitats, from the shallowest waters to the deepest abyssal depths.

Sea lilies are the most primitive echinoderms. Two groups exist today – sedentary stalked sea lilies found exclusively in deep water, and free-living mobile species, which lack a stalk and are found principally in shallow water. Both feed in the same way, by sieving particles from passing currents with their upward-pointing tube feet.

Sea urchins are globular, oval or disc-shaped creatures, densely covered with spines – poisonous in some species – and other external structures based on an underlying shell composed largely of calcium carbonate. Some are grazing herbivores, living on hard rocky surfaces, with large spines used in locomotion and defence. Others, with short spines used for burrowing, live in sand and feed on organic debris.

Starfishes or *sea stars* have five hollow arms linked to a central disc. Small spines cover the upper surface, while the arm edges are often set with large defensive plates. Most of the tube feet, arranged in five rows and surrounding the central mouth, are used for locomotion and grasping prey, but those near the arm tips are sensory. Starfishes are mostly scavengers or predators, and frequently feed on clams.

Brittle stars or *serpent stars* – so called because of their readiness to cast off arms and regrow them – are thin-armed, highly mobile animals with a compact central disc. Found in all marine habitats, often in huge numbers, they are mostly filter-feeders or scavengers.

Sea cucumbers are worm-like echinoderms that have reduced the internal skeleton to a vestige and become soft and extremely flexible. Found in all marine habitats, they use enlarged branched tube feet around the mouth for feeding, either spreading them out on a surface to pick up particles or extending them in a water current to intercept food.

Many sea slugs have conspicuous warning coloration, to signal to would-be predators that they are poisonous and best left alone. In this sea slug the protrusions at the rear end are branched respiratory gills; those at the front are sensory tentacles. (Jacana)

── MISSING LINKS? ──

Starfishes, sea urchins and other echinoderms are essentially very simple animals, without some of the organ systems that characterize more complex groups. Yet they are among the most successful of marine animals, and share certain structural and developmental features with vertebrates. Although evolving in very different ways, several obscure groups of marine invertebrates – hemichordates (acorn worms), ascidians (sea squirts) and cephalochordates (lancelets) – are thought to have developed from a single ancestral stock; and it is from this same stock that echinoderms and chordates (the group to which vertebrates belong) are believed to have evolved. For this reason the echinoderms and these other primitive animals have been seen by some as link groups between invertebrates and vertebrates.

Worms

All *flatworms* (phylum Platyhelminthes) are simple in construction and characterized by a blind-ending gut. The free-living *turbellarians* are small, flattened, leaf-like worms found in aquatic and damp terrestrial habitats, where they have a scavenging or predatory way of life. The *trematodes*, which include the flukes, are external and internal parasitic flatworms, with special attachment suckers and a complex life history involving at least two hosts. The *cestodes*, which include tapeworms, are ribbon-like gut parasites, with a complex hooked head for attachment to their host.

The *nematodes* (phylum Nematoda) – roundworms, eelworms, threadworms and hookworms – are found in soil and in both fresh and salt water. They are important crop pests, causing damage both by consumption of plant tissue and by facilitating the entry of viruses and other diseases into plants. Many have become parasitic in animals, and hookworms are thought to be among the most important causes of human illness.

Annelid (or *segmented*) *worms* (phylum Annelida) have long thin bodies with distinct head and tail ends. The body is made up of a series of separate segments, usually having external limbs or hair-like protrusions called *chaetae*. Internally, an extensive body cavity separating the gut from the body wall is a feature distinguishing them from other worms.

Of the three classes of annelids, the oldest and most diverse are the marine *polychaetes* or *bristleworms*, which include

paddleworms, lugworms and fan worms. Characterized by a pair of limbs on each segment, most live in or on the sea bed, feeding on all kinds of material. The *earthworms* and their freshwater relatives burrow their way through earth, feeding on decaying vegetable matter. They are long thin worms without external structures except retractable chaetae, which are used as anchors while burrowing. Earthworms are of considerable economic importance because of their role in recycling nutrients in the soil. The most

advanced annelids are the *leeches*, which are either predatory or externally parasitic bloodsuckers. Equipped with suckers at front and rear, they move by extending their bodies with the rear sucker attached, then attach the front sucker and draw the body forward in a characteristic looping fashion.

Molluscs

Molluscs (phylum Mollusca) make up a highly varied group of unsegmented animals. Classic mollusc characteristics include a broad locomotory foot, a protective shell, a tongue-like feeding organ (*radula*), and a special respiratory gill (*ctenidium*). Although some or all of these characteristics are found in all molluscs, each class has specialized very differently.

Gastropods – land and sea snails and slugs – form the largest group of molluscs and are the most diverse in feeding habit. All gastropods have a foot for walking or swimming and a radula, and most also have an external shell. The radula is a broad tongue in limpets, with iron-hardened teeth to rasp rocks, while in carnivores it has sharp pointed teeth.

Bivalves, which include cockles, mussels, oysters and clams, are essentially living filter pumps. Enclosed within the two-valved shell are massive gills, which pump water through themselves, sieving out particles as they do so. Most bivalves have a large foot for burrowing into sand or mud, while others glue themselves to rocks.

The *cephalopods* include squid, cuttlefishes and octopuses. They are highly specialized predators, with well-developed sensory faculties and the ability to change colour instantly. They are also capable of versatile and rapid movement, and – with their complex brains – even possess powers of learning and memory. Their tentacles have developed from the modified foot, and in the mouth behind

the beak is found a classic mollusc radula. Despite their sophistication, present-day cephalopods are only the remnant of a previously superabundant group, which in the Cretaceous period (135–65 million years ago) included a vast array of ammonites and belemnites.

A giant squid, the largest invertebrate known, sometimes growing to over 5 m (16 ft) in length. They live in deep water, however, and are rarely seen.

SEE ALSO

● OCEANS (CORAL REEFS) p. 76
● AQUATIC ECOSYSTEMS p. 130
● INFECTIOUS DISEASES p. 154

Arthropods

Judged by the number and variety of species, the arthropods are the most successful of all living organisms on earth. Crustaceans such as crabs and shrimps are the dominant arthropods in the sea, while on land insects can be found in most available habitats. Albeit to a lesser degree than insects, the other important arthropod groups – arachnids and myriapods – are highly successful land animals.

The arthropods alive today represent a highly diverse collection of animals. As a group they are characterized by having external segmented skeletons and pairs of jointed limbs.

Success and limitations

The success of the arthropods lies in the external skeleton (*exoskeleton*), which both supports and protects the animal. The exoskeleton is formed by a protective layer known as the *cuticle*, which covers the animal's soft underlying parts. The arthropod skeleton shows remarkable versatility, varying from the soft elastic bag that surrounds a caterpillar to the immensely hard claws of a lobster. The cuticle is largely composed of a complex substance called *chitin*, which is based on long-chain molecules of the sugar acetyl glucosamine; these become cross-linked to give tough fibres, which are embedded in a protein matrix. Movement is possible only where the exoskeleton is not hardened, hence the need for joints. These are composed of flexible cuticle, and allow as varied a set of movements as that found in animals with internal skeletons.

Despite its obvious success, the exoskeleton has its drawbacks. The most important of these is that the hard, external skeleton limits the size of the animal. Growth can take place only if the old skeleton is discarded and a new, larger one grown in its place. This process, known as *moulting*, has to occur a number of times in all arthropods as they grow to full adult size. At each moult the animal is vulnerable to attack by predators, parasites or disease, and – in the case of terres-

SEE ALSO

● CRUSTACEANS AND
   ARACHNIDS p. 97
● INSECTS p. 98

MYRIAPODS

There are four groups of myriapods, totalling some 10 000 species. Their principal characteristic is a body composed of a head and a long trunk with many leg-bearing segments. The various groups are probably not closely related, however, and only two groups are of significance.

Centipedes (class Chilopoda) are secretive predatory animals found throughout the world in damp terrestrial habitats (beneath bark, logs, stones, etc.). They are confined to such habitats by their vulnerability to water loss in dry air. The head has large jaws concealed beneath the modified first pair of legs, which form poison fangs. Following this are 15 or so similar segments with strong walking legs. Nocturnal in habit, centipedes are able to move very quickly, killing their prey by means of their poison fangs.

Millipedes (class Diplopoda) are herbivorous scavengers found in similar habitats to centipedes. They appear to have two pairs of legs on each segment but in reality these are fused segments, which may number as many as a hundred. They move slowly over the ground, but their legs and movement pattern are suitable for burrowing. Rapid escape from predators is impossible, so millipedes have chemical defences in the form of poisons and are heavily armoured.

---

trial species – there is also a danger of dehydration.

Arthropod evolution

The evolutionary history of the arthropods has long been an area of active debate. The fact that all arthropods have segmented exoskeletons and jointed limbs was once thought sufficient to show that they had evolved from a single ancestral stock in which these features occurred. However, recent comparative analyses of the chemical composition of arthropod exoskeletons and of the detailed structure of joints, mouthparts and legs suggest that this may not be so – that several distinct evolutionary lines may have branched off from a segmented worm-like ancestor and that the basic arthropod features evolved several times over.

According to this theory, one evolutionary line (Uniramia) gave rise to the insects, the myriapods, and the velvet worms. These all have simple (uniramous) legs that operate in essentially the same way. A second line (Biramia) gave rise to the crustaceans, in which the legs are two-branched (biramous), and in addition to the normal leg there is an outer part, often involved in feeding or swimming. A third line gave rise to the chelicerates (spiders, scorpions and mites) and the now extinct trilobites. Marine species of this group have biramous limbs, but of a different design to those of crustaceans, while land species have uniramous legs.

This view is not universally accepted, however. Current research into the molecular basis of arthropods suggests that the idea of a three-line evolution may be wrong, and that arthropods do constitute a single group after all. With persuasive evidence on either side, it will be some time yet before a clear picture of the evolutionary history of the arthropods emerges.

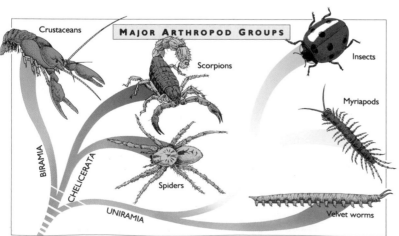

MAJOR ARTHROPOD GROUPS

Crustaceans
Scorpions
Insects
Myriapods
Spiders
Velvet worms
BIRAMIA
CHELICERATA
UNIRAMIA

Crabs and other Crustaceans

Crustaceans – the 'insects of the sea' – form a very varied group of arthropods (▷ opposite) and are extremely abundant throughout the sea. The freshwater species, though numerous, suffer competition from insects and are less abundant. A very few – woodlice and land crabs – have successfully adapted to life on land.

The subphylum Crustacea contains some 42 000 species and is divided into 10 classes. The most important of these are fairy shrimps, copepods, barnacles, decapods (crabs, shrimps and prawns), sand hoppers, and woodlice.

General features

The elongated bodies of crustaceans have many segments, each bearing a pair of limbs, and are clearly divided into a head/thorax region and a tail or abdomen. In primitive forms the head segments, bearing the antennae and mouthparts, are followed by a series of similar limbs, often fringed with hairs for food sifting. In more advanced forms the various limbs differ in function and structure – thorax limbs being used for walking and swimming, abdominal limbs usually for respiratory purposes and in reproduction.

SEE ALSO

● ARTHROPODS p. 96
● INSECTS p. 98
● AQUATIC ECOSYSTEMS p. 130

In most crustaceans the sexes are distinct. All crustaceans have the same basic larva – the *nauplius* – but later stages may be different.

Major groups

Barnacles are highly modified for feeding on tiny planktonic plants. As larvae they resemble other crustaceans, but they later settle on a carefully chosen surface and attach themselves by means of head glands. The animal secretes a protective shell complete with closing lid, from which the thorax limbs, fringed with hairs, are protruded to catch plankton.

Copepods are small crustaceans of immense importance in the economy of the sea. They feed on planktonic plants and are themselves the food of commercially important fish such as herring. Shrimp-like crustaceans called *krill*, which feed in a similar way to copepods, form the main food source of the whales of the southern oceans and are harvested by man as food for domestic animals and as fertilizer.

The *fairy* (or *brine*) *shrimps* live in temporary pools where they escape predation. They are classic primitive crustaceans, with rows of similar limbs used for movement and feeding, and they feed by sieving particles from the water.

The group known as the *decapods* includes most of the many commercially important crustaceans such as crabs, lobsters, shrimps and prawns. It is the most numerous crustacean group with around 10 000 species, and includes the largest crustacean – the giant spider crab, which commonly has a claw span of around 2.5 m (8 ft). Most are scavengers or predators, but the fiddler crabs feed on organic debris.

ARACHNIDS

The arachnids (class Arachnida) constitute the largest group of arthropods after the insects, with over 60 000 species. They include scorpions, ticks and mites, and spiders.

Scorpions were among the earliest terrestrial animals, appearing on land in the Carboniferous period (355 to 300 million years ago). Nocturnal and secretive, they hide under stones or logs by day, and are found in most warm habitats, including deserts. Waiting for their prey to move into range, they grip it with their massive claws and inject a paralysing venom with the sting in their tail. The venom of some species may cause death in humans.

Ticks and *mites* are economically important as plant and animal parasites, as carriers of disease in both animals and humans, and as food pests. Mites are found in enormous numbers in all environments. Most ticks and mites are tiny – adult mites are often less than 1 mm ($^1/_{25}$ in) in length, although some ticks are larger.

Spiders are compact specialist predators, with a body clearly divided into two parts. The front section, combining head and thorax, bears four pairs of walking legs and two other pairs of limbs. One is a pair of hollow fangs; the other pair is leg-like in females, and a complicated reproductive structure in males. As many as eight large eyes may be seen at the front end.

Spiders feed mainly on insects and have evolved an amazing variety of techniques for capturing their prey. Silk is secreted by many spiders to construct a variety of webs to catch different insects: orb webs slung across gaps catch flying insects, while sheet and hammock webs trap insects that crawl or hop onto them. Spiders are often not particular about their prey, and as the female is usually larger, elaborate rituals are gone through by the male to avoid being eaten and to allow successful mating.

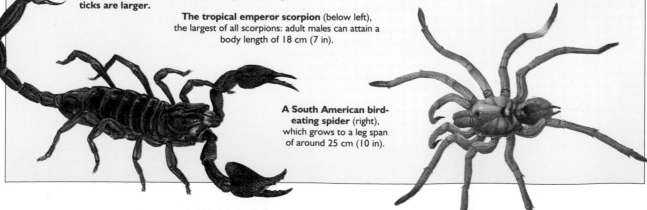

The tropical emperor scorpion (below left), the largest of all scorpions: adult males can attain a body length of 18 cm (7 in).

A South American bird-eating spider (right), which grows to a leg span of around 25 cm (10 in).

Insects

Insects form by far the largest class of animals, accounting for over 80% of all animal species on earth. There are more insect species than all other animal and plant species put together – well over a million species are recognized, with hundreds of new ones discovered each year. Insects are of immense economic importance to humans – many are animal or plant pests, while others play a central role in crop pollination or in pest control.

Adult insects are instantly recognizable as arthropods (▷ p. 96), with a body clearly divided into three parts. The head houses a large brain; within the central section (*thorax*), there is a mass of muscles and associated respiratory structures; and the rear section (*abdomen*) contains the organ systems responsible for digestion, excretion and reproduction. Most variation in insect structure is found in the form of the legs, the wings and the mouthparts, which are all carefully adapted for particular ways of life.

Although the African goliath beetle, for instance, may grow to as much as 20 cm (8 in), most insects are small, many species being less than 1 mm (1/25 in). Small size is indeed an advantage to insects, in that individuals are inconspicuous and can readily satisfy their food requirements.

Classification and reproduction

Two major groups of insects are recognized (▷ illustration): winged insects (*pterygotes*) and wingless insects (*apterygotes*). The latter, believed to be the most primitive surviving insects, fall into four orders, familiar examples being silverfish and springtails. There are 25 orders of winged insects, commonly divided by their method of development into the *exopterygotes* and *endopterygotes*, but 85% of all species belong to just four orders: Coleoptera (beetles); Lepidoptera (butterflies and moths); Diptera (flies); and Hymenoptera (bees, wasps and ants).

Insects develop from egg to adult in two distinct ways. In exopterygote forms, such as cockroaches and grasshoppers, the young live in the same environment and hatch as *nymphs* – miniature adults without reproductive structures. If the insect is a winged form, wing buds are present and grow proportionately larger at each moult. The final moult, in which external reproductive structures appear, transforms the animal to a functional adult. The alternative method, found in endopterygotes, involves larval and pupal stages (▷ illustration).

Insect habitats

Of all invertebrates insects are the most suited to existence on land. This is chiefly due to the nature of the cuticle, the material from which the exoskeleton is made (▷ p. 96). This is so resistant to water loss that insects can exist even in the driest environments. Water loss is also minimal in excretion and in respiration, the latter taking place by means of small closable pores or *spiracles* located along the thorax and abdomen. The cuticle has also allowed the evolution of very strong mouthparts, capable of tackling tough terrestrial plants.

Although rare in the sea because of competition with crustaceans (▷ p. 97), insects are the dominant invertebrate group in fresh water. Many insects, including dragonflies and mayflies, live as larvae in water, exploiting the massive food resources of that environment but abandoning

THE ORDERS OF INSECTS

			Bugs (Hemiptera)	Thrips (Thysanoptera)	Sucking lice (Anoplura)	Biting lice (Mallophaga)	Bristletails, silverfish (Thysanura)
Beetles (Coleoptera)	Ants, bees, wasps (Hymenoptera)	Stylopids (Strepsiptera)	Booklice, barklice (Psocoptera)	Stick insects, leaf insects (Phasmida)	Grasshoppers, crickets (Orthoptera)	Cockroaches, mantids (Dictyoptera)	Proturans (Protura)
Flies (Diptera)	Fleas (Siphonaptera)	Butterflies, moths (Lepidoptera)	Webspinners (Embioptera)	Earwigs (Dermaptera)	Termites (Isoptera)	Zorapterans (Zoraptera)	Diplurans (Diplura)
Caddisflies (Trichoptera)	Scorpionflies (Mecoptera)	Lacewings, dobsonflies (Neuroptera)	Stoneflies (Plecoptera)	Grylloblattids (Grylloblattodea)	Dragonflies, damselflies (Odonata)	Mayflies (Ephemeroptera)	Springtails (Collembola)

ENDOPTERYGOTES	EXOPTERYGOTES	
PTERYGOTES (Winged insects)		**APTERYGOTES** (Wingless insects)

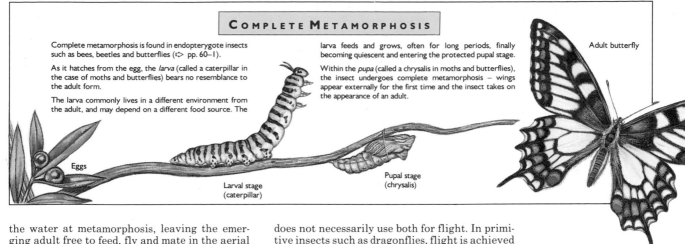

COMPLETE METAMORPHOSIS

Complete metamorphosis is found in endopterygote insects such as bees, beetles and butterflies (▷ pp. 60–1).

As it hatches from the egg, the *larva* (called a caterpillar in the case of moths and butterflies) bears no resemblance to the adult form.

The larva commonly lives in a different environment from the adult, and may depend on a different food source. The larva feeds and grows, often for long periods, finally becoming quiescent and entering the protected pupal stage.

Within the *pupa* (called a chrysalis in moths and butterflies), the insect undergoes complete metamorphosis – wings appear externally for the first time and the insect takes on the appearance of an adult.

Eggs

Larval stage (caterpillar)

Pupal stage (chrysalis)

Adult butterfly

the water at metamorphosis, leaving the emerging adult free to feed, fly and mate in the aerial environment. Other insects, such as water boatmen and pond skaters, are 'incompletely aquatic' – although highly adapted for life in water, they have to return to the surface to breathe.

Insect senses

Visual, chemical and auditory sensory abilities are all well developed in insects. They are capable of producing and perceiving sounds in and beyond the range of human hearing. Insects' compound eyes are capable not only of perceiving the environment as we know it, in colour, but also of perceiving polarized light patterns in the sky and using them in navigation.

Chemical signals (pheromones) are perceived with extraordinary sensitivity by insects, and are used for many purposes. Female moths, for example, release a pheromone that can be detected by males over several kilometres at extremely low concentrations. When a bee stings, it produces an alarm pheromone that causes other bees to fly rapidly to the source of the pheromone, ready to attack.

Insects and plants

The dependence of insects on plants for food has led over millions of years to a high degree of coevolution, resulting in much interdependence and anatomical modification on both sides. Two thirds of flowering plants are insect-pollinated (▷ p. 92), and insects such as bees and butterflies have evolved specialized mouthparts to enable them to reach nectar. Most insects, however, attack plants, which may supplement structural defences with chemical ones. Some produce highly toxic chemicals, others high levels of indigestible material. Insects have responded in various ways, some evolving enzymes to combat the toxic chemicals, others adapting their life history to take advantage of the limited periods when plants are more easily digestible.

Many insects avoid predation by camouflaging themselves, often so that they resemble plant material such as leaves or twigs. Not all insects hide, however. Many caterpillars, butterflies and wasps, for instance, are brightly coloured and obvious, to warn potential predators that they are dangerous and to be avoided. Other species, such as hover flies, which are harmless in themselves, mimic the coloration of dangerous species.

Insect flight

Flight is a major factor in the success of insects. Every flying insect has two pairs of wings but does not necessarily use both for flight. In primitive insects such as dragonflies, flight is achieved by raising and lowering the two pairs of wings by means of muscles attached to the wings. The wings beat out of phase in such a way as to give maximum efficiency. In more advanced insects, the wings are either linked together and beat as one, or – as in the case of beetles – one pair is stiff, held out as an aerofoil, while the other provides the propulsive force. In flies one pair of wings is reduced to a pair of fast-vibrating knobs that function as gyrostabilizers.

Flying is very energy-consuming, and insects in flight have a very high metabolic rate, using large amounts of energy stored in the thorax. Flying can, however, be highly energy-efficient, and has to be for migratory species such as monarch butterflies and locusts: the nature of locust thorax cuticle is such that as much as 90% of the energy exerted in one wing movement is stored by the cuticle and used in the next movement.

Social insects

Two orders of insects – wasps, bees and ants (Hymenoptera) and termites (Isoptera) – exhibit social organization in which closely related individuals live together in large groups. Individuals differ both in function and structure, and cannot survive outside the colony. The development of the colony is controlled by one or more reproductive individuals.

Ants are always social and every colony is founded by a single fertilized female of large size (the queen), who produces eggs that develop into wingless sterile individuals. These workers and soldiers are all female and any males present do not work. Winged males and females develop at appropriate times to leave the nest and found a new generation. Bees and wasps, only some of which are colonial, are broadly similar to ants: all workers are female and the sole purpose of male bees is to mate with the queen. All individuals have wings, and queens are either just a little larger or distinctive only by their behaviour. In most respects termites behave in a similar way to ants.

Honeybees have a single queen whose role is to lay eggs. The workers that emerge from the eggs have different roles in the function of the colony: they start as cell cleaners; graduate to feeding either larvae or the queen and to building combs; and finally become food foragers. Many individuals are usually idling in the hive, ready to respond if a large food source is found or if the hive is threatened. Individuals returning to the hive are able to communicate information about a valuable food source (▷ p. 124).

SEE ALSO

● FLOWERING PLANTS (POLLINATION) p. 92
● ARTHROPODS p. 96
● CRUSTACEANS AND ARACHNIDS p. 97

Fishes

DEFENCE BEHAVIOUR

Fishes may use their teeth or their speed to avoid predators. Many have spiny scales or fin supports, which are capable of inflicting severe damage. Others, such as stonefishes, can inject poison through their spines. The stingray lashes out with its tail and injects poison through a sharp spine, sometimes causing death in humans.

The members of the pufferfish family have an astonishing array of defences. Trigger-fishes have three stout spines on their dorsal fin, which help lock them into crevices, while boxfishes are protected by a bony shell. Pufferfishes swallow water or air until they are spherical, turning into balls of spines; many species also contain a powerful nerve poison. Despite this, a Pacific species of pufferfish is considered a great delicacy in the Far East, where several deaths a year result from incorrectly prepared fish.

Fishes, the vertebrates with the longest ancestry, inhabit the largest ecosystem on earth – the water. Fishes spend all their life in water, and unlike aquatic mammals, such as whales and dolphins, they are cold-blooded and (with a few exceptions) can only use oxygen if it is dissolved in water.

Modern fishes are of diverse origins, and do not form a single evolutionary group. The 22 000 living species are commonly classified in four classes, containing a total of more than 40 orders. The most primitive class, Agnatha, comprises around 60 species of lamprey and hagfish – soft-bodied fishes that lack jaws and are barely vertebrate. All other fishes have jaws; of these, two classes are of pre-eminent importance.

The smaller class – the *cartilaginous fishes* (Chondrichthyes) – is a predominantly marine group of nearly 600 species, including sharks, skates and rays. The great majority of species, however – over 21 000 – are *bony fishes* (class Osteichthyes); these include the fleshy-finned fishes (the coelacanth and lungfishes) and the ray-finned fishes, almost all of which are *teleosts*. The teleosts are the dominant fishes of the world today, accounting for over 95% of all living species. In terms of diversification, they are the most successful of all vertebrate groups, with more species than all other vertebrates put together. They are widely distributed in fresh and salt water from Arctic to Antarctic regions.

Anatomy

The characteristic adaptations of fishes are related to propulsion through water and extraction of oxygen from water. Typically, fishes have well-muscled paddles called *fins*, and the tail is well developed, to provide power and aid steering.

In cartilaginous fishes, the skeleton is formed from gristly, partially calcified cartilage, and the body is solidly muscled. Like most other fishes, their body fluids have a lower salt content than that of their environment, and – because they lack the swim bladder or lungs possessed by bony fishes – they must keep moving to maintain their chosen position. Generally their skins are rough and leathery, with many minute toothed scales, and their fins are fleshy. The bodies of rays and skates are flattened, with the mouth and gill slits on the underside, and the eyes and two gill spiracles (modified gill slits) on the upper surface.

Bony fishes have internal skeletons made of true bone. The head and shoulder regions are covered by large bony plates, while the rest of the body is typically covered in iridescent bony scales. There is flexibility in both body and tail, and the fins are supported by bony rays, usually movable and often bearing sharp spines. Their pelvic fins are generally well developed.

The coelacanth, found only off the Comoro Islands near Madagascar, is virtually a living fossil, scarcely changed in 90 million years. It was once thought that its fleshy bone-supported fins were used to walk on the sea bed. In fact these fins are used primarily for balance and for putting on the occasional burst of speed. However, the coelacanth and the related lungfishes move their fins alternately – just like salamanders walking on land – and it is thought that these fins are the precursors of land-vertebrate limbs.

Lampreys and hagfishes lack jaws, but they have rasping horny teeth. Many species attach themselves to other fishes by means of their suckerlike mouths, and feed on their blood and tissues.

Gills and lungs

Almost all fishes take in water through the mouth and expel it to the exterior across their *gills* – internal blood-rich organs that extract oxygen from the water. Jawless and some cartilaginous fishes have visible gill slits on each side of the neck region, while bony fishes have a pair of hard bony flaps covering their gill exits.

Lungs are found in the most primitive bony fishes, but in teleosts they have been transformed into the *swim bladder*, a gas-filled buoyancy aid. Some fishes, typically mud, estuary and swamp dwellers, use the swim bladder in addition to the

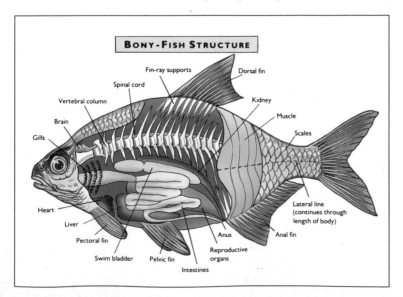

BONY-FISH STRUCTURE

Fin-ray supports
Dorsal fin
Spinal cord
Kidney
Vertebral column
Muscle
Brain
Scales
Gills
Heart
Lateral line
(continues through
length of body)
Liver
Anus
Anal fin
Pectoral fin
Reproductive
organs
Swim bladder
Pelvic fin
Intestines

gills for gas exchange, gulping in air when at the surface. Lungfishes have one or two lungs, which they use when they spend drought periods dormant in their dried-up burrows.

Fish senses

Most fishes have large well-developed eyes, with a reflective layer inside the eye and more cells in the retina sensitive to low light than land animals. This allows fishes to make maximum use of light filtering through water or generated by other fishes. The sense of smell is very important for migratory fishes, leading them back to their beach or river of origin.

Fishes can detect magnetic and electrical fields, as well as vibration and sound. Changes in their environment can be sensed by means of specialized organs – mucus-filled pits with sensory hairs – located on the head and within the lateral lines (⊳ diagram).

Diet

Some fishes are vegetation-eaters, feeding on fallen fruit, plants or bottom detritus. Most, however, are predatory carnivores, taking crustaceans, invertebrates such as jellyfish, and any vertebrates they can catch, including mammals, birds and other fishes.

The basking shark is one of the largest fishes, and the whale shark is the biggest of all, sometimes growing to around 18 m (60 ft). Despite their great size, however, they live on plankton and small fishes, sieved from sea water as it passes across their gills. Their passive feeding behaviour contrasts sharply with the aggression shown by other sharks and the active hunting of smaller fishes by barracuda and other ocean fishes such as tuna, swordfish and sailfish.

The life cycle of fishes

The eggs of most bony fishes are fertilized externally – the male sprays the eggs with sperm after they have been laid by the female. Eggs are provided with a supply of yolk and a protective coat. Where eggs are internally fertilized, as in the coelacanth, the young usually develop inside the female, hatching at or soon before expulsion. Internal fertilization is normal in cartilaginous fishes, the males of which have the pelvic fins adapted as *claspers*, to help maintain contact during copulation and to assist in funnelling in sperm.

Adult fish generally desert their eggs, but there are examples of guarding and nursing behaviour. The Nile mouthbrooder carries its newly hatched young inside its mouth, while the European stickleback uses plant material to make a nest and the male guards the eggs until they hatch.

SEE ALSO

- RIVERS AND LAKES p. 74
- OCEANS p. 76
- AQUATIC ECOSYSTEMS p. 130

Most hatched young are miniatures of their parents, but there are exceptions. The young of flatfishes – such as flounders and plaice – are round-bodied, but as they mature, the body twists to the left or right (depending on the species), so that both eyes end up on one side, with the mouth at the edge. Males and females of most fishes differ in appearance, if only in size and sometimes in brightness of colour.

Distribution and habitats

Fishes are 'cold-blooded' (poikilothermic) – their body temperatures are variable and their metabolic systems are adapted to the temperature of their surroundings. Fast swimmers such as tuna maintain their body temperatures 3–12 °C (5–22 °F) higher than the surrounding water by eating almost constantly. Antarctic cod survive water temperatures of −2 °C (28 °F) using a protein-based blood antifreeze.

In the twilight zone at depths of 200–1000 m (660–3300 ft), biologically generated light (bioluminescence) becomes relatively common as location of mates, prey or predators by sight is impossible: up to 80% of fish species carry 'lights' of some kind, often as lures to trap prey. In the deepest parts of the oceans, below 2000 m (7000 ft), fishes have evolved bizarre adaptations to their habitat. Many anglerfishes have luminous 'fishing rods' formed from a ray of the dorsal fin, which extends above the mouth and attracts prey with its fleshy 'bait'.

Perhaps the richest habitats for colourful fishes are the tropical coral reefs. Many of these fishes have beaks as well as teeth, which they use to graze on coral and seaweed. The clownfish lives in a symbiotic relationship with stinging sea anemones, thereby gaining protection from predators.

The ocean-swimming sailfish, generally believed to be the fastest species of fish over short distances: in one test, a speed of 109 km/h (68 mph) was recorded over a three-second burst. Extremely popular as sport fishes, sailfishes are known for making spectacular leaps out of the water.

Amphibians

LIFE IN THE DEEP-FREEZE

Only recently has it been discovered that some North American frogs – the grey tree frog, the spring peeper, the wood frog and the chorus frog – can survive periods of freezing between 0 and −8 °C (32 and 18 °F). When freezing starts, there is an extremely rapid accumulation in their blood of glucose – or glycerol in the case of the grey tree frog – which acts as a kind of antifreeze. The vital internal organs are insulated from further cooling by the frog's frozen exterior and its glucose- or glycerol-rich cell fluids.

The ancestors of modern amphibians such as frogs and salamanders were the first vertebrates to move from water to land, over 350 million years ago. Despite their long history, however, the members of this group have never achieved a total separation from water. They usually spend at least one stage of their life in water, and retain various features necessary for an amphibious life style.

SEE ALSO

● REPTILES p. 103
● ANIMAL BEHAVIOUR p. 124
● AQUATIC ECOSYSTEMS p. 130

The class Amphibia contains about 4000 species and is subdivided into three orders (▷ illustration). The majority of living species are frogs or toads.

Anatomy and physiology

Amphibians generally breathe through gills as larvae, and through lungs and/or gills as adults, but for many 'skin-breathing' is also important. The structure of their skin allows oxygen dissolved in water to pass through it and to be absorbed directly into the bloodstream. On land the skin is kept moist by glandular secretions, so that some oxygen from the air can also be absorbed.

Frogs and toads have well-developed fore legs and fingers, adapted for digging or holding, while the hind limbs are elongated for leaping or running. Tree frogs have adhesive discs on their toes, making landing more secure. All frogs and toads have large eyes and eyelids, which they blink when they swallow. Many also have a functional 'third eyelid', which lubricates and cleans the eye surface.

The skeleton of frogs and toads is highly modified, with a single neck vertebra, a short trunk and very short fused ribs. The lower spine and pelvis are fused to form a double-arched structure that gives adults their squat shape and acts as a shock absorber for leaping. Adult frogs and toads are tailless. By contrast, newts and salamanders have well-developed necks and tails, and up to 100 vertebrae. In general, they spend more of their lives in water than frogs and toads, and keep internal gills into adulthood. Fully aquatic species (most notably the Mexican axolotl) are often *neotenous* – they retain juvenile features such as external gills even when sexually mature.

Amphibians are poikilothermic ('cold-blooded'). They rely on external heat to maintain normal activity, and this fact is reflected in their habitats and behaviour.

Life cycles

Stimulated by climatic changes, adult frogs and toads migrate to ponds, streams and other breeding sites, whereupon rival males compete in call battles to win the best territories. Females identify males of their own species by their calls, and may carry them on their backs for weeks before laying eggs. The gel-covered eggs are then fertilized externally as they are expelled, resulting in the familiar masses of eggs or *spawn*. Once the eggs have been laid, the adults generally take no further interest in them, leaving them and the hatching tadpoles to develop on their own.

Some frogs and toads keep their eggs in the oviduct within their bodies, releasing metamorphosed young as the eggs hatch. The male may carry the eggs, wrapped round the hind legs in the case of the European midwife toad, in the vocal sac in the case of Darwin's frog of South America. The female Surinam toad implants fertilized eggs in her back, where the young develop before finally erupting through the skin.

In most other amphibians, fertilization is internal. Male newts and salamanders perform elaborate courtship displays and use chemical signals (pheromones) to attract females and make them relax during mating. This allows the transfer of a gel-covered sperm package from male to female. The immature forms of newts and salamanders typically resemble adults more closely than do frog tadpoles.

MODERN AMPHIBIANS

South American caecilian (below). Caecilians (order Gymnophiona) are the most specialized amphibians, found exclusively in the equatorial belt. They are primarily burrowers, feeding on earthworms and other soil-dwelling invertebrates.

American bullfrog (below). Frogs and toads (order Anura) are found on all continents except Antarctica, with a concentration of species in warmer regions. They typically feed on fast-moving prey such as insects and spiders, which they catch by flicking out their long saliva-laden tongues.

Red-backed salamander (above). Newts, salamanders and sirens (order Urodela) are well represented in more temperate regions, especially in the northern hemisphere. They generally favour less open situations than frogs and toads, and feed on slower-moving invertebrates, such as worms, slugs and snails.

Reptiles

Although the first vertebrates to emerge from water to walk on land were the early amphibians, the full conquest of the earth was left to the reptiles. Perhaps the single most important factor in the success of the reptiles in exploiting a wide range of terrestrial habitats was their ability to reproduce by means of shelled yolk-bearing eggs.

The class Reptilia is divided into four orders: Crocodilia (crocodiles, alligators and the gavial, or gharial); Chelonia (turtles and tortoises); Squamata (lizards, snakes and amphisbaenians); and Rhynchocephalia (the tuatara). Of the 6250 or so species of reptile, over 95% are lizards or snakes.

Anatomy and physiology

Reptilian scales are developments of skin keratin (the protein also found in hair, nails, etc.). Scales are small and granular in many lizards, smooth and iridescent in snakes, and large, thick and shield-like in tortoises and crocodiles. Scales may be periodically shed in flakes, or – in the case of snakes – cast off in a slough of the whole skin. Amphisbaenians or worm lizards have their scales arranged in rings; they are limbless and blind, and live in burrows in forest floors or sandy, dry areas.

The vertebral column of reptiles is well developed, with snakes having up to 450 vertebrae, each with a pair of ribs, and almost all have tails. Most lizards and all crocodilians have four well-developed limbs, with up to five toes on each. Turtles and tortoises have powerful limbs, often heavily clawed for digging, or beautifully adapted as paddles for life in the ocean.

The distinguishing feature of turtles and tortoises is their box-like shell, which protects the soft inner organs. It is composed of an upper section, the *carapace*, and a lower plate, the *plastron*. In many species the head, tail and limbs can be withdrawn into the shell for safety.

An obvious feature of snakes and some lizards is the forked tongue. This is flicked rapidly in and out of the mouth, carrying odour molecules to a special sense gland in the roof of the mouth.

The tuatara of New Zealand is the most archaic reptile, with little change in structure since it first appeared in the Triassic period, over 200 million years ago. Lizard-like in appearance, tuataras have a third eye underneath the skin in their forehead. They also have a much lower metabolic rate than other reptiles: they have been known to live for over 75 years, and their eggs take 15 months to hatch.

Reptiles are poikilothermic ('cold-blooded'). Largely dependent on their surroundings to maintain their normal body temperature, they actively seek warmth when they are cold and avoid it if there is a danger of overheating. If the body temperature of a reptile falls below the optimum (between 25–30 °C/75–85 °F for most reptiles), metabolic functions are reduced and the animal becomes sluggish. Many reptiles, including certain turtles, tortoises, snakes and lizards, hibernate during the colder months, slowing their metabolism dramatically.

Reptiles are typically very efficient at limiting water loss during excretion. For instance, various species of lizard, snake and turtle have salt glands on the snout through which they shed unwanted body salts, so reducing the amount of urine that has to be produced. They are therefore generally able to live in colder, hotter and drier conditions than amphibians.

Life cycles

Fertilization in reptiles is internal, and often follows a courtship ritual in which female

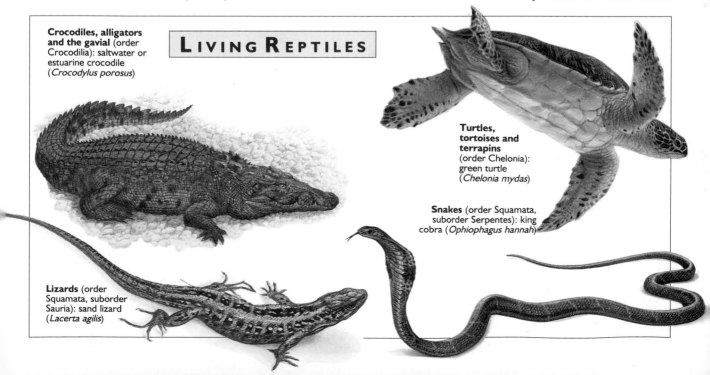

LIVING REPTILES

Crocodiles, alligators and the gavial (order Crocodilia): saltwater or estuarine crocodile (*Crocodylus porosus*)

Turtles, tortoises and terrapins (order Chelonia): green turtle (*Chelonia mydas*)

Snakes (order Squamata, suborder Serpentes): king cobra (*Ophiophagus hannah*)

Lizards (order Squamata, suborder Sauria): sand lizard (*Lacerta agilis*)

The first known reptiles, dating back some 340 million years to the early Carboniferous period, were small animals about 20 cm (8 in) long. Initially the dominant group was the synapsids (the mammal-like reptiles), the lineage that gave rise to the mammals and eventually ourselves. However, these were subsequently eclipsed by the diapsids, the group that comprised the dinosaurs on land, the plesiosaurs in the seas, and the pterosaurs in the air.

Dinosaurs

The dinosaurs, the most advanced reptiles of all time, first appeared in the Triassic period, about 230 million years ago, and were to dominate the earth for over 160 million years. Nearly 1000 species have been identified, and many of these grew to gigantic proportions.

From the beginning there were two different orders of dinosaurs, the *saurischians* ('lizard-hipped') and the *ornithischians* ('bird-hipped'). The first ornithischians – the *ornithopods* ('bird-footed') – were initially small bipedal herbivores about 1 m (40 in) long, while the first saurischians were the *theropods* ('beast-footed'), a group of bipedal carnivores about 2 m (6½ ft) in length. Of the latter there were two contrasting kinds: the heavily built, large-headed *carnosaurs*, and the lightly built *coelurosaurs*, which had small heads and long necks. It was from this second group that the birds are thought to have evolved.

During the Jurassic period, 205–135 million years ago, giant *sauropods* were the dominant herbivores. These included several massive quadrupedal types such as the brontosaur and the diplodocus, while the largest was the brachiosaur, 25 m (80 ft) long and weighing 100 tonnes (tons). These giants spent much time browsing

in lakes and rivers, where the water helped to support their great weight. While many ornithopods remained little changed as small herbivores to the very end of the age of the dinosaurs, the Jurassic is nevertheless marked by the appearance of large ornithopods, such as the herbivorous iguanodon. These dinosaurs are thought to have lived in herds of up to 30 individuals, which presumably afforded protection against predators. An alternative method of defence was seen in the stegosaurs ('plated reptiles'), which had two pairs of sharp spikes at the end of the tail. They also had a double row of vertical bony plates or spines running down the back and tail, but these are thought to have been primarily for display.

A more solidly armoured type of ornithischian developed in the Cretaceous period (135–65 million years ago). These were the ankylosaurs ('fused lizards'), so called because thick bony plates covering the back and tail were often fused into a solid sheet over the pelvic region. From the small bipedal ornithopods there eventually evolved such giants as the three-horned triceratops, with its huge bony frill extending over the vulnerable neck region. Other descendants of the small ornithopods included the pachycephalosaurs ('thick-headed reptiles'), the tops of whose skulls were to up to 30 cm (12 in) thick. The most successful of the herbivorous dinosaurs at this time were the hadrosaurs or duck-billed dinosaurs, which evolved from the large ornithopods. They also lived in herds, and maintained communal 'dinosaur nurseries', with adults caring for the young in much the same way as crocodiles do today.

As the herbivores became more advanced, so too did the carnivores. The best known of these was the fearsome-looking tyrannosaur, a bipedal scavenger 6.5 m (21 ft) tall, but by far the most formidable carnivores – although only 3 m (10 ft) long – were the deinonychosaurs or clawed dinosaurs. Hunting in packs and capable of leaping onto their prey, these bipedal predators bore a sickle-like claw on the hind foot for ripping open their victims.

Aquatic and flying reptiles

As well as dominating land habitats, several groups of reptiles returned to the water. Amongst the first of these were the ichthyosaurs ('fish-lizards'), which appeared at the start of the Triassic period. These looked rather like sharks, with a triangular dorsal fin and an enlarged vertical tail fin, and they fed on fish and squid; some species grew to lengths of up to 12 m (40 ft). In the succeeding Jurassic period, the seas were dominated by plesiosaurs, which swam by means of four hydrofoil-like paddles; the long-necked plesiosaurs were fish-eaters, while the short-necked species (also known as pliosaurs) fed on squid.

The first vertebrates to take to the air are found amongst the reptiles. The earliest of these, dating back to Permian times (300–250 million years ago), were gliding lizards in which the 'flight' membrane was supported by elongated ribs. True flight was achieved towards the end of the Triassic by the pterosaurs, which had full flight membranes extending from the wrists to the tail. While early forms had long bony tails and numerous teeth, later forms reduced their weight (like the birds) by developing air-filled bones and by losing their teeth and tails.

The great extinction

One of the greatest unsolved problems relating to the dinosaurs and these other reptilian groups is why they suddenly vanished 65 million years ago. Numerous theories have been put forward, from changes in plant life that made the dinosaurs constipated, to small mammals eating up their eggs. One of the most popular theories is that the earth was struck by a large meteorite, 15 km (9 mi) in diameter. If such an object had struck the earth, it would have thrown up a cloud of dust that could have obscured the sun for several years. This would explain the disappearance of large land-dwellers while smaller animals survived.

The major difficulty with this theory is that these reptilian groups seem to have gone into decline several million years before their final extinction. And while other forms of life also became extinct at around this time, these various extinctions were not only separated by tens of thousands of years but were highly selective. To date no theory has been able to give an adequate account of all the known factors, and the cause of these extinctions remains a mystery.

A pterosaur, one of a group of flying reptiles that dominated the skies until their extinction 65 million years ago. Some species grew to gigantic proportions, with wing spans of up to 11 m (36 ft).

The chicken-sized *Compsognathus,* one of the coelurosaurian dinosaurs from which birds are thought to have evolved.

SNAKE VENOM

A number of snakes have a pair of glands in the snout in which venom is produced. The chemical composition of this is very complex and varies from species to species. The usual effects of snakebite are paralysis of muscles and breathing, and damage to blood and body tissues. However, although thousands of people die each year as a result of snakebite, most snakes are in fact more likely to flee humans than to attack them.

In front-fanged snakes, two very large teeth swing down like the blades of a penknife as the mouth opens wide, and the snake stabs its prey and injects venom in a single movement. The front-fanged cobras are particularly feared because – in addition to biting – they can spit their venom accurately over distances of 2 m (6½ ft) or more. Rear-fanged snakes inject venom through grooved teeth closer to the throat, and are less dangerous to humans.

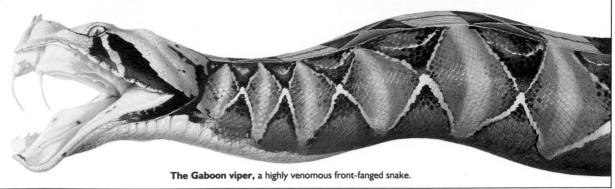

The Gaboon viper, a highly venomous front-fanged snake.

chemical signals (pheromones) and tactile stimulation are important. Clutches of eggs are laid, usually in holes in the earth or in mud. Unlike amphibians, reptiles do not pass through an aquatic larval stage, and the hatchlings are essentially miniatures of the parents. Many species of lizard and snake retain their eggs in the oviduct during the development of the young, which hatch as the eggs are laid.

While most reptiles abandon their eggs, there are some notable exceptions. All crocodiles provide nests for their eggs and protect them until they are ready to hatch. A female may also respond to the call of her young at hatching time, and help them to emerge from the eggs. Some species of crocodile also provide parental care after hatching.

Feeding

Most reptiles are carnivorous, eating invertebrate and vertebrate prey, their particular diet being related both to size and to habitat. Some are herbivores, including many land tortoises and the marine iguana of the Galápagos Islands. Snakes can open their mouths very wide, owing to elastic ligaments between the lower jaw and the skull, which enables them to swallow large prey whole; anacondas and pythons can swallow prey the size of young deer and goats.

Mainly found in East Africa and Madagascar, chameleons are bizarre-looking lizards that have adapted superbly to life both in trees and on the forest floor. Capable of remaining immobile for hours on end, chameleons vigilantly watch for prey, gauging the distance to an insect or small bird by means of their turret-like eyes, which can move independently of one another. The chameleon's hollow tongue, usually kept collapsed on the floor of the mouth, is then shot out, mucus-laden, and retrieves the prey, returning to the mouth like a piece of elastic.

Rattlesnakes and other pit vipers locate their prey at night using a pair of sense organs in pits on their snouts, and are able to detect temperature differences of as little as 0.2 °C (0.36 °F). They

can pinpoint the position of prey at distances of around half a metre (20 in) by comparing signals from left and right pits.

Movement

Snakes move on the ground or in trees or water by using their ribs, side muscles and body scales in various combinations. The sidewinder of southern USA and Mexico moves over shifting sandy terrain by swinging forward successive loops of its body. Some snakes, such as the black mamba of Africa, can exceed 16 km/h (10 mph) for short bursts by lifting the front of their bodies off the ground and 'running' on their ribs.

Lizards are generally agile, and the South American basilisk can even run on its hind legs on water – hence its local name, the Jesu Cristo lizard. With their streamlined shape, marine turtles make graceful and powerful swimmers. Using their strong fore limbs as synchronized paddles, they travel many thousands of kilometres a year.

Escape and defence

Although lizards generally rely on their agility to escape predators, a varied repertoire of other defence strategies is also found. Some chameleons resemble dead leaves, while others alter their skin colour in response to changes in their surroundings. The frilled lizard of Australia stands on its hind legs, opens its brightly coloured mouth, and expands its neck ruff to intimidate predators or rivals. Only two species of lizard – the Gila monster and beaded lizard of the drylands of the southern USA and Mexico – have poisonous bites, with venom glands located in the lower jaw.

A defensive mechanism known as *autotomy* allows some lizards to cast off a length of tail, which breaks off at a fracture plane running through the tail vertebrae. The discarded tail continues to wriggle as the lizard makes its escape. The soft part of the tail regrows, although never to the original length, but the vertebrae are not replaced.

SEE ALSO

● EVOLUTION p. 84
● AMPHIBIANS p. 102
● ANIMAL BEHAVIOUR p. 172

Birds

The power of flight has made birds among the most ubiquitous of animals – they are to be found in virtually every habitat in every continent; and their continent-spanning migrations have undoubtedly made them the best-travelled.

There are over 9500 living species of bird (class Aves). Conventionally they have been arranged in various modifications of a classification that recognizes 28 orders, but recent comparative analysis of DNA has suggested a rearrangement into just 23 orders, five being merged with others.

Wings, flight and feathers

Birds' wings are highly modified fore limbs: the digits are reduced in size, and the wrist bones are elongated and fused, to provide the supporting structure for the flight feathers. The wings are attached to the skeleton by mobile shoulder-joints and by the *furcula* (wishbone), which increases the spring of the wing beat. The power needed for flight is provided by two pairs of massive pectoral muscles anchored to the large keeled breastbone (*sternum*).

Feathers are made of the protein keratin, the same material as in the hair and nails of mammals. Closest to the skin is a layer of soft, fine

SEE ALSO

● EVOLUTION p. 84
● ANIMAL BEHAVIOUR p. 124

feathers (*down*), which is the principal insulating cover, and above this are the *contour feathers*, which serve to streamline the bird's body. The *tail feathers* and the *flight feathers* on the wings have the strongest shafts or *quills*, in order to withstand the tremendous stresses of flight and steering. As feathers are a bird's prime asset, it spends much time and effort *preening* – carefully cleaning and arranging its plumage with the bill.

Beaks, feet and claws

Like its feathers, a bird's beak or bill is composed of hardened keratin, but it is not dead tissue – nerves and fine blood vessels are present throughout. All living birds lack teeth, so the beak is the principal means by which most birds gather food (▷ illustration). Ocean-living birds are generally fish-eaters, and their bills are sharp and strong, often with serrated edges and hooked tips to hold slippery fish. Waders such as the oystercatcher and avocet probe with their beaks for invertebrates such as shellfish and worms on intertidal mud flats and shores. Most water birds – ducks, geese, divers and others – dabble and dive for plants, insects, molluscs and crustaceans. Birds of prey have strong hooked beaks and are almost exclusively carnivorous, feeding on birds, reptiles, mammals, and sometimes fish. Seed- and nut-eaters usually have short, robust bills that may be sharply curved.

A bird's hind limbs – the legs – are usually covered in scales and armed with curving nails, the *claws*. Ground birds use their claws to dig and gather food, while perching birds use them to grip branches. Three digits face forwards for propulsion, and one faces backwards as a support, but the latter is not always fully developed. In owls and tree-living birds such as woodpeckers the

THE ORDERS OF BIRDS

The 23 orders of birds, according to a recent classification based on DNA analysis. All the named groups are orders, except in the case of the Ciconiiformes (coloured light blue), where the complexity of the order is shown in greater detail.

Ostrich, rheas and relatives (Struthioniformes)

Tinamous (Tinamiformes)

Typical gamebirds: partridges, etc. (Galliformes)

Curassows, guans and relatives (Craciformes)

Waterfowl: swans, ducks, geese, etc. (Anseriformes)

Buttonquails (Turniciformes)

Woodpeckers and barbets (Piciformes)

Jacamars and puffbirds (Galbuliformes)

Hornbills (Bucerotiformes)

Hoopoes (Upupiformes)

Trogons (Trogoniformes)

Rollers, kingfishers, bee-eaters (Coraciformes)

Colies (Coliiformes)

Cuckoos (Cuculiformes)

Sandgrouse

Shorebirds: gulls, waders, etc.

Birds of prey

Grebes

Parrots (Psittaciformes)

Swifts (Apodiformes)

Hummingbirds (Trochiliformes)

Turacos (Musophagiformes)

Cormorants, boobies, gannets

Herons

Flamingos

Ibises and spoonbills

Owls and nightjars (Strigiformes)

Pigeons (Columbiformes)

Cranes and rails (Gruiformes)

Songbirds (Passeriformes)

Pelicans

Storks and New World vultures

Frigate birds

Divers, penguins, shearwaters, petrels, albatrosses

— FLIGHTLESS BIRDS —

The 10 species of flightless birds (or ratites) are the most primitive birds, and are the remnants of a group once found worldwide. They have flat breastbones, often large legbones, and wings that are reduced in size. It is now thought that such birds were probably never capable of flying. Apart from the kiwi of New Zealand, 50 cm (20 in) tall, flightless birds range in size from 1.5 m (5 ft) to the largest living bird – the ostrich of Africa, towering above humans at up to 2.75 m (9 ft). The group also includes the cassowaries of Australia and New Guinea, the rheas of South America, and the emu of Australia.

third toe also faces backwards, increasing the strength of their grip.

Physiology and senses

Like mammals, birds are 'warm-blooded' (homoiothermic) – they maintain their body temperatures at a constant level by means of internal (metabolic) mechanisms. In order to provide energy for powered flight, birds need to maintain an extremely high metabolic rate; their body temperatures are higher than those of mammals, and they have large, powerful hearts.

A high metabolic rate also demands an efficient respiratory system, to keep the blood well supplied with oxygen; birds have a unique arrangement of air sacs attached to the lungs that allow a one-way flow of air through the system. At the base of the trachea (windpipe) is a bird's singing organ, the *syrinx*, which is particularly well developed in the songbirds. Characteristically avian features of the digestive system are the *gizzard*, which is used to fragment food, and the *crop*, which serves as a food-storage chamber.

For most birds vision is the key sense, and their eyes are typically large and well developed. Hunting birds such as hawks, eagles and owls have eyes set towards the front of the head, so providing good forward and binocular vision, which is vital in pinpointing prey and judging distances when striking. The sense of hearing is also well developed in most birds. Owls have left and right earflaps in slightly different positions on their heads, allowing them to fix the position of noises more accurately. Smell is generally poorly developed, but a notable exception is the kiwi of New Zealand. It has very small eyes and detects earthworms and grubs by smell, having nostrils at the very tip of its long flexible beak.

Life cycles

In order to secure essential resources such as food, nesting material and a nesting site, male birds typically become territorial in the breeding season, actively defending a particular area against rivals. Many stake their claim to a territory and advertise their presence by means of song, bigger and better sites being taken by older, more experienced birds.

Song may also be used to attract and impress females, but often some form of visual display is required. In some cases this has led to such spectacular extravagances as the peacock's tail and the magnificent plumage of the birds of paradise. Birds such as the ruff and the prairie chicken mate in communal display grounds called *leks*, while others, including the Australasian bowerbirds, build special structures to attract females. Courtship displays may also be

BEAKS

Caribbean flamingo (left). Towering on their long thin legs, flamingos hold their beaks upside down to sieve water fleas and small fish from shallow lakes and ponds.

Toco toucan (right). Toucans have huge beaks, almost as long as their bodies. The beak is used to pluck fruit from branch tips, and may be important in display.

Gold-and-blue macaw (left). Parrots have powerful beaks, enabling them to lever themselves up trees and to break open the hardest nuts; however, they can also be used with great delicacy in grooming and courtship.

Goshawk (right). Birds of prey have sharp beaks ideally suited to slashing and dismembering their prey. Their nostrils are protected from clogging with blood by tufts of feather.

Black skimmer (left). Skimmers feed on the wing, with the lower jaw cutting the surface water and the upper jaw ready to snap down on any aquatic life that is channelled in.

Rufous hummingbird (right). Hummingbirds use their bills to reach to the bottom of tubular flowers, from which they suck nectar through their tube-shaped tongues.

important in bringing the female into a state of readiness to mate, and in monogamous species such as grebes, where both parents are required to rear the young, such displays may help to establish and reinforce pair-bonds.

Birds mate by bringing their genital openings (cloacas) into contact. As the fertilized ovum passes down the female's oviduct to the exterior, it is gradually coated in various layers. First it is provided with a food supply (the *yolk*), and then robed in *albumen* (the egg white), which acts as a cushion and supplies water. The albumen is then coated in protective membranes, and finally covered in several shell layers.

The eggs are incubated in a nest, usually by the female. Most birds gain added security against predators and the elements by nesting clear of the ground. Such nests are usually set in a forked branch, and are made by interweaving flexible stems or twigs, and are often lined with feathery down, moss, soft leaves and other materials. Many species of cuckoo are parasitic – they lay their eggs in the nest of a bird of another species, leaving the young to be reared by the foster parent.

In *nidicolous birds*, such as birds of prey, woodpeckers and songbirds, the newly hatched chicks are naked, blind and defenceless; they are entirely dependent on their parents for food and protection, and must remain in the nest for several weeks until fledged. In *nidifugous birds*, such as gamebirds, wildfowl, grebes and divers, the chicks hatch in a relatively advanced state – their eyes are open and they have a covering of fluffy down.

Archaeopteryx, the first known bird, dating back some 154 million years to the Jurassic period. Birds are generally believed to have evolved from one of the small, lightly built, flesh-eating coelurosaurian dinosaurs (▷ p. 103).

Mammals

In terms of numbers alone, the class Mammalia, with a little over 4000 species in total, is not particularly large – there are roughly five species of fish to every mammalian species. But many of the larger marine animals and most of the larger land animals – including ourselves – are mammals, and as such their importance far outstrips their numbers.

Although the earliest mammals appeared over 200 million years ago, for the first two thirds of their history they were overshadowed by the mighty dinosaurs and other reptiles. It is only during the last 65 million years that mammals have come increasingly to the fore.

The evolution of mammals

The first reptiles that dominated the land over 300 million years ago were the synapsids or mammal-like reptiles (▷ p. 103). Although typically reptilian in appearance, it is now believed that they belonged to the group from which the mammals arose. From their first appearance during the later Triassic, about 220 million years ago, throughout the age of the dinosaurs, the mammals remained small. They were shrew- or rat-like in appearance and life style, and probably managed to subsist side by side with the dinosaurs because – unlike the latter, which were cold-blooded – they could adapt to nocturnal activity.

When the dinosaurs became extinct at the start of the Tertiary period (65–1.6 million years ago), the ecological niches they had occupied became vacant, and the mammals began to extend their range and to adapt themselves to a wider range of habitats. Although not closely related, similar-looking mammals evolved independently on the different continents to fill the same kinds of niche. In Australia, which was isolated throughout much of the Tertiary, there evolved marsupial cats and dogs, marsupial flying squirrels, and even marsupial moles (▷ p. 110). On the grasslands of South America there were animals resembling modern camels, horses, rhinoceroses and elephants, and even a large marsupial cat; there were also unique creatures, such as the giant ground sloths and armoured glyptodonts (closely related to the living armadillos), which survived into historical times.

Mammalian characteristics

The name 'mammal', derived from the Latin *mamma* meaning a 'breast', points to one of the most fundamental features of the group – the production of milk from mammary glands in the female. Milk is a nutritious fluid containing varying amounts of protein and fat, and its production is not found in any other group of animals. Another unique feature of mammals is the possession of three sound-conducting bones (*ossicles*) in the middle ear (▷ p. 144).

Unlike reptiles, mammals are 'warm-blooded' (homoiothermic) – they maintain a constant internal temperature by means of a high metabolic rate. This is not unique to mammals – birds are also warm-blooded (▷ p. 106) – but their external 'lagging' is: the insulating covering of hair or fur is peculiar to mammals, just as feathers are to birds.

As one of the principal means by which mammals gather their food, the teeth have been greatly

ICE AGE MAMMALS

During the successive ice ages of the Pleistocene epoch (1.6 million to 10 000 years ago), the ice caps spread from the polar regions into central Europe, and the permafrost and tundra vegetation reached as far south as the Alps and the Himalaya. The great plains of Eurasia and North America were inhabited by woolly mammoths and woolly rhinoceroses, which grazed on the relatively rich plant life that the tundra supported at this period. These large mammals were preyed upon by carnivores such as sabre-toothed cats, which were armed with long stabbing canine teeth. Caves became

important as shelters for many animals, including humans and the large cave bears that they hunted.

Why are most of these great mammals of the Pleistocene no longer around? The disappearance of the plant-rich tundra at the end of the last ice age 10 000 years ago may have played a part in their extinction, but it is more likely that these giant animals were victims of man's improving technology and were simply hunted to extinction.

ICE AGE MAMMALS
1.6 million–10 000 years ago

WOOLLY MAMMOTH
(*Mammuthus primigenius*)

SABRE-TOOTHED CAT
(*Machairodus latidens*)

WOOLLY RHINO
(*Coelodonta tichorhinus*)

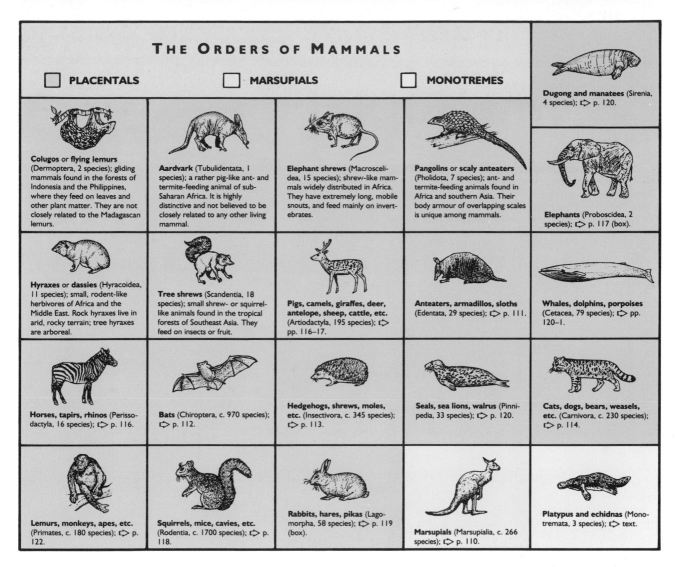

THE ORDERS OF MAMMALS

☐ **PLACENTALS** ☐ **MARSUPIALS** ☐ **MONOTREMES**

Colugos or **flying lemurs** (Dermoptera, 2 species); gliding mammals found in the forests of Indonesia and the Philippines, where they feed on leaves and other plant matter. They are not closely related to the Madagascan lemurs.

Aardvark (Tubulidentata, 1 species); a rather pig-like ant- and termite-feeding animal of sub-Saharan Africa. It is highly distinctive and not believed to be closely related to any other living mammal.

Elephant shrews (Macroscelidea, 15 species); shrew-like mammals widely distributed in Africa. They have extremely long, mobile snouts, and feed mainly on invertebrates.

Pangolins or **scaly anteaters** (Pholidota, 7 species); ant- and termite-feeding animals found in Africa and southern Asia. Their body armour of overlapping scales is unique among mammals.

Dugong and manatees (Sirenia, 4 species); ⊳ p. 120.

Hyraxes or **dassies** (Hyracoidea, 11 species); small, rodent-like herbivores of Africa and the Middle East. Rock hyraxes live in arid, rocky terrain; tree hyraxes are arboreal.

Tree shrews (Scandentia, 18 species); small shrew- or squirrel-like animals found in the tropical forests of Southeast Asia. They feed on insects or fruit.

Pigs, camels, giraffes, deer, antelope, sheep, cattle, etc. (Artiodactyla, 195 species); ⊳ pp. 116–17.

Anteaters, armadillos, sloths (Edentata, 29 species); ⊳ p. 111.

Elephants (Proboscidea, 2 species); ⊳ p. 117 (box).

Whales, dolphins, porpoises (Cetacea, 79 species); ⊳ pp. 120–1.

Horses, tapirs, rhinos (Perissodactyla, 16 species); ⊳ p. 116.

Bats (Chiroptera, c. 970 species); ⊳ p. 112.

Hedgehogs, shrews, moles, etc. (Insectivora, c. 345 species); ⊳ p. 113.

Seals, sea lions, walrus (Pinnipedia, 33 species); ⊳ p. 120.

Cats, dogs, bears, weasels, etc. (Carnivora, c. 230 species); ⊳ p. 114.

Lemurs, monkeys, apes, etc. (Primates, c. 180 species); ⊳ p. 122.

Squirrels, mice, cavies, etc. (Rodentia, c. 1700 species); ⊳ p. 118.

Rabbits, hares, pikas (Lagomorpha, 58 species); ⊳ p. 119 (box).

Marsupials (Marsupialia, c. 266 species); ⊳ p. 110.

Platypus and echidnas (Monotremata, 3 species); ⊳ text.

---

modified from those of reptiles. They have increased in size and been reduced in number, and they have also become specialized in different parts of the jaws for different functions. At the front, *incisors* have developed for biting and *canines* for stabbing, while at the back cusped teeth (*molars* and *premolars*) are adapted for chewing and grinding. The pattern of tooth replacement in mammals, with a set of milk teeth followed by a permanent set of teeth in the adult, is also unique to mammals.

Among the most significant characteristics of mammals – though the hardest to quantify – is their intelligence. The cerebral cortex (the part of the brain concerned with intelligent behaviour) is better developed in higher mammals than in any other group of vertebrates.

The classification of mammals

The class Mammalia, to which all mammals belong, is divided into three groups on the basis of the different ways in which the members of each reproduce. The smallest group, the *monotremes*, includes a single order with just three species, all of which are confined to Australasia – the semi-aquatic duck-billed platypus and the echidnas or spiny anteaters. Although now generally accepted as true mammals, they retain a number of primitive features. Even though they are furry

and feed their young on milk, they lay eggs that are structurally very similar to those of a bird, and – like birds – they incubate them in a nest or burrow.

All other mammals bear live young, but reproductive differences within this group allow further division into two subgroups. The first of these again includes just a single order, which comprises the *marsupials* or 'pouched mammals' (⊳ p. 110). These too are best known from Australasia, but they have a significant representation in South America. Although marsupials give birth to live young, the young are born at a very early stage of development. The tiny offspring typically makes its way from the birth canal to the pouch, where it attaches itself to a nipple and remains for a protracted period until capable of feeding itself.

The great majority of living mammals belong to the second subgroup – the *eutherians* or *placental mammals* (⊳ pp. 111–23). The name of the group is derived from the *placenta*, a special organ by which the embryo is fed directly from the mother's blood supply and by which waste products are removed. The length of time that the young grow within the mother (the *gestation period*) varies considerably from species to species, but no placental mammal produces offspring as undeveloped as that of a marsupial.

SEE ALSO

● EVOLUTION p. 103
● MARSUPIALS p. 110
● PLACENTAL MAMMALS pp. 111–23
● HUMAN PREHISTORY p. 226

Marsupials

The marsupials include the possums and opposums, bandicoots, wombats, kangaroos and wallabies, the numbat and the koala. Altogether there are some 266 species belonging to 18 different families. Although immensely varied in form, they are united as a group and distinguished from all other mammals by various features of their reproduction (⇨ p. 108).

SEE ALSO

● MAMMALS p. 108

Male red kangaroos sparring. The red kangaroo of the arid plains of central Australia is the largest of the marsupials, growing to a height of 1.5 m (5 ft) or more.
(Jacana)

Australia separated from other landmasses (⇨ p. 62) before placental mammals were able to establish themselves, so it is chiefly in Australia that marsupials have realized their full potential. In the absence of competition from other mammals, marsupials have filled most of the ecological niches occupied by 'true' mammals elsewhere, and range from tiny shrew-like insectivorous species to wolf-like carnivores. Thus, for instance, there is a marsupial mole, remarkably similar in appearance and life style to placental moles, while the wombat shares the burrowing life of the placental badgers and resembles them in shape and size. Although less diverse outside Australia, marsupials are found in other parts of Australasia and are represented in the Americas by the opossums.

Kangaroos

The kangaroo family (Macropodidae) comprises over 50 species and includes the largest living marsupials (⇨ photo). They are mainly grazers, filling the niche occupied by sheep or antelope in other parts of the world. The smaller kangaroos known as wallabies fill some of the niches occupied elsewhere by rabbits and hares.

A kangaroo's fore limbs are small and generally held clear of the ground, while the enlarged, well-muscled hind limbs provide the propulsive force for jumping. The larger kangaroos attain considerable speeds as they move forward in huge leaps of 6 m (20 ft) or more. The long powerful tail acts as a counterweight, providing stability on landing. The tail also serves as a balance for the handful of species – the tree kangaroos – that live in the tropical forests of New Guinea and Queensland.

Dasyurid marsupials

The main group of carnivorous and insectivorous marsupials, the dasyurids (family Dasyuridae), contains nearly 50 species, most of which are nocturnal. They range in size from tiny marsupial 'mice' (dunnarts) to native 'cats' such as the quoll, nearly 1 m (39 in) long. The smaller species, such as the shrew-like planigale and the antechinus, are voracious predators, often killing prey almost as big as themselves.

The powerful and heavily built Tasmanian devil was formerly found over much of Australia, but is now confined to Tasmania. Its squat body supports a massive head with powerful hyena-like jaws that enable it to smash through the bones of carrion.

Until its extinction, the largest carnivorous marsupial was the thylacine, or Tasmanian wolf, which grew to a length of over 1.5 m (5 ft). Formerly occurring on the Australian mainland also, thylacines were persecuted and ultimately exterminated by Tasmanian sheep farmers, the last probably dying in the 1930s.

The koala

The koala of eastern Australia superficially resembles a small thick-set bear. It is a highly specialized tree-climbing species, lacks a tail, and feeds almost exclusively on eucalyptus trees, eating as much as 1.5 kg (3¼ lb) of leaves a day. The koala's single offspring remains in the mother's pouch for as long as six months, and then rides around on her back until it is about a year old. Until recently koalas were threatened with extinction through a combination of hunting for the fur trade, loss of habitat and epidemic disease. Now under strict protection, the koala is now once again fairly abundant.

New World marsupials

Three families of marsupial, containing around 83 species, are found in the Americas – the only marsupials found outside Australasia. About 70 of these species belong to the opossum family (Didelphidae), and most of the others resemble opossums. The majority of opossums live in forests and are rat-like in appearance, although some are more reminiscent of shrews.

The Virginia opossum – the largest species of opossum, and the only one found north of Mexico – has adapted well to life with man, following the spread of agriculture and often scavenging in urban refuse. It is a prodigious breeder, with up to three litters a year. The young are smaller than honeybees at birth, and litters of 18 have been recorded, but fewer than this survive.

Anteaters, Sloths and Armadillos

Armadillos, anteaters and sloths together form the order Edentata. The scientific name means 'toothless', although in fact only the anteaters are entirely lacking in teeth – armadillos and sloths have simple, peg-like cheek teeth.

SEE ALSO

● MAMMALS p. 108

The species of edentate mammal alive today are the remnants of a once much larger group of South American mammals, many of which became extinct in prehistoric and historic times. These included a number of giant forms, including giant sloths and heavily armoured armadillo-like animals.

Anteaters

The four species of anteater occur in tropical forests and savannah from southern Mexico as far south as northern Argentina. All species have long tapering snouts and sticky tongues to trap ants or termites. The fore limbs are armed with powerful claws for ripping open insect nests, the claw on the middle digit being especially long and sharp. The largest species is the giant anteater, which is ground-dwelling and grows to over 2 m (7 ft) long (▷ illustration).

The two species of lesser anteater, or tamandua, and the silky (or pygmy) anteater are tree-dwelling, and have prehensile tails. The latter, growing to a body length of just 15 cm (6 in), has hind feet with jointed soles, allowing it to grasp branches both with its tail and with its claws.

Armadillos

The 20 species of armadillo (family Dasypodidae) occur throughout much of South and Central America, and even extend into the southern USA and some of the West Indies. They have a highly distinctive appearance, with bony armour shielding both the head and the body. This protective covering is arranged as a series of hard, rigid plates covered by horn and connected to the underlying flexible skin. Even the tail and upper surfaces of the limbs are armoured, but not the belly, which is soft and hairy. In addition to this defence, some species, including the three-banded armadillo, can roll into a ball when threatened. Armadillos are fast burrowers, loosening the soil with the fore limbs and then kicking it clear with the hind legs.

Armadillos are adaptable animals with an omnivorous diet, which has allowed them to exploit a wide range of habitats. They feed on a variety of invertebrates as well as some plant matter. The common long-nosed armadillo has successfully spread into and colonized much of the southeastern USA, and can be a pest in arable land, where it causes damage to crops by digging and feeding. This species normally produces quadruplets, all of the same sex, which have developed from a single fertilized egg and are thus identical.

Sloths

There are two groups of living sloths – three species of three-toed sloth (family Bradypodidae) and two species of two-toed sloth (family Megalonychidae). All are adapted for life in the trees of the tropical rainforests of Central and South America, where they feed on a diet of leaves. They have rounded heads with rather flattened faces, and their feet are highly modified, with five toes on the hind feet and either two or three on the fore feet, each possessing a huge, hook-like claw used to grip branches. Unlike other arboreal mammals, they hang from the branches, and they rarely come to the ground.

Sloths have thick coats made up of a short, dense undercoat overlaid with longer, coarser hairs. The coat often assumes a greenish hue caused by blue-green algae that grow in grooves running the length of the hairs, and this provides excellent camouflage. The three-toed sloths are very unusual in having eight or nine neck vertebrae instead of the usual seven found in most other mammals (even giraffes); this gives extra flexibility in the movement of the head. Female sloths produce a single youngster at a time, which is carried for six to nine months by its mother.

The giant anteater can extend its narrow, sticky tongue some 60 cm (2 ft) into the nests of ants and termites. It then flicks it in and out at an astonishing rate of up to 150 times a minute. In this way it satisfies its appetite for around 30 000 insects a day.

Bats

DECLINING NUMBERS

In parts of the world where there is intensive farming, bat populations have undergone catastrophic declines in the past few decades. Damage to habitat has been a significant factor, but the widespread use of persistent pesticides in agriculture and of highly toxic insecticides for treating building timbers has also played a major part. Although most bats produce only one offspring a year, this low rate of reproduction is normally balanced by the fact that they are long-lived animals, with even small bats known to live 20 years or more in the wild. As a result, declines in numbers can take a long time to be noticed – and even longer to be reversed.

Although certain other mammals are capable of gliding, bats are the only mammals capable of true flight. A bat's flying membrane consists of skin stretched between the four extremely elongated fingers of each hand; only the thumb remains free, and is used for grooming. The elastic membrane is attached to the bat's ankles, and in many species it is also connected to the tail.

SEE ALSO

● MAMMALS p. 108

Bats (order Chiroptera) occur all over the world except the colder regions, above the tree line, and on some remote oceanic islands. Two distinct groups are recognized: the Megachiroptera, consisting of a single family of about 170 fruit bats; and the Microchiroptera, which includes all other bats – around 800 species in 18 distinct families. Bats vary in size from one of the smallest known mammals, Kitti's hog-nosed bat of Thailand, which is about the size of a bumblebee, to the fruit bats, which may have wingspans in excess of 1.5 m (5 ft).

Fruit bats

The fruit bats, or flying foxes, are found in the tropical and subtropical regions of Australia and the Old World. As their name suggests, they mostly eat fruit, but some feed on nectar as well. Most have large eyes and rely principally on their sight, and are therefore usually active at dusk or dawn, flying up to 70 km (44 mi) in search of fruit.

Fruit bats often live in the tops of trees in communal roosts. They frequently occur in huge numbers, a single colony sometimes numbering over a million members. They often move in flocks of a thousand or more to suitable feeding sites, as figs or other fruit ripen on a particular tree. These feeding movements play an important part in the dispersal of the seeds of trees in tropical forests. Fruit bats sometimes feed in citrus and other plantations, but since they normally eat fruit that is ripe or over-ripe, they actually cause little damage. Despite this, they have been extensively persecuted by fruit farmers.

Echolocation

With the exception of most fruit bats, the majority of bats are dependent for navigation on *echolocation* – an extremely sophisticated form of sonar. Echolocation involves emitting high-pitched squeaks (mostly above the range of human hearing) and measuring how long it takes for the noise to bounce back from intervening objects. By this means bats are able to fly and to locate prey in total darkness. Many species, including the horseshoe and leaf-nosed bats, have elaborate folds of skin on the nose and face that are used to project and focus the squeaks used in echolocation.

Feeding techniques

Bats have evolved a wide variety of feeding techniques. While some species feed on pollen and nectar (▷ photo), most are insectivorous, often consuming huge numbers of tiny insects such as midges and mosquitoes in the course of a single night.

The three species of vampire bat, confined to the New World, are the most specialized of all bats, feeding entirely on the blood of warm-blooded vertebrates. Their front teeth are modified into two triangular razors, which they use to make a small incision, rarely felt by the victim. Although vampires are a problem in some parts of the New World, particularly in cattle-rearing areas and where rabies is common, the dangers are often greatly exaggerated. A few species of bat are carnivorous; the largest of these is the Australian giant false vampire, which feeds on mice, small marsupials, birds and even other bats.

Bat roosts

Many species of bat roost in caves or crevices, and some of the larger roosts are among the biggest known concentrations of any one mammal. A single colony of free-tailed bats in Eagle Creek, Arizona, once contained some 50 million members. This number subsequently fell to about 600 000, probably as a result of the widespread and often indiscriminate use of insecticides in North America in the 1960s.

While roosting, most bats hang upside down by their feet, and may even give birth in this posture. The dung, or *guano*, of cave-dwelling bats has been mined in many parts of the world as a rich source of agricultural fertilizer.

Most species of bat living in temperate regions either migrate in winter to areas where food is available or hibernate. During hibernation bats use about a tenth of the oxygen needed when active, and can rely on energy stored as fat.

A South American long-tongued bat, one of the many tropical species that feed on nectar and pollen. In so doing they are often extremely important pollinators of night-flowering trees, cacti and other plants (▷ p. 92).
(Jacana)

Insectivores

The insectivores, which include such familiar animals as hedgehogs, shrews and moles, form a diverse and highly successful group of mammals. The order to which they belong (Insectivora) contains around 345 species, and with the exception of Australasia and Antarctica there are representatives on every continent, where they occupy all kinds of terrestrial and semi-aquatic habitats.

SEE ALSO

● MAMMALS p. 108

Insectivores are generally small, with long narrow snouts and simple peg-like teeth. They have five clawed digits on each limb, and usually have minute eyes and flat feet. Most species eat insects, as their name implies, but some are carnivorous.

Hedgehogs

The hedgehog family (Erinaceidae) consists of two main groups, the moonrats or gymnures of Southeast Asia (5 species) and the true hedgehogs (12 species). The moonrats lack spines, but have long blunt-nosed snouts like true hedgehogs; they are among the largest insectivores, weighing up to 2 kg (4½ lb).

The true hedgehogs are native to Africa and Eurasia. They are covered in spines, and when alarmed can curl into a defensive ball. They feed on a wide range of small invertebrates, and have adapted well to suburban gardens. In the northern part of its range the European hedgehog and its close relative, the Romanian hedgehog, hibernate.

Shrews

The most numerous and widespread family of insectivores is the shrews (Soricidae), with around 270 species found in all parts of the world except the colder regions, Australasia, and most of South America. They are generally small mouse-like animals, with dense fur and pointed snouts; the pygmy white-toothed shrew is one of the world's smallest mammals, weighing about 2 g (1/14 oz). Although mostly ground-dwelling, a few species have adapted to an aquatic life, and several species of water shrew have fringes of stiff hairs on their feet to aid swimming.

Shrews are very active, feeding in short bursts, then resting. In order to meet its energy requirements, the common shrew may eat well over its own weight in food in a period of 24 hours. Shrews never hibernate, as it would be impossible for them to build up sufficient reserves of food. A number of shrews have poisons in their saliva powerful enough to incapacitate invertebrates such as earthworms.

Moles and golden moles

All of the 27 or so species of mole (family Talpidae) are confined to the northern hemisphere. They are adapted to life underground and to digging, and so are generally restricted to habitats with soft soil. Their shovel-like forepaws are permanently turned outwards, and they have short thick arms with powerful muscles. The fur is short and velvety, and can brush in any direction, thus allowing the mole to move backwards and forwards through its tunnels with equal ease. They have very small eyes and are virtually blind, but have long sensitive snouts. The diet of Old World moles is principally made up of earthworms, which are trapped as they fall into the mole's system of burrows. One species, the star-nosed mole of North America, has highly sensitive tentacles on its snout with which it searches for food. Desmans are aquatic moles and have webbed hind feet to aid swimming. The Russian desman is the largest of the moles, growing to around 40 cm (16 in).

The 18 species of golden mole (family Chrysochloridae) are confined to Africa, where they are found from Cameroon and Uganda to the Cape. Although similar in structure to the true moles, they are only distantly related. Their thick woolly fur has a lustre often giving them a golden or bronze appearance. Some species – despite being blind – hunt on the surface, but usually only after rain or at night. Most species feed on invertebrates, but some also eat legless lizards up to 20 cm (8 in) long – over twice their own length.

Tenrecs and solenodons

All but 3 of the 34 species of tenrec (family Tenrecidae) are confined to Madagascar and the nearby Comoro Islands. In the absence of other insectivores, they have adopted the life styles of insectivores elsewhere. The common (or tailless) tenrec has rather spiny fur, while the hedgehog tenrecs are so spiny as to be superficially very similar to the true hedgehogs. The three other species of tenrec – the otter shrews – are found in western Africa. The largest, the giant otter shrew, found in the rainforests of central Africa, grows to around 75 cm (2½ ft); it has a flattened muzzle covered with stiff whiskers and a powerful flattened tail.

The two living species of solenodon (family Solenodontidae) are confined to the islands of Cuba and Hispaniola in the Caribbean. They resemble large robust shrews, and can weigh up to 1 kg (2.2 lb). Although they mostly eat insects and fruit, they also feed on reptiles and poultry. Both species are legally protected, but are in imminent danger of extinction, particularly as a result of deforestation and predation by introduced cats and dogs.

Hedgehogs are mostly ground-dwelling, but they are also accomplished swimmers and climbers. If they fall while climbing, they use their spines to absorb the impact.
(Jacana)

Carnivores

Although the name 'carnivore' is applied generally to any carnivorous, or flesh-eating, animal, the term is used specifically to describe the group of mammals belonging to the order Carnivora. This large and highly diverse order contains around 230 species in seven families, including cats, dogs, bears, raccoons and weasels.

The natural range of living carnivores is very broad, encompassing virtually all parts of the world except Australasia and Antarctica. Carnivores are most readily distinguished as a group by the structure of their teeth: the canines are usually enlarged and dagger-like, while highly carnivorous species such as cats and weasels have well-developed cheek teeth (*carnassials*) that interlock in a scissor-like action to cut through tough flesh and sinew.

Cats

The 34 species of cat (family Felidae) are all perfectly adapted to the life of the hunter. As well as specialized teeth, all species (except the cheetah) have claws that can be withdrawn into sheaths, thus keeping the claws razor-sharp and allowing the animal to stalk noiselessly on its pads. All senses, especially sight, scent and hearing, are well developed.

The tiger is the biggest of the cats, with a head-and-body length sometimes in excess of 2.5 m (8 ft). Formerly ranging widely over most of southern Asia, it is now almost entirely restricted to parks and reserves, with fewer than 5000 left in the wild. The lion has also been exterminated from much of its former range and is now virtually confined to the savannah of sub-Saharan Africa. Unlike most cats, lions are typically active by day and live together in groups called prides, which usually contain about nine individuals.

The leopard is still relatively common throughout southern Asia and much of Africa. It typically grows to around 1.5 m (5 ft) excluding the tail. Most leopards have spots but they can be entirely black (in which case they are known as panthers). The jaguar – the largest of the New World cats – is of slightly heavier build than the leopard and is not quite so agile. The cheetah is now largely confined to the African savannah. It is the fastest land animal, with long legs and a slender, supple body; to run down its prey it relies on bursts of speed that may exceed 80 km/h (50 mph).

Among the smaller cats, the wildcat is one of the most widely distributed. It occurs in a wide range of habitats, from forest to semi-desert, in many parts of the Old World. The name 'wildcat' is sometimes applied to other medium-sized cats, including the Old World caracal, the North American bobcat, and the lynx, which is widespread throughout the northern hemisphere.

Civets and their relatives

The civet family (Viverridae) contains some 66 species, including civets, genets, mongooses and linsangs. They have a wide distribution from southern Europe across southern Asia, down through Africa and into Madagascar. Viverrids typically have long lithe bodies, short legs, pointed snouts, and very long tails. Many are boldly spotted or stripped with banded tails.

Viverrids have adapted to a wide range of habitats, from tropical forest to savannah. Most are solitary in behaviour, but a few, such as meerkats, are highly social. Mongooses are famous for their ability to prey on cobras and other venomous snakes. Contrary to popular belief, they are not immune to snake venom but rely for protection on their agility and coarse fur.

Hyenas

Three of the four species in the hyena family (Hyaenidae) – the spotted, brown and striped hyenas – are rather dog-like in appearance, with a distinctive sloping gait, massive heads, and powerful jaws capable of crushing bones. Whereas the brown and spotted hyenas are confined to sub-Saharan Africa, the striped hyena occurs in dry habitats across northern Africa and into Asia. Although noted as scavengers, the hyenas are also effective predators. The other member of the family – the aardwolf of sub-Saharan Africa – is of lighter build and feeds on termites and other insects.

Dogs and their relatives

The 35 species of the dog family (Canidae) occur in almost all habitats and – even excluding the domestic dog – in virtually all parts of the world. They are typically long-legged, with a muscular torso, bushy tail, and long muzzle. Their senses, particularly smell and hearing, are acute. Most canids are strictly terrestrial and are excellent runners.

The African hunting dog, a formidable predator of African savannah and open woodland. Hunting success, particularly when pursuing large and swift prey, is based on co-operation between members of the pack.

Canids are principally meat-eaters. Species such as the African hunting dog and the dhole (or Asiatic wild dog) are quite strictly carnivorous, while others, including the foxes, are generally more omnivorous, feeding on both animal and vegetable matter as available. Several canids, including the jackal of Asia and Africa, obtain much of their food by scavenging.

The ancestor of the domestic dog is the wolf. The grey wolf was once widespread and abundant throughout most of the northern hemisphere, but it has been ruthlessly persecuted ever since humans first started herding animals. Like most other canids, wolves are highly social, living and hunting in family groups, or packs. The North American coyote has been far more successful at surviving human persecution; like the red fox, it has even managed to colonize towns and cities.

Bears

Within historic times, the eight species of the bear family (Ursidae) occurred throughout almost the entire northern hemisphere, extending as far south as North Africa and into South America. They are now distributed patchily over their range. Bears are characteristically large and heavily built, with stocky bodies, flat feet, and long curved claws. Most bears are omnivorous and opportunistic in their feeding, eating a wide range of food; the only exception is the polar bear, which is largely carnivorous, feeding mostly on seals.

Among the bears are the largest living carnivores – the brown bears and the polar bear of the Arctic regions. An adult male polar bear weighs on average about 400 kg (880 lb) and grows to a length of 2.5 m (8¼ ft), but much heavier specimens have been reported. There are several subspecies of brown bear, including the Old World brown bears and the giant North American grizzlies; the largest are those found on Kodiak Island in Alaska (▷ illustration).

The giant panda is confined to mountainous bamboo forest in western China, where it feeds almost exclusively on bamboo shoots. The front paw has a special pad – the so-called sixth finger – that enables the panda to hold bamboo stems.

Raccoons and their relatives

The raccoon family (Procyonidae) comprises 16 species of small to medium-sized mammal, including not only raccoons but also the coatis, olingo, kinkajou, and red panda. The red panda is found from the Himalaya to southern China, but all other procyonids are confined to the Americas.

There are six species of raccoon proper, all growing to a body length of around 50 cm (20 in). The most widespread and one of the commonest mammals in North America is the common raccoon. Like other procyonids, the raccoon is an active and inquisitive animal, and a good climber. It can also use its forepaws with extraordinary dexterity, and is very adept at fishing. It has proved highly adaptable to urban life, and it is often seen rummaging among garbage cans.

Weasels and their relatives

The weasel family (Mustelidae) contains 67 species, including weasels, skunks, badgers and otters. Mustelids occur on nearly all landmasses except Australasia, and have adapted to a wide variety of habitats. They typically have long supple bodies, often arched near the hindquarters; at the front the body typically tapers into a long neck supporting a relatively small pointed head. The tail is usually long, and sometimes bushy. Mustelids are generally highly carnivorous, and most species are skilled hunters.

The least weasel of the temperate northern hemisphere is the smallest living carnivore, growing to a total length (including tail) of about 20 cm (8 in). In the northern parts of its range, its fur turns white in winter, as does that of the slightly larger stoat. Another close relative, the mink, is now farmed for its luxuriant fur, while the martens (which include the sable) are also prized for their dense, soft pelts.

All mustelids have well-developed anal scent glands, which are generally used for marking the boundaries of their territory. In the polecats and the skunks of North and Central America these glands are also used to eject a foul-smelling liquid at would-be intruders.

Badgers are found throughout Eurasia and North America. Typically they are stockily built with distinctive black-and-white facial markings. They are usually active by night, emerging from their burrows to feed on a wide diet of animal and plant material. The American badger is mostly solitary, whereas the Eurasian badger is social.

All otter species show adaptations for life in water, typically having streamlined bodies and webbed feet, as well as broad tails to give propulsion when swimming. Most specialized of all are the sea otters, which are capable of living their entire life without ever coming on shore.

SEE ALSO
● MAMMALS p. 108
● ANIMAL BEHAVIOUR p. 124

The Kodiak bear of Alaska, usually considered to be the largest member of the Carnivora. Adult males measure around 2.5 m (8¼ ft) from nose to tail.

Hoofed Mammals

The hoofed mammals or *ungulates* are divided into two orders, distinguished by the number of toes their members possess. The smaller order (Perissodactyla), with just 16 species, includes three families of odd-toed ungulates or *perissodactyls* – horses, rhinoceroses and tapirs. The larger order (Artiodactyla) – with nearly 200 species in 10 families – comprises the even-toed ungulates or *artiodactyls*, and includes deer, cattle, pigs and others. With the exception of pigs, peccaries and hippopotamuses, all artiodactyls are ruminants (▷ box).

RUMINATION

With the exception of pigs, peccaries and hippopotamuses, all artiodactyls ruminate or 'chew the cud'. They have complex multi-chambered stomachs (four-chambered except in the camels) incorporating a large fermentation chamber (rumen), which contains bacteria that help to break down the tough vegetable matter on which they feed. As food is cropped, it is swallowed and stored in the rumen, where it is moistened, softened and subjected to bacterial action. The partially digested food ('cud') is then regurgitated in small quantities into the mouth for more thorough fragmentation by the grinding cheek teeth, and mixed with saliva. It is swallowed for a second time and enters the other chambers of the stomach, where it is subjected to further action by acids and digestive enzymes.

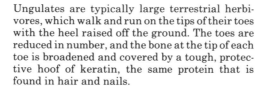

The okapi, restricted to the dense tropical forests of Zaïre, is the giraffe's only living relative. Such is the okapi's unobtrusive life style that – despite being the size of a large zebra – it remained unknown to science until 1901.

Ungulates are typically large terrestrial herbivores, which walk and run on the tips of their toes with the heel raised off the ground. The toes are reduced in number, and the bone at the tip of each toe is broadened and covered by a tough, protective hoof of keratin, the same protein that is found in hair and nails.

Horses, rhinoceroses and tapirs

The seven species of horse, ass and zebra (family Equidae) are fast-running ungulates with slender limbs and long heads and necks. They typically inhabit grasslands and semi-arid lands, where they live in herds and feed on grasses. The tarpan, believed to be the ancestor of the domestic horse, is now extinct in the wild, while the ancestor of the donkey – the African wild ass – is on the brink of extinction. South of the Sahara, four species of zebra were once widespread. The southernmost – the quagga – is now extinct, but the common zebra is still relatively widespread in eastern and southern Africa.

The five species of rhinoceros (family Rhinocerotidae) are massively built animals, with large bodies, short stocky legs, and huge heads. The simple horns on the top of the snout (one or two, depending on species) are composed of densely compacted hair. The biggest species is the white rhinoceros of Africa, weighing over 3.5 tonnes (tons) and reaching 2 m (6½ ft) high at the shoulder; it is a grazer and has square lips for cropping grasses and herbs. The other African species, the black rhinoceros, is primarily a browser, as are the three Asian species. The skin of Indian and Javan rhinoceroses is heavily folded at the joints, giving an armour-plated appearance, while the Sumatran species has a covering of bristly hairs. All rhino species are endangered, through a combination of habitat loss and hunting for their horn, which is mistakenly thought to have aphrodisiac qualities.

There are four species of tapir (family Tapiridae), three occurring in South and Central America, and one in Southeast Asia (▷ illustration). As forest-dwellers, they are sturdily built to push their way through the dense undergrowth. Their most distinctive feature is the sensitive, flexible trunk, which is used to probe about in the forest for shoots, leaves and other food.

Pigs, peccaries and hippos

The eight species of pig or hog (family Suidae) are primarily woodland- or forest-dwellers, widely distributed throughout the Old World. They are stockily built animals with short necks and long heads, and their thick skins are sparsely covered by coarse bristly hairs. Wild pigs have well-developed canines, which in males form elongated, curved tusks. A pig's most distinctive feature is its long, muscular, flexible snout, which is used to turn over the soil and sniff out food on the forest floor. Pigs have notably high reproductive rates – females may have two or more litters a year, each with six or more young. Pigs generally live in family groups of four to six individuals, although the African wart hog and the Eurasian wild boar (ancestor of the domestic pig) often occur in much larger groups.

The three species of peccary (family Tayassuidae) are confined to Central and South America. They are similar to pigs in appearance and habits, and occupy the same kinds of niche as pigs do in the Old World.

There are two species of hippopotamus (family Hippopotamidae), both restricted to Africa. Weighing up to 4.5 tonnes (tons), the common hippopotamus is one of the heaviest terrestrial mammals. It is amphibious, spending most of the heat of the day resting partially submerged in rivers or lakes and emerging at night to graze on grasses and herbs. The pygmy hippopotamus is found only in the forests of West Africa, and is much smaller, weighing just 225 kg (500 lb). Unlike its larger relative, it is not aquatic and is less social.

Camels, giraffes and the pronghorn

The family Camelidae is today represented by just six species – the two Old World camels and four related species from South America. All have long, thin necks, small heads, slender snouts and cleft upper lips. The one-humped Arabian camel or dromedary is native to North Africa and the Middle East, but it survives today only in its domesticated form. The Bactrian camel of Central Asia has also been domesticated, and wild populations are now found only in the remote deserts of Mongolia and western China. Both species are adapted to arid desert conditions and are able to go for long periods without drinking – a week or so when working, several months at other times. Contrary to popular belief,

Brazilian tapir

Malaysian tapir

SEE ALSO
- MAMMALS p. 108
- ANIMAL BEHAVIOUR p. 124
- FARMING p. 132

The three species of musk deer (family Moschidae) are mainly found in high-altitude forest in central and eastern Asia. They do not have antlers but have long upper canine teeth that project down below the lips. The four species of chevrotain or mouse deer (family Tragulidae) are like tiny deer in appearance, growing to between 20 and 35 cm (8 and 14 in) at the shoulder. They are generally found near water in the tropical forests and swamps of Africa and Asia.

Bovids

The family Bovidae is a highly diverse group containing 128 species of antelope, cattle, sheep and various related species. Bovids are most numerous and diverse in Africa, but they are well represented in most parts of Eurasia and North America. Although bovids have adapted to a wide range of other habitats, the majority of species favour open grassland, scrub or desert. All species are ruminants and almost exclusively herbivorous. The males of all bovid species and the females of most carry horns, which have bony cores covered in a sheath of horny material; they are unbranched and never shed. The ancestors of the various species of domestic cattle – banteng, gaur (or Indian bison), yak and water buffalo – are generally rare and endangered in the wild, while the aurochs (the ancestor of the domestic cattle of Europe) is extinct.

Antelopes are typically long-legged, fast-running species, often with long horns that may be laid along the back when the animal is in full flight. They are mainly grassland species, but many have adapted to flooded grasslands. Sheep and goats, together with various relatives such as gorals, serows, takins and tahrs, are typically woolly or long-haired. Several species, such as chamois and ibex, are agile cliff- and mountain-dwellers. The duikers of Africa are generally small and solitary, often living in thick forest.

a camel's hump or humps are not used to store water but are composed of fatty tissue, providing an energy store that can be used in times of food shortage. The South American camelids are the vicuna and guanaco, and the latter's domesticated descendants, the llama and alpaca. The wild species are adapted to the high altitudes and difficult rocky terrain of the Andes.

The giraffe family (Giraffidae) consists of only two living species – the okapi (r⊳ illustration) and the giraffe. With its long slender legs and enormously elongated neck, the giraffe of sub-Saharan Africa is by far the tallest land animal, males growing to a height of about 5.5 m (18 ft). Giraffes have long tongues – nearly 45 cm (18 in) in length – enabling them to browse on the tops of bushes and trees.

The pronghorn of North America is the sole survivor of a New World family of herbivorous ruminants (Antilocapridae), similar in habits and appearance to the Old World antelopes. Males and most females carry horns that are rather like branched cattle horns, but the surrounding sheath is shed after each breeding season.

Deer

The thirty-eight species of the deer family (Cervidae) are widespread throughout the northern hemisphere and in South America. They have adapted to a broad range of habitat, from tropical forest to arctic tundra. Typically, deer are delicately built, with long legs terminating in cloven (split) hooves, and all are swift and elegant runners. All deer are ruminants, feeding mainly on leaves.

In most species the characteristic feature of deer – branching antlers – are carried by males alone. They consist of bone and grow yearly from knobs on the skull. While growing, they are covered in soft velvety fur, but once fully grown, the blood supply is cut off and the fur peels off, leaving only the hard bony core. During the breeding season (*rut*), the males of many deer species become territorial and defend harems of females. Once the rut is over, the antlers are shed.

ELEPHANTS

Within the geologically recent past, giant mastodons and mammoths occurred in the New World and across northern Eurasia. Today, the order Proboscidea is represented by just two species – the Asian elephant of India and Southeast Asia and the African elephant of sub-Saharan Africa. Both African and Asian species live in herds in habitats from forest to savannah, and are entirely vegetarian.

The African elephant is the largest living land animal: a large male may stand over 3.5 m (11½ ft) at the shoulder, and weigh around 7 tonnes (tons). The Asian elephant is smaller, with a shoulder height of 3 m (10 ft) and weighing up to 6 tonnes. The African elephant is further distinguished by its larger ears and tusks, sparser hair and less domed head. Asian elephants have long been tamed and used in forestry and as ceremonial beasts.

An elephant's trunk is formed by an enormous elongation of the nose and upper lip. The nostrils are at the tip, and the sensitive grasping lip can be used to pluck foliage or to pick up objects as small as a nut. As well as for gathering food and drinking, the trunk is used in communication. An elephant's tusks are highly modified teeth – continuously growing upper incisors. The largest tusks measure around 3.5 m (11½ ft), but relentless hunting has meant that huge 'tuskers' are now rare.

African elephant

Indian elephant

Rodents

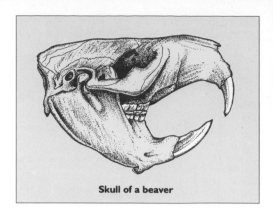

Skull of a beaver

Rodents are easily the most numerous mammals in the world, with many species having populations running into millions. Because species such as rats and mice live alongside humans, they also have the widest distribution of any wild mammals.

SEE ALSO

● MAMMALS p. 108

The order Rodentia is by far the largest order of mammals, containing almost 1700 species in some 30 families. Rodents account for about 40% of all known mammal species, and occur on all continents except Antarctica.

Common features

Despite the large number of species, rodents are remarkably uniform in structure. All have a similar arrangement of the teeth, with two pairs of incisors, one above and one below, then a gap before the cheek teeth – the canines and the anterior premolars are missing (▷ illustration). In all species the characteristic incisors grow continuously throughout the animal's life. They are coated with enamel on the outside surface only, and therefore wear down faster on the inside; and because the upper pair grow over the lower pair and constantly work against them, the incisors are self-sharpening. Many species of rodent have cheek pouches, used for carrying food.

Rodents are primarily vegetarian, feeding on seeds, leaves, roots and other plant matter. Although some species are extremely specialized, rodents in general eat a remarkable variety of foods. Many desert-dwelling species – the Australian native mice, for example – can live their entire lives without ever drinking. They manage to derive all the water they need from the seeds and grains upon which they feed.

Most rodents are relatively small. The largest – the capybara – grows to the size of a sheep (▷ photo), but the majority of species weigh less than 1 kg (2.2 lb) and there are many weighing less than 10 g (⅓ oz).

Squirrels and squirrel-like rodents

Squirrels are found in most parts of the world except Australia, but are particularly diverse in Asia, where the majority are tree-dwelling and very agile. Squirrels are generally keen-sighted, and most species are active by day and often extremely brightly coloured. Some species – the flying squirrels – are capable of gliding on a membrane stretched between the front and hind feet.

Ground squirrels are particularly widespread in North America, and some species – the prairie dogs – are often highly gregarious. Prairie dogs live in huge colonies known as 'towns', which sometimes have populations running into millions and in which a complex system of social organization operates. At the turn of the 20th century a single town in Texas was estimated to cover 64 000 km² (25 000 sq mi) and to contain 400 million individuals.

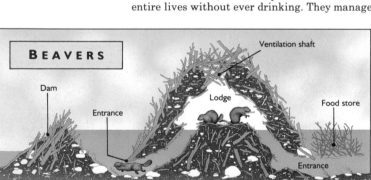

BEAVERS

Ventilation shaft

Dam

Entrance

Lodge

Food store

Entrance

With the exception of man, no mammal is capable of modifying its environment as dramatically as the beavers of North America and northern Eurasia. The aim of these accomplished engineers is to construct a family home, complete with moat, that is proof against predators and the rigours of winter.

To create an artificial lake, beavers obstruct the course of a stream by building a dam. This is made of felled logs, branches and twigs, shored up by layers of mud, gravel and larger stones. The upper surface of the dam is then waterproofed with a coating of mud, but the task of maintaining and raising the dam is continuous and may spread over several generations.

Beavers may live in burrows dug into the banks of a stream, but frequently they construct special living quarters known as lodges within their artificial lakes. These are built along the same lines as their dams, but ventilation is provided by looser construction on the top of the mound. The floor of the lodge is above the level of the water, while access is provided by underwater tunnels. Nearby is a larder of branches and stems harvested during the summer and autumn. Beavers choose the site for their dam with care, ensuring that their lake is sufficiently deep that it does not freeze to the bottom even in the coldest days of winter. In this way they are certain to have uninterrupted access to their cache of food.

RODENTS AND ECONOMICS

The impact of rodents on humankind has chiefly been negative. The brown rat, black rat and house mouse in particular cause billions of dollars' worth of damage to crops, stored foodstuffs and property. In the USA alone the damage caused by the brown rat has been put at a billion dollars a year.

Rats also spread disease. Fleas carried by rats in turn carried the bacterium responsible for bubonic plague, the disease that killed a third of the population of Europe in the 14th century and 11 million people in India between 1892 and 1918. Other diseases passed to humans by rats include Rocky Mountain spotted fever and leptospirosis (sewerman's disease).

Rodents have proved useful in some ways, however. Several rodents, such as the cane rat in West Africa and the cavy (or guinea pig) in South America, are important food animals. Others are important fur-bearers, the chinchilla being the most valuable. The domesticated brown rat is one of the most important laboratory animals, used extensively for research and in testing products such as medicines, cosmetics and poisons.

The largest of the squirrels are the marmots, which can grow to 7.5 kg (16 lb). They are found over much of the northern hemisphere, particularly in mountainous areas. Unlike the majority of rodents, marmots hibernate, and several species make hay in summer and store it underground for use in winter during spells of mild weather.

The two species of beaver are among the larger rodents. They are well adapted to their semi-aquatic life style: the ears and nostrils can be closed when the animal is submerged, while the webbed hind feet and paddle-shaped tail provide excellent propulsion and control when swimming (⊳ illustration).

Rats, mice and their relatives

Rats and mice are found in almost all parts of the world and have been introduced into regions where they do not occur naturally. Characterized by their long snouts and naked scaly tails, they are among the most successful and adaptable of all mammals. Their impact on humans has chiefly been negative, spreading diseases and causing damage to crops and property (⊳ box).

Because of their large numbers, rodents such as voles and lemmings are important prey for owls, foxes and many other predators. In northern areas rodent populations are often cyclical, building up over periods of three to four years into plague proportions, before crashing when they overexploit their food supply. This population crash is often followed by that of their predators.

Many Norway lemmings perish in the course of mass emigrations triggered every four years or so by soaring populations: hence the myth of the lemming's suicidal instincts.

Perhaps the most bizarre rodents are those belonging to the African mole rat family. Living entirely in underground burrows and feeding on plant roots and bulbs, they are virtually blind, but they are superb diggers and can even gnaw their way through soil. Naked mole rats work together in teams, and are unique among mammals in showing a system of social organization similar to that of social insects such as bees and ants.

Cavies and porcupines

The cavies, or guinea pigs, are ground-dwelling rodents found only in South America. Most species are social, and have the rather thick-set body form of the domestic guinea pig. Although in a separate family, the capybara of South America – the largest of the rodents – has the appearance of a giant guinea pig (⊳ photo). It is semi-aquatic and has partially webbed feet; it too is a social animal, always living in family groups.

RABBITS, HARES AND PIKAS

The order Lagomorpha is made up of just two families: some 44 species of rabbit and hare (Leporidae) and 14 species of pika (Ochotonidae). Unlike rodents, the lagomorphs have two pairs of incisors in the upper jaw, although only one is functional, the other being tiny and undeveloped. All lagomorphs are herbivorous, and have the curious habit of eating their own fecal pellets, thus gaining extra nutritional value from their food. They live in a wide variety of habitats, including woodlands and swamps, but generally favour open grassy habitats.

Rabbits and hares are highly successful and adaptable mammals. The hind limbs are strong and disproportionately large, giving these animals their swift bounding movement. Although the names are often used loosely, 'rabbit' is usually used to describe those species that live in burrows and give birth to small undeveloped young. Hares, on the other hand, live in shallow surface depressions known as forms, and their young are well developed at

birth, with eyes already open and a full coat of hair. As well as enhancing hearing, the large ears typical of rabbits and hares help species that live in dry, hot areas to disperse excess heat.

One species, the European rabbit, has been domesticated. It has been introduced into areas of the world where it is not native and has become a serious pest, causing widespread damage to grasslands and crops. Attempts to control it have included the introduction of the myxomatosis virus, a disease originally found in a South American species of rabbit.

Pikas, or conies, have short rounded ears, a rounded body, and a stubby tail. All species live on rocky slopes, mostly in the mountainous parts of northern and central Asia, with two species occurring in western North America. They collect green plants in summer, which they dry and store away for use in the colder months, but they do not hibernate. The Tibetan pika occupies one of the highest habitats of any mammal – up to 6000 m (20 000 ft) in the Himalaya.

Most species of porcupine are active by night, and feed on a variety of plant matter. They are characterized by the long spines (formed from modified hair) that grow thickly on the back and sides. The African and Asian species have particularly long spines, which can grow to 35 cm (14 in) in length. The New World porcupines are broadly similar in appearance to the Old World species, but – unlike the latter – most of them are tree-dwelling.

A capybara surrounded by caymans. Weighing up to 66 kg (146 lb) and growing up to 1.3 m (4 ft 3 in) in length, the capybara of South America is the largest living rodent.
(Jacana)

Marine Mammals

In the course of evolution, some mammals returned to the sea, where millions of years previously their fish ancestors had lived. Some, such as seals, have to return to land to breed, but whales, manatees and others are entirely aquatic: they eat, sleep and give birth in water.

SEE ALSO

● MAMMALS p. 108
● AQUATIC ECOSYSTEMS p. 130

Internally the bones and organs of marine mammals all closely resemble those of land mammals, and – although superficially fish-like – their paddles are in fact modified limbs. Like other mammals, they breathe by taking in oxygen from the air, and so have to return to the surface at intervals to breathe.

Manatees and the dugong

The order Sirenia contains just four species – a single species of dugong (family Dugongidae), and three species of manatee (family Trichechidae). The sirenians are also known as sea cows, as they are the only herbivorous marine mammals, feeding mainly on seaweed and other marine plants. Manatees are found in the tropical and subtropical coastal waters of the Atlantic and adjacent river systems, while the dugong is found at similar latitudes in the Indian Ocean, the Red Sea and the western Pacific.

Sirenians have heavy but streamlined bodies, and grow to about 4 m (13 ft) in length. The fore limbs are modified into paddles, and the hind limbs are absent. The tail is horizontally flattened – the dugong's into a crescent-shaped fluke, the manatees' into an oval fluke. Although the body is virtually hairless, the muzzle is covered in thick stiff whiskers. The dugong has a flexible overhanging upper lip, which it uses to uproot clumps of seaweed and other plants, and males have tusks formed from the incisor teeth. Manatees have a deeply split upper lip, allowing each half to be moved independently.

Seals and the walrus

The order Pinnipedia includes three families: the eared seal family (Otariidae) – distinguished by the possession of external ears – which includes 14 species of fur seal and sea lion; 18 species of earless or 'true' seals (family Phocidae); and the single species of the walrus family (Odobenidae). All species are predatory, feeding mainly on fish and squid.

The hands and feet of pinnipeds are flattened into flippers, and the body is streamlined. All species have thick layers of insulating blubber, and most species have a covering of coarse hair to protect the skin when on shore. Although pinnipeds are more at home in water, all species are capable of moving on land, and they have to return to the shore to breed. Most pinnipeds gather annually at traditional breeding grounds, where males (generally much larger than females) become highly territorial and seek to defend harems of females.

Walruses are usually found in the shallow coastal waters of the Arctic. Male walruses can grow to around 3.5 m (11½ ft) and weigh around 1.5 tonnes (tons). Tusks formed from the upper canine teeth are present in both sexes, and they are particularly large in males, which use them to spar with rivals in the breeding season.

Toothed whales

The order Cetacea is divided into two groups: one of toothed whales (dolphins, porpoises and most of the smaller whales); the other of baleen whales, which contains most of the giants of the sea. The cetaceans spend their entire lives in water, and are found in all oceans as well as a few of the larger river systems. They have an insulating layer of blubber and their fore limbs are modified into paddles, and instead of hind limbs they have a horizontally flattened tail fluke.

The five families of toothed whales include the dolphin and porpoise family (Delphinidae, 40 species); the river dolphin family (Platanistidae, 6 species); and three families of whales – sperm whales (Physeteridae, 3 species), white whales (Monodontidae, 2 species), and beaked whales (Ziphiidae, 18 species). All species have teeth, ranging from a single pair in some of the beaked whales to as many as 260 in some dolphin species, and they feed mainly on fish, octopus and squid. In order to gauge the position of surrounding objects, including prey, most species use a sonar system similar to the echolocation used by bats (▷ p. 112), monitoring the echoes from the high-pitched squeaks and clicks that they emit.

Most dolphins are characterized by their streamlined form and beaked snouts. They are extremely gregarious, forming schools sometimes of over a hundred individuals. Dolphins generally grow to between 2.5 and 4 m (8¼ and 13 ft) and the largest of them – the killer whale – can grow to over 9 m (30 ft). Porpoises are very similar to dolphins, but are generally shorter and stockier, and do not have a beaked snout. They are usually found in coastal waters, often venturing up rivers for several kilometres.

The blue whale, the largest animal ever to inhabit the earth. A blue whale calf grows up to 9 m (30 ft) in 7 months, and may finally reach a length of around 35 m (115 ft) and a weight of up to 130 tonnes (tons). These gigantic creatures feed only during the summer months, but during this time they may consume over 2 tonnes of food a day.

Franciscana (*Pontoporia blainvillei*), a very long-beaked species from the shallow coastal waters of eastern South America.

Vaquita (*Phocoena sinus*), an extremely rare species not sighted since 1986 and now possibly extinct. In the past thousands of these porpoises became accidentally ensnared in fishermen's nets.

Commerson's dolphin (*Cephalorhynchus commersonii*)

...mon dolphin (...phinus delphis), ...dwide in ...perate and tropical seas. ...e intelligent animals often congregate in large ...ols of several hundred individuals, and they ...e expert use of sonar (echolocation) when ...ing fish or squid.

...r whale (*Orcinus orca*), the largest of the dolphin ...y at up to 9.5 m (31 ft) in length. Killer whales ...lso the largest predators of warm-blooded ..., moving in packs to hunt for seals, ...uins and even other ...e species.

Bottlenose dolphin (*Tursiops truncatus*), the species widely known for its appearances in zoos and on TV and film.

Dall's porpoise (*Phocoenoides dalli*), one of the larger and heavier porpoises, growing to over 2 m (6½ ft) in length.

A SELECTION OF DOLPHINS AND PORPOISES

River dolphins are found in the major river systems of India, South America and China. They have long slender beaks and domed foreheads. Because their native rivers are muddy and murky, they are heavily dependent on echolocation to avoid obstacles and detect prey.

The largest of the toothed whales is the sperm whale. Males formerly grew to about 24 m (79 ft), but intensive hunting has led to a considerable decrease in size. The most striking feature of the sperm whale is its huge squarish head, which contains the largest brain of any animal – weighing around 9.2 kg (over 20 lb). The majority of the head, however, is filled with spermaceti wax – nearly 2000 litres of it – which gives the whale its name. The precise function of this wax is not known, but it may be involved in sound transmission, or help to regulate buoyancy during dives.

The two species of white whale are restricted to Arctic coastal waters. One of them, the narwhal, has an extraordinary spiral tusk, which may grow to over 2.5 m (8¼ ft). It is in fact a hugely elongated upper incisor, the precise function of which is unclear.

Baleen whales

There are three families of baleen whales: the single species of the grey whale family (Eschrichtidae) of the coastal waters of the northern Pacific; three species of right whale (Balaenidae); and six species of rorqual whale (Balaenopteridae). Despite their great size, all baleen species feed by filtering krill (tiny planktonic crustaceans) and other planktonic animals from sea water. Their teeth are replaced by hundreds of sheets of horny brush-like material known as *baleen* (or *whalebone*), which hang from the upper jaw. The inner edges of these sheets are fringed with long fibres, which mat together to form a sieve.

Rorquals are distinguished from other baleen whales by the many grooves – up to 94 in the case of the blue whale – running along the throat. Humpback whales are usually seen in family groups of three or four members, and are great migrants, moving from their summer feeding grounds off Alaska to spend the winter in the tropical waters off Hawaii. Here they produce calves conceived during the previous breeding season, mate, and indulge in their famous singing. Their complex songs usually last for about 10 minutes, and may be repeated for hours on end. Their purpose is not clear, but they may aid identification and help to coordinate movement during migration.

Right whales are so called because they were regarded by whalers as the 'right' whales to kill: they are stockier and less streamlined than other baleen whales, and so more easily overtaken. They lack throat furrows and have enormous heads, which accommodate 700 baleen plates. Like other large whales, right whales have been hunted commercially to the point of extinction.

Crabeater seals are found in enormous numbers on the desolate brink of the Antarctic pack ice. In spite of their name, they in fact feed on krill (planktonic crustaceans) strained from the water by means of their sieve-like teeth.

Primates

Although the similarity between humans and apes had long been recognized, in the past the likeness was regarded by many as purely coincidental and of no great significance. Only after Darwin (▷ p. 84) was the true relationship between man and apes generally accepted.

The order Primates consists of around 180 species, the majority of which are confined to the tropical regions of the world. Within the order, two groups or suborders are recognized: the *lower primates* (or *prosimians*), which include lemurs and lorises, and the *higher primates* (also known as *simians* or *anthropoids*), which include tarsiers, monkeys, apes and man.

Primate characteristics

Although highly varied in form, primates are distinguished as a group by certain common characteristics. While smell is the most important sense for most ground-living mammals, the primates typically have a well-developed visual system, with forward-facing eyes and binocular vision, and a highly refined sense of touch, with sensitive tactile pads on fingers and toes and flat nails rather than claws. The large brains of primates, notable for the complexity and elaboration of the cerebral cortex, has resulted in the development of intelligence and flexible patterns of behaviour, particularly in the higher primates.

Another characteristic primate feature is their prehensile (grasping) hands and feet, vital for moving around safely in trees, and the opposable thumb and big toe, which are capable of being moved freely and rotated. Primates usually have single births or twins, and all have a long life cycle and gestation period relative to their size. Even more remarkable is the length of time the young remain psychologically dependent on their parents – 2½ years in lemurs, 3½–4 years in monkeys, 3–5 years in apes, and 12–14 years or more in humans.

Lower primates

There are five families of lemur with a total of 21 species. Most are confined to the forests of Madagascar, although some have been introduced into the nearby Comoro Islands. Lemurs are primarily arboreal but may come down to the ground to look for food. Their diet includes insects, small vertebrates, fruit buds, shoots, leaves and bark. Many species are nocturnal.

The smallest are the mouse lemurs, with a head-and-body length of 12.5–15 cm (5–6 in), while the true lemurs grow to around 45 cm (18 in). The largest lemur is the indri, which grows up to 90 cm (3 ft) long; unlike other lemurs, which have long tails, it is almost tailless. The closely related sifakas are around half their size, and can leap considerable distances from tree to tree – up to 10 m (33 ft) – aided by gliding membranes. The extremely rare aye-aye has large naked ears and long, slender fingers, particularly the third one. It taps on tree trunks to locate insect larvae, listens for movement, and then uses its long finger to extract its prey.

The 10 species of the family Lorisidae – the lorises, pottos and galagos (or bushbabies) – are found in Africa and southern Asia. They are largely nocturnal and arboreal, with large, round eyes. The lorises and pottos are small (less than 40 cm / 16 in long), and have no tails. Although slow-moving and not known to leap or jump, they are skilled climbers. Feeding largely on insects, they approach their prey stealthily and then seize it with their hands. The galagos, by contrast, are agile leapers and have long furry tails. The largest species, the greater galago, grows to 37 cm (14½ in) plus a tail of 47 cm (18½ in). Galagos eat a wide variety of insects and other small animals, as well as gums and nectar.

Tarsiers

The three closely related species of tarsier (family Tarsiidae) are found in the forests and other thickly vegetated habitats of the Philippines and Indonesia. They are at the most 16 cm (6½ in) long, with a naked tail up to 27 cm (11 in). Their most obvious features are their huge eyes, which are 16 mm (⅔ in) in diameter. They have short arms and long legs, and the fingers and toes are all tipped with soft round pads enabling them to grip almost any surface. They are excellent jumpers – they can leap distances of 1.7 m (5½ ft) on the ground and can make even greater leaps from tree to tree.

New World monkeys

The only non-human primates found in the New World are the marmosets and tamarins (family

Verreaux's sifaka, a leaping lemur of western and southern Madagascar. These lemurs live in small troops with well-defined territories. They are active by day, spending their time feeding, resting and sun-bathing. (Jacana)

Callitrichidae) and the cebid monkeys (▷ below). In contrast to the Old World monkeys, these species are characterized by flat noses with widely spaced nostrils. The 20 species of marmoset and tamarin are the smallest of the higher primates, with a body length of 13–37 cm (5¼–14½ in) and long tails. Many have tufts or ruffs of fur round their heads, and all have claws on hands and feet, with a flat nail only on the big toe. They live mostly in tropical forest, and like most higher primates they are active by day; they are mainly arboreal, bounding swiftly through the trees rather like squirrels. They have a varied diet including nuts, insects, bark and sap, and are sociable animals, living in small family groups.

The 31 species of the family Cebidae include capuchins, howlers, spider monkeys and woolly monkeys. They are mostly confined to the tropical forests of South America and are largely arboreal. Apart from the uakari, they all have long, often strongly prehensile tails, which serve as a fifth limb when swinging through the forest. They range in size from the squirrel monkeys, which are around the size of marmosets, to the massive howler monkeys, with a body length of 80–90 cm (32–36 in). Howlers are noted for their powerful voices, which can be heard up to 3 km (1.9 mi) away. All cebids are social, living in family-based groups with much visual and vocal communication. Their diet is largely vegetarian.

The Old World monkeys

The 70 or so species of Old World monkey (family Cercopithecidae) include the macaques, mandrills, mangabeys and others. They are found in Africa, Asia and Indonesia, in a much greater range of habitats than the South American monkeys. All walk on all fours and have thin noses with forward-pointing nostrils, and none have prehensile tails. Some species, such as baboons, are found in open, often rocky, arid areas, and spend most of their time on the ground.

The Old World monkeys are generally larger than the South American primates, and often have heavy manes and bare buttock pads, sometimes brightly coloured. The male proboscis monkey of Borneo has a huge pendulous nose that straightens out when it makes its loud honking call. The females are generally smaller – sometimes only half the size – and less brightly coloured, with lighter manes or none at all. Old World monkeys are primarily vegetarian, but some may supplement their diet with insects and small animals.

Apes

All apes have protruding jaws and lack tails, but the slender, agile gibbons – the lesser apes – are otherwise very different from the sturdy, powerful great apes. The nine species of gibbon (family Hylobatidae) are all found in the forests of Southeast Asia and Indonesia. They are perhaps the best adapted of all mammals for moving swiftly through the forest canopy, using their extremely long arms and hooked hands to swing from branch to branch. The largest is the siamang, with a body length of 90 cm (3 ft) and a spread of 1.5 m (nearly 5 ft) from hand to hand. Most male gibbons have an inflatable throat sac used to amplify their voice. The loud calls are important both for communicating within the family group and for defining their territory. Gibbons are primarily fruit eaters, and live in family groups of two to six.

The four species of great ape are our closest living relatives in the animal kingdom. The arboreal orang-utan (family Pongidae) is confined to the rainforests of Borneo and Sumatra; it is the second largest primate, weighing up to 90 kg (almost 200 lb). Males are much larger and heavier than females, and as they grow old they develop distinctive cheek flaps. Orang-utans live alone or in small family groups. Fruit is their staple diet.

The common chimpanzee is found in Africa, having a relatively wide range in woodland and forest south of the Sahara and north and east of the Zaïre River, while the pygmy chimpanzee is found only in Zaïre. Like gorillas and man (the other members of the family Hominidae), chimpanzees are largely terrestrial, and both chimpanzees and gorillas walk on the knuckles of their hands. Chimpanzees are intelligent and social animals, using a wide range of gestures and sound for communication. They live in groups of varying composition, sometimes having as many as 50 members. When standing, the male can measure up to 1.7 m (5 ft 8 in) and is strongly built with long powerful arms. They eat a wide range of food, basically vegetarian, but also including insects, birds' eggs, and small birds and mammals. They use sticks as tools to winkle termites or ants from their mounds, hurl stones at intruders, and use leaves as sponges to soak up water.

The largest of the primates is the gorilla (▷ photo), found in the forests of the Zaïre basin, with isolated populations of mountain gorillas on the slopes of the mountains between Rwanda and Zaïre. A male gorilla may measure up to 175 cm (70 in) around the chest and weigh up to 275 kg (605 lb). Although females and young gorillas climb trees, males rarely do so because of their size. Gorillas are almost exclusively vegetarian in their diet; like chimpanzees, they build a nest each night to sleep in.

SEE ALSO

● EVOLUTION p. 84
● MAMMALS p. 108
● ANIMAL BEHAVIOUR p. 124
● THE HUMAN ORGANISM pp. 134–57
● HUMAN PREHISTORY p. 226

A mature male gorilla or 'silverback'. Gorillas live in social groups, usually presided over by a silverback, but very little aggression is shown. If another group is encountered, the silverbacks first stare at their rivals; if this fails to deter them, they display by uttering loud cries, throwing leaves in the air, beating their chests, and finally running sideways, tearing up vegetation, and banging their hands on the ground. Only if this intimidation fails do the rivals come to blows.

Animal Behaviour

In order to survive and thrive, animals must successfully perform a number of vital activities. At various times an animal may have to find and gather food, defend a territory or nest site, find and court a mate, contest a position within a social hierarchy, and ward off the unwelcome attentions of predators.

Most animals are born with at least some of the responses appropriate to the various stimuli they encounter in their environment 'built in' to their nervous system: bees construct combs, male sticklebacks mate, and female mice care for their young, all without previous experience. Such behaviour is *instinctive* and must be encoded in the animal's genetic material (▷ p. 86). *Learning* occurs when an animal shows a beneficial change of behaviour as a result of experience: for example, birds learn to avoid unpleasant-tasting insects, and rats learn to avoid food that makes them ill. Learning involves interaction with the environment and allows animals to modify their behaviour to suit changing or variable conditions.

Animal communication

An astonishing array of communication signals are to be seen in the animal kingdom. One of the most important functions of such signals is to bring the sexes together for reproduction: it is the means by which the species, sex, reproductive state and sometimes even the particular individuals concerned are identified. *Courtship* often involves complex displays in which one or both partners posture and perhaps call to each other. Such displays enable partners to learn to recognize each other and to assess each other's suitability as mates. Communication is also important in spacing out animals, in marking territorial boundaries and in establishing a position within a social hierarchy. Size or pitch of voice may indicate competitive status, as may the possession of weapons such as antlers or tusks.

The form of communication signal differs depending on the information to be conveyed, the distance over which it has to travel, and the habitat of the animals concerned. *Chemical signals* depend on the sense of smell and sometimes on the sense of taste; they may be used for long-term signalling, as when mammals such as hyenas and deer mark their territory, while the food trails left by ants are a form of short-term signalling. The main advantage of *acoustic signals* is that they can change very rapidly in pitch and intensity, and so can be used to convey a wide range of information. *Visual signals* can be turned on and off very rapidly but can generally only be used in daytime and are easily blocked by objects such as trees; such signals are often bright or consist of jerky movements to make them more conspicuous. *Tactile signals* can only be used close at hand. They are particularly important among primates as indications of friendship and appeasement. *Vibration signals* are effective over short distances; male orb-web spiders indicate their presence to females by vibrating their webs in a characteristic way, thus dissuading females from treating them as prey.

Territory, mating and social organization

All animals require an adequate supply of various essential resources, such as shelter, food and nesting materials. In order to secure these in sufficient quantities, it may be necessary for one or more animals to keep a particular area for their sole use and to keep out other members of the same species. An area in which vital resources are defended in this way is known as a *territory*.

Whether a male mates with one or more females, or vice versa, often depends on the type of parental care the male provides. In *polygynous species*, such as red deer and elephant seals, each male mates with a number of females and generally shows no parental care after mating; males are often highly territorial, fighting with one another to defend groups (*harems*) of several females. Where the male is needed to help feed the young, as is the case with many birds, the common mating system is *monogamy*, where one male mates with a single female.

THE DANCE OF THE HONEYBEE

One of the most astonishing feats of communication in the whole of the animal kingdom is the 'dance language' of honeybees. When a worker bee finds a rich supply of food, she communicates a variety of information about it to her fellow workers by performing a dance inside the dark hive. If the food is within about 50 m (164 ft) of the hive, she performs a *round dance* – she dances in a circle, first one way, then the other. Other workers follow the dance, keeping in touch with the dancer by means of their antennae. They pick up the odour of the flowers she has visited by her scent and their taste from small amounts of food that she regurgitates. The recruits then fly out of the hive and search for the right smell within a 50-metre radius.

If the food is more distant, the returning worker performs a *waggle dance*, in the form of a figure-of-eight with a straightened central bar. During the straight part of the dance, she waggles her abdomen to and fro, producing bursts of sound. The further away from the hive the food is, the slower the rate at which the bee dances; the richer the food supply, the more intense the waggle and the sound produced. The angle at which the straight part of the dance is performed indicates the direction of the food source. The top of the comb is equivalent to the position of the sun outside, and the dance is performed at the same angle to this vertical position as the food source is to the sun. This symbolic dance can therefore code for the direction, distance and abundance of the food source, and – as in the round dance – odour cues indicate its nature.

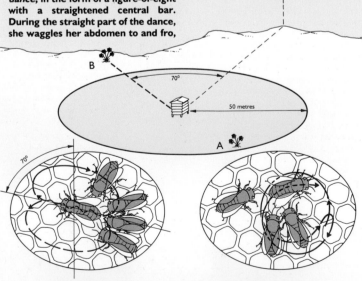

Living in social groups has many advantages. Important among these is that some degree of cooperation is possible – in finding and collecting food, in looking out for danger, and in defence against predators. One of the simplest types of social group is the *family*, where both parents remain with the young for a given period of time. Examples of this kind of family are the groups formed by jackals, swans and many songbirds. Social insects – some bees and wasps, ants, and termites (⊳ illustration) – live in large groups and show extreme division of labour, with only one individual, the queen, reproducing. Most members of a colony are sterile and do not reproduce; instead they devote themselves to foraging and to building, maintaining and defending the colony.

Finding food

Obtaining food of an appropriate kind and in adequate quantities is an essential activity for all animals. Many animals are *specialist feeders*, taking either a single kind of food or a narrow range of foods: koalas feed exclusively on the leaves of a few species of eucalyptus, pandas mainly on bamboo shoots. At the other extreme, there are *generalist feeders*, such as rats, pigs and raccoons, which feed opportunistically on a wide range of foods.

In order to obtain food, many animals rely solely or partly on *predation* – killing and eating a member of another species. *Sit-and-wait* or *ambush predators* (e.g. praying mantises) conceal themselves in places that are likely to be visited by their prey and then seize the unsuspecting victim as it comes into range. Predators such as lions and cheetahs normally have to reveal themselves to their prey before launching a final attack, but they often minimize the extent of open pursuit by stalking and thereby greatly increase their chances of success.

Defence

For many animals the first line of defence is to remain inconspicuous and so avoid detection. Usually this is achieved by blending in with the environment by means of some form of *camouflage*. However, various animals that are dangerous or unpleasant to eat (e.g. wasps, sea slugs) may advertise their unpalatability by adopting bright *warning coloration*. Some harmless animals such as hoverflies benefit by mimicking the warning colours of dangerous animals.

Once detected by a predator, relatively slow-moving or immobile animals with body armour or some similar means of protection (e.g. snails, turtles) may sit tight, withdrawing or hiding vulnerable parts if possible. Others (e.g. under-wing moths) attempt to startle their assailants by exposing areas of bright *flash coloration*. When cornered, animals such as rattlesnakes and toads may attempt to intimidate a predator by some form of *threat display*. Many predators lose interest in dead prey, so a number of animals, including various snakes and opossums, may escape attack by pretending to be dead (*death-feigning*). If an attack cannot be avoided, an animal may yet save itself by some system of damage limitation. Many butterflies have small eye-spots near the tips of their wings, which deflect bird pecks away from the head or body, while some lizards shed their tails.

Parasitism and symbiosis

Virtually all living organisms, plants as well as animals, are involved in highly intimate associations with members of other species. Such associations typically result in clear-cut patterns of harm and benefit for the organisms concerned. In *parasitism*, one species (the *parasite*) lives in or on another species (the *host*). The host is harmed by the presence of the parasite, and generally survives less well and/or produces fewer offspring. The parasite, on the other hand, benefits from the relationship, usually gaining food or other resources from the host's body. *Symbiosis* or *mutualism* is a more balanced kind of partnership in which the participating species usually survive and reproduce more successfully when living symbiotically than when living apart.

Migration and hibernation

Many animals make movements between different habitats known as *migrations*; these display a cyclical pattern, and are usually triggered by seasonal or other factors that recur at more or less fixed intervals. Some animals migrate to escape harsh winters or hot summers, others to find suitable breeding or feeding grounds. Some migrants such as birds move annually between summer breeding grounds and overwintering sites, often returning to the same areas each year, while salmon and eels take several years to complete their migrations. The most significant mammal migrants are large herbivores such as caribou, wildebeest and zebra.

Some amphibians, reptiles and mammals endure harsh winter conditions by *hibernating*. Such animals build special nests or find shelter, and become torpid – they enter a sleep-like state in which both heart rate and respiration are slowed, and in mammals the body temperature falls. Many hibernators remain inactive for several months, living on fat stores built up before hibernation.

SEE ALSO

● INVERTEBRATES pp. 94–9
● FISHES p. 100
● AMPHIBIANS p. 102
● REPTILES p. 103
● BIRDS p. 106
● MAMMALS pp. 108–23

TERMITE MOUNDS

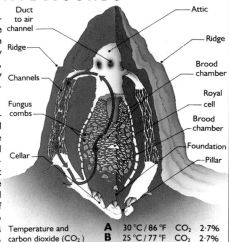

Termites are the true masterbuilders of the insect world. The enormous mounds of the African *Macrotermes* species may measure over 8 m (26 ft) in height, and even an average colony may number around two million individuals.

The walls of the mound of *Macrotermes bellicosus* are made of soil particles mined from below by the tiny worker termites and mixed with saliva to form a hard, brick-like substance, resistant to all but the most persistent assailant. The nest proper, lying in the central part of the mound, consists of a maze of passages giving access to innumerable chambers of various kinds, each with a special function in the running of the colony: brood chambers where the larvae hatch and are nourished; special 'gardens' where fungi are cultivated on combs of wood particles to provide food for the colony; and a royal cell, where the queen lives with the king, laying thousands of eggs to ensure the continuance of the colony.

Labels: Duct to air channel, Attic, Ridge, Ridge, Brood chamber, Channels, Royal cell, Fungus combs, Brood chamber, Cellar, Foundation, Pillar

Temperature and carbon dioxide (CO_2) content of circulating air:		
A	30 °C / 86 °F	CO_2 2·7%
B	25 °C / 77 °F	CO_2 2·7%
C	24 °C / 75 °F	CO_2 0·8%

As well as affording protection against intruders, the mound is so constructed as to provide a perfectly balanced 'microclimate', essential to the survival of its vulnerable inhabitants. The temperature, humidity and freshness of the atmosphere are all precisely regulated. The air within the nest, warmed by the metabolic activity of both termites and fungi to a steady temperature of around 30 °C (86 °F), moves by convection upwards into the attic area. It then passes down narrow channels within ridges in the mound walls, losing heat to the exterior and exchanging carbon dioxide for oxygen as it does so. Finally the air – now cooler and fresher – enters the inhabited area from below, to be circulated anew.

The Biosphere

The biosphere is the layer around our planet in which all living organisms exist. It contains all the different ecosystems, and all the water, minerals, oxygen, nitrogen, phosphorus and other nutrients that living things need in order to survive. It surrounds the earth like a blanket, regulating the temperature by allowing the sun's rays to enter and by letting waste heat back into space.

Everything in the biosphere is interrelated. The atmosphere helps to purify water by recycling it in the hydrological cycle (⊳ p. 75), and also provides carbon dioxide for plant photosynthesis (⊳ p. 88) and oxygen for respiration in both plants and animals. Plants provide food for animals as well as releasing oxygen (the waste product of photosynthesis) for them to breathe. The soil provides nutrients and water for plants, and when the plants die they release the nutrients back into the soil.

Niches, communities and ecosystems

All the millions of different species of plant and animal exist within the biosphere in an orderly and precise fashion. Each species has evolved to take advantage of a particular habitat and a particular position in a food chain, and this is called its *ecological niche*. By remaining in its ecological niche a species maximizes its chance of survival, for within its niche it will usually find all requirements necessary for life. In theory, each species will occupy a separate niche, so minimizing competition with other species. In practice, however, different niche spaces may overlap, and where this occurs competition for resources takes place.

Each part of the biosphere contains particular combinations of climate and soil. These areas provide life-support conditions for groups of species that have adapted to those environments, and so may be said to have broadly similar ecological niches. Such groups of species are called *communities*. There are many thousands of different communities, but they can broadly be divided into terrestrial (forest, grassland, desert) and aquatic (frestwater and marine); ⊳ pp. 128–31.

An *ecosystem* is a self-regulating natural community of living organisms (the *biotic* components) interacting both with one another and with the non-living (*abiotic* or physical) environment that surrounds them. Ecosystems are simplified models of the real world, but by studying them we can often gain a better idea of how, for example, forests, lakes and grasslands actually function as complex groups of interrelated species.

The energy for life

Energy is the driving force behind all life in the biosphere. The sun provides 99.99% of all the radiant energy required for life on earth; the remaining 0.01% comes from heat contained within the planet (⊳ p. 60). Because the sun's energy has existed for at least 4600 million years and will probably continue as far again into the future, it is described as an *infinite resource*. The sun's radiant energy arrives at the outer edge of the atmosphere as very high-energy short-wave radiation. As this radiation travels through the atmosphere about half of its energy is absorbed, scattered and reflected by water vapour. At the outer edge of the atmosphere the ozone layer (⊳ p. 61) plays a crucial role in trapping the bio-

---

ENERGY FLOW IN THE BIOSPHERE

SOLAR ENERGY

Green plants — PRODUCERS

Herbivores

Carnivores

Top carnivores — CONSUMERS

Death and defecation

Scavengers (Woodlice, millipedes, etc.) — CONSUMERS

Death and defecation

ENERGY LOST THROUGH NATURAL PROCESSES

Decomposers (Fungi and bacteria) — CONSUMERS

Energy enters the biosphere in the form of solar energy, which is used by the primary producers – predominantly green plants – to fuel the photosynthetic reactions by which atmospheric carbon dioxide is converted into organic sugars. Virtually all other organisms – animals, fungi and most bacteria – are consumers, ultimately relying on the organic matter of plants for their support.

ECOSYSTEM PRODUCTIVITY

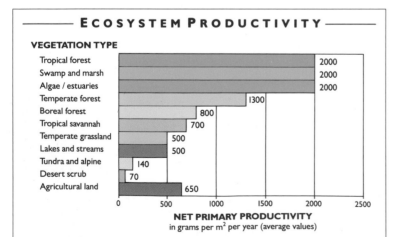

VEGETATION TYPE

Vegetation type	Net primary productivity
Tropical forest	2000
Swamp and marsh	2000
Algae / estuaries	2000
Temperate forest	1300
Boreal forest	800
Tropical savannah	700
Temperate grassland	500
Lakes and streams	500
Tundra and alpine	140
Desert scrub	70
Agricultural land	650

NET PRIMARY PRODUCTIVITY
in grams per m^2 per year (average values)

Different ecosystems vary greatly in their net primary productivity – the total amount of material assimilated by autotrophs, minus the material lost its repiration. Forests, swamps and estuaries are the most productive systems, and there is a strong productivity gradient from the tropics (high) to the poles (low).

logically harmful ultraviolet radiation emitted by the sun. This layer is currently under threat from man-made chemicals (⊳ p. 186). Of the energy that reaches the surface of the earth, 95–99% is absorbed by the oceans, leaving at most 5% available to green plants for photosynthesis.

The input of energy into an ecosystem is measured by recording the gain in weight by vegetation in a particular area over a measured period of time. This is called the *primary productivity* of that vegetation. The quantity of material present in an ecosystem at any given time (per unit ground area) is called the *biomass*. This term can be used of either plant or animal matter. Different types of ecosystem vary greatly in their productivity (⊳ box).

Primary and secondary producers

Living organisms have two remarkable properties: firstly, they can replicate themselves (that is they can *reproduce*), and secondly, the green plants and cyanobacteria (blue-green algae; ⊳ p. 82) can manufacture their own food supply from inorganic materials by the process of photosynthesis. The products of photosynthesis – the plants themselves – are then consumed by animals, thus forming the beginning of a *food chain*.

As the photosynthesizing organisms make their food from inorganic materials, they are called *autotrophs* ('self-feeders') or *producers*. All other organisms (in particular, the animals) are known as *heterotrophs* or *consumers*, as they consume other living organisms. The heterotrophs can be divided into several subgroups. Those animals that eat plants are the *herbivores* or *primary consumers*. In turn, they are preyed upon by *carnivores*, which are the *secondary* and *tertiary consumers*.

Eventually, when plants and animals die, they are broken down by the *decomposer organisms* (mostly bacteria and fungi) and their nutrients are released into the soil, whereupon the nutri-ents can be re-used by new living organisms. This process is called *nutrient cycling*.

Nutrient sources for life

Nutrient cycling is necessary because, unlike solar energy, the nutrients held within the soil are scarce commodities existing in fixed quantities. Hence they are called *finite resources*. Nutrients are scarce because the biosphere only includes the topmost 2–3 m (6–10 ft) of the earth's surface – plant roots and soil microorganisms cannot penetrate much beyond this depth.

The bodies of plants and animals consist mainly of the elements carbon, oxygen, hydrogen, nitrogen, phosphorus and sulphur, in various chemical compounds. These are the so-called *macroelements*. About 97% of human bodies are made from these elements. The remainder is made up of *microelements*, which may include between 14 and 24 different elements, depending on the organism.

When a plant or animal dies, the chemical compounds locked in its body are gradually released back to the soil and the oceans via the decomposer organisms. Most of these compounds become locked into vast, slow-moving *biogeochemical cycles*. Two nutrient cycles – involving the elements carbon and nitrogen – are of particular importance because they are concerned with elements needed in large quantities (⊳ illustration).

The entire cycle of nutrient movement may take many millions of years to complete. It is a sobering thought to realize that the chemical elements in our bodies may have previously formed part of some ancient organism such as a dinosaur living at least 65 million years before the present, and may already by then have been recycled several times in the history of life on earth.

SEE ALSO

● THE EARTH'S STRUCTURE AND ATMOSPHERE p. 60
● CLIMATE p. 80
● PLANTS (PHOTOSYNTHESIS) p. 88
● TERRESTRIAL ECOSYSTEMS p. 128
● AQUATIC ECOSYSTEMS p. 130
● THREATS TO THE ENVIRONMENT p. 186

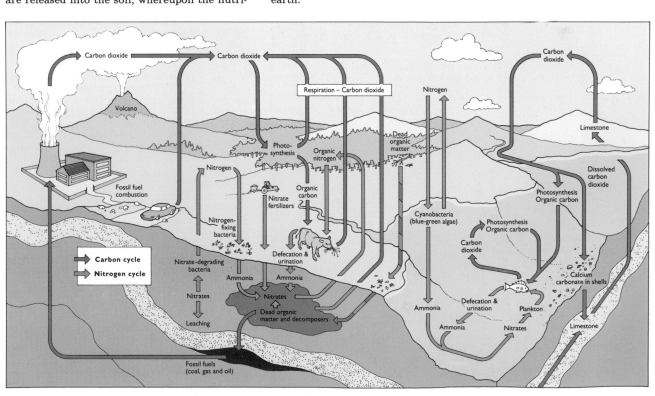

Terrestrial Ecosystems

The richness of *tropical forests* is proverbial. Such forests occupy about one fifth of the earth's land surface, and probably contain in excess of 1.5 million species of plant and animal.

True tropical rainforest is confined to a narrow belt around the equator, from 4° N to 4° S. Here there is little seasonal change in climate, and temperature and rainfall are always high. The tropical forests contain the largest bulk of living material per unit area of ground found in any type of ecosystem, often amounting to over 45 kg/m². This huge quantity of biomass is arranged in a complex spatial structure (▷ illustration).

Logging for timber and destruction by burning for farming are both taking their toll on the world's dwindling tropical forests. The area of forest lost each year probably lies between 75 000 and 140 000 km² (29 000 and 58 000 sq mi). This is over 1% of the total area, and the rate is accelerating each year. Apart from the loss of species, the destruction of the forests by burning puts large quantities of carbon dioxide into the atmosphere, adding to the greenhouse effect and global warming (▷ p. 186).

Tropical grassland

Tropical grassland (savanna) is most characteristic of central and eastern Africa and South America south of the Amazon basin. High temperatures persist throughout the year in such areas, but rainfall is mainly confined to the five-month wet season. The savannahs are dominated by grasses, which have the remarkable property of growing from the leaf bases, so that if the tips are grazed off they can continue growing from below. The trees of the savannah, such as acacias and baobabs, are equally well adapted to the sequence of wet and dry seasons.

The most remarkable feature of the animal life is the abundance and diversity of plant-feeding animals. In the African savannah the browsers include the giraffe, elephant and black rhinoceros, while wildebeest, zebra and others graze the grasses. The abundance of herbivorous life provides the basis for complex food webs, at the summit of which are the large cats, such as lions and cheetahs.

One of the most serious threats to the savannah is its exploitation for cattle grazing. Ultimately this can lead to the invasion of the grasslands by scrub vegetation and the loss of its potential productivity.

Deserts

Deserts cover more than one third of the earth's land surface. Hot deserts, such as those in Africa, the Middle East and central Australia, fall within the subtropical high-pressure belts north and south of the equator; they experience high temperatures throughout the year and very low rainfall. The dry climate of other deserts, such as the Gobi Desert of central Asia, is due to their geographical isolation from the sea, which prevents moisture-bearing winds from reaching them.

The density of vegetation in arid lands is sparse. Many plants have developed elaborate methods of protecting themselves from excessive heat and drought. Some have deep and extensive root systems, while the New World cacti form a fibrous mat in the surface soils to catch the dew and store water in their fleshy, evergreen stems. Most desert animals are nocturnal or active during the cooler periods of dawn and dusk.

Temperate forest

The temperate zone is wide and contains many different types of forest. In much of Europe and eastern America the characteristic forest is dominated by deciduous broad-leaved trees, while further north there is an admixture of conifers. There is usually a period unfavourable for growth during the temperate year. This may be due to summer drought in the warm temperate zone, or winter cold and frost in the higher latitudes. A plant's characteristic response to the latter is the dropping of leaves. Although the structure of temperate forest is simpler than that of tropical forest, it is still sufficiently complex to permit diverse assemblages of animals (▷ illustration).

The greatest problem facing the temperate forests is their fragmentation following thousands of

A cross-section through a Southeast Asian forest.

Upper-air community: mostly insectivorous birds and bats; also birds of prey.

Main-canopy community: birds, fruit bats, and mammals such as monkeys and squirrels.

Mid-zone flying animals: insectivorous birds and bats.

Mid-zone climbing animals: mostly mammals such as squirrels and monkeys, but also snakes and amphibians such as tree frogs. These animals may spend some time on the ground.

Large ground animals: mainly mammals (deer, pigs, elephants and some predatory carnivores) and also some flightless birds (such as jungle fowl) and large reptiles.

Small ground animals: a huge group of insectivores and mixed feeders.

TROPICAL FOREST

Serpent eagle

Great-eared nightjar

Red giant flying squirrel

Emerald dove

Great hornbill

Fruit bat

Common pigtail monkey

Lar gibbon

Palm civet

Tree frog

Sun bear

Asian elephant

Tiger

Lesser chevrotain

Malayan tapir

Bush pig

Malayan porcupine

HEIGHT ABOVE THE GROUND

EMERGENTS / CANOPY / UNDERSTOREY / SHRUB LAYER/FOREST FLOOR

years of human pressure. In Europe there remains only a tiny proportion of the original forest cover.

Temperate grassland

Some temperate areas receive too little rainfall to carry forest cover. These areas usually have a vegetation dominated by grasses and herbaceous plants, and a fauna in which grazing animals form a conspicuous part. The temperate grasslands mostly lie in the central parts of the major continents, far from the sea, where rainfall is low and where there is a wide seasonal range of temperature. Such grasslands have been given different names in various parts of the world: steppes in Asia, pampas in South America, prairie in North America, and veld in South Africa.

In their natural state these grasslands were rich in large herbivores, such as the European and North American bisons, the pronghorn, the rheas and the guanaco. Many of these animals have been severely reduced in numbers by human farming activity. Overgrazing can reduce the grasslands to a desert condition, and a similar result has occasionally been achieved by the conversion of prairies to arable agriculture.

Mediterranean climate

A number of warm-temperate areas of the world are characterized by a mediterranean climate, in which hot, dry summers alternate with mild, wet winters. This type of climate is found not only in the Mediterranean basin, but also in parts of California, Chile, South Africa and southern Australia. Such areas typically have sufficient water resources to support tall scrub or even forest vegetation, but a high frequency of fire, often accompanied by overgrazing, has generally reduced them to low scrub or open heath, variously called chaparral, maquis, garrigue or fynbos in its different geographic locations.

The plant life of mediterranean areas is dominated by a mixture of deciduous and evergreen shrubs. Historically the greatest problem in mediterranean habitats has been forest clearance, but now intensive grazing and repeated fires probably have the greatest impact on the environment.

Boreal forest

The colder regions of the temperate climatic zone, north of about latitude 55° N, are not able to support broad-leaved deciduous forest, but are clothed instead with needle-leaved coniferous trees (▷ p. 91), most of which (apart from larch) are evergreen. Such regions are called boreal forest or *taiga*. Only a few broad-leaved trees, such as birch and aspen, can cope with the extremely cold winters and the abundance of snowfall, conditions to which pine, spruce and most other conifers are well adapted. The evergreens are able to begin their photosynthesis as soon as conditions become warm enough in spring; there is no need for the delay entailed in the development of new foliage. The hard winters restrict the number of animal species that can survive in this habitat. Hibernation is the answer for animals such as bears, but many birds, for example, migrate south to avoid the winter stress.

Over-exploitation by man for forestry is a major threat to the survival of natural boreal forest. This kind of forest is also particularly sensitive to the effects of acid rain (▷ p. 186).

Tundra and alpine

In the polar regions the winters are long, dark and very cold, and throughout the year there is very little precipitation. These conditions lead to the development of tundra vegetation, consisting of low shrubs and perennial herbs, and there is a low biological diversity. Nevertheless, the habitat is remarkable for the adaptations found among plants and animals to cope with such a stressful environment.

In many respects high mountains in lower latitudes – the so-called alpine areas – have a very similar climate to the tundra. However, some features are quite different. In the alpine habitat days are shorter in summer and longer in winter. Because the sun is higher in the sky, daytime temperatures can rise much higher, so there is a greater daily fluctuation in temperature. Precipitation is also usually higher, so a substantial snow cover may accumulate in winter, protecting plants and animals from the worst of the low temperatures.

SEE ALSO

- MOUNTAINS p. 68
- DESERTS p. 72
- WEATHER p. 78
- CLIMATE p. 80
- PLANTS pp. 88–93
- THE BIOSPHERE p. 126
- AQUATIC ECOSYSTEMS p. 130
- FARMING p. 132
- THREATS TO THE ENVIRONMENT p. 186

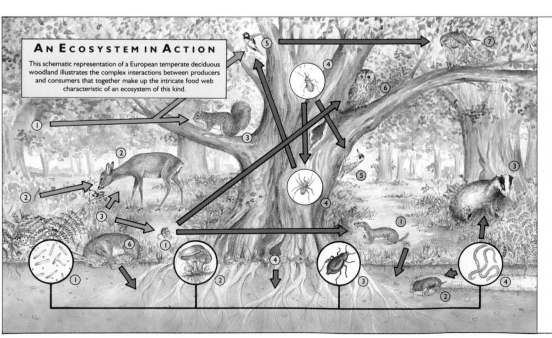

AN ECOSYSTEM IN ACTION

This schematic representation of a European temperate deciduous woodland illustrates the complex interactions between producers and consumers that together make up the intricate food web characteristic of an ecosystem of this kind.

Producers
1 Trees 2 Shrubs
3 Grasses 4 Leaf litter

Herbivores
(primary consumers)
1 Mice 2 Deer
3 Squirrel
4 Plant-feeding insect
5 Great tit 6 Rabbit

Carnivores
(secondary and higher consumers)
1 Weasel 2 Mole
3 Badger 4 Spider
5 Woodpecker 6 Owl
7 Sparrowhawk

Decomposers and Scavengers
1 Bacteria 2 Fungi
3 Beetle 4 Earthworms

▷ Producer to primary consumer
▷ Primary to secondary consumer
▷ Other consumer-to-consumer transfers
▷ Defecation and dead material to decomposers and scavengers

Aquatic Ecosystems

Water covers 71% of the surface of the earth. This fact, combined with the great depth of many of the oceans (average depth 3700 m/ 12 140 ft), provides a living space estimated to be 200 times larger than all the land ecosystems.

Aquatic ecosystems are better able to support life than the terrestrial ecosystems. However, because of the constancy of the water environment when compared to the land environment, the diversity of life in the vast aquatic ecosystems is relatively small.

The aquatic environment

A watery environment was almost certainly the original source of all life on this planet (▷ p. 82). Water provides a protective shield around plants and animals, preventing cells from drying out, providing buoyancy, transporting food, and carrying away waste products. Water also makes fertilization much easier than on land, preventing the developing young from becoming dry, maintaining an even temperature, filtering out harmful ultraviolet light from the sun, and dispersing the young after birth.

One of the most remarkable properties of water is its dissolving power. Because rainwater is nearly neutral (it is in fact slightly acidic), chemical compounds can be dissolved, transported, and precipitated out with virtually no chemical alteration. In some places, however, acid rain has increased the natural acidity of water bodies, with harmful consequences for the organisms living in them (▷ p. 186).

The buoyancy of water means that aquatic plants and animals can reduce or dispense with rigid structures (woody tissues in plants, bones in animals). The density of protoplasm – the jelly-like substance within all living cells – is in fact identical to that of sea water, which is why we float in sea water more easily than in fresh water.

Controlling factors

Various factors control the nature of different aquatic ecosystems. The most important is *salinity* (the saltiness of water), which depends principally upon the amount of sodium chloride dissolved in it, along with small amounts of bromides, carbonates and sulphates of the elements sodium, potassium, calcium and magnesium. In the marine environment salinity is lowest – typically 30 parts per thousand (ppt) – near the estuaries of large rivers, where the addition of fresh water dilutes the concentration of salts. High salinity (70 ppt) is recorded where rainfall is low and evaporation rate is high – in the Red Sea, for example. The amount of salinity divides aquatic ecosystems into two main groups.

The first group, the *freshwater ecosystems*, includes standing water such as reservoirs, lakes, ponds, marshes and wetlands, and the flowing water of rivers and streams. These ecosystems are normally of very low salinity, usually between 15 and 30 ppt. By contrast, the waters of the second group, the *marine* or *saltwater ecosystems* (which include oceans, estuaries, mangrove swamps and coral reefs), contain considerably more salts, typically between 35 and 70 ppt. The saltiness of the oceans is ultimately derived from minerals and salts eroded and washed away from rocks and soils, and eventually transported to the sea by rivers.

The temperature of the water in aquatic ecosystems is also critically important for life forms. Of the ultraviolet light that reaches the surface of the planet, about 95% is absorbed as heat by the oceans. The effect of this is to make the seas behave like giant radiators that warm the northern hemisphere in winter and cool it in summer (and vice versa in the southern hemisphere). On average, the annual variation in surface-water temperature of the oceans is about 10 °C (18 °F), but at a depth of 20 m (66 ft) the annual variation may be as little as 1 or 2 °C (2 or 4 °F). Because of the evenness of temperatures, most aquatic life forms have little or no need for temperature-control mechanisms such as those found in land-based life forms.

The third controlling factor is oxygen. Most oxygen is found at the surface of water bodies, especially in turbulent streams or where waves break. The amount of dissolved oxygen in water can be severely altered by human activity. In particular, the dumping of untreated sewage and industrial wastes directly into seas and rivers has caused a huge increase in the demand for oxygen by the organisms (bacteria and scavenger organisms) that feed on the effluents (▷ p. 186). The increase in the numbers of such organisms results in most or all of the dissolved oxygen being used up, and this leads to the death of other aquatic life forms.

A fourth factor is the rate at which sunlight disappears with depth. This depends upon the quantity of suspended materials and floating

INTERTIDAL ZONE · COASTAL OR NERITIC ZONE · OCEANIC ZONE

Depth in metres (feet)

Wave action

Seaweeds and major commercial fishing shoals

EUPHOTIC ZONE

0

Continental shelf

Benthic environment

Pelagic environment

Continental slope

100–200 (330–660)

BATHYAL ZONE

2000 (6600)

ABYSSAL ZONE

6000 (20 000)

MARINE ECOSYSTEMS

The scale in this diagram is extremely distorted: in fact the euphotic zone accounts for only 8% of the total volume of the oceans, the bathyal 14%, and the abyssal a staggering 78%. Sometimes the abyssal zone is divided into two, that part below 6000 m (20 000 ft) being referred to as the hadal zone.

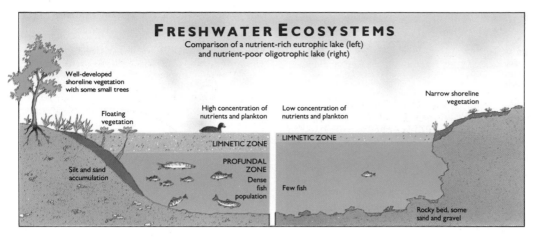

FRESHWATER ECOSYSTEMS

Comparison of a nutrient-rich eutrophic lake (left)
and nutrient-poor oligotrophic lake (right)

Well-developed
shoreline vegetation
with some small trees

Floating
vegetation

High concentration of
nutrients and plankton

Low concentration of
nutrients and plankton

Narrow shoreline
vegetation

LIMNETIC ZONE

LIMNETIC ZONE

PROFUNDAL
ZONE

Dense
fish
population

Few fish

Silt and sand
accumulation

Rocky bed, some
sand and gravel

SEE ALSO

● RIVERS AND LAKES p. 74
● OCEANS p. 76
● BEGINNINGS OF LIFE p. 82
● PRIMITIVE ANIMALS p. 94
● CRUSTACEANS p. 97
● FISHES p. 100
● AMPHIBIANS p. 102
● MARINE MAMMALS p. 120
● THE BIOSPHERE p. 126

organisms in the water. Usually some 50% of red, orange and yellow light is absorbed in the top 2 m (6½ ft) of water, and by 20 m (65 ft) only small amounts of blue-green light remain to give water its typical 'colour'. The rapid removal of sunlight means that all aquatic ecosystems that are more than several metres deep are dark, cool environments. Even at the equator, the temperature of deeper water does not exceed 4 °C (39 °F).

Marine ecosystems

Ocean ecosystems can be divided into two main types: the *coastal* or *neritic zone*, and the *oceanic zone* or *ocean deeps*. Coastal ecosystems extend from low water to the edge of the continental shelf and they do not exceed 200 m (660 ft) in depth. This zone represents less than 10% of the ocean area yet contains 98% of marine life forms. It is the location of most commercial fishing, and increasingly for offshore oil platforms. Unfortunately, it is also the most heavily polluted part of the oceans.

Most of the oceanic zone is remote from landmasses, and so for the most part it is relatively unpolluted. Three distinct zones or subzones can be found: a surface or *euphotic zone* to 200 m (660

ft), which contains most life forms, a middle *bathyal zone* (200–2000 m/660–6600 ft), and a cold, dark, bottom layer or *abyssal zone* (below 2000 m/ 6600 ft). Surprisingly, about 98% of the species in the ocean deeps are in the deepest zone, but most are bacteria involved in decomposition.

Freshwater ecosystems

Freshwater ecosystems are highly variable and their characteristics depend upon the surrounding geology, land use, and pollution levels.

Most freshwater ecosystems are *eutrophic*, i.e. there is an accumulation of nutrients and organic matter. This accumulation takes place over time and can be thought of as an 'ageing' process, particularly in lakes. Unfortunately, extreme eutrophication can also occur when raw sewage or agricultural wastes are allowed to enter fresh water, with a resulting depletion in oxygen (⊳ above). In contrast, fresh water that flows off ancient acid rocks or that drains from peaty areas often has a very low nutrient content. Such freshwater ecosystems are described as *oligotrophic*. They have clear water (apart from brown staining from peat) and usually have very few life forms.

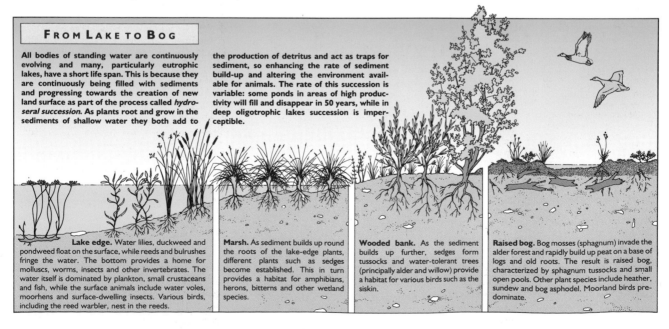

FROM LAKE TO BOG

All bodies of standing water are continuously evolving and many, particularly eutrophic lakes, have a short life span. This is because they are continuously being filled with sediments and progressing towards the creation of new land surface as part of the process called *hydroseral succession*. As plants root and grow in the sediments of shallow water they both add to

the production of detritus and act as traps for sediment, so enhancing the rate of sediment build-up and altering the environment available for animals. The rate of this succession is variable: some ponds in areas of high productivity will fill and disappear in 50 years, while in deep oligotrophic lakes succession is imperceptible.

Lake edge. Water lilies, duckweed and pondweed float on the surface, while reeds and bulrushes fringe the water. The bottom provides a home for molluscs, worms, insects and other invertebrates. The water itself is dominated by plankton, small crustaceans and fish, while the surface animals include water voles, moorhens and surface-dwelling insects. Various birds, including the reed warbler, nest in the reeds.

Marsh. As sediment builds up round the roots of the lake-edge plants, different plants such as sedges become established. This in turn provides a habitat for amphibians, herons, bitterns and other wetland species.

Wooded bank. As the sediment builds up further, sedges form tussocks and water-tolerant trees (principally alder and willow) provide a habitat for various birds such as the siskin.

Raised bog. Bog mosses (sphagnum) invade the alder forest and rapidly build up peat on a base of logs and old roots. The result is raised bog, characterized by sphagnum tussocks and small open pools. Other plant species include heather, sundew and bog asphodel. Moorland birds predominate.

Farming

Arable farming is principally concerned with growing food crops. Although there are about 80 000 edible plants, just four plants (rice, wheat, maize and potatoes) make up more of the world's total food production than all the others combined. Some crops are grown for purposes other than food: for example, cotton and jute are turned into fabrics, esparto grass is used in the manufacture of paper and rope, and tobacco is used for smoking materials.

SEE ALSO

- CLIMATE p. 80
- PLANTS pp. 88–93
- BIRDS p. 106
- HOOFED MAMMALS p. 116
- FOOD, DIET AND DIGESTION p. 138
- POPULATION AND HUNGER p. 185
- TEXTILES p. 200

Livestock farming is concerned with the rearing of animals for a variety of useful products. Meat and meat products are used for both human and animal consumption. Dairy products are based on milk, and include butter, cream, cheese and yoghurt. Hides and skins are mostly processed (tanned) into leather, which is used for clothing and footwear. Wool is spun into yarn and then woven or knitted into garments. Glue and gelatin are made by boiling bones, skin and horns, while fertilizers can be made from ground hoof and horn.

The development of farming

The first agricultural animal to be domesticated was the sheep: this occurred in the Middle East around 9000 BC. Goats, cattle and pigs soon followed, and livestock farming started to spread to Europe in around 6000 BC. The domestication of draught animals (such as horse, ox, camel) allowed the mechanization of agriculture to begin.

Arable agriculture first emerged in the Middle East in the period 9000–7000 BC, shortly after the last Ice Age. The crops grown were primitive forms of wheat and barley. Between 6000 and 4000 BC agricultural development also began in many of the fertile river valleys of the Far East, India and the Nile Valley, and in Central and South America.

Initially, farming was largely at a subsistence level, i.e. producing just enough crops for survival. With gradual improvements in techniques, surpluses could sometimes be sold for a profit, or put aside for hard times. A major agricultural revolution took place in Western Europe in the 18th century, when several new techniques increased productivity and helped to feed the growing populations of the towns. A four-field system of crop rotation, with one fallow year, helped to maintain the fertility of the soil, and ploughing and sowing techniques were improved. Extra fodder crops, such as turnips, were grown, enabling more animals to be kept alive during the winter, and farmers began to experiment with selective breeding of livestock, leading to hardier and more productive animals.

Modern livestock farming

Meat is too expensive for most of the world's people to consume, because large herbivores are

---

THE MAIN FOOD CROPS OF THE WORLD

WHEAT
Distribution: non-tropical regions throughout the world, extending to about latitude 60 °N and 50 °S.
Uses: flour for bread-making and baking.

Wheat can hybridize with ease, and there are a great many varieties. There are two main groups of modern wheat. *Spring wheat* is sown in March and harvested in September (in the northern hemisphere), and is usually found in higher-latitude locations such as Canada and Russia. It produces a hard grain well suited to bread making. *Winter wheat* is slower growing and less tolerant of winter cold. It is planted in September and harvested the following July (in the northern hemisphere). It is a softer grain more useful for general baking.

RICE
Distribution: any region where growing-season temperatures exceed 21 °C (70 °F) and irrigation is possible.
Uses: boiled as a staple food, and milled to rice flour.

More than half the world's population depends on rice for sustenance. Most rice in Asia is of the 'paddy' variety, that is, grown in standing water. Elsewhere, 'upland rice' is grown, which relies on abundant rainfall. Paddy rice gives the highest yields, and up to three crops per year can be obtained.

MAIZE (CORN)
Distribution: originally from the Americas, but now extensively grown in all tropical, sub-tropical and warm temperate regions.
Uses: consumed by humans in the form of maize

flour and breakfast cereals, and as a vegetable ('sweetcorn'). Milled for animal feed, and used as a source of oils, vitamins and industrial starch. Also fermented for maize beer.

Under optimum growth conditions maize is three times as productive as wheat. Experiments have shown it to be ideally suited for the production of industrial alcohol, and the plant residue can be decomposed to produce methane gas (biofuel).

BARLEY
Distribution: northern hemisphere mid-latitudes.
Uses: animal feedstock. In its 'malted' (germinated) form it is used in the manufacture of beer and whisky.

Barley is the fourth most important cereal in terms of world production.

PULSES (PEAS AND BEANS)
Distribution: worldwide.
Uses: oils for human and industrial use and increasingly as alternative sources of high-quality protein in meat-free diets. Extracts from pulses are used in putty, paint, waterproofing materials and leather dressings.

The most important pulse today is the soybean, and now 40% of world soybean output comes from the USA. The bean produces valuable oil, and the residue is fed to animals.

POTATOES
Distribution: originally from South America, but now extensively grown at temperate and high latitudes throughout the world.
Uses: as a vegetable for humans.

The potato is particularly rich in carbohydrate and also supplies protein, iron, vitamins B and C, as well as 50% of phosphorus and 10% of calcium requirements. Their natural variety makes them ideal subjects for genetic engineering, and new varieties have already been developed for tropical latitudes – potentially revolutionizing the diets of many Third World populations.

SWEET POTATOES
Distribution: originally from tropical South America, and now grown extensively in the tropics, and increasingly in temperate latitudes.
Uses: as a flavoursome staple food.

The swollen root is rich in starch, sugar, iron, calcium and a vitamin A substitute.

CASSAVA
Distribution: originally the tropics of the New World, but now more extensive in Africa.
Uses: fried, roasted, boiled, sun-dried or fermented for human consumption.

Cassava is a versatile crop, and will tolerate drought conditions. It contains virtually no protein (at best 1%) and people who eat mainly cassava develop kwashiorkor, a protein-deficiency disease.

OATS AND RYE
Distribution: cool, damp climates of the higher latitudes.
Uses: mainly as cattle and horse feed, but oats are used for porridge and rye as a specialist bread flour.

These two cereals are of lesser importance than formerly. The advantages of both are that they can grow in poor soils in poor climates. They are also extremely nutritious.

too inefficient at converting plant material into meat for human consumption. In an attempt to make livestock farming a more productive method of producing food, various new approaches have been adopted in the developed world. Breeding has been made more efficient by the use of artificial insemination, and totally new varieties have been made possible by the genetic engineering of specific animal types to suit particular locations. Factory farming is widely used for intensive rearing, although this method has been criticized as cruelty to animals, and also for the practice of feeding growth hormones and chemical additives to animals in an effort to boost the quantity and quality of the product. However, if we continue to demand large quantities of meat, eggs and dairy products then we shall be forced to rely upon factory-farming methods, as free-range methods are too inefficient to provide sufficient food.

Modern arable farming

In the early 1900s the mechanization of farming began to speed up, and in the 1930s the first large-scale use of artificial fertilizers and pesticides began. There were dramatic increases in productivity levels, although wider environmental problems have sometimes resulted.

By the 1960s plant geneticists were able to breed crops for specific environments, and by the 1970s they were able to recombine the genetic structure of plants to produce new varieties with greater yields and increased disease resistance. In the 1980s the cloning of plants allowed the mass production of young plants that all had identical properties; as a result, harvesting costs have been reduced and yield increased.

A 'Green Revolution' has occurred over the last three decades with the application of genetic techniques to plant breeding. Here the growing characteristics of different strains of maize (corn) are being studied under greenhouse conditions. (SPL)

THE MAIN TYPES OF DOMESTICATED ANIMAL

CATTLE
Distribution: worldwide.
Uses: meat, meat products, milk, dairy products, leather; draught animals (oxen).

Many different varieties exist, some bred principally for beef, others for milk production; in addition different varieties have been bred for different climatic conditions. Cows can be bred at any time of the year. Following the birth of the calf, the mother remains in milk for up to 10 months. Good cows can be kept in an almost continuous cycle of calf production and milk yield from about 18 months of age to 10 years. Most male calves are castrated and reared for beef, being ready for slaughter at 18 months. In contrast, animals destined for veal production are fed only on milk, and slaughtered at about 14 weeks.

PIGS
Distribution: worldwide.
Uses: every part of the pig can be used, and products include meat, meat products, leather, hair for brushes, fat for industrial use.

Traditionally, pigs have been allowed to range freely, but nowadays in the developed world pigs are generally kept in purpose-built buildings. Pigs intended for pork are slaughtered at 40–50 kg (88–110 lb) body weight, while for bacon, a weight of 80–100 kg (176–220 lb) is acceptable.

SHEEP
Distribution: mainly Old World, Australia and New Zealand.
Uses: wool, meat, skins; locally milk for cheese making.

An amazing variety of domestic types have been bred. Two major categories can be identified, the *hairy sheep* kept for milk and meat (especially in Africa), and the *woolly sheep* with fluffier hair and found mainly in the higher latitudes. Sheep can generally survive on poorer pasture than cattle. Male lambs are usually castrated and reared for slaughter.

HORSES
Distribution: worldwide.
Uses: transportation, sport.

The domesticated horse shows a great variety of types, but is often divided into two main groups. The *Arabian stock* produces a fine-boned, smooth-skinned animal, well suited for running and pulling light carriages but with a nervous disposition. The so-called *cold-blooded stock* is characterized by a heavy frame, a shaggy coat, and a quiet temperament, making such animals suitable for farm work.

ASSES AND MULES
Distribution: mainly Africa, Asia and South America.
Uses: human transport, agricultural work and to power machines (especially water wheels and grinding apparatus).

No other domesticated animal will perform so much work for so little food as the ass (or donkey). Mules are crosses between horses and asses, and are more versatile and less flighty than horses. Mules are sterile, and therefore each generation has to be bred afresh from horse and ass parents.

GOATS
Distribution: principally Africa and Asia.
Uses: milk, wool, skins, fine leather, meat, horns.

Unfortunately, goats are destructive foragers and will overgraze an area if their population is too high. The Cashmere and Angora varieties are valued for their high-quality wool.

CAMELS
Distribution: North Africa, Middle East, Central Asia.
Uses: transportation, hides, dung for fuel, meat in emergencies.

The camel is the ideal animal for use in dry environments. Females lactate for 11–15 months and yield between 1–7 litres of milk per day.

WATER BUFFALO
Distribution: mostly in southern Asia.
Uses: draught animal; meat; skins and horns used commercially.

Water buffalo are still widely used to work the rice fields, where they pull ploughs and carts, and can even be ridden. The water buffalo exceeds all other cattle in terms of strength, resistance to disease, and intelligence.

POULTRY
Distribution: worldwide.
Uses: meat, eggs, feathers.
Types: chickens, turkeys, ducks, geese.

Poultry are mostly low-grade grazers and foragers. In developed countries, poultry rearing has been revolutionized by the breeding of smaller birds that can be kept in small cages (battery farming).

Reproduction and Development

Every human being begins life as a single cell no bigger than the dot above the letter i and grows to be an individual composed of 6 million million cells. Growth begins at conception and proceeds at an increasing rate during the first six months of pregnancy.

From the sixth month of pregnancy, however, there is a slowly decelerating rate of growth through infancy and childhood, with a brief increase in rate during puberty.

Sperm and ova

Even before birth a female baby possesses her full quota of *ova* or eggs, each of which contain 23 chromosomes – half the complement of other body cells. The ova develop in the *ovarian follicles*, which are stored in the *ovaries* – two glands that in adults are about the size of pigeons' eggs. Each month one ovum ripens, breaks free from its protective follicle and is swept up by the fringe-like endings (*fimbriae*) of one of the *fallopian tubes*. Its journey down the fallopian tube to the *uterus* or womb lasts four days. For a few hours only it is in a state of readiness to be fertilized by a sperm. Unfertilized, it will pass on and out of the woman's body. The enriched blood supply lining the uterus in preparation for receiving a fertilized ovum is shed soon after. This loss of blood is *menstruation*, often referred to as a 'period'.

The human male, too, is born with cells that will produce sperm in adult life. Sperm are manufactured in *seminiferous tubules* in the testes (testicles) at the rate of 1000 per second, and stored in the *epididymis*. Each sperm starts with 46 chromosomes but sheds 23 as it matures (a process

that takes 74 days). If it loses its Y chromosome and goes on to fertilize an egg, the resulting baby will be a girl; if the X chromosome has been shed the child will be a boy (⊳ also p. 86). A mature sperm is still less than 0.05 mm ($^1/_{500}$ in) long.

Coitus and fertilization

During sexual intercourse or *coitus*, the erect penis is inserted into the vagina and rhythmical movements lead to orgasm and the ejaculation of *semen* – some 2–3 million sperms in a nutrient fluid. A sperm swims by using rapid movements of its long, threadlike tail, and the head of the sperm contains stores of glucose to provide energy for its long swim to the ovum. The first sperms to reach the ovum will pair its 23 chromosomes with the 23 chromosomes of the ovum.

Within hours of conception a fertilized ovum, called a *zygote*, begins to divide. To do this it needs to be surrounded by the hormone *progesterone*, which is supplied by cells that develop in the egg's discarded follicle – the *corpus luteum*. Progesterone also prevents any further ovulations. Three days after fertilization, the zygote has divided three times, producing eight cells. Four days later, containing 16 cells, the zygote reaches the uterus.

Three days after that, the zygote implants itself into the uterine wall. Now called a *blastocyst* and 0.1 mm ($^1/_{250}$ in) in size, its cells change into two types – *embryoblast* cells that will eventually become the baby, and *trophoblast* cells that will form the *placenta* and nourish the growing foetus. The embryo cells themselves soon change into an inner and an outer layer.

The developing embryo

By the start of the third week, a third layer develops between the other two. As the third week ends two tiny tubes covered by muscle cells merge into one, forming the heart. By week 4 it is already pumping blood through tiny arteries and veins to reach inner cells. In the first month, the embryo grows to a length of 4 mm ($^1/_6$ in) with one end bigger than the other. Groups of cells have clustered in readiness to become specific organs or limbs. The middle layer has begun to lay down what will be the spine and the nervous system, heart and blood vessels.

By the fifth week, the eyes, ears, nose and nerve cells have started to appear. Arms and legs are beginning to emerge with translucent flipper-like plates showing the forerunners of fingers and toes. One week later the 10 mm ($^2/_5$ in) embryo is already bending its elbows and moving its hands, which have clearly defined fingers. The face is forming recognizable eyes, mouth and ears. The brain has divided into its various parts responsible for thinking, memory, reflexes and emotions. Throughout the embryo cartilage begins to turn to bone. By the fourteenth week the foetus is completely formed, and from this time on – until week 40 when it is ready to be born – it grows in size rather than complexity.

Birth

When the foetus reaches maturity or outgrows its food supply from the placenta it triggers off the start of labour. The hormone *oxytocin* begins to circulate in the mother's blood, softening the *cervix* (the neck of the womb) so that it will be able to stretch and accommodate the baby's head. There are three clearly defined stages of labour. In the *first stage*, the muscular wall of the uterus gradually builds up the force and frequency of its contractions as it draws up the edges of the now

REPRODUCTIVE ORGANS

FEMALE

Fimbriae
Fallopian tube
Ovary
Uterus
Cervix
Bladder
Pubic bone
Clitoris
Urethra
Vagina
Vulva
Rectum
Anus

MALE

Rectum
Ureter
Bladder
Seminal vesicle
Pubic bone
Ejaculatory duct
Prostate gland
Urethra
Erectile tissue
Epididymis
Testis
Anus
Cowper's gland
Vas deferens
Scrotal sac

thinned and softened cervix until it is fully dilated (i.e. widened). The first stage of labour is the longest, taking an average of 8–10 hours for a first baby. At the end of the first stage the membranes rupture, releasing the *amniotic fluid*, which surrounds the foetus in the uterus – this is known as the breaking of the waters.

The *second stage* is shorter (½–2 hours) but harder. This is the stage where the baby is moved down the birth canal (the cervix and vagina) and is born. The uterus contracts forcefully and the mother experiences an overwhelming desire to 'bear down' or push with her abdominal muscles to help the baby to be born. The *third stage* is the delivery of the placenta or 'afterbirth'.

Growth in childhood

Growth in the first year of postnatal life is determined by nutrition. Towards the end of the first year, the control of the growth process switches from nutrition to growth hormone secretion (▷ p. 143). Growth hormone is released from the pituitary gland and the rate at which children grow depends on the amount of growth hormone secreted. Growth continues at a slowly decelerating pace until the deceleration is interrupted by puberty.

Puberty

During the 12th year of life secondary sexual characteristics will have become apparent in 50% of girls and boys. These include development of breasts in girls, enlargement of the testes and, later, deepening of the voice in boys, and growth of axillary (underarm) and pubic hair in both sexes. Such developments occur before the age of 9 years in 3% of children, and 97% show some secondary sexual characteristics by the age of 14.

As soon as the ovary begins to secrete sufficient oestrogen to promote breast enlargement (the earliest change in female puberty), the growth rate increases as a result of an increase in the secretion of growth hormone. A girl starts her pubertal growth from an average height of about 140 cm (4 ft 7 in), and pubertal growth adds approximately 20 cm (8 in). As puberty progresses, girls grow increasingly quickly for about 18 months and then the growth rate begins to fall. By this time menstruation – controlled by cyclical changes in oestrogen levels – will have commenced. The timing of the first period has relatively little biological importance but has occurred in 97% of girls by the age of 15. After the onset of the first period, most bleeding occurs at irregular intervals because ovulation does not become reliably established for at least 18 months.

Boys continue growing along the childhood (decelerating) curve during the first two years of their pubertal development, and reach an average height of about 150 cm (4 ft 11 in) before the pubertal growth spurt starts. It adds approximately 25 cm (10 in) in height and the final height of adult men is consequently an average 12.6 cm (5 in) greater than that of adult women. This is mainly due to the prolongation of childhood growth in men and not to the contribution of the pubertal growth spurt. As soon as testosterone secretion occurs in the testes, *spermatogenesis* (the production of sperm) begins in the seminiferous tubules (▷ diagram). Testosterone also promotes muscle development and the growth of body hair, for instance on the chest.

The menopause

In women between the ages of 45 and 55 the follicles in the ovaries stop producing ova (eggs),

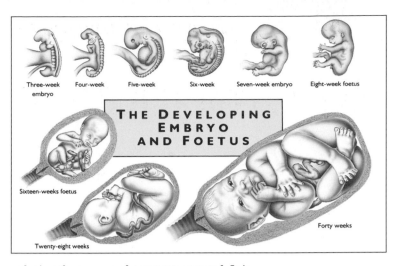

THE DEVELOPING EMBRYO AND FOETUS

Three-week embryo · Four-week · Five-week · Six-week · Seven-week embryo · Eight-week foetus

Sixteen-weeks foetus · Twenty-eight weeks · Forty weeks

reducing the amount of oestrogen secreted. It is this reduced level of oestrogen that produces the menopause. The sudden decline in oestrogen secretion has been blamed for many symptoms, but the only symptoms clearly associated with oestrogen deficiency are hot flushes, vaginal dryness and skin changes, *osteoporosis* (loss of bone density, making them more liable to fracture), and an increase in the rate of development of *atherosclerosis* (hardening of the arteries). These changes can cause severe psychological and physical symptoms, which is why the question of hormone replacement therapy for post-menopausal women is so important. Men are less severely affected by hormonal changes, since the decline in male sex hormone concentrations occurs over a much longer period.

Old age

The physical changes associated with old age have been much less intensively studied than those of childhood. It is obvious that old people become thinner, more wrinkled through loss both of skin elasticity and of subcutaneous (under-skin) fat, shorter through vertebral compression, and more vulnerable to disease. However, there are no standards comparable to those established in childhood.

SEE ALSO

- GENETICS p. 86
- GLANDS AND HORMONES p. 143
- LEARNING, CREATIVITY AND INTELLIGENCE p. 148

CONTRACEPTIVE METHODS

Hormonal The Pill is the best-known hormonal contraceptive. Millions of women have used it since it became widely available in the 1960s. The Pill is highly effective and may protect woman against some gynaecological cancers, such as ovarian cancer. Older versions of the Pill with higher doses of oestrogen and progesterone carried a slightly increased risk of circulatory disease and breast cancer.

Sterilization In women sterilization involves blocking the fallopian tubes by either cutting or tying them. Male sterilization – *vasectomy* – involves cutting the *vas deferens*, the channel that transports sperm.

Barrier Barrier methods of contraception consist of the condom (sheath) worn over the man's penis, the female condom worn inside the woman's vagina, and the diaphragm, which covers the woman's cervix. They are less reliable than the Pill in preventing pregnancies, but have no effects on other body systems. The spread of AIDS has made the condom a popular choice since it forms a complete barrier. The diaphragm may give some protection against cancer of the cervix.

IUDs The *intra-uterine device* (IUD or 'coil') is a small object made from plastic and metal wire, often copper, inserted into the uterus. It probably works by preventing a fertilized egg from implanting into the uterine wall. IUDs have lost popularity since they have been associated with infections and infertility in some women and heavy, painful periods in others.

Rhythm This is one of the oldest methods of contraception and relies on restricting intercourse to the days in a woman's menstrual cycle when she is unlikely to become pregnant. It is the least reliable way to prevent unwanted pregnancies. More recently, other signs of fertility such as an increase in clear mucus or body temperature have been used by couples to either increase or reduce their chances of conceiving.

How People Move

Bones, joints, muscles and nerves are the essential requirements for human movement, whether for top athletes or just ordinary people going about their daily lives. Normally, people are born with the same set of anatomical equipment – bones, joints and voluntary muscles supplied with an almost identical network of nerves and blood vessels. Bones account for one sixth of body weight, and muscles make up two fifths.

SEE ALSO

● FOOD, DIET AND DIGESTION p. 138
● RESPIRATION AND CIRCULATION p. 140
● THE BRAIN AND NERVOUS SYSTEM p. 146

The speed and control with which individuals move and the suppleness of their bodies depend partly on luck in inheriting the right genes from parents. The length and thickness of bones and the laxity of joint ligaments are determined to a great extent before birth, but regular exercise can strengthen muscles and improve skill in movement.

Bones

Without the rigid support provided by bones we would all be shapeless bags of organs. But the skeleton performs a number of important functions besides giving the body shape and form.

Bones such as the skull, ribs and vertebrae encase vital organs such as the brains, lungs, heart and spinal cord, protecting them from injury.

Other bones such as the femur, tibia and fibula – the long bones of the legs – and the humerus, radius and ulna in the arms serve primarily as levers providing attachments for muscles that propel the body forward or allow it to reach and retrieve objects.

Some bones, including the ribs, pelvis and sternum (the breast bone), contain bone marrow. This is the substance responsible for manufacturing the millions of red blood cells essential to life (⊳ p. 140). Bones also act as reservoirs for calcium and other minerals needed to maintain health.

At birth bones are made up of two thirds fibrous material and one third mineral, while in old age they are two thirds mineral and one third fibrous. Broken bones in children are called *greenstick fractures* – children's bones are more flexible and do not break completely. In old people bones contain less calcium and break more easily.

Joints

Bones meet one another to form joints, of which there are six main types (⊳ below). The degree of movement possible at a joint is determined by the surface of the bone ends and the joint space and fluid between them.

The hip joint is an example of a *ball-and-socket joint*, where both bone ends have a large area of smooth surface covered in cartilage and lubricated by *synovial fluid*. Movement is possible in all directions.

The knee and elbow are *hinge joints*, with movement mostly in one plane. The joint between the thumb and hand is a *saddle joint* permitting

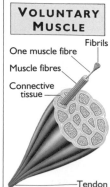

VOLUNTARY MUSCLE

Fibrils
One muscle fibre
Muscle fibres
Connective tissue
Tendon

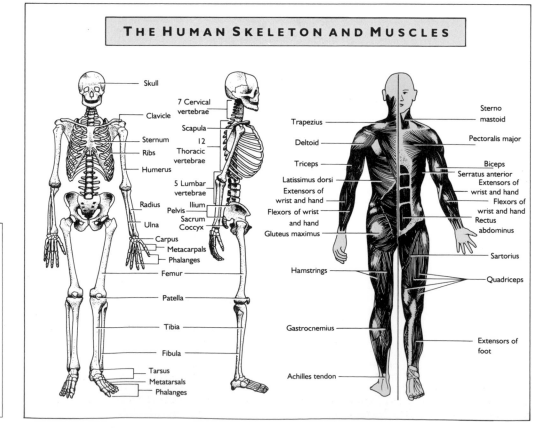

THE HUMAN SKELETON AND MUSCLES

Skull
7 Cervical vertebrae
Clavicle
Scapula
Sternum
12 Thoracic vertebrae
Ribs
Humerus
5 Lumbar vertebrae
Radius
Ilium
Pelvis
Ulna
Sacrum
Coccyx
Carpus
Metacarpals
Phalanges
Femur
Patella
Tibia
Fibula
Tarsus
Metatarsals
Phalanges

Trapezius
Deltoid
Triceps
Latissimus dorsi
Extensors of wrist and hand
Flexors of wrist and hand
Gluteus maximus
Hamstrings
Gastrocnemius
Achilles tendon

Sterno mastoid
Pectoralis major
Biceps
Serratus anterior
Extensors of wrist and hand
Flexors of wrist and hand
Rectus abdominus
Sartorius
Quadriceps
Extensors of foot

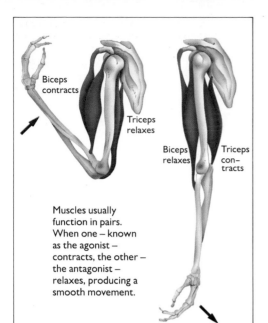

Muscles usually function in pairs. When one – known as the agonist – contracts, the other – the antagonist – relaxes, producing a smooth movement.

movement in a number of directions, while the joint between the base of the spine and the pelvis – the sacro-iliac joint – is a *plane joint* where very little movement is possible except during pregnancy, when the pelvis expands to accommodate the growing foetus.

Where the first vertebra – the *atlas*, so named because it holds the weight of the head – joins the next vertebra, the *axis*, a *pivotal joint* is formed. Movement occurs between the ring of the atlas and the toothlike peg of the axis, allowing rotation or turning of the head to look over the shoulder.

Condyloid joints are those between the bones of the hand and the fingers, and between those of the foot and the toes.

Muscle types

Muscle is basically of two types: the sort we can control, known as *voluntary*, *striped*, or *skeletal muscle*, and the sort we cannot control, otherwise known as *smooth*, *autonomic* or *involuntary muscle*. Although the heart muscle is not under our direct control it is usually classed separately as *cardiac muscle*.

All types of muscle are influenced by psychological factors. Most people have experienced how feeling nervous can make the hands and legs tremble and the heart beat faster. There may also be a need to rush to the lavatory as the urinary and digestive tracts empty faster than they would under more relaxed circumstances. Some people learn to control unwanted muscle actions using meditation and relaxation techniques.

Voluntary muscle

Voluntary muscle is composed of long thin cells or fibres enclosed in an outer coat. Under the microscope the fibres show alternate light and dark bands, which is why they are sometimes referred to as striped. The dark bands contain the protein *myosin* while the light ones contain *actin*. In the middle of the dark bands is a lighter area called the H band. In the middle of the light bands is a slim dark band called the Z area and the space

between two Z areas is known as a contractile unit or *sarcomere*.

When a message to move is sent by the brain to a muscle via the nerves (⊳ pp. 146–7) or if an electrical stimulus is applied to a muscle fibre, it will contract – the light bands shorten and the actin and myosin filaments slide past each other. When a muscle contracts it can shorten and become thicker – an *isotonic* contraction – or it can remain the same length but increase in tension – an *isometric* contraction. If a weight is picked up and the elbow bent, the biceps contract isotomically. If we try to bend the elbow while applying pressure with the other hand to prevent it actually bending, the biceps contracts isometrically.

Although we can directly cause voluntary muscles to contract, we rarely do so. The usual course is to direct a movement like walking upstairs. Such a command initiates action in whole groups of muscles that act in harmony to perform a coordinated manoeuvre. Some of the muscles perform the more obvious actions like bending the hip and knee, while others come into play to stabilize the trunk and increase strength in the opposite leg, which temporarily bears the entire body weight.

Habitual movement patterns are so well established that the way we move is largely performed unconsciously. Only the dedicated few – for example, tennis players wanting to improve their backhand stroke – study precisely which muscles are working and develop the conscious ability to make fine adjustments to the way they perform.

Involuntary muscle

Involuntary or smooth muscle is found in the walls of the digestive tract, in the respiratory system and in the urinary and reproductive tracts. It is the main tissue in the middle coat of the smaller arteries and determines the diameter of these vessels. By regulating the resistance of the vessels it controls the distribution of blood to the various tissues and organs and helps control the blood pressure.

In the eye, involuntary muscle controls the amount of light entering by adjusting the size of the pupil (⊳ pp. 144–45) and in the skin it causes the hair to stand erect when we are cold or frightened.

Involuntary muscle is the simplest type of muscle in construction, consisting of spindle-shaped fibres each with a single nucleus. But it is capable of very strong contractions. During birth the smooth muscle of the uterus contracts powerfully to expel the foetus, and the act of defecating or vomiting brings smooth muscle in the digestive tract into play with considerable force.

Cardiac muscle

The heart muscle is unique in construction, consisting of long cylindrical fibres arranged in sheets and bundles. Certain special fibres in the heart muscle make up the conducting system by which electrical impulses spread to the other fibres and bring about the rhythmical sequence of contraction and relaxation that allows the heart to empty itself of blood and then refill (⊳ pp. 140–1).

TYPES OF JOINT

Ball and socket

Saddle

Hinge

Condyloid

Pivotal

Plane

Food, Diet and Digestion

Unlike plants, which can synthesize everything they require using energy from the Sun (▷ p. 6), animals, including humans, must obtain their nutrients and energy from food. Digestion is the process in which the energy and nutrients contained in food are broken down into a suitable form to be absorbed by the body and utilized as a source of energy, or to synthesize substances such as proteins, enzymes and hormones that are required for the normal functioning of the body.

The nutrients required by the body are proteins, carbohydrates, fats, minerals and vitamins. Water is not a nutrient but an adequate intake is essential to replace the water that is lost each day through the skin and lungs and in urine and faeces.

Proteins

Proteins are made up of large numbers of *amino acids*. There are about 20 amino acids and they can be arranged in any order to produce a larger number of different proteins. Eight amino acids must be provided by the diet – these are called the *essential amino acids*. The others can be synthesized from one of the other amino acids.

Proteins provide cell structure, help fight infections, transport substances around the body and form enzymes and hormones. They can also provide energy. Meat, eggs, milk and pulses (peas, beans, lentils, etc.) are all rich in proteins.

Carbohydrates

Carbohydrates contain carbon, hydrogen and oxygen and provide energy. The simple carbohydrates are the *monosaccharides* (glucose, fructose and galactose) and the *disaccharides* (sucrose, lactose and maltose). A disaccharide consists of two molecules of a monosaccharide. Sucrose (table sugar) contains a molecule of glucose joined to a molecule of fructose. Good sources of simple carbohydrates are fruits, honey, milk and table sugar.

Complex carbohydrates (*polysaccharides*) contain many hundreds of monosaccharides. Starch is a polysaccharide of glucose. Good sources of complex carbohydrates are bread, rice and potatoes. *Dietary fibre* consists mainly of complex carbohydrates that cannot be digested. It provides bulk and aids bowel function. Sources include unrefined cereals, fruit and vegetables.

Fats

Fats are made up of *triglycerides*. A triglyceride has a backbone of *glycerol* with three *fatty acids* attached to it. Fatty acids can either be *saturated* or *unsaturated*. Fats provide twice the amount of energy as carbohydrates and proteins. A diet high in fat, particularly 'saturated fat' (as found in, for example, red meat and dairy products), has been linked to the development of coronary heart disease. Most people would benefit from reducing their total fat intake, particularly if it contains a lot of saturated fatty acids.

Minerals

Mineral salts are essential for many of the body's chemical reactions. *Sodium* in the fluid surrounding the cells regulates the cells' external environment, while *potassium* plays the same role inside the cell. Haemoglobin, which transports oxygen, contains *iron*; many enzymes contain *zinc*; the transmission of nerve impulses requires sodium and potassium, and the mineral salts *calcium* and *phosphorus* are found in bone.

Vitamins

Vitamins are complex chemical compounds that are essential in small quantities for many chemical reactions (▷ box). If a vitamin is lacking in the diet a deficiency disease arises – for example, lack of vitamin C leads to scurvy. An excess of certain vitamins can also be dangerous.

Digestion and absorption

The gastrointestinal tract is a long tube about 9 m long, which passes through the body from the mouth to the anus. Here the complex structures present in food are mixed with *enzymes* (proteins that act as catalysts in certain biochemical reactions) and broken down into their simple constituents. These are small enough to be absorbed through the wall of the intestine into the bloodstream.

Food is chewed in the mouth and mixed with saliva. It passes through the *oesophagus* into the

KIDNEY NEPHRON

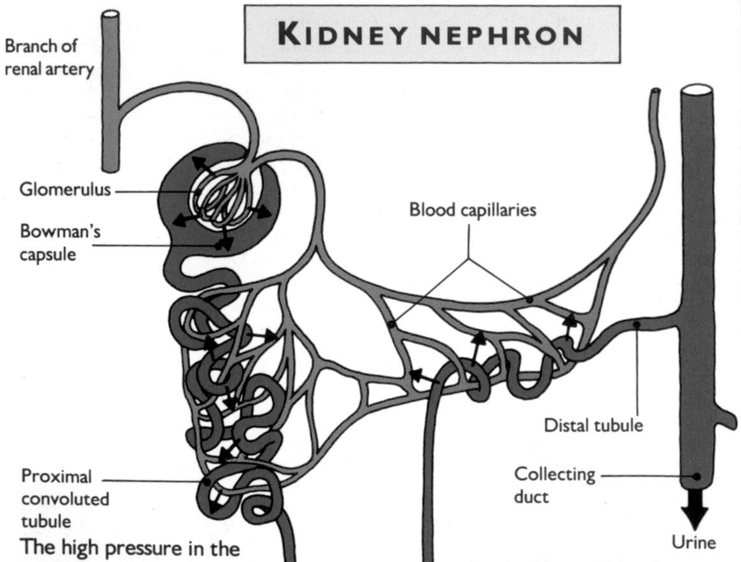

Branch of renal artery

Glomerulus

Bowman's capsule

Blood capillaries

Distal tubule

Collecting duct

Urine

Proximal convoluted tubule

The high pressure in the capillaries of the *glomerulus* forces the fluid part of blood through the capillary walls into the *Bowman's capsule*. Proteins and blood cells are too large to squeeze through the gaps in the capillary wall and remain behind.

Loop of Henle

As the filtered blood passes through the nephron, glucose, amino acids, most of the mineral salts and most of the water are reabsorbed into the bloodstream. Urea and other waste products pass through unabsorbed and are excreted as urine.

GASTROINTESTINAL TRACT

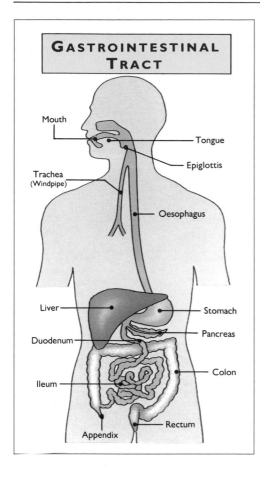

Mouth
Tongue
Epiglottis
Trachea (Windpipe)
Oesophagus
Liver
Stomach
Duodenum
Pancreas
Ileum
Colon
Appendix
Rectum

SEE ALSO
● FARMING p. 132
● REPRODUCTION AND DEVELOPMENT p. 134
● RESPIRATION AND CIRCULATION p. 140
● THE SENSES p. 144
● NON-INFECTIOUS DISEASES p. 152

Amino acids are stored as proteins, which can be broken down to release the amino acids when they are required. Excess amino acids are converted to carbohydrate by the removal of the 'amino' group, and used as an energy source. The 'amino' group is converted to *urea*, a waste substance that is excreted in the urine.

Fatty acids are also an energy source. When the supply of glucose begins to fall, triglycerides are broken down in the liver and adipose tissue, and fatty acids are released into the blood to be taken up by other cells.

Energy is produced by the oxidation of either glucose or fatty acids and is stored in the high-energy molecule ATP (*adenosine triphosphate*). ATP can later release this energy to drive other chemical reactions in the cell. The oxidation of fatty acids produces more than twice as many molecules of ATP as the oxidation of glucose. Carbohydrates and proteins provide 4 kilocalories (17 kilojoules) of energy per gram, and fat 9 kilocalories (39 kilojoules) per gram.

Excretion

Many of the chemical reactions that take place in the body produce compounds that would be toxic if allowed to accumulate. Blood must therefore be purified and the toxic waste products excreted. This takes place in the *kidney nephron*. There are many hundreds of nephrons in each kidney (▷ diagram).

stomach. The stomach acts as a temporary store and mixes the food until it is in a semi-fluid state called *chyme*. This is then released slowly into the *duodenum*.

Most digestion takes place in the duodenum. Enzymes, secreted by the pancreas into the duodenum, split proteins into amino acids, fats into fatty acids and glycerol, and polysaccharides into glucose and fructose. These are then absorbed through the walls of the *ileum* (part of the small intestine). Glucose, fructose and amino acids are absorbed into the bloodstream and carried to the liver (▷ below). Fatty acids and glycerol are absorbed into the lymphatic system (▷ p. 142), and enter the bloodstream later.

Substances that cannot be digested pass into the *colon* (the large intestine). Some compounds are fermented by the bacteria there and others are excreted as waste products in the faeces via the *rectum*.

Storage and use of nutrients

The blood carries the absorbed nutrients from the intestine to the liver. After a meal the liver prevents the levels of glucose and amino acids in the blood from rising too much by removing them from the blood. Glucose is stored as *glycogen* and can be converted back into glucose when the blood levels of glucose begin to fall. Any excess glucose is converted into *triglyceride* and is stored in *adipose tissue* – connective tissue packed with fat cells.

VITAMINS

VITAMIN A (Retinol)
Functions: Essential for growth; vision in poor light; health of cornea and resistance to infection. Deficiency causes stunted growth, night blindness and susceptibility to infection. **Sources:** Dairy products, fish-liver oils, egg yolks. Carotene, found in carrots and green vegetables, can be converted by the body into retinol.

VITAMIN B1 (Thiamin)
Functions: Essential for carbohydrate metabolism and nervous system functioning. Deficiency causes beriberi, with symptoms either of fluid retention or of extreme weight loss. **Sources:** Yeast, egg yolks, liver, wheatgerm, peas and beans.

VITAMIN B2 (Riboflavin)
Functions: Essential for tissue respiration. Deficiency causes inflammation of tongue and lips. **Sources:** Yeast, yeast and meat extracts, milk, liver, kidneys, cheese, eggs, green vegetables.

FOLIC ACID
Functions: B vitamin essential for maturing of red blood cells in bone marrow. **Sources:** Spinach, liver, broccoli, peanuts.

NICOTINIC ACID (Niacin)
Functions: B vitamin essential for metabolism of carbohydrates; functioning of digestive tract and nervous system. Deficiency causes pellagra, characterized by scaly skin, diarrhoea and depression. **Sources:** Yeast, yeast and meat extracts, fish, meat, cereals, peas and beans.

VITAMIN B6 (Pyridoxine)
Functions: Essential for metabolism of fat

and protein. **Sources:** Liver, egg yolks, meat, peas and beans.

VITAMIN B12 (Cyanocobalamin)
Functions: Essential for maturing of red blood cells in bone marrow. **Sources:** Liver, fish, eggs, meat.

BIOTIN
Functions: B vitamin essential for metabolism of fat. **Sources:** Egg yolks, liver, tomatoes, raspberries, artichokes.

VITAMIN C (Ascorbic acid)
Functions: Essential for formation of red blood cells, antibodies and connective tissue; formation and maintenance of bones; maintenance of strength of blood capillaries. Deficiency causes scurvy, with symptoms of swollen bleeding gums, weakness and dizziness. **Sources:** Blackcurrants, citrus fruits, green vegetables, potatoes.

VITAMIN D
Functions: Essential for absorption of calcium and phosphorus. Deficiency causes rickets. **Sources:** Fish-liver oils, eggs, butter, cheese. Humans can synthesize vitamin D from sunlight.

VITAMIN E
Functions: Has antioxidant properties, thought to prevent oxidation of unsaturated fatty acids in cells. **Sources:** Vegetable oils, cereals, green vegetables, eggs, butter.

VITAMIN K
Functions: Associated with clotting mechanism of blood. **Sources:** Green vegetables, liver; can be synthesized in the human gut.

Respiration and Circulation

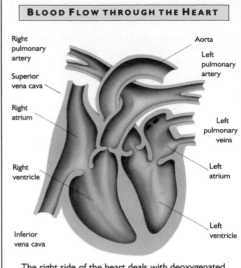

BLOOD FLOW THROUGH THE HEART

Right pulmonary artery

Aorta

Left pulmonary artery

Superior vena cava

Right atrium

Left pulmonary veins

Left atrium

Right ventricle

Left ventricle

Inferior vena cava

The right side of the heart deals with deoxygenated blood, while the left side deals with oxygenated blood.

Every cell of the body requires a constant supply of oxygen and nutrients. The immediate source of these is the interstitial fluid, which surrounds the cell and is continuously replenished by the blood supply. Carbon dioxide and other waste produced by the cells are then carried away by the blood.

Carrying gases is one of the many functions of blood, which consists of three types of cell. Suspended in a liquid called *plasma* are red corpuscles, white corpuscles and platelets. The main function of white corpuscles is to fight infection (▷ p. 142) and the platelets initiate the clotting mechanism, which ensures that when a blood vessel is damaged the wound is sealed before much of the 5 litres (8 pints) of blood that the average person possesses is lost.

Each litre of blood contains about 5×10^{12} red blood corpuscles containing *haemoglobin* – a substance which combines with oxygen in the lungs and carries it to the tissues, where the oxygen is exchanged for carbon dioxide. This carbon dioxide is then carried to the lungs, where it is exchanged for more oxygen. If a person has a reduced number of red corpuscles or if the corpuscles have a reduced amount of haemoglobin, they are said to be suffering from *anaemia* and not

enough oxygen is carried to the tissues. This results in tiredness and breathlessness, particularly on exertion.

Respiration

The oxygenation of blood in the lungs, the use of oxygen and production of carbon dioxide by the tissues and the removal of carbon dioxide from the blood in the lungs is called respiration.

Air enters the respiratory system through the nose or mouth and passes down the *trachea*, which branches in the lungs into smaller and smaller tubes or *bronchioles* and finally into *alveoli*, where blood and gas are in close contact and gases can exchange freely. This occurs as a result of muscle contraction. Breathing in (*inspiration*) occurs when two sets of muscle contract – the *diaphragm*, which separates the chest from the abdomen, and the *intercostals*, which lie between each rib. Contraction of these muscles increases the volume within the *thoracic cavity* (chest). This causes the lungs to expand and air to rush in. When the muscles stop contracting, they relax passively and the lungs deflate again, forcing the air out (*expiration*).

Circulation

William Harvey (▷ pp. 156–7) proved that the heart and blood vessels formed a closed system, with the blood continuously circulating around it. The centre point of this system is the heart – the pump which forces the blood through the blood vessels to every part of the body. The heart is in fact a double pump – a right and a left pump, each consisting of two chambers, an *atrium* and a *ventricle*. The right atrium receives blood from all parts of the body and passes it on to the right ventricle, which then pumps it to the lungs (*pulmonary circulation*). The oxygenated blood then returns to the left atrium and into the left ventricle, which pumps it to all parts of the body (*systemic circulation*). The heart is a very powerful muscle, contracting between 60 and 200 times a minute depending on the level of activity. To ensure that the blood moves in only one direction through the heart, the openings between the atria and ventricles and between the ventricles and blood vessels are guarded by valves.

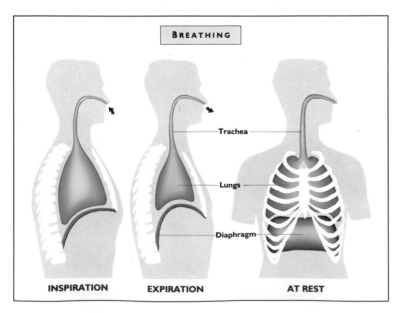

BREATHING

Trachea

Lungs

Diaphragm

INSPIRATION   **EXPIRATION**   **AT REST**

The blood vessels leaving the heart are called arteries, with the *pulmonary artery* going to the lungs, and the *aorta* to all the organs and tissues of the body. As they get further from the heart, they branch into smaller and smaller arteries. Arteries appear circular in cross section, with thick muscular walls. The smaller arteries eventually become *capillaries* – thin-walled vessels through which the transfer of oxygen and other substances between the blood and interstitial fluid occurs. At the same time, carbon dioxide and other waste products leave the interstitial fluid and enter the blood. The capillaries then converge, forming larger and larger vessels known as *veins*, which are thin-walled and of indefinite shape. Veins contain valves, which aid the movement of blood from the lower parts of the body against gravity. Eventually they merge into two large veins, the *superior vena cava* and *inferior vena cava*, which return blood to the right atrium.

The effects of exercise

As the body changes from a state of rest to one of activity, its requirements alter. At rest the body uses about 0.25 litres of oxygen each minute, and this can rise to three litres a minute in heavy exercise. To make this possible, both the heart and the respiratory system must increase their level of activity. At rest the heart pumps about five litres of blood per minute to the lungs and the same amount around the rest of the body. In heavy exercise, this volume is increased to about 30 litres per minute – the heart rate increases from about 60 to 200 beats per minute and the amount of blood pumped out with each beat is doubled. Because the amount of blood passing through the lungs increases about six times, more air must be brought into the lungs to provide the necessary oxygen, and this is achieved by breathing more frequently and more deeply. The circulatory and respiratory systems can be finely controlled in this way to meet the prevailing requirements of the body.

Other functions

Nutrients, eaten and digested (▷ p. 138), are absorbed into the bloodstream and transported to the liver and tissues which need them. Water, which accounts for about 60% of the body, is constantly moving around the body and this is brought about by movement into and out of the bloodstream. Hormones are secreted into the bloodstream by the endocrine glands and transported to their target tissues (▷ p. 143). Waste products are carried to the kidneys for excretion in the urine (▷ p. 139). Drugs taken by mouth or injected enter the bloodstream and are carried to the organs on which they are expected to act.

Injury or infection causes inflammation – local blood vessels dilate and the increased flow of blood brings microphages, macrophages and antibodies to the area (▷ p. 142). Blood also plays a part in regulating body temperature: in hot weather vessels in the skin dilate allowing heat to escape and in cold weather they contract, conserving body heat.

SEE ALSO

● HOW PEOPLE MOVE p. 136
● FOOD, DIET AND DIGESTION p. 138
● GLANDS AND HORMONES p. 143
● NON-INFECTIOUS DISEASES p. 152

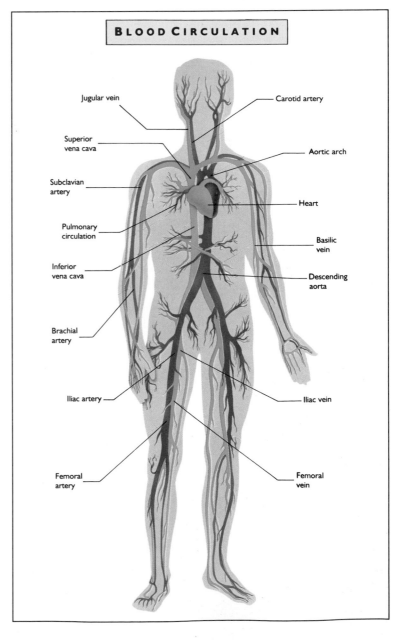

BLOOD CIRCULATION

Jugular vein
Carotid artery
Superior vena cava
Aortic arch
Subclavian artery
Heart
Pulmonary circulation
Basilic vein
Inferior vena cava
Descending aorta
Brachial artery
Iliac artery
Iliac vein
Femoral artery
Femoral vein

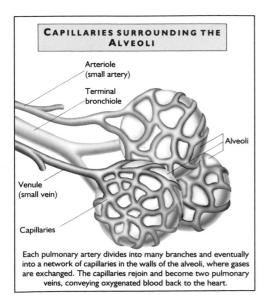

CAPILLARIES SURROUNDING THE ALVEOLI

Arteriole (small artery)
Terminal bronchiole
Alveoli
Venule (small vein)
Capillaries

Each pulmonary artery divides into many branches and eventually into a network of capillaries in the walls of the alveoli, where gases are exchanged. The capillaries rejoin and become two pulmonary veins, conveying oxygenated blood back to the heart.

The Immune System

Every day of our lives there is a constant battle between our bodies and a multitude of microbes. To bacteria, viruses and fungi, many of which cause disease, the human body represents a warm haven where food is plentiful.

SEE ALSO

● RESPIRATION AND CIRCULATION p. 140
● GLANDS AND HORMONES p. 143
● NON-INFECTIOUS DISEASES p. 152
● INFECTIOUS DISEASES p. 154

Before a microorganism can install itself, however, it has to breach the body's first line of defence. Waterproof skin affords some protection, enhanced by the secretions of the sebaceous glands that contain *lysozyme*, which kills bacteria and viruses. Mucus, lining the tubes to the lungs, acts as a physical barrier to bacteria reaching the lungs, as mucus will be coughed up or swallowed and destroyed by acidic stomach juices. Microorganisms that can enter the body via the urinary openings are often flushed out by urine. Harmless bacteria resident in the gut and vagina also help prevent disease-causing microorganisms from establishing themselves.

However, bacteria, viruses and fungi sometimes manage to evade these defences and begin to multiply in the body. It is then that the immune system comes into play.

The immune system

White blood cells known as *lymphocytes* form one of the most important components of the immune system. The cells destined to become lymphocytes originate in the bone marrow. Some of them travel in the blood to the *thymus gland* in the neck, where they mature into *T-lymphocytes*. The thymus gland seems to have a role in ensuring that only those T cells that recognize foreign proteins (as opposed to the body's own proteins)

are released into the circulation. Some of the immature cells remain in the bone marrow for the rest of their development, however, and they become *B-lymphocytes*. Once mature, the T and B cells migrate in the blood to the *spleen*, the *lymph nodes* and other components of the *lymphoid tissue*, such as the tonsils. The spleen is an organ found on the left side of the body, just below the diaphragm. One of its functions is to filter circulating microorganisms from the blood. Lymphocytes present in the spleen are ready to respond to any foreign microbe that appears.

The lymph nodes, present throughout the body, filter the *lymph* – a clear fluid that drains from the body tissues. The lymph collects in the vessels of the *lymphatic system*, and eventually returns to the blood. It first passes through the lymph nodes and any microorganisms or cancer cells are filtered out. If an infection is present, lymphocytes respond by multiplying, which accounts for the swelling of the nodes – for example, in the armpits and under the lower jaw – that sometimes occurs. Vast numbers of other types of white blood cell, e.g. *microphages* (neutrophils) and *macrophages*, can engulf and destroy microorganisms. They also destroy red blood cells that have reached the end of their 120-day life span. These so-called *phagocytic* cells are found in the tissues, lymph nodes and spleen.

Antigens and antibodies

An *antigen* is any foreign substance – for instance, the protein on the coat of a bacterium – that can stimulate an immune response. When T cells meet antigens they respond by multiplying and dividing, releasing molecules that stimulate other cells of the immune system (including other T cells) to grow.

There are may different kinds of T cells. *Cytotoxic T cells* can recognize and kill cells infected with viruses. *T-helper cells* can help macrophages to kill microorganisms. T-helper cells also have an important role in stimulating B cells.

Once stimulated, a B cell multiplies. Its offspring mature into *plasma cells*, which secrete *antibodies*. These are specialized molecules that can latch on to antigens and help the rest of the immune system eliminate the foreign particle. There is potentially an infinite variety of antibodies, one for every conceivable antigen. Once a B cell is stimulated, the result is a *clone* of plasma cells, all dedicated to manufacturing the antibody that recognizes the antigen in question.

Immunity and memory

A few of the cells that result when a B cell divides in response to an antigen are so-called *memory cells*. These remain in the body for life: when the individual meets the same antigen again, they are ready to respond, faster and with more force than before. This explains why people who have one attack of rubella (German measles), for example, are immune to subsequent infections by this virus. Immunization works on this principle. Vaccines aim to prime the immune system to recognize disease-causing organisms, so that it will spring into action when it encounters the microorganisms concerned. Several vaccines consist of bacteria or viruses that have been killed or weakened; they provoke a protective immune response, but no longer have the capacity to cause the disease.

T-lymphocytes seen through a false-colour scanning electron micrograph. These 'killer' white blood cells recognize antigens on foreign microorganisms and destroy them by releasing enzymes that disrupt their cell membranes. (SPL)

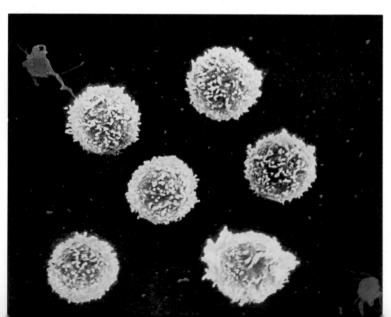

Glands and Hormones

Cells within the human body communicate with one another through two basic mechanisms: the nervous system (⊳ p. 146) and the *endocrine system*. The latter consists of the endocrine glands, scattered throughout the body. The endocrine glands produce chemicals (*hormones*) that are transported in the blood to distant tissues (*targets*) whose activities they modify.

SEE ALSO

- REPRODUCTION AND DEVELOPMENT p. 134
- FOOD, DIET AND DIGESTION p. 138
- RESPIRATION AND CIRCULATION p. 140
- NON-INFECTIOUS DISEASES p. 152

THE ENDOCRINE SYSTEM

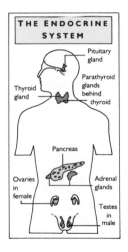

Pituitary gland

Parathyroid glands behind thyroid

Thyroid gland

Pancreas

Ovaries in female

Adrenal glands

Testes in male

Hormones exert their effects in four broadly defined biological areas: reproduction, growth and development, control of the internal environment, and regulation of energy production.

The anterior pituitary

The *pituitary* gland consists of two lobes, anterior and posterior. It sits in a cavity of the skull, underneath the brain, and despite its small size – less than 1 cm (¹/₅ in) in diameter and 0.5 g in weight (¹/₅₀ oz) – it is crucial to the endocrine system. In particular, by their actions on other glands throughout the body, the hormones of the anterior pituitary play a fundamental role in the control of reproduction and metabolism. The anterior pituitary is itself controlled by the *hypothalamus*, an area of the brain that receives information about the body's internal environment and adjusts pituitary output accordingly.

Reproduction

Reproductive function in both sexes is controlled by the anterior pituitary *gonadotrophins* (FSH and LH) and the *steroid hormones* from ovary or testis (testicle). In women, fluctuations of these hormones govern each menstrual cycle, stimulating ovulation and preparing the uterus (womb) for pregnancy (⊳ p. 134). After delivery, *prolactin* and *oxytocin* control milk production and expression. In men, pituitary gonadotrophins are responsible for sperm production and fertility. The sex steroids also bring about the development of secondary sexual characteristics – beard growth, deep voice and muscle increase in males, and breast development in females (⊳ p. 134).

Growth

Many hormones participate in the coordination of growth, both of individual organs and of the whole body. *Growth hormone* (GH) is particularly important for growth of the skeleton during childhood, while *thyroid hormone* (TH) is crucial for the maturing of the central nervous system. In the absence of thyroid function during early infancy, physical and mental development fail, giving rise to *cretinism* – restricted height and mental retardation. An excess of GH in adult life leads to *acromegaly*, characterized by abnormal thickening of bones and soft tissues.

The internal environment

A multitude of hormones participate in the regulation of the body's internal environment. *Antidiuretic hormone* from the posterior pituitary and *aldosterone* from the cortex of the adrenal gland regulate the excretion of water and salt by the kidney; *parathyroid hormone*, together with vitamin D, controls the level of the minerals calcium and phosphorus in the blood, while the functions of liver, muscle and fat are influenced by GH, insulin, glucagon, adrenaline, sex steroids and cortisol.

Metabolism

The pancreatic hormones *insulin* and *glucagon* help the body convert food into usable and stored energy. Insulin deficiency leads to diabetes (⊳ box, p. 152). The thyroid gland produces *thyroxine*, which stimulates metabolism, helping to generate large amounts of energy in the form of heat. People with thyroid insufficiency suffer a variety of metabolic disorders – including extreme cold sensitivity and mental slowing – while in Graves disease (overactive thyroid) metabolic rate is elevated and the patient loses weight and feels hot, hyperactive and anxious.

Hormone secretion

The output of a hormone is usually regulated so as to allow a response to a biological need without a prolonged high level of secretion. Hormones or the effects they produce often inhibit their own output by negative feedback – their secretion is self-limiting. Many hormones are released in response to stress, while some show a daily (*circadian*) pattern. *Adrenocorticotrophic hormone* (ACTH) and the adrenal cortical hormones show such a 24-hour rhythm, with a peak occurring in the early morning, probably to prepare the body for the stress of getting up.

MAJOR GLANDS AND THEIR HORMONES

Hypothalamus (brain) Produces releasing hormones responsible for controlling output of anterior pituitary hormones, e.g. thyrotropin releasing hormone (TRH), which stimulates secretion of TSH (⊳ below).

Anterior pituitary Produces gonadotrophins (luteinizing hormone, LH; follicle-stimulating hormone, FSH), which targets the gonads (ovaries and testes); prolactin, which targets breast tissue; adrenocorticotrophic hormone (ACTH), which targets the adrenal cortex; thyroid stimulating hormone (TSH), which targets the thyroid gland; growth hormone (GH), which targets most cells.

Posterior pituitary Produces antidiuretic hormone (ADH), which targets the kidney; oxytocin, which targets breast tissue.

Thyroid gland Produces thryoxine, which targets most cells.

Adrenal cortex Produces cortisol steroid, which targets most cells; and aldosterone steroid, which targets the kidney.

Ovaries and testes Produce sex steroids (oestrogens, progesterone and testosterone), which all target the reproductive system.

Placenta Produces sex steroids and human chorionic gonadotrophins (HCG), which target the uterus and breast.

Pancreas Produces insulin and glucagon, which target most cells.

Parathyroid glands Produce parathyroid hormone (PTH), which targets the bone tissue and kidney.

Adrenal medulla Produces adrenaline and noradrenaline, which target the heart and blood vessels.

The Senses

The prime senses in the human being are sight, hearing, touch, taste and smell. They give us vital information about what is going on in the world around us, allowing our bodies to react appropriately.

Sensing is not affected by experience and learning; a sensation produced by a specific stimulus remains essentially unchanged from one time to another. What can change, however, is our *perception* of that sensation, which may alter in the light of something we have learnt.

Vision

The eyes function as a pair, each seeing a slightly different version of the object being looked at. This 3-D or stereoscopic vision is particularly important in order to judge distances, and hence to judge at what speed things are travelling.

The *sclera*, or white of the eye, is a firm membrane that forms the outer layer of the eyeball. At the front of the eye it continues as the *cornea*, a transparent convex membrane that refracts the light rays to focus on the retina (▷ below). The eyelids form a pair of protective shutters and also spread tears over the cornea, keeping it moist and free from infection. The *iris* – the part of the eye that regulates the amount of light that enters – lies behind the cornea in front of the lens. It forms a pigmented muscular body with a central aperture, the *pupil*, which varies in size depending on the intensity of light; the pupil will constrict in bright light and dilate in dim light.

The *lens*, a transparent crystalline structure, is enclosed in a thin clear capsule and situated behind the pupil. It is able to fine-tune the focusing performed by the cornea. It is highly elastic, changing focus by increasing or decreasing its thickness – this is brought about by contraction of the muscle in the *ciliary body*. The nearer the object, the thicker the lens needs to be in order to bring it into focus. The *retina* is the

VISUAL IMPAIRMENT

The most common reasons for visual impairment are *myopia* (short sight) and *hypermetropia* (long sight). Short-sighted people find that objects get progressively more blurred the further away they are because parallel light rays are brought to a focus in front of the retina. The condition can be corrected by spectacles with concave lenses. In the case of long sight, parallel light rays are brought to a focus behind the retina, so that close objects appear blurred. Wearing spectacles with convex lenses can restore normal sight. *Presbyopia*, a condition common in later life, is caused by a gradual loss of elasticity in the lens – it becomes less able to increase its curvature in order to focus on near objects.

Cataract is also a common cause of poor sight. The lens begins to become opaque, and the condition may eventually prevent any light coming through at all. *Glaucoma*, or tunnel vision, is an inherited condition in which the pressure of fluid within the eye builds up, thus destroying the nerve cells in the retina. Eventually only a small patch of nerve cells in the centre of the retina remains, giving the sufferer the sensation of constantly looking down a tube.

light-sensitive layer lining the inside of the eye. It contains nerve fibres and specialized cells – *rods* and *cones*. The rods, numbering about 125 million, are essential for seeing in dim light. The 6–7 million cones function in bright light and are necessary for sharp vision; they are most concentrated in the *fovea* – a small depression in the retina. Certain types of cone cells are colour-sensitive and are responsible for colour vision.

The human eye is similar in structure to a camera (▷ p. 204) and the principles of vision lie within the basic physical theories of optics (▷ p. 24). The light image focused by the lens onto the retina is converted into electrical impulses, which are then transmitted to the brain via the *optic nerve*.

Once inside the brain, the electrical image of what the eyes are looking at must be interpreted and 'recognized' according to the brain's past experience. If the eye is shown a table, for instance, the brain will receive electrical messages telling it that something with a horizontal surface and four legs is present. The brain sorts through all the other images it has seen that resemble this – four-legged animals, beds, etc. – eventually matching it up with a table seen in the past and giving it a label. Although complicated, the process takes only a fraction of a second.

Hearing and balance

The ability to hear has two elements – a mechanical element and an element involving electrical nerve impulses. Sound enters through the *external ear* or *auricle* – that part of the ear that is visible. Its scalloped shape ensures that as much sound as possible is reflected into the inside of the ear. Inside the ear, sound travels down a short tube, the *external auditory canal*, until it hits a very thin sheet of skin called the *eardrum* or *tympanic membrane*. The mechanical force of the sound waves (▷ p. 22) sets the eardrum vibrating. This vibration is then transmitted across the cavity, or *middle ear*, on the other side of the eardrum by a series of tiny bones (*auditory ossicles*), which form a series of movable joints with each other. The *stapes* is a stirrup-shaped bone; the *incus*, an anvil-shaped bone, is situated in the middle; and the *malleus*, a hammer-shaped bone, is in contact with the tympanic membrane.

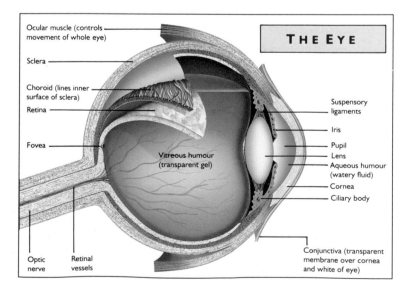

THE EYE

Ocular muscle (controls movement of whole eye)

Sclera

Choroid (lines inner surface of sclera)

Retina

Fovea

Vitreous humour (transparent gel)

Suspensory ligaments

Iris

Pupil

Lens

Aqueous humour (watery fluid)

Cornea

Ciliary body

Optic nerve

Retinal vessels

Conjunctiva (transparent membrane over cornea and white of eye)

Beyond the middle ear is the *inner ear* or *cochlea*. This helix-shaped structure is basically a fluid-filled tube lined with nerve endings. Like many musical instruments, it is wider at one end in order to pick up low-pitched sounds and narrower at the other in order to pick up high-pitched ones.

The *semicircular canals*, three tubes that open into the inner ear, are not concerned with hearing but with balance. Each canal registers movement in a different plane and sends nerve impulses to the brain. They are thus essential in establishing our sense of physical position.

If the vibrations passing through the ear are at any stage impeded – perhaps by a burst eardrum, by damage to the ossicles of the middle ear or by degeneration of the nerves taking the sound messages to the brain, then the individual will become partially or completely deaf in that ear.

The skin and sense of touch

The skin is composed of two layers – the epidermis and the dermis – with a *subcutaneous layer* of fatty tissue underneath. The *epidermis*, or outer layer, itself consists of several layers. At the lowest layer living cells are constantly dividing, providing new cells that rise through the layers. When they reach the outermost layer, the cells are flat, thin and filled with fibrous protein, *keratin*. The *dermis* is the layer of living tissue, and consists of connective tissue with blood capillaries, lymph vessels, sensory nerve endings, sweat glands and pores, hair follicles and sebaceous glands. The old cells within *hair follicles* are converted to keratin and form the root and shaft of a hair. *Sebaceous glands* – associated with hair follicles – produce *sebum* or oil, which lubricates the hair and skin. The skin continues in a modified form in the *mucous membrane*, which lines the nose, mouth and digestive tract.

Buried within the skin and other exposed surfaces are the *sensory nerve endings*, which have lost their protective myelin sheath (▷ p. 147) and branch out into fine filaments. These are responsible for telling the brain what the body is in contact with and alerting it to specific sensations – pressure, warmth, cold and pain. An electrical response is produced in the stimulated nerve ending, and this travels up the sensory fibres of a nerve to the outer layer of the brain (▷ p. 146). Certain areas have a far greater concentration of nerve endings than others, such as the lips, palms of the hands, soles of the feet and the genitalia.

Pain stimuli travel at different speeds within the nerve fibres, hence the sensation of 'double pain'. If a finger is put in scalding water there will be sudden, sharp 'first pain', carried quickly in one sort of nerve fibre, followed a few moments later by duller 'second pain', carried more slowly in another sort of nerve fibre. Pain receptors in the brain respond very quickly to the chemicals that are released from damaged cells. The sensitivity to chemicals allows pain to be treated using pain-killing drugs (analgesics).

Another function of the skin is to regulate body temperature. The *eccrine* sweat glands, present throughout the skin but more numerous in the palms of the hands, soles of the feet, armpits and groin, produce sweat, which is released through the sweat pores. The evaporation of sweat from the skin cools the body. Sweat also carries out some waste products.

Smell

In humans, the sense of smell is relatively under-developed when compared to most animals. The

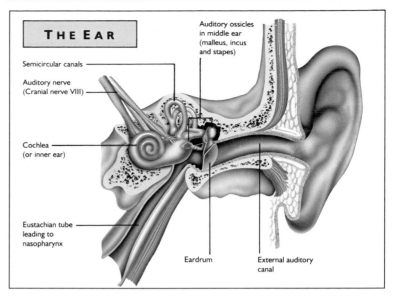

THE EAR

Auditory ossicles in middle ear (malleus, incus and stapes)

Semicircular canals

Auditory nerve (Cranial nerve VIII)

Cochlea (or inner ear)

Eustachian tube leading to nasopharynx

Eardrum

External auditory canal

sense of smell is derived from tiny nerve endings that pass from the *olfactory nerve* at the base of the brain into the damp lining of the nose, known as the *nasal mucosa*. This mucous membrane contains thousands of tiny glands whose job it is to produce the wet, sticky *mucus*. Odorous substances give off molecules, which are present in the air and are breathed in. They dissolve in the nasal mucus, thereby stimulating the olfactory nerve. This information is then passed back to the olfactory lobes in the brain and also to a primitive part of the brain, the limbic system (▷ p. 146).

Taste

Taste is a complex sensation. The tongue can distinguish between only four basic tastes: sweet, sour, salt and bitter – and nothing else. The surface of the tongue is covered with small projections called *papillae*, which contain the nerve endings concerned with the sense of taste. These specialized sensory receptors – the *taste buds* – are stimulated by particles of food dissolving in the saliva. Nerve impulses are sent to the brain via the facial nerve and the glossopharyngeal nerve. The range of tastes normally associated with food depends, in fact, more on the sense of smell than on that of taste.

SEE ALSO

● ACOUSTICS p. 22
● OPTICS p. 24
● THE BRAIN AND NERVOUS SYSTEM p. 146
● LEARNING, CREATIVITY AND INTELLIGENCE p. 148

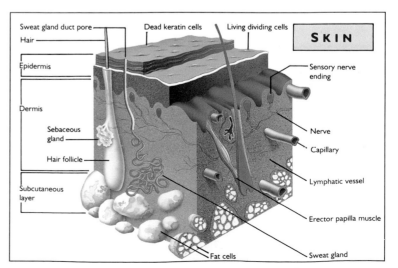

Sweat gland duct pore

Hair

Epidermis

Dermis

Sebaceous gland

Hair follicle

Subcutaneous layer

Dead keratin cells

Living dividing cells

SKIN

Sensory nerve ending

Nerve

Capillary

Lymphatic vessel

Erector papilla muscle

Sweat gland

Fat cells

The Brain and the Nervous System

The brain is a highly developed, dense mass of nerve cells that forms the upper end of the central nervous system. Together, the brain and nervous system provide a complex network that regulates every aspect of human life and endeavour, from breathing to running a marathon, from feeling emotion to mathematical calculation.

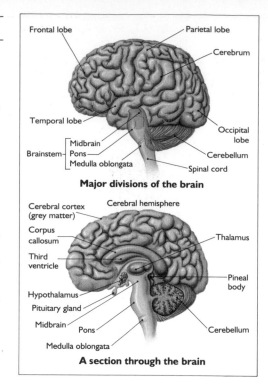

Major divisions of the brain

A section through the brain

The nervous system comprises two major divisions: the *central nervous system* (CNS), which consists of the brain and spinal cord, and the *peripheral nervous system*. The CNS deals largely with sensations and voluntary movement. Messages passing to and from the CNS are carried by way of the branching fibres of the peripheral nervous system, which reaches all the way to the body extremities.

The brain itself has three major divisions. The *brainstem* and *cerebellum* are basic structures concerned with life-support, posture and coordination of movement. The *forebrain* is relatively more developed in humans than in other species.

Nerve cells

The basic functional unit of the brain and nervous system is the nerve cell or *neurone*. From the cell body containing the nucleus, branching outgrowths called *processes* trail in all directions. The cell's longest process – its 'main cable' – is the *axon*, which carries outgoing signals. An axon may extend all the way from the central nervous system to a finger or toe to connect with the muscle on which it acts. Processes known as *dendrites*, which vary in number, pick up messages from other cells.

There are billions of neurones in the CNS. They vary greatly in shape and size, but all communicate electrochemically with their neighbours, forming an intricate network that far outstrips in complexity the circuitry of the most advanced electronic computer.

Nerve signals, sent along the axons, are in the form of discrete all-or-nothing, on-or-off electrical impulses (as in a digital computer). The axon terminates at the *synapse* – the junction where it makes contact with the dendrites or cell bodies of other neurones, or with secretory cells or muscle cells (▷ diagram). At the synapse, the electrical signal in the axon causes the release of a small amount of a chemical transmitter which communicates information to other cells.

The brainstem and cerebellum

The brainstem – the oldest structure in evolutionary terms – forms the stalk of the brain, where

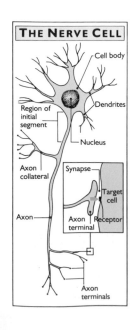

THE NERVE CELL

Cell body
Dendrites
Region of initial segment
Nucleus
Axon collateral
Synapse
Target cell
Axon
Axon terminal
Receptor
Axon terminals

vital functions such as breathing and circulation are integrated. The cerebellum consists of two hemispheres, one on either side. It has a grey outer covering (*cortex*) with a core of white matter. The cerebellum is chiefly involved with the coordination of movement. It ensures coherent muscle function and tone and helps to maintain posture.

The forebrain

Overlying the brainstem and cerebellum is the forebrain (▷ diagram), consisting of a central core (the *diencephalon*) and the *cortex*. Key landmarks in the diencephalon include the *thalamus*, a relay station and integrating centre for sensory messages on their way to the cerebral cortex (▷ below). Below it lies the *hypothalamus*, which is responsible for regulating the body's internal environment (▷ p. 143).

In human beings the great mass of the brain is formed by the *cerebrum*, separated by a deep cleft into two *cerebral hemispheres*, which are linked at the bottom by a communicating bridge, the *corpus callosum*. The left and right cerebral hemispheres have different specializations (▷ box, p. 148). The cerebrum is the most recently evolved part of the brain, responsible for intelligence, intellectual and creative skills and memory. The *cerebral cortex* (or 'grey matter'), the fissured outer layer of the cerebrum, processes information that reaches it from the thalamus and other lower centres.

The higher centres

The cerebral cortex, then, is the most sophisticated part of the brain, where incoming information of all kinds is processed. The cortex sifts, sorts and generally makes sense of the vast mass of stimuli flooding in from the periphery. It organizes these data into the intelligible sights, sounds, impressions and thoughts that are needed to cope with daily living. It is here that decisions are taken and instructions are issued for their implementation.

Anatomists divide the cerebral cortex into four lobes – the frontal, parietal, temporal and occipital lobes, all named after the skull plates beneath which they lie. The *frontal lobe*, extending back behind the forehead and temples, is the largest of the four, as well as the newest in evolutionary terms. Not surprisingly, therefore, it bears the greatest responsibilities and is regarded as the seat of the most advanced mental processes. The frontal lobe governs all voluntary actions, from the simplest physical movements to the intricate matters of thought, language and speech.

Behind the frontal lobes are the *parietal lobes*, straddling each hemisphere towards the rear. Within the parietal lobes are the primary reception areas for the sensation of touch, as well as zones associated with spatial perception (recognition of body position). Damage in these areas would plunge us into a topsy-turvy world.

Running along the base of the parietal lobes, the *temporal lobes* lie approximately on a level with the ears. They contain the centres for auditory perception, with both ears represented on each side of the brain. If one of the temporal lobes is damaged, hearing is not lost, as vision is if one of the *occipital lobes* comes to harm. The smallest of the four, at the rear of the cortex, the occipital lobes receive and process visual images.

Since the information from one sense alone does not always give us a complete picture, all incoming signals are supplemented by, and integrated with, other data being processed simultaneously. This integration process, fulfilled by what are known as *association areas* in the cortex, gives us total awareness of our surroundings.

Instinctive behaviour and emotions

The *limbic system* is the oldest part of the forebrain and consists of a rim of cerebral cortex around the stalk of each central hemisphere, together with a group of deeper structures concerned with instinctive behaviour and the emotional and physical changes that accompany them. These include sexual drive, thirst, hunger, fear and anger.

The peripheral nervous system

The central nervous system communicates with the peripheral nervous system through 12 pairs of cranial nerves and 31 pairs of spinal nerves, which leave the brain and spinal cord. It is these fibres that eventually make their way to the body extremities.

Individual fibres in a nerve may arise from either afferent or efferent neurones. *Afferent neurones* are those carrying signals towards the CNS, while outgoing signals are conducted by *efferent neurones*. Groups of afferent fibres enter the spinal cord at the rear, where they form the dorsal roots; efferent fibres leave the spinal cord at the front, by way of the ventral roots.

The efferent fibres of the peripheral nervous system are divided into the *somatic* (bodily) *nervous system* and the *autonomic* (self-regulating) *nervous system*. Somatic fibres activate skeletal (voluntary) muscle control, whereas autonomic fibres act on smooth or involuntary muscle (such as that found in the gut), as well as cardiac muscle and the various internal organs and glands (⊳ pp. 136 and 143).

Because the activity of the neurones in the somatic nervous system leads to contraction of muscles, they are often called *motor neurones*. Damage to the cell bodies of motor neurones, which are present in clusters in the brain and spinal cord, results in impaired movement.

The autonomic system

The autonomic nervous system, concerned with involuntary function, breaks down further into the *sympathetic* and *parasympathetic nervous systems*. These two components, often present in the same gland or organ, keep each other in check. Broadly, the sympathetic division takes over when rapid action is needed. It enables the appropriate circulatory, metabolic and other adjustments to be made in order to engage in 'fight, flight or fright'.

The autonomic system has been called the 'involuntary nervous system' because of its role in controlling physiological events in which normally there is no conscious input. These include routine matters of body maintenance, such as breathing, heart rate, blood flow, temperature control, digestion, glandular secretion and excretion.

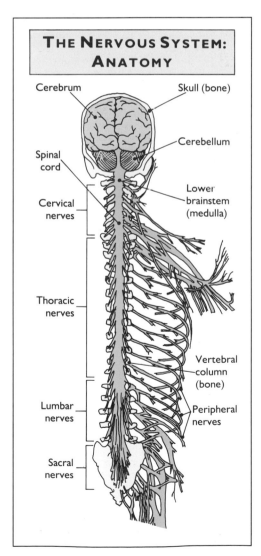

THE NERVOUS SYSTEM: ANATOMY

Cerebrum

Skull (bone)

Cerebellum

Spinal cord

Lower brainstem (medulla)

Cervical nerves

Thoracic nerves

Vertebral column (bone)

Lumbar nerves

Peripheral nerves

Sacral nerves

SEE ALSO

● THE SENSES p. 144
● LEARNING, CREATIVITY AND INTELLIGENCE p. 148
● MENTAL DISORDERS p. 150

Learning, Creativity and Intelligence

Learning, creativity and intelligence are all concerned with the acquisition and use of knowledge. Philosophers have argued about the nature of knowledge, and how we come by it, for thousands of years. Psychologists have now begun to answer more modest – but solvable – questions. Why is it that some people seem to learn faster than others? Are differences between people due to genetic or environmental influences? What factors make someone creative?

If the kinds of thinking involved in different subjects or *knowledge domains* – for example, how we solve problems in mathematics or how we

remember events in history – are analysed we find that they are found to be specific to that domain. A child's understanding of the world seems to be very different from that of an adult: for example, a child might think that the wind is made by trees moving. Such observations led to the idea that intelligence is simply a random collection of independent pieces of knowledge and thinking skills. Yet there are striking regularities in the data that suggest that intelligence and knowledge are not the same thing.

Intelligence

Our ability to think and reason improves as we become older, and this improvement follows the same pattern for all abilities. The major improvements take place in early childhood and end by the late teens.

Everyone has differences between their abilities. However, when individuals of the same age are compared, someone who is relatively good at one kind of thinking will also tend to be good at others. In other words intelligence is general.

Despite the obvious and large changes in our knowledge over the years, IQ (intelligence quotient) is relatively stable throughout life. So what is it that gives rise to these regularities? One explanation is that although different subjects require different kinds of thinking and reasoning skills, all thought processes are influenced by the biological properties of the brain. Alternatively, it could be that general intelligence is a result of our environment rather than a property of our brains. In other words, it may be that the en-

---

ILLUSIONS

The brain experiences the world of objects through information from the senses. This experiencing of sensations is called *perception*. However, sometimes the brain misinterprets the information, and this misinterpretation produces illusions.

Optical illusions can be divided into four types – ambiguities, distortions, paradoxes and fictions. Many of these phenomena of perception are not simply physiological in origin; it is far more likely that many are due to cognitive misreading of the available sensory data.

Ambiguities are spontaneous perceptual changes, the result of searching for the best bet when there are two (or more) equally likely kinds of objects out there. *Distortions* can be caused by

errors of physiological signalling, but most are due to misreading size and distance. Errors are made in judging size, distance, shape or curvature. Objects indicated by perspective, or other cues, as being distant are perceptually expanded in pictures. *Paradoxes* are figures or objects that appear impossible. They are also related to depth perception, as when near and far features happen to line up and touch. *Fictions* – edges and surfaces that are not actually there but are clearly seen – lead to the assumption of the presence of an object or a surface. The ghostly surface, though seen, is not really there. Indeed, this going beyond the sensory data to see what 'ought' to be there could be the cause of many reported apparitions.

Ambiguities: a meaningful picture will probably be perceived when the drawing above is first seen, but it may then be abruptly replaced by another image. It is not known why the image of a vase first appears to some people and that of two faces to other people, nor is the reason for the sudden change clear.

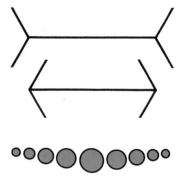

Distortion: in the diagram above, two lines of equal length are made to appear unequal by the addition of the lines at each end, which lead the eye either inward or outward. The tops of the circles above seem to form a curved line, but in fact are aligned in a straight line. The brain is misled because of the strong curve formed by the bottoms of the circles.

Fictions: the edges of the white triangle overlapping the circles are not physically present, but are clearly perceived. Perception goes beyond the sensory data to see what 'ought' to be there.

vironmental circumstances of some individuals provide better learning opportunities.

Nature versus nurture

The study of twins has been the most common method for estimating the relevance of genetic factors to intelligence. *Monozygotic* (identical) twins have the same genetic constitution (*genotype*), whereas *dizygotic* (non-identical) twins have only 50% of their genotype in common (i.e. no more than any two offspring of the same biological parents). The extent to which identical twins are similar in intelligence compared to the extent of similarity in non-identical twins gives us an estimate of the degree to which intelligence is inherited. Because twins have more than their genotype in common – they often have similar environments for example – studies concentrate on twins reared apart.

Identical twins reared apart are more similar in intelligence than non-identical twins reared apart, and so there is little doubt that there is some genetic contribution to intelligence. The best estimate is that at least 50% of the total variance in intelligence is due to inherited differences. Of course, this leaves at least 50% that could be environmental in origin. Heritability estimates apply to populations and tell us that, on average, genes contribute half of the variation in intelligence. However, we cannot say that half of any particular individual's intelligence is due to genes and half to environment. Either the environmental circumstances or the genetic history of an individual, if extreme enough, could totally determine the level of intelligence.

Learnability

It is also interesting that some things that have proved impossible for computers to learn seem remarkably simple for all human beings, irrespective of the level of general thinking ability. For example, there is no computer that has fully mastered the ability to understand human language (as opposed to specially designed computer languages), and yet almost all human beings can do so. Similarly, the process of constructing our perception of the visual world from a retinal image – the image projected on to the light receptors in our eyes – is beyond the capability of any computer but is within the mastery of the human infant. This suggests that evolution has furnished us with specialized brain structures that are unrelated to our ability to think. Occasionally such structures may go wrong, producing people with anomalous abilities (see below).

Specific learning disorders

Undoubtedly some individuals perform less well than we would expect from their level of general intelligence. For example, dyslexic children usually have great difficulty with reading, writing and spelling and yet are of normal intelligence. In such cases a complex brain process usually involved in the analysis of words may not be working. There are also cases in which a brain structure is spared the consequences of general brain damage and a spectacular anomalous ability occurs, where some individuals of very low measured intelligence display a single isolated – sometimes remarkable – ability. These abilities range from knowledge of numbers and number systems (for example, being able to say almost immediately what day of the week it was or will be on any given date) to musical and artistic abilities. Some of these individuals appear so talented

that they have been used as evidence that creativity is independent of intelligence.

What is creativity?

Creativity is usually thought of as depending on some special talent that some people are born with. It has been suggested that creativity depends on properties of the right, as opposed to the left, cerebral hemisphere. While it is true that the two hemispheres of the brain seem to be specialized for different kinds of thinking (box), there is no evidence to suggest that one is specialized for any creative abilities. If we analyse the life history of creative individuals there are few, if any, that would be regarded as unintelligent.

It is also clear that many factors such as personality, motivation, parental involvement and practice contribute to an individual's creativity. In addition, because much of creativity may be in the eye of the beholder, many social factors determine whether someone will be called creative or not. Perhaps here, more than in any area related to human intelligence, we see the limitations of analysing the brain independently of the environment in which it develops.

SEE ALSO

- GENETICS p. 86
- ANIMAL BEHAVIOUR p. 124
- THE SENSES p. 144
- THE BRAIN AND NERVOUS SYSTEM p. 146
- EDUCATION p. 162
- HOW LANGUAGE WORKS p. 354

THE HEMISPHERES OF THE BRAIN

When the eyes focus on a spot (*fixation point*) in the middle of the field of view, everything to the right of that spot (*right visual field*) will be projected on to the left cerebral hemisphere and everything to the left (*left visual field*) will be projected to the right cerebral hemisphere. Since both eyes receive information from both visual fields this means that half of the fibres from each eye must cross over on their way to the projection centres of the brain. They do this at the *optic chiasma*.

Scientists can take advantage of this anatomical feature of the visual system to test the specialization of the cerebral hemispheres. Although the cerebral hemispheres communicate with each other by sending messages through the *cerebral commissures*, presenting information in each visual field for a shorter time than it takes to change fixation (about one fifth of a second) ensures that it is only projected on to the one hemisphere. Any systematic differences in the kinds of information that are processed in each hemisphere can be seen.

The adjacent diagram illustrates an experiment in which people are shown on a screen a series of pictures, of which half are cars and half are other objects, and a series of words, of which half are 'car' and the remainder other words. They are asked to focus on a fixation point in the middle of their field of view. The images are flashed on to the screen at random, in either the right or left field of vision, very briefly so that there is no time to change fixation.

They are asked to press a red button if they see a picture of a car or the word car, and an orange button if

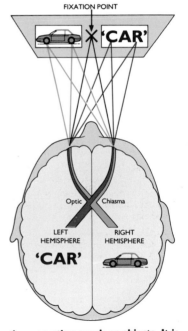

they see other words or objects. It is found that when a *picture* is presented to the left field of vision (right hemisphere) the response is faster than when it is presented to the right; when a *word* is presented to the right field of vision (left hemisphere) the response is faster than when it is presented to the left.

This has led scientists to suppose that the right hemisphere is more specialized for visual imagery and the left for verbal processing. Some believe that the difference is more general than this, with the right hemisphere dealing with more intuitive forms of reasoning and the left with more analytical and sequential thinking.

Mental Disorders

Throughout history people have explained mental disorders in ways that have suited their particular culture and society. In some societies people with mental disorders were regarded as being possessed by devils and were tortured to drive them out, while in others, such people were thought to be divinely inspired. In the case of some artistic geniuses – such as Vincent van Gogh – there appears to have been a link between mental illness and creativity.

In general, however, the mentally ill were badly treated. In the 19th century large asylums were built for the mentally ill as places of safety, although these too have been the sites of some appalling treatment. Not until recently, with the introduction of powerful drugs and new pyschological theories, has medicine had the means of effectively treating mental illness.

Unchaining the insane from their manacles at La Salpêtrière, Paris, in the 18th century. Fear and lack of understanding produced a long history of violence and ill-treatment towards the mentally ill. (AR)

Classification

Mental disorders can be broadly divided into psychosis, neurosis, organic and other disorders. *Psychosis* is perhaps what most people think of when they talk of madness. It means being out of touch with reality, and is characterized by frequently bizarre behaviour in a seemingly normal setting. The mental symptoms are of a severe disturbance of beliefs and perceptions – the psychotic person may have delusions (false beliefs) and hallucinations (seeing things that are not there, or hearing imaginary voices). Psychotic people are often not aware – at least during severe episodes – that they are ill. The two psychotic disorders are schizophrenia and affective illness.

Schizophrenia can affect every aspect of a person's mind and personality. One of the most distressing symptoms is the belief that one's thoughts are not one's own, and even that one's physical actions are initiated by someone else. The term schizophrenia ('split mind') was first used in 1911 to describe this splitting of mental functions.

Affective or *mood disorder* can take two forms: mania and depression. *Mania* is characterized by excessive cheerfulness, overactive behaviour and impaired judgement. *Depression* is classified as psychotic when beliefs and perceptions are distorted.

A *neurosis* is a psychological illness that causes distress but is understandable in terms of more normal mental processes. In *anxiety neurosis* anxiety is the predominant emotion, to the extent that it becomes impossible to live a normal life. An *obsessive-compulsive disorder* can involve long complicated rituals, frequently related to the fear of contamination – repeatedly washing the hands, for example. The ritual is omitted only at the cost of unbearable anxiety. In the case of *phobias*, anxiety is focused on particular objects or situations. Usually these are objects that we have an instinctive capacity to fear, such as

snakes or confined spaces. *Depressive neurosis* involves depression as the principal emotion and, unlike psychotic depression, perceptions are not distorted. *Hysteria* is a complicated problem that can take many forms. It involves symptoms with no physical cause that enable the sufferer to escape from an intolerable situation – these can be connected with memory, as in amnesia, or with the body, as in hysterical paralysis or blindness.

In *organic disorders*, mental illness is caused by physical disease. *Delirium* is an acute, short-term clouding of consciousness, as with a high fever or in delirium tremens (DTs or alcohol withdrawal). *Dementia* is a chronic or long-term brain dysfunction, which is most commonly seen in old age. It can also be a result of tertiary syphilis (general paralysis of the insane) or of brain damage caused by illness or drugs. There are other mental disorders treated by psychiatrists, but which are not necessarily termed mental illness. These include personality disorders and problems such as drug abuse and sexual dysfunction.

Causes

Many factors are involved in the origins of mental disorder, including heredity. Exactly what form the inheritance takes is only poorly understood, but some disorders have been shown to be more prevalent in family members of afflicted individuals. Such disorders include schizophrenia, manic-depressive psychosis and alcoholism.

Upbringing too plays its part. It was once thought that mothers were the cause of severe mental illness (such as schizophrenia), but this theory is no longer accepted. The odd ways in which families with a mentally ill member behave are now seen as understandable, given the stress these families live with. Cruelty or neglect, however, do have serious implications for mental health, and family patterns of behaviour may contribute to the development of neuroses.

Precipitating factors are easier to identify than original causes. Perhaps the best way to view the development of a mental breakdown is to see people as being more or less vulnerable because of their genes, early life and personality. Stress in their environment, such as leaving home or starting a new job, can be the final straw. In particularly vulnerable people the actual stress may be very minor indeed.

Treatment

Drug therapy came of age in psychiatry in the early 1950s with the introduction of anti-psychotic drugs called *phenothiazines*. Until then the old asylums were overcrowded with psychotic patients for whom little could be done, but with the introduction of phenothiazines vast numbers of people have been helped to lead normal lives.

Anti-depressant drugs have also proved effective in many cases. Tranquillizers – *benzodiazepines* – have a place in short-term treatment, but they are only rarely useful in the longer term, and can be addictive.

Most of the old physical treatments have now fallen into disrepute. One, however – *electroconvulsive therapy* (ECT) – is still useful. For a specific, selected group of patients ECT can bring about a recovery more rapidly than any other treatment, although it is not known how it works. These people may be severely depressed, unable to eat or sleep, hearing accusatory voices, and genuinely believing that they are totally worthless – perhaps even thinking that they are dead. It

FREUD, JUNG AND PSYCHOANALYSIS

At the turn of this century the Austrian neurologist Sigmund Freud (1856–1939) and Swiss psychiatrist Carl Gustav Jung (1875–1961) pioneered a new technique, psychoanalysis, to help people with mental disorders. Fundamental to their treatment was the understanding of the unconscious.

According to Freud and Jung, dreams are the most obvious manifestation of the unconscious, which they conceived of as a vast repository of hidden instincts, memories, ideas and emotions that exists in all of us. Freud thought that unpleasant experiences or guilt-provoking desires were *repressed*, or banished from the conscious mind, but gave rise to such symptoms as anxiety, depression, phobias and 'hysterical' paralysis. Psychoanalysis aims to enable the analyst and the patient to gain access to the unconscious mind through discussion, free association – in which the patient says whatever comes into his or her mind – and dream analysis. Through this method the patient remembers the experience and the emotions associated with it, and is cured.

Freud grew to believe that the experiences, wishes or emotions that were repressed were often sexual and could be traced back to early childhood. He believed that these repressed impulses affected our thoughts and actions, and that dreams are disguised fulfilments of repressed, usually sexual, wishes, with disturbing ideas represented by symbols. Patients could be cured of their symptoms by a successful interpretation of their dreams, their slips of the tongue and of their neurotic behaviour itself.

Freud identified five stages in sexual development: the *oral* stage (during the first year); the *anal* stage (1–3 years); the *phallic* stage (3–4 years); the *latency* period before puberty; and finally the mature *genital* stage at puberty. In addition to these stages Freud put forward the concept of the *Oedipus complex* experienced by most male children at age 4 or 5. It describes the erotic feelings a son has for his mother, which leads to aggressive feelings towards his father.

Freud thought that the mind was divided into three parts – the *id*, concerned with basic, inherited instincts, the *ego*, concerned with the tasks of reality and the sense of self within the world, and the *superego*, a kind of conscience that represents ideals and values derived from parents and society, and that controls the impulses of the id and ego.

According to Jung, dreams are communications from the unconscious but are not necessarily concerned with wishes. Jung divided the unconscious life into two parts – the personal and the collective. The *personal unconscious* consists of contents that have been forgotten or repressed, while the *collective unconscious* is an inherited pattern of memories, instincts and experiences common to everyone. He formed his theory of the collective unconscious when he noticed that delusions and hallucinations in different patients seemed to contain similar themes, and often could not be explained as products of the patients' own experiences.

Jung also developed the idea of dividing people into *extroverts*, or outward-looking personalities, and *introverts*, or inward-looking personalities – although he recognized that most people combine aspects of both types.

Few of the theories of Freud and Jung are now seen as being capable of scientific testing. However, they had a profound effect on the way we look at the human mind and opened the way for modern psychiatry and psychotherapy.

is clear then that a recovery as soon as possible is important.

Psychotherapy is a form of treatment that is aimed at helping patients to understand themselves. It is a broad term that covers therapies from classic psychoanalysis (▷ box) to counselling, drama therapy, music therapy and art therapy. These treatments can be used to help people with almost all forms of mental disorder. They can be combined with drug therapy, as drugs and counselling can be aimed at different facets of the same problem.

As well as individual psychotherapy sessions, people can attend group or family therapy. Group therapy is especially beneficial for a number of people with the same problem. Family therapy is a particularly useful tool as it acknowledges that individuals are affected by their families and vice versa. It is widely used by therapists working with children and adolescents.

SEE ALSO
● THE BRAIN AND NERVOUS SYSTEM p. 146
● CRIME AND LAW p. 164

Non-Infectious Diseases

A patient undergoing radiotherapy to treat Hodgkin's disease – a cancer of the lymphatic system. The illuminated discs over the patient's chest indicate the areas that are to receive radiation. (SPL)

Diseases that are not transmitted have now replaced infections as the primary health problem – at least in developed countries. Infectious diseases such as smallpox, tuberculosis and diphtheria have been ousted from their positions as major killers by cancer, heart disease and strokes.

While factors such as an inappropriate diet, lack of exercise, excessive intake of alcohol and tobacco smoking have to take the blame for many of these diseases, they are not the only culprits. The genes that each of us inherits from our parents may also put us at risk of developing heart disease, schizophrenia, rheumatoid arthritis or certain types of cancer, for example.

The role of heredity

There are many different types of inherited disease. Some are apparent from birth, while others may take decades to reveal themselves. Abnormalities of the chromosomes (▷ pp. 86 and 134) may be to blame. In *Down's syndrome*, for example, the affected child has an extra copy of chromosome number 21.

More than 4000 genetic diseases result from the inheritance of a mutant gene. They include achondroplasia (dwarfism), cystic fibrosis, Huntington's chorea and the blood disorders sickle-cell disease and thalassaemia. Affected couples may seek genetic counselling in order to assess their risk of passing on the disease to their children.

Many common diseases such as heart disease, diabetes (▷ box) and some types of cancer may result from the inheritance of a blend of 'predisposing' genes, particularly when combined with environmental factors such as diet.

Physical and chemical causes of disease

Environmental hazards such as radiation and pollutants account for some types of disease. People normally encounter only small doses of radiation, from diagnostic X-rays or perhaps as a treatment for cancer. In addition, everyone is exposed to low background levels of natural radiation from the Sun and from some types of rock. However, excessive doses of radiation may follow accidents at nuclear reactors or the detonation of nuclear weapons.

People who experience such high exposures develop radiation sickness, with loss of cells from their bone marrow and the lining of their intestine. The person loses appetite and suffers diarrhoea, sickness, chills, fever and extreme tiredness. Death may follow because of the damage to the bowel and bone marrow resulting in loss of resistance to infection and severe

SEE ALSO

● GENETICS p. 86
● FOOD, DIET AND DIGESTION p. 138
● THE IMMUNE SYSTEM p. 142
● INFECTIOUS DISEASES p. 154

CANCER

Cancer occurs when cells grow out of control. A single cell can accumulate changes in its genes that allow it to replicate in an uncontrolled way. Such a cell can give rise to a *tumour*, which may manifest itself as a palpable lump or a mass. Once cells become cancerous they lose the function that they once had: they simply reproduce themselves indefinitely.

A tumour is considered to be *benign* if it remains localized in the place where it originated. Nevertheless, benign tumours can be life-threatening if they jeopardize normal structures. Benign tumours of the brain, for example, can be fatal.

Malignant tumours have the capacity to spread around the body. Individual cells, or groups of cells, can detach themselves from the *primary tumour*, migrate via the blood or the lymph (▷ p. 142) around the body and become deposited in other organs such as the brain, the bones or the lungs. There they form *secondary tumours*. This process is called *metastasis*, and the secondary tumours are known as *metastases*.

In many cases the cause of cancer is unknown, and will vary according to the type of cancer. Studies of women who have had breast cancer suggest that – in some cases at least – genetic influences are at work. Breast cancer

is also more common in women who begin their periods early, who have their first child later in life and who have a late menopause. This suggests that hormonal influences on the breast are important. Environmental factors undoubtedly play a part in the development of some cancers. Excessive exposure to ultraviolet light in sunlight seems to be responsible for *melanoma*, or cancer of the skin. Almost a third of all deaths from cancer could be avoided if people abandoned smoking tobacco.

Treatment for cancer varies according to the type of tumour, the site of the primary tumour and the extent of the spread of cancerous cells. *Chemotherapy* (drug therapy) can produce long remissions in some forms of the disease, but side effects occur as normal cells are also damaged and the white blood cells (▷ p. 142) become depleted. *Radiation therapy* uses ionizing radiation – including X-rays and gamma-rays – to destroy cancer cells. Chemicals can be used to sensitize malignant cells to radiation, leaving healthy cells undamaged. Surgery is used to remove malignant growths, but is only completely effective if cancer cells have not migrated into other parts of the body.

anaemia. Long-term survivors are at increased risk of developing cancers, including cancers of the blood, and cataracts.

Chemical hazards are probably more often encountered at work than at home. The list of industrial diseases is a long one and includes poisoning by lead, mercury and other heavy metals. Many industrial diseases result from inhaling some harmful substance. *Asbestosis*, for example, results from inhaling fibres of asbestos. The lungs become fibrous and the affected person not only experiences increasing breathlessness, with failure of the heart and lungs, but also has an increased risk of developing cancer of the lung.

Autoimmune disease

Some diseases result from the immune system (▷ p. 142) attacking the body's own tissues or other components. In *thyrotoxicosis*, antibodies produced by the immune system bind to cells of the thyroid, stimulating them to produce excessive amounts of thyroid hormone. In *rheumatoid arthritis* (▷ box), there is evidence that the damage to the lining of the joint results from a faulty immune response within the joint.

Diet

The Western diet has been criticized for being too low in fibre and too high in sugar and other refined carbohydrates and in fat. Heart disease, diabetes, bowel cancer, constipation, haemorrhoids and obesity are among the many diseases that may result.

A diet too high in saturated fat may result in an elevated level of blood cholesterol leading to *atheroma* – degeneration of artery walls due to the formation of fatty deposits. People with this disease are prone to *angina* (severe pain in the chest on exertion) and heart attacks, which may be fatal.

Obesity can also encourage unwanted health problems. People who are overweight are more likely to suffer from heart disease, diabetes and strokes.

Alcohol

Apart from the social cost of alcohol-related diseases, excessive intake of alcohol exerts a huge toll on physical health. The long-term effects of alcohol taken to excess include cirrhosis of the liver (in which liver cells are replaced by scar tissue), alcoholic hepatitis (inflammation of the liver) and liver cancer. Alcohol can damage the heart, brain and nerves. Cancers of the larynx, oesophagus and pancreas are also associated with excessive consumption of alcohol.

Smoking

Cancer of the lung is 10 to 15 times more common in regular tobacco smokers than in people who have never smoked, and up to 40 times commoner in very heavy smokers. Smoking also increases the risk of cancer of the pancreas, oesophagus and larynx. Smokers are more likely than non-smokers to suffer heart attacks, chronic bronchitis and *emphysema*, a condition in which the sufferer commonly experiences increasing breathlessness.

DIABETES MELLITUS

Diabetes is an extremely common and – as yet – incurable metabolic disease. In Western societies 1–2% of the population are affected, while the incidence can reach 15% in certain subpopulations, e.g. Australian Aboriginals and North American Indians.

In many cases the disease is genetically determined, but it can also be precipitated by certain viral infections, toxins, chronic disease or pregnancy. In all cases, the primary defect is a deficiency of *insulin*, a hormone that plays a pivotal role in the control of the metabolism (▷ p. 143).

Insulin deficiency results in profound metabolic derangements, the most consistent of which is *hyperglycaemia* (blood glucose levels above the normal range). As blood sugar rises, glucose appears in the urine, carrying water with it and giving rise to the increased urine output and thirst that characterize the disorder. Fat metabolism may also be enhanced, leading to the accumulation of acidic by-products (keto-acids) which, if unchecked, can result in coma or death.

Many diabetic patients are treated by dietary restrictions and the use of drugs, but some are dependent upon daily administration of insulin to control their symptoms. Although the major clinical manifestations of diabetes can usually be controlled, it is difficult to maintain blood glucose levels within the normal range. Consequently, diabetics become susceptible to degenerative complications involving the nerves, eyes, kidneys and blood vessels, and it is these secondary problems that make diabetes such a devastating disease.

ARTHRITIS

Arthritis is a common condition caused by the inflammation of a joint, usually with swelling, redness, pain and restriction of movement. Most people with arthritis suffer from *osteoarthritis*. Originally ascribed to general wear and tear because it affects so many old people and people who have suffered joint injuries, it is now thought some other unidentified factor is also involved. In osteoarthritis the cartilage covering joint surfaces becomes thinner and bony outgrowths proliferate around the edges of the bone ends. Usually only one joint is affected.

Rheumatoid arthritis is a more crippling disease, believed to be an autoimmune condition (▷ main text). It affects people earlier in life than osteoarthritis, and usually several joints are involved at any one time. The disease begins in the *synovial membrane*, which lines the joint capsule and provides lubrication. This membrane becomes eaten away by an inflammatory substance that spreads over the bone ends destroying cartilage, bone and even affecting surrounding muscles. This arthritis is extremely painful and causes sufferers a general illness during times when the condition flares up. Damage to the joints can lead to deformity.

Arthritis is usually treated with anti-inflammatory drugs and pain killers, and antibiotics if an infection is present. Rest is important during attacks but otherwise exercise and physiotherapy is advised to keep the joints from stiffening.

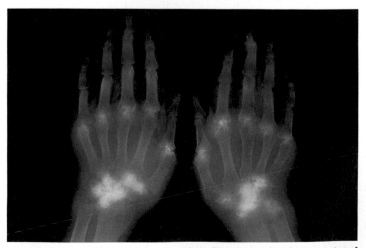

An arthritic hand shown in a false-colour X-ray. The deformation and destruction of the first joints of the fingers can be seen clearly. (SPL)

Infectious Diseases

An infectious disease is one in which one living organism inhabits and multiplies on or within another, harming it in the process, either by the production of toxic substances or by damaging, digesting or destroying part or all of its cellular structure. Such harmful organisms are mostly microscopic – viruses, bacteria and protozoans – but also include various larger organisms such as various kinds of fungi, worms and arthropods.

SEE ALSO

● BEGINNINGS OF LIFE p. 82
● THE IMMUNE SYSTEM p. 142
● THE HISTORY OF MEDICINE p. 156

The vast majority of microorganisms are harmless; some live with human beings in harmony, each helping the other in a *symbiotic* relationship. However, many organisms are harmful, and such organisms are called *pathogens*. Pathogens are divided into four main groups: viruses, bacteria, fungi and parasites.

Viruses

Viruses (▷ p. 82) are by far the smallest of the pathogens. They need to live inside the body cells of other organisms to survive, and in reproducing themselves they destroy the host cell. Our only natural defence against viruses is the formation of antibodies from B cells manufactured in the bone marrow (▷ p. 142). One other natural substance that is effective against viruses is interferon, but this has proved difficult to pro-

duce commercially. Only two or three drugs are of any use, and these only against a limited number of viruses. Treatment at the moment has to be by prevention in the form of immunization, which produces the antibodies in our system before the virus itself attacks (▷ p. 142). Considerable research has recently been going on into cancer-causing viruses.

Bacteria

Bacteria (▷ p. 82) are bigger structures than viruses, and have four main shapes: round (*cocci*), straight rods (*bacilli*), curved rods (*vibrios*), and coils (*spirochaetes*). Two groups of drugs are used to treat bacterial infection. The first group, the *bacteriostats*, prevent the multiplication of bacteria. The second group, the *antibiotics*, either disrupt the cell membranes or metabolic pathways of bacteria, or act as direct poisons. Antibiotics, first developed in the mid-20th century (▷ p. 157), have proved effective against a host of previously incurable bacterial infections. Immunization is also effective in many cases.

Fungi

Very few fungi (▷ p. 90) infect human beings, and those that do mostly colonize the surface (skin, nails and hair), causing diseases such as athlete's foot, ringworm and thrush. However, there are geographical differences: in North America, for example, there are many deeply invasive fungi, causing such diseases as pneumonia.

Parasites

Parasites are divided into three groups – protozoans, worms and arthropods. *Protozoans*, although still microscopic, are generally larger than bacteria and possess a more evolved cell structure (▷ p. 82). They include the amoeba that causes amoebic dysentery. Protozoans are not damaged by antibiotics in the concentrations that would be lethal to bacteria. Some, such as the malaria parasite, go through complicated life cycles.

Parasitic *worms* affect human intestines in various ways, and in some cases migrate to various other organs of the body, sometimes causing large cysts or swelling of limbs as in elephantiasis. They include threadworms, roundworms, hookworms, flatworms, flukes and tapeworms.

Arthropods (▷ p. 96) such as lice, fleas and mites not only infest or infect humans, but some also act as carriers (*vectors*) of microorganisms, such as those that cause typhus and plague.

Transmission of infections

There are six main channels for the transmission of infectious diseases. *Airborne* diseases are transmitted through infected droplets in the air from the nose, throat/lungs or saliva, or from dust particles from fallen skin. *Contamination* occurs through food or water supplies usually by infected faeces or urine. Diseases may be passed through *direct contact* (or contagion), in close contact with an infected person. *Sexual transmission* of diseases through vaginal or anal intercourse or oral sex can be reduced by the use of condoms. *Blood-borne* diseases are transmitted by the injection of contaminated blood or blood products or by improperly sterilized instruments. The bites from *animal carriers* (or vectors) transmit their contaminated saliva as in malaria and the bubonic plague (flea bites).

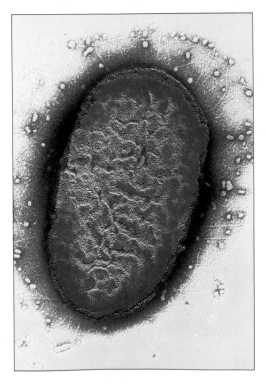

A whooping cough bacterium (*Bordetella pertussis*) seen through a false-colour transmission electron micrograph. These bacteria live only in humans, causing an infection in the respiratory tract. It is highly infectious and the condition can be fatal in infants. (SPL)

AIDS
Cause HIV virus. **Transmission** Sexual; transfusion; contact with infected blood. **Characteristics** Destruction of immune system. Always fatal. **Prevention** Avoidance of unprotected sex and infected blood. **Treatment** Antiviral drugs (of limited use).

CHOLERA
Cause Bacterium. **Transmission** Faecally contaminated water. Largely restricted to tropics. **Characteristics** Vomiting and diarrhoea leading to dehydration. Often fatal. **Prevention** Clean water supply. Vaccination effective 6–9 months. **Treatment** Antibiotics.

COMMON COLD
Cause Viruses. **Transmission** Airborne; direct contact. **Characteristics** Inflammation of nose and upper respiratory tract causing sneezing, coughing, sore throat. **Prevention** Avoidance of direct contact. **Treatment** Rest. Proprietary medicines may relieve some symptoms.

DIPHTHERIA
Cause Bacterium. **Transmission** Airborne. **Characteristics** Infection of pharynx; breathing obstructed; heart inflammation. Often fatal. Now rare in developed countries. **Prevention** Immunization. **Treatment** Antibiotics.

DYSENTERY
Cause Amoeba or bacteria. Amoebic dysentery confined to tropics. **Transmission** Contaminated food or water. **Characteristics** Diarrhoea, weight loss, dehydration. With amoebic dysentery, liver abscesses. **Prevention** Hygiene, clean water supply. **Treatment** Antibiotics, emetine, rehydration.

FOOD POISONING
Cause Bacteria, including *Salmonella*, *Listeria* or more rarely *Clostridium botulinum*. Viruses. **Transmission** Contaminated food or water. **Characteristics** Vomiting and diarrhoea. Botulism affects central nervous system and is often fatal. **Prevention** Food hygiene, clean water supply. **Treatment** Antibiotics, rehydration.

GLANDULAR FEVER
Cause Virus. **Transmission** Direct contact. **Characteristics** Swollen lumph nodes, fever, sore throat, fatigue. **Prevention** Avoidance of direct contact. **Treatment** Rest.

GONORRHOEA
Cause Bacterium. **Transmission** Sexual. **Characteristics** Discharge, pain on urinating; if not checked can cause sterility and inflammation of heart valves. **Prevention** Avoidance of unprotected sex. **Treatment** Antibiotics.

HEPATITIS A and B
Cause Virus. **Transmission** Contaminated food or water (A); sexual or blood-borne (B). **Characteristics** Inflammation of liver causing fever, sickness and jaundice; hepatitis B can be fatal. **Prevention** Immunization; avoidance of unprotected sex and infected blood (B). **Treatment** No effective anti-viral drug.

HERPES SIMPLEX
Cause Virus. **Transmission** Direct contact. **Characteristics** Small blisters on mouth or genitals. Virus lies dormant and symptoms may recur. **Prevention** Avoidance of close contact. **Treatment** Acyclovir.

HERPES ZOSTER (SHINGLES)
Cause Reactivation of virus that causes varicella (chickenpox). **Characteristics** Virus affects a nerve of the face, abdomen or chest causing severe pain and blisters in surrounding skin. **Treatment** Acyclovir.

INFLUENZA
Cause Virus. **Transmission** Airborne. **Characteristics** Fever, loss of appetite, weakness. In elderly people can be fatal. **Prevention** Immunization against certain viruses. **Treatment** Rest.

LEPROSY
Cause Bacterium. **Transmission** Prolonged or close contact. **Characteristics** Thickening of skin and nerves, numbness, deformity and disfigurement. **Prevention** Avoidance of direct contact. **Treatment** Control with sulphone drugs.

MALARIA
Cause Parasite. **Transmission** Mosquito bites. **Characteristics** Destruction of red blood cells causing fever and anaemia. Can be fatal. **Prevention** and **Treatment** Anti-malarial tablets.

MEASLES
Cause Virus. **Transmission** Airborne. **Characteristics** Fever, rash, possible middle-ear infection or bronchopneumonia. **Prevention** Immunization. **Treatment** Antibiotics if infections present.

MENINGITIS
Cause Virus or bacteria. **Transmission** Airborne or direct contact. **Characteristics** Inflammation of membranes surrounding brain causes headache, fever, convulsions. Can be fatal. **Prevention** Avoidance of direct contact. **Treatment** Bacterial meningitis antibiotics. Viral meningitis rest.

MUMPS
Cause Virus. **Transmission** Airborne. **Characteristics** Fever, swelling of parotid salivary glands. In adults, testicular and ovarian inflammation. **Prevention** Immunization (immunity short-lived). **Treatment** Rest.

PLAGUE
Cause Bacterium. **Transmission** Airborne or via flea bites. **Characteristics** Fever, weakness, delirium, painful buboes (swelling of lymph nodes). Often fatal. **Prevention** Immunization (partial protection). **Treatment** Antibiotics.

PNEUMONIA
Cause Bacteria or viruses. **Transmission** Airborne; direct contact. **Characteristics** Inflammation of lung causing pain and breathing difficulty. Can be fatal. **Treatment** Antibiotics if caused by bacteria.

POLIOMYELITIS
Cause Virus. **Transmission** Direct contact. **Characteristics** Infection of central nervous system causing fever, headache, stiffness of neck. Possible paralysis in minority of cases. **Prevention** Immunization. **Treatment** Use of respirator if respiratory paralysis occurs.

RUBELLA (GERMAN MEASLES)
Cause Virus. **Transmission** Direct contact. **Characteristics** Headache, sore throat, fever, swelling of neck, pink rash. Can damage developing foetus if caught by pregnant woman. **Prevention** Immunization. **Treatment** Rest.

SCHISTOSOMIASIS (BILHARZIA)
Cause Parasitic flatworm *Schistosoma*. **Transmission** Flatworm larvae released by snails penetrate skin of person bathing in infected water and colonize blood vessels of intestine. **Characteristics** Diarrhoea, enlarged spleen and liver, cirrhosis of the liver. Can be fatal. **Prevention** Clean water supply. **Treatment** Various drugs.

SCARLET FEVER
Cause Bacterium. **Transmission** Airborne. **Characteristics** Fever, sore throat, scarlet rash, possible ear and kidney infections. **Prevention** Avoidance of contacts. **Treatment** Antibiotics.

SYPHILIS
Cause Bacterium. **Transmission** Sexual; can also be passed to foetus via placenta. **Characteristics** Hard ulcer on genitals followed by fever, malaise, rash on chest. Eventual heart and brain damage, blindness, general paralysis of the insane. **Prevention** Avoidance of unprotected sex. **Treatment** Antibiotics.

TAPEWORMS
Transmission Through infested meat. **Characteristics** Weakness, hunger, weight loss. **Prevention** Avoiding undercooked meat. **Treatment** Antithelmintics.

TETANUS (LOCKJAW)
Cause Bacterium. **Transmission** Bacterium entering wounds. **Characteristics** Muscle stiffness, spasm and rigidity, high fever, convulsions, extreme pain. Can be fatal. **Prevention** Immunization. **Treatment** Penicillin and antitoxins.

THREADWORMS
Transmission Direct contact. **Characteristics** Anal itching caused by female worm emerging at night to lay eggs. **Prevention** Hygiene. **Treatment** Piperazine.

THRUSH
Cause Fungus *Candida albicans*. **Transmission** Fungus lives in alimentary tract and vagina; thrush arises when growth of fungus increases, in some cases following course of broad-spectrum antibiotics. Can be passed to baby at birth. **Characteristics** White patches in mouth or irritation of vagina. **Prevention** Avoidance of broad-spectrum antibiotics. **Treatment** Antifungals.

TUBERCULOSIS
Cause Bacterium. **Transmission** Airborne; unpasteurized milk. **Characteristics** Bacteria inhaled into lungs cause a *tubercle* or lesion leading to fever, weight loss, coughing up blood. Bacteria in milk affect abdominal lymph nodes. Formerly often fatal. **Prevention** Immunization, pasteurizing milk. **Treatment** Antibiotics.

TYPHOID
Cause Bacterium. **Transmission** Faecally contaminated food or water. **Characteristics** Infection of digestive system causing high fever, red rash, possible inflammation of spleen and bones. Formerly often fatal. **Prevention** Immunization. **Treatment** Antibiotics.

TYPHUS
Cause Parasite *Rickettsia*, spread by lice, fleas or ticks. **Characteristics** Severe headaches, rash, high fever, delirium. **Prevention** Hygiene. **Treatment** Antibiotics.

VARICELLA (CHICKENPOX)
Cause Virus. **Transmission** Airborne. **Characteristics** Mild fever, itchy blistering rash. **Prevention** Immunization. **Treatment** Rest.

WHOOPING COUGH
Cause Bacterium. **Transmission** Airborne; direct contact. **Characteristics** Infection of trachea and bronchi producing coughs followed by involuntary intakes of breath. **Prevention** Immunization. **Treatment** Rest.

The History of Medicine

Disease is as old as life itself. Medicine, on the other hand, is of quite recent origin. In most early civilizations medicine was closely linked to religion. Diseases were believed to be caused by gods who might also effect cures, and treatment involved rituals and incantations.

Papyrus fragments show that Egyptian medicine was sophisticated in observation and diagnosis, if not in treatment. In ancient Babylon the Code of Hammurabi contained laws regulating a large and well-organized medical profession. Many herbal remedies were known in ancient India.

Greek medicine

At its peak Greek medicine was rational, scientific and clearly separated from religion. The Greek philosopher **Hippocrates of Cos** (c. 460–370 BC) is regarded as the 'father of modern medicine'. Hippocrates believed that moderation in all things is the key to health. He also set out a code of ethics for physicians, and the *Hippocratic Oath*, taken by doctors, is based on this code.

The Greek theory of the elements and the humours – which originated with the philosophers **Empedocles** (c. 490–430 BC) and **Aristotle** (384–322 BC) – influenced the shape of medicine for many centuries. It was based on the belief that everything was made out of combinations of four *elements* – air, water, earth and fire – and that these corresponded to four *qualities* – cold, wet, dry and hot. They thought that in the body the

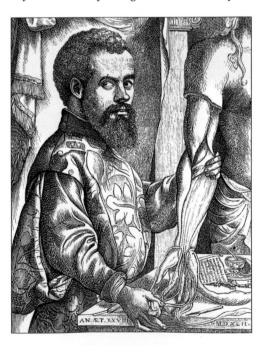

Andreas Vesalius laid the foundations of modern anatomy when he published detailed descriptions and drawings of the dissected human body. (AR)

elements blend to form four *humours*: blood (hot and wet), yellow bile (hot and dry), black bile (dry and cold) and phlegm (cold and wet). Good mental and physical health was supposed to depend on the correct balance of the humours.

At the time of the Roman Empire the Greek physician **Galen of Pergamum** (Latin name Claudius Galenus, AD 130–201) carried out dissections on animals but not on humans, and this led to many errors in his anatomical descriptions. Galen combined the theory of the humours with his own studies in anatomy and physiology to produce an erroneous system of medicine, which nevertheless lasted more than 1000 years.

Medieval medicine

After the fall of the Roman Empire, Greek learning was preserved and developed by Arab scholars such as **Razes** (al-Rhazi, AD 860–932) and **Avicenna** (Ibn Sinna, AD 980–1036). From about AD 1000 ancient knowledge began to return to the West via centres such as the medical school at Salerno. Later, medicine was taught in new universities such as Montpellier and Bologna – two places where, in the 14th century, anatomy lessons included the public dissection of corpses. However, the Church prohibited clerks from shedding blood and this meant that the universities did not teach surgery. In this field students had to be trained by a practising surgeon. In general, medieval medicine was a mixture of ancient physiology, empirical knowledge of the effects of some drugs, and superstitious incantation. By the 14th century thousands of hospitals had been founded in Europe.

The 16th century

Individual doctors had frequently doubted Galen's authority on specific points, but it was only after the invention of printing (▷ p. 202) that such doubts could become widely known. For example, in his book *De Humani Corporis Fabrica* ('On the Fabric of the Human Body') the Flemish anatomist **Andreas Vesalius** (1514–64) showed the inadequacies of Galen. It is the first accurate anatomy book, based on the dissection of human corpses, and laid the foundations of modern anatomy. Surgery was advanced at the same time by the Frenchman **Ambroise Paré** (1517–90), who opposed the use of *cauterization* (the application of red-hot irons or boiling oil) to treat wounds.

The Italian **Girolamo Fracastoro** (Latin name Fracastorius, 1484–1553) speculated that epidemic diseases might be caused by minute germs, invisible to the naked eye. He argued that germs are *specific*, i.e. that each kind causes a particular disease, but his theory was not proved until the 19th century. The idea that specific diseases required specific treatments was pioneered by a Swiss physician and alchemist, **Philippus Aureolus Paracelsus** (real name Theophrastus Bombastus von Hohenheim, 1493–1541). He also introduced the use of chemicals into medicine, pioneering the use of mercury and laudanum.

The 17th and 18th centuries

The main medical event of the 17th century was the discovery by **William Harvey** (1578–1677), an English physician, of the true nature of the heartbeat and the circulation of the blood. His book *De Motu Cordis* ('On the Movement of the Heart') laid the foundation of all modern physiology.

A further aid to the study of physiology – and to medical science generally – was provided by the invention of microscopes (⊳ p. 25). The Dutchman *Anton van Leeuwenhoek* (1632–1723) showed the value of these fundamental research tools by using them to investigate blood cells, spermatozoa and even microbes.

During the 18th century a number of great medical schools, including Vienna and Edinburgh, were founded. Surgery was established on firm scientific principles by the Scot *John Hunter* (1728–93), and the science of neurology was pioneered by the Swiss physiologist *Albrecht von Haller* (1708–77), with his theory that nerve fibres acted on 'irritable' muscle to produce movement.

Giovanni Battista Morgagni (1682–1771), an Italian anatomist, argued that disease is localized in parts of the body rather than spread throughout, while the invention of the stethoscope by the French physician *René Théophile Hyacinthe Laennec* (1781–1826) was to prove a major aid in the diagnosis of disease.

One of the first scientific steps in preventing disease was the introduction of vaccination by the English physician *Edward Jenner* (1749–1823), when he discovered in 1796 that inoculation with the cowpox virus gives immunity to smallpox. Immunization against various other diseases was to be introduced over the next two centuries (⊳ p. 142).

The 19th century

The 19th century was the century of progress in medicine. One of the most important discoveries was the demonstration by the Frenchman *Louis Pasteur* (1822–95) and the German *Robert Koch* (1843–1910) that diseases such as rabies and tuberculosis are caused by microorganisms called *bacteria* (⊳ pp. 82 and 154). They showed precisely which bacteria cause which disease, and between 1875 and 1906 over 20 fatal diseases were made preventable through immunization.

Although by the 19th century many kinds of surgical operation had been successfully carried out, patients died in large numbers from infections entering their bodies during operations or childbirth, or through wounds. They also had to endure the agony of being fully conscious during operations. Pain control by *anaesthesia* (loss of feeling induced by drugs) was pioneered by the Americans *Horace Wells* (1815–48), using nitrous oxide, and *William Thomas Green Morton* (1819–68), using ether. In Britain general anaesthesia – rendering the patient unconscious – by means of chloroform was introduced by the Scottish surgeon *Sir James Young Simpson* (1811–70). In the 1840s the Hungarian *Ignaz P. Semmelweiss* (1818–65) showed the crucial importance of *asepsis* (a germ-free environment) in childbirth wards, and in 1865 the Scottish surgeon *Joseph Lister* (1827–1912) introduced *antisepsis* (the destruction of bacteria), spraying the area being operated on with carbolic acid.

The century also saw many measures introduced to improve public health. Chief among these were improved sewage and sanitary conditions, and such preventive measures improved the life expectancies of millions.

Finally, the century saw the emergence of modern nursing, largely due to Englishwoman *Florence Nightingale* (1820–1910), who showed that good nursing had a dramatic effect on reducing death rates in hospitals.

Edward Jenner inoculates a child with cowpox to give immunity from smallpox. Jenner's discovery was violently opposed at first, but within five years the practice of vaccination was widespread. (AR)

The 20th century

The 20th century has been an era of technological innovation in medicine, particularly in diagnosis. In 1895 the German physicist *Wilhelm Konrad Röntgen* (1845–1923) discovered X-rays (⊳ pp. 27 and 210), the medical applications of which had been realized by the turn of the century. Other inventions of the early part of the century included the *electrocardiograph* (for measuring heart activity) and the *electroencephalograph* (for measuring brain activity). The introduction of ultrasound scanning (⊳ p. 210) in the 1970s allowed even more accurate pictures than X-rays.

Work on the chemistry of nutrition by the German *Emil Fischer* (1852–1919) gave rise to *biochemistry* (the study of the chemistry of living organisms), and the chemical study of disease is now a basic medical approach. Subsequently British biochemist *Sir Frederick Gowland Hopkins* (1861–1947) discovered that certain substances – later called *vitamins* (⊳ p. 138) – are essential to the diet in minute amounts, and that disease occurs if these are absent.

Chemotherapy, treatment by chemicals that attack disease agents with minimum harm to the body, was pioneered by the German scientist *Paul Ehrlich* (1854–1915), who discovered that synthetic dyestuffs could kill bacteria. The *sulphonamides*, derived from dyestuffs and introduced in 1932, greatly reduced the number of post-operative infections. Ehrlich also initiated the study of the body's immune system (⊳ p. 142). A large number of bacterial infections – many of which were previously fatal – were rendered curable by a new range of drugs, the *antibiotics*. These drugs were developed from the accidental discovery by the British microbiologist *Sir Alexander Fleming* (1881–1955) that a growth of penicillin mould had destroyed a bacterial culture he was working on.

Surgery has also been aided by technology, and now lasers are sometimes used for very precise work. The greater understanding of the immune system has led to the possibility of transplants of organs from one body to another. Kidney transplantation, first attempted in 1902, is now a well-established operation. Heart transplantation was first performed by the South African surgeon *Christiaan Barnard* (1922–) in 1967.

SEE ALSO

● THE HISTORY OF SCIENCE p. 48
● MENTAL DISORDERS p. 150
● NON-INFECTIOUS DISEASES p. 152
● INFECTIOUS DISEASES p. 154

The Family

A family is a group of people who are related to each other by blood (for instance a brother and sister), or by marriage (for instance a husband and his wife's sister). A wider group of related families is referred to as a *kinship system*.

SEE ALSO

● SOCIAL STRATIFICATION AND DIVISIONS p. 160
● RELIGIONS pp. 284–301

Everyone has blood relatives, but the patterns of family, marriage and kinship relationships vary both geographically and historically.

Marriage

Marriage is the bond that makes families possible. Typically it involves a legal agreement between a man and a woman to enter into a long-term socio-sexual relationship for the purposes of establishing a home, satisfying sexual needs and raising children. Marriage also creates rights and responsibilities, such as the economic support of spouse and offspring.

Marital relationships are usually formalized and solemnized by a wedding ceremony, often with relatives of the couple in attendance. In Western societies, marriage is the final stage in a social process that involves dating, courtship and engagement. In many non-Western societies, for example in rural China, marital partners are selected by parents or other matchmakers rather than the couple themselves.

Although all known societies prohibit marriage and/or sexual relations between certain categories of relatives (*incest*), the categories themselves differ according to the culture in question. Exceptionally, in ancient Egypt brother-sister marriages were permitted within the family of the pharaoh to preserve the blood purity of the ruling dynasty. By contrast, the traditional family system of China prohibits marriage among a wide range of relatives, including distant cousins.

Similarly, rules concerning the number of husbands or wives a person is allowed at one time vary between societies. Basically, there are two types of marriage: *monogamy*, where the individual has only one spouse at a time; and *polygamy*, where two or more spouses are recognized socially. Polygamy can involve husbands having two or more wives (*polygyny*) or, more rarely, wives having two or more husbands (*polyandry*). Polygyny is particularly widespread in Islamic areas of Africa, where Muslim men are allowed to

AGE ROLES

Age is an important marker of social differences in families as well as in societies. Some people are treated differently from others according to their age, and are expected to behave in a socially approved way. These expectations define the *age roles* that people play. Age roles are the product of a people's shared history and experience and therefore they vary from society to society and over time.

Societies differ in the importance they attach to age roles and changes in social status. Until recently, traditional tribal societies in Africa and elsewhere attached great significance to age as a determinant of social position. The Masai of East Africa, in common with many other pastoral, nomadic societies, organize their social, political and economic life around age groupings, which typically span 10–15 years. However, the spread of new ideas and technologies from the developed world produces new ways of living in traditional Third World societies. Most significantly, men and women become less dependent on traditional structures for their opportunities in life, and age roles and rites of passage cease to be dominant features.

Although modern societies stress individualism and personal achievement, social relations are still frequently recognized by age. Age is formally and legally significant in many areas of life in modern societies. It determines when people go to school, when they may leave school, when they may marry, when they may enter full-time employment, when they have to leave employment and so on. Age is often used as the basis for assigning rights and duties to people in society.

In recent times the term *ageism* has been used to describe the assessment of people solely in terms of age. It implies criticism of the use of unchangeable (*ascribed*) characteristics as a criterion of assessment by a society that purports to judge people according to what they have achieved.

have up to four wives. Monogamy, which is characteristic of Western societies, is spreading under the influence of Western culture. However, due to the increasingly high incidence of divorce and remarriage in Western societies, the practice of having many spouses consecutively is becoming more common.

Divorce rates vary considerably in different societies. Where marriage is essentially regarded as a civil contract, as in Britain, the USA and Russia, the divorce rate tends to be high. However, in countries dominated by the Catholic Church (which officially forbids divorce), such as Ireland, Spain, Italy and Mexico, the divorce rate is either not calculated or is very low. There are also many other ways of ending a marriage, including deser-

The male-dominated family was regarded as the central institution of 19th-century Western society. Families were typically large, but after 1875 the gradual spread of contraception led to a decline in the birth rate in Europe and North America. (Popperfoto)

A Hindu marriage in India. Marriage ceremonies often include visible signs of the new social status of the bride and groom, such as distinctive jewellery, garments and headdress. (Gamma)

tion, separation and annulment (legal cancellation). Consequently, divorce rates are an imperfect measure of marital breakdown.

A person who marries leaves the *family of origin* to set up his or her own *family of procreation*. In the process he or she simultaneously becomes a member of a kinship system consisting of three families: the family of origin, the spouse's family of origin and the new family of procreation. A family comprising two generations only, namely parents and children, is known as a *nuclear family*. A family of three or more generations living together, namely parents, children and grandparents, is known as an *extended family*.

Family functions

The family performs the same range of functions to a greater or lesser extent in all societies: regulating sexual activity; ensuring economic survival; preparing young people for adulthood; and providing emotional security. As societies have developed economically and have grown in size and complexity, the family has lost its monopoly regarding these social functions. For example, although no society allows total sexual freedom, in Western societies there has been a tendency during the 20th century to relax the norms and rules governing sexual behaviour. As a result, sex outside marriage is now more common and more widely accepted. In the case of its economic and socialization functions, the family no longer operates alone in training young people to produce or supply goods and services. It does so indirectly in conjunction with schools, colleges, factories and offices. However, in Western societies, people still consume goods and services in a family context (for instance, eating meals) and the majority of children are born within marriage, even if many are conceived outside it.

Disharmony and alternatives

The model of family life in which parents and children live together is generally considered to be the ideal. But the increasing emotional weight that the modern family has to bear, along with other factors such as inequalities within the family and the pressure to be economically successful, have caused problems. For example, a high rate of marital breakdown and a corresponding increase in *single-parent families* is apparent in many industrial societies. Also, the social and economic limitations of two-generation households, often revealed by the problem of caring for very young or very old family members, has been largely responsible for the persistence of extended family households. The emotional intensity of family relationships, combined with other pressures on the modern family, is also thought to be responsible for the increasing prevalence of family conflict and violence. This includes child and wife abuse, and family murder.

RITES OF PASSAGE

Within the family and in society, rites of passage are rituals or ceremonies that mark the movement of individuals or groups from one social status to another (such as birth, puberty, marriage, and death). The French anthropologist Arnold van Gennep (1873–1957) demonstrated that all rites of passage involve three phases: *separation*, *transition* and *incorporation*. As individuals change status they are separated from their old associations and relationships. They move into a transitional phase, having left the old status but not yet assuming the new. Finally they take on their new status and join others of like status. Different rites of passage stress different phases, though all are present within each ritual or ceremony. In funeral ceremonies the emphasis is on the separation of the deceased and the bereaved. In Christian baptism the emphasis is on incorporation – the joining of a religious community.

'Coming of age' parties in Western societies celebrate the transition in time from child to adult. In tribal societies the rituals that mark the movement into adult status are sometimes called *puberty rites*, and mark a movement into a sexual world from a non-sexual one. Sometimes this transition is marked physically by ritual scarring or body mutilation. Puberty rites amongst Australian Aborigines involve a symbolic re-enactment of death in order to achieve new life as an adult. The Jewish ritual of *bar mitzvah* can be seen both as a puberty ritual and as a ceremony of religious transformation. Bar mitzvah transforms a boy into a full member of the Jewish male religious community.

Wedding ceremonies display separation, transition and incorporation. In Christian wedding ceremonies in Britain the relatives and friends of the bride and groom are physically separated; the bride is 'given away' by her father or senior male relative to the groom (separated from her family to be incorporated into a new family); the bride and groom leave the ceremony together (separate from both sets of relatives and friends as they form a new union); after the ceremony relatives and friends of the couple mingle together, symbolizing the restructuring of their relationships brought about by the marriage.

Pregnancy and *childbirth* are traditionally seen as dangerous and polluting, especially to men. Pregnant women are in a transitional phase between being one person and being two or more. Transitional phases are confusing because the people who inhabit them do not belong to the ordered categories of society – they are between them. Until quite recently it was common in Western societies for women who had given birth to be *churched* – ritually cleansed and received back into the community of the Christian Church.

In most societies *death* is marked by elaborate ritual, generally of a religious nature. In traditional China, the dying were specially prepared for death, having their heads shaved and their bodies washed and placed in a sitting position to allow the soul to leave the body easily. In Catholic Christianity, the dying make a last confession of their sins to a priest, and receive absolution.

The actual disposal of the body displays varying degrees of complexity and religious significance in different societies. In ancient Egypt, the dead underwent ritual embalming (mummification) to prepare them for a proper afterlife. In most societies, burial or cremation are the favoured methods of disposing of the dead. However, the Parsis of India expose their corpses on 'towers of silence' to be devoured by crows, kites and vultures. This is to avoid polluting by burial or cremation the sacred divine creations of earth and fire. In Western countries, despite a tendency for funerals to become less elaborate (simple cremation rather than burial), religious rites and customs surrounding death continue to be observed even though the beliefs that inspired them have been discarded. In all societies funeral ceremonies mark the movement from life to death and help the bereaved adjust to the loss of a member of the community.

Whatever their form and content, rites of passage and age roles are ways in which human beings try to structure and organize their relationships with one another. Rites of passage provide an ordered framework for individuals in which their rights and obligations are made clear to them in a public context.

Some people choose to reject conventional domestic arrangements and set up alternative household groups. Multi-family households such as communes or kibbutzes, frequently inspired by political or religious ideas, continue to exist in Western societies as a minority pattern.

Social Stratification and Divisions

The hierarchical classification of social differences in terms of one or more dimensions of social inequality – such as wealth, power or prestige – is known as *social stratification*. The particular pattern that predominates in any one society tends to vary over time. In preliterate societies, membership of a *clan* (a group tracing its descent from a common male ancestor) or *tribe* (a distinctive ethnic and cultural group) is the main determinant of social inequality.

As well as the hierarchical classification of social differences that divides societies into horizontal layers, it is also possible to divide societies vertically into blocks or pillars. Physical and cultural divisions based on factors such as sex/gender, race, ethnic identity, language and religion tend to cut across hierarchically ranked social groups, thereby fragmenting a society even further.

The caste system of social stratification

Caste is found in its most developed form in the Hindu-based system of social stratification in India. Its origins are obscure, although it is known to have existed for over 2000 years. Social groups known as *castes* are separated from each other by religious rules of ritual purity and are ranked hierarchically on a scale that ranges from pure to impure – each caste is 'purer' than the one below it. Contact between castes is prohibited in case lower castes 'pollute' higher ones. Membership of caste is inherited and regarded by Hindus as divinely ordained. Members are required to marry within their caste. Traditionally, castes are associated with particular kinds of work, and this reinforces social segregation. Because caste

membership is permanent and unchangeable, social mobility – the ability to move up (or down) the social ladder via marriage or individual effort – is impossible within a rigid caste system.

The main castes and their associated occupations are:

1. Brahmin (priests)
2. Kshatriya (warriors and landlords)
3. Vaishya (farmers and traders)
4. Sudra (rural and urban labourers)

Subsequently, another caste was added to the bottom of the classification; *Harijans* or *'untouchables'*, who undertake the most menial of tasks such as cleaning streets and toilets. In addition to the main castes, several thousand subcastes (*jatis*) exist at the local village level. As in the wider caste system, jati membership is inherited, permanent and unchangeable. Legal discrimination based on caste has been abolished in modern India and industrialization has created many new occupational groups. This has led to an increase in both individual and collective social mobility, which in turn has loosened some of the rigidities of the caste system.

The estate system

Social groups known as *estates* existed in Europe from the time of the Roman Empire to as late as 1789 in France. The estate system reached its zenith during the feudal era in Europe (▷ p. 246) and there was a similar system in Japan. Estates were created by laws that provided for a clear structure of rights and duties, privileges and obligations. Estates were also related to the prevailing economic division of labour, but an estate system was not an entirely closed system of social stratification. Social mobility was possible but not very widespread.

The main estates were:

1. The nobility
2. The clergy
3. The commons (also known as serfs and peasantry)

The decline of the estate system in Europe coincided with the rise in the economic and political power of the urban *bourgeoisie* (merchants, manufacturers, financiers, etc.), a distinctive social group that developed within the system. According to some theories, this group played a major part in transforming and overthrowing the estate system of social stratification.

Class systems

Class systems of social stratification are characteristic of industrial capitalist societies. *Classes* are defined in economic rather than religious terms (as in caste systems), or political-legal terms (as in estate systems). There are no formal barriers to economic achievement in modern democratic societies, hence class systems tend to be less characterized by inherited factors and are correspondingly more open than other types of social stratification. In a class system, social mobility is the norm rather than the exception. Following the pioneering sociological theories of the Germans Karl Marx (▷ p. 168) and Max Weber (1864–1920), there are two main models of class – Marxist theory and Weber's occupational status system.

In Marxist theory, a class is a group of people who have the same relationship to capital (property, such as land, factories or money, used for profit). Marx's classification, which is strictly economic, recognizes two main and two minor classes:

Violence at Ayodhya, India, in 1990. Since partition (1947), India has experienced periodic communal clashes between Hindus and Muslims. Although the Hindus are numerically and politically dominant, the division cuts across normal class structure. (Gamma)

1. Bourgeoisie (large-scale owners of capital / employers)
2. Workers (non-owners of capital / employees)
1a Petty bourgeoisie (small-scale owners of capital / employers)
2b New middle class (managers and professional employees)

The relationship between workers and employers, and the conflict that it inevitably gives rise to, is the key point of Marx's theory of class. With industrialization, Marx expected the petty bourgeoisie to decline and the new middle class to expand, which has in fact happened. He also expected conflict between the two main classes to increase, resulting in the revolutionary overthrow of the dominant class, the owners, by the much larger subordinate class, the workers. This did not happen in the most economically developed Western societies, but it did in several other societies, such as China, Cuba, and the former USSR.

In addition to those differences based on the individual's relationship to capital, Weber suggested that class is also determined by a person's relationship to the market (▷ p. 170). People have qualifications or skills for which there is a large or small demand depending on the situation. Weber's theory of class tends to have more class categories than the Marxian one because it includes the ownership/non-ownership of knowledge as well as that of capital. Weber also emphasized the concept of *status*, which he defined as social prestige. Social status is not unique to modern societies and can be influenced by many factors, including birth, education, occupation and lifestyle.

The occupational status system

As a result of the increased economic and social significance of work in modern societies, *occupational status* (also sometimes called *occupational class*) is often used as an alternative to class models of social stratification. The rank order of occupations can vary between societies and alter over time. For example, since the 19th century, nursing has increased in skill and has therefore moved up the ranking, whereas clerical work has been deskilled and has declined in status.

The main occupational status groups are:

1. Higher managerial and professional (e.g. doctor, lawyer)
2. Lower managerial and professional (e.g. teacher, nurse)
3. Skilled non-manual (e.g. insurance agent, secretary)
4. Skilled manual (e.g. carpenter, hairdresser)
5. Semi-skilled manual (e.g. bus driver, cashier)
6. Unskilled manual (e.g. cleaner, labourer)

Market research companies in Britain, the USA and many other industrial capitalist societies use a comparable *social grading of occupation*:

A Upper middle class (higher managerial and professional)
B Middle class (lower managerial and professional)
C1 Lower middle class (routine white-collar)
C2 Skilled working class (manual)
D Semi-skilled and unskilled working class (manual)
E Residual (including those dependent upon the state)

In these classifications, the terms *middle class* and *working class* are widely used by sociologists and market researchers to refer to non-manual and manual occupational groups respectively.

SEE ALSO

- THE FAMILY p. 158
- GOVERNMENT AND THE PEOPLE p. 166
- POLITICAL IDEOLOGIES p. 168
- CIVIL AND HUMAN RIGHTS p. 182

Poor working class residents of Stepney, east London, celebrate King George V's Silver Jubilee of 1935. Particularly in large cities, social divisions are reflected by rich, middle class and poor neighbourhoods. (Popperfoto)

OTHER SOCIAL DIVISIONS

Such social distinctions as gender, race, ethnic identity, language and religion have been widely used as the basis for discrimination, both official and unofficial, in many societies. In the 19th century, for example, in many countries women were not allowed to own property or to enter certain professional occupations (▷ p. 183). Under the apartheid system in 20th-century South Africa, political, economic and social discrimination was officially practised by the dominant White race in relation to the non-White races. When discrimination is legally abolished, it often persists informally. Consequently, disadvantage in the competition for wealth, education, work, power and prestige continues to be experienced by certain groups, notably women and Blacks.

The term *plural society* refers to one that is divided into different racial, ethnic, linguistic, and/or religious groups. The degree of segmentation varies between societies and depends on several factors, such as the extent to which different groups have their own social institutions. Modern Dutch society is a particularly good example of advanced pluralism. In the Netherlands there are Catholic, Calvinist and non-religious political parties, trade unions, education organizations and broadcasting institutions. Many other societies are similarly divided, sometimes to such a degree that conflict between the major social groups occurs. Such tensions exist between Catholics and Protestants in Northern Ireland, Hindus and Muslims in India, Greeks and Turks in Cyprus, and Muslims and Christians in Lebanon. The USA is highly pluralistic – as was the former USSR – in that it is made up of many large ethnic groupings, some of which coexist harmoniously, others less so.

Extreme tensions between groups with different cultural traditions can lead to political movements for *separatism*. Groups such as the Basques in Spain and the French-speaking nationalists in Quebec in Canada have at times campaigned for their own separate state. Protestants in what is now Northern Ireland chose to stay outside the newly independent Irish Free State in 1922, agitating for the six counties where their communities are concentrated to remain a part of the United Kingdom. In India, extreme violence between Muslims and Hindus led to the partitioning of the country on independence in 1947 into two separate states – predominantly Hindu India, and predominantly Muslim Pakistan.

Education

Education is the process that allows each new generation to learn and sometimes challenge the knowledge, skills, values and behaviour that have been developed by previous generations. It may be acquired formally, in schools, colleges, universities and workplaces, or informally, in the home, on the streets, or in places of leisure. Although some people educate themselves, most learn from others, either from teachers who are paid to teach them, or from parents, relatives, friends and workmates.

Without education even advanced societies would sink back into a primitive state within a few years. We rely on education to ensure a supply of doctors, engineers, scientists and teachers, as well as to provide all citizens with a good foundation of basic knowledge and skills. In order to achieve this most countries have established a formal system of schooling. Children usually start attending school on a regular basis at the age of 5 or 6, although nursery and other forms of pre-school education may begin earlier.

The history of education

Accounts of many early civilizations contain descriptions of teaching. In ancient societies it was crucial to be able to hunt, cook, make weapons and utensils, and to know important rituals such as tribal dances and songs. Such skills and knowledge were passed on to children by their elders.

When societies became more advanced they needed teachers. Teachers were sometimes paid by the community out of taxes, or by parents. Some became well known. In the 5th century BC Kongfuzi (Confucius; ▷ p. 292) wandered round China with his disciples, who in turn became teachers, and wrote down his philosophy of teaching in the *Analects*. One of his sayings was 'If out of the four corners of a subject I have dealt thoroughly with one corner and the pupils cannot find out the other three for themselves, then I do not explain any more.'

In ancient India knowledge of the sacred texts was regarded as very important for teachers. They would live with and follow their own teachers or *gurus* until they had acquired enough wisdom to be teachers themselves. This was also the pattern adopted by Jesus and his disciples.

In Classical Greece and Rome, mastery of *rhetoric* (the skill of persuasion and communication in debate and public speaking) was highly valued. Athenian parents were willing to pay well-known teachers, such as Protagoras, as much as 10 000 drachmas to turn their sons into successful orators and men of affairs within three or four years. In Rome Cicero and Quintilian (▷ p. 356) analysed teaching methodology in considerable detail, and taught their pupils how to deliver a talk on a subject, or how to write in the style of different authors.

From about AD 1200 education gradually began to be made available to the ordinary people, not just the children of the wealthy (▷ p. 248). The Church played a big part in this: in many European countries the first schools for the poor were run by the local church, with the priest doubling up as teacher. As countries became industrialized there was political pressure to have a better educated workforce, and in the 19th century the first forms of official public education for all began to emerge (▷ p. 258).

During the 20th century the formal education of children in schools has spread throughout the world. In cities like New York the schools are huge and cater for thousands of pupils. In contrast, rural primary schools may only have a teaching staff of one and just a handful of children. Some schools simply teach their country's national curriculum (if it has one), while others may be founded on less conventional principles and adopt radically different teaching styles. Summerhill, founded in England in 1921 by the Scottish educationalist A.S. Neill (1883–1973), stresses freedom of choice for children, with optional attendance at lessons and a 'parliament' of teachers and pupils. Gordonstoun, founded in Scotland in 1935 by the German Kurt Hahn (1886–1974), emphasizes the benefits of a spartan outdoor regime and the achievement of ambitious intellectual and physical objectives. Hahn had established a similar school in Germany, but was forced to flee by the Nazis.

Aims and methods

Most official documents on education would claim that the aim of schooling is to develop children's talents to the full. In reality, however, there is some variety in what different schools try to achieve.

The primary or elementary phase of education usually covers the period from the start of compulsory schooling up to the age of 11 or 12. This is a time when pupils receive a general education and a basic grounding in foundation subjects – especially in their own language and mathematics – often, though not always, from a single teacher. Many primary schools have been influenced by the philosophy of European thinkers on education, such as the German Friedrich Froebel (1782–1852) and the Italian Maria Montessori (1870–1952), who both stressed the importance of creative play, self-motivation and practical activ-

A ragged school in London in the 1850s. The ragged schools were charitable institutions that provided elementary schooling, industrial training and religious instruction for nearly 300 000 destitute children. The schools died out after the introduction of compulsory education in Britain in 1870. (AR)

A school classroom in Communist China. The Chinese state lays down that the education system should follow the principles of Marxist-Leninism. There is an emphasis on technical skills that are perceived to benefit China's economic development. (Gamma)

ity. In parts of the United Kingdom, and in a few other countries, children attend middle schools from the age of 8 or 9 to 12 or 13.

Certain countries, especially the less wealthy, do not provide any education beyond the primary level. Even in Britain it was not until the Education Act of 1944 that secondary education was made available to all children. In some countries, such as Germany, children undergo a selection procedure to determine which type of secondary school they should attend. In others, like the United States and most of the United Kingdom, all pupils in an area attend the same secondary or high school.

During the secondary phase pupils usually study a variety of subjects taught by specialist teachers. The curriculum in some countries consists entirely of traditional academic subjects such as mathematics, history, science and both their native and a foreign language. In other countries there may be a more vocational bias. Pupils in the USA, for example, may be able to have classes in such fields as journalism.

Further and higher education

Once the compulsory years of education are over, those who wish to continue learning can choose either to teach themselves, learn in their workplace, or attend an institution of further or higher education. Colleges of further education usually provide a wide range of courses for people wanting to study either part or full time. Most of these courses are below degree level, often leading to a professional or technical qualification, but such colleges may offer courses of general education or 'second chances' to those who were not able to obtain academic qualifications earlier in their careers.

Institutions of higher education include universities (and, in some countries, polytechnics), which offer courses at first-degree level or beyond. Students either attend for their general education, or they may pursue a course related to a

future career in, for example, medicine, engineering or law. Numbers attending degree-level courses may vary from a tiny percentage of the population in less wealthy countries, to one in three in Japan and parts of the USA.

Issues in education

There are few parts of the world where education is not a contentious issue. In countries with high unemployment it may be a passport to one of the few good jobs available, so parents will be anxious to secure the best opportunities for their children. Particular controversy attaches to the question of equal opportunities for all. Do children of all backgrounds get a fair deal? Do boys have a better education than girls? Are children from different religious, ethnic and social groups given the same opportunities as others? Should children attend selective schools according to their ability, or should all attend a common high school or comprehensive school? And within the school should they be grouped according to their ability – in streamed classes – or be taught in 'mixed ability' classes? All these questions are commonly asked.

In addition, the speed of technological change is such that education is having to change rapidly. The development of radio, television, the microcomputer and the interactive videodisc have already influenced the way people learn and will continue to do so. With a source of electrical power and a telephone link, even the remotest areas can have access to the greatest stores of information in the world.

Furthermore, the many rapid changes in society and the realization that human beings are capable of learning throughout their lives – even into old age – have combined to produce a demand for permanent educational opportunities. In the 21st century people will need to be able to learn and retrain throughout their lives, not just during the brief years of compulsory schooling.

SEE ALSO

● LEARNING, CREATIVITY AND INTELLIGENCE p. 149
● MEDIEVAL AND RENAISSANCE CULTURE p. 248

EDUCATION AROUND THE WORLD

The organization of education varies considerably from one country to another. In some countries, such as France, there is a national system and curriculum controlled by the central government. Other countries favour local control, as in Germany, where the regional government in each *Land* (state) decides how schools are run. In the USA there is even more decentralization, with hundreds of school districts, some quite small, organizing local education.

The United Kingdom has a number of different systems. England and Wales have a mixture of local and national control, the curriculum, since 1988, being prescribed by the government but most day-to-day decisions about teachers, methods, books and buildings being decided at school level. Since 1988 schools have been able to 'opt out' of local authority control and receive their funding direct from the central government. In Scotland the Scottish Education Department exercises central control of the curriculum and examinations.

In many countries the state or the Church exerts a powerful influence on schooling. Before 1989–91, in Eastern bloc countries such as the USSR and Bulgaria, the state determined that education was provided according to the principles laid down by Marx and Lenin. In some Islamic countries such as Saudi Arabia and Pakistan, education is dedicated to promoting the principles of the Muslim religion, and much time in schools is devoted to the teachings of the Qur'an (Koran). In Ireland the Roman Catholic Church controls the administration of the vast majority of the country's schools.

Though the predominant form of schooling in most countries is that provided by the state, many countries have a private sector. Most private schools charge fees, although some are free, and the number varies from none at all in countries where independent schools are not permitted, to parts of the USA where there may be more private than public provision.

Law and Crime

At the root of all systems of law is the notion of justice. *Justice*, associated with the principles of fairness and impartiality, is often personified as a blindfolded figure holding a pair of scales, to symbolize the impartiality of the law. It is said that justice must be done and be seen to be done. Judges should be neutral and have no personal interest in the outcome of the case. No person should act as both prosecutor and judge. With a few exceptions, anyone can be called as a witness, and be required to give evidence.

Ancient legal systems, particularly those of Greece and Rome, still influence the modern law. There are now four distinct 'schools' of law in the world. The first is based on *Roman law*, which is the chief influence on the legal systems of many Western European countries. Roman-law systems are characterized by the writing down of laws in the form of general codes. Perhaps the most famous of these is the French Napoleonic Code. The second type is based on *common law*, and is found in Britain and in those countries – such as the USA and Commonwealth countries – whose legal systems are modelled on British law.

SEE ALSO

● GOVERNMENT AND THE PEOPLE p. 166
● CIVIL AND HUMAN RIGHTS p. 182

The public execution of a rapist in Saudi Arabia, where the death penalty is carried out by beheading or stoning, depending on the nature of the crime. Over 100 countries retain capital punishment, many by means of a firing squad. In the USA, 39 states retain the death penalty by hanging, gas chamber or injection by poison. (Gamma)

The third type is *socialist law*, strongly influenced by Marxism-Leninism (▷ p. 168), and found in some Asian countries and, until the early 1990s, in Eastern Europe and the former USSR, where the legal system is under review. Fourthly, *Muslim law* is based on the Qur'an (Koran; ▷ p. 300).

The sources of the law

The first and most important source of the law is *statute law*. In Britain a statute is an Act of Parliament passed by both Houses of Parliament; similarly, in other countries, laws are passed by a majority in the representative assembly (*legislature*; ▷ p. 166). European Community laws are having an important effect in standardizing the laws of EC member-countries (▷ p. 178). In the USA, statutes may apply at either state or federal level, but the most important statute is the US Constitution itself. Sometimes the wording of a statute may be unclear, in which case a judge must give a ruling (*statutory interpretation*) on the meaning of the new law. In Roman-law systems, the main task of the judge is to apply the codes.

The second source of the law is previous court decisions. The doctrine of *precedent*, which is found in all legal systems, says that the judge must generally follow an earlier decision of any higher court on the same point of law that he is considering. A *litigant* who wants to challenge that law must take his or her case on appeal to a court high enough to overturn the earlier decision. The system of precedent means that a legal system must have detailed accounts (*law reports*) of previous cases.

Common-law systems are *adversarial*, which means that lawyers on each side put opposing arguments to the judge, who then decides which argument wins. The role of the judge is rather like an umpire – he or she ensures fair play and then announces the result. In some kinds of cases, the

── WHAT IS CRIMINAL BEHAVIOUR? ──

As societies evolve and become more complex, views on what constitutes crime may change. Although the central core of criminal wrongdoing – offences such as murder, theft and assault – has remained more or less unchanged over the centuries and from country to country, other behaviour may be regarded as criminal at one time or place but not at another. In Britain, for instance, suicide was a crime until 1961 and eavesdropping until 1967, and homosexual behaviour was legalized in some situations in the same year.

On the other hand, many new crimes have been created. Insider dealing – the unfair use of information about stocks and shares to make a personal profit – was made a crime in several countries in the 1980s, and some countries have made computer 'hacking' a crime. In South Africa, the apartheid system, which segregated people according to their skin colour, was enforced by criminal law until the early 1990s. In countries with a strict system of Islamic law, it is a criminal offence to commit adultery, or to drink alcohol.

Generally crimes can be classified in four broad groups: firstly there are crimes against the person, such as murder, manslaughter, assault and sexual offences; secondly crimes against property, such as theft, burglary and criminal damage; thirdly crimes against public order, such as riot, affray and incitement to racial hatred; and fourthly crimes against the state, such as treason and sedition. Some laws are designed to protect health, such as quarantine laws and laws against the possession and use of dangerous drugs, or to protect people's feelings and beliefs, such as the laws of libel and blasphemy.

The notion that the criminal law always enforces morality is a mistaken one. While the criminal law can be used to enforce the Ten Commandments, for example, it can also be used to bolster the most repressive political regimes, such as Nazi Germany. For the society that has made the law, crimes are wrongs committed not just against an individual victim, but also against society as a whole. Thus prosecutions are almost always brought by the state and only rarely by individual citizens. In most countries the prosecution must prove an accused person's guilt beyond reasonable doubt.

For all serious crimes, the prosecution must prove that the accused committed the wrongful act, such as killing the victim, and that this was done with a guilty mind – that is to say on purpose rather than by accident. Even if the prosecution can prove these elements of the crime, the accused person may be able to rely on a defence – such as insanity or duress – to show the court that in the circumstances he or she should not be found guilty after all. However, if pleading insanity the accused may be detained in a mental institution.

jury has the role of deciding the result (▷ criminal law, below). A quite different system, the *inquisitorial* one, operates in Roman-law, socialist and Islamic systems. Here, the judge or magistrate actively investigates the case and questions the witnesses in court before reaching a decision.

Civil law

Civil law governs rights and duties between citizens. The law of *contract* deals with important business matters such as trade, credit and insurance, but also governs more commonplace agreements (for example, a bus ticket is a contract between the passenger and the bus company). The law of *tort*, or *delict*, governs liability following breach of a duty of care between citizens, such as a case in which a person is injured by another's negligent driving, or where a person's reputation is damaged by defamatory statements in a published work.

In civil cases the person injured (known in England and Wales as the *plaintiff*) will use the law to bring an action against the *defendant* in a civil court, probably seeking the remedy of *damages*, which is a payment of compensation. Another civil remedy is an *injunction*. This might be used where one neighbour sues another to stop them having noisy parties. In such cases the plaintiff does not want compensation; the court is being asked to order the offending behaviour to be stopped. Civil law covers other important areas of life, such as the purchase of a house, the disposal of property where a marriage ends in divorce, and the care and custody of the children of that marriage.

Criminal law

Criminal law deals with the situation where the *accused* person is said to have broken a law that has caused an injury not just to another individual, but also to the state. This law covers offences that range from murder, manslaughter, assault and sexual offences, to offences against property such as theft, burglary and criminal damage. The purpose of the criminal law is quite different from that of the civil law. The state prosecutes accused persons in a criminal court not in order to obtain compensation, but to punish them for what they have done.

In common-law systems, serious criminal law cases are dealt with by a judge and *jury*, but most cases can be decided by *magistrates*, or *justices of the peace*, who are not lawyers and are unpaid. With the exception of some libel cases, a jury is never used in a civil case in Britain, and juries are hardly ever used in Roman-law, socialist or Islamic legal systems. In England and Wales a jury is composed of 12 impartial people, aged between 18 and 70. At the end of the case they decide if the accused is guilty or not guilty. In most countries that have a jury system a unanimous verdict is needed, but in England and Wales a majority verdict, with up to two dissenters, is allowed. If the jury cannot agree, there may be a retrial. In Scotland, juries consist of 15 people, and a bare majority verdict of 8:7 is acceptable.

The accused's guilt in a criminal case must be proved by the prosecution beyond reasonable doubt. The rules governing what evidence can be heard in court are complex and vary between different legal systems. In Britain the accused's previous convictions cannot be discussed, nor can *hearsay* evidence, where one person testifies as to what another person told him. Opinion evidence is not allowed, unless it is the opinion of an expert, such as a forensic scientist.

──PUNISHMENT──

After a person is convicted of an offence by a criminal court, the court proceeds to sentence him or her. Judges often have a wide discretion over which sentence to impose. Under many legal systems their decision is subject to an appeal by the offender, if he or she thinks the sentence is too severe, and conversely by the prosecution if they think the sentence is too lenient.

Capital punishment (the death penalty) was once widely used in Britain, for offences as diverse as defacing the coinage and sheep stealing. It was effectively abolished in 1965, although theoretically it can still be imposed for a crime of treason. The death penalty still exists in other countries, such as China, the USA and South Africa. A death sentence is often not carried out immediately, and prisoners on 'Death Row' may face months or years of uncertainty until they know whether an appeal against their sentence will be successful, or whether the government will commute their sentence to one of imprisonment.

Imprisonment was not originally designed as a punishment. Prisons were places used to hold people securely until they paid their debts, were executed, or transported overseas. In many countries imprisonment is now the most severe sentence a court can impose. It may be for a fixed term stated by the judge, or for life. In either case the actual period served may be reduced, sometimes quite considerably, by the prisoner's good behaviour and a decision by the authorities to release a prisoner early, under supervision. Prison sentences, and the equivalent sentence of detention in a youth-offender institution for those under 21, are used in about half the cases sentenced in the British Crown Courts.

Courts can opt for non-custodial sentences as alternatives to prison. Prison sentences can be suspended, which means that the offender will only serve the sentence if he or she commits a further offence within a specified time. In Britain fines are the most frequently imposed non-custodial sentence, though in the USA they are seldom used. In Germany and Sweden a system exists whereby offenders are fined a percentage of their income, rather than being fined a fixed amount for the crime committed.

Community service – introduced first in Britain in 1972 and in many countries since – requires the offender to do up to 240 hours of unpaid work in the community to repay his or her debt to society. This may be hard physical labour, such as clearing derelict land, or social work alongside professional carers and volunteers with the disadvantaged or handicapped. A probation order places the offender under the supervision of a probation officer for a period of up to three years. In the USA some offenders on probation are required to wear an electronic anklet or tag, so that the probation officer can check their whereabouts by radio monitoring.

In many cases where the offender can afford to pay, he or she will be required by the criminal court to pay money in compensation to the victim of the crime. Alternatively, a victim who has suffered physical injury may be able to claim some compensation from the state. The first scheme of this type started in New Zealand in 1960 and most countries now have one.

A demonstration against the Mafia in Palermo, Sicily, in 1992. The Mafia – an international secret criminal society originating in Sicily – was responsible for an upsurge of violent crime in the 1990s. The scale of Mafia operations in Italy outraged public opinion and threatened the stability of state institutions. (Gamma)

Government and the People

The word 'government' comes from the Latin word *gubernator*, meaning helmsman. Well before Roman times, early societies started to develop special institutions to look after their common well-being. Government is needed to make decisions on matters affecting the people of a state as a whole. Effective government means the ability to arrive at a balance between conflicting pressures, and to steer the state towards shared community goals.

SEE ALSO

● SOCIAL STRATIFICATION AND DIVISIONS p. 160
● POLITICAL IDEOLOGIES p. 168

The original purposes of government were to protect a people from external aggressors, and to provide them with a body of laws to bring order to their everyday lives. Since the 19th century, the tasks of government have grown to cover education, health and pensions (the 'welfare state'). Some people think that modern governments take on too wide a range of tasks.

The ancient Athenian city-state (▷ p. 230) is often viewed as the basic model of democracy. It was certainly more democratic than anything that had come before it; but, by modern standards, Athenian democracy was limited by the inferior status of women, the reliance on slavery, and an unequal sharing of power among male citizens. The Roman republican system (▷ p. 232) saw a further development of popular control of government, in particular in the acceptance of the idea that sovereignty rests in the people as a whole rather than in one small group.

In the medieval period, government was effectively divided between the state and the Church,

The Democratic Party national convention in 1992, part of the complex electoral process in the USA. Delegates to the national conventions of the Democratic and Republican parties are chosen by a series of state elections. To receive the party nomination for president, a candidate must gain the majority of the votes of delegates. US electors do not directly choose a president, but vote for members of the Electoral College, who, in turn, vote for the nominee who gets the largest number of votes in their particular state. (Gamma)

with each claiming their own set of rights. The medieval view was that the authority of one person to rule over another came from God – the so-called 'divine right of kings'. The Italian political theorist Niccolò Machiavelli (1469–1527) rejected this in favour of a secular view of the state. He favoured a popular form of government that he saw as having existed in the Roman Republic.

The social contract

The emergence of the idea of the *social contract* in the 16th century reintroduced the notion that government rests on the consent of the people. In his treatise *Leviathan* (1651), the English political philosopher Thomas Hobbes (1588–1679) described the chaos in which he believed people lived when they did not have a proper government. His doctrine is that men can only live together in peace if they agree to obey an absolute sovereign, and this agreement Hobbes called 'the social contract'. Hobbes's concern about what happened when government broke down, as in the English Civil War during his lifetime, led him to suggest that considerable power should be placed in the hands of the sovereign. In his two *Treatises of Government* (1690), the English philosopher John Locke (1632–1704; ▷ p. 304) also proposed the idea of a social contract. However, Locke opposed absolutism, and saw the free consent of the governed as the basis of legitimate government. Obedience depends on governments ruling for the good of the governed, who have the right to rebel if they are oppressed. This idea is quite acceptable today, but was seen as radical at the time – being adopted, for example, by the American Revolutionaries of 1776 (▷ p. 260).

The French philosopher Jean-Jacques Rousseau (1712–1778; ▷ p. 304) faced the question that had troubled all social-contract theorists since the decline of the idea of a God-given authority. If laws are made by citizens, why should other citizens obey them? Rousseau made it clear that citizens must exist within a system of law, but citizens can only be bound by those laws if they take part in making them. In his *Social Contract* (1762), Rousseau defined the ideal democracy based on popular sovereignty. The exercise of power, he argued, should accord with the 'general will' and have the consent of all the people.

Types and tasks of government

By developing the idea of *separation of powers*, the French enlightenment philosopher Montesquieu (1689–1755; ▷ p. 304) pointed the way to the modern view of the three branches of government. The *legislature* is responsible for the making and amending of laws; the *executive* is responsible for carrying out laws and the *judiciary* is responsible for administering justice. This division of governmental powers provides a basis for popular control. For example, a supreme court (the highest court of the judiciary) can rule whether the government (executive) has broken the law. In the USA, the constitution is based on a system of 'checks and balances' between the different branches of government.

Liberal or western democracies take a number of forms, but have in common the regular election of governments by free choice between competing parties. Countries such as France and the USA have *presidential* systems in which executive power is vested in an elected president. A president's power is usually limited to some extent by the legislative assembly, which is responsible for the day-to-day running of the government. In a *parliamentary* system, a *Prime Minister* – usually the leader of the majority party in the legislative assembly – heads the executive branch of government. In a *constitutional monarchy*, such as Britain, the prime minister serves under a sovereign who has only ceremonial powers (⊳ box).

Communist states, such as the Soviet Union until 1990–91, depended on one-party rule by the Communist Party. In 1989–91, the power of the Communist Party was eroded in the countries of Eastern Europe, which moved towards democratic political systems. Many countries, particularly in the Third World, are governed by the military. However, since the 1970s, there has been a trend for military regimes to be replaced by democracies, first in southern Europe, later in Latin America and most recently in Africa.

A *federal* system, as in Germany, divides power between central government and a number of regional governments. A *unitary* system concentrates executive authority in the hands of central government.

Political participation

Modern democracy has developed as a system in which the people are able to take part in government decision making. The most basic form of political participation is voting to elect public officials. This may be direct or indirect. In the system of indirect election in the USA, the people choose a body of electors – an *electoral college* – which then elects a president. Some countries, such as Britain, have a first-past-the-post electoral system in which the candidate with the most votes in a constituency (i.e. a particular area) is elected. France uses a two-stage system, while most other European countries use a variety of systems of *proportional representation* intended to ensure that parties are represented in parliament in relation to the number of votes they receive from the electorate as a whole. In Australia and Belgium it is illegal not to vote in a general election. Some countries, such as Switzerland, make extensive use of referenda to allow the electorate to decide directly on current issues. Referenda have been used in Britain on the issues of membership of the European Community and devolution for Scotland and Wales.

The administration

The German sociologist Max Weber saw bureaucracy as a more efficient form of administration than, for example, the earlier system based on the members of a monarch's court. However, the very efficiency of bureaucracy, and the permanent status of most civil servants, raises serious questions about the accountability of bureaucrats to the people.

The civil service, particularly its senior members, is important both in terms of offering advice on policy, and putting policies into operation. The central position of bureaucracy in modern government has created a need for new ways of dealing with complaints from citizens about unfair treatment. In Britain, the *ombudsman* is an official who investigates claims of maladministration against national and local government. Reforms such as this can help to deal with complaints from individuals, but they do not solve the more general problem of the accountability of bureaucrats. The power of the bureaucracy – which Montesquieu did not anticipate when writing about the separation of powers – poses the most serious problem for popular control.

Guerrilla forces from the province of Tigray seized power in Ethiopia in 1991, toppling a Marxist-Leninist government that had itself come to power in a military coup. The peaceful transfer of power associated with free multi-party elections was unknown in Africa between 1960 and 1990, when Zambia became the first of a growing number of African countries to adopt a democratic system. (Gamma)

GOVERNMENT IN BRITAIN

The United Kingdom uses a 'first-past-the-post' system for electing Members of Parliament. Each constituency elects one MP, the person gaining the most votes being elected. In a contest between four parties, it would be possible for an MP to be elected with less than a third of the total vote. At national level, it is possible for the party that obtains the largest number of votes not to win the election, as happened in 1951 when the Labour Government lost office to the Conservatives.

The first-past-the-post system favours parties that appeal to a particular social class (such as the Conservative and Labour parties) or to a region (such as the Nationalist parties in Wales and Scotland). Parties that have an appeal across the electorate gain fewer seats. The British system tends to produce majority governments that do not have to rely on coalition partners to govern. Systems of proportional representation, such as those of Germany and Italy, can give a lot of influence to very small parties whose support is needed by larger parties to enable them to form a government.

The monarch is head of the United Kingdom, although the *crown* is seen as a symbol above and beyond the monarch. Legislative power is vested in Parliament, with the *royal assent* needed for a bill to become law. The Commons is elected for a term of not more than five years. Parliament is *dissolved* by the monarch on the advice of the Prime Minister. After a general election, the monarch appoints the head of the winning party as the new prime minister, although if no one party had a working majority, the monarch would have to seek advice on who to ask first to try to form a government. Britain operates a system of *cabinet government* in which ministers in charge of departments are drawn from the two Houses of Parliament, largely from the Commons (lower house) rather than the Lords (upper house). If the government loses a vote of confidence in the House of Commons, even by only one vote, as happened to the Labour Party in 1979, it has to resign.

Because modern governments have so much to do, the Cabinet increasingly works through a system of committees. Some are permanent committees dealing with tasks such as managing the economy, while others are formed to deal with particular problems. The whole Cabinet is crucial in shaping the general policy of the Government, although the Prime Minister is clearly its most important single member.

Much of the work of governing Britain is done by local government. Local authorities (county councils and district councils in England and Wales, regional and district councils in Scotland) are responsible for services such as education, social services, local authority housing, and the fire brigade. There has been some loss of tasks by local government in the 1980s, with some metropolitan authorities (notably the Greater London Council) being abolished and schools being allowed to opt for direct funding by central government. A review of the structure of local government in Britain began in 1992.

Political Ideologies

A Soviet political poster of 1920 urges 'Long live the struggle of farm and industrial workers against the capitalist yoke. Long live socialism!' (AKG)

The political terms *left*, *right* and *centre* originated in the French Revolution of 1789 (▷ p. 262). In the French Estates General the aristocracy sat on the King's right, whereas the commoners (or 'third estate') sat on his left. Subsequently, in French and other European assemblies, radical democrats, radical liberals and socialists sat on the left of the president's or speaker's chair; conservatives, Christian democrats and other right-wing parties sat on the right.

The French revolutionary commitment to 'liberty, equality and fraternity' lie at the centre of the Left's arguments.

The Left

The tensions between liberty, equality and fraternity help explain much of the internal debate and fragmentation within the Left. However, all these values and tensions are subsumed within a broad philosophical commitment to 'political rationalism'. The Left – especially its liberal and demo-cratic components such as the socialist, labour and social democratic parties of Western Europe – are distinguished by their fundamental commitment to democracy, understood as government based on popular consent and popular participa-

---

POLITICAL THEORIES OF THE LEFT

Socialism

Socialism is a political and economic theory advocating the ownership and control of the means of production, distribution and exchange by the entire community or by the state, and the equal distribution of wealth. The term was first used by the French political theorist Claude Saint-Simon (1760–1825) and the British manufacturer and reformer Robert Owen (1771–1858). Parties describing themselves as 'socialist' range from extreme left-wing Communist parties (▷ Marxism) advocating political change by violent revolution, to moderate social democrat or labour parties embracing the institutions of representative democratic government.

The Communist 'state socialist' tradition has never been universal on the Left. Western democratic socialists have argued that markets can be regulated to achieve socialist ends (i.e. liberal, egalitarian and fraternal outcomes) without supplanting them by state planning. They have agreed with the Right that monopolistic state ownership and planning endanger liberty and reduce efficiency without necessarily producing either greater equality or solidarity. In the 1980s the fundamental failures of the planned economies of the Communist bloc totally discredited the 'state socialist' tradition. This discrediting has permitted the democratic socialist Left in Western Europe, such as the Swedish and German Social Democrats, the British Labour Party, and the French Socialists, to clarify their commitment to economic pluralism, i.e. a mixed economy in which markets are regulated by governments to maximize liberty, equality and community.

Marxism

The economic and political doctrine known as Marxism was outlined by the German theorists Karl Marx (1818–83) and Friedrich Engels (1820–95). Their most famous joint work was *The Communist Party Manifesto* (1848), and Engels helped finish Marx's major work *Das Kapital* (1867–94). According to Marx and Engels' theory of *dialectical materialism*, human history has seen the existence of a number of progressive modes of production, each characterized by fundamental class division and exploitation. They believed that changes in modes of production occurred through *class struggle* and were always signalled by revolution. They

thought that the socialist revolution would be characterized by a temporary 'dictatorship of the proletariat (working class)' – in which the means of production would be owned by the state – which would build the conditions for a classless communist society, with the means of production collectively owned by all members of society, and goods and services distributed justly according to people's needs.

Through its profound influence on revolutionary Communists such as Lenin (1870–1924; ▷ p. 270) and Mao Zedong (1893–1976; ▷ p. 276), as well as its lesser influence on evolutionary socialists and social democrats, Marxism has had a dramatic impact on the history of the 20th century. Lenin advocated the creation of an elite party of professional revolutionaries to hasten violent proletarian revolution, and argued for the dictatorship of this party rather than the working class as a whole. His revolutionary philosophy – Marxist-Leninism – became the guiding doctrine of the Soviet Union and spread throughout the world. Mao Zedong's interpretation of Marxist-Leninism was based on the revolutionary potential of the rural peasantry, and on guerrilla warfare, and adapted Marx and Lenin's ideas to Chinese conditions. In practice, Marxist-Leninism or Communism has meant the dictatorship of the Communist Party and the regulation of every aspect of human life. States under Communist control have been characterized by centralized economies and vast administrative bureaucracies, and by the suppression of free speech and competing political parties. Communist parties have monopolized state power in the Soviet Union and Eastern Europe (until 1989), and in China, Indochina and Cuba.

Social Democracy

A number of left-of-centre political parties are described as *social democrat*. Before 1919 the term described socialist political parties usually subscribing to a Marxist analysis of society. Between 1919 and 1945 the label was used for those left-wing parties which, whilst often avowedly Marxist, rejected the leadership of the Soviet Union. In the postwar period, the term has come to be applied to democratic left-wing parties committed to redistribution of wealth, extension of welfare and social security schemes, and limited state management of the economy.

tion in the formation and exercise of political authority. The Left hold that human freedom requires political freedom – freedom to choose the government and to dissent from it – and regards the civil rights of assembly, expression and participation essential to the realization of such freedom. However, they have always been divided over how and to what extent to increase democracy (⊳ box).

The Right

The Right are defined as the political opponents of the Left. Like the Left, the Right encompasses a wide range of beliefs. However, four core values lie at the heart of right-wing political thought: authority, hierarchy, property and community. Though there is much disagreement amongst right-wing political theorists over their interpretation and justification, these four values are generally subsumed under a 'common-sense' political philosophy that rejects the idea that human beings can be made perfect. Varying degrees of commitment on the Right to these values are reflected in different right-wing political ideologies (⊳ box).

Liberalism

Political liberals – non-socialist upholders of tolerance, freedom of expression and individual liberty – occupy the centre ground of politics between Left and Right, and are found in such parties as the British Liberal Democrats and the German Free Democratic Party. The writings of John Locke (1632–1704) were an early source of liberal political thought, and many of the principles of political liberalism were enshrined in the Constitution of the USA. In the 19th century 'classical liberalism' embraced an economic philosophy insisting on a laissez-faire economy untrammelled by state intervention. In the late 19th century the social inequalities created by unfettered industrial capitalism produced a new type of liberal thinking, given practical expression by the reforming administrations of Herbert Henry Asquith (1852–1928) and David Lloyd George (1863–1945) in Britain. Henceforth, however, the cause of political and social reform was to be more successfully championed by the emerging social democrat and socialist parties and, in most countries, liberal parties went into decline.

Nationalism

National parties belong to both the Right and the Left, but all are characterized by a feeling of common identity shared by a group of people with the same language, culture, ethnic origins and history. It manifests itself in a sense of loyalty to a 'mother country', particularly where that country has not yet become a state in its own right, in which case nationalist parties often advocate secession. Fascism contains elements of extreme nationalism.

Other trends

Set somewhat apart from the main political traditions are various other trends. *Anarchism* – first outlined by Pierre-Joseph Proudhon (1809–65) – advocates the abolition of formal government and the state. The influence of anarchism has now largely waned. *Libertarians* may have loyalties to either left or right – or neither. They are anti-authoritarian, opposing any state restriction on the liberties of the individual, for example calling for the legalization of banned drugs and the lifting of anti-obscenity laws. Those on the Right are also extreme economic liberals (⊳ box). *Green* political parties – dedi-

—— **POLITICAL THEORIES OF THE RIGHT** ——

Conservatism

Conservatives share with all liberals a firm commitment to individuals' rights to private property – in contrast with socialists and Communists. They cite two arguments for the justice of strong private-property rights. The first, deriving from the English philosopher John Locke (⊳ main text), suggests that individuals have a natural right to property on which they have worked, and that this right is transferable. The second, best developed in the work of the German philosopher G.W.F. Hegel (1770–1831; ⊳ p. 304), suggests that private property rights are essential if individuals are to be free, and able to exercise their freedom.

Economic liberalism – based on the doctrine of the 18th-century Scottish economist Adam Smith (1723–90) – has been on the ascendant amongst the Right in the last two decades. Political exponents of this philosophy, known as the 'New Right', have been especially active in the English-speaking democracies. Supporters of Margaret Thatcher in Britain and Ronald Reagan in the USA have vigorously pursued tax-cutting, privatization (selling public enterprises into private ownership) and the freeing of business from governmental restrictions, arguing that leaving people free to exploit their property is the best means to advance general prosperity.

Christian Democracy

The term *Christian democrat* is used to describe a number of conservative European political parties, especially the Christian Democracy Parties of Germany and Italy. They emphasize Christian values, a community ethic and social reform. Christian democracy developed after 1945 and remains one of the main political forces in Western Europe.

Fascism

An ancient Roman symbol of authority, the *fasces*, provides the origin of the name Fascism, one of the most significant ideologies of the 20th century. Fascism grew out of the unstable political conditions that followed World War I. Its mass appeal derived from its promises to replace weak democratic governments with strong leadership and to rectify the grievances of individuals and states arising out of the postwar settlement (⊳ p. 269). In the 1920s Fascist dictators began to gain power in several countries and by the end of the following decade Italy, Germany, Japan and Spain had Fascist governments.

Fascism was not a coherent doctrine like Marxism, but all Fascists believed in a strong, nationalist, authoritarian state, ruled by a charismatic dictator backed by a single paramilitary party. Fascists were fanatically opposed to democracy, socialism, Marxism and liberalism, and were often racist and antisemitic. Some elements of Fascism have been revived in recent years by extreme right-wing parties in a number of European countries.

Neo-Nazi demonstrators in Dresden, Germany, in 1991. Since the demise of the Communist governments of the former Soviet bloc (1989–91), various Fascist and extreme nationalist movements have appeared in Germany, Russia and the Balkans. (Gamma)

cated to environmental protection and opposed to nuclear power – first emerged in the 1970s and had some electoral success in the 1980s, forcing other parties to adopt more environmentally aware policies. Many Greens believe that the promises of unlimited economic growth held out by the mainstream political parties are unsustainable, and will lead to environmental degradation and collapse.

SEE ALSO

● GOVERNMENT AND THE PEOPLE p. 166
● ECONOMIC SYSTEMS p. 170
● CIVIL AND HUMAN RIGHTS p. 182

Economic Systems

Economics is concerned with the problem of using the available resources of a country as efficiently as possible to achieve the maximum fulfilment of society's unlimited demands for goods and services. The ultimate purpose of economic endeavour is to satisfy human wants for products. The problem is that although wants are virtually without limit, the resources – natural resources, labour and capital – available to produce goods and services are limited in supply.

Since resources are scarce – relative to the demands they are called upon to satisfy – mechanisms are required in order to allocate resources between individual end uses (*microeconomics*; p. 172) and to ensure that all the available resources are fully employed (*macroeconomics*; p. 174). An economy can be organized in a number of ways. These are usually described as market, command and mixed economies.

The stock exchange in Los Angeles, California. The USA's largest stock exchange is Wall Street, New York. Other major international exchanges are London, Tokyo, Paris, Hong Kong and Frankfurt. Computerization has revolutionized international dealings in stock and shares.
(Images)

Market economies

In a *market* or *private enterprise* economy the means of production are privately held by individuals and businesses. Economic decision-making is highly decentralized, and resources are allocated through a large number of individual markets for goods and services. The *market* brings together buyers and producers. By establishing prices for products and suitable profit rewards for suppliers, the market will determine how much of a product will be produced and sold.

Proponents of enterprise systems highlight the inefficiencies and rigidities usually associated with state bureaucracies (command economies), and suggest that competition, far from being wasteful, acts as an important spur to efficiency and encourages enterprise, leading to lower prices and better goods and services.

Command economies

In a *command*, *centrally planned* or *state* economy, economic decision-making is centralized in the hands of the state. The means of production – except labour – are under collective ownership. The state bureaucracy decides which products – and how many of each – are to be produced in accordance with some centralized national plan. Resources are allocated between producing units by quotas.

Advocates of this system emphasize the benefits of synchronizing and coordinating the allocation of resources as a unified whole, avoiding the 'wastes' of duplication inherent in competition. However, the fundamental failure of the planned economies of the Communist bloc in the late 1980s has totally discredited the theories behind command economies.

Mixed economies

In a mixed economy the state provides some goods

FINANCIAL INSTITUTIONS AND MARKETS

Financial institutions can be classified into two broad groupings – *deposit-taking institutions* and *longer-term savings institutions*.

Deposit-taking institutions comprise the commercial banks, savings banks, merchant banks, building societies (called savings and loan societies in the USA) and finance houses. Such institutions rely mainly on deposits from individuals and businesses for their funds. They pay interest on deposits and make a profit on their operations by lending out money or buying securities at higher rates of interest.

The *commercial banks* provide a money-transmission service for their depositors (for instance redeeming cheques and paying standing orders) and are involved in all three categories of short-term finance, as well as mortgage finance (▷ box on Capital). The other deposit-taking institutions operate in narrower areas. *Building societies* specialize in mortgage finance (loans for buying houses); *finance houses* specialize in instalment loans (i.e. hire purchase) and leasing (buying business assets such as machinery and cars, which are then hired out to companies); *savings banks* invest most of their funds in loan and share capital and government stocks; *merchant banks* specialize in business loans and 'underwrite' new share issues on the stock market (i.e. agree to buy up shares that are not sold on the open market).

Longer-term savings institutions include: *pension funds* (institutions that collect personal savings from contributors to provide them with pension payments in their retirement), *insurance companies* (companies that collect funds from individuals and businesses on a long-term basis, providing insurance to cover loss of life and injury, or to cover personal and business property against loss or damage), *unit trusts* and *investment trust companies* (institutions that issue, respectively, 'units' and shares, principally for purchase by small investors).

The financial markets comprise two main channels for bringing together borrowers and lenders, and savers and investors. These are the *money market*, which deals primarily in short-term financial securities (such as bills of exchange and Treasury bills) and inter-bank loans; and the *stock market*, which deals mainly in company stocks and shares and government stocks. The stock market performs two important functions: it provides a 'new-issue' market where companies and the government can raise capital by the sale of new stocks and shares, and it provides a secondary market for the day-to-day buying and selling of existing stocks and shares.

Shares provide a permanent source of finance for as long as the company continues to exist. The shareholders of a company are its legal owners and are entitled to a share in its profits. During the 1980s, the growth of multinational companies and financial institutions led to an opening-up of stock markets around the world and a greater interdependency between them. Shares in companies can now be traded simultaneously across stock markets based in New York, London and Tokyo, using new satellite and computerized communication systems for transmitting deals.

LABOUR

Labour represents people's contribution to productive activity; it includes both manual tasks such as laying a pipeline, and mental and organizational skills such as managing a business. The labour force of a country consists of employers, employees and the self-employed, together with those registered as unemployed. An economy is working near to its maximum productive capabilities when there is full employment; *unemployment* represents 'wasted' labour resources and thus 'lost' output potential.

Notable trends in the labour forces of the major Western industrialized countries over the past two decades include an increase in the proportion of women in the labour force, a decline in the average number of hours worked per week and an increase in the number of part-time employees, especially women. A significant trend in the distribution of labour has been the fall in the proportion of the labour force employed in manufacturing industry and a continuing expansion of the service industries. Generally, this is consistent with a change in the pattern of demand and the composition of output in favour of services, but in some countries, notably Britain, employment in the manufacturing sector has been adversely affected by foreign competition.

People who take on a particular job are required to accept the terms and conditions specified by their employers in an employment contract. Failure to meet the requirements of that contract, either through non-compliance or incompetence, may result in dismissal. Individually, workers tend to be in a relatively weak position in relation to their employers, especially in large companies. For this reason, workers have found it expedient to organize themselves into *trade unions* to increase their bargaining power.

Trade unions are organizations of workers whose primary objective is to protect and advance the economic interests of their members by negotiating pay deals with employers (*collective bargaining*), and coming to agreements on hours and conditions of

The Jarrow marchers – unemployed shipbuilders – walked 430 km (270 mi) in 1936 from Tyneside, northern England, to London to make their cause heard in Parliament. They were led by their Member of Parliament, Ellen Wilkenson, and trade union leaders. Trade unions – called labour unions in the USA – undertake collective action to improve pay, working conditions and employment prospects. (Fox)

work (including paid holidays, and redundancy and dismissal procedures). Trade union membership has declined in many countries in recent years, owing to a lack of interest in and dissatisfaction with trade union policies, and most importantly the structural shifts in the labour force away from the manufacturing industries, the traditional strongholds of union power, towards the less unionized service sector. However, unions continue to play a significant role in the functioning of national economies, in particular by influencing the level of wage rates and, through this, supply costs and prices.

CAPITAL

Capital refers to investment in such things as factories, training and research; *money capital* constitutes the means of financing such investment. The three main types of capital investment are capital stock, human capital and research and development.

Capital stock is investment in business and social assets. This comprises investment by private businesses and public corporations in factories, offices, machinery and equipment, etc., and investment by the government in the provision of *social capital* – roads, railways, schools, hospitals, etc. *Capital formation* (the process of adding to capital stock) expands the productive capacity of an economy, enabling a greater quantity of goods and services to be supplied. This, together with similar investments in the provision of social capital, contributes significantly to improving a country's general standard of living.

Human capital refers to investment by governments in general education and by government and businesses in vocational training. A better educated and skilled workforce not only helps to increase productivity (output per employee) in the economy, but also assists in the more rapid development and introduction of new, superior technologies and products.

Research and development (R & D) is investment in the invention and introduction of new technologies and products. Technological advance frequently involves the removal of existing capital and its replacement by superior production processes and equipment (which help to reduce supply costs), while the introduction of new, more sophisticated and reliable products benefits the consumer.

Investment has to be financed, and this requires savings and borrowing facilities. In some cases a business, individual or

government may be able to finance investment out of their own resources: a business might use its retained profits (*corporate savings*) to buy a new machine. In a large number of cases, however, businesses, individuals and governments have to use other people's money, raising the finance they need by borrowing or issuing *financial securities* such as *stocks and shares* (⊳ box on Financial Institutions and Markets). It is in this latter capacity that a country's *financial system* plays an important role, by channelling savings and other funds into investment uses, as well as financing spending on personal consumption (such as loans to purchase a new car).

The three main types of short-term finance are: a *loan* (a specified sum of money advanced to a borrower by a lender to cover, for example, personal consumption and the day-to-day financial requirements of a business), an *overdraft* (a credit facility offered by banks that allows an individual or business to 'overdraw' their bank account up to an agreed limit), and *commercial bills of exchange* and *Treasury bills* (fixed-interest securities issued respectively by businesses and the government, and purchased by discount houses and banks).

There are four main types of long-term finance: a *mortgage* (a specified sum of money advanced to a borrower, to be used to purchase a house, factory, land, etc.), *loan capital* (fixed-interest securities such as *loan stock* and *debentures* issued by a company as a means of borrowing money for a specified period of time, usually upwards of 10 years), *share capital* (money subscribed to a company by shareholders), and *government bonds* or *stocks* (fixed-interest stocks issued by the government).

and services (for example, postal services, medical care, education, etc), while others are provided by private enterprise. The precise 'mix' of private enterprise and state activities to be found in particular countries varies substantially and is influenced by the political philosophies of the government concerned (⊳ pp. 168–9). The formation of the European Community (⊳ p. 180), programmes of privatization in Britain, France, and many other countries, and the collapse of the command economies of the countries of the former Soviet bloc, bear testimony to the current ascendancy of the 'free' market economy and the mixed economy.

SEE ALSO

- POLITICAL IDEOLOGIES p. 168
- MICROECONOMICS p. 172
- MACROECONOMICS p. 174
- TRADE p. 176

Microeconomics

Microeconomics is concerned with how resources that are scarce are allocated to produce a multitude of goods and services to meet the demands of consumers for these products. In capitalist economies the allocation of resources is dealt with through exchange mechanisms known as *markets*. Markets provide opportunities for buyers and sellers to communicate with one another and exchange their goods and resources. Markets also send out signals that help consumers decide which products and how much of them to buy, and help producers decide which products and how much of them to make.

At the heart of a market system are the forces of *demand* and *supply*. The interplay of these forces determines the prices of products, how much of a product will be produced and sold, the prices of resources, and how each product will be made.

Consumers' demand for goods and services depends on several factors. The most important of these are the number of potential customers, their tastes or preferences for products, how much of their income is available to spend on products (*disposable income*), the price of the product, and the prices of other products that consumers could buy.

The amount of a product that producers are prepared to supply (i.e. sell at a given price) depends on the prices that they pay for the materials, labour and capital (⊳ p. 170) needed for making the product. Producers need to cover these production costs if it is to be worthwhile for them to make the product. They will also bear in mind alternative products that they could make with their resources, and will only continue to supply a particular product if its price covers supply costs, including a 'fair' profit on the capital investment made and the risks taken.

The following simple example explains how the interplay of demand and supply works.

The price system

Let us assume two products, chicken and beef, and that initially prices are such as to equate supply and demand for these products in their respective markets. If there is a change in consumer demand away from beef and towards chicken, the increased demand for chicken – coupled with an unchanged supply of chicken in the short run – results in an *excess demand* for chicken at the prevailing price. This extra demand causes the price of chicken to rise. By the same token, the fall in demand for beef – coupled with an unchanged beef supply in the short run – results initially in an *excess supply* of beef at the prevailing price and a fall in the price of beef as suppliers seek to clear unsold stocks.

These changes in prices will affect the profits of chicken and beef suppliers. The rising price of chicken will increase the profitability of supplying poultry and the falling price of beef will decrease the profitability of supplying beef. In the long term, existing poultry farmers will expand production and new producers will enter the market, causing the price of chicken to fall until a new *equilibrium price* – at which supply will again equal demand – is reached. Similarly, the falling price of beef will drive less efficient suppliers out of the market, while other suppliers will cut their output. The resulting decline in beef

SEE ALSO

- POLITICAL IDEOLOGIES p. 168
- ECONOMIC SYSTEMS p. 170
- MACROECONOMICS p. 174
- TRADE p. 176

Inner city renewal schemes have been undertaken by many governments to promote the revival of old urban industrial areas. Here in London Docklands, a government-funded development corporation has encouraged new office, industrial and commercial schemes to create employment opportunities. Public finance has also been made available to help establish the necessary infrastructure, for example, the light railway (centre). (Spectrum)

MICROECONOMIC POLICY

Because of the problems involved in responding to market mechanisms (⊳ main text), governments often attempt to improve the allocation of resources by using a variety of industrial, competition, regional and labour policies. *Industrial policy*, for example, can be used to reorganize industries beset by excess capacity, by compensating firms for leaving the industry or encouraging firms to merge and close down redundant plant. Industrial policy can also be used to foster innovation by providing grants and tax benefits to firms investing in research and development and to provide retraining facilities to improve occupational mobility.

Competition policy can be used to prevent dominant firms from profiteering at the expense of consumers and to outlaw price-fixing agreements between firms. Similarly, competition policy can be used to prevent mergers and takeovers likely to have anti-competitive consequences.

Regional policies can be used alongside macroeconomic policies (⊳ p. 174) to stimulate employment opportunities by encouraging new firms and industries to invest in areas of high unemployment to replace declining industries. It is also possible for a government to improve the functioning of resource markets through *labour policies* – for example, attacking restrictive labour practices and reducing the monopoly power of trade unions.

supply will continue until beef supply adjusts to the lower level of demand and prices stabilize, restoring the equality of supply and demand.

The diagram shows how farmers and firms would respond to changes in demand for chicken and beef and the resulting changes in the prices of these products, the profitability of their producers and the prices of resources used in these two markets. Such forces can affect the regional distribution of industries and employment within a country. If beef production was concentrated in the north of a country and chicken production in the south, the effects on unemployment of the mechanism traced in the diagram would be considerable.

The market mechanism

In the diagram, market changes were initiated by changes in consumer demand for products, which in turn led to changes in the demand for, and price of, resources. But changes in the relative scarcity and price of resources can also affect markets. For example, if beef is produced through labour-intensive grazing, while chickens are reared in mechanized battery units needing little labour, then overall increases in wage rates caused by labour shortages would affect beef and chicken production differentially. Chicken producers would find their production costs hardly affected and so would need to raise their prices very little; while beef producers would have a strong incentive to mechanize production and substitute capital for comparatively expensive labour to keep production costs down, or would be forced to raise beef prices substantially to cover increased costs and lost sales as demand declined.

The response to supply within the price system to changes in consumer demand may be very slow and painful, because less efficient producers are not eliminated quickly but linger on making low profits or losses. In addition, resources cannot always be easily switched from one activity to another. For example, in the case of labour, a significant amount of retraining may be required or workers may be required to move from one area of the country to another. Thus, occupational and geographical immobilities may inhibit effective resource redeployment.

Monopolies

The market forces depicted in the diagram will only operate properly where markets are competitively structured. Without numerous sellers to provide competition, suppliers have no incentive to keep prices down to levels that just cover costs and offer a normal profit or return on the capital employed. Furthermore, in market situations with only a single supplier (*monopoly*) or only a few large suppliers (*oligopoly*), there exists a number of barriers to market entry of new suppliers. Such factors as heavy advertising (causing strong consumer preferences for existing brands), and the control of raw materials and market outlets by established firms, may prevent new firms from moving into the markets. Increased consumer demand in such markets may simply lead to higher prices and profits for the monopolist or oligopolists, without any increase in the resources deployed there.

To counter potential exploitation of consumers by monopolies, most governments have regulatory bodies such as the Office of Fair Trading (OFT) and the Monopolies and Mergers Commission (MMC) in Britain, and the Anti-Trust Division of the Supreme Court in the USA. Such bodies monitor the behaviour of monopolists and investigate mergers between suppliers.

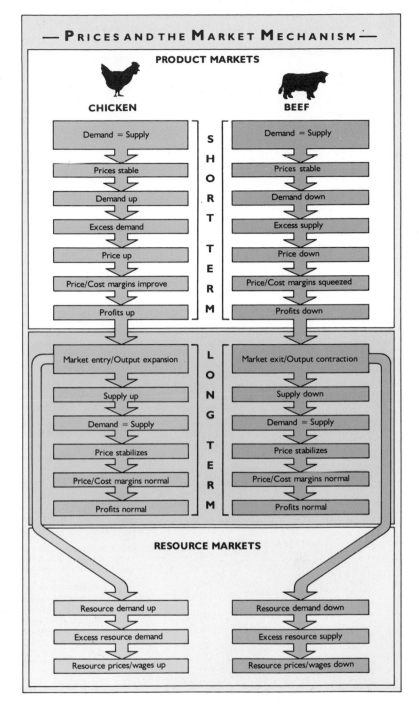

— PRICES AND THE MARKET MECHANISM —

PRODUCT MARKETS

CHICKEN | BEEF

SHORT TERM

CHICKEN	BEEF
Demand = Supply	Demand = Supply
Prices stable	Prices stable
Demand up	Demand down
Excess demand	Excess supply
Price up	Price down
Price/Cost margins improve	Price/Cost margins squeezed
Profits up	Profits down

LONG TERM

Market entry/Output expansion	Market exit/Output contraction
Supply up	Supply down
Demand = Supply	Demand = Supply
Price stabilizes	Price stabilizes
Price/Cost margins normal	Price/Cost margins normal
Profits normal	Profits normal

RESOURCE MARKETS

Resource demand up	Resource demand down
Excess resource demand	Excess resource supply
Resource prices/wages up	Resource prices/wages down

— ADAM SMITH —

The workings of the market mechanism (▷ main text) were first outlined by the Scottish economist and philosopher Adam Smith (1723–90) in his influential book *An Inquiry into the Nature and Causes of the Wealth of Nations* (1776). Smith emphasized the benefits of specialization and exchange. His contention was that if producers were free to seek profits by providing goods and services, then the 'invisible hand' of market forces will ensure that the right goods and services are produced. Provided that markets remain free of government regulation, competition will ensure that production is dictated by what buyers want.

The theory of *economic liberalism* (▷ p. 168) – based upon the doctrine of Adam Smith – rose to prominence on the political Right during the 1980s. Political exponents of this philosophy, known as the 'New Right', have been especially active in English-speaking democracies. The adoption of the market by most of the former Communist states has added to current interest in the theories of Adam Smith.

Macroeconomics

Macroeconomics is concerned with how the economy as a whole 'works'. It seeks to identify the factors that determine the levels of national income, output and spending, employment and prices, and the balance of payments.

The premise of macroeconomics – and the rationale for governments 'managing the economy' – is that there are certain 'forces' at work in the economy that transcend individual markets (▷ p. 172). The level of spending in the economy affects all markets to a greater or lesser degree as well as affecting the overall levels of employment and prices in the economy. Thus, if total spending (i.e. *aggregate demand*) is too low relative to the output potential of the economy (i.e. *aggregate supply*) the result is likely to be rising unemployment. If total spending is too high, causing the economy to 'overheat', the result may be inflation (▷ box) and/or rising levels of imports, leading to balance of payments problems.

Income and expenditure

'Households' purchase goods and services from 'businesses', using incomes received from supplying economic 'resources' (their labour and/or capital) to businesses. Businesses produce goods and services using resources supplied to them by households. This basic model can be developed to incorporate a number of 'injections' to and 'withdrawals' from the flow of national income (▷ box on Gross National Product).

Businesses not only produce *consumer goods*, they also produce *investment* or *capital goods* (factories, machines, etc). Investment injects funds back into the income flow. Part of the income received by households is taxed by the government and serves to reduce the amount of income that consumers have available to spend. *Taxation* is a withdrawal from the income flow. However, when governments spend their taxation receipts by providing public goods (schools, roads, etc.) and benefits such as old-age pensions and unemployment benefit, they inject income back into the flow.

Households spend part of their income on goods and services produced abroad. Imports are a withdrawal from the income flow. On the other hand, some output is sold to overseas customers. Exports represent spending by foreigners on domestically produced goods and services and so constitute an injection into the income flow (▷ p. 176).

Macroeconomic policy

Governments attempt to manage or control income and spending flows in the economy in order to ensure that they are consistent with their overall economic objectives. Typically, governments are concerned to secure four main macroeconomic objectives:

Full employment – unemployment is to be avoided not only because of its social consequences but also because it results in 'lost' output to the country;

Price stability – inflation is to be avoided because it produces harmful effects, for example people on fixed incomes – such as pensioners – suffer a fall in their standard of living;

Economic growth – growth enables the economy to produce more goods and services over time, serving to increase living standards;

Balance of payments equilibrium – a persistent excess of imports over exports is to be avoided since this is likely to lower domestic income and lead to job losses.

SEE ALSO

● ECONOMIC SYSTEMS p. 170
● MICROECONOMICS p. 172
● TRADE p. 176

EXCHANGE RATES

Exchange rates are *fixed* when countries use specific measures of a metal, for example gold, or some other agreed standard to define how much the currency is worth. When supply and demand (▷ p. 172) or speculation determines the value of a currency, it is said to be *floating*. Most currencies – including the Russian rouble since 1992 – are allowed to float but do so within limits managed by individual governments.

The *ERM* (Exchange Rate Mechanism) is an agreement between most of the members of the European Community (EC; ▷ p. 178) to limit movement in the value of their currencies. ERM members agree a set of exchange rates against each other's currencies and a margin on either side of these *central rates* to allow for daily movement in the markets. Within such a system, a currency may become overvalued, leading to pressure upon the government concerned to *devalue* the currency.

When the currency of a country is devalued it becomes worth less in terms of other currencies. The goods and services offered by that country therefore become cheaper on the international market and the *terms of trade* are said to be in its favour, at least in the short term. However, imports, including raw materials from abroad, will be more expensive and the cost advantage enjoyed by exports may not last long. If a currency is *revalued* – becoming worth more in terms of other currencies – its exports become more expensive, but its imports become cheaper.

German children playing with virtually worthless banknotes in November 1923. During the early 1920s Germany experienced rampant inflation, with the value of the mark falling to 4 200 000 000 000 to the US dollar. The causes of, and cures for, inflation are the subjects of economic and political debate, but contributory factors include an increase in the money supply, excess spending and unsatisfied demand. (AKG)

Governments use four main methods to control the level and distribution of spending in the economy – fiscal policy, monetary policy, prices and incomes policies and management of the exchange rate.

Fiscal policy

Fiscal policy involves the use of various taxation measures to control spending. If spending needs to be reduced, the authorities can, for example, increase *direct taxes* on individuals (raising *income tax* rates) and companies (raising *corporation tax* rates). Spending can also be reduced by increasing *indirect taxes* – an increase in the *value-added tax* (VAT) on products in general, or an increase in *excise duties* on particular products such as oil or beer will, by increasing their prices, lead to a reduction in purchasing power. Alternatively, the government can use changes in its own expenditure to affect spending levels; a cut in current purchases of products or capital investment by the government, for example, will reduce total spending in the economy.

Taxation and government expenditure are linked together in terms of the government's overall fiscal or budget position. A *budget surplus* (with government taxation and other receipts exceeding expenditure) serves to decrease total spending, while a *budget deficit* (where expenditure is greater than taxation receipts) serves to increase total spending in the economy.

Monetary policy

Monetary policy involves the regulation of the *money supply* (notes and coins, bank deposits, etc.), and of credit and interest rates in the economy. If, for example, the authorities wish to reduce the level of spending they can seek to reduce the money supply by an *open market operation* such as selling government securities to the general public. Buyers pay for these securities by running down their bank deposits – an important component of the money supply. This forces the banks in turn to reduce the amount of bank loans to personal and business customers.

The authorities can also seek to reduce spending by making borrowing more expensive, i.e. by increasing interest rates on loans used to buy cars, televisions, houses, etc. This is done by direct government intervention in the money markets to reduce the availability of monetary assets relative to the demand for them, and so forcing up base lending rates. The authorities may use more direct methods to limit credit by, for example, 'instructing' the banks to limit or reduce the amount of loans they make available.

Prices and incomes policies

Prices and incomes policies are statutory controls on costs and prices of goods, raw materials, wages and salaries. In Britain, Germany and the USA policies to restrain increases in prices and in incomes have been implemented through voluntary agreements with trade unions and business. In Scandinavian countries, wage increases have been arrived at through centralized collective bargaining. Communist governments, for example in the former USSR, controlled the prices of staple items of food, heating costs and rent.

Exchange rates

The management of the exchange rate – the price of the currency of one country against the price of the currency of another country – influences a country's external trade and payments position (▷ box).

Homeless unemployed people sleeping outside an employment bureau on the streets of London. Full employment is a major macroeconomic objective. During a recession, labour is laid off as demand for goods and services falls. Homelessness increased sharply in Britain and the USA in the early 1990s when the loss of employment meant that some people were no longer able to keep up their mortgage payments. (Gamma)

GROSS NATIONAL PRODUCT

Gross National Product (GNP) is generally considered the best way of measuring the economic power of a country. GNP comprises the GDP (▷ below) plus property income received from abroad, less payments made abroad (profits, dividends, rent and interest). *Gross Domestic Product* (GDP) is the total money value of the output of goods and services produced in a country over a one-year period. *National income* is the sum of all income received in an economy during one particular period of time, usually one financial year. It is equal to GNP less depreciation.

The GNPs of the major industrial countries in 1989–90 were as follows:

Country	GNP in US dollars
USA	5 237 707 000 000
Japan	2 920 310 000 000
Germany	1 272 959 000 000
France	1 000 866 000 000
Italy	871 955 000 000
United Kingdom	834 166 000 000
Russia	649 000 000 000[1]
Canada	500 337 000 000

[1] 61% of the GNP of the former Soviet Union.

ECONOMIC DOCTRINES

For most of the period since 1945, monetary policy has been widely used as a short-term measure but has largely taken second place to fiscal policy – the regulation of taxation and government spending as a means of controlling the level and composition of spending in the economy (▷ main text). This reflects the dominance of the ideas of the British economist John Maynard Keynes (1883–1946). However, in a number of countries, the recent influence of *monetarist* ideas has led to long-term control of the money supply taking centre stage in government economic policy. The depression of the early 1930s led Keynes to argue that unemployment can only be avoided by government spending on public-works programmes. His advocacy of government intervention in the economy caused several nations to adopt spending programmes in the 1930s, for example Roosevelt's 'New Deal' in the USA. Despite the current popularity of monetarist policies, *Keynesian economics* continues to influence many governments today.

Monetarism as an economic doctrine emphasizes the role of money – in particular the money supply (▷ main text) – in the functioning of the economy. Unlike Keynesian economists, monetarists believe that with the exception of managing the money supply, governments should not intervene in the economy. The historical roots of modern monetarism – associated with the work of the American economist Milton Friedman (1912–) – lie in the *quantity theory of money*, which indicates that excessive increases in the money supply will lead to inflation. In policy terms, this means that the amount of money in the economy used to finance purchases of goods and services (*aggregate demand*) has to be 'balanced' with the economy's ability to produce goods and services (*aggregate supply*). If the money supply is increased at a faster rate than the supply capacity of the economy, then the excess demand created will result in inflation. Monetarist policies were adopted by the governments of a number of countries in the 1970s and 1980s, including Britain, the USA and Argentina.

Trade

All countries to a greater or lesser degree are dependent on international trade. Trade is a two-way process involving imports and exports. Countries receive payment from trading partners for domestic goods and services exported; they make payments to trading partners for goods and services imported.

International trade can be divided into two main groups of products: trade in goods, consisting of agricultural produce, minerals and manufactured goods; and trade in services, consisting of earnings from shipping and air freight, banking, insurance and management services, as well as receipts and payments from foreign investments and government transactions.

In 1990 Western Europe accounted for about 45% of total world trade, followed by Asia (20%) and North America (17%). The 'top ten' exporters of goods are Germany, the USA, Japan, France, the UK, Italy, Russia, Canada, the Netherlands and Belgium (with Luxembourg). The 'top ten' exporters of services are the USA, the UK, France, Germany, Japan, Belgium (with Luxembourg), Italy, the Netherlands, Switzerland and Spain. Both sectors are dominated by the older developed countries, although in the goods trade a number of 'newly industrializing' countries (Taiwan, Hong Kong and South Korea) are also becoming significant exporters.

In recent years, international trade flows have become increasingly complex, with the continued rapid growth of *multinational companies*. Ford Motors, for example, make car engines in Britain and gearboxes in Germany. These – along with other parts – are then shipped to Spain and assembled into complete vehicles for export to other European markets.

International trade grew at an annual rate of around 8% from the late 1950s until 1973. During this period trade was stimulated by high rates of economic growth and the pursuit of 'free trade' policies (▷ below). Although the major oil price increases of 1973 and 1979 reduced economic growth rates and created balance of payments and debt problems for many countries (▷ box), international trade has continued to expand at an annual average rate of around 4% since 1973.

The benefits of international trade

Countries trade with one another for the same reasons that individuals, firms and regions within a country engage in the exchange of goods and services – to obtain the benefits of specialization. By exporting its own products in exchange for imports of products from other nations, a country can enjoy a wider range of goods and services (many of which, such as scarce

TRADE AND THE BALANCE OF PAYMENTS

A country's balance of payments represents the *net* results over a particular time period (usually one year) of its trade and financial transactions with the rest of the world. The *current account* shows a country's profit and loss in day-to-day dealings. The *visible trade balance* indicates the difference between the value of a country's exports and imports of goods (raw materials, fuel, foodstuffs and manufactures). The *invisible trade balance* includes earnings from and payments for such services as shipping, banking, insurance and tourism; interest, profits and dividends on investments and loans; and government receipts and spending on defence, overseas administration, etc. A country's balance of payments also includes the *investment and other capital transactions account*, which covers the purchase of physical assets (such as new factories) and financial assets (such as stocks and shares) by individuals, companies and governments, and a variety of interbank dealings. An overall balance of payments deficit is financed by a fall in the reserves (and/or increased borrowing), while a surplus leads to an addition to the reserve position.

Surplus vegetables dumped on the pavements of Nantes by French farmers protesting about reduced state support for farming under the EC Common Agricultural Policy. French opposition to free trade in agricultural products was a major factor in delaying the conclusion of a new GATT accord in the early 1990s (▷ main text). (Gamma)

SEE ALSO

● ECONOMIC SYSTEMS p. 170
● MICROECONOMICS p. 172
● MACROECONOMICS p. 174
● DEVELOPMENT p. 184

raw materials or high technology products, may be unobtainable from domestic sources), and obtain them more cheaply than would otherwise be the case. An international division of labour in which each country specializes in the production of only some of the goods that it is capable of producing enables total world output to be increased. It can also help to raise countries' standards of living.

A country's choice of which products to specialize in will be determined to a large extent by the *comparative advantages* it possesses over others in the production of particular products. Such advantages occur largely as a result of differences between countries in their *factor endowments* (the availability and cost of raw materials, labour and capital) and their level of economic sophistication and skills.

Free trade and protectionism

The achievement of the potential benefits of international trade is best secured by conditions of *free trade*, that is, the absence of any form of restriction on the free movement of goods and services from one country to another. Countries have attempted to promote free trade both by the General Agreement on Tariffs and Trade (GATT; ⇨ p. 179) and the formation of various regional free trade blocs. GATT has achieved significant tariff cuts on many products, and in the case of some items the complete elimination of tariff and quota restrictions. Free trade blocs are more limited in scope. While they promote free trade between member countries, they also involve trade restrictions against non-members. There are three main types of trade bloc:

A *free trade area* (such as EFTA; ⇨ p. 178), where members eliminate trade barriers between themselves but each separately continues to operate its own particular barriers against non-members.

A *customs union*, where members eliminate trade barriers between themselves but establish uniform barriers against non-members.

A *common market* (such as the EC; ⇨ p. 178), a customs union that also establishes common rules, standards and practices so that members' economies are harmonized into a 'single market'. It also allows the free movement of labour and capital across the national boundaries.

In practice the benefits of international trade are often unequally divided between countries and this tends to produce situations where national self-interest is put first. *Protectionism* occurs when governments take measures to protect their domestic industries from foreign competition or seek to reverse a balance of payments deficit. The most direct forms of protectionism are:

Tariffs, the imposition of taxes or duties on imported products. This raises their prices in the domestic market, thereby encouraging buyers to switch to domestically produced substitutes;

Quotas, the use of physical controls to limit imports of a product to a specified number of units;

Exchange controls, the limitation by the monetary authorities (central banks) of the amount of foreign currency made available for the purchase of imported products.

Indirect forms of protectionism include complex import documentation requirements and customs procedures, local market standards requiring imported products to be modified, and government subsidies to domestic firms to lower their costs and compete more effectively with imports.

PRODUCTION AND TRADE

A country's economy is made up of a complex amalgam of industries – some produce goods and services such as cars, soap and banking services for the *final consumer*, while others are engaged in the provision of *intermediate* products. These include raw materials such as farm products (wheat, livestock, etc.), natural products (crude oil, timber, etc.) and component parts (steel, textiles, etc.). The passage of goods from raw materials to consumers requires a business *infrastructure* consisting of factories, offices, road and rail networks and a range of facilitating services, including finance, distribution, insurance and marketing. In fact, the manufacture and distribution of a typical consumer product involve a long chain of related activities. These start with the extraction and processing of raw materials, then move through various component and manufacturing stages and via a number of distribution channels before reaching the consumer.

The diagram illustrates the various end products produced in the chemical and petrochemical industries from the basic raw materials of oil and natural gas. Crude oil is extracted from oil wells and then transported by pipeline or shipped to an oil refinery, located either close to the oil wells or in a major industrial centre. At the refinery crude oil is broken down into various 'primary' base materials such as ethylene and propylene. These primary derivatives are processed and combined with chemicals and other materials to form 'secondary' materials, such as polyethylene and phenol, to produce a wide range of products, including pharmaceuticals, cosme-

tics, paint, detergents, tyres and clothing.

To take the example of a plastic bread bin, a firm engaged in plastic fabrication might use ethylene as a basic raw material in the processing of various chemicals to produce secondary materials such as polyethylene and polystyrene. These materials in turn would be processed further, combined with other materials and subjected to various treatments and assembly operations before finally emerging as finished products. Each of these activities may be undertaken by firms specializing at a particular level, or combined and performed as part of a vertically integrated operation. For example, oil companies such as BP and Shell are involved in oil exploration and extraction, and in refining and manufacturing, as well as in retailing petrol.

Products reach markets through distribution channels. These incorporate a sequence of value-adding activities that assist the passage of goods from raw materials to the consumer. Manufacturers typically produce large quantities of a limited variety of goods, while consumers normally want a limited quantity of a broad range of goods. Therefore, a number of distribution tasks must be undertaken to ensure that goods of appropriate quality and form are provided to customers in the right quantities, at the right time and at convenient locations. Market information must be gathered, storage provided for goods, and large quantities broken down into smaller lots. Also, retail outlets need to be set up close to consumers, and credit and service facilities established.

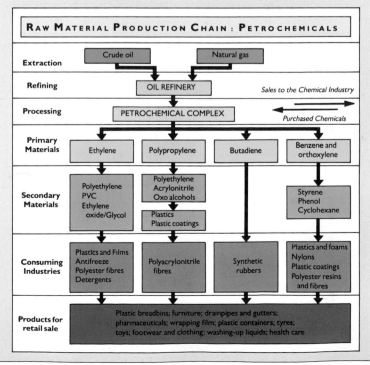

International Organizations

The world today consists of nearly 200 states. Each state has a defined territory, a people or peoples and a sovereign government, with the result that humanity is represented politically by numerous individual state governments. The growth in the number and functions of all types of international organizations since 1945 has been very marked – so much so that they have sometimes been seen as superseding the state, or indeed as changing the whole character of international relations.

The largest international organization – the United Nations Organization (UNO) or simply the United Nations (UN) – was formed in 1945 by

EUROPE: MAIN ECONOMIC GROUPINGS

EUROPEAN COMMUNITY (EC)

EUROPEAN FREE TRADE AREA (EFTA)

ORGANIZATION for ECONOMIC COOPERATION and DEVELOPMENT (OECD)

OECD also includes Australia, Canada, Japan, New Zealand and the USA.

THE UN SYSTEM

The UN has six principal organs – listed below – together with an outline of their size and role. All are based in New York, with the exception of the International Court of Justice, which is based in The Hague.

The General Assembly is composed of all member-states and can discuss anything within the scope of the Charter. It takes decisions by a qualified majority (two-thirds) of those present on 'important' questions, and by a simple majority on other issues, each member having one vote.

The Security Council is the main organ for maintaining international peace and security. It has 5 permanent members – China, France, Russia, the UK and the USA, states that constituted the 'great powers' at the end of World War II – and 10 other seats taken by other member-states in turn. Decisions are reached through 9 out of 15 members voting for a measure. However, any one of the permanent members can invalidate a decision by exercising its right of veto. This system therefore institutionalizes the world authority of the great powers.

The Economic and Social Council has 54 members. It has acted as a coordinating body for the numerous specialized agencies created by the UN with the aim of achieving international cooperation in the economic, social and related fields.

The Trusteeship Council has effectively been wound up as all but one of the territories – mostly former German and Japanese colonies – placed under its supervision have achieved independence.

The International Court of Justice is the UN's principal judicial organ, available to offer legal rulings on any case that is brought before it.

The Secretariat acts as a sort of international civil service. Its head is the **Secretary General**, who combines the task of being the organization's chief administrative officer with that of being an international mediator. The post has had six incumbents so far: Trygve Lie (Norway) 1946–53; Dag Hammarskjöld (Sweden) 1953–61; U Thant (Burma) 1961–72; Kurt Waldheim (Austria) 1972–81; Javier Perez de Cuellar (Peru) 1982–92; Boutros Boutros Ghali (Egypt) 1992– .

The Specialized Agencies are intergovernmental agencies related to the UN and attached to it. Among the agencies reporting to the Economic and Social Council are: FAO (Food and Agriculture Organization), IBRD (International Bank for Reconstruction and Development – the World Bank), ILO (International Labour Organization), IMF (International Monetary Fund), UNESCO (United Nations Educational, Scientific and Cultural Organization), and WHO (World Health Organization). Additional agencies are IAEA (International Atomic Energy Agency, which reports to the General Assembly and, as appropriate, to the Security Council), and GATT (General Agreement on Tariffs and Trade, which lays down rules for international trade). Subsidiary UN organs include UNHCR (United Nations High Commissioner for Refugees) and UNICEF (United Nations International Children's Emergency Fund).

the victorious anti-Axis (⊳ p. 274) nations. Today, apart from Taiwan (the Republic of China, which was displaced as the representative of the Chinese people by the People's Republic of China in 1971), Switzerland (which maintains its strict interpretation of neutrality), and a number of small countries in Europe and the Pacific, all sovereign states are members of the UN.

The UN

The founders of the UN gave their creation three basic purposes: primarily, to maintain international peace and security; secondly, to 'develop friendly relations among nations based on respect for the principle of equal rights and self-determination of peoples . . .'; and, thirdly, to 'achieve international cooperation in solving international problems of an economic, social, cultural, or humanitarian character' and promote and encourage 'respect for human rights and for fundamental freedoms for all without distinction as to race, sex, language, or religion . . .'.

The founders gave the UN the authority to discuss and to make recommendations for the settlement of disputes, and, if necessary, to order collective measures to enforce the peace. This authority was vested primarily in two of the Organization's principal organs, the *General Assembly* and the *Security Council* (⊳ box). The Assembly was empowered to discuss disputes and make recommendations on matters of international peace and security. The Security Council could go further, being entitled not only to make recommendations for the peaceful settlement of disputes but also, if these efforts proved ineffective, to direct member-states to impose diplomatic or economic sanctions, or even take military action, against a target government or regime. The Assembly was also entitled to discuss and make recommendations on virtually any matter falling within the scope of the Charter. All UN activities (except enforcement) were subject to the proviso that the organization should not 'intervene in matters which are essentially within the domestic jurisdiction' of any state.

The record of the UN

The UN's efforts to give effect to its main purpose of keeping the peace have been undermined by deep political divisions, especially those associated with the Cold War (▷ p. 280), and the General Assembly's meetings have as often reflected disunity as harmony among nations. The Security Council has similarly been hampered by a lack of unanimity among the great powers, and has rarely exercised its enforcement powers. The only exceptions are its decision to give military assistance to South Korea in June 1950 (▷ p. 280) – the Soviet delegation was absent from the Council at the time – and its decisions to impose diplomatic and economic sanctions against Southern Rhodesia in 1966 and against Iraq in 1990, an arms embargo against South Africa in 1977, and an arms and economic embargo against Serbia and Montenegro in 1992.

The Security Council has mounted several 'peacekeeping' operations, in which forces drawn from member-states have acted as buffers between warring states or factions, at the request of the government(s) concerned, so as to make a resumption of hostilities less likely. UN peacekeeping forces have been deployed in various combat zones, including Cyprus, the Golan Heights, the Lebanon, Cambodia and the former Yugoslavia. In 1990–91, increased cooperation among the five permanent members of the Security Council led to the Security Council authorizing armed action by a US-led coalition to liberate Kuwait from Iraqi occupation (▷ p. 283).

Successive Secretary Generals (▷ box) have played a significant part in arbitrating international disputes, and the *International Court of Justice* has contributed, providing an opportunity for states to take their disputes to legal settlement. The UN has also helped to accelerate the progress towards self-government of the peoples of former colonies and has done much to make the private cruelties of states a matter for the whole international community. It has endeavoured to alleviate economic, social, educational, health and related problems in the Third World, particularly through specialized agencies such as the WHO and UNICEF (▷ box).

European organizations

Representatives of many European states attended the Congress of Europe in 1948, which resulted in the creation of the *Council of Europe* in May 1949. The Council of Europe aims to foster greater unity between member-states, and their economic and social progress. One of the Council's major achievements was the establishment in 1950 of the *European Convention for the Protection of Human Rights*. Most democracies in West and Central Europe are members of the Council.

The establishment of the *European Coal and Steel Community* (ECSC) by the Treaty of Paris (1951) paved the way for a measure of economic and political integration in Europe. Belgium, France, Italy, Luxembourg, the Netherlands and West Germany – the founder members of the ECSC – went on to create the *European Economic Community* (EEC or Common Market) and the *European Atomic Energy Authority* (EAEA or

CONSTITUENT BODIES OF THE EC

The EC's equivalent of an executive body is the *Council of Ministers*. Meetings of the Council are attended by government ministers with responsibility for the issue under consideration. These ministers represent national interests, but are supposed to arrive at unanimous decisions. In addition, heads of government meet regularly to discuss EC policy matters and foreign affairs.

The Council acts mainly on legislative proposals provided by the *European Commission*, whose members are duty-bound to act in the interests of the Community as a whole rather than those of individual countries. The Commission is based in Brussels and has 17 members, two appointed by France, Germany, Italy, Spain and the UK, and one by the other member-states. They are appointed by member governments for a four-year renewable term.

The Commission is answerable to the *European Parliament*, which can vote the former out of office. Based in Strasbourg, the Parliament has 567 members elected to serve for five-year periods. The allocation of seats per state varies according to population ratios. Germany has 99 members, France, Italy and the UK have 87 members, Spain 64, the Netherlands 31, Belgium, Greece and Portugal 25, Denmark 16, Ireland 15 and Luxembourg 6. The Parliament is split along party lines similar to those in the national parliaments of member-states.

The *European Court of Justice* – based in Luxembourg – consists of 13 independent judges, whose task is to settle disputes arising out of the application of Community Law.

EURATOM). The EEC aimed to abolish import and export duties on goods in general, and EURATOM to promote a common effort in the development of nuclear energy for peaceful purposes. Both bodies were authorized by the treaties signed in Rome in 1957. The 'Six' were joined in these organizations by Denmark, Ireland and the UK in 1973, by Greece in 1981, and by Spain and Portugal in 1986. These 12 states form what is now known as the *European Community* (EC; ▷ box), whose 345 million people provide a market larger than the USA, Russia or Japan. The enlarged Community – in accordance with the stated intention of the Rome treaties of an 'ever closer union' – decided to move towards economic integration ('the single market') by 1993, allowing free movement of capital, labour, goods and services within the Community. The EC looks set to expand again in the mid-1990s with applications for membership from Austria, Sweden, Finland, Malta, Cyprus and Turkey. ▷

Famine relief in Chad, where UN bodies, such as UNHCR and UNICEF, work with organizations such as the Red Cross to distribute food to drought victims. As well as coordinating relief for the victims of natural and other disasters, the neutral International Red Cross and Red Crescent movement (founded in 1864) negotiates between warring parties, protects casualties of armed conflict and – through the terms of the Geneva Convention – protects prisoners of war. (UN)

UN peace-keeping forces escort a supply convoy in Dobrinja near the Bosnian capital, Sarajevo, in 1992. The early 1990s saw UN forces committed in 12 countries – more concurrent operations than at any time in its history. (Gamma)

SEE ALSO

- NUCLEAR DISARMAMENT AND DISARMAMENT p. 181
- CIVIL AND HUMAN RIGHTS p. 182
- DEVELOPMENT p. 184
- DECOLONIZATION p. 278
- THE COLD WAR p. 280
- THE MIDDLE EAST p. 282

OTHER MAJOR ORGANIZATIONS

The *Association of South East Asian Nations* (ASEAN), founded in 1967 to promote economic development. Membership: Brunei, Indonesia, Malaysia, the Philippines, Singapore and Thailand.

The *Caribbean Community* (CARICOM), founded in 1973 as a West Indian common market.

The *Commonwealth* is an association of sovereign states that have been at some time ruled by the UK. Membership: over 50 states, predominantly in the Third World.

Economic Community of West African States (ECOWAS), founded in 1975 to promote trade and cooperation between member-states.

The *Latin American Intergration Association* (ALADI), founded in 1980 to encourage trade. Membership: nearly all Latin American states. Three regional Latin American economic organizations have also been formed – the *Central American Common Market* (CACM), *Mercosur* (with Argentina, Brazil, Paraguay and Uruguay as members) and the *Andean Pact* (Bolivia, Colombia, Ecuador, Peru and Venezuela).

The *League of Arab States* or *Arab League*, founded in 1945 to promote economic and cultural links, and to minimize conflict between Arab states. Membership: all Arab states as well as the Palestine Liberation Organization (PLO; ➪ p. 283), which the League regards as the representative of a legitimate state.

The *Non-aligned Movement*, founded in 1961 to create a new force in international politics, outside the two major power blocs (➪ p. 280) and to promote the principles of non-alignment, peaceful co-existence and national self-determination. Membership: nearly 110 countries, most of them African or Asian.

The *North American Free Trade Agreement* (NAFTA), founded in 1992 to eliminate tariffs, quotas and import licences between member-states. Membership: Canada, Mexico and the USA.

The *Organization of African Unity* (OAU), founded in 1963 to eradicate colonialism and to promote economic and political cooperation between member-states. Membership: all the African states except South Africa and Morocco (a founder member, which withdrew in 1985).

The *Organization of American States* (OAS), founded in 1948 to promote solidarity among the states of the Americas. Membership: 35 members including the USA and Canada, Latin American and Caribbean countries.

The *Organization of Petroleum Exporting Countries* (OPEC) set up to safeguard the collective interests of Third World petroleum-exporting states. This oil cartel sprang into world prominence during the October 1973 Arab-Israeli War, when members restricted the supply and quadrupled the price of their oil exports, causing serious economic problems for the consumer nations of the West. Membership: Algeria, Ecuador, Gabon, Indonesia, Iran, Iraq, Kuwait, Libya, Nigeria, Qatar, Saudi Arabia, the United Arab Emirates and Venezuela.

Three of the more recent members of the EC – Denmark, Portugal and Britain – had formerly been members of an economic association called the *European Free Trade Association* (EFTA). Formed in 1959 by Austria, Denmark, Norway, Portugal, Sweden, Switzerland and Britain, EFTA's underlying aim was to achieve free trade in industrial products between member-states. Although the 'Seven' were to lose Denmark, Portugal and Britain, they gained Iceland (1970), Finland (1986) and Liechtenstein (1991). The EC and EFTA have negotiated the creation of a single market for goods, services, capital and labour – the *European Economic Area* (EEA).

All the member-states of the EC and EFTA (except Liechtenstein) are also members of a wider economic grouping called the *Organization for Economic Cooperation and Development* (OECD). The organization developed from a body set up in 1948 to further European economic recovery after World War II using aid supplied from the USA by the Marshall Plan. It became the OECD in 1961, when Canada and the USA joined the 16 European members and economic development was added to its original purpose of economic coordination. Since 1961, Australia, Canada, Finland, Japan, New Zealand and Turkey have also joined the OECD. In effect, the OECD is the West's vehicle for harmonizing economic and development policies.

The West's main military alliance is the *North Atlantic Treaty Organization* (NATO). In 1948 Belgium, France, Luxembourg, the Netherlands and Britain agreed to help each other in the event of an armed attack. These five signatories to the Brussels Treaty were joined in 1949 by the USA, Canada, Denmark, Norway, Iceland, Italy and Portugal as signatories to the North Atlantic Treaty, which established NATO. These 12 states agreed that an attack against any of them would be regarded as an attack against all, and that if such an attack occurred they would take appropriate measures, including armed force if necessary, to assist the party attacked. The original 12 were joined by Greece and Turkey (1952), West Germany (1955) and Spain (1982). French forces were withdrawn from NATO's integrated military structure by President de Gaulle (1966). NATO was set up principally to defend the West against the perceived threat from the USSR, which in 1955 established the Warsaw Pact, a military alliance with its East European allies. With the dissolution of the Warsaw Pact in 1991, NATO has been obliged to re-examine its role.

The aims of the *Conference on Security and Cooperation in Europe* (CSCE) – established in 1975 by a security conference held in Helsinki, Finland – were formulated by the Charter of Paris (1990), which has been described as the formal end of the Cold War (➪ p. 280). Members affirm an adherence to democracy and human rights, and a commitment to settle disputes by peaceful means. Its members comprise over 50 North American, European and former Soviet states.

Following the dissolution of the USSR (December 1991; ➪ p. 281), 11 of the former Soviet republics – Russia, Armenia, Azerbaijan, Belarus, Kazakhstan, Kyrgyzstan, Moldova, Tajikistan, Turkmenistan, Ukraine, and Uzbekistan – formed the *Commonwealth of Independent States* (CIS). The CIS maintains some elements of the economic, military and political coordination that existed within the former USSR.

Nuclear Weapons

On 16 July 1945 scientists in the USA successfully tested the world's first atomic device. It was an awesome spectacle, producing an explosion equivalent to thousands of tons (kilotons) of conventional TNT. On 6 August a B-29 Superfortress bomber dropped an atomic bomb on Hiroshima, killing some 80 000 people instantaneously; three days later Nagasaki was hit, killing 35 000. These attacks hastened the Japanese surrender and the end of World War II (▷ p. 275). The atomic age had dawned.

These early atom bombs were based on the theory, first proposed by the German chemist Otto Hahn (1879–1968), that if the atoms of a heavy element such as uranium were bombarded with neutrons, they would split and create a chain reaction – nuclear fission – releasing an enormous burst of energy. The destructive power of the atom bomb was, however, dwarfed by that of the thermonuclear or hydrogen bomb, which was first tested by the USA in 1952. In the thermonuclear bomb the hydrogen nuclei of deuterium and tritium are fused together – nuclear fusion – under the pressure of a fission explosion.

No one has used a thermonuclear device in anger, for possession of such weapons forced a change of attitude to war. In the past force had often been used to gain a political objective, but now the results of such a policy would be so damaging as to be self-defeating. Instead, the superpowers began to use their weapons to deter war, threatening nuclear attack to force an opponent to

SEE ALSO

- ATOMS AND SUBATOMIC PARTICLES p. 30
- WORLD WAR II p. 274
- THE COLD WAR p. 280

THE NUCLEAR RACE

1945 Scientists in the USA successfully tested the world's first atomic device (▷ main text).

1949 The USSR test-exploded a nuclear device.

1950s Disarmament groups, such as CND (the Campaign for Nuclear Disarmament) in the UK, began pressure for unilateral nuclear disarmament, in which one side gives up its nuclear weapons hoping that the other will follow.

1952 The UK exploded a nuclear device.

1952 The first thermonuclear (hydrogen) bomb was tested by the USA.

1960 France exploded a nuclear device.

1960s A rough US-Soviet nuclear parity emerged. Both superpowers experimented with ABMs (anti-ballistic missiles) – rockets that could intercept and destroy incoming weapons.

1964 China exploded a nuclear device.

late 1960s The Americans experimented with MRVs (multiple re-entry vehicles), which enabled missiles to carry up to five separate warheads. The Soviets followed suit. As technology threatened the nuclear balance, the Americans and Soviets discussed control.

1972 An ABM Treaty, limiting deployment to two systems only in each superpower, was signed as part of the SALT I (Strategic Arms Limitation Talks) package.

1974 US-Soviet agreement to impose 'ceilings' on the number of nuclear delivery vehicles (bombers, intercontinental ballistic missiles and submarines) that each superpower deployed.

1979 The SALT II agreement reduced the ceilings, but the Soviet invasion of Afghanistan prevented ratification by the US Senate.

early 1980s START (Strategic Arms Reduction Talks) – the follow-up to SALT – made slow progress.

1983 President Reagan announced his decision to fund a space-based defensive system – SDI (the Strategic Defense Initiative) or 'Star Wars'.

1987 US-Soviet agreement to abolish land-based INF (intermediate nuclear forces).

1990 Under the START agreement both superpowers agreed to cut strategic arsenals to 6000 weapons on each side by 1998.

1991 The superpowers agreed to eliminate all land-based tactical missiles and nuclear artillery shells. The dissolution of the USSR left strategic nuclear weapons stationed not only in Russia but also in Belarus, Ukraine and Kazakhstan, which agreed to the eventual transfer of the weapons to Russia for destruction.

early 1990s Several states without nuclear weapons (e.g. Iraq and North Korea) pursued nuclear capability (*nuclear proliferation*).

Anti-nuclear demonstrators in Hyde Park, London, in 1987 formed the shape of the international warning symbol for radioactivity. The peace movement grew in strength in Europe during the 1980s when the decision to station American Cruise and Pershing II missiles in several NATO countries led to protests. (Gamma)

reconsider a particular course of action. If one side had gained the means to carry out a devastating first strike that deprived the other of its retaliatory capability, or developed defensive systems that left it substantially protected against attack, the deterrent power of 'mutually assured destruction' (MAD), deterrence would have failed. The superpowers strove to improve the accuracy of their warheads, making them capable of seeking out and destroying more targets.

There was, of course, an alternative approach – to negotiate mutual disarmament. But the chances of this happening in a distrustful world affected by the Cold War (▷ p. 280) were poor. Instead, the superpowers approached the problem through arms control, designed to create and maintain the central balance. That balance was destroyed when the break-up of the USSR left the USA as the only remaining superpower (▷ box).

Human Rights

Although the terms 'human rights', 'civil rights' and 'civil liberties' are often used interchangeably, there are differences in emphasis. 'Human rights' is used mostly in international law to mean the rights to which all human beings are entitled. These are often divided into 'civil and political rights' (such as the right to free speech and to vote) which governments should not restrict, and 'economic, social and cultural rights' (such as the right to health care and education) which governments should strive to provide. 'Civil rights' and 'civil liberties' are expressions used more often to describe freedoms protected by the laws of a particular country.

SEE ALSO

● LAW AND CRIME p. 164
● GOVERNMENT AND THE PEOPLE p. 166
● POLITICAL IDEOLOGIES p. 168
● INTERNATIONAL ORGANIZATIONS p. 178

In the West, the development of the concept of human rights can be traced to the writings of Greek and Roman philosophers, but they also have a religious foundation in the Judaeo-Christian tradition. Thomas Aquinas developed a religious theory of 'natural law' based on Christian principles against which secular law – the actual law of the state – was to be measured. In the 17th and 18th centuries the philosophers of the Enlightenment (▷ p. 302) attempted to develop theories of natural law that could be discovered by the exercise of reason rather than by divine revelation. They suggested that government derived its authority from the consent of the governed rather than from divine authority. This revolutionary idea carried with it the possibility that such consent could be withdrawn, and was used to justify the American and French revolutions at the end of the 18th century (▷ pp. 260 and 262).

Three important milestones in the establishing of basic rights in Britain were the Magna Carta of 1215, a charter defining certain limitations on royal power; the Habeas Corpus Act of 1679, a law requiring that a prisoner be brought before a court to determine whether his detention is lawful; and the Bill of Rights of 1689. But none of these has the same fundamental status as the Declaration of the Rights of Man (1789) in France or the Bill of Rights (1788) in the USA.

During the 19th century, human rights began to be enshrined as articles of international law. The anti-slavery movement was one example of a growing conviction that human beings have basic rights according to a higher law to which all nations are subject. From around the middle of the 19th century many states began to agree that prisoners of war and non-combatants had rights that other states were bound to respect. The Geneva Conventions, a series of treaties signed by many countries between 1864 and 1949, provided for humane treatment of civilians in wartime, the protection of sick and wounded soldiers, and the fair treatment of prisoners of war.

Human rights in the 20th century

The systematic atrocities of World War II inspired the United Nations to adopt the Universal Declaration of Human Rights (1948). This has been repeated with variations in conventions such as the European Convention on Human Rights. The rights defined include rights of personal security against arbitrary state treatment, rights of conscience, rights of fair trial, rights to privacy and a family, political rights, economic rights, and rights of equality. Since the Universal Declaration, emphasis has been laid on the difference between civil and political rights on the one hand, and economic, social and cultural rights on the other.

Civil and political rights, such as freedom of expression and the right to travel, are essentially limits on what the state can do to individuals. In this sense, the right to life is the right not to be killed by the state. Economic, social and cultural rights, such as the right to education, housing or health care, are more likely to require action on the part of the state. But the differences between them are not clear-cut: the right to life, for example, can also mean the right to be protected from ill-health by the state through access to food and health care. Non-governmental bodies such as Amnesty International (which works to free political prisoners and prisoners of conscience) and the Red Cross are important in promoting human rights. These organizations owe much of their influence to their independence of governments, and, because they have no legal authority, their influence is based on careful documentation and publicizing of human-rights abuses.

In some countries, human rights are called civil rights or civil liberties. In the USA and many other countries they are enshrined as doctrines in written constitutions and have a higher status than ordinary legislation. Britain has no written constitution, and many basic rights, such as freedom of speech, are not protected by statute, but are rights in common law. In recent years, however, legislation has been passed to protect the rights of certain minorities, notably in cases of racial and sex discrimination.

Many countries still deny their citizens basic human rights. In South Africa, under the apartheid system, the dominant white minority denied the majority black population many rights. Communist countries such as the former USSR and China stressed the importance of social rights, such as the right to work, but often at the expense of human rights, such as freedom of speech. The implementation of human rights in national and international law has been one of the most important legal and constitutional developments of this century.

Ku Klux Klan members burning crosses at Waco, Texas, in 1992. The 20th-century version of the Ku Klux Klan is an extreme right-wing terrorist organization that seeks to deny civil rights in the USA to blacks, Roman Catholics, Jews and the representatives of organized labour. Membership exceeded 4 000 000 in the 1920s but had shrunk to under 1% of that total by the 1990s.

(Gamma)

The Women's Movement

The women's movement in its organized form is a comparatively modern development. Over the past 150 years, organized feminism has been responsible for obtaining significant improvements in the lives of women. However, although much has been achieved by the women's movement, women are still living in a society largely governed by men.

SEE ALSO

● POLITICAL IDEOLOGIES p. 168
● HUMAN RIGHTS p. 182

In the first half of the 19th century in the newly industrialized societies of the USA and Europe, the lives of middle-class women were circumscribed by social constraints. Emphasis was placed on their domestic duties and on voluntary religious and charitable work, but paid employment was discouraged. Working-class women – who were barred from the better paid and tradi-

French suffragettes invade a polling station. In France, Britain, the USA and some other Western countries, the more militant members of the women's suffrage movement attacked property, staged demonstrations, refused to pay taxes and were repeatedly sent to prison. (AR)

MILESTONES IN THE WOMEN'S MOVEMENT

1792 Mary Wollstonecraft (1759–97) wrote one of the great classics of feminist literature, *A Vindication of the Rights of Women*, advocating an education for girls that would enable them to fulfil their human potential.
1848 Seneca Falls Convention (New York State, USA) – the first women's rights meeting.
1850s and 1860s British feminists began to organize, at first concentrating on employment opportunities.
1865 Elizabeth Garrett Anderson (1836–1917) qualified as the first woman medical practitioner in the UK.
1866 The British suffrage movement began when John Stuart Mill (1806–73; ▷ p. 302) presented the first female suffrage petition to parliament.
1869 The National Woman Suffrage Association was founded in the USA by Susan B. Anthony (1820–1906) and Elizabeth Cady Stanton (1815–1902).
1878 London University became the first university to admit women to all its examinations and degrees.
1882 British married women obtained the right to own property.
1893 Women's suffrage in New Zealand – the first country to grant women the vote.
by 1900 The National Union of Women's Suffrage Societies, led by Millicent Garrett Fawcett (1847–1929), was the largest UK suffrage organization; its members campaigned peacefully.
1900 Frenchwomen entered the legal profession.
1903 A more militant association of 'suffragettes' was formed – the Women's

Social and Political Union – led by Emmeline Pankhurst (1858–1928) and her daughter Christabel (1880–1958).
1906 The (British) National Union of Women Workers was formed.
1907 French married women won the right to control their own earnings.
1917 An Indian Women's Association was founded to campaign for suffrage, education and Hindu law reform.
1918 Women's suffrage in Germany and in the UK (initially only for women aged 30 and over).
1920 Women's suffrage in the USA.
1923 The Egyptian Feminist Movement was formed to campaign for suffrage, educational opportunities and an end to purdah and the veil.
1945 Women's suffrage in France, Italy and Japan.
1949 Publication of *The Second Sex*, an analysis of woman's condition by Simone de Beauvoir (1908–86).
1960 In Sri Lanka, Sirimavo Bandaranaike (1916–) became the first woman head of government.
1963 Betty Friedan (1921–) wrote *The Feminine Mystique*, which together with *The Female Eunuch* (1970) by Germaine Greer (1939–) presented a feminist critique of women's subordinate role in society.
1970 The Equal Pay Act was passed in the UK.
1974 In Argentina, Isabel Perón (1931–) became the first woman president.
1980 In Iceland, Vigdis Finnbogadottir (1930–) became the first democratically elected woman president.

tionally male jobs – frequently worked in unskilled sectors of the labour market or in workshops where employees worked long hours in poor conditions for very low wages. All women were denied access to higher education and professional training, and were legally prevented from the right to vote. In response, the women's movement emerged, working for change through publications, suffrage societies, and trade unions (▷ box). By the early 20th century, women were also campaigning for social reforms such as birth control information and baby clinics.

The widespread use of female labour during World War II, often in the traditionally male-dominated industries, was short-lived. After 1945 many women returned to the home. In the 'baby boom' years of the 1950s, traditional ideas about women's role in society regained a strong foothold, particularly in the Western world, and the achievements of the first feminists were largely hidden from history. The women's movement re-emerged in the late 1960s and early 1970s. Women were still conditioned to accept their feminine, domestic and maternal role as paramount. They found it difficult to be active in the men's world of public and political affairs and to enter male-dominated sectors of the economy such as business, industry and banking.

The contemporary women's movement has emphasized issues of childcare, sexuality, male violence and the role of men and women in the home. It has raised questions as to how and why men and women are different in the 'nature versus nurture' debate – in other words, apart from physical differences, are women different from men because of their genetic make-up or because of their upbringing?

The Third World

The tragedy of the 20th century is that, while some countries have developed, many more states – the Third World – still lack both the social organization and the surplus capital to be able to advance economically. The Third World comprises virtually all the countries of Asia, Africa and Latin America, the majority of which – apart from the Latin American states – have gained independence since World War II.

SEE ALSO

- TRADE p. 176
- INTERNATIONAL ORGANIZATIONS p. 178
- DECOLONIZATION p. 278
- THE COLD WAR p. 280

The term 'Third World' was coined in France to evoke a comparison with the three 'Estates' of French society before the revolution of 1789. The Third Estate – the great majority of the French people – had very few political rights, and was considerably impoverished. Similarly today, the Third World experiences great economic difficulties, and lacks political power in the world's financial and trading institutions.

Third World debt

The common feature of the Third World countries is that they are poorer than the developed world. Many Third World countries are heavily in debt to the developed world or its banking institutions. Unfortunately, because of this link to the 'First World' (the Western capitalist economies), the Third World catches cold every time the developed world sneezes. Increases in Western interest rates, for example, are reflected directly in the interest payments on Third World debt. Because the economies of Third World countries are weak, development has been difficult. Moreover, there seems to be no way in which they can escape poverty and debt.

Third World debt – a relatively recent problem – involves very large sums. Because some Western commercial banks lent excessive amounts to Third World countries in the 1970s and early 1980s, the interest payments constitute a severe drain on the economy of these countries. Since the late 1980s, some African countries have used more convertible currency in debt repayments than for any other purpose, leaving little even to maintain current facilities and infrastructure (schools, hospitals, transport systems, etc.). Because of the reluctance on the part of Western commercial banks to undertake major new investments in the Third World, the International Monetary Fund (IMF; ⇨ p. 178) is increasingly approached for loans. The IMF makes finance available only if a country organizes its financial planning with the IMF's approval, but local development may thereby be compromised, causing major social problems. This has led to the accusation that the IMF has eroded the financial independence of many states.

Third World trade

Trade has been suggested as a means towards greater economic health for Third World countries. However, the price of commodities – the primary products that account for the majority of Third World exports – tend to be fixed in Western financial centres, and may be driven up or down according to Western market requirements. This often results in severe income fluctuations for the producer countries, and because many Third World countries are mono-economies – dependent on exports of a single commodity – they have very little flexibility to cope with any fall in the prices of primary products.

Apart from the NICs ('newly-industrialized countries') in some parts of Southeast Asia (for example, Taiwan and South Korea) and Latin America, Third World countries have little industrial capacity. Indeed, industrial development is often hampered by the reluctance of Western states to accept Third World manufactured exports for fear of undercutting Western manufacturing industries. The terms of trade appear to be stacked against the Third World. The high price of imported oil, for example, has hampered every aspect of Third World debt repayment, manufacturing and transportation, the mechanization of farming, and the maintenance of urban life.

Third World countries are in an invidious position in trade negotiations. They seek at least a free market for their exports, and resist the

AID TO THE THIRD WORLD

The most comprehensive plan for confronting both the problems of debt and slow development was proposed in the *Brandt Report* (1979), prepared by the Independent Commission on International Development Issues chaired by former West German Chancellor Willy Brandt (1913–92). The Report recommended a global programme to stimulate food production; a global energy programme; greater participation for Third World countries in organizations such as the IMF and World Bank; and, most importantly in the immediate term, increased financial aid to the Third World, in the form of grants and low-interest loans, and in the reduction or cancellation of many existing debts, to allow Third World states to recommence development. Although the Report argued that its proposed plan was in Western self-interest, Western governments have paid little attention to it, though Western aid has been forthcoming to help meet emergency conditions. Famine in Ethiopia and Mozambique brought disaster relief from both governments and the public. In many countries voluntary charities are deeply involved in raising money for the starving in the Third World. The problem with emergency aid, however, is that it often does not address fundamental problems.

At some time in the future, the West will need to discuss exactly what its relationship with the Third World should be. The danger is that the Third World will be marginalized, with development concentrated on basic facilities for citizen survival and agriculture. However, development that integrates the Third World into the international economic system will require measures to alleviate existing debt and a massive programme of investment.

During the Cold War (⇨ p. 280), the USA and the USSR attempted to secure allies through large-scale aid programmes. The USSR sought to use aid to win over recently independent African countries, initially spending most money on those thought likely to develop along socialist lines and later tending to confine significant aid to countries of strategic value, such as Ethiopia. The USA has developed a very large aid budget, but the largest portions of this aid go firstly to Israel and secondly to Egypt, to maintain influence in the Middle East. Aid (much of which is directly military) has often been given, therefore, not for the sake of development within a Third World country, but for the sake of political advantage.

Aid by itself usually forms only a small part of the finance a country needs to operate properly. The economic domination of the Third World by developed Western industrial nations is sometimes referred to as *neo-imperialism*. The 24 richest Western states together account for 60% of world industrial production, 73% of world trade, and 80% of all aid to developing countries. More importantly, all of the great commercial banks – as well as the IMF and the World Bank – are found in the West.

POPULATION AND HUNGER

Somewhere between 24 June and 11 July 1987, the human population of the planet Earth reached 5 billion. Yet, around 1800, the world's population was barely over one billion. Despite predictions – most notably by Thomas Malthus (1766–1834) – that the human species would breed itself into starvation, the population keeps increasing – but so too does the food supply. Two contending views have emerged concerning the extent to which burgeoning populations affect food supply. The first is that population must be controlled if persistent malnutrition and starvation are not to become inevitable over much of the globe. The second is that, even with a projected global population of 10 billion by the year 2070, there is sufficient food to feed everyone.

These views reflect differing assumptions. Those who – like Malthus – link hunger directly with overpopulation believe that in a world of relatively finite resources, increases in human numbers lower the demand for labour. This in turn lowers the wages of labour, leaving many people unable to purchase food. Unless human beings restrict their numbers, through voluntary celibacy, late marriages, abortion and contraception, so the neo-Malthusians argue, only war, epidemics and starvation will control the balance between population and food availability. Such assumptions were challenged by Karl Marx (⊳ p. 168), who believed that the ways society was structured and its resources allocated were more important than population and finite resources. Others consider hunger to be more related to the way that people are deprived of access to food rather than due to its insufficiency. Although the debate continues, increasing evidence would seem to support the struc-

tural view. Over the past 25 years, increases in food production have outstripped unprecedented global population growth by about 16%. Based upon this figure, it can be deduced that there is sufficient food in the world today to supply every individual with a daily intake of 3600 calories, although 900 million people live on the precipice of malnutrition (2100 calories per day for adult maintenance).

The greatest increases in population are in countries that are the poorest. Many Third World countries depend upon subsistence agriculture, have limited social services and lack most forms of advanced agricultural technology. Under such conditions, rural families tend to be large, ensuring an adequate rural labour force as well as support for members of the family in their old age. Hence, large families are an essential norm for the poor, who represent the majority in Third World states. Ironically, the emphasis placed upon eliminating disease amongst the young – for example through mass immunization – has lowered levels of infant mortality, increased the population and eventually decreased the prospects for work. Thus cities are seen as havens for alternative employment, although urban centres in underdeveloped countries offer limited job opportunities, and migration to cities has done little to break the poverty cycle.

The forces of nature are generally blamed for the hunger that threatens much of humanity. Yet the effects of nature cannot be divorced from man-made poverty. In the USA in 1987, much of the southeast of the country was stricken by drought. No one died, no lives were threatened. At the same time, drought-affected Ethiopia needed over 1.3 million tonnes of emergency food

to save the lives of over 4 million affected people. The differences between the two situations underscore the relationship between poverty and hunger. In the USA, resources had been invested in irrigation and water schemes, and insurance and loan schemes protected farmers. In Ethiopia, the resources required to develop such support systems are not available. Without them, people become more vulnerable to the forces of nature, and their poverty intensifies. Ecological degradation demonstrates this well. With few resources, Third World farmers must till their fields continuously, leaving no respite for their recovery. Fertilizers are expensive, and therefore not readily available. The topsoil of these lands may have been held in place by trees that have now been felled to be used as fuel for which the poor have no real alternatives. Rain washes away valuable topsoil and the farmer gets less and less for his efforts.

If the world produces sufficient food to feed itself but the poor are increasingly exposed to threats of malnutrition and starvation, the issue seems to be how to give them access to the food that is available rather than one of population reduction. Greater access can be achieved through effective development either to help rural families to farm more effectively for profit – enabling them to purchase more food – or to allow them to find other means of earning income. Although with increases in family incomes the size of families decrease, this does not diminish the fact that poverty rather than population size lies at the heart of hunger. Whether a population is large or small, there is little evidence that size in itself influences the way societies are structured or the way resources are allocated. In short, population is related to hunger but it is far from being its necessary cause.

imposition of tariff boundaries (⊳ p. 176) or quotas on their products. They have sought guaranteed access and guaranteed prices for their exports, but some Third World nations have, at the same time, placed restrictions on Western imports in order to protect their own infant industries. The infrastructure of Third World countries is deficient. The attempts of these states to create a national unity have not always been successful and are not helped by underdevelopment, poverty and problems linked with rapid population growth (⊳ box). Particularly in Africa, very few local inhabitants had been properly trained by the colonial powers to become the skilled administrators and technicians of these new states. Seen in this light, the achievements of many Third World countries since independence – the establishment of transport, education and health networks, and the extension of public administration – are impressive.

A village deserted owing to drought in Mauritania. The development of many countries in the Sahel region of West Africa and the Horn of East Africa has been set back since the early 1980s by persistent drought, which has devastated crops and nomads' herds, and contributed to soil erosion. (UN)

Threats to the Environment

Perhaps the most disturbing surprise of the late 20th century has been the discovery of the frailty of the world's environment. The tropical rain forests, which provide much of the oxygen we breathe, are disappearing at an alarming rate in Africa, South America and particularly in Southeast Asia (▷ map). The ozone layer, which protects us from harmful radiation, is being eaten away. As the threat of a nuclear war recedes with the end of the Cold War (▷ p. 281), the new battle is to protect the Earth's biological and natural systems from human exploitation.

The rise of industry in the northern hemisphere has brought with it material wealth at the expense of the local environment. Opencast mining has scarred the countryside; cities and factories have spread, and the smoke from their chimneys has released harmful chemicals into the air. Cars are multiplying, adding their pollutants to the atmosphere. The source of modern environmental problems lies in the lifestyle of the industrialized nations. The widespread use of disposable convenience goods that are 'energy inefficient' is wasteful of scarce resources; the batteries that power personal stereos, for example, take 50 times more energy to manufacture than they produce. A developed Third World that follows such damaging practices could propel the Earth into an ecological holocaust within decades.

Air pollution

The internal combustion engine that powers the motor car produces carbon monoxide, an odourless, highly poisonous gas. Car engines also emit hydrocarbons and nitrogen oxides, which, under the influence of sunlight, form *low-atmosphere ozone*, a major irritant and air pollutant. It is the main ingredient in the photochemical smog that afflicts Los Angeles, Tokyo and Athens. Lead, which is added to petrol to improve performance, is also a threat. Excess lead levels in the atmosphere can damage the brain and nervous system, especially in children. Lead-free petrol is becoming more popular, but the switch to unleaded fuel has brought its own problems. In America, the aromatic hydrocarbon content of petrol – benzine, toluene and xylene – has been doubled to help performance. These compounds are known carcinogens (causes of cancer).

But the major form of air pollution comes from another source. Coal-fired power stations and other industrial processes emit sulphur dioxide and nitrogen oxides, which, when combined with atmospheric moisture, create *acid rain* (dilute sulphuric or nitric acid). Acid rain (or snow) is the main atmospheric fallout of industrial pollutants, although these may also occur as dry deposits (such as ash). Acid rain damages forests, plants and agriculture, raises the acid level in lakes and ground water, killing fish, and contaminating drinking water.

Temperate forests have been seriously damaged by acid rain. The Black Forest in Germany has been steadily losing its trees through *Waldsterben* (tree death). But Britain has the highest percentage of damaged trees in Europe – 67%. In southern Norway 80% of the lakes are devoid of fish life, and Sweden has 20 000 acidified lakes. Acid rain upsets the fine chemical balance in lakes that are home to numerous species of fish. Even a slight increase in acidity causes heavy metals such as aluminium and mercury to become more concentrated, decreasing the amount of oxygen the fish can absorb and eventually causing their death. The absence of large fish destabilizes the ecosystem and the effects are felt throughout the food chain. Only some smaller creatures, such as water beetles, seem able to survive.

Acid rain also causes damage to the soil. High levels of acid rain in the soil cause lead and other heavy metals to become concentrated and interrupt the life-cycles of microorganisms. The bacteria and fungi that help break down organic matter into nutrients are disturbed (▷ the nitrogen cycle, p. 126), and soils can lose their ability to support forests or agriculture.

There are various methods of reducing the amount of pollutants reaching the atmosphere, such as lead-free petrol, catalytic converters attached to car exhausts (which destroy some of the harmful gases), and filter systems that reduce dangerous emissions from power stations and industry.

Water pollution

Rivers and seas are also used as dumping grounds for waste products. Excessive amounts of domestic sewage, fertilizers and other toxic chemicals thus disposed of can destroy the life forms that live in water. (Oil spills at sea such as the *Exxon Valdez* disaster off Alaska in 1989 can cause the deaths of thousands of sea birds and fish.) Water itself is also used to cool industrial factories, but when returned to rivers can cause an increase in the temperature, so destabilizing the natural habitat. Industrial waste products can also contaminate drinking water. Some of the most toxic materials used by man are *polychlorinated biphenyls* (PCBs), which are widely used in light

SEE ALSO

- SMALL MOLECULES p. 42
- WEATHER p. 78
- CLIMATE p. 80
- THE BIOSPHERE p. 126
- TERRESTRIAL ECOSYSTEMS p. 128
- FARMING p. 132
- ENERGY p. 188
- MINERALS AND MINING p. 196

TROPICAL RAIN FORESTS OF SOUTHEAST ASIA AND AUSTRALASIA

CHINA, INDIA, BURMA, VIETNAM, PHILIPPINES, MALAYSIA, Sarawak, PAPUA NEW GUINEA, INDONESIA, AUSTRALIA

Area covered by tropical rain forests in 1900

Area covered by tropical rain forests in 1990

fittings, commercial cooling systems and transformers. PCBs are water-soluble but find their way into the food chain through their propensity to dissolve in fats, eventually reaching the higher mammals at the top of the food chain.

Pesticides

Increasingly high levels of pesticides are also present in the bodies of most creatures. More than 2 300 000 tonnes (tons) of pesticides were produced in the world in 1986, and their use is increasing worldwide by nearly 13% per year. Like PCBs they become concentrated in the bodies of animals at the top of the food chain (including humans). Producers claim that without pesticides humanity would starve, but there is little evidence to support this. Pests tend to become immune to pesticides, while their predators are contaminated by them and decline in population. The resulting imbalance creates more pests rather than fewer because their natural enemies have been poisoned.

Global warming

Pollution can have subtler but potentially more devastating effects on the environment than just poisoning. Many scientists believe that carbon-dioxide emissions threaten the world's climate, by causing a gradual warming of the planet – the so-called *greenhouse effect*. Average temperatures on Earth have increased by 0.5 °C (0.9 °F) in the last century. 'Greenhouse' gases (particularly carbon dioxide) – produced by burning fossil fuels – are accumulating in the atmosphere, and it is thought that these are trapping heat that would normally escape into space, rather like the glass in a greenhouse. If this is the case, the weather will become hotter as a result, and the polar ice caps will release more water into the oceans, raising sea levels worldwide. It has been estimated that the temperature may rise by 1.5–4.5 °C (2.7–8.1 °F) by the year 2050. Estimates of the resulting rise in sea level vary from 0.3–1.8 m (1–6 ft). The larger projected rise could result in the disappearance of low-lying islands such as the Maldives in the Indian Ocean and would threaten cities such as London, New York and Venice.

Nuclear power

The nuclear industry has always maintained that its reactors are safe and clean, but accidents, such as the one at Chernobyl in Ukraine in 1986, have cast doubt on these claims. Some agencies estimate that up to 40 000 people will develop cancer over the next 50 years because of the accident at Chernobyl. The Chernobyl accident was the result of an experiment involving the deliberate switching-off of the safety systems. Power rose to 480 times the normal levels before the reactor exploded, contaminating vast tracts of Eastern Europe and Scandinavia.

The nuclear industry produces waste, much of which will remain highly toxic and radioactive for tens of thousands of years. In the USA, high-level waste is stored in stainless steel tanks, which are cooled and buried. But in Britain high-level waste undergoes vitrification, which involves solidifying the radioactive material in glass to facilitate handling. Lower-level waste is usually buried in shallow sites, or in abandoned mines. The problem of nuclear waste disposal has not been solved, only delayed. Most methods involve moving the waste to safer places ready for the future.

THE OZONE LAYER

Ozone is a gas made up of three oxygen atoms (O_3). It is inherently unstable, and is formed partly by the action of sunlight on normal oxygen, which is made up of pairs of oxygen atoms (O_2). Ozone is a minor constituent of the atmosphere, found in varying concentrations between sea level and a height of 60 km (37 mi). Most ozone is in the layer of the atmosphere called the stratosphere ($\rhd$ p. 60), which extends from around 10–12 km (6–7.5 mi) to about 45–50 km (28–31 mi) above the Earth's surface. The ozone layer filters out harmful ultraviolet radiation from the Sun. Ultraviolet radiation can cause skin cancer and eye cataracts, and can damage crops. During every southern-hemisphere spring since the 1970s, holes have developed in the ozone layer above Antarctica. There the effects are minimal, but there are signs that similar holes are appearing over the heavily populated northern latitudes, which include Europe, North America and Russia.

The culprits are chlorofluorocarbons (CFCs) – man-made gases used in air conditioning, fridges, many aerosols and some foam-blown cartons. The gases released from these products collect in the upper atmosphere and there decay into chlorine gas, which destroys the ozone. The development of safe substitutes for aerosols, plastic-foam materials and for refrigeration and air-conditioning systems is lagging behind the need for a rapid phasing-out of CFCs. Even if all production of CFCs was banned immediately, the chemicals would take centuries to fall to the levels of the mid-1970s, and until 2050 even to drop to the level of 1985.

Environmental awareness

Awareness of environmental threats is increasing, but while governments may accept that there is a serious problem, it is quite another thing to adopt unpalatable economic policies to rectify the situation. Governments have failed to agree on reductions in the carbon-dioxide emissions that accelerate global warming because they say this would hamper economic growth. While CFC production ($\rhd$ box) has not yet been phased out, the Montreal Convention (1989) commits the international community to a 100% reduction by the year 2000. Public opinion will determine whether economic growth continues to be put before the environment. 'Green' politics have become a major force in modern society ($\rhd$ p. 168). Consumers are increasingly opting for goods that are environmentally less damaging (such as non-toxic washing-up liquid), and are prepared to pay more for them. When industry finds that it is not economically viable to be environmentally irresponsible then the tide will have turned.

Air pollution from factory chimneys in Japan. The burning of fossil fuels, and certain industrial smelting processes, causes the emission of sulphur dioxide. In 1989 it was estimated that some 150 million tonnes (tons) of sulphur dioxide were released into the atmosphere in this manner. A much smaller amount of the gas is also emitted naturally during volcanic eruptions. (WHO)

Energy
1. Coal, Oil and Nuclear

In the industrialized world, the vast amount of power that we demand is most often provided by means of electricity. However, in deciding how best to generate electricity in ever-increasing quantities, we are confronted with an unenviable choice. On the one hand, there is the gradual but inevitable damage to the environment caused by burning coal and oil; on the other, the unlikely but potentially catastrophic risks associated with nuclear power.

Today, almost all electricity in the developed world is generated from burning coal, oil or from nuclear fission. In each case the heat produced by the fuel is used to raise steam, which turns the blades of a steam turbine (⊳ p. 192). The turbine rotor is connected to the shaft of an electrical generator (⊳ p. 28).

Pollution

The burning of fossil fuels in power stations leads to the emission of several by-products that are potentially damaging to the environment. *Fly ash*, which results from burning pulverized coal, is effectively removed by passing the flue (or waste) gases from the furnace through an *electrostatic precipitator* – a series of electrically charged plates that hold back the tiny particles of ash.

However, other by-products pass straight from the chimney to the atmosphere, including sulphur dioxide and nitrogen oxides, major causes of acid rain, and carbon dioxide, which contributes to the greenhouse effect (⊳ pp. 186–7). Some of the biggest power stations are fitted with burners to minimize the production of nitrogen oxides, and major coal-fired stations are likely to include desulphurization equipment.

Nuclear power

Uranium-235 (U-235) is the form (or isotope) of the element uranium used as the fuel in most nuclear reactors. However, it is only present in tiny quantities – less than 1% – in mined uranium. The rest is made up of uranium-238. For many reactors, the proportion of U-235 has to be increased by a complex and very costly process known as *enrichment*. The fuel – enriched or natural uranium as required – is packed into fuel rods, which are placed in the core of a nuclear reactor.

The nuclei of U-235 atoms sometimes break apart when struck by neutrons, in a process known as nuclear fission (⊳ p. 31). As the nucleus splits, two or three more neutrons are released. These go on to bombard other nuclei and may cause them to split, thus setting off a chain reaction. The reaction is essentially a controlled version of what happens when an atomic bomb explodes. To increase their chance of fissioning U-235 (rather than being captured without fission by U-238), the neutrons are slowed down using a *moderator* such as graphite. So much energy is released as the fuel is fissioned that a single tonne (ton) of uranium is equivalent to 25 000 tonnes of coal.

The vessel in which the fuel rods are placed is filled with a *coolant*. As nuclei split, energetic fragments fly off and are brought to rest in the surrounding coolant, so causing its temperature to rise. The coolant is constantly circulated through the core, so preventing the core from overheating and at the same time acting as the medium by which heat is channelled away from the core to raise steam. The nuclear reaction can be slowed down or stopped altogether if control rods containing a material that absorbs neutrons, such as boron, are lowered into the reactor core.

Types of nuclear reactor

The first commercial nuclear power station, opened in 1956 at Calder Hall in Cumbria, England, was a *magnox reactor*. Magnox reactors are so called because their fuel – natural (unenriched) uranium – is clad in an alloy of magnesium and aluminium called magnox. They are cooled by carbon dioxide gas. In the 1970s a new generation of much bigger gas-cooled reactors

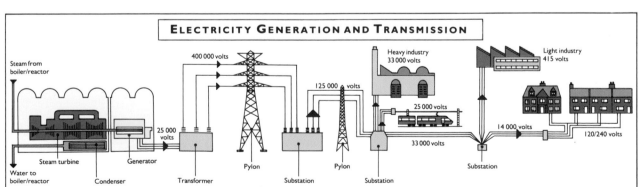

ELECTRICITY GENERATION AND TRANSMISSION

Heat is produced by burning oil or coal in the furnace of a conventional power station, or by nuclear fission in a nuclear reactor. In the case of a coal-fired power station, the fuel is first pulverized to a fine powder, which is then pumped in a stream of air through jets into the furnace. The heat is used to boil water circulating through tubes in the boiler/reactor, so creating steam. The steam is then superheated until it reaches temperatures of up to 600 °C (1112 °F).
The superheated steam is channelled to a steam turbine,

where it is used to drive the turbine shaft at high speed. The steam is then passed through a condenser, where it is turned back into water, thus creating a partial vacuum and so improving the flow of steam through the turbine. The condensed water is pumped back to the boiler/reactor under pressure.

The turbine shaft is linked to a generator, where – in the case of the largest modern generators – electricity is generated at around 25 000 volts of alternating current. For efficient transmission, the voltage is stepped up by transformers to

very high voltages, typically as high as 400 000 volts – otherwise, significant amounts of energy would be lost through resistance in the transmission cables.

In many countries, the output is fed into a national grid system, by means of overhead cables suspended from pylons. A single row of pylons is able to carry the entire output from an average power station. At substations at various points on the grid, the supply is stepped down to suitable levels for distribution to consumers, typically at around the voltages shown in the diagram.

was developed in Britain – the *advanced gas-cooled reactors* or AGRs (⊳ diagram). Meanwhile, the Canadians have developed reactors that use 'heavy water' (deuterium oxide). Because heavy water (unlike ordinary water) absorbs few neutrons itself, reactors using it as moderator and coolant can operate with unenriched (and thus cheaper) fuel. The economy in fuel costs is offset, however, by the additional expenditure involved in producing heavy water.

Today, the most widespread nuclear power plants are *light-water reactors*. The coolant and moderator – ordinary ('light') water – is readily available and cheap, but the uranium fuel has to be highly enriched. In the case of *boiling-water reactors* (BWRs), the water is allowed to boil to make steam, which is less efficient at cooling and moderating the reactor, and so must be prevented from building up in the reactor core. In *pressurized-water reactors* or PWRs (⊳ diagram), the water must remain at even higher pressure than is required in a BWR, so that it can reach useful temperatures without boiling.

The world's reserves of uranium will not last for ever, but one sort of reactor could make them go a lot further – the *fast breeder reactor* or FBR (⊳ diagram). The drawback of fast reactors is that they require the reprocessing of spent nuclear fuel both to extract plutonium (its main fuel) in the first place and to recover it from the uranium blanket. Reprocessing is a highly complex and expensive operation – as well as being unpopular with environmentalists. Reservations about fast reactors have led some countries to halt FBR programmes and research. The UK has abandoned its FBR research, and the fast reactor in Dounreay, Scotland, will close.

Nuclear safety

In April 1986 a nuclear power plant at Chernobyl in Ukraine suffered the world's worst nuclear accident. The reactor – a design of BWR peculiar to the former USSR – was operated in such a way that water was allowed to boil to steam inside the reactor. This led to a reduction in cooling and a build-up of pressure. Finally steam reacted with the graphite moderator in the reactor core, producing hydrogen, which exploded. Thirty-three people died of radiation sickness, but many more throughout northern Europe may ultimately suffer cancer caused by radiation exposure.

As a result of Chernobyl, many countries have slowed or halted their nuclear programmes. Italy and Sweden have decided to abandon their nuclear programmes. France and Russia, however, continue to build new nuclear plants, and Britain has decided to go ahead with a PWR at Sizewell, Suffolk. More are planned, but all arouse intense public debate.

Nuclear fusion

The ultimate dream of the nuclear industry is not to split big nuclei as at present, but to combine small ones – to exploit nuclear fusion (⊳ p. 31) rather than nuclear fission. In principle nuclear fusion sounds the perfect answer. The fuel required – deuterium and tritium, isotopes of hydrogen – can be produced relatively simply and in almost unlimited quantities. Although parts of the reactor will be made radioactive by energetic neutrons, the fuel produces no radioactive waste.

There is a problem, however: to produce a continuous fusion reaction would effectively involve mimicking conditions in the core of the Sun or in

NUCLEAR REACTORS

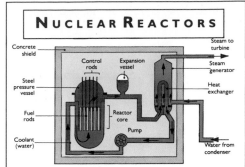

The pressurized-water reactor (PWR). A PWR is essentially a closed loop in which the combined coolant and moderator – ordinary ('light') water – is pressurized to about 150 atmospheres, and pumped through the reactor core. The core, made up of fuel rods containing pellets of enriched uranium dioxide, heats the coolant to around 325 °C (617 °F), which then passes through a heat exchanger, where it transfers heat to a separate reservoir of water. This water is vaporized to steam, which is piped off to drive the turbine.

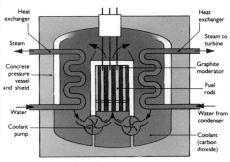

The advanced gas-cooled reactor (AGR). In an AGR, the heat exchangers are located within the pressure vessel itself. The carbon-dioxide coolant is pressurized and heated up to 600 °C (1112 °F) or more as it is pumped through the core, which is made up of fuel rods filled with enriched uranium dioxide.

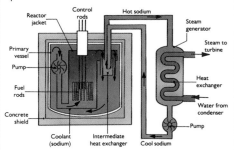

The fast breeder reactor (FBR). In an FBR, the neutrons released from the highly enriched fuel (uranium-235 and plutonium) convert a surrounding blanket of uranium-238 into more plutonium – the reactor 'breeds' plutonium. The reactor is 'fast' because no moderator is used to slow down the neutrons in the core. The coolant is liquid sodium, which is efficient at conducting heat away from the compact core and capable of dealing with the high temperatures involved. The coolant flow is isolated from the steam generator by a second, entirely independent sodium flow.

a hydrogen bomb explosion (⊳ p. 181). The hydrogen isotopes must be heated to such high temperatures that electrons are stripped off their nuclei, and the nuclei collide at such high energy levels that they fuse to form helium, releasing energy in the process. Temperatures of hundreds of millions of degrees will probably be required, so that the materials involved will have to be contained by laser beams or strong magnetic fields. Technologies have been stretched to the limits to make experimental reactors, but it is unlikely that power from nuclear fusion will become a commercial reality until the mid-21st century.

SEE ALSO

- ELECTRICITY IN ACTION p. 28
- ATOMS AND SUBATOMIC PARTICLES p. 30
- NUCLEAR WEAPONS p. 181
- THREATS TO THE ENVIRONMENT p. 186
- ENERGY 2 p. 190

Energy
2. Other Sources

Even the biggest man-made power stations are dwarfed by the Earth's principal source of energy – the Sun. Directly or indirectly, it provides nearly all the energy we need, for the Sun warms the planet and ultimately drives the wind and waves. Even the chemical energy of the world's coal, oil and gas came originally from plants and algae, which themselves derived their energy from sunlight.

SEE ALSO

- THE SUN AND THE SOLAR SYSTEM p. 6
- ELECTRICITY IN ACTION p. 28
- THE FORMATION OF ROCKS p. 66
- THE OCEANS p. 76
- ENERGY I p. 188

The Earth intercepts hundreds of billions of megawatts of power from the Sun. Although most of this is radiated back into space and is not available for use, the amount of solar energy that is absorbed by the Earth in a single year is still far greater than the energy that could be derived from the world's entire recoverable reserves of fossil fuels. If we made full use of just a tiny fraction of this solar energy, we would satisfy our present needs. The Sun will continue to shine for billions of years, so the energy forms derived from it on a daily basis are called *renewable sources*.

Biomass

On a global scale, *biomass* – vegetable matter used as a source of energy – meets a significant proportion of our energy needs. In most developing countries, wood, crop residues and animal dung provide over 40% of the fuel burnt. The wood used as fuel comes mainly from unmanaged forestry, in which trees are felled but not replanted. There are developments under way, however, that will make both the production

and the combustion of biomass more efficient. Crop residues such as straw can now form the fuel for compact boilers used to heat farms or factories, to generate power, or to fuel industrial processes. Farmers, particularly in the Third World, are beginning to plant fast-growing tree species in forests or between rows of crops to provide a regular supply of firewood.

Many tractors in Africa are being converted to run on sunflower oil instead of diesel. Crops rich in starch and sugar can be fermented to make alcohol, which in some countries, particularly Brazil, is added to petrol to produce what is known as 'gasohol'.

Rubbish

Domestic and commercial waste is expensive to dispose of in dumps, yet it could form a valuable fuel. A dry weight of 100 million tonnes (tons) of rubbish could replace about 15 million tonnes of coal. In Sweden, roughly half the country's domestic refuse is burnt to produce energy, which is used to heat homes and offices.

Where waste is dumped into the ground, it can still yield useful energy. As rubbish decomposes, it produces methane (the principal component of natural gas). There are many schemes in the USA in which gas is extracted from buried refuse dumps, and the technology is being introduced elsewhere. Even sewage can be used as a source of energy. Millions of rural homes in the developing world have *biogas plants*. At their simplest, these consist of cement-lined tanks buried in the ground; these receive human waste or animal manure, and bacterial action produces methane, or 'biogas'.

Sunshine

Direct solar energy is one of the simplest sources of power. Building designs, old and new, take advantage of it for heating and lighting. Today, more active designs are becoming widespread. Each square metre (11¾ sq ft) of a solar collector in northern Europe receives roughly 1000 kilowatt-hours of solar energy in the course of a year, and can use about half of this energy to heat water. A similar collector in California receives twice as much energy as this.

Solar or 'photovoltaic' cells (▷ p. 29), which use the Sun's radiation to generate electrical energy, are also becoming cheaper and more efficient. Earlier cells, made from large slices of crystalline silicon, were very expensive, but new materials, such as amorphous silicon and gallium arsenide, are bringing the price down towards the goal of about one dollar per watt. The latest experimental solar cells are able to convert about a third of the energy in sunlight into electricity. Solar cells are already proving the best option for producing electricity reliably in remote locations.

Wind and water power

The traditional windmill has tapped the energy of the winds for centuries. Modern windmills have blades resembling giant aircraft propellers up to 60 m (200 ft) across, and can generate 3 MW of electricity. Two such machines provide much of the electricity for the Orkney Islands, and several 'wind farms' have been built at coastal sites both in Europe and in the USA. Another approach,

Wind power farm in California. Several large wind farms have been built in Europe and the USA to produce electricity, usually at windy coastal sites. Modern designs have chiefly been of two types: horizontal-axis turbines, which resemble gigantic aircraft propellers; and vertical-axis turbines, which have the advantage that they do not need to be orientated towards the wind. (Spectrum)

pioneered in Britain, is a wind turbine with blades like a giant letter H, which rotate around a vertical axis. The blade tips are tilted inwards in high winds, thus regulating the supply.

The average power in waves washing the North Atlantic coast of Europe is 50 kW per metre of wave front. Many ingenious techniques have been devised to harness this power, ranging from systems of rafts or floats known as 'ducks', rings of air bags known as 'clams', or columns in which water is forced up and down. However, it has proved difficult to design structures capable of withstanding the force of the waves without excessive maintenance. It has become clear that wave power will not easily produce the hoped-for quantities of cheap energy.

The power of running water has long been exploited by water mills. In some countries, *hydroelectric power*, or 'hydropower' (▷ box), is the most important source of energy. Hydropower provides 8% of Western Europe's energy, and worldwide it provides roughly as much energy as nuclear power. Major projects can be controversial as they may involve flooding environmentally sensitive areas. However, the latest design of low-head water turbines has reduced the necessary height difference (the 'head') between the turbine and the surface of the reservoir, so making it possible to build smaller barrages or even to place turbines directly into river beds.

Tidal movements – ultimately derived from the Earth's rotation (▷ p. 76) – are potentially a vast source of energy. The energy can be harnessed as the tidal currents funnel into river estuaries. There are currently only a few tidal power stations in the world.

Geothermal power

Just 30 km (19 mi) beneath our feet, the rock has a temperature of around 900 °C (1650 °F). This heat comes primarily from the gradual radioactive decay of elements within the Earth. Strictly speaking, this source of power is not renewable, but it is immense. There is enough heat in the top 10 km (6 mi) of the Earth's crust, at depths accessible with current drilling techniques, to supply all our energy needs for hundreds of years.

In some parts of the world, including Iceland, the amount of geothermal heat reaching the surface is distinctly greater than elsewhere, and can be used directly as a means of domestic heating. In other countries, blocks of flats are heated by hot water from wells 2 to 3 km (1 to 2 mi) deep.

The biggest reserves of geothermal heat, however, are to be found deeper still, at 6 km (4 mi) or so. As the rocks at this depth are dry, it is harder and more costly to get the heat out, because it is necessary to pump down water in order to bring the heat up. In an experimental project in Cornwall, England, three boreholes drilled to a depth of 2 km (1¼ mi) have been interconnected with a system of cracks, allowing water to be pumped from one borehole to another. There are plans to drill holes to three times this depth, but even at current depths the water returns to the surface hot enough to produce steam to drive turbines. Some estimates suggest that in Cornwall and other areas where the rocks are hotter at shallower depths, schemes of this kind could ultimately yield energy for Britain equivalent to 10 billion tonnes (tons) of coal.

Energy in the future

No single form of renewable energy is likely to be as dominant in the future as oil and coal have been in the past. Taken together, however, such sources could answer most of the world's needs, replacing finite and environmentally unacceptable fossil fuels. If fuel-saving measures such as waste-heat recovery are also widely implemented, it may be that our energy needs will fall even as our prosperity grows.

HYDROELECTRIC POWER

In a typical hydroelectric power plant, a river is dammed to create a reservoir that can provide a steady and controllable supply or running water. Water from the reservoir is channelled downstream to the power plant, where it causes a turbine to rotate, which in turn drives an electric generator. The electricity generated is then stepped up by transformers at a substation to the high voltages suitable for transmission.

In areas where there are considerable fluctuations in electricity demand, pumped-storage plants may be installed. The surplus power available at off-peak periods is used to pump water to a separate reservoir. At peak times, the stored water is released to generate extra electrical power.

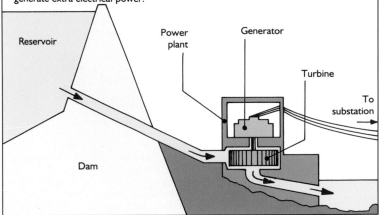

TIDAL POWER

The tidal power station at La Rance in Brittany, France, opened in 1966, consists of a barrage blocking the 750 m (2460 ft) wide estuary of the River Rance. The tidal waters are channelled through 24 tunnels in the barrage (seen in cross-section below). Each tunnel houses a reversible turbine generator that can operate efficiently both on the flood tide (when the water flow is from sea to basin) and on the ebb tide (from basin to sea). At high tide, the sluices are closed, trapping the water in the tidal basin. The water can then be released to turn the turbines when the tide is low but when demand for power is high. Each of the 24 turbines can generate up to 10 MW – the total output of the plant being sufficient to satisfy the needs of around a million consumers.

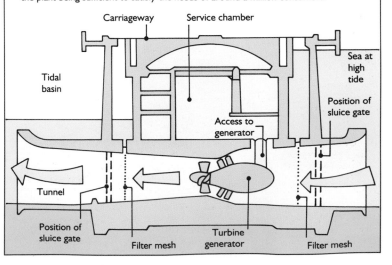

Engines

The steam engine greatly extended mass production in factories and provided power for railways and ships. The internal-combustion engine greatly increased personal mobility through the motor car, and the jet engine has made long-distance travel an everyday occurrence.

The first steam engines – developed in England by Thomas Savery (c. 1650–1715), and improved by Thomas Newcomen (1663-1729) – pumped water from mines. In Newcomen's atmospheric engines, steam from a boiler was admitted to the lower part of a cylinder, so driving a tightly fitting piston upwards. The steam was then condensed (turned back into water) by cooling the cylinder itself, thus creating a partial vacuum and allowing atmospheric pressure to force the piston down in the power stroke. The piston was attached to a beam pivoted in the centre, the other end of which was connected to the pumping rod.

The power of steam

The Scottish inventor James Watt (1736–1819) introduced a condenser separate from the cylinder into Newcomen's basic design. This meant that the cylinder did not need to be alternately heated and cooled; the result was a big reduction in fuel consumption and operating costs. Watt's invention of the 'sun-and-planet' gear allowed the reciprocating (up-and-down) motion of the cross-beam to be used to drive a wheel. He later improved the design of his engine by making it

double-acting (▷ diagram). Steam engines were applied first in mining and manufacturing, and then in transport. By the early 19th century, commercially successful steamboats were operating. Richard Trevithick (1771–1833), who built steam engines operating at much higher pressures than Watt's, installed an engine in a locomotive that could pull a load of 10 tonnes on a tramway in Wales, at a speed of 8 km/h (5 mph).

Today the only important form of steam power is the *steam turbine*. Instead of driving a piston (in a reciprocating motion) the steam in a turbine expands past a series of sets of blades mounted on a single axle, generating power without vibration. It was developed by Charles Parsons (1854–1931) for his yacht *Turbinia* which in 1897 achieved the unprecedented speed of 34 knots or 63 km/h (39 mph). Steam turbines found their ideal function in generating electricity. Fed by steam from coal, oil or nuclear boilers, and attached directly to alternators, huge steam turbines produce almost all the electricity we use (▷ p. 188).

Petrol, gas and rocket engines

In steam engines the fuel is burnt outside the engine – they are external-combustion engines. But *internal-combustion engines* – in which the fuel is burnt inside the cylinder, expanding to drive the piston – have proved more versatile. Their combination of lightness and power made possible the motorcar, the aeroplane, the tractor and the tank. The first practical internal-combustion engine, built in 1860 by the Belgian Étienne Lenoir (1822–1900), ran on coal gas, had a single cylinder, and consumed a lot of fuel. A better engine was built in 1876 by a German engineer, Nikolaus August Otto (1832–91), who re-invented the four-stroke principle (*Otto cycle*) first proposed in 1862 but then forgotten. The *four-stroke*

SEE ALSO

● SPACE EXPLORATION p. 12
● HEAT AND ENERGY p. 18
● TRANSPORTATION pp. 216–23
● THE AGRICULTURAL AND INDUSTRIAL REVOLUTIONS p. 258

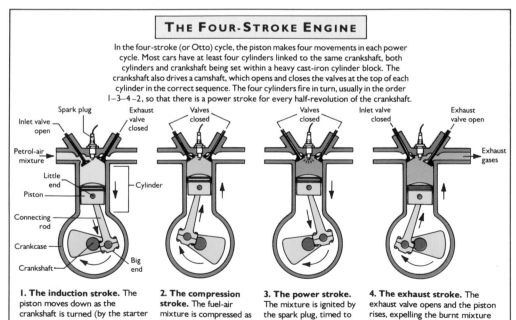

THE FOUR-STROKE ENGINE

In the four-stroke (or Otto) cycle, the piston makes four movements in each power cycle. Most cars have at least four cylinders linked to the same crankshaft, both cylinders and crankshaft being set within a heavy cast-iron cylinder block. The crankshaft also drives a camshaft, which opens and closes the valves at the top of each cylinder in the correct sequence. The four cylinders fire in turn, usually in the order 1–3–4–2, so that there is a power stroke for every half-revolution of the crankshaft.

Spark plug · Exhaust valve closed · Inlet valve open · Petrol-air mixture · Little end · Cylinder · Piston · Connecting rod · Crankcase · Big end · Crankshaft · Valves closed · Valves closed · Inlet valve closed · Exhaust valve open · Exhaust gases

1. The induction stroke. The piston moves down as the crankshaft is turned (by the starter motor, in a car), causing a reduction in pressure inside the cylinder. The partial vacuum thus created draws petrol and air (mixed in the carburettor or by a fuel-injection system) through the open inlet valve into the cylinder.

2. The compression stroke. The fuel-air mixture is compressed as the piston ascends with both valves closed.

3. The power stroke. The mixture is ignited by the spark plug, timed to produce a brief spark at the top of the compression stroke. The piston is driven down as the burning fuel expands.

4. The exhaust stroke. The exhaust valve opens and the piston rises, expelling the burnt mixture from the cylinder to make room for fresh fuel on the next induction stroke.

THE DOUBLE-ACTING STEAM ENGINE

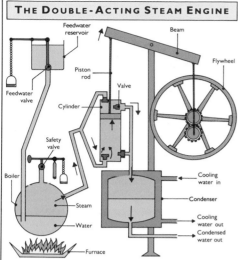

The principal components of a typical Watt double-acting steam engine, as built c. 1790. Steam from a boiler was introduced alternately on either side of the piston, so that the engine was 'double-acting' – both the upstroke and the downstroke were powered by steam. After passing through the cylinder the steam was condensed to water, which was extracted by means of an air pump. As the steam condensed, a partial vacuum was created in the part of the cylinder into which the piston was moving. Thus – although the steam pressure in Watt's engines did not exceed 1½ atmospheres – the relative pressure difference within the cylinder increased the effective power of the engine.

REFRIGERATION

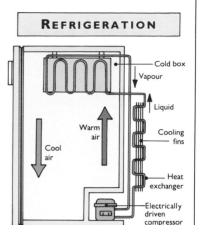

The operation of a domestic refrigerator is based on the fact that the working fluid – the *refrigerant* – becomes cooler as it expands and changes from liquid to vapour while circulating through pipes within the cold box. As it does so, it takes in heat from the warmer air within the fridge, so cooling the interior. The refigerant – now vapour – is withdrawn by a pump. The pump then compresses the refrigerant, so raising its temperature above that of the room and allowing it to transfer heat through a heat exchanger into the air outside the fridge. Becoming liquid again as it cools, the refigerant is then ready to pass into the cold box to repeat the cycle. This system – the *vapour-compression* cycle – is the basis of most domestic and industrial refrigeration. A commonly used refrigerant is the chlorofluorcarbon (CFC) Freon-12. Otherwise inert and ideally suited for refrigeration and other uses, this and other CFCs react with ozone and are responsible for depleting the ozone layer (⊳ p. 186).

engine has had a greater impact than any other type of engine, and is used to drive most modern cars on the road today (⊳ box).

The *two-stroke engine* is a simpler version of the four-stroke. It dispenses with valves and uses the rotation of the crankshaft inside a pressurized crankcase to force the fuel into the cylinder. It has essentially the same ignition system as the four-stroke, however, and it too is fuelled by petrol and air (although it requires a proportion of oil in the fuel). Such engines are still used in some motorbikes and in chainsaws. Some engines dispense with spark plugs, relying on the increase in temperature caused by the compression stroke to ignite the mixture. They are called *compression-ignition engines*, or *diesel engines*, after their German inventor Rudolf Diesel (1858–1913). Air is fed into the cylinder, and compressed so that it reaches a temperature higher than the ignition temperature of the fuel. The fuel is then injected by a pump, and ignites. More economical than petrol engines, they are used in ships, trucks, taxis and increasingly in private cars.

Like the steam engine, the internal-combustion engine also has a turbine equivalent – the *gas-turbine* (or *jet*) *engine* (⊳ box). Very high speeds and temperatures are reached in these engines, making great demands on the materials used. The first efficient gas turbines were installed at an oil refinery in the USA in 1936 by the Swiss firm Brown Boveri. In Britain Frank Whittle (1907–) realized that the gas turbine could be used to power aircraft if the exhaust gases were forced through a nozzle to produce a powerful jet. The first aircraft powered by jet engines were flying by the end of World War II, and the jet has gone on to transform air travel (⊳ p. 222). An easier way to produce a jet is to burn fuel in a container with a single nozzle through which the exhaust is driven. This is the principle of the *rocket engine*, first demonstrated in 1200 in China. The first long-range rocket, the V-2, was developed by a team led by Wernher von Braun (1912–77) and used by the Germans to bombard London (1944–5). Rocket fuels may be either solids that burn steadily rather than exploding, or liquids (such as liquid hydrogen and oxygen) that react with each other. Unlike jet engines, rockets need no external source of oxygen, so they can work in space.

THE JET ENGINE

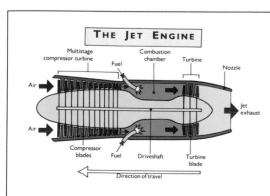

The *turbojet* is the simplest form of gas-turbine (or jet) engine. Forward thrust is created by the rapid expulsion of high-pressure exhaust gases through the nozzle at the rear of the unit. The compressor turbine, initially set in motion by an electric motor, acts like a series of fans to compress air drawn in at the front of the engine. The hot compressed air passes into the combustion chambers, where it is mixed with fuel (kerosene) and ignited. Once ignited, the temperature within the engine – typically in excess of 450 °C (840 °F) – is sufficient to keep the fuel-air mixture burning. Before exiting through the tail nozzle, the exhaust gases pass through a second turbine, which itself drives the compressor turbine via the driveshaft. The basic turbojet has been modified. In a *turboprop* engine, the driveshaft is used to rotate a conventional propeller mounted in front of the compressor. The *turbofan* engine, used to power the biggest aircraft, has a large fan in the air intake at the front of the engine. This fan takes in extra air, most of which is channelled around the combustion chambers and out through the tail nozzle, so increasing efficiency and reducing noise.

Oil and Gas

For hundreds of millions of years before humans first trod the Earth, plants and simple single-celled organisms had flourished. After they had died and decayed, they gradually formed deposits of coal, oil and natural gas – the fossil fuels upon which modern society largely relies. We live, quite literally, upon the reconstituted rubbish of the past.

SEE ALSO

● ENERGY pp. 188–91
● CHEMICALS AND BIOTECHNOLOGY p. 201
● SEEING THE INVISIBLE p. 210
● SHIPS p. 216

Oil and natural gas are hydrocarbons – organic compounds built from just two elements, hydrogen and carbon (▷ p. 46). Hydrocarbons range from light gases like methane to heavy solids like asphalt. Crude oil is a mixture of hydrocarbons – some light, some heavy – and is often found in conjunction with natural gas. Three types of rock are needed to form an oil reserve: the sedimentary rocks in which the hydrocarbons form; porous rocks that can store the oil and gas like a sponge; and an impervious layer of rock over the top, ideally in the form of a dome, to form a trap.

Exploration and drilling

Three surveying techniques are used to pinpoint areas where oil and gas are likely to have formed. In *gravimetric* and *magnetic surveys*, small variations in the force of gravity or in the Earth's magnetic field give clues to the type of rock in an area. *Seismic surveys* use shock waves, usually created by detonating small explosions (▷ pp. 22 and 210). These waves are reflected from the various layers of rock beneath the ground and measured at the surface. Computer analysis of the reflected waves enables a cross-section of the subterranean rocks to be drawn.

When a likely area has been identified, exploratory drilling begins. The first oil well was drilled in 1859 in the USA, at Titusville, Pennsylvania, by Edwin Drake. He was attracted to the spot by a stream whose water was often contaminated by oil seeping to the surface. He found oil 21 m (69 ft) down, using a drill that pounded away at the ground in an up-and-down motion. Today's drilling rigs work by rotary action and must drill much deeper to strike oil, often to depths of several kilometres (▷ diagram).

If economic amounts of oil are found, production wells are drilled. From a single derrick, many holes can be drilled, fanning outwards to reach all corners of the reserve. This is done with a tool called the *whipstock*, which forces the flexible drillstring to bend slightly. A large field may be drilled from several different platforms. Each hole is lined with steel casing embedded in concrete, and explosives are used to punch holes through the casing, to allow the oil to get into the hollow casing from the surrounding rock.

Once the well has been drilled, an arrangement of

ROTARY DRILLING RIGS

Modern drills (▷ diagram) work by rotary action. The rock is cut by the *drill bit*, which is attached to a *drillstring* made up of 9 m (30 ft) sections of steel piping. The top piece of the string – the *kelly* – is usually square-shaped, and fits into the *rotary table*, which is powered by a motor and causes the whole drillstring to rotate. In order to concentrate weight on the bit, an extra-heavy section of piping called the *drill collar* is fitted immediately above the bit. As the well gets deeper, fresh sections of pipe are added to the top of the drillstring. The chips of fragmented rock are carried to the surface by pumping 'mud' (actually a mixture of water, clay and added minerals) through the hollow drillstring. The mud is forced out through the bit and returns to the surface, where it is filtered before being recycled. The mud helps to keep the bit cool, and its weight prevents blowouts and gushers – uncontrollable escapes of oil and gas – if the drill should encounter a region of oil and gas under high pressure. Drilling speeds vary with the type of rock, from 60 m (200 ft) an hour in soft shales to only 6 m (20 ft) a day in the hardest rocks. When the bit is blunt, the whole drillstring must be removed section by section, and a new bit fitted. The process of removal and reassembly can take as long as 10 hours if the well is deep.

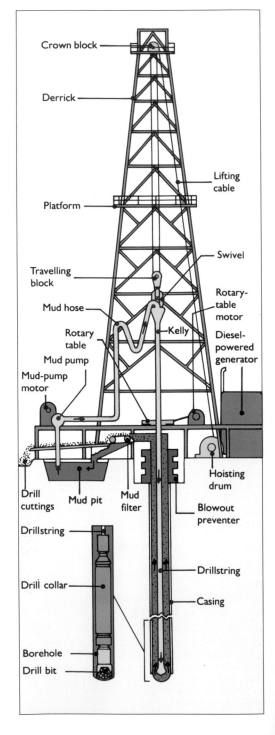

Crown block
Derrick
Lifting cable
Platform
Swivel
Travelling block
Rotary-table motor
Mud hose
Kelly
Rotary table
Diesel-powered generator
Mud pump
Mud-pump motor
Hoisting drum
Drill cuttings
Mud pit
Mud filter
Blowout preventer
Drillstring
Drillstring
Drill collar
Casing
Borehole
Drill bit

During the 19th century coal was the dominant fuel, but in the 20th century coal has been eclipsed by oil. Although renewable sources of energy are becoming increasingly significant, the dominance of fossil fuels in the global picture is still largely undiminished. Oil and natural gas meet about half the world's energy needs, while coal still accounts for more than a quarter. By contrast, nuclear power provides just 5% of global requirements. In addition, oil is the principal raw material from which plastics and polymers are produced (▷ p. 199). Without it, modern society could not long continue to flourish.

How long will oil last? Although very large, supplies cannot be inexhaustible. The difficulty is that we cannot simply divide the world's known reserves by its annual production to work out how many years' supply is left. If we do that, the figure comes to no more than 20 years or so. In reality, however, as stocks diminish and prices rise, many new sources of oil are discovered, always keeping reserves ahead of production. While geologists accept that there must be a limit eventually, it remains a long way off. So far we have used no more than a quarter, and perhaps as little as a tenth, of all the oil that can be extracted.

During the 1970s the producer nations, particularly in the Middle East, realized that their mineral wealth was being used up by the developed economies of the USA, Europe and Japan, and that the price these countries were paying did not reflect the true value of the product. The oil-producing nations therefore got together to form OPEC (Organization of Petroleum Exporting Countries; ▷ p. 180) – a cartel, or 'producers' club', intended to gain a greater share of the wealth derived from oil for those who were fortunate enough to have territory containing it.

In 1973 and again in 1979, OPEC was strong enough to enforce huge increases in the price of oil, placing a big burden on the world economy and sparking off worldwide inflation. The extra burden imposed by higher oil prices led to a slump in industrial output and world trade, and although the oil producers became rich, the fall in the value of the dollars they had earned eliminated much of the gain. Today the growth of oil production outside OPEC has reduced the organization's hold over the market, and oil prices have fallen back to values lower in real terms than they were before the second 'oil shock' of 1979.

pipework and valves – called a 'christmas tree' because of its shape – is installed at the surface to control the flow. The pressure of the oil may be enough to drive it to the surface, but pumps can also be used. As pressure falls, it may be artificially increased by pumping water down other holes. Even with such techniques no more than 30 to 40% of the oil in place can be recovered.

From production to refining

Oil is seldom found exactly where it is needed. In most cases, the biggest oil-producing countries – principally in the Middle East, Africa and Latin America – are not themselves major consumers, and are therefore able to export much or most of the oil they produce. Russia and the USA also possess large oil reserves, but both are major consumers as well, the latter being by far the greatest single consumer. At the other extreme, Japan – another big consumer – has virtually no reserves of its own. This geographical imbalance between production and consumption has meant that the transportation of oil has become a vast business in itself.

The easiest way to transport oil overland is through pipes. Pipelines are made up of welded steel sections, and may be up to 1.2 m (4 ft) in diameter. Pumping stations are installed at regular intervals to maintain pressure. For sea transport, huge tankers are used (▷ p. 216). Natural gas can also be carried in ships, if it is first liquefied by refrigeration.

To turn crude oil into useful products it must be refined. Two basic processes are used. *Fractional distillation* allows lighter fractions to be separated from heavier ones (▷ diagram). *Catalytic cracking* uses heat, pressure, and certain catalysts to convert or 'split' some of the heavier fractions obtained by distillation into lighter, more useful ones. Today the most valuable product is petrol (gasoline), used to drive the world's cars, so a growing proportion of each barrel is converted into that.

Gas

Natural gas is often found together with oil, because it is formed in the same way and collects in the same kind of geological formations. The development of long-distance pipelines and ships that carry liquefied natural gas has greatly increased the market for gas, which is both an excellent fuel and a useful raw material for the chemical industry (▷ p. 201). Gas flows more

readily than crude oil, so as much as 80% of the gas in place may be recovered. The processing of gas involves separating it from any liquids and 'sweetening' it by removing gases such as hydrogen sulphide and carbon dioxide. The end product consists mostly of methane (more than 80%) combined with smaller amounts of ethane, propane and butane (▷ p. 46).

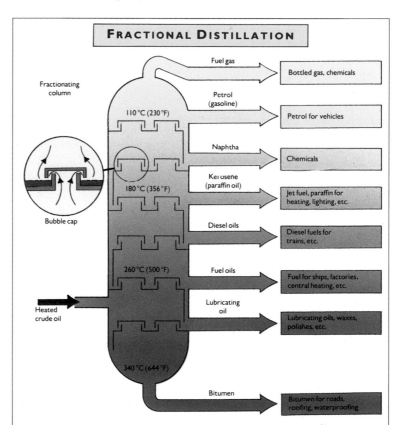

FRACTIONAL DISTILLATION

Fractionating column

Fuel gas → Bottled gas, chemicals

110 °C (230 °F) — Petrol (gasoline) → Petrol for vehicles

Naphtha → Chemicals

Bubble cap

180 °C (356 °F) — Kerosene (paraffin oil) → Jet fuel, paraffin for heating, lighting, etc.

Diesel oils → Diesel fuels for trains, etc.

260 °C (500 °F) — Fuel oils → Fuel for ships, factories, central heating, etc.

Heated crude oil

Lubricating oil → Lubricating oils, waxes, polishes, etc.

340 °C (644 °F)

Bitumen → Bitumen for roads, roofing, waterproofing

In order to yield useful products, the various liquids and dissolved solids of which crude oil is composed must be separated. The principal method by which this is achieved is fractional distillation. Crude oil is heated in a furnace to around 350 °C (660 °F), and the oil vapours passed into the lower part of a *fractionating column*, a cylindrical tower about 50 m (165 ft) high, in which 30 or so perforated trays are placed at regular intervals.

As the vapours rise up the column, the temperature falls. Constituents (or *fractions*) of the oil with high boiling points, such as lubricating oils, condense lower down the column, while fractions that boil at lower temperatures, such as petrol, continue to rise until they reach a level cool enough for them to condense.

Modern distillation units generally have a capacity well in excess of 100 000 barrels a day. The *barrel* is the unit most commonly used in the oil industry and is equivalent to 160 litres (42 US gallons, or 35 imperial gallons).

Mining, Minerals and Metals

The Earth's crust, a thin layer that accounts for only about 0.6% of the planet's total volume (⊳ p. 60), provides the fuels, metals and minerals upon which developed societies depend. The quantities of most metals in the crust are small – only iron, aluminium and magnesium are really plentiful. We are able to extract them only because they are not evenly distributed but occur in local concentrations where mining is economically possible.

The first metals that people used were those that occurred in their natural state and appeared in outcrops on the surface – gold, silver, iron (in the form of fallen meteorites) and copper. However, supplies of elemental iron and copper soon ran out. During the Bronze and Iron Ages (⊳ p. 227) it was discovered how to extract metals from their ores, in which they are chemically combined with other elements, most often oxygen or sulphur. Many techniques have been developed for finding and recovering ores and other minerals.

Mining methods

There are basically two kinds of mine – underground mines and opencast (or surface) mines (⊳ diagram). In an underground mine, horizontal tunnels several kilometres long are cut to get at a seam containing the desired mineral. Various techniques are then used to remove the material that is mined from the seam. In *room-and-pillar mining*, a common technique in coal mines in the USA, the coal is broken up by means of explosives and drills, and then removed to form large underground caverns, with the roof supported by pillars of unmined material. *Longwall mining* is more suitable for deeper deposits, such as those generally found in Europe. A working face of 100 m (320 ft) or more is cut by huge machines, and the coal is transported back along roadways by automatic conveyors. Powered roof supports are used to prevent falls of rock at the working face. Some deep mines are very deep indeed: gold is mined in South Africa at depths of more than 3500 m (11 500 ft), where the temperature of the rock may reach 49 °C (120 °F). In opencast mining, the desired material is first exposed by removing any overlying material (the *overburden*) by means of scrapers, excavators or draglines (huge buckets pulled along by steel cables). Relatively soft materials, such as coal, may then be removed by draglines, while for harder minerals the rock must first be broken up by blasting.

Alluvial mining, often used to recover tin and gold, makes use of the erosion of ores by water. Carried down by the flow of water, the ores (or native metal in the case of gold) can be recovered from the bottom of lakes and rivers by dredging or suction. The most primitive version of this is the

---

COAL

Coal is a carbon-based mineral that formed over many millions of years as a result of the gradual compacting of partially decomposed plant matter. Three basic types of coal are found: lignite, bituminous coal and anthracite. Lignite (brown coal) has the lowest heat value, since it was formed more recently and contains less carbon and more water than the other varieties. About half the coal mined is used for generating electricity (⊳ p. 304), with another quarter going to the steel industry as coking coal. The remainder is used in other industries or for home heating. In the past, coal was the chief raw material for the plastics industry, but in this function it has been largely superseded by crude oil.

SEE ALSO

- ELEMENTS AND THE PERIODIC TABLE p. 36
- THE EARTH'S STRUCTURE AND ATMOSPHERE p. 60
- THE FORMATION OF ROCKS p. 66
- ENERGY 1 p. 188
- OIL AND GAS p. 194
- IRON AND STEEL p. 198
- THE AGRICULTURAL AND INDUSTRIAL REVOLUTIONS p. 258

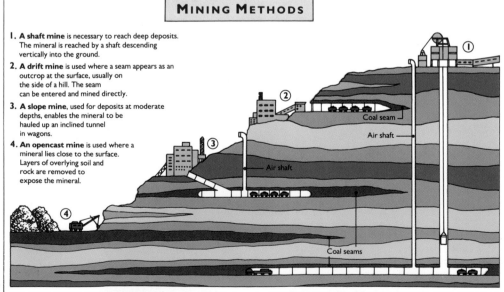

MINING METHODS

1. **A shaft mine** is necessary to reach deep deposits. The mineral is reached by a shaft descending vertically into the ground.

2. **A drift mine** is used where a seam appears as an outcrop at the surface, usually on the side of a hill. The seam can be entered and mined directly.

3. **A slope mine**, used for deposits at moderate depths, enables the mineral to be hauled up an inclined tunnel in wagons.

4. **An opencast mine** is used where a mineral lies close to the surface. Layers of overlying soil and rock are removed to expose the mineral.

Coal seam
Air shaft
Air shaft
Coal seams

The mining method chosen to extract coal or other minerals depends principally on the depth of the seam or deposit. **Opencast mines** (also called **open-pit** or **strip mines**) are appropriate for deposits close to the surface. Various types of **underground mine** – drift, **slope** or **shaft mines** – are suitable for deeper deposits.

A deep surface copper mine in Utah, USA. The ore is dug out in series of terraces, or 'benches', that gradually expand and enlarge the pit. Roadways spiralling to the surface are provided for trucks to carry away the ore. (Zefa)

panning technique used by gold prospectors. In Malaysia, huge dredges are used to pick up the tin-bearing gravels from the bottom of lakes.

An unusual method – the Frasch process – is used for mining sulphur, an element vital to the chemical industry (▷ p. 201). The system uses three tubes of different diameters, one inside another, that are drilled down into reserves of naturally occurring sulphur. Water under pressure and at a temperature of 160 °C (320 °F) is pumped down the outer pipe, melting the sulphur. Compressed air is then pumped down the centre tube, driving the molten sulphur up through the middle tube. Sulphur obtained in this way is 99% pure. Today a considerable proportion of the world's sulphur is produced as a by-product of the purification of natural gas.

Common salt (sodium chloride) is found as salt deposits and in sea water. The salt deposits can be mined, while salt is recovered from sea water by evaporation in shallow pools. Magnesium chloride is also found in sea water in small but consistent amounts, and is extracted by reacting the sea water with lime, causing the magnesium to be deposited as a precipitate.

Discovering minerals

Fortunately for humanity, metals and minerals occur unevenly. Copper, tin, nickel, zinc, lead, mercury, silver and gold are in fact extremely rare. Copper makes up only 100 parts per million of the Earth's crust, and lead only 20 parts per million. But the availability of metals does not depend so much on their abundance as on how easy it is to find and exploit their ores. Sometimes bodies of ore advertise their presence by appearing at the surface, perhaps where erosion has scoured the rocks on a cliff face. Hidden reserves can be found by *magnetic* or *gravimetric* surveys – a mountain rich in iron ore will affect the Earth's magnetic field and the force of gravity in the immediate vicinity. Seismic and satellite surveying and knowledge of the local geology may also indicate the likelihood of a particular ore occurring (▷ p. 332). The mere presence of an ore – even a valuable one – is no guarantee that it can be

exploited economically. If such a deposit is too far from its final market, it may not be able to compete with poorer ores that are more favourably placed. In Brazil there are huge iron-ore reserves, but because they are remote they have only begun to be used since the early 1970s.

Hundreds of stones are mined as gems. The most important is diamond (a form of carbon) because its great hardness makes it important for tools in industry. The major source of diamonds is South Africa, where they are recovered from rock by deep mining. Where gemstones have been eroded from rocks by water, they may be found in gravel deposits. Sapphires and rubies, for instance, occur in such deposits in Sri Lanka.

METALS

Element (mineral)	Abundance in crust (parts per million)	Major uses
Aluminium (bauxite)	81 000	Conductors, aircraft, ships, cars, foil
Chromium (chromite)	under 700	Chromium-plating, stainless steel
Copper (many)	100	Conductors, alloys (brass, bronze), coinage, plumbing
Gold (naturally occurring)	under 0.005	Source of value, jewellery, some electronic uses
Iron (hematite, magnetite, etc.)	50 000	Structures, machines
Lead (galena)	20	Batteries, roofing, radiological protection
Magnesium (magnesite, etc.)	25 000	Low-density alloys for aircraft, machinery, etc.
Mercury (cinnabar)	under 1	Explosives, scientific instruments, dentistry
Nickel (garnierite, pentlandite)	under 80	Nickel-plating, steel alloys, gas-turbine engines, coinage
Platinum (naturally occurring sperrylite)	under 0.005	Catalyst in chemical processes and in car exhausts
Silver (many)	under 1	Jewellery, silverware, photographic emulsions
Tin (cassiterite)	1.5	Tin-plating, alloys (bronze and pewter)
Tungsten (wolframite, scheelite)	1.5	Lamp filaments, electronics, steel cutting tools
Uranium (pitchblende)	under 7	Nuclear power stations
Zinc (sphalerite)	under 80	Alloys (brass), galvanizing steel

Iron and Steel

Iron and steel account for almost 95% of the total tonnage of all metal production. Iron is extracted industrially from naturally occurring ores, the two most important of which are iron oxides – hematite and magnetite. Mixed with carbon and heated to 1500 °C (2730 °F), iron oxides are reduced to metallic iron, the carbon combining with the oxygen to form carbon dioxide, in the process called *smelting*.

BLAST FURNACE

Charge of iron ore, coke and limestone

Exhaust gas (cleaned and used to heat hot-air blast)

Receiving hopper

Charging conveyor

Distributing chute

800 °C (1472 °F) Water-cooled lining

Bustle main

1900 °C (3452 °F)

Hot air

Tuyère

Slag

Molten slag

Molten iron

'Hot metal'

Slag ladle

Charcoal was first used to provide the carbon, but in 1709 Abraham Darby (1677–1717) of Coalbrookdale, England, succeeded in smelting iron with coke, which could be produced from coal. This made possible a huge increase in iron production during the Industrial Revolution (r> p. 258).

Iron smelting

The first link in the production of iron is the *blast furnace*, in which iron ore is reduced to iron (r> diagram). The biggest modern blast furnaces are up to 30 m (100 ft) tall, with walls over 3 m (10 ft) thick, and capable of making more than 10 000 tonnes (tons) of iron a day. The iron produced in the furnace is still contaminated with residual impurities. Depending on the ore, it usually contains some 3 to 5% carbon, 1% manganese and 3% silicon. The iron tapped from a blast furnace is a raw material, not a finished product. To be useful, it must be converted either into cast iron or into steel. *Cast iron* is produced by remelting pig iron (iron that has been cast into moulds and allowed to cool) and carefully adjusting the proportions of carbon, silicon and other alloying elements. Strong and resistant to wear, cast iron can be machined and is easily cast into complex shapes. The shape to be cast is impressed into sand moulds, and the molten iron poured into them. When solid, the casting is removed and the sand re-used to make a fresh mould.

Steel production

The great bulk of the iron produced in a blast furnace is converted into steel by greatly reduc-

SEE ALSO

- ELEMENTS AND THE PERIODIC TABLE p. 36
- THE EARTH'S STRUCTURE AND ATMOSPHERE p. 60
- THE FORMATION OF ROCKS p. 66
- MINING, MINERALS AND METALS p. 198
- THE AGRICULTURAL AND INDUSTRIAL REVOLUTIONS p. 258

ing the carbon content. Henry Bessemer (1813–98) discovered a way of removing carbon economically from pig iron. In the *Bessemer process*, air blown through the molten iron combined with some of the carbon, carrying it away as carbon monoxide and carbon dioxide. It also oxidized some of the iron, which then combined with the silicon and manganese to form a slag. After 15 minutes, several hundred tonnes of iron had been converted into steel. The entire converter rotated on an axle like a cement mixer to pour out the molten steel. The slower and more controllable *open-hearth process* was invented in the 1860s. In this process gas from low-grade coal was used to heat pig iron in a shallow furnace. The chemical changes were the same as in the Bessemer converter, but the process had the advantage that scrap steel could be added to the mixture. The process took up to 12 hours to produce steel, allowing very careful control of the final composition.

Today both the Bessemer and the open-hearth processes have been superseded in most countries by a process that combines the merits of both. In the Linz-Donawitz or *L-D process*, a jet of almost pure oxygen is blown through a lance onto the surface of molten iron. The process is quick and can absorb up to 20% scrap, while producing steel of very high quality. The addition of lime to the oxygen enables iron of higher phosphorus content to be converted, and in this form the process is known as the *basic oxygen furnace*. For more expensive steels, including alloy and stainless steels, *electric-arc furnaces* are used. Heat is provided by three carbon electrodes, which are lowered into a mixture of scrap and alloying additions. Silicon, manganese and phosphorus are removed as slag, and carbon is removed by adding some iron ore, which reacts just as in the blast furnace. An electric-arc furnace can melt a charge consisting entirely of scrap.

TYPES OF STEEL

Steel is sold in cast slabs, or rolled into plates, strips, rods (for nails, screws and wire) or beams (for buildings, bridges, etc.). To make it suitable for a particular use, the characteristics of a steel can be altered by a number of processes, including heat treatment and alloying. The most important factor in any steel is the carbon content. High-carbon steels are harder and stronger, but also more brittle and cannot be welded. For adequate weldability, carbon contents below 0.2% are needed. The characteristics of any steel also depend on heat treatment, which determines the microstructure of the steel. Steel can be hardened by heating it to red heat – around 850 °C (1560 °F) – and then quenching it in water, but such a steel is also brittle. Hardness can largely be retained and brittleness reduced by a second heating to a lower temperature – around 250 °C (480 °F). Such steel – which is then allowed to cool in air – is said to be *tempered*.

Alloying steel with other elements in addition to carbon is also important. A steel containing 3% nickel, for example, is very tough, and is used for gears and shafts that have to take strain. Steels containing up to 13% manganese have very hard edges, and are used for items such as rock-breaking machinery. Molybdenum is added to alloy steels to reduce brittleness. *Stainless steels*, containing around 14% chromium and sometimes nickel, do not rust because of the formation of an impermeable oxide layer on their surface. Such steels are now widely used for cutlery, kitchen sinks and the cladding of buildings.

Rubber and Plastics

The natural product of a tropical tree and the man-made creations of a chemical factory could hardly have more different origins. But rubber and plastics play similar and equally important roles in modern life.

Rubber is made from the whitish milky latex that flows from the bark of the rubber tree. The latex is heated until it coagulates. Raw rubber had few uses until 1770 when the chemist Joseph Priestley gave rubber its name, observing how useful it was

Polypropylene manufacture. Polypropylene is a tough flexible thermoplastic made by polymerizing propylene. It is used to make pipes, bottles and a variety of moulded articles, as well as fibres for carpets, ropes and bristles. (Zefa)

SEE ALSO

● CHEMICAL BONDS p. 38
● CHEMICAL REACTIONS p. 40
● SMALL MOLECULES p. 42
● TEXTILES p. 200
● CHEMICALS AND
  BIOTECHNOLOGY p. 201

for rubbing out pencil marks. In 1823, the Scottish chemist Charles Macintosh (1766–1843) invented the 'mackintosh' – a waterproof coat made from a fabric produced by sandwiching a layer of sheet rubber between two pieces of cloth. An American hardware merchant, Charles Goodyear (1800–60) looked for a way of preventing rubber going sticky when hot and hard when cold. He mixed it with sulphur and heated it, producing a product that was tougher and more consistent in its properties although it retained its natural resilience. The name *vulcanization* was given to this process. Vulcanized rubber manufactures include conveyor belts, hoses, valves, insulation of electrical cables, and – the biggest use of all – pneumatic tyres for road vehicles.

Most of the world's rubber originates in cultivated plantations of *Hevea brasiliensis*, a tree native to Brazil. Hevea seeds were brought to England in 1876 and exported to parts of the British Empire where the climate was suitable. Nearly 5 million tonnes (tons) of rubber is now produced annually, 85% of it from Southeast Asia, principally from Malaysia. Latex is still tapped from the trees in the traditional manner.

At the factory the latex is first caused to coagulate (usually by adding chemicals) and then masticated – kneaded and worked between rotating steel rollers – to break it down and make it flexible. Next, the rubber is mixed with various compounding agents – such as carbon black to reinforce it or antioxidants to prolong its life. The sulphur for vulcanizing is also added at this stage. The rubber is then shaped into its final form, and only then is it vulcanized, usually by heating it in a metal mould. For tyres, the final shaping and vulcanization are carried out at the same time, by applying heat and pressure in metal moulds. Artificial substitutes for rubber have been made, but for all but a few specialist purposes they are not as good as natural rubber.

PLASTICS

Chemically, rubber is a *polymer* – a compound containing large molecules that are formed by the bonding of many smaller, simpler units, repeated over and over again. The same bonding principle – *polymerization* – underlies the creation of a huge range of plastics by the chemical industry. The first plastic was developed in the 1860s in the USA as a result of a competition to replace ivory for making billiard balls. The prize was won by John Wesley Hyatt with a material called *celluloid*, which was made by dissolving cellulose, a carbohydrate obtained from plants, in a solution of camphor dissolved in ethanol. Celluloid rapidly found many other uses, including knife handles, spectacle frames and photographic film. Celluloid can be repeatedly softened and reshaped by heat, and is known as a *thermoplastic*.

In 1907 a Belgian chemist, Leo Baekeland (1863–1944), invented a different kind of plastic, by causing phenol and formaldehyde to react together. He called it *Bakelite*, and it was the first of the *thermosets* – plastics that can be cast and moulded while hot but cannot be softened by heat and reshaped once they have set. Bakelite was a good insulator, and was resistant to water, acids, and moderate heat. With these properties it was used to make switches, household items, and electrical components for cars.

Chemists began to look for other small molecules that could be strung together to make polymers. In the 1930s British chemists discovered that the gas ethylene would polymerize under heat and pressure to form a thermoplastic they called *polythene*. *Polypropylene* followed in the 1950s. Both are used to make pipes, bottles, and plastic bags. By replacing a hydrogen atom in

ethylene with a chlorine atom, *PVC* (polyvinyl chloride) – a hard, fireproof plastic used for drains and gutters – was produced. Additional chemicals produce a soft form of PVC, suitable as a substitute for rubber in items such as waterproof clothing. A closely related plastic is *Teflon* or PTFE (polytetrafluoroethylene), which has a very low coefficient of friction, making it ideal for bearings, rollers, and non-stick frying pans.

Polystyrene, developed during the 1930s in Germany, is a clear glass-like material, used in food containers, domestic appliances and toys. Expanded polystyrene – a white rigid foam – is widely used in packaging and insulation. *Polyurethanes*, also developed in Germany, found uses as adhesives, coatings, and – in the form of rigid foams – as insulation materials. All these plastics are produced from chemicals derived from crude oil, which contains the same elements – carbon and hydrogen – as many plastics.

In the 1930s Wallace Carothers (1896–1937) invented the first man-made fibre – *nylon*. He found that under the right conditions two chemicals – hexamethylenediamine and adipic acid – would form a polymer that could be pumped out through holes and then stretched to form long glossy threads that could be woven like silk. Its first use was to make parachutes for the US armed forces in World War II. Since then it has completely replaced silk in the manufacture of stockings. Many other synthetic fibres joined nylon, including Orlon, Acrilan, and Terylene. Today most garments are made of a blend of natural fibres, such as cotton and wool, and man-made fibres that make fabrics easier to look after.

Textiles

The history of textiles is a long one. More than 3000 years before the birth of Christ, Egyptian mummies were laid in their tombs wrapped in linen, a fabric woven from flax. The Chinese were weaving delicate patterns in silk by about 1000 BC.

The creation of textiles requires two processes: the spinning of yarn, and the weaving of cloth. The basic principles of these two crafts have not changed since the earliest times, although the materials used have been supplemented in the 20th century by man-made fibres (▷ Plastics, p. 199).

Natural fibres come from a variety of sources: wool from sheep, cotton from the seed pod of the cotton plant, flax from the stem of the flax plant, silk from the delicate webs spun by silkworms. Among the more specialized fibres, the Angora goat produces mohair, while cashmere comes from the Kashmir goat. Camel hair and the fleece of the vicuña, a relative of the llama, are used in rugs and overcoats. Jute, a plant fibre, is used for making sacks and carpet backings, while hemp, another plant fibre, is used in sailcloth and canvas.

WEAVING ON A LOOM

Warp
Reed
Roller
Heddle
Shuttle
Weft
Harnesses

Although modern looms are fully automated and electrically driven, the basic weaving operations performed are the same in principle as in earlier looms.

Two separate yarns are used, the warp and the weft. The *warp* runs along the length of the cloth, while the *weft* runs crosswise, alternately under and over the warp threads. The warp is mounted on a roller as wide as the bolt of cloth will be, and each warp passes through an eyelet at the midpoint of a fine wire called a *heddle*, all the heddles being supported in frames called *harnesses*. As the harnesses are raised and lowered, they separate the warp threads, allowing the weft to pass through the gap created. The weft is carried by a hollow boat-shaped object called a shuttle. After each pass, the weft is beaten down by a hinged, comb-like device called the *reed*, so that the most recent thread is pressed close to the previously woven cloth.

FROM FIBRE TO FABRIC

No natural fibres are very long. Wool fibres may be up to 20 cm (8 in) long, and flax a metre or more, but cotton fibres are rarely more than a few centimetres and are often as short as 3 mm ($\frac{1}{8}$ in). In order to make a continuous strand or *yarn*, the fibres have to be laid out in parallel lines and twisted together in *spinning*.

Spinning

Having first been cleaned, the fibres are carded (laid parallel) by rolling them between two surfaces faced with points. Then they are combed to remove short fibres, and rolled in machines that pull out the yarn and give it a twist, which helps to hold the fibres together. Stronger yarns are created by twisting two or more yarns together. The finished yarn is dyed and wound on *bobbins* (spools).

Spinning was originally done on a simple *spindle* – a hanging stick, weighted to make it spin round. Mechanization began with the *spinning wheel*, but the process was not industrialized until the late 18th century. The *spinning jenny*, invented around 1764 by James Hargreaves (c. 1719–78), allowed several strands to be spun simultaneously. Within a few years Richard Arkwright (1732–92) had brought mechanical power to spinning in the form of the *water frame*. Samuel Crompton (1753–1827) combined the advantages of both earlier machines in his spinning mule of 1779, which increased the speed and improved the quality of yarn production. Unlike natural fibres, man-made fibres like nylon are continuous. In principle, therefore, they can be used without spinning to make items such as net curtains or tights. For more substantial garments, however, several filaments are wound together to make a thicker yarn. Synthetic fibres may also be blended with natural ones.

Weaving

Two techniques are available for turning yarn into fabric: weaving and knitting. Weaving is used to create *bolts* (rolls) of cloth. Hand looms have been in use since ancient times, but it was not until 1785 that Edmund Cartwright (1743–1823) invented a power loom, in which the shuttle was moved across the warp mechanically (▷ illustration). In 1801 Joseph-Marie Jacquard (1752–1834) mechanized the weaving of complex fabrics by controlling the loom with a series of punched cards that allowed warp threads to be lifted and lowered in the correct sequence. The pattern of the weave can be altered to produce different effects. *Satin* gets its glossy appearance because the warp threads are interwoven not with every weft thread, but with every fourth or fifth. In *damask*, the same technique is used, but places where the warp lies on top are alternated with places where the weft does, producing subtle variations of shading. *Twill weaves* are used to produce gaberdine, serge and whipcord, and *pile weaves* for corduroy, plush, velour and velvet. The pile in such fabrics is created by cutting some of the threads after weaving, so that they stand out vertically from the surface of the fabric.

Knitting

Traditionally knitting has been used for hosiery (including nylon stockings), for sweaters, and for dresses. In knitting, the yarns are not interwoven with one another but knotted. The range of patterns is more limited, but with modern knitting machines far more ambitious designs can be achieved than had previously been possible.

Chemicals and Biotechnology

The chemical industry turns readily available raw materials – such as coal, oil, limestone, and salt – into thousands of useful products, including drugs, fertilizers and pesticides, soap and detergents, cosmetics, plastics, acids and alkalis, dyes, solvents, paints, explosives and gases.

SEE ALSO

● CHEMISTRY pp. 34–47
● THREATS TO THE
   ENVIRONMENT p. 186
● OIL AND GAS p. 194
● RUBBER AND PLASTICS p. 199
● TEXTILES p. 200

The first chemical produced on a large scale was *soda* (sodium carbonate), which was used mainly in glass and soap manufacture. The French chemist Nicolas Leblanc (?1742–1806) mixed common salt (sodium chloride) with sulphuric acid to produce sodium sulphate, which was then mixed with coal and limestone and roasted. The resultant 'black ash' was dissolved in water and then evaporated to extract the soda. A process using salt, carbon dioxide and ammonia was adopted later. Soda is typical of most products manufactured by the chemical industry in that it requires further processing to make useful products. Other early chemical products were bleaching powder and synthetic dyes. The first artificial fertilizers, *superphosphates*, were produced in 1834. The use of electrolysis to extract valuable

Pharmaceutical research is an important part of the fine chemicals sector (⊳ text). Drugs – the term includes any substance that acts on living cells – may treat or prevent a disease or condition, or may support a stressed or failing organ. Since the beginning of the 19th century, and particularly since World War II, drugs have been discovered and developed to treat every body system. (Zefa)

chemicals by passing electrical currents through salt solutions began in 1894 with the Castner–Kellner process for making pure caustic soda.

The modern chemical industry has been defined in three categories: the heavy inorganic sector, which includes fertilizers and other chemicals produced in large amounts; the fine chemicals sector, which includes drugs and dyes; and the heavy organic sector, which includes plastics, man-made fibres and paints. The term 'organic' was originally used to designate any chemical found in living organisms, but today the term refers to any chemical containing carbon. Because of the facility with which carbon atoms link to form molecules, the variety of such compounds is enormous – literally millions of carbon compounds can be synthesized.

The heavy inorganic sector

Sulphuric acid is by far the largest single product in this sector. Nearly half is used to produce superphosphate, with the rest going to a variety of chemical processes, including the production of explosives and artificial fibres. In 1908 the German chemist Fritz Haber (1868–1934) developed a catalytic method for combining the nitrogen in air with hydrogen to form *ammonia*, which is chiefly used in the manufacture of explosives and nitrate fertilizers.

The fine chemicals sector

In the fine chemicals sector, chemical substances are produced in much smaller quantities than is the case with, say, fertilizers, but higher prices are charged. Dyes are produced in a huge range of colours, originally from coal but now mostly from crude oil. Many drugs are also synthesized using the methods of organic chemistry, and some are produced biochemically.

The heavy organic sector

In this sector, materials are produced in large quantities, usually as raw materials for further processing into plastics, fibres, films or paints. Typical examples are benzene, phenol, toluene, vinyl chloride and ethylene. The raw material generally used is crude oil, which contains a range of hydrocarbons – chemicals made up of carbon and hydrogen. From crude oil individual hydrocarbons can be extracted by distillation or catalytic cracking. The hydrocarbons obtained in this way are then used to build more complex molecules by polymerization.

BIOTECHNOLOGY

Biotechnology also produces useful products, but by biological rather than chemical methods. Living organisms – or substances produced from them – are used to make drugs, to improve crops, to brew alcohols, and even to extract minerals. Some of its methods are ancient, while others are so new that they are barely out of the research laboratory.

The technique of *fermentation*, in which microorganisms such as yeast convert raw materials into useful products, has been known since earliest times. By the middle of the 19th century, industrial alcohol was being produced by fermentation in much the same way as beer or wine. After the price of crude oil went up in the 1970s, alcohol produced in this way has been able to compete under some circumstances with petrol. A number of acids can also be produced by fermentation, vinegar (dilute acetic acid) and citric acid being important examples. Fermentation has proved equally useful in the drug industry. Following the discovery of the

antibiotic penicillin in 1928, large-scale fermentation methods were developed in the 1940s to produce the drug commercially. Today a large number of drugs are produced in this way, as well as other biochemicals such as enzymes (biochemical catalysts), alkaloids, peptides and proteins.

Genetic engineering has greatly increased the range of possible products. By altering the genetic blueprint of a microorganism, it can be made to produce a protein quite unlike anything it would produce naturally. For example, if the short length of the genetic material DNA responsible for producing growth hormones in humans is inserted into cells of a certain bacterium, the bacterium will produce the human hormone as it grows. It can then be extracted and used to treat children who would otherwise not grow properly. The same methods can be used to produce insulin for diabetics, while sheep have been genetically engineered so that they produce a human blood-clotting agent in their milk.

Printing

Books spread knowledge and ideas, make universal education possible, and provide access to techniques invented by others. When the first printed books appeared in Europe in the 15th century, the progress of learning began to gather pace. The information revolution that still dominates our lives was under way.

By the end of the 2nd century AD the Chinese had invented paper, ink and a wood block with a picture or letters carved out in relief – the basic requirements for printing. By the 14th century, individual blocks had been carved for each of the 80 000 Chinese characters. They could be arranged in any order to make up a page – the principle of *movable type*.

Typesetting

The really decisive advances, however, were made in Europe in around 1450, by two goldsmiths, Johannes Gutenberg (c. 1398–1468) and Johann Fust (c. 1400–66). They used metal-alloy type – far longer lasting than wooden blocks – and a vice-like press to transfer the ink from the blocks to the paper. Each letter was separately cast, and the letters were then arranged side by side along a strip of wood to form words, and the lines were *justified* (made to fit a fixed width or *measure*) by inserting small pieces of lead between the words. By 1448 they had printed the Bible in Latin, each page taking a printer a day to set in type. A similar process was adopted by the Englishman William Caxton (c. 1422–91), who printed his first book – the first printed in English – in 1475.

Printing using 'hot metal' lasted more than 500 years. In 1884, its speed was improved by the *Linotype machine*, which could cast a whole line at once from individual letters typed by the operator on a keyboard. Its rival was the *Monotype machine*, invented in 1887. The Monotype

SEE ALSO

● PHOTOGRAPHY AND FILM
  p. 204
● COMPUTERS p. 211
● MEDIEVAL AND RENAISSANCE
  CULTURE p. 248

INKS AND PAPER

Water-based inks are unsuitable for printing, since they tend to collect in droplets on metal type and smudge when pressed on paper. The solution, quickly discovered, was to use inks made of pigments dissolved in oil. Vegetable or mineral oils may be used, depending on the type of printing. The black pigment used is generally carbon black.

The earliest documents were written on clay tablets, and then on parchment, made from sheep- or goatskin, or vellum, made from calfskin. A writing material prepared from the stem of the papyrus plant was also known to the Ancients. These materials, however, were quite inadequate for the huge volume of printed matter that was made possible by Gutenberg's inventions.

The answer was paper, invented by the Chinese nearly 2000 years ago, but not widely known in Europe until after 1100. Paper can be made from virtually any fibrous material. The commonest in use today is wood pulp, but recycled material such as rags or waste paper are also used. After felling, trees are turned into chips and then digested into pulp using sodium sulphate. The pulp is bleached and then flows through a narrow slit onto a moving screen that allows the water to drain away. The paper is then pressed to remove more water and dried by steam-heated cylinders. Finally the paper is treated with pigments such as clay to give it a smoother finish, or given a glossy surface with chalk or titanium dioxide.

operator keyed in the text, which was coded into a punched tape, together with information about the spaces between words needed to justify the line. Today typesetting, and the other stages in the production of printed material, has been almost entirely taken over by computers (⊳ box).

Printing methods and presses

Three methods of printing are of particular significance (⊳ diagram). In *letterpress printing*, the method used by Gutenberg, the raised surfaces of the typeset page are covered in ink by rollers, and

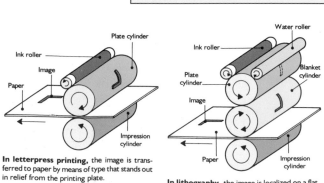

PRINTING PROCESSES

In letterpress printing, the image is transferred to paper by means of type that stands out in relief from the printing plate.

In lithography, the image is localized on a flat printing plate by means of chemicals that attract ink, while blank areas are covered by a film of water.

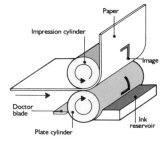

In photogravure, the image is etched into depressions on the printing plate. The plate is then inked, and the ink removed from blank (i.e. non-recessed) areas by means of a blade.

paper is pressed against it in a press to transfer the image.

The principle of *lithography* (or 'litho'), which has now almost entirely taken over from letterpress, was invented in 1796 by a Bavarian, Aloys Senefelder (1771–1834). The technique depends on the fact that water and grease do not mix. The images to be printed are transferred to flexible metal plates photographically, in such a way that the areas to be printed consist of chemicals that attract ink and repel water, while the blank areas attract water and repel ink. First water and then ink is applied to the plate; all the ink congregates in the areas of the image, and can be transferred to paper in a rotary press (⊳ below). A better image is achieved if the cylinder carrying the plate first transfers the image to a rubber-coated cylinder, which in turn transfers it to paper. This rubber 'offset' cylinder gives the method its name – *offset litho*.

A third technique is widely used for printing colour supplements and magazines. In *gravure* (short for 'rotogravure' or 'photogravure') the image is etched on the plate photographically, forming cells whose depth depends on the intensity of the colour. As the plate rotates, it picks up ink, which is wiped off blank areas by a blade. When the paper passes between the cylinders of the press, the deeper cells produce denser images, while the shallower ones produce lighter ones. In a related process, known as *copperplate gravure* or *line intaglio*, the image consists of discrete lines that vary in depth and width. It is the preferred method for printing stamps and banknotes.

Several designs of printing press have been developed over the centuries. Historically, the various kinds of press were all designed chiefly for the purposes of letterpress printing. The methods that have largely superseded letterpress – gravure and litho – are carried out almost exclusively on some variant of rotary press. In *platen presses*, the type is carried in a flat bed and pressure is applied by the platen – a second flat surface, which is fed by sheets of paper. In *flat-bed* or *cylinder presses*, the type is carried in a mobile flat bed that moves back and forth beneath an

impression cylinder, around which a sheet of paper is wrapped. Greater printing speed, particularly important for newspaper production, was achieved by *rotary presses*, which operate cylinder to cylinder. Letterpress type was formed into a curve by a process known as *stereotyping*, invented in 1727. An impression was taken of the typeset page using papier mâché, which was then curved into a half circle and used as a mould to cast copies of the typeset page. The curved page was fitted together with another page around a cylinder and locked in place. Rotary presses may be sheet-fed or web-fed; in the latter case a continuous roll (or *web*) of paper passes between the cylinders. Rotary printing allows much more rapid production than flat-bed methods.

SCREENING AND COLOUR REPRODUCTION

In lithography and letterpress (⊳ main text), it is impossible to produce gradations in tone by varying the thickness of ink deposited at different points of the printed image. Areas of different tone in an illustration are therefore reproduced by a process known as *screening* (also known as the *halftone process*). The image is photographed through a fine screen, so dividing the image into a series of evenly spaced dots; the size of the dots determines the density of the ink at a given point – the larger the dot, the darker the tone.

To print in colour, paper must successively pass over a number of printing cylinders, a different colour being transferred to the paper at each stage. The process is made simpler by the fact that any colour can be made by mixing three basic colours in the right proportions. Separate plates are made for printing in cyan (bluish green), magenta (purplish red) and yellow, and the images from each printing are superimposed exactly on top of one another. A fourth printing is then made in black, principally to add definition and contrast, as well as to print the text and captions for the colour page.

FOUR-COLOUR SEPARATION

The four printing plates necessary for full-colour reproduction are prepared from four separate pieces of film, or *separations*. The separation is achieved by means of a *colour scanner*: a computer-guided laser beam moves back and forth across a rotating drum to which the original is attached, measuring the quality and intensity of each of the basic colours at every point of the image.

1. Magenta separation.

2. Yellow separation.

3. Cyan separation.

4. Black separation.

5. Full–colour image.

THE COMPUTER REVOLUTION

Computer technology has revolutionized every stage in the production of printed matter. In a fully computerized system, it is entirely feasible that

The layout of a page being designed on screen.

the material to be printed will never have been set down on paper before it finally passes through the printer's press. Text may be keyed directly into the computer typesetting system, or an author's word-processed disks may be made compatible with a particular system. The text is displayed on screen, where it may be edited or corrected; typesetting commands – specifying the desired typeface, type size and so on – are also added at this stage. A designer may then assemble the page on screen, juggling pictures and text into the final layout.

Next the text is set in type by a laser guided by the computer. The laser scans to and fro across a sheet of film or photographic paper ('bromide'), tracing the shapes of all the characters according to the instructions prepared at the page-layout terminal. After development, the result is a positive or negative film, or a bromide; in the latter, the characters traced by the laser appear black against a white background. The film or bromide can then be used to prepare printing plates.

Photography

At least as early as the 4th century BC, the ancient Greeks were familiar with the principle of the camera obscura – a darkened chamber in which an inverted image of the world outside is projected through a small opening onto a flat surface within. However, it was not until the first half of the 19th century that a process was developed by which an image could be made permanent.

A camera is essentially a box that is lightproof except where the optical component, the lens ($\triangleright$ p. 24), projects an image onto a sheet of material inside the camera. This material, usually film, is coated with an emulsion whose chemical properties are changed by exposure to light, and which – after appropriate processing – can reproduce the image.

The *emulsion* is made of silver halide grains (often silver bromide or iodide), suspended in gelatin. After exposure to light and chemical processing (*development*), the grains become black metallic silver. When the unexposed silver halide in the parts wholly or partially untouched by light is dissolved away, the picture becomes permanent, or *fixed*. It is, however, a reversed, or *negative*, image, with the original light areas reproduced as dark areas, and vice versa. The conversion of the negative to a true, or *positive*, picture was at first a problem, until a negative/positive technique was evolved ($\triangleright$ below), which brought the bonus that an unlimited number of positive prints could be produced from a single negative.

The early pioneers

In 1826 the Frenchman Nicéphore Niepce (1765– 1833) produced the world's first photographic image. In 1839 Niepce's partner Louis Daguerre (1789–1851) marketed his *daguerreotype*, which used a copper plate coated with light-sensitive silver chloride, and required a half-hour exposure. There was no development in the modern sense, but by using mercury vapour to whiten the exposed silver and common salt to fix it, Daguerre produced a positive picture.

In 1841 the Englishman William Fox Talbot (1800–77) patented his negative/positive process (the *calotype* process). The paper negative was placed face-to-face against another, unexposed, piece of sensitized paper, and then light was passed through the back of the negative. The sensitive paper, when developed, became a positive print.

Later developments

The growth of photography as a profession was greatly assisted by the introduction of a *wet-plate* process in 1851. A jelly-like solution called collodion was poured onto a glass plate, which was then dipped in silver nitrate solution. The plate was then exposed in the camera and developed before it dried. Portrait and landscape pictures could now be made to order, and intrepid photographers set off on expeditions laden with darkroom tent, glass plates, and chemicals.

The invention of a *dry-plate* process in the 1870s led to the commercial manufacture of glass plates in which dry gelatin replaced wet collodion. The emulsion was also very much more sensitive. Using a spring-operated shutter, exposure times could therefore be reduced to $\frac{1}{25}$ second, thus making a tripod unnecessary.

In 1888 the American George Eastman (1854– 1932) produced his first Kodak camera with the slogan 'You press the button, we do the rest.' It was in the well-tried form of a box, but instead of plates used a roll of sensitive paper (later nitrocellulose, or 'film'), which could be wound on between exposures. It took 100 shots, after which the camera was sent back to the manufacturer for development and replacement of the film.

In the 1920s the Leica camera was introduced – the first commercially successful 'miniature' camera able to use 35 mm cinema film. This and subsequent miniature cameras became extremely popular with professionals as well as amateurs.

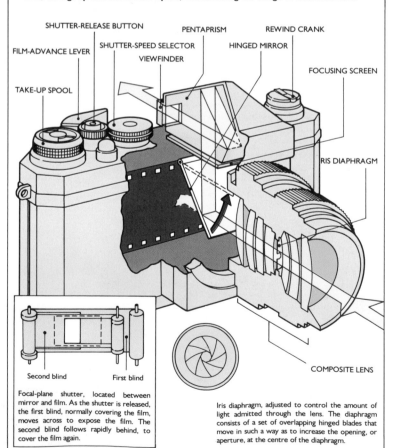

THE SINGLE-LENS REFLEX CAMERA

In a single-lens reflex (SLR) camera, a single lens is used both for viewing and for taking the picture. A hinged mirror set at 45° directs the image projected through the lens onto a ground-glass focusing screen above the mirror. The laterally reversed image on the screen is then reflected off the sides of a pentaprism (five-sided prism), so that the image – upright and the right way round – is seen through the viewfinder. The image is then focused on the screen, and the iris diaphragm is set to contract automatically to the correct aperture as the picture is taken. As the shutter-release button is pressed, the mirror swings up and the shutter opens, thus allowing the image to strike the film.

SHUTTER-RELEASE BUTTON
PENTAPRISM
REWIND CRANK
FILM-ADVANCE LEVER
SHUTTER-SPEED SELECTOR
VIEWFINDER
HINGED MIRROR
TAKE-UP SPOOL
FOCUSING SCREEN
IRIS DIAPHRAGM
COMPOSITE LENS

Second blind   First blind

Focal-plane shutter, located between mirror and film. As the shutter is released, the first blind, normally covering the film, moves across to expose the film. The second blind follows rapidly behind, to cover the film again.

Iris diaphragm, adjusted to control the amount of light admitted through the lens. The diaphragm consists of a set of overlapping hinged blades that move in such a way as to increase the opening, or aperture, at the centre of the diaphragm.

Even smaller cameras were later introduced for the mass market, but were not favoured by professionals.

In the mid-20th century the Polaroid camera was invented by the American Edwin Land (1909–91), making 'instant' pictures by processing the film inside the camera itself. This was achieved by incorporating developing agents in the film, activated by bursting a pod containing alkaline solution as the exposed film was pressed between rollers. In the 1990s the electronic camera, in which the image is captured and stored in digital form, became a practical possibility.

Modern cameras

Unlike more traditional 35 mm cameras, which have a simple see-through view-finder, the 35 mm single-lens reflex camera allows the user to see the exact picture being taken (▷ box). Larger cameras may also use the reflex viewfinder. In the case of the twin-lens reflex, the mirror is fixed and has its own lens, of the same characteristics as the taking lens. Although the 35 mm film size is the most popular, larger formats, using sheet film or roll film, are still used where convenience of use is less important than final picture quality.

More sophisticated 35 mm cameras have their own *exposure meters*, which measure the amount of light falling on the subject and adjust the shutter speed and lens aperture accordingly. They may also incorporate electronic controls and automatic focusing: the user is required only to frame the picture and press the trigger.

Film and colour photography

Emulsions have improved continuously. An early step was the introduction of *panchromatic* film, which was sensitive to red and therefore gave a better tonal rendering. Subsequent films of still greater sensitivity enabled pictures to be taken in poor light, but tended to be less sharp because the silver grains were larger – although this problem was itself solved by the later introduction of sensitive fine-grain films.

Cumbersome ways of making colour pictures were evolved in the late 19th century, but it was the appearance of Kodachrome and Agfacolor in the 1930s that introduced modern colour films. These were multi-layer films in which three separate emulsions recorded the blue, green and red parts of the image. They were then processed by dyeing each layer with the corresponding complementary colour (yellow, magenta and cyan), thus producing three positive images one

Faster than the human eye: a bullet travelling at 450 m (1476 ft) per second is captured as it strikes a strawberry. High-speed photography generally uses shutter speeds of less than $^1/_{1000}$ second, and has many applications in science and technology. (SPL/Dr Gary Settles and Stephen McIntyre)

THE MOVIE CAMERA

The movie camera incorporates a number of mechanical components that allow a sequence of still pictures, or *frames*, to be shot on a strip of film – usually 24 frames per second. The *claw* alternately engages and disengages with the sprocket holes in the film, ensuring that the film advances at the correct speed and that the film remains stationary during exposure. Synchronized with the claw is a *rotating shutter*: the movement of the shutter is timed so that the light path to the film is blocked as the claw advances the film. While the exposure gate is blocked, the mirrored surface of the shutter reflects the image, via a prism, into the viewfinder.

FEED SPOOL

CLAW

ROTATING SHUTTER

VIEWFINDER

GATE

PRISM

SPROCKET WHEEL

LENS

The illusion of movement is created when each frame is projected for a fraction of a second onto a viewing screen. A *projector* works like a movie camera in reverse. A light source at the rear of the projector is channelled through a gate, projecting each frame through a lens and onto a screen. A claw moves the film through the gate, holding each frame stationary as it is projected, while a rotating shutter is timed to cut off the light source as the film is moving between frames.

above the other, which together reproduced the original colours of the image (▷ p. 203). The final picture was a transparency, to be looked through or projected, but a negative/positive system was soon introduced to produce colour prints.

Applied photography

Photomicrography produces enlarged pictures of tiny objects, and is achieved either by using a short-focus lens on a long-bodied camera, or by taking photographs through a microscope. It has applications in biology and criminology, among other fields.

High-speed photography shows successive phases of movement too fast to be observed by the human eye. Apart from the use of high-speed shutters, a technique known as *stroboscopy* may be used, in which cameras with open shutters register successive images of a moving object illuminated by intermittent flashes. Such techniques can be used for studying phenomena as disparate as a dancer's movements, explosions, or fracturing metal.

Photography has numerous other specialized applications that have widened the possibilities of many activities and revolutionized others. Using lens filters and special film, for instance, it is possible to select parts of the electromagnetic spectrum (▷ p. 26) other than visible light as the illuminant. X-ray and infrared photography are among the important applications of this technique (▷ p. 210).

SEE ALSO

● OPTICS p. 24
● RADIO, TV AND HI-FI p. 206
● SEEING THE INVISIBLE p. 210
● CINEMA p. 328

Radio, TV and Hi-Fi

The use of electromagnetic waves to carry sound and pictures has revolutionized 20th-century communications. The media used to carry information are *radio waves*, which occur naturally in space, but which, for broadcasting purposes, are generated by accelerating electrons inside an *aerial* (or *antenna*) – a device used both to emit and receive radio waves. Like all electromagnetic waves, radio waves travel at the speed of light – 300 000 km (186 000 mi) per second in a vacuum.

Long, *medium* and *short* radio waves, with wavelengths between 2 km and 10 m (1¼ mi and 33 ft), can diffract or 'bend' around obstacles such as hills and are therefore suitable for local radio broadcasting. They are reflected by the Earth and by the ionosphere (▷ p. 61), and thus can 'bounce' between the two and be transmitted over very long distances. Short waves are reflected best, and are generally used for international broadcasting. *VHS* (very high frequency) and *UHF* (ultra-high frequency) waves have shorter wavelengths. They can only travel in a straight-line path, and pass through the ionosphere. They are chiefly used for television and local radio.

Radio

The simplest form of radio transmission is to use a radio *transmitter* to create a radio wave of a fixed frequency, and a receiver tuned to that frequency to pick it up. By turning the wave on and off, a series of dots and dashes can be transmitted, sending a message in Morse code (▷ p. 208). In 1894 the Italian Guglielmo Marconi (1874–1919) put together the discoveries of others to create radio. In the attic of his parents' house he made a bell ring by sending a radio message across the room. By 1901 he had transmitted the letter S in Morse code across the Atlantic from Cornwall, England, to Newfoundland, Canada.

A more sophisticated system is needed to transmit voices and music. A *carrier wave*, instead of being turned on and off like a tap, must have a second signal imposed on it. This is the process known as *modulation* (▷ box). A microphone produces a small electrical current representing the sounds made into it. The wave profile corresponding to this current is then superimposed on the carrier wave, broadcast, and finally separated out again at the other end by the radio *receiver*. An amplifier increases the power of the signal, so that it can operate a loudspeaker, re-creating the original sounds made into the microphone.

Television

Radio waves were first used to carry visual information in 1926 when the Scottish inventor John Logie Baird (1888–1946) demonstrated television based on a mechanical method of scanning an image into lines of dots of light. The basic principle is to break up the image into a series of dots, which are then transmitted and displayed on a screen so rapidly that the human eye perceives them as a complete picture. This system was rapidly superseded by an all-electronic system developed by Vladimir Zworykin (1889–1982), a Russian-born engineer, whose first practical camera, made in 1931, focused the picture onto a mosaic of photoelectric cells. The voltage induced in each cell was a measure of the light intensity at that point, and could be transmitted as

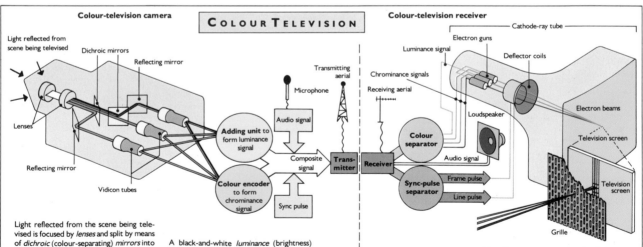

COLOUR TELEVISION

Colour-television camera — Light reflected from scene being televised; Dichroic mirrors; Reflecting mirror; Lenses; Reflecting mirror; Vidicon tubes; Adding unit to form luminance signal; Colour encoder to form chrominance signal; Audio signal; Sync pulse; Microphone; Composite signal; Transmitting aerial; Transmitter.

Colour-television receiver — Cathode-ray tube; Electron guns; Deflector coils; Luminance signal; Chrominance signals; Receiving aerial; Receiver; Colour separator; Sync-pulse separator; Audio signal; Frame pulse; Line pulse; Loudspeaker; Electron beams; Television screen; Grille.

Light reflected from the scene being televised is focused by *lenses* and split by means of *dichroic* (colour-separating) *mirrors* into three separate images, one in each of the three primary colours – blue, green and red. Each beam of coloured light is then directed into one of three identical *vidicon tubes*. The pattern of light falling on a photoconductive layer within each tube causes a varying pattern of electrical resistance; as an electron beam scans the photoconductive area from behind, a varying electric current is induced in a circuit connected to the conductive layer. The pattern of dark and light in each primary-colour image is thus converted into one of three varying electrical signals.

A black-and-white *luminance* (brightness) *signal* is created in the adding unit, by combining information from each of the three colour signals. At the same time, the colour encoder produces a single *chrominance signal*, which defines the hue and saturation of each primary colour. The luminance and chrominance signals are combined into a composite *video signal*. Prior to transmission, the *audio signal* is incorporated, together with a *synchronizing pulse* ('sync pulse'), which ensures that the electron scanning in the receiving system matches that of the transmitting system.

The composite signal picked up by the receiving aerial is decoded, separating out the various constituent signals. The luminance signal controls the overall output of three electron guns in the cathode-ray tube of the receiving set, so determining the balance of light and shade in the final picture. The chrominance signal – now split into the three primary-colour signals – regulates the relative strength of each electron beam. The sync pulse, divided into line and frame components, controls the deflection of the beams across and down the screen.

The television screen is coated with stripes of different phosphors, which glow red, blue or green when struck by electrons. Immediately behind the screen is a *grille*, or *shadow mask*, which contains many perforations. Travelling at slightly different angles as they pass through the perforations, the electron beams are caused to diverge before striking the screen, in such a way that the electrons from each gun can only reach phosphor stripes of the appropriate colour. Each image on the screen thus consists of stripes of varying brightness and colour that merge together to form the complete picture.

a signal. A modern TV camera operates in essentially the same way, measuring the light intensity at each point of the image. This information is then encoded on the radio wave and transmitted. At the receiving end, the signal has to be decoded. A TV set is basically a *cathode-ray tube*, in which a 'gun' fires a beam of electrons at a luminescent screen. As they strike it, the screen lights up. To make up the picture the beam is scanned to and fro in a series of lines (625 in modern sets), covering the entire screen in 1/25 second.

Because the VHF and UHF wavebands on which television signals are transmitted are not significantly reflected by the ionosphere, many transmitters are needed to cover most countries. For intercontinental TV, satellites above the Earth are used to pick up the signals and broadcast them back to Earth. The satellite signals are not powerful enough to be picked up by ordinary TV aerials, so they are re-broadcast by ground transmitters. Special dish-shaped aerials can pick up satellite signals, however, making possible continent-wide direct broadcasting by satellite (DBS). TV signals can also be fed down cables.

Video

TV programmes can be recorded on magnetic tape. The principle is the same as that of an audio tape recorder, but the technology is more complex. The signals are recorded as magnetic patterns on the tape. Because a video signal contains much more information than an audio one, it is necessary to pack it more efficiently onto the tape. Today's *video tape recorders* (VTRs) use a recording head that rotates as the tape runs past it, so that the information is effectively laid out diagonally across the tape, reducing the length of tape needed. *Video discs* use compact disc technology (▷ below) to record images in digital form.

Hi-fi

In 1877 the American inventor Thomas Edison (1847–1931) introduced his *phonograph*, which converted sound vibrations, channelled through a horn, into grooves on the surface of a cylinder covered in tinfoil. In 1888 Emile Berliner (1851–1929) invented flat *gramophone records*, where the groove ran in a spiral from the edge of the disc towards the centre, and the vibrations were recorded and played by side-to-side movements of the needle.

In the 1920s, the introduction of electrical recording methods improved the quality of recordings. *Microphones* were used to convert sounds into electrical currents, which could then be used to drive cutting machines to create the grooves. In playback, the vibrations picked up by the stylus were used to generate an electrical current, which could be amplified by electronic circuits and played through loudspeakers that converted the electrical signals back into sound (▷ below). Long-playing records (LPs), made of vinyl plastic, were first produced in 1946. They required much lighter stylus pressures and finer points, usually provided by using diamond or sapphire. LPs increased the maximum playing time per side from about 4 to over 20 minutes. High fidelity or *hi-fi* – the accurate reproduction of sound quality – became possible.

Recording on tape

The *telegraphone*, introduced in 1898, recorded sound by the alternating magnetization of a steel wire, replaced in the 1930s by steel tape. After 1935 strong plastic tape covered with iron-oxide powder made tape recording widely available.

─── **MODULATION** ───

Radio waves can be used to carry sound waves by superimposing the pattern of the sound wave onto the radio wave. This is called *modulation*, and is one of the basic forms of radio transmission. There are two ways of modulating radio waves. In *amplitude modulation* (AM) the amplitude of the radio *carrier wave* is made to vary with the amplitude of the sound signal. For *frequency modulation* (FM) the frequency of the carrier wave is made to vary so that the variations are in step with the changes in amplitude of the sound signal.

Domestic *tape recorders* using such tape appeared in the 1950s. Sounds are recorded by passing the tape in front of a recording head that consists of an electromagnet fed by electrical signals from a microphone. A magnetic pattern corresponding to the sounds is created on the tape as iron oxide fragments align themselves with the magnetic field. In playback, the tape passes in front of a second head, inducing an electrical current that is proportional to the magnetization of the tape. The current is then passed through an amplifier to loudspeakers. The most common type of tape is the *compact cassette*, introduced in 1963.

Stereo

Stereophonic recordings became widely available after 1958. In making a stereo recording, two microphones are set up at a distance from one another, and each of them records its own set of sound signals. The aim is to simulate the way in which we hear sounds: having two ears, we simultaneously hear two sounds, which are slightly different and come from slightly different directions. Two signals recorded on separate strips along a tape are played back through two speakers. To a listener placed in the right position this creates an illusion of the left-to-right spread of the music.

Amplifiers and loudspeakers

At the heart of any hi-fi system is the *amplifier*. An amplifier is essentially a set of electronic circuits that boost the signal from the stylus or tape deck to operate the loudspeakers. The circuits are made from transistors, and amplifiers are designed to produce the minimum distortion of the signal. *Loudspeakers* convert the electrical signal from the amplifier back into sound. The current from the amplifier flows around a coil of wire inside the field of a permanent magnet. Interaction between the field produced by the current flowing through the coil and that of the permanent magnet makes the coil vibrate. The coil is attached to a cone of stiff lightweight material that vibrates with it and creates the sounds.

Digital recording

Sounds are now recorded digitally, as a series of binary digits, or *bits* (▷ pp. 55 and 211). In a *digital system*, the sound is 'sampled' 40 000 times a second, and its amplitude and frequency (volume and pitch) are recorded as a binary number. Recordings made in this way can be turned into ordinary discs, but the advantages of low distortion and a good signal-to-noise ratio are better preserved in the form of digital ('compact') discs. *Compact discs*, which were launched commercially in 1982, record the bits as a series of minute pits or blank spaces in the surface of the disc. The pits are 'read' by a laser device (▷ p. 25) that scans the record, picking up a series of signals that are the original binary digits of the recording. The signals are converted to analogue currents that can be amplified and fed to loudspeakers. *Digital compact cassettes* and *recordable compact discs* are being developed.

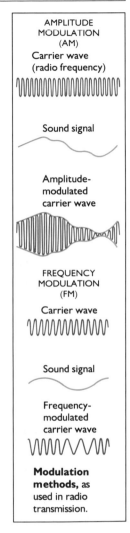

AMPLITUDE MODULATION (AM)

Carrier wave (radio frequency)

Sound signal

Amplitude-modulated carrier wave

FREQUENCY MODULATION (FM)

Carrier wave

Sound signal

Frequency-modulated carrier wave

Modulation methods, as used in radio transmission.

SEE ALSO

- WAVE THEORY p. 20
- ELECTROMAGNETISM p. 26
- ELECTRICITY IN ACTION p. 28
- PHOTOGRAPHY AND FILM p. 204
- TELECOMMUNICATIONS p. 208

Telecommunications

The transfer of information by wire or by radio waves is the basis of telecommunications, which is now one of world's biggest and fastest-growing industries. Currently, the most important systems are the telephone, the telegraph, telex, facsimile, and information systems based on the telephone or television.

Letters have long been the principal form of communication over a distance. The British 'Penny Black' – introduced in 1840 – was the first postage stamp. Before the penny post, 82 million letters a year were sent, but within 30 years the number had risen to 917 million. Other countries soon followed suit with their own postage stamps.

Telegraphy

Efficient as the 19th-century postal system was, a quicker method of communication was needed, particularly to coordinate the movements of the rapidly growing railways. The answer was the *electric telegraph*. This resulted from the work of a number of pioneers, following the publication by the Danish physicist Hans Christiaan Oersted (1777–1851) of his discovery that a magnetized needle could be deflected by an electric current flowing in a wire (▷ pp. 26–7). The electric telegraph was put into a practical form by two Englishmen, Sir Charles Wheatstone (1802–75) and William Cooke (1806–79), who were granted a British patent in 1837.

The following year the American inventor Samuel Morse (1791–1872) – in partnership with Alfred Vail (1807–59) – devised the *Morse code*, in which individual letters of the alphabet and digits are represented by different sequences of dots and dashes. This enabled messages to be sent using a single circuit at a rate of 10 words a minute. The operator tapped a key to send the message as a series of electrical impulses. At the other end it was printed out as pen marks on paper tape and decoded. The pen was soon replaced by a *sounder* when it was found that operators could decode messages faster by hearing the sounds of the pen making dots and dashes than by reading the marks on paper.

A telegraph cable was laid across the English Channel in 1851 and across the Atlantic in 1858, although the latter soon failed. In 1866 a more successful transatlantic cable was laid, and by 1872 the majority of the world's great cities were in contact with one another by telegraph. Telegraphy remained the principal form of telecommunication until just before World War I, when the telephone began to take over.

Telephones

Transmitting the sound of the human voice required further inventions – the *microphone* and the *receiver*. A microphone controls the current in a circuit operating a receiver, which generates a sound similar to that received by the microphone. The first successful telephone was made by the Scottish inventor Alexander Graham Bell (1847–1922) in 1876. The introduction of automatic exchanges early in the 20th century made possible a huge growth in the telephone system (▷ box). However, because even high-quality metal conductors show electrical resistance, it is difficult to send a signal over a long distance. For this reason, amplifiers – known as *repeaters* – had to be installed at regular intervals to compensate for the loss of power. The cost of providing and maintaining repeaters was considerable, and long-distance telephony only became effective once long-lived repeaters had been developed.

During the 1960s *electronic exchanges* began to be introduced. Dialled numbers are stored electroni-

---

THE STROWGER SWITCH

Early telephone subscribers had to rely on human operators to connect their calls by means of a plug-and-socket arrangement. The first practical automatic switching device was invented in 1889 by a Kansas undertaker, Almon B. Strowger. Fearing that his local operator – the wife of a business rival – was diverting his calls, he devised an automatic exchange – a 'girl-less, wait-less' telephone. The Strowger system proved so successful that it formed the basis of subsequent mechanical exchanges. A series of electrical pulses, produced by means of a dial, caused a contact arm to rise and rotate through a corresponding number of steps, so making the desired connection. It was not until the 1960s, with the emergence of electronic exchanges, that the dominance of the Strowger system began to be challenged, and some Strowger exchanges are still in use today.

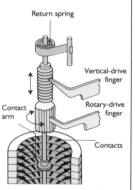

A simple Strowger switch, providing a connection to number 34.

Labels: Return spring, Vertical-drive finger, Rotary-drive finger, Contact arm, Contacts

---

Alexander Graham Bell. Bell's interest in transmitting the sound of the human voice grew out of his research into speech mechanics while training teachers for the deaf. Bell filed in his caveat (patent) for his telephone at the US Patent Office just two hours before another inventor, Elisha Gray. (AKG)

cally and routed to their destination automatically and at great speed. Such exchanges have few moving parts, less noisy lines because there are no mechanical switches, and can operate quickly enough for push-button rather than dial phones to be used.

Multiplexing

In the early days of telephony, each subscriber telephone was connected to the exchange by an individual circuit, and every link between exchanges was achieved by cables transmitting single calls. The result was chaotic, unsightly, and also expensive as telephone wires are costly to install and maintain. From 1910, this problem was resolved by the introduction of *multiplexing*, which allowed more than one call to be sent down the same set of wires at the same time. At its simplest, this is achieved by allocating carrier waves of different frequencies (⊳ pp. 206–7) to different calls. These waves are then separated out at the receiving exchange by a tuning arrangement rather like that used in radio sets.

In modern telephony, multiplexing is achieved by *pulse-code modulation*. The continuous waveform of the human voice is converted into a digital signal by means of sampling at fixed intervals – normally 8000 times a second. These samples are transformed by an *encoder* into a code that is transmitted in a series of regular pulses and pauses. At the other end, the pulses are separated again into individual conversations, and converted back into a form that is analogous to the human voice so that they can be heard on the telephone. In this method, numerous calls can be transmitted on the same line by using the gaps between the samples.

Optical cables

An even better way of transmitting more calls along the same line is to replace electrical currents with microwaves (⊳ p. 27) or with light. The amount of information that can be carried is higher for high-frequency carrier waves, but very-high-frequency carrier signals are quickly weakened by ordinary wires. Both microwaves and light produced by lasers offer much higher frequencies, with the capacity to handle thousands of calls along a single link. Cables made of optical fibre, which can transmit laser light over long distances without loss (⊳ p. 25), are now replacing the old copper cables. Optical cables are cheaper to make, tough, flexible, and immune to electrical interference. Each glass fibre in the cable can handle thousands of telephone calls at once, each one at a different frequency.

Microwaves and satellites

Radio waves at very high frequencies – *microwaves* – may be focused into beams and used for the transmission of telephone messages over middle-range distances. Unlike other radio waves with longer frequencies, microwaves are not reflected by the ionosphere (⊳ pp. 60 and 206) and so cannot be used for long-distance telecommunications unless they are transmitted via satellites. The first effective telecommunications satellite was *Telstar*, launched in 1962. Orbiting the Earth in 150 minutes, the satellite was used to transmit a single television link or a limited number of telephone calls for 20 minutes in each orbit. Telecommunications satellites now orbit the globe high above the Equator in 24 hours. By this means the satellites are always in the same location relative to stations on Earth and can therefore be used constantly. Satellite telecommunications are largely regulated by half a dozen

Eutelsat II telecommunications satellite. One of the two antennae of the satellite undergoing testing in an inflatable 'clean room'. The plastic walls of the clean room are designed not to interfere with radio transmissions between the antenna and distant calibration towers, which measure signal coverage and strength. (Roger Ressmeyer, Starlight/SPL)

international organizations, such as Intelsat. Each of Intelsat's satellites can link over 30 000 telephone calls and 60 television channels.

Radio waves are used in mobile telephones in cars; these are commonly called *cordless telephones*, but more accurately referred to as *cellular radio*. Because the number of users is greatly in excess of the number of radio channels available for this service, the area over which cellular radio operates is divided into cells in each of which there is a low-power radio transmitter whose operations are confined to the users in its area. By this means the number of calls on the system can be multiplied by the number of cells. Calls between cells are transmitted via a central control.

SEE ALSO

● WAVE THEORY p. 20
● OPTICS p. 24
● ELECTROMAGNETISM p. 26
● RADIO, TELEVISION AND VIDEO p. 206
● COMPUTERS p. 211

DATA TRANSMISSION

Telephones are not restricted to communication by voice. Increasingly they are being used to send data from computer to computer, and images of documents by facsimile transmission (fax). In many Western countries telephones are widely used to send information for display on a TV set. These services are known generically as *viewdata*. They offer a great range of information, which is stored centrally on a computer database and covers topics as varied as stock-market prices, sports and general news, holiday information, job advertisements, weather forecasts and entertainment guides.

For transmission of computer data, a *modem* – modulator-demodulator – is needed at each end of the line. A modem converts the digital signals from the computer into a form that can be transmitted by telephone and reconverts them at the other end. Provided the telephone lines are good enough, portable computers can now be connected up to the telephone system anywhere in the world, and used to send information elsewhere. Where lines are poor, *telex systems* – the descendants of the telegraph – survive. These send images of documents along the line, letter by letter, to be printed out at the far end.

Facsimile transmission – fax – is one of the fastest growing of the new telephone services. It has been available for many years – particularly in Japan, where the language, with its many symbols, makes telex too complex. Fax has only really begun to grow rapidly, however, with the availability of much cheaper machines. Fax works by scanning a sheet of typed or handwritten material, and turning the result into a digital signal that can be sent over the telephone network to a designated fax machine somewhere else. It is by far the quickest way to transmit images of drawings or typed documents.

The telephone network can also be used to send electronic mail from terminal to terminal, and to replace the use of cash for purchasing goods. *Electronic funds transfer* (EFT) is a system for automatically debiting a customer's bank account and transferring money to that of the store, without handling cash, cheques or credit cards. EFT is still in its infancy, but offers great economies over the existing paper-laden systems and is likely to grow.

Seeing the Invisible

Sound, beams of electrons, and radiation in various parts of the electromagnetic spectrum, such as X-rays and radio waves, are used to detect, measure and observe things. By these means we can penetrate outer space and gain access to a hidden world inside our own bodies, deep in the oceans and under the Earth's crust.

These forms of radiation exhibit wave-like properties and travel in straight lines (▷ p. 20). They can be used to provide images of objects that would otherwise be invisible. *Image intensifiers* are used to amplify electronically the image or shadow produced by detection techniques using various types of radiation.

X-rays – a form of short-wave electromagnetic radiation – were discovered by Wilhelm Röntgen (1845–1923) in 1895 and were almost immediately used to diagnose broken bones. By directing X-rays through the body of a living person, the bones within the flesh – which absorb X-rays – can be seen as shadows cast on photographic emulsions or fluorescent screens. If a patient is 'fed' with a chemical such as barium sulphate that absorbs X-rays, and therefore shows up when scanned, the digestive tract can be seen. As more than momentary exposure to X-rays damages tissue, they are used in radiotherapy to destroy cancers. Ultrasound scanning (▷ box) and magnetic resonance imaging (▷ below) provide safer alternatives to X-ray diagnosis in some circumstances. X-rays are also used at airports to check baggage and to detect subsurface defects in materials.

Beams of electrons – typically with wavelengths 10 000 times shorter than that of visible light – are

SEE ALSO

● THE HISTORY OF ASTRONOMY p. 10
● WAVE THEORY p. 20
● ACOUSTICS p. 22
● OPTICS p. 24
● ELECTROMAGNETISM p. 26
● ATOMS AND SUBATOMIC PARTICLES p. 30

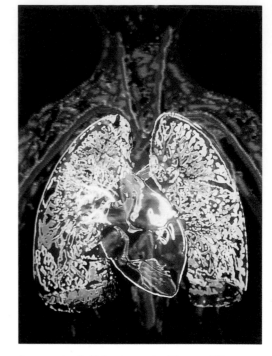

Computerized axial tomography. The use of X-rays in diagnosis was revolutionized by the development in 1973 of computerized axial tomography. The patient is placed inside a machine in which the body is scanned by a rotating source of X-rays. Variations in the density of the tissues are detected, and assembled by a computer into a cross-section of the brain or body. (Zefa)

focused (by means of electric or magnetic fields) to form images in *electron microscopes*, in which thin slices of material are examined. An alternative is the *scanning electron microscope*, in which the beam scans across the surface of the object, producing a detailed three-dimensional image.

In *magnetic resonance imaging* brief radio impulses, emitted within a very powerful magnetic field around the body, cause the nuclei of atoms first to spin and then to emit signals as they realign themselves to the magnet. Each tissue gives off characteristic signals, which are converted by computer to produce clear images.

Devices sensitive to emissions of *infrared radiation* can be used for a variety of detection and imaging purposes. Because infrared devices can operate in complete darkness, photographic emulsions sensitive to infrared light can be used at night or in conditions of poor visibility. The Landsat satellite programme has provided a wealth of geographical information. The visible and invisible parts of the electromagnetic spectrum in sunlight are reflected with varying intensity by different areas (arable land, woods, sea, etc.) of the Earth's surface. Landsat's scanning devices measure different types of reflected radiation. From the digital data transmitted by the satellites, computer 'map' images are assembled.

In astronomy, detection of radio waves, X-rays and other forms of electromagnetic radiation emitted by distant objects has provided scientists with an enormous amount of new knowledge about the universe, which would not have been possible using optical telescopes (▷ p. 11).

ULTRASOUND, SONAR AND RADAR

Bats, dolphins and whales have long been known to use high-pitched sounds to locate objects in the dark. In the 1920s *sonar* or *ultrasound devices* – closely mimicking the ultrasonic technique used by animals – were developed, primarily for detecting submarines. A series of pulses of ultrasonic sound – above the range of human hearing – are sent out and their reflections detected. From the time taken for the pulses to return, the position of intervening objects can be determined. Such techniques are also commonly used to measure the depth of water and to study the sea bed. Ultrasound has applications in medicine, where it has distinct advantages over X-rays. Whereas X-rays cannot be used on pregnant women for fear of injuring the foetus, *ultrasound scanning* has no damaging effects.

The fact that radio waves are reflected off solid objects led to the development of *radar* (short for 'radio detection and ranging') in the 1930s. Radar was installed in the UK in time to provide early detection of German aircraft in the Battle of Britain (1940). The shortest wavelengths then attainable were used to give beams of adequate intensity, able to offer accurate location of objects. In the early 1940s microwaves came into use. These are transmitted in the form of pulses, with the gaps between pulses chosen so that there is time for the reflected pulse to return and be detected before the next is sent out. From the time taken for the pulse to bounce back, the distance to the object can be calculated. If the object under surveillance is moving, the frequency of the echo will change, and from this variation it is possible to determine the object's speed and its direction of movement. Radar has many uses, including marine and aerial navigation, mapping, weather forecasting, and missile advance warning systems. By sending signals to the ground and measuring the time it takes for them to return, *radar altimeters* in aircraft calculate altitude.

Computers

A computer is a machine that manipulates data according to a predetermined sequence of commands to produce a desired result. Initially computers were seen solely as devices for performing mathematical calculations, but they have far exceeded the expectations of their original designers. Almost any kind of information can be represented in a form that can be handled by a computer – letters of the alphabet, dots that form pictures, telecommunication signals and graphs, to name but a few.

In order to manipulate information, computers are fed instructions known as *programs* (⊳ below). There are many different types of computer program (collectively known as *software*), all of which tell the *hardware* (the machinery of the computer) precisely what to do at some point in the process of communication or data handling. The computer does exactly what it is instructed to do by the software, only much quicker than a human.

The essential parts of any computer are: input and output devices to get data into and out of the machine; a storage device to record data; a processer to manipulate data; and a program to control the process.

Storage and processing

All data in a *digital computer* is stored and manipulated in *binary* – a number system that uses just 1s and 0s (⊳ pp. 54–5). Each of the binary digits, or *bits*, is represented by a device that can only have one of two positions, either 'on' or 'off'. This binary digit counting system has proved to

be faster and more reliable than any alternative. A group of eight bits is called a *byte*, and is used as the unit of computer memory. One alternative to the digital computer is the *analogue computer*, which works using continuously varying electrical voltage levels rather than with numbers. Analogue computers cannot be easily reprogrammed and are usually designed for specialized tasks that must be performed very quickly.

Modern machines use *integrated circuits* (ICs; ⊳ p. 29), which pack millions of devices, each handling one bit into a tiny slice of silicon. The action of each portion of a computer is simple; the complexity arises because of the number of devices, the ways in which they can be connected, and the way that the program uses them.

When the program is read in, the computer works on each set of instruction bytes in turn. These instructions are simple (mainly copying and arithmetic), so that the program must contain a large number of steps to carry out anything complicated. When the program ends its run, another program can be started, though some machines can run more than one program at a time.

Most of the memory of a computer is *Random Access Memory* (*RAM*) which retains data only while power is switched on. A small amount of *Read-Only Memory* (*ROM*) retains data permanently. It is used to hold a short program that will read further programs from the backing-storage system within the computer, usually in the form of a magnetic disk (the *hard disk*). Additional storage for information or programs is afforded by *floppy disks*, magnetic tape or optical disks (*CD-ROMs*) that can be removed from the computer. The magnetic disks store information in the same way as a tape recorder (⊳ p. 207), and CD-ROMs in the same way as audio compact disks (⊳ p. 207). ⊳

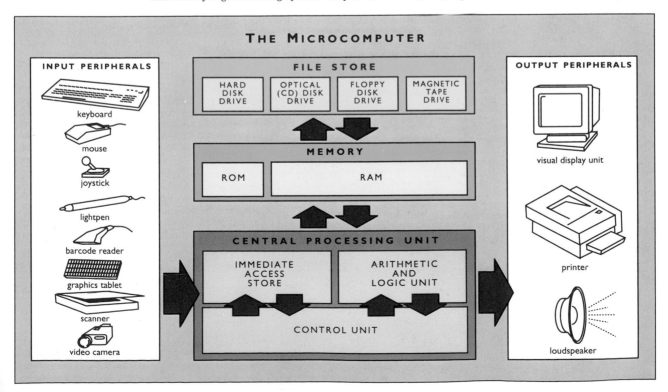

THE MICROCOMPUTER

INPUT PERIPHERALS
keyboard
mouse
joystick
lightpen
barcode reader
graphics tablet
scanner
video camera

FILE STORE
HARD DISK DRIVE
OPTICAL (CD) DISK DRIVE
FLOPPY DISK DRIVE
MAGNETIC TAPE DRIVE

MEMORY
ROM
RAM

CENTRAL PROCESSING UNIT
IMMEDIATE ACCESS STORE
ARITHMETIC AND LOGIC UNIT
CONTROL UNIT

OUTPUT PERIPHERALS
visual display unit
printer
loudspeaker

A computer graphics image of the airflow over an F-16 jet fighter, produced by the Cray Supercomputer. Determining the airflow over aircraft bodies is a complex task, requiring many related computations. Supercomputers are able to perform such calculations at very high speed.
(SPL/NASA/Dale Boyer)

Input and output

The information to be processed is input into the computer from the peripherals, usually a keyboard, but also from other units such as barscanners, picture scanners, tracers (graphics tablets), microphones, video cameras and others. A printer is needed to allow words and numbers to be printed on paper, and a visual display unit to see what a program is doing. Modern machines also use a mouse, a small trolley that moves a pointer on the screen, allowing selection and drawing actions.

Types of computers

Between 1950 and 1990 computer performance increased about one million times. The speed of the basic circuitry improved only about 10 000 times; the remainder of the improvement came from changes in the internal organization of computers.

Computers are now classified into the following categories: microcomputer, minicomputer, mainframe and supercomputer. The most familiar computer is the fast-developing *microcomputer*. It has a single-chip processor, and all the main parts of the processor are in the one device. This allows for greater reliability, smaller size and lower power consumption. The integrated circuit is connected to the memory and so allows the processor to work with a limited amount of information at high speed, using disks to hold other information. The best known are the PC, originated by IBM, and the Macintosh, originated by Apple.

Minicomputers are the next size up, often used to control networked sets of microcomputers. They are intermediate in capacity between a microcomputer and a mainframe. *Mainframe computers* are used to deal with vast amounts of information, such as house valuations for local taxation. *Supercomputers* are used where both speed and the amount of information are important, as in weather forecasting. However, the speed of even a supercomputer is limited by the heat that it generates internally, and by the time taken for a signal to travel within it. Research is currently being conducted into replacing electronic signals within computers by laser light beamed down optical fibres (▷ p. 25). If successful, this promises to produce even more powerful computers.

Software programming

Originally, programs were written directly in 0 or 1 bits. This was very tedious, and software was written to translate ordinary numbers into bits. The next step was to write *assemblers* to convert simple instruction words like ADD into the bits, the *machine code*, that the processor requires. This was the second-generation type of language, but each different design of computer required a different set of commands.

Later, high-level languages were developed. These use words similar to English language, and a *compiler* program converts the instructions into machine code. This allows programs to be written that can be used on different machines, provided a compiler has been written for each different type of machine.

The first important third-generation programming languages were FORTRAN, ALGOL and COBOL. FORTRAN (FORmula TRANslator) was intended for scientific and engineering work, ALGOL (ALGOrithmic Language) for working with logic and symbols, and COBOL (Commercial Business Orientated Language) for data processing programs. BASIC (Beginners All-purpose Symbolic Instruction Code) was originally devised as a method of teaching FORTRAN, but has developed into a widely used language in its own right. ALGOL has developed into PASCAL, C, and MODULA-2 of which C is currently the most popular language for writing applications (▷ below).

Fourth-generation languages (4GL) are programs that write programs. Most 4GLs are intended to write data-processing programs, and require the user to specify the type of information and what has to be done with it. Most 4GLs generate inefficient code and no single 4GL can be used to write every possible type of program. The latest Visual Basic for PC machines is the nearest approach to universal 4GL.

Software applications

'Off the shelf' programs are called *applications*. The most common type on larger computers is the database, but small computers are predominantly used for word processing (▷ below). A *database* allows information to be collected, stored, classified and looked up at random. These types of actions require a large mass of information to be stored in an organized way so that the correct information can be retrieved on request. Modern database programs use some form of standard 'structured query language' (SQL) to express what information is required from a database. Financial programs (book-keeping, accountancy and financial planning) are a specialized form of database.

Word processing allows you to type on the keyboard with the words appearing on the screen rather than on paper. This allows you to alter the arrangement as much as you like before printing on to paper, and to keep a store of older documents on disk, using any parts you need for new documents. A further development is desktop publishing (DTP), which allows printed pages to be produced, complete with illustrations.

Another popular type of program is the *spreadsheet*, a method of working with numbers

SEE ALSO

- OPTICS p. 24
- ELECTRICITY IN ACTION p. 28
- NUMBER SYSTEMS AND ALGEBRA p. 54
- TELECOMMUNICATIONS p. 208
- THE BRAIN AND THE NERVOUS SYSTEM p. 146
- LEARNING, CREATIVITY AND INTELLIGENCE p. 148
- HOW LANGUAGE WORKS p. 354

A computer simply carries out orders and cannot think for itself. In the 1940s and 1950s computer scientists pioneered Artificial Intelligence (AI) with the aim of creating a thinking machine. So far they have failed, but in the process they have taught us much about the way that humans think.

The British mathematician Alan Turing (1912–54) designed an experiment to test whether a machine shows intelligence. In Turing's experiment a human conducts a dialogue – by means of a computer terminal – with both a machine and another human, hidden behind a screen. Both respondents must answer every question put to them. Turing argued that if the questioner could not decide which of the two respondents was the machine, then the machine would have demonstrated intelligence.

AI researchers have adopted two very different approaches to building intelligent machines. Some have tried to build machines that use the same principles as biological intelligence, while others have chosen examples of intelligent behaviour (such as chess playing or language) and tried to build machines that copy it. Since research began AI scientists have attacked a wide range of problems. These include problem solving, natural language and vision.

Problem solving

The first attempts to tackle problem solving (often used as a measure of intelligence) produced the Logic Theorem program in the 1950s. As its name suggests, it was capable of proving theorems. Later came a more advanced program called the General Problem Solver, which was able to tackle more complex mathematical problems.

Since then computer scientists have made great strides in improving the problem-solving abilities of computers, but these are still confined to those problems that lie within the realms of logic.

Language

A major goal of AI research is to enable humans to interact with computers using natural language – language that is written and spoken by humans, as distinct from computer-program languages ($\triangleright$ text).

To understand and interpret such language, much more knowledge is needed than was once thought. Computers have to be able to work out the context in which a word is uttered in order to interpret what is being said; for example, there is a huge difference between 'close the door' and 'stay close to me'. To this end AI researchers have made use of the ideas of the linguist Noam Chomsky ($\triangleright$ p. 354), who suggested that language obeys a set of rules that can be expressed in mathematical terms.

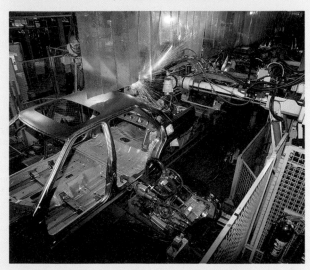

Industrial robot welding a body shell on the Rover 800 production line at Cowley, near Oxford. (SPL/Rover/James Holmes)

Running parallel with this work on natural language, research has been undertaken into speech recognition. Speech-recognition systems use information about the structure and components of speech and are typically 'trained' in on one person's voice. The challenge is to develop a machine that can recognize what any one of a variety of speakers is saying – even if their voice is affected by, for instance, a cold – and distinguish speech from background noise.

Expert systems

The most tangible and practical result of AI research has been in the area of expert systems. These are designed to help humans make decisions, typically in solving problems where it would otherwise be necessary to call in an expert in a particular area.

Many early expert systems tackled medical diagnosis, but industry and commerce have now begun to take them seriously. An expert system has three components: a *knowledge base*, in which the knowledge and experience of an expert are summarized in the form of rules; an *inference engine*, which is a program that searches the knowledge base for the best possible answer to a question; and a *user interface*, which allows the user to 'talk' to the system.

Experts often find it difficult to explain to a computer engineer exactly how they reach their decisions, and translating the mechanics of these decisions – which may rely heavily on experience and intuition – into the exact mathematical logic required by a computer is a complex task. In fact expert systems are of no use where intuition or common sense is necessary – they can only be used where the decision-making process follows a simple, well-defined logic path. But such systems are very valuable where experts are scarce, or as a means of preserving knowledge and transferring it to others as individuals retire or change jobs.

Neural computing

The most promising approach to the creation of artificial intelligence has used the structure of the brain as the basis for computer architecture. *neural networks* are connected microprocessors that mimic the complex network of interlinking neurones in the brain ($\triangleright$ p. 146). The idea of neural networks has been around since the 1940s, but only since the early 1980s has interest been rekindled. Neural networks offer big advantages over conventional computers in searching large databases for close matches, or storing and accessing data. They consist of a large number of processors (*nodes*) – the points at which the information is processed – linked by communication channels. Neural computers learn by example; they are not programmed like conventional computers, which means that they are not simply given a series of instructions to carry out. They use the concept of *feedback* – where part of the output of a node is returned as input for another process, for self-correction – and hence they can interact with their environment. However, they are still a long way from a thinking machine.

Robotics and vision

Another major branch of AI is robotics. While robots are used on the production lines of most car-manufacturing plants – for assembly and simple spot welding – they are very primitive. They inhabit a 'perfect' world, and have no sense of touch or vision to adapt to their environment, such as dealing with misplaced, faulty or missing components.

Three-dimensional vision is crucial to developing practical systems. A wide range of techniques is being developed for extracting the salient features of an image; this would allow a robot to recognize and pick up an object from the production line, for example, even if the object were not in its correct position.

Thinking machines?

The road to the thinking machine is proving longer and more difficult than the AI pioneers of the 1940s and 1950s believed. There is still much debate in the AI community about whether computers will ever be able to think, or to display the traits normally considered essential for intelligence. While the debate continues, research into AI is bringing a better understanding of brain function and our own intelligence, and an insight into such things as speech disorders and learning problems.

in rows and columns that allows you to see results of elaborate calculations, with answers changing each time a number is changed in the sheet.

Some varieties of graphics programs are designed to create line drawings of the type that once required a drawing board and a set of rulers; these are known as *CAD* (*computer-aided design*) programs. Others are aimed more at illustration, allowing the drawing of free-hand shapes and colouring.

More recent developments include: *route-finding programs*, allowing you to find a suitable road route between any two towns; *planning programs* for organization of projects; and educational programs that combine sound, words and visual displays (*multimedia*).

Construction

Construction is the most ancient of human activities. Buildings provide shelter, not only in the form of dwellings, but also for other human activities in the form of schools, offices, factories, and so on.

Construction is also concerned with altering the natural environment for the benefit of humans. This is the province of *civil engineering*, which includes the building of roads, bridges, dams, canals, tunnels, harbours and airports.

Parts of a building

The part of a building above ground level is called the *superstructure*; the part falling below ground level is referred to as the *substructure*. The stability of a building depends on its load-bearing components. There are three kinds of load: *dead*, resulting from the weight of the building itself; *live*, the result of furnishing, equipment and bodies; *lateral*, the result of sideways pressure, typically due to wind.

In a typical house, the load is borne principally by load-bearing walls. Internal dividing walls or partitions may or may not carry loads. Larger buildings may also use columns, arches and domes to support loads. The load-bearing substructure is known as the *foundations*, or *footings*, and for a house this is usually concrete supports for the load-bearing walls. Where the ground is soft, raft foundations may be used,

which distribute the load evenly over the area occupied by the building. For larger buildings, piles may be driven through the ground to connect the substructure with ground of sufficient strength to support the building.

Early building techniques

The post-and-lintel technique, in which vertical posts support horizontal lintels, has a long history; its basic form is seen in the ancient stone circle at Stonehenge in England. The method has been used from antiquity for supporting roofs, the posts taking the form of pillars in Egyptian and Greek temples. It is suitable for timber as well as masonry construction.

A way of spanning larger openings is provided by the arch (developed by the Romans). The pointed arch, a feature of Gothic architecture, foreshadowed modern skeleton building in that loads were transferred to load-bearing ribs, buttresses, shafts and piers. This enabled walls to be pierced for large openings.

In most countries timber was the favoured material for dwellings. Where wood was plentiful, planks or split trunks could form walls, but elsewhere the spaces between the wooden frame were filled with wattle (intertwined sticks and twigs) covered in clay and, later, with brick or tile. By about 1600 – when good wood was already becoming scarce – most town houses in Europe were half-timbered, having a load-bearing oak frame filled in with various materials.

The large floor area needed by the factories of the 18th and 19th centuries was provided by timber or cast-iron pillars supporting beams and floors. The construction of London's Crystal Palace in 1851 encouraged the design of buildings with cast-iron

---

ROADS

The Romans were probably the first road-builders with fixed engineering standards. *Roman roads* were constructed with a deep stone surface for stability and load-bearing. They had straight alignments and therefore were often hilly. The Roman roads remained the main arteries of European transport for many centuries, and even today many roads follow the Roman routes. New roads were generally of inferior quality, and the achievements of Roman builders were largely unsurpassed until the resurgence of road-building in the 18th century.

The 18th-century engineers, with horse-drawn coaches in mind, preferred to curve their roads to avoid hills. The road surface was regarded as merely a face to absorb wear, the load-bearing strength being obtained from a properly prepared and well-drained foundation. The Scottish engineer John McAdam (1756–1836) typically used a surface layer of only 5 cm (2 in), composed of crushed stone compacted with a mixture of stone dust and water, and then rolled. McAdam's later roads were surfaced with a layer of *tarmacadam* (or *tarmac*) – hot tar on

which a layer of stone chips were laid. Roads of this kind were known as *flexible pavements*.

By the early 19th century men such as John McAdam and Thomas Telford (1757–1834) had created a British road network totalling some 200 000 km (125 000 mi). However, in the 20th century the ever-increasing use of motor vehicles threatened to break up roads built to 19th-century standards, so new techniques had to be developed. On routes with heavy traffic, flexible pavements were replaced by *rigid pavements*, in which the top layer was concrete, 15 to 30 cm (6 to 12 in) thick, laid on a prepared bed. Nowadays steel bars are laid within the concrete. This not only restrains shrinkage during setting but also reduces expansion in warm weather.

The demands of heavy traffic led to the concept of high-speed, long-distance roads with access or slip lanes spaced widely apart. Mussolini's autostradas and Hitler's autobahns were the predecessors of today's motorways.

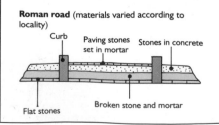

Roman road (materials varied according to locality)

Curb — Paving stones set in mortar — Stones in concrete — Flat stones — Broken stone and mortar

Flexible pavement

Bituminous surface (bitumen with sand or gravel) — Base course (sand, gravel or crushed stone, often mixed with cement or bitumen) — Subgrade — Sub-base course

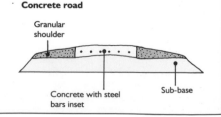

Concrete road

Granular shoulder — Concrete with steel bars inset — Sub-base

BRIDGES

The arrows indicate the forces exerted on or away from the foundations.

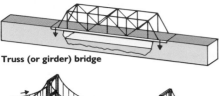

Truss (or girder) bridge

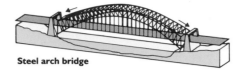

Steel arch bridge

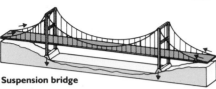

Suspension bridge

Cantilever bridge

SEE ALSO
● RAILWAYS p. 218
● ARCHITECTURE p. 326

The development of the *arched bridge* in Roman times marked the beginning of scientific bridge building. Absorbing the load by compression, arched bridges and viaducts are very strong. They were usually built of stone, but brick and timber were also used. In modern times, metal and concrete arched bridges have been constructed.

Steel, with its superior strength-to-weight ratio, soon replaced iron in metal bridgework. In the railway age the *truss* (or *girder*) *bridge* became popular. Built of wood or metal, the truss beam consists of upper and lower horizontal booms joined by vertical or inclined members. The truss thus formed is designed to resist the three forces of tension, compression and shear.

The *suspension bridge* has a deck supported by suspenders that drop from one or more overhead cables. It requires strong anchorage at each end to resist the inward tension of the cables, and the deck is strengthened to control distortion by

moving loads or high winds. Such bridges are nevertheless lightweight, and therefore the most suitable for very long spans.

Cantilever bridges exploit the potential of steel construction to produce a wide clearwater space. The spans have a central supporting pier and meet in mid-stream. The downward thrust where the spans meet is countered by firm anchorage of the spans at their other ends. Although the suspension bridge can span a wider gap, the cantilever offers better stability, which was important for 19th-century railway-builders.

In the 20th century, new forms of construction have been facilitated by the use of *prestressed concrete* – concrete surrounding tensioned steel cables that counter the stresses that occur under load. The *box girder* – a massive hollow box-shaped girder, which is both strong and light – has become a key component of concrete bridges.

frames, which in turn encouraged steel-framed multistorey buildings and led finally to the sky-scraper. The latter became possible with the introduction of steel-skeleton construction.

Modern building techniques

After World War II, skeleton-frame buildings became increasingly popular, especially for offices. Walls could be thin and light, thereby allowing the frames to support a greater weight of floor. Domestic dwellings saw fewer changes in the postwar years. Skeleton-frame construction, however, was used in the form of timber-framed housing, in which the timber members carried the loads and were covered by curtain walls on the outside, and by plasterboard or other finishing materials on the inside. In many countries pre-fabricated or industrialized building systems were introduced, in which the main components were made in factories for easy assembly on site.

In recent years building innovation has centred around the use of new materials and the potential for saving energy by means of refined insulation and ventilation techniques. The dome has also been resurrected as a means of covering the greatest area at the least cost. The stressed-skin dome, in which thin aluminium is stretched over a ribbed framework to form a combined curtain wall and roof, has been successful in specialized uses. Another trend is towards the development of tensile structures, in which the roof is supported by means of cables stretched from pylons. This frees the space beneath the roof from any supporting structure, thereby increasing the usable area.

CANALS AND DAMS

Canals and dams have a long history, although it was not until the invention of the mitre gate in the 16th century that extensive canal-building was undertaken. The *mitre gate*, formed by two leaves meeting at an angle and pointing upstream, greatly simplified the construction of locks, which are used where canals pass over rising ground. In the 19th century, inland waterways suffered from railway competition, but canals for ocean-going ships remained practicable, and the Suez Canal of 1869 and the Panama Canal of 1914 shortened key shipping routes.

The crescent (horizontally arched) dam, which first appeared in the Byzantine Empire in the 6th century AD, enabled a much greater weight of water to be held than was possible with earlier constructions. Concrete is now the preferred material for dam-construction, but earth, rock, stone and brick have been used.

The Thames Barrier at Woolwich, London, is the world's largest tidal barrier. (Zefa)

Ships

Over the last 50 years the design of commercial and naval ships has undergone radical changes both as a result of advances in technology and as a response to changing economic pressures and military threats. In all types of ship, automation has helped to reduce crew size and the cost of construction and operation.

Advances in technology have both posed threats and provided opportunities to commercial shipping. Since 1945 the main influences have been the growth in air travel, the huge increase in demands for energy, the need to transport large volumes of cargo around the world, and the increase in leisure time in the affluent West.

Passenger shipping

After World War II a few large liners such as the *Queen Elizabeth II* were built, but as the greater speed and convenience of air travel became apparent, liners were either scrapped or con-verted to cruise ships. However, on shorter sea crossings, car and passenger ferries have expanded their activities to cope with the growth of demand for holidays abroad. The *roll-on/roll-off* design – which facilitates fast boarding and unloading – is now common. This type of design can pose special stability problems should water get on to the vehicle deck. The *Herald of Free Enterprise* tragedy in 1987 highlighted this and has led to new safety standards.

Cargo shipping

The rapid growth in demand for energy has meant that large volumes of oil need to be shipped around the world. To keep the price per tonne (ton) of oil as low as possible, the size of tankers has grown dramatically. Several accidents involving large tankers have led to severe marine and coastal pollution. Design changes have been proposed to limit oil spillage but a risk remains. Liquefied Natural Gas (LNG) carriers have been developed to transport natural gas. In order to exploit gas and oil deposits in deep, exposed areas, such as the North Sea, stationary drilling ships have been developed.

Bulk carriage of grain and metal ores was influenced by the need to keep transport as cheap as possible, with minimum manpower and minimum time in port. Bulk carriers therefore grew in the same way as tankers, and like them had machinery and accommodation aft with holds or tanks forward. Some large ships are designed to be able to take different cargoes (say oil or ore) on different occasions. Load distribution is then important to ensure that the strength limits of the hull are not exceeded. Other cargoes carried in bulk bring their own problems. For instance, the bulk movement of cars has been facilitated by the use of roll-on/roll-off ships (▷ see above).

For general cargoes, there is the same need to reduce loading and unloading time to maximize the use of the ships. This led to the development of *container ships*, which carry a large number of 'standard' containers stacked in special holds. Special facilities are needed at the docks to load and unload, this being more economical than providing such facilities on each ship. The ship in this case is only one element in an integrated transport system. Containers can be loaded at the factory or source point and then carried by road and/or rail to the docks. Large ships, usually around 60 000 tonnes (tons), carry the containers between major ports, where they are transferred to road, rail or smaller vessels for transfer to smaller ports or their final destination.

Warships

With developments in materials, electronics and computers, the growing complexity of the threats posed to warships has been matched by the sophisticated means used to combat them. One example is the threat posed by *influence mines*, which are triggered by the magnetic, acoustic and/or pressure 'signature' of the target. The result of the development of mines and homing weapons (such as missiles and torpedoes, which use similar sensor devices) is that great emphasis has been placed on reducing ship signatures and thus their susceptibility to attack. The radar reflection of modern warships is reduced by using special materials, and attention is paid to shaping and minimizing the above-water profile. The magnetic signature of a ship can be significantly

---

SPECIAL SHIPS

A number of special ship types have evolved to meet new demands or to utilize some advance in technology. *Twin hulls* provide a large deck area together with great stability. This is useful for helicopter operation, for towing a variety of hydrographic equipment, or as a base for operating small submersibles. When a large part of the hull is kept well below the sea surface, the ship is known as a *semi-submersible*. Such vessels are much less affected by waves than conventional hulls and are therefore suitable for oil exploration. The *hydrofoil* uses fins to create sufficient hydrodynamic lift to raise the hull clear of the water. Hydrofoils are suitable for small high-speed ferries, as they provide a comfortable ride in moderate sea conditions. The *hovercraft* is also used for ferries. The hull is carried on an air cushion, and in some variants there are no elements of the ship in the water. Such craft can run over flat areas of land such as mudbanks and beaches as easily as they can over water. In other variants the craft has sidewalls that remain partly submerged and an underwater propulsor. These are not amphibious.

The LNG carrier *Khannar*. LNG (liquefied natural gas) carriers have special insulated tanks in which the gas is carried under pressure and at low temperature (−100 °C / −148 °F). (BP)

SEE ALSO

- ENGINES p. 192
- WEAPONRY p. 224
- ANCIENT GREECE p. 230
- THE INVASIONS p. 242
- THE AGRICULTURAL AND INDUSTRIAL REVOLUTIONS p. 258
- WORLD WAR I p. 268
- WORLD WAR II p. 274

reduced by *degaussing*, a process in which an opposing magnetic field (▷ p. 26) is produced. The acoustic signature can be reduced by specially designed propulsion units and by isolating noise sources within the ship. The susceptibility to infrared detection can be decreased by reducing hot spots in the ship. Ships must be robust enough to withstand some damage and still remain effective. Vulnerability is reduced by using protective plating against splinters, duplication of important systems, and subdivision of the ship. The hulls of vessels designed to hunt out mines are made of glass-reinforced plastic to ensure that their magnetic signature is minimized.

A modern battle fleet has a 'layered' defence. Aircraft carriers can deploy early-warning aircraft and intercept enemy aircraft at a distance with their fighters. Carriers, destroyers and frigates can deploy helicopters to combat submarines at a distance. Long-range missile systems

that can defend a given area of sea provide the next layer of defence. The inner ring is a self-defence capability provided by close-range weapons. Small specialized ships allow modern fleets to combine with land forces in amphibious operations. The need to support large fleets at great distances from base led to the 'fleet train', comprising tankers, and supply and repair ships.

A five-masted schooner in full sail, photographed in 1906. By the end of the 19th century, as steam engines became more reliable, sails were finally dispensed with, although a few sailing ships remained afloat. (AKG)

THE DEVELOPMENT OF SHIPS

THE ANCIENT WORLD
The Egyptians, Phoenicians and Greeks in the Mediterranean, and the Chinese in the East, built large fleets for trade, exploration and war. The differing needs of commerce and warfare created two distinct types of ship – warships with long, narrow hulls (usually oar-powered), designed with speed and manoeuvrability in mind, and shorter, broader, sail-powered trading vessels with carrying capacity as the major consideration. The oared fighting ship, or *galley*, with its lateen-rigged (i.e. triangular) sail was supreme in the Mediterranean. Some had a single bank of oars but others two or three (these were known as *biremes* and *triremes* respectively).

THE MIDDLE AGES
The Viking *longship* appeared sometime in the 7th or 8th centuries AD. Its bow and stern were formed nearly at right angles to the keel, and the hull planking tapered to form distinct stem- and sternposts. Although relying upon oars for fighting, the longship had a much larger and efficient sail than the galley, the longer keel and pointed ends providing a more stable and efficient sailing form. Faster and more seaworthy than the Mediterranean galley, the longship enabled the Vikings to sail as far as North America. The rise of the north German Hanseatic (trading) League in the 14th century led to the development of the *Hansa cog*, a broad, sturdy vessel, with a square sail on a single mast, built-up 'castles' at the stem and stern, and a good cargo-carrying capacity.

Early ships were manoeuvred by means of a steering oar or paddle on the quarter (i.e. the side near the stern). Between 1200 and 1500 the gradual replacement of the steering oar by the wooden *rudder* brought about a great improvement in ship-handling. Warships grew much bigger – up to 1000 tonnes (tons) or more – during the 15th century. Guns were used at sea in English ships from about 1340 and gunports were provided in French and Spanish ships before 1500.

THE AGE OF SAIL
As ships grew larger the single mast gave way to two, three or even four masts. These features were incorporated in the Mediterranean *carrack*, which became the standard large ship in the 15th and 16th centuries. A smaller version of the carrack, the *caravel*, was used along with the carrack by the Spanish and Portuguese to make their epic voyages of discovery (▷ p. 247). The caravel was easy to handle and large enough for ocean voyages, yet small enough to be rowed if there was no wind. In northern Europe the cog was expanded, while Spain and Portugal continued to develop the carrack. By the time England faced the Spanish Armada in 1588, *galleons* – sailing ships with three or more masts, lateen-rigged on the after masts, square-rigged on the main- and foremasts – were the new model of fighting ship on both sides.

In the 17th and 18th centuries, the warship developed into a vessel of considerable strength, with massive double-planked sides. Under the rating system that evolved, only 1st to 3rd rates, mounting at least 64 heavy cannon, were designated as *ships of the line*, which fought sea battles. Smaller ships, the 4th, 5th (*frigates*) and 6th (*sloops*) rates, were for 'cruising' or independent operations. Merchantmen were built on broadly similar lines, but speed was not crucial. Small merchant vessels adopted improvements to rigging to save manpower. Only the 19th-century *clipper* used a finer form, sacrificing cargo space to speed in order to dominate trade in perishable commodities such as tea, but their huge spread of canvas required large crews.

STEAM AND IRON
The invention of an efficient steam engine towards the end of the 18th century made major improvements possible. The first practical and commercially successful steamer was the *Charlotte Dundas*, launched in Scotland in 1802. By 1816 there was a steamer service running across the English Channel and in 1821 the Royal Navy ordered its first class of paddle steamers for auxiliary missions, such as towing ships of the line. Not being dependent on the wind, steam tugs made movement in restricted areas easier and safer. Steam also meant that time schedules could be maintained. In 1838 the *Sirius* and the *Great Western*, the latter designed by the English engineer Isambard Kingdom Brunel (1806–59), crossed the Atlantic, proving that steam power on its own was also suitable for long voyages.

The introduction of steam put excessive weight into wooden hulls that were already reaching their maximum size, with warships approaching 7000 tonnes (tons). The first iron steamer operated successfully from 1820, but navies were reluctant to build large warships with iron hulls and paddle engines. The iron hull was found to affect the compass on long voyages, and solid shot could fracture on impact with wrought iron. The paddle wheel was inefficient, restricted armament and was vulnerable to enemy shot. These drawbacks were overcome by the invention in 1836 of the screw propeller, by the Swedish-American John Ericcson and by the Englishman Francis Pettit-Smith. In 1840 the Royal Navy ordered its first screw steamer (HMS *Rattler*), and Brunel redesigned the SS *Great Britain* for screw propulsion. The Royal Navy converted sailing ships of the line to steam.

Iron for large warships did not find favour until the Crimean War (1853–6), when the threat from explosive shells forced the development of armour-plated 'floating batteries'. Line-of-battle ships acquired armour, and heavily armoured ships, known as *ironclads*, became the focus of ship technology. Until the end of the 19th century, the use of heavier and heavier armour-plating was matched by the ever-increasing power of naval guns, some in turret mountings. As steam engines became more reliable, auxiliary sailing rig became redundant, and by 1900 sail-and-steam ships were a thing of the past. Cheap steel replaced wrought iron.

20th-CENTURY DEVELOPMENTS
By 1900, liners were plying a regular transatlantic trade. The demand for higher speeds forced engineers to look for alternative to the reciprocating steam engine. The Parsons steam turbine offered reduced vibration at maximum power, and after experiments in destroyers, the Royal Navy adopted steam turbines for the revolutionary battleship *Dreadnought* (1905), the first all-large-gun fast battleship. Prior to World War I the major naval powers embarked upon building large fleets of similar vessels.

Advances in technology brought the submarine from a virtual toy to become a major factor in both World Wars. Aircraft carriers, designed to carry and operate aircraft, started as primitive auxiliary vessels in World War I, but by the 1940s they had displaced the battleship. Between 1900 and 1939 transatlantic liners increased in size, speed and standards of comfort culminating in the *Queen Mary* and *Queen Elizabeth*. Oil tankers grew in size and number as the demand for oil increased. The diesel engine was widely adopted as a cheap propulsion unit, initially for merchant ships and minor naval craft. Steam turbines were largely phased out, and nuclear power was also used for some warships – the first nuclear-powered warship was the submarine *USS Nautilus*, launched in 1954.

Railways

The ancient Babylonians and Greeks laid short lines of grooved stones, while in medieval Europe horse-drawn wagons running on wooden planks were occasionally used in mining. But railways as we know them resulted from the combination of two elements – mechanical traction, provided by the steam engine (▷ p. 192), and the flanged metal wheel running on metal rails.

SEE ALSO

● ENGINES p. 192
● INDUSTRIAL REVOLUTION p. 258

In 1812, steam locomotives began regular service in England on the industrial Middleton Railway near Leeds, and in 1814 the English engineer George Stephenson introduced his first steam locomotive at the Killingworth Colliery, near Newcastle-upon-Tyne. Stephenson went on to complete the Stockton & Darlington Railway, the first public steam line, in 1825. In 1830 the first intercity railway, the Liverpool & Manchester, was opened, and in the same year the initial length of the first US public steam line, the Baltimore & Ohio Railroad, was completed.

Many continental European countries built their first railways in the 1830s, often using Stephenson locomotives. Canada built a line in the same decade, but more distant parts of the British Empire waited longer. In Europe and North America the great period of railway building was the second half of the 19th century. However, competition from road transport has since caused many lines in developed countries to close, but elsewhere in the world new railways are still being built.

Technical progress

Nineteenth-century innovations included automatic train brakes controlled from the locomotive and, in passenger service, corridor trains with toilet and dining facilities, steam heating, and electric lighting. Luxury trains, including sleeping cars with a high degree of personal service, have been successfully operated, mainly by the Pullman company in the USA and Wagons-Lits in Europe.

In the 20th century, the steam locomotive was gradually replaced by electric and diesel traction. Electrification enabled trains to run more cheaply, more cleanly, and in practice more often, while the greater power of electric locomotives allowed heavier trains and higher speeds. Diesel traction was particularly advantageous on lines where traffic was not heavy enough to justify the cost of electrification.

To keep up with the image created by aircraft and racing cars, railways introduced streamlined trains – or 'streamliners' – in the 1930s, with trains such as the *Silver Jubilee* in England averaging 112 km/h (70 mph) or more. In the USA many of the streamliners were diesel-powered.

In some countries, including Britain but not the USA, freight traffic has diminished since the 1920s. Freight trains tended to become faster and more specialized. 'Piggyback' (road trailers carried on flatcars) and removable containers were widely used from the 1950s to combine the long-haul advantage of the train with the door-to-door advantage of the motor vehicle.

In 1964, high-speed trains, running on special track, appeared in Japan. The French TGV service between Paris and Lyon began in 1981, and has running speeds of up to 270 km/h (168 mph), although during trials in 1990 the TGV reached speeds of 515 km/h (320 mph). In Britain the 200 km/h (125 mph) High-Speed Train (HST) differs from the Japanese and French examples in that it has models that use diesel as well as electric, and runs on existing track. Maglev (magnetic levitation) trains, which dispense with the steel rail and flanged wheel, became technically feasible in the 1970s, but seem unlikely (at least in the short term) to prove economic except for specialized short-haul transit.

Gauge

The *gauge* of a railway track – the distance between the two rails – is partly a matter of convention but can also be varied to suit particular purposes. The gauge used by Stephenson – 1435 mm (4 ft 8½ in) – became known as *standard gauge*, and has been used for more than half of the railway track ever laid. The advantage of narrow gauge is that it is cheaper to build, especially in hilly terrain, and allows the use of smaller and lighter rolling stock, which is cheaper to operate. Broad gauge, on the other hand, is suitable for larger rolling stock and generally allows higher running speeds, because of greater lateral stability. Sometimes, to accommodate trains of different gauges, a third rail is laid to create *mixed gauge*.

The impact of railways

Railways revolutionized economic and social life. They enabled industries to be located far from their fuel sources and to enjoy nationwide markets for their products. The cheap mass movement of people and commodities that was now possible caught the popular imagination and encouraged new enterprise, thus changing static agrarian communities and nations into dynamic industrialized societies.

A Japanese bullet train. The Shinkansen high-speed line from Tokyo runs to all the major destinations on Honshu and even Kyushu. The fastest trains, called Hikari ('Light'), are able to make the 1069 km (664 mi) trip from Tokyo to Hakata in just under seven hours, travelling at a maximum speed of 257 km/h (160 mph). (Zefa)

Cars

In 1885 the German inventor Karl Benz (1844–1929) announced his Motorwagen, a single-cylinder, petrol-engined tricycle. The immediate impact of this invention was not great, but its significance cannot be overestimated. Within 10 years, many manufacturers had appeared; the first motor race – Paris–Bordeaux–Paris in 1895 – had been run; and the rich were buying cars as status symbols and as a means of transportation.

After 1900, the development of the car gathered pace. Within 10 years, the 'horseless carriage' had replaced the horse as the preferred form of transport – at least for those who could afford it. The awkward tiller steering with which the first cars were equipped was abandoned in favour of the steering wheel, which was easier to operate. Engines grew in size, and the speed of the fastest cars was well in excess of what any team of horses could muster. Even those who had dismissed the car as a passing craze began to realize that the day of horse-drawn vehicles was over.

A major landmark in the history of the car came in 1906, when Rolls-Royce produced the 'Silver Ghost'. A seven-litre, six-cylinder luxury tourer, it was capable of travelling practically unlimited distances with complete reliability, often at speeds of over 100 km/h (62.5 mph). It also offered unrivalled comfort, looks and quietness.

Mass production

At first, the car was the toy of the rich, far beyond the reach of the less affluent. In 1908, this situation was dramatically changed by the American industrialist Henry Ford (1863–1947), with the introduction of mass production. Instead of individually hand-crafting each car, he designed a car – the famous Model T Ford – that could be made on a production line with standardized parts. Available only in a single colour (black),

each car came off the line in around 90 minutes. Over 15 million Model Ts were made in its 19-year career, many being sold for as little as $250. By 1920, every major manufacturing country had begun to produce cars for general transport, rather than for the use of a privileged minority.

The age of innovation

Many of the features that make modern cars comfortable and safe were developed in the years between 1908 and 1939. Independent front suspension, which no modern family car would be without, was first introduced in a practical form on the 1922 Lancia Lambda, although it was not common practice to fit such systems until after 1945. Supercharging was pioneered in the 1920s by Mercedes, who also put the first diesel-engined production car (the Mercedes-Benz 260D) on the road in 1936. The French company Citroën produced the first successful front-wheel-drive car in 1934, when it launched the Traction Avant. The majority of cars now use their front wheels to transmit power to the ground. The only real advance during World War II was the further development of four-wheel drive in the form of the Jeep, which – thanks to its power being driven through all four wheels – could traverse terrain that would be unpassable in a normal car. After the war, manufacturers found themselves making 10-year-old designs; it was only as the 1950s approached that innovation began to return.

Modern cars

In 1959, Austin Morris launched the Mini Minor, which has profoundly influenced all subsequent small-car design. By mounting the engine *across* the chassis, its Greek-born designer, Sir Alexander Issigonis (1906–88), created a small car with more interior space than many large saloons of the day. The Mini also used the then relatively unusual technology of front-wheel drive, which obviated the need for a bulky transmission tunnel. Today virtually all small cars use this layout. Cars have now evolved to the extent that most can reach speeds in excess of 160 km/h (100 mph) and achieve over 50 km (31 mi) per gallon. Standards of reliability have also improved dramatically, so that cars generally give thousands of kilometres of trouble-free motoring – and all for a fraction of what it would have cost (in real terms) to buy an equivalent car in the 1920s. At the upper end of the market, many cars are turbocharged, fuel-injected, have four-wheel drive and are capable of around 240 km/h (150 mph).

In recent years Japanese cars have made the greatest technical progress, and the Far East is now the world-leader in engine design. US manufacturers have had trouble shedding their reputation for producing 'gas-guzzlers', but are now designing economy-conscious cars with more international appeal. Europe, the traditional breeding ground of car innovation and design, will have to change direction as the car evolves further. The move is now towards cars that give out less toxic waste and do less damage to the environment. This has led in many countries to legislation enforcing the use on cars of *catalytic converters*, which detoxify many of the harmful substances in the exhaust gases. Concern about the burning of fossil fuels and the consequent environmental damage is sure to continue, and it seems clear that the car will have to change radically in the coming decades if it is to survive.

The first motorcar patented by Karl Benz (⊳ main text). With a horizontal, water-cooled single-cylinder engine, Benz's petrol-engined tricycle was capable of speeds up to 15 km/h (10 mph) (AKG)

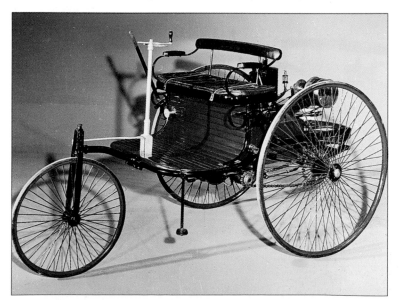

SEE ALSO

● ENGINES p. 192
● OIL AND GAS p. 194

How cars work

The engine (▷ pp. 192 and 221) is the power unit of a car, providing the motion that is ultimately transmitted to the driven wheels. However, a series of interconnected mechanisms, including the clutch, the gearbox and the differential, is required to transmit the power of the engine to the wheels in a usable form. At the same time, a number of subsidiary systems, including steering and brakes, are necessary in order to give adequate control over the movement of the car. Most cars today are fitted with an overhead-valve, four-stroke, petrol engine, with four or six cylinders (▷ p. 221). Although the main function of the engine is to spin the flywheel (the first link in the chain by which the engine's power is transmitted to the wheels), the rotary motion of the crankshaft is also used to turn the *alternator*, which generates the current needed by the car's electrical systems. At the same time, the rotation of the camshaft, again dependent on the crankshaft, drives both the oil pump and the distributor.

The ignition system

The purpose of the ignition system (▷ p. 221) is to produce a spark of sufficient strength to ignite the petrol–air mixture at the exact moment when each piston in turn is nearly at the top of the compression stroke (▷ p. 192). The spark is produced as an electric current jumps (arcs) between the two electrodes of a spark plug; however, the voltage supplied by the battery is insufficient for this purpose. The voltage from the battery is first boosted by the *coil* to around 15 000 volts before passing to the *distributor*, in which a spinning rotor (driven by the camshaft) directs the current to each spark plug in turn.

The fuel system

For efficient and economical combustion within the engine, the precise proportions of petrol and air in the fuel mixture entering the cylinders must be carefully regulated. This is generally achieved by a *carburettor*. Although different types of carburettor exist, nearly all are in the form of a tube into which air is drawn by the downward movement of the pistons on their successive induction strokes (▷ p. 192). As the air accelerates through the narrowed middle section of the carburettor, its pressure falls, so causing a jet of fuel to be drawn through a nozzle from a reservoir, which is itself fed by a pump from the petrol tank. Within the carburettor, on the engine-side of the fuel jet, a circular flap (known as a butterfly valve) is actuated by the accelerator pedal in such a way as to control the volume of air–fuel mixture drawn into the engine, thus regulating engine speed. In most designs, a similar valve (the *choke*) on the air-intake side of the fuel jet regulates the amount of air entering the carburettor and thus the richness of the fuel mix.

Increasingly, direct *fuel injection* is being used in place of the carburettor. This is more efficient and economical than the carburettor, since accurately metered and appropriate amounts of fuel can be delivered to each cylinder's combustion chamber. There are several systems – both mechanical and electrical – but the basic principle is that fuel is injected at high pressure into the combustion chamber from a point behind the inlet valve.

Transmission

The term 'transmission' embraces all the components that are responsible for transferring the engine's power from the flywheel to the driven wheels. The spinning motion of the flywheel is transmitted to the *gearbox* via the *clutch* (▷ p. 221). When the clutch pedal is depressed, the spinning flywheel is disconnected from the shaft transmitting power to the gearbox, so allowing the car to move off gently and smooth gear-changes to be made.

A gearbox is necessary because – unlike (say) an electric motor – most internal-combustion engines develop their full power and torque (turning effort) within a relatively narrow band of engine speeds (usually between 3000 and 5000 revolutions per minute). By means of the gearbox (and partly by the differential; ▷ below), the engine speed is kept within these limits while allowing the car to operate at widely varying speeds and in a wide range of driving conditions. For example, a steep hill requires a low gear, because it is only at high engine speeds that the engine is able to deliver enough torque to keep the wheels turning. On the other hand, where little torque is required, as when travelling at speed on a level road, a high gear may be used, thus matching high road speed with (relatively) low engine speed. In this way engine life is prolonged, passenger comfort enhanced, and fuel consumption kept to a minimum.

After passing through the gearbox-and-clutch assembly, the drive is transferred to the *differential*. In front-wheel-drive cars, transmission from gearbox to differential is direct; in rear-wheel-drive cars, if the engine is mounted at the front of the car, the differential is driven by a crown wheel and pinion at the end of a propeller shaft.

The rotation rate of the shaft from the gearbox is further stepped down by the differential (normally to about a quarter of the gearbox speed). However, the differential's distinctive function is to allow power to be divided between the driven wheels in whatever proportion is required. Such a mechanism is necessary when cornering, because the outside driven wheel needs to be turned more rapidly than the inside wheel.

PERFORMANCE AND POWER

The *performance* of a car is normally assessed on the basis of its top speed and its acceleration – how fast it can go and how long it takes to reach a given speed. The *power* of a car's engine may be expressed in several ways. The power (as a physical quantity – the rate at which mechanical work is done) may be expressed in brake horsepower or kilowatts (1 bhp being equivalent to 0.746 kW). The power and the performance of a car are sometimes confused, but one is not always a reliable guide to the other. Even with a seemingly advantageous power-to-mass ratio, the performance of a vehicle is largely dependent on how effectively its power is developed and then delivered to the wheels.

Basically, the efficiency of an engine depends on the mass of fuel–oxygen mixture that can be pumped through it and effectively combusted in a given period of time. This factor is known as the *volumetric efficiency*. To this end a number of systems have been developed to increase the power output of engines without increasing their size. For example, *supercharging* and *turbocharging* both force the fuel–air mixture into the combustion chamber at high pressure. Multi-valve cylinder heads have also been developed to improve the volumetric efficiency or 'breathing' of an engine.

Engine. Four pistons fit tightly in four cylinders bored into the cylinder block. Each piston is driven downwards in a fixed sequence on the power stroke of the four-stroke cycle. A *connecting rod* from each cylinder is attached to a cranked (dog-legged) shaft (the *crankshaft*), which is turned a half-revolution by each successive power stroke. To one end of the crankshaft is bolted a heavy disc called the *flywheel*, which provides the drive to the gearbox via the clutch; at the other end, a belt-and-pulley system causes the *camshaft* to rotate at half the speed of the crankshaft. Pear-shaped lobes (*cams*) along the length of the camshaft act on a series of rocker mechanisms that cause the inlet and exhaust valves on each cylinder to open and close in exact timing with the four strokes of the piston.

Air cleaner
Carburettor
Valve spring and inlet valve
Camshaft
Exhaust valve
Spark plug
Timing belt (camshaft drive)
Water pump
Crankshaft pulley
Exhaust gases
Alternator
Oil sump
Piston
Crankshaft
Flywheel
Connecting rod
Exhaust mainfold
Thermostat housing
Distributor
Cam
Valve rocker

Rack-and-pinion steering is a simple and effective system used in many cars. A toothed pinion at the base of the steering column acts on a toothed rack, moving it to left or right and thus converting the rotary motion of the steering wheel into linear motion. At each end of the rack, track rods act on pivoted steering arms, so altering the angle of the front wheels.

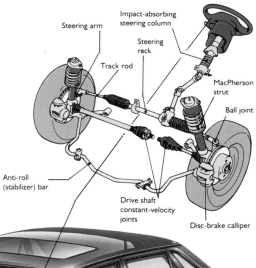

Steering arm
Impact-absorbing steering column
Steering rack
Track rod
MacPherson strut
Ball joint
Anti-roll (stabilizer) bar
Drive shaft constant-velocity joints
Disc-brake calliper

MacPherson strut
Coil spring
Shock absorber
Suspension lower arm pivot

Brake drum
Fluid in
Wheel cylinder (piston housing)
Brake shoe
Handbrake cable
Pivot plate

Suspension. The *MacPherson strut* is a very common suspension arrangement, consisting of a spring mounted on an arm that runs from the wheel to a secure place on the bodyframe. The arm moves up and down with road irregularities, so compressing the spring and absorbing bumps.

To counteract the compressed spring's tendency to rebound, a *shock absorber* is fitted (within the spring, in the case of the MacPherson strut). This is essentially a fluid-filled piston-and-cylinder assembly. The piston moves in and out to the same extent as the spring, so forcing the thick fluid back and forth through channels in the piston and thus deadening the bounce of the spring.

1st gear
Clutch housing
Reverse gear
Final-drive gear
Gear-change rod
Constant-velocity joint
Clutch release lever
Engine flywheel
Clutch assembly
Starter-motor pinion housing
Clutch release bearing
Reverse-gear idler
Selector forks
2nd gear
3rd gear
4th gear
5th gear
Output shaft
Input shaft

Disc
Hub carrier
Outer-drive shaft joint
Fluid in
Piston
Brake calliper
Brake pads

Brakes. A *drum brake* (fitted here to rear) consists of a drum, which is attached to the hub and therefore rotates at wheel speed. Within the drum are two shoes covered in a friction lining, which are attached to the axle and do not rotate. Depression of the brake pedal operates a hydraulic system that actuates a piston, which forces the shoes outwards and thus against the inner surface of the drum.

A *disc brake* (fitted here to front) consists of a steel disc, which is attached to the wheel and rotates at wheel speed. A hydraulic system operated by the brake pedal actuates a piston housed in a stationary calliper that straddles the disc, causing two brake pads to be forced onto each side of the disc. As with the drum brake, the resulting friction causes the car to slow down.

Clutch-and-gearbox assembly. The clutch consists of the flywheel (driven round by the crankshaft), a clutch (or friction) plate and a pressure plate. When the clutch is engaged (i.e. with the pedal released), powerful springs force the clutch plate against the flywheel, thereby linking the flywheel to the shaft transmitting power to the gearbox. When the clutch is disengaged, levers work against the springs to separate the clutch plate from the flywheel, so disconnecting the transmission. The friction linings on the clutch plate allow the plate to slip before becoming fully engaged, so preventing a shuddering jerk on starting.

The gearbox allows optimum (i.e. high) engine speed to be matched to a wide variety of driving conditions. By means of selector forks actuated by the gearstick, different-sized gears linked to the input shaft can be engaged with different-sized gears on the shaft transmitting power to the differential. A (relatively) small gear on the input shaft engaged with a large gear on the transmission shaft produces low speed but high power; high speed and low power are achieved by reversing the gear ratios on the input and output shafts. In top gear, no gears are engaged and transmission passes directly through the gearbox to the differential.

Aircraft

The term 'aircraft' includes every man-made device that flies in the atmosphere. Aircraft today are divided into two groups, aerostats and aerodynes. *Aerostats* are naturally buoyant, that is lighter than air. Those without power are called balloons (gas-filled or hot-air), while those with propulsion and some means of steering are called airships or dirigibles. The second and most important aircraft group, however, are the *aerodynes*, which are heavier than air, and obtain their lift in a variety of ways: by jet thrust; by means of rotating blades; or by means of fixed wings, with a separate propulsion system to make the wings move through the air.

Before the invention of the first aerodyne aircraft by the Wright brothers in 1903 (▷ box), the only method of sustained ascending flight was by balloons and dirigibles (airships). However, the heyday of airships was shortlived, eclipsed by the invention of the aeroplane. The technological advances of aeroplanes over the century have made an immense difference to long-distance travel, trade and warfare.

The principle of flight

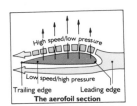

High speed/low pressure

Low speed/high pressure

Trailing edge   Leading edge

The aerofoil section

When the *weight* of an aircraft (due to the force of gravity) is exceeded by the *lift* (the upward force created by the wings or by hot air or lighter-than-air gases), the aircraft will rise in the air. In the case of aeroplanes and gliders, lift is produced as a result of the characteristic profile – the *aerofoil section* – of the wing. The wing is rounded and thicker at the front (the *leading edge*), and tapers away to a sharp edge at the back (the *trailing edge*).

Lift is created as the wings move through the air at speed and relies on the fact that air pressure drops as air speed increases. As air passes over the wing, it has to move further, and thus faster, over the more curved upper surface than the lower surface. This causes a considerable reduction in pressure above the wing, especially at the front, where the wing is thickest and the upper surface most sharply curved. Lift can be increased both by increasing the speed of airflow over the wing and by increasing the curvature of the upper wing surface.

Any aircraft with propulsion also experiences *thrust* – the resultant force pulling or pushing it through the air; and *drag* – the equal and opposite force caused by the resistance of the air to the frontal surfaces of the aircraft. Drag is effectively wasted energy, so the aim of aircraft designers is to reduce drag without sacrificing lift.

Gliders, lacking an independent source of propulsion, have to fly downhill from the moment they are cast off after take-off. The pilot thus seeks columns of rising warmer air, called *thermals*. Modern gliders are so efficient that they have climbed to nearly 15 000 m (49 200 ft) and flown 1460 km (907 mi).

Aircraft stability

In the absence of other forces, an aircraft's centre of gravity would have to be at the same point as

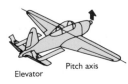

Pitch axis

Elevator

Rudder

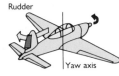

Yaw axis

Roll axis

Aileron

To control an aircraft, the pilot must direct the plane's movement on three axes. In conventional aircraft, changes of altitude are achieved by moving the nose up or down (on the *pitch axis* by means of elevators. Directional control (on the *yaw* axis) is provided by the *rudder*, while lateral control on the *roll* axis) is effected by trailing-edge flaps called *ailerons*.

its centre of lift for the craft to remain in equilibrium. In practice, however, because of thrust and drag, nearly all aeroplanes are designed to be naturally stable in the longitudinal plane, but with the centre of gravity ahead of the centre of lift. This causes a downward movement of the nose, which is counteracted by a constant download on the horizontal tail. Any disturbance tending to tilt the aircraft nose-up or nose-down is countered automatically by the change in the angle of the wings and of the horizontal tail.

Aircraft controls

Aeroplanes and gliders are controlled in the longitudinal (*pitch*) axis by *elevators* on the tailplane, or by having a fully powered pivoted tailplane. A few modern designs have a foreplane instead of a tailplane, and a very few have both. Directional control is provided by a vertical *rudder*, which is usually located on the tailplane as well. The rudder is also an important control surface if a multi-engined aircraft should suffer failure of an engine mounted far out on a wing.

Lateral (*roll*) control was formerly provided only by *ailerons* – pivoted portions of the trailing edge near the tips of the wings – but today roll control can be effected by asymmetric use of the tailplanes or by asymmetric deflection of *spoilers*. The spoilers are door-like surfaces hinged along the top of the wing. Differentially they control roll, and symmetrically they serve as airbrakes by increasing drag. Spoilers can also be used in *direct lift control* to enable the aircraft trajectory to be varied up or down without changing the attitude of the fuselage. On landing, spoilers act as 'lift dumpers', instantly killing wing lift and thus increasing the weight on the wheels and the effectiveness of the brakes.

All early aircraft used cables in tension or push/pull pivoted rods to convey pilot commands to the control surfaces. From about 1950 powered controls were widely introduced, in which the surfaces were moved by hydraulic actuators, the pilot's controls being provided with some form of artificial 'feel' so that he could sense what was happening. By 1970 *fly by wire* was rapidly becoming common, in which the pilot's controls send out small electrical signals, which are carried through multiple wires to the surface power units. Today *fly by light* is being introduced: pilot signals are conveyed as variable light output along optical fibres (▷ p. 25), thus offering colossal bandwidth and data-handling capacity.

The high-lift system

An aircraft has to work hardest during take-off and landing, when airspeed is at its lowest and yet maximum lift is required. To facilitate these manoeuvres, most aircraft have a *high-lift system*, brought into action for the approach and landing, and usually also for take-off.

Along the leading edge of the wing there may be *slats*, slender portions of the wing moved out and away on parallel arms, or alternatively *Krüger flaps*, which swing down and around from underneath the leading edge. These full-span devices greatly increase the available lift, especially from a thin wing suitable for fast jets.

Along the trailing edge are fitted *flaps*. These again come in many forms, but all swing back and down from the wing. When selected to a take-off setting, such as 15°, they increase lift and slightly increase drag; when fully down, at the landing setting of perhaps 40°, they increase lift even more but also greatly increase drag.

Aircraft propulsion

Until 1939 virtually all aeroplanes were powered by piston engines driving a *propeller*, which provides thrust by accelerating air through aerodynamic rotating blades. Almost all modern propellers are of the variable-pitch type – the angle at which the blades attack the air can be altered. The blades are set to fine pitch for take-off to match high engine speed with low aircraft speed, and then automatically adjusted to coarse pitch for cruising flight, to match economical low engine speed to high forward speed. After landing, some propellers can be set to reverse pitch to help brake the aircraft.

During World War II, engines grew rapidly in power. The Spitfire Mk I, for example, had a two-blade propeller, while the Mk XIV had five blades, in order to absorb the increased power within the limited available propeller diameter. Today some turboprop airliners (⇨ p. 193) have six-blade propellers, turning at relatively low speed for minimum noise. During and after World War II, the propeller eventually gave way to the turbojet for most purposes. The turbojet itself was largely eclipsed by the turbofan, which offers better fuel economy and reduced noise levels (⇨ p. 193).

Helicopters and autogyros

A helicopter is lifted by a *rotor* (sometimes two rotors), which is constructed of between two and eight slender blades, which effectively act as rotating wings. Lift is created as the rotor is driven round under power, forcing the air obliquely downwards. Because the rotor can create lift even when the aircraft itself is station-

The B-2 stealth bomber. The shape and the materials used to make the B-2 have made it almost undetectable to hostile radars and other sensors. The low, flat shape was designed to reflect radar energy in directions other than back to the radar, and the materials used in construction are of the lowest possible reflectivity. Moreover, masked engine emissions reveal only a small infrared signature. (Rex)

ary, a helicopter is able to hover, and to take off and land vertically. In forward flight, the airflow through the rotor is complex. In order that the greater lift produced by the advancing blade does not destabilize the aircraft, the blades are hinged at the rotorhead, so that they flap up and down once every revolution.

An autogyro has no mechanical drive to the rotor but uses a separate propulsion system, usually driving a propeller. This propels the machine forward, the airflow through the rotor causing it to spin of its own accord. The air flows obliquely up through the rotor disc.

SEE ALSO
● ENGINES p. 192
● WEAPONRY p. 224

MILESTONES IN AVIATION

1783 First manned balloon flight by Joseph (1740–1810) and Jacques-Étienne (1745–99) Montgolfier in a hot-air balloon in Paris.

1783 First hydrogen-balloon flight by the French physicist Jacques Charles (1746–1823). He travelled 26 km (16 miles), beginning in Paris.

1852 Henri Giffard (1825–82) of France manned the first flight of a mechanically propelled airship – a *dirigible*. It travelled 27 km (17 mi).

1900 Count Ferdinand von Zeppelin (1838–1917) of Germany flew the first of his rigid-frame airships. With an internal combustion engine and aluminium frame, it reached a speed of 29 km/h (18 mph).

1903 The first successful flight by a 'heavier-than-air machine' by Orville Wright near Kitty Hawk, North Carolina, USA. During a later flight that day his brother Wilbur Wright sustained flight for 59 seconds.

1907 Paul Cornu of France manned the first free vertical flight of a twin-rotor helicopter, but it took another 30 years before a successful model was developed.

1909 The Frenchman Louis Blériot (1872–1936) made the first cross-Channel flight, from Calais to Dover in 37 minutes.

1910 The Zeppelin airship entered commercial service in Germany.

1915 The first all-metal cantilever-wing aircraft, the German Junkers J1, was built.

1919 Britons John Alcock (1892–1919) and Arthur Brown (1886–1948) made the first direct non-stop transatlantic crossing in 16 hours 27 minutes.

1927 The American Charles Lindbergh (1902–74) made the first solo transatlantic flight, from New York to Paris.

1933 The Boeing Model 247 made its maiden flight: it was the first all-metal monoplane airliner with cantilever low-mounted wings and retractable undercarriage.

1935 The Douglas DC-3 'Dakota' – conceived as an airliner – made its maiden flight.

1936 The first entirely successful helicopter, Heinrich Focke's Fa-61, made its maiden flight.

1937 The world's largest airship, the *Hindenburg*, burst into flames in New Jersey, USA, ending the age of airship travel.

1939 The German Heinkel He-178 was the first aircraft to fly solely on the power of a turbojet engine. Igor Sikorsky (1889–1972) designed the prototype modern helicopter, with a single main rotor and a small tail rotor.

1944 Britain's Gloster Meteor and Germany's Messerschmitt Me 262 jet fighters ushered in the age of the turbojet.

1947 The American Bell X-1 exceeded the speed of sound in level flight. The largest ever built flying boat, the Hughes H4 Hercules, made its first and only flight. The age of the flying boat was virtually over.

1949 The De Havilland Comet became the first jet airliner. It entered service in 1952.

1958 The first US jet airliner – the Boeing 707 – entered commercial service.

1968 The first flight of the Soviet supersonic airliner, the Tupolev Tu-144.

1969 The first operational V/STOL (vertical/short take-off and landing) aircraft – the Harrier – entered service with the Royal Air Force.

1970 The Boeing 747 became the first wide-bodied 'jumbo' jet to enter service.

1976 The supersonic Anglo-French airliner Concorde entered commercial service, seven years after its maiden flight.

1989 The Bell-Boeing V-22 Osprey flew for the first time. Its tilt rotor concept combines the advantages of the aeroplane with those of the helicopter.

1991 Stealth bomber used in the Gulf War. The aircraft has been successful in avoiding detection by radar.

Weaponry

Throughout recorded history, man has searched for ways to gain advantage over his opponents on the field of battle. As new weapons have been developed, countermeasures have been sought, so invariably initiating further change and technological advances.

THE BOLT-ACTION MAGAZINE RIFLE

In the second half of the 19th century muzzle-loaded rifles were replaced by weapons in which a cartridge fed from a magazine was loaded into the breech by working a bolt. Such bolt-action rifles remained standard infantry issue until generally displaced by automatic weapons after World War I.

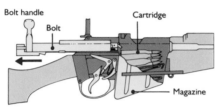

As the bolt is withdrawn, a cartridge is fed by the spring-loaded magazine into line with the bolt.

As it is pushed forward, the bolt engages with the cartridge and moves it into the breech.

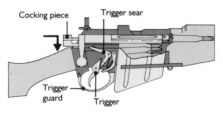

In the final stage of the forward movement of the bolt, a protruding piece of the bolt assembly catches the trigger sear, so cocking the weapon. The bolt is rotated to lock the cartridge in the breech. The weapon can now be fired by pressure on the trigger.

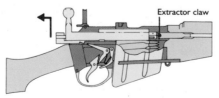

When the bolt is released and drawn backwards, a claw on the bolt engages with the rim of the spent cartridge, so removing it from the breech. Once clear, the cartridge is ejected.

SEE ALSO

- NUCLEAR WEAPONS p. 181
- SHIPS p. 216
- AIRCRAFT p. 222
- WORLD WAR I p. 268
- WORLD WAR II p. 274

Until the 14th century, technology played a limited role in warfare. Before then, weapons were little more than hunting tools – spears, axes, sling-shots and swords – put to a different use. Technology was confined to weapons that depended on tension to project missiles over distance. The Roman *ballista*, a catapult, used ropes to pull back a wooden pivot, the release of which threw large rocks against enemy defences. The same principle was used by the *longbow* and the more mechanical *crossbow*, both dependent on human muscle to tauten a string, which projected an arrow when released.

Early firearms

The real breakthrough came with the use of gunpowder to provide projectile power. Invented by the Chinese, *gunpowder* is a mixture of salt-petre (potassium nitrate), sulphur and charcoal, which – when ignited in an enclosed space – explodes. A weapon was produced when this explosion took place in a tube closed at one end, with a projectile, such as a ball or a bullet, introduced at the other end. The result was the gun, examples of which were in use in European armies by the 1320s.

Although early guns were not very accurate, improvements came steadily, and by the late 17th century the *flintlock* had appeared. A soldier armed with a flintlock musket would bite the end off a paper cartridge, empty a small amount of powder into the pan above the trigger, tip the remainder down the barrel, add a ball and the cartridge case as wadding, ram it tight and cock the weapon. When he pulled the trigger, a piece of flint struck a 'steel' that covered the pan to produce sparks, which ignited the main charge and sent the ball out of the barrel at speed. Cannon worked on the same principle, except that a match needed to be applied to the touch-hole to produce the explosion.

Breech-loaded weapons

Major changes occurred in the 19th century. In the 1830s the flintlock began to be replaced by *percussion firing*, whereby a hammer struck a detonator to produce the necessary spark. This allowed the development of self-contained cartridges of detonator, gunpowder and projectile. This in turn dispensed with the need for muzzle-loading and led to the introduction of *breech-loaded weapons*, in which the cartridge was fed directly into the breech, or firing chamber.

By the 1880s breech-loading had been refined to incorporate the use of magazines, each containing a number of cartridges, fed into the breech as the soldier worked a bolt (▷ box). Artillery also benefited from these developments, using self-contained breech-loaded shells that could be fired rapidly one after another. The invention of smokeless powder, such as cordite, also allowed firing to take place from concealed positions.

Automatic weapons

In terms of infantry weapons, the logical next step was to eliminate the working of the bolt by hand, by harnessing the explosive action of the gun to do the job automatically. Early machine guns such as the Maxim did this by using the recoil of the weapon to open the breech, eject the used cartridge and feed the next one in.

In other designs, automatic loading was achieved by diverting gases produced by the explosion back into the weapon. Experiments during World War I enabled the same system to be incorporated into much lighter weapons, producing the submachine gun and, eventually, the automatic rifle (⊳ box). Modern assault rifles such as the British SA-80 and the Soviet AK-47 work on this principle (known as 'blow-back') and give the ordinary soldier unprecedented firepower.

Tank warfare

On the ground, the face of battle was changed by the introduction of the tank and its antidotes. The tank was invented by the British in 1915 as an armoured caterpillar-tracked machine designed to cross the mud and trenches of a World War I battlefield. It was later developed into a war-winning weapon by the Germans, who recognized its potential to break through enemy lines and produce rear-area paralysis. *Blitzkrieg* ('lightning war'), dependent on a mixture of mobility and air support, was effective in the early years of World War II, but was slowly countered by new technology. Tanks proved vulnerable to other tanks, especially those armed with bigger guns and special anti-tank shells. Infantry soldiers were also equipped to deal with the threat, using spring-loaded weapons such as the British PIAT ('projectile, infantry, anti-tank') or the German Panzerfaust.

Long-range warfare

During the two World Wars the ability to hit distant targets improved dramatically, culminating in the development of pilotless bombs and surface-to-surface missiles – the German V1 and V2 weapons. The V1 was a pulse-jet-powered machine, fired from a special ramp towards its target, which it hit when it ran out of fuel. The US-produced *Cruise missile* of the 1970s owed its origins to V1, but was far more sophisticated. It incorporated an on-board 'terrain contour-matching (TERCOM) guidance system', which 'read' the ground over which the missile was flying, compared it to a pre-set computer memory, and corrected the flight path to ensure pin-point accuracy.

The V2 had a liquid-fuelled rocket engine that burned for about 70 seconds, during which the missile shot vertically to an altitude of 96 km (60 mi). It then fell back to Earth in a predetermined arc, hitting its target at a speed of 3840 km/h (2386 mph). It was the forerunner of the nuclear-armed ballistic missiles of the modern era (⊳ p. 181).

Since 1945 missiles have been preferred both for anti-tank and for anti-aircraft roles. By the early 1970s, wire-guided anti-tank missiles such as the Soviet AT-3 Sagger and British Swingfire had been developed. They were guided onto their targets by electronic signals transmitted down a command wire trailing behind. Since then, the wire has been discarded and the missile fired down a pre-set laser beam: the missile has a sensor in its nose, which – when locked onto the beam – carries it unerringly to its destination.

Current developments take this further, with the on-board sensor homing in on infrared or heat emissions from the target. As such missiles will seek out their own targets, they are known as 'fire-and-forget' weapons. Similar developments have affected surface-to-air missiles (SAMs), which home in on the heat and light emitted by the jet exhausts of modern aircraft.

AUTOMATIC RIFLES

Most modern automatic rifles work on the 'blow-back' principle, in which gases produced by the explosion of the propellant charge within the weapon are diverted to work the bolt automatically.

Spring · Muzzle · Cylinder · Piston · Port

Some of the expanding gases within the barrel are drawn off through a port near the muzzle into a cylinder, where they force back a piston against the pressure of a spring.

Bolt · Hammer · Breech · Spent cartridge

The bolt-and-hammer mechanism is pushed backwards by the cylinder, removing the spent cartridge from the breech as it does so. Once clear, the empty cartridge is ejected.

Magazine · Fresh cartridge

As the cylinder moves forward under the action of the spring, a fresh cartridge from the spring-loaded magazine is forced into the breech.

US Navy Harpoon missile fired from *USS New Jersey*. The Harpoon was designed specifically for submarines and ships, and can be fired from underwater. It is an anti-ship weapon with a range of 129 km (80 mi), and is programmed with its target coordinates before launch. When it is close to its target, it uses radar homing to lock on. It is programmed to attack the lighter armour of the deck and upperworks rather than the heavy side armour, causing maximum damage. (Zefa)

Human Prehistory

Prehistory is the period of time before written documents, the normal means by which historic events are recorded and dated. Before the development of scientific dating methods after World War II, dating methods were largely *relative* – in other words, definite dates were not assigned, but instead it was simply indicated whether a period came before or after certain important technological developments of unknown date.

The division of human prehistory into the *Stone Age*, *Bronze Age* and *Iron Age*, based on the materials used for tools, was introduced in the early 19th century. This 'Three Age System' was further developed in the late 19th century by subdividing the Stone Age into the *Palaeolithic* ('Old Stone'), *Mesolithic* ('Middle Stone'), and *Neolithic* ('New Stone') Ages. These technologically based divisions remain useful for European prehistory, but they are not always valid in other parts of the world.

The Palaeolithic

Most of the Palaeolithic developments in Europe, and in Asia outside the tropics, occurred against a background of a much colder climate, associated with the growth of vast ice sheets in northern latitudes, and extensive glacier development in more southerly latitudes, including the Alps and the Balkans. This was the last Ice Age (▷ p. 70). The causes, and exact number, of the cold periods, which were separated by warmer phases, are not clearly understood; nor is their age well established, since scientific methods have as yet not been very successful in dating this geological time span. However, the last cold phase ended about 10 000 years ago and the different warm and cold phases can be recognized archaeologically because of the preservation of the bones of characteristic animals and even the pollen of particular trees, which indicate warmer

or colder periods. They thus provide a useful *relative chronology* in which to place human developments. Archaeologists also use developments in stone-tool types to subdivide the Palaeolithic into *Lower* (i.e. earliest), *Middle*, and *Upper* phases.

The Lower Palaeolithic

No certain finds of human fossils at the australopithecine stage of evolution, dated between 2 and 5 million years ago, have appeared outside Africa. The earliest human fossils in Europe and Africa belong to the *Homo erectus* evolutionary stage, dated between 1.5 million and 200 000 years ago, although in Europe and Asia outside the tropics there is no good evidence for human occupation before 1 million years ago. *Homo erectus* fossils have been discovered in France, Germany, China and Java.

The *industries* (i.e. tool types) used by *Homo erectus* belong to the Lower Palaeolithic. The most characteristic tool is the hand axe, a general-purpose implement made by striking off pieces of stone (*flakes*) from a lump of stone until the correct shape and cutting edge were produced. Simple tools made of flakes removed from a lump of stone (a *core*) were also used, sometimes improved by further flaking of the edges. Tools in materials other than stone very rarely survive. Even at this early stage humans used fire, as exemplified by the fire hardening of the spear. While Lower Palaeolithic tools continued until about 100 000 years ago, it seems that between 300/200 000 and 100 000 years ago *Homo erectus* evolved into a more developed stage, at least in Europe. However, there is little evidence of this stage.

The Middle Palaeolithic

The Middle Palaeolithic stage, from 100 000 to as late as 30 000 years ago, is associated with the remains of Neanderthal man (*Homo sapiens neanderthalensis*, named after the Neandertal, a valley in Germany where remains were first found). While *Homo erectus* only occupied Eurasia during relatively warm periods, Neanderthals could exploit the arctic environments of the full glacial phases, living in caves and in skin tents held down by mammoth bones.

Middle Palaeolithic stone tools, made mainly from flakes, were more specialized than earlier tools, and included spear heads, knives and scraping tools for wood and hides. Neanderthals

THE THREE AGES OF NEAR-EASTERN AND EUROPEAN PREHISTORY

AGE	STONE AGE					BRONZE AGE	IRON AGE
	PALAEOLITHIC			MESOLITHIC	NEOLITHIC		
	LOWER	MIDDLE	UPPER				
PERIOD BEGAN (approximately)	1 million years ago	100 000 years ago	30 000 BC	10 000 BC	9000-4000 BC (spreading from Near East to W Europe)	3000-2000 BC (both periods earliest in Near East and SE Europe, spreading to W and N Europe)	1200-500 BC
DOMINANT HOMINID	*Homo erectus*	Neanderthal man (*H. sapiens neanderthalensis*)	Modern man (*Homo sapiens sapiens*)				
TECHNOLOGY	Simple stone tools, e.g. hand axes Use of fire	More specialized stone tools, e.g. spear heads, knives	Development of stone blades and bone tools Beginnings of art	Use of bow and arrow	Beginnings of agriculture First towns in Near East	Bronze artefacts First cities	Iron artefacts

were the first humans to bury their dead, and they also had a sense of beauty: scientific analysis shows that at Shanidar cave in Iraq a Neanderthal was buried on a bed of spring flowers.

The Upper Palaeolithic

There is still much scientific debate about the date of the first appearance of anatomically modern humans (*Homo sapiens sapiens*, also called Cro-Magnon man, after a cave in the Dordogne, France). However, it seems likely that in Europe and northern Asia they appeared relatively late – perhaps as late as 30 000 BC in Western Europe – although in some other parts of the world they had appeared before 40 000 BC.

In Eurasia, Upper Palaeolithic tools, associated with modern humans, have a number of characteristic features: stone tools were now based on *blades* (long, thin flakes), which were made into an even wider variety of specialized tools than previously. Bone tools also appear regularly for the first time. Another Upper Palaeolithic cultural achievement is the Ice Age art found, for example, in the prehistoric cave sites of France and Spain.

The achievements of these early modern humans include the peopling of the previously unoccupied continents of Australasia and the Americas (▷ pp. 388–90). A less positive achievement is the extinction of a number of large mammal species (▷ p. 108) towards the end of the last Ice Age (about 8000 BC), at least partially as a result of the efficient hunting methods of Upper Palaeolithic peoples.

The Mesolithic

The end of the Ice Age saw significantly increased temperatures and rainfall in Europe and parts of Asia. A largely treeless environment was replaced by forest, especially in Europe north of the Alps, and mammal species adapted to tundra and steppe environments were replaced by forest species. Humans adapted to these changes by living in smaller groups and exploiting the increased numbers of wildfowl and fish. In Eurasia, use of the bow and arrow became important in this period.

The Neolithic

The earliest Neolithic cultures, defined by the appearance of agriculture as a way of life, are found in the Near East, in an area between Turkey and Israel in the west and Iran in the east. In this area the wild ancestors of wheat and barley, and of sheep, goats, pigs and cattle, all occurred. The earliest Neolithic sites date to the period 9000–7000 BC, contemporary with the Mesolithic period in Europe. But in the Near East the climatic changes associated with the end of the Ice Age were far less marked than in Europe, and population pressure is a more likely explanation for the beginnings of agriculture than climatic change. By 6000 BC some substantial towns existed in the Near East.

The spread of agriculture was relatively rapid: Neolithic sites in Greece start before 6000 BC and appear in Britain by 4000 BC. During the 2000–3000-year lifespan of the Neolithic, considerable social distinctions emerged along with increasingly centralized political power. These developments are associated with the building of large

burial and ceremonial monuments in earth and stone that began in many parts of Europe at this time. Specialized production of, and widespread trade in, a variety of objects and materials also developed.

The Bronze Age

Copper and gold were the main metals used during the Bronze Age (bronze is an alloy: a mixture of copper with a little tin). The production of metal objects is a complex process, but the discovery of metallurgy probably occurred independently in several places, including the Near East, southeast Europe and southwest Asia. In parts of Europe and the Near East, small numbers of simple copper objects were in use many centuries before the beginning of the Bronze Age: this transitional period is called the *Chalcolithic* ('copper-stone') Age.

Social distinctions increased as more powerful individuals displayed their status via bronze weapons and gold jewellery. The status and power of certain individuals was particularly marked in the Later Bronze Age, as shown by various imposing grave monuments and offerings, such as the Mycenaean shaft graves (▷ p. 230), and bronze weapons and armour in a number of central European graves.

The Iron Age

The development of iron working in the Near East and its spread, starting at about 1000 BC, had little immediate effect on late Bronze Age cultures. The recognizably Celtic societies of Iron Age temperate Europe developed directly out of later Bronze Age cultures. European Iron Age societies had increasing contacts with Greece and Rome, first through trade, but later through the invasion of much of Celtic Europe by the Romans. This put an end to prehistory in those areas. However, the peripheries of Europe (Ireland, Scotland, Scandinavia, northern Germany) were never colonized by the Romans. The emergence of these areas from prehistory only occurred gradually, within the last 1500 years, after their conversion to Christianity.

The standing stones at Carnac in France, erected around 2000 BC. This megalith ('giant stone') monument consists of nearly 3000 standing stones or *menhirs* arranged in several long, parallel rows – some over 1 km (0.6 mi) in length. The amount of manpower involved in constructing such megaliths as Carnac and Stonehenge indicates the strong social and cultural cohesion of local Neolithic societies. (Images)

SEE ALSO

- THE ANCIENT NEAR EAST p. 228
- ANCIENT GREECE p. 230
- PREHISTORY OUTSIDE EUROPE AND THE NEAR EAST pp. 234–39

The Ancient Near East

The Near East comprises the countries on the eastern shores of the Mediterranean, together with modern Turkey, Iran (ancient Persia), Egypt (▷ box), and Iraq (ancient Mesopotamia). The world's first cities arose between 4000 and 3000 BC in Mesopotamia (Greek, 'land of the two rivers'). These rivers, the Tigris and Euphrates, flooded their banks during the spring and made the surrounding plain extremely fertile. The Mesopotamian farmers had to build a complex system of canals, dikes and reservoirs to control the annual floods. This required a great deal of organization and cooperation. Variations in the fertility of the soil led to differences in individual wealth – and hence to the emergence of social classes. Food surpluses allowed some people to give up farming and become craftsmen, labourers, merchants and administrators. These developments created a need for centralized decision making, regulation and control: the beginnings of urban civilization.

In southern Babylonia, between 3500 and 3000 BC, buildings became progressively larger and more elaborate. The wheel was invented around the same period. The earliest writing – simple pictures drawn on clay – developed probably because of the need for record keeping in an ever more complex society (▷ p. 350). We call these people Sumerians, from the ancient name for southern Babylonia, 'Sumer'. Each Sumerian city had a king, whose power was believed to come from the gods. Throughout the so-called Early Dynastic period (c. 2900–2370 BC) the Sumerian rulers fought each other for supremacy over their land.

About 2370 BC, Sargon of Akkad conquered Babylonia. He and his successors spoke a Semitic language, Akkadian. Akkadian was written in the cuneiform script (▷ p. 350) borrowed from Sumerian, and it replaced Sumerian as the official language. The Akkadian empire expanded rapidly, but was overrun about 2200 BC by foreign invaders. The Third Dynasty of Ur (c. 2113–2006 BC) brought a century of prosperity. Its warrior-kings created an efficient administrative system, and encouraged a renaissance in Sumerian culture.

Babylonians and Hittites

The end of Sumerian rule was marked by the sack of Ur in c. 2006 BC by the Elamites (a people of ancient Iran). The small kingdoms of Mesopotamia fought for sovereignty for 200 years. Many were ruled by Amorites, originally nomads from the Syrian desert. Eventually one of these Amorite kings, Hammurabi of Babylon (c. 1792–1750 BC; best known for his law code) conquered the whole of Mesopotamia. After his death, the empire was weakened, and Babylon was plundered by the Hittites (▷ below) in c. 1595 BC.

The period from c. 1600 to 1200 BC in the Near East saw powerful empires struggling for control. There was a balance of forces between the Kassites in Babylonia, the Mitannians in Palestine and eastern Syria, the Egyptian empire in Palestine and southern Syria, and later the Assyrians in northern Mesopotamia and the Hittites in Anatolia (modern Turkey) and northern Syria.

The Hittite empire was founded in about 1650 BC and reached its peak under Suppiluliumas I (c. 1380–1350 BC), who extended its frontiers and clashed with the Egyptian empire in Syria. In c. 1283 BC the Hittite king, Hattusilis III, signed a treaty with Ramses II of Egypt. Cuneiform was still the international script during this period, although the first alphabet was invented in Syria or Palestine in the 16th century BC (▷ p. 350). About 1200 BC many of the Near Eastern kingdoms collapsed. A major cause were the 'Sea Peoples', marauders from the eastern Mediterranean, who were eventually defeated by the Egyptian pharaohs Merenptah and Ramses III.

After c. 1200 BC there was a new look to the Near East. The Philistines, on the coast of southern Palestine, were originally one group of the Sea Peoples. Their battles against the Israelites are recorded in the Old Testament. The Phoenicians, on the Lebanese and Syrian coast, became great seafaring traders and founded colonies such as Carthage in North Africa. Carthage in turn grew to dominate the western Mediterranean, until finally defeated by the Romans in the 3rd century BC (▷ p. 232).

The Aramaeans occupied Syria and frequently fought the Assyrians and Israelites. Aramaic became the international language and script of the Near East, and was the original language of some of the later books of the Old Testament. The Old Testament records the exodus of the Jews from Egypt under Moses, and their conquest of Canaan (Palestine) under Joshua. About 1000 BC a united kingdom of Israel arose, with Saul and David as its first kings. Following the death of David's son and successor, Solomon, the kingdom divided into two – Israel in the north and Judah in the south.

Assyrians, Neo-Babylonians and Persians

The kingdom of Assyria, with its traditional capital at Ashur, was located in northern Mesopotamia. From the 9th century BC, its kings campaigned to the west against the Aramaeans.

ANCIENT MESOPOTAMIA

ASSYRIA
NINEVEH
NIMRUD
ASHUR
SAMARRA
MARI
GUTIUM
AKKAD
BABYLON
KISH
ISIN NIPPUR
SUMER UMMA
LARSA LAGASH
URUK
ERIDU UR
BABYLONIA
ELAM
Mediterranean Sea
Red Sea
Persian Gulf

SEE ALSO

● HUMAN PREHISTORY p. 226
● ANCIENT GREECE p. 230
● ANCIENT ROME p. 232

Eventually they reached the Mediterranean Sea and even briefly invaded Egypt. Tiglathpileser III (744–727 BC) proclaimed himself king of Babylon, and for the next hundred years Babylonia struggled for independence from Assyria. However, towards the end of the 7th century BC Assyrian cities fell one by one. Nineveh was destroyed in 612 BC by an alliance of Medes and the Chaldaean kings of Babylonia.

The Babylonian success was short-lived. Nebuchadnezzar defeated the Egyptians at Carchemish in 605 BC and campaigned extensively in Syria and Palestine. He captured Jerusalem in 587 BC and deported thousands of Jews to Babylonia. However, his successors were weak. In 539 BC Babylon fell without resistance to the Persian ruler Cyrus, of the Achaemenid dynasty.

The empire of the Persian Achaemenids became the largest yet known in the Near East. From their homeland in what is now Iran, the successors of Cyrus conquered Egypt, northern India and Asia Minor (modern Turkey), and frequently came into conflict with the Greeks (▷ p. 230). Darius I (521–486 BC) reorganized the provinces (*satrapies*) and the army, and introduced coinage, legal and postal systems. His successor, Xerxes (486–465 BC), crushed rebellions ruthlessly and suppressed foreign religions, reversing the religious tolerance of Cyrus. Economic decline,

revolts, murder and harem conspiracies weakened the Persian throne. The capital Persepolis fell to Alexander the Great in April 330 BC (▷ p. 231), and the last Achaemenid, Darius III, was murdered in the same year.

THE PERIODS AND DYNASTIES OF ANCIENT EGYPT

Dates (BC)	Period	Dynasties	Main events
3100–2725	Early Dynastic Period	1–3	Unification of Upper and Lower Egypt under Menes. Foundation of Memphis. Building of Step Pyramid.
2575–2134	Old Kingdom	4–8	Centralized administration. Building of Great Pyramids at Giza.
2134–2040	First Intermediate Period	9–11	Egypt divided. Political fragmentation. Control by local monarchs.
2040–1640	Middle Kingdom	11–13	Reunification under Mentuhotep II. Foundation of Itj-towy. Administrative reforms. Co-regencies. Conquest of Nubia.
1640–1552	Second Intermediate Period	14–17	Hyksos rule. Theban dynasty liberates Egypt.
1552–1070	New Kingdom	18–20	Imperial Egypt: empire extends from Syria to southern Sudan. Capital at Thebes. Great building programme.
1070–712	Third Intermediate Period	21–24	Egypt divided: priesthood of Amun rule in Thebes, while pharaohs rule in Tanis.
712–332	Late Period	25–30	Reunification of Egypt under 26th Dynasty. Persian invasion. Conquest by Alexander the Great: end of the line of native pharaohs.

ANCIENT EGYPT

Ancient Egypt consisted of the Nile Valley – a long and narrow strip of land extending some 600 miles from Aswan to the area south of modern Cairo, where the river opened up into the Delta. On either side of the valley stretched vast expanses of desert. The Nile was not only the unifying feature of the country, it was also its main source of life. In Egypt rainfall is negligible, but in antiquity the regular annual inundation of the Nile between July and October covered most of the land in the valley and in the Delta, laying down a rich layer of fertilizing silt. Agriculture involved careful management of the waters of the river through the creation of irrigation basins and channels. The main crops were cereals, but pulses, vegetables and fruit were also grown. Flax was used for clothing, sails and ropes, and the pith of the papyrus plant to produce a type of paper. Ancient Egypt was also rich in mineral resources – gold, copper and turquoise – and building and semi-precious stones were also quarried.

It is customary to divide the history of ancient Egypt into thirty dynasties of pharaohs (as the kings of ancient Egypt were known; ▷ table). The history of Pharaonic Egypt begins around 3100 BC with the unification of Upper and Lower Egypt. During the Early Dynastic (or Archaic) Period, a considerable administrative organization of the state took place. A new capital, Memphis, was founded at the junction of Upper and Lower Egypt. There was a dramatic development in the science of writing, no doubt to keep pace with the requirements of a centralized bureaucratic government. Burial customs became more complex, and the first pyramid was built – the Step Pyramid at Saqqara.

The Old Kingdom was the great pyramid age of Egypt. Written records indicate that all aspects of government and administration were controlled by the pharaoh from the royal residence at Memphis. The monumental size of the Great Pyramids at Giza – in which the pharaohs were buried – shows that the pharaoh was the dominant

figure of the state, acting as an intermediary between the gods and mankind. The construction of these enormous monuments is also evidence of the degree of state organization that the Egyptians had achieved. At the same time the horizons of the Egyptians expanded, with trading expeditions to Nubia, Sinai, Libya and the Levant.

A relaxation of the strong personal authority of the pharaohs towards the end of the 5th and during the 6th dynasty resulted in a complete breakdown of royal power during what is been called the First Intermediate Period. For about a hundred years, a number of rival princes claimed the kingship of Upper and Lower Egypt. Mentuhotep II of the 11th dynasty finally succeeded in taking control of the whole country. The period that followed this reunification of Egypt is known as the Middle Kingdom, later regarded as the 'classical' period of Pharaonic civilization. Under the strong kings of the 12th dynasty, Egypt once again became a highly centralized and well-administered state, and a new capital, Itj-towy, was founded south of Memphis. The practice of co-regency was instituted at the very beginning of the dynasty, whereby the ruling pharaoh nominated his successor as co-regent and reigned with him for the last years of his rule. In foreign affairs, contacts with the Levant were re-established and in Nubia a series of fortresses was constructed along the Nile, to secure the southern boundaries and to regulate all trade into Egypt. A series of short-lived reigns during the 13th dynasty was followed by the Second Intermediate Period, during which the political control of the land was once again fragmented. The 15th and 16th dynasties are allotted to foreign Asiatic rulers, the Hyksos, who were remembered later as hated foreign usurpers, and were eventually expelled by a new Theban dynasty.

The memory of the Hyksos domination of Egypt was largely responsible for shaping the policies of the New Kingdom rulers. The pharaohs of the 18th and 19th dynasties were true war leaders,

extending their territories from Syria to southern Sudan. Egypt became the largest empire of the ancient Near East. Diplomatic contacts were established with other great powers of the period – the Hittites, Babylonians and Assyrians (▷ text) – and peace treaties were concluded between them.

Enormous wealth poured into Egypt from the various regions of the empire. From the ancient capital of Memphis and their new religious centre of Thebes, the New Kingdom pharaohs undertook a large number of building projects. The grandiose temple complex of Karnak was built as the main cult temple for the state god Amun-Ra. The royal tombs were situated, for security reasons, in the 'Valley of the Kings', a remote canyon on the west bank of the Nile at Thebes.

However, around the late 19th and 20th dynasties, Egypt once again went into decline. Weakened by invasions, notably by the 'Sea Peoples', Egypt's control over her empire disintegrated. A series of weak kings resulted in much of royal power being usurped by the high priest of Amun. The final collapse of the New Kingdom saw the country again divided into two halves, with Upper Egypt ruled by the priests of Amun in Thebes, while the pharaohs governed from their new capital at Tanis in the Delta. This period is usually referred to as the Third Intermediate Period.

It was not until the 26th dynasty that Egypt was reunited under the Saite kings, who restored order and re-created some of the splendour of the past. But in 525 BC the Persians under Cambyses invaded Egypt. The conquest by the Achaemenid Persians meant the end of Egypt's independence. In 332 BC Alexander the Great defeated the Persians and was crowned pharaoh of Egypt (▷ p. 231). At his death, his general Ptolemy took control of the country, founding a line of kings who were to rule for some three hundred years until Egypt was annexed as a province of the Roman Empire.

Ancient Greece

The first two great civilizations in the area of the Aegean Sea were the Minoans (named after the legendary King Minos), and the Mycenaeans, whose name derives from one of the main centres of their culture, the city of Mycenae, home of Agamemnon, the mythological king who led the Greeks against Troy.

SEE ALSO

● THE ANCIENT NEAR EAST p. 228
● ANCIENT ROME p. 232
● PHILOSOPHY p. 302
● GREEK AND ROMAN ART p. 306
● CLASSICAL LITERATURE p. 356

From about 2200 BC, a series of major palaces were built in Crete, notably at Knossos and Phaestos, and at the same time writing appeared. The script, Linear A, is as yet undeciphered, but it is clearly not in Greek. Power was partially centralized, and the most important king was based in the largest palace at Knossos. The Minoans were great seafarers; they dominated some Aegean islands, and imported fine goods from all over the Eastern Mediterranean. The palace at Knossos was a huge, complex structure, with a courtyard and hundreds of rooms. Its many storage rooms suggest that its rulers collected tribute in kind and redistributed it to allies and friends. Minoan art gives vivid pictures of ships, marine and animal life, and of scenes of courtly games and religious activities. The palace suffered many phases of destruction, but their precise chronology, and their relation to events such as the volcanic eruption of Thera or hostile Mycenaean activity, are controversial. Palace records after a destruction c. 1450 BC are in the Greek Linear B script, which suggests that Mycenaeans were by then in control in Crete.

The Mycenaeans' palace-based civilization dominated the Aegean from c. 1450 BC. It is unlikely that any one king controlled the whole of Greece in this period, although some palaces, above all Mycenae, were richer than others; the gold and other metals found in their graves indicate their wealth and power, and the spread of Mycenaean pottery and goods, and the variety and luxury of their imports, suggest wide contacts throughout the Eastern Mediterranean and elsewhere. Cities like Mycenae, Tiryns, Pylos and Thebes were protected by massive walls, while the palaces were more monumental and simpler in design than those of Minoan Crete. The Linear B records from these palaces show detailed supervision of large estates and many slaves. These palaces were destroyed c. 1200–1000 BC, and Mycenaean culture went into decline. The causes remain a mystery, though internal revolts and invasions from the north may have played a part.

The Archaic Period (c. 800–500 BC)

After a period of relative poverty a new form of political and social organization, the *polis* or independent city-state, took shape in most of Greece. A city-state consisted of an agricultural territory and a walled town centre. Geographical factors (small plains surrounded by high mountains) encouraged this development, but the separate identity of each city-state was strengthened by its own dialect and cults, and by community involvement in political and legal decisions.

From about 750 BC aristocratic dominance in these cities was steadily undermined. Expansion of trade and the establishment of a large number of new Greek settlements around the Mediterranean and the Black Sea, with new laws and a fresh distribution of land, also encouraged radical questioning in mainland Greece. The introduction of heavier armour and more cohesive tactics (*hoplite* warfare) helped to give political self-confidence to peasant-soldiers. In consequence, hereditary nobles saw their powers restricted, and many cities experienced temporary rule by *tyrants* – usurpers who seized power with the support of hoplites. In the longer term, power often came to be held by oligarchies defined by wealth rather than by birth.

By the end of the Archaic period two city-states, Sparta and Athens, had become the most powerful in Greece. However, they developed in wholly contrasting ways. The Spartans won control of most of the southern Peloponnese, and the majority of the defeated peoples became 'state-serfs' (*helots*), compelled to work the land for the Spartans under brutal conditions. After a helot revolt, and simultaneous agitation by Spartan citizens organized in a hoplite army, Sparta transformed itself into a state that was politically more equal, and socially much more tightly regimented and authoritarian. During the 6th century BC Sparta created a network of alliances (the Peloponnesian League), and became the chief military power in Greece.

Athens led the way in developing democracy. In 594 Solon created a new political and legal system. His reforms established many peasant-citizens in ownership of their lands, and encouraged them to share in the assembly and legal processes. He defined rights to hold offices in terms of divisions of wealth, not birth. A period of

ATHENS AND SPARTA c.450 BC

ILLYRIANS
KINGDOM OF MACEDON
THRACIANS
EPIROTES
THESSALY AND DEPENDENCIES
ATHENIAN
AETOLIANS
BOEOTIANS
EMPIRE
PERSIAN
EUBOEA
Delphi
ACHAEANS
Plataea
Thebes
EMPIRE
Olympia
ATTICA
ATHENS
Ephesus
Corinth
ARCADIANS
Argos
Delos
Samos
Miletus
MESSENIANS
SPARTA
Naxos

Thera

ATHENIAN EMPIRE

SPARTA and ALLIES

OTHER GREEKS

Battlesites of the Greek–Persian wars (490–479BC)
1 MARATHON 490 BC   3 SALAMIS 480 BC
2 THERMOPYLAE 480 BC 4 PLATAEA 479 BC

CRETANS

'tyranny' under Peisistratos and his sons (c. 545–510 BC) further helped to secure the peasants on their lands. The reforms of Cleisthenes (d. 508 BC) introduced more democratic means of decision-making at local and city level, including the new 'Council of Five Hundred', selected by lot from newly defined local units or 'demes'. Finally, Cleisthenes introduced *ostracism*, whereby Athenians could vote for a politician to be banished from the city for ten years; its purpose was to prevent tyranny, and to resolve serious disputes.

The Classical Period (c. 500–338 BC)

The growing power of the Persian Empire had led by c. 500 BC to its control over the Greek cities of Asia Minor (modern Turkey). In 490 and 480–479 BC the Persians attempted the conquest of mainland Greece. The first invasion was repulsed by the Athenians in the land battle at Marathon. The second and more serious invasion, under Xerxes (485–465), was defeated by an anti-Persian grand coalition led by Sparta. The combined Greek forces defeated the Persians at sea at Salamis (480) and on land at Plataea (479). These victories confirmed Athens and Sparta as the major Greek powers. Themistocles was the main driving force behind the development of the Athenian navy and the strategy adopted in 480–79.

The Greeks went on to liberate many Aegean cities from Persian control, and a new and successful alliance, the Delian League, was created under Athenian leadership. By c. 450 BC the League had become an Athenian empire, as Athens insisted on tribute-payments and increasingly interfered in the politics and economies of its 'allies'. During this period Athens completed the development of its democracy. The popular juries heard almost all law suits, and the scrutiny of all office-holders was shared between the Council of Five Hundred, the assembly and the juries. Under the leadership of Pericles, between c. 462–429 BC, Athens was at its most prosperous and powerful, and used profits from its empire in a spectacular programme of public buildings, such as the Parthenon. Women, thought by Greek men to be inferior, were excluded from political life, as were the many slaves in Athens, the vast majority of whom were non-Greeks, and regarded as naturally suited for slavery.

The immediate reasons for the destructive Peloponnesian War (431–404 BC) lay in areas where the interests of Athens and the Peloponnesians overlapped. In 431 the complaints of its allies, especially Corinth, led the Spartans to declare war. But a more fundamental reason was Spartan fear of Athenian power, and of losing control over its allies. Sparta was strong on land and Athens at sea, and for long each avoided a decisive battle. Since one side tended to support democracies and the other oligarchies, and each tried to win over the other's allies, the war greatly intensified political and economic conflicts inside many Greek cities. A peace made in 421 BC did not last, once Athens had made the serious mistake of committing large forces in a disastrous attempt to conquer Sicily. Sparta then pursued a more aggressive strategy by attacking the Athenian empire in the Aegean. Decisively, the Persians contributed to the Spartan fleet. In 404 BC the war ended in victory for Sparta, though many Greek cities found themselves ruled once more by the Persians, or by narrow, Spartan-

backed oligarchies. Such an oligarchy, the 'Thirty Tyrants' (404–403), ruled briefly in Athens, but a moderate and stable form of democracy soon returned.

The defeat of Athens did not bring peace. Aggressive Spartan policies led to a coalition against it of former allies (Corinth and Thebes) and old enemies (Athens and Argos), supported by Persian gold. Thebes gained in military strength, and in 371 inflicted a serious defeat on Sparta. Sparta failed to recover as its economic and social system gradually broke down. Athens recovered a little of her former power, creating a new Aegean Confederacy. In general, however, the Greek states were steadily weakened by wars and internal conflicts. From 359 BC Philip II of Macedon reorganized his kingdom and army and by a combination of diplomacy and force achieved a position of dominance in mainland Greece, culminating in the decisive victory at Chaeronea (338 BC). After this the Greek city-states maintained a degree of self-government for centuries, but power in Greece came to depend ultimately on outsiders (⊳ box and p. 232).

ALEXANDER THE GREAT AND THE HELLENISTIC KINGDOMS

Alexander (356–323 BC) became king of Macedon when his father Philip II was assassinated in 336 BC. Having secured his position in Europe, he embarked on the major offensive against the Persian Empire, which had been planned by his father. This was explicitly portrayed as revenge for the desecrations of Xerxes (⊳ text) and liberation for the Greeks of Asia Minor; in practice it meant the replacing of Persian rule with Macedonian rule by right of conquest. Between 334 and 323 BC Alexander and his army travelled vast distances and created the largest empire yet known. He conquered the whole of the Persian Empire and beyond, defeating the Persian forces in three major battles (Granicus in 334, Issus in 333 and Gaugamela in 332). He campaigned from Egypt to the Himalaya and northern India, founding new Greek-style cities as he went. After a mutiny by his exhausted army, he returned to Babylon in 324, and died there, still planning further conquests. Increasingly, and to the dismay of many of his officers and troops, he had begun to use Persian soldiers and Persian nobles in his service, and to develop shared rule between Macedonians and Persians. Alexander became the model of the charismatic and successful conqueror and king, to be emulated by innumerable commanders, and the subject of many myths.

Alexander left no heir, and for decades the leading Macedonian generals fought ferociously to win the inheritance, or to carve out viable kingdoms for themselves. Three main dynasties were eventually established, by Ptolemy (Egypt), Seleucus (Asia) and Antigonus (Macedonia and Greece); smaller vassal kingdoms existed within their territories, and in time several of these achieved independence. The Antigonids in Macedonia maintained a type of monarchy comparable to their predecessors, but often found it difficult to maintain control over the Greek cities. From c. 240 onwards two federations of city-states, Achaea and Aetolia, were dominant. In Egypt, the Ptolemies ruled their native subjects like Pharoahs (⊳ p. 228), while giving privileged positions to immigrant Macedonians and Greeks. They maintained a strong foreign policy and a lavish court, financed by heavy taxation in a centralized economy. The Seleucids controlled a huge area through local governors (satraps) and the support of the ruling classes in the many cities founded by Alexander or themselves; increasingly areas broke away to form separate kingdoms, such as the small but prosperous kingdom of Pergamon in the west, or Bactria or Armenia further east. The cities throughout the Hellenistic world were centres of wealth and power, and displayed in their buildings and activities the ideas of the dominant Greek culture.

The Hellenistic Age was marked by a highly competitive spirit. Kings constantly fought, or negotiated, with each other for territory, wealth and glory. The constant wars came to weaken the kingdoms, and they all fell victim, during the 2nd and 1st centuries BC, to outside powers, above all to the growing might of Rome (⊳ p. 232).

A Hellenistic footsoldier

Ancient Rome

According to tradition the city of Rome was founded by Romulus in 753 BC, although archaeology has shown that the site was occupied from at least the beginning of the Iron Age (10th century BC). Romulus is a figure of legend, but the kings who are said to have ruled after him may be historical.

Literary and archaeological evidence shows that in the 6th century BC Rome was a powerful city-state that dominated the Latin communities on its southern borders and was strongly influenced by the Etruscan cities to the north.

The Republic

By 500 BC the monarchy had been replaced by a Republic dominated by the aristocratic *patricians*. But in the 5th and 4th centuries BC the patrician monopoly of power was broken by the *plebeians* (the lower-class citizens) who, through a series of reforms proposed by their leaders (the *tribunes*), gained relief from oppression as well as equal political rights, in particular the right to hold one of the *consulships* (the two annually elected *consuls* governed the state and commanded its armies, and were advised by a council of elders – the *Senate*).

During this same period the Romans were continually at war with their Italian neighbours, whom they compelled, one by one, to become allies and to contribute to further wars. Rome became the centre of an increasingly powerful alliance, and was driven to undertake ever greater military commitments. The first war overseas occurred in Sicily, where Rome clashed with Carthage (the First Punic War, 264–241 BC). The Second Punic War (218–202 BC) became a life-and-death struggle when the Carthaginian general Hannibal (247–c. 183 BC) invaded Italy in 218 BC and for a time placed Rome in mortal danger.

But the Romans eventually emerged victorious, defeating Hannibal at Zama in 202 BC, and taking over the former Carthaginian provinces in Spain. In the decades that followed, they decisively defeated the major Hellenistic kingdoms in Greece and Asia Minor (▷ p. 231). These and other imperialistic ventures led to the formation of new provinces in Greece and Macedonia in 146 BC, 'Africa' (i.e. roughly modern Tunisia) also in 146, Asia (i.e. western Turkey) in 133, southern Gaul (Provence) in 121, Cilicia (southern Turkey) in 101, and Cyrenaica (eastern Libya) in 96.

These overseas conquests vastly increased the wealth of the upper classes, and led to the growth of large landed estates in Italy, worked by war captives imported as slaves. Slave labour replaced the small peasant proprietors, who formed the backbone of the Roman army but found that prolonged service in distant lands made it increasingly difficult to maintain their farms. Many peasants were thus driven off the land to a life of penury and unemployment. Peasant displacement led not only to impoverishment and discontent, but also to problems of military recruitment, since the law laid down a property qualification for service in the army.

The widening gulf between rich and poor eventually gave rise to social conflict and political breakdown. Attempts at reform by the brothers Tiberius and Gaius Gracchus (plebeian tribunes in 133 and 123–2 BC respectively) ended in failure and the violent deaths of both brothers; other would-be reformers suffered a similar fate in the decades that followed. Meanwhile the empire was menaced by external attacks and internal revolts. The ruling oligarchy showed itself corrupt and incompetent in responding to these crises, which were only overcome by allowing able and ambitious individuals to take control of the government and by creating a professional army from the proletariat.

These measures solved the military problems, but had fatal political consequences, because they provided the poor with a means to redress their grievances, and ambitious nobles with the chance to gain personal power by means of armed force. The first civil war was between Gaius Marius (c. 157–86) and Lucius Sulla (c. 138–78). In 81 Sulla set himself up as dictator and tried to reform the political system. His efforts were ineffectual, however, and the same lethal trends continued. New military crises in the 70s enabled the popular general Pompey (Gnaeus Pompeius, 106–48) to gain a position of pre-eminence in the state: but he was unable to prevent other leaders from doing the same thing. In 49 BC, Julius Caesar (100–44), the conqueror of Gaul, invaded Italy at the head of an army. After defeating Pompey at Pharsalus in 48 he became consul and dictator for life.

Caesar's assassination on 15 March (the 'Ides of March'), 44 BC, once again plunged the empire into civil war, the main contenders being his former aide, Mark Antony (Marcus Antonius; 83–31) and his heir, Caesar Octavian (63 BC–AD 14). The issue was finally settled at the battle of Actium in 31 BC, when Octavian emerged victorious, and gained complete control of the Roman empire. Under the honorary title Augustus he became the first emperor, and ruled unchallenged until his death in AD 14.

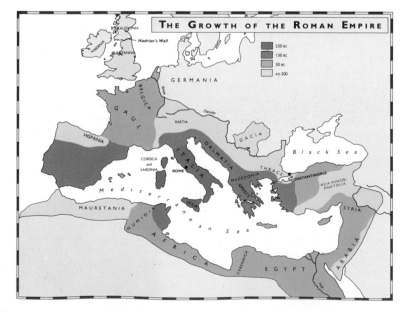

The villa of the Emperor Hadrian at Tivoli, near Rome, gives some idea of the luxury and elegance of life for wealthy Romans. Built in the early 2nd century AD, the villa complex amd its gardens cover some 18 km² (7 sq mi). As well the villa itself, there were theatres, pavilions, baths and libraries.
(Spectrum)

The Empire

Augustus' great achievement was to reconcile traditional republican opinion with the fact of personal rule. His powers, which gave him overall command of the army and the right to appoint senior officers and the governors of the major provinces, were formally conferred upon him by the votes of the Senate and people.

In general the new regime, which guaranteed stability and the chance of prosperity, was welcomed by the upper classes. In the provinces, which had suffered dreadfully from civil war, Augustus was hailed as a saviour. He received the adulation of the people of Rome, who were given free grain rations, cash hand-outs, and lavish entertainments ('bread and circuses'). He secured the loyalty of the army by settling veterans in colonies in the provinces and establishing a permanent standing force, with fixed terms of service and regular wages, with the guarantee of a retirement bonus on discharge. This reform took the army out of politics, made it dependent on the state, and guaranteed its loyalty to the emperor. Under Augustus the expansion of the empire continued, and its frontiers were extended to the Rhine and Danube rivers in central Europe. Victories abroad and peace at home were the hallmarks of Augustus' long reign. Agriculture and trade benefited, city life flourished, and literature and the visual arts flourished in what has come to be regarded as the high point of Roman civilization.

However, the rule of Augustus' successors – especially that of Tiberius (AD 14–37), Caligula (37–41), Nero (54–68) and Domitian (81–96) – became increasingly autocratic. Wars of conquest virtually ceased apart from the invasion of Britain under Claudius (41–54), and of Dacia (modern Romania) under Trajan (98–117). The stability and concord of Trajan's reign continued in the second century, under the benign rule of emperors such as Hadrian (117–138) and Antoninus Pius (138–161), but signs of strain began to appear in the reign of Marcus Aurelius (161–180).

The death of Marcus was later considered the end of a golden age. The reigns of his successors saw rising taxes, increasing military pressures and political upheavals. Septimius Severus (193–211) maintained order through military despotism, but after the death of the weak Alexander Severus (222–235) the empire lapsed into anarchy. Civil war, foreign invasions and rampant inflation were accompanied by political break-down, as emperors succumbed one after another to assassination or military revolt.

In the 270s the military threat temporarily receded, and political stability returned under Diocletian (284–304) and Constantine (312–337). But the recovery was only partial, and was achieved at the price of more oppressive government and bureaucracy, heavy taxation and the reduction of the peasantry to serfdom. A notable development was the rise of the Christian Church, which gained many converts during the 3rd-century troubles, but also attracted the hostility of the state. Official persecutions were instigated, especially by Diocletian in 303, but Constantine reversed this policy and officially recognized the Church. All subsequent emperors were nominally Christians, with the exception of Julian the Apostate (361–363), who staged an abortive pagan revival. Under Theodosius I (379–395) Christianity became the official religion of the Empire and other cults were banned.

Theodosius was the last emperor to rule over the whole Empire. In the 5th century the eastern and western parts had separate rulers and their histories diverged. The West was menaced by foreign invaders (Rome itself was sacked by the Visigoths under Alaric in 410), and in 476 the last Roman emperor, Romulus Augustulus, was deposed by the Gothic ruler Odoacer. The Byzantine Empire, as the Eastern Empire became known, although steadily reduced by Arab and then Turkish conquests, was to survive until the 15th century (▷ p. 240).

SEE ALSO

- THE ANCIENT NEAR EAST p. 228
- ANCIENT GREECE p. 230
- THE SUCCESSORS OF ROME p. 240
- ANCIENT RELIGIONS p. 286
- GREEK AND ROMAN ART p. 306
- CLASSICAL LITERATURE p. 356

WHY DID ROME FALL?

Historians have long puzzled over the causes of the decline and fall of the Western Empire, and have offered a bewildering variety of explanations. Excessive taxation, military weakness and population decline were all relevant factors, but were themselves symptoms of the condition that needs to be explained, and cannot be considered causes in their own right. The same is true of such explanations as moral corruption, while supposed environmental factors such as climate change or poisoning from lead water pipes seem contrived and unconvincing.

Much depends on the subjective view of the historian. For instance, Edward Gibbon (1737–94) in his monumental *Decline and Fall of the Roman Empire* deeply lamented the disappearance of an enlightened and rational culture, swept away on a tide of barbarism and superstition. Christians have not unnaturally challenged this view of the triumph of their faith. Modern academic historians are more neutral. They tend to emphasize the prosaic fact of the German invasions, which arose from external causes. Barbarian pressure on the frontiers had not existed under the early Empire, but built up in the 3rd century and became irresistible in the 5th. The implication of this view is that the Roman empire did not fall – it was pushed.

China to the Colonial Age

Since the fall of the Roman Empire, China has been the largest state in the world, and until the European Renaissance, technologically the most advanced. The Chinese continue to call their country the Middle Kingdom, and for long they thought of it as the centre of the world. The historic core of China was the area around the middle reaches of the Yellow River (Hwang He). There, on the fertile, easily worked soil that colours the river, the domestication of millet resulted in well-established Neolithic farming by 4000 BC. From this heartland, farming spread out in all directions, reaching the other great river basin, that of the Yangtze (Chang Jiang), by 2500 BC. As agriculture reached the warmer south, it adopted a more suitable local staple crop: rice. By 1500 BC, fully developed rice farming had spread south into Indochina and, by 500 BC, northeast into Korea.

The Great Wall of China, the largest single construction ever made. Begun in the 3rd century BC to keep out nomadic invaders from the north, it was largely rebuilt in the 15th and 16th centuries AD. On average some 9 m (30 ft) high, it stretches 2400 km (1490) mi across northern China. (AKG)

In the Yellow River heartland, the scale and organization of the farming communities increased and their technology improved. By 2000 BC, they had developed bronzeworking and ceremonial centres of some size. Around 1500 BC the first historical rulers emerged, the kings of the Shang dynasty. The remains of Shang cities and tombs reveal a civilization clearly ancestral to classic Chinese culture. Its script was of the ideographic type still used by the Chinese today, and its capital cities were laid out on a grid system oriented to the points of the compass, as all subsequent Chinese capitals have been. In addition, its bronze, pottery, jade and silk artefacts conformed to a style that the Chinese have held to ever since.

Civilization gradually spread outwards from the core area ruled by the Shang. To the west, the rulers of the Zhou acquired their essentials effi-ciently enough to displace the Shang as overlords of the Chinese heartland around 1000 BC. The Zhou expanded their power north as far as Manchuria and south over the Yangtze basin. Within those boundaries, advances in agriculture (irrigation) and technology (ironworking) made it possible to support powerful local rulers, their courts and warriors. As the centuries passed, power devolved to these smaller states which eventually – from the mid-5th century BC – became the 'Warring States'. When they were not making war, the rulers of the fiefs of Zhou China found time to consider the nature of power and government. At their courts, the essentials of Chinese views on the good society were developed. The most prominent administrator-philosopher was Kongfuzi (Confucius; 551–479 BC) who, around 500 BC, set out the basis of an ethic of civilized life that was to influence Chinese society down to the 20th century.

The beginnings of empire

The westernmost of the Warring States, Qin, emerged the final victor. In 221 BC, its ruler became Shi Huangdi (259–210) – 'the First Emperor' – and in the 11 years of his reign established the framework of the greatest state the world had so far seen. His empire spread out to touch the South China Sea and Central Asia. In the north, its boundary with the nomads was defined by the largest single human artefact ever made: the Great Wall. The laws, administration, script, currency, weights and measures of the empire were all reorganized and standardized.

Qin rule did not long outlast Shi Huangdi, but the foundations of empire had been firmly laid. Under the succeeding Han dynasty, the Chinese empire defined its traditional bounds. At the end of the 2nd century BC, it spread west into Central Asia, south into Vietnam, and east into Korea. However, these lands were too far away to be held for long, and though they always remained under strong Chinese influence they subsequently went their own way politically. One result of the expansion of the Han empire and its contacts with other societies was the arrival of Buddhism (▷ p. 290), which spread from India along the Central Asian trade routes that flourished in this period. Buddhist beliefs became and remained a major component of popular religion and culture in China. The Han empire also set the pattern of Chinese government. At the centre was the emperor and his court. He ruled through a highly educated bureaucracy selected by rigorous examination. The emperor also had a religious role: the welfare of the empire and its people was bound up with his well-being and correct performance of ritual duties. The carefully planned imperial city was the focus of ritual, bureaucracy, wealth and culture. The Chinese capitals – with populations of up to half a million – were the largest cities in the world between the fall of Rome and the rise of London. The history of the Han empire and of the later dynasties followed a similar pattern. Each dynasty started with a period of efficient government and imperial expansion. Then, slowly and inevitably, decline and disintegration set in. In the provinces, generals and governors built up separate local centres of power. Peasants rebelled as the burdens of tax and conscription weighed more heavily. Nomads pressed on the northern frontiers and sometimes broke through.

A pattern of dynasties

The next longstanding dynasty, the Tang, saw the empire rise to a classic perfection in the 7th, 8th and 9th centuries AD, ruled with rigid efficiency from Changan. Song China, between the 10th and 12th centuries, had a more complex structure. It was larger, too, containing over 100 million subjects at its peak. Among its most prosperous parts were the great new commercial cities along the Yangtze and the southern and eastern coasts, with trading links well beyond the traditional bounds of empire. These cities marked a drift of the centre of gravity of imperial China away from the Yellow River and towards the south.

The south proved sufficient to sustain a reduced 'southern Song' empire when the Yellow River basin fell under the rule of the Jin nomads from Manchuria in 1126. The northern Jin empire in turn succumbed to more powerful nomads, the Mongols under Genghis Khan (c. 1162–1227), who swept over northern China in a devastating campaign between 1211 and 1215. In the mid-13th century the Mongol attack was renewed and, by 1280, after more destruction, all China was under the rule of the Mongol Kublai Khan (1215–94).

The Yuan (Mongol) dynasty lasted a century. Although it adopted many of the trappings of traditional empire, it was overthrown in 1368 by a nationalist revolt. The first emperor of the new dynasty, the Ming, was Hongwu (1328–98), who had started life as a peasant. The Ming re-established the empire in its old form, and this empire flourished for over two centuries, then collapsed in the face of a peasant revolt in the mid-17th century. Order was restored by another nomad dynasty, the Qing, originating in Manchuria.

The last empire

The Qing (Manchu) dynasty, which ruled for two and a half centuries from 1659, formed an alien veneer on an empire that remained in its essential workings the traditional Chinese state. Under the Qing the empire expanded to include Tibet, Turkestan and Mongolia. The population within its borders rose past the 400 million mark. Its capital, Beijing, with a population approaching a million, remained the largest city in the world until the end of the 18th century. The collapse of Qing authority in the 19th century was in part a repetition of the old cycle. Population pressure, official corruption and increased taxation made peasant life a misery and revolt an attractive alternative. Thus far the old patterns held – but the barbarians pressing on the empire were different: this time they were Europeans. The Europeans did not want to rule; they wanted to trade at a profit. The Chinese empire was unwilling to expand its trade with the West, partly from a desire to remain self-sufficient, and partly out of incomprehension. However, trade was forced on the empire, in particular the import of opium from British India. Following the two Opium Wars (1839–42 and 1856–58), the conditions of trade were imposed by the European powers (c> p. 266).

In exchange, the Western powers helped to put down the most formidable peasant rebellion of the 19th century, in which several million people died. The Taiping ('heavenly peace') movement controlled much of the south of China during the 1850s. However, European arms and generalship brought it to a blood-soaked end in 1864. The Boxer Rebellion, which was turned against the Europeans by the Qing court, was equally effectively suppressed by Western forces in 1901. The court was punished for its complicity by being obliged to make further trading and other concessions. With China divided into Western (and Japanese) spheres of influence, the stage was set for the final act (c> p. 276).

SEE ALSO

● THE PEAK OF EMPIRE p. 266
● CHINA IN THE 20TH CENTURY p. 276
● RELIGIONS OF CHINA AND JAPAN p. 292
● NON-WESTERN ART p. 308

JAPAN TO THE 20TH CENTURY

Japan was first peopled from Asia in one of those periods in the last Ice Age when lowered sea levels joined offshore islands to the mainland. Over tens of thousands of years, hunting and gathering communities thrived on the Japanese islands. The techniques of fully developed rice farming reached the southern island of Kyushu from Korea, the nearest point on the Asian mainland, around 400 BC and spread up the island chain to reach the east coast of the central island of Honshu by AD 100. Links with the Asian mainland brought technical skills and cultural ideas, including the Chinese script, Confucianism and the then popular Chinese form of Buddhism (c> p. 292). By the 17th century AD the Japanese were also borrowing Chinese concepts of government, and a Chinese-style emperor was established at Nara (710–84) in a Chinese-style imperial city. However, the emperor became a religious figurehead, with power held by members of an aristocratic court family, the Fujiwara. Power in turn slipped away from the Fujiwara and into the hands of provincial governors and landowners. By the 12th century, much of the real power in Japan was exercised by the provincial barons (daimyos) through bands of warriors (samurai). After 1185 Yorimoto Minamoto ruled Japan from Kamakura (near Tokyo), eventually under the title of shogun, in the name of a powerless emperor who remained in courtly isolation at Kyoto. The Kamakura shogunate lasted a century and a half. For much of that time, the shogun himself was a figurehead, the real power being exercised by regents. In the 14th century, the Ashikaga family instituted a new shogunate based at Kyoto, but this fell apart into warring provincial baronies.

In the 16th century, Western ideas, particularly Christianity, made a significant impact on Japan, but the impact that really mattered was that of European firearms. Three military leaders in turn – Odo Nobunaga (1578–82), Toyotomi Hideyoshi (1582–98) and Tokugawa Ieyasu (1600–16) – used muskets to fight their way out of the impasse of feudal anarchy and into control of a united Japan. Under Ieyasu, the shogunate was established at Edo (Tokyo) in the control of the Tokugawa family. The Tokugawa shogunate was built on feudal concepts but governed as a military bureaucracy. The daimyos were subject to close supervision and their local power diminished by long periods of compulsory residence at the court of the shogun. Loyalty to the shogunate was further encouraged by excluding foreign influences. Christianity was suppressed, and the only foreign traders permitted were the Dutch. Hermetically sealed from outside influences, Japan went its own way between the mid-17th and the mid-19th centuries. Tokugawa Japan was a stable and, in many ways, a prosperous pre-industrial society, able to sustain great cities and a complex bureaucracy.

The industrial West arrived with an American fleet in 1853. Japan was forced into the global trading system. The impact of the outside world destabilized an already weakening Tokugawa regime. In 1867–8, power was seized at Kyoto by a group representing daimyos from western Japan together with reforming imperial courtiers. The last Tokugawa shogun was overthrown and, in 1869, Emperor Mutsuhito was installed with executive power at Edo, renamed Tokyo. The emperor adopted 'Meiji' ('enlightened government') as his throne name, and the term is also applied to the period of his reign (1867–1912). The privy councillors who exercised power on behalf of the emperor proceeded to transform Japan. Virtually all vestiges of feudalism were removed: the daimyos and samurai were pensioned off and the peasants given ownership of the land they worked (and then heavily taxed). Western systems of law, administration and taxation were introduced in 1889, followed by a constitution and parliament along Western lines. Developing a Western-style economy was a little more difficult to achieve, but industrialization was well underway by the beginning of the 20th century. By then Japan had been accepted as an equal by the Western powers. Japan even began to fight and win Western-type wars, against China in 1894–95 and Russia in 1904–5, coming away with the beginnings of a colonial empire in Taiwan, Korea and the south of Manchuria.

India and Southeast Asia to the Colonial Age

The history of civilization in the Indian subcontinent begins in the northwest (now mainly Pakistan). This region formed an extension of the Middle-East/Iranian cultural zone and it was from there that it acquired Neolithic farming techniques by 5000 BC. The techniques spread on, first to central India and then to the far south by 2000 BC.

SEE ALSO

- THE RISE OF ISLAM p. 242
- THE VOYAGES OF DISCOVERY p. 247
- EUROPEAN EMPIRES IN THE 17TH AND 18TH CENTURIES p. 257
- THE PEAK OF EMPIRE p. 266
- THE RELIGIONS OF INDIA p. 288
- BUDDHISM p. 290
- NON-WESTERN ART p. 308

A Mogul miniature of the late 17th century, depicting a nocturnal encounter between a Mogul prince and a young woman. The artistic tradition that the Moguls brought with them to India derived from the ancient civilization of Persia, but as time passed, local craftsmen and artists made an increasing contribution. The mature Mogul style was a blend of Indian and Persian elements. (AKG)

In the northwest settlements became larger, bronze working was introduced, and ruling elites emerged. The Harappan civilization, focused on the two cities of Harappa and Mohenjo-Daro, flourished in the Indus Valley between 2300 and 1700 BC. In these cities the full repertoire of Bronze Age urban society was displayed: a literate elite, carefully organized and controlled water and food supplies, and densely packed artisan quarters. The Indus Valley civilization flourished for 600 years and then collapsed for reasons that remain unclear. By 1500 BC the northeast of India, the Ganges basin, had evolved a Bronze Age culture of its own and had succeeded the Indus Valley as the core area of Indian civilization.

The shift from the Indus to the Ganges is associated with the entry into the subcontinent of the Aryans – Indo-European pastoralists from the Iranian steppe. The Aryans imposed themselves on the native Dravidians, and the resulting amalgam became the Hindu society that has been the majority community of India ever since.

The Hindu kingdoms of the Ganges valley entered the Iron Age in around 800 BC. Some 300 years later the region produced one of history's great religious teachers, the Buddha (⊳ p. 290). The dominant kingdom then and for several centuries subsequently was Magdalha; its pre-eminence

increased with the advent of the Mauryan dynasty. Chandragupta Maurya (321–297 BC) conquered most of northern and central India, and his grandson Ashoka (272–232 BC) placed inscriptions even further afield. However, an Indian empire of this extent was exceptional. Mostly the Indus valley belonged to empires that lay to the west – to Persia between the late 6th and 4th centuries BC and to Alexander the Great at the end of the 4th century BC. After Ashoka the Greeks returned to the upper Indus basin and a rich Indo-Greek society developed in the area; they in their turn were supplanted by nomad rulers from Central Asia. The decline of the Mauryan dynasty saw the north and centre of the subcontinent revert to a glittering mosaic of regional kingdoms.

The expansion of Hindu culture

Hindu expansionism was mercantile and cultural rather than imperial, although Ceylon (Sri Lanka) was brought within its influence by invasion from the north of India around 500 BC. First the tribal areas of southern India were brought into contact with the centre and north, and then overseas trading links were developed to the east. By the 3rd century AD, Hindu kingdoms were beginning to spring up all over previously tribal Southeast Asia – in Burma, Thailand, Cambodia, Java and Sumatra.

Buddhism followed Hinduism into Southeast Asia at a time when its influence at home in India was declining, and established itself as the dominant faith in Burma, Thailand and Cambodia. The splendour of Indian culture in Southeast Asia was to reach its climax between the 9th and 13th centuries in the great Buddhist Khmer empire of Cambodia and the wide Hindu maritime kingdom of Shrivijaya, centred on Sumatra.

Islam in India

In the 8th century an Arab army marched in from Iran and made Sind (southern Pakistan) a province of the Caliphate. In the 11th and 12th centuries Muslim princes in Afghanistan launched campaigns that eventually brought down the Hindu kingdoms of the Ganges valley and replaced them with an Islamic state, the Sultanate of Delhi (1206). Temporarily, under Muhammed bin Tughluq (1325–1351), then more permanently under Akbar (1556–1605) and Aurangzeb (1658–1707) of the Mogul dynasty, the sultanate expanded until it embraced almost the entire subcontinent. The Moguls came from Central Asia, but they created a culture which, in buildings such as the Taj Mahal, stamped its image on India forever.

After Aurangzeb, Mogul power declined and provincial governors, some of them Hindus, began asserting their independence. By this time European trading companies had arrived in India – the Portuguese in the 16th century, and the Dutch, French and British in the course of the 17th. At first the companies stuck to trading, then they became involved in local politics, and in wars between themselves and against native rulers. By the 1760s the British East India Company had emerged as the dominant power on the subcontinent (⊳ p. 257). It was the beginning of a new phase of empire building that ultimately brought all India under British rule (⊳ p. 266).

Africa, Australasia and Oceania to the Colonial Age

Africa south of the Sahara is the cradle of the human race: the first man-like creatures evolved there, as did the first men (▷ p. 200). As the millennia passed, early man (Homo erectus) evolved into modern man (Homo sapiens), who in turn developed different varieties to suit different environments. Sub-Saharan Africa produced four: the Negroes in the West African bush, the Pygmies in the equatorial rain forest, the Nilo-Saharans of the middle Nile, and the Bushmen of the open lands in the east and south.

SEE ALSO

● THE ANCIENT NEAR EAST p. 228
● THE RISE OF ISLAM p. 242
● THE PEAK OF EMPIRE p. 266
● DECOLONIZATION p. 278

The relatively small area of Africa north of the Sahara belonged, then as now, to a different world; its peoples are relatives of the Semites of the Middle East, and their history belongs largely to that of the Mediterranean and the Middle East (▷ pp. 228, 232 and 242).

AUSTRALASIA AND OCEANIA

The first men arrived in New Guinea and Australia around 50 000 BC when the last Ice Age lowered the sea level sufficiently to make island-hopping along the Indonesian archipelago relatively easy. After the last Ice Age, the waters finally rose to divide New Guinea and Australia sometime around 5000 BC, and the two islands went their separate ways. Both developed advanced Stone Age cultures. That of New Guinea was based on horticulture, that of Australia on hunting and gathering. The Aboriginal culture of Australia was largely isolated from this time. Neither internal pressures nor sporadic contacts with the rest of the world led to the development of agriculture. Instead, roving hunter-gatherers reacted in sophisticated ways to a wide variety of environments. The rich cultural life of the Aborigines has all but disappeared under the destructive impact of European settlement, leaving little more behind it than a fading legacy of rock paintings.

Melanesian horticulturalists from New Guinea reached the New Hebrides and New Caledonia by 2000 BC. At the same time, other peoples – originally of east Asian stock – were moving east from the Philippines and surrounding islands to settle Micronesia and the northern and eastern fringes of Melanesia. These newcomers to the area brought with them a different language and cul-ture from those previously developed in Melanesia. But they also brought a similar Neolithic horticulture which, combined with fishing, was well suited to the smaller islands of the Pacific. Settlers from such a background had reached Fiji by 1500 BC, spreading from there to Tonga and Samoa. It was in this area over the next millennium that the language and culture of the Pacific islanders developed the traits we recognize as Polynesian. Polynesian culture boasted a magnificent tradition of seafaring. Time and again, Polynesians set out into the unknown on outrigger canoes loaded with the essentials of their life and used their skill and luck to colonize islands as distant as Easter Island and Hawaii. In the south, the main islands of New Zealand were much larger than the other Polynesian islands and lay in the temperate zone. In this different environment, Maori culture developed its own variations. At first, the peculiar fauna of New Zealand made hunting an important part of life. Later, the Maori turned to an agriculture founded on sweet potatoes and fern rhizomes, and developed a warrior culture based on fortified villages. They were to become the only Pacific people to offer major armed resistance to European advances in the 19th century, and peace between the Maoris and the British colonists was only finally achieved in 1871.

Early Africa

Farming spread from the Middle East through Egypt to the middle Nile valley sometime before 3000 BC. Beyond the Nile valley the environment was more suited to specialized pastoral farming. Soon, Nilo-Saharans and their herds were moving west along the open savannah south of the Sahara, and into West Africa. In the final millennium BC, the Negro peoples of the settled village communities of West Africa developed the ability to smelt iron. The combination of agriculture and iron created a potent force in prehistoric society. Around the beginning of the Christian era, Bantu farmers began to spread east and south out of West Africa. By AD 500 they had reached as far as the east coast of southern Africa, leaving only the deep rain forest to the Pygmies and the Kalahari Desert to the Bushmen.

Settled Black Africa of the Iron Age had contacts with the world to the north and east. That world was to bring trade in exchange for Africa's gold, ivory and slaves, and eventually offered monotheistic religion as well. Egypt had always been in touch with Nilo-Saharan Nubia (northern Sudan), and had even been briefly ruled by a Nubian dynasty in the century around 700 BC. Later, Christianity found its way up the Nile to Nubia and to Ethiopia (later Abyssinia), as early as the 4th century AD. The eastern coast of Africa had longstanding contacts with the Arabian peninsula. Arab expansion (▷ p. 242) brought Islam to the northeast coast, as far south as Somalia, by the 12th century, and the establishment of trading settlements along the coast down to Mozambique between the 9th and 13th centuries. In West Africa, trade began to reach across the Sahara from Muslim North Africa in the 8th century and Islam followed into the Sahel in the 11th century.

The profit from Black African contact with the Arab world – particularly from the gold trade – enabled some African kingdoms to establish themselves on a much more lavish scale than before. In West Africa, the kingdoms of Ghana (8th–12th centuries) and Mali (13th–14th centuries) dominated the routes between the goldfields and the desert trails to North Africa. Similarly, the eastern kingdom of Zimbabwe (13th–15th centuries) controlled that region's goldfields and its trade with the coastal Arabs.

From the later 15th century, the Portuguese took over much of the east-coast Arab trade and went on to establish a similar trade on the west coast (▷ p. 252), where they were largely replaced by the Dutch in the 17th century, who in turn were replaced by the British and French in the 18th (▷ p. 257). Inland African kingdoms in West Africa lived in symbiosis with the coastal traders, supplying them with gold and slaves to work the plantations of the Americas in exchange for textiles, iron goods and guns (▷ p. 257).

In the far south Dutch colonists, the Boers, began to settle in the second half of the 17th century. By the end of the 18th century Boer expansion had led to clashes with the southernmost of the Bantu kingdoms and begun a pattern of war and colonization that was to bring about the fall of all black African kingdoms except Abyssinia by the end of 19th century (▷ p. 266).

Pre-Columbian America

America was the last of the habitable continents to be colonized by man, an event that occurred during the last Ice Age. Two opposing geographical changes made it possible. First the sea level fell because of the amount of water locked up in the icecaps: this led to the appearance of a land bridge connecting Asia and Alaska. Then the melting of the North American icecap removed the barrier to movement between Alaska and the rest of North America. There was just enough time for a few families of Siberian mammoth hunters to make the journey before the rising sea level obliterated the land bridge.

This happened in around 10 000 BC, and within 1000 years the descendants of these few families had spread over North and South America. Nearly all the American Indians derive from this stock: the only exceptions are the Athapascan tribes of Canada and western North America, and the Inuit (Eskimo) of the far north; these two peoples arrived by boat five or six thousand years later.

As the climate improved and the mammoths disappeared from the American scene, the early Americans found it difficult to support themselves by big-game hunting alone; many of them turned to smaller game, and to the gathering of edible seeds and fruit. In the end, around 2500 BC, this led to the appearance of agricultural communities in Meso-America (Mexico and Central America) and the central Andean region of South America (Equador, Peru and Bolivia).

The Warriors' Temple at Chichén Itzá, from the 10th to the 12th centuries the main Toltec city of Yucatán. Stepped pyramids were built by various Meso-American cultures, including the Mayans, Toltecs and Aztecs, and were often the site of human sacrifices. (Spectrum)

The early agriculturalists

In Meso-America the staple crop was maize. In the Andes, and on their western side, a number of crops were domesticated, including the potato, and, after 1500 BC, maize. By 1000 BC a third area of farming – relying largely on manioc – had developed in the tropical area now covered by Colombia and Venezuela.

Later in the first millennium BC maize farming reached what is now the southwest USA and spread from there into the Mississippi basin around AD 500. By that time, the whole western part of the continent between Mexico and northern Chile was occupied by maize farmers, while tropical farmers were settled on river banks along the whole length of the Amazon river system and had reached the Caribbean islands as well. Tropical farming continued to spread after this, reaching south to the Paraná basin by AD 1000 and then moving north up the Brazilian coast.

Not all Americans turned to agriculture, however. Along the coastline, on the open plains of both North and South America and in the deep tropical jungle of the Amazon basin, specialist fishers, hunters and gatherers maintained rich and varied ways of life up to the 19th or 20th centuries.

The development of civilization

As in the Old World, the acquisition of agriculture was only the beginning of a sequence of developments which culminated in civilization. Settled farmers can support settled places of worship. After a while, by coming together in sufficient numbers, they can build temples of some size and maintain the priestly elites to go with them. This development had taken place separately by 1500 BC in both of the core areas of temperate agriculture, Meso-America and the central Andes, and spread as far as the Mississippi basin by the 8th century AD (the Temple Mound culture).

The steps in the organization of society beyond tribal farming and local religious centres were

MAJOR
TRIBES
OF
NORTH
AMERICA
AD 1500

ESKIMO HUNTERS AND FISHERS	PLAINS HUNTERS AND GATHERERS	DESERT HUNTERS AND GATHERERS
FOREST HUNTERS AND GATHERERS	PLAINS FARMERS	PUEBLO FARMERS
SETTLED FISHERS AND GATHERERS	MISSISSIPPIAN FARMERS	PENINSULAR AND ANTILLEAN FARMERS AND FISHERS

The following period was one of warring local states, none of which established more than a brief regional dominance. Then from the mid-14th century the Aztecs, based on their great island city of Tenochtitlan in Lake Texcoco (the site of Mexico City), spread out to bring a large part of Meso-America under their rule. Theirs was the most impressive empire Meso-America had seen – and the last native one, falling to Spanish invaders under Cortez in 1519–21 (▷ p. 252).

In South America, the first military hegemony of some size was that established from Huari between the 9th and 12th centuries AD. It was succeeded, after a period in which regional states reasserted themselves, by the coastal power of Chimu from the late 14th to mid-15th centuries, and then by the highland rule of the Incas of Cuzco.

By the end of the 15th century, Inca power spread over virtually the whole of the area from modern Ecuador to northern Chile. The Inca empire was another first and last empire, scarcely established before it was overthrown by Spanish forces under Pizarro in 1532–33 (▷ p. 252).

The Aztec and Inca empires fell in unequal struggles. They were at a cultural level roughly equivalent to the Old World Bronze Age (▷ p. 227). They had built their first proper cities and had begun to organize themselves to collect tribute efficiently from the tribes and chiefdoms they dominated. The Incas had also built a system of roads and forts to control their domains more effectively. None of these could protect them against such instruments of advanced Old World civilization as the iron sword, the firearm and the horse-borne warrior.

SEE ALSO
● THE SPANISH AND PORTU-GUESE EMPIRES p. 252
● THE BIRTH OF THE USA p. 260

AZTEC

INCA

taken only in Meso-America and the central Andes. The initial focus of the development of civilization in these two areas was religious, centring on the building of increasingly grandiose temples and then temple-cities. This phase reached its peak in the Maya cities of lowland Meso-America, at Teotihuacán in the Mexico valley, and at Tiahuanaco high up in the Andes, all at the height of their splendour in the first millennium AD. At the heart of these ceremonial cities were great artificial temple mounds ('pyramids') set within rigid geometric layouts that had astronomical significance. In Meso-America, an obsession with the calendar led to complex mathematical calculations and the development of hieroglyphic means of record. Another obsession of Meso-American religion was human sacrifice, presumably intended to appease the gods and maintain the pattern of the seasons.

In the 7th century Teotihuacán was abandoned and the same fate gradually overtook all the other pyramid cities of Mexico and Yucatán. No one knows why – perhaps the rituals had simply become too onerous to sustain. The setback was not permanent, however, and by 900 new cities were under construction, notably Tula, the capital of the Toltecs, just to the north of present-day Mexico City.

Toltecs, Aztecs and Incas

These temple-cities were not primarily the capitals of political states. They were the religious and social centres of agricultural peoples – organized into tribes and chiefdoms – who periodically came up to their temples to worship and celebrate. States grew out of the dominance that the warriors of certain tribes established over their neighbours during this period.

In Meso-America, the earliest warrior state of major importance was probably Teotihuacán, which in the 6th century AD was sending armed embassies far afield. The next was that built up by the Toltecs, who dominated a large part of central Mexico and the Yucatán between the 10th and 12th centuries AD from their base at Tula and Chichén Itzá.

THE NORTH AMERICAN INDIANS

It is difficult to get back beyond five centuries of disruption (and destruction) to obtain a clear picture of the life of the native Americans north of the Rio Grande before 1492. It is even difficult to separate the Indian brave from his horse – a European import which the Plains Indians took over with great enthusiasm in the 18th century.

The million or so inhabitants of North America in 1492 were scattered across the whole continent and gained their living in a wide variety of ways. In and around the Mississippi basin and over to the east coast were well-established farmers living in villages of solid wooden houses. They relied largely – but not exclusively – on agriculture for their subsistence. In the southwest were other farmers, living in a more hostile and arid environment, but occupying even more solid, stone-built pueblos. Along the northwest coastline were prosperous villagers who relied on the ample resources of the sea and rivers for their main food supply.

Elsewhere, life was more mobile: following game on the Plains or gathering plants in the deserts and hills west of the Rockies. There were hunters in the forests beyond the Great Lakes and then up towards the Arctic were the Inuit (Eskimo) fishers and hunters.

The villagers and some of the more organized bands of hunter-gatherers were grouped into tribes. Tribes shared a local language and culture and often claimed a common descent. They were governed by meetings of tribal elders and came together from time to time to worship and socialize. Tribes further distinguished themselves from other tribes by a readiness to fight them.

War called for individual leadership. Among the villagers of the east and the northwest, this had led to the grouping of some of the tribes into more permanent confederations under the rule of chiefs. Chiefs could claim more extensive rights of government and a greater share of resources for themselves and their warriors than was possible among the individual tribes – and they took them. However, with the coming of the Europeans, the Indians were forced further and further west, until by the end of the 19th century all their lands had been lost (▷ p. 261).

The Successors of Rome

The Roman Empire has had many imitators. After AD 400 the western part of the Empire began to disintegrate into various kingdoms ruled by Germanic peoples (⊳ p. 233). Around 800, Charlemagne reunited many of them to create a Frankish empire in Rome's image. This later became known as the Holy Roman Empire. The eastern Roman Empire was based on Constantinople (modern Istanbul) and ruled separately from 380 onwards. Here decline was slower. This empire became known as the Byzantine Empire, after Byzantium, the Greek name for Constantinople.

The sack of Rome by the Goths in 410 (⊳ p. 233) was an act more symbolic than significant. Germanic peoples had been pressing on Roman borders for centuries and had already broken through once, in the 3rd century. However, the conquest of the 5th century was to prove permanent. By around 500, successor states were established by the Visigoths in Spain, the Vandals in North Africa, the Ostrogoths in Italy, and the Franks in Gaul (France; ⊳ map). It was the Franks who were to survive and attempt to re-create Rome's empire. The others fell either to Justinian's 'reconquest' in the mid-6th century (⊳ below) or to Islam (⊳ p. 242).

THE BARBARIAN KINGDOMS
AT THE DEATH OF CLOVIS, KING OF THE FRANKS AD 511

DANES
IRISH
ANGLES
ANGLO-SAXONS   FRISIANS
BRITISH   SAXONS
SLAVS
THURINGIANS
KINGDOM OF THE FRANKS   LOMBARDS   HUNS
BAVARIANS
AUSTRASIA
BRETONS   NEUSTRIA
KINGDOM OF THE BURGUNDIANS   KINGDOM OF THE OSTROGOTHS   GEPIDS
KINGDOM OF THE SUEVES   Poitiers
AQUITAINE
BYZANTINE EMPIRE
Constantinople
GALICIA   BASQUES
Rome
CORSICA
KINGDOM OF THE VISIGOTHS
SARDINIA
BALEARIC ISLANDS
KINGDOM OF THE VANDALS   SICILY
Carthage

From the Carolingian to the Holy Roman Empire

The Carolingian dynasty was based in northern France. It was named after Charlemagne ('Charles the Great'), king of the Franks from 768 to 814. Charlemagne's father, Pepin the Short (751–68), had ousted the old Merovingian dynasty that had ruled the Franks from c. 500 to 751. The Carolingian rise to power was due to military success. Charlemagne's grandfather, Charles Martel, had checked the Muslim advance at Poitiers in 732, and Charlemagne himself went on to conquer Italy, Hungary and Germany. He created the largest state in the West for 400 years. More than that he consciously declared it Roman and Christian.

Charlemagne had himself crowned emperor of the West by the pope in Rome on Christmas Day 800. His court at Aix-la-Chapelle (Aachen) became the centre of a cultural renaissance without which much classical learning would have been lost. Charlemagne also did much to strengthen the administration of the Empire. But a combination of the Frankish system of partible inheritance (division amongst heirs) and external attack worked against the Empire's survival. Charlemagne's son Louis the Pious (814–840) divided the Empire between his three sons. In the late 9th century, the imperial leadership proved itself ineffective against Muslim, Viking and Magyar (Hungarian) raids. The result was that power slipped into the hands of regional aristocracies.

The East Frankish (German) aristocracy became particularly prominent. In the early 10th century, its leaders – the dukes of Saxony – replaced the Carolingians as kings east of the Rhine. By first checking and then defeating the Magyars (Battle of the Lech, 955) and by keeping the Vikings at bay, Henry I (919–936) and his son Otto I 'the Great' (936–973) established claims to empire. Otto entered Italy with his army in 951 and was crowned emperor at Rome in 962. The ending of the custom of partible inheritance meant that this empire lasted until the end of the Middle Ages and beyond. When the Ottonian dynasty died out (1024), first the Salians took over (until 1125), then the Hohenstaufens (until 1254).

The efforts these rulers made to keep control over Italy led to a series of quarrels both with the increasingly wealthy and independent cities of northern Italy – and with popes intent on asserting the 'liberty of the Church' against secular interference. The quarrels with popes led to the emperors insisting on the God-given dignity of their own position; thus in the 13th century the term 'Holy Roman Empire' came into vogue.

In theory the Empire had become an elective (rather than a hereditary) monarchy in the 12th century, and in 1356 the procedure by which a college of seven electors chose the emperor-to-be was laid down. Yet – apart from a period from the mid-13th to the mid-14th century – in practice the electors were content to elect the dynastic heir. Thus Charles IV (1346–78) was succeeded by his heirs until they died out in 1437. From then on until the end of the Empire in 1918 the Austrian Habsburgs remained firmly on the throne.

By far the most prominent of the Habsburg emperors was Charles V. Holy Roman Emperor from 1519 until his abdication in 1556, and combining the Habsburg, Burgundian and

SEE ALSO
- ANCIENT ROME p. 232
- THE RISE OF ISLAM p. 242
- CHRISTIANITY RESURGENT p. 244
- THE SPANISH AND PORTU-GUESE EMPIRES p. 252

A Byzantine mosaic adorns the dome of the 12th-century Capella Palatina in Palermo, Sicily. The image of Christ Pantocrator (the Almighty) was a prominent one in Byzantine church decoration (⊳ p. 307). Byzantine art spread to Italy and Sicily by trade and conquest, and – through the expansion of the Orthodox Church – to Slav countries such as Russia, where its traditions flourished long after the Byzantine empire had collapsed. (AKG)

Spanish inheritances in a single pair of hands, he ruled over the largest European empire since Charlemagne (⊳ p. 252).

The Byzantine Empire

Secure within the walls of Constantinople the Eastern Empire weathered the storm of the 5th century. During the reign of Justinian (527–565) it underwent an intellectual, administrative, architectural and military revival. Justinian's most ambitious project was to reconquer the Empire's lost western provinces. In the 530s his great general Belisarius achieved some stunning triumphs: the reconquest of Africa, Sicily and most of Ostrogothic Italy. But in 542 bubonic plague struck, with devastating economic and financial consequences, and the Ostrogoths took the opportunity to fight back. Yet by the early 560s Justinian's armies had once again gained control of Italy and reconquered southern Spain from the Visigoths.

In 568 new invaders, the Lombards, entered Italy. Conceivably they might have been thrown out, but Justinian's over-confident successors chose this moment to break with Rome's ancient enemy, Persia. In 626 the Persians, in alliance with the Avars, laid siege to Constantinople itself. The soldier-emperor Heraclius (610–641) reacted by launching a counterattack on the Persian heart-lands, and while Constantinople's walls held firm, the Persian Empire crumbled. But the emperor's conjuring trick was in vain. In the 630s and 640s his exhausted empire was unable to prevent the loss of its richest provinces – Syria, Egypt, Mesopotamia and then Africa – to the Arabs (⊳ p. 242). This was a blow from which the Empire never entirely recovered.

The 7th century also saw the Lombards make further advances in Italy, while the Danube frontier collapsed as Slavs moved in and settled the Balkans in increasing numbers. This was a century that left its mark on the map: from now on the Middle East was to remain a Muslim preserve, and the Balkans a largely Slav one. Constantinople was threatened by Arab sieges in the 670s and 717–718, as well as by the incessant pressure of Arab raids into Asia Minor (modern Turkey) in these and subsequent decades. In the 8th and 9th centuries the traumas of religious disunity further weakened the empire.

In the 10th century there was something of a revival. Talented military emperors pressed east into Armenia and even campaigned in Syria again. In the 960s Crete and Cyprus were recovered – although in the West the Arabs completed their conquest of Sicily. The main achievement of this period was the combination of Byzantine military power and Greek cultural influence, which led to the acceptance of Orthodox Christianity by the Bulgars and Russians.

The mid-11th century, however, found the Empire once again on the retreat. Normans occupied southern Italy (⊳ p. 243) and, more seriously, Seljuk Turks overran the interior of Asia Minor. Disaster followed in 1204 when the Fourth Crusade, diverted from its original goal by Venetian policy, ended by sacking Constantinople, the greatest city of the Christian world. Although the Latin Empire set up by the Crusaders in Constantinople lasted only until 1261, the re-established Byzantine Empire was to be but a shadow of its former self. The last two centuries of Byzantine history are a record of decline in the face of pressure from the Ottoman Turks. The final fall of Constantinople to the Ottomans in 1453 was a case of an elephant crushing a flea.

Yet Byzantium had always meant more than merely its territories. It created Orthodox Christianity and it preserved Greek culture. For centuries this preservation of Greek culture was to be a source of inspiration to the West, either directly or indirectly through the Arabs (⊳ p. 242). In the end its Turkish conquerors were themselves captured by the image of Byzantium. They chose to rule, in Byzantine manner, from the place they called simply 'Stamboul' – the city.

THE ANGLO-SAXONS

From the 2nd to the 5th centuries AD Britain was ruled as a Roman colony. The native Britons, who were Celts, were largely Romanized, and Christianity was established. However, in 407, pressure from barbarians on other parts of the Roman Empire led to the final withdrawal of Roman forces from Britain, leaving a power vacuum that other peoples were eager to exploit.

Between c. 450 and c. 600 southern Britain was the target of a series of invasions by pagan Germanic invaders – principally Angles, Saxons and Jutes, but also Frisians and Franks (⊳ map). Collectively, these peoples are known as Anglo-Saxons, and it is from their language that modern English derives.

By the first half of the 7th century Anglo-Saxon control had reached the Firth of Forth in the north and the borders of Wales in the west. However, in the southwest (Cornwall) and northwest (Strathclyde) the British retained their independence. Throughout the 7th and 8th centuries there was a fluctuating number of Anglo-Saxon kingdoms, sometimes as many as a dozen. Gradually, however, a 'big three' emerged: Northumbria, Mercia and Wessex – the three kingdoms that were the cutting edge of expansion northwards and westwards.

It is possible that Wessex, Mercia and Northumbria were mixed British and Anglo-Saxon societies in which Anglo-Saxon (English) culture came to be dominant – except in one respect. Christianity – the religion of the Britons – had been reintroduced. In 597 St Augustine had been sent from Rome to convert the English and to bring the British Churches under Roman authority.

During the 7th and 8th centuries Anglo-Saxon kings were more concerned with a struggle for supremacy over each other than further expansion at the expense of the Welsh. This internal struggle was interrupted by raids carried out by fierce seafarers from across the North Sea – the Vikings (⊳ p. 243).

The Rise of Islam

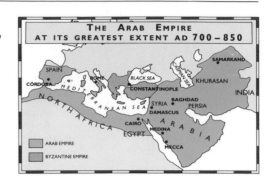

In the early 7th century of the Christian era a charismatic figure united the tribes of the Arabian Peninsula, who then embarked on a century-long campaign of conquest. The man was Muhammad, called the Prophet, and his religion was Islam – meaning 'submission to the will of God' (▷ p. 300).

Before he died in 632, Muhammad urged a *jihad* ('holy war') against unbelievers. The first targets of Arab expansion were areas adjacent to Arabia belonging to the Byzantine and Sassanid (Persian) Empires. These two great powers had exhausted themselves after decades of continuous warfare. In addition the Christians of the region belonged to sects that had no love for the Byzantine Empire. In a decade Arab armies conquered Syria (636–638), Egypt (640–642) and Mesopotamia (639–646). Persia collapsed within the same timescale. Muslim tolerance of Christians and Jews meant that many welcomed their rule.

The early caliphates

The Umayyad dynasty (651–749), reigning in Syria, created a strong, flexible state, under its *caliphs* (successors of the Prophet). However, Islam was split when a combination of dynastic and theological issues produced the breakaway Shiite sect. This consisted of followers of the Prophet's son-in-law Ali, who had been murdered in 661.

In 749 regional separatism and Shiite opposition produced a revolution and the establishment of the Abbasid dynasty. The new caliphs moved to a new capital – Baghdad. The Umayyads held on only in their most recent conquest, Spain.

The political unity of the Muslim world was further fractured in the 9th and 10th centuries. The Shiite Fatimids (claiming descent from the Prophet's daughter, Fatima) established another caliphate in Tunisia. In 969 they conquered Egypt. Meanwhile within the Baghdad caliphate real power had fallen into the hands of Turkish army commanders. Although the Abbasid dynasty was to survive until 1258, the power of the caliphs was considerably diminished.

Dealing with the 'barbarians'

Between the 11th and 13th centuries the Islamic world suffered a series of shocks at the hands of peoples it regarded as barbarians: Seljuk Turks, Western Europeans, and Mongols. However, whereas both Seljuks and Mongols were in time converted to Islam, the European Crusaders remained Christian, and indeed saw themselves as fighting a holy war of their own (▷ p. 244).

By the early 13th century the Muslims had lost nearly all of Spain to the Christians (▷ p. 244),

and this loss was to be permanent. In Syria, Christian conquests – the Crusader states – were more short-lived. In 1187 Saladin, sultan of Egypt and Syria, recaptured Jerusalem and in the late 13th century his work was completed by the Mamluk sultans of Egypt (▷ p. 244). The Mamluk sultans, moreover, had managed to keep their independence when much of the Muslim world collapsed before the Mongol advance in the mid-13th century. Once converted, however, the Mongols took Islam even further afield, into India and China.

Ottoman expansion

From small beginnings around 1300, the Ottoman Turks emerged as the foremost Muslim power. They made Anatolia (Asian Turkey) the centre of attacks on the Byzantine capital, Constantinople, which had withstood Arab sieges in the 670s and in 717–718 (▷ p. 241). By the end of the 14th century, Ottoman raids into the remaining Byzantine territory had reduced the Byzantine Empire to the walls of Constantinople. Invaders from Central Asia under the fearsome Tamerlane provided the city with a brief respite. Tamerlane (or Timur; c. 1336–1405) had led his armies from his capital in Samarkand in an orgy of conquest and destruction across Mongolia, India, Russia and the Middle East, and in 1402 he defeated and captured the Ottoman sultan. But Constantinople was finally overwhelmed by the artillery and huge forces of Sultan Mehmed II in 1453.

From their new capital, now named Istanbul, the Ottoman sultans embarked on campaigns of expansion. In 1517 Selim I conquered Egypt, and under his successor, Suleiman the Magnificent (1520–66), the Ottoman Empire reached its peak. Certainly the Ottomans did much to encourage the spread of Islam. The northern boundary of their conquests in Europe was marked by the failed sieges of Vienna in 1529 and 1683, but the Ottomans were to hold on to most of southeast Europe until the 19th century (▷ p. 265). The naval defeat at Lepanto in 1571 (▷ p. 253) meant that Mediterranean expansion was effectively over by 1600. Christian Spain expelled its Muslim population – the Moriscoes – in the mid-17th century.

Despite this check in Europe, overall the picture was still one of expansion. Just as the Christian Spanish and Portuguese spread their religion along the trade routes (▷ p. 252), so Ottoman venturers carried Islam to Africa and Southeast Asia. During the 14th and 15th centuries Malaya and Indonesia were converted to Islam, and its status as a worldwide religion was assured.

SEE ALSO

● THE SUCCESSORS OF ROME
  p. 240
● CHRISTIANITY RESURGENT
  p. 244
● NATIONALISM IN EUROPE
  p. 264
● THE MIDDLE EAST p. 282
● ISLAM p. 300
● NON-WESTERN ART p. 308

Vikings and Normans

The Vikings (or 'Norsemen') came from three distinct parts of Scandinavia – Norway, Sweden and Denmark. They were brilliant seamen, their longships taking them from the Black Sea in the east to America in the west. Viking armies were small, usually to be numbered in hundreds, and were not militantly anti-Christian – by the end of the 11th century they had all been converted to Christianity. The Vikings shared many values with the rulers of the societies they attacked in western Europe and found it easy to stay as settlers.

The Norwegians were active on both shores of the Irish Sea, ultimately settling in eastern Ireland, western Scotland, the Isle of Man and northwest England, as well as the Orkney, Shetland and Faeroe Islands. They also colonized Iceland. It was from there that Eric the Red sailed west in c. 986 to discover Greenland, where a settlement survived into the 15th century. In around 1000 the Norwegians, under Leif Eriksson, also briefly settled in northeast North America, which they called *Vinland* (possibly Newfoundland).

The Swedes went east into Russia, where they formed the first organized states. Sailing down the great river systems to the Black Sea, they also traded with – and even assaulted – the Byzantine capital, Constantinople.

The Danes directed most of their energies against the Anglo-Saxon and Frankish kingdoms (▷ p. 240). By the end of the ninth century the kingdoms of Northumbria, East Anglia and Mercia

SEE ALSO

● THE SUCCESSORS OF ROME
p. 241
● THE HUNDRED YEARS WAR
p. 245
● THE STORY OF ENGLISH
p. 352

had been taken over. These Viking kingdoms in the area known as the *Danelaw* were shortlived, but they were to have an important impact on the culture and language of England. Only Wessex (England south of the Thames) survived the onslaught, under a remarkable king, Alfred the Great (871–899). By 960 his successors had conquered the rest of England, forming one kingdom for the first time. Ironically the elimination by the Vikings of Wessex's Anglo-Saxon rivals had paved the way for the unification of England. Viking attacks were renewed during Ethelred II's reign (978–1016). After prolonged resistance the English kingdom finally capitulated to the Danish king, Cnut, in 1016. However, this conquest did not involve a major new settlement of Scandinavians in England, and in 1042 Ethelred's son, Edward the Confessor, recovered his throne.

The Normans

In 911 a Viking leader named Rollo was granted control of the lower Seine valley by the West Frankish king. In the following decades Rollo's descendants and their followers extended their grip on the Channel coast. Thus they created the duchy of Normandy, 'the land of the Northmen', but in the process lost their Viking character and merged into the aristocracy of northern France.

In the 11th century the Normans were one of the most successful peoples in Europe. Norman mercenaries carved out territories for themselves in southern Italy, ultimately seizing the whole area from its Greek and Lombard rulers, and then taking Sicily from the Arabs.

The Norman conquests in southern Italy were acts of private enterprise. The conquest of England, on the other hand, was organized by the duke of Normandy himself, with all the resources of his duchy behind him. In 1051 Duke William (later known as 'the Conqueror') had been made heir to his cousin, the childless Edward the Confessor. But in England the most powerful man after the king was Harold Godwinson, and when Edward died (January 1066), the English acclaimed Harold king.

Harold's defence of his crown was complicated by the need to repel a Norwegian invasion under Harold Hardrada, which he crushed in a great battle at Stamford Bridge near York. Meanwhile William landed on the southeast coast. In a daring campaign (September–December 1066) he demonstrated his superior military skill, defeating and killing Harold at the Battle of Hastings. He was crowned king on Christmas Day 1066.

William had seized control of a richer and more powerful kingdom by a bold and well-organized coup. Until 1071 the Norman grip on England was severely tested by revolts and Danish invasions, but this opposition hastened the destruction of the English ruling class and its replacement by a new Norman-French nobility. For more than 300 years the language of the rulers of England was to be a form of French, which left a lasting impact on the English language (▷ p. 352). Yet initially only some 10 000 newcomers were involved; there were many things that they were neither able nor willing to change. The more sophisticated administrative structures of Anglo-Saxon England were taken over virtually unchanged, and these formed the framework of English government not just in the Middle Ages, but down to the present day.

VIKING AND NORMAN INVASIONS

COMMONWEALTH OF ICELAND

To Greenland

FAEROES

NORWAY

SHETLANDS

ORKNEYS

SWEDEN

Baltic Sea

Neva

Novgorod

Volga

SCOTLAND

DENMARK

PRINCIPALITY OF RUSSIA

IRELAND

Dublin

DANELAW

Kiev

Dnieper

To the Caspian Sea

NORMAN KINGDOM OF ENGLAND

DUCHY OF NORMANDY

Seine

Noirmoutier

Loire

SETTLED BY NORWEGIANS

THE THREE SCANDINAVIAN KINGDOMS

SETTLED BY DANES

Constantinople

NORMAN PRINCIPALITY OF ANTIOCH

CONQUERED BY SWEDES

BYZANTINE EMPIRE

Antioch

SEA AND RIVER ROUTES OF THE VIKINGS

CONQUERED BY NORMANS

NORMAN KINGDOM OF SICILY

CALABRIA

SICILY

The Crusades

The era of the Crusades saw Christian Europe once more on the offensive. Inspired by a reformed and revitalized papacy, knights flocked to rescue Jerusalem from Islam. Even though in the long run the Crusader states that they set up in the Holy Land were to prove vulnerable to the Muslim 'counter-crusade', elsewhere the crusading spirit was to achieve more permanent results.

In Eastern Europe missionaries and warrior monks extended Christendom into previously pagan areas. In a process known as the *Reconquista*, Spain was recovered from the Islamic Moors after four centuries of conflict. And in the motives of men like Prince Henry the Navigator, organizer of the Portuguese exploration of Africa, the crusading outlook moved out into a wider world (➤ pp. 247 and 252).

The Crusades

No sermon has ever had greater impact than that delivered by Pope Urban II at Clermont in 1095. It set in motion the whole crusading movement. All that had been intended was to send some military assistance to the Byzantine Emperor, Alexius I, who was battling against Turkish nomads in Asia Minor. In the west, however, men believed that these Turks were making life intolerably difficult

SEE ALSO

- THE SUCCESSORS OF ROME p. 240
- THE RISE OF ISLAM p. 242
- CRISIS IN EUROPE p. 245
- THE SPANISH AND PORTU-GUESE EMPIRES p. 252

for pilgrims on their way to Jerusalem – the Holy City – and in consequence the response to Urban's preaching was on a totally unexpected scale. In 1096 several huge armies set out on the long march to Jerusalem. Their intention was to free the Christian churches in the East and recapture the Holy City, which had been in Muslim hands since the 7th century.

Despite great difficulties the knights of the First Crusade took Jerusalem and established a handful of small states. These were vulnerable to Muslim counterattack and Saladin (?1137–93, sultan of Egypt and Syria) recaptured the Holy City in 1187. All military attempts to recover the city proved futile – even Richard the Lionheart failed (➤ picture). Only the diplomacy of Emperor Frederick II brought about its temporary recovery (1228–44).

For much of the 13th century the Crusaders held on to the coast of Syria and Palestine, but this too gradually fell into the hands of the powerful Mamluk sultans of Egypt. When the port of Acre fell in 1291 the Crusaders lost their last base in the Holy Land. In the 14th century, crusades were little more than raids. The last one, in 1396 – which took a French and Burgundian army as far as Nicopolis (on the Danube) – was ignominiously defeated by the Ottoman sultan.

Although the primary motive of most Crusaders was religious fervour, there was also a good deal of self-interested adventurism involved. At times quarrels broke out between the various European contingents. The Fourth Crusade never even reached the Holy Land. Instead, at the instigation of Venice, the Crusaders captured Christian Constantinople, the capital of the Byzantine Empire, Venice's rival in the eastern Mediterranean.

In the 13th century, crusades were mounted within Christendom, both against heretics (such as the Cathars in southern France; ➤ p. 245) and against the papacy's political enemies, such as Emperor Frederick II. In the 15th century crusading became limited to Eastern Europe, against the Turks or the Hussite heretics of Bohemia – generally without success.

The Reconquista

In the Iberian Peninsula it was a different story. In the mid-11th century the small Christian kingdoms of northern Spain, principally Castile and Aragon, began to expand at the expense of the Muslim states that had long dominated their peninsula (➤ p. 242). In 1139 the kingdom of Portugal was founded but initially the progress of reconquest was by no means irreversible. On two occasions, in 1085 and 1145, Islam was reinforced by waves of Berber tribesmen from North Africa. They defeated Christian armies and briefly united the Muslims.

Towards the end of the 12th century, however, the tide was turning inexorably in favour of the Reconquista. The Castilian victory at Las Navas de Tolosa in 1212 set the seal on this process, and swift advances followed. By the mid-13th century Muslim rule was confined to the Emirate of Granada. This state survived until 1492, when it was finally snuffed out by the dual monarchy of Ferdinand of Aragon and Isabella of Castile (➤ p.252).

Richard I 'the Lionheart', king of England (1189–99) and warrior hero of legendary prowess. As a leader of the Third Crusade (1189–92) Richard won brilliant victories to wrest Acre and Joppa from Muslim hands. But the recapture of Jerusalem – the chief aim of the Third Crusade – eluded him. Shown here is a detail of Richard's tomb effigy in the abbey church of Fontevraud l'Abbaye in northern France. (AKG)

Crisis in Europe

In the 14th century Europe was dealt a series of calamitous blows. Early in the century appalling weather resulted in harvest failures and famine (1315–17). In mid-century, bubonic plague – the Black Death – wiped out a significant proportion of the population, and demand for basic foodstuffs contracted sharply. For many landowners, accustomed to seeing their products eagerly sought after, this was a rude awakening.

In some regions the miseries of war added to the sense of confusion. Criticism of the Church, the appearance of new heresies and a series of popular uprisings all added to the fundamental challenges faced by medieval society.

The Black Death

Bubonic plague was brought to Europe in 1346–47 by Italian merchant ships from the ports of the Crimea on the Black Sea. As well as Ukrainian grain they carried the rats whose fleas spread the disease. The plague spread rapidly from the Mediterranean ports, reaching southern England in 1348. Victims developed fever and hard black *buboes* (swollen lymph nodes in the groin and armpits). More than half of those infected died. Contemporary medicine knew no treatment for this terrifying affliction.

SEE ALSO

- CHRISTIANITY RESURGENT p. 244
- MEDIEVAL AND RENAISSANCE ECONOMY AND SOCIETY p. 246
- MEDIEVAL AND RENAISSANCE CULTURE p. 248
- THE REFORMATION p. 250

Death rates are difficult to calculate. In some pockets mortality was light, while small parts of southwest France, Flanders and northern Italy, and most of Silesia and Poland, escaped the Black Death altogether. Elsewhere it is accepted that one third of the population perished in the 1348–49 epidemic. Recovery from even this severe blow might have been quick had it not been for recurrent epidemics in the 1360s and 70s. These attacked children in particular and so the future breeding stock was reduced. An age of population decline set in and plague became a fact of European life for more than three centuries.

The first onslaught of the Black Death was followed by labour shortages and disruption of production. Wages and prices both rose sharply. Long-term effects were more marked. Consumption and production of basic foodstuffs declined as the population did. Within a few decades acute labour shortages meant that serfdom (▷ p. 246) had to be abandoned and that real wages for rural labourers reached levels unmatched for centuries to come. For the surviving peasantry the plague was thus a blessing, inaugurating a golden age of improved conditions and relative plenty.

Popular revolts

Economic change and the burdens of warfare inspired widespread challenges to authority. The popular French revolt of 1358 followed the humiliating defeat of the French aristocracy at the Battle of Poitiers (▷ box). The Peasants' Revolt in England (1381) was sparked off by the weight of taxation at a time when the Hundred Years War was going badly for the English. Its deep-rooted cause, however, was anger at the government's attempts to keep wages at pre-plague levels and to prevent men moving to lords offering better terms.

Anticlericalism and heresy

The wealth and worldliness of the Church attracted criticism from those who believed in a simpler and more devout way of life. Demands that the Church be stripped of its land were often inspired by a feeling that it did not pay its share of taxation. The authority and repute of the Church was further undermined by the Great Schism of 1378–1417, which saw first two, then three concurrent popes.

Some critics transgressed into heresy. The alternative Cathar (or Albigensian) Church in southern France had been broken in the 13th century by crusades and persecution. During the Great Schism two new heresies surfaced. In England the Oxford theologian John Wyclif (?1330–84) based his criticism on a fundamentalist study of Scripture, rejecting the authority of the papacy and the doctrine of transubstantiation in the Eucharist. Despite persecution, his followers – insultingly known as 'Lollards' – survived until the next century and the Reformation (▷ p. 250). The Czech scholar Jan Hus (?1372–1415) shared some of Wyclif's ideas and rejected the authority of the Church. He was condemned and burned in 1415, but his ideas became far more of a threat than Wyclif's owing to their connection with Bohemian nationalism. Under the able command of John Zizka the Hussites defeated crusaders from Germany, Austria and Hungary. Their resistance ended only in 1436 after a compact that recognized their distinctive beliefs.

THE HUNDRED YEARS WAR

Ever since 1066, when the duke of Normandy became William I of England (▷ p. 243), the Norman kings of England and their successors had continued to hold vast territories in France. By the 1330s, however, only Gascony in the southwest of France was retained by the English king. But even these reduced dominions provided cause for conflict, since as duke of Gascony the English king owed allegiance to the French crown. When the French Capetian dynasty died out in the direct male line in 1328, Edward III of England (1327–77) had an excellent claim to the French throne through his maternal grandfather, Philip the Fair (1285–1314). But the crown went to his cousin, Philip of Valois, who became Philip VI (1328–50). Soon the two kings were fighting a kind of border war in Scotland and Flanders – the Scots having made common cause with France in the 'Auld Alliance', the Flemish cloth towns being drawn by economic self-interest to the English side. The English won the naval battle of Sluys off the Flemish coast in 1340 to put paid to a threatened French invasion. At Crécy (1346) and Poitiers (1356) the over-confident French knights were routed by the firepower of the English archers. The

Treaty of Brétigny in 1360 gave England large tracts of French land in return for Edward renouncing his claim to the French throne. In 1369, however, Edward formally resumed his claim; in renewed hostilities the French regained much of their lost territory.

Richard II (1377–99) agreed to a 28-year truce in 1396, but English claims to France were revived by the warrior-king Henry V (1413–22). Taking advantage of the troubles caused by the mental illness of Charles VI of France (1380–1422), he invaded Normandy and won a stunning victory at Agincourt (1415). By 1419 Charles had named Henry his successor and an Anglo-Burgundian regime was in control of Paris and much of northern France. As it turned out, however, Henry died two months before Charles VI. In 1429 a French revival, in part inspired by Joan of Arc, recaptured the initiative. By 1435 England's Burgundian allies had swung back to the French side. England held on stubbornly, but between 1450 and 1453 Normandy and Gascony were lost forever. From now on the French and English monarchies, bound together in a troubled relationship since 1066, went their separate ways.

Medieval and Renaissance Economy and Society

The medieval world was essentially a rural one. It depended on a hard-working peasantry, fair weather and good harvests. At first, in the centuries after the fall of Rome, both people and money were in short supply. There then followed a long period of economic, commercial and population growth. This growth was slow at first – in the 9th and 10th centuries – but then accelerated through the 12th and 13th centuries. The catastrophe of the Black Death brought a century of uncertainty before expansion was resumed in the later 15th century.

Even though the population of Europe in 1600 may have been no greater than in 1300, the basic fact remains that for most of the Middle Ages the population of Europe was a growing one. This meant pressure to bring more land into cultivation and to improve the processing and distribution of basic necessities: food, fuel and clothing. Water mills proliferated, and in the 12th century a new invention, the windmill, provided a supplementary source of power. Bulk-carrying ships were developed and, on land, improved harness design enabled the much faster horse cart to replace the ox cart.

Slaves, serfs and freemen

Throughout these centuries the greater part of the work was done by small tenant farmers (i.e. peasants) and their servants – though initially, as in the ancient world, slave labour was employed on many estates. By 1200, however, slavery and the slave trade had both died out in Europe north of the Alps. Some tenants were obliged by the terms of their tenure to work their lord's land as well as their own; those whose obligations were particularly burdensome tended to be called *serfs* or *villeins*, and after the demise of slavery it was these men who were regarded as 'unfree'. Then the long period of labour shortage following the Black Death in the 14th century (⊳ p. 245) led to the end of serfdom. From then on virtually all tenants either owed a share of their harvest or a money rent; as the volume of coinage in circulation increased, the latter became more common. Thus in northwestern Europe the Middle Ages witnessed the end of both slavery and serfdom – two important moments in the history of liberty.

The 'feudal system'

Most of Europe was dominated by landlords throughout these centuries. Small local landlords owed rent or service or both to greater landlords, and so on all the way up the social hierarchy to the ruler. At each level tenants owed the kind of service – financial, administrative or military – appropriate to their status. Thus tenants of knightly status might be expected to perform 'knight service' in return for *fiefs*, estates granted them by their lords. Historians have often called this kind of society 'feudal' – from the latin *feudum* meaning a fief – though neither the word nor the concept 'feudal' existed in the Middle Ages.

Moreover the 'feudal system' was not a static one. From the 12th and 13th centuries onwards lords increasingly secured men's service by paying them in cash. At the same time the demand for administrators rose sharply – for men who were both literate and numerate. To meet this demand schools were founded all over Europe (⊳ p. 248). For men who gave their lords good service there were plenty of opportunities to rise in the world.

Town life

From the 11th century onwards a rising population led to a massive growth in the number and size of towns throughout Europe, most of them functioning principally as local markets. Most towns were small by today's standards –

A sailing vessel prepares to discharge its cargo in a woodcut of 1493. Europe's trade grew remarkably from around 1450, the recovery of its population after the Black Death stimulating food production and trade in foodstuffs, wool and cloth. The establishment of overseas settlements by Spain and Portugal in the 16th century created new markets for European goods, while the gold and silver obtained in return stimulated European trade with the Far East (which depended on the export of precious metals). (AR)

THE VOYAGES OF DISCOVERY

Marco Polo (c. 1254–1324)
Trade between Europe and China along the Silk Route (⊳ p. 234) had long been established, and in 1260–69 Marco Polo's father and uncle made a trading expedition there. Marco Polo accompanied them on their second expedition, reaching China in 1275. There he entered the service of the emperor, Kublai Khan, and remained in China until 1292.

Prince Henry the Navigator (1394–1460)
Son of John I of Portugal, Henry was the leading patron of Portuguese exploration in the early 15th century. By his death his ships had discovered the Cape Verde Islands, and advanced down the west coast of Africa as far as Sierra Leone.

Zheng He (or Cheng Ho; died c. 1433)
In the early 15th century China was also expanding its horizons and Admiral Zheng He led several expeditions to India, Arabia and the coast of East Africa. At this point, however, the Chinese government decided against further exploration.

Bartolomeu Dias (?1450–1500)
In 1488 the Portuguese navigator Bartolomeu Dias rounded the Cape of Good Hope and could report that a sea route to the spices and other wealth of the East now lay open.

Vasco da Gama (1469–1524)
Setting out from Portugal in 1497, da Gama followed a slightly different course to that of Dias and reached Calicut on the southwest coast of India, returning home in 1499. The route from Portugal to the East was now confirmed.

Christopher Columbus (1451–1506)
Because the Italian navigator Christopher Columbus believed that the world was much smaller than it is, he was confident that he could reach the East by sailing west. It had been known for centuries that the world is round, but for a long time Columbus' schemes were rejected by experts who had a much more accurate idea of the actual size of the globe. Not until 1492 was he given the backing of the Spanish Crown. His flotilla of three ships led by the *Santa Maria* reached the Bahamas in 33 days. On subsequent voyages Columbus reached the American mainland. He died still convinced, however, that he had reached the East, or the Indies, hence the name 'West Indies'.

John Cabot (c. 1450–?98)
A navigator in the service of Henry VII of England, Cabot discovered Cape Breton Island in 1497, and is sometimes credited with the discovery of North America – though the Vikings had reached there, via Iceland and Greenland, five hundred years earlier.

Ferdinand Magellan (c. 1480–1521)
A Portuguese navigator sponsored by Spain, in 1519 Magellan set off with five ships to seek a western route to the East Indies. He negotiated the strait named after him between Tierra del Fuego and the South American mainland. The expedition crossed the Pacific and reached the East Indies in 1521, where Magellan was killed. Only one ship returned to Spain in 1522, so completing the first circumnavigation of the world.

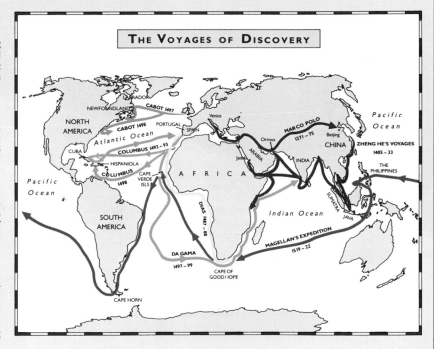

THE VOYAGES OF DISCOVERY

though by 1300 London may have had a population of 100 000 and Paris twice as many.

Townspeople struggled to win certain freedoms, notably the right to supervise their own markets and to elect their own magistrates. Successful towns obtained charters from the king – in England and Scotland such towns became known as *boroughs*. A characteristic feature of towns everywhere was the existence within them of a number of associations and clubs, known variously to contemporaries as *guilds*, *fraternities*, *companies* or *crafts*. Some of them were based on particular trades or crafts and were responsible for regulating their members' economic activities, but they also performed a wide range of social, religious and charitable functions.

In the more urbanized parts of Europe many towns – such as Milan, Florence, Cologne and Bruges – were able to become *communes*, self-governing municipalities capable of independent political action. This was particularly so in northern Italy, where a fiercely competitive society of rival city-states, not unlike the society of Classical Greece (⊳ p. 230), had emerged by the 13th century. This was the seedbed of the Italian Renaissance.

The commercial revolution

By the 13th century Italian businessmen had developed a sophisticated system of credit finance and were acting as international bankers. These facilities helped to make Italy the hub of international trade. Venice, Pisa and Genoa fought each other for control of the highly lucrative commerce of the Mediterranean. Italian merchants like Marco Polo's father travelled overland to China, but it was to be the increasing volume of seaborne trade between the Mediterranean and northern Europe that led to the crucial improvements in ship design (⊳ p. 216) that made possible the voyages of discovery (⊳ above).

SEE ALSO
● THE 14TH-CENTURY CRISIS p. 245
● MEDIEVAL AND RENAISSANCE CULTURE p. 248
● THE SPANISH AND PORTUGUESE EMPIRES p. 252

Medieval and Renaissance Culture

After the fall of the western Roman Empire, people in Western Europe gradually lost touch with the centres of culture in the eastern Mediterranean. Much of the learning of the ancient world was lost. What survived the 'Dark Ages' – the 7th to 10th centuries – did so because it was preserved in monasteries. For centuries formal education was not much more than a by-product of religion.

In the 12th and 13th centuries all that changed. Through a variety of channels, classical learning (in philosophy, law and the sciences) was recovered. Schools and universities, medical schools and hospitals (▷ p. 156) were founded. At the same time there was a new architecture – Gothic (▷ p. 326) – and a flowering of vernacular literature (▷ p. 358). In the most urbanized region in Europe – northern Italy – a rather different style took root, and by the 16th century Renaissance Italy was setting the fashion for the rest of Europe, a development assisted by a powerful new invention: the printing press.

The monastic centuries

Christianity was adopted as the official religion of the Roman Empire in the 4th century AD, and Christians found that they had become part of the imperial establishment – an experience which was not to the liking of all of them. Many preferred to turn their backs on the material comforts and pleasures that society now offered. In Egypt and Syria – the most urbanized and prosperous parts of the Roman world – so many followed this course that hundreds of new communities dedicated to religious self-denial were established, often in the desert. These were the first monasteries. During the 5th and 6th centuries this style of religious life caught on in the West, and while the Roman cultural world collapsed, monasteries survived, islands of stability, quiet, and traditional learning (▷ box).

For four or five hundred years there were few men who learned to read and write anywhere but in a monastery school. Moreover, the accumulation of pious gifts over the centuries meant that many monasteries became great landowning corporations, and could afford to employ the finest builders, sculptors and artists. In these circumstances it was probably inevitable that early medieval culture should come to have a distinctly ecclesiastical tinge.

Schools and universities

By the 12th century Western Europe was a more populous and more complex society (▷ p. 246). All over Europe, teachers began to set up new schools, including some in quite small towns and villages. The 'lost' learning of the ancient world was translated out of Arabic into Latin and so made generally available to European scholars.

It was in this receptive and expansionist educational environment that the earliest universities – Paris, Bologna and Oxford – were established (by around 1200), and they set a trend that was to last for centuries. By 1500 more than 70 more universities had been founded, among them Cambridge, Prague, Heidelberg and St Andrews. Most students were *clerks* – in other words, they were nominally churchmen. Relatively few, however, chose to become theologians or parish priests. Most studied for the 'arts' degree; of those who went on to take a higher degree most chose one of what were known as the 'lucrative sciences' – law or medicine. Their ambitions were professional and worldly.

SEE ALSO

- THE HISTORY OF SCIENCE p. 48
- THE HISTORY OF MEDICINE p. 156
- PRINTING p. 202
- MEDIEVAL AND RENAISSANCE ECONOMY AND SOCIETY p. 246
- THE REFORMATION p. 250
- MEDIEVAL AND RENAISSANCE ART pp. 310–14
- MEDIEVAL AND RENAISSANCE LITERATURE pp. 358–61

WAR AND FORTIFICATION

Throughout this period battles were rare and war largely revolved around control of strongpoints, castles or towns. Thus an important aspect of the great rebuilding that took place in the 12th and 13th centuries was the replacement of basic earthwork and timber fortifications (including the motte-and-bailey castle) by vastly more expensive stone walls. High stone walls and towers were designed to counter the high-trajectory siege catapults of the period.

But from the 1370s onwards the advent of effective siege guns – capable of delivering a massive horizontal blow – presented military architects with a new problem. Their solution was the bastion. It was low, and was built of rubble and brick so that it absorbed cannon shot, instead of fracturing on impact as stone did. Above all it was itself a gun platform, enabling the defenders to hit back at any attacker. Everywhere in Europe – though rarely in Britain – the old town defences were pulled down and a new wide ring of bastions built. Every European city from the Baltic to North Africa took on a new appearance, and wherever Europeans settled overseas, from Havana to Goa, they built towns on this new plan.

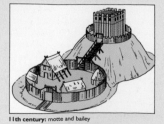

11th century: motte and bailey

12th–13th centuries: stone castle

14th century onwards: bastion

Chivalry and secular culture

Outside the Church there had always of course been another culture – even in the 'Dark Ages'. The Church might have been a rich patron, but the nobles were even richer. However, in the early Middle Ages the culture of the European aristocracy was essentially an illiterate one. Except in Anglo-Saxon England, its ideas and values were rarely fixed in writing and in consequence we know little about them.

But the vernacular literature of the 12th and 13th centuries throws a whole new flood of light on the upper levels of secular society. It shows us the world of chivalry – a society that valued knightly prowess, courage, loyalty, generosity and courtesy (particularly when in the company of ladies). The ideal nobleman was expected not only to be a warrior and huntsman, but also a fine musician, a graceful dancer, an eloquent and shrewd speaker in several languages, and to possess polished manners. The idea of the all-round 'Renaissance man', embodied in *The Book of the Courtier* by Baldassare Castiglione (1478–1529), had in fact been around long before the Renaissance, and one of the reasons for the book's success across Europe was that it was preaching – and with rare eloquence – to an audience that had been converted for centuries.

In the 12th and 13th centuries it became normal for members of the upper classes – gentry as well as business people, women as well as men – to be able to read. Many of them employed clerks to do their writing for them. By the 15th century a reading public existed that was large enough to absorb the enormous increase in books produced by the new printing presses (▷ below).

Humanism and the Renaissance

In the 14th century, the Italian poet Petrarch (1304–74) inspired a new kind of enthusiasm for the writings of ancient Greece and Rome – an enthusiasm for their style as well as for their content. Following this lead, a diverse group of scholars, known as the *humanists*, came to regard classical texts as models for public speaking, writing and conduct. Initially based in northern Italy, by 1500 humanist ideas began to spread to northern Europe, where Erasmus (▷ below) was the most important scholar.

Because the humanists laid weight on being able to speak and write like the Roman orator and writer Cicero, this tended to make them despise those who had not even tried to do so. Thus they popularized the idea of the 'Dark Ages', a period of supposed barbarism stretching between the ancient world and their own time. Undoubtedly their enthusiasm for antiquity led them to discover previously unknown texts, notably some works by the Greek philosopher Plato. By translating such texts into Latin – knowledge of Greek remained rare throughout the Renaissance – they made them more widely available. Whether their enthusiasm for classical models led them to a new or 'modern' view of the world and of man's place within it, is a question that historians still debate. In 15th-century Florence, humanist language was used to encourage active citizenship and loyalty to the state – but these were qualities of which rulers everywhere approved. Although humanism did not involve a rejection of Christian doctrine, it did undoubtedly focus on man's – as opposed to God's – role in the world, but so also did the 'old-fashioned' secular ideals of chivalry and good lordship.

A BENEDICTINE MONASTERY

The Benedictine order of monks was founded by St Benedict of Nursia (c. 480–c. 550) – the 'father' of western monasticism – who built his monastery at Monte Cassino in Italy c. 525. With minor variations, Benedictine monasteries were built to the same plan all over Europe during the Middle Ages.

At the centre of the monastery is the abbey church (1). Next to the abbey is the cloister (2), which links together the important elements of the monastery and provides the monks with a place to walk, study, and meditate. On the side of the cloister adjoining the church is the library (3). On the upper floor of the eastern side of the cloister, built over the dining-room or *refectory* (4), is the monks' dormitory or *dorter* (5). The north transept (6) of the

abbey church continues into a passage leading to the chapterhouse (7), where meetings were held.

On the western side of the cloister is the cellarer's range (8), including storerooms for food. On the northern side of the cloister are the kitchens (9), brewhouse (where ale was brewed) and buttery (where it was stored) (10), and workshops for smiths, shoemakers and saddlers (11).

The buildings around the courtyard (12) provide for dealings with the outside world. There is the almonry (13), where food and clothing would be distributed to the poor, guest-houses (14 and 15) and stables (16). The abbot's house (17) is positioned near the gatehouse (18). The infirmary (19) has its own chapel, kitchen and refectory.

The importance of printing

In 1450 the first printing press was set up at Mainz in Germany by Johannes Gutenberg (?1398–1468; ▷ p. 202). The new technique spread rapidly, particularly in the urbanized regions of the Rhineland and Italy. In 1475 William Caxton (c. 1422–91) introduced the technique into England. Printing – pictures as well as words – meant that writers could reach a much larger international audience than ever before.

When the Florentine Niccolò Machiavelli (1469–1527) argued in his book *The Prince* that the need to ensure the survival of the state justified acts that otherwise might be regarded as immoral, he was not doing much more than laying bare the way governments had always acted – but in the new world of the printed book this was enough to make his name synonymous with duplicity. More importantly, when the Dutch scholar Desiderius Erasmus (1466–1536) edited the Greek New Testament, and when in letters and tracts such as *In Praise of Folly* he called for Church reform, his words, now in print, reached minds and hearts that earlier writers had failed to reach. This anticipated the crucial role that printing was to play in the spread of the Reformation (▷ p. 250).

The Reformation

The Reformation was the outcome of dissatisfaction with abuses within the Roman Catholic Church, and also with the role of the clergy and with the direction of the Church. The close link which often developed between Protestant reformers and secular rulers resulted in the development of national churches and the appropriation of Church property. The publication of the Bible in various national languages was also a very important effect of the Reformation.

The success of the reformers transformed the Catholic Church. From the late 16th century a revitalized Catholic Church was making great efforts to recover lost ground. However, the success of the Counter-Reformation depended ultimately on the power of Catholic rulers. They made a determined effort to turn the clock back in the early 17th century, but with only partial success. Protestantism for its part had lost much of its dynamism by 1650 – but had survived.

The background

The desire for reform was not new. The weakness of the papacy in the late 14th and early 15th centuries had stimulated the progress of Lollardy in England and Hussitism in Bohemia, both of which anticipated the Reformation (▷ p. 245). However, their success was limited and the late 15th century saw a revival of papal authority.

The popes had St Peter's rebuilt so that Rome should be a fitting capital, and they paid for this and other projects by exploiting their headship of the Church to raise money throughout Europe. They sold indulgences (remissions of the penance imposed on confessed sinners), dispensations and cardinalships, and at the same time resisted calls for reform in an increasingly corrupt and secular Church. In Germany this provoked a strong anti-Italian feeling based on the belief that the papacy was extorting great sums from the Germans.

The humanists' new scholarly work on the texts of the Bible (▷ p. 248) drew attention to the great gulf between the early and contemporary Church, and gave added strength to the growing hostility to the clergy and the papacy. The invention of printing played a crucial role in the spread of the ideas both of the humanists and of the new reformers (▷ p. 249).

Martin Luther and Protestantism

In 1517 Martin Luther (1483–1547), a German monk and theologian, published his opposition to indulgences and other abuses in the Church. Luther believed that the foundation of all faith must be the Bible, and that all people should have access to it, not just those who understood Latin. Those religious doctrines and practices not founded in Scripture, such as monastic orders and the cult of Mary and the saints, he regarded as abuses; only faith in God brought salvation. Luther also denied the special status of the clergy administering the sacraments: to him the priesthood comprised all true believers, and each believer stood alone and equal before God. Following his excommunication in 1520 Luther rejected papal authority.

Luther's protest, spread by the new printing presses and by preachers, was popular in Germany. The poor thought it meant freedom from some of their burdens. However, Luther urged the brutal suppression of the Peasants' Revolt (1525) by the German princes, whom he needed to defend the Reformation against the hostility of Charles V, the Holy Roman Emperor. Yet Charles's commitments elsewhere prevented him from having time or strength enough to root out Protestantism in Germany. In 1555 he had to agree to the Peace of Augsburg, which allowed

Ego ſum Papa.

Alexander VI (1492–1503) caricatured as the devil in a 16th-century French woodcut. A corrupt and extravagant pope, his lifestyle exemplified the worldliness and neglect of spiritual values that fuelled the development of the Protestant Reformation. (AKG)

each prince, Lutheran or Catholic, to decide the religion of his subjects.

By that time Lutheran Churches had been established in a number of states in Germany, and in Sweden and Denmark, while the new state Church emerging in England (⊳ p. 254) was influenced by Lutheran doctrines. A number of rulers ordered Reformation in their states because they profited from the seizure of Church property, and increased their authority by creating a clergy subject to them and not to Rome.

Calvin and Calvinism

Reform was also effected in Zürich by Ulrich Zwingli (1484–1531). But the most influential of the other reformers was John Calvin (1509–56), a French lawyer. Calvin, like Luther, based his ideas firmly on Scripture, but went beyond Luther in believing that salvation was predestined or determined by God. He also went further than Luther in rejecting religious ceremonial and imagery. Calvin reformed both the Church and the government of Geneva, ensuring a closer link between the two and a greater supervision of the religious and moral life of its citizens. Geneva provided a model for Calvinists, who in the late 16th century took the lead in the reform movement. However, their different beliefs often meant conflict with Lutherans as well as with Catholics.

In Scotland, a successful revolt against the Catholic Mary Queen of Scots was followed by reform of the Church on Calvinist lines by John Knox (?1514–72). In France the Huguenots (as French Calvinists were known) became involved in the rivalries of the noble factions in the French Wars of Religion (1559–98). The strength of the Huguenots fell considerably after the St Bartholomew's Day Massacre of their leaders (1572). Yet they were strong enough to obtain toleration in 1598 under the Edict of Nantes.

Calvinist resistance contributed to the success of the Dutch revolt against Philip II (⊳ p. 252), a Calvinist Church being set up in the Dutch Republic. Calvinist Churches were also established in Bohemia, Hungary, Poland, and parts of Germany (where Calvinism was not included in the settlement of 1555). Not surprisingly, Calvinism was associated with rebellion.

The Counter-Reformation

The success of the Reformation increased the pressure for a council to reform the Roman Catholic Church from within. Such a council was indeed established, and met at Trent between 1541 and 1563. Yet the Council of Trent made few concessions to Protestant criticisms. Instead it restated traditional doctrine regarding the sacraments, the Bible and papal supremacy. It also declared that Catholics should be better instructed in their faith, and provided for a trained clergy to do this.

The Council was followed by a great missionary effort to recover the areas lost to Protestantism. A leading part in this was played by the Jesuits (the Society of Jesus), founded by a Spaniard, Ignatius Loyola (1491–1556). The Jesuits were distinguished both as missionaries in Europe, America and Asia, and as teachers in their European colleges. As royal confessors they urged Catholic rulers to ignore Protestant rights as a limitation on their power. This reflected the dependence of the Counter-Reformation on the support of monarchs such as Mary of England (1553–58), who tried to recatholicize her kingdom (⊳ p. 254), and Philip II of Spain (⊳ p. 253).

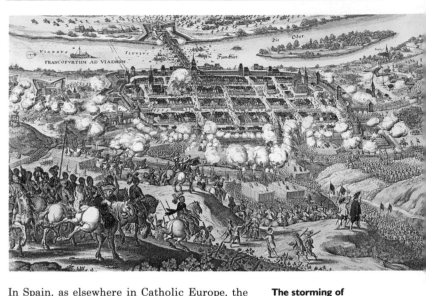

In Spain, as elsewhere in Catholic Europe, the Inquisition investigated suspected heretics, passing serious offenders to the secular authorities for punishment. It also enforced the 'Index' of books whose content was regarded as heretical and not to be read by Catholics. The Index was constantly revised, and was not abandoned until 1966.

The Thirty Years War

The religious tensions that had built up over the previous 60 years or more finally erupted in a complex series of struggles known as the Thirty Years War. The war began with a revolt in 1618 in Bohemia against the anti-Protestant and centralizing policies of the Austrian Habsburg emperor, Ferdinand II. By 1620 this revolt had been crushed, but the struggle quickly became entangled with wider European conflicts.

Spain, the ally of the Austrian Habsburgs, resumed its war with the Dutch in 1621. During the course of the war the Spanish occupied the Palatinate – in western Germany – whose ruler had led the Bohemian revolt. By 1629 Habsburg power seemed dominant in Germany, and in that year Ferdinand II attempted to reimpose the religious settlement of 1555, thus ending the unofficial toleration of Calvinism. Fear of Habsburg and Catholic power led Gustavus Adolphus, king of Sweden (1611–32), to invade Germany in 1630. After some brilliant successes he was killed at the battle of Lützen in 1632.

The war was now becoming an essentially political struggle, especially with the entry of France, the greatest anti-Habsburg power, in 1635. The growing difficulties of both the Spanish and Austrian Habsburgs led in 1648 to the Peace of Westphalia, which confirmed the 1555 Augsburg settlement, and now included the Calvinists.

In parts of Germany up to a third – and in a few areas up to two-thirds – of the population may have died during the war, mainly through disease and famine brought about by economic disruption. The struggle between France and Spain went on until 1659, but the age of religious, or partly religious, wars was over. The religious divisions of Europe (⊳ map) were now fixed essentially as they are today.

The storming of Frankfurt an der Oder by the Swedes under Gustavus Adolphus, 13 April 1631. Between his invasion of Germany in 1630 and his death at Lützen in 1632, Gustavus turned the tide against the forces of the Habsburg emperor and the German princes of the Catholic league with a series of stunning victories. His intervention in the Thirty Years War ensured the survival of Protestantism in Germany. (AKG)

DIVIDED EUROPE
RELIGIOUS FAITHS IN 1650

LUTHERAN   ROMAN CATHOLIC
REFORMED/CALVINIST   ORTHODOX
ANGLICAN   ISLAM

SEE ALSO

● THE 14TH-CENTURY CRISIS p. 245
● MEDIEVAL AND RENAISSANCE CULTURE p. 248
● THE SPANISH AND PORTUGUESE EMPIRES p. 252
● THE RISE OF BRITAIN p. 254
● WORLD CHRISTIANITY p. 298

The Spanish and Portuguese Empires

The 16th century saw the creation of the first large colonial empires by European powers. The empires of Spain and Portugal resulted from their sponsorship of the great voyages of discovery (▷ p. 247). In the case of Spain its empire would not have been created without the achievement of political unity at home. This came about in 1469, when Isabella of Castile married Ferdinand of Aragon. With his support she restored order and royal authority in Castile. In 1492 they completed the conquest of the Moorish kingdom of Granada, bringing to a conclusion the Reconquista, the reconquest of Islamic Spain (▷ p. 244).

The achievement of Ferdinand and Isabella rested on the cooperation of their two realms. Aragon feared being swallowed up by the far richer Castile and made little contribution to

Spain's subsequent greatness. Yet the union was held together, first by Ferdinand and Isabella, and then from 1516 by the Habsburgs, initially in the person of Charles V. Charles inherited both realms and was also elected Holy Roman Emperor in 1519. Spain's incorporation into the Habsburg Empire offered it the opportunity to use its own resources and those of its American empire on a wider stage. Spain assumed the role of leading power in Europe until well into the 17th century.

Spain and Portugal divide the world

Following Columbus's successful voyage of 1492, Isabella needed to establish her right to colonize the Americas. After arbitration by the pope, Spain and Portugal came to an agreement at the Treaty of Tordesillas in 1493. All lands west of an imaginary north-to-south line drawn 370 leagues west of the Azores and Cape Verde Islands were to go to Spain, and all those east of it to Portugal. The result of this was that Portugal got Brazil, and Spain virtually all of the rest of South and Central America, and even parts of North America.

The Spanish impact on native life

Before settlement of the Americas could begin, the existing native empires (▷ p. 239) had to be subdued. This was the achievement of the conquistadores. In a short time and against vastly greater numbers – but aided by an overwhelming technological superiority – Cortez overthrew the Aztec empire in Mexico (1519–21), Alvardo conquered the Mayas in Yucatán (1524), and Pizarro subdued the Inca empire in Peru (1531–33).

Spanish colonization accelerated, and the native Indians were subjected to a colonial administration headed by two viceroys – in Mexico and Peru – responsible to the king in Spain. The Indians were obliged to work on the Spaniards' lands and in the gold and silver mines. The Spanish missionaries destroyed the Indians' temples and idols, established mission churches, and began a process of wholesale, sometimes forcible, conversion. The Roman Catholic Church thereby acquired massive numbers of believers in the Americas. The disruption of the Indians' way of life, together with the introduction of diseases to which they were not immune, contributed to a massive decline in their numbers – from perhaps 25 million in Mexico alone in 1519 to just over 1 million in 1600.

Trade, gold and silver

Gold had been the original attraction of the Americas for the conquistadores, and tales of El Dorado, a fabled city rich in gold, continued to fuel exploration. However, silver soon made up 90% of the precious metals sent back to Spain. These metals went as taxes and to pay for the goods the colonists received from Spain. Spain tried to prevent foreigners trading with their colonies, but this proved difficult. The silver stimulated the Spanish economy, and then that of the whole of Europe, contributing to the general

Charles V, Habsburg king of Spain (1516–56) and Holy Roman Emperor (1519–56), was by far the most powerful ruler of his day. In America his dominions were extended by the brutal conquests of Cortez and Pizarro, while in Europe he organized Christendom against the Turks and successfully defended Spanish and imperial rights in Italy against French aggression. Titian's portrait (1548) shows him at the battle of Mühlberg (24 April 1547). (AKG/Prado, Madrid)

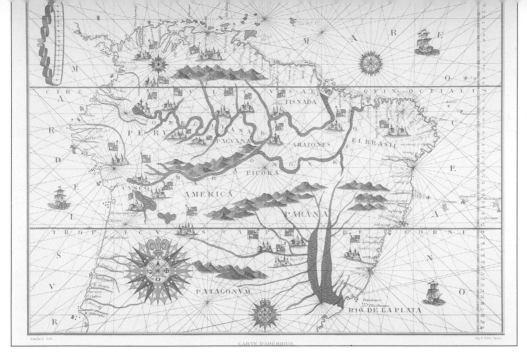

A map of South America, 1582, based on a Spanish atlas of the period. Gold and silver from the New World made Spain the richest country in the world in the 16th century. (AKG)

inflation in the 16th century. However, in the 17th century, colonial self-sufficiency and economic recession, combined with a fall in silver exports, all contributed to a depression in the European economy.

Portugal's empire in Africa and Asia

Portugal's empire was much more dispersed than that of Spain. Limited to a few coastal settlements in Brazil, the Portuguese also had a handful of forts and 'trading' factories in West Africa and along the Mozambique coast, and a scattering of settlements between India and the Pacific.

This pattern reflected the importance of trade with the East. Portugal drew from the East an impressive range of spices, which then attracted high prices in Europe. The Portuguese also obtained gold from China and silver from Japan. Some of these goods were traded locally, but many were carried back to Lisbon, and on to Antwerp for European distribution. Since the only way to Portugal from the East was round the Cape of Good Hope, the forts and factories along the African coast protected this trade. Africa also provided gold – particularly from the Gold Coast (now Ghana) – and slaves. The latter were especially valued as labour on the developing sugar plantations of Brazil.

The number of White settlers in both the Portuguese and Spanish Empires was always far inferior to the number of non-Whites, but many Whites, including missionaries, were attracted to the colonies. The Portuguese, like the Spanish, condoned conversion of the native populations by force, so it is not clear how genuine the conversions were.

Spanish power in Europe

In 1556 Charles V abdicated. His brother had long ruled the Habsburg lands in Austria, and now kept them. Everything else went to Charles's son, Philip II (who ruled 1556–98). Spain now dominated much of Italy and therefore the whole of the western Mediterranean. It also surrounded France – and threatened England – through its possession of the Netherlands. Spain also led the Christian fight against the Turks at sea: it was a largely Spanish fleet that defeated the Turks at Lepanto in 1571, although this did not end Turkish power in the Mediterranean (▷ p. 240).

Following the death of the king of Portugal in battle in Morocco in 1578, Philip added the Portuguese Empire to that of Spain. Apart from making Spain a major power in the East, this made Philip much stronger in Europe. The Spanish Empire in 1600 was the biggest the world had ever seen.

Spain's great military strength was used in a long struggle to suppress the revolt of the Protestant Netherlands from 1567. However, Philip was unable to devote himself wholly to ending the revolt, and his enemies aided the rebels in order to weaken Spain.

The failure of Philip's Armada against England in 1588 (▷ p. 254) meant that these distractions continued. Warfare on this scale was too expensive even with the silver of the Americas, and Spain was unable to beat the Dutch rebels.

The decline of Spain

The recovery of France from the weakness inflicted by the Wars of Religion (▷ p. 250) proved disastrous for Spain. Spanish troops proved very successful in the first half of the Thirty Years War (▷ p. 251), but their victories ended after France's entry into the war in 1635. At the same time Castile was less able to carry the cost of empire alone, largely owing to decline in its population, agriculture and industry, and to the American recession. Yet the non-Castilian realms refused to shoulder more of the costs. Catalonia revolted in 1640 when Castile attempted to pass on some of the burden, as did Portugal, whose empire Spain had proved incapable of defending.

Spain recovered Catalonia but was obliged to recognize Dutch (1648) and Portuguese (1668) independence. Portugal then rebuilt its colonial empire around Brazil.

Although Spain continued to decline, the support of other states, now concerned to resist France rather than Spain, meant that the Spanish Empire was still vast enough to be worth fighting over when the last Habsburg king of Spain died (the War of the Spanish Succession; ▷ p. 256).

SEE ALSO

● PRE-COLUMBIAN AMERICA p. 238
● CHRISTIANITY RESURGENT p. 244
● THE VOYAGES OF DISCOVERY p. 247
● THE REFORMATION p. 250
● THE RISE OF BRITAIN p. 254
● LOUIS XIV p. 256
● EUROPEAN EMPIRES IN THE 17TH AND 18TH CENTURIES p. 257

The Rise of Britain

Between the end of the 15th and the middle of the 18th centuries England became Great Britain. By 1763 Britain had emerged as a leading power in Europe and the world, with a vast colonial empire. This position was achieved by the development of political stability after the upheavals of the 16th and 17th centuries. Stability was associated with the establishment of a Protestant, parliamentary monarchy from 1688. The achievement of effective control over the previously independent realms of Scotland and Ireland (Wales had been subjugated in the 13th century) contributed to the success of that new system.

England's future success was not obvious when Henry Tudor defeated Richard III at Bosworth in 1485, so becoming Henry VII (1485–1509). It remained to be seen whether Henry could end the cycle of civil war known as the Wars of the Roses, which had started in 1455. These wars did little real damage to the wealth of England, but reduced the prestige and authority of the Crown, which had often proved incapable of enforcing obedience from the great nobles. The Crown had become the plaything of factions, being claimed by the Houses of York (the white rose) and Lancaster (the red rose). Scotland remained an independent kingdom inclined to ally with France against England.

The early Tudor achievement

Henry married Elizabeth, daughter of Edward IV, ensuring that their children were heirs of both Lancaster and York. He defeated Yorkist attempts to seize his throne, and gained foreign support by a policy of marriage alliances and

Henry VIII (1509–47) in a painting (1540) by Hans Holbein the Younger. Henry's divorce of Catherine of Aragon marked the beginning of the English Reformation. After the execution of his second wife, Anne Boleyn, he subsequently married Jane Seymour, Anne of Cleves, Catherine Howard and Catherine Parr. (AKG/ National Gallery, Rome)

peace. Henry had no police or army and could restore royal authority only by channelling patronage (grants of land and offices) to those who obeyed him.

Henry VII's success was such that Henry VIII (1509–47) succeeded without question to a rich and powerful Crown, financially independent thanks to Henry VII's careful exploitation of the Crown's extensive landed estates. Henry VIII revived the traditions of the Hundred Years War (▷ p. 245), invading France in 1513. In his absence the Scots invaded England, but were defeated at Flodden. The man who organized the French expedition, Cardinal Thomas Wolsey (1473–1530), became Henry's chief minister.

The English Reformation

Henry VIII's wife, Catherine of Aragon, had five children, but only Princess Mary survived. The security of the Tudor dynasty required that Henry be followed by a son. The pope, not wishing to offend Catherine's uncle, Emperor Charles V, refused Henry a divorce. Henry therefore declared himself Supreme Head of the Church in England, which then granted him a divorce. Henry and his new chief minister, Thomas Cromwell (1485–1540), then dissolved the monasteries – thereby increasing the landed revenue available to the Crown – and reformed the Church. Opposition to Henry's policies was brutally suppressed. In the interests of security, Wales was incorporated into the English Crown (1536, 1543), Henry was declared king of Ireland (1541), and efforts were made in the 1540s to subject the Scots.

Under Edward VI (1547–53), Henry VIII's son by his third wife, Jane Seymour, the Reformation continued. However, Edward was succeeded by his half-sister, Mary (1553–58), who hoped to restore Catholicism and papal authority in England, burning nearly 300 Protestants in the process. Mary might have been successful, but died in 1558 leaving no children to carry on the work. She was succeeded by Elizabeth I (1558–1603), Henry's daughter by his second wife, Anne Boleyn.

Elizabeth re-established the Church of England (also known as the Anglican Church) on the basis of the Thirty-Nine Articles (1559), disappointing those 'Puritans' who wished for a purer Protestant Church. Fear of Spanish power led her to support the Dutch rebels against Philip II (▷ p. 252). Following the discovery of plots against Elizabeth's life by Philip and Mary Queen of Scots (held prisoner by Elizabeth since 1570), Mary was executed in 1586. In 1588 Philip attempted the conquest of England by means of the Armada. It failed, but Philip continued to threaten Elizabeth, aiding the Catholic Irish chiefs who rebelled against Elizabeth in 1599. Ireland was not reconquered until 1603, the year of Elizabeth's death. Elizabeth never married and so left no heir. Instead she left the Crown to her Stuart relative, James VI of Scotland, who became James I of England (1603–25).

Parliament, the Stuarts, and the English Civil War

Elizabeth's wars, and the great inflation of the 16th century, eroded the financial achievement of the early Tudors. The Crown sought Parliamentary help since Parliament's consent was

The defeat of the Spanish Armada, 1588, as depicted around 1600 by Hendrik Cornelisz Vroom. Among the commanders of the English fleet were Sir John Hawkins and Sir Francis Drake, under the Lord High Admiral, Howard of Effingham. After their defeat at Gravelines, the Spanish fleet tried to escape round Scotland and Ireland, suffering further losses by storm and shipwreck. Of the 130 Spanish ships that originally set out, only 86 returned. (AKG/Landesmuseum, Innsbruck)

necessary for full-scale taxation. This gave MPs the opportunity to criticize the Crown, and to attempt to influence its policy. The ending of the war with Spain by James I did not end these problems, but the situation was far worse under James's son Charles I (1625–49).

Charles expected to be obeyed, and after fierce arguments over his efforts to pay for an expensive foreign policy, he ruled without Parliament from 1629, raising money on his own authority. This, and the religious policies of Archbishop Laud – which seemed to threaten the return of Catholicism – were unpopular. However, Charles succeeded until Presbyterian Scotland rebelled against his efforts to impose an English-style Church there. The Scots invaded England, and Charles's need for money obliged him to call Parliament. Parliament's distrust of Charles and its efforts to obtain a share of government led him to begin the Civil War in 1642. The creation of the successful New Model Army helped Parliament to victory by 1649.

The Parliamentarians felt that Charles could not be trusted. He was therefore beheaded, and England was declared a republic (1649). The Parliamentary commander, Oliver Cromwell (1599–1658), then asserted the authority of the Parliamentary regime in Ireland and Scotland by force. English foreign policy in the 1650s was more aggressive and successful than under the Stuarts. However, the problem of a permanent replacement for the monarchy proved insoluble. Cromwell ruled as 'Lord Protector' (1653–58), but on his death the only solution seemed to be the restoration of the Stuart monarchy, stripped of the powers that had proved so offensive under Charles I.

The Glorious Revolution and parliamentary monarchy

Exploiting the widespread fear of another civil war, Charles II (1660–85) advanced towards an absolute monarchy, supported by a small standing army. He also used this fear to defeat attempts to exclude his Catholic brother James from the succession. However, the efforts of James II (1685–88) to recatholicize England led supporters of the Anglican Church to invite William of Orange, husband of James's daughter Mary, to come to save them. William and his army landed in England in November 1688, and James fled to France. No blood was spilt, and the 'Glorious Revolution' had been achieved.

In the Bill of Rights of 1689 Parliament declared some of the royal powers used by James illegal, and offered the Crown jointly to William (1689–1702) and Mary (1689–94), obliging them to call Parliament regularly. Aided by Louis XIV, James led a revolt in Ireland, but was defeated by William at the Battle of the Boyne (1690). This laid the foundations of effective British control of Ireland. Scotland also rejected James's political and religious policies in 1688–89, offering the Scottish Crown to William and Mary, but retaining its own parliament. Under William and Mary, and then Anne (1702–14), England's growing army and navy played a major part in defeating Louis XIV (⊳ p. 256), obliging him to recognize the Revolution settlement.

These wars required enormous loans – often raised by the Bank of England, founded in 1694 – which in turn contributed to the growth of the national debt. These loans were secured by regular grants from Parliament, to which governments became more accountable for their policies. Ministers controlled Parliament by the use of patronage (basically a form of bribery), a system perfected by Sir Robert Walpole, the first 'Prime Minister' (1721–42).

Anne, the last Stuart monarch, left no surviving heir, so the Elector George of Hanover, in virtue of his descent from a daughter of James I, became king as George I. The most obvious threat to the new Hanoverian dynasty came from the Jacobites, supporters of the son (Prince James Francis Edward Stuart, the 'Old Pretender') and grandson (Prince Charles Edward Stuart, the 'Young Pretender') of the exiled James II. In Scotland – which had lost its separate parliament by the 1707 Act of Union – Jacobite sympathies remained strong, particularly in the Highlands. These sympathies broke out in two major revolts, in 1715 and 1745–46, which were, however, defeated. The final defeat of the Jacobites was followed by the collapse of the old Gaelic-speaking society and culture of the Scottish Highlands.

Secure at home, Great Britain had triumphed abroad by 1763 with its victories in the Seven Years War and acquisition of vast new colonial territories (⊳ p. 257). This stability, combined with its growing empire, enabled Britain to embark on a process of industrialization that was to make it the world's most powerful country in the 19th century (⊳ pp. 258 and 266).

SEE ALSO

● VIKINGS AND NORMANS p. 243
● THE HUNDRED YEARS WAR p. 245
● THE REFORMATION p. 250
● EUROPEAN EMPIRES IN THE 17TH AND 18TH CENTURIES p. 257
● THE INDUSTRIAL REVOLUTION p. 258
● THE REVOLUTIONARY AND NAPOLEONIC WARS p. 263
● THE PEAK OF EMPIRE p. 266

Louis XIV

Between the end of the Thirty Years War and the French Revolution the most typical form of government in Europe was absolute monarchy. In this style of government kings were unhindered by the need to refer to representative assemblies, and also developed ways of controlling their states more firmly. The archetype of the absolute monarch was Louis XIV, king of France (1643–1715).

Louis XIV, king of France (1643–1715), depicted in martial pose by Jean-Baptiste Martin around 1688. The territorial ambitions of *le Roi Soleil* (the 'Sun King') dominated the affairs of Europe for nearly fifty years. (AKG)

For much of the first half of the 17th century, France had been ruled by two chief ministers. Louis XIII (1610–43) had given great power to Cardinal Richelieu (1585–1642), and when Louis died his widow acted as regent for his son Louis XIV – then a child – though much power was in the hands of another chief minister, Cardinal Mazarin (1602–61). Resentment of Mazarin's influence contributed to the outbreak of civil war in France (the so-called 'Frondes') in 1648–53.

Louis' personal rule in France

When Mazarin died in 1661, the 22-year-old Louis declared that henceforth he would rule personally. He did so until his death in 1715. His persistence owed a great deal to his belief (commonly held at that time) that kings ruled by divine right, receiving their power from God, and so must rule justly and in person. This belief is summed up in the famous words attributed to Louis, *'L'état c'est moi'* ('I am the state').

Louis had a number of very capable ministers, notably Jean Baptiste Colbert (1619–83) and the Marquis de Louvois (1641–91), but made it clear that they were his servants and dependent on his favour. Royal academies were set up to promote and direct the arts and sciences. Colbert set up state trading companies and state-subsidized factories to boost the economy. This growing cultural and economic regulation stimulated the development of a centrally controlled bureaucracy.

The nobles, who had been so unruly during the Frondes, were encouraged to attend Louis' court at Versailles. Far away from their power bases in the provinces, and under the watchful eye of the king, they were less likely to cause mischief. The king's power to suppress dissent was increased once Louvois had completed the creation of a large standing army. Religious division was strongly disapproved of, and in 1685 Louis revoked the Edict of Nantes (c> p. 250), which had declared toleration for Protestantism in France. Louis also asserted his authority over the Church in France against the pope, but subsequently allied with him to suppress the Jansenists, a radical and anti-papal school of thought within the French Church.

Louis and Europe

Louis' identification of himself with the state was most evident in his foreign policy. He saw his personal reputation, or *gloire* ('glory'), as inseparable from that of France. But Louis' main concern was France's vulnerability, and for this reason he had fortresses built along the eastern and northeastern borders. Louis also believed in

dynastic right, and asserted his claim to the Spanish Empire that ringed France (c> p. 252).

Between 1667 and 1713 Louis fought a series of increasingly large-scale and expensive wars in an effort to strengthen France's frontiers and assert his own prestige and dynastic rights. The fear he aroused led to the formation of large coalitions against him; and the fact that after the Glorious Revolution of 1688 (c> p. 254) England finally joined his enemies was a serious setback. The peace of 1697 saw Louis forced for the first time to return some of his previous gains, while the War of the Spanish Succession (1701–13) brought France close to collapse. When Louis died in 1715, he left France territorially strengthened, but at a heavy economic and social cost.

Yet French influence remained great. Other rulers envied Louis' authority in France and his success abroad. Those who had not already introduced absolutist measures copied his bureaucracy, his tax system, his standing army, his academies, and his style of personal rule.

The limits of absolutism

Yet despite greater central control, a large number of individuals, groups and provinces enjoyed privileges restricting Louis' authority. Since Louis had neither the resources nor the inclination to end these privileges, the administration of France was by no means completely centralized or uniform. Much of it remained in the hands of independent officials. Louis therefore depended on the cooperation of the privileged groups, and their desire for order. His government also depended increasingly on huge loans from private financiers. These limits were made clear in the 1690s and 1700s, when Louis' wars demanded more money. More offices were sold, and the tax burden and government debt vastly increased.

Nevertheless absolute monarchy was still intact in 1715. It declined under Louis XIV's successors because neither Louis XV nor Louis XVI had the same capacity to run the machine. Even so, its survival until the Revolution in 1789 (c> p. 262) contributed to the long-term centralization of French government.

SEE ALSO

● THE SPANISH AND PORTU-
  GUESE EMPIRES p. 252
● THE RISE OF BRITAIN p. 254
● EUROPEAN EMPIRES IN THE
  17TH AND 18TH CENTURIES
  p. 257
● THE FRENCH REVOLUTION
  p. 262

European Empires

in the 17th and 18th Centuries

European expansion overseas in the 16th century had been limited to Spain and Portugal (▷ p. 252), and the Spanish colonial empire remained the largest in the world in the 17th and 18th centuries. However, in the 17th century new colonial empires were created by the maritime states of northwest Europe – Britain, France and the Dutch Republic. Much of this was at the expense of Spain and Portugal, but Europeans were also making their presence felt in new areas. These new empires provided Europe with a wide range of colonial products and stimulated the demand for and production of European manufactured goods.

SEE ALSO

- THE SPANISH AND PORTU-
  GUESE EMPIRES p. 252
- THE RISE OF BRITAIN p. 254
- THE BIRTH OF THE USA
  p. 260
- NATIONALISM IN EUROPE
  p. 264
- THE PEAK OF EMPIRE p. 266

Europe's overseas trade boomed in the 17th and 18th centuries owing to growing demand for a wider range of goods: timber and other naval stores, furs, tobacco, rice and fish (all from North America), tea, cotton and silk (from the East), coffee (from Java, the Americas and the East), but above all sugar (from Brazil and the West Indies). The sugar, tobacco, and coffee plantations depended on regular supplies of African slaves. A trade 'triangle' developed. Traders from Europe would buy slaves in West Africa, carrying them to the Americas. There they traded them for colonial products with which they returned to Europe. In Europe processing industries refined those products for re-export to other parts of Europe.

The attitude of the governments of the period towards their colonies was influenced by the theories of *mercantilism*. These theories assumed the amount of wealth in the world to be fixed, and therefore that individual states had to ensure that their subjects achieved the largest share possible of world trade. Since success depended on a favourable trade balance, governments felt that their policies should encourage manufactured exports, and discourage their import. It was thought that a country's trade should be monopolized by its own subjects, and that colonies existed only to benefit the mother country.

The Anglo-Dutch Wars

In the first half of the 17th century the Dutch seized most of Portugal's scattered East Indian empire, along with its valuable spice trade. They also captured many of its African forts, and temporarily held part of Brazil. The Dutch were therefore the target for the mercantilist policies of their rivals. From 1651 the Navigation Acts reserved the produce of England's colonies for England, and their carriage to English shipping. The Acts led to a series of Anglo-Dutch Wars (1652–54, 1665–67, 1672–74) fought out – mostly at sea – in many parts of the world. England ousted the Dutch from North America and West Africa (and so from the slave trade) and gradually excluded them from its foreign and colonial trade. Expensive land wars against France overstrained Dutch resources, and by 1713, when the wars of Louis XIV ended (▷ p. 256), the Dutch were being overtaken by both Britain and France.

The Anglo-French colonial struggle

Britain and France now increasingly felt that each was the other's natural trading and colonial rival. French colonization had begun in a number of West Indian islands and Canada early in the 17th century, and in Louisiana (which then comprised much of the Mississippi basin) at the end of the 17th century. In 1713 Britain took advantage of victory in Europe to secure her position in North America, gaining Nova Scotia, Newfoundland and Hudson's Bay. The two countries were on opposing sides during the War of the Austrian Succession (1740–48), when for the first time the British and French East India Companies fought each other in India. Neither country gained a decisive advantage in this war, and the struggle continued.

Fighting in North America contributed to the outbreak of the Seven Years War (1756–63). While Prussia distracted France in Germany, the British navy achieved dominance over the French at sea. Most of France's main colonies were captured, including Canada, thanks to the victory of General James Wolfe (1727–59) at Quebec. In India, under the generalship of Robert Clive (1725–74), victories over Indians and French made the British East India Company a large private colonial power, which dominated the subcontinent. France renewed the struggle during the American War of Independence (1776–83; see p. 260). Yet, despite Britain's loss of its American colonies, the war did not reverse Britain's long-term victory in the colonial struggle.

▷ p. 252

▷ p. 252

▷ p. 256

see p. 260

THE NON-COLONIAL EMPIRES
OF EUROPE

While the maritime states sought wealth and power overseas, new great powers emerged in 18th-century Europe without the aid of colonial wealth. The Baltic empire that Sweden had built up during the 17th century collapsed during the Great Northern War (1700–21). That war saw the first appearance of Russia as a European power. Russia had been emerging in the later 17th century, a process greatly accelerated by Peter the Great (1682–1725). He created a large Russian army and navy and gave Russia a Baltic outlet. Russia continued to expand into Siberia in the 18th century, and in the reign of Catherine the Great (1762–96) exploited Turkish decline to expand southwards – a process continued in the 19th century (▷ p. 264).

Austria had reconquered Hungary from the Turks by 1700 and had been revitalized after losing Silesia to Prussia in the 1740s. Prussia had been a small and scattered kingdom in 1740. However, a superb administration and a large and effective army enabled Frederick the Great (1740–86) to seize Silesia in 1740, and to resist Austrian efforts (supported for most of the Seven Years War by Russia) to recover it. In 1772 Prussia, Russia and Austria agreed to the first partition of Poland, which for most of the 18th century had been a Russian satellite. Subsequent partitions, in 1793 and 1795, saw the disappearance of independent Poland and the further enlargement of Austria, Prussia and Russia.

The Industrial Revolution

The Industrial Revolution began in Britain during the 18th century and spread to much of the northern hemisphere throughout the 19th and early part of the 20th centuries. The advent of mechanized mass production heralded the transformation of the countries of Europe and North America into predominantly industrial rather than agricultural nations, with their populations increasingly concentrated in the cities.

Why did the Industrial Revolution begin in Britain? Britain had the advantage of being a united country with a relatively stable internal political situation, free from internal customs duties and with well-established banking and insurance facilities. In the 18th century Britain became the dominant international trading power (▷ p. 257), and many British merchants had accumulated large sums of capital. In addition, new and more efficient farming methods – developed to feed the increased numbers after a rapid population rise in the second half of the 18th century – produced huge profits for some farmers. Thus ambitious new schemes could be financed at very low rates of interest.

Britain's secure position as an island, and its proximity to the principal sea routes between northern Europe and the rest of the world, gave it great natural advantages. In addition, Britain's large numbers of natural harbours and navigable rivers – many linked by new canals in the 18th century – meant that internal and overseas trade were easily linked. Acquisition of a colonial empire became vitally important for Britain and later for other powers, so as to provide markets and raw materials (▷ pp. 257 and 266).

Rapid industrial development was also precipitated by a need to tackle Britain's fuel crisis. By the mid-18th century it was apparent that the forests were seriously depleted; opencast and shallow underground coal mines were nearing exhaustion and existing technologies for draining deeper mine shafts were inadequate. The invention of steam pumps as a far more efficient way to drain mines and the discovery of a process for smelting iron using coke made possible a more intense exploitation of Britain's mineral resources. The geology of Britain – with sources of coal and iron ore close to each other – also played its part.

A goods train on the Liverpool and Manchester railway, 1831. As a cheap and rapid method of long-distance transport – carrying workers and materials to where they were needed – railways provided a great impetus to the process of industrialization in virtually every country in the world. (AR)

Textiles

Woollen cloth had long been one of Britain's most important products, but as the 18th century progressed, it became difficult to fulfil the greatly increased demand. Inventions such as the spinning jenny produced larger quantities of thread more quickly, especially cotton. Cotton was imported in increasing quantities from the USA, and became vital to the British textile industry. Further mechanical spinning devices such as the water frame and the spinning mule appeared in the 1770s, and in 1785 the introduction of Cartwright's power loom, capable of being operated by relatively unskilled labour, marked the end of handloom weaving. The initial development of mechanized textile industries in the USA and much of continental Europe was dependent on many of these British inventions.

Only those with capital could invest in the new machinery, and those without it could not produce thread or cloth as cheaply. Thus mechanization of the textile industry gave rise to the factory system. Instead of being self-employed and working at home, women and children – and later men as well – went 'out to work' for wages in the factories, where steam engines set the pace. Attempts to destroy the new machinery by disgruntled weavers ('Luddites') were severely repressed.

Iron, steel, steam and coal

The breakthroughs in iron smelting and production in the 18th century were vital to early industrialization. Iron was used for machinery, ships, and railways. Although high-quality cast steel was produced from the 1740s, it was not until 1857 that a cheap method of mass producing mild steel was discovered (the Bessemer process). This process was developed and improved by others, and large-scale production of steel using these techniques was an important factor in the rapid industrial growth of Germany and the USA.

Experimental attempts to drain water from mines led to the early steam engines of Savery (1698) and Newcomen (1712). However, it was not until James Watt redesigned Newcomen's device (patented in 1769) that a cheaper and more efficient steam pump became available. With the addition of rotary motion, achieved by Watt in 1781, steam engines quickly became ubiquitous. As well as pumps, steam engines powered all kinds of factory machinery, railway locomotives, and ships. Without steam many of the later developments of the Industrial Revolution would have been impossible.

Coal production was dramatically increased as a direct result of the availability of practical steam pumps and other technological innovations. However, deeper, more mechanized mining proved more dangerous to the mineworkers, who included children of 4 years old and upwards. Coal was the basic fuel for steam engines, and

Saltaire, a model textile factory and town near Bradford, Yorkshire, founded in 1851 by the industrialist Titus Salt (1803–76). Built on the banks of the Leeds and Liverpool Canal for ease of transport, the settlement provided shops, libraries and other services for the factory's employees. There were, however, no public houses, since Salt was a teetotaller. (AR)

throughout Europe and the northeast USA heavy industry grew up in areas close to rich coal seams. Such areas included the Scottish lowlands, South Wales, the Ruhr and Silesia.

By the 1880s, the development of electrical energy as a power source, pioneered by Michael Faraday (1791–1867), heralded the introduction of a rival that was eventually to supersede steam. British industries, unlike those in Germany and the USA, did not abandon steam engines until well into the 20th century. Other industries, such as the potteries of Josiah Wedgwood (1730–1795), were transformed in the 18th century by the invention of new chemical processes. Development of accurate and standardized machine tools was another important aspect of the Industrial Revolution.

Industrialization outside Britain

Although Britain initiated the Industrial Revolution, other European nations, notably Belgium, were close behind. In France, industrialization proceeded more slowly, but was still impressive. In the late 19th century superior expertise in the key technologies of electricity and the internal combustion engine would result in Germany overtaking Britain as Europe's leading industrial power. In the USA the difficulties of developing an adequate transport system to cover vast distances held industrialization in check for a while. But rapid growth would make the USA the world's leading industrial power by the beginning of the 20th century (⊳ p. 260).

For Russia and Japan, industrialization during the later part of the 19th century was a result of deliberate government policy. In the 1850s both powers were largely agricultural societies dominated by ancient feudal systems, but by the start of the 20th century Japan had emerged as a serious industrial, military and economic rival to the world's industrial giants. Russia's industrialization was hampered by the country's vast size and poor communications, and even more so by the backwardness of a society still run as a feudal system, and by the inertia of the autocratic rule of the Tsars. A succession of foreign loans and internal reforms gradually made it possible to increase production and build up a railway network, and in the early years of the 20th century state aid was used to encourage growth. Indus-

trialization continued following the Bolshevik Revolution, but under circumstances of extreme difficulty (⊳ p. 270).

The effects of industrialization

Industrialization radically altered the face of European society. The demographic shift away from the countryside led to an explosion of large cities in which slum housing, low wages and the use of child labour created social and economic problems on a massive scale. The growth of industrial capitalism in Western Europe also produced a more complex political society, in which the new social and economic classes spawned by the Industrial Revolution began to organize themselves and to wield greater political influence. The industrial and commercial middle class played a crucial role in the development of 19th-century liberalism (⊳ p. 264), while the new urban proletariat of skilled and semi-skilled workers began to organize themselves in trade unions from the mid-19th century onwards.

SEE ALSO

- FARMING p. 132
- ECONOMICS pp. 172–5
- ENGINES p. 192
- MINERALS AND BIOTECHNO- LOGY p. 196
- TEXTILES p. 200
- CIVIL ENGINEERING p. 214
- SHIPS p. 216
- RAILWAYS p. 218

TRANSPORT

The need for reliable and cheap access to raw materials and markets made improvements in transport an essential part of the Industrial Revolution. Road building enjoyed a long overdue revival in the 18th century, pioneered in Britain by such men as John McAdam (1756–1836) and Thomas Telford (1757–1834). Initially more important, however, were canals, which provided the cheapest way of transporting goods and materials in bulk. A massive canal-building programme got under way in the 18th century, and by 1830 there were over 6400 km (4000 mi) of canals in Britain alone, linking all the main industrial areas. However, with the advent of the railways, the canals fell rapidly into disuse.

After the opening of the first public steam line in 1825 (the Stockton & Darlington line, designed by George Stephenson; 1781–1848), private rail-

way companies in Britain proliferated rapidly, with the result that a national network evolved with little attempt at planning. In continental Europe the railways were subject to a greater degree of state regulation and control. This was especially true of Belgium and Germany.

By providing a rapid means of transporting in bulk both raw materials and manufactured goods (⊳ picture), the growth of railway networks greatly assisted the process of industrialization. The railways also provided an impetus for other developments, such as the electric telegraph, and in the USA they played a key role in opening up the interior after the Civil War (⊳ p. 261). The railways also played a social and cultural role: by providing a means of cheap and swift long-distance passenger transport they opened up a wider world to millions of people.

The Birth of the USA

Continuous European settlement of North America dates from the beginning of the 17th century. The first British plantation, Virginia, was established in 1607, with its centre at Jamestown. In November 1620 Protestant separatists (Puritans) reached Cape Cod after sailing from Plymouth in the *Mayflower* two months earlier. Their Massachusetts Bay colony became a refuge for Puritans fleeing religious strife in England. Other British settlements followed, notably New York (formerly Dutch New Netherland) and Quaker Pennsylvania. In the South the tobacco plantations were worked by imported African slaves. By 1700 most of the colonies possessed governors appointed by the Crown and had been integrated into Britain's Atlantic empire.

In 1756–63 Britain won mastery of the continent by defeating the French in the Seven Years War (▷ p. 257). France surrendered Louisiana (then comprising much of the Mississippi basin) to Spain (regaining it in 1800) and Spain in turn gave up Florida to Britain but retained its own settlements in the southwest. The British victory was a costly one, for the national debt almost doubled during these years. It was time, the British Parliament concluded, that the colonists made a greater contribution to their own defence.

The American Revolution

During the first half of the 18th century Americans became used to a good deal of self-government. Although they regarded themselves as British, they resented their lack of representation in Parliament and their economic subordination within the Empire. In 1765 Parliament's imposition of a stamp duty on legal documents and merchandise unleashed the cry of 'no taxation without representation'. Although widespread opposition to these measures forced the British government to back down, Parliament insisted that it had full power to make laws for the colonies and left a tax on tea as proof of its authority. In 1773 it allowed the struggling East India Company to dump its tea on the American market, still retaining the controversial duty. When the first consignment reached Boston, Massachusetts, a group of American radicals, disguised as Indians, threw the tea chests into the harbour. The incident became known as the 'Boston Tea Party'.

Britain instituted repressive measures against Massachusetts, and Americans reacted by sending delegates to the First Continental Congress in September 1774, which banned imported British goods. Colonial pamphleteers insisted that traditional freedoms were being threatened by a corrupt and tyrannical enemy. In April 1775, when British troops moved to seize a store of arms outside Boston, they were confronted at Lexington by armed farmers, and retreated without achieving their objective.

King George III and his government now regarded the Americans as traitors who must be suppressed. British troops and German mercenaries were sent across the Atlantic. The Americans themselves were divided as to how they should react. Most of those in the patriot movement, however, believed Britain's policy of coercion had severed the ties of empire. In mid-1776 a Virginia planter, Thomas Jefferson (1743–1826), drafted a formal Declaration of Independence. This also announced a potentially revolutionary new doctrine: 'that all men are created equal, that they are endowed by their Creator with certain unalienable rights, that among these are life, liberty and the pursuit of happiness'. Congress approved the document on 4 July.

In the eight-year-long struggle for independence the Americans had a number of crucial advantages. They were fighting in conditions familiar to them but not to the British, and they had interior lines of communication, whereas the enemy was dependent on a long supply route from Europe. Moreover the rebels owed much to the leadership of George Washington (1732–99), a cautious but inspiring commander. Finally, France's decision to support the American cause after 1777 diverted much of Britain's resources and threatened the Royal Navy's mastery of the seas. When a British army under Cornwallis found

The Battle of Gettysburg, July 1863, is generally seen as the turning-point of the American Civil War. The three-day engagement, which cost the Union 23 000 casualties and the Confederacy over 20 000, put a halt to Southern General Robert E. Lee's invasion of the North. From then on the Confederacy was on the defensive. (AKG)

itself besieged by Washington at Yorktown in 1781 a French fleet in Chesapeake Bay cut off the only avenue of escape. Cornwallis surrendered on 19 October, and Yorktown turned out to be a decisive victory. Two years later, in 1783, Britain recognized American independence.

In May 1787 delegates from 12 of the states gathered in Philadelphia to draft a new constitution. The Articles of Confederation, which delegated very restricted powers to Congress, were no longer enough to cope with the needs of the new republic. The Constitution that was finally agreed upon was a compromise between the various regional interests in the Convention. In spite of serious flaws it was a remarkably democratic document for its time. Critics who disliked its strengthening of central government were placated in 1791 by the passage of the Bill of Rights, which formed the first amendments to the Constitution.

The expansion of the USA

Although a majority of Americans welcomed the creation of a stronger national government in 1787, the initial unity was quickly undermined by a debate over the future of the country. On the one hand the Federalists, followers of Secretary of the Treasury Alexander Hamilton (1755–1804), demanded a sound system of public finance that would attract capital for commerce and manufacturing. On the other hand Democratic-Republicans, supporters of President Thomas Jefferson, hailed the virtues of an agrarian republic in which the states would check the excesses of federal power. New England Federalists flirted with treason during the War of 1812 (fought against Britain over Canada), thereby hastening the demise of their party. By the mid-1830s most Jeffersonians had become members of President Andrew Jackson's new pro-Southern Democratic Party, which endorsed the idea that the US had a 'Manifest Destiny' to expand over the whole of North America.

In spite of increasing industrial growth the USA remained a predominantly agricultural nation, and during the 19th century millions of Americans moved westward hoping to settle on the fertile soils of the Mississippi basin and the Pacific coast. This process resulted in the displacement and settlement on separate, economically depressed reservations of most of the native Indian tribes.

Slavery and the territorial issue

The US military defeat of Mexico in 1846–48 added a vast tract of land to the national domain and unleashed a bitter debate over whether slavery should be excluded from the new territories (notably California). In 1854 the Kansas-Nebraska Act repealed the previous ban on slavery in the northwest. This appeared to open up all the new territories to slave labour, and Northern and Southern hotheads became embroiled in a vicious guerrilla war to make Kansas a state in their own image.

The crisis deepened as Northerners perceived the South's ruling planter class as a threat to their own freedoms and began voting for the new Republican Party. This organization, which represented Northern evangelical sentiment and economic interests, demanded Federal prohibition of slavery expansion. Southerners, on the other hand, believed their slave-based society to be under attack from abolitionists. When the Democratic Party split into Northern and Southern factions over the slavery issue, the

Republican candidate, Abraham Lincoln (1809–65), won the 1860 presidential election. The seven Deep South states responded by seceding from the Union to form an independent Confederacy. In April 1861 the Confederates bombarded Federal troops at Fort Sumter, South Carolina, and civil war broke out (▷ box).

Reconstruction

The North's triumph in the Civil War preserved the Union, ended slavery, and confirmed the dominance of the North's free-labour system. But it also created new problems. Radical Republicans hoped that after Lincoln's assassination on 14 April 1865 his successor, Andrew Johnson, would join them in seeking to reconstruct Southern society before readmitting Southern delegates to Congress. In fact Johnson, a Tennessean, proved to be an ally of the defeated planter class. A fierce political struggle evolved during which moderate and Radical Republicans united to give Southern Blacks the vote.

During the 1870s Deep South states with large Black populations sent Black delegates to Congress. However, after the onset of economic recession in 1873, the Northern electorate lost interest in Reconstruction, and the Republicans abandoned their Southern allies to the racist White majority. During the 1890s Southern Blacks were deprived of the vote by state laws, and they remained second-class citizens until the mid-20th century.

The industrial giant

Between 1880 and 1900 the USA emerged as a major industrial power. Large corporations took advantage of new urban markets for manufactures and raw materials. Unprecedented numbers of immigrants, many from southern and eastern Europe, journeyed to the USA to take up jobs produced by postwar economic growth. Between 1870 and 1900 the nation's population more than doubled to a total of 76.1 million.

The USA was now on the threshold of claiming an imperial role. This had been hinted at as early as 1823 by the Monroe Doctrine (enunciated by President James Monroe), which had warned European nations not to seek further colonies in the New World. In 1867 the USA purchased Alaska from Russia, and in 1898 assumed control over Puerto Rico, Cuba, and the Philippines after winning a brief, jingoistic war against Spain. The USA had at last arrived on the world stage.

SEE ALSO
- GOVERNMENT AND THE PEOPLE p. 166
- EUROPEAN EMPIRES IN THE 17TH AND 18TH CENTURIES p. 257
- PEAK OF EMPIRE p. 266
- WORLD WAR I p. 268
- WORLD WAR II p. 274
- COLD WAR p. 280

THE CIVIL WAR

The Upper South's decision to join the Confederacy when war broke out in April 1861 bolstered the region's military effort. Until 1863 Southern generalship as a whole was markedly superior to the North's. The Virginian general Robert E. Lee (1807–70) was the most talented strategist.

For most of 1861–63 the Northern cause looked bleak. Union armies suffered a string of serious reversals. Lincoln himself was attacked by fellow Republicans for his tentative approach to the war, and particularly for his reluctance to alienate the loyal slave states (Maryland, Delaware, Kentucky, and Missouri) by tackling the slavery question. However, on 1 January 1863 Lincoln signed the famous Emancipation Proclamation declaring that all slaves outside Union lines were free.

On 4 July 1863 the Union army of General Ulysses S. Grant (1822–85) finally broke through in the west by taking the Confederate stronghold of Vicksburg. The previous day Lee had been repulsed at Gettysburg, Pennsylvania. These two defeats sealed the fate of the Confederacy. Over the next two years the armies of Grant and William T. Sherman (1820–91) ground down the rebels in Virginia, Georgia, and the Carolinas. On 9 April 1865 Lee surrendered at Appomattox. The dream of an independent Southern nation was over.

The French Revolution

Between 1789 and 1791 the political and social institutions that had characterized France for the previous century and more were overthrown. In 1792 France became a republic, and between 1793 and 1794 experienced a revolutionary dictatorship (the 'Reign of Terror'). Thereafter a reaction set in, culminating in the military dictatorship under Napoleon Bonaparte (1769–1821). With the overthrow of the republic, many of the institutions and practices of pre-Revolutionary France were reintroduced. In 1815, following Napoleon's final defeat (▷ p. 263), the Bourbon dynasty was restored.

SEE ALSO

● LOUIS XIV p. 256
● REVOLUTIONARY AND NAPOLEONIC WARS p. 263
● NATIONALISM IN EUROPE p. 264

The execution of Louis XVI, 21 January 1793. Louis failed to come to terms with the fact of the Revolution and continued to plot with both French and foreign counter-revolutionaries. Evidence of his intrigues led to his conviction and execution for treason. (AKG)

The France of the *ancien régime* – the political and social system prior to the Revolution – was a centralized, absolute monarchy ruled by Louis XVI (1774–92; ▷ p. 256). The great mass of taxation was paid by the unprivileged urban poor and peasantry. The wealthiest non-nobles (the *bourgeois*), although by no means unprivileged, had fewer legal and social rights than the aristocracy. Some nobles and bourgeois agreed that merit should be the true basis of social status. They were also critical of royal absolutism, and the corruption of the court.

The immediate background to the revolution was the government's bankruptcy following French intervention in the American War of Independence (▷ p. 260), and a trade recession coinciding with harvest failure. At a time of growing discontent among the poor, Louis XVI was obliged to call the States-General to consider reform of the tax system, including a reduction in privileges. The Third Estate (the commoners) of the States-General declared itself a National Assembly, intending to introduce reform. Louis ordered troops to Paris and Versailles. On 14 July, fearing an attack on Paris and the Assembly, the Paris mob seized the Bastille (a royal fortress and prison) in order to obtain arms. An independent municipal government (commune) and National Guard were established in Paris and other towns. Since the army was divided and unreliable, royal authority collapsed, and the Assembly survived. Following a wave of peasant revolts, the Assembly abolished feudal and other privileges. This abolition was confirmed in the Declaration of the Rights of Man, which stated that that natural rights of man and the citizen could never be given up. All men were free and equal, and equally liable to taxation, and the king derived his authority solely from the will of the people.

The Assembly prepared a 'modern' constitutional government, in which legislative power lay with a new elected assembly, and local government and the legal system were completely reorganized. Religious toleration for Protestants and Jews ended the privileges of the Catholic Church, and the confiscation and sale of Church lands paid off the national debt while a fairer tax system was being devised. After a failed attempt to flee the country in 1791, Louis XVI was obliged to approve the new constitution. By the end of 1791 the Revolution had put an end to absolute monarchy and transformed French society. In 1792 foreign powers invaded France (▷ p. 263), stimulating suspicions of plots to betray the Revolution. A thousand suspected counter-revolutionaries were massacred in the prisons of Paris, and France was declared a republic. In 1793 Louis XVI and Marie Antoinette were tried for treason and guillotined.

The Reign of Terror

Not all Frenchmen supported the Revolution. In 1793 revolt broke out in the Vendée, Normandy and the south. Against the background of civil and foreign war some people called for a revolutionary dictatorship. This was brought about by the Jacobins in the summer of 1793. Virtually dictatorial powers were assumed by the Committee of Public Safety, of which Maximilien Robespierre (1758–94) was the most prominent member. The Committee unleashed a 'Reign of Terror' against suspected counter-revolutionaries. At least 300 000 people were arrested, and of these about 17 000 were executed. In the spring of 1794 the Terror intensified. Fearing for their own lives, and that Robespierre's power was too great, his enemies had him arrested on 27 July 1794 and executed. A new regime, a group of five known as the Directory, was established.

The Terror was brought to an end, the Jacobin club closed, and the Paris commune abolished. The more democratic constitution of 1793 was replaced. The Paris mob resented these moves but was powerless against the army, who supported the Directory. Frequent military interventions in politics culminated in a coup on 8 November 1799, bringing General Napoleon Bonaparte to power. In 1800 Bonaparte became first Consul, and in 1804 Emperor Napoleon I, so ending the First Republic. His military dictatorship saw the restoration of central control of local government, the end of representative assemblies, and the creation of a new aristocracy.

The French Revolution was the first 'modern' revolution, in that it attempted to transform the whole social and political system. It put into circulation modern notions of democracy, nationalism, and even socialism.

The Revolutionary and Napoleonic Wars

From 1792 the French were obliged to defend their Revolution (▷ p. 262) against a series of foreign enemies, who feared the spread of revolutionary ideas to their own countries. The French appealed to peoples everywhere to rise up against their rulers. The war became an ideological crusade on both sides. France was soon on the offensive, and its expansion meant the end of some old-established states.

SEE ALSO

- THE FRENCH REVOLUTION p. 262
- NATIONALISM IN EUROPE p. 264

In 1792 the Austrians and Prussians invaded France, but were repulsed, and France went onto the offensive. French success alarmed Britain, which declared war in 1793. By offering cash subsidies Britain built up the First Coalition against France. The Coalition included most of Europe, but it lacked an effective strategy. The French introduced conscription, which gave France the largest army in Europe (750 000 men in 1794), and in 1794–5 French armies carried all before them. One by one the allies settled with France. The brilliant French campaign in Italy in 1796–7 – led by a young general, Napoleon Bonaparte (1769–1821) – forced Austria to surrender Belgium in exchange for Venice. The French established 'sister republics' in the United Provinces, Italy and Switzerland.

Britain built up the Second Coalition, again using subsidies, which consisted of Russia, the Ottoman (Turkish) Empire, Austria, Portugal and Naples. Despite the defeat of the French fleet at the Nile (1798), Napoleon returned to Europe, and seized political power in France (▷ p. 262). The Austrians were forced to accept French domination of Italy after their defeat at Marengo (1800). Britain's other allies were soon forced to settle with France. But Britain found it too expensive to carry on alone, and settled with France (the Peace of Amiens, 1802).

However, in 1803 Britain declared war again. Napoleon declared himself Emperor in 1804 and proceeded to assemble an army to invade England, but his plans were frustrated by Horatio Nelson's (1758–1805) defeat of the Franco-Spanish fleet at Trafalgar (1805). Yet Britain again depended on European allies. Napoleon's proclamation of himself as king of Italy led Austria, Russia and Naples to join the Third Coalition. Britain again provided subsidies. In a lightning campaign, Napoleon defeated the Austrians at Ulm (October 1805) and defeated an Austro-Russian army at Austerlitz (December). Austria was forced to recognize French supremacy in Italy and Germany. Prussia decided to restrain Napoleon, but suffered a disastrous defeat at Jena (1806). Napoleon reorganized Germany into the French satellite organization, the Confederation of the Rhine. In 1807 Russia too was beaten, settling with Napoleon and declaring war on Britain. Austria, defeated again in 1809, decided to join France. Napoleon, having divorced Josephine, married an Austrian princess.

Napoleon was determined to destroy Britain by ruining its export trade – the basis of its wealth and thus of its continued opposition to France. Napoleon banned the import of British goods into all parts of Europe under French control. This blockade (the Continental System) created serious difficulties for Britain. However, the System was not effective, and its unpopularity contributed to growing resentment of French occupation in Europe.

The collapse of Napoleon's Empire

In 1808 Napoleon imposed his brother as king of Spain, sparking off a popular revolt. Henceforth large numbers of French troops were tied down in Spain. Britain sent a force to the Iberian Peninsula, precipitating years of fighting in the Peninsular War. After the British victory at Vitoria (1813), British troops entered France in 1814.

In 1812 Napoleon invaded Russia. Despite defeating the Russians at Borodino and reaching Moscow, the bitter winter and Russian attacks forced Napoleon to retreat with heavy casualties. The fiasco stimulated the formation of a Fourth Coalition. This included Prussia and Austria, and was again financed by British subsidies. In France there was growing resistance to conscription, and to Napoleon's rule in general. Fighting on two fronts, Spain and Germany, Napoleon was defeated at Leipzig (1813). In 1814 he abdicated and was exiled to Elba. However, in March 1815 Napoleon exploited the unpopularity of the new Bourbon king, Louis XVIII, to return to France, seize power and renew the war. His 'Hundred Days' ended with his defeat at Waterloo (June 1815) by allied forces under the Duke of Wellington (1769–1852) and the Prussian general von Blücher. Napoleon was sent to St Helena, and Louis XVIII was restored.

The Congress of Vienna peace settlement of 1814–15 rewarded the victors and prevented France from again dominating Europe. A ring of strong states was established around France, including a new kingdom of the Netherlands and a Prussian presence in the Rhineland. The Confederation of the Rhine was abolished, but not all the small states were restored. Austria kept Venice, and Russia acquired most of Poland.

NAPOLEON'S MILITARY REVOLUTION

In the 18th century warfare had largely been a matter of siege and manoeuvre, because troops were too expensive to lose in battle. With their massive conscript armies, the French developed – and Napoleon perfected – new formations and tactics. Napoleon concentrated his troops against his enemy's weakest point. He divided his armies into corps of 25–30 000 men. These could be deployed over a wide front (keeping the enemy guessing as to where the attack would come) and then be reunited before the decisive battle. Napoleon was a master of rapid manoeuvre, and developed an appropriately flexible logistic system, including living off the land as his troops marched on.

The success of Napoleon's approach was founded on good communications and supply, a vast reservoir of new conscripts, and on his popularity with his troops. This popularity was helped by a system of promotion through the ranks, and many of Napoleon's generals – such as the great Marshal Ney (1769–1815) – had risen in this way.

Nationalism in Europe

Nationalism is based on a feeling of common identity shared by a large group of people with the same language, culture, ethnic origins and history. During the 19th century, nationalist sentiment sprung up throughout Europe, and provided the ideological cement for the construction of two new powers in Europe: Germany and Italy. Conversely, the effect of nationalism among such peoples as the Hungarians, Serbs, Poles and Greeks was to encourage rebellion against the larger and more powerful empires that controlled them.

Liberalism and Romanticism (▷ pp. 318 and 366) were often closely associated with nationalism. Some, although by no means all, 19th-century nationalist movements combined their demands for national freedom or unity with the demands of the middle classes for a liberal form of government.

The revolutions of 1848

Many of the European revolutions of 1848 were associated with nationalist demands. The uprising in Paris on 22 February 1848 led to the overthrow of the Orléans monarchy and the installation of a republican government, and was to inspire revolts right across Europe.

In Italy outbreaks of revolution occurred throughout the Italian peninsula, leading to wholesale expulsion of the Austrians occupying the north. However, disunity among the nationalists led to the Austrians (and the Spanish Bourbons in the south) regaining control. In the vast, multilingual Austrian Empire, the revolutionaries of 1848 set their sights on overthrowing Austrian rule. The Hungarians, Croats and Czechs all managed to assert their independence from the Austrians and set up their own states for a brief period. However, the old rulers soon returned to power, partly by exploiting the divisions between the various national groupings. Popular uprisings also occurred in many of the German states, and a liberal 'German National Assembly' met in Frankfurt in May, but by the end of 1849 the attempt to construct a constitutional unified German state had ended.

Italian unification

At the Congress of Vienna in 1815 (▷ p. 263), Napoleonic Italy was divided into 13 separate states, of which only two, the Papal States and the kingdom of Sardinia (including Piedmont), were ruled by Italians. Austria dominated the penin-sula. Nationalist secret societies such as the Carbonari ('charcoal burners') staged several risings and conspiracies during the 1820s and 30s, but none succeeded in dislodging Austrian rule. Other groups, including the Young Italy movement of Giuseppe Mazzini (1805–72), fared little better.

At the forefront of the Risorgimento ('resurrection') – as the movement for Italian unification came to be known – was Piedmont, which was by far the most industrialized and economically prosperous Italian state. Camillo di Cavour (1810–61), Piedmont's prime minister from 1852, seized every opportunity to advance the cause of Italian unification, and successfully solicited French help in driving the Austrians out of most of northern Italy in 1859. In 1860 the nationalist guerrilla leader Giuseppe Garibaldi (1807–82) landed in Sicily with an army of 1000 volunteers, and swiftly took control. He crossed to the mainland and swept aside minimal Bourbon resistance in southern Italy. Cavour moved troops to the Papal States in order to assert Piedmontese control of the newly united Italy.

In 1861 the 'Kingdom of Italy' comprised the entire peninsula, with the exceptions of Venetia

The uprising in Paris in February 1848 was the catalyst to revolution on a European scale. Disturbances spread quickly to central Europe, where the political situation had long been volatile. Demonstrations were held throughout the German Confederation and there were uprisings in Berlin, Vienna, Prague and Budapest. (AKG)

North German Confederation in an economic alliance. In the final stage, the fears of the southern Germans of possible French aggression were exploited by Bismarck as a means of compelling them to draw closer to Prussia. Bismarck manoeuvred France into declaring war on Prussia in 1870 (the Franco-Prussian War). Following the swift and humiliating French defeat, the whole of the 'German' area of Europe was finally unified under Prussian control, and Prussia also gained Alsace and Lorraine from France. The new German Empire was proclaimed on 18 January 1871, with the Prussian king declared Kaiser Wilhelm I of Germany.

SEE ALSO

- POLITICAL IDEOLOGIES p. 168
- THE RISE OF ISLAM p. 242
- THE FRENCH REVOLUTION p. 262
- THE REVOLUTIONARY AND NAPOLEONIC WARS p. 263
- THE PEAK OF EMPIRE p. 266
- WORLD WAR I p. 268

Giuseppe Garibaldi, whose popular charisma led many to follow him in the cause of Italian unification. With his Redshirts – a band of irregular guerrilla fighters – he was responsible for many of the military successes of the Risorgimento, but his radical republicanism put him at odds with the more conservative Italian leaders. (AKG)

(in the northeast) and Rome. Venetia was eventually acquired from Austria after Italian help had been given to Prussia in the 1866 'Seven Weeks War' (▷ below). Rome, with the exception of the Pope's own territory of the Vatican, was taken over when the French garrison left in 1870.

German unification

One man, Otto von Bismarck (1815–98), Prussian prime minister (1862–71) and then German chancellor (1871–90), is credited with masterminding the process of German unification. Germany at the close of the Napoleonic Wars existed only as a loosely grouped, weak confederation of 39 states. Economic unity preceded political unification, with the Prussian-led Zollverein ('customs union') being established in 1818. The 1848 revolutions rocked the rulers of states throughout Germany. However, by 1851, having crushed its own revolutionary unrest, Austria rather than Prussia had reverted to the position of dominant power within the reinstated German Confederation. Bismarck determined to change this through a policy of 'blood and iron', which unfolded in three main stages.

The first stage involved Prussia allying with Austria against Denmark over the thorny and complicated question of who should control the duchies of Schleswig and Holstein. In 1864 Prussia invaded and swiftly defeated Denmark, and then took control of Schleswig, while Austria took Holstein. In the second stage Bismarck isolated Austria by means of skilful diplomacy and then provoked a war with Austria and various north German states in June 1866. This 'Seven Weeks War' culminated in a decisive Prussian victory over Austria at Sadowa (Königgrätz). Austria was forced to accept that Prussia was now pre-eminent in north German affairs. The still independent south German states (Bavaria, Württemberg and Baden) were associated with the new, Prussian-dominated

THE EASTERN QUESTION

In Eastern Europe, the nationalist aspirations of the various peoples under foreign domination became confused with the attempts by various of the great European powers to fill the power vacuum being created by the decline of the Ottoman (Turkish) Empire. This was particularly so in the Balkans, where the Turks had ruled a variety of mostly Slavic peoples for centuries, and which were seen by Russia, France and Britain as the key to dominance of the strategically important eastern Mediterranean.

The first crisis arose in Greece, where a popular uprising was put down by the Turks in 1821. The following year a National Greek Assembly declared Greece independent, and liberal and nationalist sympathizers from all over Europe pledged their support. The governments of the European powers remained officially uninvolved, until massacres perpetrated by the Turkish Sultan's troops goaded Russia into declaring its intention to intervene. In 1826, in order to forestall Russian domination in the area, Britain and France put pressure on the Sultan to grant a measure of autonomy to Greece, and when he refused, a joint British and French naval force sunk his fleet in Navarino Bay in 1827. Greek independence was eventually guaranteed by Britain, France and Russia in 1830.

In the previous year Russia had gained some territory and considerable rights and privileges in the Balkans from Turkey. The Russians also turned nationalist sentiments in the region to their advantage with the doctrine of 'Pan-Slavism', by which Russia took upon itself the right, as the largest Slav nation, to promote the desires of other Slav peoples for independence. Help to Balkan nationalists tended to coincide with Russian foreign-policy aims, particularly for power in the eastern Mediterranean, and control of the strategically vital entrance to the Black Sea. In other areas, where Russia's own interests were not likely

to be furthered by the promotion of local nationalist aspirations, any such stirrings were quickly and firmly crushed – as happened in Russian-ruled Poland in 1830 and 1863.

Although liberal opinion in Britain and France was very much in sympathy with the national aspirations of the Balkan peoples, the governments of those two countries were more concerned by Russian territorial ambitions in the region. Russian interest in and encroachment on Afghanistan and Persia (present-day Iran) also caused tension with Britain, as it appeared to threaten the security of British India.

British and French fears of Russian ambitions were confirmed when Russia occupied the eastern Balkan territories of Moldavia and Walachia in 1853. The following year the Russians sank a Turkish fleet, and Britain and France sent an expeditionary force to the Crimea, a Russian peninsula in the Black Sea. The Crimean War (1854–6) cost the lives of half a million men, largely owing to disease and military incompetence, and did not in the end forestall Russian ambitions.

Further Russian encroachments into Turkish territory in the Balkans were halted at the Congress of Berlin in 1878. In return, Turkey recognized Serbia, which became the largest independent Slav state in the region. However, Slav nationalists – encouraged by Russia and Serbia – greatly resented having to exchange Turkish for Austro-Hungarian control, as happened in Bosnia-Herzegovina. The Balkan Wars of 1912 and 1913 led to success for Slav nationalist aspirations: the territory of the Ottoman Empire was much reduced, and Serbia increased its size and strength. Austria was their next target. It was a Slav nationalist who assassinated the Austrian Archduke Franz Ferdinand in Sarajevo in 1914 – an event which precipitated the outbreak of World War I and the final break-up of the Austro-Hungarian Empire into independent nation-states following its defeat in the war (▷ p. 269).

The Peak of Empire

In 1800 most people in the world were self-governing. By 1914 about one-quarter of the globe had been taken over as colonies by half a dozen states. At the time many people argued that imperialism was needed to increase trade and find new materials for the economies of Europe. Others wanted to gain more territories to increase their strategic power in relation to other states. In the 19th century the various motives of the imperialists – economic, political and strategic – came together and encouraged the drive for Empire.

By the late 18th century various European empires had been established (▷ pp. 252 and 257), but these had either been in relatively under-populated areas, such as Canada and Australia, or had already shown signs of growing independence, as in the United States (1776; see p. 260) and South America in the early 19th century. The one serious exception was the rule of the British East India Company.

The British in India

By 1805 the East India Company was dominant in India. Wars against Nepal (1814–16), Sind (1843) and the Sikh kingdom of the Punjab (1849) extended the frontiers to the natural boundaries of the subcontinent in the north. To the east the British had annexed the Burmese empire by 1886. Within India the traditional system of landholding was destroyed and the British introduced private ownership. Production of food did not keep pace with the growth in population (some 190 million in 1871) and famine was a continuous threat. As a result the land quickly passed into the hands of relatively few large landowners, creating a large number of landless peasants.

The Indian Mutiny was the last effort of traditional India to oppose British rule. Princes, landlords and peasants were all united by the speed and tactlessness of the changes imposed by the British. The revolt began in 1857 as a mutiny of the Company's Indian soldiers. This spark ignited into rebellion all those who resented the growing British interference in Indian customs and believed that the introduction of Western education would destroy the indigenous culture of India. Opposition to the British centred around the large number of rulers, including the Mogul emperor himself, who had been dispossessed by the Company. The British brutally ended the revolt in 1858 after 14 months of bitter struggle.

After the Indian Mutiny the British government took direct control of India, and embarked on a programme of modernization. By 1927 92 000 km (57 000 mi) of roads had been built; education in English was introduced; and, most importantly, a railway network was constructed. The railways made possible the exploitation of Indian raw materials and the introduction of cash crops, such as tea. On the other hand, the British refused or failed to modernize industry, destroying, for example, the Indian cotton industry so that it could not compete with the British.

Fears of a Russian threat to the Indian subcontinent led to ill-fated British expeditions to Afghanistan in 1839–42 and again in 1878–80. The

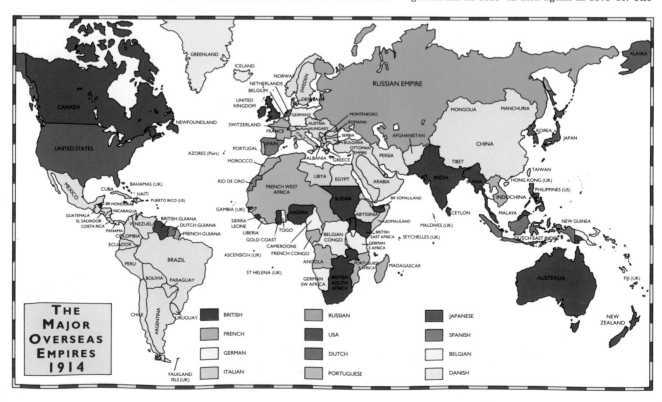

THE MAJOR OVERSEAS EMPIRES 1914

BRITISH · FRENCH · GERMAN · ITALIAN · RUSSIAN · USA · DUTCH · PORTUGUESE · JAPANESE · SPANISH · BELGIAN · DANISH

THE SCRAMBLE FOR EMPIRE

Before the 1880s the Africans had largely resisted European conquest, even forcing the Portuguese out in 1690. Even in the late 19th century the Ashanti, the Zulu and the Abyssinians were capable of strong resistance, but the balance of military technology was now decisively in favour of Europe. Large areas of the globe, particularly in Africa and Oceania, were carved up between the Western powers (⊳ map).

The French gained most of north and west Africa as well as Madagascar and Indochina. Germany acquired an empire in the Cameroons, Togoland, South West Africa, Tanganyika, China, part of New Guinea and some Pacific islands (all lost to the Allies after World War I). Italy obtained Libya, Eritrea and part of Somaliland, but failed in 1896 to conquer Abyssinia (⊳ p. 273). The British made the greatest gains, including Egypt (although nominally still part of the Ottoman Empire), the Sudan, Uganda, Kenya, British Somaliland, Nigeria, Ghana, the Rhodesias and Nyasaland, as well as strategically important areas of the Pacific such as Singapore, Malaya and

Fiji. The British also consolidated their rule of South Africa with their victory in the Boer War (1899–1902) over the Boers (or Afrikaners: settlers of Dutch descent).

The old empire of the Dutch remained in Indonesia, while the Portuguese reasserted control of Angola, Mozambique and Guinea, although their largest colony, Brazil, had become independent in 1822. What remained of the Spanish Empire after the successful wars of independence in its South American colonies (1810–29), however, was largely taken over by the USA after a brief war in 1898. The Americans acquired Puerto Rico, Guam and the Philippines from Spain, and also the Panama Canal, Hawaii and other Pacific bases.

The imposition of colonial rule varied. In the Congo the personal rule of King Leopold of Belgium led to horrific atrocities. In South West Africa the Germans massacred the Hereros to impose their rule. Many Africans revolted against colonial rule: for example, the Ndebele and Shona rebelled in Rhodesia (1896–97) and the Zulus in South Africa (1906).

The French explorer and colonial administrator Savorgnan de Brazza (1852–1905) – founder of the French colony of the Middle Congo (now the Republic of Congo) – on his last mission to West Africa in 1905. (AR)

fiercely independent Afghan tribesmen managed to oust the British, and their country remained as a buffer between the British and Russian Empires.

European imperialism

After 1870 there was a rush to acquire colonial possessions by the major European powers (⊳ box). There were a number of reasons for this 'scramble for empire'. The development of commerce in the 19th century created a global economic system. Many formerly remote areas of the world were being settled and developed: Canada, the USA west of the Mississippi, Australia and New Zealand. Ancient civilizations – such as Persia (Iran), China and Japan (⊳ p. 234) – were being opened to European penetration. In Africa and Asia missionaries and traders were arguing the enormous potential value of colonies as a treasure house of souls and raw materials.

New technologies were developing that depended on raw materials found mostly in remote places – the motor car depended on oil and rubber, and copper from Africa and South America was needed for the new electrical industry. In addition the new mass consumption of sugar, tea, coffee, cocoa and fruit led to the development of tropical plantation economies. So the scramble for natural resources provided a fresh impetus for expansion.

In Europe there was increasing competition between the old imperial powers – Britain and France – and the emerging nations, especially Germany and Italy. Each feared being left behind by its rivals. Missionaries, traders, military and naval men and the public came together in the European capitals to press for imperial advances. The drive for empire and control of the world economy created new antagonisms between the major powers. The rivalries between the powers, formerly confined to Europe, became global and imperial.

China

Once a great empire, by the 19th century China was politically weak and corrupt. It remained closed to outsiders until in the first Opium War of 1839–42 the British forced the Chinese to allow the traffic of drugs into China, and established five British-dominated treaty ports. British and French victory in the second Opium War (1856–60) forced the Chinese to open further ports. China seemed doomed to disappear under colonial rule. Russia exercised influence in Manchuria, the Germans carved out bases in the north, Britain enlarged its Hong Kong colony, and the rising power of Japan annexed Taiwan in 1894–95 and Korea in 1910 after defeating the Russians in the Russo-Japanese War of 1905.

The Western powers were able to unite to put down the Boxer Rising and to occupy and loot Beijing (Peking) in 1900, but they were unable to agree how to divide the immense Chinese empire. As a result China remained independent, but the strains of foreign interference helped cause the final collapse of the world's most ancient civilization in 1911 (⊳ p. 276).

The legacy of imperialism

Imperialism was both a massive movement and a very brief experience for those involved. The entire experience of colonialism in many parts of the world can be fitted within a single life – decolonization started after World War II, accelerated in the 1960s and was virtually complete by the 1980s (⊳ p. 278). For most people the cultural impact of imperialism was very limited, though a minority did have Western education and many of these later became the leaders of anti-imperialism. Perhaps the most significant long-term impact of imperialism is continuing resentment against the imposition of Western ideas and against the economic dominance of the West over large areas of the Third World (⊳ p. 184).

SEE ALSO

● THE THIRD WORLD p. 184
● THE SPANISH AND PORTUGUESE EMPIRES p. 252
● EUROPEAN EMPIRES IN THE 17TH AND 18TH CENTURIES p. 257
● DECOLONIZATION p. 278

World War I

By 1914 Europe was divided into two armed camps based upon political, territorial and economic rivalries. In the centre of Europe was a recently unified Germany, allied to Austria-Hungary since 1879 and Italy since 1882, fearful of attack from France and Russia (allied since 1894), yet threatening expansion against either or both. Britain, traditionally aloof, viewed German industrial development, naval expansion and colonial ambitions (⊳ p. 266) with distrust and since 1904 had been associated with Germany's rivals.

Exhausted British troops awaiting the signal to attack at Passchendaele, October 1917. Field Marshal Alexander Haig's preliminary bombardment of the German positions around Ypres turned the area into a swamp, and the British offensive became bogged down in a nightmare of mud. Despite the deadlock of trench warfare, both sides continued to throw millions of men into attacks that might only gain a few hundred metres – at the cost of hundreds of thousands of casualties.
(Image Select)

On 28 June 1914 the Archduke Franz Ferdinand, heir to the throne of Austria-Hungary, was assassinated in Sarajevo, capital of Bosnia, a region of the Balkans then part of the Austro-Hungarian Empire (⊳ p. 265). The Austrians – supported by the Germans, who feared the disintegration of their ally – blamed the newly independent neighbouring state of Serbia and threatened to attack. The Serbs in turn appealed for aid from their fellow Slavs in Russia, who began to mobilize their vast army. Fearing attack, Germany put into action a strategy known as the *Schlieffen Plan*, and declared war on both Russia and France. The Plan was designed to knock out France (Russia's ally) before the Russians completed mobilization, so avoiding a two-front war. As German troops crossed into neutral Belgium as a preliminary to their attack on France, Britain (which had guaranteed Bel-

gian independence) declared war on Germany. The battle lines were drawn. On the one side were the *Allies* (Britain, France and Russia), and on the other the *Central Powers* (Germany and Austro-Hungary). Italy held back. By 4 August Europe had been plunged into a conflict that was to last for over four years, killing an estimated 20 million people.

Opening moves

The French, intent on recovering the provinces of Alsace and Lorraine (lost to the Germans in 1870, see p. 265) mounted a major attack around Metz on 14 August, only to suffer enormous casualties. Meanwhile the Germans swept into Belgium towards northeastern France, aiming to take Paris in a huge outflanking movement. However, the Germans, with large distances to cover, lost momentum in the broiling heat of summer. This allowed the French to scrape together a new army to defend Paris, counterattacking across the River Marne in early September to force the Germans back. Both sides then tried to outflank the other to the north, but neither could gain advantage. The rival armies dug in and, by October, had created a line of trenches from the Channel to the Swiss border.

By then the Germans had been forced to divert armies to the east. The Russians had advanced into East Prussia in August, but were defeated in a series of battles around Tannenberg. Further south the Russians were more successful, pushing the Austrians back in Galicia, necessitating a German reinforcement to prevent defeat. By Christmas 1914 a two-front war had become a reality for Germany.

The trench nightmare

Warfare on the Western Front was characterized by the trench system. This emerged to a large extent because of new weapons that gave the advantage to the defender. If one side wished to attack – as Britain and France did in order to liberate northeastern France and Belgium – their soldiers had to do so through mud, across barbed wire and into the teeth of machine guns and quick-fire artillery. In 1915, as casualties mounted alarmingly, the nature of the war changed, forcing all the major combatants to raise large armies and to mobilize their societies to produce new armaments. Anglo-French offensives failed to break the deadlock in the west, while on the Eastern Front the situation, although more fluid, similarly denied victory to either side.

Instead, the war expanded. In October 1914 the Turks declared war on the Allies, and in May 1915 Italy – in return for Allied promises of territorial gains from Austria-Hungary – declared war on the Central Powers, opening up new fronts that drained resources. In mid-1915 the Germans forced the Russians back through Poland, taking pressure off Germany's eastern border, and in October Bulgaria joined the Central Powers. Only in Serbia was a decisive campaign fought: by December 1915 the country had been conquered by the Central Powers.

The nightmare deepened in 1916. In February the Germans made an attack around Verdun on the River Meuse, designed to 'bleed France white'. The French obliged by pouring in reserves until, by December, the fighting had cost each side

about 700 000 men. On 1 July the British tried to break through on the River Somme, losing 57 000 soldiers in the first few hours; by November this figure had risen to 460 000. On the Eastern Front it was even worse: a Russian offensive in June enjoyed initial success near the Carpathian Mountains, only to be turned back three months later at a cost of a million men. Things were no better in 1917: a French offensive in Champagne failed in April, while at Passchendaele in July the British entered a nightmare of mud that cost a further half million casualties. Only on the Austrian-Italian front was there a break in the stalemate, with the defeat of the Italians at Caporetto.

Alternatives to trench deadlock

In such circumstances alternatives to attritional deadlock were sought. Britain, for example, devoted part of her effort to attacks against the outer edge of the Central Powers, searching for weaknesses. As early as 1914 British forces had seized many of Germany's colonies in Africa, but a greater opportunity arose when Turkey came into the war.

It was argued that a knock-out blow against Turkey – the 'sick man' of Europe – would open up the southern flank of the Central Powers. In April 1915 a seaborne attack was made on the Gallipoli peninsula, on the Dardanelles Straits between the Aegean and Black Seas, with the main aim of taking Constantinople (now Istanbul). It failed, at a cost of 265 000 Allied troops, many of them Australian and New Zealand volunteers. A similar campaign in Mesopotamia (now Iraq) ended in disaster at Kut, on the road to Baghdad, in April 1916. Only later, in Mesopotamia and Palestine (the latter aided by an Arab revolt coordinated by T.E. Lawrence, 1888–1935), was success achieved.

Other alternatives were tried, using the sea and air to reinforce the pressures of conflict on land. At sea, fleet actions were rare – the only major engagement between the British and Germans, at Jutland in May 1916, ended in stalemate – but from the start of the war both maritime powers attempted to impose blockades on their rivals. Britain was successful, but Germany was not.

The German U-boat (submarine) offensive caused heavy British losses, but in 1917, with a declaration of unrestricted warfare against any ships suspected of trading with Britain, it helped to trigger a declaration of war against the Central Powers by the USA. Using protected convoys and new anti-submarine weapons, the British gradually gained the initiative. By late 1918 the British blockade of Germany had led to starvation and social unrest, but that year the Central Powers gained the Ukraine with its rich harvests. Germany mounted bombing raids on England by Zeppelin airships and aircraft, but they had little effect on the war effort. In the end, whoever won the land battles would prevail, and this meant looking to new weapons and tactics to break the trench deadlock.

In 1915 the Germans used poison gas at Ypres, and the British soon reciprocated, but generally gas led to no major breakthroughs. On the Somme in 1916 Britain first deployed the tank as a means of crossing the mud and barbed wire of no-man's-land between the trenches and countering the effects of machine guns. However, it was not until Cambrai in November 1917 that the full offensive potential of massed tanks began to be seen. On this occasion the Germans counterattacked using select groups of 'stormtroops' to infiltrate rather than attack head on. By late 1917 the ingredients for tactical success were emerging.

Allied victory

By the end of 1917 the balance of power between the two sides had shifted. In late 1917 Russia dissolved into revolutionary chaos (▷ p. 270) and the Germans took the opportunity to attack with decisive results: by March 1918 a peace treaty between the two countries had been signed. This enabled the Germans to concentrate their forces in the west for a major assault on the British and French before American troops arrived in Europe in large numbers.

The German offensive enjoyed some success in March, using the new storm-trooper tactics tried out at Cambrai, but by the middle of April Allied forces had rallied and stopped the advance. In August they moved onto the offensive, using tanks supported by ground-attack aircraft and, significantly, involving the first of the newly arrived American divisions. Elsewhere, the Central Powers began to crumble, first in the Middle East, where British troops took Jerusalem and Damascus and defeated the Turks, then in Italy, where the Austro-Hungarians were defeated at Vittorio Veneto and forced to seek terms. By November the Germans were isolated. With public confidence in the government evaporating, Communism spreading from the East and the Allies closing in, the German Kaiser fled to Holland and an armistice was arranged. At 11 AM on 11 November 1918 the fighting ceased.

A German postcard encouraging Germans to help the war effort by buying government war bonds. (AKG)

SEE ALSO

- NATIONALISM IN EUROPE p. 264
- THE PEAK OF EMPIRE p. 266
- THE RUSSIAN REVOLUTIONS p. 270
- THE GROWTH OF TOTALITARIANISM p. 272

THE POSTWAR SETTLEMENT

Two months after Germany was forced to ask the Allies for an armistice to end World War I, the Paris Peace Conference opened. Although 32 states (but neither Germany nor Russia) sent representatives, most of the major decisions were taken by the 'Big Three' – the British and French prime ministers (David Lloyd George and Georges Clemenceau) and the US president (Woodrow Wilson). As well as concluding the Treaty of Versailles with Germany, the Allies signed other treaties with Austria-Hungary, Bulgaria and Turkey. The terms of these treaties were to lay the foundations for the future of the world.

Under the *Treaty of Versailles* (28 June 1919), the state of Poland was created and awarded the 'Danzig Corridor' – a belt of former German land that gave the Poles access to the sea and separated East Prussia from the rest of Germany. Germany also had to return the provinces of Alsace and Lorraine (seized in 1870, ▷ p. 265) to France. The Rhineland was to be demilitarized and occupied by Allied troops. German colonies overseas passed to the Allies as 'mandates' of the League of Nations, whose Covenant was included in the peace settlement. The size of the German army was limited to 100 000 men, conscription was forbidden, and Germany was banned from possessing tanks, military aircraft and large naval vessels. In addition, heavy reparations were imposed.

Under the *Treaty of St Germain* (10 September 1919) Austria lost Bohemia (including the Sudetenland) and Moravia to the newly created state of Czechoslovakia, and ceded territory to Poland and Italy. By the *Treaty of the Trianon* (4 June 1921) Hungary, the other half of the old Dual Monarchy, was stripped of two-thirds of its territory to help form Czechoslovakia, the new state of Yugoslavia and Poland. Under the *Treaty of Neuilly* (26 November 1919) Bulgaria ceded land to Greece.

The *Treaty of Sèvres*, signed with Turkey in August 1920, gave substantial parts of the old Ottoman Empire as mandates to France (which received 'Greater Syria') and Britain (which gained Palestine, Iraq and Transjordan; ▷ p. 282). However, following a nationalist revolt led by a distinguished Turkish general, Kemal Atatürk (1881–1938), the *Treaty of Lausanne* (1923) gave Turkey much improved terms.

The seeds of future conflict were sown by these treaties. The various peoples of Europe were too mixed up to be neatly separated into nation-states, and the territorial settlement caused resentment and strife. Germany emerged from the postwar settlement weakened and embittered but still the strongest power in central Europe. The grievances of both Italy and Germany – exacerbated from 1929 by the economic and political strains of the Depression – were to help undermine the fragile democratic systems in those countries (▷ p. 272).

The Russian Revolutions

At the turn of the 20th century Russia was a feudal state. Tsar Nicholas II ruled, as his ancestors had ruled before him, as an autocratic monarch. Nicholas had the backing of a large and inefficient bureaucracy, but remained supreme. His will was enforced by the state police and the army, and his officials controlled education and censored the press. Dissent was ruthlessly crushed. It was a situation ripe for revolution.

The vast majority of Russian subjects were poverty-stricken peasants, controlled through 'land captains' appointed by the government. Although serfdom (virtual ownership of the peasants by the land-owning classes) had been abolished in 1861, the peasants were closely bound to the land by a communal system of land holding.

Lenin, the leader of the Bolshevik Revolution and founder of the Soviet Union. This painting by Valentin Alexandrovich Serov depicts him with fellow revolutionaries in December 1905. (AKG)

Nevertheless, increasing numbers migrated to the cities, for Russia began to industrialize rapidly in the first decade of the 20th century with the aid of Western, particularly French, capital. Life for the 15 million or so members of the urban working class was harsh. Housing and conditions in the factories were poor, providing fertile ground for the growth of radical and revolution-

ary political parties. The two most important such parties were the Social Democrats and the Social Revolutionaries. The effective leader of the former was Vladimir Ilyich Ulyanov, better known as Lenin (1870–1924).

The roots of revolution

In 1904–5 Russia fought and lost a war with Japan. Even before this, unrest had been growing in both urban and rural areas. The defeat at the hands of the Japanese precipitated a revolution. On 'Bloody Sunday' (22 January 1905) troops opened fire on a peaceful demonstration near the Tsar's Winter Palace in the capital, St Petersburg. About 1000 protesters – including women and children – were killed. This was followed by a general strike, peasant uprisings in the countryside, rioting, assassinations and army mutinies. In October 1905 the Tsar agreed to elections to a *Duma*, or parliament. This rallied moderate political reformers to the side of the government, which was able to crush the revolt.

The first two Dumas proved to be too radical for the Tsar's taste, but in 1907 a conservative Duma was elected after electoral changes. Some reforms did take place under the chief minister, Petr Arkadievich Stolypin (1863–1911), who curbed the power of the land captains and helped to create a small class of peasants who owned their own land. However, Stolypin was unpopular with both Left and Right, and was assassinated.

World War I placed Russian society under tremendous strain. After three years of war the army had suffered 8 million casualties and over 1 million men had deserted. Inflation was rife and the peasants began to stop sending their produce to the cities, leading to food shortages. Respect for the Imperial government – which was seen to be dominated by the corrupt and debauched monk Grigori Efimovich Rasputin (c. 1872–1916) – had crumbled and revolutionary propaganda began to spread among the soldiers and workers.

On 8 March 1917 revolution broke out in Petrograd (as St Petersburg had been renamed in 1914). *Soviets* (councils) of soldiers, workers and peasants were set up all over Russia. On 15 March the Tsar abdicated and a moderate provisional government was set up. In the summer of 1917 Aleksandr Fyodorovich Kerenski (1881–1970) became the chief minister, but the powerful Petrograd soviet was controlled by Lenin's Bolsheviks. On 7–8 November (25–26 October in the old Russian calendar) Kerenski was ousted in a coup led by Lenin.

Lenin and the Bolsheviks

Lenin had studied the ideas of Karl Marx (▷ p. 168) and aimed to replace capitalism with a Communist workers' state. He decided that the Russian people needed to be led by a well-educated, dedicated revolutionary elite. His opponents in the Social Democratic Party, who wished to build a mass party, were dubbed *Mensheviks* (or the minority), although in fact it was the followers of Lenin, the *Bolsheviks* (or majority), who formed the smaller group.

When the March revolution began, Lenin was in exile in Switzerland, but in April 1917 he was allowed by the Germans to return to Russia in a sealed train. He immediately began to plot the downfall of the provisional government, which had misguidedly decided to continue the war with

Germany and was slow in introducing land reform. Lenin's promise of 'bread, peace and land' won many to the Bolshevik cause. After he seized power in November 1917, Lenin moved against rival socialist groups, using the Cheka (secret police) as a weapon, and executed the deposed Tsar and his family.

The Bolsheviks were forced to accept a harsh peace with Germany at Brest-Litovsk in March 1918, but this allowed the Bolsheviks to turn their attention to the civil war that had begun in Russia. The 'Reds' were opposed by the 'Whites' – a loose coalition of democrats, socialists and reactionaries, united only by their opposition to Lenin – and by armies sent by Britain, France, Japan and the USA.

However, the various White factions were unable to coordinate their strategy, and they were defeated piecemeal by the Red Army created by Leon Trotsky (1879–1940), a former Menshevik. By mid-1920 it was clear that the Bolsheviks had triumphed. Russia was then attacked by Poland, which was intent on seizing territory in western Russia. The Red Army weathered the attack and then advanced as far as Warsaw before suffering a defeat on the Vistula. During the civil war the Red Army also reconquered the various non-Russian areas of the former Tsarist empire; these had formed their own republics in 1918. The Union of Soviet Socialist Republics was formally established in 1922.

Economic problems and the NEP

In November 1917 the new Bolshevik government faced many economic problems. They divided up the old estates, giving the land to peasants, which gained them considerable support. In June 1918 Lenin was forced to introduce 'War Communism', by which there was wholesale nationalization and state control of agriculture. This led to the collapse of industrial production and serious food shortages. In March 1921, after a serious naval mutiny at Kronstadt, the New Economic Policy (NEP) was introduced. This returned small businesses to private hands and allowed farmers to sell their crops. Previously, surplus produce had simply been requisitioned by the state, but now a class of *kulaks* (affluent peasant farmers) emerged. The NEP improved both industrial and agricultural output.

The death of Lenin in 1924 initiated a power struggle among his successors. By 1929 Joseph Stalin had emerged victorious and he remained the unchallenged ruler until his death in 1953. His chief rival had been Trotsky, who had advocated spreading revolution across Europe. In the mid-1920s Trotsky was eased out of power and eventually went into exile in Mexico, where he was murdered in 1940 by a Spanish Communist, probably acting for Stalin.

Stalin's policy of building 'socialism in one country' was undoubtedly more realistic, given the weakness of the USSR. Stalin aimed to catch up with the Western capitalist powers by a crash programme of industrialization and agricultural collectivization. This policy was to cause untold suffering to the Soviet people.

In 1928 Stalin ordered that land be taken away from its peasant owners and used to create collective farms, which were supposed to be more efficient as well as egalitarian. In the process the

kulak class was destroyed, with perhaps 10 million deaths in 10 years. The disruption caused by the collectivization programme led to famine.

The first of the Five-Year Plans to improve Soviet heavy industry also began in 1928. Generally, the targets were too ambitious; nonetheless Soviet industry did begin to catch up with the West. As in pre-revolutionary days, such rapid industrial growth caused much hardship. Living standards plummeted as the industrial workforce swiftly doubled to 6 million, and Soviet officials were quick to punish underproduction by imprisonment in labour camps.

The USSR and Europe

Although European governments feared that the USSR was bent on spreading revolution to their countries, the Soviets played relatively little part in European affairs in this period. The 1922 Treaty of Rapallo brought the USSR together with Germany, but with the emergence of Hitler, the Soviets began a bitter war of propaganda against the Nazis.

From 1934 onwards Stalin moved towards Britain and France. However, disillusioned by the policies of appeasement and worried at the prospect of Soviet isolation, Stalin signed a non-aggression pact with Hitler in 1939, agreeing to partition Poland between their two countries. This gave the Soviets a breathing space, but it was only to last until June 1941, when Hitler invaded the USSR (▷ p. 274).

A Bolshevik propaganda poster commemorating the second anniversary of the Revolution of November 1917. Bolshevik supremacy was finally assured by the defeat of the counter-revolutionary 'White' Russian forces by Trotsky's Red Army in 1920. (AKG)

SEE ALSO

● POLITICAL THEORIES p. 168
● THE INDUSTRIAL REVOLUTION p. 258
● WORLD WAR I p. 268
● THE GROWTH OF TOTALITARIANISM p. 272
● WORLD WAR II p. 274
● THE COLD WAR p. 280

The Growth of Totalitarianism

From an ancient Roman symbol of authority, the fasces, is derived the name of one of the most significant ideologies of the 20th century – Fascism. Fascism grew out of the unstable political conditions that followed World War I. Its mass appeal derived from its promises to replace weak democratic governments with strong leadership and to rectify the grievances of individuals and states arising out of the postwar settlement (▷ p. 268). In the 1920s Fascist dictators began to gain power in several countries. Once they did, tensions arose between themselves and the democratic states – tensions that would lead eventually to war.

Fascism was not a coherent doctrine like Marxism (▷ p. 168), but all Fascists believed in a strong, nationalist, authoritarian state, ruled by a charismatic dictator backed by a single paramilitary party. Fascists were fanatically opposed to democracy, socialism, Marxism and liberalism, and were often racist and antisemitic. Both in opposition and in power, Fascists made effective use of propaganda and terror to win support and to dispose of political rivals.

Mussolini gains power

Italy appeared to be threatened by Communist revolution after World War I. One of the many extremist right-wing groups that was formed in response was the Fasci di Combattimento (usu-ally shortened to 'Fascists'), led by Benito Mussolini (1883–1945). By 1922, largely through Mussolini's brilliant oratory and shrewd political sense, the Fascists had gained enough support to attempt to seize power. In October, 25 000 Fascist 'Blackshirts' marched on Rome and King Victor Emmanuel III was forced to ask Mussolini to form a government. In 1926 Mussolini made himself dictator, awarding himself the title 'Il Duce' ('the Leader'). His most notable achievement was the Lateran Treaty of 1929, which ended the hostility between the Catholic Church and the Italian State.

The rise of the Nazis

In Germany the weak Weimar Republic (set up in the aftermath of World War I, and named after the town where its parliament first met) came under attack in 1919 from Communist 'Spartacist' revolutionaries, and in 1920 right-wing paramilitary units launched an abortive coup – the 'Kapp Putsch'. In 1923 Adolf Hitler (1889–1945), leader of the small National Socialist German Workers' (or Nazi) Party, tried to overthrow the Bavarian government. The 'Beer-Hall Putsch' was unsuccessful and Hitler, a former army corporal, was arrested, serving a short prison sentence. During his imprisonment he wrote *Mein Kampf* ('My Struggle'). In it he set out his beliefs on race: that 'Aryan' Germanic peoples were superior to Slavs, Negroes and, above all, Jews, and that the German 'Master Race' must conquer territory in the east to achieve *lebensraum* ('living space').

The Depression rang the death knell of the Weimar Republic. In 1930 a political crisis developed over plans to cut government spending on welfare services and President von Hindenburg (1847–1934) began to rule by decree. The Nazis were well placed to exploit the crisis. Hitler was a masterly orator and one of his principal lieutenants, Josef Goebbels (1897–1945), had a genius for propaganda. Hitler denounced demo-

Flag-bearing Nazis at a party gathering in September 1933. One of the features of totalitarian states is the highly regimented mass rally of party members. Those held annually by the Nazis at Nuremberg involved huge open-air gatherings in a specially built stadium. The leaders used these occasions to rouse their followers to a frenzy of devotion and to deliver important policy statements. (AKG)

cratic politicians for stabbing the undefeated German Army in the back at the end of World War I by signing the Treaty of Versailles (▷ p. 268), and blamed the Depression on Jewish financiers. Nazi tactics were ruthless but effective: the brown-shirted 'Stormtroopers' of the SA (Sturmabteilung) intimidated and murdered opponents. The Nazis began to receive support from all classes who longed for firm government.

In the 1932 election the Nazis won 230 seats, becoming the largest party in the Reichstag (the German parliament), and on 30 January 1933 Hitler became chancellor (prime minister). The move to totalitarianism was swift. The Nazis used the burning of the Reichstag on 27 February 1933 – which was probably the work of the Nazis themselves – as an excuse to arrest opposition politicians. The Nazis also forced through a law giving Hitler dictatorial powers.

Hitler in power

After von Hindenburg's death in August 1934 Hitler became 'Führer' ('Leader') with the powers of chancellor and president. The Nazis outlawed all other political parties, banned trade unions, and tightened their grip by the use of censorship and by establishing a hierarchy of Nazi officials down to the lowest levels. Hitler's will was enforced by the SS (Schutzstaffel, 'protection squad') and Gestapo (Geheime Staatspolizei, 'secret state police'), both under the authority of Heinrich Himmler (1900–45). Ernst Roehm, the head of the SA and a potential rival to Hitler, was murdered along with 150 of his followers on the 'Night of the Long Knives' (30 June 1934).

In accordance with Hitler's hatred of the Jews, the 1935 Nuremberg Laws stripped German Jews of their remaining rights; eventually 6 million Jews were murdered in concentration camps. By reintroducing conscription and rearming in defiance of the Treaty of Versailles, Hitler not only reduced unemployment but also restored national pride – both of which made him genuinely popular in Germany in the 1930s.

Totalitarianism in Japan

Japanese governments in the 1920s tended to be weak, and even before the Wall Street Crash the country suffered from serious economic problems. Faced with the power of big business on the one hand and the development of left-wing movements on the other, Fascist-style ideas began to influence army officers. Many sections of Japanese society supported the idea of strong military government and military expansion at the expense of Japan's neighbours – particularly the European colonial powers.

The army began to demonstrate increasing independence from the government. In 1931, following a clash with Chinese troops at Mukden, the army occupied Chinese Manchuria on its own initiative. Four years later it attempted to seize power in Tokyo. Although the coup failed, the army came to have a dominating influence on the government, with General Hideki Tojo (1884–1948) becoming prime minister in 1941. Domestic policies began to resemble those of European Fascist states.

The failure of the League of Nations

The League of Nations proved unable to prevent war. When in 1933 a League commission denounced the Japanese attack on Manchuria the Japanese simply left the League and began a war of

Goering and Hitler look on as French prime minister Edouard Daladier signs Hitler's guest book during the Munich conference, 29 September 1938. Franco-British hopes that the Munich agreement would put an end to Germany's territorial demands proved short-lived. Within two years France was in German hands, and a beleaguered Britain under threat of German invasion. (AKG)

conquest in China proper in 1937. Similarly, in 1935–6 Mussolini invaded and conquered Abyssinia (Ethiopia). All the League of Nations did was to impose – for a brief period – ineffective economic sanctions on Italy. Three years later, in March 1939, Mussolini struck again, attacking and occupying Albania.

Meanwhile Hitler began to threaten the peace of Europe. In 1934 Germany left the League and in 1935 Hitler announced his rearmament programme. The following year he marched into the demilitarized zone in the Rhineland. This was a gamble: German forces were still very weak and the French might have driven them back. However, Britain and France did nothing. Also in 1936 Mussolini and Hitler became allies in the Rome–Berlin Axis, and Japan joined Germany in the Anti-Comintern Pact, aimed against the USSR.

Appeasement and the road to war

British and French policy towards Hitler has been called 'appeasement' – that is, they gave way to what they believed to be Hitler's reasonable demands in the hope that he would be content and not go to war. In March 1938 German troops marched into Austria and the Anschluss (union of the two countries) was proclaimed. Hitler next began to threaten Czechoslovakia, using the alleged ill-treatment of German-speaking peoples in Czech Sudetenland as a pretext. Britain and France at first supported the Czechs, but at the Munich conference in September 1938 the British and French prime ministers agreed to Hitler's demands, and the Sudetenland was handed over to Germany. The British prime minister returned to Britain announcing that he had achieved 'peace in our time'.

This peace lasted for approximately 12 months. In March 1939 Hitler seized what was left of independent Czechoslovakia, in defiance of the Munich agreement. He then turned his attention to Poland, demanding the return of Danzig and access across the Polish Corridor to East Prussia. War once again seemed inevitable and the British and French began half-heartedly negotiating with the USSR. But on 24 August Germany signed a 'non-aggression pact' with the USSR. Hitler, convinced that the British and French would do nothing, attacked Poland on 1 September 1939. World War II had begun.

SEE ALSO

● POLITICAL IDEOLOGIES p. 168
● WORLD WAR I p. 268
● THE RUSSIAN REVOLUTIONS p. 270
● WORLD WAR II p. 274

World War II

Between September 1939 and September 1945 the world experienced a 'total war', fought by countries that devoted their full human and material resources to the complete destruction of their enemies. In the process the fighting spread to almost every continent and ocean, and all the ingenuity of man was used to produce new weapons of mass destruction. By the end of it all, over 50 million people had died.

The conflict began in Europe when, on 1 September 1939, Germany invaded Poland in pursuance of its territorial demands (▷ p. 272). Britain and France declared war on Germany two days later but could do nothing to help the Poles. On 17 September, following the Nazi-Soviet Non-Aggression Pact, Soviet units advanced from the east to link up with Hitler's armies. Poland ceased to exist.

Europe and the Mediterranean

After a pause known as the 'Phoney War', Hitler turned towards the west. In early April 1940 German forces invaded Denmark and Norway, then on 10 May turned their *blitzkrieg* ('lightning war') tactics on the Netherlands, Belgium and France, spearheading their attacks with dive bombers and fast-moving tank units. Anglo-French forces moved into Belgium, but found that the Germans had advanced across their rear. Trapped on the coast the British rescued over 300 000 men from Dunkirk, leaving the French to fight on alone. France surrendered on 22 June, and a pro-German French government was set up in the town of Vichy.

By then Britain was besieged. Since September 1939 the Germans had been conducting a naval campaign against British merchant shipping, and the German U-boats (submarines) were beginning to have an effect. After Dunkirk this threat was reinforced by air attacks on Britain. Initially the Germans tried to destroy the RAF as a preliminary to invasion, but were defeated in the Battle of Britain in the summer of 1940. They then tried to undermine British resolve by bombing cities in the 'Blitz' (September 1940–May 1941).

Nor was the fighting confined to Europe. On 10 June 1940 Italy declared war on Britain and France, taking the opportunity of their weakness to seize Somaliland (Somalia) and invade Egypt. In the event both attacks were defeated, with British counterattacks to take Italian-held Abyssinia (Ethiopia) and eastern Libya. This triggered a German response to prevent Italian humiliation. In North Africa General Erwin Rommel (1891–1944) pushed the British back to the Egyptian border, while in the Mediterranean the key island of Malta came under air attack. In the Balkans, where an Italian invasion of Greece (October 1940) had come close to disaster, German forces swiftly overran Yugoslavia, Greece and Crete (April–May 1941). British fortunes were at a low ebb, boosted only by a growing friendship with the USA. This resulted in the provision of war materials to the UK under 'Lend-Lease'.

The war spreads

The war suddenly escalated on 22 June 1941, when Hitler's forces attacked the USSR. As German tanks thrust deep into western Russia, massive pockets of Soviet troops surrendered. But Hitler could not make up his mind about objectives, first of all shifting forces to the north, then to the south. It was not until October that a major drive on Moscow began. As German units approached the city the winter snows began, enabling the Russians to recover. In December they counterattacked, forcing the Germans into winter enclaves.

By then the war had spread to the Pacific. On 7 December 1941 Japanese aircraft struck Pearl Harbor in the Hawaiian islands, crippling the US Pacific Fleet. In the next few weeks Japanese forces attacked the Philippines, Malaya, Hong Kong and the Dutch East Indies. By May 1942 all these colonies, together with Burma and Singapore, had been lost, and even Australia was under attack.

These escalations were to spell long-term disaster for the Axis powers (Germany, Italy and Japan), for a Grand Alliance (including Britain, the USA and the USSR) now emerged. Cooperation between the three main Allies was not always smooth, but a series of meetings, initially between British prime minister Churchill and President Roosevelt of the USA, then including the Soviet leader Stalin, gradually developed a concerted strategy for the defeat of the Axis, based on a demand for unconditional surrender.

The tide turns in the west

The first priority was the defeat of Germany. The Americans favoured an immediate cross-Channel invasion, but Britain was not enthusiastic. By early 1942 North Africa had still to be cleared, and Allied shipping in the Atlantic was still under heavy attack by German U-boats. Churchill therefore persuaded the Americans to concentrate on these two areas first, together

Motorized German infantry advancing through a devastated Polish town in September 1939. Polish resistance was brushed aside in three weeks of *blitzkrieg* campaigning by German panzer divisions. By the end of September – in accordance with the secret protocol contained in the Nazi-Soviet Non-Aggression Pact of 23 August – Poland had been partitioned between Germany and the Soviet Union. Eastern Poland remained in Soviet hands until the German invasion of Russia in 1941.
(AKG)

with a combined bombing offensive against German cities.

By early 1943 new tactics and weapons had given victory to the Allies in the Atlantic. In North Africa, the tide was turned at Alamein in October 1942 by British forces under General (later Field Marshal) Bernard Montgomery (1887–1976). Simultaneously Anglo-US forces invaded French North Africa and, although the Axis forces fought stubbornly for Tunisia, victory was attained by May 1943.

The Americans called again for a cross-Channel assault, but the Mediterranean still took priority. In July 1943 Allied forces invaded Sicily then, in September, southern Italy. Mussolini was overthrown and the Italians surrendered, but German units rushed south to fill the breach. The Allied advance soon stalled in mountains to the south of Rome, centred on Monte Cassino. Despite an amphibious landing at Anzio (January 1944), Cassino was not taken until May. Rome was liberated on 4 June.

The defeat of Germany

The build-up of Allied forces in Britain was now complete. On 6 June 1944 (D-Day) they crossed the Channel under the overall command of General Dwight D. Eisenhower (1890–1969) to seize beachheads on the coast of Normandy. Bitter fighting ensued, but by early September Paris had been liberated, an invasion of southern France had taken place and Anglo-US forces were closing in on Germany. An attempt to use airborne forces to 'jump' the lower Rhine at Arnhem in the Netherlands failed in September, and an autumn stalemate developed.

The Soviets meanwhile, under Marshal Georgi Zhukov (1896–1976), had advanced from the east. Their victory was hard-won, beginning in early 1943 when a German push towards the Caucasus had been stalled in the shattered streets of Stalingrad (now Volgograd). This enabled the Soviets to push westwards and by July 1943 their forces had re-entered the Crimea and advanced as far as Kursk, where a major German counterattack was decisively defeated. In 1944 a series of coordinated attacks all along the Eastern Front pushed the Germans out of the Ukraine in the south, to the gates of Warsaw in the centre (where an uprising by Polish resistance fighters was put down brutally by the Germans) and to the former Baltic provinces in the north. Leningrad, under German siege since 1941, was relieved in January 1944, having cost over one million Russian lives. Advances into the Balkans finally cleared the Germans from Soviet territory in late 1944.

The end came swiftly for Germany. Attacked from the air by massive fleets of Anglo-US bombers, its cities lay in ruins and, despite a desperate German counterattack through the Ardennes in December 1944, the Allies closed in. In the east the Russians drove from Warsaw to the gates of Berlin; in the west the Anglo-Americans crossed the Rhine and reached the River Elbe; in Italy the Germans were pushed over the Alps. Hitler committed suicide in late April 1945 and Berlin fell to the Soviets in early May. On 8 May Germany surrendered unconditionally.

The defeat of Japan

This left the Japanese. Their initial wave of success had been halted at the Battle of Midway (June 1942) as well as in New Guinea and Guadalcanal (Solomon Islands). The Americans immediately went on to the offensive, conducting

THE WAR IN EUROPE 1939-45

US, BRITISH, COMMONWEALTH & OTHERS
SOVIET
ALLIED COUNTERATTACKS 1942-45
MAXIMUM EXTENT OF AXIS EMPIRE, NOVEMBER 1942
UNOCCUPIED ALLIED POWERS
NEUTRAL

Siege of LENINGRAD 1941-44
MOSCOW
Battle of STALINGRAD 1942-43
Fall of BERLIN MAY 1945
D-DAY 6 JUNE 1944
BERLIN
GERMANY
POLAND
PARIS
CZECHOSLOVAKIA
FRANCE
SWITZERLAND
HUNGARY
YUGOSLAVIA
ROMANIA
BULGARIA
Invasion of south of FRANCE AUGUST 1944
ROME
ALBANIA
TURKEY
OPN TORCH Invasion of N W AFRICA NOV 1942
SICILY
GREECE
Invasion of ITALY SEPT 1943
CRETE
TUNISIA
Invasion of SICILY JULY 1943
Battle of ALAMEIN OCTOBER 1942
TOBRUK
CAIRO Suez Canal
ALGERIA
LIBYA
EL ALAMEIN
EGYPT

a two-pronged advance – under General Douglas MacArthur (1880–1964) in the southwest and under Admiral Chester Nimitz (1885–1966) in the central Pacific. Simultaneously British forces prepared to counterattack in Burma in conjunction with Chinese units. The Solomons/New Guinea campaign achieved success by late 1943, enabling MacArthur to prepare for the liberation of the Philippines; at the same time forces under Nimitz began an 'island-hopping' campaign, aiming for Taiwan.

By early 1944 it had been decided that both prongs should converge on the Philippines. As Nimitz closed in, taking the Marshall and Mariana Islands by June, he defeated a major Japanese naval force at the Battle of the Philippine Sea; as MacArthur invaded Luzon in October, he did the same at the Battle of Leyte Gulf. Both victories enabled the Americans to step up the pressure, fighting to liberate the myriad islands in the Philippines while initiating a bombing campaign on Japan from the Marianas. In Burma a Japanese attack towards Imphal was defeated and the British went on to the offensive, liberating Rangoon by May 1945.

By then Iwo Jima had been captured and Okinawa invaded, although as US troops got closer to Japan the level of resistance grew more fanatical. Presented with the means to knock Japan out of the war and thereby save thousands of US soldiers, the new US president, Harry Truman, authorized the use of the newly developed atomic bomb on Hiroshima (6 August) and Nagasaki (9 August; ▷ p. 181). The latter coincided with a Soviet invasion of Manchuria and this finally broke Japanese resolve. The Pacific war ended on 15 August, although the surrender was not formally signed until 2 September. It was the end of six years of war.

SEE ALSO

● NUCLEAR ARMAMENT AND DISARMAMENT p. 181
● WORLD WAR I p. 268
● THE GROWTH OF TOTALITARIANISM p. 272
● CHINA IN THE 20TH CENTURY p. 276
● THE COLD WAR p. 280

China in the 20th Century

At the beginning of the 20th century China was in turmoil. Despite a remarkable continuity of civilization dating back to at least 2000 BC, the authority of the emperor had been weakened in the 19th century by outside powers greedy for trade, and by huge rebellions which had left large areas of the country beyond the control of central government (▷ pp. 234 and 266). In 1911 a revolution, led by the *Guomindang* (*Kuomintang* or Nationalists) under Sun Zhong Shan (Sun Yat-sen; 1866–1925), overthrew the last of the Manchu emperors. Strong in the south (where Sun established a republic in 1916), the Nationalists faced problems in the north, which was ruled by independent warlords resentful of central interference.

By the time of Sun's death in 1925 it was obvious that if the republic was to be extended to the whole of China, force would have to be used: indeed, Sun's successor, Jiang Jie Shi (Chiang Kai-shek; 1887–1975), gained his new position primarily because he commanded the Nationalist armies. Some inroads were made into the north, only to be undermined by the emergence of another, potentially powerful political force – the Communists.

Mao Zedong

The Chinese Communist Party (CCP) was formed in Beijing (Peking) in 1921, taking as its model the Bolshevik revolution in Russia four years earlier (▷ p. 270). But the Russian Communists had based their revolution on the discontented urban working class, and this the Chinese – an overwhelmingly peasant people – lacked. By 1928, after a series of disastrous urban uprisings, easily

and brutally suppressed by Jiang, the CCP seemed doomed to extinction. However, a relatively unknown member of the CCP, Mao Zedong (Mao Tse-tung; 1893–1976), had been experimenting with new ideas. Recognizing that any successful revolution needed popular support and that in China such support could only come from the peasants, he concentrated on the rural areas, setting up 'safe bases' as a foundation for future action against the Nationalist government. Operating initially in his own home province of Hunan, in south-central China, then in the remote and inaccessible mountains of neighbouring Jiangxi, Mao proved so successful that by the early 1930s he was posing a direct challenge to Jiang's authority.

Jiang responded with military action, gradually reducing the Jiangxi base until, in October 1934, Mao was forced to withdraw. During the next 12 months he led his followers on a 9000 km (5600 mi) trek known as the 'Long March', moving from Jiangxi to the even more remote northwestern province of Shaanxi. Jiang, convinced that he could do no more damage, let him go.

The Sino-Japanese War

But by this time Jiang was facing a much more immediate threat – that of Japanese expansion. This had begun in 1931 with the Japanese seizure of Manchuria (one of the few centres of Chinese industry), and this was followed six years later by an all-out attack that led to the Japanese occupation of Beijing as well as of substantial parts of the Chinese coast (▷ p. 273).

Despite an alliance between Jiang and Mao, the Nationalists could do little to counter Japanese aggression. Only after the extension of the war to the Pacific and Southeast Asia in 1941–42 (▷ p. 274) could Jiang be guaranteed the outside support he needed, especially from the USA, but even then the record of the Nationalists was poor. They were still facing the Japanese occupation of large parts of China when Japan surrendered to the Allies in August 1945.

Part of the pressure exerted on Japan in the final days of the war was a Soviet invasion of Manchuria. In its aftermath the Soviets tried to ensure that Mao's Communists took over the area, hoping to accelerate the revolution. During the Sino-Japanese War Mao had extended his influence and gathered strength, waiting for an opportunity to attack the weakened Nationalists. In 1946 he marched into Manchuria.

The civil war

This began a civil war in China that was to last for three years. At first the Nationalists held on to Manchuria, but gradually lost their grip in the face of guerrilla attacks. By 1948 Manchuria was in Communist hands, and when this was followed by attacks on Beijing, Jiang's forces began to collapse. On 1 October 1949 Mao proclaimed a People's Republic in Beijing. Jiang fled to the

Nationalist gunners in action in Jiangsu province during the Chinese Civil War (1946–9). Jiang Jie Shi's Nationalist (Guomindang) forces enjoyed early successes against their Communist rivals, but 1947 saw a shifting of the tide in the latter's favour. The establishment of Communist control over Manchuria and large areas of northeastern China in the second half of 1948, culminating in the capture of Beijing, sealed the fate of the Nationalists. (Popperfoto)

offshore island of Taiwan, where a Nationalist government was set up. The Communists periodically exerted military and political pressure against the Nationalists. However, the Nationalist government in Taiwan still exists today.

Meanwhile, in 1949 Mao's first priority was to ensure Communist control over the whole of mainland China, sending the newly created People's Liberation Army (PLA) to root out 'class enemies' and the remnants of the Nationalist armies. This led in 1950 to the first of a series of moves beyond the borders of China, when PLA units entered Tibet, an independent state since 1916. Repressive Communist rule alienated the native Tibetans, loyal to their religious leader, the Dalai Lama, and in 1959 they rose in revolt, only to be ruthlessly suppressed. Tibet has remained under Chinese control ever since.

Border wars

Expansion such as this highlights one of the chief priorities of the Chinese Communists – to secure the borders of China against outside interference. From late October 1950 PLA 'volunteers' saw action in Korea, triggered by an advance by United Nations forces into Communist North Korea after the North Koreans had been pushed back from their invasion of the South (⊳ p. 280). As the UN advance seemed to be approaching the border with China, Mao felt justified in committing his troops. At the end of the Korean War in 1953 all of the North had been restored to Communist control and the threat to China's border removed. Similar intervention in the Himalayan border region against India in 1962 prevented what was seen as a threat from that direction, while in 1979 an incursion into northern Vietnam, albeit less successful militarily, continued the trend.

The Sino-Soviet split

The incursion into Vietnam had its origins in a Chinese fear of Soviet encirclement, for by then Vietnam was supported by the USSR. Relations between China and the USSR had deteriorated in the late 1950s, with ideological clashes over the true nature of Communism and border clashes in Manchuria. One result was an acceleration of Chinese research into atomic weapons – they test-exploded their first device in 1964 – but more significant were the effects of the split on Chinese domestic and foreign policy. In foreign policy, Mao mended fences with the USA in the early 1970s, playing the West against the East in a new twist to the Cold War (⊳ p. 280), while at home he tried to radicalize the revolution to ensure its ideological strength.

The Cultural Revolution and after

The process of radicalization had begun in the 1950s, when the PLA (always primarily a political rather than a military instrument) had been sent into the countryside to spearhead the 'Great Leap Forward', an ambitious programme of land collectivization and education. It had largely failed, suggesting to Mao that the PLA had lost its revolutionary zeal.

After appropriate reforms in the PLA, Mao tried again in the mid-1960s, determined to spread more radical revolutionary ideas to the people in the so-called Cultural Revolution. He stirred up a

Mao Zedong, the former teacher and son of a prosperous farmer. By bringing Communist rule to China, he transformed the lives of a quarter of the world's inhabitants. He is shown here with his Defence Minister and designated successor, Lin Biao, in 1969. Lin Biao was to disappear in bizarre circumstances two years later. Having organized an abortive coup against Mao, he is alleged to have died in a plane crash while fleeing to the USSR. (AKG)

hornets' nest, with militant students forming groups of 'Red Guards' to attack the existing hierarchy, which they regarded as bourgeois and over-Westernized. Thousands died, and thousands more bureaucrats and intellectuals were sent to work in the fields. Mao was lucky to survive, having to turn to the PLA for support against the Red Guards when they went out of control. The power struggle that ensued between the militants and the now influential PLA was still being played out when Mao died in 1976.

After Mao's death China – under the leadership of Deng Xiaoping (1904–) – followed a more careful course both at home and abroad. Border disputes were settled more peaceably, and relations with the USSR were cautiously re-established in 1989. Foreign affairs generally were characterized by more open friendship with previously hated enemies. The agreement to negotiate the future of Hong Kong, which is to cease to be a British colony and revert to Chinese control in 1997, is a case in point.

The reason for this opening up to foreign countries is that the Party leadership had recognized the need for industrialization and modernization if China was to compete in the world, and this would be impossible if foreign crises occurred. Western technology was needed, and for this to be available and effective in China, less extreme policies had to be introduced. Economic liberalization and the opening up to Western cultural influence has led to internal pressures for political change, culminating in the massive pro-democracy demonstrations by students and workers in early 1989. These were brutally repressed by an ageing leadership unwilling to loosen its hold on political power. In the face of an international outcry, China seemed to be turning inwards again.

China is currently at a crossroads: if it succeeds in modernizing its industry it has great potential; if it reverts to repression and international distrust, the record of violence and war so characteristic of its history in the 20th century could continue.

SEE ALSO

● POLITICAL IDEOLOGIES p. 168
● CHINA TO THE COLONIAL AGE p. 234
● WORLD WAR II p. 274
● THE COLD WAR p. 280

Decolonization

In 1945 there were some 70 independent sovereign states in existence, and much of the globe – especially vast tracts of Africa, the Indian subcontinent, Southeast Asia and the Middle East – was controlled by European colonial powers, either as colonies and protectorates or 'mandates' from the now defunct League of Nations (▷ p. 269). Thirty years later there were more than 170 independent states on the map, the increase being accounted for almost entirely by decolonization, and there were hardly any non-self-governing areas left. The age of European colonialism was over, the nationalist revolution having wrought a massive change in the international political system.

That such a transformation came about has been explained by some historians in terms of a 'push-pull' concept – in other words, that the colonial powers abandoned their empires both because of the 'push' provided by the rise and spread of nationalism within their colonies, and because of the 'pull' provided by liberal opinion in the home countries. The two processes coincided with dramatic effect during the second and third quarters of the 20th century to produce the wholesale withdrawal from empire.

Pressures for change

The 'push' – rising demand for self-government and independence – may be explained by a number of factors. One of these, the basis for the growth of nationalist sentiment within colonial territories, was the tendency of the colonial powers to provide Western-style education to their colonial subjects, albeit a minority of those subjects only and usually no more than a small elite. Education was provided for reasons of self-interest as well as altruism – an educated elite was a valuable asset in terms of local administration and development. But the consequences were the same: the emergence of a group of people who understood Western ways and who were imbued with notions such as freedom, self-determination and equality, and determined to enjoy such advantages themselves.

Another equally significant factor was the development in many colonies of an economic infrastructure (roads, railways, schools, etc.) and even some commerce and industry. This helped to stimulate 'detribalization' (the breaking down of barriers between different groups of people within a colonial area) and, allied to the spread of education, this produced groups of colonial subjects susceptible to the nationalist message.

Finally, the clash of cultures brought about by imperialism created upheaval. The imperialists were alien in terms of race and religion in most cases, and local people – often for the first time – became aware of their own unique characteristics. In the Middle East, for example, the importance of the Islamic religion and the steady growth of an awareness of the Arab race as a distinct social and cultural grouping undoubtedly fuelled the rise of Arab nationalism – a force of some potential as early as the 1920s and 1930s (▷ p. 282).

The myth of White invincibility

If the effect of these factors could be seen from such an early stage, World War II gave a tremendous boost to the growth of nationalist feeling – especially in areas occupied by Axis forces or cut off from the imperial power.

In Southeast Asia, for example, French and British territories were exposed to revolutionary ideas following the Japanese conquests of 1941–2 (▷ p. 274). Having shattered the myth of White invincibility, the Japanese encouraged local anti-colonial movements. After the war, these movements were superseded or enlarged by anti-Japanese nationalists – many of them Communists. Winning considerable popular backing, these elements were able to persuade or coerce the returning imperialists into granting independence – in Burma with minimal violence but in the Dutch East Indies (Indonesia) and French Indochina (Vietnam, Laos and Cambodia) only after prolonged and bloody conflict in the late 1940s and early 1950s (▷ p. 280).

In Africa, too, nationalist sentiment developed rapidly as a result of World War II. Its rise was fuelled by a variety of factors: the humiliation of France and Britain in 1940 and of Italy by 1943; economic and commercial development during the war; and, of course, by inspiration offered by

THE DECOLONIZATION OF AFRICA

Key to abbreviated countries
G   GAMBIA 1965
G-B   : GUINEA-BISSAU 1974
C.A.R. : CENTRAL AFRICAN REPUBLIC
R   RWANDA 1962
B   BURUNDI 1962

MOROCCO 1956
TUNISIA 1956
SPANISH SAHARA (To Morocco) 1976
ALGERIA 1962
LIBYA 1951
EGYPT (Formal independence 1922. British military presence ends 1965)
MAURITANIA 1960
MALI 1960
NIGER 1960
CHAD 1960
SUDAN 1956 (Anglo-Egyptian condominium until 1956)
ERITREA (to Ethiopia 1952)
DJIBOUTI 1977
SENEGAL 1960
G
UPPER VOLTA 1960
NIGERIA 1960
SOMALIA (united 1960)
G-B
GUINEA 1958
IVORY COAST 1960
C.A.R. 1960
ETHIOPIA 1941
SIERRA LEONE 1961
LIBERIA
TOGO and DAHOMEY 1960
CAMEROON 1960
GHANA 1957
EQUATORIAL GUINEA 1968
GABON 1960
ex Belgian CONGO 1960
UGANDA 1962
KENYA 1963
R
B
ex French CONGO 1960
TANGANYIKA 1961 (united as Tanzania 1964)
ZANZIBAR 1963
ANGOLA 1975
ZAMBIA 1964
MALAWI 1964
MOZAMBIQUE 1975
NAMIBIA 1990
ZIMBABWE 1980
MADAGASCAR 1960
BOTSWANA 1966
SWAZILAND 1968
SOUTH AFRICA (British Dominion until 1961)
LESOTHO 1966

Possessions and protectorates of the colonial powers in 1940

FRANCE
BELGIUM
BRITAIN
SPAIN
ITALY
SOUTH AFRICA
PORTUGAL
INDEPENDENT

Asian countries such as India and Pakistan, which gained their independence (albeit to the accompaniment of widespread sectarian violence) in 1947. By then, the Philippines had gained independence from the USA (in 1946), Britain had given notice of her intention to withdraw from the mandate of Palestine (in 1947; ⊳ p. 282), and Indonesia formally became independent of the Dutch in 1949.

World War II, or more accurately the effects of that war, also encouraged the growth of anti-imperialist feeling in the mother countries themselves. Many of these countries, notably Britain, France, Belgium and the Netherlands, had been devastated or virtually bankrupted by the war and were finding it difficult to provide the necessary resources to rebuild their shattered economies, provide greater living standards at home and, at the same time, continue to bear the 'White man's burden' of empire. Imperial glory began to feel like imperial strain.

Moreover, the colonial powers began to find themselves overstretched not only economically and militarily but also, in a sense, morally. West European leaders and public opinion in general became responsive to the idea that colonial peoples should be allowed, indeed encouraged, to achieve the same rights of self-determination that Europeans had claimed for themselves long before. In short, the colonial powers began to lose the will, as opposed to just the power, to hang on to their empires indefinitely. The 'push' and the 'pull' thus came together and the imperial powers withdrew from empire in the third quarter of the 20th century almost as systematically as they had rushed into it in the latter half of the 19th. The days of empire, for better or worse, were over.

The end of empire

Setting the pace of decolonization were the British, who had established the largest of the overseas empires. Britain had begun the process long before World War II, granting independence to the countries of White settlement – Canada, Australia, New Zealand and South Africa – and this was followed in 1947 by the concession of independence to the largest non-White territory, India (split along religious lines into predominantly Hindu India and Muslim Pakistan).

Then, under successive governments, colonies in Asia, Africa, the West Indies and Oceania followed suit, the process being greatly accelerated by the Suez Crisis of 1956, when Britain, having invaded Egypt (in conjunction with the French and Israelis) in an effort to reverse President Nasser's decision to nationalize the Anglo-French Suez Canal Company, was forced to withdraw under intense diplomatic and economic pressure from the USA (⊳ p. 282). The implication was that, even if Britain wished to maintain an empire, it could no longer do so in a superpower-dominated world.

Decolonization gathered pace in the 1960s, presaged by Prime Minister Harold Macmillan's recognition of a 'wind of change' blowing through Africa. Empire was replaced by the concept of a multiracial Commonwealth, formed for the most part from states that had gained independence without recourse to violence, although the British did have to fight in places

such as Malaya (1948–60), Kenya (1952–60), Cyprus (1955–9), Borneo (1963–6) and Aden (1964–7) to ensure, or try to ensure, the emergence of friendly governments.

The French also withdrew from empire, though only after two protracted and bitter conflicts against nationalists in Indochina (1946–54) and Algeria (1954–62) had persuaded them to abandon the concept of an indivisible French Union. The Portuguese, too, tried to preserve an indivisible empire, but gave up in 1974–5 after prolonged insurgencies in their three African territories of Angola (1961–74), Mozambique (1964–74) and Guinea–Bissau (1963–74).

In contrast, the Dutch accepted more quickly that they could not reassert their authority in the East Indies (Indonesia), while the Belgians granted independence to their main overseas holding, the Congo (Zaïre) in 1960, although this was followed by a bitter civil war. Even Spain decided to abandon her African colonies, Guinea and the Spanish Sahara, in 1968 and 1976 respectively.

By the late 1970s the world had changed dramatically, producing new political, territorial and economic rivalries as well as new opportunities for alliances and trade. One significant political development was the establishment in 1961 of the non-aligned movement (mostly consisting of African and Asian states), which encouraged foreign policies independent of the Eastern and Western superpower blocs (⊳ p. 280). However, despite the technical independence of Third World states, many of them continue to be influenced strongly – politically and economically – by either the superpowers or a former colonial power – a situation sometimes described as *neo-imperialism* or *economic imperialism* (⊳ pp. 184–5).

Congolese troops attempt to beat information out of captured villagers. The Belgian Congo (now Zaïre) experienced a particularly chaotic and bloody process of decolonization. Independence in 1960 was followed by a vicious civil war between tribal factions, in which UN, Belgian and mercenary forces also became involved. (Popperfoto)

SEE ALSO

- THE THIRD WORLD p. 184
- THE PEAK OF EMPIRE p. 266
- WORLD WAR II p. 274
- THE COLD WAR p. 280
- THE MIDDLE EAST p. 282
- COUNTRIES OF THE WORLD p. 378

The Cold War

After the Allied victory in World War II, the USA and the USSR emerged as the world's superpowers. Two new opposing military alliances emerged in Europe: NATO in the West, and the Warsaw Pact in the East (▷ p. 180). The Cold War is the name that has been given to the confrontation between the superpowers and their respective allies that continued for four decades after 1945. The term 'Cold War' derives from the fact that the superpowers themselves were never in direct military conflict, partially for fear of nuclear war. Instead there was a conflict of ideologies – Western capitalism versus Eastern Communism – exacerbated by what each side believed was the other's desire for economic and political domination of the world.

SEE ALSO

- POLITICAL IDEOLOGIES p. 168
- INTERNATIONAL ORGANI-
  ZATIONS p. 178
- NUCLEAR ARMAMENT AND
  DISARMAMENT p. 181
- THE RUSSIAN REVOLUTIONS
  p. 270
- WORLD WAR II p. 274
- CHINA IN THE 20TH
  CENTURY p. 276
- THE MIDDLE EAST p. 282

In February 1945 Roosevelt, Churchill and Stalin met at Yalta to decide on the fate of postwar Europe. It was implicitly agreed that the USSR should maintain its influence in the areas occupied by the Red Army in Eastern Europe. Germany itself was to be divided into four zones of military occupation, with the UK, USA and France in the West and the USSR in the East. Berlin, lying within the Soviet sector, was to be split along the same lines.

By 1949 Soviet-dominated Communist governments ruled East Germany, Romania, Bulgaria, Poland, Czechoslovakia, Hungary and Albania. Yugoslavia too was Communist. All opposition was suppressed, and many freedoms curtailed.

Europe was effectively divided from the Baltic to the Adriatic, and the so-called Iron Curtain had fallen. Until 1989, only Yugoslavia, Albania and Romania had managed to break with the Moscow line. When other Eastern European countries tried to implement independent policies the USSR quickly reasserted its domination. The reforming governments of Hungary (1956) and Czechoslovakia (1968) were overthrown by military invasion.

Early confrontations

Once Hitler had been defeated, the wartime friendship and cooperation between the Allies quickly crumbled, and the old ideological hostility re-emerged. In 1947 President Truman declared the intention of the USA to resist Communist expansion. This policy – the Truman Doctrine – has been pursued by all subsequent US governments. European reliance on the USA was ensured by the Marshall Plan, which pumped $13 billion of aid into Western Europe. When the Western Allies proposed currency reform throughout occupied Germany, the USSR vetoed the idea. The Western Allies unilaterally instituted the reforms in their own occupation zones. In retaliation, Soviet forces blocked off all land links to West Berlin (June 1948). However, the USA and the UK organized an enormous airlift of supplies, and the blockade was lifted in May 1949.

Anti-Communist feeling in the West was further intensified by the explosion of the first Soviet atom bomb, the Communist victory in China (both in 1949), and the outbreak of the Korean War in 1950. In the USA the 'Red Scare' came to a head with Senator Joseph McCarthy's witch-hunt of suspected Communists (1950–54).

The Korean War

Korea, which had been a Japanese territory, was divided in 1945 into two occupation zones, with the Soviets to the north of the 38th parallel of latitude and the Americans to the south. The eventual reunification of Korea was planned, but in each zone the occupying forces set up governments that reflected their own ideologies.

The occupation ended in 1948, and in 1950 North Korea launched a massive invasion of the South. The UN Security Council, which was then being boycotted by the USSR, sent armed forces to intervene. The UN forces rapidly pushed the North Koreans back over the 38th parallel, and continued to advance northwards, ignoring Chinese warnings. China attacked in response, and the UN forces retreated back into South Korea. Fighting continued for another two years along the border. In 1953, after the USA threatened to use nuclear weapons, an armistice was signed, restoring the status quo.

Latin America and the Caribbean

Since the formulation of the Monroe Doctrine (▷ p. 261) the USA has regarded the Americas as its sphere of influence. With the onset of the Cold War this policy was adapted to resist Communist penetration of the region. Sometimes this has led to covert American involvement in the overthrow of democratically elected governments that the

Peaceful demonstrators on board a Soviet tank in the streets of Prague in August 1968, when Soviet forces suppressed the so-called 'Prague Spring' reform movement.
(Popperfoto)

USA considers dangerously left-wing, as in Chile in 1973. It has also led the USA to support authoritarian governments of the right.

In 1959 Castro's left-wing government came to power in Cuba. His nationalization of American-owned property led the US government to back an unsuccessful invasion by Cuban exiles at the Bay of Pigs (1961). Castro then adopted full-blooded Communism, and allowed the USSR to build missile bases on the island in 1962. The USA saw this as a direct threat, and told the Soviets to withdraw the missiles or face nuclear attack. The brinkmanship succeeded; the missiles were removed. Cuba attempted to export its revolution to various Third World countries. In the 1980s Cuba supported the left-wing Sandinista government of Nicaragua, while the USA supplied extensive aid to the right-wing 'Contra' rebels.

Towards détente

Following the Cuban Missile Crisis both the USA and the USSR realized how close they had come to mutual annihilation. Both sides sought thereafter to defuse tensions between them and to try to achieve a measure of 'peaceful coexistence'. Although the most dangerous phase of the Cold War was over, both sides were to become embroiled in local conflicts, carefully avoiding direct confrontation with the other. Without doubt the worst of these conflicts was in Vietnam (⊳ box). The beginning of the Vietnam peace talks in 1968 coincided with a broader effort at détente – the term applied to a reduction in tensions between states.

Friendly relations were re-established between the USA and Communist China, which by this time had established itself as the third super-power. China had broken with the USSR in the 1950s (⊳ p. 276), since when relations between the two had steadily deteriorated. With China making friends with the USA, the USSR saw the need to improve relations with the Americans. The results of détente included the SALT and ABM agreements in the 1970s at which the USA and USSR agreed to limitations in the nuclear arms race (⊳ p. 181). There was also the Helsinki Conference of 1973–75, which was designed to reduce tension and increase cooperation within Europe.

A major setback to détente occurred in 1979 with the Soviet invasion of Afghanistan. The West immediately condemned the invasion and sent military aid to the anti-Soviet Afghani guerrillas in the subsequent civil war. For several years East–West relations were extremely frosty, with both sides accelerating the arms race.

The end of the Cold War

With the advent of Mikhail Gorbachov as the Soviet leader in 1985 the climate began to change. Gradually Gorbachov initiated liberalizing reforms at home, and made a series of initiatives on arms reductions (for example, agreeing the INF Treaty with the USA in 1987; ⊳ p. 181). Like the Americans in Vietnam before them, the Soviets realized they could not win the war in Afghanistan without unacceptable losses, and in 1989 all Soviet forces were withdrawn.

Gorbachov also encouraged change in Eastern Europe, making it clear to the old-guard Communist leaderships that they should give way to reformers. By the beginning of the 1990s all the former Soviet satellites were on the path to multi-party democracy. The Berlin Wall was opened in November 1989 and, in October 1990,

WARS IN VIETNAM

US troops in action at Dak-To, South Vietnam, in 1967. (Popperfoto)

French colonial involvement in Indochina came to an end with defeat by Ho Chi Minh's Communist Viet Minh at Dien Bien Phu in May 1954. The Geneva Accords of July 1954 gave independence to Laos, Cambodia and Vietnam. Vietnam was split along the 17th parallel of latitude, with a Communist government in the north and a pro-Western government in the South.

The North was intent on reunification under Communist rule, and Communist guerrillas in the South known as Viet Cong (VC) began to mount attacks in rural areas with support from fellow-Communists in Laos and Cambodia. The USA, which saw South Vietnam as a bulwark against the spread of Communism in Asia, committed advisers to train the South Vietnamese army. In August 1964, after an alleged North Vietnamese attack on US warships in the Gulf of Tonkin, the US Congress approved an expanded US military commitment to Vietnam. Although the Americans attempted to avoid full-scale commitment of their forces, they were drawn deeper and deeper into the struggle. Co-ordinated attacks throughout the South by the North Vietnamese army (NVA) and VC in January 1968 (the Tet Offensive), although eventually defeated, created a deep sense of shock in the USA. Richard Nixon, who replaced Lyndon Johnson as President in 1969, sought to hand responsibility for the war to the South Vietnamese army, so that US

troops could be withdrawn. However, US incursions into neighbouring Cambodia and Laos, culminating in a successful US-backed coup against Prince Sihanouk of Cambodia, spread the war and left both countries vulnerable to their own indigenous Communist groups (the Khmer Rouge in Cambodia and the Pathet Lao in Laos).

A North Vietnamese invasion of the South in March 1972 was halted by US airpower. After renewed US air attacks on the North, the North Vietnamese agreed to a ceasefire that left their forces in place in South Vietnam. The Americans completed their withdrawal; they had lost over 47 000 servicemen in the conflict. However, the USA proved unable to maintain support for the South. The South Vietnamese army collapsed in the face of a North Vietnamese invasion in early 1975, and by April Saigon was in Communist hands. Cambodia and Laos also fell to the Communists in what was a massive defeat for US policy.

The violence did not end. Cambodia endured the nightmare of dictator Pol Pot's 'reconstruction' programme in which 1.4 million died. Following a Vietnamese invasion of Cambodia in 1978, China tried to help Pol Pot by attacking northern Vietnam (which was Moscow-oriented). Vietnam eventually withdrew from Cambodia in 1989, and in 1991 Cambodia's warring factions agreed on a UN-supervised peace plan.

West and East Germany were reunified. A month later, the Charter of Paris for a New Europe, signed by 34 countries representing the old East–West divide, marked the official end of the Cold War. In September 1991, following the abortive coup by hardliners in the USSR, the Soviet Communist Party was suspended and major political reforms were implemented. However, with the USSR breaking up and Yugoslavia embroiled in civil war, Europe was clearly still subject to internal conflict.

The Middle East

The Middle East has long been a centre of tension and conflict. Lying astride some of the most important trade routes of the world – linking Africa, Asia and Europe – and containing valuable deposits of oil, it has attracted interference from a variety of outside powers. As a centre of three major religions – Judaism, Christianity and Islam – it has endured a high level of internal discord, fuelled in more recent times by nationalist and territorial disputes.

Until the end of World War I in 1918, much of the region was under Ottoman (Turkish) rule, but Western colonial powers – Britain, France and Italy – had already established their influence there, particularly since the opening of the Suez Canal in 1869 had offered a much shorter route from Europe to the Far East. After World War I major parts of the Ottoman Empire were given as 'mandates' of the League of Nations (▷ p. 269) to Britain and France, with the intention of preparing them for eventual independence. France received 'Greater Syria' (part of which became the predominantly Christian state of Lebanon in 1920), while Britain received Iraq, Transjordan and Palestine.

The creation of Israel

From the time of the Roman Empire, the majority of Jews had been dispersed from Palestine. Since the late 19th century Palestine had been claimed by the Zionists, a group of Jews who demanded a revived Jewish homeland on the basis of biblical rights. In November 1917, in an effort to ensure Jewish support for the war effort, the British foreign secretary, Arthur Balfour, had pledged his government to 'view with favour' the establishment of such a homeland once the Turks

SEE ALSO

- DECOLONIZATION p. 278
- THE COLD WAR p. 280
- JUDAISM p. 294
- ISLAM p. 300

had been defeated. To the British in the 1920s and 1930s, the 'Balfour Declaration' meant no more than permitting restricted Jewish immigration to Palestine. But to the Arabs it was a first move in a Jewish seizure of their land and to the Zionists it was the first step in the creation of an independent Jewish state.

Britain faced growing Arab and Jewish unrest. Violence, particularly from extremist Jewish groups, increased after World War II, leading Britain in 1947 to hand the area over to the United Nations (UN) as successor to the League of Nations. Palestine was partitioned between Arabs and Jews, allowing the state of Israel to emerge in 1948. The response of neighbouring Arab countries – newly independent from Western rule and imbued with a growing sense of nationalism – was immediate. Five armies – from Egypt, Jordan, Iraq, Syria and Lebanon – invaded the new state, but were defeated. By early 1949 Israel had secured its existence, but in order to survive with slender resources it evolved remarkably capable armed forces.

The Arab–Israeli Wars

The prowess of these forces was shown in October 1956 when Israel, in collusion with Britain and France – angry at Egypt's nationalization of the Suez Canal Company (▷ p. 279) – invaded the desert region of Sinai, the area of Egypt east of the Canal. It was a short, sharp war, with the Israelis quickly occupying Sinai, and French and British forces attacking the area round the Canal. There was an international outcry, and the USA in particular exerted pressure that led to a withdrawal. A UN peacekeeping force moved into Sinai to keep the two sides apart.

After 1956 Arab nationalism grew, particularly under the leadership of the Egyptian president, Gamal Abdel Nasser (1918–70). His contacts with Syria and Jordan alarmed Israel and when, in May 1967, he moved troops into Sinai and demanded that the UN force withdraw, it looked to Israel as if an attack was about to take place. The Israelis responded with a shattering strike against the Arab air forces on 5 June, followed immediately by a rapid campaign. In six days Israel defeated the Egyptians in Sinai, the Jordanians on the West Bank (that part of Jordan west of the River Jordan) and the Syrians on the Golan Heights overlooking northern Galilee. This time, however, Israel had the backing of the USA – which was concerned about Soviet friendship with Egypt and Syria – and refused to withdraw. Israel's territorial gains placed it behind more defendable borders but ensured continued Arab enmity.

Intent on recovering lost territory, Egypt and Syria aimed to force Israel to the conference table on the terms of UN Resolution 242, which called for a return to the borders of 1949. A war of attrition was fought along the Suez Canal in 1969–70, and on 6 October 1973 Egypt and Syria simultaneously mounted major attacks, under

Victorious Israeli soldiers after the fierce battle for the Golan Heights during the 1973 Arab–Israeli War. A Syrian attack on the Golan Heights on October 6 dislodged the Israelis from territory they had occupied since 1967, but by October 10 an Israeli counterattack had restored the area to Israeli hands and pushed the Syrians back towards Damascus. (Popperfoto)

cover of the Jewish religious holiday Yom Kippur. Caught by war on two fronts, the Israelis were hard pressed, but they devised tactics to counter new Soviet weapons and defeated Egypt and Syria after 16 days of hard fighting. During the war, a US nuclear alert – triggered by apparent Soviet moves to commit troops to the support of Egypt and Syria – reminded the world of the volatile nature of the Middle East and helped to initiate a peace process that culminated at Camp David in the USA in 1979. In exchange for promises of peace, Egypt regained Sinai.

The Palestinians and Lebanon

Since 1948 Palestinian Arabs had opposed the loss of their homeland to the Israelis, initially by looking for Arab support and then, with the creation of the Palestine Liberation Organization (PLO) in 1964, by recourse to guerrilla warfare and terrorism. By 1970 the PLO, organized as a 'state in exile', was threatening the internal stability of Jordan, forcing King Hussein to commit his army aginst them. In response many Palestinians fled to Lebanon, taking advantage of the internal chaos of that country, which was split between Christian and Muslim sects.

A civil war between these sects in 1975–6 caused the Syrians (who had never accepted the creation of a separate Lebanon) to intervene, moving forces into the Beqa'a Valley to the east of Beirut. The Israelis regarded this as another threat to their security, made worse by increasing attacks by the PLO. In June 1982 Israeli forces invaded southern Lebanon, intent on destroying PLO forces based there. They also aimed to create a buffer of Christian Lebanese between Israel and the Syrian positions.

The Israelis advanced to Beirut in less than six days, but the lack of an immediate UN-sponsored ceasefire condemned Israel to a war of attrition. A local ceasefire in August allowed the PLO to withdraw from Lebanon. However, a subsequent Israeli move into Muslim-controlled West Beirut (during which pro-Israeli Lebanese forces massacred Palestinian civilians at the Sabra and Chatilla refugee camps) revived the fighting.

By June 1985 the Israelis, weakened by the seemingly endless commitment to Lebanon, had withdrawn, leaving a buffer zone on their border in the hands of the South Lebanese Army. Lebanon disintegrated into ungovernable chaos, within which various extremist factions emerged. The situation was made worse by splits in the Muslim ranks, brought about by the rise of Islamic fundamentalism in Iran (▷ box) and by the return to Lebanon of elements of the PLO.

In 1988 the Palestinian Arabs in the occupied territories began widespread demonstrations against continued Israeli rule. This generally unarmed uprising has become known as the *Intifada*. Violence on the streets was a new experience for the Israeli armed forces and their often brutal response led to condemnation abroad. Israel looked increasingly isolated. Exploiting this development, the PLO Chairman, Yasser Arafat (1929–), shifted the emphasis of his campaign and went as far as to recognize the state of Israel. However, he lost international sympathy by supporting Iraq in the Gulf War. The large influx of Soviet Jews into Israel since 1990 has given extra impetus to the Intifada. Israel came under increased international pressure in 1991 to contribute to a Middle East settlement and attempts were made to organize a peace conference.

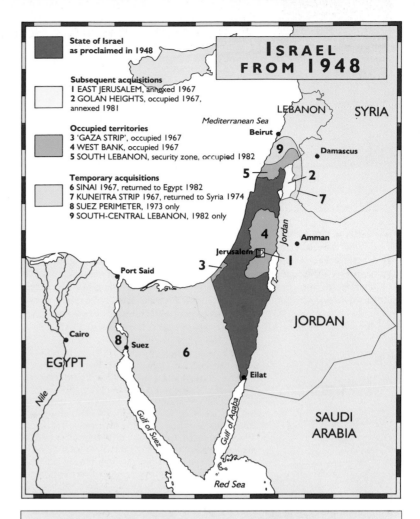

ISRAEL FROM 1948

State of Israel as proclaimed in 1948

Subsequent acquisitions
1 EAST JERUSALEM, annexed 1967
2 GOLAN HEIGHTS, occupied 1967, annexed 1981

Occupied territories
3 'GAZA STRIP', occupied 1967
4 WEST BANK, occupied 1967
5 SOUTH LEBANON, security zone, occupied 1982

Temporary acquisitions
6 SINAI 1967, returned to Egypt 1982
7 KUNEITRA STRIP 1967, returned to Syria 1974
8 SUEZ PERIMETER, 1973 only
9 SOUTH-CENTRAL LEBANON, 1982 only

LEBANON SYRIA
Mediterranean Sea
Beirut
Damascus
Amman
Jerusalem
Port Said
Cairo
Suez
EGYPT
JORDAN
Eilat
Nile
Gulf of Suez
Gulf of Aqaba
SAUDI ARABIA
Red Sea

WARS IN THE GULF

In early 1979 the Shah of Iran was overthrown by Shiite Muslims under the Ayatollah Khomeini (1900–1989), intent on a fundamentalist Islamic revival. This inevitably led to tensions with Arab countries in the Middle East ruled by more secular Sunni Muslims. In its most dramatic form it led to the Iran–Iraq War.

Territorial disputes over the Shatt-al-Arab waterway, coupled to religious and ethnic differences, led to an Iraqi invasion of Iran in September 1980. The fighting was to continue for eight years, and it is estimated that 1 million people died. As each side tried to starve the other of valuable oil revenues, the war spilt over into the waters of the Gulf, both sides mounting air and naval attacks on predominantly Western-owned oil tankers. Eventually American, Russian, French and British warships were deployed in the Gulf to protect shipping, despite the possibility of escalation to more general war. A ceasefire in 1988 imposed a shaky peace, but the world had been reminded yet again of the potential dangers of the Middle East. What had been intended by Iraq as a quick victory resulted in the virtual bankruptcy of the country.

In an attempt to restore Iraq's economic fortunes, President Saddam Hussein ordered the invasion of neighbouring oil-rich Kuwait (2 August 1990). The international community was almost unanimous in its condemnation of the invasion and UN sanctions against Iraq were imposed. Iraq annexed Kuwait, declaring the emirate to be its 19th province, and refusing to withdraw despite repeated UN demands. The UN Security Council authorized armed action by a US-led coalition to liberate Kuwait from Iraqi occupation, and on 16 January 1991 the Gulf War began with a massive air campaign. The following month, coalition forces entered Iraqi and Kuwaiti territory in a short ground war that put an end to the occupation of Kuwait.

When the future of the Ba'athist Party dictatorship of Saddam Hussein appeared to be in danger, Iraq accepted all the UN resolutions regarding Kuwait and agreed to a ceasefire. During March and April – with coalition forces occupying part of southern Iraq – Saddam suppressed revolts by Shiites in the south and Kurds in the north. International efforts were made to feed and protect over 1 million Shiite and Kurdish refugees who fled to Iran and Turkey.

What is Religion?

Religion is one of the most universal activities known to humankind, being practised across virtually all cultures, and from the very earliest times. However, no universally accepted definition of religion exists. Religion appears to have arisen from the desire to find an ultimate meaning and purpose in life, and this is usually centred around belief in a supernatural being (or beings). In most religions the devotees attempt to honour and/or influence their god or gods – commonly through prayer, sacrifice or right behaviour.

The question arises as to what can be included in what we call religion. Can we, for example, call Marxism-Leninism a religion, or humanism (the belief in humanity and reason rather than a god)? Some people would be willing to include such beliefs in a modern definition of religion as 'anything to which we give ultimate allegiance'; however, such beliefs do not normally include any reference to a supernatural or ultimate being

SEE ALSO

● POLITICAL IDEOLOGIES p. 168
● RELIGIONS OF THE WORLD pp. 286–301
● PHILOSOPHY p. 302

(or god). It is therefore better to describe them as ideologies, rather than religions, though they may share many of the characteristics of religion.

Beliefs and practices

Religion is made up of both beliefs and practice. The academic discipline of theology (especially in the West, and in relation to Christianity) has tended to concentrate on belief. It is important to realize, however, that in some societies there is no word for religion. It is not a separate compartment of life – it is a way of understanding and living life itself. Nevertheless, it is possible to distinguish several different aspects in most religions. One widely accepted classification identifies four aspects: faith, cult, community, creed and code. *Faith* is the internal part of religion; what people believe, their feelings of awe and reverence, individual prayer, etc. *Cult* is all that is involved in worship – buildings, images, altars, rituals, holy songs, community gatherings and so on. *Community* is the social aspect of religion – the worshippers at a particular church or temple, the wider denomination or sect, monks and nuns, etc. *Creed* involves all the beliefs and ideas held by the religion as a whole. It includes scriptures, and ideas about God, angels, heaven, hell and salvation. *Code* involves the way people behave because of their religious beliefs, and includes ethics, taboos, and ideas of sin and holiness.

Families of religions

The religions of the world can be divided into two major groups – primal and universal. *Primal religions* include the traditional religions of Africa, Australasia, Oceania, some parts of Asia and the original peoples of the Americas (▷ box). They also include the pre-Christian religions of Europe and the religions of other ancient peoples (▷ p. 286). These religions, though differing in detail, have several features in common. They all tend to be local – they are tailored to the particular tribe or people who practise them and their practitioners do not generally regard them as relevant to other peoples. Thus many of the myths and stories of such religions deal with the origin of one particular tribe. Modern primal religions tend to depend largely on oral traditions rather than on written scriptures and are generally non-missionary, i.e. they do not seek converts.

Universal religions, as this name implies, see themselves not as local but as potentially universal – i.e. they have significance for the whole world. To varying degrees, therefore, they try to make converts. In addition, they have usually developed written scriptures that play a central part in the religion. Islam and Christianity are characteristic examples of this type of universal religion. Within the universal group certain main families can be identified. The *Semitic family* includes Judaism, Christianity and Islam (▷ pp. 294–301), all of which share a common historical

A West African mask used by witch doctors. Among many peoples – particularly in Africa –there is a widespread belief in magic, the ability to change the physical world through ritual action. Although magic shares some of the characteristics of religion, it differs in at least one major respect. In most religions, there is a belief that ultimately people cannot hope to command the divine being, but merely to influence it in their favour. In magic, however, the world is understood in such a way that certain ritual actions automatically bring about the desired result. (Paysan)

The Festival of the Supreme Being in Revolutionary France, 1794. At the outset of the French Revolution there was considerable anti-Christian feeling. However, within a few years the Revolutionary leadership had come to believe that religion was necessary for social stability, and introduced a cult of the Supreme Being.
(Explorer)

and geographical background. The *Indian family* is made up of Hinduism, early Buddhism, Jainism and Sikhism (⊳ pp. 288–91). The *Far Eastern family* includes Confucianism, Daoism (Taoism) and Shinto (⊳ p. 292). Though any given religion will normally claim to have been inspired by God, it is important to remember that all religions begin and develop in particular historical, geographical and cultural situations that influence and mould the form that religion takes.

Another way of classifying groups of religions is to distinguish those with a single god (*monotheistic*) and those with several gods (*polytheistic*). Monotheistic religions include Judaism, Christianity and Islam. Polytheistic religions include Hinduism, the ancient Greek and Germanic religions, and many modern primal religions.

Religion and secularism

In the present century, particularly in the West, some people have seen evidence of a decline in religion, and its replacement by *secularism* (a belief that the physical world is self-contained, and can be perfectly well understood by the insights of modern science, without reference to any supernatural explanations). While it is true that in some societies there is a decline in organized religion, there is little evidence of a decline in religiosity (religious feeling). Thus, while fewer people in many Western countries regularly attend church, most still claim to believe in God. This may indicate changing patterns of religiosity, rather than its decline. One example of this is the growth of new religious movements in Western societies, offering alternative religious traditions not previously available. Thus groups such as Transcendental Meditation, the Unification Church (Moonies), the Hare Krishna movement and others attract followers because at a time of rapid change many people are disillusioned with traditional religions, yet retain a basic religiosity.

MODERN PRIMAL RELIGIONS

The primal religions that survive today are the religions of non-literate, usually tribal, societies. Although they have no written sources, this does not mean that primal religions are without history or are in some way 'fossilized' remnants of a past age. Like the universal religions, most have long and complex histories. The word 'primal' is used to convey the idea that these religions came first in human history, and underlie all the major religions of the world. It is wrong to think of these religions as primitive. They often contain beliefs and ideas about the world that achieve high levels of sophistication.

There are many thousands of primal societies scattered throughout the world – in North and South America, Siberia, the Arctic, Central Asia, Australia, Southeast Asia and the Pacific Islands. Every primal society has its own culture and its own unique religion. However, these religions have enough in common in terms of beliefs and practices to make it possible to group them together as primal religions. In almost all primal religions there is a conception of a supreme god, sometimes prominent in religious life, sometimes remote and uninterested in human affairs. Belief in a supreme god is found throughout Africa, but in many parts he is considered so great and remote that he is not worshipped. Powerful named spirits, each with their own specific characteristics, and ancestors, who act as intermediaries between people and the supreme god, are worshipped instead. Only in times of extreme distress is the god directly approached by people. In West Africa, the Americas, Asia and Polynesia, people believe in a multitude of divinities other than the supreme god.

Virtually all primal peoples believe in spirits or souls of ancestors that survive the body after death and are capable of interfering in the lives of the living for good or ill. They have the power to do harm (for example, sending illness), but at the same time they are honoured through ritual offerings and prayers, and thought of with affection. As well as powerful divinities and ancestor spirits, most primal peoples believe in numerous minor spirits, who may be good, malevolent or capricious. They may be the souls of the forgotten dead, who haunt the living and play tricks on them. Spirits live in all sorts of places – in rocks, caves, mountain passes, river crossings, even in animals and insects. They are unpredictable and people are careful not to offend them.

Mana is a spiritual power or life force that is believed to permeate the universe. Originally a Melanesian word, it is now applied by anthropologists to spiritual power in other primal religions. Mana is not a spirit, and it has no will or purpose – it is impersonal and flows from one thing to another, and can be manipulated to achieve certain ends. Charms, amulets and medicines contain this power for the benefit of the wearer or user. It can be used for good or evil purposes.

There are a whole range of religious specialists, from the priests, prophets, diviners and sacred kings of Africa to the medicine men of North America and the shamans of Siberia and the Arctic. Their role is to mediate – often in an ecstatic trance – between people and the spirit world. A priest's role is to serve a divinity or divinities, and to carry out specific ritual and ceremonial duties.

Most primal peoples today have been profoundly influenced by contact with more 'sophisticated' and powerful societies and their religions. This has led to the development of new movements within primal religions, and in some cases to new religions. Most of these movements have developed out of interaction with Christianity. In Papua New Guinea and some other Pacific islands, for instance, primal and Christian elements have combined in movements, often called 'cargo cults', to create a new society.

BAHA'ISM

Baha'ism is a modern universal religion that emphasizes the unity of all religions and the spiritual unity of humanity. It evolved from the teachings of two 19th-century Persian visionaries – Mirza Ali Muhammad (1820–50), known as the Bab ('gateway'), and Mirza Husain Ali (1817–92), known as Baha'ullah ('Glory of God'). Baha'ullah announced in 1863 that he was the latest of a series of divine manifestations – including Jesus, the Buddha, Muhammad and Zoroaster – sent to redeem the world. Baha'ullah was imprisoned and exiled many times, eventually setting up his headquarters in Palestine. He developed his teachings into a religion, based on a new scripture the *Kitab Akdas*. His followers see him as a manifestation of God and a divine healer, relieving suffering and uniting mankind. Today, Baha'ism has over 5 000 000 members worldwide. Baha'ism has been persecuted in Iran since 1979.

It must also be remembered that while organized religion may seem to be declining in the West, in most other parts of the world the major universal religions (especially Christianity and Islam) are increasing at a considerable rate. Thus religion – always living and changing – remains the near universal phenomenon it has always been.

Ancient Religions

The earliest evidence of what seems to be religious activity dates from 30 000–10 000 BC. Cave paintings dating from 15 000–11 000 BC found in France appear to show rituals connected with hunting, and figurines as old as 25 000 BC suggest a mother goddess or fertility figure. The development of writing systems in the ancient Near East from around 3000 BC reveals a considerable variety of religious beliefs and practices.

SEE ALSO

- HUMAN PREHISTORY p. 226
- THE ANCIENT NEAR EAST p. 228
- ANCIENT GREECE p. 230
- ANCIENT ROME p. 232
- WHAT IS RELIGION? p. 284
- JUDAISM p. 294
- PHILOSOPHY p. 302
- CLASSICAL LITERATURE p. 356

All the ancient cults – apart from Zoroastrianism and Judaism (▷ p. 294) – were polytheistic, and gods and goddesses tended to be rationalized into hierarchical or family groups.

The Near East

The peoples of the Levant honoured a pantheon of gods under the control of El, the 'Creator of Created Things', and his counterpart, Asherah (the mother goddess). Baal (the storm god) is aided by his sister and vindicator Anat (goddess of fertility and war) in his struggle with Yam (the ruler of the sea) and with Mot (death and sterility). A third goddess associated with fertility is Astarte, the Canaanite version of Ishtar, the Semitic mother goddess. Religious practice seems largely to have consisted of animal and occasionally human sacrifices, the dramatization of myths, and enactments of sacred marriage. Kings were regarded as divine.

In Mesopotamia (southern Iraq), the cities of the Sumerians (▷ p. 228) each had their own pantheon of deities, though many were assimilated to

dominant types (Nanna – Moon, Utu – Sun, An – sky, Ea – storm, Enki – Earth, Inanna – the mother goddess, equivalent to the Semitic Ishtar). Sacred marriage myths and rites were popular. The religions of the successive empires of Akkad, Babylon and Assyria (▷ p. 228) preserved many Sumerian features, although adapted to the new cultures. Superficially nature deities, the gods of Mesopotamia were complex beings who also symbolized moral and social values. Temple cult consisted largely of sacrificial offerings to divine images. In temples (usually tiered mounds known as *ziggurats*), the creation myth was narrated, proclaiming the victory of Marduk (Babylon) or Asshur (Assyria) over Tiamat (the primordial deep).

In Anatolia (modern Turkey), the Hittite empire of the second millennium BC (▷ p. 228) has left little clear information on religious matters. Many of its myths were translations of Semitic or other texts. The kingdom of Phrygia, which succeeded the Hittites, was the centre of the cult of Cybele, an Earth goddess whose priests were eunuchs. This cult later spread to Greece and Rome. By the second millennium BC, the great empire of Mitanni was established in Syria and northern Mesopotamia. Its religion appears to have been eclectic, incorporating various features met with in the Vedas of India (▷ p. 288). These in turn influenced local cults. A religion akin to that of the Vedas was also practised in ancient Persia, where the same deities are found.

Egypt

The pharaohs of ancient Egypt (▷ p. 228) were regarded as divine, and were called 'Horus' and 'Son of Re'. Re was the Sun god and the ruler of gods. As 'Son of Re' the pharaoh embodied the life-giving power of the Sun. Horus was the son of Isis, the Divine Mother, and of Osiris, the god of the inundation, vegetation and the dead. As Horus, the pharaoh embodied the renewal of life and fertility borne on the annual inundation of the land by the Nile. To augment their powers, local deities were often linked with national ones; the most significant was Amun, the god of invisibility. From c. 2000 BC he was combined with Re to become Amun-Re of Thebes, whose temple at Thebes was to become the wealthiest in Egypt. The short-lived 'Amarna revolution' (c. 1350 BC) under Akhenaton promoted the cult of the Aten (a sole god represented by the sun disc), in opposition to Amun-Re.

The Egyptians could not imagine death to be different to Egyptian life and so the preservation of the body was essential for survival in the afterlife. Food, clothes and luxuries accompanied the body in the tomb. The deceased were judged by the gods of the underworld but, armed with the Negative Confession, a denial of 49 possible offences contained in the Book of the Dead – a collection of spells and prayers – a safe and prosperous afterlife was assured.

Zoroastrianism

In northeast Persia in the late second millennium (possibly c. 1200 BC) a religious reformer named Zarathustra (Zoroaster) preached a simplification of the old polytheistic cosmology. Life meant a choice between Ahura Mazda ('wise lord') and Angra Mainyu ('hostile spirit'), embodying good and evil respectively. Ahura Mazda was assisted by angels, the Amesha Spentas ('bountiful immor-

Cernunnos, the Celtic 'lord of the animals'. This relief is a detail from the Gundestrup Cauldron, a masterpiece of Iron Age metalwork dating from around 100 BC. (AKG)

tals'). A person's destiny after death (heaven or hell) was determined by his or her choice. Zoroastrianism, which appears to be the earliest 'salvation religion', became the national cult of the Persian Achaemenid Empire (▷ p. 228). Zoroastrian dualism (i.e. seeing the world as a struggle between good and evil) may have influenced Greek and early Jewish thought. It survives in the religion of the Parsis of India (▷ p. 288).

Greece

The Linear B texts of Mycenaean civilization (▷ p. 230) – the first written evidence of religion in Europe – show the importance of Poseidon the sea god and of 'the Lady' (presumably a mother goddess). Some other divine names occur, including Zeus and Hera. In the epic poetry of Homer (▷ p. 356), the gods lived ageless and immortal on Mount Olympus, but acted like humans – and not the best-behaved humans. They could change shape, intervene in human life, and might respond to gifts and prayers to change human destiny (but not human nature). The Olympian gods (▷ box) were incorporated into the workings of secret societies, and into healing and divination cults (for example, the oracle of Delphi). By the 6th century BC they were part of the official worship of the Greek city-states. But ancient Greek religion had little to do with morality, and the moral, metaphysical and scientific concerns of the 5th- and 4th-century Athenian philosophers (▷ p. 302) challenged popular religion with different ideas of God. The conquests of Alexander the Great (▷ p. 230) spread Greek language and ideas through the Near East. The resulting Hellenistic civilization fused Greek and Oriental cultures. Worship of the Olympians spread, but the cults of the Egyptian Isis and the Phrygian Cybele spread too.

Rome

Early Roman religion was probably shaped by Etruscan culture (▷ p. 232) and was concerned with the farming year. Two forms of religious expression developed. Domestic piety recognized household gods (*lares* and *penates*), while the state cult – conducted by a high priest (the *pontifex maximus*) and other officials – ensured corporate wellbeing. As Rome encountered Greek culture, the state deities were identified with Olympian equivalents. As the empire expanded, its armies brought back foreign cults. The most important of these – until the adoption of Christianity in the 4th century AD – was Mithraism, based on worship of Mithra or Mithras (the Persian god of light, truth and justice), whose killing of a cosmic bull was echoed by his devotees in ritual sacrifices. A male-only mystery cult, Mithraism reached Rome in the 1st century BC, and became particularly popular in the army.

Roman official religion resisted innovations, or admitted them only when of proven worth. Divine honours were accorded to Julius Caesar after his death, and to Augustus, most of his successors, and various members of the imperial family at death. In the Eastern provinces of the Roman Empire living emperors were saluted as divine.

The temple to the goddess Athena on the island of Lindos in the Aegean Sea. A Greek temple was basically a house for the deity, who was represented by a statue. The focus of worship was an altar, generally at the eastern end of the building. The elongated plan of the temple and the outer pillared colonnade were special features to distinguish a divine house from a secular one. (Spectrum)

THE TWELVE GODS OF MOUNT OLYMPUS

Zeus (Roman Jupiter), the sky deity, ruler of the immortals. 'Father of gods and men' (but not creator).

Hera (Roman Juno), consort of Zeus, guardian of marriage and childbirth.

Poseidon (Roman Neptune), 'the earthshaker', ruler of the sea.

Demeter (Roman Ceres), goddess of corn and crops.

Apollo (no direct Roman equivalent), averter of evil, source of prophecy and divination; sometimes associated with the Sun, music and poetry.

Artemis (Roman Diana), virgin goddess of hunting and wild animals; originally a mother goddess, and sometimes associated with the Moon.

Ares (Roman Mars), god of war.

Aphrodite (Roman Venus), goddess of love and beauty.

Hermes (Roman Mercury), messenger of the gods, guardian of the market place.

Athena (Roman Minerva), goddess of wisdom and virgin protector of the household; patron of Athens.

Hephaestos (Roman Vulcan), god of fire and volcanoes; patron of smiths.

Hestia (Roman Vesta), goddess of the hearth; patron of the city of Rome.

Divinities not among the Twelve but important in popular religion included: **Dionysus** (Roman Bacchus), associated with wine and crops, and worshipped at orgiastic rituals; and **Asklepios** (Roman Aesculapius), source of healing.

CELTIC AND GERMANIC RELIGION

We have no 'insider's' account of pre-Christian Celtic religion and much remains uncertain. Some Irish stories hint at a Celtic High God, but the commonest Celtic religious image is a male figure with horns – evidently a fertility figure. Sometimes the horned god has an 'earth mother' consort. Traces of places of worship occur close to fertility-giving water – at springs, wells and river sources. Human sacrifice seems to have been common, and the human head to have had special significance. Several observers mention 'druids' conducting sacrifices and divination ceremonies.

The religions of the Germanic peoples survived into the Middle Ages: Scandinavia did not become Christian until the 10th–12th centuries. We know most about the later forms, especially from Norse literature; but the Norse stories were written down in Christian times and give an incomplete picture of Viking and Anglo-Saxon religion. Germanic religion had many divinities. In early times, three in particular were worshipped: Wotan or Woden (Norse Odin), father of the gods and the slain; Tiw or Tiwaz (Norse Tyr), the giver of law; and Thor, the thunder deity. (These gods gave their names to Wednesday, Tuesday and Thursday respectively.) Odin and Thor belong to the Aesir, who defeated the Vanir, another race of gods. Aesir and Vanir became reconciled, and the Vanir Frey and his female counterpart Freya, closely associated with fertility, are major figures. There is no High God, only a chaos of divine energy. The worshipper chose the divinity thought most likely to serve him. Odin was the natural patron of warriors, and his Valkyries (female warriors) took dead heroes to his great hall, Valhalla. Thor seems to have been the most popular divinity.

The Religions of India

India is home to what is – alongside Judaism – the world's oldest surviving religion. Hinduism, generally referred to as *sanatana dharma* or 'eternal tradition' by Hindus themselves, has a history of some 4000 years. Although officially a secular state, India is still a highly religious country, with over 700 million Hindus, over 90 million Muslims (▷ p. 300), and 25 million Christians, together with smaller numbers of Sikhs, Buddhists, Jains, Parsis, Jews and those following tribal religions.

Hinduism, Buddhism, Jainism and Sikhism, though differing, have some common themes. They all share the idea of a continuing cycle of birth, death and rebirth (*samsara*), and the belief that individuals suffer the consequences of their actions (*karma*). Both of these ideas are linked to the idea of *transmigration* – that the soul is continually reincarnated in different bodies (human or animal) after the last body dies, and that what form this body takes depends on actions in the previous incarnation.

Hinduism

All the religions speak of *dharma*, usually said to mean 'law', 'duty', 'way' or 'nature'. Both Hindus and Sikhs refer to their religious leaders and teachers as *gurus*, and all the religions except Sikhism hold up celibacy and asceticism (the renunciation of pleasure and luxury) as ideals.

An elderly Sikh in Amritsar, Punjab, India. All Sikh males wear the symbols of their faith, the so-called 'five K's': *kesh* (uncut beard and hair, the latter worn in a turban); *kangha* (comb, to keep the hair clean); *kara* (metal bracelet); *kaccha* (knee-length undershorts); and *kirpan* (dagger). (Gamma)

The earliest scriptures, the *Vedas*, were compiled by the Aryans (▷ p. 236). In these texts sacrificial rituals and the role of the *brahman* priest are described. The authority of the *brahmans* in Indian religion has continued to be significant – despite the many movements that have challenged it, such as Buddhism (▷ p. 290) and Jainism (▷ below). Between 500 BC and AD 500, in addition to the rise of Buddhism and Jainism, India saw the growth of the Hindu tradition, building on the Vedic tradition. The great epics, the *Ramayana* and the *Mahabharata* (incorporating the *Bhagavadgita*) were compiled. They told the stories of Rama and Krishna, both of whom were seen as *avataras* or incarnations of the great god, Vishnu. These gods became increasingly popular along with Shiva (the destroyer god) and the goddess Devi, and later became the inspiration for religious sects.

All these gods and goddesses (▷ box) have innumerable manifestations, i.e. they appear in many different forms and with different names. There are also a large number of minor gods, spirits and demons. Reflecting this, within Hinduism there are a large number of different sects worshipping a particular god or goddess, or even a particular manifestation. Some are known only to people in a particular area and may be worshipped to ensure local protection. Hindus believe that the divine can be manifested in any number of gods, objects or people, which then become worthy of worship.

Closely bound up with Hindu belief and practice is the *caste* system, a hierarchical system of social and religious stratification (▷ p. 160). Everyone is born into a particular caste, and for Hindus, this determines how they live. Most homes set aside a corner for worship at which family members offer food, flowers, incense and the light of a candle.

A Hindu temple (*mandir*) may be a huge, ornate building dedicated to the worship of a major deity – visited particularly during festivals and pilgrimages – or it may be a small roadside shrine to a local spirit. The Hindu calendar celebrates the anniversaries of deities and saints, seasonal events, and the new year. At these times, many Hindus undertake pilgrimages. At the major pilgrimage centre Varanasi (Benares), Hindus immerse themselves in the sacred waters of the River Ganges. It is here that a Hindu may go to die with the hope of achieving final liberation (*moksha*) from the cycle of death and rebirth. After death, the body is cremated.

The brahman priests are required to keep a high level of purity and a knowledge of the ancient Sanskrit language and of ritual practice. They lead the rites of passage at times of initiation, marriage and death. In a village there may be other specialists who are responsible for communicating with local spirits for such purposes as healing, blessings or exorcism.

Jainism

Founded by the ascetic Mahavira in the 6th century BC at around the same time as Buddhism, Jainism shares with Buddhism a belief in no god. With the rise in popularity in India of the gods Vishnu and Shiva, Buddhism gradually declined. Jainism, however, has not died out and remains strong in the west of India. Non-violence or *ahimsa* is central to Jain life and has influenced

MAJOR FESTIVALS IN INDIA

The principal Hindu festivals are the New Year (celebrated in April), the beginning of the monsoon (July), Krishna's birthday (*Janamashtami*; August), *Shradh* (remembering ancestors; September), *Durga Puja* (the celebration of goddesses; October), *Dashera* (Rama's victory over Ravana), *Divali* (the festival of lights; November), *Kumbha Mela* (pilgrim fairs; January), *Mahashivaratri* (the festival for Shiva; February), and *Holi* (the spring harvest celebration; March).

Major Sikh festivals include the New Year (April), *Divali* (▷ above), Guru Nanak's birthday (November), Guru Gobind Singh's birthday (December), and *Holi* (▷ above).

Jains celebrate the beginning of the monsoon (▷ above), Mahavira's birthday (April), and *Divali*. The Parsi New Year (*No Ruz*) is celebrated in March.

The Hindu festival of the Kumbha Mela (pilgrim fairs) is held every three years. The Kumbha Mela rotates between four traditional sites on the Ganges, Sipra and Godavari rivers. Pilgrims bathe in the rivers during the festival to cleanse their bodies and souls. (Gamma)

SEE ALSO

● INDIA AND SOUTHEAST ASIA p. 236
● BUDDHISM p. 290
● ISLAM p. 300
● NON-WESTERN ART p. 308

those of other religions too, like Mahatma Gandhi. Jains believe that all living creatures have souls and must not be harmed. They are therefore strict vegetarians. Many are nuns or monks, the ascetic life being encouraged as the true path to non-violent, personal liberation.

The Parsis

Parsiism is a monotheistic religion derived from Zoroastrianism (▷ p. 286), whose adherents fled Persia in the 8th century AD to escape Arab persecution. Most Parsis are now found in western India, particularly Bombay. Parsi worship is centred in fire temples where a sacred fire – the representative of God or Ahura Mazda – burns continuously. Rather than burying or cremating their dead, which they believe would contaminate earth, fire and water, Parsis expose the bodies in circular 'towers of silence', where they are eaten by vultures and other birds.

Parsis have maintained their communal identity by keeping the symbols of the sacred shirt (*sudre*) and cord (*kusti*), by encouraging marriage within the faith and by supporting Parsi business and educational ventures, charitable concerns and housing colonies.

The Sikhs

The Sikhs, like the Jains, are comparatively small in number in India. Sikhism, however, is an important religion, particularly in the north. Sikhs are proud of their history and still remember, in their prayers and festivals, many of the events in the lives of their ten gurus. Sikhism is a monotheistic religion, and was founded by the first of the ten gurus, Nanak (1469–1539). The Sikh gurus were critical of the ritual and social aspects of Hindu tradition, rejecting the caste system. They were political as well as religious leaders, evolving the idea of the warrior-saint and standing up against the rule of the Muslims who had dominated north India since the 13th century.

The foundations of Sikh life are the teachings of Nanak on how to lead a good life and seek final union with God. Also of fundamental importance was the formation by the last guru, Gobind Singh (1666–1708), of the Sikh community, with its shared symbols (▷ photo) and the names 'Singh' and 'Kaur' for men and women respectively.

Equality is an important Sikh ideal, and this is symbolized by the sharing of food in the *gurdwara*. This is the place of worship where Sikhs meet and where they are in the presence of their holy book, the *Guru Granth Sahib*. The most important Sikh temple is the Golden Temple at Amritsar, built in the late 16th century. Many Sikhs begin and end the day with prayers from the holy book. Their aim is to sanctify ordinary life, keeping the mind and heart set on God. Of the four major religions of India, it is only Sikhism that has turned away from the ideals of asceticism and celibacy and focused instead on the householder.

HINDU GODS AND GODDESSES

GODS OF THE VEDAS
Indra Thunder god, god of battle.
Varuna Guardian of order; divine overseer.
Agni God of fire.
Surya God associated with the Sun.

MAJOR GODS OF HINDUISM
Brahma The creator; linked with goddess Saraswati.
Vishnu The preserver; with Shiva, one of Hinduism's great gods. Vishnu has ten incarnations or *avataras*, and is married to Lakshmi (▷ below). Vishnu's ten avataras are: **Matsya**, the fish; **Kurma**, the tortoise; **Varaha**, the boar; **Narasimha**, the man-lion; **Vamana**, the dwarf; **Parasurama**, Rama bearing the axe; **Ramachandra**, (otherwise known as **Rama**), the god of the *Ramayana* epic, married to Sita, and identified by his bow and quiver of arrows; **Krishna**, (the important god featured in the *Bhagavadgita*) who is worshipped particularly as a baby and as a flute-playing cowherd and lover of Radha; **the Buddha**, the great teacher from the 6th–5th century BC and founder of Buddhism (▷ p. 290); **Kalki**, 'the one to come', a future avatara.
Shiva A great god, associated with destruction. In Hindu mythology, Shiva is married to Parvati and is the father of Ganesh.
Ganesh The elephant-headed god, worshipped as the remover of obstacles and god of good luck.
Hanuman The monkey warrior-god associated with the god Rama.

THE GODDESSES
The goddesses are manifestations of the great creative spirit or **Shakti**. The most popular are:
Parvati Wife of Shiva; also known as **Uma.**
Durga All-powerful warrior goddess, also known as **Amba**, and linked with Shiva.
Kali Goddess associated with destruction.
Lakshmi Goddess of beauty, wealth and good fortune, wife of Vishnu.
Saraswati Goddess of learning, arts and music, and wife of Brahma.

Buddhism

Buddhism originated in India around 500 BC with the life and teaching of Gautama the Buddha ('enlightened one'). According to tradition, Prince Gautama (?563–483 BC) was born into luxury, but after seeing an old man, a sick man and a corpse he realized that he too would grow old, become decrepit, and die. A meeting with a wandering religious seeker inspired Gautama to leave home and seek liberation from the endless cycle of birth and death through *yoga* or meditation.

After unsuccessfully attempting to gain liberation by depriving the body of food and comfort, Gautama rejected asceticism and sought a *middle way* between luxury and self-mortification. He sat in meditation through the night, and attained awakening or *nirvana* (literally the 'blowing out' of the flames of passion and craving), overcoming the attachments that would have caused him to be reborn in the world.

The Buddha attracted disciples, and these formed the nucleus of the Buddhist community or *sangha*. Initially a wandering religious order, their resting places later developed into Buddhist monasteries.

Propagated throughout India as a creed of righteousness and non-violence by the great Mauryan king Ashoka (272–232 BC), Buddhism spread through southern and eastern Asia. Two main branches developed, Theravada and Mahayana (▷ below). However, in India itself, Buddhism had virtually died out by the 13th century AD.

Images of the Buddha at Wat Suthat temple in Bangkok, Thailand. Statues or pictures of the Buddha – usually depicted in a meditative position – are important in Buddhist worship. However, the ritual use of such images indicates reverence for the Buddha's teachings and example, and does not necessarily imply a recognition of his divinity.
(Spectrum)

The nature of Buddhism

Buddhist teachings (called *dharma*) are distinctive because the Buddha taught that there is no permanent 'self'. Indeed, Buddhist teachings stress that nothing at all exists permanently – there is only perpetual change. Family, friends, possessions, even our own mind and body – all the things cherished as 'me' or 'mine' – are subject to perpetual change and decay. Yet people become mentally and emotionally attached to them as if they were permanent, so when any of them changes – for instance if someone dies – people suffer. Even moments of happiness are unsatisfactory, because they never last.

The Buddha taught that since impermanence is an unalterable fact of life, we can be truly happy only by becoming detached from the delusive notions of 'me' and 'mine'. Such detachment may be achieved through techniques of meditation.

Buddhism shares with Hinduism the concepts of *samsara*, an eternal cycle of death and rebirth, and *karma*, the idea that individuals suffer the effects of past actions (▷ p. 288).

Theravada Buddhism

Theravada ('Teaching of the Elders') is found mainly in Sri Lanka, Cambodia, Thailand, and other countries of Southeast Asia. Theravadins view Gautama as a human being who achieved nirvana after many lifetimes of moral and spiritual development (inspiring tales of the Buddha's previous human and animal lives are a favourite method of teaching about Buddhism). To imitate the Buddha by becoming a monk is the best way to attain enlightenment.

A Theravadin monk follows a strict discipline, eating only donated food, remaining celibate, and not harming living beings. The monastic routine

sometimes by Zen masters to shock the monk's mind into 'awakening'. Japanese Zen profoundly influenced the martial arts and the tea ceremony.

Esoteric, Tantric or *'Diamond'* Buddhism became popular in Tibet and Japan. It holds that enlightenment is fully present within the disciple and with the correct spiritual technique passed on privately by a master, enlightenment can be had here and now.

Nichiren Buddhism, named after a 13th-century Japanese monk, contains esoteric elements such as a *mantra*, a repeated phrase with special power (▷ p. 293).

Festivals in Mahayana countries vary according to the tradition and are often a blend of Buddhism and other religions. There are numerous Mahayana cults focusing on different Buddhas and bodhisattvas to whom people pray for help with problems. In Japan, Buddhist priests are mainly responsible for funeral and memorial services for the ancestors.

The contemporary relevance of Buddhism

Buddhism has now spread worldwide, with Buddhist centres in most Western countries, and Buddhists today are debating the future role and direction of Buddhism. Some hold that Buddhism necessarily involves withdrawing from the world and social involvement is contrary to the 'middle way'. Others feel that the Buddha's teaching provides a blueprint for a better society, and Buddhists should therefore engage in social-reform movements.

The appeal of Buddhism in modern industrial society may lie in its emphasis on individual well-being, its non-exploitative approach to life, and its inner-directed philosophy. A Buddhist would say that people are drawn to Buddhism in this life because they performed acts of merit in a previous life.

A **Theravadin Buddhist novice monk** (left). Theravadin Buddhists believe that to imitate the Buddha by becoming a monk is the best way to attain enlightenment. In some Theravadin cultures – particularly in Thailand and Myanmar (Burma) – virtually all young males spend a period as a novice in a monastery. (Popperfoto)

helps monks forget worldly concerns, so enabling them to concentrate on Buddhist teachings and to control the mind through meditation.

Monasteries depend entirely on the goodwill of the wider community. People give generously to the monastery, believing that such acts of merit will help them gain a better rebirth, perhaps become a monk in a future life. In return, lay people receive spiritual guidance from the monks and emulate them by following some of the rules of the Buddhist life. Lay Buddhists pray to local gods and spirits for mundane benefits such as a good harvest – for although gods, like people, are impermanent, they may still be able to help.

Theravada Buddhist festivals vary from country to country, but typically celebrate the Buddha's birth and enlightenment and important events in the history of Buddhism in that country.

Mahayana Buddhism

Mahayana ('Great Vehicle') is a strand of Buddhism originating in India which spread to China, Korea, Japan and Tibet. According to Mahayana scriptures, the Buddha is not Gautama but an eternal, formless, cosmic principle, constantly acting to liberate us from suffering existence. The eternal Buddha uses wise and compassionate 'skilful means' (such as appearing in human form as the Buddha Gautama) if this will help deluded beings out of the cycle of rebirth.

Mahayanists recognize several Buddhas and many *bodhisattvas* ('enlightenment-beings'), near-Buddhas who have delayed entering final nirvana to help all beings attain enlightenment. Underlying Mahayana Buddhism are two important religious concepts. One is the idea of *emptiness* – that nothing at all has any permanent substance; even Buddhist doctrines are 'empty' and one should not become attached to them. The other is 'mind-only', meaning that the world we experience is a product of the mind, like a dream. The task of the Buddhist is to 'awaken' from the dream of existence.

Mahayana takes several forms. In *Pure Land,* by visualizing the Buddha Amida's beautiful form or chanting his name, a devotee is assured of rebirth in Amida's 'Land of bliss', where conditions are better for attaining final nirvana.

Zen ('meditation') Buddhism emphasizes the hard discipline of silent meditation, with unusual methods such as shouting and slapping used

SEE ALSO

● THE RELIGIONS OF INDIA p. 288
● THE RELIGIONS OF CHINA AND JAPAN p. 292
● NON-WESTERN ART p. 308

THE FOUR NOBLE TRUTHS

Buddhists believe that Gautama's teaching can be expressed succinctly in the Four Noble Truths.

1. To exist is to suffer.

2. Suffering is caused by attachment to impermanent things.

3. Suffering ceases once attachment ceases.

4. There is a 'Way' to end suffering.

This 'Way' varies with different kinds of Buddhism. Pure Land Buddhists rely on the power of Amida to help them (▷ main text); Zen Buddhists rely on meditation. Theravadin Buddhists have a formula that describes the Way – the **Noble Eightfold Path**:

1. Perfect understanding or knowledge.

2. Perfect attitude or resolve.

3. Perfect speech.

4. Perfect action.

5. Perfect occupation or living.

6. Perfect effort.

7. Perfect mindfulness.

8. Perfect composure or meditation.

Some Buddhists believe that these 'perfections' can only be obtained by long meditation and by living a strictly moral life. Others believe that the Buddha helps those who turn to him for assistance, or that these perfections are complete and innate within all of us.

Religions of China and Japan

Chinese religion comprises a basic belief in the power of gods, fate, spirits and ancestors, and three great religions with separate origins: Confucianism and Daoism (Taoism), which originated in China between 500 and 300 BC, and Buddhism, which entered China about AD 100 (▷ p. 290). In practice these religions are thoroughly blended in the rites and festivals of Chinese religion.

Buddhism is also important in Japan, where it takes three main forms: Zen and Pure Land (▷ p. 290), and Nichiren. Japan's oldest religion, however, is Shinto, which has always been the religion of the emperors. Many new religions have also emerged in Japan in the last hundred years. Some offer totally new teachings, while others aim to revitalize the practices and values of older traditions.

Confucianism

Confucianism is an approach to life and way of thinking based on the teachings of Kongfuzi (Confucius; 551–479 BC). Kongfuzi was a scholar-official who taught that man's duty and happiness lay in conforming to the 'Will of Heaven' – a supreme spiritual principle that is believed to regulate the course of events and relationships between people. When people live according to

Dragons, known as *Lung*, played an important role in state Confucianism in Imperial China. 'Collective sacrifices' were made to the gods by mandarins (members of the senior grades of the bureaucracy of the Chinese Empire). Perhaps the most popular sacrifices were local ceremonies of offerings to the Lung. (Images)

the Will of Heaven, society is stable and people are happy and prosperous. However, if people follow their selfish desires and contravene the Will of Heaven, conflicts and natural disasters occur, and the whole universe becomes disordered.

Kongfuzi himself is considered to represent the Confucian ideal of the 'noble man'. Gradually through diligent training and study ('self-cultivation'), he was able to remould his own character to conform to the Will of Heaven. Proper respect, family love, reciprocity among friends, benevolence to strangers and loyalty to the state are the five noble Confucian qualities to be cultivated.

Kongfuzi's teachings were developed by Mengzi (Mencius; 372–289 BC) and became the basis of Chinese ethics and behaviour, in which there is an emphasis on the preservation of the family and the state, and the performance of proper rites for the ancestors.

Daoism (Taoism)

Dao or *Tao* ('the Way') is a word of deep significance in Chinese thought. It refers to the mystical power behind all events, the flow of events themselves, and the religious path one should follow. The central text of Daoism is the *Dao de jing (Tao Te Ching)*, dating from the 4th century BC but traditionally ascribed to Lao Zi (Lao-tzu), a semi-legendary philosopher of the 6th century BC. Also dating from the 4th century BC are the writings of Zhuang Zi (Chuang Tzu). In these texts the Dao is described as unfathomable and indescribable. It includes good and evil, darkness and light, stillness and motion. Another text normally regarded as a blend of Daoist and Confucian thought is the *Book of Changes (Yijing* or *I Ching)*, an oracular work that claims to predict the future from chance events, such as throwing sticks in a pattern.

Unlike Confucianism, Daoism advocates spontaneity and naturalness, abandoning oneself to the current of the Dao. Everything, good or bad, is the sublime operation of the Dao and should not be interfered with. Daoists naturally tended to solitude, meditation and simple living. Their techniques of quiet contemplation were similar to Buddhist meditation. Indeed, the Chinese word later used for Buddhist enlightenment was 'Dao'.

Oneness with the Dao was believed to confer immortality, and Daoist alchemy originated as an attempt to find an elixir that would transmute the perishable self into an Immortal. Though seemingly opposed to Confucianism in its advocacy of 'non-action', Daoists shared the Confucian aim of a harmonious existence, and most Chinese combine Daoism and Confucianism in their way of thinking.

Chinese religion in practice

Chinese festivals follow the cycle of the agricultural year and reflect concern for ancestors, health and prosperity. The Daoist rite of cosmic renewal (*jiao*) is carried out in early winter, and the Ch'ing Ming ('clear and bright') festival in the spring involves repairing ancestors' graves and offering food and paper 'spirit' money to the souls of the ancestors. Daoist and Buddhist priests as well as *shamans* (intermediaries between this world and the spirit world) assist in these festivals and in the rituals marking events in the life cycle, such as birth, marriage and death.

Rural people in mainland (Communist) China tend to be more religious than Chinese living in capitalist countries such as Hong Kong and Taiwan, but practising any religion has been difficult in China since Marxism became the official belief system in 1949 (⊳ p. 277). A more liberal policy towards religion emerged in the late 1970s, but Chinese rulers throughout history have suppressed religions that do not support the government.

Shinto

Shinto ('the Sacred Way') is the native religion of Japan. Shinto existed in Japan long before the introduction of writing from China (5th century AD), but its earliest texts date from the 8th century. These texts include semi-mythological histories of Japan, tracing the line of emperors back to Amaterasu, the Sun goddess, so bestowing divine status on the imperial line.

Adherents of Shinto seek vitality, growth and prosperity through the worship of *kami* ('deity' or 'sacred energy'). The many Japanese gods are described as kami, and kami may also be found in sacred trees, rocks, waterfalls, mountains, and in the emperor and other outstanding individuals. Shinto shrines throughout Japan house the kami of the locality. Shinto priests perform rituals of purification and renewal, and during festivals the kami is ceremonially carried through the streets in a *mikoshi* or portable shrine and entertained with a ceremony or a strenuous contest among the young men.

Shinto coexisted peacefully with other religions in Japan until the 1870s, when the modernizing government suppressed other religions and adapted Shinto teachings for government propaganda. Up to the Japanese defeat at the end of World War II, *State Shinto* taught that a citizen's religious duty was obedience to the divine emperor. In 1946 Emperor Hirohito renounced all claims to divinity, and the new postwar constitution safeguards religious freedom and prohibits any association between religion and state.

Modern Japanese religions

With freedom of religion, many new religions appeared in postwar Japan, while others, suppressed before the war, expanded rapidly. Some so-called 'new' religions actually began in the 19th century but had been restricted until 1945. The new religions are usually lay movements based on the personality and teaching of a founder, who may be a female shaman (⊳ above). Founders may reveal new truths about the meaning of life, or may simply renew people's faith in more traditional teachings. Some new religions offer magical solutions to difficulties, while others encourage positive thinking as the solution to life's problems.

Several new religions teach that family problems are caused by selfishness and by neglect of the spirits of the family ancestors, who make their anger felt by disrupting life. Religious rites are prescribed to pacify the ancestors and thus solve the problem. These new Japanese religions are continuing ideas and practices dating back to the earliest known forms of Chinese religion.

Praying to 'Golf Kannon', the golf *kami* (⊳ main text), in Tokyo. There are Shinto ceremonies for most aspects of modern social and working life, for example purification ceremonies for new factory equipment or completion ceremonies for a new office block. Today, Shinto is often an aspect of everyday life and behaviour rather than a structured system of religious belief. (Gamma)

SEE ALSO
● CHINA TO THE COLONIAL AGE p. 234
● THE GROWTH OF TOTALITARIANISM p. 272
● CHINA IN THE 20TH CENTURY p. 276
● BUDDHISM p. 290
● NON-WESTERN ART p. 308

MODERN JAPANESE BUDDHISM

Nichiren (AD 1222–82) was a Japanese monk who preached faith in the *Lotus Sutra*, a major scripture of Mahayana Buddhism. Unusually for a Buddhist, Nichiren violently criticized all other forms of Buddhism as heresy. Civil war, famine and disease were threatening Japan in Nichiren's time. He believed these calamities were due to people's lack of faith in the *Lotus Sutra*, for the sutra warns those who scorn it that they will suffer.

Though Nichiren failed to convert all Japan to his cause, his form of Buddhism eventually became very popular in Japan. One group of followers was called *Nichiren Shōshū* (the 'True Nichiren Sect'). Nichiren Buddhists chant the Japanese title of the *Lotus Sutra*, 'Namu-myō-hō-renge-kyō'. Nichiren taught that this chanting has the power to make one enlightened, by awakening one's already-present Buddha-nature.

Sōka Gakkai ('The Society for the Creation of Value') was founded in the 1930s by Makiguchi Tsunesaburo, a schoolmaster who intended to combine Nichiren Buddhist practice with his own progressive educational theories. Although the movement was suppressed and Makiguchi died in prison during World War II, his successors Toda Josei and Ikeda Daisaku built up Sōka Gakkai membership in the 1960s to approximately 10 million members – the most successful lay religious movement in Japan.

Sōka Gakkai attracted converts by promising healing, business success and happiness, and in the 1970s the movement began to spread to other countries under the name *Nichiren Shōshū*. Many people – including pop stars and business and professional people – have been attracted to this accessible form of Buddhism. It teaches that chanting can bring anything one desires, from a new job to a Rolls-Royce. People who chant for material goods, however, discover that having everything one desires is not the same as being happy. They begin to study the deeper meaning of Buddhism taught by Nichiren.

Despite its rapid growth since 1945, Sōka Gakkai points out that it is not a 'new' religion but a lay movement attached to the 'True Nichiren Sect', and that it regards Nichiren himself as the Buddha for the present age.

Judaism

The biblical account of the origin of the Jewish religion traces its history back to the revolt by Abraham against the idol-worship of his native Mesopotamia (now Iraq), when he smashed his father's idols and fled to Canaan (present-day Israel). His fundamental belief in one God is enshrined in God's covenant 'with you and your descendants, to be a God to you and your descendants after you' (Genesis 17:7).

Temple Mount in Jerusalem is sacred to Jews, Muslims and Christians. In the foreground, Jews pray at the Western (Wailing) Wall, all that is visible of the Temple of Solomon. Orthodox Jews pray daily for the reconstruction of the Temple, which was built on the site where – according to tradition – Abraham prepared to sacrifice his son Isaac. The Dome of the Rock mosque (centre background) was built in the 7th century over the place from which the Prophet Muhammad was believed to have ascended to Heaven. (Gamma)

RITES OF PASSAGE

As a sign of the covenant between God and the Jews, the Torah lays down that every baby boy must be circumcised. The service is performed by a specially trained person, a *mohel*, on the eighth day after birth. Girls are named by their father in the synagogue.

When a Jewish boy is 13 years old, he is regarded as being old enough to take responsibility for himself and for his observance of the Law. He is then *bar mitzvah* (Hebrew for 'son of the commandment'), an adult in religious terms. He can then take an active part in services, be counted in the minyan and may be called to read a passage of the Torah, in Hebrew, in a synagogue service – the first occasion he can do this is often made the pretext of a party.

A Jewish marriage ceremony takes place under a canopy, the *chuppah,* and can be held anywhere, but is usually held in a synagogue or out of doors. After the bridegroom places a ring on the bride's forefinger, the ketubah or marriage contract is read out, and seven blessings are recited. At the end of the ceremony, the bridegroom breaks a glass underfoot, recalling the destruction of the Temple in Jerusalem. In Orthodox circles, the celebrations continue for a week.

Jewish law requires that a body must be buried in consecrated ground as soon as possible after death. It is first washed, anointed with spices, wrapped in a white sheet, and placed in a plain wooden coffin. Orthodox Jews regard cremation as a denial of belief in bodily resurrection. At the funeral, mourners tear their clothes, and for the next year – and annually on the anniversary of the death – they recite the *Kaddish*, a declaration of faith.

When Canaan was struck by famine, Abraham's grandson Jacob (who was renamed Israel by an angel) was forced to take his twelve sons to find food in Egypt, where they were enslaved. God's promise to Abraham to make his descendants into a nation and to give them the land of Canaan in perpetuity was fulfilled when the twelve tribes of Israel, the descendants of Jacob's sons, were led out of Egypt by Moses (c. 1300 BC). During their 40-year journey to the Promised Land, the Ten Commandments were revealed to Moses by God on Mount Sinai, along with the foundations of the legal and moral system of the Jewish religion.

The Written Law and the Oral Law

Orthodox Judaism regards all religious authority as deriving from this revelation, as embodied in the *Torah*, the first five books of the Hebrew bible. The Jewish bible (known to Christians as the Old Testament) also contains the historical books of the Prophets, and the 'Writings' which include such poetical and ethical books as Psalms and Proverbs. The word 'Torah' literally means 'instruction' or 'law', and the term is also used to refer to the 613 commandments that tradition identifies in the Five Books of Moses, and to the whole body of social and religious law developed around them.

Tradition holds that an *Oral Law* containing the key to the interpretation of the Written Law was revealed to Moses together with it. After the destruction of the Jewish state by the Romans in AD 70, this was codified as the *Mishna*, whose 63 'Tractates' are grouped into six 'Orders' dealing with agricultural law (in the land of Israel), sabbaths and festivals, family law, damages, temple ritual and dietary laws, and laws of purity. In the following centuries debate amongst the Rabbis continued, and much of this is recorded in the *Gemara*. The *Talmud*, the great encyclopedia of Jewish teaching, consists of the interwoven texts of the *Mishna* and *Gemara*, usually printed with later commentaries around the page.

Beliefs

The Jewish religion is based on the belief in one God, Creator and Lord of the Universe, whose special relationship with the Jewish people consists in their undertaking to keep God's laws faithfully. Although Judaism expects non-Jews to observe certain basic ethical laws, it does not regard Jewish ritual as obligatory and does not seek converts. In fact, God promises the righteous of all people a place in the world to come when the *Messiah* (meaning 'anointed') inaugurates an age of universal peace and security.

Ritual and worship

Jewish law lays down a complex set of laws of *kashrut*, which distinguishes permitted (*kosher* or *kasher*) from prohibited (*treifa*) foods. Only mammals that have both cloven hoofs and chew the cud, such as cows and sheep, are permitted as food. They must be killed by a skilled *shochet* in a way that minimizes pain to the animal and drains as much blood as possible. Fish must have fins and scales (so that eels and sturgeon are forbidden). Shellfish and birds of prey are prohibited. In addition, milk and meat and their derivatives must be strictly separated and must not be cooked or prepared together, nor eaten at the same meal.

The Jewish day starts at sunset, and the week on Sunday, so that *Shabbat*, the day of rest ordained by the Torah, is observed from dusk on Friday to nightfall on Saturday. This day of rest derives from the account of the creation in the Bible, where God rested on the seventh day. During Shabbat, productive work, kindling fire, carrying, writing, cooking and travelling (except a limited distance on foot) are prohibited.

Synagogues were first built to serve as temporary places of worship after the destruction of the Temple in Jerusalem by the Babylonians in 586 BC. Although the Jews did rebuild the Temple, the practice of local houses of prayer continued. However, the second Temple was also destroyed, this time by the Romans, and never rebuilt, and to this day the synagogue service is modelled upon, and refers to, the Temple service.

The central role of the synagogue in Jewish religious life is attested by its Hebrew names, which translate as 'house of meeting' and 'house of study', as well as 'house of prayer'. Although there are no requirements for a specially built building, and prayer can take place anywhere, many synagogues incorporate such ancient Jewish symbols as the Star of David, the *Menorah* (the seven-branched Temple candlestick), and the two tablets containing the Ten Commandments (Exodus 20) in their decoration. The congregation usually faces the Ark, a cupboard containing the Torah scrolls, which are handwritten by a specially trained scribe. Above the Ark, which is usually in the wall facing Jerusalem, a light is kept burning as a sign of God's eternal presence.

Services are held in the evening, morning, and afternoon. Each service has at its centre a silent prayer, which is recited standing and facing Jerusalem. Morning and evening prayers contain the *Shema*, the central declaration of Jewish faith, which is also the last rite of a Jew on his deathbed. For a formal service to take place, a *minyan* or quorum of ten men is required; otherwise the Torah is not read and certain prayers cannot be said. Any of the minyan may lead the prayers and read the Torah, not only the rabbi, whose main function is as teacher and interpreter of the Law.

Jewish traditions and sects

For the Orthodox Jew, all authority derives from the divine will as expressed in the Torah and interpreted in the rabbinic tradition; the main role for human reason is in working out the precise details of that law. Ritual observance and the obligation to study are not thought of as different from ethical behaviour. Nonetheless, there are diverse traditions within Orthodox Judaism: the *Ashkenazi* tradition developed in the communities of Germany and Poland; while the *Sephardic* tradition is traced back to the Jews who lived in the lands of the Near East and Mediterranean (particularly Spain) under Muslim rule in and before the Middle Ages. When the Sephardic Jews of Spain and Portugal were expelled in 1492 they settled in various countries, but have preserved different traditions from the Jews of northern Europe. The *Hassidic* sects of eastern Europe and some of the Oriental and North African communities also evolved their

---

MAJOR JEWISH FESTIVALS

The normal Jewish year consists of 12 lunar months of 29 or 30 days. An extra month is added to 7 years of every 19-year cycle to bring the calendar back in time with the solar year. The Jewish months are as follows: Nisan (March–April), Iyyar (April–May), Sivan (May–June), Tammuz (June–July), Av (July–August), Ellul (August–September), Tishri (September–October), Cheshvan (October–November), Kislev (November–December), Tevet (December–January), Shevat (January–February), Adar (February–March).

Pesach (Passover), 15–22 Nisan. Formal meal to commemorate the Exodus from Egypt; also originally a thanksgiving for the barley harvest. No leaven bread is eaten.

Shavuot (Pentecost), 6–7 Sivan. Commemorates the giving of the Torah; also originally a thanksgiving for the wheat harvest.

Fast of Av, 9 Av. A 24-hour fast to commemorate the destruction of the Temple in Jerusalem by Nebuchadnezzar in 586 BC and by the Romans in AD 70.

Rosh Hashana, 1–2 Tishri. New Year; commemorates the 'Birthday of the World'. White is worn for repentance, and a ram's horn is blown to commemorate Abraham's covenant with God.

Yom Kippur, 10 Tishri. Day of Atonement, marked by 24 hours of fasting and prayer for forgiveness of past sins.

Sukkot (Tabernacles), 15–22 Tishri. The 40 years of wandering in the desert are commemorated by eating and sleeping in huts roofed with branches.

Simchat Torah, 22–23 Tishri; ▷ picture.

Chanukah or *Hanukkah* (Festival of Lights), 25 Kislev–3 Tevet. Candles are lit in a nine-branched Menorah or Chanukiah to commemorate the rededication of the Temple in Jerusalem by Judas Maccabeus in 165 BC.

Purim, 14 Adar. Readings of Book of Esther, giving of charity and sending of gifts all commemorate the deliverance of the Jews of Persia from destruction.

Two new dates are observed by many Jews: *Yom Ha'atzma'ut* (5 Iyyar) celebrates the establishment of the State of Israel, and *Yom Hashoah* (27 Nisan) is a memorial for the 6 million Jews who died in the Nazi Holocaust.

Simchat Torah (22–23 Tishri) is celebrated by the procession of the Torah scrolls through the synagogue. The festival marks the completion of the annual cycle of Torah readings and the commencement of a new cycle. Children, waving flags, play an important part in the joyful ceremonies, symbolizing a new cycle of life. (Gamma)

---

own rites. These groups, however, recognize each other's legitimacy in so far as they subscribe to the traditional concept of divine authority.

In the 19th and early 20th centuries various trends in Europe and America moved away from traditional or Orthodox observance, giving rise to Reform, Liberal, Conservative, Reconstructionist and other forms of Judaism. They reject the divinity of the Torah and rabbinic authority, and believe, to varying degrees, that Jewish practice must adapt to changing circumstances. They have introduced changes such as holding services partly in the vernacular (rather than Hebrew).

SEE ALSO

- THE ANCIENT NEAR EAST p. 228
- THE GROWTH OF TOTALITARIANISM p. 272
- WORLD WAR II p. 274
- THE MIDDLE EAST p. 282
- ANCIENT RELIGIONS p. 286
- CHRISTIANITY: BELIEF AND PRACTICE p. 296

Christianity: Belief and Practice

The Western calendar, shaped and determined by Christianity, sees the birth of Jesus of Nazareth, known as the Christ, as the turning point of history. In dating the modern era from the supposed date of his birth (it seems likely Jesus was actually born c. 4 BC), Christianity was making a profound statement about the significance of Jesus Christ.

For Christians, the Jewish child born in Bethlehem was no ordinary human. He was and is, both human and divine, the Son of God. While it is possible to say that a historical person named Jesus lived between c. 4 BC and AD 30, it is only faith that can claim that he was the Christ, the anointed one of God, the long awaited Messiah of the Jews.

The nature of God

Christians believe that God is the creator of the universe and all life. They believe that Jesus Christ is the only Son of God, who has existed with God the Father from before time began. Jesus was incarnated (given human form) when, by the power of the Holy Spirit, his human mother, Mary, gave birth to him. The purpose of his incarnation was to reconcile humanity with

God, as human sinfulness had broken the relationship with God. Through Jesus' death upon the cross God broke the power of sin and evil, and through the rising of Jesus from the dead on the third day God showed the triumph of life over death, of good over evil, and gave the promise of everlasting life to those who believe in Jesus.

After his death, Jesus appeared to his disciples a number of times, and then ascended to heaven. He promised to send the Holy Spirit to guide and enlighten the Church. Christians believe that Jesus will return at the end of time to judge the world. The *Trinity* expresses the Christian belief that there are three persons who are of the same substance – God, namely the Father who created, the Son who revealed God's love and purpose to humanity and creation, and the Holy Spirit, through which God seeks to guide and instruct the world today.

The teachings of Jesus

What we know of Jesus' teachings and life is recorded in the Gospels and in several quotes and stories found in the other books of the New Testament. These were all written by Christians who believed Jesus to be in some way both human and divine. Our knowledge of Jesus therefore comes through the pens of believers. Jesus taught that God was like a father who cares for every person on Earth. He taught that through repentance and forgiveness, God calls all humanity to him in love and seeks for every individual to do his will on Earth. Jesus taught that through living as God wishes, the Kingdom of God – justice, love, mercy and peace – could come upon Earth, either in individual lives or possibly to the world as a whole. What we cannot be sure of is quite how Jesus understood his role. He certainly rejected the model of the *Messiah* that the Jews of his day had. They longed for a righteous warrior who would free them from Rome and give them their own country again. But whether Jesus understood himself to be divine is a hotly debated issue. He certainly talked of the kingdom to come – but not a political or military one, rather one established in people's hearts and minds.

The Church holds that through the twelve key disciples of Jesus, the apostles, authority on Earth was given to the Church, which is to be seen as the body of Christ on Earth. The Church is therefore held to be essential to salvation – to being freed from sin and to the possibility of everlasting life.

The Church and ritual

The life of the Church has been formed by both the Bible (▷ box) and by Christian teachings and doctrine. Through a dynamic interaction between Bible and tradition the Church has developed its teachings, beliefs and creeds as well as liturgies, sacraments and festivals. These impart to the believer the essence of the Christian faith and imbue the significant stages of life with Christian meaning and purpose. The following account draws primarily upon Roman Catholic and Anglican practices; there is in fact a wide divergence of belief and practice within the Christian faith.

There are two rites or *sacraments* that were instituted by Jesus himself, namely baptism and the eucharist. Other rites celebrated at times of grace or blessing include confirmation, marriage,

The Eucharist (or Holy Communion) is a commemoration of the action of Jesus at the Last Supper, and a central rite of worship in many Christian denominations. The majority of Christians believe that Christ is present in the Eucharist in some way, but there is considerable disagreement between Churches concerning the nature and the effects of that presence (▷ text).
(Gamma)

MAJOR CHRISTIAN FESTIVALS

Of the Christian festivals, the following are the most significant – although every day of the year has its saints, and there are many minor festivals.

Advent and Christmas

Advent runs for some four or five weeks prior to 25 December (Christmas Day) and is a time of preparation for the coming of Jesus in the past, in the present and in the future. Christmas Day celebrates the birth of Jesus and is traditionally followed by the twelve days of Christmas, ending with Epiphany, which celebrates the visit of the wise men to the child Jesus.

Lent and Easter

This is the major festival of the Church. For 40 days before Holy Week and Easter – a period known as Lent – Christians fast or go without certain foods to remind themselves of Jesus' 40 days in the wilderness and of the sufferings he endured on the cross. Holy Week begins with Palm Sunday, which recalls Jesus' entry into Jerusalem when the people covered the road with palm leaves to celebrate his arrival. Good Friday – so called because it brought redemption to humanity – is the day Christians commemorate the death of Jesus upon the cross. Easter Sunday celebrates the rising from the tomb by Jesus and his first appearance to his disciples and friends.

Ascension Day

Ascension Day comes 40 days after Easter and celebrates the ascension of Jesus into heaven – the last earthly appearance of Jesus.

Pentecost

Pentecost (or Whitsunday) comes ten days later, and celebrates the gift of the Holy Spirit upon the disciples and the founding of the Church.

The Nativity (the birth of Jesus), a 15th-century German book illustration of the arrival of the three kings. The Gospels recount how the Angel Gabriel announced to Mary that she was to conceive the Son of God by the Holy Spirit, and that, although married to Joseph, she remained a virgin. In both the Orthodox and Roman Catholic Churches, Mary is regarded as a mediator between God and man. (AKG)

---

ordination to the priesthood, confession, and extreme unction just before death.

The *Eucharist* (or *Holy Communion*) – in which bread and wine is consecrated and offered to the congregation – is the central service of many Churches, because Jesus at the Last Supper (just before the Crucifixion) told his disciples to remember him when they broke bread and drank wine. There is a wide diversity of understanding of the role of the bread and the wine. In Roman Catholic theology it is believed that the bread and the wine become the body and blood of Christ – a process known as *transubstantiation*. In Protestant thought the term *consubstantiation* covers one understanding – that the body and blood of Christ are present in the bread and the wine. Protestant thought also has the idea that the bread and wine are simply a memorial to the blood and body of Christ.

Baptism (or *christening*) marks the acceptance of a new member into the Church, and involves sprinkling holy water on the head of the person concerned, or may, in some traditions, involve total immersion. The ritual recalls the baptism of Jesus by John the Baptist, and Jesus' own baptizing of his disciples.

Many Churches have professional clergy. These fall into two main types, priests and ministers. The role of the *priest* in, say, the Orthodox or Roman Catholic tradition is to act as an intermediary between God and the world. The priest has a formal, liturgical role that does not necessarily involve a pastoral dimension. In contrast, the *minister* in many Protestant Churches does not act as an intermediary, as each person is believed to be in direct communication with God, or capable of being so. The minister's role is to guide reflection on the Word of God and to help Christians in the daily conduct of their lives according to Christian principles. In such Churches there is a belief in the priesthood of all believers.

The term 'church' needs to be explored, for it has two distinct meanings. With a capital 'C', it is applied to the whole body of believers, as in the Church of England. It does not just mean the clergy, but all who profess Christ's name and belong to him through the Church. The second meaning, with a lower-case 'c', is the physical place of worship for the community of believers. Most churches have their sanctuary, where the altar is kept, and provide places for communal worship, reading of the Bible, preaching and administration of the eucharist and other sacraments such as baptism. In certain traditions the church faces towards Jerusalem.

The different forms or traditions of Christianity are described on pp. 298–9.

SEE ALSO

● ANCIENT ROME p. 233
● THE SUCCESSORS OF ROME p. 241
● CHRISTIANITY RESURGENT p. 244
● MEDIEVAL AND RENAISSANCE CULTURE p. 248
● THE REFORMATION p. 250
● WHAT IS RELIGION? p. 284
● JUDAISM p. 294
● WORLD CHRISTIANITY p. 298

THE BIBLE

The Jewish Bible is called the *Old Testament* by Christians, and the Gospels, Acts of the Apostles, Letters and Revelation are called the *New Testament*. In so doing, the Church shows that it considers itself to be the true heir of Israel, to whom the Old Testament or covenant was given (▷ p. 294). But Christians believe Israel failed to recognize Jesus as the fulfilment of the Old Testament, and so the special relationship with God enjoyed by Israel passed to the Church. Some Christians believe the Bible is a factual, historical and scientific account of life on Earth, its purpose and meaning. Other Christians hold that it reveals, through story and myth, the nature of humanity's relationship with God and with one another. For both, the Bible plays a central role in helping to determine Christian responses to moral, social and spiritual issues.

The Bible the first Christians knew was the Jewish one, in which Christians see Jesus foretold. The Jewish Bible was known to the early Christians in two forms, the original Hebrew and the Greek translation known as the *Septuagint*. This was because Christianity started amongst Jews – Jesus appears to have had few non-Jewish (Gentile) followers during his life on Earth. Very soon, however, Christians were attracted from non-Jewish groups and they read the Jewish Bible in the common language of their time, Greek. The New Testament was entirely written in Greek, showing how the Gentile world became more important to the Church than the Jewish world. Jesus himself spoke Aramaic (a Semitic language), and a few words of this remain in the New Testament.

The earliest history of the Church is captured in the Acts of the Apostles, while the four Gospels portray the life of Jesus in different ways. The New Testament also contains letters from St Paul and others to the early churches, in which Christian theology and reflection on Jesus begins to develop. At the end of the New Testament is the Book of Revelation, which envisages the end of the world and the Second Coming of Jesus. The early Church seems to have expected Jesus to return very soon and to establish God's rule on Earth. When this did not happen, this Second Coming became an event in the distant future, when all would be judged and the just rule of God would come on Earth.

World Christianity

In every form of Christianity the same scriptures are used, the God of Israel is worshipped, and Jesus Christ is seen as having ultimate significance. The differences in expression and forms of worship among Christians are immense, as Christianity has adapted to different cultures and historical circumstances. To understand this diversity it is necessary to consider how Christianity has spread.

The earliest Christians were all Jews. The belief that Jesus was Israel's Messiah led to a rethinking of Israel's history and scripture. Many Gentiles (non-Jews) were attracted already to the monotheism of Judaism and found in Christianity a way that brought Jewish and Greek thought together. Crucially, the Christians decided that non-Jewish followers of Jesus should not become converts to Judaism. This meant that the new Christians (who were soon the majority) had a different lifestyle from the first followers of Jesus.

Greco-Roman Christianity

Christianity spread in all directions from Palestine, but most rapidly in the Roman Empire, where it had to adapt to Greek philosophy and popular (and later official) hostility. Though local forms of Christianity developed, a process of consensus produced statements of teaching regarded as *catholic* (universal) and *orthodox* (right thinking). The methods of Greek philosophical debate were employed to define and state Christian teaching. After 313 the Roman state began to favour Christianity and eventually made it the official religion (▷ p. 232).

The Emperors generally wanted religious uniformity and so 'catholic' and 'orthodox' formulations came to have state sanction. In the Empire's eastern provinces, Christians were thinking about Christ not only in terms of Greek philosophy, but also in terms of Syrian and

SEE ALSO

- ANCIENT ROME p. 233
- THE SUCCESSORS OF ROME p. 241
- CHRISTIANITY RESURGENT p. 244
- MEDIEVAL AND RENAISSANCE CULTURE p. 248
- THE REFORMATION p. 250
- JUDAISM p. 294
- PHILOSOPHY p. 302

Egyptian thought. *Monophysitism* and *Nestorianism* are names given to teachings about Christ rejected at Empire-based councils in the 5th century. The issues are complex, but the basic conflict was probably between mainstream Greco-Roman and non-Greek ways of thinking. Most Syriac and Coptic Christians formed Monophysite or Nestorian Churches, and Churches of these types spread in the Middle East and northeast Africa, across Central Asia, and over to southern India (▷ Oriental Churches, below).

Christianity and Europe

By 400, Christianity was established in Roman-Greek culture. After the collapse of Rome (▷ p. 232) the Empire continued in the east at Constantinople until 1453 (▷ p. 241), but its eastern provinces were gradually conquered by Muslims (▷ p. 240). By 1000 the majority of tribal peoples from Ireland to Russia had become Christian, some under Roman, some under Greek influence. Roman or Greek culture was added to tribal heritages to form new, distinct Christian civilizations in Western Europe and Russia. The linguistic and cultural differences meant that Eastern and Western Christians increasingly grew apart. Western Christians used Latin and looked to Rome; Eastern Christians used Greek or Slavonic languages and looked to Constantinople. Despite various attempts at reconciliation, the breach between Eastern and Western Christianity had hardened by the 11th century.

Christianity expands again

From the late 15th century, Western Europeans learned of new routes and hitherto unknown lands; and, from the 16th century, Russia explored its vast Asian hinterland. Both thought it a duty to bring Christianity to their new neighbours. In Spanish America, Christianity was enforced by conquest (▷ p. 252). In most other areas, conquest was out of the question. The result was missionary endeavour on the part of the Roman Catholic Church in Africa and Asia from the 16th century. Orthodox missions in Siberia and Protestant missions elsewhere developed in earnest in the 18th century. Though missions sometimes profited from colonial ventures, many preceded the major imperial expansions of the late 19th century (▷ p. 266). However, until the 20th century the success of the missions appeared modest.

The Eastern Churches

Most of the Churches called Orthodox derived from the ancient Greek Christianity of the Eastern Mediterranean. A direct link with Churches founded by apostles and the memory of a Christian Roman Empire (the Byzantine Empire) that lasted until 1453 heighten the importance of tradition as the guide of the Church. Tradition includes the scriptures, the early Church councils and the writings of the Church Fathers (the

An Ethiopian priest with a ceremonial umbrella. The Ethiopian Church underwent a difficult period with the Marxist regime in Ethiopia (1976–91), but has held its place as the major humanitarian agency in the famine-struck country. The Ethiopian Church and the Coptic Church in Egypt are the oldest in Africa. Elsewhere in Africa, various independent Churches have developed, the largest of which are the Kimbanguist Church in Zaïre and the Zion Church in South Africa. (Spectrum)

early medieval writers on Christian doctrine), the liturgy and the veneration of holy pictures (icons). The Ecumenical Patriarch of Constantinople is the senior figure, but each autonomous Church – the Russian is the largest – has its own patriarch and is self-governing. Apart from Russia, Orthodox Christianity is particularly important in Ukraine, Greece, Cyprus, Romania, Bulgaria and Serbia.

The Oriental Churches

The Oriental Churches include the surviving parts of the ancient Monophysite and Nestorian Churches (▷ above). The Monophysite Churches include the Coptic Church of Egypt – one of the earliest Churches; the Ethiopian Church founded in the 4th century; the Syrian Church – again one of the earliest, and which includes the Thomarists of India; and the Armenians – who became the first nation to officially adopt Christianity, at the end of the 3rd century.

The Roman Catholic Church

Rome was the only Western Church founded by an apostle (St Peter). From Ireland to the Carpathians, Christians came to acknowledge the bishop of Rome as pope (from Vulgar Latin *papa*, 'father'), and used Latin for worship, scripture-reading and theology. In the 16th century most of northern Europe broke the link with Rome to form reformed Protestant Churches (▷ p. 250 and below). This division of Western Christianity led to the terms 'Protestant' for these northern Churches and 'Roman Catholic' (though to its members it was simply 'the Church') for Latin Christianity. Supreme in southern Europe, Catholic Christianity was extended to the Americas and to parts of Asia and Africa. Missions in the 19th and 20th centuries extended it further, and the Roman Catholic Church today is found worldwide, forming the largest single Christian body. It has a strong central authority based on the idea of the Church as the possessor and interpreter of the tradition of Christ. Since the Second Vatican Council (1962–65) Latin has for most purposes given way to local languages. Some smaller non-Latin Churches, such as the Ukrainian Church and the Lebanese Maronites, accept the leadership of the pope. These are known as 'Uniate' Churches.

The Protestant Churches

In 16th-century Europe, movements to reform the Church accompanied fresh interpretations of the Bible and the use of everyday language in place of Latin. These movements rejected Roman authority and established reformed national forms of Christianity in the various states of northern Europe, such as Lutheranism in Sweden and parts of Germany, Calvinism in Geneva and Scotland, and Anglicanism in England. This process is known as the Reformation (▷ p. 250). The majority Protestant movement aimed to reform the Church within each state while keeping the idea that the Church embraced the whole community. The Radical (or Anabaptist) movement insisted that the Church consisted solely of those who made a commitment to Christ, and broke the link with the state. A minority in Europe, this movement produced the dominant Christian forms in North America.

The 18th century saw movements for spiritual renewal in Protestant countries – Pietism in Germany and the Evangelical Revival in Britain, North America and elsewhere. These brought the majority and radical Protestant streams closer together. European emigration brought all the Protestant traditions to America, including the Pietist and Evangelical movements. They took new life and new shapes in a huge community – largely Christian, but multi-ethnic and with no national Church. Some completely new forms of Christianity also arose – notably Pentecostalism, with its stress on gifts of tongues and healing. Today the American religious scene is characterized by a large number of denominations.

The Megachurch in Houston, Texas. In the USA, the second half of the 20th century has seen the growth of many new Churches, particularly those of an evangelical or Pentecostal nature. There has also been a widespread development of the charismatic movement, which is characterized by an emphasis on communal prayer and speaking in tongues. (Gamma)

CHRISTIANITY TODAY

In 1900, about 83% of the world's professing Christians lived in Europe or North America. Today between 50% and 60% live in Africa, Asia, Latin America and Oceania, and the proportion is rising – in Africa alone there are now 230 million Christians, where there were only 10 million in 1900. In the West, especially in Europe, Christian belief has declined, making Christianity increasingly a religion of the southern continents.

New expressions of Christianity are appearing in the southern continents as Christians there meet situations not encountered in the West. There are some signs that a tradition of Christianity is developing that may be as distinctively African as Catholicism and Protestantism have been Western, in that African Independent Churches reflect African ways of worship and address issues of African life. In India, united Churches of South India and North India have developed, and these replace the denominational Churches of Western origin. Latin America has produced new developments such as 'liberation theology' and 'basic Christian communities' (radical movements within the Roman Catholic Church that work for social justice), and a surge of Pentecostalist Christianity.

One characteristic of Christianity today is the increased understanding and cooperation both between Christians in different parts of the world and between Christians of different backgrounds and traditions. The word *ecumenical* is used to describe such spirit and action. Though sometimes used in a narrower sense to refer to the movement associated with the World Council of Churches (founded in 1948), the word simply means 'worldwide' (from the Greek *oikumene*, 'inhabited world'). It is a sign that Christianity is a world faith to a greater extent than ever before, and that in itself means diversity. While traditional missionary activities continue today, a new feature has arisen – the interest in dialogue and cooperation with non-Christian religions. This, along with issues of justice, peace and ecology, concerns many of the major Churches as they move into the third Christian millennium.

Islam

Islam is an Arabic word meaning 'submission'. Muslims are those who submit themselves to Allah – whom they regard as the one true God – by accepting the faith of Islam. The sacred book of Islam is the Qur'an (Koran), the word of God revealed to the Prophet Muhammad. Five basic beliefs are central in Islam. These are the Articles of Faith and consist of belief in the oneness of God; the holy books he has revealed for the guidance of humanity; the prophets; the angels; and the hereafter.

Islam was founded by the Prophet Muhammad. Born around AD 570 at Mecca in western Arabia, Muhammad received his call to prophethood when he was about 40 years old. He claimed that he had been sent to bring good news and to warn his people against idolatry, so that they might turn to the true God. Those who believed and obeyed the laws in the Qur'an would be rewarded in paradise, whereas those who rejected the message would be punished in hell. Gradually opposition built up against him, especially among the rich merchant class, and he and his followers migrated from Mecca to Medina, a city 450 km (280 mi) to the north of Mecca. This migration – known as the Hijra – took place in July 622, marking the beginning of the Islamic calendar. At Medina, Muhammad became the head of a new religious community. He fought his Meccan opponents until his final conquest of Mecca in 630. He died in 632, having spread the message of Islam through much of Arabia.

God, revelation and the Qur'an

Muslims insist on God's oneness and believe that no one and nothing should be worshipped alongside him. God is seen as the creator, the giver and taker of life, present everywhere in the universe and quite unlike any other being. He is described by many 'beautiful names' such as All-Powerful, All-Seeing, All-Hearing, Merciful, Compassionate, Forgiving. From a Muslim viewpoint God can be known most reliably through his revelation of himself in the Qur'an.

According to Islamic doctrine, the Qur'an is the collection of God's revelations to the Prophet Muhammad through the medium of the angel Gabriel. Revealed in Arabic over 22 years from AD 610 to 632, it is seen not as an earthly-inspired book but as the exact words of God, taken from a heavenly tablet. It is regarded as a miracle and great care has been taken to preserve it without change.

Muslims maintain that in the Qur'an God speaks of his own nature, of his relationship with human beings, and of how they will be held accountable to him at the Last Judgement. Although the Qur'an refers directly to Muhammad and the early Islamic community, it offers moral guidance to people of all times and all races. In addition, earlier prophets – including Abraham, Moses and Jesus – are recognized.

Religious leaders

Prayers in the mosque are led by an *imam*. Any male Muslim can act as an imam, but there are usually professional imams attached to mosques and they may also preach, teach and conduct marriages and funerals. The word 'imam' can also be used to mean the leader of all the Muslims. After Muhammad's death, the Sunni Muslims used the word in this way, but no longer have such a leader. The Shiite sects have varying beliefs about the imam as head of the community, but stress the importance of his spiritual leadership. Scholars of religion provide guidance for the community in matters of theology and the Holy Law. Among the Twelver Shiites the senior theologians, known in Iran as *ayatollahs*, exercise great authority in the absence of the Imam. The title of *mullah*, also used in Iran, is a general term for a Shiite religious scholar.

Sufism is the name given to the mystical movement in Islam. Sufi *shaikhs* provide leadership for their followers in the mystical brotherhoods, guiding the initiates on their spiritual journey. In some areas of the Islamic world, for example in parts of West Africa, they remain a powerful influence.

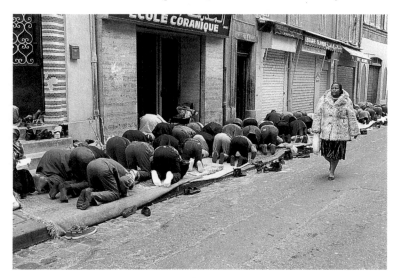

Muslims at prayer in a street in Marseille, France. Migration from North Africa, the Indian subcontinent, Turkey and the former Yugoslavia – as well as a small but growing number of conversions – has increased the Muslim population of Western Europe. There are estimated to be 2 500 000 followers of Islam in France, over 1 800 000 in Germany and at least 1 300 000 in the UK. (Gamma)

WOMEN AND ISLAM

The status of women in Muslim countries is changing rapidly. A man is allowed up to four wives, but this is rare nowadays and most men have only one. Traditionally, a man can divorce his wife by saying three times that he intends to divorce her, but she cannot divorce him. However, reform in the law in some countries now allows a woman to divorce her husband in some circumstances – for example, if he takes another wife after writing in their marriage contract that she would be his only wife.

Some women wear strict Islamic dress covering all parts of the body, including face, hands and hair. Others allow just their face and hands to show, and some wear modest Western dress, keeping Islamic dress for attendance at the mosque and prayers at home. These variations can even be seen within one family. Many younger married women work, and some run their own companies or have attained senior positions in government.

THE PILLARS OF ISLAM

Certain essential religious duties, described as the 'Five Pillars', are intended to develop the spirit of submission to God. They are:

Profession of the faith. 'There is no god but God, and Muhammad is God's messenger' is the fundamental creed of Islam.

Prayer. The act of worship is performed five times a day – at dawn, midday, mid-afternoon, sunset and before bed. After washing themselves, Muslims face in the direction of Mecca and pray communally at the mosque or individually in any place that is ritually clean, often using a prayer rug. Each prayer consists of a set number of 'bowings', for example, two at dawn, four at midday. The 'bowing' is composed of a prescribed succession of movements, in which the worshipper stands, bows, kneels with forehead to the ground, and sits back on the haunches. Recitations in Arabic, mostly words of praise and verses of the Qur'an, accompany each movement. Attendance at the mosque is not compulsory, but men are required to go to the special congregational prayers held every Friday at noon. For women, all attendance is optional. The mosque also has an educational role, and teaching ranges from advanced theology to religious instruction for children.

Almsgiving. An offering, known as *zakat*, is given by those Muslims with sufficient means as a yearly charitable donation.

Fasting. Muslims fast from shortly before sunrise until sunset every day during the Islamic month of Ramadan, the month in which they believe the Qur'an was first revealed. The person fasting may not eat, drink or smoke. However, there are several categories of people who are exempted from the Ramadan fast, including the elderly, the sick and children.

Pilgrimage. Pilgrimage to Mecca (the *hajj*) is to be undertaken at least once in a lifetime by every Muslim who can afford it. The pilgrimage takes place every year in the Islamic month of Dhu'l-Hijja. The ceremonies begin at Mecca with the pilgrims walking seven times round the cube-shaped building called the Kaaba – for Muslims the most ancient house of worship of the One God. Other observances follow in Mecca and its vicinity, ending with the Great Feast, when goats, sheep and camels are sacrificed.

Jihad. Jihad (c> p. 240) is sometimes regarded as another pillar of the faith. It means 'striving' and is commonly used to describe the duty of waging 'holy wars' to spread Islam or to defend Islamic lands. It may also be used to mean the struggle for spiritual improvement.

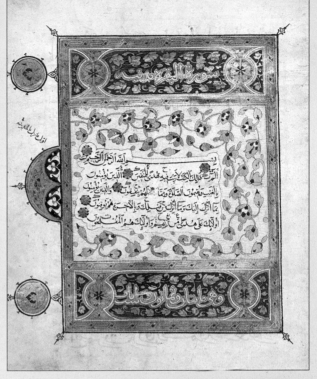

A 14th-century copy of the Qur'an. The Qur'an is divided into 114 *surahs* ('chapters') of unequal length. The first surah is a short opening prayer; the remaining surahs are arranged according to length, beginning with the longest. As many of the first surahs revealed to the Prophet are among the shortest, much of the Qur'an is in reverse chronological order. (AKG)

The sects of Islam

The *Sunnis*, who form about 90% of Muslims, are known more fully as 'the People of the Sunna and Collectivity'. Their name derives from their claim to follow the *sunna* or 'trodden path' (the name given to the words and actions of Muhammad and his first four successors), and also from their claim to adhere to the ways of the 'collectivity' of Muslims.

The *Shiite* sects originated in a dispute as to who should head the Islamic community after the Prophet's death. Supporters of his cousin and son-in-law, Ali, became known as the *Shiat Ali* or 'Party of Ali'. All Shiites recognize lines of Ali's descendants as imams. They are divided into three main subsects.

The first of the Shiite subsects consists of the *Zaidis*, who differ little from Sunni Muslims, but recognize a line of imams possessing no supernatural qualities. The Zaidi imams ruled Yemen until their overthrow in 1962.

The majority of Shiites are *Twelvers* or *Imamis*. This subsect forms most of the population of Iran, with considerable numbers in Iraq, Lebanon, Pakistan and India. They recognize twelve imams, the last of whom disappeared in AD 878 and is expected by them to return as the *Mahdi*, a Messiah-like figure who will usher in an age of justice before the end of the world. The Twelvers regard the imams as perfect and sinless, partaking of divine qualities through the emanation into them of the Divine Light. In modern times the title 'imam' has also been given to other major religious leaders of the Twelvers, such as Imam Khomeini of Iran.

The last main Shiite subsect is formed by the *Ismailis*, who recognize a continuing line of infallible imams descended from Ismail, the eldest son of the sixth Twelver imam. The doctrines of the Ismailis are strongly influenced by neoplatonic and Indian thought, introduced especially in their interpretation of the Qur'an, in which they saw inner truths different from the external meanings. The Fatimid caliphs of Egypt (c> p. 240) were Ismailis. Modern branches are the Khojas, led by the Aga Khan (mainly in India and East Africa), and the Bohras of India and Yemen.

Life under the Holy Law

Islamic law is called the *Sharia*, the 'highway' along which God commands the Muslims to walk. The scope of the Sharia is wider than that of Western secular law and covers all aspects of life. Religious duties are specified in detailed regulations for performing prayer, pilgrimage, etc. Punishments are laid down for certain offences, for example, the amputation of a hand for theft, 80 lashes for drinking alcohol. Family organization is determined by laws dealing with marriage, divorce, custody of children and inheritance.

SEE ALSO

● ANCIENT ROME p. 233
● THE SUCCESSORS OF ROME p. 241
● CHRISTIANITY RESURGENT p. 244
● MEDIEVAL AND RENAISSANCE CULTURE p. 248
● THE REFORMATION p. 250
● JUDAISM p. 294
● PHILOSOPHY p. 302

Philosophy

The word 'philosophy' is derived from the Greek, meaning 'love of wisdom'. Broadly speaking, 'philosophy' can be taken to mean any questioning of or reflection upon the principles underlying all knowledge and existence. Philosophy differs from religion since its quest for underlying causes and principles does not depend on dogma and faith; and it differs from science, since it does not depend solely on fact. Its interrelation with both science and religion can be seen in the large number of philosophers who were also either theologians or scientists, and the few who were all three.

SEE ALSO

● HISTORY OF SCIENCE p. 48
● THE BRAIN AND NERVOUS SYSTEM p. 146
● LEARNING, CREATIVITY AND INTELLIGENCE p. 148
● POLITICAL IDEOLOGIES p. 168
● CIVIL AND HUMAN RIGHTS p. 182
● WHAT IS RELIGION? p. 284
● MAJOR PHILOSOPHERS p. 304

Philosophy developed from religion, but became distinct when thinkers sought truth independent of theological considerations. Until the 19th century the term 'philosophy' was used to include what we now distinguish as 'science'. Eventually all the branches of science, from physics to psychology, broke away. Philosophy is traditionally divided into three sectors: ethics, metaphysics and epistemology.

Ethics

Ethics is the study of how we should decide how people ought to live and act. Philosophers' opinions about ethics tend to resolve into an opposition between two main schools: the idealists and the utilitarians. The *idealists* consider that the goodness or badness of a course of action must be judged by standards derived from outside the everyday world: from God, or heaven, or from a human higher self. The *utilitarians* hold that the effects that a course of action produces in this world are all that is relevant to its ethical value.

The Idealist school began with the Greek philosopher Plato, who wrote in the 4th century BC. Plato, in a series of dialogues, depicts his former teacher Socrates discussing the problems of philosophy with friends and opponents. In the dialogues, Socrates' procedure is to draw out wisdom from those with whom he is discussing the question. He rarely makes a statement of his own – rather he asks questions that compel others either to discover the truth for themselves or else to appear foolish.

Leibniz in the garden of the ruler of Hannover's Herrenhausen Palace demonstrating that no two leaves are alike. Leibniz was a historian and political adviser to the Hannoverian dynasty. As well as being an influental philosopher, he was also a scientist and mathematician who worked on windmills, submarines, clocks and hydraulic presses, and independently invented differential and integral calculus. (AKG)

In these dialogues, especially the *Republic*, the *Protagoras*, the *Phaedo* and the *Gorgias*, Plato developed a system of ethics that is essentially idealistic. Plato argued that the good comes from the realm of 'Ideas' or 'Forms'. This is a perfect world of which the world of ordinary experience is only a pale replica. For Plato, individual conduct is good in so far as it is governed by the form or idea of the good, which is to be discovered only after a thorough philosophical education.

Another important work that has to be classed as idealist is Aristotle's *Nicomachean Ethics*. Aristotle was a pupil of Plato and he also thought of the good as divine, but his ethics had a more practical bent. He equated happiness with the good and was responsible for the doctrine of the *golden mean*. This stated that every virtue is a middle-point between two vices. Generosity, for instance, is the mean between prodigality and stinginess. The same tendency to give idealism a practical turn is found in the works of the 18th-century philosopher Immanuel Kant. The most famous part of Kant's ethics is that connected with the phrase 'categorical imperative'. In Kant's own words: 'Act only according to a maxim of which you can at the same time will that it shall become a general law.' In other words, before acting in a certain way, the individual must ask himself: 'Would I wish everyone to behave like this?'

The utilitarians are more directly concerned than the idealists with earthly welfare. The earliest Western philosopher in this tradition was Epicurus, a Greek of the 4th century BC. Instead of deriving ideas of right and wrong from transcendant ideals, Epicurus maintained that 'we call pleasure the beginning and end of the blessed life'. The term *epicurean* is often used to describe one who indulges in excessive pleasure, but this usage is not just. Epicurus did not condone excesses. On the contrary, he said that pleasure was only good when moderate and calm.

The utilitarian tradition has on the whole had more adherents than the idealistic tradition in modern philosophy. Jeremy Bentham, for example, writing in the 18th century, acknowledged his debt to Epicurus. Bentham agreed that pain and pleasure were the 'sovereign masters' governing human conduct. He added to this a doctrine of utility, which argued that 'the greatest happiness of the greatest number is the measure of right and wrong'. John Stuart Mill is perhaps the most famous of the utilitarians. He extended Bentham's doctrines by arguing that 'some kinds of pleasure are more valuable than others'. This doctrine is explained in his essay *Utilitarianism*.

Metaphysics

The term 'metaphysics' originated as the title of one of Aristotle's treatises. 'Metaphysics' initially covered philosophy as a whole, but eventually the term was restricted to that branch of the subject concerned with speculation as to the ultimate nature of reality, what sort of things exist and how they are related. Metaphysics is concerned with the meaning, structure and principles of reality as a whole. It is, therefore, highly theoretical, and its inquiries are rooted in reason rather than in observation. Arguments concerning the existence of an immortal soul, free will, a life force, or a creator of the universe are central metaphysical problems.

Epistemology

Epistemology is the study of the nature, grounds and validity of human knowledge – how we come to know; how far we can rely on different kinds of belief; how science can be separated from superstition; and how conflicts between rival scientific theories can be resolved. Those epistemologists who are usually called *rationalists* assert that knowledge is inherent in reason and has only to be drawn forth. By contrast, *empiricism* holds that at birth the mind is a passive blank sheet on which knowledge is then imprinted by experience. The Rationalist school is represented classically by Plato, who discussed various theories of knowledge and discarded those built on the shifting sands of sense perception. The senses are, he thought, too fallible. True knowledge comes from general notions derived from the realm of the Forms or Ideas, which the soul possesses prior to birth.

The 17th-century French philosopher René Descartes, although not a Platonist, was a rationalist in that he regarded sensory knowledge as a bad foundation for science. Its certainty, he argued, could never equal that of mathematics or of our own knowledge of our thoughts. This inalienable certainty is expressed in his famous statement 'I think therefore I am': however deep my doubt, I must exist in order to doubt. The classic representative of Empiricism was John Locke (1632–1704). Locke defined an opposite point of view to Plato and Descartes. He regarded the mind at birth as comparable to an empty cabinet. As we live, 'experience' fills it with 'ideas' either of our inner states (*ideas of reflection*) or of external objects (*ideas of sensation*). He argued that human knowledge could never get beyond the limits of such ideas.

Modern philosophy

The main movements of modern philosophy – Hegelianism, analytic philosophy, and phenomenology – would regard the division of the subject into metaphysics, ethics and epistemology as outmoded.

Hegelianism is derived from the theories of Georg Wilhelm Friedrich Hegel, who, at the beginning of the 19th century, criticized all previous conceptions of philosophy as being lifeless, one-sided and unhistorical. Hegel proposed that philosophy is always rooted in history, but at the same time always strives for a conception of reality as a single developing whole, every part of which is animated by all the others.

The movement known as *analytic philosophy* was founded at the beginning of the 20th century by Bertrand Russell, building on the work of Gottlob Frege. Analytic philosophy – which, like Hegelianism, is highly critical of philosophical tradition – is based on the idea that authentic philosophy is essentially the study of logic, that is to say of formal patterns of reasoning abstracted from their metaphysical, ethical, epistemological or historical contexts. Ludwig Wittgenstein, who studied with Russell, has been a major influence on 20th-century British philosophers. He produced two systems of philosophical thought exploring the relationship of language to the world.

At about the same time as the foundation of analytic philosophy, the German philosopher Edmund Husserl established *phenomenology*. The phenomenological movement has come to dominate 20th-century European philosophy just as the analytic school has dominated philosophy in the English-speaking world. This movement claims that philosophers always tend to miss the one fundamental question – why our experience should be framed in terms of a distinction between an objective world and our subjective experience of it. Heidegger and Derrida have developed this line of thought by arguing that, so far from trying to build on past philosophy, we should attempt to 'destroy' or 'deconstruct' it.

PHILOSOPHICAL SCHOOLS AND THEORIES

Since the days of the early Greeks, philosophers have been divided into different schools and have advanced opposing theories, including:

absolutism the theory that truth is absolute and universal.

altruism the principle of living and acting in the interest of others rather than for oneself.

analytic philosophy ⟡ main text, Modern Philosophy.

asceticism the belief that withdrawal from the physical world into the inner world of the spirit is the highest good attainable.

atomism the belief that the entire universe is ultimately composed of interchangeable indivisible units.

critical theory a philosophical version of Marxism associated with the Frankfurt School (founded 1921).

criticism the theory that the path to knowledge lies midway between dogmatism and scepticism.

determinism the belief that the universe and everything in it (including individual lives) follows a fixed or pre-determined pattern.

dialectical materialism the theory that reality is strictly material and is based on an economic struggle between opposing forces.

dogmatism the assertion of a belief without arguments in its support.

dualism the belief that the world consists of two radically independent and absolute elements, e.g. good and evil, or (especially) spirit and matter.

egoism the belief that serving one's own interests is the highest good.

empiricism the doctrine that there is no knowledge except that which is derived from experience.

existentialism the doctrine that the human self and human values are fictions, but inevitable ones, and that it is bad faith to deny one's own free will, even in a deterministic universe.

fatalism the doctrine that what will happen will happen and nothing we can do will make any difference.

hedonism the doctrine that pleasure is the highest good.

humanism any system that regards human interests and the human mind as paramount in the universe.

idealism any system that regards thought or the idea as the basis of knowledge or existence.

interactionism the theory that physical events can cause mental events, and vice versa.

materialism the doctrine that asserts the existence of only one substance – matter – thus denying the existence of spirit.

monism a belief in only one ultimate reality, whatever its nature.

naturalism a position that seeks to explain all phenomena by means of strictly natural (as opposed to supernatural) categories.

nominalism the doctrine that general terms are, in effect, nothing more than words. Compare realism.

operationalism the doctrine that scientific concepts are tools for prediction rather than descriptions of hidden realities.

pantheism the belief that God is identical with the universe.

personalism the theory that ultimate reality consists of a plurality of spiritual beings or independent persons.

phenomenology ⟡ main text, Modern Philosophy.

pluralism the belief that there are more than two irreducible kinds of reality.

positivism the doctrine that there is no knowledge outside science.

pragmatism a philosophical method that makes practical consequences the test of truth.

predestination the doctrine that the events of a human's life are ordained beforehand.

rationalism the theory that reason alone, without the aid of experience, can arrive at truth.

realism the doctrine that general terms have a real existence. Compare nominalism.

relativism the rejection of the concept of absolute and invariable truths.

scepticism the doctrine that nothing can be known with certainty.

sensationalism the theory that sensations are the ultimate and real components of the world.

stoicism a philosophical school that believed that reason (God) was the basis of the universe and that humanity should live in harmony with nature.

structuralism the doctrine that language is essentially a system of rules; or the extension of this idea to culture as a whole.

theism the belief in a God.

transcendentalism the belief in an ultimate reality that transcends human experience.

utilitarianism ⟡ main text.

voluntarism the theory that will is a determining factor in the universe.

PHILOSOPHERS AND THEIR THEORIES

THE ANCIENT WORLD

Thales of Miletus (624–550 BC), Greek. An exponent of monism, he is regarded as the first Western philosopher.

Anaximander of Miletus (611–547 BC), Greek. He continued Thales' quest for universal substance, but reasoned that universal substance need not resemble any known substances.

Heraclitus of Ephesus (533–475 BC), Greek. He opposed the concept of a single ultimate reality and held that the only permanent thing is change.

Empedocles of Acragas (c. 495–435 BC), Greek. He believed that there were four irreducible substances (water, fire, earth and air) and two forces (love and hate).

Parmenides of Elea (c. 495 BC), Greek. A member of the Eleatic school, he formulated the basic doctrine of idealism.

Zeno of Elea (c. 495–430 BC), Greek. He argued that plurality and change are appearances, not realities.

Protagoras of Abdera (481–411 BC), Greek. An early relativist and humanist, he doubted human ability to attain absolute truth.

Socrates (c. 470–399 BC), Greek. He developed the Socratic method of enquiry (⊳ main text, Ethics). Socrates was the teacher of Plato, through whose writings his idealistic philosophy was disseminated.

Democritus of Abdera (460–370 BC), Greek. He began the tradition in Western thought of explaining the universe in mechanistic terms. He believed that all matter was made up of tiny indivisible particles called atoms.

Antisthenes (c. 450–c. 360 BC), Greek. The chief of the group known as the Cynics, he stressed discipline and work as the essential good.

Plato (c. 428–347 BC), Greek. The founder of the Academy at Athens, he developed the idealism of his teacher Socrates and was the teacher of Aristotle. (⊳ also main text.)

Aristotle tutored Alexander the Great for three years. Aristotle taught his Macedonian pupil to model himself on the classical Greek hero. He stressed the importance of philosophy and urged Alexander to dominate the non-Greeks. Relations between the two men were soured by Alexander's execution of Aristotle's nephew, Callistenes of Olynthus. After the death of Alexander, the philosopher fell victim to an anti-Macedonian campaign and was accused of impiety. Certain of condemnation, he withdrew from the city and died the following year. (AR)

Aristotle (384–322 BC), Greek philosopher and scientist, whose works have influenced the whole of Western philosophy. Aristotle taught that there are four factors in causation: form; matter; motive cause, which produces change; and the end, for which a process of change occurs. (⊳ also main text.)

Pyrrho of Elis (c. 365–275 BC), Greek. He initiated the sceptical school of philosophy. Pyrrho believed that man could not know anything for certain.

Epicurus (341–270 BC), Greek. A proponent of atomism (⊳ Democritus, above) and hedonism, he taught that the test of truth is in sensation.

Zeno of Citium (c. 335–263 BC), Greek. Chief of the stoics – so called because they met in the *Stoa Poikile* or Painted Porch at Athens. Zeno taught that man's role is to accept nature and all it offers, good or bad.

Plotinus (AD 205–270), Roman. The chief exponent of neo-Platonism, an interpretation of the teachings of Plato that was later to be blended with Christian ideas.

St Augustine of Hippo (AD 354–430), North African. One of the greatest influences on medieval Christian thought, Augustine believed that God transcends human comprehension.

Boethius (c. AD 480–524), late Roman statesman. In *The Consolations of Philosophy* Boethius proposed that virtue alone is constant.

THE MIDDLE AGES

Avicenna (980–1037), Arabic follower of Aristotle and neo-Platonism whose works revived interest in Aristotle in 13th-century Europe.

Anselm (1033–1109), Italian Augustinian and realist who was famous for his purported proof of God's existence.

Peter Abelard (1079–1142), French theologian and philosopher whose nominalism antagonized the Church.

Averroës (1126–98), a great philosopher of Muslim Spain, and a leading commentator on Aristotle. Averroës regarded religion as allegory for the common man and philosophy as the path to truth.

Maimonides (1135–1204), Jewish student of Aristotle who sought to combine Aristotelian teaching with that of the Bible.

St Thomas Aquinas (1225–74), Italian scholastic philosopher who evolved a compromise between Aristotle and Scripture, based on the belief that faith and reason are in agreement. His philosophical system is known as Thomism.

THE EARLY MODERN PERIOD

Desiderius Erasmus (1466–1536), Dutch. The greatest of the humanists, he helped spread the ideas of the Renaissance throughout northern Europe.

Niccolò Machiavelli (1469–1527), Italian. Machiavelli placed the state as the paramount power in human affairs. His book *The Prince* brought him a reputation for amoral cynicism.

Francis Bacon (1561–1626), English statesman and philosopher of science. In his major work, *Novum Organum*, Bacon sought to revive the inductive system of logic in interpreting nature.

Thomas Hobbes (1588–1679), English materialist who believed the natural state of man is war. In *Leviathan* Hobbes outlined a theory of human government whereby the state and man's subordination to it form the sole solution to human selfishness (⊳ p. 166).

René Descartes (1596–1650), French dualist, rationalist and theist whose 'Cartesian' system is the base of much modern philosophy. Descartes evolved a theory of knowledge that underlies modern science and philosophy, based on the certainty of the proposition 'I think, therefore I am' (⊳ main text).

Blaise Pascal (1623–62), French theist who held that sense and reason are mutually deceptive, that truth lies between dogmatism and scepticism.

Benedict de Spinoza (1632–77), Dutch rationalist metaphysician who developed the ideas of Descartes while rejecting his dualism.

John Locke (1632–1704), English empiricist whose influence in political, religious, educational and philosophical thought was wide and deep (⊳ p. 166). In his great *Essay Concerning Human Understanding* he sought to refute the rationalist view that knowledge derives from innate principles of reason.

Gottfried Wilhelm von Leibniz (1646–1716), German idealist and absolutist whose optimism was ridiculed by Voltaire in *Candide*. Leibniz held that reality consisted of units of force called monads.

George Berkeley (1685–1753), Anglo-Irish idealist and theist who taught that things exist only in being perceived and that the very idea of matter is contradictory.

David Hume (1711–76), Scottish empiricist, philosopher and historian who developed the ideas of Locke into a system of scepticism. According to Hume, human knowledge is limited to the experience of ideas and sensations whose truth cannot be verified.

Jean-Jacques Rousseau (1712–78), French social and political philosopher who advocated a 'return to nature' to counteract the inequality brought about by civilized society.

Immanuel Kant (1724–1804), German founder of Critical Philosophy. At first influenced by Leibniz, then by Hume, Kant sought an alternative approach to the rationalism of the former and the scepticism of the latter. In ethics, he formulated the 'categorical imperative', which states that what applies to oneself must apply to everyone else unconditionally.

Jeremy Bentham (1748–1832), English utilitarian who, like Kant, believed that the interests of the individual are at one with those of society. He regarded pleasure and pain rather than basic principle as the motivation for right action.

Johann Gottlieb Fichte (1762–1814), German. Fichte formulated a philosophy of absolute idealism based on Kant's ethical concepts.

THE 19th CENTURY

Georg Wilhelm Friedrich Hegel (1770–1831), German. His metaphysical system was rationalist, historicist and absolutist, based on the belief that thought and being are one, and nature is the manifestation of an Absolute Idea (⊳ main text).

Arthur Schopenhauer (1788–1860), German idealist who gave the will a leading place in his metaphysics. The foremost expounder of pessimism, he rejected absolute idealism as wishful thinking, and taught that the only tenable attitude lay in utter indifference to an irrational world. He held that the highest ideal was nothingness.

Auguste Comte (1798–1857), French founder of positivism, a system which denied transcendent metaphysics and stated that the Divinity and man were one, that altruism is man's highest duty, and that scientific principles explain all phenomena.

Ludwig Feuerbach (1804–72), German. Feuerbach argued that religion was no more than a projection of human nature. He was an important influence on Marx.

John Stuart Mill (1806–73), English exponent of utilitarianism who differed from Bentham by recognizing differences in quality as well as quantity in pleasure. His most famous work is *On Liberty* (1859).

Søren Kierkegaard (1813–55), Danish religious existentialist whose thought is the basis of modern (atheistic) existentialism. He taught that only existence has reality, and that the individual has a unique value.

Karl Marx (1818–83), German revolutionary thinker who, with Friedrich Engels, was the founder of modern Communism. Marx (⊳ also p. 168) was a critical follower of Hegel.

Herbert Spencer (1820–1903), English evolutionist whose 'synthetic philosophy' interpreted all phenomena according to the principle of evolutionary progress (⊳ p. 84).

Charles S. Peirce (1839–1914), American physicist, mathematician and founder of the philosophical school called pragmatism. Peirce regarded logic as the basis of philosophy and taught that the test of a belief is whether it works.

William James (1842–1910), American psychologist and pragmatist who held that reality is always in the making and that each man should choose the philosophy best suited to him.

Friedrich Wilhelm Nietzsche (1844–1900), German. Nietzsche held that the 'will to power' is basic in life and that the spontaneous is to be preferred to the orderly. He attacked Christianity as a system that fostered the weak, whereas the highest value belonged to the 'overman' or 'superman'.

Nietzsche was an outstanding poet and novelist as well as being one of the most influential modern philosophers. Forced by ill health to resign a university post in Switzerland in 1879, he spent the following decade writing his major works at the rate of one book a year. His creative life was ended by a mental breakdown in 1889. After his death in 1900, Nietzsche's sister, Elizabeth Förster, deliberately misrepresented his thought for nationalist and anti-Semitic purposes. (AR)

THE 20th CENTURY

Gottlob Frege (1848–1925), German mathematician who revolutionized formal logic and thus paved the way for analytic philosophy.

Henri Bergson (1859–1941), French evolutionist who asserted the existence of a 'vital impulse' that carries the universe forward, with no fixed beginning and no fixed end. He believed that the future is determined by the choice of alternatives made in the present.

John Dewey (1859–1952), American pragmatist who developed a system known as instrumentalism. He saw man as continuous with, but distinct from, nature.

Edmund Husserl (1859–1938), German founder of phenomenology. He sought to ground knowledge in pure experience without presuppositions.

Alfred North Whitehead (1861–1947), British evolutionist and mathematician who held that reality must not be interpreted in atomistic terms, but in terms of process. He held that God is intimately present in the universe – a view called pantheism.

Benedetto Croce (1866–1952), Italian. Croce was noted for his role in the revival of historical realism.

Bertrand Russell (1872–1970), British agnostic who adhered to many systems of philosophy before expounding logical positivism – the view that scientific knowledge is the only factual knowledge.

George Edward Moore (1873–1958), British moral philosopher who developed the doctrine of ideal utilitarianism.

Martin Heidegger (1889–1976), German student of Husserl who furthered the development of phenomenology and greatly influenced atheistic existentialists.

Gabriel Marcel (1889–1973), French. Initially a student of the English-speaking idealists, Marcel was preoccupied with the Cartesian problem of the relation of mind and matter.

Ludwig Wittgenstein (1889–1951), Austrian. The most influential philosopher of the 20th century, Wittgenstein developed two highly original but incompatible systems of philosophy, both dominated by a concern with the relations between language and the world (⊳ main text).

Herbert Marcuse (1898–1979), German-American philosopher who attempted to combine existentialism and psychoanalysis with a libertarian Marxism that was critical of Communism.

Gilbert Ryle (1900–76), British. Ryle studied the nature of philosophy and the concept of mind as well as the nature of meaning and the philosophy of logic.

Sir Karl Popper (1902–), British critical rationalist who held that scientific laws can never be proved to be true and that the most that can be claimed is that they have survived attempts to disprove them.

Theodor Adorno (1903–69), German philosopher who combined Marxism with avant-garde aesthetics.

Jean-Paul Sartre (1905–80), an influential French philosopher who developed the existentialist thought of Heidegger. An atheistic supporter of a subjective, irrational human existence, his slogan was 'existence before essence'.

Maurice Merleau-Ponty (1907–61), French phenomenologist who insisted on the role of the human body in our experience of the world.

Simone de Beauvoir (1908–86), French existentialist who founded modern feminist philosophy.

Claude Lévi-Strauss (1908–), French anthropologist and proponent of structuralism whose writings investigate the relationship between culture (exclusively an attribute of humanity) and nature, based on the distinguishing characteristics of man – the ability to communicate in a language.

Willard van Orman Quine (1908–), American philosopher who combined pragmatism with logical positivism and destroyed many of the dogmas of early analytic philosophy.

Sir Isaiah Berlin (1909–), British moral and political philosopher and historian who emphasized the importance of moral values, and the necessity of rejecting determinism if the ideas of human responsibility and freedom are to be retained.

Alfred J. Ayer (1910–89), British. Ayer was the principal advocate of logical positivism, developed from Russell.

Donald Davidson (1917–), American philosopher of language, and a follower of Quine.

Jurgen Habermas (1929–), German. Habermas is a critical Marxist with strong Kantian and liberal affinities.

Jacques Derrida (1930–), French founder of deconstruction, a development of Heidegger's technique of interpreting traditional philosophers with great care in order to reveal their constant incoherence.

Greek and Roman Art

The arts of Greece and Rome are characterized by a sense of proportion, harmony and balance. Since the Renaissance, Classical decoration, whether ornate or simple, has frequently provided architects with a fruitful source of ideas, and Classical imagery has enriched the work of poets, painters and sculptors. In general, Classical form has exerted a largely civilizing influence over the past two and a half millennia.

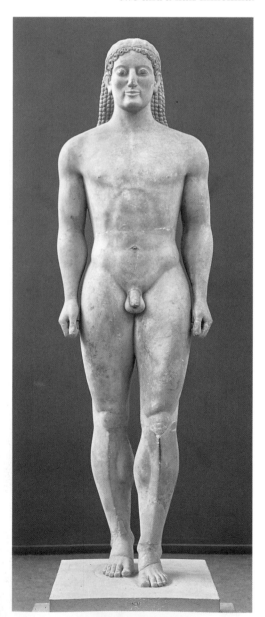

Marble kouros of Archaic Greece. Derived from Egyptian examples, the naked youths were typically carved in a walking position with clenched fists. (AAAC)

This influence has been achieved in part by the surviving architecture, sculpture and ceramics (which have been surveyed, collected and catalogued with mixed success since the 18th century), and in part by the writings of ancient Roman scholars. Among these scholars were Vitruvius (1st century BC), whose writings on architecture inspired Palladio (▷ p. 326) in the 16th century; and Philostratus (?2nd/3rd century AD), to whom Mantegna and Rubens looked for their knowledge of the lost works of the Greek painters Apelles and Zeuxis.

The concentration on what has survived, and the elevation of some of it to the first rank of artistic excellence in modern eyes, have tended to obscure the fact that we now possess very little of what ancient Greeks and Romans might have considered to be artistically important. Although today even fragments of Greek pots, for example, are highly valued, the Greeks and Romans themselves were more materialistic, and tended rather to appreciate highly wrought works in gold and silver. Since articles of precious metal were the first to be seized or melted down in times of war or hardship, such works have virtually all vanished, but contemporary accounts of shrines and temples, as well as of the houses of rich individuals, speak of great amounts of sculpture and vases made of gold and silver, and it was in these media that eminent craftsmen preferred to work.

The Archaic period

What remains of Archaic Greek art (of the 6th and early 5th centuries BC) consists mostly of marble and pottery, with a little bronze. Luxury arts are represented by seals cut in semiprecious stones, jewellery, and coins. Apart from the silver ox at Delphi, perhaps the most impressive surviving object of the period is the huge (1.64 m / 5 ft 5 in high) Vix crater (a wine-mixing bowl). The figurine of a woman on the lid and the warriors on the frieze on the neck display the famous 'archaic smile' – Lucian's 'holy and forgetful' smile – that characterized much Archaic sculpture well into the 5th century. We are used to seeing it on the anonymous marble *kouroi* (youths) and *korai* (maidens) that have survived in considerable numbers, or on the painted decoration of archaic Greek pottery.

If, however, we consider the artefacts thought worthy of note by contemporaries, we get a rather different picture. One of the most sought-after artists in the 6th century was Theodore of Samos. He made a gold wine crater and a vine set with jewels for the bedroom of Darius, the king of Persia. He made the ring of the tyrant Polycrates, and a silver bowl that was among the gifts sent by Croesus, king of Lydia, to Delphi. Other gifts included a statue of a woman in gold, 1.8 m (6 ft) high. This object may have been of solid gold, but it was more usual for temple sculpture to be of wood or marble covered with gold sheathing. Thus a statue of Apollo at Sparta was considered to be unfinished until it was gilded. A statue stolen by a Persian from Delos in 490 is said to have been covered with gold, and the same is true of one of the earliest statues carved in Greek marble presented by an Egyptian pharaoh to a temple at Lindos in the mid-6th century BC. The practice seems to have had its origins in the Near East, and continues today in the modern Greek custom of covering icons with precious metal.

The Classical period

In the Classical period (5th and 4th centuries BC) there is again a marked discrepancy between

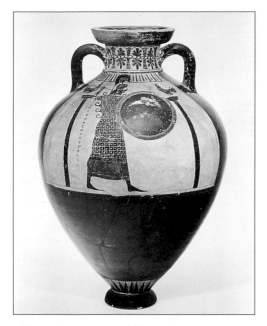

Black and red pottery of Classical Greece, painted by Exekias (fl. c. 550–525 BC), one of Greece's finest painters.
(AKG/Badisches Landesmuseum, Karlsruhe)

what there is and what we know there was. The marble sculpture that once adorned the Parthenon in Athens is rightly regarded as exemplifying the Classical ideal, but it is frequently forgotten that it only cost about 4% of the total cost of the building, and that 50% went on Phidias' gold and ivory cult-figure of Athena Parthenos. More than 10 m (33 ft) high, and incorporating gold worth some $20 million at today's prices, this and Phidias' other great masterpiece, the Zeus at Olympia, are what the Greeks would have considered to be the greatest works of their time. The Zeus was still being tended by Phidias' descendants in the 2nd century AD, but was stripped of its precious metal by the first Christian emperor, Constantine, and its remains taken to Constantinople, where they were destroyed by fire in the 5th century. However, the image of a majestic seated and bearded deity survived, and was adopted by Byzantine Greek artists as the model for Christ Pantocrator (Christ had hitherto been shown beardless), thus providing the basis for a potent image that has lasted until today.

Painted pottery appears prominently in today's picture of Classical Greece, but its role in antiquity is currently being reassessed. Most of it comes from the graves of rich Etruscans, who seem to have had the pots as substitutes for silver table vessels. Black and red pottery evokes the appearance of vases of patinated ('oxidized') silver decorated with gold-figure ornament. The imagery preserves something of the imagery on the few pieces of Classical plate that have escaped the melting pot. Of the major Classical paintings, nothing survives except awestruck contemporary accounts of the ability of the greatest painters to mimic nature. Classical paintings presented an idealized vision of the past, retold in the light of the Greeks' recent victories over the Persians. Allegory in art was another major Greek contribution.

The Hellenistic period

Alexander the Great's conquests (which included the capture of 4680 tons of gold and silver from the Persians) led to an emphasis on the aggrandizement of the ruler, rather than that of the city-state. There was even a plan to carve the Athos peninsula (some 32 km / 20 mi long) in the shape of a reclining Alexander. Alexandria in Egypt, Antioch in Syria, and Pergamon in western Asia Minor (modern Turkey) were major artistic centres. The Great Altar of Zeus from Pergamon (now in Berlin) gives us some idea of Hellenistic splendour. The 'Tazza Farnese' (now in Naples) is one of the few pieces of court art of the period to have survived. The red mould-made pottery reflects the use of gold vessels on the tables of the rich.

Roman art

Rome was the successor to all of this. Republican simplicity gave way to the flamboyant luxury of the Caesars, but once more we only have the husks of a few great buildings, which would once have been covered with exotic marbles and rich mosaics. The frescoes and mosaics from Pompeii and Herculaneum are but a pale reflection. Sculptors were commissioned to make portraits of the emperor that would be set up throughout the Empire, and to decorate public monuments such as Trajan's Column or the Arch of Constantine with idealized renditions of imperial triumphs and expressions of official propaganda. Occasional finds, such as the Hildesheim Treasure, give us an idea of the great artistry that went into the production of gold and silver plate. Glass has survived in some quantity, but it was rarely a luxury item, and pottery never was. Arretine pottery does, however, preserve something of the appearance of lost work in gold.

SEE ALSO

● ANCIENT GREECE p. 230
● ANCIENT ROME p. 232
● ANCIENT RELIGIONS p. 286
● RENAISSANCE ART p. 312
● ARCHITECTURE p. 326
● CLASSICAL LITERATURE p. 356

Seven actors backstage, a Roman mosaic from Pompeii. (AKG/National Archaeological Museum, Naples)

Non-Western Art

The arts of the non-Western world have the oldest histories in the world. As in the West, religion has played a major part in shaping them. Often underestimated, the technical skill and artistic detail of African, Islamic and Asian art, particularly from China and Japan, is considerable.

SEE ALSO

- CHINA TO THE COLONIAL AGE p. 234
- INDIA AND SOUTHEAST ASIA p. 236
- AFRICA, AUSTRALASIA AND OCEANIA p. 237
- RELIGIONS OF INDIA p. 288
- BUDDHISM p. 290
- RELIGIONS OF CHINA AND JAPAN p. 292
- ISLAM p. 300

Some innovative branches of art in the West owe much to the non-Western world. Picasso (⊳ p. 324) was greatly influenced by African sculpture, believing it to be free of the constraints of naturalism and realism, and Japanese *Ukiyo-e* prints inspired the Post-Impressionist painters (⊳ p. 321).

Islamic art

The word 'Islamic' reflects a culture and society united by Islam (⊳ p. 300), but as artistic influences from Arabia (the birthplace of Islam) were minimal, Islam can in some ways also be seen as a catalyst for the development of existing Byzantine, Persian and later Indian styles that prevailed when the conquering Muslim armies arrived.

The traditional ban on the representation of living figures in a religious context directed Muslim artists towards ornamental styles based on plants and flowers, geometrical shapes, and actual Arabic script. It also accounts for the virtual absence of sculpture. Calligraphy became ornate and decorative, and in turn became closely associated with architecture. In Spain and Persia especially, entire surfaces were often covered with verses from the Qur'an or with sayings of the Prophet.

An extension of calligraphy was book illustration. Initiated by the Mongol Il Khans in Persia, book illustration became the starting point of miniature painting. The miniature reached its peak under the Safavids in Persia and the Moguls in India.

The minor arts of Islam reached maturity under the Abbasids. In pottery the emphasis was on decoration rather than shape. The best surviving metalwork is Iranian silver dishes and ewers, but the dearth of silver in the 11th century made bronze and brass popular. While Iranian metalwork focused on courtly scenes, the Mamluks preferred heraldic statements.

The most important textiles are silks and carpets, the former usually for ceremonial use. The earliest surviving carpets are 13th-century Anatolian. Later carpets are best represented by vivid Safavid scenes of the 16th century.

South Asian art

India's earliest civilization flourished in the Indus Valley between 2300–1700 BC, centred on the cities of Harappa and Mohenjo-Daro. Its architecture was utilitarian, but some fine statues in sandstone and slate were produced. Little survives between the time of the Harappa civilization and that of the Mauryas (321–185 BC), who initiated a revival in sculpture. During their rule Persian and Greek influences are apparent, notably in architecture.

Essentially traditional and religious, Buddhist and Hindu works of art are symbols and manifestations of gods. One of the most distinctive Buddhist architectural forms is the *stupa* – an ornate burial mound. Another distinctly Indian form is the man-made cave, such as the finely carved cave-temples at Ajanta (2nd century BC–7th century AD) and those at Ellora (5th–8th centuries AD). In the 7th century fresco painting and rock sculpture in India had reached a peak and by the 13th century erotic carvings had become popular. With the spread of Islamic influence Indian painters turned to miniatures and book illustration in the Persian style (⊳ above).

Chinese art

China has an art history stretching back at least 4000 years. The distinctiveness of Chinese art has been complemented by very high technical skills, and for many centuries ceramics, bronzes, jade carvings, silk and lacquer were produced at standards surpassing all other cultures.

Under the Shang and Zhou dynasties (1480–221 BC), very sophisticated bronze vessels were manufactured. The art of the Qin and Han dynasties (221 BC – AD 220) was characterized by ceramic tomb sculptures, silk weaving, murals, glazed pottery and lacquering. The introduction of Buddhism (1st century AD) encouraged religious art in China, in particular sculptures of Buddha in stone, marble and gilt bronze.

The Tang dynasty (AD 618–907) was a golden age for Chinese art. Buddhist sculpture was made on a monumental scale. The invention of porcelain (about 1000 years before its discovery in Europe) meant that ceramics became highly prized abroad. Calligraphy and painting, using brush, ink and paper, began to flourish, and landscape painting emerged as an important genre.

Chinese ceramics reached perfection under the Song dynasty (960–1279), but became much more

Hokusai's *Fujiwara Bridge*, an Ukiyo-e print from the Japanese Edo period. (AKG/Staatl. Kupferstichkabinett, Dresden)

An Indian miniature painting (left) showing the Mogul Emperor Babur (c. 1593). (AKG/Guimet Museum, Paris)

elaborate under the Ming (1368–1644), being manufactured in huge industrial complexes. During the Qing dynasty (1644–1911) technical perfection began to take precedence over innovations.

Japanese art

Japanese art has throughout its history borrowed inspiration and techniques from China. However, different requirements and technical skills resulted in a creative originality distinct from that of China. Japanese colour prints and pottery, influenced by Western culture in the 19th century, have in turn been an important influence on 19th- and 20th-century Western art.

In the Heian period (794–1185) Buddhist sculptured figures possess an elegance and mysticism more characteristically Japanese than Chinese. The period also saw the development of a Japanese school of scroll painting combining decorative and narrative features. The Samurai dominated the arts in the Kamakura period (1185–1392), when wooden sculpture became more realistic, and Buddhist painting more emotionally expressive. The horizontal scroll paintings depict historical tales and legends in an animated style with few Chinese precedents.

In the 16th and 17th centuries the demands of the warlords and rising middle classes resulted in lacquer ware, ceramics and textiles, famous for their brilliance of design and technical perfection. The *Ukiyo-e* prints (pictures of the floating world) of the Edo period (1615–1868) were produced by artists such as **Katsushika Hokusai** (1760–1849) and **Kitagawa Utamaro** (1753–1806). They drew their subject matter from the entertainment life of Edo (modern Tokyo), depicting the courtesans and actors of the time. This popular art was mass-produced in coloured woodblock prints. Sculptural art was now often directed towards miniatures such as *netsuke* carving – ornamental toggles used to fasten purses or tobacco pouches to garments – but lacquer ware, often decorated with gold dust, flourished, as did ceramics. By the late 19th century European influence began to transform Japanese art and many of its native traditions had exhausted themselves.

African art

The earliest paintings and engravings in the Sahara may date from c. 6000 BC, and depict giant masked figures, hunters and animals now extinct in the area, such as hippopotamuses and buffalo. The San (Bushman) rock art of South Africa and Namibia may be even more ancient. The tradition continued into the 19th century AD.

The earliest known sculptural tradition of sub-Saharan Africa emerged c. 500 BC in northern Nigeria. Its products are grouped together as the 'Nok culture', and consist of naturalistic terracottas of animals and more stylized terracottas of human figures; the figures often have simplified bodies, disproportionately large heads and distinctive eyes.

Nok sculpture may have influenced the art of the kingdom of Ife in southwest Nigeria (c. AD 1100–1600). The Ife terracottas and bronzes are in the form of realistic, if idealized, heads and figures, some of which may portray local rulers. The famous bronzes of the kingdom of Benin (1500–1700) similarly depict full figures and heads, but include plaques decorated in high and low relief with scenes of warriors, chiefs and Portuguese traders.

Carved wooden masks and sculptures have come to typify African art. Although many of the most famous works were collected in the 19th and early 20th centuries, the tradition is very ancient and persists in certain regions even today. Both masks and figures were created for specific occasions, such as initiation and healing rites, or to communicate with spirits. They tend to face forward and to be symmetrically arranged around a vertical axis. Figures are usually carved from a single piece of wood, while masks are often embellished with beads, feathers, hair or fibre.

Bronze Benin head, from the end of the 17th century. (AKG)

Medieval Art

The period between the Classical Age and the Renaissance has sometimes been described dismissively as the 'Dark Ages'. This is both inaccurate and misleading. These centuries formed an essential artistic bridgehead, when new approaches to pictorial form were worked out and deeper spiritual values attached to works of art.

The art of the early Christians is a branch of late Roman art and it first resembled – in style and subject matter – its pagan counterpart. Because Christians were initially persecuted, it was not until the 4th and 5th centuries that a specifically Christian *iconography* (a vocabulary of images) developed, and scenes from the Old and New Testaments became widespread on the walls of churches and in illuminated manuscripts. The move away from Classical naturalism, already evident in late Roman art, was hastened as more emphasis was given to story-telling and simple iconic images.

BYZANTINE ART

In the early Byzantine Empire the interiors of the major churches – the *basilicas* – were painted or covered in mosaic pictures. The 6th-century Hagia Sophia at Constantinople (now Istanbul) is an outstanding example of the brilliant artistic innovations that flourished under the patronage of the Byzantine emperors. Much of the mosaic decoration in the church is now covered over, but some idea of its former richness is conveyed by the nearly contemporary mosaics in the church of San Vitale in Ravenna.

After a period of iconoclasm (726–843), when all representations of people in religious art were banned in the East, through to the fall of Constantinople to the Turks in 1453, Byzantine art is notable for its continuity. Right across the Empire there was a remarkable similarity of style, which also spread outwards to neighbouring regions, so that similar schemes of mosaic decoration may be seen, for example, in Venice (St Mark's) and Sicily.

The Magi in the 6th-century mosaic from S Apollinare in Classe, Ravenna typifies the stylized Byzantine approach in the depiction of the human figure. (AKG)

Romanesque art

In Western Europe prior to 1000 some of the most brilliant art is to be found in illuminated manuscripts, such as the Anglo-Saxon Lindisfarne Gospels and those produced at the court of Charlemagne. However, large-scale sculpture was rare before the advent of Romanesque architecture (▷ p. 326), when the art was revived to decorate the inside and outside of the new churches. Special attention was paid to the embellishment of capitals surmounting columns and to doorways – the *tympanum* (the semicircular space between the door and the arch) was usually elaborately carved, often with a figure of Christ in Majesty.

The Romanesque style spread quickly throughout Europe in the 11th and 12th centuries, and despite regional variations there is a certain uniformity of style. An especially popular decorative device – found in sculpture, metalwork and manuscript illumination – is the *inhabited scroll*, where men and animals are found amongst foliage.

Gothic painting and sculpture

Romanesque art was succeeded by Gothic art in Europe, which developed first in the architecture and sculpture of churches and cathedrals in northern France in the 12th century. It placed a new emphasis on nature and humanity's place within its hierarchy. This is shown in a more human relationship between God and the individual and the expression of human emotions. There are obvious stylistic variations, but it is often characterized by elegant, sometimes elongated figures, decorative surface treatment, and an attention to detail.

Gothic figure sculpture became more naturalistic and less dependent on its architectural support as time progressed. By the mid-13th century, at Rheims Cathedral, the sculptures of the Visitation and Annunciation groups (c. 1224–45) are well proportioned and the drapery is used to create a greater sense of form as the figures appear to move freely in front of the columns. In Germany too, naturalism was accentuated by an expression of contemplation in the faces, as seen in the Rider at Bamberg (mid-13th century). Most medieval sculptures were originally painted, making them even more realistic.

Italian Gothic

Towards the end of the 13th century the anatomical realism of classical sculpture was taken up by the Pisan sculptor *Nicola Pisano* (active 1258–84), who, with his Florentine assistant *Arnolto di Cambio* (active 1265–1300), began the move into the realm of the Gothic. However, it was in the hands of Nicola's son, *Giovanni Pisano* (active 1265–1314), that the style blossomed, especially on his pulpit in S Andrea, Pistoia (1301), where a wealth of human emotions are expressed, and the human form beneath the drapery is clearly delineated.

This sculptural approach was paralleled in the works of the painters, particularly the Florentine *Giotto di Bondone* (c. 1267–1337). The first attempts at this type of realism are in works attributed to an earlier Florentine, *Cimabue* (active 1272–1302), although the artist still produces the iconic image of his Byzantine predecessors. It is dramatically developed by Giotto, whose solid figures are more convincingly set into space. In contrast, the early work of the Sienese painter *Duccio di Boninsegna* (active 1278–1319) concentrates on a two-dimensional decorative surface treatment that was to continue in Sienese art.

However, other concerns often governed an artist's approach – the need to produce a clear narrative, for example. In the frescoes of the Arena Chapel (Padua, 1304–13), Giotto's figures are mainly ranged along the front of the picture plane, and this, while unnaturalistic, assists in the story-telling.

During this period the identity of artists became more publicly known and their status increased. Similarly the importance of the patrons and their requirements must also not be overlooked. Major decorative schemes were commissioned by the Church, the guilds, wealthy individuals and city governments. An especially important project was the decoration of the double church of S Francesco at Assisi, where virtually all the painters of note were employed. Among them was the Sienese *Simone Martini* (active 1315–44), whose linear rhythms, sensitive use of colour and graceful figure style create a spirituality that obviously appealed to many different types of patron.

The Sienese painters *Ambrogio* and *Pietro Lorenzetti* (active c. 1319–48) produced works which marry Sienese tradition with sculptural, Giottesque form. Their expression of emotion clearly illustrates Gothic humanism and especially the close mother-and-child relationship.

International Gothic

At the end of the 14th and the beginning of the 15th century a new development in art, aptly known as International Gothic, combined the French court style, Sienese tradition and Central European features. It is characterized by a preciousness and delicacy of handling, and attention to detail, particularly evident in the illuminated manuscripts of the *Très Riches Heures* of the *Limbourg Brothers* (Paul, Jean and Herman; d. c. 1416). It is also seen in the monumental figures of the Flemish sculptor *Claus Sluter* (active c. 1380–d. 1405/6), whose use of naturalistic facial expression and swaying drapery is typical of the style.

In Italy International Gothic existed alongside the growing development of Renaissance classicism. The bronze doors of the Baptistery in Florence, begun by Ghiberti in 1403, retain a Gothicism in figure style and layout while demonstrating a greater awareness of the antique.

The influential *Adoration of the Magi* (1423) by the Venetian painter *Gentile da Fabriano* (c. 1370–1427) displays a clear knowledge of Simone Martini's figure style. This painting appears to have been used as a model by *Lorenzo Monaco* (c. 1370/2–1422/5) for his *Adoration* (c. 1424). The linear contours and colourism in his elongated figures betrays his Sienese background.

The close relationship between International Gothic painting and tapestries (produced mainly in Flanders) is clearly shown in the work of the Veronese *Antonio Pisanello* (c. 1395–1455/6). In the *Vision of St Eustace* (1435–38) the subject is treated in a largely two-dimensional way, with detailed plant and animal life dotted about the surface.

Giotto di Bondone's painting of the dream of St Jerome from the fresco cycle *The Lives of the Virgin and Christ* (1305–8) in the Arena Chapel, Padua. The grandeur of the simple figures within a setting of bare essentials dramatically tells a story and concentrates on human feeling. Giotto's break from the Byzantine tradition was a major influence on other painters. His concern with the pictorial representation of space was in advance of many of his contemporaries. (Giraudon)

SEE ALSO

● MEDIEVAL AND RENAISSANCE CULTURE p. 248
● GREEK AND ROMAN ART p. 306
● RENAISSANCE ART p. 312
● ARCHITECTURE p. 326

Claus Sluter's *The Well of Moses* at the Chartreuse de Champmol, Dijon (1395–1404). Six prophets are sculpted in full three-dimension with facial expressions and expansive gestures. The figures were originally painted, so heightening their realism. (Giraudon)

Renaissance Art

The term Renaissance ('rebirth') was first coined in the 19th century to describe a period of intellectual and artistic renewal that lasted from about 1350 to about 1550. The dominant theme of this period is the revival of interest in Classical literature and art by 14th- and 15th-century humanists (▷ p. 248) and the rediscovery by artists of their cultural past. Florence was the first centre of this rediscovery, which rapidly spread to other Italian cities, and then, after 1500, to northern Europe.

This flowering was accompanied by a change in the status of artists – from craftsmen to honoured members of cultured society – and was aided by enlightened civic, private, royal and papal patronage. Although the demand for paintings and sculpture of religious subjects was as great as before, the choice widened to include mythological, historical and allegorical subjects.

Early Renaissance

The growing interest in *perspective* – a mathematical method of depicting three-dimensional space in two dimensions – and in the use of Classical motifs is clearly revealed in the early work of both **Filippo Brunelleschi** (1377–1446) and **Lorenzo Ghiberti** (1378–1455). The panels from Ghiberti's second set of doors (1426–52) for the Florence Baptistery are important landmarks in Renaissance art, and include highly sophisticated representations of space and form.

An advance in the realistic depiction of the draped figure can be seen in the sculpture of **Donatello** (c. 1386–1466), which probably influenced the figures of **Masaccio** (1401–c. 1428), including those in the frescoes for the Brancacci Chapel. In his fresco of the Trinity (1426–27) the

Botticelli's *Primavera* ('Spring'; 1478) reflects contemporary interest in esoteric Neoplatonist philosophy. In the 19th century, Botticelli's wan female figures influenced the Pre-Raphaelites (▷ p. 319), and the Art Nouveau movement (▷ p. 321) was inspired by his flowing line. (AKG/Uffizi, Florence)

— **LEONARDO DA VINCI**

Leonardo da Vinci (1452–1519) represents the true Renaissance artist: not only was he proficient in all the arts, but he was also an engineer, inventor, scientist, mathematician and philosopher. His inventions include designs for a parachute and flying machines.

As a painter, he developed the use of *aerial perspective*, in which colours are paled and tones cooled towards blue with receding distance. He also evolved monochrome effects in such paintings as the *Mona Lisa* (1503), and yet his technical experiment in *The Last Supper* (1495–98) resulted in the immediate decay of one of his great masterpieces. His reputation was enormous during his lifetime, and has continued to be so. One of his greatest legacies is a vast collection of compositional and technical drawings.

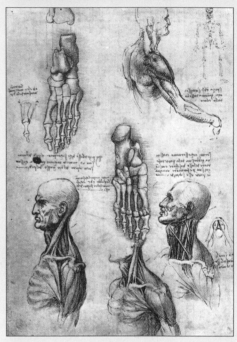

Leonardo da Vinci's anatomical studies were initially undertaken for artistic training but soon grew into an independent area of research. (AKG/Windsor Castle)

realism of the architectural setting for the figures owes much to Brunelleschi's architectural designs.

As popular to contemporary tastes were the paintings of **Fra Angelico** (c. 1399–1455) and **Fra Filippo Lippi** (c. 1406–69), which retain many of the refined features of Gothic religious painting, yet show an awareness of the need for a realistic depiction of space and form. The crowded space of Lippi's Virgin-and-Child compositions are like painted depictions of high-relief sculpture.

Paolo Uccello (c. 1397–1475) was one of the first of the Florentine painters to experiment in perspectival compositions. He employed this new method in his fresco of the *Deluge* to produce dramatic foreshortening and distant *vanishing points* (the points at which all receding parallel lines appear to meet). The application of mathematical rules in painting was pursued by **Piero della Francesca** (?1420–92). His compositions and figures, as seen in the frescoes illustrating the *Story of the True Cross* in Arezzo, have a monumentality and geometric purity unequalled by his contemporaries.

EARLY NETHERLANDISH AND GERMAN ART

The Netherlandish and German art of the period from around 1400 to 1570 is often described under the blanket term 'Northern Renaissance'. While this label recognizes the originality and vitality of the northern contemporaries of the Italian Renaissance masters, it obscures the very important divide between the 15th and 16th centuries. In the earlier century the rediscoveries of the Italians aroused little interest north of the Alps, but in the 16th century Netherlandish and German artists became increasingly fascinated by Classical antiquity.

The new realism in the Netherlands

The Flemish painter *Jan van Eyck* (active 1422–41) is remembered as the 'father' of the early Netherlandish painting. A court painter, he excelled both as a portraitist and as a painter of altarpieces. By contrast, almost nothing is known about his elder brother and co-painter of the Ghent Altarpiece, *Hubert van Eyck* (d. 1426). This altarpiece, completed in 1432, abounds in innovations, including portraiture, nudes, meticulously accurate details and distant landscapes, spatial illusionism and the careful depiction of light and shadow. The brothers Van Eyck were the first to grasp fully the capacity of oil paint to render effects of light, colour and texture. This new realism invested the age-old motifs of Christian art with a powerful new impact, permitting ever more complex levels of meaning. After Jan van Eyck, the Flemish painter most praised by contemporaries was *Rogier van der Weyden* (c. 1399–1464). Aided by a brilliant sense of abstract design, he explored the emotive possibilities of the new style in his masterpiece, the Madrid *Descent from the Cross*.

The spread of the new style

By the mid-century collectors as far afield as Italy and Spain were eagerly acquiring paintings by the Netherlandish pioneers. Inspired by their example, German masters from *Steven Lochner* (active 1442–51) in Cologne to *Konrad Witz* (c. 1400–46/7) in Basel formulated local variants of the new style. In Colmar in Alsace *Martin Schongauer* (active 1469–91) translated Rogier van der Weyden's figure style into the new technique of engraving, and so the style was widely disseminated through prints. In the low countries, *Dierick Bouts* (active 1448–75) and *Hans Memling* (active 1465–94) also took their starting point from Rogier, while *Hugo van der Goes* (active 1467–82) turned repeatedly to the monumental grandeur of Jan van Eyck.

The impact of Italy and the Reformation

During the early 16th century many northern artists developed an essentially traditional style to ever increasing levels of complexity. Among such artists, the Flemish painter *Hieronymus Bosch* (active 1480/1–1516) is particularly notable. Bosch specialized in large, panoramic compositions peopled with myriad tiny figures and creatures. Although his paintings frequently utilize the triptych (triple-panel) format usual in altarpieces, it is more likely that they were intended as moral allegories for the entertainment and edification of private collectors.

The German painter *Grünewald* (Mathis Neithardt-Gothardt, active 1501–28) is the most expressionist of Renaissance artists, concentrating on religious themes. His masterpiece, the shutters of the Isenheim altarpiece (1515), vividly embodies the poetic mysticism of late medieval theology.

Other painters followed the lead of the German *Albrecht Dürer* (1471–1528). Dürer studied perspective and the theory of human proportions in Italy, and his paintings display an immensely fertile imagination and brilliant technical skill. He also elevated printmaking to the status of a major medium with such works as the humanist-inspired *Melancholia* of 1513.

The Germans *Albrecht Altdorfer* (c. 1480–1538), *Hans Baldung Grien* (1484/5–1545), and *Lucas Cranach* (1472–1553) consolidated Dürer's foundation of the greatest school of painting and printmaking in German history. Artists in Catholic regions continued the traditional subject matter of altarpieces, while others such as Cranach and the German *Hans Holbein the Younger* (1497/8–1543) played a major role in the spread of the Reformation through their Protestant paintings and book illustrations. Holbein was also the principal portraitist of his day and, became court painter of the English king, Henry VIII.

Despite Dürer's visit to Antwerp in 1520–21, the growth of an Italianate style in the low countries was on the whole an independent development. *Quentin Massys* (1464/5–1530) had access to drawings by Leonardo da Vinci, who moved to France in 1517, and *Jan Gossaert* (also known as *Mabuse*; active 1503–32) visited Rome in 1508–09. *Lucas van Leyden* (c. 1489–1533) studied Italian and German prints, and his own engravings were celebrated as the equal of Dürer's own work. In contrast to such transplanted Italianism, *Joachim Patenir* (c. 1480–1524) developed the 15th-century fascination with landscape until it became an independent subject.

Although *Pieter Bruegel the Elder* (c. 1525–69) mainly painted scenes of peasants and the countryside, his works often illustrate moral themes. Thus the famous *Peasant Dance* is best interpreted as a criticism of the lust and hypocrisy of the peasants who abuse a saint's day by regarding it as an excuse for a party. Some multi-figure landscapes such as his *Procession to Calvary* (1564) treat traditional religious themes. The breathtaking naturalism of Bruegel's paintings also marks the birth of a new, secular outlook, which was to flourish in the Golden Age of Dutch painting (▷ p. 316).

Bruegel's *The Blind Leading the Blind* (1568) elevated the genre of proverb painting. It reveals the artist's interest in the rendering of movement, particularly the image of the falling figure. (AKG/Galleria Nazionale di Capodimonte, Naples)

The antiquarian pursuits and application of artificial perspective in the work of the North Italian *Andrea Mantegna* (c.1430–1506) led him to depict Classically clothed figures and sculpture in steeply foreshortened scenes in the Overtari Chapel (Padua, Eremitani Church, 1459).

The desire to decorate private palaces with secular narratives of historical or mythological subjects gave painters new areas for exploration. The mythological paintings of *Sandro Botticelli* (c. 1445–1510), such as *Primavera* ('Spring', 1477–78) and the *Birth of Venus* (c. 1485–90), reflect contemporary interest in esoteric Neoplatonist philosophy. In these enchanted visions Botticelli explores his distinctively linear style to the full.

High Renaissance

The focus of artistic activity in Italy shifted during the early 16th century from Florence to Rome, under the patronage of a succession of popes. This period is known as the High Renaissance, when harmony and proportion were combined with a new found freedom and mastery of technique.

Michelangelo Buonarroti (1475–1564) started his artistic career in the humanist environment of Florence, where the Medici had been his patrons. On his first visit to Rome he carved his first great sculptures, such as the *Pietà* (1499), and on returning to Florence produced his giant marble *David* (1501–4). On his return to Rome in

SEE ALSO

● MEDIEVAL AND RENAISSANCE CULTURE p. 248
● THE REFORMATION p. 250
● MEDIEVAL ART p. 310
● THE DUTCH SCHOOL pp. 315–16

Michelangelo's *Creation of Sun and Moon* (above) on the ceiling of the Sistine Chapel (1508–12). Working totally unaided, Michelangelo demonstrated his skill as draughtsman and colourist, creating painted figures of sculptural presence. The *Ignudi* that corner the central scene are examples of what Michelangelo regarded as perfect human beauty. (AKG/Sistine Chapel)

Mannerism

Mannerism is a style of exaggerated sophistication and virtuosity – sometimes combined with a heightened emotionalism and religiosity – that grew out of the example of High Renaissance art and was partly a reaction to it. In Florence, *Jacopo Pontormo* (1494–1556) and *Agnolo Bronzino* (1507–1572) perfected a style that featured figures posed in elegant tension, contrasts of colours, and dense, complicated compositions. In sculpture this tendency is represented by the brilliant goldsmith's work and bronzes of *Benvenuto Cellini* (1500–71) and in the work of *Giambologna* (1529–1608), such as the spiralling group of the *Rape of the Sabines* (1579–83).

In Mantua, Raphael's assistant, *Giulio Romano* (1492–1546), combined architecture and painting in his witty application of Mannerist details in the designs for the Palazzo del Tè, begun in 1526. *Antonio Correggio* (c. 1495–1534) developed a rich painterly style in his altarpieces and frescoes, based on knowledge of Mantegna, Michelangelo and Raphael. Influenced by Correggio, *Parmigianino* (1503–40) evolved a style that delighted in elegant, if bizarre, distortion of the human figure, for instance in his *Madonna of the Long Neck* (c. 1535). In Spain, *El Greco* (1541–1614) produced a highly personal Mannerist style characterized by acid colours, elongated figures and mystical visions, seen for instance in his *Burial of Count Orgaz* (1586).

Mannerism became popular all over Catholic Europe. However, the Counter-Reformation (▷ p. 251) brought in restrictions on both subject matter and treatment of religious art and by the end of the 16th century Mannerism had lost much of its vigour.

El Greco's *The Resurrection of Christ* (below) (1594). The elongated figures, harsh colours and elaborate composition are typical of El Greco's distinctive Mannerist style. (AKG/Museo del Prado)

1505, Michelangelo began work on Pope Julius II's tomb, a project that lasted 30 years. Of the carved figures originally planned only the monumental *Moses* was finally placed on the much modified tomb. His next major project was the ceiling of the Sistine Chapel (1508–1512). In scenes from the Old Testament Michelangelo demonstrated his powers as a draughtsman and innovative colourist, and as the creator of painted figures of almost sculptural presence and beauty. Michelangelo worked in Florence from 1516 to 1534, but on his return to Rome he painted the *Last Judgement* (1536–41) on the altar wall of the Sistine Chapel.

Raphael (1483–1520), who had been based in Florence in 1504–8, was also involved in extensive decorative schemes in Rome: in paintings for the *Stanze* and loggias of the Vatican Palace (1509–14), such as *The School of Athens*, and on the series of cartoons (drawings) for a set of tapestries for the Sistine Chapel (1517–18). These richly classical works, together with other works such as his portraits and Virgin-and-Child paintings, form the basis for High Renaissance art. Their wealth of invention and harmonious compositions were copied by artists for centuries.

During the absence of Michelangelo, Raphael and Leonardo (see box), the artistic scene in Florence was dominated by *Fra Bartolommeo* (c. 1474–c. 1517) and *Andrea del Sarto* (1486–1530), whose altarpieces and frescoes represent the epitome of the harmonious and quietly classical Florentine style prior to the advent of Mannerism.

VENICE

Venetian painting reflected the impact both of Byzantine decoration and of north European painting, particularly in the use of oil painting. Its surface brilliance and sumptuous colour was more important than the inclusion of Classical forms. *Giovanni Bellini's* (c. 1430–1516) oil painting – probably learnt from *Antonello da Messina* (c. 1430–79) – profoundly affected the direction of Venetian art. His still, contemplative altarpieces and portraits, later became increasingly saturated with colour and light, a quality he also brought to his landscape compositions.

At the beginning of the 16th century *Giorgione* (c. 1476/8–1510) introduced a new category of paintings depicting esoteric subjects – such as *The Tempest* – into Venetian art. Giorgione also pioneered dream-like pastorals, in which figures and landscape became harmoniously integrated. This genre was also taken up by *Titian* (c. 1487/90–1576), considered to be the greatest of the Venetian painters. He established an influential style of court portraiture, and his sensual allegorical works contain a lyrical richness that relies more on colour and tone than drawing and line.

Mannerism in Venetian painting is represented by the darkly dramatic, sharply foreshortened compositions of *Jacopo Tintoretto* (1518–94) in his series decorating the confraternity headquarters of the Scuola di San Rocco. In contrast are the large canvases of *Veronese* (1528–88) depicting religious, historical and allegorical events in sumptuous Venetian settings.

Art in the 17th and 18th Centuries

Classicism and the Baroque were the two dominant trends in the visual arts of the 17th century. Although frequently divergent and opposed, they both originated in the reaction against the aridity of Late Mannerism (▷ p. 314). A return to the naturalism, harmonious equilibrium and compositional coherence of the High Renaissance was combined with a new physical realism, emotional immediacy and dynamic vigour. Classicism was soon diluted by the 18th-century desire for the informal and the undemanding, which found its artistic expression in the style known as Rococo.

SEE ALSO

● EUROPEAN EMPIRES IN THE
  17TH AND 18TH CENTURIES
  p. 257
● RENAISSANCE ART
  pp. 312–14
● ART IN THE 19TH CENTURY
  p. 318
● ARCHITECTURE p. 326
● EARLY MUSIC p. 332
● THE CLASSICAL PERIOD
  (MUSIC) p. 334
● CLASSICISM IN LITERATURE
  p. 362

The Baroque style combined the dramatic effects of energetic movement, vivid colour and decorative detail with expressive originality and freedom. Classicism deployed more restrained qualities of directness and precision to enliven traditional ideas of balance and decorum.

The Early Baroque

The most remarkable painter of the Early Baroque was *Michelangelo Merisi da Caravaggio* (1573–1610). His earlier works were controversial, celebrating sexually ambiguous low-life characters and representing holy figures as ordinary people, aspects combined in the *Calling of St Matthew* (c. 1599). His religious imagery was powerful, expressed in gestures, shadowed backgrounds and dramatic use of light and shade (*chiaroscuro*). The altarpieces he painted in Naples, Malta and Sicily were among his finest

creations, increasingly sombre, poignant and dramatic.

Ludovico Carracci (1555–1619) and his cousins *Agostino* (1557–1602) and *Annibale* (1560–1609) represented the orthodox side of the Early Baroque revolution, founding the first true example of the modern artistic academy, in Bologna in the 1580s. Their works revived the dignity of the Renaissance, enhanced by richer contrasts and colours, weightier figures and complex compositional relationships.

Annibale's most talented pupils were *Guido Reni* (1575–1642) and *Domenichino* (1581–1641). In their companion frescoes of *Scenes from the Martyrdom of St Andrew* (1608–9), Reni's decorative elaboration contrasts with Domenichino's concentration on narrative. Reni's developed towards idealized beauty, rhythmic grace and surface elegance. Domenichino, on the other hand, created an austerely original Classicism, with simplified and static compositions, grandiose figures and archaeologically accurate details.

The great Flemish painter *Peter Paul Rubens* (1577–1640) studied in Italy, but subsequently transformed his Italian influences through a vigorous imagination and a brilliant technique. His paintings embody all the energy, colour and sensuality of the Baroque. But he was equally capable of tenderness and sensitivity, particularly in portraiture; and his landscapes, allegorical schemes and altarpieces show a marvellous animation. The most distinguished of Rubens' assistants were *Jacob Jordaens* (1593–1678), who coarsened the master's style, and *Anthony Van Dyck* (1599–1641), who refined it in his superbly elegant portraits.

Portraiture also became the chief medium of expression for the Spanish painter *Diego Velasquez* (1599–1660). His early works of everyday life, and his religious and mythological pictures, are charged with a sober naturalism. In his portraits too his level gaze never faltered as he moved from the power-mongers of the Spanish government to the pathetic court dwarfs and frail royal children.

The High Baroque

Perhaps the greatest figure of the Italian High Baroque was *Gianlorenzo Bernini* (1598–1680). The brilliant naturalistic forms of his sculpture expressed ideas of daring originality. He went on to combine sculpture with architecture and painting. An equal contrast is provided by the sensuous richness and formal harmony of the painting of *Pietro da Cortona* (1596–1669). The pictorial lightness of his later works indicates an increasing awareness of the new Classicism.

The challenge of Classicism

Despite Bernini's dominance there was an important group of artists who were opposed to the emotional drama and formal licence of the Baroque. Instead they combined Baroque colour and solidity with a revival of antique forms. Dominating the group was the Frenchman *Nicolas Poussin* (1593/4–1665), who was strongly influenced by Domenichino. The increasingly sober, abstract qualities of his later mythologies and religious pictures appealed to the more rigorous intellectual climate of Paris. As part of this

The Garden of Love (1630–34) by Rubens. The luminosity of colour characterizes the paintings of Rubens. (AKG/Museo del Prado)

In the 17th century a sudden flowering of painting in the Netherlands coincided with the overthrow of Spanish rule and Dutch mercantile success throughout the world. The Dutch wanted a calm reflection of their vision of reality. To achieve this their artists concentrated on the types of painting in which they had long specialized – still life, genre, landscape and portraiture.

Still life

Early 17th-century Dutch still lifes faithfully render domestic objects and flowers in brilliant colour and light, but almost haphazardly against dark backgrounds. More subtle compositions were gradually developed, using restricted colour harmonies and more atmospheric tones and settings. In the second half of the century, lower viewpoints, combined with greater depth in the composition, produced a naturalistic effect. The works of *Willem Kalf* (1619–93) – daringly composed arrangements of sculpted silver, blue and white Delft ware and ripe fruit – are typical.

Genre

Genre painting is the depiction of scenes of everyday life, originally with an allegorical intention. It was popularized by *Hendrick Terbrugghen* (1588–1629) and *Gerard van Honthorst* (1590–1656). They founded the Utrecht School, which produced paintings of colourful groups of low-life characters in fancy dress, distinguished by Caravaggesque use of dramatic light and shade. More realistic were the works of *Adriaen Brouwer* (1605/6–38), a Fleming working in the Netherlands. In his tavern scenes, boorish men carousing or snoring are sympathetically depicted in delicate colour harmonies with subtle lighting. Also related to the Flemish tradition were Dutch pictures of butchers' shops and market stalls, which combined still life with picturesquely vulgar figures. Vulgarity, ostensibly with a moralizing message, was also the keynote of the boisterous, colourful and highly detailed scenes of *Jan Steen* (1626–79).

Quite different was the quiet atmosphere of the genteel interiors of *Gerard Terborch* (1617–81), which often feature precise renderings of silks and carpets. Far subtler and more daring in the handling of light and perspective were the interior and exterior views of *Pieter de Hooch* (1629–84). An air of mystery is often added to the realism of his homely rooms and courtyards by the interpolation of further, gently lit views into subsidiary background spaces. *Jan Vermeer* (1632–75) of Delft is best known for his domestic interiors, whose restricted colours, simplified

forms, delicate rendering of light effects and skilful compositions built up from geometrical shapes transformed the humdrum into the poetic.

Landscapes

The earliest Dutch landscapes combined the artificial compositions of Mannerism (▷ p. 314) with a minute description of realistic detail, but a more naturalistic style later developed. In the 1630s and 1640s, parallel with changes in still life painting, atmosphere and tonal subtleties created a new sense of light and space. After 1650 these achievements were gradually combined with a richer colour range, and a greater feeling for natural drama.

The most accomplished figure of this last period was *Jacob van Ruisdael* (1628/9 –82), whose works are as varied and as inventively composed as Claude's, though less idealized. Those of *Meindert Hobbema* (1638– 1709) concentrate on decorative, sunlit forest scenes, while his best-known work, *The Avenue at Middelharnis* (1689), derives its strong central focus from an avenue of tall trees. Contrastingly Italianate are the golden light and warm tonalities of *Aelbert Cuyp* (1620–91), which lend his simple groupings of trees, cows or ships a poetic monumentality.

Portraits

Portraiture, the most popular branch of Dutch painting, developed at a rapid pace. This was due to the brilliant talent of *Franz Hals* (1580/85–1666). The immediacy of his group portraits gives life to potentially static compositions, while single sitters are portrayed directly, with apparently spontaneous handling of paint providing visual excitement. His technique became even freer, and his colours more limited, during the 1640s and 1650s. His final works, painted when he was destitute, show a more sensitive approach that may indicate an awareness of the late Rembrandt.

Rembrandt van Rijn (1606–69) stands apart from the rest of the Dutch School not only through his imagination and depth of human sympathy, but also because of the variety and originality of his subject matter and his superlative technical skills. However, Rembrandt made his name through his success in portraiture. Subtle illusionistic effects and an ambitious compositional use of light appeared in the so-called *Night Watch* (1642); this extraordinary picture combines an almost abstract disposition of its naturalistic parts with a Baroque sense of dramatic movement. This was the high point of Rembrandt's worldly success.

His interest in Old Testament subjects had begun early, as shown by the *Jeremiah* of 1630, opulently coloured and richly detailed, with only the dramatic fall of light illuminating the prophet's sorrow. Subsequent examples, such as *Bathsheba* (1654), are more direct in composition, more restrained in colour and comparably deeper in psychological insight. More conventional religious feeling was expressed in Rembrandt's etchings, though with unconventional means – vast sweeps of light, tense groupings of figures and sudden detail create great emotional dramas, often in a tiny area. His technical mastery is equally evident in the range of his drawings.

Rembrandt's range and development can most clearly be seen in his series of self-portraits. These were painted over forty years and charted his personal journey from unconventional beginner to young master, disillusioned middle-aged bankrupt to weary sage, by which time he had achieved an extraordinary freedom and expressiveness in his handling of paint.

Rembrandt's series of self portraits spanned 40 years. In his final years Rembrandt lived alone and in poverty, and the later self-portraits are among the most moving portraits ever painted. (AKG/Louvre, Paris)

Vermeer's *Lady Reading a Letter at an Open Window* (1657). (AKG/Gemäldegalerie Alte Meister)

THE BRITISH PORTRAITISTS

The 18th-century interest in rational philosophy and in the development of personal taste contributed to the importance of the individual, and this was reflected in the rise of portraiture as a pictorial genre – a genre that particularly flourished in Britain. **Allan Ramsay** (1713–84) created images of delicacy and directness. The same qualities appear in the technically more original works of **Thomas Gainsborough** (1727–88), which, frequently set against a melting landscape background, often seem to capture a fleeting moment. The Classical allusions and solid technique of **Joshua Reynolds** (1723–92) attempt to bring the allegorical values of history painting to portraiture. His influence can clearly be seen in many compositions by **Henry Raeburn** (1756–1823). The precocious talent of **Thomas Lawrence** (1769–1830) effectively captured the flamboyance of the Regency period.

development Poussin often turned to pure landscape as an expression of mathematical order and contemplative grandeur.

A new spirit was infused into landscape painting by another Frenchman, **Claude Lorraine** (1600–82). His sensitivity to nature and magical light effects transformed the stylizations of northern European landscape artists into poetic evocations of the changing moods of the Italian countryside. The wild and rocky scenes of the Italian **Salvator Rosa** (1615–73) were seen in the 18th century as precursors of the Sublime.

Rococo

Rococo began in France as an interior design style of extravagant decoration, characterized by foliage, sunbursts, grotesques, and shellwork (or *rocaille*, giving rise to the later, contemptuous name 'Rococo'). During the 18th century Rococo spread to all the fine and decorative arts. Some of the most original creations of French Rococo were in the applied arts of furniture, porcelain and silverware.

Decorative elegance also characterized contemporary French painting, although neither of its two greatest figures, **Antoine Watteau** (1684–1721) and **Jean-Baptiste-Siméon Chardin** (1699–1779), can be thought of properly in terms of Rococo. While Watteau refined the Flemish mythologies of Rubens and Van Dyck into scenes of melancholy charm, Chardin poeticized the prosaic Dutch gentleness of de Hooch and Ter Borch. More in harmony with Rococo interiors were the paintings of **François Boucher** (1703–70), and the even frothier confections of **Jean-Honoré Fragonard** (1732–1806). The Venetian **Giambattista Tiepolo** (1696–1770) – perhaps the greatest genius of the Rococo – brilliantly enhanced the Kaisersaal and Treppenhaus at Würzburg with his illusionistic ceiling frescoes (painted 1750–52).

The other masters of Venetian Rococo were Tiepolo's brothers-in-law, **Gianantonio** (1699–1760) and **Francesco** (1712–93) **Guardi**. The real and imaginary views of Venice painted by Francesco evoke the changing hues of water and sky as freely as the Impressionists. But even the more precise scenes of **Antonio Canaletto** (1697–1768)

were imbued with a poetry only partly due to the decorative fantasy of Venice itself.

Neoclassicism

The intellectual and philosophical basis of Neoclassicism originated and was developed in Rome and Paris. The ideas of various French theorists and the accurate recording of Greek and Roman antiquities provided food for thought as well as matter for stylistic change. The Louis XVI style of decoration (actually begun under Louis XV) replaced curves with straight lines, sculptural movement with low-relief restraint, and natural and abstract forms with stylized Antique detail.

Neoclassicism in painting is best represented by the severely noble canvases of **Jacques-Louis David** (1748–1825). Lacking Antique examples of his art, David relied on the achievements of Nicolas Poussin; but his forms were more simplified and his details more archaeological. At his height he could achieve the poetic realism of the *Death of Marat* (1793) without losing his Classical poise. The leading Neoclassical sculptor was the Italian **Antonio Canova** (1757–1822), who, in contrast to David, tended towards the sentimental, setting the style for much 19th-century sculpture.

Poussin's *Landscape with Diogenes* (1648). The Classical landscape contained an almost mathematical order, conveying an impression of simplicity and calm. Motifs of trees, rivers and Classical buildings or ruins were typical of the genre. (AKG/ Louvre, Paris)

Jacques-Louis David's *The Intervention of the Sabine Women* (1799). The painting displays clear references to the Antique, within a rigorously formalized Neoclassical structure. (Giraudon/Louvre, Paris)

Art in the 19th Century

The 19th century was the age of industrialization, and artists, no longer in service to Church, court, or community, sought new standards and justifications for their art. Romanticism emerged as an expression against the ugliness and materialism of the Industrial Revolution, while Realism sought to portray everyday life in detached, objective observation.

SEE ALSO

● ART IN THE 17TH AND 18TH CENTURIES p. 315
● MODERN ART p. 324
● ARCHITECTURE p. 326
● ROMANTICISM IN LITERATURE p. 366

Impressionism took an innovative look at nature, particularly in its use of light. However, it was the new ground broken by the Post-Impressionists, Symbolists and Secessionists that heralded the modern art of the 20th century.

Romanticism

Romanticism flourished as a movement in art from the late 18th to the middle 19th century. The movement was a reaction both against the aesthetic and ethical values of Classical and Neoclassical art, and against the Industrial Revolution. The influence of Romantic writers (▷ p. 366) was particularly important in providing both subject matter and a philosophy for the Romantic painters. Indeed it is the content of Romantic painting and the attitude of the artists themselves that give the movement coherence, as in terms of style and technique there are enormous variations.

The Romantic landscape

For the Romantics, landscapes contained a meaning beyond and above its mere visual appearance, and many painters attempted to imbue their landscapes with this sense of transcendent mean-ing. The German painter **Caspar David Friedrich** (1774–1840) used an almost photographic technique to bring out every detail in his landscapes. Mountains, forests, oceans, skies and ruins dominate tiny figures, evoking a melancholy sense of the infinite. Friedrich saturates his scenes with the light of storm or moon or dawn or sunset to give the sense of visionary experience.

The Romanticism in the landscapes of **John Constable** (1776–1837) is found in his honesty to his own experience of nature. Changing moods in the weather, the play of light on clouds and trees and water – all these Constable captured on canvas with unprecedented directness and skill. He had no desire to idealize or generalize the particular scene before him, and if it contained a broken-down old cart (as in *The Hay Wain*, 1821), in it would go.

Like Constable, **Joseph Mallord William Turner** (1775–1851) was far more concerned with the business of painting nature as he saw it than with any Romantic philosophy. Initially inspired by the landscapes of Claude and the 17th-century Dutch masters, Turner gradually introduced more obviously Romantic subject matter into his work. His exploration of the visual effects of great elemental forces such as Alpine storms was accompanied by increasingly free brushwork. In *Rain, Steam and Speed* (1844), light and atmospheric effects dominate the picture to such an extent as to make it virtually abstract.

Explorers of the irrational

Henry Fuseli (1741–1825) was a Swiss painter who settled permanently in England in 1788. In his most famous work, *The Nightmare* (1782), a grotesque demonic dwarf squats on the body of a sleeping woman, while through the curtains bursts the head of a fearsome horse. Although not an outstanding painter, his explorations of the darker side of human nature were highly influential within the Romantic movement.

A far greater painter was **Francisco de Goya y Lucientes** (1746–1848). His dislike for the reactionary establishment led him to such works as the *Caprices* (1799), a series of prints intended to mock the follies and superstitions of society. The result was a series of nightmare images. In *Saturn Devouring One of his Children* (c. 1820–23), hideous giant figures loom out of the frenzied

Géricault's *The Raft of the Medusa* (1818–19). Based on a recent event, the painting depicts the dead and dying abandoned on a raft following a shipwreck. Transcending the sensationalism of the subject, Géricault transforms the terrible scene into one of timeless drama. (AKG/ Louvre, Paris)

paintwork, giving a more symbolic expression to the dark forces within humanity.

The French Romantics

In 1812 *Théodore Géricault* (1791–1824) virtually overthrew the dominance of Neoclassicism in France with one picture, his *Charging Chasseur*. This gallant cavalry officer on his wild, rearing horse represented the epitome of untamed Romantic power, and they feature in many of his finest paintings. *Eugène Delacroix's* (1798–1863) sympathy for liberal and nationalist aspirations – shared by many Romantic artists – is reflected in works such as *Liberty Leading the People* (1830), a celebration of the revolution in that year. What was striking about this picture was its lack of idealization: the revolutionaries at the barricade – and even Liberty herself – are far from genteel or classically heroic. Delacroix was also attracted by more exotic subjects – often featuring sex and violence – which he painted in brilliant clashes of vibrant colour. Delacroix often gave his compositions an apparently random structure, suggesting an extraordinary sense of movement and actuality.

Medievalism

The nostalgia for things medieval that first emerged in the architecture of the Gothic Revival (▷ p. 326) was given expression by the *Pre-Raphaelite Brotherhood* (founded 1848). The English group tried to re-create what they saw as the innocent naturalism of 15th-century Italian painting. Leading members of this group were *Dante Gabriel Rossetti* (1828–82), *John Everett Millais* (1829–96) and *William Holman Hunt* (1827–1910). Their work lacked the vigour of the original, and the subjects chosen often veered towards the pious or the sentimental.

Realism

In the 1840s, a group of French artists reacted against the subjectivity, individualism and historical obsessions of many of the Romantics, adopting instead a style of art based on truth to nature. The movement, known as Realism, flourished until 1880, during which time it spread throughout Europe and America. The Realists replaced the grand, heroic subject matter of the Romantic movement with simple views of everyday life, and Romantic emotionalism was abandoned in favour of detached, objective observation. Realists usually avoided the vivid, dramatic brushstrokes of the Romantics, preferring to make their paintings distinct and precise, with straightforward subjects.

The Frenchman *Gustav Courbet* (1819–77) was deeply influenced by the ideals and aims of democracy and socialism that followed the Revolution of 1848 (▷ p. 264). He was inspired to represent the new ideas in his art, and in 1850 he created a scandal in Paris with the exhibition of his paintings *The Peasants at Flagey Returning from the Fair*, *The Burial at Ornans* and *The Stonebreakers*. In these works he showed humble villagers, peasants and labourers, rather than the gods, heroes and biblical figures that the Parisian public was accustomed to as subjects for paintings. However, Courbet invested these humble figures with monumental dignity.

Realism also had an impact on landscape. The French painter *Camille Corot* (1796–1875) was an important link with Romanticism. As his style developed, he began to exhibit sketches that he had made out of doors. This move was particularly controversial because landscape painters

Turner's *Venice: Sunset over the Grand Canal* (1840–50). Turner was one of the most original landscape painters, and his use of light anticipated the development of Impressionism. (AKG/British Museum, London)

traditionally made sketches out of doors, but finished the painting in the studio.

Corot was especially influential on the *Barbizon School* – a group of artists who moved to Barbizon in the Forest of Fontainebleau, southeast of Paris. There they immersed themselves in the study of nature and painted *'en plein air'* (out of doors), in order to represent nature as faithfully as possible. Perhaps the most unusual member of the Barbizon group was *Jean-François Millet* (1814–75). From a peasant background, Millet studied painting in Paris, but settled into his own distinctive and unusual style. His subjects consisted mainly of peasants working in the fields, sowing, gleaning (gathering left-over corn) or mowing, endowed with grace and dignity by Millet's cool classical style.

The Realists' desire to be modern, rather than historical, led to a series of paintings representing scenes of middle-class life. *Eugène Boudin's* (1824–98) paintings of the beach resorts of Trouville and Deauville depicted French middle-class, bourgeois society. *Honoré Daumier's* (1808–79) series of caricatures combined fantasy with Realism. These often bitter satires attacked both political evils and social foibles, and was the cause of his arrest and imprisonment in 1832.

The spread of Realism

In 1855 the display of Realist paintings in the Exposition Universelle (Universal Exhibition) in Paris ensured the spread of Realism to Britain, Russia, Italy, Germany and Scandinavia. In England, *William Powell Frith* (1819–1909) adopted the fashionable beach scene for his painting of *Ramsgate Sands* (1854). In Germany, the first great Realist was *Adolph von Menzel*

Courbet's *The Stonebreakers* (1851). Courbet did not seek to portray ugliness, as he was accused, but the reality and dignity of the working man. (AKG/Gemäldegalerie, Dresden)

Monet's *Palazzo da Mula, Venice* (1908). Monet was the most consistent Impressionist painter, in that he sought always to portray the 'impression' of a scene and not the reality. The effect of light, in particular, was paramount in his work. (AKG/National Gallery of Art, Washington)

MANET

The French artist *Edouard Manet* (1832–83) is frequently linked with the Impressionist group although he declined ever to exhibit with these artists and shared few of their artistic aspirations. He produced large-scale canvases painted entirely in the studio using heavy earth colours and rich, velvety blacks, all of which were to be abandoned by the Impressionist group.

In 1863 Manet's paintings were rejected by the official Salon, and were shown instead at the *Salon des Refusés* – the counter-exhibition. His painting *Déjeuner sur l'herbe* ('Picnic on the grass') evoked strong feelings in its viewers because he had chosen to rework a classical theme – the nude in a landscape – and place it within a clearly identifiable modern setting. Because of the presence of the two men in modern dress and the direct gaze of the seated woman, the painting was seen to portray two prostitutes with their clients. A similar scandal was caused by *Olympia* (1863).

While the Impressionist painters did not by and large share Manet's subject matter nor his techniques, they recognized that in the late 1860s and 1870s he was the leader of the artistic avant-garde in Paris, both because of his forceful painting style and also because of his uncompromising stance against hallowed art institutions.

OTHER MAJOR ARTISTS OF THE 19TH CENTURY

John Martin (1789–1854), British Romantic painter and engraver, noted for his sensationalist apocalyptic scenes: *The Deluge* (1834).

Samuel Palmer (1805–81), English Romantic painter and etcher of pastoral scenes.

Théodore Rousseau (1812–67), French landscape painter of the Barbizon School: *Descent of the Cattle* (1835).

Charles-François Daubigny (1817–78), French landscape painter of the Barbizon School.

Ford Madox Brown (1821–93), English painter in the Pre-Raphaelite style: his social beliefs were reflected in his famous painting *Work* (1852–65).

James McNeill Whistler (1834–1903), American painter, who worked in England. Briefly associated with the Realists, his later, more Impressionist work became abstract.

Auguste Rodin (1840–1917), French sculptor, whose work shows an extra-

ordinary technical skill and a deep understanding of the human form; *The Thinker* (1880), *The Kiss* (1886).

Mary Cassatt (1844–1926), American Impressionist painter, noted for her paintings of mothers and children.

Max Liebermann (1847–1935), German painter and founder of the Berlin Secession.

Walter Sickert (1860–1942), key English painter in the Camden Town Group. He concentrated on paintings of lower-class London life: *Ennui*.

Henri de Toulouse-Lautrec (1864–1901), French painter and draughtsman, famous for his lithographs and posters of dance halls and cabarets: *Le Moulin Rouge*.

Pierre Bonnard (1864–1947), French Intimist painter of middle-class interiors and nudes.

Edouard Vuillard (1868–1940), French Intimist painter, noted for his domestic scenes of bourgeois life.

(1815–1905), whose style anticipated that of the Impressionists. The main exponents of Realism in America – also known as *Naturalism* – were **Thomas Eakins** (1844–1916) and **Winslow Homer** (1836–1910). In the 1860s and 1870s Homer painted scenes of rural America, which were influenced by *plein air* paintings he had seen in France. After a visit to England in 1881, he became fascinated by the sea, and spent the rest of his life painting views of the coastal life.

Impressionism

Impressionism was neither a school nor a movement with a clearly defined programme, but can be better regarded as an ill-defined association of artists who joined together for the purpose of mounting independent group exhibitions from 1874 to 1886. While they had no stated aims or manifesto their work shared some techniques and certain subjects.

In the summer of 1869 the French painters **Claude Monet** (1840–1926) and **Pierre Auguste Renoir** (1841–1919) worked together at a popular bathing spot just outside Paris. Painting in collaboration, they produced a series of canvases that are generally regarded as being the first examples of the fully developed Impressionist style.

Artists began to produce finished paintings *en plein air*, resulting in smaller and more intimate canvases. In order to represent the effect of sunlight on water they used the characteristic 'broken' brushstroke, in which dabs of pure pigment were laid side by side on the canvas rather than smoothly modelled as had previously been the case. They eliminated all the earth colours, particularly black, from their palettes and concentrated instead on the three primaries (red, yellow and blue) and their immediate derivatives. They observed that the colours of objects were modified by their surroundings and introduced colour reflections into the shadows.

Rejected by the Salon and in need of some commercial success, the Impressionist artists held their first exhibition in 1874. The 39 artists exhibiting included not only Monet and Renoir but also Paul Cézanne (▷ below), **Edgar Degas** (1834–1917), **Berthe Morisot** (1841–95), **Camille Pissarro** (1831–1903) and **Alfred Sisley** (1839–99). By the time of the last exhibition in 1886, the character had changed fundamentally with the inclusion of artists such as Gauguin (▷ below), **Georges Seurat** (1859–91) and **Paul Signac** (1863–1935), whose contributions were not always admired by some of the older artists.

Neoimpressionism

At the final Impressionist exhibition, Seurat, Signac and Pissarro all showed canvases using the latest *divisionist* (or *pointillist*) techniques. This involved the use of pure colours applied in such small patches (often dots) that they appeared to fuse to form an intermediary tone when viewed from an appropriate distance. Hence grass might be composed of touches of blue alongside areas of yellow. These ideas were not new, but had been used in a much less systematic way by the Impressionists. However, the static quality of works such as Seurat's *Bathers at Asnières* (1884) and its large format marked a departure from orthodox Impressionism.

Post-Impressionism

Just as the Impressionists reacted against the established art of their day, a succession of artists later reacted against Impressionism itself. The

Post-Impressionists, as they became known, were active mainly in France between about 1880 and 1905. They included artists who painted in a wide variety of styles but who shared a desire to go beyond pure naturalism and to give more emphasis to colour, emotions and imagination.

The term Post-Impressionism was first used in 1910 by the British critic and artist Roger Fry when he arranged an exhibition entitled 'Manet and the Post-Impressionists'. The principal artists in this exhibition were Cézanne, Gauguin and van Gogh; according to Fry these were the three great artists who had moved beyond Impressionism in the search for a new art. Also included were paintings by the Neoimpressionists Seurat and Signac, together with Redon (▷ box), Picasso, Matisse, Derain, Vlaminck, Rouault, and Marquet (▷ p. 324).

The Frenchman *Paul Cézanne* (1839–1906) painted dark romantic pictures, often using a palette knife to depict scenes of violence and eroticism. In the early 1870s, encouraged by the Impressionist Camille Pissarro, he began to work out of doors and gradually lightened his palette. Cézanne soon developed away from the Impressionists and their depictions of a fleeting moment in time, which he felt resulted in a lack of structure. Like the Impressionists he wanted to paint directly from nature, but also to recapture the grandeur and order of the masters of Classicism such as Poussin (▷ p. 315). Part of his greatness lies in his struggle to combine these two aims and to achieve a monumental, timeless fusion of forms. Cézanne spent most of his life in the south of France, where he mainly painted still lifes and landscapes – often depicting Mont Sainte-Victoire, a mountain near his native town of Aix.

The most powerful works of *Vincent van Gogh* (1853–90) were painted after 1888, when he moved to Arles in Provence. In numerous self-portraits and landscapes his emotions are conveyed through brilliant colours, thick paint and strong rhythmic brushstrokes. He was subject to periodic fits of depression and eventually committed suicide.

Paul Gauguin (1848–1903) gave up his life as a prosperous Parisian businessman to become a painter. In monumental compositions such as *Nevermore* (1897), forms are portrayed as broad flat areas of rich colour surrounded by sinuous lines. Like van Gogh, Gauguin used colour for emotional rather than naturalistic effect. However, Gauguin was closer to the Symbolists in his use of bold, rhythmical outlines and arbitrary colours, and the air of ambiguity and mystery in his figure compositions (▷ box).

The turn of the 19th century was a period of great development in art. Cézanne, van Gogh and Gauguin all influenced subsequent art movements, including Symbolism (▷ box), Expressionism, Fauvism and Cubism (▷ p. 324). In the last of these Cézanne's influence was central. However, individualism also flourished and many artists cannot easily be grouped into schools.

Van Gogh's *Wheatfields* (1890), executed in the typically turbulent brushstrokes and expressive colours of his late works. (AKG/Rijksmuseum Vincent van Gogh, Amsterdam)

SYMBOLISM AND SECESSION

The Symbolist movement emerged in the 1880s as a reaction against the idea that art was an imitation of nature and against modern industrialism and materialist values. The Symbolists sought to escape into the past or into the world of fantasy, including dreams. They believed that art existed alongside, not in direct relation to, the real world, and that it had its own rules. The anti-naturalism of the Symbolists was also shared by many of the artists of the German and Austrian Secessions of the 1890s.

Symbolism in art was linked to a legacy of Romanticism in art and literature. The subject of Sâlomé – used by the poet Charles Baudelaire (▷ p. 372) – was depicted many times by *Gustave Moreau* (1826–98) in pictures such as *The Apparition*. Its jewel-like colours and extravagant, ornamental details, together with its atmosphere of mystery and menace, were characteristic of his anti-naturalistic approach. The *femme fatale* – seductive, exotic and evil – was to become a recurrent theme in Symbolist art of the so-called 'decadent' kind.

The work of *Odilon Redon* (1840–1916) dealt with fantastic subject matter, dream or nightmare imagery and strange, hallucinatory beings in a mixture of the emotional and the irrational. He worked almost exclusively in black and white until around 1890, when he began making pastels and oil paintings in radiant colours. Moreau and Redon pioneered the way to Symbolism in art in France. In England, the paintings by Dante Gabriel Rossetti (▷ text) were a major influence on *Sir Edward Burne-Jones* (1833–98) and *Aubrey Beardsley* (1872–98), among others.

In Austria and Germany in the 1890s the growing revolt against the academicism of conventional painting led to the formation of *Secessions* – breakaway groups of artists. It was the Vienna Secession (1897), led by *Gustav Klimt* (1863–1918), that was the most radical. It was successful in its aim of promoting and encouraging Austrian painters, architects and craftsmen. The major styles of the artists of the Vienna Secession were Symbolism and *Jugendstil*, the German and Austrian form of the highly decorative Art Nouveau.

Cézanne's *The Chateau Noir* (1900–04). Cézanne's works – embodying his aim to 'treat nature in terms of the cylinder, the sphere, the cone ' – were a crucial influence on the Cubists. (AKG/National Gallery of Art, Washington)

Modern Art

In the first half of the 20th century a revolution occurred in the practice of art. The convention that art should provide a faithful representation of the world was challenged by the Fauves and broken completely by Cubism. The greater emphasis on colour and form led to pure abstraction.

SEE ALSO

● ART IN THE 19TH CENTURY
p. 318
● ARCHITECTURE p. 326
● MODERN MUSIC p. 338
● MODERN LITERATURE
pp. 372–7

The writings of Darwin, Marx and Freud, together with the horrors of World War I, fostered a revolt against traditional values. Dada and Surrealism were two movements that grew out of this climate. They were deliberately provocative in their rejection of existing social and artistic order. Since then various new approaches to art have continued to shock, although some artists have returned to work in more traditional styles.

Fauvism

The Frenchmen *Henri Matisse* (1869–1954) and *André Derain* (1880–1954) were the founders of Fauvism, the first modern movement of the 20th century. The movement derived its name from a French critic who in 1905 called them *fauves* ('wild beasts'), referring to their bold, shocking colours.

Matisse was one of the most important and influential artists of the early 20th century. He was a master of colour and line as well as a major sculptor and illustrator. In his paintings of female nudes, still lifes and interiors, Matisse combined a sensitivity of line with decorative pattern and rich flat colour. His colours became brighter after he painted with the Neoimpressionist painter Signac (▷ p. 319) in 1904. The following year he worked in the south of France with Derain and their paintings were trans-

formed into explosions of bold brushstrokes and brilliant colours. Another major Fauvist was the professional cyclist *Maurice de Vlaminck* (1876–1958), whose love of speed was reflected in the immediacy of his paintings – he frequently used thick pigment squeezed directly from the tube on to the canvas.

Expressionism

Expressionism as a movement reached a peak around 1910. It attempted not just to depict the visual, but to express the emotional. Expressionist styles varied, although there was a general tendency towards distorted forms and unnaturalistic colours. Van Gogh (▷ p. 321) was an important influence. The paintings of the Norwegian *Edvard Munch* (1863–1944) are early examples of Expressionism. He produced paintings and prints whose subject matter and its treatment could be described as hysterical, neurotic and intense. In *The Scream* (1893) he portrayed anxiety, fear and despair, not only in the shrieking figure, but also in the tortured sky.

The Austrian Expressionists *Egon Schiele* (1890–1918) and *Oskar Kokoschka* (1886–1980) were strongly influenced by the work of Gustav Klimt (▷ p. 321). Schiele became one of the major Austrian Expressionists, noted for his contorted and often sexually explicit nudes, which convey a psychological tension. Kokoschka's *The Tempest* (*Bride of the Wind*) (1914) is treated with a nervous linearity through which he reveals the subject's intimate feelings and neuroses.

The German Expressionists

The group known as *Die Brücke* ('The Bridge') was formed in Dresden in 1905, and lasted until 1913. Its members included *Ernst Ludwig Kirchner* (1880–1938), *Erich Heckel* (1883–1970), *Karl Schmidt-Rotluff* (1884–1976), *Max Pechstein* (1881–1955) and, for a short time, *Emil Nolde* (1867–1956). They were influenced by Gauguin (▷ p. 321) and the Fauves, and also by African sculpture and German medieval woodcuts (a medium they revived). Though similar to Fauvism, their work was deliberately rougher and cruder, with broken, unnaturalistic colours and heavily expressive, stylized forms. German Expressionism was given further impetus by *Der Blaue Reiter* ('The Blue Rider'), formed in 1911. The members included the Russian *Wassily Kandinsky* (1866–1944), *August Macke* (1887–1914) and *Franz Marc* (1880–1916). The group encouraged artists to achieve an individual style, but shared a use of bold colours and a tendency towards abstraction.

Cubism

Cubism, one of the most important movements in 20th-century art, was originated in France by the Spanish artist *Pablo Picasso* (▷ box) and the Frenchman *Georges Braque* (1882–1963). The movement lasted from about 1907 into the 1920s, and following the example of Cézanne (▷ p. 321), the Cubists sought new answers to the age-old question of how to depict the three-dimensional real world on a flat two-dimensional canvas. They were also influenced by the recently discovered African tribal sculpture. Picasso and Braque began to analyse objects, breaking them down into their geometrical shapes and restructuring them in order to show each form's many facets in a single image. They were therefore representing what is known about an object rather than what is actually seen. These early *Analytical Cubist* works, as they became known, generally depict

Matisse's *Harmony in Red* (1908–09). Matisse was fascinated by the patterns of furnishing, and his figures are often absorbed into the background to make a deliberately two-dimensional composition. (BAL/Hermitage, St Petersburg)

either single figures or still lifes and were painted in a restricted range of greys and browns.

By 1910–11 the paintings by Picasso and Braque were almost abstract meshes of colour and line – the subject was identifiable only by a few clues, such as a pipe, a moustache or the indication of a chair back. To combat this move towards abstraction the artists began to add references to the real world, firstly by adding lettering or by simulating actual textures such as wood or fabric. Eventually even sand and newspaper cuttings were glued to the canvas to make a *collage*. Brighter colours were used in this phase, which was known as *Synthetic Cubism*.

Futurism

Futurism was founded in Italy by the poet Filippo Marinetti (1876–1944). In 1909 he urged artists to seek inspiration from industrial society and the dynamism of modern life, particularly speed. In order to realize their aim of depicting objects in motion, the Futurists made use first of Divisionist (⊳ p. 320) and later of Cubist techniques. By painting successive movements simultaneously, artists such as *Giacomo Balla* (1871–1958) and *Carlo Carra* (1881–1966) were able to suggest dynamic movement.

The *Rayonist* movement in Russia owed a considerable debt to the Futurists. Between 1912 and 1914 artists such as *Natalia Goncharova* (1881–1962) combined the influences of Cubism and Futurism in their works, which are characterized by almost abstract diagonal rays of colour. The *Vorticists* shared some of the revolutionary aims of the Futurists, and the crisp geometrical forms and jagged lines of their works reflect the aggressive nature of this British group led by *Wyndham Lewis* (1882–1957).

Abstraction

By about 1910, a greater emphasis on colour and form rather than subject matter had led many artists to move towards abstraction. Some, such as Wassily Kandinsky (⊳ above), approached abstraction through Expressionism. Others, like *Piet Mondrian* (1872–1944), developed through Cubism, abstracting from a tree or a windmill until the original subject almost completely disappeared. Mondrian gradually restricted his colours and used only vertical and horizontal lines in his compositions. The other members of the Dutch *De Stijl* movement, to which Mondrian belonged, also worked in geometrical abstract shapes, as did the artists of the Russian *Suprematist* movement, founded in 1915.

It was another Russian artist, *Naum Gabo* (1890–1977), who, with his brother *Antoine Pevsner* (1886–1962), co-founded the abstract movement *Constructivism*. Gabo used plastic and other new man-made materials to construct completely abstract sculptures that have something of the character of mathematical models. Far less rigorous in his abstraction was the Swiss painter *Paul Klee* (1879–1940), whose playful, witty works are rarely entirely abstract. The Romanian sculptor *Constantin Brancusi* (1876–1957) took a shape, such as a head or a bird, as a starting point and gradually simplified it until he had eliminated all inessential details, arriving at an almost abstract form of great purity.

Dada

The aftermath of World War I brought a crisis of faith in society. Dada and Surrealism grew out of this climate, and although they were essentially

PICASSO

Pablo Picasso (1881–1973) was the outstanding artistic genius of the 20th century. His inventiveness in discovering new ways of expression were unparalleled, dominating art for the first half of the century and influencing numerous artists worldwide.

Picasso was born in Malaga in Spain, and although he lived for most of his life in France he remained conscious of his origins. His horror at the Spanish Civil War inspired the violent and monumental *Guernica* (1937).

Because of the great diversity of his work, it is usual to divide Picasso's career into various stages. His first important works are the melancholy depictions of social outcasts, such as *The Old Guitarist* (1903), from his 'Blue Period' (1901–04), and the softer depictions of circus people from his 'Rose Period' (1905–07). These were followed by his brilliant contributions to the development of Cubism (⊳ main text).

At various times Picasso worked simultaneously in different styles. In the early 1920s he painted massive classical figures of bathers, and in the 1930s he exhibited with the Surrealists. His most emotionally distorted images date from the pre-war and war years: in *Weeping Woman* (1937) he savagely tears the subject apart in a manner quite unlike the careful dissection of the Cubist years.

Picasso's genius was not confined to painting; his prints and sculptures also demonstrate a great originality. He assembled some of them from found objects, which he imaginatively transformed. In the late 1940s Picasso added the production of ceramics to his activities. His late paintings were executed with great vigour in a summary, sketchy style and were sometimes based on famous works by Velasquez, Rembrandt and Manet.

Picasso's *Man with a Pipe* (1916). (AKG/Art Institute of Chicago)

Erich Heckel's *Scene from Dostoevski* (1912). This woodcut, with its angularity and strong contrasts, is typical of the Expressionism of Die Brücke.

different in purpose and character, some common ground existed, and a number of Dada artists later joined the Surrealist movement.

Dada was born in Zürich in 1916 where a group of young writers, poets and artists had converged. It embraced literature, the visual arts and performance, and was more a 'state of mind' than a coherent art movement. Deliberately provocative, it aimed to shock people out of a state of complacency, and create an art freed from the values and ideas that had preceded it. The Alsatian artist **Jean (Hans) Arp** (1887–1966) experimented with torn pieces of coloured paper scattered randomly on a paper background, emphasizing the laws of chance.

In 1915 the Frenchmen **Marcel Duchamp** (1887–1968) and **Francis Picabia** (1879–1953) moved to New York, and became the focus of a proto-Dada movement that was joined by the American **Man Ray** (1890–1976). Duchamp worked on his masterpiece *The Bride Stripped Bare by her Bachelors, Even* (1915–23), which is partly a fantastic and ironic mechanical diagram of sexual intercourse. He also continued to designate selected everyday objects – such as a hat rack or a urinal – as works of art, terming them 'ready-mades'.

The influence of Cubist collage is evident in the Dadaists' development of photomontage, a collage technique using photographs and words. It was used by **Raoul Hausmann** (1886–1971), **George Grosz** (1893–1959) and **John Heartfield** (Helmut Herzfelde, 1891–1968). In Hanover **Kurt Schwitters** (1887–1948) collected rubbish – such as cigarette wrappers, tickets, and newspapers – to incorporate into his collages, known as *Merzbilden*. **Max Ernst's** (1891–1976) work was rooted in Late Gothic fantasy drawn from Grünewald and Bosch (▷ p. 313).

Surrealism

Surrealism was founded in Paris in 1924 in reaction to the rationalism and materialism of Western society. The potential of the subconscious mind as a source of fantastic and dreamlike images was central to the Surrealists' interests. Art and literature were viewed as a means of expressing the fusion of the seemingly contradictory states of dream and reality into a 'sort of absolute reality, a surreality'.

In the visual arts Surrealism took two directions. The first adapted the automatic writing techniques of the Surrealist poets in order to liberate the mind from conscious control and produce a flow of ideas from the subconscious. The works produced in this way could be either abstract or figurative. The other stream was based on elaborate, meticulously detailed reconstructions of a dream world in which objects were often placed in unexpected juxtaposition. Both reflected the Surrealists' interest in the use of chance. The pioneer of this approach in painting was the Italian **Giorgio de Chirico** (1888–1928), whose early work of about 1912–17 was highly influential. De Chirico painted dreamlike visions of Italian piazzas, in which he introduced enigmatic imagery – classical statues, tailor's dummies, trains, gloves.

In 1925, the former Dadaist Max Ernst (▷ above), invented the technique of *frottage*. Rubbings were taken from textured surfaces such as wooden floorboards or leaves and used to suggest fantastic images. Many of his paintings employed the *decalomania* method of placing paint on a surface

such as glass, metal or shiny paper and then pressing this on to a canvas or paper support. The shapes in the resulting impression could then be developed imaginatively.

In *The Harlequin's Carnival* (1924–5), the Spanish painter **Joan Miró** (1893–1983) crossed the boundary between observation of the 'external model' and freely invented signs flowing from the subconscious. Though based on drawings made in a state of hallucination induced by hunger, its composition is highly organized through the intervention of conscious control.

René Magritte (1898–1967) rejected as unauthentic the supposed spontaneity of automatism. Instead he began to work with images that appeared stiffly conventional at first sight, but which were given a bizarre, dreamlike character by wildly impossible juxtapositions or changes of scale.

In 1929 **Salvador Dali** (1904–89) became an official member of the Surrealist group and gave it a new impetus with his method of *paranoiac-critical activity*, which combined the delusions associated with paranoia with a certain degree of objective detachment and control. Dali was particularly interested in abnormal mental conditions and, in particular, hallucinations. His strange dream imagery was depicted in sharp focus and as realistically as possible in a mode of painting that resembled colour photography.

Movements in art since 1945

The postwar period is characterized by extremely varied approaches to the problems of art. Although much of the best work has been abstract, some artists have continued to work in more traditional styles.

The first new movement to emerge after the war was **Abstract Expressionism**, which placed emphasis on spontaneous personal expression. A group of American painters, including **Jackson Pollock** (1912–56), began to make abstract pictures in much freer, more improvisatory styles. Pollock went on to develop a technique known as **Action painting**. It involved spattering the canvas in a semi-random fashion, so recording the action of the painter at the moment of painting as well as his emotional state.

Performance art – also known as *Happenings* – began in the late 1950s, and involves the artist in

Lichtenstein's *The Melody Haunts my Reverie* (1965) (right). On huge canvases, Lichtenstein parodied the style of popular comics. The enlarged images gained an almost abstract quality. (AKG/Sothebys)

Pollock's *Enchanted Wood* (1947) (left). Pollock's rhythmical dripping of paint on the canvas sought to record the action of the painter as well as his emotional state at the time of painting. (AKG/Peggy Guggenheim Collection, Venice)

Photo-Realism, a mainly American movement, began in the late 1960s. It developed as a return to realism, but painters worked from photographs instead of directly from nature. Most, like *Richard Estes* (1936–), painted street scenes with buildings and shop fronts depicted with great clarity and as if frozen in a moment of time.

In the 1980s *Neo-Expressionism* became prominent, particularly in Germany. Paintings are executed with great vigour in styles sometimes reminiscent of German Expressionism. It marks a return to myths, religion and mysterious symbolism as subject matter for painting.

(spontaneously) directing or performing an entertainment. It has a strong visual element and may also include theatre, music, film, and the participation of the audience. Performance can take many forms, and includes *Gilbert and George's* (1943– and 1942–) 'Singing Sculpture', where artists mimed, robot-like, to a piece of music.

Pop art developed in the late 1950s from the rejection of Abstract Expressionism by younger artists. They felt that it had become unrelated to the reality of contemporary life. In contrast, Pop art uses the images of mass media, advertising and pop culture, presenting the common everyday object as art. *Andy Warhol's* (1928–87) *Coca-Cola Bottles* and *Marilyn* series (1962) expressed the essence of the American dream where both products and celebrities were the icons of contemporary life.

The 1960s saw the peak of *Op art* (short for 'optical art'), a type of abstract art that exploits the optical effects of patterns. Its chief exponent, *Victor Vasarély* (1908–), explored expanding and contracting space using grid-like compositions in dazzling juxtapositions of black and white. Whereas some Op art works create an illusion of movement, *Kinetic art* works actually move, either by means of an electric motor or through outside forces such as air currents.

From the mid-1960s, various sculptors developed an awareness of the 'literalness' of objects and materials in *Minimal art*. *Donald Judd* (1928–) and *Sol LeWitt* (1928–) pioneered the use of industrial manufacturing techniques and materials in the creation of art. Much Minimal art is characterized by repeated geometric forms such as cubes. *Conceptual art* grew partly out of Minimal art as artists started to make works of a temporary character utilizing different types of process and system, inscribing imaginary geometric patterns on the landscape, and working with photographs and texts.

OTHER MAJOR ARTISTS

James Ensor (1860–1949), Belgian painter, a major influence on Expressionism and Surrealism.

Alexej Jawlensky (1864–1941), Russian painter loosely associated with *Der Blaue Reiter*: *Head of a Young Girl*.

George Rouault (1871–1958), French painter, noted for his Expressionist religious work.

Kees van Dongen (1877–1968), Dutch painter. His work developed along Fauvist lines, but his later works were principally of Parisian society.

Raoul Dufy (1877–1953), French painter briefly with the Fauves. Noted for his colourful scenes of racecourses and the seaside.

Kasimir Malevich (1878–1935), Russian painter, founder of Suprematism.

Jacob Epstein (1880–1959), English sculptor (born USA). Vorticist works include *The Rock-Drill* (1913–14); later work was more representational.

Fernand Léger (1881–1955), French painter, famous for his distinctive semi-abstract monumental style, often depicting people and machines.

Umberto Boccioni (1882–1916), Italian Futurist painter and sculptor: *Dynamism of a Dog on a Leash* (1912).

Max Beckmann (1884–1950), German Expressionist painter: *The Night* (1919).

Amedeo Modigliani (1884–1920), Italian painter and sculptor, famous for his elongated figures and erotic nudes.

Robert Delaunay (1885–1941), French painter, influenced by Cubism.

Juan Gris (1887–1955), Spanish painter, noted for his development of the Cubist style: *Homage to Picasso* (1911–12).

Marc Chagall (1887–1985), Russian-born French painter; although not a Surrealist his work has a dreamlike style with irrational juxtapositions.

Paul Nash (1889–1946), British painter, whose visionary landscapes and war paintings show Surrealist influences.

Henri Gaudier-Brzeska (1891–1915), influential French Vorticist sculptor.

Ben Nicholson (1894–1982), British abstract painter, some of whose works involve carved relief.

André Masson (1896–1987), French Surrealist painter. He made spontaneous drawings while in a trance.

Henry Moore (1898–1986), British sculptor, draughtsman and graphic artist, well known for his rounded forms.

Alberto Giacometti (1901–66), Swiss sculptor, well known for his elongated bronze human figures.

Barbara Hepworth (1903–75), English abstract sculptress.

Graham Sutherland (1903–80), British painter whose early landscapes had a dreamlike surreal quality; his later works include well-known portraits.

Mark Rothko (1903–70), American Abstract Expressionist, noted for his vast expanses of colour that fill the canvas.

Willem De Kooning (1904–), American Abstract Expressionist: *Woman* series.

Barnett Newman (1905–70), American Abstract Expressionist painter, noted for his large, coloured canvases broken by 'zips' (bands) of colour.

Francis Bacon (1909–92), British painter (born in Dublin), noted for the disturbing quality of his twisted figures: *Three Studies at the Base of a Crucifixion* (1944) and *Study after Velasquez*.

Nicolas de Stäel (1914–55), French-Russian abstract painter, whose works is characterized by broad patches of paint: *The Roofs* (1952).

Robert Motherwell (1915–), American Abstract Expressionist painter, also noted for his collages.

Joseph Beuys (1921–86), influential German Performance artist: *Coyote* (1974), a week-long 'dialogue' with a live coyote.

Richard Hamilton (1922–), English Pop artist, his work reflects his interest in marketing styles: *$he* (1958–61).

Roy Lichtenstein (1923–), American Pop artist, best known for his enlarged comic strip paintings: *Whaam!* (1963).

Robert Rauschenberg (1925–), American artist best known for his combination of Pop art and Abstract Expressionism.

Jasper Johns (1930–), American painter, printmaker and sculptor, best known as the founder of Pop art; *Target* and *Flags* paintings.

David Hockney (1937–), English painter and draughtsman, initially prominent in Pop art, but notable for his innovations in many styles: *Peter getting out of Nick's pool* (1966).

Anselm Kiefer (1945–), German Neo-expressionist painter, his work concentrates on Germany's history.

Architecture

Architecture is the art and science of designing and erecting buildings that are both functional and aesthetically pleasing. A building's design will depend upon many factors, including the technology and materials available along with their cost, the function of the building, and the taste of the building's architect, its owner and its user.

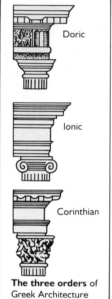

Doric

Ionic

Corinthian

The three orders of Greek Architecture

In ancient times buildings were monumental in scale, constructed to the greater glory of a deity or the dead. Secular architecture developed more slowly with an emphasis upon grandeur and security, rather than comfort.

Ancient Near East and Egypt

The earliest architecture known to us are the buildings of the civilizations that flourished along the banks of the rivers Nile, Tigris and Euphrates from the 5th millennium BC. In all these cultures the staple building material was mud brick. From the 3rd millennium BC the temple pyramids with stepped sides appeared in Mesopotamia. Egyptian pyramids developed around 2700 BC out of *mastaba*, tombs consisting of mazes of corridors surmounted by a mud-brick superstructure. The first millennium BC saw increasing use of vast columned halls – in Egypt at Thebes (Luxor) – and sprawling palace complexes of courtyards, halls and corridors.

Greece and Rome

Temples were the most important buildings of Classical Greece (5th and 4th centuries BC), and designers contented themselves with refining the simple formula of a rectangular structure surrounded by columns in one of the three orders (▷ illustration). Roman architecture fused the Greek discipline of columnar architecture with the structural innovations of vaults and arches of the Etruscan civilization of Italy (8th to 6th centuries BC). The Romans used these in many new buildings and shapes including circular temples, triumphal arches, amphitheatres, aqueducts and basilicas, which were made possible by new materials, including concrete.

Byzantine and Islam

From the 4th century AD Byzantine architects inherited and developed the Romans' structural innovations and combined them with a variety of decorative influences, especially mosaic work, from Greece and Asia. Where the Romans always built the domes over cylindrical bases, the Byzantines perfected building them over square bases, creating vast and complex many-domed palaces and churches.

As Muslims took over former Byzantine areas the many-domed style of Byzantine architecture was adopted as particularly suitable to mosque building. This style superseded the original mosques, based on the prophet Muhammad's house, but kept the minarets and mihrab (recess in the wall towards Mecca). The widespread proscription of figure representation in Islamic art partly accounts for the vividly coloured, intricate, often floral-based decoration found in Islamic architecture from Spain to Iran. Islamic cities are also characterized by careful town planning.

Romanesque

Buildings during the European 'dark ages' were relatively small and simple. However, during the 11th and 12th centuries many new, larger churches began to be built across Europe in a style known as Romanesque (also known as 'Norman' in Britain). The Roman basilica evolved with the addition of transepts into the cross-

---

MAJOR ARCHITECTS

Alvar Aalto (1898–1976), Finnish: Säynätsalo town hall (1950–52).

Robert Adam (1728–92), Scottish: the south front and interior of Kedleston Hall, Derbyshire.

Leon Battista Alberti (1404–72), Florentine: founder of Renaissance architectural theory.

Francesco Borromini (1599–1667), Italian: the façade of the church of S Carlo alle Quattro Fontane (1665–67), Rome.

Richard Boyle, Earl of Burlington (1694–1753), English: Chiswick House (1729).

Donato Bramante (1444–1514), Italian: rebuilt part of the Vatican and St Peter's, Rome.

Filippo Brunelleschi (1377–1446), Florentine: the dome of Florence Cathedral (1436).

Sir William Chambers (1723–96), English: Somerset House (1856), London, Kew Gardens pagoda.

Le Corbusier (Charles-Édouard Jeanneret; 1887–1965), Swiss-born French: Notre-Dame-du-Haut (1950–55), Roncamp (France).

Antonio Gaudi (1852–1926), Spanish (Catalan): Casa Batlló (1904–06), Church of the Holy Family, Barcelona.

Walter Gropius (1883–1969), German: founder of the Bauhaus (1928).

Hector Guimard (1867–1942), French: Art Nouveau stations on the Paris Metro.

Nicholas Hawksmoor (1661–1736), English: several London churches (with Wren), Blenheim Palace, Castle Howard (with Vanbrugh).

(Baron) Victor Horta (1861–1946), Belgian: the Hotel Tassel (1892–93).

Inigo Jones (1573–1652), English: the Queen's House, Greenwich (1616), Banqueting Hall, Whitehall (1619).

William Kent (1685–1748), English: Horse Guards Building, Whitehall, London (1750–58).

Louis Le Vau (1612–70), French: the Louvre, Paris; also planned Versailles.

Sir Edwin Lutyens (1869–1941), English: the plan and principal buildings of New Delhi, India.

Charles Rennie Mackintosh (1868–1928), Scottish: Glasgow School of Art (1909).

Carlo Maderna (1556–1629), Italian: determined the style of early Baroque.

Jules Hardouin-Mansart (1646–1708), French: Palace of Versailles.

John Nash (1752–1835), English: Regent's Park and Regent Street, Marble Arch, London.

Balthasar Neumann (1687–1753), German: The Residenz in Würzburg (Germany).

Andrea Palladio (1508–80), Italian: founder of the Palladian style: Villa Rotonda near Vicenza.

Sir Joseph Paxton (1801–65), British: Crystal Palace (1851).

Praxiteles (fl. 5th century BC), Greek: Parthenon on the Acropolis in Athens.

Augustus Welby Northmore Pugin (1812–52), English Gothic Revival church architect.

Richard Rogers (1933–), English: Pompidou Centre, Paris (1977), Lloyds' Building, London (1986).

Ludwig Mies van der Rohe (1888–1969), German-born American: Seagram Building, New York (1958).

Sir George Gilbert Scott (1811–78), English: the Albert Memorial (1863–72), London.

Sir John Soane (1753–1837), English: the Bank of England (1792–1833) in London.

Louis Sullivan (1856–1924), American: Wainwright Building, St Louis, Missouri.

Sir John Vanbrugh (1664–1726), English: Blenheim Palace and Castle Howard (with Hawksmoor).

Eugène-Emmanuel Viollet-le-Duc (1814–79), the leading French Gothic Revival architect.

Vitruvius (fl. 1st century BC), Roman: *De architectura*, 10 books on architecture.

Sir Christopher Wren (1632–1723), English: St Paul's Cathedral (1710), many London churches.

Frank Lloyd Wright (1869–1959), American: Guggenheim Museum, New York (1959).

shaped plan, with massive piers and rounded arches, and towers at the west end. Mouldings and attached columns became large and simple.

Gothic

The Gothic, which flourished from the 12th century in Spain, Britain, France, Germany and Central Europe, was a sophistication of the Romanesque, typified by pointed arches. Structural thrusts were increasingly carried on rib vaults and down piers and attached columns to the ground. This complex stone framework meant walls were merely infill and allowed vast areas of stained glass to be introduced. Ribs, mouldings and colonettes became more complex and decorative in later Gothic.

Renaissance

The Renaissance was a conscious attempt to revive the arts and literature of Classical Rome. It appeared first in 15th-century Italy, which contained the greatest concentration of Classical remains. By the early 16th century Italian architects had thoroughly studied these and were building churches and palaces with carefully proportioned Classical Roman features such as pediments and loggias. In France and Britain the Renaissance style first appeared mixed with the Gothic in a rather haphazard and decorative way in 16th-century country houses and palaces.

Mannerism, Baroque and Rococo

The Classical styles dominated architecture in Western Europe, and later the USA, from the 16th to the 19th centuries. Mannerist architecture emerged in mid-16th-century Italy, when architects began combining Classical architectural elements in a manner never seen in Ancient Rome: broken pediments; giant orders which rose through two or more storeys of a building; and dropped keystones. Baroque architecture avoids such obvious visual perversity but invests Classical architectural elements with a new sense of movement; undulating façades, bristling grouped pilasters and expressive sculpture often feature. The Baroque flourished in Italy and Spain and more restrainedly in Britain and France. The Rococo (▷ p. 317) was an exuberant and frothy style of usually interior decoration which flourished in 18th-century France and Germany, often contrasting with a more restrained Classical exterior.

Palladianism and Neoclassicism

Andrea Palladio's (▷ box) theories and buildings greatly influenced building in Britain two centuries after he lived. Country houses show this in the sparseness of decoration and the geometry of planning derived from his Vicenza villas. Patrons travelled to Italy to study the originals and, increasingly, the Classical buildings and remains that had inspired Palladio himself. The result of this was the flourishing of Neoclassicism throughout Western Europe from the mid-18th to the early 19th century. All types of buildings, religious and domestic, were influenced and show this in the archaeological correctness of their details, proportions and decoration.

The 19th century

Until the late 18th century all Classical revivals had been based on Roman originals. The new taste for archaeology resulted in a spreading taste for Classical Greek buildings. The simplicity and severity of the originals appealed to many French, British and American architects tired of endless variations on 'decadent' Roman originals, and the period c. 1775–1850 saw many

FEATURES OF A GOTHIC CATHEDRAL
Based on Amiens (13th century)

churches, public buildings and country houses with massively simple Greek porticoes. The taste for archaeology spread later in the century to medieval buildings, long despised as 'barbaric'. During the Gothic Revival in Britain, France and the USA, architects regarded the Gothic as the only way to build with structural – to them therefore moral – integrity. They regarded Classical styles as deceitful, often unChristian, as the outward appearance did not directly reflect how the structure worked. One method of building that did this, but avoided the retreat into the past, was to use new materials such as iron and glass for railway stations and bridges. The battle between Classical and Gothic culminated at the century's end in Art Nouveau, with its asymmetrical, exuberant decoration based on natural and fantastical forms.

The 20th century

The greatest impact on 20th-century architecture has been new technology and the subsequent International Modernist style. Architects for most of the century believed that a building's appearance should reflect its function and how it worked structurally. Decoration was therefore undesirable and with the development of steel framing – where the structural forces in a building are carried by a steel frame – and reinforced concrete, buildings of great size and simplicity were made possible. In the 1970s Hi-Tech, a sophisticated variation of Modernism, emerged with buildings expressing their technological as well as structural function through exterior display of brightly coloured electrical conduits – even plumbing. By the close of the 20th century widespread disillusionment had occurred with the 'inhumanity' of modern buildings. Post-Modernism is an imprecise term coined to cover the wide variety of building styles presently used, from careful pastiches of Neoclassical buildings to 'fun' buildings that play with simplified Classical forms, often in bright colours.

SEE ALSO

● CONSTRUCTION AND ENGINEERING p. 214
● GREEK AND ROMAN ART p. 306
● RENAISSANCE ART p. 312

Cinema

There are several claims to the invention of cinema. The American Thomas Edison (1847–1931) was the first to market a successful film machine, but it was in Europe, during the first years of the 20th century, that the potential of cinema was first recognized. Then came World War I and the American film industry, uninterrupted by the conflict that held back development in Europe, began its long dominance. However, indigenous cinema has always been important in preserving national identity and in offsetting foreign cultural dominance.

SEE ALSO

● PHOTOGRAPHY p. 204
● RADIO AND TV p. 206

Perhaps the first great artist of the cinema was the American **D.W. Griffith** (1875–1948), a director who began to make more adventurous use of the camera. He experimented with lighting, long-shots and close-ups, takes of different lengths, different camera setups and angles within a scene, appreciating that all these affect audience reaction. Realizing that close-up acting demands skills different from the flamboyant style of many stage actors, he built up a team of cinema actors. His epic *The Birth of a Nation* (1915) amazed the world with what films could do.

The silent comics

Mark Sennet (1884–1960) was a younger director who learned rapidly from Griffith and founded the Keystone company in California. His most famous films featured cleverly edited, speeded-up antics of the Keystone Cops, and were made to a regular formula of chases and slapstick, using stop and reverse action filming combined with carefully planned stunts. Keystone films also featured such famous names as Roscoe 'Fatty' Arbuckle, Charlie Chaplin and Buster Keaton.

European silent classics

In the years after World War I the European cinema could not compete with Hollywood

Ingmar Bergman's *Seventh Seal* (1956). Death comes to claim a knight. Bergman's vision of death has become part of the iconography of modern cinema. (Kobal)

commercially but led in terms of experiment. **Robert Weine's** (1881–1938) use of expressionist settings in *Cabinet of Dr Caligari* (1919) drew attention to German cinema. It produced many films notable for their distinctive style and social awareness, such as **Fritz Lang's** (1890–1976) *Metropolis* (1927). In France intellectuals experimented with the film as a serious art form, an example of which is **Luis Buñuel's** (1900–83) *Un Chien Andalou* (1928), made in collaboration with Salvador Dali. The greatest of the Russian directors, **Sergei Eisenstein** (1898–1948), emerged after the Russian Revolution. He used symbols to reinforce ideas and edited shots to make a 'collision' of images, emphasizing conflict in the subject. His *Battleship Potemkin* (1925) is a virtuoso demonstration of these skills.

The coming of sound and colour

Sound was added to motion pictures in 1927 with the release of *The Jazz Singer*. It included songs and a snatch of dialogue and is generally accepted as the first 'talkie'. The problems of sound recording brought back the static shorts of very early cinema. Technical limitations on movement, however, were soon overcome, and directors soon began to use dialogue, sound effects and background music creatively. Technicolor, a three-colour process, was developed in 1932, but it was not until Eastman Color (1952) that colour was used universally.

Hollywood genres

Historical romances and adaptations of novels and stage successes were among the earliest feature films, but soon films began to be produced that were recognizable as belonging to particularly cinematic genres. Hollywood is particularly associated with the musical, the gangster film and the western, but also produced thrillers, horror films, detective stories, war and action films, romances, comedies and films dealing with social problems.

The western, with its emphasis on action, was ideal for the silent cinema. The roles of 'goodie' and 'baddie' were usually clear-cut, whether the conflict involved outlaws or Indians. Chases, stunts and often comedy were regular elements, and in the 1930s, after the coming of sound, there was a vogue for singing cowboys. After World War II distinctions between good and bad become more blurred, and the traditional folk hero was replaced by more complex characters. Gunfight violence became more realistic and a more balanced view of 'Wild West' life was presented.

After the advent of sound and the American experience of prohibition, gangster films became a popular genre, often based on identifiable real-life criminals. Later films often showed social problems as a reason for turning to crime. In the 1960s and 70s films such as *Bonny and Clyde* (1967) and *The Godfather* (1971) were sophisticated treatments of the gangster film.

With the talkies came the musical. *The Broadway Melody* (1929), the first 'all-talking, all-singing, all-dancing' film, was so successful that over 70 musicals appeared within a year. Its use of a stage story as an excuse for revue-style numbers was repeated in subsequent films. Others echoed the styles of operetta and stage musical comedies. *42nd Street* (1933) introduced the spectacular dance sequences of **Busby Berkeley** (1895–1976). He produced dazzling dance routines often featuring kaleidoscope-like effects, but the cost of making musicals had soared and in the years that followed most musicals were film versions of big box office stage shows.

The popularity of television in the 1940s and 50s dramatically reduced cinema attendance. Hollywood retaliated with spectacular epics and innovations such as ultra-wide Cinerama, 3-D and stereophonic sound. Recently there has been an emphasis on elaborate special effects and on films aimed at the American teenage market.

However, economic problems have seen the decline of some of the big studios. Independent companies are now responsible for a larger proportion of film releases, although finance and distribution may still come from the big studios, which are now part of multinational companies such as Coca-Cola. Much production in Hollywood is now designed for television.

World cinema

Freedom from some of the pressures of Hollywood has enabled non-American film makers to be more personal and often more thoughtful in their films, and to reflect the societies in which they work. It has allowed them to risk experiment and to explore subjects unacceptable to the US film industry's Production Code.

In Britain *John Grierson* (1898–1972) pioneered the creation of a documentary tradition, which flourished in the 1930s. He made his name with *Drifters* (1929). After the war Italy's Neorealist movement produced films that emphasized real life – including poverty. *Vittoria de Sica's* (1901–74) *Bicycle Thieves* (1948) is remarkable in its ability to develop from a simple story so much frustration and pathos. Neorealism influenced many later Italian directors such as *Federico Fellini* (1920–) and *Bernardo Bertolucci* (1940–) and has been incorporated into cinema from India to Brazil.

In the mid-1950s international attention focused on the work of the Swedish director *Ingmar Bergman* (1918–). His work deals with complex moral, psychological and metaphysical problems. Combining his existential quest with a deft cinematic hand, Bergman is considered one of the greatest film artists.

Influential in the late 1950s was a group of French critics turned directors, led by *François Truffaut* (1932–84), *Jean-Luc Godard* (1930–), *Claud Chabrol* (1930–) and *Alain Resnais* (1922–). Collectively dubbed the *Nouvelle Vague* (New Wave), they emphasized personal style rather than conventionally 'well-made' films in successes such as *Les Quatre-cent Coups* (Truffaut, 1959), *Hiroshima Mon Amour* (Resnais, 1959) and *A Bout de Souffle* (Godard, 1960). Many of the films were characterized by a spirit of spontaneity, improvisation, and freedom.

Charlie Chaplin (1889–1977) revolutionized early farces by introducing mime, characterization and slapstick pathos. His immense popularity allowed him to set up a company independent of the powerful studios.

OTHER MAJOR DIRECTORS

Woody Allen (1935–), American: *Annie Hall* (1977) and *Hannah and her Sisters* (1986).

Richard Attenborough (1923–), English: *Gandhi* (1982).

Bernado Bertolucci (see text): *Last Tango in Paris* (1972), *The Last Emperor* (1988).

Robert Bresson (1907–), French: *Les Anges du péché* (1943) and *Un condamné à mort s'est echappé* (1956).

Frank Capra (1897–91), American: *Mr Deeds Goes To Town* (1936), *You Can't Take It with You* (1938) and *It's a Wonderful Life* (1946).

Marcel Carné (1909–), French: *Le Jour se Lève* (1939) and *Les Enfants du Paradis* (1945).

René Clair (1898–1981), French: *Le millin* (1931), *À nous la liberté* (1932), *The Ghost Goes West* (1936).

Jean Cocteau (1889–1963), French: *Beauty and the Beast* (1946).

Francis Ford Coppola (1939–), American: *Patton* (1969), *The Godfather* (1972) and *Apocalypse Now* (1979).

George Cukor (1899–), American: *Little Women* (1933), *A Star Is Born* (1954) and *My Fair Lady* (1964).

Cecil B. De Mille (1881–1959), American: *The Ten Commandments* (1923), *King of Kings* (1927) and *The Greatest Show on Earth* (1952).

Rainer Werner Fassbinder (1946–82), German: *Despair* (1977).

Frederico Fellini (see text): *La Dolce Vita* (1959), *8½* (1963).

John Ford (1895–1973), American: *Stagecoach* (1939), *The Grapes of Wrath* (1940).

Milos Forman (1932–), Czech: *The Fireman's Ball* (1967).

Bob Fosse (1925–88), American: *All That Jazz* (1979).

Werner Herzog (1942–), German: *Aguirre, Wrath of God* (1973) and *Fitzcarraldo* (1982).

Alfred Hitchcock (1899–1980), English: *Rebecca* (1940), *Psycho* (1960) and *The Birds* (1963).

John Huston (1906–87), American: *The Maltesc Falcon* (1941), *The African Queen* (1951).

Elia Kazan (1909–), Greek-born American: *A Streetcar Named Desire* (1951), *On the Waterfront* (1956).

Stanley Kubrick (1928–), American: *2001: A Space Odyssey* (1968) and *A Clockwork Orange* (1971).

Akira Kurosawa (1910–), Japanese: *Seven Samurai* (1954) and *Rann* (1986).

David Lean (1908–91), English: *Oliver Twist* (1948), *The Bridge on the River Kwai* (1957) and *Lawrence of Arabia* (1962).

Joseph Losey (1909–84), American: *The Servant* (1963) and *The Go-Between* (1971).

Ernst Lubitsch (1892–1947), German-born American: *Heaven Can Wait* (1943).

Louis Malle (1932–), French: *Les Amants* (1958) and *Au revoir les enfants* (1987).

Friedrich Murnau (1888–1931), German: *Nosferatu* (1922).

Nagisa Oshima (1932–), Japanese: *Ai No Corrida* (197), *Max Mon Amour* (1987).

Pier Paolo Pasolini (1922–75), Italian: *Gospel According to St Matthew* (1963).

Sam Peckinpah (1926–84), American: *The Wild Bunch* (1969).

Roman Polanski (1933–), Polish: *Rosemary's Baby* (1968), *Chinatown* (1974), *Tess* (1979).

Otto Preminger (1906–86), Austrian-born American: *Exodus* (1961).

Satyajit Ray (1921–92), Indian: *Pather Panchali* (1955).

Carol Reed (1906–76), English: *The Third Man* (1949).

Jean Renoir (1894–1979), French: *La Grande Illusion* (1937) and *La Règle du Jeu* (1939).

Nicholas Roeg (1928–), British: *Performance* (1970) and *Bad Timing* (1980).

Eric Rohmer (1920–), French: *Ma Nuit Chez Maud* (1969), *Le Rayon Vert* (1984).

Roberto Rossellini (1906–77), Italian: *Rome, Open City* (1945).

Ken Russell (1927–), English: *Women in Love* (1969) and *Tommy* (1975).

John Schlesinger (1926–), British: *Midnight Cowboy* (1969).

Steven Spielberg (1947–), American director and producer: *E.T.* (1982) and *The Color Purple* (1986).

Josef von Sternberg (1894–1969), Austrian-born American: *Blue Angel* (1930).

Andrei Tarkovsky (1932–88), Soviet: *Andrei Rublev* (1966) and *Solaris* (1971).

King Vidor (1894–1982), American: *The Big Parade* (1925), *Hallelujah!* (1929) and *The Citadel* (1938).

Luchino Visconti (1906–76), Italian: *Ossessione* (1942) and *Death in Venice* (1970).

Andrzej Wajda (1926–), Polish: *Ashes and Diamonds* (1958).

Peter Weir (1944–), Australian: *Picnic at Hanging Rock* (1975) and *Green Card* (1991).

Orson Welles (1915–85), American: *Citizen Kane* (1940).

Wim Wenders (1945–), German: *The American Friend* (1977), *Paris, Texas* (1984), *Wings of Desire* (1987).

Billy Wilder (1906–), Austrian-born American: *Double Indemnity* (1944), *Sunset Boulevard* (1950) and *Some Like it Hot* (1959).

William Wyler (1902–81), American: *The Best Years of our Lives* (1946).

Fred Zinneman (1907–), Austrian-born American: *High Noon* (1952), *A Man For All Seasons* (1966).

What is Music?

If asked to define music, most of us would find it hard to answer. Surprisingly, the multi-volume *New Grove Dictionary of Music and Musicians* takes the subject so completely for granted that it does not attempt a definition. The *Collins English Dictionary* calls it 'an art form consisting of sequences of sounds in time, especially tones of definite pitch organized melodically, harmonically, rhythmically and according to tone colour'.

But not all music aspires to being an art form, and not all music is melodic, harmonic, or rhythmic. Music is difficult to tie down. Its components may include melody, rhythm, harmony, pitch and timbre (tone colour), not necessarily all at the same time.

The origins of music

The sophisticated evolution of music – even the notes of a simple scale or chord – took place over a period of centuries. There was certainly a rich musical tradition in the years before Christ – for example in India, China, Egypt and Greece, much of it tantalizing because it was passed on orally, not written down.

In the West, much of what we today call music emerged through the spread of Christianity, particularly through medieval *plainsong* chants sung in churches (⊳ p. 332), and through *Gregorian chant*, named after Pope Gregory I, in whose time (around AD 600) it was systematized. This still forms part of Roman Catholic musical ritual. However, its *modes* (or 'scales') gradually gave way to the modern scale.

The components of music

A musical *note*, therefore, is more than just a 'noise'. It is a single sound of definite pitch and duration, which can be identified in writing. The *pitch* of a note is its height or depth in relation to other notes, or in relation to an absolute pitch. This absolute pitch has internationally been set at A = 440 Hz (hertz); that is, the A above middle C has a frequency of 440 cycles or vibrations per second (⊳ also Wave Theory, p. 20, and Acoustics, p. 22).

SEE ALSO

- WAVE THEORY p. 20
- ACOUSTICS p. 22
- HIFI p. 207
- WESTERN MUSIC p. 332–9
- THE SYMPHONY ORCHESTRA AND ITS INSTRUMENTS p. 340
- BALLET AND DANCE p. 346

TIME VALUES OF NOTES

Each note has half the duration or time value of the note above. The symbol for each note is followed by the symbol for the equivalent rest. The breve is rarely used. A dot after a note increases its value by half.

Note symbol	Rest symbol	British name	US name
		semibreve	whole note
		minim	half note
		crotchet	quarter note
		quaver	eighth note
		semiquaver	sixteenth note
		demisemiquaver	thirty-second note
		hemidemisemiquaver	sixty-fourth note

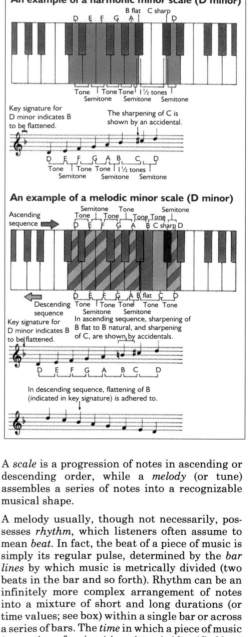

MAJOR AND MINOR SCALES
Showing the intervals between notes.

An example of a major scale (D major)

Key signature for D major indicates F and C are to be sharpened.

An example of a harmonic minor scale (D minor)

Key signature for D minor indicates B to be flattened.

The sharpening of C is shown by an accidental.

An example of a melodic minor scale (D minor)

Ascending sequence

Descending sequence

Key signature for D minor indicates B to be flattened.

In ascending sequence, sharpening of B flat to B natural, and sharpening of C, are shown by accidentals.

In descending sequence, flattening of B (indicated in key signature) is adhered to.

A *scale* is a progression of notes in ascending or descending order, while a *melody* (or tune) assembles a series of notes into a recognizable musical shape.

A melody usually, though not necessarily, possesses *rhythm*, which listeners often assume to mean *beat*. In fact, the beat of a piece of music is simply its regular pulse, determined by the *bar lines* by which music is metrically divided (two beats in the bar and so forth). Rhythm can be an infinitely more complex arrangement of notes into a mixture of short and long durations (or time values; see box) within a single bar or across a series of bars. The *time* in which a piece of music (or section of a piece) is written is identified by a *time signature* at the beginning of the piece or section. Thus 3/4 time (three-four time), which is waltz time, represents three crotchets to the bar.

This means that the main beat comes every three crotchets: 1 2 3, 1 2 3, etc.; 4/4 time, which is march time, has four crotchets: 1 2 3 4, 1 2 3 4, etc.; 3/8 and 6/8 represent three and six quavers, respectively.

A melody may have *harmony*. This means that it is accompanied by *chords*, which are combinations of notes, simultaneously sounded. It may also have *counterpoint*, whereby another melody, or succession of notes with musical shape, is simultaneously combined with it. 'Rules' of harmony and counterpoint, stating which notes could be acceptably combined and which could not, have been matters of concern to scholars, teachers and pupils in the course of musical history. But as with any other grammar, progressive composers have known when to break or bend the rules to the benefit of their own music.

Tonality

The old modes, or scales, employed in the Middle Ages gradually gave way in the 17th century to a modern *tonality* – scales laid out in 12 major and minor *keys*, each consisting of a sequence of seven notes, divided into tones and semitones. Each of the 12 major and minor scales starts on one of the 12 semitones into which an octave is divided (▷ illustration). Melodies in a specific key use the notes of that scale, and the order in which the notes are used determines the nature of the melody. On a piano the scale of C major consists entirely of white notes, starting on C.

The notes from C to the next C, either above or below, form an *octave*. A note and another note an octave above sound 'the same' because the higher note has double the frequency (▷ above). For example, the A above middle C is 440 cycles per second, and the A above that is 880 cycles.

From C to D (the first 'white' note above) represents an interval of a tone, from C to C sharp (the first 'black' note) an interval of a semitone, so called because it represents half a tone. But from E to F, and from B to C, also forms a semitone (on a piano there is no black note between them). A scale therefore consists of a mixture of tone and semitone intervals. A *chromatic scale*, on the other hand, employs nothing but semitones, and thus requires all 12 of the white and black notes to be used.

In musical terminology, a sharp (♭) indicates a semitone rise in pitch, and a flat (♯) a semitone fall. A natural (♮) is a note that is neither sharp nor flat, though the indication sign needs only to be used in special circumstances.

The first note of a scale is known as the *tonic*, or 'keynote'. The tonic of the scale of C is therefore the note C. All other scales require one or more black notes to be played in order to produce the same sequence of intervals. The sequence of intervals between the notes in a major scale is therefore as follows (using C major as an example):

C [tone] D [tone] E [semitone] F [tone] G [tone] A [tone] B [semitone] C.

Minor scales employ a different sequence of notes from major, and incorporate, in particular, a flattened third (in the scale of C minor the note E, a 'third' higher than the note C, is 'flattened' to the black note immediately below, i.e. E flat). It is this that gives minor keys what listeners traditionally identify as their element of 'sadness' compared with major ones. There are two commonly used forms of the minor scale, and the

sequence of intervals is as follows (using A minor as an example):

Harmonic Minor: A [tone] B [semitone] C [tone] D [tone] E [semitone] F [1½ tones] G sharp [semitone] A.

Melodic Minor: A [tone] B [semitone] C [tone] D [tone] E [tone] F sharp [tone] G sharp [semitone] A.

There is a different descending sequence in melodic scales:

A [tone] G [tone] F [semitone] E [tone] D [tone] C [semitone] B [tone] A.

It is important to remember that these scales are conventions – conventions to which our ears are attuned through familiarity. The modes of ancient Greece and medieval Europe employed different sequences of tones and semitones, and the scales used in Indian music and some modern jazz, for example, may use quarter tones.

In the course of a piece of music, a composer may often *modulate*, or change key, in order to avoid monotony. In Bach's time, and beyond, an established and logical change was to the key based on the fifth note of the scale, known as the *dominant* (the note G in the key of C). Harmonically this is closely related to the tonic note, so the transition could be made from one key to the other, and back to the home key, without difficulty. But modulations to harmonically more 'distant' keys, though at one time frowned on for pedantic reasons, were soon found to be a source of dramatic effects, as also was the sudden contrast between a minor key and a major, exploited by composers such as Beethoven with increasing freedom. By the time Wagner composed *Tristan and Isolde* (1865), modulation had become so fluid that it was only a step away from *atonality*, or the composition of music in no fixed key at all. Atonality was systematized by Schoenberg (▷ p. 338) in what he described as *dodecaphonic* or 'twelve-note' music. In this method of composition, one of the major influences on 20th-century music, the twelve notes within an octave were employed in such a way that there was no home key and no reliance on modulation in the old sense, though key relationships did often remain implied, even if not specifically stated.

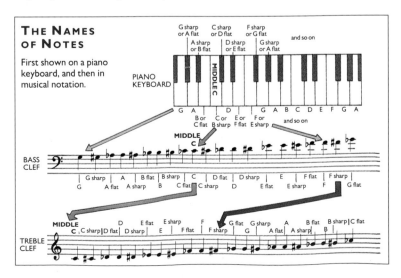

THE NAMES OF NOTES

First shown on a piano keyboard, and then in musical notation.

Early Music

The beginnings of Western music lie in the cultures of the ancient Near East, where music is believed to have been used as an accompaniment to religious worship, dance, and work. The musical culture of the Eastern Mediterranean was transplanted to the Western Mediterranean by the Romans, and after the decline of the Roman Empire, it was the Christian Church that perpetuated and extended the musical heritage of antiquity.

SEE ALSO

- ART IN THE 17TH AND 18TH CENTURIES p. 315
- WHAT IS MUSIC? p. 330
- THE CLASSICAL PERIOD p. 334
- THE SYMPHONY ORCHESTRA p. 340
- OPERA p. 342
- BALLET AND DANCE p. 346

Two of the crucial developments in the early history of Western music were *plainsong* and *polyphony*, both of which came about through the spread of the Christian religion. Plainsong, consisting of a single line of vocal melody in 'free' rhythm that was not divided into metred bar lengths, reached its peak in Gregorian chant, still used in the Roman Catholic Church today.

Plainsong falls into the category of *monophonic* music (Greek for 'single sound'). *Polyphony*, conversely, means 'many sounds', and indicates the simultaneous sounding of two or more independent melodic lines to produce a coherent musical texture. Polyphony began to emerge in Europe in the 12th and 13th centuries. The early polyphonic style, involving the addition of parts to a plainsong melody, was described by early 14th century writers as 'Ars Antiqua' (Latin 'old art'). Its successor, 'Ars Nova' (Latin 'new art'), flourished in France and Italy in the 14th century, and incorporated significant innovations in rhythm and harmony. Its most celebrated practitioner, *Guillaume de Machaut* (c. 1300–77), also pioneered the polyphonic setting of poetry in fixed song forms, known as *chansons*. Compositions such as these were influenced by the medieval tradition of monophonic secular song as practised, for instance, by the *troubadours* (▷ p. 358) – itinerant poet-musicians active in Provence in the 11th and 12th centuries.

The Renaissance

The Renaissance brought significant developments in both religious and secular musical forms. In religious music, composers concentrated their efforts on the mass and the motet (▷ box). Plainsong melodies had formed the basis of earlier polyphonic settings for the mass, but *Guillaume Dufay* (c. 1400–74) used secular songs for the same purpose. Musicians from the Low Countries dominated the European musical stage in the second half of the 15th century. The polyphonic style established by *Johannes Ockeghem* (c. 1425–c. 1495) and *Josquin Desprès* (1440–1521), adding further parts to increase the breadth of sound, persisted to the beginning of the 16th century, but gradually different national styles and forms began to emerge. In Germany the Lutheran chorale took root, while in England the anthem (the Protestant equivalent of the Latin motet) took its place in the liturgy of the Church of England. The polyphonic mass reached its apogee in the work of three great composers: the Italian *Giovanni Palestrina* (c. 1525–84), the Spaniard *Luis de Victoria* (c. 1548–1611), and the Fleming *Roland de Lassus* (1532–94). In Venice, a more flamboyant polychoral (multi-choir) style was developed by the Venetians *Andrea Gabrieli* (c. 1510–86) and his nephew and pupil *Giovanni Gabrieli* (1557–1612).

The European polyphonic tradition was introduced into England by *Thomas Tallis* (c. 1505–85). His compatriot *William Byrd* (1543–1623) – a Catholic – wrote masses and motets for the Roman Catholic Church, as well as anthems and psalm settings for the Anglican Church. Byrd's music for virginal (a keyboard instrument similar to the harpsichord) and his fantasias for viol consort established an English style of intrumental composition. His secular songs, unlike the madrigals of his contemporaries, show little Italian influence.

The madrigal was a secular polyphonic composition for several voices. By the late 16th century, in the hands of composers such as *Carlo Gesualdo* (c. 1560–1613) and Claudio Monteverdi (▷ below), it had become a highly sophisticated and dramatic genre. Italian madrigals began to appear in England in the late 16th century, and a native English tradition of madrigal composition was established by composers such as *Thomas Weelkes* (c. 1576–1623) and *John Wilbye* (1574–1638). The *ayre*, a less contrapuntal form, was usually performed to lute or consort accompaniment. Pre-eminent among England's school of lutenist song composers was *John Dowland* (1563–1626).

In the Middle Ages instruments were principally used to double voices in vocal polyphony or to provide music for dancing. The real burgeoning of instrumental music took place in the 16th century. Dance forms such as the stately *pavan* and vigorous *galliard* emerged, and were often composed in pairs, prefiguring the instrumental suites of the 17th century. Instrumental music in the 16th century was performed mainly on the lute, the organ, the virginal or harpsichord, and by instrumental ensembles. The lute in particular enjoyed immense popularity as a domestic instrument. Instrumental ensembles of the Renaissance never became standardized, but consorts of viols, and groups of wind instruments such as cornetts and sackbuts were common.

The Italian *Claudio Monteverdi* (1567–1643) is chiefly celebrated today as the composer of three innovative operas (▷ p. 342) and the *Vespro della Beata Vergine* ('Vespers of the Blessed Virgin'; 1610). His church music displays two contrasting trends: one following the traditional polyphonic style, the other tending towards the newer Ba-

---

MASSES AND MOTETS

The Mass is the principal service of the Roman Catholic Church, which composers set to music as part of their duty to God and to their employers. The first known integrated setting of the 'Ordinary' of the Mass (*Kyrie, Gloria, Credo, Sanctus* with *Benedictus* and *Agnus Dei*) was Machaut's *Messe de Notre Dame*. By the 18th century, masses with instrumental accompaniment had established themselves, as Bach's great B minor Mass confirms. Requiem masses for the dead consisted of a different sequence of movements, including an opening *Requiem Aeternam* ('Grant them eternal rest') and a *Dies Irae*.

A motet is a short choral work, often unaccompanied, whose origins go back to the 13th century. The early motet was a polyphonic composition for three voices, two accompanying voices being added in counterpoint to a plainsong or other melody sung by a tenor. The Renaissance motet, for four to six voices, reached its apogee in the works of Victoria , Palestrina, Byrd and Tallis.

Johann Sebastian Bach, the German composer and organist, whose output was described by Richard Wagner as 'The most stupendous miracle in all music'. During his lifetime, however, his music was only known to a comparatively narrow circle, and his highest aspiration was to become organist and choirmaster of St Thomas's Church in Leipzig. Bach was in fact only the second choice for this post, the job originally being offered to his friend Telemann, who turned it down. (AKG)

roque style of brilliant and expressive writing for solo voices and chorus (⊳ below). The German *Heinrich Schütz* (1585–1672) encountered the new Italian style while a pupil of Giovanni Gabrieli in Venice. In his compositions for the Lutheran Church, he married the polychoral style of the Gabrielis, the operatic style of Monteverdi, and the emerging *concertante* style of his Italian contemporaries with the native German polyphonic tradition.

The Baroque

In the 17th century revolutionary change took place both in composition and in the formal organization of music: the medieval modes that had been the basis of polyphonic composition in the 16th century giving way to a system involving the use of modern scales (⊳ p. 330). Innovations such as the *concertante* style – in which instrumental or vocal parts were accompanied by a *basso continuo* (involving a low-pitched instrument such as a cello or bass viol combined with a harpsichord, organ or lute) – distinguish the Baroque from the Renaissance.

The development of the two major new instrumental genres of the Baroque – the sonata and the concerto – was largely the work of Italian composers. The 12 *Concerti Grossi* (1714) of *Arcangelo Corelli* (1653–1713) established the form of the concerto grosso and were imitated all over Europe. The composer-priest *Antonio Vivaldi* (1678–1741) is chiefly known for his development of the solo concerto; his set of violin concertos known as *The Four Seasons* – representing but four concertos out of an output of more than 460 – has become perhaps the best known of all Baroque compositions. The three-movement structure of his concertos became a model for many composers of concertos, including J.S. Bach. Unlike his sonatas and concertos, Vivaldi's operas have never been successfully revived. A similar fate has befallen the 115 extant operas of the prolific Neapolitan *Alessandro Scarlatti* (1660–1725). One of Scarlatti's important innovations was the three-movement form of the Italian opera overture or *sinfonia*, regarded by many as being the earliest forerunner of the

Classical symphony (⊳ p. 334). The new freedom of expression Scarlatti imparted to opera was given to harpsichord music by his son *Domenico Scarlatti* (1685–1757) in his 550 sonatas for that instrument.

Harpsichord music and opera brought the best out of composers of the French Baroque. The Italian-born Frenchman *Jean-Baptiste Lully* (1632–87) established the form of the French opera (⊳ also p. 342), which was to reach its peak in the operas of Rameau. So-called French overtures on the Lullian model were used by numerous composers of opera and oratorio, while the stylized dance movements that Lully incorporated in his operas became an integral part of the Baroque orchestral suite. *François Couperin* ('Le Grand'; 1668–1733) is best known for his elegant harpsichord pieces, many of which bear fanciful titles and characterize people or objects. The early career of *Jean-Philippe Rameau* (1683–1764) was dominated by harpsichord composition, but he was to enjoy a second and highly successful career as a composer of opera (⊳ p. 342).

In his concertos, sonatas, cantatas and keyboard music the German composer *Johann Sebastian Bach* (1685–1750) took to a summit of achievement the forms that had developed in Italy during the 17th century. Although he never left his homeland, he was aware of musical trends elsewhere, as his *French Suites* and *Italian Concerto* for harpsichord testify. Lutheran hymn tunes were a further influence on his style, whose components included an exhilarating use of rhythmic syncopation, along with an unrivalled grasp of counterpoint (polyphonic composition) that was later to influence composers such as Mozart, Beethoven and Mendelssohn. A number of Bach's many sons were also distinguished composers. The symphonies and concertos of *Carl Phillip Emanuel Bach* (1714–88) show a reaction against his father's counterpoint, while in his sonatas can be detected the growth of the thematic treatment of different keys, which was to develop into Classical sonata form (⊳ p. 335). Posterity has accorded *Georg Phillipp Telemann* (1681–1767) a lowlier status than his friends Bach and Handel. However, Telemann wrote with a keen sense of the possibilities of individual instruments, and his concertos and orchestral suites are distinguished by engaging melody and buoyant rhythms.

In England, *Henry Purcell's* (1659–95) odes, theatre music, church music, string fantasias and sonatas display a sublime gift for melody and a mastery of counterpoint. His best-known work is the miniature opera *Dido and Aeneas* (⊳ p. 342). The greatest composer working in England during the late Baroque was the German-born *George Frideric Handel* (1685–1759). Handel drew on a range of influences – Italian solo and instrumental style, German counterpoint and the English choral tradition he encountered in Purcell – to create a brilliant, highly individual style of writing in his operas, oratorios, concertos and suites. When Italian opera went into a decline in London, Handel turned his attention to the oratorio. Of his many oratorios, *Messiah* (1741) has always held pride of place at the expense of his other masterpieces in the form, notably *Saul* (1739), *Solomon* (1748) and *Jephtha* (1751).

MUSICAL FORMS OF THE BAROQUE

CONCERTO
A work for one or more solo instruments and orchestra, usually in three movements following a quick-slow-quick pattern. A concerto grosso (*grosso* in Italian means 'big') incorporates an interplay between a large body of instruments and a smaller one.

CANTATA
From the Italian word *cantare*, 'to sing', this is a vocal work with solo voices or chorus (or sometimes a combination of both), accompanied by a solo instrument or orchestra.

SONATA
From the Italian *suonare*, 'to sound or play an instrument', the sonata developed from its 16th-century origins into a major musical form, employing one or more solo instruments and structured usually in three or more movements.

SUITE
An instrumental work consisting of a group of dance movements, usually in the same key. Traditionally the Baroque suite comprised a sequence allemande–courante–sarabande–gigue with 'galant' French movements such as minuets and gavottes.

ORATORIO
An unstaged dramatic composition, usually on a biblical theme, for soloists, chorus and orchestra, first developed in Italy.

The Classical Period

If the music of J.S. Bach represents the summit of the Baroque era, that of his sons, particularly Carl Philip Emanuel and Johann Christian (▷ p. 333), provides a link with the period loosely known as Classical. It was a time of new developments in the art of the symphony and concerto, of the birth of the string quartet and piano sonata, and of the humanizing of opera.

SEE ALSO

● ART IN THE 17TH AND 18TH CENTURIES p. 315
● WHAT IS MUSIC? p. 330
● EARLY MUSIC p. 332
● MUSIC OF THE ROMANTICS p. 336
● THE SYMPHONY ORCHESTRA p. 340
● OPERA p. 342
● CLASSICISM IN LITERATURE p. 362

Vienna, the capital of the Austrian Habsburg Empire, now became the centre of musical progress, with *Franz Joseph Haydn* (1732–1809), *Wolfgang Amadeus Mozart* (1756–91) and, before long, *Ludwig van Beethoven* (1770–1827) as its principal representatives. In the next generation *Franz Schubert* (1797–1828) was to sustain Vienna's musical pre-eminence. Both Beethoven and Schubert were to extend the Classical forms and infuse them with a Romantic sensibility (▷ p. 336). All four composers collectively became known as the First Viennese School (for the Second Viennese School, ▷ p. 338).

By 1790 Haydn and Mozart were both resident in Vienna. The Salzburg-born Mozart had settled there in 1781 after a quarrel with his employer, the Archbishop of Salzburg, while Haydn had only just arrived after his retirement at the age of 58 from the post of resident composer with the Esterházy family. At the palace of Esterháza, Haydn had had the privacy to work in peace – yet

Wolfgang Amadeus Mozart, portrayed by Joseph Silfrede Duplessis (1725–1802). Although Mozart had a huge success as a child prodigy, as an adult he experienced continual financial difficulties, and was finally buried in an unmarked pauper's grave. (Scala)

he was famed throughout Europe. Beethoven, born in Bonn in Germany, did not make Vienna his home until two years later, by which time Mozart was dead at the age of 35.

Classicism in music

Classicism, in musical terms, has been defined as a style accepting certain basic conventions of form and structure (▷ box), and using these as a natural framework for the expression of ideas. Unlike Romantic music (▷ p. 336), which developed out of Classicism, it saw no need to break the set boundaries, although in a discreet way its greatest practitioners did so more often than not.

Only in pedantic hands did Classicism lead to rigidity of structure. Its strength derived from the ability of composers to concentrate the intensity of their inspiration within a formal framework, and to express themselves with clarity through the use of moderate resources. The Classical period also saw the development of the symphony – and thereby the symphony orchestra – as a vehicle for well-argued musical discourse.

The symphony

The word *symphony* derives from the Greek word for 'consonance' (i.e. pleasing harmony). In the Baroque period the symphony was no more than a prelude or interlude. But out of the three-section form of many operatic overtures (or *sinfonias*) came the basic structure of what was subsequently to establish itself as the self-sufficient symphony, intended for concert performance.

The three short, usually interconnected movements grew in scale and became more clearly separated from each other; in due course a fourth movement was added. The Classical symphony orchestra was somewhat larger than Bach's orchestra, although less expansive than those of the later Romantics. It drew extra colour from the woodwind family (usually pairs of flutes, oboes, bassoons and the then novel clarinets), from horns, and from the 'pompous' combination of trumpets and kettledrums. Most of these instruments had already been employed by Bach and Handel, but not normally together. Haydn, with his own orchestra and a benevolent patron at Esterháza, was ideally placed to perfect symphonic form the way he wished. In the end he produced over a hundred symphonies remarkable for their terseness of structure, harmonic and rhythmic verve and warmth of expression.

But elsewhere, too, the symphony was spreading like wildfire. The 'Mannheim School' of composers – including *Johann Stamitz* (1717–57) and his son *Karl* (1745–1801) – established brilliant scale passages ('Mannheim rockets') as a symphonic feature, along with startling contrasts between soft and loud, and pioneered the disciplined orchestral *crescendo* and *decrescendo* (increases and decreases in volume). The young Mozart, on a visit to Mannheim, benefited from what he heard there. Mozart also reacted in his own way to the 'Paris style', with its fashionable *premier coup d'archet* (the arresting bowstroke signalling the start of a symphony), which he encountered during his visit to France in 1778 and commemorated in his *Paris* symphony (no. 31 in D).

More important than such gestures was the actual structure of the symphony (▷ box). Although this structure seems rigid, the Classical symphony nevertheless gave composers considerable scope for self-expression. The last 6 of Mozart's 41 symphonies, and the last 12 of Haydn's 104, represent the summit of the Clas-

Rehearsing a string quartet in the late 18th century. During the Classical period the string quartet became the most sophisticated vehicle for musical expression in the domain of chamber music, matching the achievement of the symphony in orchestral music. (Giraudon)

sical style. Beethoven, in his 9 symphonies, built on the work of his predecessors, but was to extend the form considerably in scale and take it into the beginnings of the Romantic era (▷ p. 336), as was Schubert in the last 2 of his 9 symphonies.

Other forms

But what was achieved symphonically at this time was also reflected in the progress of the concerto, the string quartet, the piano trio and the piano sonata. Mozart, on leaving the security of Salzburg, found himself living by his wits in Vienna as the world's first major 'freelance' composer. Up to that point composers generally worked full time either for a wealthy patron or the Church. Mozart attempted to earn money by giving public subscription concerts, the first of their kind, incorporating new piano concertos written for himself (or star pupils) to play. But if the initiative was commercial, the works themselves were epoch-making, achieving a perfection that was only to be equalled by Beethoven.

What Mozart did for the concerto, Haydn (and, under his influence, Mozart also) did for the string quartet, entrusting a group of four players (two violinists, a viola player and a cellist) with his most intimate musical thoughts. Haydn wrote sets of quartets all his life, and these sublime conversation-pieces now form the basis of the quartet repertoire, along with those of Mozart, Beethoven (▷ p. 336) and Schubert. Haydn's piano trios, too, set a standard other composers could emulate but never surpass, and his keyboard sonatas, along with Mozart's, paved the way for Beethoven's 32 unparalleled masterpieces in the form.

Church music was also an important part of a Classical composer's workload, just as it was in Bach's and Handel's time. To their Masses and other choral works, Haydn and Mozart brought a distinctively Austrian flavour that was at times almost operatic, quite different from those of Bach. But then – thanks to Mozart – opera itself had changed personality (▷ p. 342).

CLASSICAL STRUCTURES

The three-movement (fast – slow – fast) concerto had already been established in the Baroque period (▷ p. 333), and in the Classical period the sonata for one or two solo instruments typically had a similar three-movement structure. The Classical symphony, however, had four movements, each of which employed one of the prevailing structural forms of the day: a first movement in *sonata form* (with or without a slow introduction), a slow movement either similarly structured or perhaps in *variation form*, a *minuet and trio*, and a final *rondo*. These structural forms were also utilized in sonatas, concertos and other works.

SONATA FORM

Sonata form (so called because it was commonly used for the first movements of sonatas) was an elaboration of the 'rounded binary' form found in the more extended Baroque suite movements. Like these movements, the sonata-form movement proceeded from the tonic key to the dominant (or relative major, if it was a minor-key movement), then, after a double bar and a repeat of all the music so far, passed through several more remote keys before presenting again all the material before the double bar, but without the key change – so that the movement ended in the tonic. The section before the double bar was later termed the *exposition*, its recurrence without change of key the *recapitulation*, and the part in between the *development*. There was usually a theme or motive of strong character at the beginning, and sometimes other themes and episodes marked the successive stages. These successive stages consisted of the 'transition' (the passage during which the key changed) – if there was one – the section in the dominant key, the 'closing' section (which rounded off the expo-

sition), and even the development. Occasionally there was an extra passage at the end called a *coda*. The most notable feature of the sonata style was its sectionality: the tendency for each small part to be rounded off with a cadence, and to be distinguished from its surroundings by contrasts of texture and mood.

THEME AND VARIATIONS

A theme and variations offered the opportunity to concentrate on all the melodic, harmonic, rhythmic and decorative possibilities of a theme (usually, though not necessarily, heard at the outset). The slow movement of Haydn's *Surprise* symphony wittily uses a nursery tune as its inspiration.

MINUET AND TRIO

The minuet and trio, usually intended to add light relief, used the old French dance-metre as the basis of a simple three-section structure, in which a minuet led to a contrasted trio section (so called because originally using fewer players) and then to an abbreviated repeat of the minuet. Sometimes the format included two trio sections, and ultimately it gave way to the *scherzo and trio*, pioneered by Haydn and perfected by Beethoven, which employed the same 3/4 beat at a usually considerably faster tempo. This resulted in greater musical excitement, and also provided opportunities for heightened humour (*scherzo* is Italian for 'joke').

RONDO

The rondo could also be employed to witty and often brilliant effect. Its essential idea was the periodic recurrence of the main theme, interspersed with contrasted *episodes*. Essentially clear-cut, rondo form could be made more intricate by being combined with sonata form, the resultant hybrid being identified as a *sonata-rondo*.

Music of the Romantics

Romanticism in music was not necessarily born in 1800. But the first year of the 19th century, when Beethoven had just produced the first of his nine symphonies, is as good a time as any by which to commemorate the establishment of composers as individual artists – rather than as servants of rich patrons, which had been the case throughout the Baroque and Classical periods.

Mozart had pointed the way by provoking the Archbishop of Salzburg into dismissing him, and later by composing (purely for himself) his 40th symphony, a work of dark and passionate Romanticism, albeit within a Classical format. His opera, *Don Giovanni*, with its swashbuckling but doomed hero, provided another pointer (▷ p. 342). Significantly it was this more than any other 18th-century masterpiece that fired the Romantic 19th-century imagination by demonstrating how it was possible to break the bounds of 18th-century formality.

The beginnings of Romanticism

So when in 1800 *Ludwig van Beethoven* (1770–1827; ▷pp. 334–5) produced not only his first symphony (which in size and appearance seemed quite Mozartian but had the explosiveness of a time bomb) but also his C minor piano concerto (which had a startling assertiveness absent from his two previous works in the form), it was clear that winds of change were sweeping through music in Vienna. This was confirmed in 1803 by the unleashing of the *Eroica* symphony, origin-

LITERARY INFLUENCE

The age of Romanticism increased the influence of literature on music. Beethoven's 'An die ferne Geliebte' ('To the Distant Beloved', 1816) was the first song cycle of importance, paving the way for 'Die schöne Müllerin' ('The Beautiful Maid of the Mill', 1823) and 'Winterreise' ('Winter Journey', 1827) by *Franz Schubert* (1797–1828; ▷ pp. 334–5), the most gifted and one of the most prolific of all song-writers. The art of the song cycle, which required songs to be grouped in a particular order and to possess some specific literary theme, was nourished in Germany after Schubert's early death by *Robert Schumann* (1810–56) in his 'Dichterliebe' ('Poet's Love') and 'Frauenliebe und -Leben' ('Woman's Love and Life'), both written in 1840, and by Berlioz in his 'Nuits d'été' ('Summer Nights', 1841).

Though composers of the period were often attracted to high-quality texts – Berlioz chose Théophile Gautier's poetry for his 'Nuits d'ete' and Schumann chose Heinrich Heine for 'Dichterliebe' – great songs were not necessarily dependent upon great poetry for their inspiration. Schubert, through his music, raised minor verse to the level of Goethe (▷ p. 366). Wagner wrote his own operatic texts, employing alliteration to bring flow and cohesion to such works as 'Tristan and Isolde' and 'The Ring'.

ally intended by Beethoven to be a homage to Napoleon. This in itself was a Romantic act – Napoleon for a time being regarded as the champion of republican liberty – just as was the composer's subsequent decision to delete Napoleon's name when the French general declared himself emperor. But the special achievement of the *Eroica*, Beethoven's third symphony, was that it finally shattered the bounds of Classicism. It was not only the biggest symphony ever written until that time, it was also recognized to be a personal testament in music, the first of its kind, symbolizing Beethoven's battle with the growing deafness that was to destroy his career as a public performer, but which intensified his inspiration as a composer.

The crucial role played by Beethoven in the progress of symphonic form, and of the art of the string quartet and piano sonata, was something no later composer could ignore. In his last quartets in particular, Beethoven explored the most profound emotional and spiritual tensions with a musical daring not seen again for another century. In Italy, Verdi (▷ p. 342) slept with Beethoven's quartets by his bedside. In France, *Hector Berlioz* (1803–69) stated Beethoven to be a primary influence on his style. In Germany, the symphonic structure employed by *Richard Wagner* (1813–83; ▷ p. 343 and below) in his music dramas had Beethoven's ninth symphony as source.

Programme music

As well as being influenced by literary models (▷ box), composers of the period were also attracted to representational or *'programme music'* – music that evokes pictorial scenes or finds some way to tell a story in purely musical terms. As early as 1808, Beethoven wrote his *Pastoral* symphony, describing its often quite precise imagery rather cautiously as 'the expression of feelings rather than painting'. His E flat piano sonata (opus 81a) of the following year was also an expression of feelings; its three movements were entitled 'Farewell', 'Absence'

Robert Schumann's career as a pianist was cut short when he damaged his hand with a device intended to strengthen his fingers. But as a composer he was to enrich the piano repertoire with pieces that successfully combine Classical structure with Romantic expressiveness. His long-delayed marriage to Clara Wieck (1840), the daughter of his piano teacher, inspired an outpouring of songs and song-cycles that rank with the greatest of the Romantic period. (Scala)

and 'Return', the sonata being dedicated to the Archduke Rudolph on his departure from Vienna during the siege by Napoleon's troops. But that Beethoven's piano music often seemed to evoke pictures, in a way that Haydn's or Mozart's did not, cannot be denied – hence, for example, the nickname *Moonlight* given by a critic to Beethoven's C sharp minor piano sonata.

In Germany, **Felix Mendelssohn** (1809–47), in such works as *The Hebrides* (1830–32) and his *Scottish* and *Italian* symphonies, evoked landscapes within conventional forms, while Schumann evoked scenes of sentiment, chivalry and humour in his piano music. More significant in terms of breaking traditional formal boundaries was the piano music of **Frédéric Chopin** (1810–49), a Pole who settled in France. Chopin's nocturnes, ballades, mazurkas, polonaises, preludes, studies, waltzes and scherzos inspired all sorts of poetic responses in their listeners, although Chopin himself, it is true, seldom supplied these pieces with 'programmes', and indeed, as his sonatas disclose, he was a far more rigorous composer than he has been given credit for. Bach, rather than raindrops, was the source of his 24 preludes, Op 28, though the undeniable 'poetry' of his music – along with the fact that he was tubercular – was bound to enhance his reputation in Romantic terms.

Berlioz's *Symphonie fantastique* (1830) contained a far more deliberate 'programme', each movement depicting a scene from a tragic imaginary love affair, inspired by Berlioz's own unhappy love affair with the actress Harriet Smithson. However, it was **Ferencz** or **Franz Liszt** (1811–86) who developed the art of programme music into a heavy industry. Born in Hungary, Liszt subsequently toured all over Europe as a hugely popular piano virtuoso. Liszt coined the term *symphonic poem* for his series of 13 descriptive orchestral works, each written in a single 'symphonic' movement, and also wrote numerous piano pieces inspired by poems, paintings and places. Through his symphonic poems, and above all through his single-movement piano sonata in B minor (1852–53), he developed the idea of musical *metamorphosis*, whereby the transformations of a single theme, through changes of tempo, rhythm, contour and harmony, could form the argument of an entire piece.

Nationalism in music

The rise of nationalist feeling all over Europe in the 19th century (▷ p. 264) inspired many Romantic artists, including composers. Folk rhythms, folk dances, folk songs, folk legends and folk harmonies served as important sources of inspiration to such composers as **Bedřich Smetana** (1824–84) and **Antonín Dvořák** (1841–1904) in what is now Czechoslovakia, **Edvard Grieg** (1843–1907) in Norway, and **Modest Musorgsky** (1839–81) and **Pyotr Ilyich Tchaikovsky** (1840–93) in Russia. These composers often employed nationalist subjects for their operas while their symphonic works gained an intensity and identity of their own by combining recognizably nationalistic colouring with the established structural procedures of the German mainstream.

Wagner, Brahms and after

But that mainstream itself was undergoing change. On the one hand Wagner was abandoning all constraints of scale and conventional

musical structure in his vast music dramas (▷ p. 343). In these complex tapestries of interwoven themes he built on Liszt's ideas of metamorphosis, and cultivated tonal chromaticism – the frequent introduction of notes foreign to the key of the music. On the other hand, composers such as Berlioz in France and **Johannes Brahms** (1833–97) in Germany were exploring the tensions arising from containing Romantic emotions within strict Classical structures. It was inevitable that Brahms and Wagner in their time were considered to represent opposite musical poles, and that listeners tended to take sides.

In the long term, however, it was Wagner who proved the major influence. The nine symphonies of the Austrian **Anton Bruckner** (1824–96) employ Wagnerian harmony yet have roots in Schubert's *Great* C major symphony (1825), an Austrian masterpiece written on a similarly spacious scale. Wagner and Schubert also provided the foundations of the ten symphonies (the last unfinished) of Bruckner's fellow-Austrian **Gustav Mahler** (1860–1911), who exploited elements of anguish and ecstasy beyond anything previously attempted in symphonic music. In Germany, **Richard Strauss** (1864–1949) absorbed aspects of both Liszt and Wagner into his operas and symphonic poems, though his opera, *Der Rosenkavalier* (1911), reveals a degree of Mozartian nostalgia. At heart Strauss remained a Romantic: a year before he died in 1949, he wrote his *Four Last Songs* for soprano and orchestra, an almost unbearably poignant farewell. However, it was Wagner's tendency towards atonality rather than his high Romanticism that was at the root of mainstream musical development in the 20th century.

Niccolò Paganini (1782–1840), the Italian composer and violin virtuoso, who revolutionized the art of violin playing. In 1833 he rejected *Harold in Italy*, a viola piece he had commissioned from Berlioz, on the grounds that its viola solo did not present enough of a challenge. Paganini's flamboyant lifestyle and Mephistophelian appearance gave rise to stories that he had acquired his virtuosity through a pact with the devil. (ME)

SEE ALSO

● ROMANTICISM (IN PAINTING) p. 318
● THE CLASSICAL PERIOD p. 334
● MODERN MUSIC p. 338
● THE SYMPHONY ORCHESTRA AND ITS INSTRUMENTS p. 340
● OPERA p. 342
● BALLET AND DANCE p. 346
● ROMANTICISM (IN LITERATURE) p. 366

Modern Music

Symphony (1924), *Chamber Concerto* (1934) and sets of tiny yet intense orchestral pieces, Op 6 and 10 (1910 and 1913).

The decades around 1900 marked the beginnings of Modernism. Wagner's *Tristan and Isolde* (1865) was the German fountainhead, with Debussy's *Pelléas and Mélisande* (1892–1902) as its French counterpart. From these two operas, the major trends in 20th-century music all flowed. Modernism in music – as in the visual arts and literature (⊳ pp. 322 and 372–6) – involved a radical break with existing conventions. It also involved what often appears as a greater distancing between the artist and audience – certainly audiences in all the arts have tended to find Modernist works 'difficult'. However, although Modernism has been at the intellectual forefront of music in the 20th century, many composers have followed more accessible paths.

Wagner's chromaticism (⊳ p. 337) had a powerful influence on the young Austrian composer **Arnold Schoenberg** (1874–1951). In early works such as *Verklarte Nacht* ('Transfigured Night') for string sextet (1899), the ties of conventional tonality begin to be loosened, a process continued by Schoenberg and his disciples **Alban Berg** (1885–1935) and **Anton Webern** (1883–1945). These three composers formed what has become known as the Second Viennese School (for the First Viennese School, ⊳ p. 334). The music of Schoenberg and his German and Austrian contemporaries is sometimes described as 'Expressionist'. This term (⊳ also p. 324) is particularly applicable to works such as Schoenberg's *Erwartung* ('Waiting', 1909) for soprano and vast orchestra, which displays the nightmarish despair of a woman awaiting an absent lover who may or may not be dead, and to Berg's operas *Wozzeck* (1922) and *Lulu* (1935; ⊳ p. 342). Schoenberg moved away from Expressionism towards a sparer, more abstract music, and by the 1920s he had formulated *dodecaphony*, or *twelve-note music*, a method of composition whereby all 12 notes within the octave (the 7 white and 5 black keys on a piano keyboard) are treated as equals, with no chords or groups of notes dominating as in conventional harmony. Webern, who also adopted dodecaphonic techniques has, like Schoenberg, exercised a profound influence on later composers, notably through his *Chamber*

Debussy, Stravinsky and others

Claude Debussy (1862–1918), although admiring Wagner's achievement, regarded him as a dead end. Debussy's *Pelléas and Mélisande*, a setting of Maurice Maeterlinck's Symbolist play, is in essence a triangular drama about two half-brothers involved with the same woman. Its fastidiously pared-down music transforms its dreamlike subject almost into an anti-opera from which anything as vulgar as a melody has been ruthlessly excluded. But what gives this masterpiece its cool yet extraordinary intensity is what goes on in the orchestra pit.

Debussy's sense of instrumental colour was what earned him his 'impressionist' label: much to his annoyance, critics characterized him as a musical equivalent of Claude Monet (⊳ p. 320). Many of Debussy's works, such as his three orchestral *Nocturnes* (1901), had visual associations, but poetry – particularly that of Symbolists such as Mallarmé (⊳ p. 372) – also influenced Debussy and his fellow French composers, **Gabriel Fauré** (1845–1924) and **Maurice Ravel** (1875–1937). Although Fauré is best known today for his *Requiem* (1887), he was to develop more modern idioms, and both he and Ravel wrote exquisite songs as well as sharing Debussy's delight in instrumental colour. This was particularly so of Ravel in works such as *Rapsodie espagnole* (1907), *La Valse* (1920) and *Bolero* (1928). The strain of ironic playfulness detectable in some of the music of these French composers is also apparent in the piano miniatures of **Erik Satie** (1866–1925) and the output of his six disciples – nicknamed **Les Six**, and including **Francis Poulenc** (1899–1963) and **Darius Milhaud** (1892–1974). Satie's *Vexations* (1893), requiring a few bars of music to be repeated 840 times over a period of a whole day, are an early example of what came to be known as 'minimalism' (⊳ box). Dadaism, the movement that had invaded French visual arts with its irrationality and irreverence (⊳ p. 323), found in Satie its musical champion.

Debussy also influenced the Russian-born **Igor Stravinsky** (1882–1971) and the Hungarian **Béla Bartók** (1881–1945). The opening notes of Stravinsky's sensational ballet, *The Rite of Spring* (1913), have their roots in Debussy's *Prélude à l'après-midi d'un faune* (1894), even if the bludgeoning rhythms of the rest of the work do not. Stravinsky, who spent a vital part of his career in Paris and ended up, like Schoenberg, in Los Angeles, can now be seen to have straddled the 20th century like nobody else. He was aware of, and responsive to, all the modern trends, and capable of transforming them into pure Stravinsky. His changes of direction can all be seen as revelations of different aspects of one and the same formidable mind. First came the blockbuster early ballets for Diaghilev's Ballets Russes (⊳ p. 347) – their rich orchestration influenced as much by his fellow-Russian **Nikolay Rimsky-Korsakov** (1844–1908) as by Debussy. Then came Stravinsky's more ascetic 'neoclassical' period represented in the 1920s by *Apollon-Musagète* and *Pulcinella*, and these in turn led to his even more pared-down later works.

Bartók's study of Hungarian folk music liberated him from the influence of the German Romantics, and he went on to develop a very individual

Claude Debussy, one of the key figures in the birth of musical Modernism. In 1913 he declared 'A century of aeroplanes needs its own music. As there are no precedents, I must create anew.' (Giraudon)

MINIMALISM

Minimalism in music was first evolved by the American **Terry Riley** (1935–) in the late 1960s. Minimalist music involves the extensive repetition of the simplest of melodies or rhythms over slowing changing harmonies, and the overall effect, for those with the patience to listen, can be compellingly hypnotic. The style continues to be vigorously exploited by such composers as **Steve Reich** (1936–), **Philip Glass** (1937–) and **John Adams** (1947–).

approach to composition – with sometimes forbiddingly dissonant but always compelling results. His works ranged from exciting orchestral scores to the severe abstractions of piano music such as *Mikrokosmos*, and his six string quartets were the first to extend the possibilities of the form since Beethoven.

Britain and Scandinavia

Britain found itself largely – and willingly – shut off from these continental trends. The musical voice of **Edward Elgar** (1857–1934) was that of his native Worcestershire (of which his *Introduction and Allegro* for strings, of 1905, is redolent). However, the influence of Schumann and Wagner was strong, and there were times when he seemed to carry the pain and the glory of Victorian England on his shoulders, as in his two symphonies and concertos, and the touching *Enigma Variations*. **Benjamin Britten** (1913–76) was actively prevented as a young man from studying under Alban Berg in Vienna, because it was feared this would do him harm – although he was the one British composer of his period who might have benefited from such exposure. Despite this, Berg's operas, with their psychological concerns, were to prove a major influence on those of Britten, especially *Peter Grimes* (1945), *The Turn of the Screw* (1954) and *Death in Venice* (1973). **Ralph Vaughan Williams** (1872–1958), after a brief period in Paris when he flirted with the music of Ravel, returned home to produce the intensely English, often folk-song inspired, music for which he was revered. Each of these composers, like **Frederick Delius** (1862–1934) and **Gustav Holst** (1874–1934), succeeded in discovering his own individually English voice, but it was Britten above all who found an idiom, at once English and international, which enabled his music to cross boundaries more freely than that of the others.

Also set apart from the European mainstream was the Finnish composer **Jean Sibelius** (1865–1957), whose tone poems and seven symphonies possess their own lonely grandeur and integrity. The Dane **Carl Nielsen** (1865–1931) was another very individual symphonist. His first symphony (1892) was novel in its introduction of 'progressive tonality' (in other words it began in one key and ended in another).

America and Russia

Charles Ives (1874–1954), was largely ignorant of musical developments in Europe, but in the first two decades of the 20th century he was experimenting with note clusters (produced by pressing a piece of wood across the keys of the piano), chance elements and improvisation, and even evolving a form of dodecaphony. Other experimenters at work in America in the early 20th century include Ives's great champion **Carl Ruggles** (1876–1971), **Henry Cowell** (1897–1965), and

the French-born **Edgard Varèse** (1865–1965). More conventional was the music of **Aaron Copland** (1900–90), much of it based on American folk idioms.

Before the Revolution, the mystical and voluptuous music of **Alexander Skryabin** (1872–1915) proved a dead end, while **Sergey Rakhmaninov** (1873–1943), who spent several years abroad before his final departure from Russia in 1917, was content to exploit his own vein of Romantic nostalgia. More Modernist in spirit was **Sergey Prokofiev** (1891–1953), who also left Russia during the Revolution and lived in Paris from 1922 until his return to the Soviet Union in 1934. It was left to Prokofiev and **Dmitri Shostakovich** (1906–75) to compose progressive and individual music conforming with political pressures to produce easily accessible works for the masses. Shostakovich's increasingly bleak and inward-turning music was a poignant testimony to how compromise could actually be made to work, because, in Shostakovich's case, enforced jollity could never hide the skull beneath the skin.

SEE ALSO

● WHAT IS MUSIC? p. 330
● MUSIC OF THE ROMANTICS p. 336
● THE SYMPHONY ORCHESTRA p. 340
● OPERA p. 342

THE NEW MUSIC

Music since 1945 has evolved in many different ways. For many composers – especially in the 1950s – the once revolutionary twelve-note techniques of Schoenberg (▷ text) became the new orthodoxy, while the avant-garde in the 1960s and 1970s enthusiastically embraced the novel sound possibilities offered by the development of electronic instruments. Another notable development was *aleatory music* – music that deliberately involves random or chance elements, so no two performances are ever the same. For a while it seemed as though conventional tonality had been banished from any music aspiring to be 'serious'; indeed tonality still tends to be the exception rather than the rule.

However, the advent of Minimalism in the late 1960s – a movement that came to maturity in the 1980s (▷ box) – saw the restoration of tonality (and even of melody) to respectability, at the same time finding a wider audience for serious music, verging as it does on the fringes of certain developments in jazz and rock. There has also, in recent years, been a decline in interest in electronic music, as the sounds offered by the new medium have become commonplace, rather than strange and exciting. With the reversion to conventional instruments (and voices) there has often come an opening up to influences from further back in the Western musical tradition, and also to influences from non-Western traditions. The following are some of the most individual composers to have emerged since 1945:

Luciano Berio (1925–) Italian composer: *Sinfonia* (1969), an instrumental work; *Sequenze* for instrumental soloists and orchestra; *A-Ronne* (1974), a radiophonic documentary for 8 actors.
Pierre Boulez (1925–), French composer, many of whose works employ twelve-note technique: *Le Marteau sans maître*, ('The Hammer without a Master') for voice and chamber orchestra (1953–55); *Pli selon pli* ('Fold upon Fold') for soprano and chamber orchestra (1957–62).

John Cage (1912–92), US composer of aleatory and electronic music: *Music of Changes* (1951); *Imaginary Landscape No 4* (1951); *HPSCHD* (1969).
Elliott Carter (1908–), US composer: *Symphony of 3 Orchestras* (1976–7).
Peter Maxwell Davies (1934–) English composer: the theatre pieces *Vesalii Icones* (1969) and *Eight Songs for a Mad King* (1969).
Hans Werner Henze (1926–), German composer: the oratorio *The Raft of the Medusa* (1968); the war opera *We Come to the River* (1976).
Gyorgy Ligeti (1923–), Hungarian composer: *Requiem* (1965); *Lux aeterna* (1966); the opera *Le Grand Macabre* (1978); *San Francisco Polyphony* (1974).
Witold Lutoslawski (1913–) Polish composer: three symphonies; cello concerto (1970).
Olivier Messiaen (1908–92), French composer, mainly of organ music: the piano piece *20 Regards sur L'Enfant Jésus*; *Turangalîla-symphonie* (1946–8).
Luigi Nono (1924–), Italian composer: the opera *Intolleranza 1960*.
Krzysztof Penderecki (1933–), Polish composer: *Threnody for the Victims of Hiroshima* for 52 solo strings (1960); *St Luke Passion* (1966); the opera *The Devils of Loudun* (1969).
Alfred Shnittke (1934–), Russian composer: an oratorio *Nagasaki* (1958); three violin concertos.
Karlheinz Stockhausen (1928–), German composer of electronic music: *Prozession* (1967); *Stimmung* (1968); *Jubilaeum* (1977); a seven-part opera cycle *Licht* (from 1984).
Michael Tippett (1905–), English composer of orchestral and chamber works and operas: *The Midsummer Marriage* (1955) and *The Knot Garden* (1970), and the oratorio *A Child of our Time* (1980).
Iannis Xenakis (1922–), Romanian-born Greek composer. Mathematics has played an important role in his music, which he has often written with the aid of a computer.

The Symphony Orchestra

The rise of the symphony orchestra, consisting of 80 or more instrumentalists performing for a conductor in a concert hall, was one of the great musical developments of the 19th century. Its roots lay in the much smaller groups of players that formed the opera orchestras of the 17th and 18th centuries, and in the ensembles that took part in performances in cathedrals and churches. In the Baroque period, these tended to be based on a small body of strings, supported by keyboard continuo (either harpsichord or organ), and sometimes with woodwind players in addition.

SEE ALSO

● WAVE THEORY p. 20
● ACOUSTICS p. 22
● WHAT IS MUSIC? p. 330
● WESTERN MUSIC p. 332–9

The arrival of the classical symphony, via Haydn and Mozart, brought larger forces into play: more strings and woodwind (with the clarinet gradually added to the flute, oboe and bassoon), a pair of horns, plus ceremonial trumpets and kettledrums. Throughout the 19th century these forces continued to be augmented: Beethoven's fifth symphony (1808) incorporated trombones, a piccolo and a double bassoon (all new to the concert hall), and Berlioz's *Symphonie Fantastique* (1830) added cornets, tubas and extra percussion. By the start of the 20th century, the range of instruments at a composer's disposal had grown still larger. Stravinsky's *Rite of Spring* (1913) required eight horns and quintuple woodwind, while Strauss's *Alpine Symphony* (1915) included wind and thunder machines.

In general, the 19th-century structure of the orchestra has been maintained, though seating positions have been altered since Haydn's day. The first and second violins, formerly placed to the left and right of the conductor, are now massed together on the left. This achieves greater brilliance of sound, but at the expense of spatial interplay between the two sets of instruments –

an effect that was deliberately built into Classical scores.

For some idea of how Classical symphonies were meant to sound, however, one can turn to the increasing number of specialist 'period' ensembles that have grabbed for themselves a large slice of the symphonic repertoire. But whether an orchestra uses modern or 'original' placings and instruments, these instruments fall into four families: strings, woodwind, brass and percussion.

Strings

Of the string instruments, the *violins* produce the highest sound, with the violas, cellos and double basses following in descending order (the larger the instrument the deeper the sound). Their forerunners, employed until about 1700, were the *viols* and were likewise of various sizes.

The *viola* is a larger, lower-pitched relative of the violin, and is likewise placed beneath the player's chin. Its mellow, often gravely eloquent tone blends into the string ensemble and in solo passages achieves high expressiveness. The *cello* (whose full name is *violoncello*) has a still darker tone, though its lighter upper register can be exploited to magical effect. All these are four-stringed instruments; so, too, is the *double bass*, though five-string basses, giving the instrument an even deeper register, are also found.

Woodwind

The woodwind are so called because they were all originally made of wood – although most flutes today are actually made of metal. The woodwind are of two types: those that are blown directly (flutes and recorders) and those that are blown by means of a single or double reed.

The highest, most piercing flute is the *piccolo*. Pitched an octave lower is the standard *flute* (often, like the other woodwind instruments, employed in pairs in the orchestra), with a compass from middle C upwards for three octaves. Unlike the rest of the woodwind, the flute is played sideways, the sound being produced by blowing across an aperture cut into the top of the tube at one end.

The oboe and its lower-toned relative, the cor anglais, are both blown through a double reed, as also is the bassoon. The *oboe*, 'reedier' in sound than the pure-toned flute, has a range from the B flat below middle C upwards for more than 2½ octaves. The *cor anglais* ('English horn') is neither English nor a horn but a large oboe, recognizable by its bulb-shaped bell and darker tone quality. It is pitched a fifth lower than an oboe. The *bassoon* – the bass member of the woodwind family – consists of a long tube doubled back on itself. Though sometimes employed to comic effect, its nasal tone is capable of eloquence and, at the top and bottom of its compass, which stretches from the B flat below the bass stave upwards for 3½ octaves, it can also sound sinister.

The *clarinet*, which looks like an oboe, differs by being blown through a single reed. Its creamy tone was much loved by Mozart, who was the first composer to realize its full potential, both as a member of the woodwind and as a solo instrument. The clarinet family is a large one, the instruments originally being made in several sizes to facilitate playing in different keys. But by the time the symphony orchestra was fully established, only two sizes – the B flat (with a compass

---

KEYBOARD INSTRUMENTS

The *organ* is the oldest of the keyboard instruments, being known to the ancient Greeks and Romans. The organ grew in size over the years, the medieval portative (i.e. transportable) and the gentle Baroque organ being much smaller than the multi-keyboard 19th-century organs. But whatever the size, the operation – involving bellows blowing air through pipes to sound the notes – is the same. The modern electronic organ has done away with the need for pipes, but is regarded as a feeble substitute for the real thing.

The *harpsichord*, roughly akin to the grand piano in shape, originated in the 15th century – or earlier – but acquired its most developed from in

the Baroque period (⊳ p. 333). The harpsichord may have one, two or (exceptionally) three keyboards. The strings, unlike those of the piano, are plucked mechanically rather than struck.

From the harpsichord and the related softer-toned *clavichord* there developed the *pianoforte* (so named, in Italian, because it could play both softly and loudly). At first it was sometimes called the *fortepiano*, and the name is nowadays abbreviated to 'piano'. The terms fortepiano and pianoforte are now used principally to differentiate the silvery-toned 19th-century instrument from the larger and weightier concert grand built from the 19th century.

stretching three octaves from the D below middle C) and the A (with a compass a semitone lower than the B flat) – were in regular use. These, however, were merely the 'standard' clarinets, and to them were added the high E flat clarinet; the *basset horn*, a low-toned clarinet adored by Mozart; and the *bass clarinet*, pitched an octave lower than the B flat clarinet and shaped like a saxophone.

The *saxophone* itself, though of more recent vintage (it was invented in 1840), is also a type of clarinet, using a single reed, but producing a more vibrant, wailing tone. It too comes in several sizes and plays a vital role in jazz, though Classical composers have also used it.

Brass

Brass instruments are made of metal and their sound is produced by vibration of the lips against a cup-shaped mouthpiece. The horn, trumpet, trombone and tuba are the brass instruments most commonly used in the symphony orchestra, though the *cornet* (resembling a trumpet but with a wider bore and an expressiveness all of its own) also appears.

The *horn*, distinguished by its coiled shape, was at one time capable of producing only a limited number of notes. But in its modern form, through the addition of valves, it is more versatile and provides a complete chromatic compass from B below the bass stave upwards for 3½ octaves. Of the brass instruments it is the most mellow, though it can also be assertive and agile. In Britain, the horn is often referred to as the 'French horn', because it was in France that the instrument was perfected.

The modern *trumpet*, like the horn, has valves and considerable versatility. Originally, however, it was a straight tube with a limited number of notes at its disposal, and its use was primarily ceremonial. The more familiar type of folded trumpet first appeared in the 15th century, and the addition of 'crooks' – detachable sections of tubing

---

PERCUSSION

Percussion instruments are either struck or shaken, and may be either pitched or non-pitched. The copper-bottomed *timpani*, or *kettledrums*, are the most important and versatile of all the instruments in this section. Of Arab origin, they were first used orchestrally in the 17th century, when they were played in pairs and were capable of only two notes, one tuned to the tonic and the other to the dominant of whatever key was being performed, the pitch being adjusted by screws on the rim of the drums. From Beethoven's time onwards, however, the instruments gained other tunings – in the 20th century with the help of foot pedals.

Side drum, tenor drum, bass drum, cymbals, triangle and *castanets* are the instruments of indefinite pitch most frequently seen in the symphony orchestra, though today the variety of such instruments is endless. Keyed percussion instruments, such as the *xylophone, glockenspiel, vibraphone* and *marimba*, are tuned to a definite pitch, and have proved increasingly popular with modern composers. The *piano* is also, technically, a percussion instrument (in that it is struck) and even the *harp* is sometimes listed as a member of the percussion family, even though its strings, encompassing seven octaves, are plucked.

---

that altered its pitch – gave it greater scope. The modern trumpet uses valves to open up different sections of tubing, and in the case of the B flat trumpet has a compass from E below middle C upwards for about three octaves.

Trombones, which come in tenor and bass versions, operate with the help of valves and U-shaped slides that move along the length of the instrument and provide a compass from E below the bass stave upwards for about three octaves in the case of the tenor trombone, and from the lower D flat in the case of the bass. The solemnity of trombone tone was effectively used by Mozart in *The Magic Flute*. The *tuba*, an instrument of more recent invention, underpins the trombones and comes in tenor, bass and other versions (though the bass is the one most regularly employed in the symphony orchestra). Its great girth, and its upward-facing bell, make it instantly recognizable. Its compass, founded on the F an octave below the bass stave, stretches upwards as high as three octaves.

From left to right: **Oboe, cor anglais and clarinet.**

The London Symphony Orchestra. As with most modern symphony orchestras, the cellos and double basses are placed to the right of the platform, instead of more centrally. Some would argue that this arrangement destroys the original sense of balance and the solidity of tone that the basses provided when they stretched round the back of the platform facing into the audience. However, most of today's star conductors prefer the modern arrangement, and orchestras have become accustomed to it. (LSO)

Opera

Opera is the Italian word for 'work'. But, as an abbreviation of *opera in musica* (a 'musical work'), it began to be used in 17th-century Italy for music dramas in which singers in costume enacted a story with instrumental accompaniment. The narrative element was what differentiated these pieces from earlier entertainments known as *intermedii*, or 'interludes', which were written to celebrate weddings, birthdays and similar events at the Italian courts, and incorporated lavish balletic and vocal sections.

The first true operatic masterpieces were by the Venetian composer *Claudio Monteverdi* (1567–1643; ▷ p. 332). Monteverdi's *Orfeo* of 1607, followed by *The Return of Ulysses* (1640) and *The Coronation of Poppea* (1642), gradually took opera out of the court and into the public domain with music of great beauty and sophistication. Brief arias (solo songs), madrigals (part songs), declaimed recitatives (sung speeches), duets and ensembles were the materials Monteverdi worked with, and he used them with a freedom that his successors might have envied.

Many prominent opera composers of the late 17th and early 18th centuries came from Naples, giving rise to the term the *Neapolitan School*, though their operas tended to be first performed in Rome or Venice. One such composer was *Alessandro Scarlatti* (1660–1725), in whose work the conventions of *opera seria* (▷ below), including the *da capo* aria, were established.

In France a native form of opera was developed by *Jean-Baptiste Lully* (1632–87), who reduced the extended Italian aria to shorter 'airs' and introduced a declamatory style of recitative, and assigned a major role to ballet interludes and choruses (▷ pp. 332 and 346). The operatic style established by Lully reached its high point in the operas of *Jean-Philippe Rameau* (1683–1764) – especially *Hippolyte et Aricie* (1733) and *Castor et Pollux* (1737) – with their complex and brilliant orchestration and pervasive atmosphere of languid melancholy.

Just as in France the acceptance of opera was hampered by the strength of the tradition of the court ballet, so in England its development was delayed by the popularity of the masque (▷ p. 360). But England did produce a miniature masterpiece in *Dido and Aeneas* (1689) – the one 'true' opera of *Henry Purcell* (1659–95; ▷ p. 332) – which offers an astonishing range of dramatic expression and depth of human understanding.

From Handel to Mozart

The greatest operas of the first half of the 18th century were written in England – but their composer was German-born, and the language of their texts (because of the rage for *opera seria*) was Italian. By the time *George Frideric Handel* (1685–1759; ▷ p. 332) arrived in London from Italy in 1710, opera had become more formalized. The *da capo* aria (so called because its introductory section was repeated *da capo*, or 'from the beginning', after a contrasting middle section) reigned supreme. For all the melodic beauty Handel was able to bring to such arias in his 39 operas, the unhurried progress of the music demands a degree of patience on the part of a modern audience. Nevertheless the rewards provided by a sympathetic performance of operas such as *Giulio Cesare* (1724), *Orlando* (1733) or *Alcina* (1735) speak for themselves. *Opera seria* ('serious opera') was the apt title later given to the form favoured by Handel and his contemporaries, and Italian remained the favoured language. The term *opera seria* was strictly applied to operas whose subjects were taken from Classical and medieval history, but it is more loosely used to include operas on mythological themes. The principal roles in *opera seria* were usually taken by *castrati* (male sopranos or contraltos).

Even though the brilliant, florid-voiced *castrati* were the stars of their day, they ultimately provoked composers such as the German *Christoph Willibald von Gluck* (1714–87) to

Orphée aux enfers
('Orpheus in the Underworld'; 1774) by Christoph Willibald von Gluck, in a scene from Paris Opera's 1988 production. Handel once said rather unkindly of Gluck that he knew 'no more of counterpoint than my cook'. However, Gluck's successful attempts to inject more drama into opera, especially in *Orpheus and Eurydice* (the original Italian version of the opera illustrated here), have ensured him a lasting place in opera history.
(Explorer)

rebel against what seemed the increasingly rigid conventions of *opera seria,* and to demand a complete reform of the art. *Orpheus and Eurydice* (1762) and *Alceste* (1767) were the first fruits of Gluck's determination to make opera more genuinely dramatic, and to 'restrict music to its true office by means of expression and by following the situations of the story'. Working in Paris as well as in Vienna, Gluck fell victim to the French capital's rival operatic factions, which had already (in 1752) prompted the so-called *Guerre des Bouffons,* or 'war of the comedians', between supporters of Italian comic opera and the stately French tradition of Lully and Rameau.

If in the end Gluck was a disillusioned man, his operatic beliefs were soon to find inspired expression in the masterpieces of **Wolfgang Amadeus Mozart** (1756–91; ▷ pp. 334 and 336). Mozart's operas straddled the worlds of comedy and *opera seria,* and of Italian and German opera, in a way nobody else achieved. Whether in *Idomeneo* (1781), the most human *opera seria* ever written, or in his penetrating human comedies – *The Marriage of Figaro* (1786), *Così fan tutte* (1790), *Don Giovanni* (1787) and *The Magic Flute* (1791) – Mozart was the supreme operatic genius of his age. He accepted the convention of the 'number' opera (in which the music is divided into arias, duets, ensembles and so forth) but provided a new continuity that found its high-water marks in the finale of Act Two of *The Marriage of Figaro* and the climax of *Don Giovanni.*

From Beethoven to Wagner

With Mozart as an example, operatic structure became increasingly continuous. In *Fidelio* (1814), **Ludwig van Beethoven** (1770–1827; ▷ pp. 334 and 336) used the methods of a traditional German *Singspiel* ('song-play', employing speech and song in alternation) to create a sublime music drama on the subject of love and liberty.

With its Romanticism and its open-air scenario, *Der Freischütz* (1821) by **Carl Maria von Weber** (1786–1826) was a milestone on the road to Wagner's *Ring,* completed half a century later. By then the German **Richard Wagner** (1813–83; ▷ p. 337) had expanded and transformed the art of opera into what he himself preferred to describe as 'music drama'. Laid out in four parts, intended to be spread over four nights, *Der Ring des Nibelungen* ('The Nibelung's Ring') is the longest opera ever written. *The Ring* was the outcome of some 20 years of its composer's life, culminating in its first complete performance in 1876. By the time he completed it, having already produced *The Flying Dutchman* (1843), *Lohengrin* (1850), *Tristan and Isolde* (1865) and *Die Meistersinger* (1868), Wagner had made each act of his operas wholly continuous. He wrote the words as well as the music of each of his works, and built his own revolutionary theatre at Bayreuth in Bavaria, complete with a covered orchestra pit.

In Italy, **Giuseppe Verdi** (1813–1901) was following a parallel, if more cautious, course. Verdi inherited the tradition of the 'number opera' from his Italian predecessors. Notable among these were **Gioacchino Rossini** (1792–1868), whose operas include *The Barber of Seville* (1816) and *William Tell* (1829); and the prolific **Gaetano Donizetti** (1797–1848), whose most famous works, *Maria Stuarda* (1834) and *Lucia di Lammermoor* (1835), are based on works by the Romantic writers Schiller and Scott respectively (▷ p. 366). Verdi gradually rebelled against this tradition, while retaining a lyrical Italian feeling for the art of *bel canto* ('beautiful singing'). *Il Trovatore*

(1853) marked the turning point. While it may sound like just another number opera, it nevertheless represents a conscious effort on Verdi's part to escape from what he regarded as dead traditions. *La Traviata* (1853) took him farther along the road to structural freedom. The two sublime masterpieces of his old age, *Otello* (1887) and *Falstaff* (1893) – both based on Shakespeare – demonstrated that Verdi had reached Wagner's goals by his own route, without sacrificing his abiding gift for melody.

The second half of the 19th century saw the increasing use by composers of realistic subjects. *Carmen* (1875), by the French composer **Georges Bizet** (1838–75), tells of the fickle affections of a girl who works in a cigarette factory. In Italy a move towards down-to-earth representation of contemporary life (*verismo*) is registered in *Cavalleria rusticana* (1890) – a one-act opera by **Pietro Mascagni** (1863–1945). *Pagliacci* (1892) – a brief *verismo* opera by **Ruggero Leoncavallo** (1858–1919) is often performed with Mascagni's opera as a double bill.

The 20th century

From Verdi to **Giacomo Puccini** (1858–1924) in Italy – as from Wagner to **Richard Strauss** (1864–1949) in Germany – was inevitably a downhill progress. But the theatricality of Puccini's *La Bohème* (1896), *Madama Butterfly* (1900) and *Tosca* (1904) has kept them in the repertoire, as has the bitter-sweetness of *Der Rosenkavalier* (1911), with its application of a vast Wagnerian scale to a Viennese chocolate-box story.

Opera's real genius of this period, however, emerged from Czechoslovakia, as audiences have only recently come to realize. In operas such as *Jenufa* (1904) and *The Cunning Little Vixen* (1924), **Leoš Janáček** (1854–1928) showed himself to possess a deep compassion for his characters.

To state, as some have done, that the history of opera ended with Puccini's unfinished *Turandot* in 1926 suggests that he manipulated his admirers all too well. Yet as early as 1902, **Claude Debussy** (1862–1918; ▷ p. 338) had shown in the dreamlike shadowy world of *Pelléas and Mélisande* that opera was capable of taking new directions. The same was proved by the Expressionist dramas *Wozzeck* (1925) and *Lulu* (1937) by the Austrian **Alban Berg** (1885–1935; ▷ p. 338).

More recently, Benjamin Britten (1913–76), Michael Tippett (1905–), Harrison Birtwistle (1934–) and Peter Maxwell Davies (1934–) in Britain, Hans Werner Henze (1926–), Karlheinz Stockhausen (1928–), Bern-Alois Zimmermann (1918–70) in Germany, Luciano Berio (1925–) and Luigi Nono (1924–) in Italy, Olivier Messiaen (1908–) in France and John Adams (1947–) in America are among those who have demonstrated opera to be alive and kicking. (For more details on some of these composers, ▷ p. 339.)

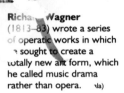

Richard Wagner (1813–83) wrote a series of operatic works in which he sought to create a totally new art form, which he called music drama rather than opera. (la)

SEE ALSO

● EARLY MUSIC p. 332
● CLASSICAL MUSIC p. 334
● MUSIC OF THE ROMANTICS p. 336
● MODERN MUSIC p. 338
● BALLET AND DANCE p. 346
● CLASSICISM IN LITERATURE p. 362
● ROMANTICISM IN LITERATURE p. 366

Popular Music in the 20th Century

Popular music shares some features in common with folk music. Both types of music have a wider appeal than classical music, and have in many cases been disseminated by oral means. Unlike folk music, however, popular music is produced by professional musicians and predominantly from an urban milieu. The 20th century has witnessed an increasing uniformity of styles of popular music, largely because of the powerful cultural influence of the USA.

From the mid-19th century onwards, serious and popular music increasingly flowed down separate channels. Operetta (i.e. 'light opera') and dance music were purveyed to perfection by *Johann Strauss* (1825–99) in Vienna, by *Jacques Offenbach* (1819–80) in Paris, and by the so-called Savoy Operas (really operettas) of *W.S. Gilbert* (1836–1911) and *Arthur Sullivan* (1842–1900) in Victorian London. Musical comedy and the Broadway musical were the 20th-century offspring of operetta, and of the old German *Singspiel* (⊳ p. 342).

These works had as their common factor the alternation between spoken words and sung ones, and were capable of considerable subtlety and melodic distinction. The musical and verbal wit of *The Mikado* (1885) by Gilbert and Sullivan has proved indestructible. Musical comedy, in compa-

Charlie 'Bird' Parker (1920–55) was one of the leading exponents of the 'bebop' movement in jazz, which revolted against the dominance of swing in the 1940s. His harmonic and rhythmic innovations exerted a potent influence on practitioners of 'modern' jazz such as John Coltrane and Miles Davies.
(Redfern)

rison, tended to be more lyrical, especially in the works of the Irish-born American *Victor Herbert* (1859–1924) and *Jerome Kern* (1885–1945), whose *Show Boat* (1927) contained some of the best American songs of the period.

Broadway

The Broadway musical preserved the lyricism of musical comedy in such successes as *Oklahoma!* (1943) by Rodgers and Hammerstein, and *My Fair Lady* (1958) by Loewe and Lerner, but also brought new edge and vitality to the form. With *Lorenz Hart* (1895–1943) as his sardonic literary partner, *Richard Rodgers* (1902–80) proved an infinitely sharper composer in *Pal Joey* (1940) than with the more sentimental *Oscar Hammerstein II* (1895–1960) in *The Sound of Music* (1959). But for sheer punch and incisiveness, *West Side Story* (1958) – a New York updating of Shakespeare's *Romeo and Juliet* with music by *Leonard Bernstein* (1918–91) and lyrics by *Stephen Sondheim* (1930–) – remains unsurpassed.

The popular song, whether written in isolation or for a stage production, has always been an American speciality. Notable exponents of the genre include *Irving Berlin* (1888–1988), composer of 'White Christmas' and 'Alexander's Ragtime Band'; *Cole Porter* (1893–1964), whose songs include 'Let's do it', 'You're the top', and 'I get a kick out of you'; and above all *George Gershwin* (1898–1937), whose melodic perfection reached its high-water mark in 'The man I love' and in his opera *Porgy and Bess* (1935).

Blues and jazz

At its best, whether in Gershwin or in the often despairing music of the 12-bar blues, which follows a precisely set sequence of chords, the American popular song achieved the status of an art form, with the Black singers *Bessie Smith* (1898–1937) and *Billie Holiday* (1915–59) as its greatest exponents. The blues has been Black America's most eloquent gift to the world of music – a major influence on jazz and, since the 1950s, on rock.

The roots of jazz lie in the music that began to develop in the Black communities of the southern states of the USA towards the end of the 19th century. In New Orleans, the fusion of Black and European cultures enabled jazz to formulate and gain its own identity, at first in saloon bars and brothels but also in the street parades that were part of New Orleans life. Ragtime, an early form of jazz that was sometimes composed rather than improvised, was particularly associated with solo piano performance, its most famous exponent being the Black pianist and composer *Scott Joplin* (1868–1917). In the early days the form and harmony of jazz were simple; the complexity came from the way the performers improvised collectively upon the simple melodies, and from their command of syncopation.

Jazz music soon swept northwards to Chicago and other cities, before spreading abroad. *Louis Armstrong* (1900–71) was one of the first to carry the message beyond New Orleans, where he was born. As a solo cornet player and singer, by the 1920s Armstrong had created his own instantly recognizable style, basing his improvisations on the harmonic sequence of tunes rather than the melodies themselves. This would lead, in the 1940s, to jazz performances in which the original melody was sometimes never stated at all, but merely implied by its underlying harmonies. Though jazz in Armstrong's early days was predominantly the music of Black Americans, White musicians – such as **Bix Beiderbecke** (1903–31), another brilliant cornet player – proved that it was not exclusively a Black preserve.

As the popularity of jazz began to spread, so the bands, which had tended to comprise five, six or seven players, grew larger. During the 'swing' era before World War II, bands such as that of **Benny Goodman** (1909–86), with brass and reed sections blowing against each other over a solid beat, grew fashionable. Crucial to the success of such bands were their virtuoso instrumentalists, including Goodman (an outstanding clarinettist), the trombonist **Glenn Miller** (1904–44), and the tenor saxophonist **Lester Young** (1909–59). Miller formed his own band and achieved a phenomenal success during World War II with such hits as 'Moonlight Serenade' and 'In the Mood'. Young – a member of **Count Basie's** (1904–84) band – was to prove influential on the development of 'modern' jazz (▷ below).

The major jazz watershed occurred at the end of World War II, when 'traditional' jazz, with its simple harmonies, gave way to the complexity, tension, abrasiveness and virtuosity of 'modern' jazz, whose key figures have included the saxophonists **Charlie 'Bird' Parker** (1920–55) and **Ornette Coleman** (1930–   ), and the trumpeters **Dizzy Gillespie** (1917–93) and **Miles Davis** (1926–91). Whether identified as 'bop', 'bebop' or 'rebop', modern jazz gains much of its intensity of expression from the contrast between a steady beat and a convoluted, often agonized, solo line. Traditionalists tend to say that jazz came to an end in 1945, and continue to perform or listen to traditional jazz as if modern jazz had never been invented, but at least one of the greatest jazzmen, the pianist and band leader **Duke Ellington** (1899–1974), succeeded in straddling both camps.

Rock

Although some people claim that jazz no longer forms part of popular music at all, because it has become much too specialized, it has nevertheless exerted a powerful influence on more obviously popular music. 'Rhythm and blues', an offshoot of the blues, featured an ensemble rather than a solo voice, and produced its own Negro-spiritual-inspired offshoot known as 'soul music'. 'Reggae', an Afro-Jamaican hybrid, originated in the 1960s and employs topical lyrics. 'Country and western' is America's modern equivalent of the European country dances of previous centuries. But above all jazz has inspired rock, a hybrid of American popular forms: blues, rhythm and blues, gospel, and country and western. Since the advent of 'rock 'n' roll' in the 1950s, rock music – usually performed by groups using electronically amplified instruments – has established itself as the major force of present-day popular music.

In the 1950s Black artists such as the guitarist **Chuck Berry** (1926–   ) vied for popularity with Whites such as **Buddy Holly** (1936–1959) and, most notably, **Elvis Presley** (1935–77), whose physicality and tremulous baritone delivery inspired an almost religious devotion in his millions of fans. The most significant developments in rock music in the 1960s took place in Britain, where the **Beatles** introduced a more sophisticated lyricism to the genre, and the **Rolling Stones** brought an overt sexuality to

their vigorous dance numbers. The 'Mersey Sound' associated with the Beatles was a skilful brew of British and American trends of the period, and combined genuine melodic flair with words of real literary merit. A similar literary distinction has stamped the songs of the American **Bob Dylan** (1941–   ), who achieved a synthesis of elements of rock and roll and folk in his songs of protest. Other 1960s rock trends were the drug-influenced 'acid rock' of such performers as the American guitarist **Jimi Hendrix** (1942–70), and the highly amplified, rhythmic style of rock and roll, known as 'hard rock', practised by such bands as **The Who**. A significant development in the late 1960s was the use of rock music in stage works or 'rock operas' such as *Hair*, *Jesus Christ Superstar* and The Who's *Tommy*.

In the early 1970s the progressive rock of British bands such as **Pink Floyd** and **Genesis** involved longer tracks, more advanced harmonies, and more complicated instrumental solo passages. It was partly in response to what some perceived as the pompous self-indulgence of such music that 'punk rock' exploded on to the scene in Britain in the mid-1970s. Punk rock gave vivid and sometimes anarchic expression to working-class discontent, most notably in the abrasive and nihilistic anthems of its most notorious practitioners, the **Sex Pistols**. The 1980s saw an increasing divergence of styles and a growing use of electronic equipment. An increasingly influential role was played by production teams in the creation of rock music.

Elvis Presley (1935–77), the American rock and roll singer. His highly charismatic performing style – typified by sexually suggestive gyrations of the hips and trembling baritone delivery – raised his female fans to a fever pitch of adulation. Graceland – his ostentatious mansion in Memphis, Tennessee – was besieged by thousands of mourning fans after his death from a heart attack in 1977, and has since become a place of pilgrimage for his admirers. (Redfern)

SEE ALSO

● OPERA p. 342

Ballet and Dance

Forms of dance vary from those that employ the whole body in free and open movement to those in which movement is restricted to certain parts – just to the eyes in the case of one Samoan courtship dance. It can be a simple expression of pleasure in the movement of the body or an art form of complex patterns and significant gestures.

Many folk dances originate in the rituals and folklore of particular regions, and social dances (▷ box) have developed from courtship dances. Classical ballet, however, is a theatrical dance that has become a major art form. In a reaction against the formal rules of ballet, modern dance has developed freer styles.

Classical ballet

Ballet is a theatrical dance form based upon a set of positions, steps and expressive gestures that demand considerable skill and training. Ballet may tell a story or offer abstract patterns of movement. Though generally aiming at an appearance of effortless grace, it can also be highly dramatic. There are several ways in which ballet differs from other forms of dance. Most obvious is the 90° 'turned-out' position of the feet,

which permits a remarkable degree of balance in all positions. Ballet also requires a tension and arching of the foot and Achilles tendon to provide a powerful jump and to cushion landing. Dancers begin training at an early age to achieve the positions required, and must continue to exercise daily.

In 1661 the French king, Louis XIV, established a group of dancing instructors, the Académie Royale de Danse, to codify court dances. Its director, **Charles Louis Beauchamp** (1636–1705), is credited with inventing the 'five positions' (▷ box), though he may just have followed existing practice. As greater skills were needed, trained professionals began to replace the aristocratic amateurs who had previously participated in courtly entertainments.

The early ballets had consisted of a succession of dances with music and poetry, and dancers wore heavy court costume and masks. However, interest grew in making ballet a dramatic form in which the dance itself carried the story and emotion. The greatest instigator of change was **Jean Georges Noverre** (1727–1810), who became ballet master at the Opéra in his native Paris in 1776. He tried to get rid of the heavy wigs, masks and big padded skirts, and also to introduce more natural gestures along with a greater emphasis on dramatic action. There was considerable resistance to Noverre's reforms in France, which were adopted most fully in Denmark in the work of **August Bournonville** (1805–79).

However, long before Noverre's arrival some changes had been initiated. **La Camargo** (Marie Anne de Cupis de Camargo, 1710–70) danced in heel-less slippers to aid her famous footwork, which she displayed to better effect by shortening her skirts to mid-calf. Her contemporary and rival **Marie Sallé** (1707–56) placed more emphasis on plot and interpretation.

Sometime after 1800 women began to dance 'on point' (on the tips of the toes), stiffening the ends of their slippers for support. Pointwork became a key feature of choreography for women. It requires strengthening of the muscles in foot and leg and can cause injury if attempted prematurely. La Scala's ballet Master **Carlo Blasis** (1797–1878) developed exercises – with deep knee bends and stretching of the feet and thighs – that still form the basis of the dancer's daily class.

As in the other arts, the fashion now was for Romanticism (▷ pp. 318, 336, 366), which in ballet took the form of stories of princes in love with nymphs and of unrequited love. Although there were still some virtuosi male dancers, in Romantic ballets men tended to be mere partners, literally supporting the women.

A French dancer and choreographer, **Maurice Petipa** (1822–1910), and a Danish teacher, **Christian Johansson** (1817–1903), were responsible for a flowering of ballet in Russia in the second half of the 19th century. Dancers achieved a distinctive national style, making ballet the equal of opera in artistic status. In 1919 the impresario **Serge Diaghilev** (1872–1929) mounted a season of Russian ballet in Paris, calling his company the Ballets Russes. His dazzling dancers and stunning stagings attracted wild enthusiasm. For the next 20 years Diaghilev toured his company in Europe and the Americas, creating a new enthusiasm for ballet and launching the careers of many international stars. Several of today's great ballet companies have their origins in

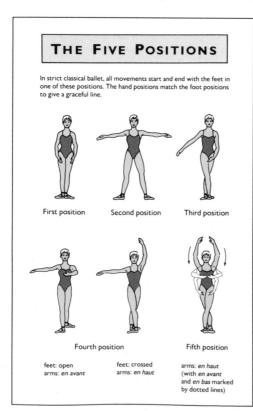

THE FIVE POSITIONS

In strict classical ballet, all movements start and end with the feet in one of these positions. The hand positions match the foot positions to give a graceful line.

First position

Second position

Third position

Fourth position

feet: open
arms: *en avant*

Fifth position

feet: crossed
arms: *en haut*

arms: *en haut*
(with *en avant*
and *en bas* marked
by dotted lines)

SEE ALSO

● OPERA p. 342
● POPULAR MUSIC IN THE 20TH CENTURY p. 344
● MODERN DRAMA p. 374

Diaghilev's company. *George Balanchine* (1904–83), *Ninette de Valois* (1898–), and *Marie Rambert* (1888–1982) are only a few of the key figures who were once members of his company.

Russia has continued to produce superb dancers such as *Galina Ulanova* (1910–) and *Maya Plisetskaya* (1929–) and several who have made their names in the West: *Rudolph Nureyev* (1939–93), *Mikhail Baryshnikov* (1948   ) and *Natalia Makarova* (1940–). Innovation and experiment, however, have shifted elsewhere. Many countries, from Canada to Japan, Cuba to Australia, now have major national companies. Choreographers like *Jerome Robbins* (1918–) in the USA, *Frederick Ashton* (1904–88) and *Kenneth Macmillan* (1929–92) in Britain, the Dane *Harold Lander* (1905–), *Roland Petit* (1924– , French), *John Cranko* (1927–73, South African) and *Jiri Kylian* (1947– , Czech) have extended the vocabulary of dance while remaining within the classical world.

Modern dance

At the forefront of a reaction against the formal constraints of classical ballet were three Americans, all influenced by the ideas of *François Delsarte* (1811–71), a Frenchman who had analysed gesture and movement. *Isadora Duncan* (1878–1927) sought to express emotion through dance based on the grace of natural movement, and to this end she danced barefoot and in a costume modelled on ancient Greek dress. She found success in Europe, where she was a major influence. *Ruth St Denis* (1879–1968) and her husband *Ted Shawn* (1891–1972) also sought a free dance form, but they explored folk and national dance for their inspiration, especially that of the Orient. Shawn's all-male company helped to break down prejudice against male dancers.

A dancer with St Denis's company for some years, *Martha Graham* (1894–1991) eventually tired of its mixture of styles. From about 1927 she developed a new style, apparently angular and abstract but rooted in the expression of emotion. Like St Denis's style it emphasized contact with the ground, rather than the constant attempt in classical ballet to escape gravity. Graham's approach celebrates the energy of muscular action. To equip dancers for the demands of her style she evolved a highly developed training system.

Although Graham's influence is still at work, some have reacted against it. *Merce Cunningham* (1919–) rejected her strong links to story and meaning to create a more abstract dance, sometimes involving elements of chance. In one piece he even breaks off a virtuoso dance sequence for some unrelated activity like riding a bike.

The Hungarian-born movement analyst and choreographer *Rudolph Laban* (1879–1958) was the theorist behind 'Labanotation', a system of symbols to record all the body's movements, which is now the most widely used way of writing down dance. He paid much attention to the relationship between the individual and the surrounding space.

Recent years have seen the creation of many modern dance companies drawing on existing styles and experimenting with new ideas. *Twyla Tharp* (1942–) is one of the best known of many innovative American choreographers. She has choreographed work for the wide spaces of New York's Central Park, and experimented with texts and songs that parallel the dance. Not only

have choreographers invented new figures within the classical discipline, but techniques from various styles have been combined. Classical purists have criticized many choreographers, such as the Frenchman *Maurice Béjart* (1927–), for breaking all the rules of formal classicism, but these have found particular favour with young audiences. All over the world many talented choreographers are extending the parameters of modern dance.

Zansa, a recent dance work performed by the Rambert Dance Company. (CA)

SOCIAL DANCING

The social dances of the nobility at first differed little from formal peasant dances. The basic medieval dance – the *basse danse* or low dance – used small gliding steps with only a lift onto the toes. With the brighter secular music of the 15th and 16th centuries came faster livelier paces. The *sarabande* involved advances and retreats and couples passing between rows of dancers. Then there was the sprightly jigging *galliard* and the twirling *volta*. Favourites at the French court in the 17th century were the lively *gavotte*, which gave couples a chance to dance on their own, and the delicate *minuet*. The latter became fashionable in Europe in the 18th century. The waltz emerged in the 19th century from a simplified version of the Austrian dance, the *Ländler*. It spread slowly because the physical contact involved scandalized so many people. Nevertheless, its popularity grew and it became the leading ballroom dance of the 19th century.

Most of the new dances of the 20th century originated in America. The most important innovators at the beginning of the century were the Americans Irene and Vernon Castle. They introduced new steps and popularized the *one step*, the *foxtrot*, the *tango*, and many other dances. The Jazz Age of the 1920s brought the *charleston*, and from South America came the *samba*, *rumba* and *cha-cha*. Popular dance crazes during and after the war included the *jitterbug* in the 1940s, the *jive* in the 1950s, the *twist* in the 1960s, *disco dancing* in the 1970s, and *robotics* and *break-dancing* in the 1980s. Dancers now often invent their own steps and body movements, and they do not necessarily mirror a partner.

The World's Languages

No one is certain how many living languages there are in the world, but it is likely that the number exceeds 5000. Each world language is unique in that each has its own system of sounds, words and structures, and yet each is related either closely or distantly to other languages found in the same part of the world. Thus English, French, Igbo and Yoruba are all distinct languages, but English and French share many linguistic features with each other and with other languages in Europe, whereas Igbo and Yoruba have more in common with each other and with other African tongues.

The world's languages are as unique as individual people, but like people they can be classified in terms of families. Tree diagrams such as that illustrated here are often used in descriptions of languages to show the relationships that are thought to exist within language families. The 'tree' shows the main branches of the *Indo-European* family of languages.

Language families

Language trees were used by 19th-century *philologists* (historical linguists). They all derive, to some extent, from the work of scholars such as the Englishman Sir William Jones (1746–94), who in 1786 described the relationship that exists – especially in the area of vocabulary – between Latin and Greek, the Germanic languages, Hindi and Persian.

In the 19th century, two further developments occurred: phonological and syntactic evidence (⊳ p. 354) was used to reinforce relationships already clear from similarities of vocabulary between languages, and other language families were established. The German philologist and folklorist Jacob Grimm (1785–1863) – also famous for his and his brother Wilhelm Carl's collection

SEE ALSO

● WRITING SYSTEMS p. 350
● THE STORY OF ENGLISH p. 352
● HOW LANGUAGE WORKS p. 354

of folk tales – formulated a law which, with certain modifications proposed by the Danish linguist Karl Verner (1846–96), gave a systematic account of the sound differences in the related Indo-European languages.

The second development in historical language study was the recognition of additional groupings of languages. Today, as well as the Indo-European family, other large families have been recognized. These include *Altaic* (e.g. Mongolian and Turkish), *Amerindian* (North American Indian languages such as Chinook and Nootka), *Bantu* (Sub-Saharan African languages such as Herero and Zulu), *Dravidian* (languages of central and southern India and Sri Lanka such as Tamil and Telugu), *Indo-Chinese* (e.g. Chinese and Tibetan), and *Semitic-Hamitic* (languages spoken in North Africa and southwest Asia such as Arabic and Hebrew).

Language types

Other approaches to the relationship between languages have also been pursued. The German philologist Wilhelm von Humboldt (1767–1835), followed by August Schleicher (1821–1868), helped to establish a branch of language study known as *typological linguistics* that classifies languages according to their structural type. According to this approach the three main groups of languages are agglutinative, fusional (or inflectional) and isolating. Von Humboldt's approach dealt mainly with *morphology*, that is, the structure and forms of words (⊳ p. 354).

Agglutinative languages, like Turkish, typically form structures by means of a string of *morphemes* (⊳ p. 354), each with a specific meaning or function. Thus in Turkish 'to love' is *sevmek* ('love' + infinitive), and 'to be loved' *sevilmek* ('love' + passive + infinitive).

Fusional or *inflectional languages*, like Latin, have words where there is not a one-to-one correspondence between a morpheme and a meaning. The Latin word *equus* fuses the features nominative case + masculine + singular as well as the meaning ('horse'). Cases change in fusional languages; for example, the nominative case *equus* would be used where the word is the subject of a sentence, and the accusative case *equum* where the word is the object of a sentence.

In *isolating languages*, each word consists of just one morpheme – and words don't change their form at all – so the distinction between word and morpheme is not very useful. There are very few pure isolating languages in the world, but Vietnamese is the best example. Some *pidginized* languages (languages based on one language but containing elements of another) are, to a large extent, isolating.

In contrast to isolating languages, in *polysynthetic* languages few words contain just one morpheme. Polysynthetic languages, including many Amerindian languages, are characterized by long, complex words that express the meanings of whole phrases or clauses.

These ways of grouping languages reveal useful information about the characteristics of languages, but no language belongs solely to one type. English has characteristics of all four types. A word such as 'unworkmanlike' is agglutinative in that one can distinguish four morphemes each with a recognizable meaning. 'Took' is fusional in that it incorporates the meaning of past tense +

GENERAL FEATURES OF LANGUAGES

1. All languages change through time because of internal pressures. These include the desire to regularize ('dived' rather than 'dove' is now used in British English as the past tense of the verb 'dive'); and changes of meaning (the word 'silly' in English used to mean 'holy'). External pressures often result in vocabulary borrowed from other languages.

2. Language change may be slow or very rapid. Icelandic has changed less in the last 1000 years than English did in 20 as it was pidginized on the sugar plantations of Queensland in the 19th century.

3. All language users use different styles of their language in different

contexts, e.g. formal and ritual occasions, storytelling and literature, within families, within peer groups.

4. Any human language can be translated into any other, although there may be losses in nuance and cultural reference in the process.

5. All languages are equal to the needs of their users. There are no inferior languages.

6. Any normal child will learn the language or languages of his or her environment irrespective of the family the language may belong to. In other words, an English child exposed to Hindi or Swahili will learn it as easily and as naturally as he or she learns English.

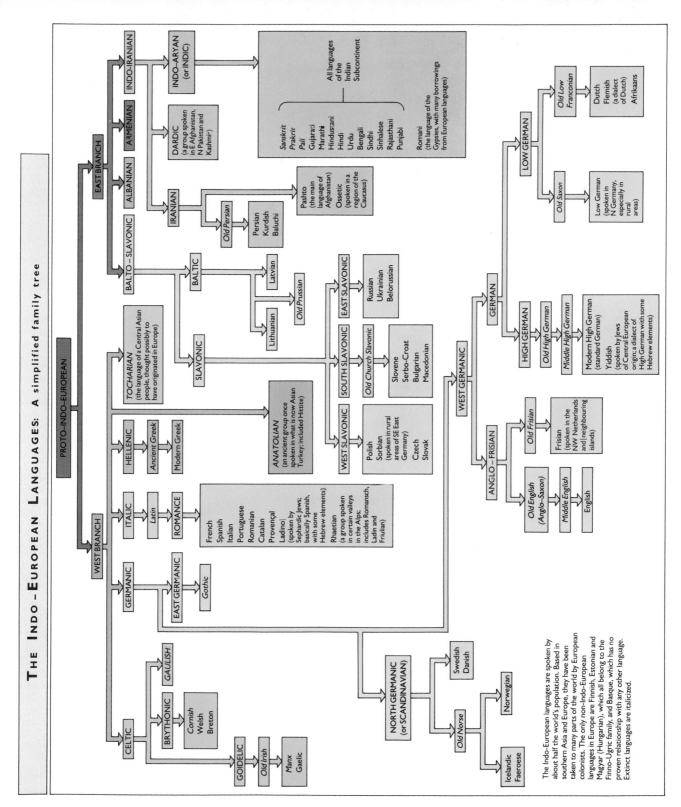

THE INDO-EUROPEAN LANGUAGES: A simplified family tree

the meaning of 'take'. The fact that 'fish' can be a singular or a plural noun as well as a verb shows that parts of English resemble isolating languages. A word such as 'disestablishmentarianism' has the complex structure of a word from a polysynthetic language.

Contemporary linguists consider other factors in identifying language groups, including phonological patterns, such as the use of tone to distinguish meaning. Chinese, for example, is a tone language. An important way of classifying language types is by word order. Typically, English has the basic order subject-verb-object ('I – ate – the apple'); it is an SVO language, as are Greek and Swahili. But Hindi, Japanese and Turkish, for example, are basically SOV ('I – the apple – ate', as it were). And Hebrew, Maori and Welsh are examples of VSO languages ('Ate – I – the apple'). Languages in each group (and these are not the only ones possible) generally have other syntactic features in common.

Writing Systems

LU	=	man
LU.MESH	=	men (with special sign for the plural form)
LUGAL	=	king (literally, 'great man')

Human beings are believed to have kept records since the last Ice Age, about 20 000 years ago. Bones and antlers have been found with regular groups of incisions thought by some archaeologists to be calendars. These may have been used to keep track of the migrating animals on which hunters of the Palaeolithic period (▷ p. 226) depended. However, true writing was not invented until much later.

The distinguishing feature of a proper writing system is that the written symbols transmit the actual words and sounds of a particular language, and not simply ideas. Thus a picture of a horse does not constitute writing since it could be 'read' in any language, for example as *cheval, hippos, equus, sisu* or *horse*. In contrast, all of the words listed express the same idea – horse – but the writing reproduces the sounds of several different languages: French, Greek, Latin, Akkadian (ancient Babylonian) and English. Writing systems are not the same as languages. One writing system, such as the Roman alphabet in which English is written, can be used to write a number of European languages. Similarly, the Arabic alphabet has been used to write Turkish and Persian as well as the Arabic language.

Logographic scripts

According to the way they work, writing systems can be classified as *logographic, syllabic* or *alphabetic*. Some writing systems use more than one of these principles simultaneously. Ancient Egyptian, for example, used all three at once.

In *logographic* writing systems each symbol stands for a whole word. In many such systems *grammatical determinatives* (symbols indicating changes in meaning or grammar such as compound or plural forms) are added to the basic signs. Below are the additions that would be made to the basic sign for 'man' in Sumerian – the oldest known script – used in southern Mesopotamia from about 3100 BC:

Logographic writing systems were principally used by ancient peoples, but some are still used by modern languages, most notably Chinese. A difficulty with logographic writing systems is that an enormous number of symbols is necessary to express every word in a language. The Chinese script consists of about 50 000 characters, though not all are in regular use.

Syllabic scripts

Syllabic writing systems use symbols to express syllables. Many early writing systems were syllabic: Babylonian and Assyrian cuneiform in the ancient Near East, two scripts of pre-Classical Greece (known as Linear A and B), Japanese, and the ancient Mayan script of Central America. Although syllabic writing systems are less cumbersome than logographic ones, they remain difficult and were generally used only by professional scribes. Babylonian cuneiform – which has over 600 symbols – was originally derived from logographic Sumerian writing. Both scripts were written by pressing wedge-shaped marks on to wet clay tablets. Words were composed by stringing syllabic signs together. Here is the composition of the words for 'father' and 'brother' in Akkadian (ancient Babylonian).

	a-bu (abu)	= father
	a-hu (ahu)	= brother

The syllabic cuneiform script lasted from c. 3100 BC to c. 100 BC. As well as Akkadian, it was also used to write other, unrelated languages such as Hittite (spoken in central Turkey; ▷ p. 228). Similarly, while Japanese is largely a syllabic writing system, the symbols it uses are derived from Chinese logographic characters (▷ box).

Alphabetic scripts

Most modern languages use *alphabetic* writing systems, in which each symbol stands for a basic sound. English and most modern European languages are written in Roman-derived alphabets. The great advantage of alphabetic systems is that many fewer symbols need to be learned than in logographic or syllabic writing systems, since most alphabets have fewer than 30 characters.

Ironically, the first alphabet may have been inspired by ancient Egyptian script, one of the most complicated writing systems ever devised. Egyptian *hieroglyphics* used logographic, syllabic and alphabetic symbols in combination. By the middle of the second millennium BC communities dwelling in the Sinai peninsula realized that all the sounds of their West Semitic tongue (related to Hebrew) could be expressed by a small number of alphabetic symbols. (They were perhaps derived from the alphabetic signs in Egyptian hieroglyphics; ▷ box.) Their innovation was to lead to the creation of the familiar alphabetic writing systems of the present.

THE EARLIEST WRITING

Writing developed independently in several areas, including the Near East, China, the Indus Valley (in what is now Pakistan) and Central America. The writing systems that evolved in each of these areas are different and not influenced by the others. The earliest known true writing system was the cuneiform (wedge-shaped) script of Mesopotamia (modern Iraq), which dates back to at least 3100 BC (▷ p. 228).

In most places where writing was independently invented, the oldest surviving written documents are labels (often on storgae jars), lists, or the names of rulers. It is usually assumed that writing was invented because the members of dominant social groups needed to monitor the movements of commodities and people in order to maintain their control over them. Written words were also powerful symbols of authority. The monumental writing of a ruler's name – for example on gigantic stone slabs in Central America – indicated the ruler's special status, and enhanced his power and control.

In many societies (though not all), writing soon came to be used for other purposes as well. In early Mesopotamia business documents, letters, laws, religious rituals and even literature were written down. Often special scribes were the only ones with the ability to read and write. In Mesopotamia temples ran special schools that trained boys (but only rarely girls) to be scribes.

CHINESE AND JAPANESE WRITING

Chinese script – reckoned to be more than 4000 years old – is the oldest script still in use today; it consists of *logograms* (signs for words) and syllabic signs. Types of Chinese script sign include picture signs (as in 1 below), symbolic pictures (as in 2), and symbolic compounds (as in 3).

Sign	Meaning	Explanation
1. 木	tree	branches above and roots beneath
2. 言	to speak, word	mouth with breath coming out
3. 炎	very hot	two fires

The Chinese writing system appeared in Japan in the 5th century AD, Chinese word-signs being taken over by the Japanese and read with Japanese rather than Chinese values. Some Chinese word-signs were given phonetic values and used as syllabic signs to express the grammatical determinatives of the Japanese language. Despite the development of a stable system of syllabic signs, the Japanese continue to make extensive use of Chinese logograms in their writing and printing today.

By 1150 BC alphabetic writing systems derived from the original Sinai script must have been widespread in the Levant (modern Israel, Jordan, Lebanon and Syria). However, because alphabetic writing was largely done on perishable materials, such as parchment (dried sheepskins) or papyrus (an early form of paper), very little original material survives.

Early examples of alphabetic writing dating from between 1450 and 1150 BC have been found on the site of the ancient Canaanite city of Ugarit (modern Ras Shamra in Syria). In order to write in Ugaritic (a West Semitic language related to Hebrew) a writing system was developed here consisting of 30 cuneiform symbols. Documents in Ugaritic script were written on clay tablets, which last almost forever once baked. The development of this script suggests that the inhabitants of Ugarit were also familiar with the more common tradition of Semitic alphabetic writing on perishable materials.

A much later and very rare example of the survival of original Semitic parchments is the *Dead Sea Scrolls*. This collection of religious texts in Aramaic and Hebrew dating from between 100 BC and AD 68 was found in a desert cave in Israel between 1947 and 1956. After 1200 BC the development of alphabets used for Semitic languages such as Phoenician, Hebrew and Aramaic becomes slightly easier to trace, since there are a few inscriptions carved in stone.

The Semitic use of alphabetic scripts differs from the modern European use of alphabetic writing in two notable ways. Firstly, the normal direction of writing in Semitic scripts was right to left (as is still the case in Hebrew and Arabic), rather than left to right. Secondly, the vowel sounds and diphthongs of the languages that use Semitic scripts (a, e, i, o, u, ou, ai, oo, etc.) are not written, and only the consonants (b, k, d, f, g, etc.) are recorded. The writing of vowel sounds seems to

have been an accident, rather than a brilliant invention. Greeks became acquainted with alphabets of the Levant when they came into regular contact with the Phoenicians between 950 and 800 BC. Some letters that represent consonants in Semitic were heard in Greek as vowels. The Greeks also seem to have been responsible for changing the direction of writing. The earliest Greek inscriptions run both right to left and left to right (sometimes both in the same text), but after about 150 years left to right became standard.

The Greeks also brought their alphabet to Italy, where it was adapted to writing Etruscan, Latin and other languages. The Roman Empire (▷ p. 232) helped spread the alphabet over much of Western Europe, though the Greek alphabet continued to be used in the eastern Empire. By the time the Western Roman Empire fell in the 5th century AD it was a Christian Empire. Writing (in Latin) had by this time become essential to the administration of the Church. Both the Roman writing system and Christianity outlasted the Empire within which they had developed. During the early medieval period the Latin alphabet was adapted for writing local spoken languages such as Gothic, Old Irish, Frankish and Anglo-Saxon (▷ p. 352). Meanwhile, in the east, Greek Orthodox Christianity spread north to the Balkans and Russia and with it went the Greek alphabet. It is reputed that two Orthodox clerics, St Cyril and St Methodius, adapted the Greek alphabet to write Slavonic languages. Hence the alphabet used today in Russia, Bulgaria and some other parts of Eastern Europe is called *Cyrillic*, after St Cyril. Thus the Semitic, Greek, and Roman alphabets were the basis of most of the alphabets now used in modern Europe, the Middle East and the Indian subcontinent.

SEE ALSO

● THE ANCIENT NEAR EAST p. 228
● ANCIENT GREECE p. 230
● THE WORLD'S LANGUAGES p. 348
● THE STORY OF ENGLISH p. 352
● HOW LANGUAGE WORKS p. 354

THE DEVELOPMENT OF THE ROMAN ALPHABET

The modern Roman alphabet, as well as the other major alphabets in use today – Greek, Cyrillic, Hebrew and Arabic – developed from a script (North Semitic) that evolved on the eastern shores of the Mediterranean during the second millennium BC. The table below traces the development of six modern Roman characters from their earliest hieroglyphic form. It is generally believed that North Semitic script took over elements from ancient Egyptian hieroglyphic script in order to reproduce the consonant sounds of the North Semitic language. According to one theory, the name of the object indicated by the hieroglyphs was translated into the North Semitic language, and the Semitic word then provided the new alphabetic value of the sign. Thus the hieroglyph for house was translated into Semitic as *bet* and used as the letter for *b*.

Egyptian hieroglyphic	Proto-Sinaitic Script	North Semitic (Phoenician)	Hebrew	Greek (with local variations)	Cyrillic	Latin
(ox)		('alep)		(alpha)	A	A
(building, house)		(bet)		(beta)	Б	B
(head)		(resh)		(rho)	P	R
		(shin [tooth])		(sigma)	C	S
(eye)		('ayin)		(omikron)	O	O
(fence)		(he)		(epsilon)	E	E

The Story of English

The English language is a rich mixture, both in its origins and in the variety of ways in which it is spoken in the world today. The origins of English lie in the *Germanic* group of languages – from which other modern languages such as German and Dutch are also descended – but its vocabulary includes a very large proportion of *Romance* words, which are derived from Latin and are related to modern languages such as French and Italian.

Britain's colonial past has ensured the extraordinary expansion in the use of English from being spoken only in a small island to becoming the most widely-used language in the world. As such, it is used worldwide for air-traffic control and is the most common language used in technical publications. It is also taught as the principal foreign language in may countries.

Old English

Before the 5th century AD, various *Celtic* languages were spoken in Britain. But the real ancestors of English began to develop in the 5th century, when the Celtic languages were displaced by successive invasions from the eastern coasts of the North Sea (▷ p. 241). These invaders spoke *Germanic* languages (Frisian, Saxon, Jutish). It is from these languages that *Old English* (the language of the Anglo-Saxons) developed. Although Old English is as different from Modern English as a foreign language, it provided the basis of modern English both in the way sentences are formed and in most of the short, non-abstract words that are used in ordinary speech. The Celtic languages did survive in the west and north, however, developing into Welsh and Gaelic.

The most obvious difference between Old English (OE) and any later form of the language is that the function of words in a sentence was indicated not by the order in which they appeared, but by *inflections* – endings that change the form of words (▷ p. 608). Furthermore, as in many modern languages, all nouns had *grammatical gender* – masculine, feminine or neuter – and adjectives changed their form to agree with the gender of nouns. OE (like Modern German) was thus a richly inflected language and the history of English is in part the history of the gradual loss of this inflectional system. Some of it remains, however, most notably in our present-day pronouns (e.g. *he*, *him*, *his*).

The 7th-century Christian missions to Britain brought learning and literacy. At first this was entirely Latin, but an OE written literature did emerge, most notably in the West Saxon kingdom of Alfred the Great (871–899). From the late 8th to the 10th century, the vocabulary was influenced by further invaders from Scandinavia – the Vikings (▷ p. 243) – whose *Norse* tongue gave us several words, including 'happy', 'husband', 'wrong' and the pronoun 'they'.

Middle English

The Norman Conquest in 1066 (▷ p. 243) not only changed the government of England – it also changed the way in which the English language developed. English now became the language of a conquered people and ceased to be the 'national language'; a Romance language – Norman French – was the language of the court, and a Normanized Latin the language of government, learning and the Church.

Mother tongue

Second language

Key to numbered countries
1 THE GAMBIA
2 LIBERIA
3 GHANA
4 UGANDA
5 ETHIOPIA
6 ISRAEL
7 SRI LANKA
8 BANGLADESH

CANADA, USA, WEST INDIES, GUYANA, SIERRA LEONE, NIGERIA, CAMEROON, ZAMBIA, NAMIBIA, SOUTH AFRICA, BRITISH ISLES, PAKISTAN, INDIA, NEPAL, SUDAN, KENYA, TANZANIA, MALAWI, ZIMBABWE, BOTSWANA, BURMA, HONG KONG, PHILIPPINES, MALAYSIA, AUSTRALIA, NEW ZEALAND

THE ENGLISH-SPEAKING WORLD

Nevertheless, literature was still written in English, with dialect forms in different parts of the country. For three hundred years after the Conquest, English and French slowly merged as the separation between Norman and Saxon became less rigid. By the end of the 14th century, English was being used for official purposes. By 1400 a language had developed that, despite its many dialect variations, was recognizably the beginnings of the English we know today. The greatest writer in Middle English was the poet Geoffrey Chaucer (?1345–1400), whose *Canterbury Tales* show the range and power of expression of the emergent language (▷ p. 358).

This language was different in two ways from Old English. Its vocabulary no longer came from a single source but showed an inextricable mixture of Germanic and Romance words. Often the more basic word today is Germanic and the derived word Romance; we take our *teeth* (Germanic) to a *dentist* (Romance). The other important difference relates to the simplification of the inflectional system. Grammatical gender was entirely lost in Middle English (and so adjectives ceased to 'agree' with nouns) and the inflectional endings of OE were already disappearing, with word order being used to signal meaning as in present-day English.

The Renaissance

By 1500 English was not very far removed from the language we use today. During the Renaissance (▷ p. 248) English was influenced, both in its vocabulary and in the sentence structure of scholarly style, by the classical models of Latin and Greek. English became accepted once again as the national language for all public purposes. Besides, as the poetry and plays of the Tudor period (notably the works of Shakespeare) had clearly shown, the language was well established as capable of literary as well as popular use (▷ p. 360).

Shakespeare's works show the language in transition. The form 'thou' and the inflection '–est' as in 'thou knowest' ('you know') were still used in speaking to one person regarded as an intimate or an inferior, though the usage was not consistent. As regards the formation of questions: in *Macbeth*, Lennox asks 'Goes the king today?' where we would use the verb 'do' as in 'Does the king go today?', though both forms were available, as shown by Polonius's question in *Hamlet* 'What do you read, my lord?' Notice also that we would say 'What are you reading?' The present-day distinction between 'I read' (simple present tense) and 'I am reading' was only just emerging at this stage.

The introduction of printing into England by William Caxton in the 15th century (▷ p. 202) brought more books in English, and printers began to regularize spelling and punctuation. Although regional dialects continued to be spoken, the idea of a standard form of written English was now accepted. The establishment of this standard and the status of English, as against Latin, was strengthened by the writings of the Reformation (▷ p. 250), notably the *Book of Common Prayer* and the *Authorized* or *King James* translation of the Bible (1611).

Modern English

From the late 17th century, English usage became more regular and consistent. Individual scholars

── ENGLISH IN THE WORLD ──

The language of Shakespeare was the language of some 5 million people, the population of Britain in the late 16th century. Since that time English has spread throughout the world, beginning with the colonies in North America (▷ p. 422). The speech of the early settlers developed into American English, with some differences in vocabulary, grammar and spelling. As the British Empire expanded during the 18th and 19th centuries (▷ pp. 416 and 432), English became the language of countries such as Canada and Australia, occupied mainly by people of British origin. It was also the official language in India, many parts of Africa and elsewhere. When these countries gained independence, they usually kept English for use in international communication and between speakers with different first languages. These speakers, like those in the USA, have adapted English for their own purposes, thereby creating new varieties of the language that are legitimate in their own right.

The variety of English known as 'British English' is in fact now spoken by a minority among the English-speaking peoples of the world. It has been estimated that there are over 300 million people for whom English is their native language, perhaps 1000 million for whom it is a second national language, and an unknown number who have learned it as a foreign language. The teaching of English as a second or foreign language, both in Britain and abroad, has greatly expanded and is now academically and commercially important. The emergence of the mainly English-speaking USA as a superpower undoubtedly played a role in the international importance of English.

British English was itself affected by world use. It has readily absorbed new words ever since the Norman Conquest and today has words from many languages: examples include *bungalow* from Hindi, *pyjamas* from Urdu, *gong* from Malay and *boomerang* from Australian aboriginal. The English that emerged about the end of the 14th century as a mixed and developing language has now a very extensive vocabulary.

and writers tried to preserve what they regarded as the 'purity' of their native language. Standards of spelling and meaning were supported by dictionaries, the most famous being that of Samuel Johnson in 1755. Grammarians made recommendations for correct English usage, based on Latin and regarded as a prescriptive set of rules for all to follow.

The grammar of English did not greatly change after the middle of the 17th century. The third-person singular of the present tense of the verb ended in -s instead of -eth, and the singular pronoun *thou* disappeared with the universal use of *you*. The main development over the last three centuries has been the growth of vocabulary. Some words have become obsolete or changed their meanings but many more have been introduced.

In the late 19th century new discoveries, inventions and ideas brought further expansion of vocabulary. This coincided with another great literary period marked by the acceptance of the novel as a serious literary medium (▷ pp. 364 and 368). Academic study of language principles brought better understanding of the history and nature of English. A notable contribution was the *Oxford English Dictionary*, begun by James Murray (1837–1915) in 1879.

In the 20th century technical advances have brought still more new words as well as adapting old ones. A word like *computer* is introduced and the word *screen* takes on a special meaning in connection with it. There have been few changes in grammar, but a tendency to drop some forms; the inflected form *whom* is seldom heard in speech today. A more significant change is the use of *they* and *them* in connection with singular common-gender words like *person* and *student* instead of the masculine form.

SEE ALSO

● THE WORLD'S LANGUAGES
  p. 348
● HOW LANGUAGE WORKS
  p. 354
● RENAISSANCE LITERATURE
  p. 360
● REALISM IN LITERATURE
  p. 368

How Language Works

Language is the most important and widespread of sign systems; all human technology, civilization and culture depend upon it. Its use demands the coordination of immensely complex physical and mental activities. Since these activities are normally subconscious, language is usually taken for granted and treated as a transparent medium through which we entertain ideas and acquire information about the world.

Language usually manifests itself in the form of writing (▷ p. 350) or speech, though not necessarily so. The sign languages used by the deaf are as complex as spoken languages. Speech develops before writing, both in societies and in individuals. There are an estimated five thousand living languages (▷ p. 348). Making this calculation is hindered by the difficulty in distinguishing languages from dialects (▷ below); distinctions are often drawn for political reasons rather than linguistic ones.

Linguistics: the study of language

The academic study of language is known as *linguistics*. Its aim is to understand how language in general works. Following the ideas of the Swiss linguist **Ferdinand de Saussure** (1857–1913), it focuses on the linguistic system ('*la langue*') underlying people's linguistic behaviour ('*la parole*'). It aims to describe the system underlying the way people actually speak their own language – rather than telling them how they ought to speak it, or teaching them foreign languages. In other words, linguistics is *descriptive*, rather than *prescriptive*. Saussure was the first to suggest that *synchronic* linguistics – the study of languages as they are at a given point in time – could be independent of *diachronic* (historical) linguistics – the study of how languages have developed through the centuries (▷ p. 348). At the centre of linguistics lies the study of *gram-*

mar, which can be divided into phonetics, phonology, morphology, syntax, and semantics.

Sounds in language

Speech is a continuous stream of sound that the speaker's mind divides into units. The physical study of such sounds, and how they are produced in the vocal tract, is called *phonetics*. Linguists use a special *phonetic script* to represent speech sounds because there is seldom a one-to-one correspondence between speech sounds and the symbols of ordinary spelling *(graphemes)*. Think, for example, how 'ough' is pronounced in 'bought', 'bough', 'enough' and 'through'.

By contrast with phonetics, which deals with the physical aspects of sound, *phonology* is concerned with the linguistic significance of sounds in a given language. Not all phonetic (physical) differences in sound are linguistically significant in a given language. In English the physical difference between [l] and [r] is significant and functional: it serves to distinguish words from one another (e.g. 'lip' and 'rip', 'light' and 'right'). 'l' and 'r' are thus different *phonemes* in English, and the difference between them is described as a *phonemic* difference. But in the Ewe language (spoken in Ghana), the distinction is not phonemic. In Ewe, no two words are distinguished from each other simply by that difference in sound: indeed speakers of Ewe find it difficult to hear the difference.

Words and sentences

Some sequences of phonemes or graphemes represent *morphemes*, which are the smallest units of meaning in the structure of words. (The study of word structure is called *morphology*.) For example, the sequence of graphemes $d + o + g$ represents the English morpheme 'dog', while the sequence $o + l + s$ represents no English morpheme. Morphemes may stand as words in their own right or combine with other morphemes to form complex words. For example, the word 'dogs' consists of two morphemes: 'dog' (a kind of animal) + '-s' (plural); and 'uninvited' divides into 'un-' and 'invited' which in turn divides into 'invite' and '-ed'. In some languages there is a tendency for morphemes to correspond to words; in others, words tend to contain more than one morpheme (▷ p. 348).

We are more conscious of using the words (the vocabulary) of our language than we are of using any other kind of linguistic unit. But words by themselves don't make a language. Languages include rules for combining words into larger grammatical units – for combining words into *phrases*, phrases into *clauses*, and clauses into full *sentences* (▷ below). These rules constitute the *syntax* of the language. The most influential present-day linguist, the American **Noam Chomsky** (1928–), emphasizes that it is these rules that allow speakers to create an infinity of new sentences from a finite stock of morphemes.

For example, 'away' can combine with 'ran' to form the phrase 'ran away'; 'poor' can combine with 'John' to form the phrase 'poor John'. In turn, those two phrases can combine to form the clause 'poor John ran away' (▷ diagram). A clause can act as a complete sentence as it stands or as a unit within the structure of another sentence as in 'She said poor John ran away'. Words are assigned to *word classes* according to

SEE ALSO

● THE WORLD'S LANGUAGES p. 348
● WRITING SYSTEMS p. 350
● THE STORY OF ENGLISH p. 352

A PHRASE MARKER

Sentence

Noun phrase — Verb phrase

Pronoun — Verb — Sentence

She — *said* — Noun Phrase — Verb Phrase

Adjective — Noun — Verb — Adverb

poor — *John* — *ran* — *away.*

Phrase markers are tree diagrams used by linguists to show the structure of sentences

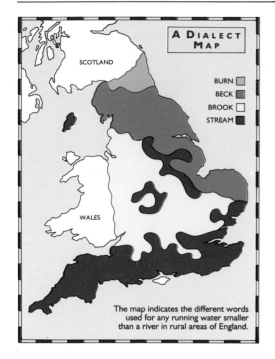

A Dialect Map

SCOTLAND

BURN
BECK
BROOK
STREAM

WALES

The map indicates the different words used for any running water smaller than a river in rural areas of England.

the ways in which they can combine with other words and phrases: *noun*, *verb*, *adjective* and so on. These classes are sometimes called the *parts of speech*.

In English (as in French and Italian) the structure and meaning of sentences are indicated by the order of words ($\triangleright$ p. 348). In other languages, such as Russian, Arabic, and Latin, the order of words is fairly free because structure and meaning are indicated by special morphemes at the end of words. These are called *inflections*. For example, the English sentence 'Brutus killed Caesar' translates into Latin as either 'Brutus Caesarem tuit' or 'Caesarem Brutus tuit'.

Meaning

For many people the most obvious point about language is that it carries meaning. The study of literal linguistic meaning is known as *semantics*. The meaning of a sentence depends not only on the meanings of its words or morphemes; it depends also on how these are combined in the structure of sentences. Although the two English sentences 'the reluctant farmer followed the noisy cow' and 'the noisy reluctant cow followed the farmer' contain exactly the same words, they have different meanings, and 'farmer cow noisy the followed reluctant' means nothing, even though each word is meaningful. Sentence meaning thus depends on how sentences are structured by the rules of language.

By contrast, and as Saussure pointed out, what meaning a morpheme has does not depend on rules, but is a matter of arbitrary convention within each language. The connection between the English morpheme 'tree' and any actual tree is no more natural or inevitable than the connection between the French morpheme 'arbre' and any actual tree.

Meaning depends on much more than morphemes and grammar, however. Speakers convey or communicate much more than the literal mean-

ings of the sentences they utter. What is communicated depends on who the speaker is, who the hearer is, and on the context in which the sentence is used. The meaning of 'I am the victor of Waterloo' depends on whether it is said by Wellington (in which case it is true) or Napoleon (false). 'It's cold in here!' will communicate that the hearer should do something about it if it is said by Lord X to his butler, but not if the butler says it to Lord X.

The study of these contextual aspects of meaning is called *pragmatics*. Since pragmatics is about meaning in context it is also concerned with how sentences are structured into coherent discourse (this aspect of pragmatics is sometimes called *discourse analysis*). Pragmatics also covers the contribution to communication made by how something is said: by stress and intonation (variations in pitch), voice quality, body movement and facial expression.

Language variation

Speakers of a given language speak it in different ways. For example, English is spoken differently in Australia, California, Jamaica, Scotland, southern England and Northern Ireland. The most noticeable difference is that of accent, but there are also differences in syntax and vocabulary. A variety of a language associated with geographical location (especially where there is variation in vocabulary) is called a *dialect* of that language. In fact, most linguists do not consider that there is a 'proper' form of a language, together with a cluster of 'non-standard' dialects, but rather that *all* forms of a language are in fact dialects. However, it may be that one dialect may be appropriate for use in a domestic or social situation, and another, more formal, dialect may be appropriate in a work situation or in writing. The subject of variation in language in general, its causes and effects, is called *sociolinguistics*.

Linguistics and cognitive science

The capacity of human beings to store and to structure information, to reason and solve problems, to engage in rational interaction with others and perceive the world in a purposeful way, is heavily dependent on their language capacity. Linguistics thus relates to psychology on the one hand and to the computer study of *artificial intelligence* and *synthetic speech* on the other. The connections between these fields are the concern of *cognitive science*. Indeed, linguistics is coming now to be seen as a branch of this relatively new science.

LANGUAGE ACQUISITION

Every human being acquires proficiency in at least one language during infancy, without conscious effort or teaching. This is their *native language*. The extreme ease and speed of language acquisition led Chomsky ($\triangleright$ text) to suggest that human beings are unique in that they are genetically programmed to develop a native language, and that certain very general principles governing all human languages are built into the human mind regardless of nationality or intelligence. The study of these principles is known as *universal grammar*. It is possible to switch languages or acquire new ones until roughly the age of puberty, but thereafter it is more difficult and requires conscious effort. In addition to the native language used at home, many people have to use a different language in the society in which they work. This is called their *second language* to distinguish it from any other *foreign language*. For example, English is used as a second language in Malaysia, as is French in Morocco.

Classical Literature

Western literature begins with the literature of Greece and Rome, and the literatures of Europe have constantly imitated, adapted, reacted against and returned to this inescapable Classical inheritance. The 1500 years from Homer to the early Middle Ages saw the birth of almost all the major forms of prose and poetry, and the very concept of literature itself as a separate activity first made its appearance.

From this varied inheritance, the Renaissance (▷ p. 360) fashioned an image of Classicism as a static entity whose values were order, unity and stability. But on closer inspection the literatures of Greece and Rome present a more varied and discordant scene.

Greek literature

The earliest extant documents in Greek are Mycenaean clay tablets of the second millennium BC written in the 'Linear B' script (▷ p. 350), but literature begins with two epics: the *Iliad* and the *Odyssey* of **Homer** (?8th century BC). These may not in fact be the work of one man; certainly a long tradition of oral poetry lay behind them. The *Iliad* describes the war waged against Troy by the Greeks to recover Helen, wife of Menelaus – Helen having been abducted by Paris, son of Priam, the king of Troy. The *Odyssey* tells of the wanderings of Odysseus (known to the Romans as Ulysses) as he returns from Troy to claim his wife and throne. Together these two poems established the form and themes of the epic genre for the West.

Homer's near-contemporary **Hesiod** (?8th–7th centuries BC) wrote the first didactic poetry in his *Works and Days* (an account of a farmer's life) and *Theogony* (an account of creation and the gods). More significant, however, is the first appearance of personal poetry in the works of **Archilochus** (mid-7th century BC) and **Alcaeus** (7th–6th centuries BC), and above all in the passionate love-songs of **Sappho** (born mid-7th century BC), the first Western poetess.

Philosophical and historical writing in the 6th century BC marks the beginning of Greek literary prose. Meanwhile **Pindar** (c. 520–445), with his choral songs for victorious athletes, continued the themes of the lyric age. But in the 5th century BC an unparalleled explosion of literary innovation occurred, particularly in Athens, the centre of a newly created empire (▷ p. 230).

Tragedy is believed to have its beginnings in primitive rituals. However, it was in the plays of **Aeschylus** (c. 525–456 BC), most notably in his great trilogy the *Oresteia* (458 BC), that tragedy acquired the intense interest in human suffering and responsibility that has marked it ever since. The same issues are to be found in the plays of **Sophocles** (c. 497–405 BC), notably *Oedipus Rex* (c. 430 BC) and *Antigone* (441 BC), whose passionately intense heroes are brought into uncomfortable proximity with the everyday world of the audience. With **Euripides** (c. 485–406 BC) the genre took an intellectual turn, exploring the ambiguous power of language. But passion was not abandoned: there is no greater representation of the extremes of emotion than Euripides' *Medea* (431 BC), in which the heroine kills her own children.

Presented at the same time as the tragedies were the riotously obscene yet politically engaged comedies of **Aristophanes** (c. 445–385 BC). The story of the wars with Persia at the beginning of the 5th century (▷ p. 230) was told by the 'father of history', **Herodotus** (c. 490–c. 425 BC), in a work that showed a sympathetic interest in the civilizations of the Middle East and Egypt. His younger contemporary **Thucydides** (c. 455–c. 399 BC) related the history of the later disastrous Peloponnesian War (▷ p. 230) in an intensely personal style.

The 4th century BC was an age of prose. The greatest writers worked in genres often now excluded from the category of literature: **Plato** (c. 427–347 BC) and later **Aristotle** (384–322 BC) in philosophy (▷ p. 302); and **Demosthenes** (384–322 BC) in oratory. But to the Greeks themselves the prose of Plato and Demosthenes ranked among their finest literary achievements, while it is to Aristotle in his *Poetics* that we owe many of the central concepts of literary theory.

The rise of Macedon and the end of traditional Greek freedom (▷ p. 231) caused yet another shift in literary fashion. The continuing vigour of

The Greek tragedian Aeschylus (c. 525–456 BC) is credited with introducing a second actor into Greek tragedy (before there had been only one actor and a chorus – a group of actors standing outside the action and commenting on it). The story that Aeschylus was killed when an eagle dropped a tortoise on his bald head (illustrated here) is almost certainly the fabrication of a later writer. (ME)

literary activity in Athens is evident in the 'New Comedy' of dramatists such as **Menander** (342–c. 292 BC), whose witty but stylized humour of situation and intrigue lacks the satirical edge of Aristophanes. But the centre of balance moved to the kingdoms of the dynasts who succeeded Alexander the Great, above all to the court of the Ptolemies in the new city of Alexandria (▷ p. 231).

The greatest figure of this 'Alexandrian' or 'Hellenistic' age was the scholar-poet **Callimachus** (c. 310–240 BC). For him, artistry in literature was all, and he railed against 'big books' and empty archaism. Also notable are the beginnings of pastoral poetry in the *Idylls* of **Theocritus** (3rd century BC).

The 2nd century BC saw the growing power of Rome (▷ p. 232) impinge more and more on Greece, but this by no means ended the story of Greek literature. In the work of figures such as **Plutarch** (c. AD 46–120) – best known for his *Parallel Lives* of eminent Greeks and Romans (much used by Shakespeare) – it displayed an assured confidence in the continuity of Greek culture. Christianity was as easily assimilated, and the flowering of the new Eastern capital of Byzantium (Constantinople; ▷ p. 233) has left us more works than survive from the rest of Greek history put together. Byzantine literature ended only with the sack of the city by the Turks in 1453 (▷ p. 241) – and by then the great works of Greek literature had once more begun to make their way to the West.

Roman literature

From its beginning Latin literature was heavily influenced by Greek. The first work of real independence was the *Annals* of **Ennius** (239–169 BC), a historical epic of which only fragments survive. Better preserved are the adaptations of Greek New Comedy by **Plautus** (c. 250–184 BC) and the North African **Terence** (c. 185–159 BC).

It was in the middle years of the 1st century BC that Latin really began to rival Greek as a vehicle for literary creativity. Both **Lucretius** (98–c. 55 BC) with his didactic poem *On the Nature of Things* and **Catullus** (c. 84–c. 54 BC) with his short poems of love and hate showed that the pressures of following Greek tradition could be a positive rather than a negative force. The backdrop to their poems was the death of the Roman Republic in war and civil strife, a demise that Rome's greatest orator **Cicero** (106–43 BC) tried to stop. When he failed, he returned to philosophy – although this did not stop Mark Antony demanding his head after Julius Caesar's murder in 44 BC.

The greatest period of Roman literature began, however, under the new emperor Augustus (▷ p. 233). Under the patronage of Augustus' minister Maecenas, **Virgil** (70–19 BC) wrote the exquisite *Eclogues* and *Georgics* and his national epic the *Aeneid* (29–19 BC), while the lyric poet **Horace** (65–8 BC) vied with Sappho and Alcaeus in his *Odes* and created new genres of colloquial poetry in his *Satires* and *Epistles*.

Though writing under Augustus, Virgil and Horace in many ways represented the end of Republican poetry. The prolific **Ovid** (43 BC–AD 17) was the first real Imperial poet, and his clever burlesques of love elegy show that the influence of Roman literature itself was now beginning to be felt as a burden and challenge. His great *Metamorphoses* (which recounts both Greek and

Roman myths and legends) is both epic and anti-epic, a reply to Virgil but also the only way possible to continue the tradition.

As the empire became established, the past became more important. Already the Augustan **Livy** (59 BC–AD 17) had used the history of Rome's past to make points about the present, but it was the cynical and sardonic **Tacitus** (c. AD 56–117) who brought this mode to perfection. Yet his style was a contemporary one, characterized by a pointed 'silver' Latin (in contrast to the Latin of the 'golden age'). 'Silver' Latin had been developed a generation earlier by writers such as the philosopher and dramatist **Seneca** (AD 4–65), whose plays of violent rhetoric exerted a potent influence on Shakespeare (▷ p. 360).

This creative tension between tradition and innovation was the main dynamic of the literature of the Empire. It revealed itself in a low-life comic novel, the *Satyricon* of **Petronius** (d. AD 65), in *The Golden Ass*, a romance by **Apuleius** (active AD 155), in the biting and often obscene miniatures of the epigrammatist **Martial** (c. AD 40–104), and in the hard-hitting verse satire of **Juvenal** (?AD 60–?140).

Latin Literature lasted even longer than Greek: late antiquity could provide in **Boethius** (c. AD 476–524) a poet to equal Ovid and at times even Virgil, and the vast Latin literature of the Middle Ages and the Renaissance cannot even be touched upon here. When Greek was rediscovered, the enthusiasm for the new wonders that discovery revealed led at first to an underestimation of Latin on grounds that it was derivative. But the same charge can be levelled at the whole of Western culture. The distinctive contribution of Latin was precisely to articulate that sense of 'coming after', and to suggest strategies for dealing with it – strategies that even today we cannot avoid as we try to come to terms with the Classical inheritance.

A Roman mosaic dating from the 1st century AD portraying the abduction of the nymph Europa by Zeus in the form of a bull. The theme of physical transformation provided the Latin poet Ovid (43 BC–AD 17) with a thread on which to hang a series of brilliantly recounted stories from both Greek and Roman mythology in his *Metamorphoses*. (AKG)

SEE ALSO

● RENAISSANCE LITERATURE p. 360
● CLASSICISM IN LITERATURE p. 362

Medieval Literature

The chief glories of Western medieval literature lie in its narratives: epics, romances, and tales composed in poetry or prose for recitation. All human life from peasant hardship to aristocratic privilege, with the rising world of modern commerce in between, was represented. In subject and technique stories ranged from comic bawdiness to scholarly wit, from pure romance to pungent satire, from folk superstition to elevated Christian doctrine. Since few outside the Church and Court could read and write, the narratives which have survived were generally preserved within religious or aristocratic communities.

The earliest surviving literature of the period is the heroic verse depicting the pre-Christian warrior culture of the Scandinavian and Germanic peoples. The *Sagas* ('Stories') of Iceland and Norway are powerful semi-historical fictions of feudal life, mostly concerned with manslaughter and revenge, but also with love, adventure and magic. The exploits of the Norse heroes and Gods are recounted in the Icelandic *Elder Edda* (before 1000) which contains an early form of the *Nibelungenlied* ('Song of the Nibelungs'; c. 1200), a long narrative poem celebrating the warrior Siegfried which inspired Richard Wagner's opera cycle *Das Ring des Nibelungen* (▷ p. 342). The Anglo-Saxon alliterative poem *Beowulf* (c. 800) is the epic masterpiece of the age. In honourable defence of his people, its hero first kills the monster Grendel, who has devoured his sleeping followers, and then the monster's mother who

comes to avenge her son. Years later, Beowulf also slays a fire-breathing dragon while in his own death-throes.

The most important early epics of France and Spain celebrate the deeds of real, historical characters. *La Chanson de Roland*, one of a series of *chansons de geste* ('songs of deeds') concerning the exploits of the knights of the Emperor Charlemagne (▷ p. 240), recounts the heroic, and fatal, rearguard action fought by Roland at the Battle of Roncevaux in the Pyrenees in AD 788. The Spanish knight Rodrigo Diaz de Vivar (c. 1043–99) achieved fame as *El Cid* ('the Lord') fighting the Moors in Spain. The *Poema del Cid* emphasizes the hero's honour as he strives successfully to prove his loyalty to his King and to obtain justice for the dishonour done to his daughters. Both poems share a similar poetic form, with verses made up of irregular numbers of lines rhyming by vowel sound only.

The world of romance

Medieval romances were verse and prose narratives dealing for the most part with chivalric adventure and the code of *Courtly Love*, a semi-religious philosophy of love in which a noble woman is placed upon an exalted pedestal and a knight ennobles himself in her service (▷ p. 248). It developed first amongst the Provençal lyric poets, the *troubadours* (▷ p. 332), in the 11th century and spread quickly to France, Germany and England. The 13th-century *Roman de la Rose* is a dream allegory of courtly love in two parts. The first 4058 lines by **Guillaume de Lorris** (d. 1237) describe the Lover's attempts to make the Lady respond, and he gets as far as kissing her despite his opponents, who represent aspects of her character such as Shame, Danger, and Fear. The remaining 17 722 lines, written by **Jean de Meun** (c. 1250–c. 1305) forty years later, extend the discussion of love into debates, supporting stories, and satire, until at last the Lover wins the Lady. The work was profoundly influential, affecting the treatment of love in such works as Geoffrey Chaucer's *Troilus and Cressida*, one of several romances set in the period of the Trojan War (▷ p. 230).

Romances written throughout Europe celebrated the exploits of King Arthur and the Knights of the Round Table. In real life Arthur may have been a Romano-British chieftain of the 5th century. His first appearance in literature was in early Welsh poetry and in Latin histories of Britain by Welsh monks. In 1155 the account of Arthur by **Geoffrey of Monmouth** (d. 1155) was expanded by the Jersey poet **Wace** (c. 1100–1171), writing in Norman-French for the court of Eleanor of Aquitaine (1122–1204). Wace's account was taken up and enormously elaborated by the French poet **Chrétien de Troyes** (active 1170–90) whose five long poems in octosyllabic couplets represent the greatest achievement in Arthurian literature. Chrétien's works inspired the German **Gottfried von Strassburg** (active 1210), author of the tragic love tale of *Tristan and Isolde*. Another aspect of the Arthurian legend was taken up by **Wolfram von Eschenbach** (c. 1170–c. 1220), whose *Parzival* (c. 1212) deals with the Quest for the Holy Grail, the sacred chalice – according to legend used by Christ at the Last Supper – which will restore spiritual happiness and earthly triumph.

Geoffrey Chaucer, author of the *Canterbury Tales*, as portrayed in the Ellesmere manuscript. Chaucer includes himself among the group of pilgrims who tell stories to shorten the journey to Canterbury, and recounts two of the 24 tales. (London, Victoria and Albert Museum/ET).

Arthurian literature also flourished in England. The anonymous manuscript of *Sir Gawain and the Green Knight* (c. 1390) begins as an adventure tale as the hero chops off the head of the Green Knight. However, Gawain is unexpectedly required to defend the honour of the Round Table when the decapitated giant reminds him of his pledge to receive a return blow the following Christmas Eve. Gawain ultimately survives this test because he preserves his chastity when the Green Knight's wife attempts to seduce him. Another Arthurian alliterative work of this period is very different in tone. The *Morte Arthure* looks back in spirit to the Norse sagas. It is a savage epic which details Arthur's military conquests and the treachery of his nephew Mordred. The various legends associated with Arthur – Excalibur and the Lady of the Lake, Lancelot's adultery with Guinevere, the magic of Merlin and Morgan le Fay, the deaths of Mordred and Arthur, the downfall of the fellowship of the Round Table – are collected and bound into unity in the prose romance *Morte D'Arthur* by **Sir Thomas Malory** (d. 1471).

Medieval tales

The *Decameron* ('The Ten Days' Work') by **Giovanni Boccaccio** (1313–75) is a collection of 100 tales supposedly told by a group of young Florentine aristocrats over a ten-day period to while away the time in a country villa where they seek to escape an outbreak of plague in the city. The tales vary enormously and in some cases incorporate material from the *Thousand and One Nights*, a collection of Indian, Arabic and Persian stories dealing with fabulous and romantic subjects in exotic oriental settings. But Boccaccio's stories are generally realistically set in his contemporary Italian world, with scandalous episodes of sex and intrigue predominating.

Geoffrey Chaucer (1343–1400) drew on the *Decameron* for certain of his *Canterbury Tales* – an unfinished collection of 24 stories extending to 17 000 lines of verse and prose. In the *Canterbury Tales* 30 pilgrims, representing the most diverse trades and social classes, gather at an inn in Southwark and agree to engage in a story-telling contest as they ride together to the shrine of St. Thomas Beckett in Canterbury. The tales they tell are preceded by a General Prologue presenting vivid and humorous character sketches, and are linked together by a variety of conversational exchanges between the pilgrims. Prologue, tales and linking passages combine together to present a unified whole, presenting a richly varied collection of different classes of person and types of story: courtly romance, fable, devotional sermon, allegory and, perhaps most memorably, bawdy *fabliau*.

The fabliau was a short verse tale, often in couplets, which dealt with farcical situations drawn from everyday life in which knockabout sex and satire of church officials were prominent. In Chaucer's *Miller's Tale* for example, a dull-witted carpenter is cuckolded by his student lodger, who – in a riotous finale – is branded on the bare behind. Chaucer also employed the form of the *beast fable*, short verse or prose tale exemplifying a particular moral, following the tradition of **Aesop's** *Fables* (c. 6th century BC). His *Nun's Priest Tale* retells the familiar fable of the Cock and the Fox in mock-heroic style: the self-important cock is persuaded by the fox to display his prowess at crowing, and is thus caught off-guard when the fox seizes him, but nevertheless succeeds in escaping by flattering the fox in turn.

DANTE

Dante and Virgil approach Limbo – supposed domain of the just who died before the coming of Christ – in a 14th-century illuminated manuscript of the *Divine Comedy*. (Venice, Biblioteca Marciana/ET)

The towering figure of medieval Italy is **Dante Alighieri** (1265–1321), whose *Divine Comedy* is one of the greatest poems of Western civilization. It is written in *terza rima* – lines of 11 syllables arranged in rhyming groups of three – and consists of three parts: the *Inferno*, the *Purgatorio* and the *Paradiso*. The *Divine Comedy* is a Christian epic in which the poet journeys through Hell and Purgatory with the Latin poet Virgil (⟡ p. 356), and reaches Paradise guided by his beloved Beatrice, who in her death has become the handmaiden of God. It is a poem of both present and future life – seen by the poet as it were through the eyes of God – and is full of Dante's passion and prodigious learning in philosophy, astronomy, natural science and history. It ends on a pinnacle of bliss, in which the poet's soul achieves salvation through his idealized love for Beatrice.

Mystery and morality plays

At religious festivals throughout medieval Europe, mystery plays were performed based on the Christian story from the Creation to the Last Judgement, and on the lives of the Saints. They were scripted by Churchmen and acted by townspeople with staging as magnificent as that of the tournaments and pageants of the nobility. Mystery plays were performed in or outside churches, often on purpose-built stages, or on huge pageant carts which moved about town to designated audience-sites. In England, four cycles of such plays survive, from York (48 plays), Chester (25), Wakefield (32), and N-town (so called since it is not known where the plays were performed). Except at N-town, the plays were put on by craft guilds (⟡ p. 246) and although the subject matter they portrayed was serious, the treatment they received was often down-to-earth and amusing. In many versions of the Nativity story, for example, Herod appears as a splendid pantomime villain.

In the 15th century, dramatized sermons called *moralities* developed. Broadly, they show mankind's fight against sin and the process by which the soul is saved. The best known are *The Castle of Perseverance* (late 15th century) and *Everyman* (c. 1510). Both plays are allegories, metaphorical narratives in which the characters represented abstract qualities, such as the Seven Deadly Sins. Later moralities, however, were more overtly political: **John Skelton** (c. 1460–1529), for example, castigated vices in public life and offered advice to rulers in his morality play *Magnyfycence*.

SEE ALSO

● MEDIEVAL ART p. 310
● EARLY MUSIC p. 332
● RENAISSANCE LITERATURE p. 360

Renaissance Literature

The literature of the Renaissance is intelligible to us in ways that medieval literature never can be, because it springs from the historical moment when humanity begins to elbow God aside to occupy the stage of its own consciousness. The poetry, prose and drama of the Middle Ages is mainly religious, reflecting Christian dogma and ritual; the literature of the Renaissance is predominantly secular, embodying the realm of human activity. A concern with the hereafter, the salvation of the individual soul, is replaced by an examination of the fate of kingdoms, countries, families and races. The Renaissance historicised literature as it secularized culture; literature, like history in Karl Marx's formulation, became 'nothing more or less than the spectacle of man pursuing his aims'.

This is not to say that there was a sudden violent break with the heritage of the Middle Ages. One of the hallmarks of the period, exemplified in the works of *Joachim du Bellay* (1525–60) in France and *Pietro Bembo* (1470–1547) in Italy, is the attempt to fuse a veneration of pagan antiquity and Classical culture with deeply held Christian faith. A similar tension between secular scholarship and religious affirmation is apparent in the career of the Frenchman *François Rabelais* (c. 1494–1553). Rabelais, a distinguished humanist and physician, was the author of *Gargantua and Pantagruel*, a voluminous prose satire extolling a responsible life of freedom and self-expression, yet he was also a devout Christian who took Holy Orders. Even as late as 1667 *John Milton* (1608–1674) was able to base his *Paradise Lost* on the biblical account of the expulsion of Adam and Eve from Eden and attempt to 'justify the ways of God to Man'; but in the event the poem is suffused with Classical lore and rhetoric, while the demonic energies of Satan and the drama of the developing human relationship between Adam and Eve dominate the narrative of this last and greatest of Christian epics.

Christian and courtly epics

Lodovico Ariosto (1474–1533) had inaugurated a fashion for the courtly romance and his *Orlando Furioso* (1532) traces vividly and humorously the erotic and chivalric adventures of the medieval knight Roland. Ariosto's successor as court poet to the Italian ducal house of Este, *Torquato Tasso* (1544–1595), believed heroic verse had a duty to instruct as well as delight and spent years composing and revising his Counter-Reformation masterpiece, *Jerusalem Delivered*, a highly romanticized but deeply serious epic of the Crusades. The English poet *Edmund Spenser* (1522–1599) drew on the example of both these Catholic poets when composing his own unfinished Protestant epic, *The Faerie Queene* (1590–96). The work sets out to exemplify the twelve Aristotelian 'moral virtues' through the

allegorical exploits of its often wayward knight-heroes in the service of Queen Gloriana, an idealized portrait of Elizabeth I. The patriotic fervour of this work is reflected in *The Lusiads* (1572), the national Portuguese epic, by *Luis de Camoëns* (1524–80). Based on Vasco da Gama's voyages of discovery, the work depicts the explorer as the contemporary embodiment of Virgil's Aeneas (▷ p. 356). Even such an ostensibly 'scientific' work as *La Sepmaine* – a long poem extolling the Creation – is coloured by the national and religious commitments of its French Protestant author, *Guillaume Du Bartas* (1544–90).

Poetic forms

Renaissance lyric forms varied from the simple and unaffected, to the extremely complex and sophisticated. Many lyrics were set to music and the traditions of song were elaborated in England by poet-musicians such as *John Dowland* (▷ p. 332) and – in very different fashion – by the guilds of professional poets or *Meistersingers* in Germany, whose most famous representative is *Hans Sachs* of Nuremburg (1494–1576).

The most celebrated lyric form was the *sonnet*, which enjoyed a Europe-wide vogue in the later 16th century. The *Rimes* of *Petrarch* (1304–74) – a series of love poems which supplied the intricate 14-line form and the persona of the unrequited poet-lover – served as models for many later writers. *Sir Philip Sidney* (1554–86) – whose reputation as soldier, scholar, poet and lover has led him to be widely regarded as the exemplar of the Renaissance courtier – recorded the passage of love with all its vicissitudes in his sonnet sequence *Astrophel and Stella* (1591). Other notable sequences include the *Amours* (1553) of the French poet *Pierre de Ronsard* (1524–85), Spenser's *Amoretti* (1595), the *Sonnets* of *Michelangelo de Buonarotti* (▷ p. 310) and those of Shakespeare (▷ box).

Poets relished complex, intricate forms such as the *sestina* (a poem of six-line stanzas), but also probed areas of complex psychology and philosophy. The 18th-century critic Dr Johnson coined the term *Metaphysical* to describe the verse of *John Donne* (1572–1631), whose early love poetry is characterized by a dazzling and often cynical wit, while his later religious poems explore the paradoxes of Christian belief. *George Herbert* (1593–1633), like Donne, was an Anglican searching out issues and problems of faith, though in a less dramatic and more reflective mode. The lyrics of another Metaphysical poet, *Andrew Marvell* (1621–78), provide the most sophisticated exploration of the seminal genre of *pastoral*, dealing with complex problems in terms of the simplicities of life in the countryside.

Renaissance drama

The Renaissance produced a body of dramatic literature that is unrivalled. The 'golden age' of Spanish drama was inaugurated by *Lope de Vega* (1562–1635), whose prodigious output – some 1500 plays of which only 500 survive – includes plots of intrigue and chivalry, biblical themes, and complex dramas drawn from Spanish history. Lope's works made flexible use of the dramatic unities, and were to exercise a profound influence over French Classical drama of the seventeenth

SEE ALSO

● EARLY MUSIC p. 432
● MEDIEVAL LITERATURE p. 358
● CLASSICISM IN LITERATURE p. 362

century (⊳ p. 362). The versatile genius of the Spanish theatre was **(Pedro) Calderon (de la Barca)** (1600–81) who wrote popular plays, religious dramas, and court spectacles. His secular tragedy *The Mayor of Zalamea* (c. 1643) contrasts the nobility with the people, and rejects the traditional assumptions of the aristocratic code, heralding honour as the prerogative of all who display moral integrity, regardless of their social class.

The purpose-built theatres which began to be built in England from the 1570s onwards were supplied with plays by a new class of professional dramatists, entirely ousting the pre-Reformation religious dramas. The plays of **Christopher Marlowe** (1564–93) offered radical reinterpretations of traditional materials. His *Tragical History of Dr Faustus* (c. 1589) took up the theme of the battle between good and evil for the fate of the Christian soul, but instead of a simple warning against transgression, the play becomes an affirmation of human desire for knowledge and freedom. Marlowe's contemporary, **Thomas Kyd** (1558–94), created out of the crude, violent, and melodramatic conventions of *revenge tragedy*, the complex plot of his *Spanish Tragedy* (1592), a work suggestive of Shakespeare's later *Hamlet* (1603; ⊳ box).

The 'citizen comedies' of **Ben Jonson** (1572–1637) and Thomas Middleton (⊳ below) teem with the working- and middle-class life of London, and satirize the follies of contemporary society. In Middleton's *A Trick to Catch the Old One* (1604) the young hero is only able to marry his virtuous and rich fiancée by exploiting the sexual and financial greed of his bourgeois elders. Similarly Jonson's *The Alchemist* (1610) and *Volpone* (1605), the latter ostensibly set in a corrupt Venetian society, ruthlessly anatomize the corrosive effect of competition and acquisition within contemporary society. Both of these playwrights were employed for a time by the 'Boys Companies' (acting troupes consisting of the children of the choir schools at St. Pauls and the Chapel Royal who specialized in citizen comedies) whose indoor theatres briefly equalled in popularity the outdoor adult companies.

By the time James I succeeded Elizabeth in 1603, the focal point of theatrical activity was no longer the public outdoor theatres but the more exclusive indoor venues such as the Blackfriar's Theatre and the Court itself. In these private theatres there developed a new kind of tragedy which, in plots of sensational intrigue and artistically refined violence, portrayed the world as hopelessly corrupt. **Thomas Middleton** (1580–1627), a playwright with a more extensive range than any of his contemporaries with the exception of Shakespeare, presented the Renaissance court as a scene of cruel sexual exploitation and violent blood revenge in works such as *The Revenger's Tragedy* (c. 1605), *Women Beware Women* (1621), and *The Changeling* (1622; with William Rowley). **John Webster** (c. 1578–c. 1632) elevated melodrama to tragedy in *The White Devil* (1612) and *The Duchess of Malfi* (1613–14) by pitting a sinister and depraved world against female heroines who display some measure of corrupt nobility.

Meanwhile the court of James I began to stage hugely expensive *masques*, a form of spectacular court entertainment involving music and dancing in which masked performers enacted allegorical plots. Masques were written by dramatists such as Ben Jonson with elaborate stagings by artists such as Inigo Jones (⊳ p. 326). Such works profoundly influenced the output of the professional theatrical companies, particularly as these had come to rely on royal protection from the hostility of the Puritans who dominated London's civic life. The leading company of the age, 'The Lord Chamberlain's Men' – with William Shakespeare (⊳ box) as their principal playwright, after Elizabeth's death became known as 'The King's Men', in effect personal servants to James I himself. The royal taste for romantic tragedy and *tragi-comedy* was satisfied by the later plays of Shakespeare and those of his successors as principal writers for the King's Men, **Francis Beaumont** (1584–1616) and his collaborator **John Fletcher** (1579–1625). **John Ford** (1586?–1639) created one of the last dramatic masterpieces of the period, '*Tis Pity She's Whore*' (1632), an exploration of the taboos surrounding the incestuous love between a brother and a sister, before the English theatres were finally closed by the Puritans in 1642.

SHAKESPEARE

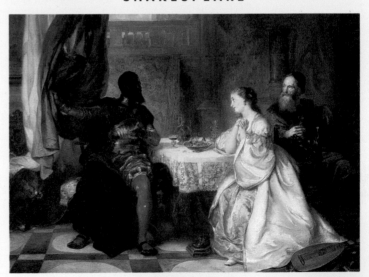

Othello and Desdemona, chief protagonists of Shakespeare's tragedy *Othello*, portrayed by Robert Alexander Hillingford (1825–1904).

(London, Christopher Wood Gallery/BAL).

No other dramatist succeeded in so many genres as **William Shakespeare** (1564–1616). In comedies such as *Twelfth Night* and *As You Like It* (both c. 1600) he excelled in a particular type of romantic comedy, depicting the maturing of a romantic hero through the help of a strong, assertive woman, within a festive 'green world' removed from everyday pressures. Shakespeare also developed the chronicle history play, constructing a huge cycle of plays covering the period of English history from the deposition of Richard II in 1399 to the death of Richard III at the Battle of Bosworth in 1485. In tragedy Shakespeare began with the materials of crude melodrama, but in later plays such as *Hamlet* (c. 1600), *King Lear* (c. 1605), and *Macbeth* (c. 1606), wrote chronicles which seem to depict the universal catastrophe of an age as well as the agonizing death of a hero. After these great tragedies, as theatrical fashion veered towards romantic tragi-comedy, Shakespeare wrote some extraordinary and complex plays, notably *The Winter's Tale* and *The Tempest* (both 1611), which re-examine within a framework of romance the conventions of comedy, history and tragedy.

Classicism in Literature

Knowledge of and interest in the works of ancient Greek and Roman authors was a key aspect of the Renaissance (▷ p. 360). After that explosive fusion of old and new ideas came a period when *Neoclassical* writers tried to imitate in modern languages what they thought was the spirit and style of the classics. *Neoclassicism* was especially strong in the French theatre during the 17th century and in England from the Restoration of 1660 to the end of the 18th century.

The virtues seen in ancient Classical writers were an appeal to reason rather than emotion; a concern with ideas and experiences of a universal validity; and a style characterized by clarity, control and dignity.

The French Classical theatre

In his *Poetics* Aristotle (▷ p. 356) discussed the unified organization of a tragedy. In the 16th century the Italian critic **Lodovico Castelvetro** (1505–71) developed Aristotle's ideas into a set of rules, known as the *unities*. The unity of *action* restricted the action to a single plot. The unity of *time* restricted the span of events on stage to 24 hours and the unity of *place* limited the action to a single spot. The unities of time and place were intended to help the audience 'believe' what they saw. When they are skilfully handled, as in the best plays of Corneille and Racine (▷ below), these constraints can produce drama of great power and concentration; less adroitly applied,

they can engender much clumsy contrivance in order to squeeze characters into one location and action into one day.

Pierre Corneille's (1606–84) celebrated tragedy *Le Cid* (1637) is based on the life of the 11th-century Spanish hero and explores the moral clash of passion and duty. The play was immensely successful, but broke the unity of action, thereby displeasing Académie française, a literary academy founded in 1634 and devoted to maintaining the standards of the French language. This controversy led to final acceptance of the unities and the exclusion of sub-plots from French Classical drama thereafter. Corneille went on to write three great plays – *Horace* (1640), *Cinna* (1641) and *Polyeucte* (1643) – which conform strictly to these rules, and deal with conflicts between family affection and public duty and the rival claims of justice and mercy.

Corneille lived to see his place as France's greatest tragic dramatist usurped by **Jean Racine** (1639–99), who drew upon Greek, Roman and biblical sources for most of his plays. The tragedies *Andromaque* (1667), *Britannicus* (1669), *Bérénice* (1670) and *Bajazet* (1672) respectively explore themes of emotional rejection, tyranny, the conflict of love and duty, and revenge. But it is in *Phèdre* (1677) that Racine's central theme of the destructive power of passion is most memorably dramatized. Racine used the formal and stylistic conventions of Neoclassicism to write tragedies of power and psychological depth unrivalled in French literature. His plays adhere rigidly to the unities; his plots are stark and simple; all is focused on a poetic language of masterly flexibility and concentration.

The greatest writer of Classical French comedy was the playwright, actor and producer **Molière** (Jean-Baptiste Poquelin, 1622–73). The ancient Greeks saw comedy as a way of ridiculing the absurdities of men, and this Molière did supremely well. But as well as exposing the foibles

A production of Molière's *Le Malade Imaginaire* in the garden of Louis XIV's palace at Versailles (▷ p. 256). A number of features of the 17th-century court theatre are clearly visible in Jean Lepautre's engraving (1676), including the proscenium arch over the stage, and the sunken orchestra pit at the front of it. (Explorer)

and falsity of a whole gallery of misfits, obsessives and hypocrites in such plays as *The School for Wives* (1662), *Don Juan* (1665) and *The Miser* (1668), he also celebrates tolerance and generosity of spirit. Molière's plots, which often involve a romantic element and clever, contriving servants, are influenced by Terence and Plautus (▷ p. 357) in their use of certain stock characters, and by the improvised farce of the Italian *Commedia dell'arte*. But Molière's characters take on an individuality and a vitality of their own. In *Tartuffe* (1664) he derided religious hypocrisy so effectively that he outraged all shades of religious opinion. Molière's greatest play, *The Misanthrope* (1666), stops only just short of tragedy in its perceptive depiction of an uncompromising and self-righteous critic of the sins of society.

The influence of French Neoclassicism throughout Europe was deep but not always beneficial. In Germany the dramatist and critic **Gotthold Ephraim Lessing** (1728–81) – who used English literature as his model in his comedy *Minna von Barnhelm* (1767) and his domestic tragedy *Miss Sara Sampson* (1755) – helped free German literature from slavish imitation of French Neoclassicism. Lessing's drama exemplified a new trend in drama to select subjects from everyday life, rather than the doings of the great.

This egalitarian trend is also evident in two plays by **Pierre-Augustin Caron de Beaumarchais** (1732–99), which take the character of the clever servant to its highest expression. *The Barber of Seville* (1775) and *The Marriage of Figaro* (1784) explore the master-servant relationship in the household to attack despotic government and hereditary privilege. The plays inspired operas by Rossini and Mozart (▷ p. 342).

Restoration drama

Exiled in France during the years of Cromwell's Protectorate (▷ p. 254), Charles II and many of his court brought back a taste for French theatre to England in 1660. This included the use of actresses to play women's parts, an innovation that introduced new possibilities for the exploration of sexual relationships into drama. Essentially Restoration comedy is a mocking view of the manners of London society. Smart rakes and fops, sexually voracious wives and tedious, jealous husbands are the chief players in a drama of sexual intrigue, often with money as the motive. The plots are complicated, the style fast, witty, and at times very bawdy.

The Country Wife (1675) by **William Wycherley** (1641–1715) makes hilarious use of ribald innuendo, and is fiercely satirical in its presentation of a society so dedicated to pleasure that it has lost touch with real human values. A more restrained and elegant approach to social satire is found in the plays of **William Congreve** (1670–1729). His comedy of deception, *The Way of The World* (1700), is distinguished by brilliant dialogue and makes serious points about the social pressures on love and marriage. This tradition of social comedy continued in milder form into the 18th century with **Richard Sheridan** (1751–1816) – with plays such as *The Rivals* (1775) – into the 19th century with Oscar Wilde and into the 20th century with Noel Coward.

Elevated heroic tragedies also played in the Restoration theatre. Influenced by French tragedies, these plays involved heroes caught in

Alexander Pope, master of irony and the heroic couplet, in a painting by Sir Godfrey Kneller (c. 1646– 1723). The most brilliant satirist of the Augustan period, Pope was the first English poet to enjoy international fame during his own lifetime. (BAC)

stock situations of conflicting loyalties. However, the rhetoric and strict form of classical tragedy never became popular in England, although the poet and dramatist **John Dryden** (1631–1700) did manage a successful adaptation of Shakespeare's *Anthony and Cleopatra* in the blank-verse play *All for Love* (1678). Dryden was much more in his element as a poet, mastering the ode and, in the allegorical poem *Absalom and Achitophel* (1681), writing some of the keenest satire in the English language. (Hugely inventive prose satire is also found in the works of Jonathan Swift, ▷ p. 364.)

The Augustan Age

The fifty or so years following Dryden's death are named after the Roman Emperor Augustus, under whom poets such as Virgil and Horace flourished (▷ p. 357). The natural successor to Dryden was **Alexander Pope** (1688–1744). Dryden had translated some of Juvenal's satire (▷ p. 357), using the heroic couplet to stinging effect. Pope began by writing pastoral verse and later translated Homer into formal English. But like Dryden he was most effective as a satirist, writing in mock-heroic vein in *The Rape of the Lock* (1712–14), and achieving a wicked elegance in his great attack on literary mediocrity, the *Dunciad* (1728–43). In his *Essay on Criticism* (1711) he laid down the rules for writing in the neoclassical manner with an emphasis on a high degree of polish and a harmony of style and sense.

Another aspect of 18th-century poetry, and one visible in early Pope, is a taste for natural description, meditation and melancholy introspection. **Oliver Goldsmith's** (?1730–74) *The Deserted Village* (1770) laments a lost golden age of English village life, despoiled by the effects of the enclosures. This introspective tendency becomes more noticeable in the poetry of **Thomas Gray** (1716–71), who produced little but wrote with great care, perfecting the *Elegy Written in a Country Churchyard* (1751) over ten years. Of one part of it Dr Johnson said that while he had seen the ideas nowhere else, 'he that reads them here persuades himself that he has always felt them'. Although the poem is of the 18th century in its language, its mood of wistfulness and gloom looks forward to the early Romantics (▷ p. 366).

SEE ALSO

● CLASSICAL LITERATURE p. 356
● RENAISSANCE LITERATURE p. 360
● THE BEGINNINGS OF THE NOVEL p. 364
● ROMANTICISM p. 366

The Beginnings of the Novel

In the early 18th century, a relatively new form, the *novel* – an extended prose narrative treating in a realistic manner the story of fictional individuals within a recognizable social context – achieved popularity with a wide audience and came to be seen as a vehicle for serious literary expression.

Up to the 16th century the dominant literary mode had been verse, often of an elevated character and dealing with high-born heroes and heroines. Even in antiquity, however, there had also been examples of prose fiction treating less exalted themes – works such as the *Satyricon* of Petronius and *The Golden Ass* of Apuleius (▷ p. 357). The Italian *novella* – a type of short tale of a humorous nature found in Boccaccio's *Decameron* (▷ p. 358) and elsewhere lent its name to the more extended prose fictions of Defoe, Richardson and Fielding.

A number of important strands can be discerned in the early novel. Some novels show a strong emphasis on *realism* – the representation of life as it is. The use of *first-person narrative* creates an impression that authentic experience is being described, underpinning the illusion of reality. *Epistolary novels* – written in the form of letters – were intended to enhance this illusion, by allowing the intimate recounting of recently lived experience. But the most important early influence on the development of the novel was the tradition of the picaresque.

The frontispiece of an 18th-century edition of *Don Quixote*. Cervantes' tale of the often absurd adventures of Don Quixote – a poor gentleman of la Mancha whose brain is addled by excessive reading of tales of chivalry – presents a vivid picture of all levels of Spanish society. (BAL)

The picaresque novel

The term *picaresque* derives from the Spanish word *picaro*, meaning a wily rogue. Picaresque tales appeared in Spain in the 16th century and typically relate the adventures of rascally servants who defraud their social superiors before repenting their ways. *Simplicissimus* (1669), by the German **J.J.C. von Grimmelshausen** (c. 1621–76), was closely modelled on the Spanish picaresque novel and presents a vivid social picture of a Germany torn apart by the Thirty Years War (▷ p. 251).

A variation on the picaresque theme is found in *Don Quixote* (1615), by the Spanish writer **Miguel de Cervantes** (1547–1616). In what is widely regarded as the first true novel, the impossible idealism of the chivalric knight Don Quixote is contrasted with the earthy pragmatism of his servant Sancho Panza. By parodying the ballads and romances of chivalric literature Cervantes helped establish the humorous prose narrative as a serious literary genre.

The rise of the English novel

The works of the English writer **Daniel Defoe** (1660–1731) were influenced by the picaresque tradition and show a similar concern with low-life characters. The first-person narrative of *Moll Flanders* (1722) emphasizes the heroine's strong personality but also dwells on the social injustices that determine her colourful story. Defoe's most famous novel, *Robinson Crusoe* (1719), has a desert-island setting, but its shipwrecked hero proves to be a resolute defender of bourgeois values, re-creating in the wilderness the ordered world of 18th-century mercantile society.

The Irish clergyman **Jonathan Swift** (1667–1745) took the tale of the shipwrecked mariner into the realms of fantasy in *Gulliver's Travels* (1726). Lemuel Gulliver's adventures take him to such fantastical locations as the island of Lilliput (inhabited by midgets) and Brobdingnag (peopled by giants). In the petty squabbles of their various inhabitants, Swift satirizes the intellectual pretentions and vanity of the philosophers, scientists and political and literary factions of the time.

Defoe's immediacy of expression and close recording of realistic detail is heightened in the novels of **Samuel Richardson** (1689–1761). Richardson employed the epistolary technique, allowing his characters to speak in their own private voices through letters that detail not just events but also the varied emotional and psychological responses of the characters to those events. Richardson's *Pamela* (1740–1) records the experiences of a young woman in domestic service who resists the lecherous advances of her unscrupulous employer (▷ picture). His later masterpiece *Clarissa* (1747–8) registers the psychological collapse of a young woman who is drugged and raped by the appropriately named rake, Lovelace. Novels such as Richardson's, in which extreme sensitivity is allied to true virtue, are sometimes known as *novels of sentiment*. But the highly emotional way in which Richardson's characters respond to life reflects a wider cult of feeling, or *sensibility*, that arose in Europe in the mid-18th century. The cult, which drew on philosophical beliefs in the innate goodness of man and prefigured Romanticism in its exalting of emotion (▷

An illustration from Samuel Richardson's *Pamela, or Virtue Rewarded* (1740–1). The novel is presented in the form of letters and journals, most of them written by the heroine. Penniless and without protection, Pamela determinedly resists the various attempts of the lecherous Mr B. to make her his mistress. Pamela's patience is rewarded when her virtue eventually leads to her suitor's rehabilitation and leads to a model marriage. The apparently simple-minded morality of Richardson was parodied in a spoof novel – *Shamela* (1741) – by Henry Fielding. (BAL)

p. 366), is also evident in the novels of Fielding, Sterne and Rousseau.

The apparently easy moral distinctions of Richardson cannot be made in the case of the novels of **Henry Fielding** (1707–54). *Tom Jones* (1749) tells the adventures of a generous-hearted foundling who is almost cheated of his rightful inheritance by mean-spirited relations. By the end of the novel he regains his legitimate fortune and captures the heart of the virtuous heroine – but not before indulging in a variety of sexual escapades along the way. The style of the novel is graphic, ironic and often bawdy, and the account of Tom Jones's journeyings allows a wide-ranging view of English society of the period.

Standing somewhat apart from the main realistic tradition of 18th-century fiction is *The Life and Opinions of Tristram Shandy* (1759–68), by the clergyman **Laurence Sterne** (1713–68). This original and idiosyncratic novel comprehensively satirizes the conventions of the youthful novel form. The novel opens at the moment of the hero's conception and his birth is not described until well into the book, even then being interrupted by the overdue insertion of a Preface. Sterne constantly reminds readers of the unreality and illusion of fiction, indulging in abrupt time shifts and obscure philosophical speculation, and at times abandoning any sense of coherent plot. Nothing comparable to *Tristram Shandy* appears in literature until the novels of James Joyce in the 20th century (⬥ p. 376).

The novel in France

The psychological realism and acute analysis of character that were to become the hallmark of the 18th-century French novel are seen for the first time in a novel by **Madame de la Fayette** (1634–93). The *Princess of Cleves* (1678) forsakes the idealized pastoral settings of its predecessors to present a tragic tale of married life and the temptations of romantic love in the realistic setting of a French court.

Character and emotion receive yet closer analysis in the novels of **Antoine-François (l'Abbé) Prévost** (1697–1763). *Manon Lescaut* (1731) is a first-person account of the mutually destructive passion of a refined but weak-willed nobleman and an alluring but amoral young woman. The novel celebrates passion with extraordinary intensity, most notably in the heroine's protracted death in the arms of her lover in the North American desert. The influence of the picaresque tradition is evident in two novels by **Pierre Marivaux** (1688–1763; ⬥ p. 626). *The Life of Marianne* (1731–41) and *The Fortunate Peasant* (1735) are first-person narratives whose heroes recount their upward progress in society. While both novels have elements of social realism strongly reminiscent of Defoe, their keynote is psychological analysis of motive and feeling. In the importance that they attach to emotion and intuition, and their rejection of authority and tradition in favour of simple morality and naturalness, Marivaux's novels, like Richardson's, look forward to the Romantic period.

The Enlightenment thinker **Voltaire** (1694–1778) professed an aversion for the novel form, but worked in the related genre of the 'philosophical tale'. In *Candide* (1759), the most famous of these, the hero sees and suffers so much that he comes to reject the belief of his optimistic tutor, Dr. Pangloss, that this is 'the best of all possible worlds'. He decides instead that the secret of happiness is to 'cultivate one's garden' – an intensely practical philosophy that rejects excessive idealism and convoluted metaphysics. **Denis Diderot** (1713–84) shared with Voltaire an enthusiasm for English culture. His novel *Jacques the Fatalist* (1773) – which marries the tradition of the picaresque novel to the philosophical tale – shows the influence of Sterne in its awareness of the artificiality of the novel form.

Acute analysis is applied to the domain of sexual psychology with consummate skill in *Dangerous Liaisons* (1782), a finely crafted epistolary novel by **Choderlos de Laclos** (1741–1803). The novel takes the form of an exchange of letters between two cynical aristocrats who use innocent youth as a pawn in their sexual and emotional power struggle. Whether it is seen as a satire on the emptiness and corruption of aristocratic society prior to the French Revolution (⬥ p. 262) or as an account of erotic psychology, *Dangerous Liaisons* is unquestionably a masterpiece.

SEE ALSO

● MEDIEVAL LITERATURE p. 358
● CLASSICISM IN LITERATURE p. 362
● ROMANTICISM p. 366
● REALISM IN LITERATURE p. 368

Romanticism

Romanticism is broadly defined as a reaction against the French Neoclassicism (▷ p. 362) that had dominated the arts in the 18th century, and the faith in human reason that had characterized the Enlightenment. It roots lie in a period of great cultural revival in Germany during the late 18th century, and, in particular, in the emergence of a new type of philosophy known as idealist thinking, which was to have a potent impact not only on literature, but also on philosophy, aesthetics and political thought.

In the late 18th century Germany was enjoying a great cultural renaissance in literature, philosophy, and music. The country was still far from being a single nation state (▷ p. 264), and there was a widespread desire to discover and affirm a national identity. The critic and cultural historian *Johann Gottfried Herder* (1744–1803) and the greatest German poet, *Johann Wolfgang von Goethe* (1749–1832), had proclaimed the need to stop imitating French culture (▷ p. 362). This had been for two centuries Neoclassical in character – based on Greco-Roman models – and therefore itself an imitation rather than truly modern; it was also associated with the kind of monarchic and repressive rule which had long prevailed not just in France but throughout Europe.

Goethe, Herder, and Schiller (▷ below) were the principal figures in a movement of young writers known as *Sturm und Drang* ('Storm and Stress'). Strongly influenced by Rousseau (▷ below), they rebelled against convention in both art and life, and exalted the free, the natural, and the spontaneous. Naturalness of emotion and a feeling for nature were the keynotes of Goethe's youthful poetry, while his plays dramatized the struggle for freedom. His novel, *The Sorrows of Young Werther* (1774), with its story of an artist's unrequited passion and suicide, made the new sensibility famous throughout Europe.

Goethe, however, after an encounter with Classical art during a stay in Italy, was to develop a Neoclassical style of his own. He did not simply suppress his former inspiration, but disciplined it to a wiser perfection. His novel, *Wilhelm Meister* (1795–6), educates its Werther-like hero to accept his place in society. *Faust*, a dramatic poem Goethe worked on all his life, finally saves the hero's restlessly striving soul. The best achievements of Goethe's 'Classical' maturity are the verse dramas of reconciliation and renunciation – *Iphigenia* (1787) and *Torquato Tasso* (1790).

The dramatist and poet *Friedrich Schiller* (1759–1805) similarly turned away from the rhetoric of rebellion towards the measured verse of a purely spiritual freedom. The moral idealism of his mature dramas, *Wallenstein* (1798–9) and *Maria Stuart* (1800), is more profound psychologically and dramatically than that of *The Robbers* (1781), a wild *Sturm und Drang* production. Schiller's philosophical essays on art and morality, and especially his concept of a beautiful soul, have been widely influential.

The German Romantics

Apart from much speculative writing about culture and the creative personality, Romantic scholars developed German philology, collected the nation's folk-songs and tales, and translated Shakespeare and other kindred spirits of the Romantic age. A host of minor talents wrote poems and even fairy stories in a folkloric manner, some of which have been immortalized by being composed into Romantic *Lieder* (▷ p. 336). The best poet of such song-like lyrics was *Heinrich Heine* (1797–1856), whose ironic intelligence, personal sufferings, and political principles lent this simple style some depth of interest. The danger facing all Romantics was escapism into self-indulgent emotions and fancies. Where this tendency was not corrected by a maturer sense of reality (as it was with Goethe), it required some unusual intensity of inwardness to raise fantasy above private make-believe.

Such intensity is present in the poetic meditations of *Novalis* (Friedrich Leopold von Hardenberg; 1772–1801) on art and death, in the elegiac laments of *Friedrich Hölderlin* (1770–1843) for the loss of the ancient gods, and in the tragic stories and plays which *Heinrich von Kleist* (1777–1811) wove out of his sense that men are enclosed in illusion. Novalis willed himself to die for love, Hölderlin went mad, and Kleist committed suicide.

None of these developments would have taken place without the all-pervading presence throughout Germany of a new kind of philosophy. Known as idealist thinking, it originates with Kant (▷ p. 302), and analyses how much the world is shaped through human understanding of it. What appears to be reality is, in truth, a projection of the human mind. The specifically Romantic philosophers, *F.W.J. von Schelling* (1775–1854) and *J.G. Fichte* (1762–1814), showed how nature therefore corresponds with the mind, being in a sense identical with it. *G.W.F. Hegel* (1770–1831) saw in human history and culture a direct manifestation of absolute spirit (or God). Coleridge learnt this view of nature from Schelling and taught it to Wordsworth (▷ box); Marx learnt his philosophical method, though not his political message, from Hegel (▷ p. 168). Few aspects of modern European culture remain untouched by the influence of this period in philosophy.

The French Romantics

French Romanticism has its roots in the works of *Jean-Jacques Rousseau* (1712–78). Rousseau argued that man's inherently perfect nature is corrupted by society. His novel *Emile* (1762) proposed a new type of 'natural' education in which the child is shielded, like the 'noble savage', from the harmful influence of civilization. From Rousseau's novel *La Nouvelle Heloïse* (1761), which shows sentiment and virtue flourishing in an idyllic setting, all Europe learned a new sensibility and appreciation of nature (▷ p. 364). From his political treatise *The Social Contract*, a new revolutionary generation learned their most radical ideas of freedom.

By the time a generation of avowed Romantics appeared in France, still further influences were at work. There was a mood of religious revival, encouraged by Napoleon, and captured by *François-René de Chateaubriand*, and there

SEE ALSO

● ART IN THE 19TH CENTURY
  p. 320
● CLASSICISM IN LITERATURE
  p. 362
● BEGINNINGS OF THE NOVEL
  p. 364
● REALISM IN LITERATURE
  p. 368

was admiration for the works of Byron and Scott (⊳ box). A more or less 'Byronic' poetry of lonely intellectual genius, isolated in an alien world, bewailing its fate and addressing nature was variously practised by such well-born poets as **Alphonse de Lamartine** (1790–1869), **Alfred de Vigny** (1797–1863) and **Alfred de Musset** (1810–57). The greatest was **Victor Hugo**, whose high-minded idealism lent his later poetry a prophetic and visionary quality, drove him into political exile and made him at last a national hero. For these writers, Romanticism also meant a chance to break with the regularities and restrictions of Neoclassical forms, both in verse and in drama. Hugo's preface to his verse play *Cromwell* (1827) rejected conventions observed in France since the 17th century and pointed to Shakespeare to justify, for instance, mixing comedy in the same play. Hugo also proclaimed complete freedom of inspiration for poetry, but the medium in which his vivid and dramatic imagination expressed itself was fiction, notably *The Hunchback of Notre Dame* (1831).

The great 'national' poets of other countries were also active at this time: **Adam Mickiewicz** (1798–55) in Poland, **Giacomo Leopardi** (1798–1837) in Italy, and **Alexander Pushkin** (1799–1837) in Russia. Their work goes beyond the typical concerns of Romanticism, though these are present too in, for instance, the folkloric material of Mickiewicz, in the solitariness and melancholy of Leopardi and in the nature scenes and yearning passions of Pushkin. The Russians found in the landscape and people of the Caucasus their image of the simple and natural, which generations of Romantics – under Rousseau's influence – longed for. The most interesting Romantic literature grew from the realization that this ideal was unattainable.

THE BRITISH ROMANTICS

In Britain the Romantic movement was largely a poetic one, but it also manifested itself in certain types of prose. Among these were Gothic novels, tales of the macabre and the fantastic set in wild landscapes of rugged mountains, haunted castles and ruins. These novels are the ancestors of the modern horror story. *The Castle of Otranto* (1765) by **Horace Walpole** (1717–97) is a pioneer of the genre; but the most popular and successful Gothic novels were those of Mrs **Ann Radcliffe** (1764–1823), of which the most celebrated is *The Mysteries of Udolpho* (1794).

The Romantic poets were to draw on this Gothic inheritance. Indeed it was Shelley's wife, **Mary Wollstonecraft Shelley** (1797–1851), who constructed one of the most enduring myths of science-fiction terror in *Frankenstein* (1818). The success of the historical novels of the Scottish writer **Sir Walter Scott** (1771–1832), such as his vivid medieval pageant *Ivanhoe* (1819), owes much to the vogue for the Gothic. Another Scot, **Robert Burns** (1759–96), collected, edited and wrote over 700 Scottish dialect songs (including such well-known lyrics as 'Auld Lang Syne').

The poet, painter and engraver **William Blake** (1757–1827) was the most consciously revolutionary and the most politically involved of the English Romantics. His most successful works were the *Songs of Innocence* (1789) and *Songs of Experience* (1794), which juxtapose the linked opposites of existence, and capture perfectly the tense and conflictory nature of the age.

The 'Lake Poets' was the collective name given to **William Wordsworth** (1770–1850), **Samuel Taylor Coleridge** (1772–1834) and their lesser associate Robert Southey (1774–1843), all of whom lived in the English Lake District for long periods after 1800. The natural landscape and peasant inhabitants of the Lake District, where he was brought up, provided the substance for much of Wordsworth's poetry. In 1795 Wordsworth had met Coleridge and, as neighbours in Dorset, the two poets worked closely together, publishing the *Lyrical Ballads* (1798), a collection of poems dealing with common life, and written in popular ballad and lyrical forms. Despite his desire to reach out towards the common people, and his image of the poet as 'a man speaking to men', Wordsworth was the great poet of the self. In his huge psychological epic *The Prelude* (1798–1805), he attempted to link the development of his own experience with the revolutionary changes of his age. Coleridge's poetic gifts were in some ways the opposite of Wordsworth's. His imagination dwelt on the strange and fantastic and on dream and hallucination. His contribution to the *Lyrical Ballads*, 'The Rime of the Ancient Mariner' – the tale of a nightmare sea-voyage and an enduring myth of psychological extremity and isolation – is regarded as one of the great poems

The funeral of Shelley by Louis Edouard Paul Fournier (d. 1857). Shelley was drowned when his yacht, the *Ariel*, overturned in a summer squall off the coast of Tuscany on July 8 1822. His body was later burnt on the beach in the presence of Byron, amongst others. (BAL)

of Romanticism. His 'Kubla Khan', supposedly half-remembered from an opium dream, creates an exotic Romantic landscape of the mind.

Lord Byron (George Gordon Byron; 1788–1824) epitomized the more flamboyant aspects of Romanticism, and lived out the fantasies of his own verse. In the triumphantly successful *Childe Harold's Pilgrimage* (1812) Byron established as a typical Romantic figure the type of the melancholy, isolated 'Byronic' hero, exiled from his native land for some nameless and mysterious crime. Having scandalized public opinion by a rumoured liaison with his half-sister (who probably bore his child), Byron left England in 1816 and lived the rest of his life in continental Europe. His most substantial achievement was in a vein of Romantic satire, combining wit and sentiment, passion and humour, that remained relatively undeveloped in England. Its most effective expression was his epic satire *Don Juan* (1819–24).

Percy Bysshe Shelley (1792–1822) and **John Keats** (1795–1821) are often linked together like Wordsworth and Coleridge, but the respective imaginative impulses of their poetry are almost opposite. Shelley's poetic search was always a quest for the unblemished purity of the eternal. In politics he was an extreme radical and a Utopian idealist: his vision of progress was realized in great Utopian poems like 'Prometheus Unbound' (1820), or channelled into harsh satirical anger against existing political conditions, as in 'The Mask of Anarchy' (1832). Keats on the other hand was fascinated by the colours, the appearances and the sensations of physical existence itself. His characteristic achievement, in poems like the great *Odes* ('To a Nightingale', 'On a Grecian Urn', 'To Autumn'; 1820), was a poetry which simultaneously achieves through a rich and sensuous language a firm grasp of physical reality, while acknowledging the elusive transitoriness of all things.

Romantic poets either died young, with their dreams and aspirations intact, or they lived on, like Wordsworth, into old age and disillusionment. The final note of Romanticism always seems to be one of melancholy disappointment, a feeling that (in Wordsworth's line) 'there hath passed away a glory from the earth'. Later poets who revived and extended the Romantic inheritance also inherited these contradictions. The poetry of the great Victorian **Alfred, Lord Tennyson** (1809–92) continually poses a set of irreconcilable conflicts between desire and duty, dream and reality, pleasure and public life.

Realism in Literature

The term Realism is commonly used to describe works of art that appear to represent the world as it is, not as it might or should be. It can be applied to literature (and painting) from almost any period, but is especially associated with those 19th-century novelists and playwrights who claimed to be giving detailed, accurate and objective descriptions of life, in sharp contrast to what they saw as the idealizing and even sentimentalizing of their 18th-century predecessors (▷ pp. 362 and 364).

To some extent this charge was unjust. Realism as a self-conscious literary movement had already appeared in early 18th-century English drama, and gathered strength in the novels of Defoe, Richardson, Fielding and Austen (▷ p. 364 and below). These writers prided themselves on truthfulness to life, strength of feeling, moral seriousness and common sense – all features which have remained the dominant conventions of Realism. The term Realism, however, first appeared in France in the 1830s when it was used to characterize the work of Balzac and Stendhal.

The French Realists

The enormously prolific *Honoré de Balzac* (1799–1850) embarked on the long series of novels collected as *La Comédie humaine* ('The Human Comedy') in 1829. His aim was to paint a comprehensive portrait of French society in the early 19th century. He does this by creating hundreds of characters and settings, some of whom recur, giving the sense of a complete world – a practice followed by many later writers. Balzac is famous for his attention to physical detail, but his main interest is in psychology; and while he delights in describing everyday life, he is also fascinated by the melodramatic and the macabre: misers, murderers, poets and madmen.

To this extent he is not only a Realist but also a Romantic, like his great contemporary *Stendhal* (Marie-Henri Beyle; 1783–1842). But where Balzac is sensational, Stendhal is ironic; where Balzac presents the world objectively, Stendhal shows it to us through the minds of his protagonists – especially in *Le Rouge et le noir* ('The Red and the Black'; 1830).

Stendhal's subtler and more disturbing notion of reality – as something conditioned by the way we perceive it – was developed by *Gustave Flaubert* (1821–80). Flaubert was an aesthete: that is to say he saw the reality of human life as a squalid business redeemed only by the beauty and perfection of art. For him Realism is not so much a matter of copying reality as of reconstructing it in language. In Flaubert's *Madame Bovary* (1857), the story of a provincial housewife who drifts into debt and casual affairs is worked into a highly finished masterpiece in which the contrast between the novelist's everyday material and his exquisite workmanship is powerfully ironic.

The Russian Realists

Irony – the perception that things are not what they seem – is perhaps the main link between the French and the Russian Realists. In other respects Russia, which had almost no literary traditions to speak of before Pushkin (▷ p. 367), is very different. Nineteenth-century Russian writers were profoundly and directly involved with the great social and political debates of their day, but they often display a freedom and scope lacking in their Western counterparts – tending to the fantastic in Gogol and Dostoevski and to the poetic and epic in Turgenev and Tolstoy.

Ivan Turgenev (1818–83) is perhaps closest in spirit to the French novel. His exquisitely polished tales of aristocratic life in the country reveal the seething moral and political torments which lie just under the surface, ranging from young love to revolutionary fervour. In *Fathers and Sons* (1862) he reveals the intrinsically tragic irony of life through an analysis of the political and social situation in contemporary Russia.

This situation was the principal theme of Russian fiction in the 19th century. For example, it is central to the works of *Nikolai Gogol* (1809–52), such as his comic masterpiece *Dead Souls* (1842), his short stories (especially 'The Overcoat'; 1842) and his play *The Government Inspector* (1836). But these works also show how the conventions of Realism (objectivity and accuracy) can be stretched to reveal the incredible lurking within the ordinary.

Gogol's fiction hovers between tragedy and farce in a way strongly reminiscent of Dickens (▷ p. 370). Both writers influenced *Fyodor Dostoevski* (1821–81), who adapted their blend of satire, fantasy, comedy, pathos and stark realism to his own lofty purposes. Like Gogol – and unlike his French and English contemporaries – Dostoevski was a profoundly religious writer and he

Nikolai Gogol, the Russian novelist, as portrayed by A.F. Muller. In Gogol's novels, Realism begins to turn into Surrealism (▷ p. 322) – this is not a simple transcription of reality, but a hallucinatory vision of it.
(ME)

soon moved on from straightforward Realism. Where French and English writers tend to focus on personal, moral and social predicaments, he has no hesitation in tackling the largest political and religious issues, most famously in *Crime and Punishment* (1866) and *The Brothers Karamazov* (1880).

These ultimate questions are also the concern of Dostoevski's great contemporary, **Leo Tolstoy** (1828–1910). But Tolstoy presents them in a very different way. In the vast *War and Peace* (1869) and in *Anna Karenina* (1877) there is none of the stylistic and narrative exuberance of Gogol and Dostoevski. These are apparently stories of ordinary people leading ordinary lives, told in a plain, lucid style, in some ways akin to that of the English novelist George Eliot (⊳ p. 370). Tolstoy's type of Realism assumes the existence of a common human nature, and this allows the author to write about his characters as universal types, while at the same time focusing on individuals.

Naturalism

Towards the end of the 19th century prose fiction assumed a new focus with the appearance of Naturalism, a specialized form of Realism based on the philosophical doctrines of materialism and determinism (⊳ p. 302). For the novelist these amount to a belief that everything in the world – including human behaviour – has observable physical causes; and that the individual is therefore shaped by society.

In his essay 'The Experimental Novel' (1880), **Émile Zola** (1840–1902) dismisses the minute pyschological and moral description typical of the traditional Realist novel in favour of sociological analysis. Zola was a political radical who believed that the writer's task is not merely to describe society but to reform it. *Germinal* (1885), set in a grim mining village, is less about individual characters than the appalling sufferings of a whole working-class community in an unjust social system.

A similar approach is seen in the work of the Russian **Maxim Gorki** (1868–1936), the American **Theodore Dreiser** (1871–1945), the German **Gerhart Hauptmann** (1862–1946) and the Italian **Giovanni Verga** (1840–1922). These writers all began as Romantic sentimentalists, turning to Naturalism in revulsion against what they saw as the trivializing, self-indulgent influence of Symbolism (⊳ p. 372) and Romanticism. Little read today, they had considerable influence – especially Gorki. The style he enshrined as 'Socialist Realism' was for decades to be the only approach to literature allowed in many Communist countries.

The novel in 19th-century Britain

With improved printing processes and the vogue for serialization in magazines, the novel became the dominant literary form in 19th-century Britain, achieving both popularity with the reading public and critical acceptance as a serious art form. Its major advances are seen in a deepening realism, both of a psychological and social nature, and in the development of regional writing. The 19th-century British novel at times reflects the optimistic energy of the age, but is also concerned with corruption, injustice, and

Émile Zola, the French novelist, in a painting by Edouard Manet (1868). His most famous novel, *Germinal*, is but one in a 20-volume cycle – the *Rougon-Macquart* novels – in which Zola set out to present 'the social and natural history of a family under the Second Empire'.
(AKG/Louvre, Paris)

the uncaring nature of capitalist industrial society. Its hallmarks are a radical questioning and probing, and a strongly moral emphasis on personal relationships. Some writers use the device of an ironic commentary that establishes a close relationship between narrator and reader.

Jane Austen (1775–1817) was the mistress of the ironic manner, though she was writing about a very different society from that of the Victorians, and for a narrower readership. Her novels *Sense and Sensibility* (1811), *Pride and Prejudice* (1813), *Mansfield Park* (1814), *Emma* (1815) and *Persuasion* (1818) are astutely observed comedies of middle-class manners. They are unpassionate romances with an emphasis on morality – balanced and witty, concisely ironic, employing natural dialogue that reveals a refined and incisive mind.

The novels of **Charlotte** (1816–55) and **Emily** (1818–48) **Brontë** both contain Gothic elements (⊳ p. 366). With their sister **Anne** (1820–49), they adopted male pen names to get their work published. Charlotte's *Jane Eyre* (1847) is the story of an independent woman who refuses to become the mistress of the man she loves. *Wuthering Heights* (1847), the only novel of Emily Brontë, is a complex and original masterpiece. It is beyond moral and literary convention, and concerns the consuming and self-destructive love of Catherine and Heathcliff. The novel combines violence, poetry, supernatural and Gothic devices, and the story is filtered through a variety of narrators.   ⊳

Mr Rochester and Jane Eyre, chief protagonists of Charlotte Brontë's romantic masterpiece, *Jane Eyre*, as portrayed in a painting by Frederick Walker (1840–75). Charlotte was the oldest of three novel-writing sisters. The failure of a collection of their poetry, *Poems by Currer, Ellis and Acton Bell* (the pen names of Charlotte, Emily and Anne), did not deter the sisters from seeking publishers for their novels. (BAL)

The social and regional novel in Britain

The social concern characteristic of the Victorian novel is manifest in a trilogy of novels by *Benjamin Disraeli* (1804–81; later prime minister, 1868 and 1874–80) – *Coningsby* (1844), *Sybil* (1845) and *Tancred* (1847) – and in two novels by **Elizabeth Gaskell** (1810–65), *Mary Barton* (1848) and *North and South* (1855). But it is in the works of the greatest mass communicator of the 19th century, **Charles Dickens** (1812–70), that social issues are given their most thorough-going examination. In *Oliver Twist* (1837–8) he attacked Poor Law administration as well as exposing criminal low life; in *Nicholas Nickleby* (1838–9) corrupt schools; in *Bleak House* (1852–3) the law and social deprivation; and in *Little Dorrit* (1855–7) debtors' prisons and financial swindling. His highly developed social conscience derived in part from his own experience of childhood poverty and deprivation, in particular his period of forced labour in a blacking warehouse. His two first-person narratives, *David Copperfield* (1848–50) and *Great Expectations* (1861), retain a strongly autobiographical flavour. Dickens's social concern is combined with a richly imaginative and intensely humane presentation of character and scene. He stands for human values against hypocrisy, crime and snobbery. His creations are vivid and often larger than life; his humour is immediate, being both verbal and pictorial in effect.

William Makepeace Thackeray (1811–63) takes as his subject matter the exploration of social and personal morality. He established himself as a major novelist with *Vanity Fair* (1846–8), which is set in the period of the Battle of Waterloo (1815), and castigates the corruptions of society.

George Eliot (Mary Ann Evans; 1819–80) scandalized conventional social prejudice by living openly with her lover and mentor, G.H. Lewes. But she retained throughout her life a high-minded sense of duty, moral responsibility and altruistic endeavour. Her chief works – *Adam Bede* (1859), *The Mill on the Floss* (1860), *Silas Marner* (1861) and her masterpiece *Middlemarch* (1871–2) – are realistic portrayals of provincial life, with ironic humour and incisive observation of human behaviour, in which she penetrates the surface of social convention and lays bare the motives of human action.

The prolific **Anthony Trollope** (1815–82) was a friend of Thackeray's who developed Thackeray's social concerns into perceptive studies in two important novel sequences; *The Barsetshire Novels* (1857–67), in which he created an imaginary county, and the political *Palliser Novels* (1864–80). Trollope is fascinated by the world of political machination and in particular with the pressures created by political responsibility.

The greatest exponent of the regional novel was **Thomas Hardy** (1840–1928). His setting is Wessex, the name he gives to Dorset and the surrounding counties. Hardy's reputation was made by *Far from the Madding Crowd* (1874), but his characteristic view of man as subject to a malign fate is seen from *The Return of the Native* (1878) onwards. This was followed by the great tragedies *The Mayor of Casterbridge* (1886), *The Woodlanders* (1887) and *Tess of the D'Urbervilles* (1891). Disgusted by the adverse reception of *Jude the Obscure* (1895), Hardy turned from fiction to concentrate on poetry and short stories.

Towards the modern English novel

The strains inherent in late 19th-century society can be discerned in the work of novelists writing at the end of the century, who often use techniques to be developed by the Modernists. Some of the most perceptive English-language writing of this later period comes from novelists springing from American and European traditions, such as the American **Henry James** (1843–1916), who eventually made his home in England, and the Polish-born **Joseph Conrad** (1857–1924). Conrad's early sea stories are in the Realist manner, but with *Heart of Darkness* (1902) he experimented with Modernist techniques to analyse the corruptions at the heart of imperialism and the

SEE ALSO

● BEGINNINGS OF THE NOVEL p. 364
● ROMANTICISM p. 366
● THE MODERN NOVEL p. 376

human psyche. In *The Secret Agent* (1907), which depicts the anarchic face of the modern industrial city as well as the underworld of international terrorism, the traditional linear narrative is disrupted by shifts in the time-sequence. In his masterpiece, *Nostromo* (1904), the façade of Western economic progress is exposed by an exploration of its effects on the imaginary South American country of Costaguana.

The last three novels of Henry James, *The Wings* of the Dove (1902), *The Ambassadors* (1903) and *The Golden Bowl* (1904), dwell on his abiding interest in the contrast of the European and American character. These are truly psychological novels in that their chief events are the thoughts and realizations that 'happen' in the minds of the protagonists. While James saw himself as working in the tradition of Charles Dickens and George Eliot (▷ p. 369), he anticipated the modern novel in his intellectual, psychological and linguistic concerns (▷ p. 376).

AMERICAN LITERATURE OF THE 19TH CENTURY

In the 19th century American literature took on a specifically national character in its treatment of certain themes and ideas. Uncontaminated by history or tradition, the New World presented exciting possibilities for the creative writer. The successful War of Independence (1775–83) gave the USA the right to set its own constitution and create its own society (▷ p. 260). The writing of a native literature was a key factor in this process. From 1861 to 1865 the country was torn apart by the Civil War (▷ p. 261) and afterwards there was an even deeper need for literature to unite the nation and re-establish a national consciousness. In Fenimore Cooper's evocation of frontier life, Whitman's celebration of American democracy, Hawthorne's analysis of New England Puritanism and Thoreau's and Emerson's American brand of Romanticism can be seen conscious efforts to create a national identity.

Washington Irving (1783–1859) was the first American author to achieve an international readership. His collection *The Sketch Book of Geoffrey Crayon* (1819–20) consists of essays, sketches of English life and American adaptations of German folk tales, including most notably 'Rip Van Winkle' and 'The Legend of Sleepy Hollow'.

James Fenimore Cooper (1789–1851) was responsible for establishing the historical novel in the United States. *The Pioneers* (1823), the first of his 'Leatherstocking Tales', introduced the character of Natty Bumppo or Hawkeye, the archetypal American pioneer or wilderness man. This, and later novels in the sequence, notably *The Last of the Mohicans* (1826), describe in detail the frontier experience of the White settlers but also present a vivid picture of the traditions and customs of the American Indians.

Ralph Waldo Emerson (1803–82) and **Henry David Thoreau** (1817–1862) were the most important members of an intellectual movement known as Transcendentalism, which insisted on the oneness of all forms of life. The interests of the transcendentalists were as broad as those of the European Romantics who so influenced them (▷ p. 366). Emerson developed the idea of an 'Over-Soul', which included God, humanity and nature, and many of his writings, including the essay *Nature* (1836), are centrally concerned with this relationship. Thoreau expressed his political radicalism in his essay *Civil Disobedience* (1840), which advocated techniques of peaceful protest taken up by Gandhi in the 20th century. His antimaterialist philosophy led him to embark on an experiment in self-sufficiency in the woods near Concord, Massachusetts. *Walden, or Life in the Woods* (1854) describes his daily physical and spiritual existence in the cabin he built himself beside Walden Pond.

Nathaniel Hawthorne (1804–64) lived in the experimental Transcendentalist community at Brook Farm for a brief period, but was at times a critic of what he saw as the excesses of Transcendentalist philosophy. He moves away from the concerns of this group in his great novel *The Scarlet Letter* (1850). Set among the original Puritan settlers in New England, the novel tells the story of a woman who is ostracized for bearing an illegitimate child, and explores the themes of sin, guilt and hypocrisy.

Edgar Allan Poe (1809–49) worked for much of his brief and difficult life as a magazine editor. His collection of stories *Tales of the Grotesque and Arabesque* (1840) established the tone of writing with which his name was to become synonymous – that of terror, mystery and the macabre. The collection includes Poe's best-known story 'The Fall of the House of Usher'. His later tale 'The Murders in the Rue Morgue' has been described as the first modern detective story.

Herman Melville (1819–91) went to sea at the age of 19 and was to bring many of his sea-going adventures into his fiction. His experience on board a whaling ship is reflected in his most ambitious novel, *Moby-Dick* (1851). On a simple narrative level, the novel is a powerful and dramatic account of Captain Ahab's obsessive and ultimately fatal quest for the giant white whale that has bitten off his leg. But behind the bare facts of the doomed voyage of the *Pequod* lies a rich pattern of symbols that have been interpreted in many different ways: the ship's multiracial crew as a microcosm of the USA and of wider humanity; the whale as nature, God and the universe.

Mark Twain (Samuel Langhorne Clemens; 1835–1910) helped define a national identity through the use of 'Yankee' humour. He made his name with a tall tale called 'The Celebrated Jumping Frog of Calaveras County' (1867), which was reprinted in newspapers across the USA. Memories of his own childhood beside the Mississippi River colour *The Adventures of Tom Sawyer* (1876) and his masterpiece *The Adventures of Huckleberry Finn* (1884). Twain used comedy and the misunderstandings arising from the naïvety of his characters as a way to attack the injustices of society, particularly the horror and cruelty of slavery.

When **Walt Whitman** (1819–92) published his first collection, *Leaves of Grass*, in 1855, a distinctive American poetry was born. His views were influenced by the work of Emerson and his work celebrates the simple fact of life, in all its forms – human, animal and the landscape of his country. Whitman was intensely patriotic and sought to encompass within his verse both the broadest of *Democratic Vistas* (1871) and the smallest of personal experiences.

Emily Dickinson (1830–86), although a prolific and brilliant poet, published only seven poems during her lifetime. She lived with her father in Amherst, Massachusetts, and rarely left home, preferring to communicate with the outside world by letter. She often defies convention in her poems, using unusual metre and punctuation and – to great effect – unexpected language. Based on a deliberately limited world in which the largest of truths can be expressed, Dickinson's poems evoke in minute detail the vividness of lived experience, and sensitively explore the spiritual relations between the individual and her maker.

Walt Whitman photographed in 1890. As well as celebrating American democracy, his poetry explores the themes of sexual liberation and the meaning of death. (AKG)

Modern Poetry

Modern poetry includes both 'difficult' poetry and poetry that is more directly accessible to the reader. The difficult poetry is obscure and highly allusive in the Modernist manner exemplified by T.S. Eliot's *The Waste Land* and Ezra Pound's *Cantos* (▷ below). The poetry that is more accessible – though not necessarily easy to understand – belongs to a tradition which does not break so abruptly with previous poetry.

Almost all Modernist poetry has its roots, however indirectly, in the poetry of the French Symbolist and Aesthetic writers whose works dominated 19th-and early 20th-century European literature. These poets shared a belief in the absolute value of art, rejecting its long-standing association with moral and religious values. And their contempt for the everyday world – dismissed as small-minded and materialistic – was often reflected not only in the use of startlingly transcendent forms and imagery but also in the deliberately shocking flamboyance of the poets' own lifestyles.

The French Symbolists

Charles Baudelaire (1821–67), seen by some as the father of Modernism, is amongst the greatest of all French poets. The inspiration for his poetry came from a rebellious and often tortured lifestyle that included drugs, drink and desperate womanizing – yet he succeeded in transforming this misery into a profound and potent symbol of the wretchedness inherent in the human condition. His verse poems of tragic intensity – focusing on the conflict between human degradation and human aspiration, death and dreams – are collected in a volume entitled *Les Fleurs du Mal* ('the flowers of evil').

The poetry of *Stéphane Mallarmé* (1842–98), *Arthur Rimbaud* (1854–91) and *Paul Verlaine* (1844–96) marked a further step in the development of Modernism beyond personal tragedies and scandals, indeed beyond personal experience altogether, towards pure intellectual preoccupation with words. These poets strove for what Mallarmé called 'the pure idea' – an essence of things that could be grasped only by allowing words to act as stimulating abstractions rather than descriptions of real situations. Their greatest works all but eliminated the lyrical 'I' and the helpful presence of the author as guide: words and images were to be experienced for themselves.

Dissimilar styles of Modernism

Although some writers were so individual that they resist classification into any one tradition – such as the Austrian poet *Rainer Maria Rilke* (1875–1926), whose poetry sought to transcend human existence to attain a spiritual vision that goes beyond the merely human – a host of new intellectual groups, styles and ideas flourished throughout Europe. A mood of innovation spread across all spheres of the arts. For example, the French poet *Guillaume Apollinaire* (1880–1918) experimented with the principles evolved by Cubist painters and produced early examples of 'concrete' poetry (▷ picture).

With the dawn of the new century, poets' attempts to represent the complexity of human existence continued to intensify. A number of philosophical influences, including psychoanalysis (▷ p. 150), Marxism (▷ p. 168) and Nietzsche (▷ p. 302), contributed to a suspicion that

A gathering of Symbolist writers, including Verlaine and Rimbaud (seated on the far left) as painted by Henri Fantin-Latour.
(AKG)

SEE ALSO

● MODERN ART p. 322
● ROMANTICISM p. 366
● REALISM IN LITERATURE
  p. 370
● MODERN DRAMA p. 374
● THE MODERN NOVEL p. 376

society's conventional view of the world was a mere façade, resting on misconception and illusion. This suspicion was intensified by the carnage of World War I and by the virtual collapse of the old social order in Europe (⊳ p. 269). Against this background of cultural and social crisis two distinct approaches to poetic form evolved. Contrasts between illusions and reality or conflicts between intellect and body might be highlighted and thrown into relief by the use of formal classically controlled metre. In this way, stylistic order could be a counterpoint to spiritual or political chaos. Conversely, the abandoning of rhyme or regular rhythm (known as 'free verse') and constant shifts in focus or tone of voice could create a verbal evocation of the complicated existence being described.

The former approach – typified by the French poet **Paul Valéry** (1871–1945) – was to permeate the work of the great Irish poet **W.B. Yeats** (1865–1939; ⊳ below). The latter approach – reflected in the works of the French poet **Jules Laforgue** (1860–87) – was to influence profoundly the *Cantos* of the American **Ezra Pound** (1865–1972) and the poetry of **T.S. Eliot** (1888–1965). In *The Waste Land* (1922) Eliot evokes the sterility and dissolution of modern civilization by means of a series of symbolic landscapes, fragmented images or snatches of dialogue and a kaleidoscopic use of literary echoes and allusions. His *Four Quartets* (1943), a series of religious meditations on time and eternity, are gentler and more profound in mood, but continue to interweave echoes and images drawn from different settings and times.

Modern poetry in Britain and Ireland

The political events of the 20th century have had a significant bearing on modern poetry in Britain and Ireland. World War I, for example, inspired poetry that was concerned less with the conventional celebrations of honour and patriotism exemplified in the works of **Rupert Brooke** (1887–1915) than with condemning the horrific realities of war and the corruption of military leadership. **Siegfried Sassoon** (1886–1967) and **Wilfred Owen** (1893–1918) wrote directly and graphically about their own experiences of trench warfare. The Irish Nationalist Movement prior to the establishing of the Irish Free State in 1921 affected profoundly the poetry of **W.B. Yeats**. The spare yet tragically powerful 'Easter 1916', a poem which meditates on the abortive Nationalist uprising in Dublin, marked a transition from the wistful nostalgia of his earlier poetry to the plainer and more muscular style that characterizes his finest work. The threat of Fascism in the 1930s prompted a movement of left-wing political poetry among writers such as **Louis MacNeice** (1907–63), **Stephen Spender** (1909–) and – most famously – **W.H. Auden** (1907–73). A prolific writer and technically one of the most skilful and innovative of modern poets, Auden addressed a wide range of political and intellectual issues (often in updated ballad forms).

Thomas Hardy (1840–1928) and **D.H. Lawrence** (1885–1930), are two outstanding poets of the early 20th century who are perhaps even better known as novelists (⊳ p. 276). The poems of both writers could be described as regional rather than metropolitan, using natural events and local settings as a stimulus for reflecting on human experience. If there is an 'English' postwar tradition, as such, it may be said to stem from their works. **Philip Larkin** (1922–85) is the chief

A concrete poem.
Modern poetry has seen attempts to extend imaginative expression beyond the normal verse range to include verbal shapes on the printed page. Known as 'concrete poetry', this form is arresting, but limited. It scarifices the possibility of developing an argument or elaborating subtle distinctions, but offers instead images that have a poster-like effect, or entertain the reader (viewer?) with witty arrangements of language. Shown here is *Target Practice, Dedicated to both sides in Vietnam* (1968) by Ronald Draper. (RD)

inheritor from Hardy, combining the provincial and the national in his faithful representations of ordinary life in the 1960s. *Ted Hughes* (1930–) shares with Lawrence a vigorous emphasis on the brute instinct of the animal world, often in order to identify archetypes within the human subconscious.

Non-English poets of the postwar years include most famously the Welsh poets **Dylan Thomas** (1914–53) and **R.S. Thomas** (1913–), the Scottish poets **Hugh MacDiarmid** (1892–1978) and **Edwin Muir** (1887–1959) and the Irish poet **Seamus Heaney** (1939–). Heaney, while far from being an imitator of Yeats, shows a similar capacity to deal realistically with the facts of a turbulent Ireland while seeing them in the perspective of history.

MODERN AMERICAN POETRY

Arguably the greatest and certainly the most widely read of 20th-century American poets, *Robert Frost* (1874–1963) exploits the distinctive rhythms of American speech in poems that can seem deceptively straightforward. His poetry may appear restrained, even detached. Typically, however, his purpose is to question and undermine the obvious, in the interests of a more tentative, cautious wisdom.

Elsewhere, American poets have been divided in their response to the affirmation of T.S. Eliot (⊳ text) that poetry should be impersonal rather than a private confession. Eliot's position was championed in the works of *Wallace Stevens* (1879–1955), an impressively elegant and original writer who makes the art of poetry a major subject of his own work. In 'Anecdote of the Jar', the placing of a jar on a hill 'in Tennessee' becomes an analogy for the way that an artist's imagination endows formless nature with form and so makes it interesting and comprehensible to the mind.

Other poets, however, have been less reticent about focusing on personal experience. In the works of *John Berryman* (1914–72), *Robert Lowell* (1917–77) and *Sylvia Plath* (1932–63) the elements of disturbance that can be seen to underlie the apparent calm of Frost's poems are brought forcefully into the foreground. These poets led difficult lives, often struggling with depression or mental illness (both Berryman and Plath committed suicide), and their writing – which came to be labelled 'confessional' poetry – confronts their inner torment without compromise. Berryman's *Dream Songs* (1964), written in an abrupt, idiosyncratic style, create the ravaged figure of a middle-aged American called 'Henry'. One of Lowell's most celebrated poems, 'Skunk Hour', confronts the poet's own psychological condition ('My mind's not right') and climaxes in a disturbing vision of moonlit skunks marching up 'Main Street'. In Plath's frequently anthologized 'Daddy', the Nazi concentration camps of Dachau, Auschwitz and Belsen are used to express her own sense of victimization by domineering males.

Modern Drama

The 20th century has witnessed an enormous expansion in experiment and innovation in European theatre. Radical developments have pushed back the frontiers of theatrical taste and fundamentally challenged the relationship between performers and spectators established in the 19th century. German Expressionism, Epic Theatre, the Theatre of Cruelty and the Theatre of the Absurd all began as experiments designed to break away from the dominant theatrical convention of Naturalism (⊳ p. 369).

European drama of the late 19th century can be seen in many ways as the final flowering of Realism (⊳ p. 368). The genre of *Naturalism* – the close observation of individuals within a domestic or family context – that had come to dominate the novels of the period was typified theatrically in the plays of the Russian *Anton Chekhov* (1860–1904), the Norwegian *Henrik Ibsen* (1828–1906) and the Swede *August Strindberg* (1849–1912).

Chekhov's work – including *The Seagull* (1896), *Uncle Vanya* (1900) and *The Cherry Orchard* (1904) – is characteristically melancholy, yet lyrical, in tone. Ibsen's plays range from those dealing explicitly with social and political problems in the claustrophobic world of the provincial bourgeoisie – such as *A Doll's House* (1879) – to later plays such as *Hedda Gabler* (1890) which employ more symbolic techniques and show greater concern with the subconscious. In the later work of Strindberg – notably *The Ghost Sonata* (1907) – the dissolution of classic Realism into Expressionism becomes apparent.

German Expressionism and Epic Theatre

Expressionism began in Germany around 1910 as a deliberate movement away from Naturalism and the creation on stage of an illusion of reality. It introduced radically different performance conventions – such as non-realistic sets and stylized movement – which, instead of attempting to imitate life, drew attention to themselves as art. Early Expressionists such as *Georg Kaiser* (1878–1945) and *Ernst Toller* (1893–1939) concentrated on expressing the universal world of human feeling rather than on depicting a specific external reality.

During the rise of the Nazi party in the 1920s, the concern of many artists to focus on collective issues rather than on individual anxieties intensified, and Expressionism developed into the militant anti-naturalistic approach that became known as *Epic Theatre*. This was pioneered by the radical socialist theatre director *Erwin Piscator* (1893–1966), whose most famous disciple was the dramatist and lyric poet *Bertolt Brecht* (1898–1956). Brecht's collaborations with the composer *Kurt Weill* (1900–50) – most notably *The Threepenny Opera* (1928) – marked a new approach to musical theatre through their cabaret-like style and social satire. In plays such as *Mother Courage*

(1937), *Galileo* (1938–9) and *The Caucasian Chalk Circle* (1944–5), Brecht sought a theory of performance and a way of writing plays that would arouse in an audience a passion for rational argument and debate. He deliberately distanced audiences emotionally from the characters and action on the stage – for example, through stylized dialogue and the use of songs – so that they might focus more intensely on understanding the political contexts of the action. Brecht later described this approach as the *Verfremdungseffekt* ('alienation effect').

Theatre of the Absurd

Between the wars a radically different form of theatrical experiment was evolving in France through the work of *Antonin Artaud* (1896–1948). His book *The Theatre and its Double* (1938) rejected – as Expressionism had done – the conventions of Naturalistic theatre as too limiting for an audience. Instead, Artaud believed, the true potential and purpose of theatre was not to appeal to the rational mind but to communicate directly through the senses. Theatre should be a powerful, even magical, event for an audience, conducted not only in conventional performance spaces but in factories, on streets, wherever life itself was happening. Artaud termed this concept a Theatre of Cruelty because he believed that the way in which it would force audiences continually to confront their deepest selves would be inevitably a painful process.

Elsewhere in Europe, other dramatists were also experimenting. In Italy, *Luigi Pirandello* (1867–1936) was writing an extraordinary series of plays – including the well-known *Six Characters in Search of an Author* (1921) – in which he explored ideas of illusion and reality, the role of performers and spectators, and the very nature of the theatrical experience itself.

The *Theatre of the Absurd* – a movement associated chiefly with dramatists writing after World War II – had its roots in these earlier experiments. The term 'absurd' as a description of the human condition as incomprehensible, bewildering and purposeless, had been given currency by the philosophical writings of the French novelist *Albert Camus* (1913–60; ⊳ also p. 376) in the 1940s. In 1961, the term 'theatre of the absurd' was coined by the theatre critic Martin Esslin to refer to the work of a number of dramatists whose plays presented a vision of mankind adrift in a meaningless universe.

The two best known of these dramatists are the Romanian-born Frenchman *Eugene Ionesco* (1912–) and the Irishman Samuel Beckett (1906–1989; ⊳ also p. 376). Both writers abandoned the comfort of familiar settings and even familiar narrative structures (such as the notion of a sequential plot) in order to dramatize sombre themes of human isolation, of communication difficulties and of the inevitability of death. However, the scope for comedy afforded by an 'absurd' view of existence is also revealed in the work of both writers. In Ionesco's anarchic early play *The Bald Prima Donna* (1948) two strangers engaged in trivial conversation are astonished to find that they are in fact man and wife; in Beckett's *Waiting for Godot* (1952) two characters stranded in an empty landscape attempt to pass the time in a series of banal activities reminiscent

SEE ALSO

- MODERN ART p. 322
- ROMANTICISM p. 366
- REALISM IN LITERATURE p. 370
- MODERN POETRY p. 372
- THE MODERN NOVEL p. 376

of the comic routines popularized in silent films or by circus clowns.

British and Irish Drama

Following the mediocrity of much late-Victorian British drama, the wit of two Anglo-Irish dramatists, **George Bernard Shaw** (1856–1950) and **Oscar Wilde** (1854–1900), reawakened the interest of theatre-goers. Both dramatists aimed to do more than merely entertain. Wilde's plays, especially *The Importance of Being Earnest* (1895), were caustic in their satire of high society. Shaw's dramas ranged more ambitiously both in social setting and in the breadth of new ideas about society that they introduced, including Socialism. Although Shaw's career spanned over half a century, his powers were probably at their height in the earlier years, when he produced plays such as *Arms and the Man* (1894), *Man and Superman* (1905) and *Major Barbara* (1905).

Over a similar period, the development of modern drama in Ireland was bound inextricably with the growth of Irish nationalism and the founding of the Irish Free State in 1921. The Abbey Theatre in Dublin fostered a distinctively Irish – as opposed to British – drama. The plays of the poet **W.B. Yeats** (1865–1939; ▷ also p. 372) drew inspiration from ancient Celtic mythology. Those of **J.M. Synge** (1871–1909) – which included *The Playboy of the Western World* (1907) – drew directly on the author's experience of peasant life on the isolated Aran Islands. The 1920s were dominated by the political plays of **Sean O'Casey** (1880–1964), including *Juno and the Paycock* (1924) and *The Plough and the Stars* (1926).

New plays in Britain prior to World War II ranged from the elegant social comedies of **Noel Coward** (1899–1973) to the verse dramas of the poet **T.S. Eliot** (1888–1965; ▷ also p. 372). In the disillusionment of the postwar period, however, a significant new movement arose in British drama. *Look Back in Anger* (1956), the first play by **John Osborne** (1929–), expressed a widespread mood of national frustration through its hero Jimmy Porter (tagged the 'angry young man'), and inspired a whole generation of writers to use the theatre to make statements about themselves and their society. The 'angry young men' among British dramatists included **John Arden** (1930–), who wrote the startlingly original *Sergeant Musgrave's Dance* (1959), and **Arnold Wesker** (1923–), whose plays of predominantly working-class domestic life were sometimes referred to as 'kitchen sink' drama. Further new writers emerging in the 1960s included the political dramatist **Edward Bond** (1934–), the anarchic **Joe Orton** (1936–67) and the enigmatic **Harold Pinter** (1930–). Pinter's plays, unlike Bond's, contain no clear social message and steadfastly resist classification – although the dark humour of his early plays, *The Birthday Party* (1958) and *The Caretaker* (1960), has caused him to be linked by some critics to the tradition of Theatre of the Absurd.

Powerful and original dramatists of recent years include **Alan Bennett** (1934–), **Howard Brenton** (1937–), **Caryl Churchill** (1938–), **Brian Friel** (1929–) and **David Hare** (1947–). In terms of popular appeal, however, two playwrights – **Tom Stoppard** (1937–) and **Alan Ayckbourn** (1939–) stand out. Stoppard's work explores philosophical ideas with immense wit and verbal skill. His early works, in particular, both parody and draw from existing works of drama. *Rosencrantz and Guildenstern are Dead* (1966) and *Travesties* (1974) use characters from Shakespeare and Oscar Wilde respectively. Ayckbourn's plays of middle-class suburban life – notably *Relatively Speaking* (1967) and *The Norman Conquests* (1974) – take comedy painfully near to tragedy in their exposure of human pretensions and weaknesses.

AMERICAN DRAMA IN THE 20TH CENTURY

It was not until after the end of World War II that a distinctive voice was heard in the American theatre. **Eugene O'Neill** (1888–1953) was never afraid to experiment with new and diverse dramatic techniques. *The Hairy Ape* (1922) used Expressionist techniques, while his other plays were influenced by Symbolism (▷ p. 372), Realist conventions and the stream-of-consciousness mode (▷ p. 376). *Mourning Becomes Electra* (1931) was the first play in a trilogy based on the *Oresteia* of Aeschylus (▷ p. 356). *The Iceman Cometh* (1946) and *A Long Day's Journey Into Night* (published posthumously in 1956) established O'Neill's international reputation.

After the end of World War II American theatre welcomed two young and highly talented dramatists whose work was to dominate the American stage for nearly three decades: **Tennessee Williams** (1911–83) and **Arthur Miller** (1915–). Williams' successes included *A Street Car Named Desire* (1947), which explored themes of sexual obsession and violence, and *Cat on a Hot Tin Roof* (1955), a study of a family in disintegration, with Freudian undertones. Critical acclaim for Miller's work has largely been reserved for his earlier dramas, notably *Death of a Salesman* (1949), *A View from the Bridge* (1955) and *After the Fall* (1963), which depict the lives of ordinary Americans whose desire for material reward is in conflict with their need for spiritual renewal and personal happiness.

Edward Albee's (1928–) *Who's Afraid of Virginia Woolf?* (1962), a savage portrayal of a marriage in crisis, raised hopes that a new and rich talent had been unleashed, but with the exception of the works of **Sam Shepard** (1943–) – notably *Fool for Love* (1979) and *Lie of the Mind* (1988) – and those of **David Mamet** (1947–) – including *Glengarry Glen Ross* (1984) and *Things Change* (1987) – American dramatic writing remains largely in the doldrums.

Death of a Salesman. Arthur Miller's Pulitzer prize-winning examination of personal and professional failure has become a classic of modern American theatre. Shown here are John Malkovitch and Dustin Hoffman in the 1985 film version of a Broadway production. (AL)

The Modern Novel

Towards the end of the 19th century and in the early years of the 20th, the dominant influence of Realist conventions (▷ p. 368) on the novel form began to disintegrate. In common with trends in modern drama (▷ p. 374) and modern poetry (▷ p. 372), the fiction of the early 20th century was characterized by a mood of experimentation – in ideas, in form and in expression.

There was, however, no instantaneous recognition of the Modernist revolution in fiction. In the period leading up to the end of World War I, those novelists now regarded as the great mainstream of modern prose fiction were struggling, neglected, or even persecuted by cultural and political authorities.

The Modernist revolution

The first great Modernist novel in English-language fiction is generally agreed to be *Ulysses* (1922) by the Irish writer *James Joyce* (1882–1941), although its roots can be seen both in Joyce's own earlier work and in the work of the English writer *D.H. Lawrence* (1885–1930). Central to the work of both writers was a re-interpretation of the notion of 'character'. This led to an intense scrutiny of the individual's inner being, often in richly-textured and highly poetic language. Both novelists also broke free from the framework of conventional morality that had formed the basis of much Realist fiction. This manifested itself not only in their re-evaluation of the importance of 'art' but also in their challenging of traditional taboos regarding sexuality. The

Marcel Proust, the French novelist, photographed in 1900. After his mother's death in 1905 Proust became increasingly reclusive, living in a cork-lined room and devoting himself to work on his massive seven-part novel, *Remembrance of Things Past.* (ME)

explicit description of sexual relationships in their fiction led not only to their writing being censored and banned by the authorities but also to their being forced to publish some of their most famous works abroad. *Ulysses* was first published in France; Lawrence's *Women in Love* (1920) and *Lady Chatterley's Lover* (1928) were first published in America and Italy respectively (the latter remaining unpublished in complete form in Britain until the 1960s, following a celebrated obscenity trial).

Ulysses, like Modernist poetry (▷ p. 372), contains many different shifts in style – ranging from polished realism, surrealist fantasy and literary and journalistic pastiche to classical allusion and 'stream of consciousness'. The latter technique – showing 'reality' as it flows, unfiltered, through characters' minds – was also exemplified in the later novels of *Virginia Woolf* (1882–1941). *Mrs Dalloway* (1925) and *To the Lighthouse* (1927) present human experience through sequences of thought associations, creating patterns of narrative that defy conventional notions of time and place. The greatest novel of this kind, however, remains *Remembrance of Things Past* (1913–27) by the French writer *Marcel Proust* (1871–1922). This immense work in seven parts explores a whole life, from childhood to middle age, not as chronological narrative, objectively reported, but as a process of ever-shifting realization, a reality constantly reborn through memory and transformed into thought.

As novelists concentrated on evoking the inner world, the image of the alienated individual lost in a nightmarish external world became an archetype of modern fiction. The classic expression of this is to be found in the writings of the Czech novelist *Franz Kafka* (1883–1924), whose post-humously published novels *The Trial* (1925) and *The Castle* (1926) have a terrifying hallucinatory quality that has since come to be described as 'Kafkaesque'. Later in the century, this sense of bewildered isolation formed the basis for the fiction of the absurd (▷ p. 374) in novels such as *The Outsider* (1942) by the Frenchman *Albert Camus* (1913–60) or *Nausea* (1938) by the French existentialist philosopher *Jean-Paul Sartre* (1905–80; ▷ p. 302). The fiction of another writer of the absurd tradition – the Irishman *Samuel Beckett* (1906–89; ▷ p. 374) – takes language to its furthest limits, dissolving the external world to the point where novels cease to be about anything 'real' at all but become (as in *The Unnameable*; 1960) a form of pure writing.

Continuities

In contrast with the formal experimentation of the Modernists, a substantial number of 20th-century writers continued to work within more traditional artistic frameworks. However, this technical conservatism did not necessarily imply a conservative approach to their subjects. Nor did it preclude incisive moral and social criticism of the world they lived in.

The potentially tragic conflict between individual aspirations and a disintegrating external world which dominated so much of Modernist fiction in the 1920s was explored by contemporary American writers from a more specifically sociological standpoint. In *The Sun Also Rises* (1926) and *A Farewell to Arms* (1929), *Ernest Hemingway* (1899–1961) wrote of the mood of disillusion of a so-called 'lost generation' of American writers. **F. Scott Fitzgerald** (1896–1940) traced the tragic decline of the 'Jazz Age' in novels such as *The Great Gatsby* (1925). And **William Faulkner** (1897–1962) and **John Steinbeck** (1902–68) chronicled respectively the declining civilization of the American South and the effects of the Great Depression on Californian agricultural workers.

In France **André Gide** (1869–1951) and in Germany **Thomas Mann** (1875–1955) explored the social alienation of the artist, the decline of European civilization and the oppressive burdens of the past. Their works included not only full-length classics like Mann's *The Magic Mountain* (1924), but also some remarkable shorter novels – such as Gide's *The Immoralist* (1930). In Britain, **E.M. Forster** (1879–1970) expressed in *Howard's End* (1910) and *A Passage to India* (1924) his concern for the imaginative life of humanity and the need for sincerity and sensitivity in human relationships against a background of social change. The Catholic writer **Evelyn Waugh** (1903–66) depicted with satirical relish the frivolous futility of the 'bright young things' of the 1920s in *Decline and Fall* (1928) and *A Handful of Dust* (1934), before introducing deeper notes of elegy and pessimism into his later *Brideshead Revisited* (1945), which traces the decline of the Catholic aristocracy. The novels of **Graham Greene** (1904–92) also expressed a difficult relationship with Catholicism, but from the perspective of a writer drawn towards Communism and the political landscape of the modern world. Greene's major novels are usually set in colonial or Third World locations. *The Power and the Glory* (1940), for example, is set in Mexico and *The Heart of The Matter* (1948) in Africa.

Other 20th-century British writers who continued to extend prose fiction along more traditional lines include **Aldous Huxley** (1894–1963) and **George Orwell** (1903–50). Huxley's *Brave New World* (1932) and Orwell's *Nineteen Eighty-Four* (1949) depicted nightmare visions of a future totalitarian society. Outstanding contemporary writers have included **William Golding** (1911–), whose classic *Lord of the Flies* (1954) pared fiction down to a modern form of the fable, and **Iris Murdoch** (1919–), who combined fiction and philosophy in highly symbolic novels such as *The Bell* (1958) and *The Sea, The Sea* (1978). In America and Australia respectively, **Saul Bellow** (1915–) in *Herzog* (1964) and **Patrick White** (1912–) in *Voss* (1957) also combined technical conservatism with a deep and painful fictional exploration of the self and civilization. In Russia, the strength of the great Realist tradition and the post-revolutionary concern with social realism (▷ p. 368) ensured the continuity of traditional fictional forms in writers such as **Boris Pasternak** (1890–1960), whose critical view of Soviet Russia, *Dr Zhivago*, was published in Italy in 1957, and – more recently – **Alexander Solzhenitsyn** (1913–) and **Mikhail Sholokhov** (1905–84).

Post-Modernist innovation

'Post-Modernist' writers have extended the Modernist search into the potentialities of human consciousness and the distinction between the individual and the objective world by means of a deliberate subversion of fictional conventions. This has made possible a whole range of new fictional techniques, opening up serious fiction to fantasy, surrealist allegory and 'Magic Realism'.

Vladimir Nabokov, the Russian-born American novelist, photographed in 1959. His most famous novel, *Lolita* (1958), charts the sexual obsession of a middle-aged European intellectual for a 12-year-old American 'nymphet'. (ME)

Vladimir Nabokov (1899–1977), an expatriate Russian, was a major and typical Post-Modernist novelist. His flexible uses of narrative and his playful linguistic inventiveness can be seen at their most exhilarating in *Pale Fire* (1962). The novels of **Marguerite Duras** (1914–) and **Alain Robbe-Grillet** (1922–) – exponents of the French *Nouveau Roman* ('New Novel') – destabilized narrative (so that it was neither realistic nor told from the viewpoint of an omniscient narrator) and avoided imposing any fixed interpretation on the subject matter. The impact of these developments on the British novel can best be seen in the work of **John Fowles** (1926–). *The French Lieutenant's Woman* (1969) is a semi-historical novel that contrasts the conventions of the Victorian novel with a more modern view of fiction. The action of the narrative is interrupted constantly by the comments of the narrator, who stands back from the characters to remind the reader that they are not real people and that fiction involves deception and manipulation.

Elsewhere, Post-Modernist fiction has moved even further away from the landscape of social realism and entered realms of dream, myth and fantasy. The Argentinian writer **Jorge Luis Borges** (1899–1986) established – in collections of short stories such as *Fictions* (1945) – the form of *Magic Realism*, based on the premise that fantasy is no less 'real' than supposed 'fact'. *One Hundred Years of Solitude* (1967) by the Colombian writer **Gabriel Garcia Marquez** (1928–) also mixed the ordinary and the fantastic, the real and the supernatural, in a manner typical of Magic Realism and in a fragmented and dispersed narrative style that is characteristically Post-Modernist.

In comic and experimental novels such as *The Tin Drum* (1959) and *Dog Years* (1965), the German writer **Günter Grass** (1927–) similarly questioned the status of truth and reality in the modern world – but from a socialist perspective and with strong political preoccupations. And a call for positive social engagement is also at the heart of the work of the Anglo-Indian novelist **Salman Rushdie** (1947–). An exponent of Magic Realism, he applied his blend of myth and reality, philosophy and fantasy to present in *Midnight's Children* (1981) and *The Satanic Verses* (1988) a provocative exploration of Eastern culture and religion. Ironically, the offence the novel caused to many Muslims led to his being sentenced to death for blasphemy by the then spiritual leader of Iran, Ayatollah Khomeini, and thus forced into hiding.

SEE ALSO

● MODERN ART p. 322
● ROMANTICISM p. 366
● REALISM IN LITERATURE p. 370
● MODERN POETRY p. 372
● THE MODERN NOVEL p. 376

Sovereign States

A country may be variously described as an area that is distinguished by its people, its geography or its culture, or as a land that enjoys political autonomy, more usually referred to as 'sovereignty'. This chapter describes the sovereign states of the world, that is the independent states that, in theory, exercise unrestricted power over their own destinies.

However, in some ways the concept of sovereignty is of limited value in the closing years of the 20th century. It could be argued that there is no such thing as a truly independent state. The overwhelming majority of sovereign states are members of one or more of the various economic, political or military alliances and groupings, such as NATO, the EC, the OAU and so on (⊳ pp. 178–80). Most states recognize that the demands of security and trade bring agreed limits upon the freedom of action of individual countries as in the case, for example, of EC membership. Conversely, Commonwealth membership – enjoyed by all former British territories except Myanmar (Burma), Fiji and Ireland – makes no such demands. Countries also rely upon their neighbours, and other states, at least economically, and are therefore restricted in their independence.

If a country is an area that may be recognized by its distinctive people, geography or culture, then many sovereign states may be said to contain other countries within their boundaries. For example, the United Kingdom comprises four distinct countries – England, Northern Ireland, Scotland and Wales – none of which has political autonomy. Conversely the states of Australia and the USA possess considerable political autonomy but have none of the characteristics of a country. Tibet (an autonomous region of China) is just one example of an area often thought of as a country, even though it is not an independent state. Poland disappeared from the map of Europe from 1795 until 1918 but it did not cease to be a country.

New countries

The number of sovereign countries is not a constant. After the Napoleonic Wars, the Congress of Vienna (1814–15) redrew the map of Europe delineating, for example, nearly 40 German-speaking states – almost as many as the total number of countries in Europe today. However, many of the ancient European countries have disappeared – the result of German and Italian unification and of two World Wars.

In the early 1990s the two German states created as a result of partition after World War II – the Federal Republic of Germany and the Democratic German Republic – achieved reunification, while in Eastern Europe separatism became a very real issue as other peoples sought to re-establish their autonomous political identity. The Yugoslav federation was destroyed by civil war, while Czechoslovakia effected a 'velvet divorce'. Following the failed coup by Communist hardliners in Moscow (1991), Estonia, Latvia and Lithuania achieved international recognition of their renewed independence. When the USSR was dissolved, the remaining 12 Soviet republics were recognized as sovereign states. Thus, even in a continent generally thought of as 'stable', countries can merge and emerge to renewed sovereignty.

In Africa, Asia, Oceania and the Caribbean over 80 countries have emerged from colonial rule since 1918, and more than one half of the countries listed in this chapter did not exist at the beginning of the 20th century.

Over 50 dependent territories remain, most of them small and not possessing that distinctive but intangible characteristic by which we may recognize a country. The dependent territories are listed as appropriate. These include colonies, associated states – which enjoy varying degrees of autonomy (Puerto Rico and the Cook Islands, for example, enjoy complete internal self-government) – and overseas territories administered in a similar manner to local government units in the country to which they belong (for example French overseas départements). Territorial claims in Antarctica and other disputed areas – for example, Macedonia – are also included.

Individual entries

Individual entries in this chapter detail:

Area: Its area in square kilometres (and in square miles). In the case of some countries, more than one figure may be found for the area of the state. This is because that country's frontiers may be disputed or not defined, or because the country may lay claim to part of a neighbouring territory (for example East Timor is claimed by Indonesia).

Population: Its population according to the latest available census or official estimate. Where there is no reliable official estimate, an estimate of the national population from UN sources is given.

Capital and major cities: In many cases the names of cities in their local languages are given in brackets. Except where noted, the population figure given for a city relates to the agglomeration or urban area; that is the city, its suburbs and surrounding built-up area rather than for local government districts.

Languages: The principal languages only are indicated.

Religions: The principal religions only are indicated. As many censuses do not question respondents concerning their religious affiliation, the percentages given are approximations.

Government: The form of government – republic or monarchy – and the nature of government – single- or multi-party, presidential or parliamentary – are indicated.

Each entry concludes with a description of the main geographical features of each country, a summary of its most important economic activities, resources and trends, and a list of the most important events of its recent history.

AFGHANISTAN

Area: 652 225 km² (251 773 sq mi). *Population:* 16 121 000 (1990 est). *Capital:* Kabul 1 425 000 (including suburbs; 1988 est). *Languages:* Pushto (52%), Dari (Persian; 30%). *Religions:* Sunni Islam (74%), Shia Islam (25%). *Government:* Republic – provisional government.

GEOGRAPHY
Highlands, dominated by the Hindu Kush, cover over 75% of the country and contain several peaks over 6400 m (21 000 ft). The N is plains; the SW is desert and semidesert. Most of the country is dry and experiences cold winters and cool summers. The deserts have hot summers.

ECONOMIC ACTIVITY
Over 60% of the labour force is employed in agriculture. Most of the usable land is pasture, mainly for sheep. Principal exports include natural gas, fresh and dried fruit, and wool.

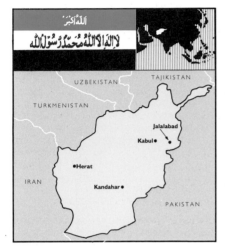

RECENT HISTORY
19th century: Rivalry between Russia and Britain for control of Afghanistan. **1921:** Independence recognized. **1933:** Stable monarchy established. **1973:** Coup; monarchy overthrown. **1978:** Revolution led to close relationship with the USSR. **1979:** Soviet invasion; civil war began. **1989:** Soviet withdrawal; left-wing government in Kabul challenged by Muslim fundamentalists who controlled the countryside. **1992:** Fundamentalists took Kabul and formed a provisional government; factional unrest continued.

ALBANIA

Area: 28 748 km² (11 100 sq mi). *Population:* 3 303 000 (1991 est). *Capital:* Tirana (Tiranë) 238 000 (1989 est). *Languages:* Albanian (Gheg and Tosk dialects). *Religion:* Sunni Islam (20%). *Government:* Republic – multi-party parliamentary system.

GEOGRAPHY
Coastal lowlands support most of the country's agriculture, but mountain ranges – rising to 2751 m (9025 ft) – cover most of Albania. Summers are hot and dry; winters are mild and wet on the coast, but colder inland.

ECONOMIC ACTIVITY
Albania is poor by European standards. The economy, which is still largely state-owned, relies on agriculture and the export of chromium. In 1990 Albania ended self-imposed economic isolation and sought foreign assistance, but much of the industrial infrastructure collapsed.

RECENT HISTORY
1912: Albania declared independence from (Turkish) Ottoman rule. **1912–13:** Balkan Wars –

independence secured. **1914:** Occupation by Italy. **1920:** Independence re-established. **1928:** President Ahmed Zogu made himself King (Zog I). **1939:** Italy annexed Albania. **1943:** German invasion. **1944:** Germans withdrew; Communist-led partisans took power. **1946:** Communist People's Republic declared. **1946–85:** Stalinist regime of Enver Hoxha; policy of self-sufficiency and isolation after 1978. **From 1990:** Social, economic and political reforms. **1992:** Former Communists lost multi-party elections.

ALGERIA

Area: 2 381 741 km² (919 595 sq mi). *Population:* 25 888 000 (1991 est). *Capital:* Algiers (El Djazaïr or Alger) 1 722 000 (including suburbs; 1989 est). *Languages:* Arabic (official), French, Berber. *Religion:* Sunni Islam (official). *Government:* Republic. Military government – constitution suspended.

GEOGRAPHY
Over 85% of Algeria is covered by the Sahara Desert. To the N lie the Atlas Mountains; in the SE are the Hoggar mountains, rising to 2918 m (9573 ft). Plains and lower mountain ranges line the coast, which has a Mediterranean climate with hot summers, mild winters and adequate rainfall. In the Sahara, it is hot and arid.

ECONOMIC ACTIVITY
Petroleum and natural gas are the main exports

and the basis of important industries. The country faces severe economic problems including high unemployment. Over 25% of the labour force is involved in agriculture, but lack of rain and suitable land mean that Algeria is dependent on imports of food. Arable land mainly produces wheat, barley, fruit and vegetables, while arid pasturelands support sheep, goats and cattle.

RECENT HISTORY
19th century: French colonization of Algeria (beginning in 1830). **1945:** Nationalist riots in Sétif. **1954:** Front de Libération Nationale (FLN) began the revolt against French rule. **1958:** Rising of French settlers in favour of integration with France. **1958–62:** War between the FLN and the OAS (the settlers' terrorist organization). **1962:** Independence. **1965–90:** One-party socialist state. **1990:** Multi-party system restored. **1992:** The military took power to prevent Islamic fundamentalists winning elections.

ANDORRA

Area: 467 km² (180 sq mi). *Population:* 55 400 (1991 est). *Capital:* Andorra la Vella 33 000 (including suburbs; 1990 est). *Languages:* Catalan (official; 30%), Spanish (59%), French (6%). *Religion:* Roman Catholic. *Government:* Co-principality – the president of France and the Spanish bishop of Urgel are joint heads of state; non-party parliamentary system.

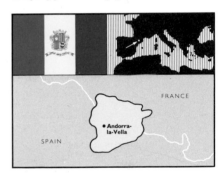

GEOGRAPHY
In the E Pyrenees, Andorra is surrounded by peaks up to 3000 m (9840 ft) high. The climate is mild, but winters are cold and snowy.

ECONOMIC ACTIVITY
The economy depends on tourism, encouraged by the development of ski resorts and by the duty-free status of consumer goods.

RECENT HISTORY
1970s–1990s: Constitutional reforms; establishment of a modern governmental system and international relations.

ANGOLA

Area: 1 246 700 km² (481 354 sq mi). *Population:* 10 284 000 (1991 est). *Capital:* Luanda 1 200 000 (1988 est). *Languages:* Portuguese (official), Umbundu (38%), Kimbundu (27%). *Religions:* Roman Catholic (over 60%), animist (20%). *Government:* Republic – multi-party system with executive presidency.

GEOGRAPHY
Behind a narrow coastal plain, plateaux, over 1000 m (3300 ft), cover most of Angola. The SW is desert. Angola is tropical, with lower temperatures in the uplands. October to May is the rainy season.

ECONOMIC ACTIVITY
Although Angola is rich in minerals (diamonds, iron ore and petroleum), development has been hampered by war. Less than 5% of the land is

arable, but over 50% of the labour force is engaged in farming. The main export crop is coffee.

RECENT HISTORY
1920s–1960s: Racial discrimination and heavy taxation by Portuguese colonial authorities stimulated nationalism. **1961–75:** Guerrilla wars against Portuguese rule. **1975:** Independence. Rival guerrilla movements fought for control – the Marxist-Leninist MPLA (backed by the USSR and Cuba) in the N; the South African-aided UNITA movement in the S. **1991:** Civil war ended. **1992:** Multi-party elections; UNITA defeated and resumed civil war.

ANTIGUA AND BARBUDA

Area: 442 km² (170.5 sq mi). *Population:* 81 600 (1991 est). *Capital:* St John's 36 000 (1986 est). *Language:* English. *Religion:* Anglican (44%). *Government:* Dominion – multi-party parliamentary system.

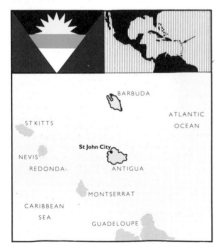

GEOGRAPHY
Antigua is a low limestone island; Barbuda – 45 km/25 mi to the N – is a flat wooded coral island. The tropical climate is moderated by sea breezes. Antigua island suffers from drought.

ECONOMIC ACTIVITY
Tourism is the mainstay of the country. In an attempt to diversify, agriculture is encouraged.

RECENT HISTORY
1981: British colonies of Antigua and Barbuda – united since 1860 – gained independence.

ARGENTINA

Area: 2 766 889 km² (1 068 302 sq mi) – excluding the Falkland Islands and various Antarctic territories claimed by Argentina. *Population:* 32 880 000 (1990 est). *Capital and major cities:* Buenos Aires 11 382 000, Córdoba 1 167 000, Rosario 1 096 000 (1990 est; all including suburbs). *Language:* Spanish (official; 95%). *Religion:* Roman Catholic (nearly 93%). *Government:* Republic – multi-party system with executive presidency.

GEOGRAPHY
The Andes, whose highest point in Argentina is Cerro Aconcagua (6960 m / 22 834 ft), extend as a rugged barrier along the Chilean border. Patagonia, in the S, comprises pastureland and semi-desert. The prairies of the central pampas form one of the world's most productive agricultural regions. The NE contains subtropical plains including the Gran Chaco prairie. Most of Argentina has a mild temperate climate, although the S is cooler and the NE is subtropical. The higher parts of the Andes have a subpolar climate. Rainfall is heavy in the Andes and the far NE, but generally decreases towards the S and SW which are dry.

ECONOMIC ACTIVITY
Argentina is one of the world's leading producers of beef, wool, mutton, wheat and wine. The pampas produce cereals, while fruit and vines are important in the NW. Pasturelands cover over 50% of Argentina – for beef cattle in the pampas and for sheep in Patagonia. However, manufacturing (including chemicals, steel, cement, paper, pulp and textiles) now makes the greatest contribution to the economy. The country is rich in natural resources including petroleum, natural gas and iron ore. Between the 1930s and 1980s, Argentina's status as an economic power declined owing to political instability and massive inflation.

RECENT HISTORY
From 1880: Large-scale European immigration to Argentina. **1930–45:** Period of economic decline and military rule. **1946–55:** Rule by the populist leader Juan Perón. **1966–73:** Military rule. **1976–83:** Military rule. **1982:** Falklands War with Britain – attempted Argentine annexation of the Falkland Islands. **1983:** Constitutional rule restored.

ARMENIA

Area: 29 800 km² (11 500 sq mi). *Population:* 3 376 000 (1989 census). *Capital:* Yerevan 1 215 000 (1989 census). *Language:* Armenian (official; 93%). *Religion:* Armenian Orthodox majority. *Government:* Republic – multi-party system with executive presidency.

GEOGRAPHY
All of Armenia is mountainous. The highest peak is Mt Aragats at 4090 m (13 418 ft). A dry continental climate has considerable local variations owing to altitude and aspect.

ECONOMIC ACTIVITY
Industries include chemicals, metallurgy, textiles, and food processing. Major projects have provided hydroelectric power and irrigation for agriculture. Steps have been taken to introduce a market economy, but an effective blockade by Azerbaijan has devastated the economy.

RECENT HISTORY
1896 and **1915:** Large-scale massacres of Armenians by Turks in W (Turkish-ruled) Armenia. **1918–22:** E (Russian) Armenia became independent until invaded by the Soviet Red Army and incorporated into the USSR. **Since 1990:** Azerbaijan and Armenia have fought over Nagorno Karabakh, an enclave of Armenians surrounded by the Muslim Azeris. **1991:** Independence regained when the USSR was dissolved.

AUSTRALIA

Area: 7 682 300 km² (2 966 150 sq mi). *Population:* 17 211 000 (1991 est). *Capital and major cities:* Canberra 310 000, Sydney 3 657 000, Melbourne 3 081 000, Brisbane 1 302 000, Perth 1 193 000, Adelaide 1 050 000 (including suburbs; 1990 census). *Language:* English. *Religions:* Roman Catholic (26%), Anglican (24%). *Government:* Federal dominion – multi-party parliamentary system.

STATES AND TERRITORIES
(with areas, populations in 1991 and capitals)
New South Wales – 801 600 km² (309 500 sq mi), 5 862 000, Sydney.
Queensland – 1 727 200 km² (666 875 sq mi), 2 939 000, Brisbane.
South Australia – 984 000 km² (379 925 sq mi), 1 448 000, Adelaide.
Tasmania – 67 800 km² (26 175 sq mi), 459 000, Hobart.
Victoria – 227 600 km² (87 875 sq mi), 4 407 000, Melbourne.
Western Australia – 2 525 500 km² (975 100 sq mi), 1 650 000, Perth.
Australian Capital Territory – 2400 km² (925 sq mi), 289 000, Canberra.
Northern Territory – 1 346 200 km² (519 750 sq mi), 158 000, Darwin.

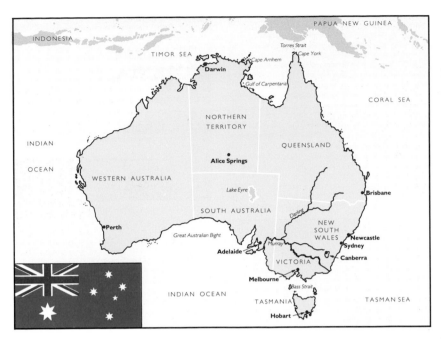

PAPUA NEW GUINEA
INDONESIA
TIMOR SEA
Cape Arnhem
Cape York
Torres Strait
Darwin
Gulf of Carpentaria
CORAL SEA
NORTHERN
TERRITORY
QUEENSLAND
INDIAN
OCEAN
Alice Springs
WESTERN AUSTRALIA
Lake Eyre
Brisbane
SOUTH AUSTRALIA
Darling
NEW
SOUTH
WALES
Perth
Newcastle
Great Australian Bight
Murray
Sydney
Adelaide
Canberra
VICTORIA
Melbourne
INDIAN OCEAN
Bass Strait
TASMANIA
TASMAN SEA
Hobart

EXTERNAL TERRITORIES
(with areas, populations in 1990–91 and capitals)
Ashmore and Cartier Islands – 5 km² (2 sq mi), uninhabited.
Australian Antarctic Territory – 6 120 000 km² (2 320 000 sq mi), uninhabited.
Christmas Island – 135 km² (52 sq mi), 1770, Flying Fish Cove.
Cocos (Keeling) Islands – 14 km² (5.5 sq mi), 600, Bantam Village.
Coral Sea Islands Territory – 8 km² (5 sq mi), uninhabited.
Heard and MacDonald Islands – 292 km² (113 sq mi), uninhabited.
Norfolk Island – 34.5 km² (13.3 sq mi), 1980, Kingston.

GEOGRAPHY
Deserts cover most of central and western Australia, a region of plateaux averaging 400–600 m (1300–2000 ft) high. This scarcely populated area covers more than 50% of the country. The majority of Australians live in the narrow coastal plains of the fertile, well-watered E coast. Behind the plains – which range from temperate forest in the S to tropical rain forest in the N – rise the Eastern Uplands, or Great Dividing Range, stretching from Cape York Peninsula in the N to the island of Tasmania. The Australian Alps rise to Mt Kosciusko (2230 m / 7316 ft). The Great Artesian Basin extends from the Gulf of Carpentaria to the Murray River and Eyre Basins. Many of Australia's rivers flow intermittently. The N is tropical with wet summers (January to March) and dry winters and, in the NW, subject to summer monsoons. The interior is extremely hot and dry. The coastal fringes in the S are either temperate or subtropical, with winter rainfall, hot or warm summers and mild winters.

ECONOMIC ACTIVITY
Minerals account for over 30% of the country's exports. Australia has major reserves of coal, petroleum and natural gas, uranium, iron ore, copper, nickel, bauxite, gold and diamonds. Manufacturing and processing based upon these resources include iron and steel, construction, oil refining and petrochemicals, vehicle manufacturing and engineering. Food-processing and textile industries are also prominent. Australia is the world's leading producer of wool. Major farming interests include sheep, cattle, cereals (in particular wheat), sugar and fruit.

RECENT HISTORY
1901: Commonwealth of Australia established by federation of six self-governing British colonies. **1914–18:** The Australian contribution in World War I included the heroic landing at Gallipoli in the Dardenelles. **1931:** Australian independence confirmed by the Statute of Westminster. **1939–45:** World War II – N Australia threatened by Japan. **Since 1945:** Migrants from all over Europe and many parts of Asia have diluted the British connection; trading partnerships have been formed with Asian countries.

AUSTRIA

Area: 83 855 km² (32 367 sq mi). *Population:* 7 812 000 (1991 census). *Capital:* Vienna (Wien) 2 045 800 (including suburbs – 1984 est). *Language:* German (official). *Religion:* Roman Catholic (84%). *Government:* Federal republic – multi-party parliamentary system.

GEOGRAPHY
The Alps – which occupy 60% of Austria – rise to the Grossglockner at 3798 m (12 462 ft). Lowland Austria – the E – comprises low hills, the Vienna Basin, a flat marshy area on the Hungarian border and a forested massif on the Czech border. The E is drier than the W, and is, in general, colder than the Alpine region in the winter and hotter, but more humid, in the summer.

ECONOMIC ACTIVITY
Austria produces about 90% of its own food requirements, but agriculture employs only 8% of

CZECH REPUBLIC
GERMANY
SLOVAKIA
Danube
Linz
Vienna
Salzburg
Innsbruck
Graz
SWITZERLAND
HUNGARY
ITALY
SLOVENIA
CROATIA

the labour force. Fertile arable land in the E grows cereals and grapes for wine. Dairy produce is an important export from the pasturelands in the E and in the Alps. The mainstay of the economy is manufacturing industry, including machinery and transport equipment, and iron and steel products. Natural resources include hydroelectric power potential and large forests. The Alps attract winter and summer visitors, making tourism a major foreign-currency earner.

RECENT HISTORY
By 1900: Nationalist movements threatened the vast multilingual Habsburg Empire. **1914:** The heir to the Habsburg throne assassinated in Sarajevo – an event that precipitated World War I. **1918–19:** Habsburg Empire was dismembered; a separate Austrian republic established. **1938:** Austria annexed by Germany (the *Anschluss*). **1945:** Austria liberated by Allied forces. **1955:** Withdrawal of Allied occupation forces; neutral Austria regained independence.

AZERBAIJAN

Area: 86 600 km² (33 400 sq mi). *Population:* 7 137 000 (1989 census). *Capital:* Baku 1 757 000 (1989 census). *Languages:* Azeri (83%). *Religion:* Shia Islam majority. *Government:* Republic – multi-party system with executive presidency

GEORGIA
RUSSIA
CASPIAN SEA
ARMENIA
Gyandzha
Kura
Baku
TURKEY
Nakhichevan
IRAN

GEOGRAPHY
Azerbaijan comprises lowlands beside the Caspian Sea, and part of the Caucasus and Little Caucasus Mountains. The republic includes the Nakhichevan enclave to the W of Armenia. The climate ranges from subtropical beside the Caspian Sea to continental conditions in the mountains.

ECONOMIC ACTIVITY
Large reserves of oil and natural gas are the mainstay of the economy and the basis of heavy industries. Agricultural exports include cotton and tobacco. Initial steps have been taken to introduce a market economy.

RECENT HISTORY
1918–20: An independent Azeri state broke away from Russia. **1920:** Invasion by the Soviet Red Army; Azerbaijan incorporated into USSR. **Since 1990:** Azerbaijan and Armenia have fought over Nagorno Karabakh, an enclave of Armenians surrounded by Azerbaijan. **1991:** Independence regained when the USSR was dissolved.

BAHAMAS

Area: 13 939 km² (5382 sq mi). *Population:* 255 000 (1990 census). *Capital:* Nassau 169 000 (1990 census). *Language:* English. *Religions:* Baptist (32%), Roman Catholic (26%). *Government:* Dominion – multi-party parliamentary system.

GEOGRAPHY
The Bahamas comprises some 700 long, flat, narrow islands, and over 2000 barren rocky islets. The climate is mild and subtropical, with no great seasonal variation in temperature.

ECONOMIC ACTIVITY
Tourism – mainly from the USA – is the major source of income, and employs the majority of the labour force. The islands have become a tax haven and financial centre.

RECENT HISTORY
1973: Independence after over 250 years of British rule.

BAHRAIN

Area: 691 km² (267 sq mi). **Population:** 516 000 (1991 est). **Capital:** Manama 152 000 (1988 est). **Language:** Arabic. **Religions:** Shia Islam (60%), Sunni Islam (33%). **Government:** Emirate – absolute monarchy.

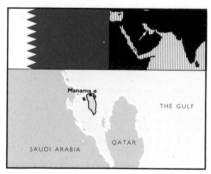

GEOGRAPHY
Bahrain Island – the largest of 35 small sandy and marshy islands – is linked to Saudi Arabia by causeway. The climate is very hot and dry.

ECONOMIC ACTIVITY
Bahrain's wealth is due to its petroleum and natural gas resources, and the oil-refining industry. As reserves waned in the 1970s, diversification was encouraged and Bahrain is now one of the Gulf's major banking and communication centres.

RECENT HISTORY
19th century: Treaties with the UK established a British protectorate of Bahrain. **1932:** Petroleum discovered. **1971:** Independence restored.

BANGLADESH

Area: 143 998 km² (55 598 sq mi). **Population:** 107 992 000 (1991 census). **Capital and major cities:** Dhaka 5 731 000, Chittagong 2 133 000 (1990 est). **Language:** Bengali (official; 97%). **Religion:** Sunni Islam (official; 87%). **Government:** Republic – multi-party parliamentary system.

GEOGRAPHY
Most of Bangladesh is alluvial plains in the deltas of the rivers Ganges and Brahmaputra. The low swampy plains are dissected by rivers dividing into numerous distributaries with raised banks. The coastal regions contain mangrove forests (the Sundarbans). The only uplands are the Sylhet Hills in the NE and the Chittagong hill country in the E. The climate is tropical. Most of the rainfall comes during the monsoon (June to October) when intense storms bring serious flooding. Rainfall totals range from 1000 mm (40 in) in the W to 5000 mm (200 in) in the Sylhet Hills.

ECONOMIC ACTIVITY
With a rapidly increasing population, Bangladesh is among the world's poorest states and is heavily dependent on foreign aid. Over 70% of the labour force is involved in farming. Rice is produced on over 75% of the cultivated land. Although the land is fertile, crops are subject to floods and cyclones. The main cash crops are jute and tea. Industries include processing jute, cotton and sugar.

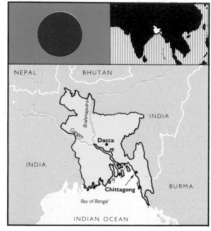

RECENT HISTORY
1947: Partition of British India – as the majority of its inhabitants were Muslim, the area became the E province of Pakistan. **1960s:** Resentment grew over rule from the Urdu-speaking, politically dominant W province of Pakistan. **1971:** Civil war – Indian aid to Bengali irregulars gave birth to an independent Bangladesh ('Free Bengal') under Sheik Mujib-ur-Rahman. **1975:** Mujib assassinated. **1977–79:** General Zia-ur-Rahman created an 'Islamic state'. **1982–90:** General Ershad in power. **1990:** Parliamentary rule reintroduced.

BARBADOS

Area: 430 km² (166 sq mi). **Population:** 257 000 (1990 census). **Capital:** Bridgetown 102 000 (city 7500; 1989 est). **Language:** English. **Religion:** Anglican (40%). **Government:** Dominion – multiparty parliamentary system.

GEOGRAPHY
Barbados is generally flat and low, except in the N where it rises to Mount Hillaby (340 m 1115 ft). The climate is tropical with heavy rainfall.

ECONOMIC ACTIVITY
Tourism – the main source of income – employs 40% of the labour force, and banking and insurance are becoming important. Sugar – once the mainstay of Barbados – remains the main crop.

RECENT HISTORY
1937: Riots led to social and economic reform in the British colony of Barbados. **1966:** Independence.

BELARUS

Formerly known as Byelorussia. **Area:** 207 600 km² (80 200 sq mi). **Population:** 10 260 000 (1989 census). **Capital:** Minsk (Mensk) 1 612 000 (1989 census). **Languages:** Belarussian (also known as Belorussian; 79%), Russian (13%). **Religion:** Russian Orthodox majority. **Government:** Republic – limited multi-party parliamentary system with executive presidency.

GEOGRAPHY
Belarus comprises lowlands covered with glacial debris in the N, fertile well-drained tablelands and ridges in the centre, and the low-lying Pripet Marshes in the S and E. Much of Belarus is flat and the highest point only reaches 346 m (1135 ft). The continental climate is moderated by the proximity of the Baltic Sea.

ECONOMIC ACTIVITY
Although Belarus has few natural resources, its economy is overwhelmingly industrial. Heavy engineering, fertilizer, chemical and related industries were established as part of the centrally-planned Soviet economy and Belarus remains dependent upon trade with other former Soviet republics. Little progress towards establishing a market economy has been made and Belarus faces

severe economic problems. Agriculture is dominated by raising fodder crops for beef cattle, pigs and poultry. Flax is grown for export and a local linen industry. Extensive forests supply large woodworking and paper industries.

RECENT HISTORY
1914–18: As part of Russia, the area suffered fierce fighting between Russia and Germany during World War I. **1919:** A Byelorussian Soviet republic proclaimed. **1940–45:** Byelorussia was devastated during World War II. **1986:** A perceived lack of Soviet concern after the Chernobyl nuclear power station accident (in Ukraine) increased a reawakening Belarussian national identity. **Late 1980s:** Large areas sealed off because of contamination from Chernobyl. **1991:** Independence gained – as Belarus – when the USSR was dissolved.

BELGIUM

Area: 30 519 km² (11 783 sq mi). **Population:** 9 849 000 (1991 census). **Capital and major cities:** Brussels (Bruxelles or Brussel) 960 000, Antwerp (Antwerpen or Anvers) 919 000 (city 468 000) (1990 est). **Languages:** Flemish (a dialect of Dutch; 58%), French (42%). **Religion:** Roman Catholic (86%). **Government:** Federal kingdom – multiparty parliamentary system

GEOGRAPHY

The forested Ardennes plateau – rising to 694 m (2272 ft) – occupies the SE. The plains of central Belgium, an important agricultural region, are covered in fertile loess. The flat, low-lying N contains the sandy Kempenland plateau in the E and the plain of Flanders in the W. Enclosed by dykes behind coastal sand dunes are polders, former marshes reclaimed from the sea. Belgium has relatively cool summers and mild winters, with ample rainfall throughout the year.

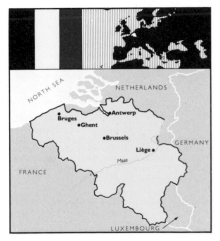

ECONOMIC ACTIVITY

Belgium is a small, densely populated industrial country with few natural resources. In the centre and the N, soils are generally fertile and the climate encourages high yields of wheat, sugar beet, grass and fodder crops. Metalworking, textiles, chemicals, ceramics, glass and rubber are major industries. Recent economic problems have mirrored Belgium's linguistic divide, with high unemployment concentrated in the French-speaking (Walloon) S, while industry in the Flemish N has prospered. Brussels has benefited from its role as the unofficial 'capital' of the EC.

RECENT HISTORY

1908: The Belgian Congo (Zaïre) acquired from King Leopold II, whose personal possession it had been since 1879. **1914–18:** Belgian neutrality ignored by German occupation during World War I. **1940–44:** German occupation during World War II; Belgium capitulated in 1940. **Since 1970:** Increased Flemish and French separatism; evolution of federalism based on linguistic regions.

BELIZE

Area: 22 965 km² (8867 sq mi). **Population:** 191 000 (1991 est). **Capital and major cities** Belmopan

4000, Belize City 50 000 (1989 est). **Languages:** English (official), Creole, Spanish (32%). **Religion:** Roman Catholic (62%). **Government:** Dominion – multi-party parliamentary system.

GEOGRAPHY

Tropical jungle covers much of Belize. The S contains the Maya Mountains; the N is mainly swampy lowlands. A subtropical climate – with heavy rainfall – is tempered by trade winds.

ECONOMIC ACTIVITY

The production of sugar, bananas and citrus fruit for export dominates the economy.

RECENT HISTORY

1981: Colony of British Honduras (formally proclaimed 1862) gained independence as Belize. **Until 1991:** Guatemala claimed Belize.

BENIN

Area: 112 622 km² (43 484 sq mi). **Population:** 4 776 000 (1991 est). **Capital and major cities:** Porto-Novo 208 000, Cotonou 487 000 (1982–83 est). **Languages:** French (official), Fon (47%). **Religions:** Animist (61%), Sunni Islam (22%). **Government:** Republic – multi-party system with executive president.

GEOGRAPHY

The NW comprises the Atacora Massif; in the NE, plains slope down to the Niger Valley. The plateaux of central Benin fall in the S to a low fertile region. A narrow coastal plain is backed by lagoons. The N is tropical; the S is equatorial.

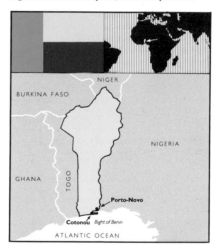

ECONOMIC ACTIVITY

Agriculture occupies over 70% of the labour force. The main food crops are cassava (manioc), yams and maize; the principal cash crop is palm oil. In the late 1980s, central planning was abandoned in favour of a market economy.

RECENT HISTORY

1890s: The area became the French colony of Dahomey. **1960:** Independence, followed by political turmoil. **1972–91:** One-party Marxist-Leninist state. **1975:** Dahomey was renamed Benin. **1991:** Multi-party system restored.

BHUTAN

Area: 46 500 km² (17 954 sq mi). **Population:** 1 442 000 (1990 UN est; 1992 Bhutanese government estimates give a population of over 700 000). **Capital:** Thimphu 60 000 (1985 est). **Languages:** Dzongkha (Tibetan; 70%; official); Nepali (30%); English (official). **Religions:** Buddhist (70%); Hindu (30%). **Government:** Kingdom – limited parliamentary system.

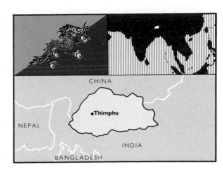

GEOGRAPHY

The Himalaya – which in Bhutan rise to 7554 m (24 784 ft) – make up most of Bhutan. The central valleys are wide and fertile. The narrow subtropical Duars Plain lies along the Indian border. Temperatures get progressively lower with altitude resulting in permanent snow cover in the N. Precipitation is heavy.

ECONOMIC ACTIVITY

Bhutan is one of the poorest and least developed countries in the world. Over 90% of the labour force is involved in producing food crops.

RECENT HISTORY

1907: Present monarchy established under British protection. **1949:** India assumed influence over Bhutan's external affairs. **1990s:** Discrimination against the Nepalese minority.

BOLIVIA

Area: 1 098 581 km² (424 164 sq mi). **Population:** 7 530 000 (1991 est). **Capital and major cities:** La Paz (administrative capital) 1 050 000, Sucre (legal capital) 96 000 (1988 est). **Languages:** Spanish (official, 55%), Aymara (22%). **Religion:** Roman Catholic (official; 93%). **Government:** Republic – multi-party system with executive presidency.

GEOGRAPHY

The Andes – whose highest point in Bolivia is Sajama (6542 m / 21 463 ft) – divide into two parallel chains between which is the Altiplano depression, containing Lake Titicaca, the highest navigable lake in the world. The E and NE lowlands include tropical rain forests (the Llanos), subtropical plains and semiarid grasslands (the Chaco). Rainfall is negligible in the SW, and heavy in the NE. Temperature varies with altitude from the cold Andean summits to the tropical NE.

ECONOMIC ACTIVITY

Bolivia is a relatively poor country, despite being rich in natural resources such as petroleum and tin. Lack of investment, political instability and the high cost of extraction have retarded develop-

ment. Farming is labour intensive, producing domestic foodstuffs (potatoes and maize), and export crops (sugar cane and cotton). The illegal cultivation of coca (cocaine) is economically important.

RECENT HISTORY
1879–83: War of the Pacific against Chile – Bolivia lost its coastal provinces. **1928–30** and **1933–35:** Chaco Wars against Paraguay – Bolivia sustained great human and territorial losses. **1935–82:** Period of political instability and a succession of military and civilian governments. **Since 1982:** Democratic civilian government restored.

BOSNIA-HERZEGOVINA

Area: 51 129 km² (19 741 sq mi). **Population:** 4 365 000 (1991 census); 2 000 000 (late 1992 est; some 2 000 000 refugees left Bosnia in 1992 and over 200 000 people were killed in the war). **Capital:** Sarajevo 526 000 (city 416 000; 1991 census). By late 1992 the population of Sarajevo was c. 200 000. **Language:** Serbo-Croat – a single language with two written forms. **Religions:** (pre-1992) Sunni Islam (44%), Serbian Orthodox (33%), Roman Catholic (17%). **Government:** Republic – in early 1993 government authority was restricted to about 10% of central Bosnia.

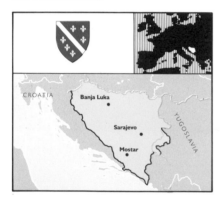

GEOGRAPHY
Ridges and arid limestone plateaux of the Dinaric Mountains, rising to over 1800 m (6000 ft), occupy most of the country. The N comprises restricted lowlands in the valley of the River Sava. The combined length of two tiny Adriatic coastlines is 20 km (13 mi). Bosnia (the N) has cold winters and warm summers; Herzegovina (the S) is milder.

ECONOMIC ACTIVITY
The economy was devastated by war in 1992. Agriculture is the major employer and sheep, maize, olives, grapes and citrous fruit, and forestry are important. Bosnia has little industry.

RECENT HISTORY
1908: Bosnia-Herzegovina – under Austrian rule since 1878 – annexed by the (Habsburg) Austro-Hungarian Empire. **1914:** Assassination in Sarajevo of the heir to the Habsburg empire helped precipitate World War I. **1918:** Bosnia became part of Yugoslavia. **1941–45:** Bosnia annexed by Axis-controlled Croatia. **1945:** Bosnia became a constituent republic of Communist Yugoslavia. **1992:** Referendum in favour of independence. Bosnian Serbs, encouraged by Serbia, seized 70% of the country, killing or expelling Muslims and Croats in a campaign of 'ethnic cleansing'. International peace and humanitarian efforts attempted.

BOTSWANA

Area: 582 000 km² (224 711 sq mi). **Population:** 1 320 000 (1991 est). **Capital:** Gaborone 130 000

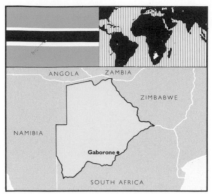

(1990 est). **Languages:** English (official), Setswana (national). **Religions:** Animist (over 50%), various Christian denominations (under 50%). **Government:** Republic – multi-party system with executive presidency.

GEOGRAPHY
A central plateau divides a flat near-desert in the E of Botswana from the Kalahari Desert and Okavango Swamps in the W. The climate is subtropical with extremes of heat and frequent drought.

ECONOMIC ACTIVITY
Nomadic cattle herding and the cultivation of subsistence crops occupies the majority of the labour force. The mainstay of the economy is mining for diamonds, copper-nickel and coal.

RECENT HISTORY
1885: British protectorate of Bechuanaland established. **1966:** Independence achieved as Botswana.

BRAZIL

Area: 8 511 965 km² (3 286 488 sq mi). **Population:** 153 332 000 (1991 est). **Capital and major cities:** Brasília 1 864 000, São Paulo 16 832 000 (city 9 700 000), Rio de Janeiro 11 141 000 (city 5 487 000), Belo Horizonte 3 446 000 (city 2 103 000) (1991 est). **Language:** Portuguese (official). **Religions:** Roman Catholic (89%), various Protestant Churches (7%). **Government:** Federal republic – multi-party system with executive presidency.

GEOGRAPHY
Nearly 50% of Brazil is drained by the world's largest river system, the Amazon, whose low-lying basin is still largely covered by tropical rain forest, although pressure on land has encouraged deforestation. N of the Amazon Basin are the Guiana Highlands. A central plateau of savannah grasslands lies S of the Basin. In the E and S, a densely

populated coastal plain adjoins the Brazilian Highlands – a vast plateau divided by fertile valleys and mountain ranges. The Amazon Basin and the SE coast are tropical with heavy rainfall. The rest of Brazil is either subtropical or temperate. Only the NE has inadequate rainfall.

ECONOMIC ACTIVITY
Agriculture employs about one quarter of the labour force. The principal agricultural exports include coffee, sugar cane, soyabeans, oranges, beef cattle and cocoa. Timber was important, but environmental concern is restricting its trade. Rapid industrialization since 1945 has made Brazil a major manufacturing country. While textiles, clothing and food processing are still the biggest industries, the iron and steel, chemical, petroleum-refining, cement, electrical, motor-vehicle and fertilizer industries have all attained international stature. Brazil has enormous – and, in part, unexploited – natural resources, including iron ore, phosphates, uranium, copper, manganese, bauxite, coal and vast hydroelectric power potential. In the last two decades, rampant inflation has hindered development.

RECENT HISTORY
1889: Military coup ended the monarchy; republic proclaimed. **1930–45:** Dictatorship of Getúlio Vargas. **1954–64:** Civilian rule restored. **1964–85:** Military rule. **1985:** Civilian rule restored.

BRUNEI

Area: 5765 km² (2226 sq mi). **Population:** 264 000 (1991 est). **Capital:** Bandar Seri Begawan 52 000 (1988 est). **Languages:** Malay (official; over 50%), Chinese (26%), English. **Religions:** Sunni Islam (official; 66%), Buddhist 12%. **Government:** Sultanate – absolute monarchy.

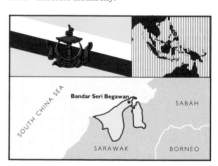

GEOGRAPHY
Brunei consists of two coastal enclaves. The (larger) western part is hilly; the eastern enclave is more mountainous and forested. Brunei has a tropical monsoon climate with heavy rainfall.

ECONOMIC ACTIVITY
Exploitation of substantial deposits of petroleum and natural gas has given Brunei one of the world's highest per capita incomes. Most of the country's food has to be imported.

RECENT HISTORY
1888–1971: British protectorate of Brunei. **1929:** Oil discovered. **1984:** Complete independence restored.

BULGARIA

Area: 110 912 km² (42 823 sq mi). **Population:** 9 005 000 (1991 est). **Capital:** Sofia (Sofiya) 1 221 000 (1990 est). **Languages:** Bulgarian (official; 89%), Turkish (11%). **Religions:** Orthodox (80%), Sunni Islam (8%). **Government:** Republic – multi-party parliamentary system.

GEOGRAPHY
The Balkan Mountains run from E to W across central Bulgaria. To the N, low hills slope down to

the River Danube. To the S, a belt of lowland separates the Balkan Mountains from a high, rugged massif, which rises to Musala at 2925 m (9596 ft). The continental N has warm summers and cold winters; the SE has a Mediterranean climate.

ECONOMIC ACTIVITY
With fertile soils, and few other natural resources, Bulgaria's economy has a strong agricultural base specializing in wheat, maize, barley, fruit (grapes) and, increasingly, tobacco. Production is centred on large-scale, mechanized cooperatives. Agricultural products are the basis of the food processing, wine and tobacco industries. Other major industries include engineering, fertilizers and chemicals. Bulgaria's trade patterns and economy have been disrupted by the collapse of the East European trading bloc. Steps towards a market economy have been taken.

RECENT HISTORY
1878: Bulgaria became an autonomous state within the Turkish empire. **1908:** Independent kingdom established. **1912–13:** Balkan Wars – Bulgaria lost territory to Greece. **1915–18:** Bulgaria allied to Germany in World War I; further losses of territory. **1942–44:** Bulgaria allied to Axis powers in World War II. **1944:** Invasion by the (Soviet) Red Army. **1946:** King exiled; Communist republic established. **1989:** Popular demonstrations against Communist rule. **1990:** Free elections held.

BURKINA FASO

Area: 274 200 km² (105 869 sq mi). **Population:** 9 261 000 (1991 est). **Capital:** Ouagadougou 442 000 (1985 est). **Languages:** French (official), Mossi (48%). **Religions:** Animist (45%), Sunni Islam (43%). **Government:** Republic – multi-party system with executive presidency.

GEOGRAPHY
The country consists of plateaux averaging about 500 m (1640 ft) high. The climate is hot and dry,

with adequate rainfall only in the savannah of the S. The N is semidesert.

ECONOMIC ACTIVITY
Burkina Faso, one of the world's poorest states, has been severely stricken by drought in the last two decades. Nomadic herdsmen and subsistence farmers – producing mainly sorghum, sugar cane and millet – form the bulk of the population. Cotton, manganese and zinc are exported.

RECENT HISTORY
1896: French colonial rule began. **1960:** Independence as Upper Volta. **Since 1960:** Succession of military coups. **1984:** Name changed to Burkina Faso. **1991–2:** Civilian multi-party rule restored.

BURMA (see MYANMAR)

BURUNDI

Area: 27 834 km² (10 747 sq mi). **Population:** 5 611 000 (1991 est). **Capital:** Bujumbura 227 000 (1990 est). **Languages:** Kirundi (majority), French – both official. **Religion:** Roman Catholic (over 60%). **Government:** Republic – military government; scheduled to become a multi-party system with executive presidency.

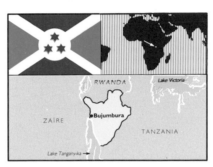

GEOGRAPHY
Burundi is a high plateau, rising from Lake Tanganyika in the W to 2685 m / 8809 ft. The lowlands are hot and humid, although the mountains are cooler.

ECONOMIC ACTIVITY
Over 92% of the labour force is involved in agriculture, producing both subsistence crops and crops for export, such as coffee.

RECENT HISTORY
1890: Semi-feudal kingdom of Burundi colonized by Germany. **1919:** Burundi became a League of Nations mandate under Belgian rule. **1962:** Independence; the minority Tutsi tribe dominated the Hutu majority. **1966:** Monarchy overthrown; republic established. **1972:** Ethnic unrest; massacre of the Hutu. There have since been further coups and ethnic unrest.

CAMBODIA

Area: 181 035 km² (69 898 sq mi). **Population:** 8 780 000 (1991 est). **Capital:** Phnom-Penh 900 000 (1991 est). **Language:** Khmer (official). **Religion:** Buddhist (majority; official). **Government:** Republic – interim council under UN auspices in partnership with provisional government.

GEOGRAPHY
Central Cambodia comprises fertile plains in the Mekong River valley and surrounding the Tonle Sap (Great Lake). To the N and E are plateaux covered by forests and savannah. The southern mountains rise to 1813 m / 5947 ft. Cambodia is

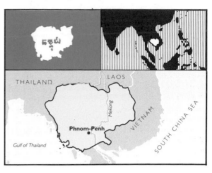

tropical and humid. The monsoon season (June–November) brings heavy rain.

ECONOMIC ACTIVITY
Invasion, civil wars, massacres of the civilian population (1976–79) and the (temporary) abolition of currency (1978) all but destroyed the economy. Aided by Vietnam since 1979, agriculture and – to a lesser extent – industry have been rebuilt slowly, but Cambodia remains one of the world's poorest nations. Rice yields – formerly exported – still fall short of Cambodia's own basic needs.

RECENT HISTORY
1863–1953: French protectorate over kingdom of Cambodia. **1941–44:** Japanese occupation during World War II. **1953:** Independence. **1955–70:** Prince Sihanouk (formerly king) attempted to maintain Cambodia's neutrality during the Vietnam War. **1970:** Sihanouk overthrown in pro-US coup. **1970–75:** Civil war – won by Communist Khmer Rouge forces. **1975–78:** The Khmer Rouge, under Pol Pot, aimed at self-sufficiency, forcibly evacuated the towns and massacred up to 2 000 000 of their compatriots. **1978:** Invasion by Vietnam; Khmer Rouge overthrown. **1989:** Vietnamese troops withdrew. **1991:** Cambodia's warring factions agreed a peace plan, including multi-party elections in 1993. **1992:** UN peacekeeping force deployed in Cambodia; the Khmer Rouge effectively withdrew from the peace plan.

CAMEROON

Area: 475 442 km² (183 569 sq mi). **Population:** 12 239 000 (1991 est). **Capital and major cities:** Yaoundé 712 000, Douala 1 117 000 (1987 est). **Languages:** French, English (both official), Fulani. **Religions:** Roman Catholic (34%), Sunni Islam (21%), animist (28%). **Government:** Republic – limited multi-party system with executive presidency.

GEOGRAPHY
In the W, a chain of highlands rises to the volcanic Mount Cameroon at 4069 m (13 353 ft). In the N, savannah plains dip towards Lake Chad. Plains and plateaux occupy the S and the centre. Cameroon is tropical, with hot, rainy conditions on the coast, but drier inland.

ECONOMIC ACTIVITY
Cameroon is a major producer of cocoa, and other export crops include coffee and cotton, rubber and palm oil. The petroleum industry is a major foreign-currency earner.

RECENT HISTORY
1884: German protectorate of Kamerun declared. **1919:** Cameroon was divided between the UK and France as a League of Nations mandate. **1960:** French Cameroons became independent. **1961:** N British Cameroons merged with Nigeria; S British Cameroons federated with the former French territory. **1966–92:** Single-party state. **1992:** Multi-party system restored.

CANADA

Area: 9 970 610 km² (3 849 674 sq mi). *Population:* 26 991 000 (1991 est). *Capital and major cities:* Ottawa 864 000 (city 301 000), Toronto 3 752 000 (city 612 000), Montréal 3 068 000 (city 1 015 000), Vancouver 1 547 000 (city 431 000), Edmonton 824 000 (city 574 000) (1990 est; cities 1986 census). *Languages:* English (62% as a first language; official), French (25% as a first language; official), bilingual (English-French; 16%). *Religions:* Roman Catholic (45%), United Church of Canada (15%), Anglican (10%). *Government:* Federal dominion – multi-party parliamentary system.

PROVINCES
(with areas, populations in 1990 and capitals)
Alberta – 661 199 km² (255 285 sq mi), 2 473 000, Edmonton.
British Columbia – 948 596 km² (366 255 sq mi), 3 139 000, Victoria.
Manitoba – 650 087 km² (251 000 sq mi), 1 091 000, Winnipeg.
New Brunswick – 73 437 km² (28 354 sq mi), 724 000, Fredericton.
Newfoundland and Labrador – 404 517 km² (156 185 sq mi), 573 000, St John's.
Nova Scotia – 55 490 km² (21 425 sq mi), 892 000, Halifax.
Ontario – 1 068 582 km² (412 582 sq mi), 9 748 000, Toronto.
Prince Edward Island – 5657 km² (2184 sq mi), 130 000, Charlottetown.

Québec – 1 540 680 km² (594 860 sq mi), 6 771 000, Québec.
Saskatchewan – 651 900 km² (251 700 sq mi), 1 000 000, Regina.
Northwest Territories – 3 379 285 km² (1 304 903 sq mi), 54 000, Yellowknife; the territory of Nunavut is to be created in the E of Northwest Territories.
Yukon Territory – 482 515 km² (186 299 sq mi), 26 000, Whitehorse.

GEOGRAPHY
Nearly 50% of Canada is covered by the Laurentian (or Canadian) Shield, a flat region of hard rocks stretching round Hudson's Bay. Inland, the Shield ends in a scarp that is pronounced in the E, beside the lowlands around the St Lawrence River and the Great Lakes. To the W, a line of major lakes (including Lake Winnipeg) marks the boundary with the interior plains, the Prairies. A broad belt of mountains – W of the plains – comprises the Rocky, Mackenzie, Coast and St Elias Mountains, which include Canada's highest point, Mount Logan at 5951 m (19 524 ft). A lower, discontinuous, chain of uplands borders the E of Canada, running from Baffin Island to Nova Scotia. Much of Canada experiences extreme temperatures, with mild summers and long, cold winters. The climate in the far N is polar. Average winter temperatures only remain above freezing point on the Pacific coast. Precipitation is heavy in the W, and moderate or light in the rest of the country. Most of Canada experiences heavy winter snow falls.

ECONOMIC ACTIVITY
Canada enjoys one of the highest standards of living in the world, due, in part, to great mineral resources. There are substantial deposits of zinc, uranium, asbestos, nickel, gold, silver, iron ore and copper, as well as major reserves of petroleum and natural gas, and enormous hydroelectric-power potential. These resources are the basis of such industries as petroleum refining, motor vehicles, metal refining, chemicals and iron and steel. Canada is one of the world's leading exporters of cereals – in particular, wheat from the Prairie provinces. Other agricultural interests include fruit (mainly apples) and beef cattle. Vast coniferous forests have given rise to large lumber, wood-pulp and paper industries. Rich Atlantic and Pacific fishing grounds are the basis of a major fishing industry. Canada has an important banking and insurance sector, and the economy is closely linked with that of the USA.

RECENT HISTORY
Late 19th century: Large-scale emigration to Canada from Europe; settlement spread rapidly W; important mineral finds, including the Klondike gold rush. **1914–18:** Canadian forces played an important role in World War I. **1931:** Statute of

Westminster recognized Canada's independence. **1939–45:** Canada played a major role in World War II. **1949:** Newfoundland joined Canada. **Since 1970s:** Increase in separatism in Québec; friction over the use and status of the French language. **Since 1982:** Attempts to redefine Québec's constitutional status.

CAPE VERDE

Area: 4033 km² (1557 sq mi). *Population:* 341 000 (1991 est). *Capital:* Praia 62 000 (1990 est). *Languages:* Portuguese (official), Crioulu (majority). *Religion:* Roman Catholic (over 92%). *Government:* Republic – multi-party system with executive presidency.

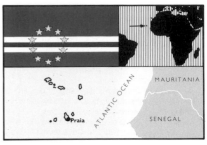

GEOGRAPHY
Cape Verde comprises ten volcanic, semiarid islands. Temperatures seldom exceed 27 °C (80 °F).

ECONOMIC ACTIVITY
Lack of surface water hinders agriculture, and over 90% of Cape Verde's food has to be imported. Money sent back by over 700 000 Cape Verdeans living abroad is vital to the economy.

RECENT HISTORY
1975: Independence from Portuguese rule. **1975–90:** Marxist-Leninist regime. **1990:** Free-market economy and multi-party system were introduced.

CENTRAL AFRICAN REPUBLIC

Area: 622 984 km² (240 535 sq mi). *Population:* 2 937 000 (1991 est). *Capital:* Bangui 598 000 (1988 est). *Languages:* French (official), Sangho (national). *Religions:* Protestant Churches (48%), Roman Catholic (32%), animist (20%). *Government:* Republic – limited multi-party system with executive presidency.

GEOGRAPHY
The country is a low plateau, rising in the E to the Bongos Mountains and in the W to the Monts Karre. The N is savannah, with little rain between

November and March. The S is equatorial with high temperatures and heavy rainfall.

ECONOMIC ACTIVITY

Subsistence farming dominates, although cotton and coffee are grown for export. Diamonds contribute over 25% of the state's foreign earnings. The country is one of the poorest in the world, largely owing to mismanagement under Bokassa.

RECENT HISTORY

1903: French colony of Oubangi-Chari established. **1960:** Independence gained as the Central African Republic. **1965–79:** Dictatorship of Jean-Bédel Bokassa, who declared himself emperor (1976). **1991:** Multi-party system restored.

CHAD

Area: 1 284 000 km² (495 750 sq mi). *Population:* 5 823 000 (1991 est). *Capital:* N'Djamena 594 000 (1988 est). *Languages:* French and Arabic (both official). *Religions:* Sunni Islam (over 40%), various Christian Churches (33%), animist (over 20%). *Government:* Republic – military government; constitution suspended.

GEOGRAPHY

Deserts in the N include the Tibesti Mountains, which reach 3415 m (11 204 ft). Savannah and semidesert in the centre slope down to Lake Chad. Plateaux in the S are covered by tropical forest. Chad is hot and dry in the N, and tropical in the S.

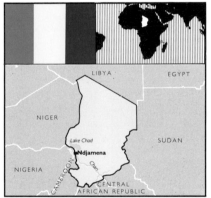

ECONOMIC ACTIVITY

Chad – one of the poorest countries in the world – has been wracked by civil war and drought. With few natural resources, it relies on subsistence farming, foreign aid and exports of cotton.

RECENT HISTORY

1890s–1916: French conquest of Chad. **1960:** Independence. **Since 1960:** Several military coups; intermittent civil war between the Muslim Arab N and the Christian and animist Black African S.

CHILE

Area: 756 945 km² (292 258 sq mi). *Population:* 13 385 000 (1991 est). *Capital:* Santiago 5 343 000, Valparaíso (legislative capital) 277 000 (1991 est). *Language:* Spanish. *Religion:* Roman Catholic (79%). *External territory:* Chile claims sovereignty over part of Antarctica. *Government:* Republic – multi-party system with executive presidency.

GEOGRAPHY

For almost 4000 km (2500 mi), the Andes form the eastern boundary of Chile. They rise to 6895 m (22 588 ft) at Ojos del Solado. Parallel to the Andes is a depression, in which lies the Atacama Desert in the N and fertile plains in the centre. Mountains run between the depression and the coast, and, in the S, form islands. The temperate climate is

influenced by the cool Humboldt Current. Rainfall ranges from being negligible in the Atacama Desert in the N to heavy – 2300 mm (90 in) – in the S.

ECONOMIC ACTIVITY

The central plains – the main agricultural region – grow cereals (mainly wheat and maize) and fruit (notably grapes). Major fishing grounds yield a large catch of fish. There are considerable mineral resources and great hydroelectric-power potential. Chile is the world's largest exporter of copper, and has major reserves of iron ore, coal, petroleum and natural gas.

RECENT HISTORY

1879–84: War against Peru and Bolivia; Chile gained territory. **1920s–1960s:** Liberal and radical governments. **1970–73:** Marxist presidency of Salvador Allende. **1973:** General Augusto Pinochet took power in a US-backed military coup; tens of thousands of leftists killed, imprisoned or exiled by the junta. **1990:** Multi-party rule restored.

CHINA

Area: 9 571 300 km² (3 695 500 sq mi). *Population:* 1 150 000 000 (1991 est), Han (Chinese) 92%, with Mongol, Tibetan, Uighur, Manchu and other minorities. *Capital and major cities:* Beijing (Peking) 10 819 000, Shanghai 13 342 000, Tientsin 8 785 000, Shenyang 4 500 000, Wuhan 3 710 000, Guangzhou (Canton) 3 540 000 (1990 census). *Languages:* Chinese (Guoyo or 'Mandarin' majority; local dialects in S and SE, e.g. Cantonese), small Mongol, Tibetan and other minorities. *Religions:* Officially atheist – Confucianism and Daoism (over 20% together), Buddhism (c. 15%). *Government:* Republic – (Communist) single-party system.

GEOGRAPHY

China is the third largest country in the world in area and the largest in population. Almost half of China comprises mountain chains, mainly in the W, including the Altaï and Tien Shan Mountains in Xinjiang Uygur, and the Kun Lun Mountains to the N of Tibet. The Tibetan Plateau – at an altitude of 3000 m (10 000 ft) – is arid. In the S of Tibet is the Himalaya, containing 40 peaks over 7000 m (23 000 ft), including Mt Everest (8863 m / 29 078 ft). In the far S, the Yunnan Plateau rises to nearly 3700 m (12 000 ft), while in the far NE, ranges of hills and mountains almost enclose the NE Plain, formerly known as Manchuria. Ranges of hills and mountains cross central China and separate the basins of the Yellow (Huang He) and Yangtze (Chang Jiang). In E and central China, three great lowlands support intensive agriculture and dense populations – the plains of central China, the Sichuan Basin and the North China Plain. A vast loess plateau, deeply dissected by ravines, lies between the Mongolian Plateau – which contains the Gobi Desert – and desert basins in the NW. In general, temperatures increase from N to S, and rainfall increases from NW to SE. NE China has a continental climate with warm and humid summers, long cold winters, and rainfall under 750 mm (30 in). The central lowlands contain the hottest areas of China, and have 750 to 1100 mm (30 to 40 in) of rainfall. The S is wetter, while the extreme

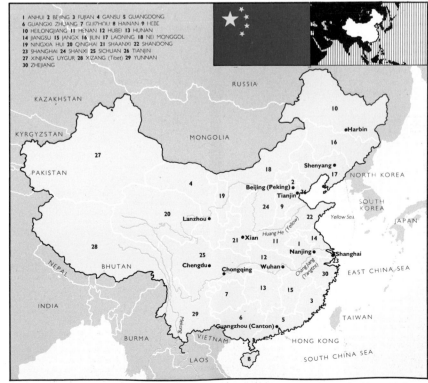

subtropical S experiences the monsoon. The continental loess plateau is cold in the winter, warm in summer and has under 500 mm (20 in) of rain. The NW is arid, continental and experiences cold winters. The mountainous W experiences an extreme climate with low rainfall; most of Tibet has ten months of frost.

ECONOMIC ACTIVITY

Agriculture occupies over 60% of the labour force. All large-scale production is on collective farms, but traditional and inefficient practices remain. Almost half the arable land is irrigated, and China is the world's largest producer of rice. Other major crops include wheat, maize, sweet potatoes, sugar cane and soyabeans. Livestock, fruit, vegetables and fishing are also important. Mineral and fuel resources are considerable and, for the most part, underdeveloped. They include coal, petroleum, natural gas, iron ore, bauxite, tin and antimony in major reserves, as well as huge hydroelectric power potential. The economy is centrally planned, with all industrial plant owned by the state. Petrochemical products account for nearly 25% of China's exports. Other major industries include iron and steel, cement, vehicles, fertilizers, food processing, clothing and textiles. Recent reforms have included an 'open-door' policy under which joint ventures with other countries and foreign loans have been encouraged, together with some small-scale private enterprise. Special Economic Zones and 'open cities' were designated in S and central coastal areas to encourage industrial links with the W. Although foreign investment temporarily diminished after the 1989 pro-democracy movement was suppressed, sustained economic progress – with growth rates in excess of 10% per annum – has been achieved, particularly in southern China and around Shanghai.

RECENT HISTORY

The recent history of China is covered on pp. 276–7.

CHINA, REPUBLIC OF (TAIWAN)

Area: 35 981 km² (13 893 sq mi). **Population:** 20 489 000 (1991 est). **Capital:** Taipei 2 720 000 (1990 est). **Language:** Chinese (northern or Amoy dialect). **Religions:** Buddhist (24%), Daoist (14%), Roman Catholic (14%). **Government:** Republic – multi-party system with executive presidency.

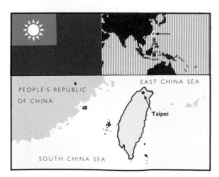

GEOGRAPHY

Taiwan is an island 160 km (100 mi) off the SE coast of China. Its mountainous interior rises to 3997 m (13 113 ft). Most Taiwanese live on the coastal plain in the W. The N is subtropical; the S is tropical. Taiwan has rainy summers and mild winters, and is subject to tropical cyclones.

ECONOMIC ACTIVITY

Despite Taiwan's diplomatic isolation, the island is a major international trading nation, exporting machinery, electronics, and textiles. Mineral resources include coal, marble, gold, petroleum and natural gas. Despite the fertility of the soil, agriculture has declined in relative importance.

RECENT HISTORY

1895–1945: Japanese rule. **1945:** Chinese rule restored. **1949:** Nationalist forces of Jiang Jie Shi (Chiang Kai-shek) were driven onto Taiwan by the Communist victory on the mainland. Under US protection, the resulting regime on Taiwan claimed to be the legitimate government of all China. **1948–71:** Taiwan (as the Republic of China) held the Chinese seat at the UN. **Since 1978:** Diplomatic isolation. **Late 1980s:** Multi-party system developed. **1991:** New constitution marked the transition to a more Taiwanese identity.

COLOMBIA

Area: 1 141 748 km² (440 831 sq mi). **Population:** 33 613 000 (1991 est). **Capital and major cities:** Bogotá 4 820 000, Medellín 2 121 000 (1990 est). **Languages:** Spanish (official). **Religion:** Roman Catholic (official; over 95%). **Government:** Republic – multi-party system with executive presidency.

GEOGRAPHY

The Andes run N to S through Colombia, rising to Pico Cristóbal Colón (5775 m / 18 947 ft). Most of Colombia lies E of the Andes in the savannah grassland plains of the Llanos and the tropical Amazonian rain forest. A coastal plain lies to the W of the mountains. The lower Andes are temperate; the mountains over 4000 m (13 100 ft) experience perpetual snow. The rest of the country is tropical. The coasts and the Amazonian Basin are hot and humid, with heavy rainfall.

ECONOMIC ACTIVITY

Colombian coffee is the main export; other cash crops include cocoa, sugar cane, bananas, flowers and tobacco. However, profits from the illegal cultivation and export of marijuana and cocaine produce much revenue. Mineral resources include petroleum, natural gas, coal and nickel. The main industries are food processing, petroleum refining and chemicals.

RECENT HISTORY

1899–1902: Civil war between centralizing pro-clerical Conservatives and federalizing anti-clerical Liberals. **1948–57:** Conservative-Liberal civil war. **1957–74:** Bipartisan rule by Liberals and Conservatives to protect a fragile democracy. **1970–89:** Widespread left-wing guerrilla activity. **Late 1980s–early 1990s:** Colombia destabilized by right-wing death squads and the activities of powerful drug-trafficking cartels.

COMOROS

Area: 1862 km² (719 sq mi) (excluding Mayotte, which is administered by France). **Population:** 479 000 (1991 est; excluding Mayotte). **Capital:** Moroni 60 000 (including suburbs; 1987 est). **Languages:** French and Arabic (both official), Comoran (majority; Arabized version of Swahili). **Religion:** Sunni Islam (official; 99%). **Government:** Federal republic – multi-party system with executive presidency.

GEOGRAPHY

Ngazidja (Grande Comore) – the largest island – is dry and rocky, rising to an active volcano. Ndzouani (Anjouan) is a heavily-eroded massif. Moili (Mohéli) is a forested plateau with fertile valleys. The tropical climate is dry from May to October, but with heavy rain for the rest of the year.

ECONOMIC ACTIVITY

Poor and eroded soils, overpopulation and few resources combine to make the islands one of the world's poorest countries. Subsistence farming occupies most of the population, although vanilla, cloves and ylang-ylang are produced for export.

RECENT HISTORY

1912: French colony proclaimed. **1974:** Independence declared by three of the four islands; Mayotte, the fourth island, remained under French rule. **1978–90:** Single-party Islamic state. **1990:** Multi-party system restored.

CONGO

Area: 342 000 km² (132 047 sq mi). **Population:** 2 411 000 (1991 est). **Capital:** Brazzaville 760 000 (1990 est). **Languages:** French (official), Lingala patois (50%), Monokutuba patois (45%). **Religion:** Roman Catholic (over 40%). **Government:** Republic – multi-party system with executive presidency.

GEOGRAPHY

Behind a narrow coastal plain, the forested plateaux of the interior rise to over 700 m (2300 ft). Congo's tropical climate is hot and humid. Rainfall exceeds 1200 mm (47 in) a year.

ECONOMIC ACTIVITY

Until 1991, Congo had a centrally-planned

economy. Privatization has begun but the country is crippled by the highest per capita external debt in Africa. Petroleum and timber are the main exports. Subsistence agriculture – chiefly for cassava – occupies over one half of the labour force.

RECENT HISTORY
1905: French colony of Moyen Congo established. **1960:** Independence. **1963–91:** Marxist-Leninist one-party state. **1991:** Multi-party system restored.

COSTA RICA

Area: 51 100 km² (19 730 sq mi). **Population:** 3 015 000 (1990 est). **Capital:** San José 1 040 000 (1990 est; including suburbs). **Language:** Spanish (official). **Religion:** Roman Catholic (official). **Government:** Republic – multi-party system with executive presidency.

GEOGRAPHY
Between Pacific and Caribbean coastal plains are a central plateau and mountain ranges that rise to 3820 m (12 533 ft). Rainfall is heavy along the Caribbean coast, but the Pacific coast is drier. Temperatures are warm in the lowlands, cooler in the highlands.

ECONOMIC ACTIVITY
Coffee is Costa Rica's major export. Bananas, sugar cane and beef cattle are also important.

RECENT HISTORY
1948: Brief civil war; army disbanded. **Since 1948:** Stable democracy; Costa Rica has adopted the role of regional peacemaker.

COTE D'IVOIRE

Formerly known as the Ivory Coast. Since 1986 Côte d'Ivoire has been the only official name. **Area:** 322 462 km² (124 503 sq mi). **Population:** 12 464 000 (1991 est). **Capital and major cities** Yamoussoukro (capital de jure) 120 000, Abidjan (legislative capital) 1 850 000 (1987 est). **Languages:** French (official), Bete (20%). **Religions:** Animist (60%), Sunni Islam (20%), Roman Catho-

lic (nearly 20%). **Government:** Republic – limited multi-party system with executive president.

GEOGRAPHY
The N is a savannah-covered plateau. In the S, tropical rain forest has largely been cleared for plantations. Temperatures are high; rainfall is heavy in the S, but decreases in the N.

ECONOMIC ACTIVITY
The country depends on exports of cocoa and coffee, and suffered in the 1980s when prices for these commodities fell. Natural resources include petroleum, natural gas and iron ore. Political stability has helped economic growth.

RECENT HISTORY
1893: French Ivory Coast colony established. **1960:** Independence. **1990:** Multi-party system permitted.

CROATIA

Area: 56 538 km² (21 829 sq mi), including the area (about one third) that is controlled by Serb forces. **Population:** 4 760 000 (1991 census) – by the end of 1992, there were over 400 000 refugees from Bosnia in Croatia. **Capital:** Zagreb 1 175 000 (city 704 000; 1991 census). **Language:** Croat (official; over 75%) – the written form of Serbo-Croat that uses the Latin alphabet. **Religion:** Roman Catholic majority. **Government:** Republic – multi-party system with executive presidency.

GEOGRAPHY
Croatia comprises plains in the E (Slavonia), hills around Zagreb, and barren limestone ranges running parallel to the Dalmatian coast. Dubrovnik is detached from the rest of Croatia. The interior is colder and drier than the Mediterranean coast.

ECONOMIC ACTIVITY
Manufacturing interests include aluminium, textiles and chemicals. Slavonia grows cereals, potatoes and sugar beet. In 1991–2 the economy was wrecked by the Yugoslav civil war, and the lucrative Dalmatian tourist industry collapsed.

RECENT HISTORY
Late 19th century: Growth of Croat nationalism against Habsburg rule. **1918:** Croatia became part of Yugoslavia. **1941:** German invasion; Axis puppet-state of Croatia founded. **1945:** Croatia became a constituent republic of Communist Yugoslavia. **1991:** Independence declared; Serb insurgents, backed by the Yugoslav army, invaded occupying one third of Croatia.

CUBA

Area: 110 860 km² (42 803 sq mi). **Population:**

10 700 000 (1991 est). **Capital:** Havana (La Habana) 2 096 000 (1990 est). **Language:** Spanish. **Religion:** Roman Catholic (39%). **Government:** Republic – (Communist) single-party system.

GEOGRAPHY
Three ranges of hills and mountains run E to W across Cuba, rising to 1971 m (6467 ft). The climate is semitropical with heavy rainfall.

ECONOMIC ACTIVITY
Sugar (the leading export), tobacco and coffee are the main crops. State-controlled farms occupy most of the land but are unable to meet Cuba's food needs. Nickel is Cuba's second most important export. The end of the Communist CMEA trade bloc and of Soviet subsidies have brought the Cuban economy to the verge of collapse.

RECENT HISTORY
1895–98: US intervention in Cuban war of independence against Spain. **1899–1901** and **1906–09:** US administration. **1902:** Independence confirmed. **1925–59:** Period of corrupt governments, dictatorships and military coups. **1959:** Guerrilla leader Fidel Castro seized power. **1961:** US-backed Cuban exiles attempted invasion. **From 1961:** Communist system established. **1962:** Installation of Soviet missiles on Cuba almost led to world war. **1970s–1980s:** Cuba encouraged revolutionary movements in Latin America and sent troops to bolster Marxist regimes in Africa. **1989–91:** Collapse of international Communism left hardline Cuba isolated.

CYPRUS

Area: 9251 km² (3572 sq mi). **Population:** 748 000 (1991 est). **Capital:** Nicosia 338 000 (including the Turkish Cypriot zone Lefkosa) (1990 est). **Languages:** Greek (80%), Turkish (19%). **Religions:** Orthodox (75%), Sunni Islam (19%). **Government:** Republic – multi-party system with executive presidency. (The 'Turkish Republic of Northern Cyprus' is unrecognized except by Turkey.)

GEOGRAPHY
The Troodos Mountains in the S rise to Mount Olympus 1951 m (6399 ft). A fertile plain runs across central Cyprus. The Kyrenian Mountains and the Karpas Peninsula occupy the N. Summers are hot and dry; winters are mild.

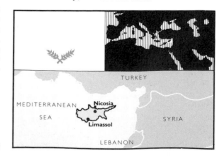

ECONOMIC ACTIVITY

Cyprus exports potatoes, fruit, wine, clothing and textiles. Tourism is important. In the Greek Cypriot area, ports, resorts and an international airport have been constructed to replace facilities lost since partition. The Turkish Cypriot area relies heavily on aid from Turkey.

RECENT HISTORY

1878–1960: Cyprus under British rule. **1950s:** Greek Cypriots, led by Archbishop Makarios III, campaigned for Enosis (union with Greece). **1963:** Power-sharing agreement between Greek and Turkish Cypriots broke down; UN intervened. **1974:** Turkey invaded N Cyprus. **1975:** Turkish Cypriot administration established in N Cyprus.

CZECH REPUBLIC

Area: 78 880 km² (30 456 sq mi). *Population:* 10 299 000 (1991 census). *Capital:* Prague (Praha) 1 212 000 (1991 census). *Language:* Czech (95%). *Religion:* Roman Catholic (39%). *Government:* Republic – multi-party parliamentary system.

GEOGRAPHY

In the W (Bohemia), the Elbe basin is ringed on three sides by uplands. The Moravian plain lies to the E of Bohemia. The climate is continental with cold winters and warm summers.

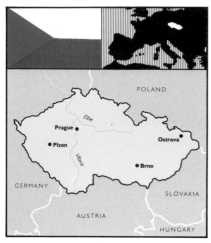

ECONOMIC ACTIVITY

The main crops include wheat, maize, potatoes, barley and sugar beet. Apart from coal, there are few mineral resources, but the country is heavily industrialized and some areas have suffered heavy pollution. Manufactures include industrial machinery, motor vehicles and consumer goods. The country is switching from a state-controlled to a free-market economy, and has increasingly attracted foreign investment (80% German).

RECENT HISTORY

1918: After the collapse of the Austro-Hungarian Empire, the Czechs joined the Slovaks to form an independent Czechoslovakia. **1938:** Hitler demanded that Germany be granted the mainly German-speaking Sudetenland; Czechoslovakia dismembered. **1939–45:** German 'protectorate' of Bohemia and Moravia. **1945:** Czechoslovakia restored. **1949:** Communist takeover. **1968:** 'Prague Spring' – political reforms crushed by Soviet invasion. **1989:** Peaceful revolution forced the Communists to renounce their leading role. **1990:** Multi-party system restored. **1993:** Division of Czechoslovakia; separate Czech Republic formed.

DENMARK

Area: 43 092 km² (16 638 sq mi) – 'metropolitan' Denmark, excluding dependencies. *Population:* 5 194 000 (1990 census; including the Faeroe Islands but excluding Greenland). *Capital:* Copenhagen (København) 1 337 000 (city 465 000) (1991 census). *Language:* Danish. *Religion:* Lutheran (91%). *Government:* Kingdom – multi-party parliamentary system.

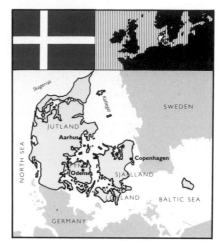

DEPENDENCIES

(with areas, populations in 1990–91 and capitals)
Faeroe Islands – 1399 km² (540 sq mi), 48 400, Tórshavn.
Greenland – 2 175 600 km² (840 000 sq mi), 55 500, Nuuk (formerly Godthab).

GEOGRAPHY

Denmark is a lowland of glacial moraine – only Bornholm, in the Baltic, has ancient hard surface rocks. The highest point – on the Jutland Peninsula – only reaches 173 m (568 ft). The islands to the E of Jutland make up nearly one third of the country. The climate is temperate and moist, with mild summers and cold winters.

ECONOMIC ACTIVITY

Denmark has a high standard of living, but few natural resources. Agriculture is organized on a cooperative basis, and produces cheese, butter, bacon and beef, mainly for export. Over 20% of the labour force is involved in manufacturing, with iron and metal working, food processing, brewing, engineering and chemicals as the major industries. Petroleum and natural gas from the North Sea have reduced the costly burden of fuel imports.

RECENT HISTORY

1914–18: Neutral during World War I. **1940–45:** German occupation during World War II. **1973:** Denmark joined the EC.

DJIBOUTI

Area: 23 200 km² (8950 sq mi). *Population:* 541 000 (1991 est). *Capital:* Djibouti 290 000 (1988 est). *Languages* Arabic and French (both official). *Religion:* Sunni Islam. *Government:* Republic – multi-party system with executive presidency.

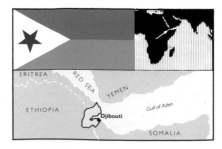

GEOGRAPHY

Djibouti is a low-lying desert rising to 2062 m (6768 ft) in the N. The climate is extremely hot and dry.

ECONOMIC ACTIVITY

Lack of water largely restricts agriculture to grazing sheep and goats. The economy depends on the expanding seaport and railway, which both serve Ethiopia.

RECENT HISTORY

1888: Colony of French Somaliland established. **1977:** Independence as Djibouti. **1981–92:** Single-party state.

DOMINICA

Area: 751 km² (290 sq mi). *Population:* 83 400 (1991 est). *Capital:* Roseau 22 000 (city 8300; 1988 est). *Languages:* English (official), French patois. *Religion:* Roman Catholic (80%). *Government:* Republic – multi-party parliamentary system.

GEOGRAPHY

Dominica is surrounded by steep cliffs. Its forested mountainous interior rises to 1447 m (4747 ft). There is little seasonal variation to a tropical climate characterized by very heavy rainfall.

ECONOMIC ACTIVITY

Dominica is a poor island. It produces bananas, timber and coconuts, and exports water to drier neighbours. Tourism is increasing in importance.

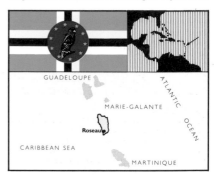

RECENT HISTORY

1978: Independence after over 210 years of British rule.

DOMINICAN REPUBLIC

Area: 48 422 km² (18 696 sq mi). *Population:* 7 320 000 (1991 est). *Capital:* Santo Domingo 1 600 000 (1986 est). *Language:* Spanish. *Religion:* Roman Catholic (official; over 90%). *Government:* Republic – multi-party system with executive presidency.

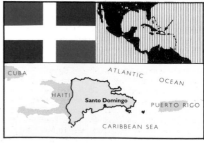

GEOGRAPHY

The republic is the eastern two thirds of the island of Hispaniola. The fertile Cibao Valley in the N is an important agricultural region, but most of the country is mountainous. The climate is largely subtropical, but it is cooler in the mountains. Rainfall is heavy, but the W and SW are arid.

ECONOMIC ACTIVITY
Sugar is the major crop, but nickel and iron ore are now the main exports. Tourism has become the greatest foreign currency earner.

RECENT HISTORY
1916–24: US administration after rule by a succession of dictators. **1930–61:** Dictatorship of Rafael Trujillo. **1965:** Civil war ended by US intervention; multi-party system restored.

ECUADOR

Area: 270 670 km² (104 506 sq mi). *Population:* 10 782 000 (1990 census). *Capital and major cities:* Quito 1 388 000, Guayaquil 1 764 000 (1990 census). *Language:* Spanish (official; 93%). *Religion:* Roman Catholic (92%). *Government:* Republic – multi-party system with executive presidency.

GEOGRAPHY
The Andes – rising to 6267 m (20 561 ft) at Chimborazo – divide the Pacific coastal plain in the W from the wet tropical Amazonian rain forest in the E. The tropical coastal plain is humid in the N, arid in the S. The highland valleys are mild, but the highest peaks have permanent snow.

ECONOMIC ACTIVITY
Petroleum is the major foreign currency earner. One third of the working population is involved in agriculture. Exports crops include cocoa, coffee and, in particular, bananas.

RECENT HISTORY
1895–1978: Long periods of military rule. **1941:** Loss of Amazonian territory in a war against Peru. **1978:** Constitutional multi-party rule restored.

EGYPT

Area: 997 739 km² (385 229 sq mi). *Population:* 54 609 000 (1991 est). *Capital and major cities:* Cairo (El-Qahira) 12 287 000, Alexandria (El-Iskandariyah) 3 170 000 (including suburbs; 1990 est). *Language:* Arabic (official). *Religions:* Sunni Islam (90%), Coptic Christian (7%). *Government:* Republic – multi-party system with executive presidency.

GEOGRAPHY
Desert covers more than 90% of Egypt. The Western Desert is low-lying. The Eastern Desert ends in the SE in mountains beside the Red Sea. The vast majority of the population lives in the Nile River valley and delta, intensively cultivated lands that rely on irrigation from the Nile. E of the Suez Canal, the Sinai Peninsula rises to Mt Catherine (Jabal Katrina) at 2642 m (8668 ft). Egyptian winters are mild and summers are hot and arid. On the N coast rainfall reaches 200 mm (8 in); beside the Red Sea rainfall is negligible.

ECONOMIC ACTIVITY
Over 40% of the labour force are involved in farming, producing maize, wheat, rice and vegetables for the local market, and cotton and dates for export. Petroleum reserves (small by Middle East standards), canal tolls and tourism are major foreign currency earners. Economic problems include rapid population growth, the demands of a large public sector and food subsidies.

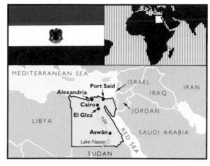

RECENT HISTORY
1914–22: British protectorate. **1922:** Independence. **1952:** Military coup. **1953:** Republic proclaimed. **1954–70:** Under President Gamal Nasser, Egypt became the leader of Arab nationalism. **1956:** Nasser nationalized the Suez Canal; Franco-British military intervention; Israel invaded Egypt. **1958–61:** Union with Syria. **1967:** Israel defeated Egypt and occupied Gaza and Sinai. **1973:** Further defeat in Arab-Israeli War. **1979:** President Anwar Sadat concluded a peace treaty with Israel. **1980–82:** Sinai regained. **1981:** Sadat assassinated. **1980s–1990s:** Egypt regained its role as a leader of the Arab world.

EL SALVADOR

Area: 21 393 km² (8260 sq mi). *Population:* 5 392 000 (1991 est). *Capital:* San Salvador 1 151 000 (city 477 000; 1987 est). *Language:* Spanish (official). *Religion:* Roman Catholic (over 90%). *Government:* Republic – multi-party system with executive presidency.

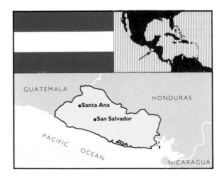

GEOGRAPHY
The country is mountainous, with ranges in the N and a high volcanic chain in the S. The coast is tropical; the interior is temperate.

ECONOMIC ACTIVITY
Coffee and sugar cane are the country's main exports. The economy has declined since the 1970s owing to the state of near civil war.

RECENT HISTORY
1932: Major peasant uprising. **1989:** War against Honduras. **Late 1970s–1992:** Virtual civil war between US-backed military and left-wing guerrillas. **1992:** Peace agreement; constitutional multi-party rule restored.

EQUATORIAL GUINEA

Area: 28 051 km² (10 831 sq mi). *Population:* 358 000 (1991 est). *Capital:* Malabo 37 000 (1988 est). *Languages:* Spanish (official), Fang, Bubi. *Religion:* Roman Catholic (over 90%). *Government:* Republic – executive presidency. Effective power exercised by military council.

GEOGRAPHY
The republic consists of the fertile island of Bioko (formerly Fernando Póo), the much smaller islands of Pagalu (formerly Annobón) and the Corisco Group, and the district of Mbini (formerly Río Muni) on the African mainland. The tropical climate is hot and humid with heavy rainfall.

ECONOMIC ACTIVITY
Mbini exports coffee and timber; Bioko exports cocoa. The economy relies heavily on foreign aid.

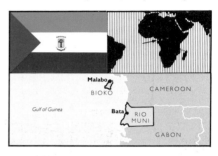

RECENT HISTORY
1968: Independence from Spanish rule. **1968–79:** Dictatorship of Francisco Macias; severe economic decline. **1979:** Military coup. **1992:** Restoration of multi-party system approved.

ESTONIA

Area: 45 100 km² (17 413 sq mi). *Population:* 1 589 000 (1991 est). *Capital:* Tallinn 505 000 (1991 est). *Languages:* Estonian (over 62%), Russian (30%). *Religion:* Lutheran (30%). *Government:* Republic multi-party parliamentary system.

GEOGRAPHY
Estonia comprises a low-lying mainland – rising in the SE to 318 m (1042 ft) – and two main islands. The moist temperate climate is characterized by mild summers and cold winters.

ECONOMIC ACTIVITY
Major industries include engineering and food processing. Gas for heating and industry is extracted from bituminous shale. The important agricultural sector is dominated by dairying. Since 1991 severe economic difficulties have resulted from Estonia's heavy dependency upon trade with Russia. Privatization of industry has begun.

RECENT HISTORY

1917: Independence from Russian rule declared; German invasion. **1919:** Independence secured. **1940:** Soviet invasion; Estonia annexed by USSR. **1941–44:** German occupation during World War II. **1945:** Soviet rule reimposed. **1991:** Estonia seceded from the USSR.

ETHIOPIA

Area: 1 223 600 km² (472 435 sq mi), including Eritrea. *Population:* 51 617 000 (1991 est), including Eritrea. *Capital:* Addis Ababa 1 739 000 (1991 est). *Languages:* Amharic (official), Arabic, Oromo (40%). *Religions:* Sunni Islam (45%), Ethiopian Orthodox (40%). *Government:* Federal republic – constitutional provision for a multi-party system with executive presidency. (Since 1991, Eritrea – see below – has *de facto* been an independent state.)

GEOGRAPHY

The Western Highlands – including Eritrea, the Tigré Plateau and the Semien Mountains (rising to over 4000 m / 13 000 ft) – are separated from the lower Eastern Highlands by a wide rift valley. The climate is very hot and dry in the N and E, but temperate in the highlands.

ECONOMIC ACTIVITY

Secessionist wars have damaged an impoverished, underdeveloped economy. The majority of the population is involved in subsistence farming. Coffee is the main foreign-currency earner.

RECENT HISTORY

1890: Eritrea became an Italian colony. **1896:** Under Emperor Menelik II, Ethiopia resisted an Italian invasion. **1936–41:** Italian invasion and occupation of Ethiopia. **1941:** Independence restored. **1947–50:** British rule in Eritrea. **1950:** Eritrea became part of Ethiopia. **1961–91:** Independence campaign by Eritrean guerrillas. **1974:** Emperor Haile Selassie overthrown. **1979–91:** Marxist-Leninist one-party state. **1980s:** Recurrent drought and famine. **1991:** An alliance of Tigrayan separatist and other forces toppled the Communist government. **1993:** Referendum on independence scheduled in Eritrea.

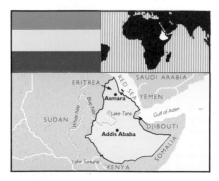

ERITREA

Area: 117 400 km² (45 300 sq mi). *Population:* 3 323 000 (1991 est). *Capital:* Asmara (Asmera) 344 000 (1991 est).

FIJI

Area: 18 376 km² (7095 sq mi). *Population:* 738 000 (1991 est). *Capital:* Suva 141 000 (city 70 000; 1986 census). *Languages:* English, Fijian (48%), Hindi (46%). *Religions:* Methodist (45%), Hindu (over 40%). *Government:* Republic – multi-party parliamentary system.

GEOGRAPHY

The mountainous larger islands are volcanic in origin. The smaller islands are mainly coral reefs.

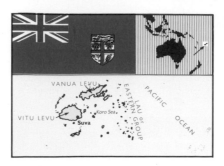

Fiji experiences high temperatures and heavy rainfall with local variations.

ECONOMIC ACTIVITY

Fiji's economy depends on tourism and agriculture – with sugar cane as the main cash crop. Copra and ginger are also exported.

RECENT HISTORY

1874–1970: British colony of Fiji. **1870s–1916:** Indian labourers imported to work plantations – their descendants became the majority community. **1970:** Independence. **1987:** Military coup overthrew an Indian-led government, following racial tension and land disputes. **1990:** New constitution entrenched the minority Fijian community in power.

FINLAND

Area: 338 145 km² (130 557 sq mi). *Population:* 4 999 000 (1990 census). *Capital:* Helsinki (Helsingfors) 994 000 (city 492 000; 1990 census). *Languages:* Finnish (94%), Swedish (6%). *Religion:* Lutheran (88%). *Government:* Republic – multi-party parliamentary system.

GEOGRAPHY

Nearly 30% of Finland lies N of the Arctic Circle and 10% of the country is covered by lakes, some 50 000 in all. Saimaa – the largest lake – has an area of over 4400 km² (1700 sq mi). During the winter months the Gulfs of Bothnia (to the W) and of Finland (to the S) freeze, and ports have to be kept open by icebreakers. The land is glaciated, and except for the NW mountains most of Finland is lowland. Finland has warm summers with long, extremely cold, winters particularly in the N.

ECONOMIC ACTIVITY

Forests cover over 60% of the country and wood products provide 40% of Finland's foreign earnings. Metalworking and engineering (particularly shipbuilding) are among the main Finnish industries, which have a reputation for quality and good design. Apart from rivers suitable for hydroelectric power, there are few natural resources. However, Finland has a high standard of living, although the collapse of trade with Russia – a major trading partner – brought severe economic difficulties to Finland in 1991–92. The agricultural sector produces enough dairy products for export.

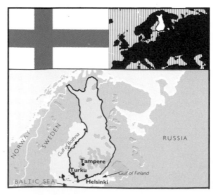

RECENT HISTORY

1906: Finland gained autonomy within Russia. **1917:** Civil war between nationalists and pro-Russians. **1919:** Independence secured. **1939:** Soviet forces invaded; territory ceded to USSR. **1941–44:** Alliance with Germany; war against USSR led to further territorial losses. **1945–91:** Policy of neutrality during Cold War.

FRANCE

Area: 543 965 km² (210 026 sq mi) – 'metropolitan' France, excluding overseas départements and territories. *Population:* 56 614 000 (1990 census) – 'metropolitan' France. *Capital and major cities:* Paris 9 063 000 (city 2 175 000), Lyon 1 262 000 (city 422 000), Marseille 1 087 000 (808 000), Lille 950 000 (city 178 000), Bordeaux 686 000 (city 213 000), Toulouse 608 000 (city 366 000) (1990 census). *Languages:* French, with Breton and Basque minorities. *Religion:* Roman Catholic (74%). *Government:* Republic – multi-party system with executive presidency.

OVERSEAS DEPARTEMENTS AND TERRITORIES

Overseas départements and collectivités territoriales: – integral parts of the French Republic (with areas, populations in 1990 and capitals) *Guadeloupe* – 1780 km² (687 sq mi), 387 000, Basse-Terre.

Guyane (or French Guiana) – 90 000 km² (34 750 sq mi), 115 000, Cayenne.

Martinique – 1100 km² (425 sq mi), 360 000, Fort-de-France.

Réunion – 2512 km² (970 sq mi), 597 000, Saint-Denis.

Mayotte – 376 km² (145 sq mi), 94 400, Dzaoudzi.

Saint-Pierre-et-Miquelon – 242 km² (93 sq mi), 6400, Saint-Pierre.

Overseas territories: (with areas, populations in 1989–90 and capitals)

French Polynesia – 4200 km² (1622 sq mi), 199 000, Papeete.

New Caledonia – 19 103 km² (7376 sq mi), 168 000, Nouméa.

Southern and Antarctic Territories – 451 598 km² (174 367 sq mi), no permanent population.

Wallis and Futuna Islands – 274 km² (106 sq mi), 13 700, Mata-Utu.

GEOGRAPHY

The plateau of the Massif Central – rising to almost 2000 m (6500 ft) – occupies the middle of France and is surrounded by four major lowlands, which together make up over 60% of the total area of the country. The Paris Basin – the largest of these lowlands – is divided by low ridges and fertile plains and plateaux, but is united by the river system of the Seine and its tributaries. To the E of the Massif Central is the narrow Rhône-Saône Valley, while to the W the Loire Valley stretches to the Atlantic. SW of the Massif Central lies the fertile Aquitaine Basin. A discontinuous ring of highlands surrounds France. In the NW is the Armorican Massif (Brittany). In the SW the Pyrenees form a high natural boundary with Spain. The Alps in the SE divide France from Italy and contain the highest peak in Europe, Mont Blanc (4807 m / 15 771 ft). The lower Jura – in the E – form a barrier between France and Switzerland, while the Vosges Mountains separate the Paris Basin from the Rhine Valley. In the NE the Ardennes extend into Belgium. The Mediterranean island of Corsica is an ancient massif rising to 2710 m (8891 ft). The Mediterranean S has warm summers and mild winters. The rest of France has a temperate climate, although the more continental E experiences warmer summers and colder winters. Rainfall is moderate, with highest falls in the mountains and lowest falls around Paris.

ECONOMIC ACTIVITY

Nearly two thirds of France is farmed. The principal products include cereals (wheat, maize, barley), meat and dairy products, sugar beet and

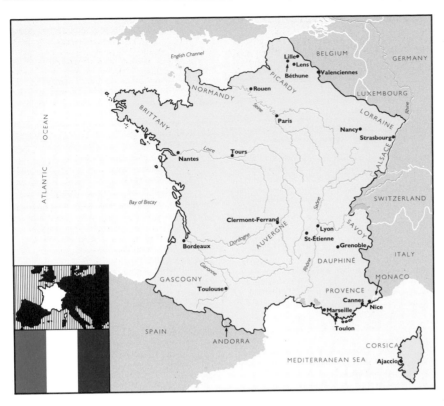

Republic – multi-party system with executive presidency.

Republic – multi-party system with executive presidency.

GEOGRAPHY
The Gambia is a narrow low-lying country on either bank of the River Gambia. The climate is tropical, with a dry season from November to May.

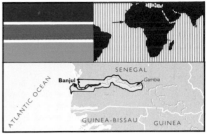

ECONOMIC ACTIVITY
The economy is largely based on the cultivation of groundnuts. Tourism is increasing in importance.

RECENT HISTORY
1965: Independence after over 120 years of British rule. **1981–89:** Confederation with neighbouring Senegal.

GEORGIA

Area: 69 700 km² (26 900 sq mi). **Population:** 5 464 000 (1991 census). **Capital:** Tbilisi 1 264 000 (1991 census). **Languages:** Georgian (69%), Armenian (9%), Russian (7%). **Religion:** Georgian Orthodox majority. **Government:** Republic – multi-party parliamentary system.

GEOGRAPHY
The spine of the Caucasus Mountains forms the N border of Georgia. The highest peak, Elbrus, reaches 5642 m (18 510 ft). The lower Little Caucasus occupies S Georgia. Lowlands occupy central Georgia. Coastal and central areas have a moist Mediterranean climate. Climate varies considerably with altitude and aspect.

ECONOMIC ACTIVITY
Despite a shortage of cultivable land, Georgia has a diversified agricultural sector including tea, citrus fruit, tobacco, vines, sheep and vegetables. Natural resources include coal, manganese and plentiful hydroelectric power. Industries include machine building, food processing and chemicals. The private sector is more highly developed than in most former Soviet republics, but the economy was damaged by civil war (1991–92).

RECENT HISTORY
1878: Russian annexation of Georgia completed. **1918–21:** Independence restored. **1921:** Invasion by Soviet Red Army; Georgia absorbed into USSR. **1991:** Independence upon the dissolution of the USSR. **1992:** Civil war; Abkhazia region attempted secession.

---

grapes for wine. France is remarkably self-sufficient in agriculture. However, the small size of land holdings remains a problem despite consolidation and the efforts of cooperatives. Reafforestation is helping to safeguard the future of the important timber industry. Natural resources include coal, iron ore, copper, bauxite and tungsten, as well as petroleum and natural gas, and plentiful sites for hydroelectric power plants. Major French industries include textiles, chemicals, steel, food processing, motor vehicles, aircraft, and mechanical and electrical engineering. Traditionally French firms have been small, but mergers have resulted in larger corporations able to compete internationally. France is now the world's fourth industrial power after the USA, Japan and Germany. During the later 1980s many of the state-owned corporations were privatized. Over one half of the labour force is involved in service industries, in particular administration, banking, finance, and tourism.

RECENT HISTORY
1871–1940: Third Republic. **End of 19th century:** Colonial expansion in Africa, SE Asia and the Pacific. **1914–18:** World War I; N France occupied by Germany; Alsace-Lorraine recovered in 1918. **1939–45:** World War II. **1940:** France defeated by Germany. **1940–44:** General Charles de Gaulle headed the Free French in exile. **1942–44:** Marshal Philippe Pétain led a collaborationist regime in Vichy. **1946–58:** Fourth Republic – marked by instability. **1950–53:** French colonial forces defeated in Indochina. **1956:** Suez Crisis – Franco-British intervention in Egypt. **1954–59:** Revolts by nationalists and by French colonists in Algeria led to the end of Fourth Republic. **1956–62:** Independence of African colonies. **1959–69:** Presidency of General de Gaulle. **Since 1959:** Fifth Republic. **Since 1981:** Presidency of François Mitterand.

GABON

Area: 267 667 km² (103 347 sq mi). **Population:** 1 133 000 (1990 est). **Capital:** Libreville 352 000

(1988 est). **Languages:** French (official), Fang (30%). **Religions:** Roman Catholic (71%), animist (28%). **Government:** Republic – multi-party system with executive presidency.

GEOGRAPHY
Apart from the narrow coastal plain, low plateaux make up most of the country. The central massif rises to 980 m (3215 ft). The climate is hot and humid with little seasonal variation.

ECONOMIC ACTIVITY
Petroleum, natural gas, manganese and uranium – and a relatively small population – make Gabon the richest Black African country, although most Gabonese are subsistence farmers.

RECENT HISTORY
1883: French colony of Gabon founded. **1960:** Independence. **1968–90:** Single-party state. **1990:** Multi-party system restored.

GAMBIA

Area: 11 295 km² (4 361 sq mi). **Population:** 883 000 (1991 est). **Capital:** Banjul 147 000 (city 44 000; 1986 est). **Language:** English (official). **Religion:** Sunni Islam (85%). **Government:**

GERMANY

Area: 357 050 km² (137 857 sq mi). *Population:* 79 096 000 (1991 est). *Capital and major cities:* Berlin 3 410 000, Bonn (capital de facto) 284 000, Essen 4 700 000 (Ruhr agglomeration – city 621 000, Dortmund 589 000, Duisburg 530 000), Hamburg 1 626 000, Munich (München) 1 218 000, Cologne (Köln) 940 000, Frankfurt 629 000 (1990 est). *Language:* German. *Religions:* Protestant Churches (mainly Lutheran; 34%), Roman Catholic (35%). *Government:* Federal republic – multi-party parliamentary system.

GEOGRAPHY
The North German Plain – a region of fertile farmlands and sandy heaths – is drained by the Rivers Elbe, Weser and Oder. In the W, the plain merges with the North Rhine lowlands which contain the Ruhr coalfield and over 20% of Germany's population. A belt of plateaux crosses the country from E to W and includes the Hunsrück and Eifel highlands (in the Rhineland), the Taunus and Westerwald uplands (Hesse), and the Harz and Erz Mountains (Thuringia). The Rhine cuts through these central plateaux in a deep gorge. In southern Germany, the Black Forest (Schwarzwald) separates the Rhine valley from the fertile valleys and scarplands of Swabia. The edge of the Bohemian uplands marks the Czech border, while the Bavarian Alps – rising to the Zugspitze (2963 m / 9721 ft) – form the frontier with Austria. The climate is temperate, but with considerable variations between the generally mild N coastal plain and the Bavarian Alps in the S, which have cool summers and cold winters. The E has warm summers and cold winters.

ECONOMIC ACTIVITY
Germany is the world's third industrial power after the USA and Japan. The country's recovery after World War II has been called the 'German economic miracle'. The principal industries include mechanical and electrical engineering, chemicals, textiles, food processing and vehicles, with heavy industry and engineering concentrated in the Ruhr, chemicals in cities on the Rhine and motor vehicles in large provincial centres such as Stuttgart. From the 1980s, there has been a spectacular growth in high-technology industries. Apart from coal and brown coal, Germany has relatively few natural resources, and the country relies heavily upon imports. Before reunification, labour was in short supply, and large numbers of 'guest

workers' (*Gastarbeiter*) – particularly from Turkey and Yugoslavia – were recruited. Since reunification in 1990 the labour shortage in the W has also been met by migration from the former GDR. Service industries employ almost twice as many people as manufacturing industry. Banking and finance are major foreign-currency earners and Frankfurt is a world financial and business centre. Reunification has proved costly to the economy. The GDR's economy had previously been the most successful in the Communist bloc, but, since 1990, many East German firms have been unable to compete with their Western counterparts. A trust (the *Treuhandanstalt*) was set up to oversee the privatization of the 8000 state-run firms in the E, but many have gone bankrupt and unemployment in the E is high. The main German agricultural products include hops (for beer), grapes (for wine), sugar beet, wheat, barley, and dairy products. The collectivized farms of the former GDR were privatized in 1991. Forests cover almost 30% of Germany and support a flourishing timber industry.

RECENT HISTORY
Late 19th century: Imperial Germany engaged in naval and commercial rivalry with Britain. **1914–18:** World War I. **1918:** German monarchies overthrown. **1919:** Defeated Germany lost territory in Europe and colonies overseas; reparations imposed; Rhineland occupied by the Allies until 1930. **1919–33:** The liberal Weimar republic could not bring economic or political stability. **1927:** Financial collapse of Germany during the Depression. **1933:** Nazi party, under Adolf Hitler, came to power. **1938:** Austria annexed. **1939:** Czechoslovakia dismembered; Poland invaded. **1939–45:** World War II; Nazis exterminated the Jews and others they regarded as 'inferior'; Germany gained control of much of Europe, before being defeated and divided into four zones of occupation by UK, France, USA and USSR. **1948–49:** USSR blockaded West Berlin. **1949:** Federal Republic of Germany formed in the W; (Communist) German Democratic Republic (GDR) proclaimed in the E. **1953:** Abortive uprising in the GDR. **1955:** West Germany gained sovereignty as a member of the Western Alliance. **1961:** Construction of Berlin Wall by E German leader Walter Ulbricht to stem the flow of refugees from E to W. **1970:** Under Willy Brandt, W German chancellor 1969–74, treaties were signed with USSR (1970) and Poland (recognizing the Oder-Neisse line as Poland's W frontier); relations with the GDR normalized. **1989:** Collapse of GDR; Berlin Wall opened; coalition government formed in GDR. **1990:** Reunification. **Since 1990:** Large-scale migration of refugees from E Europe into Germany.

GHANA

Area: 238 537 km² (92 099 sq mi). *Population:* 15 509 000 (1991 est). *Capital:* Accra 1 580 000 (1988 est). *Languages:* English (official), Asante, Ewe. *Religions:* Various Protestant Churches (30%), Sunni Islam (20%). *Government:* Republic – multi-party system with executive presidency.

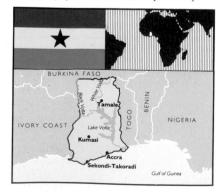

GEOGRAPHY
Ghana comprises low-lying plains and plateaux. In the centre, the Volta Basin contains the large Lake Volta reservoir. The climate is tropical with heavy rainfall on the coast, decreasing markedly inland. The N is subject to the hot, dry Harmattan wind from the Sahara.

ECONOMIC ACTIVITY
Political instability and mismanagement have damaged Ghana's economy. Nearly 50% of the labour force is involved in agriculture. Cocoa is the main cash crop. Forestry and mining for bauxite, gold and diamonds are also important.

RECENT HISTORY
1874: British colony of the Gold Coast established. **1898:** Inland kingdom of Ashanti crushed. **1957:** Independence. **1957–66:** Dictatorship of Kwame Nkrumah. **Since 1966:** Recurrent coups and periods of instability. **1992:** Multi-party system restored.

GREECE

Area: 131 957 km² (50 949 sq mi). *Population:* 10 269 000 (1991 census). *Capital and major cities:* Athens (Athínai) 3 097 000, Thessaloníki (formerly Salonika) 706 000 (including suburbs; 1991 census). *Language:* Greek (official). *Religion:* Orthodox (97%; official). *Government:* Republic – multi-party parliamentary system.

GEOGRAPHY
Over 80% of Greece is mountainous. The Pindus Mountains – extending from Albania S into the Peloponnese Peninsula – reach 2911 m (9550 ft) at Mount Olympus; the Rhodope Mountains lie along the Bulgarian border. Greece has some 2000 islands, of which only 154 are inhabited. Summers are hot and dry; winters are mild and wet. The N and the mountains are colder.

ECONOMIC ACTIVITY
Agriculture involves 25% of the labour force. Much of the land is marginal – in particular the extensive sheep pastures. Greece is largely self-sufficient in cereals, fruit and vegetables, and exports wine, olives (and olive oil) and tobacco. The industrial sector is expanding rapidly and includes the processing of natural resources including petroleum and natural gas. Tourism, a large merchant fleet, and money sent back by Greeks working abroad are major foreign-currency earners. Greece receives special economic aid from the EC.

RECENT HISTORY
1912–13: Greece gained territory in Macedonia in the Balkan Wars. **1921–22:** Greece defeated by Turkey in Anatolian War. **1924–35:** Greek

republic. **1935–73:** Monarchy restored. **1941–45:** German invasion and occupation during World War II. **1945–49:** Civil war between Communists and monarchists. **1967:** Military coup; 'colonels' junta' 1969–74. **1973:** Republic proclaimed. **1974:** Multi-party constitutional rule restored.

GRENADA

Area: 344 km² (133 sq mi). **Population:** 96 000 (1991 est). **Capital:** St George's 36 000 (city 7500; 1989 est). **Language:** English (official). **Religion:** Roman Catholic (over 60%). **Government:** Dominion – multi-party parliamentary system.

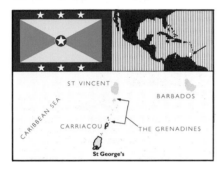

GEOGRAPHY
A forested mountain ridge covers much of this well-watered island. The island of Carriacou forms part of Grenada. The tropical maritime climate has a dry season from January to May.

ECONOMIC ACTIVITY
Spices, in particular nutmeg, are the mainstay of a largely agricultural economy. Tourism is increasing in importance.

RECENT HISTORY
1974: Independence after nearly 200 years of British rule. **1979:** Left-wing coup. **1983:** PM Maurice Bishop killed in a further coup; US and Caribbean forces intervened. **1984:** Multi-party constitutional rule restored.

GUATEMALA

Area: 108 889 km² (42 042 sq mi). **Population:** 9 454 000 (1991 est). **Capital:** Guatemala City 2 000 000 (including suburbs; 1989 est). **Language:** Spanish (official); Mayan languages (45%). **Religions:** Roman Catholic (official; 70%); Protestant Churches (30%). **Government:** Republic – multi-party system with executive presidency.

GEOGRAPHY
A mountain chain – containing over 30 volcanoes including Tajumulco (4220 m/13 881 ft) – separates Pacific and Atlantic coastal lowlands. The coastal plains are tropical; the uplands are temperate.

ECONOMIC ACTIVITY
More than one half of the labour force is involved in agriculture. Coffee accounts for over 25% of the country's exports, while the other main crops include sugar cane and bananas.

RECENT HISTORY
1898–44: Long periods of dictatorship. **1944:** Revolution. **1954:** US assistance helped the army depose reformist President Jacobo Arbenz. **1954–86:** Military rule; left-wing guerrilla armies active. **1986:** Constitutional multi-party rule restored.

GUINEA

Area: 245 857 km² (94 926 sq mi). **Population:** 7 052 000 (1991 est). **Capital:** Conakry 705 000 (1983 est). **Languages:** French (official), Fulani (40%). **Religion:** Sunni Islam (95%). **Government:** Republic – executive presidency; power is exercised by a military council.

GEOGRAPHY
Tropical rain forests cover the coastal plain. The interior highlands and plains are covered by scrubby grassland. The SW mountains rise to 1752 m (5748 ft). The climate is tropical with heavy rainfall. The highlands are cooler.

ECONOMIC ACTIVITY
Bauxite accounts for 80% of Guinea's exports. However, 75% of the labour force is involved in agriculture, producing bananas, oil palm and citrus fruits for export, and maize, rice and cassava as subsistence crops. Guinea – one of the world's poorest countries – relies heavily on aid.

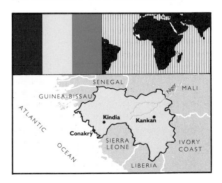

RECENT HISTORY
1890: Colony of French Guinea established. **1958:** Independence. **1958–78:** Policy of isolation under President Sékou Touré. **Since 1984:** Military rule.

GUINEA-BISSAU

Area: 36 125 km² (13 948 sq mi). **Population:** 994 000 (1991 est). **Capital:** Bissau 125 000 (1988 est). **Languages:** Portuguese (official), Crioulo. **Religions:** Animist (55%), Sunni Islam (40%). **Government:** Republic – multi-party system with executive presidency.

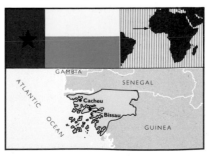

GEOGRAPHY
Swampy coastal lowlands adjoin a flat forested interior plain. The NE is mountainous. The climate is tropical with a dry season from December to May.

ECONOMIC ACTIVITY
The country – one of the poorest in the world – has a subsistence economy based mainly on rice. Palm kernels and timber are exported.

RECENT HISTORY
1879: Colony of Portuguese Guinea created. **1961–74:** Nationalists mounted a liberation war. **1973:** Independence (internationally recognized 1974). **1991:** Multi-party system introduced.

GUYANA

Area: 214 969 km² (83 000 sq mi). **Population:** 760 000 (1991 est). **Capital:** Georgetown 187 000 (1986 est). **Languages:** English (official), Hindu, Urdu. **Religions:** Hinduism (34%), various Protestant Churches (mainly Anglican; 34%), Roman Catholic (19%). **Government:** Republic – multi-party parliamentary system.

GEOGRAPHY
Dykes protect a coastal plain from the sea. Tropical rain forest covers much of the interior. The Pakaraima range rises to 2772 m (9094 ft).

ECONOMIC ACTIVITY
Guyana depends on mining bauxite and growing sugar cane and rice. Nationalization and emigration have caused economic problems.

RECENT HISTORY
1831: Colony of British Guiana formed. **1964** and **1978:** Racial violence. **1966:** Independence.

HAITI

Area: 27 750 km² (10 714 sq mi). **Population:** 6 486 000 (1990 est). **Capital:** Port-au-Prince 1 144 000 (including suburbs; 1988 est). **Languages:** Creole (90%) and French (both official). **Religions:** Voodoo (majority), Roman Catholic (official). **Government:** Republic – executive presidency; power is exercised by a military junta.

GEOGRAPHY

Haiti is the western part of the island of Hispaniola. Mountain ranges – up to 2800 m (8800 ft) – run from E to W, alternating with densely populated valleys and plains. The tropical climate is moderated by altitude and by the sea.

ECONOMIC ACTIVITY

Two thirds of the labour force is involved in agriculture, mainly growing crops for domestic consumption. Coffee is the principal cash crop. With few resources, overpopulated Haiti is the poorest country in the western hemisphere.

RECENT HISTORY

1915–35: US intervention. **1956–86:** The dictatorships of François and Jean-Claude Duvalier. **Since 1986:** Several coups have followed the violent end to the Duvalier era.

HONDURAS

Area: 112 088 km² (43 277 sq mi). **Population:** 4 708 000 (1991 est). **Capital:** Tegucigalpa 648 000 (including suburbs; 1988 census). **Language:** Spanish (official). **Religion:** Roman Catholic (85%). **Government:** Republic – multi-party system with executive presidency.

GEOGRAPHY

Over three quarters of Honduras is mountainous, with the highest point at Cerio las Minas 2849 m (9347 ft). There are small coastal plains. The tropical lowlands experience high rainfall; the more temperate highlands are drier.

ECONOMIC ACTIVITY

Over 50% of Hondurans work in agriculture, but despite agrarian reform, living standards remain low. Bananas and coffee are the leading exports. There are few natural resources.

RECENT HISTORY

1907: US intervention. **1925:** Civil war. **1925–80:** Military dictatorships. **Since 1980:** Constitutional rule restored.

HUNGARY

Area: 93 036 km² (35 921 sq mi). **Population:** 10 375 000 (1990 census). **Capital:** Budapest 2 018 000 (1990 census). **Language:** Magyar (Hungarian; 97%). **Religions:** Roman Catholic (56%), Calvinist. **Government:** Republic – multi-party parliamentary system.

GEOGRAPHY

Hungary W of the River Danube is an undulating lowland. The thickly wooded highlands of the NE rise to Kékes at 1015 m (3330 ft). The SE is a great expanse of flat plain. The climate is continental with long, hot and dry summers, and cold winters.

ECONOMIC ACTIVITY

Nearly one fifth of the labour force is involved in agriculture. Major crops include cereals (maize, wheat and barley), sugar beet, fruit, and grapes for wine. Despite considerable reserves of coal, Hungary imports more than half of its energy needs.

The steel, chemical fertilizer, pharmaceutical, machinery and vehicle industries are important. Since the early 1980s, private enterprise and foreign investment have been encouraged.

RECENT HISTORY

1918: Hungary – part of the Austro-Hungarian Dual Monarchy – defeated in World War I. **1919:** Hungary lost 60% of its territory; short-lived Communist regime. **1941–44:** Hungary, under Miklás Horthy, cooperated with Nazi Germany. **1945:** Occupation by Soviet Red Army. **1949:** A Communist People's Republic was established. **1956:** The Hungarian Uprising against Communist rule; quickly suppressed by Soviet forces who executed its leader Imre Nagy. **1980s:** Political and economic reform. **1990:** Democratic, multi-party state established; Communists lost power; Soviet troops left.

ICELAND

Area: 103 001 km² (39 769 sq mi). **Population:** 258 000 (1991 est). **Capital:** Reykjavik 146 000 (city 98 000) (1990 est). **Language:** Icelandic (official). **Religion:** Lutheran (93%). **Government:** Republic – multi-party parliamentary system.

GEOGRAPHY

Most of Iceland has a volcanic landscape with hot springs, geysers and some 200 volcanoes, some active. Much of the country is tundra. The S and centre are covered by icefields, the largest of which contains Hvannadalshnúkur – 2119 m (6952 ft) – Iceland's highest peak. The cool temperate climate is warmed by the Gulf Stream, which keeps Iceland milder than most places at the same latitude.

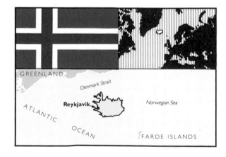

ECONOMIC ACTIVITY

The fishing industry provides 75% of Iceland's exports. Hydroelectric power is used to smelt aluminium; geo-thermal power warms extensive greenhouses. Ample grazing land makes Iceland self-sufficient in meat and dairy products.

RECENT HISTORY

1918: Independence gained under the Danish crown. **1944:** A republic declared. **1958** and **1972–76:** The Cod Wars – fishing disputes with the UK.

INDIA

Area: 3 287 263 km² (1 269 212 sq mi) – including the Indian-held part of Jammu and Kashmir. **Population:** 844 324 000 (1991 census). **Capital and major cities:** Delhi 8 375 000 (city 7 175 000), Bombay 12 572 000 (city 9 910 000), Calcutta 10 916 000 (city 4 388 000), Madras 5 361 000 (city 3 795 000), Hyderabad 4 280 000 (city 3 005 000), Bangalore 4 087 000 (city 2 651 000) (1991 census). **Languages:** Two national official languages – Hindi (31%) and English; 16 regional official languages: Assamese (3%), Bengali (6%), Gujarati (5%), Kannada (5%), Kashmiri, Malayalam (4%), Marathi (8%), Nepali, Oriya (4%), Punjabi (3%), Sanskrit, Sindhi (2%), Tamil (5%), Telugu (8%), and Urdu (5%); over 1600 other languages. **Religions:** Hindu (83%), Sunni Islam (11%), various Christian Churches (nearly 3%), Sikh (2%), Buddhist, Jain. **Government:** Federal republic – multi-party parliamentary system.

GEOGRAPHY

The Himalaya cut the Indian subcontinent off from the rest of Asia. Several Himalayan peaks in India rise to over 7000 m (23 000 ft), including Kangchenjunga on the Nepal-Sikkim border – at 8598 m (28 208 ft) India's highest mountain. S of the Himalaya, the basins of the Rivers Ganges and Brahmaputra and their tributaries are intensively farmed and densely populated. The Thar Desert stretches along the border with Pakistan. In S

India, the Deccan – a large plateau of hard rocks – is bordered in the E and W by the Ghats, discontinuous ranges of hills descending to coastal plains. Natural vegetation ranges from tropical rain forest on the W coast and monsoon forest in the NE and far S, through dry tropical scrub and thorn forest in much of the Deccan to Alpine and temperate vegetation in the Himalaya. India has three distinct seasons: a hot season from March to June, a wet season (when the SW monsoon brings heavy rain) from June to October, and a cooler drier season from November to March. Temperatures range from the cool of the Himalaya to the tropical heat in the S.

ECONOMIC ACTIVITY

Two thirds of the labour force are involved in subsistence farming, with rice and wheat as the main crops. Cash crops tend to come from large plantations and include tea, cotton, jute and sugar cane – all grown for export. The monsoon rains and irrigation make cultivation possible in many areas, but drought and floods are common. Major coal reserves provide the power base for industry. Other mineral deposits include diamonds, bauxite, and titanium, copper and iron ore, as well as substantial reserves of natural gas and petroleum. The textile, vehicle, iron and steel, pharmaceutical and electrical industries make important contributions to the economy, but India has balance-of-payment difficulties and relies upon foreign aid for development. Over one third of the population is below the official poverty line. In the 1990s, economic reforms have reduced state involvement in certain areas of the economy.

RECENT HISTORY
1919: Amritsar Massacre; nationalist demands grew after British troops fired without warning on a nationalist protest meeting. **1920:** Mahatma Gandhi began a campaign of non-violence and non-cooperation with the British authorities. **By 1940:** The Muslim League was demanding a separate state. **1947:** Independence and partition into India and Pakistan; over 70 million Hindus and Muslims became refugees and crossed the new boundaries; many killed in communal violence. **1947–49:** Border war with Pakistan. **1947–64:** Under PM Jawaharlal Nehru, India became a leader of the non-aligned Third World. **1962:** Border clashes with China. **1965:** War with Pakistan over Kashmir. **1971:** War with Pakistan in E Pakistan (now Bangladesh). **Since 1984:** An often violent Sikh campaign for an independent homeland. **1984:** PM Indira Gandhi assassinated. **Since 1990:** Increase in Hindu-Muslim violence, aggravated a dispute over a holy site in Ayodhya. **1991:** PM Rajiv Gandhi assassinated.

INDONESIA

Area: 1 919 443 km² (741 101 sq mi) – including East Timor which has an area of 14 874 km² (5743 sq mi). **Population:** 179 322 000 (1990 census) – including East Timor which had a population of 748 000. **Capital and major cities:** Jakarta 7 829 000, Surabaya 2 345 000, Medan 2 110 000 (all including suburbs; 1985 est). **Languages:** Bahasa Indonesian (official), Javanese (34%), Sundanese (14%); 26 other main languages. **Religions:** Sunni Islam (87%), various Christian Churches (10%). **Government:** Republic – multi-party system with executive presidency.

GEOGRAPHY
Indonesia consists of nearly 3700 islands of which about 3000 are inhabited. The southern chain of mountainous, volcanic islands comprises Sumatra, Java with Madura, Bali and the Lesser Sunda Islands. Java and its smaller neighbour Madura are fertile and densely populated, containing over 60% of Indonesia's people. The northern chain comprises Kalimantan (the Indonesian sector of Borneo), the irregular mountainous island of Sulawesi (Celebes), the Moluccas group and Irian Jaya (western New Guinea), which contains the highest peak Ngga Pulu at 5030 m (16 503 ft). The climate is tropical with heavy rainfall.

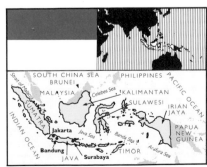

ECONOMIC ACTIVITY
Indonesia has great mineral wealth – petroleum, natural gas, tin, nickel and bauxite – but is relatively poor because of its great population. Over 50% of the labour force are subsistence farmers with rice being the major crop, but both estate and peasant farmers produce important quantities of rubber, tea, coffee and spices for export. Industry is largely concerned with processing mineral and agricultural products.

RECENT HISTORY
1908: Dutch conquest of East Indies completed. **1942–45:** Japanese invasion and occupation. **1945:** Achmed Sukarno declared Indonesian independence. **1945–49:** War of independence against reimposed Dutch rule. **1949:** Independence recognized. **1962:** Indonesia seized Dutch New Guinea (Irian Jaya). **1963–66:** Confrontation against Malaysia in Borneo. **1965–66:** Suppression of abortive Communist uprising; Sukarno replaced by T.N.I. Suharto. **1976:** Annexation of Portuguese East Timor - unrecognized internationally. **Since 1986:** Large-scale resettlement on outlying islands to relieve overcrowded Java. **Since 1991:** Increased unrest in East Timor.

IRAN

Area: 1 648 000 km² (636 296 sq mi). **Population:** 57 050 000 (1991 est). **Capital:** Tehran 6 043 000 (including suburbs; 1986 census). **Languages:** Farsi or Persian (official; 45%), Azeri (26%), Kurdish, Luri, Baluchi. **Religion:** Shia Islam (official; 98%). **Government:** Republic – effectively a non-party restricted parliamentary system with a supreme religious leader (the Wali Faqih).

GEOGRAPHY
Apart from restricted lowlands along the Gulf, by the Caspian Sea and in the W, Iran is a high plateau, surrounded by mountains. The Elburz Mountains in the N include Iran's highest peak, Demavend at 5604 m (18 386 ft); the Zagros Mountains form a barrier running parallel to the Gulf. In the E, low plateaux are covered by salt deserts. The extreme climate ranges from very hot on the Gulf to sub-zero temperatures in winter in the NW. The Caspian Sea coast has a subtropical climate with adequate rainfall but most of Iran has little rain.

ECONOMIC ACTIVITY
Petroleum is Iran's main source of foreign currency. The principal industries are petrochemicals, carpetweaving, textiles and cement. War with Iraq and the country's international isolation severely interrupted trade in the 1980s. Privatization is being encouraged and links with the West are increasing. Over 25% of the labour force are involved in agriculture, mainly producing cereals and keeping livestock, but lack of water, land ownership problems and manpower shortages have restricted yields.

RECENT HISTORY
Early 20th century: Russo-British rivalry for influence in Iran. **1921:** Reza Khan Pahlavi took power; established Pahlavi dynasty in 1925. **1979:** Pro-Western monarchy overthrown by Islamic fundamentalists led by Ayatollah Ruhollah Khomeini; Islamic republic proclaimed; Western-educated classes fled. **1979–81:** Radical students held American hostages in US embassy. **1980–88:** War with Iraq. **Since 1989:** Economic necessity brought a less militant phase of the Islamic revolution after Khomeini's death.

IRAQ

Area: 441 839 km² (170 595 sq mi). **Population:** 17 754 000 (1990 est). **Capital:** Baghdad 5 348 000 (including suburbs; 1988 est). **Languages:** Arabic (official; 80%), Kurdish (19%). **Religions:** Sunni Islam (41%), Shia Islam (51%). **Government:** Republic – single-party system with executive president.

GEOGRAPHY
The basins of the Rivers Tigris and Euphrates contain most of the arable land and most of the population. Desert in the SW occupies nearly one half of Iraq. In the NE, the highlands of Kurdistan rise to 3658 m (12 001 ft). Summers are hot and dry; winters in the N are cold. Rainfall ranges from 100 mm (4 in) in the desert to 1000 mm (40 in) in the N.

ECONOMIC ACTIVITY
Irrigated land in the Tigris and Euphrates basins produces cereals, fruit and vegetables for domestic consumption, and dates for export. Iraq depends upon its substantial reserves of petroleum but exports have been halted by international sanctions and the Gulf War (1991), during which the economy was devastated.

RECENT HISTORY
1917: In World War I, British forces took Iraq, which had been part of the (Turkish) Ottoman Empire. **1920:** Iraqi monarchy established under a British mandate. **1932:** Complete independence. **1941–45:** British occupation during World War II. **1958:** Revolution; republic declared. **1968:** Ba'athist regime came to power in a military coup. **Since 1979:** Dictatorship of President Saddam Hussein. **1980–88:** War against Iran. **1990–91:** Annexation of Kuwait. **1991:** Gulf War; Iraq defeated by UN-authorized US-led coalition; UN sanctions imposed on Iraq. **1991–93:** Exclusion zones proclaimed by coalition allies to protect Kurds and marsh Arabs from Saddam's forces.

IRELAND

Area: 70 282 km² (27 136 sq mi). **Population:** 3 523 000 (1991 census). **Capital and major cities:** Dublin 921 000 (city 478 000), Cork 174 000 (city 127 000) (1991 census). **Languages:** Irish (official; minority), English (official; universal). **Religion:** Roman Catholic (93%). **Government:** Republic – multi-party parliamentary system.

GEOGRAPHY
Central Ireland is a lowland crossed by slight

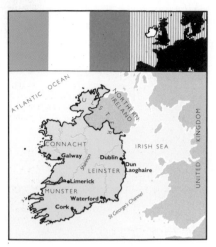

ridges and broad valleys, bogs and large lakes. Except on the E coast N of Dublin, the lowland is surrounded by coastal hills and mountains including the Wicklow Mountains, the Ox Mountains and the hills of Connemara and Donegal in the W. The highest uplands are the Macgillicuddy's Reeks in the SW, rising to Carrauntuohill (1041 m / 3414 ft). The rugged Atlantic Coast is highly indented. Ireland has a mild temperate climate. Rainfall is high, ranging from over 2500 mm (100 in) in the W and SW to 750 mm (30 in) in the E.

ECONOMIC ACTIVITY
Manufactured goods – in particular machinery, metals, chemicals and the electronics industry – account for over 80% of Ireland's exports. Agriculture – the traditional mainstay of the economy – concentrates upon the production of livestock, meat and dairy products. Food processing and brewing are major industries. Ireland suffers high rates of unemployment and emigration.

RECENT HISTORY
Late 19th century: Home Rule Bills rejected by the British Parliament. **1916:** Nationalist Easter rising in Dublin. **1918:** Irish nationalist MPs formed a provisional government led by Eamon de Valera. **1919–21:** Except in the Protestant NE, British administration in Ireland crumbled; near civil war elsewhere. **1922** Partition into (independent) Irish Free State and (British) Northern Ireland. **1922–23:** Civil war in Free State. **1937:** Free State became Republic of Eire. **1949:** As the Republic of Ireland, Eire left the Commonwealth. **Since 1968:** Relations between S and N have often been tense during the 'troubles' in Northern Ireland.

ISRAEL

Area: 21 946 km² (8473 sq mi), including East Jerusalem. **Population:** 4 821 000 (1991 est) – including East Jerusalem. **Capital and major cities:** Jerusalem (not recognized internationally as capital) 525 000, Tel-Aviv 1 157 000 (city 339 000) (1990 est). **Languages:** Hebrew (official; 85%), Arabic (15%). **Religions:** Judaism (official; 85%), Sunni Islam (13%). **Government:** Republic – multi-party parliamentary system.

OCCUPIED TERRITORIES
(with areas and populations in 1990)
Gaza – 378 km² (146 sq mi), 642 000.
Golan – 1150 km² (444 sq mi), 26 000.
West Bank (Judaea and Samaria) – 5879 km² (2270 sq mi), 955 000.

GEOGRAPHY
Israel – within the boundaries established by the 1949 cease-fire line – consists of a fertile thin coastal plain beside the Mediterranean, parts of the arid mountains of Judaea in the centre, the Negev Desert in the S and part of the Jordan Valley

in the NE. The climate is Mediterranean with hot, dry summers and mild, wetter winters. Most of Israel receives under 200 mm (8 in) of rain a year.

ECONOMIC ACTIVITY
Severe economic problems stem, in part, from Israel's large defence budget and political circumstances, which prevent trade with neighbouring countries. Israel is a major producer and exporter of citrus fruit. Much land is irrigated and over 75% of Israel's arable land is farmed by collectives (kibbutzim) and cooperatives. Mineral resources are few, but processing imported diamonds is a major source of foreign currency. Tourism – to biblical sites – is important.

RECENT HISTORY
1917: During World War I, Palestine was captured by British forces from Turkey; Balfour Declaration in favour of a Jewish homeland. **1918–1948:** British administration. **1922–39:** Increased Jewish settlement in Palestine. **1939–45:** 6 000 000 Jews murdered in concentration camps in Germany and Poland by the Nazis during World War II. **1948:** State of Israel founded. **1956, 1967** and **1973:** Arab-Israeli wars; details are to be found on pp. 282–3. **Since 1990:** Influx of Soviet Jews; Palestinian uprising (intifada) in the occupied territories.

ITALY

Area: 301 277 km² (116 324 sq mi). **Population:** 57 590 000 (1991 census). **Capital and major cities:** Rome (Roma) 3 000 000 (city 2 804 000), Milan (Milano) 3 700 000 (city 1 449 000), Naples (Napoli) 2 900 000 (city 1 204 000), Turin (Torino) 1 003 000 (1990 est). **Languages:** Italian (official), small German-, French- and Albanian-speaking minorities. **Religion:** Roman Catholic (over 83%). **Government:** Federal republic – multi-party parliamentary system.

GEOGRAPHY
The Alps form a natural boundary between Italy and its neighbours to the N and W. The highest point in Italy is at 4760 m (15 616 ft) just below the summit of Mt Blanc (Monte Bianco). A string of lakes at the foot of the Alps include Lakes Maggiore, Lugano and Como. The fertile Po Valley – the great lowland of N Italy – lies between the Alpine foothills in the N, the Apennine Mountains in the S, the Alps in the W and the Adriatic Sea in the E. The narrow ridge of the Ligurian Alps joins the Maritime Alps to the Apennines, which form a backbone down the entire length of the Italian peninsula. Coastal lowlands are few but include the Arno Basin in Tuscany, the Tiber Basin around Rome, the Campania lowlands around Naples, and

plains beside the Gulf of Taranto and in Puglia. The islands of Sardinia and Sicily are both largely mountainous. Italy has four active volcanoes, including Etna on Sicily and Vesuvius near Naples. Italy has a Mediterranean climate with warm, dry summers and mild winters. Sicily and Sardinia tend to be warmer and drier than the mainland. The Alps and the Po Valley experience colder, wetter winters.

ECONOMIC ACTIVITY
Northern Italy, with its easy access to the rest of Europe, is the main centre of Italian industry. The S, in contrast, remains mainly agricultural, producing grapes, sugar beet, wheat, maize and tomatoes. Most farms are small – and many farmers in the S are resistant to change – thus incomes in southern Italy (the 'Mezzogiorno') are on average substantially lower than in the N. Agriculture in the N is more mechanized and major crops include wheat, maize, rice, grapes (for the important wine industry), fruit and fodder crops for dairy herds. Industrialization in the S is being actively promoted. The industries of the N are well-developed and include electrical and electronic goods, motor vehicles and bicycles, textiles, clothing, leather goods, cement, glass, china and ceramics. The N is also an important financial and banking area, and Milan is the commercial capital of Italy. Apart from Alpine rivers that have been harnessed for hydroelectric power, Italy has few natural resources. Tourism and money sent back by Italians living abroad are important sources of foreign currency. Recession and a crippling public deficit have added to Italy's growing economic problems.

RECENT HISTORY
1914–18: World War I; Italian participation in the allied cause; territorial gains from Austria. **1922:** Rise of Fascism; Benito Mussolini became PM. **1936:** Italy invaded Ethiopia. **1939:** Italy invaded Albania. **1940–43:** Italy at war allied to Nazi Germany. **1943:** Italy defeated; Mussolini dismissed; Italy returned to war on the allied side. **1946:** Republic declared. **Since 1946:** Recurrent short-lived government coalitions. **1990s:** State institutions weakened by corruption, political instability and the activities of the Mafia; growth of regional separatism in the N.

IVORY COAST (see COTE D'IVOIRE

JAMAICA

Area: 10 991 km² (4244 sq mi). **Population:** 2 420 000 (1991 est). **Capital:** Kingston 662 000

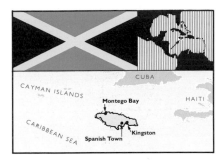

(1990 est). *Language:* English. *Religions:* Church of God (17%), Anglican (10%). *Government:* Dominion – multi-party parliamentary system.

GEOGRAPHY
Coastal lowlands surround the interior limestone plateaux (the 'Cockpit Country') and mountains that rise to 2256 m (7402 ft). The tropical lowlands are rainy; the cooler highlands are wetter.

ECONOMIC ACTIVITY
Agriculture is the mainstay of the economy, with sugar cane and bananas as the main crops. Jamaica is a leading exporter of bauxite. Tourism is a major foreign currency earner.

RECENT HISTORY
1930s: Severe social and economic problems led to rioting. **1962:** Independence after over 300 years of British rule.

JAPAN

Area: 377 815 km² (145 874 sq mi). *Population:* 123 612 000 (1990 census). *Capital and major cities:* Tokyo 18 200 000 (city 11 855 000), Osaka 8 500 000 (city 2 624 000), Yokohama (part of the Tokyo agglomeration) 3 220 000, Nagoya 2 155 000, Sapporo 1 672 000, Kobe (part of the Osaka agglomeration) 1 477 000 (1990 census). *Language:* Japanese. *Religions:* Shintoism (86%) overlaps with Buddhism (74%). *Government:* Empire – multi-party parliamentary system.

GEOGRAPHY
Japan consists of over 3900 islands, of which Hokkaido in the N occupies 22% of the total land area, and Shikoku and Kyushu in the S respectively occupy 5% and 11%. The central island of Honshu occupies 61% of the total land area and contains 80% of the population. To the S, the Ryukyu Islands stretch almost to Taiwan. Nearly 75% of Japan is mountainous. Coastal plains – where the population is concentrated – are limited. The principal lowlands are Kanto (around

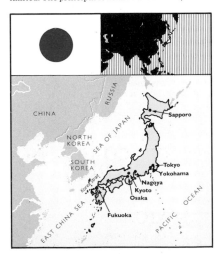

Tokyo), Nobi (around Nagoya) and the Sendai Plain in the N of Honshu. The highest peak is Fujiyama at 3776 m (12 388 ft), an extinct volcano. There are also over 60 active volcanoes in Japan. There are great variations in climate. Although the whole country is temperate, the N has long cold snowy winters, while the S has hot summers and mild winters. Rainfall totals are generally high.

ECONOMIC ACTIVITY
Despite the generally crowded living conditions in the cities, the Japanese enjoy a high standard of living. The country has the second largest industrial economy in the world, despite having very few natural resources. Japanese industry is heavily dependent on imported raw materials – about 90% of the country's energy requirements come from abroad and petroleum is the single largest import. Japan's economic success is based on manufacturing industry, which – with construction – employs nearly one third of the labour force. Japan is the world's leading manufacturer of motor vehicles, and one of the major producers of ships, steel, synthetic fibres, chemicals, cement, electrical goods and electronic equipment. Rapid advances in Japanese research and technology have helped the expanding export-led economy. The banking and financial sectors have prospered, and Tokyo is one of the world's main stock exchanges and commercial centres. Agriculture is labour intensive. Although Japan is self-sufficient in rice, agriculture is not a priority and one third of its food requirements have to be imported. The fishing industry is one of the largest in the world.

RECENT HISTORY
Late 19th century: Western-style reforms after the Meiji emperor overthrew the last shogun (1867). **1894–96:** Japan defeated China, taking Taiwan. **1904–05:** Japan defeated Russia. **1910:** Korea annexed. **1914–18:** Japan participated in World War I against Germany. **1930s:** Rise of totalitarianism and aggressive Japanese expansion in China, particularly Manchuria. **1941:** Allied to Nazi Germany, Japan attacked Pearl Harbor (Hawaii), bringing the USA into World War II. **1941–44:** Rapid Japanese military expansion across SE Asia and the Pacific. **1945:** Japan defeated after atomic weapons used on Hiroshima and Nagasaki. **1945–52:** Allied occupation of Japan. **1946:** Emperor Hirohito renounced his divinity. **Since 1950s:** Astonishing economic recovery based on an aggressive export policy and protectionism. **1980s:** Japan became the world's second economic power.

JORDAN

Area: 89 206 km² (34 443 sq mi) – excluding the Israeli-occupied West Bank. *Population:* 3 285 000 (1991 est) – excluding West Bank. *Capital:* Amman 1 160 000 (1986 est). *Language:* Arabic (official). *Religion:* Sunni Islam (over 80%). *Government:* Kingdom – multi-party system.

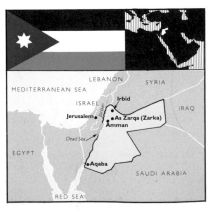

GEOGRAPHY
The steep escarpment of the East Bank Uplands borders the Jordan Valley and the Dead Sea. Deserts cover over 80% of the country. Summers are hot and dry; winters are cooler and wetter, although most of Jordan has very little rainfall.

ECONOMIC ACTIVITY
Apart from potash – the principal export – Jordan has few resources. Arable land accounts for only about 5% of the total area. Foreign aid and money sent back by Jordanians working abroad are major sources of foreign currency.

RECENT HISTORY
1917–18: Area taken from the (Turkish) Ottoman Empire by British forces during World War I. **1918–46:** British administration. **1923:** Emirate of Transjordan established. **1946:** Independence as Jordan. **1948:** Arab-Israeli war; West Bank occupied by Jordan. **1967:** Arab-Israeli war; West Bank and Jerusalem taken by Israel. **1979:** Civil war. **1988:** Jordan renounced responsibility for the West Bank. **1991:** Multi-party system legalized.

KAZAKHSTAN

Area: 2 717 300 km² (1 049 200 sq mi). *Population:* 16 793 000 (1991 census). *Capital:* Alma-Ata 1 151 000 (1991 census). *Languages:* Kazakh (40%), Russian (38%). *Religions:* Sunni Islam majority, Russian Orthodox minority. *Government:* Republic – multi-party system with executive presidency.

GEOGRAPHY
Kazakhstan comprises a vast expanse of low tablelands (steppes), which in the W descend below sea level beside the Caspian Sea. Uplands include ranges of hills in the N and mountain chains, including the Tien Shan, in the S and E, where Khan Tengri, at 6398 m (20 991 ft), is the highest point. Salt lakes include the Aral Sea, which is shrinking because of excessive extraction of irrigation water from its tributaries. Deserts include the Kyzylkum in the S and the Kara Kum in the centre. The climate is characterized by bitterly cold winters and hot summers. Rainfall is low everywhere and negligible in the deserts.

ECONOMIC ACTIVITY
Kazakhstan is a major supplier of food and raw materials for industry to other former Soviet republics, particularly Russia. The transition to a market economy is beginning. Farming employs almost 50% of the labour force. Large collective farms on the steppes in the N contributed 30% of the cereals of the former USSR. Other major farming interests include sheep, fodder crops and fruit. Rich natural resources include coal, tin, copper, lead and zinc. Iron and steel, pharmaceuticals and food processing are major industries.

RECENT HISTORY
1917–20: Major revolt against Russian rule; Kazakhs attempted to secure autonomy. **1920:** Invasion by Soviet Red Army. **1936:** Kazakhstan became a Union Republic of the USSR. **1950s:**

Widespread immigration from other parts of the USSR when 'Virgin Lands' of N Kazakhstan were opened up for farming. **1991:** Independence upon the dissolution of the USSR.

KENYA

Area: 580 367 km² (224 081 sq mi). *Population:* 25 905 000 (1991 est). *Capital:* Nairobi 1 505 000 (including suburbs; 1990 est). *Languages:* Swahili (official), English, Kikuyu (21%), Luhya (21%). *Religions:* Roman Catholic (27%), African Christian Churches (19%), other Protestant Churches (27%). *Government:* Republic – multi-party system with executive presidency.

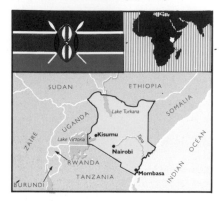

GEOGRAPHY
The steep sided Rift Valley divides the highlands that run from N to S through central Kenya and rise at Mount Kenya to 5199 m (17 058 ft). Plateaux extend in the W to Lake Victoria and in the E to coastal lowlands. The coastal areas are hot and humid; the cooler highlands experience high rainfall. The N is very hot and arid.

ECONOMIC ACTIVITY
Over 75% of the labour force is involved in agriculture. Major crops include wheat and maize for local consumption, and coffee, tea, sisal and sugar cane for export. Large numbers of beef cattle are reared and Kenya has a major dairy industry – rare in Black Africa. Tourism is an important source of foreign currency.

RECENT HISTORY
1895: British protectorate established in Kenya. **1920:** Colony of Kenya proclaimed. **1952–56:** Mau Mau rising against British rule. **1963:** Independence under Jomo Kenyatta. **1969–91:** Single-party rule. **1991:** Multi-party system restored.

KIRIBATI

Area: 717 km² (277 sq mi). *Population:* 73 000 (1991 est). *Capital:* Bairiki (on Tarawa) 25 000 (1990 census). *Languages:* English (official), I-Kiribati. *Religions:* Roman Catholic (over 50%), Kiribati Protestant (Congregational; over 40%). *Government:* Republic – effectively a non-party system with executive presidency.

GEOGRAPHY
With the exception of the island of Banaba – which is composed of phosphate rock – Kiribati comprises three groups of small coral atolls. Kiribati has a maritime equatorial climate with high rainfall.

ECONOMIC ACTIVITY
Most islanders are involved in subsistence farming and fishing. Copra is the main export.

RECENT HISTORY
1892: British rule – as the Gilbert Islands – began. **1942–43:** Japanese occupation during World War II. **1957–64:** British nuclear weapons were tested on Christmas Island. **1979:** Independence as Kiribati (pronounced 'Kiri-bass').

KOREA DPR (Democratic People's Republic of Korea)

Popularly known as North Korea. *Area:* 120 538 km² (46 540 sq mi). *Population:* 21 815 000 (1991 est). *Capital:* Pyongyang 2 640 000 (1986 est). *Language:* Korean. *Religions:* Atheist majority; Confucianism and Daoism (14%). *Government:* Republic – (Communist) single-party system with executive presidency.

GEOGRAPHY
Over three quarters of the country consists of mountains, which rise in the NE to the volcanic peak Mount Paek-tu at 2744 m (9003 ft). N Korea has long cold dry winters and hot wet summers.

ECONOMIC ACTIVITY
Over 30% of the labour force work on cooperative farms, mainly growing rice. Natural resources include coal, zinc, magnetite, iron ore and lead. Great emphasis has been placed on industrial development, notably metallurgy and machine-building. The end of barter deals with the former USSR (1990–91) brought a sharp economic decline.

RECENT HISTORY
1945: Korea divided into zones of occupation after World War II. **1948:** Communist republic established in the Soviet zone in the N. **1950–53:** Korean War; N Korea – with Chinese assistance – attempted to achieve reunification by force; S Korea aided by multi-national UN force. **1953:** Ceasefire; N–S frontier re-established close to the 38th parallel. **1972:** Kim Il-Sung – Communist Party leader since 1945 – became President. **Since 1990–91:** N Korea increasingly isolated since the collapse of Communism in the former USSR and E Europe.

KOREA, REPUBLIC OF

Popularly known as South Korea. *Area:* 99 143 km² (38 279 sq mi). *Population:* 43 520 000 (1990 census). *Capital and major cities:* Seoul (Soul) 10 726 000, Pusan 3 825 000 (1990 census). *Language:* Korean (official). *Religions:* Buddhist (24%), various Christian Churches (21%). *Government:* Republic – multi-party system with executive presidency.

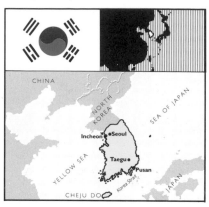

GEOGRAPHY
Apart from restricted coastal lowlands and the densely-populated basins of the Rivers Han and Naktong, most of the country is mountainous. The highest point is Halla-san (1950 m / 6398 ft), an extinct volcano on Cheju island. Korea experiences cold dry winters and hot summers during which the monsoon brings heavy rainfall.

ECONOMIC ACTIVITY
One fifth of the labour force is involved in agriculture. The principal crops are rice and barley. Industry is dominated by a small number of large family conglomerates. The important textile industry was the original manufacturing base. South Korea is now the world's leading producer of ships and footwear and a major producer of electronic equipment, electrical goods, steel, petrochemicals and motor vehicles. Banking and finance are expanding. The country achieved high economic growth rates throughout the 1980s and early 1990s.

RECENT HISTORY
1910: Korea annexed by Japan. **1945:** After World War II, Korea divided into zones of occupation. **1948:** Republic of Korea founded in the American zone in the S. **1950–53:** Korean War; N Korea attempted to reunite Korea by force; UN forces came to aid of the S. **Since 1953:** Astonishing economic transformation of the S; long periods of authoritarian rule. **Since 1987:** More open multi-party rule.

KUWAIT

Area: 17 818 km² (6880 sq mi). *Population:* 1 100 000 (1992 est). *Capital:* Kuwait City 750 000 (including agglomeration; 1992 unofficial est). *Language:* Arabic (official). *Religions:* Sunni Islam (official; about 70%), Shia Islam (30%). *Government:* Emirate – restricted parliamentary system with executive monarchy.

GEOGRAPHY
Most of the country is desert, relatively flat and low lying. Kuwait experiences extremes of heat in

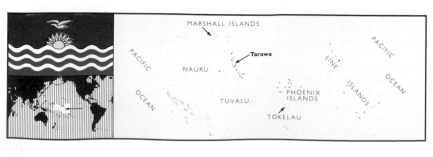

summer. Almost all the annual rainfall of 100 mm (4 in) comes during the cooler winter.

ECONOMIC ACTIVITY
The economy was devastated by the Iraqi invasion and Second Gulf War (1991), but reconstruction followed rapidly. Large reserves of petroleum and natural gas are the mainstay of the economy. Lack of water makes little agriculture possible.

RECENT HISTORY
1899–1961: Kuwait was a British-protected state. **1946:** Commercial oil production began. **1990:** Iraq invaded and annexed Kuwait. **1991:** Kuwait liberated by UN-authorized US-led coalition. **Since 1991:** Reconstruction; expulsion of the previously large Palestinian population, which was perceived to have favoured Iraq.

KYRGYZSTAN

Formerly known as Kirghizia. *Area:* 198 500 km² (76 600 sq mi). *Population:* 4 422 000 (1991 census). *Capital:* Bishkek (formerly Frunze) 626 000 (1989 census). *Languages:* Kyrgyz (53%), Russian (21%), Uzbek (13%). *Religions:* Sunni Islam majority. *Government:* Republic – multi-party system with executive presidency.

GEOGRAPHY
Most of Kyrgyzstan lies within the Tien Shan mountains, rising at Pik Pobedy to 7439 m (24 406 ft). Restricted lowlands contain most of the population. The country's altitude and position deep within the interior of Asia combine to produce an extreme dry continental climate.

ECONOMIC ACTIVITY
Agriculture is dominated by large collectivized farms that specialize in growing fodder crops for sheep and goats, and cotton under irrigation. Natural resources include coal, lead, zinc and considerable hydroelectric-power potential. The economy remains centrally planned.

RECENT HISTORY
1850: Area annexed by Russia. **1915:** Major revolt against Russian rule. **1926:** Kirghiz Soviet Republic founded. **1991:** Independence after dissolution of the USSR.

LAOS

Area: 236 800 km² (91 400 sq mi). *Population:*

4 290 000 (1991 est). *Capital:* Vientiane (Viengchane) 377 000 (1985 est). *Language:* Lao (official). *Religion:* Buddhism (over 57%). *Government:* Republic – (Communist) single-party system with executive presidency.

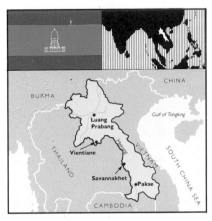

GEOGRAPHY
Except for the Plain of Jars in the N and the Mekong Valley and low plateaux in the S, Laos is largely mountainous. Phou Bia (2820 m / 9252 ft) is the highest peak. Laos has a tropical climate with heavy monsoon rains between May and October.

ECONOMIC ACTIVITY
Laos is one of the poorest countries in the world. The majority of Laotians work on collective farms, mainly growing rice.

RECENT HISTORY
1893: Laos established as a French protectorate. **1940–45:** Japanese occupation during World War II. **1953–73:** Civil war between royalist forces and the Communist Pathet Lao. **1954:** Independence. **1975:** A Communist People's Republic established.

LATVIA

Area: 64 589 km² (24 938 sq mi). *Population:* 2 686 000 (1991 est). *Capital:* Riga 917 000 (1990 est). *Languages:* Lettish (over 52%), Russian (33%). *Religions:* Lutheran (22%), Roman Catholic (7%). *Government:* Republic – multi-party system with executive presidency.

GEOGRAPHY
Latvia comprises an undulating plain, lower in the W (Courland) than in the E (Livonia), which rises to 311 m (1020 ft). Latvia has a moist, temperate climate with mild summers and cold winters.

ECONOMIC ACTIVITY
Engineering dominates a heavily industrialized economy. Latvia has relied on Russian trade and

faces severe difficulties as it introduces a free market. Agriculture specializes in dairying and meat production.

RECENT HISTORY
1918: Latvia declared independence from Russian rule. **1940:** Annexed by USSR. **1941–44:** German occupation during World War II. **1944:** Soviet rule reimposed. **1991:** Independence restored.

LEBANON

Area: 10 452 km² (4036 sq mi). *Population:* 2 745 000 (1991 census). *Capital:* Beirut (Beyrouth) 1 100 000 (including suburbs; 1990 est). *Languages:* Arabic (official). *Religions:* Shia Islam (31%), Sunni Islam (27%), Maronite Christian (22%), other Christian Churches (Armenian, Greek Orthodox, Syrian; 16%), Druze. *Government:* Republic – multi-party system with executive presidency.

GEOGRAPHY
Beside a narrow coastal plain, the mountains of Lebanon rise to 3088 m (10 131 ft). Beyond the fertile Beka'a Valley, to the E, are the Anti-Lebanese range and Hermon Mountains. The lowlands have a Mediterranean climate. The cooler highlands experience heavy snowfall in winter.

ECONOMIC ACTIVITY
Reconstruction of an economy devastated by civil war began in 1991. The principal crops are citrus fruit (grown mainly for export), wheat, barley and olives. The illegal cultivation of opium poppies is economically significant. The textile and chemical industries and the financial sector are important.

RECENT HISTORY
1916: French intervention in Turkish-ruled Lebanon. **1920:** Lebanon became a French League of Nations mandate. **1943:** Independence. **1958:** Civil war; US intervention. **1978–91:** Civil war; country plunged into ungovernable chaos; Syrian and Israeli interventions. **After 1990:** Defeat of Christian militia by Syrian troops allowed the Lebanese government to gradually reassert its authority. **1991:** Most militias disbanded.

LESOTHO

Area: 30 355 km² (11 720 sq mi). *Population:* 1 806 000 (1991 est). *Capital:* Maseru 110 000 (1988 est). *Languages:* Sesotho and English (official). *Religions:* Roman Catholic (44%), Protestant Churches (49%). *Government:* Kingdom – parliamentary system scheduled to be restored.

GEOGRAPHY
Mountainous Lesotho rises to Thabana Ntlenyana (3482 m / 11 425 ft) in the Drakensberg Mountains.

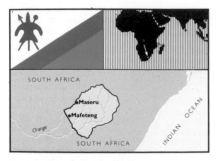

The climate is subtropical with lower temperatures in the highlands.

ECONOMIC ACTIVITY

Livestock – cattle, sheep and goats (for mohair) – are the mainstay of the economy. Natural resources include diamonds and abundant water, which is exported to South Africa.

RECENT HISTORY

1868: British protectorate of Basutoland founded. **1966:** Independence as Lesotho. **1986:** Military coup. **1990:** King deposed; replaced by his son.

LIBERIA

Area: 111 369 km² (43 000 sq mi). *Population:* 2 607 000 (1990 est). *Capital:* Monrovia 465 000 (1987 est). *Language:* English (official). *Religions:* Animist (50%), Sunni Islam (26%), various Christian Churches (mainly Methodist, Baptist, Episcopalian; 24%). *Government:* Republic – interim executive president (owing to civil war).

GEOGRAPHY

A low swampy coastal belt borders a higher zone of tropical forest. Further inland, plateaux rise to 1380 m (4540 ft). The climate is tropical with a wet season in the summer and a dry season in winter.

ECONOMIC ACTIVITY

Over 70% of the labour force is involved in agriculture, producing cassava and rice as subsistence crops and rubber, coffee and cocoa for export. Liberia is a major exporter of iron ore. The economy was disrupted by a civil war in 1990, since when Liberia's trade has been greatly diminished.

RECENT HISTORY

1878–1980: True Whig Party held power in Liberia, which was founded as a settlement for freed Black American slaves (1821). **1980:** Military coup. **Since 1990:** Civil war; ECOWAS intervention.

LIBYA

Area: 1 759 540 km² (679 363 sq mi). *Population:* 4 325 000 (1991 est). *Capital:* Tripoli (Tarabulus) 591 000 (1989 est). In 1988 some government functions were decentralized to Benghazi, Sirte (Surt) and Al Jofrah. *Language:* Arabic (official). *Reli-*

gion: Sunni Islam (over 97%). *Government:* Republic – single-party state with executive revolutionary leader.

GEOGRAPHY

The Sahara Desert covers most of Libya. In the NW (Tripolitania) coastal oases and a low plain form Libya's main agricultural region. In the NE (Cyrenaica) a coastal plain and mountain ranges support Mediterranean vegetation. The Tibesti Mountains rise to 2286 m (7500 ft). The hot dry climate is moderated near the coast.

ECONOMIC ACTIVITY

Libya is one of the world's largest producers of petroleum. Liquefied gas is also exported. Coastal oases produce wheat, barley, dates and grapes.

RECENT HISTORY

1911–42: Italian rule. **1942–51:** Libya divided between British and French administrations. **1952:** Independence as a kingdom. **1969:** Military coup led by Colonel Moamar al Gaddafi. **Since 1970s:** Cultural and economic revolutions; alleged Libyan support for terrorism.

LIECHTENSTEIN

Area: 160 km² (62 sq mi). *Population:* 29 000 (1991 est). *Capital:* Vaduz 4800 (1990 est). *Language:* German (official). *Religion:* Roman Catholic (87%). *Government:* Principality – multi-party parliamentary system.

GEOGRAPHY

To the E of the floodplain of the River Rhine, the Alps rise to the Grauspitze at 2599 m (8326 ft). The country has a mild Alpine climate.

ECONOMIC ACTIVITY

Liechtenstein has one of the highest standards of living in the world. Tourism, banking and manufacturing (precision goods) are all important.

RECENT HISTORY

1924: Customs and monetary union with Switzerland. **1990s:** Increased independent role – e.g. joining EFTA and UN.

LITHUANIA

Area: 65 200 km² (25 174 sq mi). *Population:* 3 739 000 (1989). *Capital:* Vilnius 593 000 (1990 est). *Languages:* Lithuanian (80%), Russian (9%), Polish (7%). *Religion:* Roman Catholic (over 80%). *Government:* Republic – multi-party system with executive presidency.

GEOGRAPHY

Lithuania comprises a low-lying plain dotted with lakes and crossed by ridges of glacial moraine that rise to 294 m (964 ft) in the SE. The climate is transitional between a mild temperate type and a more extreme continental climate.

ECONOMIC ACTIVITY

One fifth of the labour force is engaged in agriculture, principally cattle rearing and dairying. Much of the country is heavily forested. The engineering, timber, cement and food-processing industries are important, but Lithuania faces an uncertain future as it dismantles state control and breaks away from the former Soviet trade system.

RECENT HISTORY

1915–20: Lithuania disputed by German, Russian and, later, Polish armies. **1923:** Lithuanian independence recognized. **1940:** Lithuania annexed by USSR. **1940–44:** German occupation during World War II. **1944:** Soviet rule reimposed. **1990:** Independence declared; internationally recognized in 1991.

LUXEMBOURG

Area: 2586 km² (999 sq mi). *Population:* 385 000 (1991 census). *Capital:* Luxembourg 117 000 (city 78 000; 1991 census). *Languages:* Letzeburgish (national), French and German (both official). *Religions:* Roman Catholic (95%). *Government:* Grand Duchy – multi-party parliamentary system.

GEOGRAPHY

The Oesling in the N is a wooded plateau; the

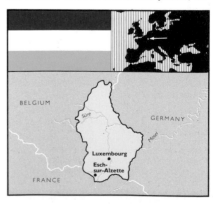

Gutland in the S is a lowland of valleys and ridges. Luxembourg has cool summers and mild winters.

ECONOMIC ACTIVITY
The iron and steel industry – originally based on local ore – is important. Luxembourg has become a major banking centre. The N grows potatoes and fodder crops; the S produces wheat and fruit, including grapes.

RECENT HISTORY
1890: End of dynastic link with the Dutch crown. **1914–18:** German occupation during World War I. **1922:** Customs union with Belgium. **1940–44:** German occupation during World War II. **Since 1957:** Luxembourg has become one of the administrative centres of the EC.

MACEDONIA (see YUGOSLAVIA)

MADAGASCAR

Area: 587 041 km² (226 658 sq mi). *Population:* 11 197 000 (1990 est). *Capital:* Antananarivo (Tananarive) 802 000 (1990 est). *Languages:* Malagasy and French (official). *Religions:* Animist (47%), Roman Catholic (26%), Madagascan Protestant (22%). *Government:* Republic – multi-party system with executive presidency.

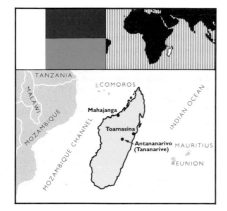

GEOGRAPHY
Massifs form a spine running from N to S through the tropical island and rise to Tsaratanana peak at 2885 m (9465 ft). The mountains are cooler. The N receives monsoon rains, but the S is dry.

ECONOMIC ACTIVITY
Over three quarters of the labour force are involved in agriculture. The main crops are coffee and vanilla for export, and rice and cassava for domestic consumption. The island is an important producer of chromite.

RECENT HISTORY
1896: Madagascar annexed by France. **1904:** End of resistance to French rule. **1947–48:** Major nationalist revolt. **1960:** Independence. **1976–90:** Virtual single-party rule. **1990:** Multi-party rule restored.

MALAWI

Area: 118 484 km² (45 747 sq mi). *Population:* 9 152 000 (1991 est). *Capital and major cities:* Lilongwe 234 000, Blantyre 403 000 (1986 census). *Languages:* English (official), Chichewa (official; over 50%). *Religions:* Animist (67%), Roman Catholic (17%). *Government:* Republic – single-party system with executive presidency.

GEOGRAPHY
Plateaux cover the N and centre. The Rift Valley

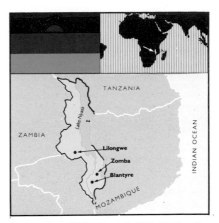

contains Lake Malawi and the Shire Valley. The Shire Highlands in the SE rise to Mount Sapitawa at 3002 m (9849 ft). The climate is equatorial with heavy rainfall from November to April.

ECONOMIC ACTIVITY
Agriculture is the mainstay of the economy, providing over 90% of Malawi's exports. Tobacco, tea and sugar cane are the main crops.

RECENT HISTORY
1891: British protectorate of Nyasaland founded. **1915:** Uprising against British rule. **1953–63:** Part of the white-dominated Central African Federation. **1964:** Independence as Malawi. **Since 1966:** One-party state.

MALAYSIA

Area: 329 758 km² (127 320 sq mi). *Population:* 17 556 000 (1990 census). *Capital:* Kuala Lumpur 1 233 000 (including suburbs; 1990 census). *Languages:* Bahasa Malaysia (Malay; official; 58%), English, Chinese (32%), Tamil (4%). *Religions:* Sunni Islam (official; 53%), Buddhist, Daoist and Christian minorities. *Government:* Federal kingdom – multi-party parliamentary system.

GEOGRAPHY
Western (Peninsular) Malaysia consists of mountain ranges running N to S and bordered by densely populated coastal lowlands. Rapidly diminishing tropical rainforest covers the hills and mountains of Eastern Malaysia – Sabah and Sarawak, the N part of the island of Borneo. The highest point is Kinabalu in Sabah (4101 m / 13 455 ft). Malaysia has a tropical climate with heavy rainfall. There is more seasonal variation in precipitation than temperature, with the NE monsoon (from October to February) and the SW monsoon (from May to September) bringing increased rainfall, particularly to Peninsular Malaysia.

ECONOMIC ACTIVITY
Rubber, petroleum and tin are the traditional mainstays of the Malaysian economy, but all three suffered drops in price on the world market in the 1980s. Pepper, cocoa and timber are also important. One quarter of the labour force is involved in agriculture, mainly growing rice as a subsistence

crop. Manufacturing industry is the largest exporter; major industries include rubber, tin, timber, textiles, machinery and cement. The government has greatly encouraged industrialization, investment and a more active role for the ethnic Malay population in industry, which – with commerce and finance – has been largely the preserve of Chinese Malaysians. Malaysia has experienced high economic growth rates since the early 1980s. The tourist industry is being actively promoted.

RECENT HISTORY
1841–1946: The British Brooke family ('White Rajas') ruled Sarawak. **1867:** British Straits Settlements administration founded. **1881:** North Borneo (later Sabah) became British. **1940–45:** Japanese occupation during World War II. **1948:** Federation of (peninsular) Malaya founded. **1948–60:** Communist insurgency in Malaya. **1957:** Independence. **1963:** Sabah, Sarawak and Singapore joined Malaya to establish Malaysia. **1965:** Singapore withdrew. **1965–66:** Confrontation against Indonesian territorial claims in Borneo. **1969–71:** Racial unrest.

THE MALDIVES

Area: 298 km² (115 sq mi). *Population:* 213 000 (1990 census). *Capital:* Malé 55 000 (1990 census). *Language:* Dhivehi (Maldivian; official). *Religion:* Sunni Islam (official). *Government:* Republic – non-party system with executive presidency.

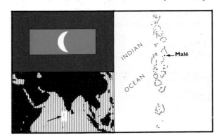

GEOGRAPHY
The country is a chain of over 1190 small low-lying coral islands, of which 203 are inhabited. The climate is tropical with heavy rainfall brought by the monsoon between May and August.

ECONOMIC ACTIVITY
Tourism is the mainstay of the economy. About 25% of Maldivians subsist on fish and coconuts.

RECENT HISTORY
1887–1965: British protectorate of the Maldives. **1965:** Independence.

MALI

Area: 1 240 192 km² (478 841 sq mi). *Population:* 8 299 000 (1987 census). *Languages:* French (official), Bambara (60%). *Religions:* Sunni Islam (90%), animist (9%). *Government:* Republic – multi-party system with executive presidency.

GEOGRAPHY
The low-lying plains of Mali rise to 1155 m (3789 ft) in the Adrar des Iforas range in the NE. The S is savannah; the Sahara Desert is in the N. Mali is hot and largely dry, although the S has a wet season from June to October.

ECONOMIC ACTIVITY
Drought in the 1970s and 1980s devastated Mali's livestock herds. Only one fifth of Mali can be cultivated, producing mainly rice, millet and sorghum for domestic use, and cotton for export.

RECENT HISTORY
1880–95: France conquered Mali, establishing the colony of French Sudan. **1960:** Independence.

1968–90: Military governments. 1979–92: Single-party state. 1992: Multi-party system restored.

MALTA

Area: 316 km² (122 sq mi). *Population:* 357 000 (1991 est). *Capital:* Valletta 204 000 (city 9200) (1991 est). *Languages:* Maltese and English (official). *Religion:* Roman Catholic (official; 98%). *Government:* Republic – multi-party parliamentary system.

GEOGRAPHY
The three inhabited islands of Malta, Gozo and Comino consist of low limestone plateaux with little surface water. The climate is Mediterranean with hot dry summers and cooler wetter winters.

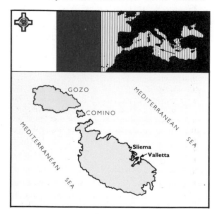

ECONOMIC ACTIVITY
The main industries are footwear and clothing, food processing and shiprepairing. Tourism is the main foreign-currency earner. Malta is virtually self-sufficient in agricultural products.

RECENT HISTORY
1939–45: Malta beseiged during World War II. 1964: Independence after over 160 years of British rule.

MARSHALL ISLANDS

Area: 180 km² (70 sq mi). *Population:* 49 000 (1991 est). *Capital:* Dalap-Uliga-Darrit (on Majuro) 20 000 (1990 est). *Languages:* Marshallese and English. *Religions:* Various Protestant Churches (over 50%), Roman Catholic minority. *Government:* Republic – effectively non-party system with executive presidency.

GEOGRAPHY
The Marshall Islands comprise over 1150 small

---

coral atolls and islands below 6 m (20 ft) high. The tropical climate has heavy rainfall.

ECONOMIC ACTIVITY
With practically no resources, the islands depend on subsistence farming, tourism and US grants.

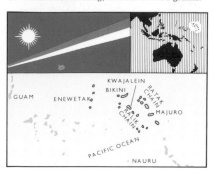

RECENT HISTORY
1885–1914: German rule. 1914–45: Japanese administration. 1945–86: Part of the US Pacific Islands Trust Territory. 1986: US administration ended. 1990: Independence; UN trusteeship terminated.

MAURITANIA

Area: 1 030 700 km² (397 950 sq mi). *Population:* 2 053 000 (1991 est). *Capital:* Nouakchott 600 000 (city 393 000; 1988 census). *Languages:* Arabic (official; 81%); French. *Religion:* Sunni Islam (official; 99%). *Government:* Republic – limited multi-party system with executive presidency.

GEOGRAPHY
Isolated peaks rise above the plateaux of the Sahara Desert that cover most of Mauritania. The climate is hot and dry, with adequate rainfall only in the S.

ECONOMIC ACTIVITY
Persistant drought has devastated the nomads' herds of cattle and sheep. Fish from the Atlantic and iron ore are virtually the only exports.

RECENT HISTORY
1903: France annexed the Arab emirates inland to the coastal colony. 1960: Independence. 1976–79: Mauritania occupied S of (former Spanish) Western Sahara. 1979–92: Military governments; single-party state. 1992: Multi-party system restored.

MAURITIUS

Area: 2040 km² (788 sq mi). *Population:* 1 087 000 (1991 est). *Capital:* Port Louis 142 000 (1990 est). *Languages:* English (official), Creole (nearly 30%), Hindi (over 20%). *Religions:* Hindu (51%), Roman Catholic (25%). *Government:* Republic – multi-party parliamentary system.

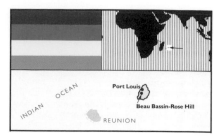

GEOGRAPHY
The central plateau of Mauritius is surrounded by mountains, including Piton de la Riviere Noire (826 m / 2711 ft). Other islands in the group include Rodrigues and the Agalega Islands. The subtropical climate can be very hot from December to April. Rainfall is high in the uplands.

ECONOMIC ACTIVITY
The export of sugar cane dominates the economy. Diversification is being encouraged, and light industry – in particular clothing – and tourism are of increasing importance.

RECENT HISTORY
1968: Independence after over 150 years of British rule. 1992: Republic declared.

MEXICO

Area: 1 958 201 km² (756 066 sq mi). *Population:* 83 151 000 (1991 est). *Capital and major cities:* Mexico City 19 480 000 (city 13 636 000), Guadalajara 3 187 000 (city 2 847 000), Monterrey 2 859 000 (city 2 522 000) (1990 census). *Languages:* Spanish (official; 92%). *Religion:* Roman Catholic (91%). *Government:* Federal republic – multi-party system with executive presidency.

GEOGRAPHY
Between the E and W ranges of the Sierra Madre mountains is a large high central plateau. Volcanoes include Volcán Citlaltepetl (Pico de Orizaba) at 5610 m (18 405 ft), the country's highest point. The coastal plains are generally narrow in the W, but wider in the E. The Yucatán Peninsula in the SE is a broad limestone lowland; Baja California in the NW is a long narrow mountainous peninsula. There is considerable climatic variation, in part reflecting the complexity of the relief. In general, the S and the coastal lowlands are tropical; the central plateau and the mountains are cooler and drier.

ECONOMIC ACTIVITY
Over one fifth of the labour force is involved in agriculture and many Mexicans are still subsistence farmers growing maize, wheat, kidney beans and rice. Coffee, cotton, fruit and vegetables are the most important export crops. Mexico is the world's leading producer of silver. The exploitation of large reserves of natural gas and petrol-

eum enabled the country's spectacular economic development in the 1970s and 1980s. An expanding industrial base includes important petrochemical, textile, motor-vehicle and food-processing industries. Economic problems remain, and high unemployment has stimulated immigration – often illegal – to the US.

RECENT HISTORY
1876–80 and **1888–1910:** Dictatorship of Porfirio Díaz. **1910:** Beginning of Mexican revolution. **1916–17:** US expeditionary force sent against the outlaw Pancho Vılla. **From 1924:** The revolution became anticlerical; persecution of the Church. **1929:** Order restored by Institutional Revolutionary Party (PRI). **1929–89:** PRI had a virtual monopoly of power. **Since 1990:** More liberal economic and political climate.

MICRONESIA

Area: 702 km² (271 sq mi). *Population:* 111 000 (1991 est). *Capital and major town:* Kolonia 6300 (1990 est). A new capital – Palikir – is under construction on Pohnpei. *Languages:* English, Trukese, Ponapean, Yapese, Kosraean. *Religions:* Various Protestant Churches. *Government:* Federal republic – effectively non-party system with executive presidency.

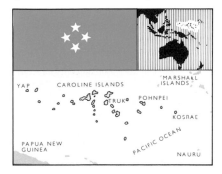

GEOGRAPHY
The 600 Micronesian islands – which are in two main groups – are mainly low coral atolls, but Kosrae and Pohnpei are mountainous. The climate is tropical with heavy rainfall.

ECONOMIC ACTIVITY
Apart from phosphate, the islands have practically no resources and depend upon subsistence agriculture, fishing, US grants and tourism.

RECENT HISTORY
1874–99: Spanish rule in what were known as the Carolines. **1899–1914:** German rule. **1914–45:** Japanese rule. **1945–86:** Part of the US Pacific Trust Territory. **1986:** US administration ended. **1990:** Independence; UN trusteeship terminated.

MOLDOVA

Formerly known as Moldavia. *Area:* 33 700 km² (13 000 sq mi). *Population:* 4 367 000 (1991 est). *Capital:* Chisinau (formerly Kishinev) 720 000 (1989 census). *Languages:* Romanian (64%), Ukrainian (14%), Russian (13%). *Religion:* Orthodox majority. *Government:* Republic – limited multi-party system with executive presidency.

GEOGRAPHY
Moldova comprises a hilly plain between the River Prut and the Dnestr valley. The country experiences a mild, slightly continental climate.

ECONOMIC ACTIVITY
Large collective farms produce fruit (particularly grapes for wine), vegetables, wheat, maize, tobacco and sunflower seed. Industries include food processing and machine building. Little progress has been made to privatize agriculture and industry.

RECENT HISTORY
1878–1918: Russian rule in Moldavia. **1918:** Short-lived Moldavian republic. **1918–44:** Part of Romania. **1944–91:** Part of USSR. **1991:** Independence upon dissolution of USSR. **1992:** Civil war; attempted secession of Slavic minorities in Trans-Dnestr; CIS forces intervened.

MONACO

Area: 2.21 km² (0.85 sq mi). *Population:* 29 900 (1990 est). *Capital and major cities:* Monaco 1200, Monte-Carlo 13 200 (1990 est). *Languages:* French (official), Monegasque. *Religion:* Roman Catholic (90%). *Government:* Principality – effectively non-party parliamentary system.

GEOGRAPHY
Monaco consists of a rocky peninsula and a narrow stretch of coast. Since 1958 the area has increased by one fifth through reclamation of land from the sea. The climate is Mediterranean.

ECONOMIC ACTIVITY
Monaco depends upon real estate, banking, insurance, light industry and tourism.

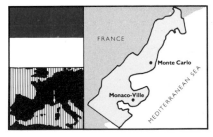

RECENT HISTORY
Since 1861: Monaco has been under French protection. **1962:** Liberal constitution granted.

MONGOLIA

Area: 1 565 000 km² (604 250 sq mi). *Population:* 2 156 000 (1992 est). *Capital:* Ulan Bator (Ulaan Baatar) 575 000 (1991 est). *Language:* Khalkh Mongolian (official; 78%). *Religion:* Buddhism (suppressed from 1924 to 1990). *Government:* Republic – multi-party system with executive presidency.

GEOGRAPHY
Mongolia comprises mountains in the N, a series of basins in the centre, and the Gobi Desert and Altai Mountains – rising to Mönh Hayrhan Uul (4362 m / 14 311 ft) – in the S. The climate is dry with generally mild summers and severely cold winters.

ECONOMIC ACTIVITY
Mongolia depends on collectivized animal herding (cattle, sheep and goats). Cereals and fodder crops are grown on a large scale on state farms. Industry is dominated by food processing, hides and wool. Copper accounts for 40% of Mongolia's exports.

The former USSR was Mongolia's principal trading partner, but trade has been disrupted since 1991, leading to severe economic difficulties.

RECENT HISTORY
1913: 'Outer Mongolia' gained autonomy from China. **1919–21:** Chinese rule restored. **1921:** Independence. **1924:** Communist People's Republic established. **1990:** Multi-party system established.

MONTENEGRO (see YUGOSLAVIA

MOROCCO

Area: 458 730 km² (177 115 sq mi), excluding the disputed Western Sahara – see below. *Population:* 25 208 000 (1990 est) excluding Western Sahara. *Capital and major cities:* Rabat 1 472 000 (including Salé), Casablanca (Dar el Beida) 3 210 000, Marrakesh 1 517 000 (all including suburbs; 1990 est). *Languages:* Arabic (official; 75%), Berber, French. *Religion:* Sunni Islam (official; 98%). *Government:* Kingdom – multi-party parliamentary system.

GEOGRAPHY
The Grand, Middle and Anti Atlas Mountains in the W and N rise at Jebel Toubkal to 4165 m (13 665 ft). The E is an arid plateau. Much of the country – including the disputed Western Sahara territory – is semiarid or desert. The N has a Mediterranean climate with hot dry summers and warm wetter winters.

ECONOMIC ACTIVITY
Over 30% of the labour force is involved in agriculture, producing mainly citrus fruits, grapes (for wine) and vegetables for export, and wheat and barley for domestic consumption. Morocco is the world's leading exporter of phosphates. Other resources include iron ore, lead and zinc. Many important industries and services are in state ownership. Tourism is growing.

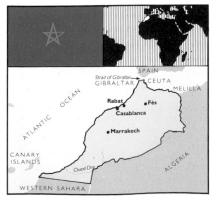

RECENT HISTORY

Late 19th century: Spain secured long-claimed coastal areas in Morocco. **1905–6** and **1911:** 'Moroccan Crises'; French interests in Morocco challenged by Germany. **1912:** French protectorate established. **1925:** Rif rebellion against French rule. **1956:** Independence. **1975:** Morocco annexed (former Spanish) Western Sahara. **1991:** Ceasefire in Western Sahara.

WESTERN SAHARA

Area: 266 000 km² (102 676 sq mi). *Population:* 185 000 (1985 est). *Capital:* El-Aaiun (Laayoune).

MOZAMBIQUE

Area: 799 380 km² (308 641 sq mi). *Population:* 15 656 000 (1991 est). *Capital:* Maputo 1 070 000 (including suburbs; 1989 est). *Languages:* Portuguese (official), Makua-Lomwe (52%). *Religions:* Animist (60%), Sunni Islam (16%), Roman Catholic (15%). *Government:* Republic – restricted multi-party system with executive presidency.

GEOGRAPHY

The Zambezi River separates high plateaux in the N from lowlands in the S where isolated mountains include Mount Bingo at 2436 m (7992 ft). The climate is tropical, with maximum rainfall and temperatures from November to March.

ECONOMIC ACTIVITY

Over 80% of the labour force is involved in farming, mainly growing cassava and maize. Fishing is a major employer – prawns and shrimps make up nearly 50% of Mozambique's exports. In terms of GDP per head, Mozambique is the poorest state on earth. Its economy has been devastated by civil war and drought, and famine is widespread.

RECENT HISTORY

End of 19th century: Portugal gained control of all of Mozambique. **1964–75:** Frelimo movement led guerrilla war against Portuguese rule. **1975:** Independence under Frelimo. **1975–90:** Marxist-Leninist one-party state. **1982–92:** Civil war; government forces confronted Renamo guerrilla movement. **1989:** Frelimo abandoned Marxism. **1991:** Multi-party politics permitted. **1992:** Ceasefire in civil war; UN presence in Mozambique agreed.

MYANMAR (BURMA)

The name Burma was officially dropped in May 1989. *Area:* 676 552 km² (261 218 sq mi). *Population:* 42 561 000 (1991 est). *Capital:* Rangoon (Yangon) 2 513 000 (1983 census). *Languages:* Burmese (official; 80%), Karen, Mon, Shan, Kachin. *Religion:* Buddhist (80%). *Government:* Republic – military government.

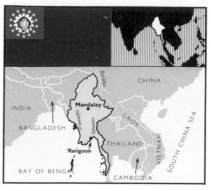

GEOGRAPHY

The N and W of Burma are mountainous, rising to Hkakado Razi (5881 m / 19 296 ft). The Shan Plateau occupies the E. Central Burma (the Irrawaddy valley) and the S are lowlands. Burma is tropical, experiencing monsoon rains – up to 5000 mm (200 in) in the S – from May to October.

ECONOMIC ACTIVITY

Burma is rich in agriculture, timber, and minerals, but because of poor communications, lack of development and serious rebellions by a number of ethnic minorities, the country has been unable to realize its potential. Subsistence farming involves the majority of the labour force.

RECENT HISTORY

1885: British annexation of Burma completed. **1940–45:** Japanese occupation during World War II. **1948:** Independence. **Since 1948:** Karen, Shan, Mon and other ethnic groups have conducted armed campaigns for autonomy. **1962:** Military coup by General Ne Win; state of official isolationism. **1990:** Multi-party elections; army denied power to winning party (led by Aung San Suu Kyi).

NAMIBIA

Area: 823 168 km² (317 827 sq mi) – excluding the South African enclave of Walvis Bay. *Population:* 1 334 000 (1991 est). *Capital:* Windhoek 115 000 (1988 est). *Languages:* Afrikaans and English (both official). *Religions:* Lutheran (30%), Roman Catholic (20%), other Christian Churches (30%). *Government:* Republic – multi-party system with executive presidency.

GEOGRAPHY

The coastal Namib Desert stretches 160 km (100 mi) inland and contains the highest point, the Brandberg, at 2579 m (8461 ft). Beyond the Central

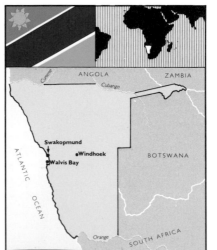

Plateau, the Kalahari Desert occupies the E. The tropical climate is hot and dry with average coastal rainfall under 100 mm (4 in).

ECONOMIC ACTIVITY

Over one third of the labour force is involved in agriculture, mainly raising cattle and sheep, but the country is prone to drought. The economy depends upon exports of diamonds and uranium, and is closely tied to South Africa.

RECENT HISTORY

1884: German protectorate of South West Africa proclaimed. **1903–04:** Massacre of three quarters of the Herero people by the Germans. **1915:** South West Africa taken by South Africa during World War I. **1919:** South African League of Nations mandate established. **1960s:** SWAPO guerrilla movement began campaign against South African rule. **1989:** Ceasefire; UN-supervised elections. **1990:** Independence.

NAURU

Area: 21 km² (8 sq mi). *Population:* 9400 (1990 est). *Capital:* No official capital; Yaren (the major settlement) is capital *de facto*. *Languages:* Nauruan (official), English. *Religions:* Nauruan Protestant Church (majority), Roman Catholic (minority). *Government:* Republic – effectively non-party system with executive presidency.

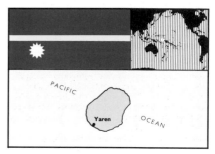

GEOGRAPHY

Nauru is a low-lying coral atoll. Its tropical climate has heavy rainfall, particularly between November and February.

ECONOMIC ACTIVITY

Nauru depends almost entirely upon the export of phosphate rock, stocks of which are expected to run out after 1995. Shipping and air services and 'tax haven' facilities are planned to provide revenue when the phosphate is exhausted.

RECENT HISTORY

1888: Nauru annexed by Germany. **1914–42:** Australian administration. **1942–45:** Japanese occupation during World War II. **1945–68:** Australian administration. **1968:** Independence.

NEPAL

Area: 147 181 km² (56 827 sq mi). *Population:* 19 379 000 (1991 est). *Capital:* Kathmandu 420 000 (city 235 000; 1987 est). *Languages:* Nepali (official; 53%), Bihari (19%), Maithir (12%). *Religion:* Hindu (official; 90%). *Government:* Kingdom – multi-party parliamentary system.

GEOGRAPHY

In the S are densely populated subtropical lowlands. A hilly central belt is divided by fertile valleys. The Himalaya dominate the N, and include Mount Everest – 8863 m / 29 078 ft – on the Chinese border. The climate varies between the subtropical S and the glacial Himalaya. All of Nepal experiences the monsoon.

ECONOMIC ACTIVITY

Nepal is one of the least developed countries in the

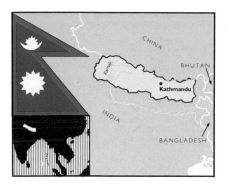

world. Most of the labour force is involved in subsistence farming, mainly growing rice, barley and maize. Forestry is important, but increased farming has led to deforestation.

RECENT HISTORY
1846–1950: Power in Nepal exercised by Rana family of hereditary PMs. **1958–60:** Constitutional rule. **1960–90:** Royal autocracy. **1990:** Constitutional multi-party rule restored.

THE NETHERLANDS

Area: 41 785 km² (16 140 sq mi), or 33 937 km² (13 103 sq mi) excluding freshwater. *Population:* 15 065 000 (1991 est). *Capital and major cities:* Amsterdam – capital in name only – 1 062 000 (city 702 000), The Hague ('s Gravenhage) – the seat of government and administration – 690 000 (city 444 000), Rotterdam 1 051 000 (city 582 000) (1991 est). *Language:* Dutch (official). *Religions:* Roman Catholic (under 30%), Netherlands Reformed Church (17%), Reformed Churches (Calvinistic; 8%). *Government:* Kingdom – multi-party parliamentary system.

DEPENDENCIES
(with areas, populations in 1990–91 and capitals)
Aruba – 193 km² (75 sq mi), 66 000, Oranjestad.
Netherlands Antilles or The Antilles of the Five – 800 km² (309 sq mi), 191 000, Willemstad.

GEOGRAPHY
Over one quarter of the Netherlands – one of the world's most densely populated countries – lies below sea level. A network of canals and canalized rivers cross the W where sand dunes and man-made dykes protect low-lying areas and polders (land reclaimed from the sea). The coast has been straightened by sea walls protecting Zeeland in the SW and enclosing a freshwater lake, the IJsselmeer, in the N. The E comprises low sandy plains, rising to 321 m (1053 ft). The maritime temperate climate gives cool summers and mild winters.

ECONOMIC ACTIVITY
Despite having few natural resources – except natural gas – the Netherlands has a high standard

of living. Agriculture and horticulture are highly mechanized with a concentration on dairying and glasshouse crops, particularly flowers. Food processing is a major industry, and the country is a leading exporter of cheese. Manufacturing includes chemical, machinery, petroleum refining, metallurgical and electrical engineering industries. Raw materials are imported through Rotterdam, which is the largest port in the world and serves much of Western Europe. Banking and finance are well developed.

RECENT HISTORY
1914–18: Neutral during World War I. **1940–45:** German occupation during World War II. **1949:** Indonesian independence recognized. **Since 1957:** Founder member of EC.

NEW ZEALAND

Area: 269 057 km² (103 883 sq mi). *Population:* 3 425 000 (1991 census). *Capital and major cities:* Wellington 325 000 (city 150 000), Auckland 885 000 (city 316 000) (1991 census). *Languages:* English (official), Maori. *Religions:* Anglican (24%), Presbyterian (18%), Roman Catholic (15%). *Government:* Dominion – multi-party parliamentary system.

DEPENDENT AND ASSOCIATED TERRITORIES
(with areas, population in 1989–91 and capitals)
Ross Dependency – 450 000 km² (175 000 sq mi), uninhabited.
Tokelau (legally part of New Zealand) – 13 km² (5 sq mi), 1700, no capital.
Cook Islands – 234 km² (90 sq mi), 19 000, Avarua.
Niue – 259 km² (100 sq mi), 2300, Alofi.

GEOGRAPHY
Mountains run from N to S through South Island, and in the SW reach the sea in the deeply indented coast of Fjordland. The Southern Alps rise at Mount Cook to 3754 m (12 315 ft). The Canterbury Plains lie to the E of the mountains. North Island is mainly hilly with isolated mountains and two active volcanoes. Lowlands on North Island are largely restricted to the coast and the Waikato Valley. The climate is temperate, although the N is warmer. Rainfall is abundant, rising to over 6350 mm (250 in) on the W coast of South Island.

ECONOMIC ACTIVITY
The majority of New Zealand's export earnings come from agriculture, in particular meat, wool and dairy products. Forestry is expanding and supports an important pulp and paper industry. Apart from coal, lignite, natural gas and gold, the country has few natural resources, although its considerable hydroelectric-power potential has been exploited to produce plentiful cheap elec-

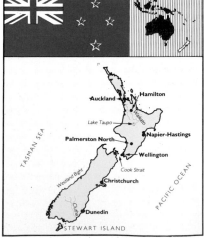

tricity. Natural gas is converted to liquid fuel. Despite its small domestic market and being remote from the world's major industrial powers, New Zealand has a high standard of living.

RECENT HISTORY
1907: Dominion status (not formally acknowledged by New Zealand until 1947). **1914–18:** Fought as a British ally in World War I; Gallipoli campaign (1915). **1939–45:** Active in World War II, in particular against Japan in the Pacific. **Since 1945:** Postwar alliance with Australia and USA in ANZUS pact. **Since 1973:** New trading links with the Far and Middle East.

NICARAGUA

Area: 120 254 km² (46 430 sq mi). *Population:* 4 000 000 (1991 est). *Capital:* Managua 979 000 (city 682 000; 1988 est). *Language:* Spanish (official). *Religion:* Roman Catholic (88%). *Government:* Republic – multi-party system with executive presidency.

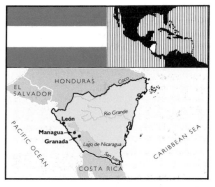

GEOGRAPHY
Most Nicaraguans live on a fertile plain on the Pacific coast. Central mountain ranges rise to Pico Mogotón at 2107 m (6913 ft). The humid tropical climate has a rainy season from May to October.

ECONOMIC ACTIVITY
The largely agricultural economy was devastated by guerrilla warfare and hurricanes in the 1980s. Strict austerity measures are in force. Coffee, cotton and sugar cane are the main exports.

RECENT HISTORY
1912–25 and **1927–33:** US intervention. **1937–79:** Dictatorship of the Somoza family. **1974–79:** Growing popular uprising led by the Sandinista guerrilla army. **1979–90:** Left-wing Sandinista government; accused of being Communist by the USA, which backed right-wing Contra guerrillas. **1989:** Ceasefire agreed. **1990:** Sandinistas defeated in multi-party elections.

NIGER

Area: 1 267 000 km² (489 191 sq mi). *Population:* 8 024 000 (1991 est). *Capital:* Niamey 398 000 (1988 census). *Languages:* French (official), Hausa (85%). *Religion:* Sunni Islam (85%). *Government:* Republic – interim government pending restoration of multi-party system with executive presidency.

GEOGRAPHY
Most of Niger lies in the Sahara Desert; the S and the Niger Valley are savannah. The central Aïr Mountains rise to 2000 m (6562 ft). Niger is dry and hot. The S has a rainy season from June to October.

ECONOMIC ACTIVITY
Livestock herds and harvests of subsistence crops – millet, sorghum, cassava and rice – have been reduced by desertification. Uranium is mined.

However, a combination of falling petroleum prices and OPEC quotas has resulted in major economic problems, although it has also encouraged diversification. There are major reserves of natural gas and coal. Industries include petrochemicals, textiles and food processing. Over 60% of the labour force is involved in agriculture, mainly producing maize, sorghum, cassava, yams and rice as subsistence crops. Cocoa is an important export.

RECENT HISTORY
1914: British coastal protectorate and inland colonies united to form Nigeria. **1960:** Independence. **Since 1960:** Regional rivalries led to instability and recurrent military coups; unwieldy federal structure constantly revised, increasing the number of states from 3 to 30. **1967–70:** Civil war; Eastern Region – the homeland of the Ibo – attempted to secede as Biafra. **1993:** Scheduled return of civilian rule.

RECENT HISTORY
1901: French territory of Niger proclaimed. **1960:** Independence. **1974–92:** Military governments; single-party state. **1992:** Multi-party system restored.

NIGERIA

Area: 923 768 km² (356 669 sq mi). **Population:** 88 514 000 (1991 census) – previous World Bank and UN estimates of Nigeria's population are 20 000 000 higher than the figure recorded in the 1991 census. **Capital and major cities:** Abuja (new federal capital) 379 000, Lagos 5 686 000 (city 1 340 000) (1991 census). **Languages:** English (official), over 150 local languages including Hausa, Yoruba and Ibo. **Religions:** Sunni Islam (48%), various Protestant Churches (17%), Roman Catholic (17%). **Government:** Federal republic – military government pending introduction of dual party system with executive presidency.

GEOGRAPHY
Inland from the swampy tropical jungles of the coastal plains, Nigeria comprises a series of plateaux mainly covered by open woodland or savannah. The far N is semi-desert. Isolated ranges of hills, rising above the plateaux, include the central Jos Plateau and the Biu Plateau in the NE. Vogel Peak (Dimlang) – near the Cameroon border – rises to 2042 m (6700 ft). The coastal areas are very humid and hot. Rainfall is heavy on the coast but decreases gradually inland – although there is a rainy season from April to October. The dry far N experiences the Harmattan, a hot wind blowing out of the Sahara.

ECONOMIC ACTIVITY
Nigeria – the major economic power in West Africa – depends upon revenue from petroleum exports.

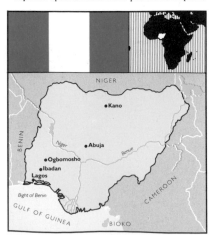

NORWAY

Area: 323 878 km² (125 050 sq mi), or 386 958 km² (149 469 sq mi) including the Arctic island territories of Svalbard (formerly known as Spitsbergen) and Jan Mayen. **Population:** 4 250 000 (1991 est). **Capital:** Oslo 462 000 (1991 est). **Languages:** Two official forms of Norwegian – Bokmaal (80%), Nynorsk (or Landsmaal; 20%); Lappish. **Religion:** Lutheran (official; 92%). **Government:** Kingdom – multi-party parliamentary system.

ANTARCTIC TERRITORIES
(with areas)
Bouvet Island – 50 km² (90 sq mi), uninhabited.
Peter I Island – 180 km² (69 sq mi), uninhabited.
Queen Maud Land – as no inland limit to the Norwegian claim in Antarctica has been made no estimate of the area can be made.

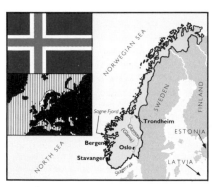

GEOGRAPHY
Norway's coastline is characterized by fjords, a series of long narrow inlets formed by glacial action. The greater part of Norway comprises highlands of hard rock. Galdhøpiggen – the highest peak – reaches 2469 m (8098 ft). The principal lowlands are along the Skagerrak coast and around Oslo and Trondheim. Svalbard is a bleak Arctic archipelago. Norway's temperate climate is the result of the warming Gulf Stream. Summers are remarkably mild for the latitude, while winters are long and very cold. Precipitation is heavy but there are marked rain shadows inland.

ECONOMIC ACTIVITY
Norway enjoys a high standard of living. Agriculture is heavily subsidized and only a small proportion of the land can be cultivated – chiefly for fodder crops for dairy cattle. Timber is a major export for Norway, over 50% of which is forested. Fishing is an important foreign-currency earner, and fish farming is taking the place of whaling and deep-sea fishing. Manufacturing is now dominated by petrochemicals and allied industries, based upon large reserves of petroleum and natural gas in Norway's sector of the North Sea. Petroleum and natural gas supply over one third of the

country's export earnings. The development of industries such as electrical engineering has been helped by cheap hydroelectric power.

RECENT HISTORY
Before 1905: Norwegian union with Sweden, although Norway had a considerable degree of independence. **1905:** Complete independence as a separate kingdom. **1940–45:** German occupation during World War II; puppet government of Vidkun Quisling. **1972:** Norway rejected EC membership. **1992:** Norway reapplied to EC.

OMAN

Area: 300 000 km² (120 000 sq mi). **Population:** 1 502 000 (1991 est). **Capital:** Muscat 380 000 (city 85 000; 1990 est). **Language:** Arabic (official). **Religions:** Ibadi Islam (75%), Sunni Islam (25%). **Government:** Sultanate – absolute monarchy.

GEOGRAPHY
A barren range of hills rises sharply behind a narrow coastal plain and reaches 3170 m (10 400 ft) at Jabal ash Sham. Desert extends inland into the Rub' al Khali ('The Empty Quarter'). A detached portion of Oman lies N of the United Arab Emirates. Oman is arid and very hot in the summer, but milder in the winter and the mountains.

ECONOMIC ACTIVITY
Oman depends almost entirely upon exports of petroleum and natural gas. Owing to aridity, less than 1% of Oman is cultivated.

RECENT HISTORY
1891–1951: British protectorate. **1970:** Palace coup; Sultan Qaboos came to power. **1970s:** Beginning of reforms to modernize Oman; left-wing separatist guerrillas in the S.

PAKISTAN

Area: 803 943 km² (310 403 sq mi), or 888 102 km² (333 897 sq mi), including the Pakistani-held areas of Kashmir (known as Azad Kashmir) and the disputed Northern Areas (Gilgit, Baltistan and Diamir). **Population:** 126 406 000 (1991 est; including the Pakistani-held areas of Kashmir – Azad Kashmir – and the disputed Northern Areas). **Capital and major cities:** Islamabad 266 000, Karachi 6 771 000, Lahore 3 850 000 (all including suburbs; 1992 est). **Languages:** Urdu (national; 20%), Punjabi (60%), Sindhi (12%), Pushto, Baluchi. **Religions:** Sunni Islam (official; 92%), Shia Islam (5%). **Government:** Federal republic – multi-party parliamentary system.

GEOGRAPHY
The Indus Valley divides Pakistan into a highland region in the W and a lowland region in the E. In the S (Baluchistan) the highlands comprise hills and low mountains running NE to SW. In the N

(the North-West Frontier Province and the disputed areas) mountain chains rise to over 7000 m (21 300 ft) and include the Karakoram, parts of the Himalaya and the Hindu Kush. The highest point is K2 (Mount Godwin Austen), at 8607 m (28 238 ft) the second highest peak in the world. The Indus Valley – and the valleys of its tributaries – form a major agricultural region and contain the majority of Pakistan's population. A continuation of the Indian Thar Desert occupies the E. The N and W of Pakistan are arid; the S and much of the E experience a form of the tropical monsoon. Temperatures vary dramatically from the hot tropical coast to the cold mountains of the far N.

ECONOMIC ACTIVITY
One half of the labour force is involved in subsistence farming, with wheat and rice as the main crops. Cotton is the main foreign-currency earner. Irrigation schemes are being encouraged, but over 50% of the cultivated land is subject to either waterlogging or salinity. Mineral reserves – including coal, gold and copper – have not been extensively developed. Manufacturing is dominated by food processing, textiles and consumer goods. Unemployment and underemployment are major problems, and the country relies heavily upon foreign aid and money sent back by Pakistanis working abroad.

RECENT HISTORY
1947: Partition of British India; Pakistan formed as a Muslim state, comprising W Pakistan (the present state) and E Pakistan (now Bangladesh). **1947–49** and **1965:** War with India over Kashmir, which was effectively partitioned. **1947–85:** Political instability; periods of military rule. **1970:** Secession of Bangladesh during civil war between Pakistan's two wings; war with India. **Since 1985:** Multi-party civilian rule restored.

PANAMA

Area: 77 082 km² (29 762 sq mi) including the former Canal Zone. **Population:** 2 466 000 (1991 est). **Capital:** Panama City 828 000 (city 585 000; 1990 census). **Language:** Spanish (official). **Religion:** Roman Catholic (85%). **Government:** Republic – multi-party system with executive presidency.

GEOGRAPHY
Panama is a heavily forested mountainous isthmus joining Central America to South America. The highest point is the extinct volcano Baru (Chiriqui) at 3475 m (11 467 ft). The tropical climate has little seasonal change.

ECONOMIC ACTIVITY
Income from the Panama Canal is a major foreign-currency earner. Panama – which has a higher standard of living than its neighbours – has become an important 'offshore' banking centre. Major exports include bananas and shrimps.

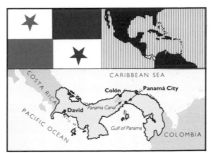

RECENT HISTORY
1903: Independence from Colombia. **1914:** Panama Canal opened. **1914–79:** USA controlled Panama Canal Zone. **1983–89:** Dictatorship of General Manuel Noriega – deposed by US invasion (1989). **1989:** Constitutional multi-party rule restored.

PAPUA NEW GUINEA

Area: 462 840 km² (178 704 sq mi). **Population:** 3 790 000 (1990 census). **Capital:** Port Moresby 193 000 (city 174 000; 1990 census). **Languages:** English (official), Pidgin English, over 700 local languages. **Religions:** Roman Catholic (33%), Protestant Churches (over 60%). **Government:** Dominion – multi-party parliamentary system.

GEOGRAPHY
Broad swampy plains surround New Guinea's mountainous interior, which rises to Mount Wilhelm at 4509 m (14 493 ft). Tropical New Guinea has high temperatures and heavy monsoonal rainfall.

ECONOMIC ACTIVITY
About 70% of the labour force is involved in agriculture – mainly subsistence farming – although agricultural exports include coffee, cocoa and coconuts. The economy depends upon the export of copper, gold and silver.

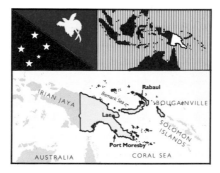

RECENT HISTORY
1884: British protectorate established in SE New Guinea; German colony founded in the NE. **1906:** British area transferred to Australia and renamed Papua. **1914:** Australia occupied German New Guinea. **1914–75:** Australian rule. **1942–45:** Japan occupied New Guinea and part of Papua. **1949:** Unification of Papua New Guinea. **1975:** Independence. **1990–92:** Bougainville rebellion.

PARAGUAY

Area: 406 752 km² (157 048 sq mi). **Population:** 4 279 000 (1990 est). **Capital:** Asunción 732 000 (city 608 000; 1990 est). **Languages:** Spanish (official; 7%), Guaraní (40%), bilingual Guaraní-Spanish (48%). **Religion:** Roman Catholic (official; 97%). **Government:** Republic – multi-party system with executive presidency.

GEOGRAPHY
The country W of the Paraguay River – the Chaco – is a flat semiarid plain. The region E of the river is a partly forested undulating plateau. The climate is subtropical with considerable variation in rainfall between the wet SE and the dry W.

ECONOMIC ACTIVITY
Agriculture – the main economic activity – is dominated by cattle ranching, cotton and soyabeans. Cheap hydroelectric power from dams on the Paraná has greatly stimulated industry.

RECENT HISTORY
1929–35: Wars with Bolivia. **1954–89:** Dictatorship of Alfredo Stroessner. **1989:** Military coup; constitutional rule restored.

PERU

Area: 1 285 216 km² (496 225 sq mi). **Population:** 22 881 000 (1991 est). **Capital:** Lima 6 405 000 (city 5 494 000; 1990 est). **Languages:** Spanish (68%), Quechua (27%) and Aymara (%) – all official. **Religion:** Roman Catholic (official; 91%). **Government:** Republic – multi-party system with executive presidency.

GEOGRAPHY
The coastal plain is narrow and arid. The Andes run in three high parallel ridges from N to S, rising at Huascaran to 6768 m (22 205 ft). Nearly two thirds of Peru is tropical forest (the Selva) in the Amazon Basin. A wide climatic variety includes semitropical desert – cooled by the Humboldt Current – on the coast, the very cold Alpine High Andes and the tropical Selva with a heavy rainfall.

ECONOMIC ACTIVITY
About one third of the labour force is involved in agriculture. Subsistence farming dominates in the interior; crops for export are more important near the coast. Major crops include coffee, sugar cane, cotton and potatoes, as well as coca for cocaine.

Sheep, llamas, vicuñas and alpacas are kept for wool. Rich natural resources include copper, petroleum and lead. The fishing industry – once the world's largest – has declined since 1971. A combination of natural disasters, a very high birth rate, guerrilla warfare and the declining value of exports have severely damaged the economy.

RECENT HISTORY
1941: War against Ecuador; Peru gained Amazonian territory. **1975–80:** Right-wing military government. **Since 1980:** Growth of extreme left-wing Sendero Luminoso ('Shining Path') guerrilla movement. **1980–92:** Constitutional rule. **1992:** Coup effected by president; constitution temporarily suspended.

THE PHILIPPINES

Area: 300 001 km² (115 831 sq mi). *Population:* 62 354 000 (1991 est). *Capital:* Manila 7 832 000 (city 1 599 000; 1990 census). *Languages:* Pilipino (based on Tagalog; national; 55%), Tagalog (over 20%), Cebuano (over 20%), English, Spanish. *Religion:* Roman Catholic (84%), Sunni Islam (5%). *Government:* Republic – multi-party system with executive presidency.

GEOGRAPHY
Some 2770 of the Philippines' 7000 islands are named. The two largest islands, Luzon and Mindanao, make up over 65% of the country's area. Most of the archipelago is mountainous with restricted coastal plains, although Luzon has a large, densely populated central plain. Mount Apo, on Mindanao, is the highest point at 2954 m (9692 ft). The country experiences high humidity, high temperatures and heavy rainfall.

ECONOMIC ACTIVITY
Almost 50% of the labour force is involved in agriculture. Rice and maize are the main subsistence crops, while coconuts, sugar cane, pineapples and bananas are grown for export. Deforestation is a problem as land is cleared for cultivation. Major industries include textiles, food processing, chemicals and electrical engineering. Mineral resources include copper (a major export), gold, petroleum and nickel. Money sent back by Filipinos working abroad is an important source of foreign currency.

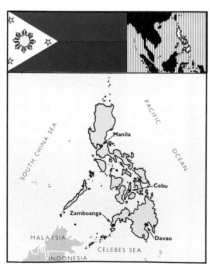

RECENT HISTORY
1898: Philippines ceded to USA after the Spanish-American War. **1898–1906:** Armed resistance to US rule. **1935:** Semi-independent 'Commonwealth' of the Philippines established. **1941–45:** Japanese occupation during World War II. **1946:** Independent Republic of the Philippines established. **1953–57:** President Ramon Magsaysay crushed

Communist-dominated guerrillas. **1965–86:** Increasingly dictatorial presidency of Ferdinand Marcos. **1986:** Marcos overthrown in a popular revolution in favour of Corazon Aquino.

POLAND

Area: 312 683 km² (120 727 sq mi). *Population:* 38 273 000 (1991 est). *Capital and major cities:* Warsaw (Warszawa) 1 656 000, Lódź 848 000, Kraków 751 000 (1990 est). *Language:* Polish. *Religion:* Roman Catholic (93%). *Government:* Republic – multi-party parliamentary system.

GEOGRAPHY
Most of Poland consists of lowlands. The Baltic lowlands and the Pomeranian and Mazurian lake districts occupy the N. Central Poland is a region of plains. In the S are the hills of Little Poland and the Tatra Mountains, which rise to Rysys at 2499 m (8199 ft). The climate tends towards continental with short warm summers and longer cold winters.

ECONOMIC ACTIVITY
Polish agriculture is predominantly small-scale and privately owned. Over 25% of the labour force is still involved in farming, growing potatoes, wheat, barley, sugar beet and fodder crops. The large industrial sector relies upon major deposits of coal and reserves of natural gas, copper and silver. Engineering, food processing, and the chemical, metallurgical and paper industries are important, but the economy has steadily deteriorated since the 1960s. Poland has crippling foreign debts. Privatization has been accelerated since 1991 but living standards have decreased.

RECENT HISTORY
1919: Polish statehood restored by reunification of Russian-, Austrian- and German-controlled areas. **1926–35:** Virtual dictatorship of Józef Pilsudski. **1939:** Poland partitioned by Germany and USSR. **1940–45:** German occupation during World War II; Poland lost 15% of its population. **1944:** Warsaw Rising. **1945:** Liberation by Soviet Red Army; Communist state established; Poland lost 50% of its territory in the E to the USSR, but gained in the N and W from Germany. **1980:** Period of unrest led to the birth of the independent trade union Solidarity (Solidarnosc), led by Lech Walesa. **1981:** Martial law declared; attempt to restore Communist authority. **1989:** Free elections; Solidarity formed a government with former allies of Communists. **1990:** Walesa became President. **Since 1990–91:** Political, economic and social reforms.

PORTUGAL

Area: 92 072 km² (33 549 sq mi) including Madeira and the Azores. *Population:* 10 421 000 (1991 est). *Capital and major cities:* Lisbon (Lisboa)

2 131 000 (city 950 000), Oporto (Porto) 1 695 000 (city 450 000) (1990 est). *Language:* Portuguese (official). *Religion:* Roman Catholic (nearly 90%). *Government:* Republic – multi-party parliamentary system.

AUTONOMOUS REGIONS
(with areas, populations in 1991 and capitals)
Azores (Açores) – 2247 km² (868 sq mi), 253 000, Ponta Delgada.
Madeira – 794 km² (306 sq mi), 273 000, Funchal.

OVERSEAS TERRITORY
Macau – 17 km² (6.5 sq mi), 402 000, Macau.

GEOGRAPHY
Behind a coastal plain, Portugal N of the River Tagus is a highland region, rising to 1993 m (6539 ft). A wide plateau in the NE is a continuation of the Spanish Meseta. S of the Tagus is mainly an undulating lowland. The Atlantic islands of Madeira and the Azores are respectively nearly 1000 km (620 mi) and 1200 km (745 mi) SW of the mainland. A mild temperate climate is wetter and more Atlantic in the N, and drier and hotter inland and in the S.

ECONOMIC ACTIVITY
Agriculture involves 20% of the labour force, but lacks investment following land reforms in the 1970s. Major crops include wheat and maize, grapes (for wines, port etc.), and cork trees. Portugal lacks natural resources. Manufacturing industry includes textiles and clothing (major exports), footwear, food processing, and, increasingly, electrical appliances and petrochemicals. Tourism and money sent back by Portuguese working abroad are major foreign-currency earners. Despite impressive recent economic development Portugal is W Europe's poorest country.

RECENT HISTORY
1910: Monarchy overthrown. **1932–68:** Dictatorship of PM Antonio Salazar. **1961–75:** Expensive colonial wars; Portugal attempted to check independence movements. **1974:** Left-wing military coup. **1974–75:** Independence of colonies. **Since 1976:** Constitutional multi-party rule.

QATAR

Area: 11 437 km² (4416 sq mi). *Population:* 456 000 (1991 est). *Capital:* Doha 272 000 (city 217 000; 1986 est). *Language:* Arabic. *Religion:* Wahhabi Sunni Islam (official; 98%). *Government:* Emirate – absolute monarchy.

GEOGRAPHY
Qatar – a low barren peninsula projecting into the Gulf – is very hot in summer, but milder in winter.

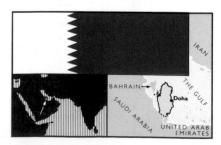

Rainfall averages between 50 and 75 mm (2 to 3 in).

ECONOMIC ACTIVITY
Qatar's high standard of living is due almost entirely to the export of petroleum and natural gas. The steel and cement industries have been developed in an attempt to diversify.

RECENT HISTORY
1872–1914: Part of the (Turkish) Ottoman Empire. **1916:** Became a British-protected state. **1972:** Complete independence regained.

ROMANIA

Area: 237 500 km^2 (91 699 sq mi). **Population:** 22 749 000 (1992 census). **Capital:** Bucharest (Bucuresti) 2 325 000 (1990 est). **Languages:** Romanian (official; 89%), Hungarian (10%). **Religion:** Orthodox (70%). **Government:** Republic – multi-party system with executive presidency.

GEOGRAPHY
The Carpathian Mountains – which run through the N, E and centre of Romania – rise to 2544 m (8346 ft) at Moldoveanu. To the W of the Carpathians is the tableland of Transylvania and the Banat lowland. In the S the Danube Plain ends in a delta on the Black Sea. Romania experiences cold snowy winters and hot summers. Rainfall is moder-

ate in the lowlands but heavier in the Carpathians.

ECONOMIC ACTIVITY
State-owned industry – which employs nearly 40% of the labour force – includes mining, metallurgy, mechanical engineering and chemicals. Natural resources include petroleum and natural gas. Considerable forests support a timber and furniture industry. Major crops include maize, sugar beet, wheat, potatoes and grapes for wine, but agriculture has been neglected, and food supplies have fallen short of Romania's needs. Economic mismanagement under Ceausescu decreased low living standards, and the country faces severe economic difficulties. Privatization of land began in 1990.

RECENT HISTORY
1916–18: Romania at war with Austria and Germany during World War I. **1919:** Bessarabia (now Moldova) and Transylvania acquired. **1938–41:** Dictatorship of King Carol II. **1941–44:** Romania – under Marshal Ion Antonescu – joined the Axis powers in World War II. **1944–45:** King Michael dismissed Antonescu; Romania at war with Germany; Soviet Red Army invaded. **1945:** Soviet-dominated government installed. **1947:** Monarchy abolished. **1967–89:** Dictatorship of Nicolae Ceausescu and his wife Elena. **1989:** Revolt against the Ceausescus; army took power; Communist Party dissolved. **1990:** Multi-party elections.

RUSSIA

Area: 17 075 400 km^2 (6 592 800 sq mi). **Population:** 148 543 000 (1991 est). **Capital and major cities:** Moscow (Moskva) 8 967 000, St Petersburg (Sankt-Peterburg; formerly Leningrad) 5 020 000, Nizhny Novgorod (formerly Gorky) 1 438 000, Novosibirsk 1 436 000, Yekaterinburg (formerly Sverdlovsk) 1 367 000 (1989 census). **Languages:** Russian (83%), Tatar (4%), over 100 other languages. **Religion:** Orthodox (27%). **Government:** Federal republic – multi-party system in formation.

GEOGRAPHY
Russia – the largest country in the world – covers over 10% of the total land area of the globe. Between the Baltic and the Ural Mountains is the North European Plain, S of which are the relatively low-lying Central Russian Uplands. The vast West Siberian Lowland – E of the Urals – is

largely occupied by the basin of the River Ob and its tributaries. The Central Siberian Plateau rises between the Rivers Yenisey and Lena. Beyond the Lena, the mountains of E Siberia include the Chersky Range and the Kamchatka Peninsula. Much of S Siberia is mountainous. The Yablonovy and Stanovoy Mountains rise inland from the Amur Basin, which drains to the Pacific. The Altai Mountains lie S of Lake Baikal, along the border with Mongolia. Between the Black and Caspian Seas are the high Caucasus Mountains which rise to Elbrus at 5642 m (18 510 ft) on the Georgian border. The Kaliningrad enclave between Poland and Lithuania on the Baltic is a detached part of Russia. There is a wide range of climatic types, but most of Russia is continental with extremes of temperature. The Arctic N is a severe tundra region in which the subsoil is nearly always frozen. The forested taiga zone – to the S – has long hard winters and short summers. The steppes and the Central Russian Uplands have cold winters, but hot, dry summers. Between the Black and Caspian seas, conditions are almost Mediterranean.

ECONOMIC ACTIVITY
Russia is one of the largest producers of coal, iron ore, steel, petroleum and cement. However, its economy is in crisis. Economic reforms in 1985–91 introduced decentralization to a centrally-planned economy. Since 1991, reform has been accelerated through the introduction of free market prices and the encouragement of private enterprise. However, poor distribution has resulted in shortages of many basic goods. Inflation is rampant – reaching 2200% in 1992 – and the value of the rouble has plummeted. Manufacturing involves 30% of the labour force and includes the steel, chemical, textile and heavy machinery industries. The production of consumer goods is not highly developed. Agriculture is large-scale and organized either into state-owned farms or collective farms, although the right to own and farm land privately has been introduced. Despite mechanization and the world's largest fertilizer industry, Russia cannot produce enough grain for its needs, in part because of poor harvests, and poor storage and transport facilities. Imports have assumed added importance. Major Russian crops include wheat, barley, oats, potatoes, sugar beet and fruit. Natural resources include the world's largest reserves of coal, nearly 30% of the world's natural gas reserves, 30% of the world's forests, major

deposits of many minerals, and plentiful sites for hydroelectric power installations. Machinery, petroleum and petroleum products are Russia's major exports and the republic is self sufficient in energy. Russia has a large trade surplus with the other former Soviet republics.

RECENT HISTORY

Early 20th century: Rapid industrialization; increased demands for constitutional reform; first elected parliament (1906). **1904–05:** Russo-Japanese War. **1914–17:** Russia at war with the Central Powers. **1917 (February):** First revolution; monarchy overthrown. **1917 (November):** Second revolution; Communists under Lenin took power. **1918–22:** Outlying parts of Russian Empire seceded; civil war between Reds (Communists) and Whites (largely tsarists). **1922:** Soviet Union formed; Red Army re-established control over most of former empire. **1924–53:** Dictatorship of Joseph Stalin. **1930:** Kulaks (rich peasants) dispossessed. **1936–38:** Purges of Stalin's political rivals. **1939:** Non-aggression pact with Hitler. **1940:** USSR invaded Poland, Finland, Romania and the Baltic states. **1941–45:** World War II; up to 20 million Soviet citizens may have died. **1945:** USSR established control of a cordon of satellite states in E Europe and challenged the West in the Cold War. **1956:** USSR put down Hungarian uprising. **1964–82:** Leonid Brezhnev in power; USSR increasingly drained by burdens of an impoverished and overstretched empire. **1968:** Soviet invasion of Czechoslovakia **1985–91:** Political and economic reforms of Mikhail Gorbachov who attempted reconstruction (*perestroika*) and greater openness (*glasnost*). **1989–91:** Abandonment of Communism in E European Soviet satellites. **1991 (August–September):** Abortive coup by hardline Communists; Boris Yeltsin and Russian parliament led resistance; republics began to renegotiate their relationship with the centre. **1991 (December):** USSR dissolved; Russia – under Yeltsin – took over the international responsibilities of the USSR. **Since 1991:** Ethnic disputes and a severe economic and constitutional crisis.

RWANDA

Area: 26 338 km² (10 169 sq mi). *Population:* 7 491 000 (1991 est). *Capital:* Kigali 300 000 (1990 est). *Languages:* French and Kinyarwanda (both official). *Religions:* Roman Catholic (63%), animist (21%). *Government:* Republic – limited multi-party system with executive presidency.

GEOGRAPHY

Rwanda is a mountainous country rising to Mount Karisimbi at 4507 m (14 787 ft). Most of the western boundary is formed by Lake Kivu. The climate is tropical but cooler in the mountains.

ECONOMIC ACTIVITY

Subsistence farming dominates Rwanda's economy. Coffee and tea are the main exports. Africa's highest population density retards development.

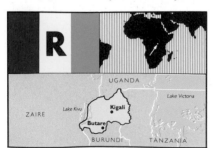

RECENT HISTORY

1890: Feudal kingdom of Rwanda became a German possession. **1916–62:** Belgian administration. **1962:** The monarchy – of the dominant minority Tutsi people – overthrown by the major-

ity Hutu people. **Since 1962:** Intermittent tribal violence. **1978–91:** Single-party state. **1991:** Multi-party system permitted.

SAINT CHRISTOPHER AND NEVIS

St Christopher is popularly known as St Kitts. *Area:* 262 km² (101 sq mi). *Population:* 43 000 (1991 est). *Capital:* Basseterre 18 500 (1986 est). *Language:* English (official). *Religions:* Anglican (36%), Methodist (32%). *Government:* Dominion – multi-party parliamentary system.

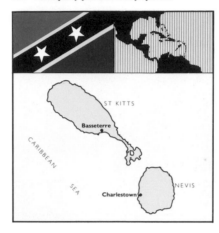

GEOGRAPHY

St Kitts and Nevis are two well-watered mountainous islands, set 3 km (2 mi) apart. The moist tropical climate is cooled by sea breezes.

ECONOMIC ACTIVITY

The economy is based on agriculture (mainly sugar cane) and tourism.

RECENT HISTORY

1967: Small island of Anguilla – a reluctant partner in the federation – proclaimed independence; UK intervened; Anguilla remains British. **1983:** Independence of St Kitts-Nevis after over 450 years of British rule.

SAINT LUCIA

Area: 616 km² (238 sq mi). *Population:* 151 000 (1990 census). *Capital:* Castries 57 000 (1990 census). *Languages:* English (official), French patois (majority). *Religion:* Roman Catholic (82%). *Government:* Dominion – multi-party parliamentary system.

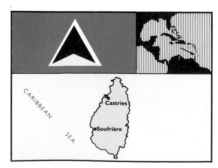

GEOGRAPHY

St Lucia is a forested mountainous island rising to 959 m (3145 ft). It has a wet tropical climate, but there is a dry season from January to April.

ECONOMIC ACTIVITY

The economy depends on agriculture, with bananas and coconuts as the main crops. Tourism is increasingly important.

RECENT HISTORY

1979: Independence after over 160 years of British rule.

SAINT VINCENT AND THE GRENADINES

Area: 389 km² (150 sq mi). *Population:* 108 000 (1991 census). *Capital:* Kingstown 34 000 (city 19 000; 1989 est). *Language:* English (official). *Religions:* Anglican (42%), Methodist (21%). *Government:* Dominion – multi-party parliamentary system.

GEOGRAPHY

The mountainous wooded island of St Vincent rises to Mount Soufrière – an active volcano – at 1234 m (4048 ft). The Grenadines – which include Bequia and Mustique – are a chain of small islands to the S of St Vincent. The climate is tropical with heavy rainfall in the mountains.

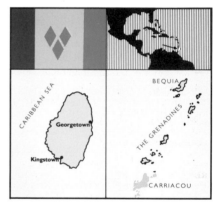

ECONOMIC ACTIVITY

Bananas and arrowroot are the main crops of a largely agricultural economy.

RECENT HISTORY

1979: Independence after over 210 years of British rule.

SAN MARINO

Area: 61 km² (23 sq mi). *Population:* 23 700 (1990). *Capital:* San Marino 9000 (city 4200). *Language:* Italian. *Religion:* Roman Catholic (official; 95%). *Government:* Republic – multi-party parliamentary system with co-regents as joint heads of state.

GEOGRAPHY

The country is dominated by the triple limestone peaks of Monte Titano at 739 m (2424 ft). The climate is Mediterranean.

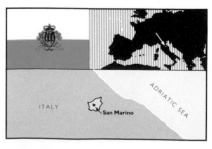

ECONOMIC ACTIVITY

Manufacturing and tourism – in particular visitors on excursions – are the mainstays of the economy.

RECENT HISTORY

1957: Bloodless 'revolution' replaced the Communist-Socialist administration.

SÃO TOMÉ E PRÍNCIPE

Area: 964 km² (372 sq mi). **Population:** 123 000 (1991 est). **Capital:** São Tomé 35 000 (1989 est). **Languages:** Portuguese (official), Fang (90%). **Religion:** Roman Catholic (50%). **Government:** Republic – multi-party system with executive presidency.

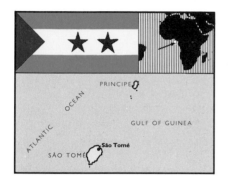

GEOGRAPHY

The republic consists of two mountainous islands about 144 km (90 mi) apart. São Tomé rises to 2024 m (6640 ft). The climate is tropical. A wet season – with heavy rainfall – lasts from October to May.

ECONOMIC ACTIVITY

Cocoa is the mainstay of a largely agricultural economy. Most of the land is nationalized.

RECENT HISTORY

Early 20th century: The islands' plantations were notorious for forced labour. **1975:** Independence from Portugal. **1975–90:** Single-party Marxist state. **1991:** Multi-party elections held.

SAUDI ARABIA

Area: 2 240 000 km² (864 869 sq mi). **Population:** 14 691 000 (1991 est). **Capital and major cities:** Riyadh (Ar Riyad) – the royal capital – 2 000 000, Jeddah (Jiddah) – the administrative capital – 1 400 000, Mecca (Makkah) 620 000 (all including suburbs; 1986 est). **Language:** Arabic (official).

Religion: Islam (official) – Sunni (92%; Wahhabi), Shia (8%). **Government:** Kingdom – absolute monarchy.

GEOGRAPHY

Over 95% of the country is desert, including the Rub 'al-Khali ('The Empty Quarter') – the largest expanse of sand in the world. The Arabian plateau ends in the W in a steep escarpment overlooking the Red Sea coastal plain. The average rainfall is 100 mm (4 in) or less, and there are no permanent streams. The country is very hot.

ECONOMIC ACTIVITY

Saudi Arabia's spectacular development and present prosperity are based almost entirely upon exploiting vast reserves of petroleum and natural gas. Industries include petroleum refining, petrochemicals and fertilizers. The country has developed major banking and commercial interests. Less than 1% of the land can be cultivated.

RECENT HISTORY

1902: Ibn Saud took Riyadh. **1906:** Central Arabia (Nejd) annexed. **1912–27:** Ibn Saud conquered the E, the SW (Asir) and Hejaz. **1932:** Ibn Saud proclaimed himself king of Saudi Arabia. **1973:** Saudi Arabia put pressure on the USA to influence Israel by cutting oil production. **1991:** Saudi Arabia played major role in allied Gulf War coalition.

SENEGAL

Area: 196 722 km² (75 954 sq mi). **Population:** 7 517 000 (1990 est). **Capital:** Dakar 1 490 000 (1988 census). **Languages:** French (official), Wolof (36%), Serer (19%), Fulani (13%). **Religions:** Sunni Islam (94%), Roman Catholic. **Government:** Republic – multi-party system with executive presidency.

GEOGRAPHY

Senegal is mostly low-lying and covered by savannah. The Fouta Djalon mountains in the S rise to 1515 m (4970 ft). The tropical climate has a dry season from October to June.

ECONOMIC ACTIVITY

Over three quarters of the labour force is involved in agriculture, growing groundnuts and cotton as cash crops, and rice, maize, millet and sorghum as subsistence crops. The manufacturing sector is one of the largest in West Africa, but unemployment is a major problem.

RECENT HISTORY

1960: Independence from France. **1960–80:** Presidency of Léopold Sedar Senghor. **1981–89:** Attempted federation with Gambia.

SERBIA (see YUGOSLAVIA)

SEYCHELLES

Area: 454 km² (173 sq mi). **Population:** 68 000 (1991 est). **Capital:** Victoria 24 000 (1987 est). **Languages:** Creole (official; 95%), English, French. **Religion:** Roman Catholic (92%). **Government:** Republic – multi-party system with executive presidency.

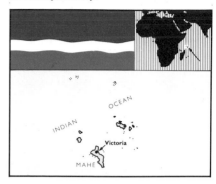

GEOGRAPHY

The Seychelles consist of 40 mountainous granitic islands and just over 50 smaller coral islands. There is a pleasant tropical maritime climate with heavy rainfall.

ECONOMIC ACTIVITY

The economy depends heavily on tourism, which employs about one third of the labour force.

RECENT HISTORY

1976: Independence after over 150 years of British rule. **1977:** Coup; one-party socialist state established. **1992:** Multi-party system reintroduced.

SIERRA LEONE

Area: 71 740 km² (27 699 sq mi). **Population:** 4 260 000 (1991 est). **Capital:** Freetown 550 000 (city 470 000; 1985 census). **Languages:** English (official), Krio, Mende (34%), Temne (31%). **Religions:** Animist (52%), Sunni Islam (39%). **Government:** Republic – military government (a return to multi-party rule is proposed).

GEOGRAPHY

The savannah interior comprises plateaux and mountain ranges that rise to 1948 m (6390 ft). The swampy coastal plain is forested. The tropical climate has a dry season from November to June.

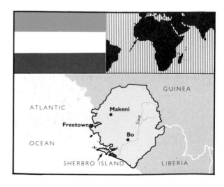

ECONOMIC ACTIVITY

Subsistence farming – mainly rice – involves two thirds of the labour force. Rutile, bauxite and cocoa are major exports. The decline of diamond mining has added to severe economic problems.

RECENT HISTORY

1961: Independence after 150 years of British rule. **1978–92:** Single-party system. **1992:** Military coup.

SINGAPORE

Area: 623 km² (240 sq mi). **Population:** 2 705 000 (1990 census). **Capital:** Singapore 2 705 000 (1990 census). **Languages:** Chinese (77%), Malay (14%), Tamil (5%), English (all official). **Religions:** Buddhist and Daoist (54%), Sunni Islam (15%), various Christian Churches (13%). **Government:** Republic – multi-party system with executive presidency.

GEOGRAPHY
Singapore is a low-lying island – with 56 islets – joined to the Malay peninsula by causeway. The tropical climate has monsoon rains from December to March.

ECONOMIC ACTIVITY
Singapore relies on imports for its flourishing industries (electronics, oil refining, rubber processing, food processing) and entrepôt trade. Finance and tourism are important. In Asia only Japan has a higher standard of living.

RECENT HISTORY
1942–45: Occupied by Japan during World War II. **1963:** Independence from UK; became part of Malaysia. **Since 1965:** Separate independent statehood. **1965–91:** Premiership of Lee Kuan Yew.

SLOVAKIA

Area: 49 025 km² (18 929 sq mi). **Population:** 5 269 000 (1991 census). **Capital:** Bratislava 442 000 (1991 census). **Languages:** Slovak (87%), Hungarian (11%). **Religion:** Roman Catholic (60%). **Government:** Republic – multi-party parliamentary system.

GEOGRAPHY
Slovakia is largely mountainous. The Tatra Mountains – in the N – rise to 2655 m (8737 ft) at Gerlachovka. The only significant lowlands are in the S adjoining the River Danube. A continental climate has cold winters and warm summers.

ECONOMIC ACTIVITY
Slovakia has a mainly agricultural economy into which heavy industry was introduced when the country was part of Communist Czechoslovakia. Wheat, maize, potatoes, barley and sheep are important. Natural resources include iron ore and

brown coal. Slovakia has slowed the privatization of its uncompetitive out-of-date factories.

RECENT HISTORY
1918: After the collapse of the Habsburg Empire, Slovaks and Czechs joined together in an independent Czechoslovakia. **1938:** Czechoslovakia dismembered by Nazi Germany. **1939–45:** Axis puppet state of Slovakia. **1944:** Slovak uprising against Germany. **1945:** Czechoslovakia restored. **1949:** Communist takeover. **1993:** After the success of Slovak nationalists in multi-party elections (1990), Czechoslovakia was dissolved; separate Slovak Republic formed.

SLOVENIA

Area: 20 251 km² (7819 sq mi). **Population:** 1 963 000 (1991 census). **Capital:** Ljubljana 338 000 (city 286 000; 1991 census). **Language:** Slovene (91%). **Religion:** Roman Catholic (over 90%). **Government:** Republic – multi-party parliamentary system.

GEOGRAPHY
Most of Slovenia comprises mountains including the Karawanken Alps and Julian Alps, which rise to Triglav at 2864 m (9396 ft). Slovenia has a very short Adriatic coastline. The S and W are Mediterranean; the N and E are more continental.

ECONOMIC ACTIVITY
Slovenia was the most industrialized and economically developed part of Yugoslavia. Industries include iron and steel, textiles and coal mining. Agriculture specializes in livestock and fodder crops.

RECENT HISTORY
1918: The Slovenes – formerly part of the (Austro-Hungarian) Habsburg Empire – became part of Yugoslavia. **1945:** Republic of Slovenia became a constituent state of Communist Yugoslavia. **1990:** Free elections. **1991:** Slovenia declared independence; short unsuccessful campaign against Slovenia by Yugoslav federal army.

SOLOMON ISLANDS

Area: 27 556 km² (10 639 sq mi). **Population:** 328 000 (1991 est). **Capital:** Honiara 35 300 (1990

est). **Languages:** English (official), Pidgin English, over 85 local (mainly Melanesian) languages (85%). **Religions:** Anglican (34%), Roman Catholic (19%). **Government:** Dominion – multi-party parliamentary system.

GEOGRAPHY
The mountainous volcanic Solomons rise to Mount Makarakomburu at 2447 m (8028 ft). The climate is tropical with temperature and rainfall maximums from November to April.

ECONOMIC ACTIVITY
Most of the labour force is involved in subsistence farming, although copra and cocoa are exported. Fishing is a major industry.

RECENT HISTORY
1893–1942: The Solomons under British rule. **1942–45:** Japanese occupation during World War II. **1945:** British rule restored. **1978:** Independence.

SOMALIA

Area: 637 657 km² (246 201 sq mi). **Population:** 7 691 000 (1991 est). **Capital:** Mogadishu 1 000 000 (1986 est). **Languages:** Somali (national), Arabic (official). **Religion:** Sunni Islam (official). **Government:** Republic – at the beginning of 1993 there was no effective government.

GEOGRAPHY
Somalia occupies the 'Horn of Africa'. Low-lying plains cover most of the S, while semi-arid mountains in the N rise to 2408 m (7900 ft). The climate is hot and largely dry.

ECONOMIC ACTIVITY
Nearly two thirds of the labour force are nomadic herdsmen or subsistence farmers. Bananas are grown for export in the S, but much of the country suffers drought. As a result of civil war, much of the economic infrastructure of the country has been destroyed and there is widespread famine.

RECENT HISTORY
1886: British protectorate established in the N; Italy colonized the S. **1960:** British and Italian colonies united as independent Somalia. **1969–91:** Dictatorship of Muhammad Siad Barre. **Since 1991:** Bitter civil war between local leaders; no effective government. **1992:** US-led UN involvement to relieve famine.

SOUTH AFRICA

Area: 2 347 661 km² (906 437 sq mi) including Walvis Bay – 1124 km² (434 sq mi) – and the 'independent' homelands – 1 125 500 km² (434 558 sq mi). **Population:** 33 140 000 (1991 est) including Walvis Bay – 21 000 (1981) – and the 'independent' homelands – 5 954 000 (1985). **Capital and major cities:** Pretoria (administrative capital) 823 000 (city 443 000), Cape Town (legislative capital) 1 912 000 (city 777 000), Bloemfontein (judicial capital) 233 000, Johannesburg 4 000 000 (city 1 726 000; Soweto 915 000) (all including suburbs; 1985 census). **Languages:** Afrikaans and English (both official), Xhosa (21%), Zulu (16%), Sesotho. **Religions:** Dutch Reformed Church, independent African Churches, with Anglican, Methodist,

Roman Catholic, Hindu and Sunni Islam. **Government:** Federal republic – limited multi-party system with executive presidency. (A new constitution was under discussion in 1993.) Four homelands – Bophuthatswana, Ciskei, Transkei and Venda – had been granted 'independence', but are unrecognized internationally.

GEOGRAPHY
The Great Escarpment rises behind a discontinuous coastal plain and includes the Drakensberg Mountains, which reach 3408 m (11 1182 ft) at Injasuti. A vast plateau occupies the interior, undulating in the W and rising to over 2400 m (about 8000 ft) in the E. Much of the W is semi-desert, while the E is predominantly savannah grassland (veld). Walvis Bay is an enclave on the Namibian coast. A subtropical climate has considerable regional variations. The hottest period is between December and February. Rainfall is highest on the E coast but much of the country is dry.

ECONOMIC ACTIVITY
The country is the world's leading exporter of gold – which forms 35% of South African exports – and a major producer of uranium, diamonds, chromite, antimony, platinum and coal (which meets 75% of the country's energy needs). Industry includes chemicals, food processing, textiles, motor vehicles and electrical engineering. Agriculture supplies 30% of South Africa's exports including fruit, wine, wool and maize. The highest standard of living in Africa is very unevenly distributed between Whites and Non-whites. The withdrawal of some foreign investors in the 1970s and 1980s increased the drive towards self-sufficiency.

RECENT HISTORY
1899–1902: Boer War; British achieved supremacy in South Africa. **1910:** Union of South Africa founded. **1912:** African National Congress (ANC) founded as a protest against White supremacy. **1914–15:** South Africa – as a British ally in World War I – took German South West Africa (Namibia). **1919–24** and **1939–48:** Premierships of Jan Christiaan Smuts; South Africa joined Allied cause in World War II despite Nationalist protests. **After 1948:** Afrikaner National Party in power; racial segregation increased by the policy of apartheid ('separate development'), which deprived Blacks of civil rights, segregated facilities, etc. **1960:** Sharpeville massacre of Black demonstrators; ANC banned. **1960s:** International pressure against apartheid increased. **1970s–80s:** Black opposition revived; Soweto uprising (1976). **1986:** State of emergency introduced; censorship and detentions. **Since 1989:** Presidency of F.W. de Klerk; ANC prisoners, including Nelson Mandela, released; legal structures of apartheid dismantled. **Since 1991:** Multi-ethnic, multi-party convention negotiating new power-sharing government and constitution.

SPAIN

Area: 504 782 km² (194 897 sq mi) including the Canary Islands, Ceuta and Melilla. ***Population:*** 39 952 000 (1991 census). ***Capital and major cities:*** Madrid 4 846 000 (city 3 121 000), Barcelona 3 400 000 (city 1 707 000), Valencia 777 000, Seville (Sevilla) 754 000 (city 684 000) (1991 census). ***Languages:*** Spanish or Castilian (official; as a first language over 70%), Catalan (as a first language over 20%), Basque (3%), Galician (4%). ***Religion:*** Roman Catholic (98%). ***Government:*** Federal kingdom – multi-party parliamentary system.

GEOGRAPHY
In the N, a mountainous region stretches from the Pyrenees through the Cantabrian mountains to Galicia on the Atlantic coast. The central plateau, the Meseta, averages around 600 m (2000 ft) high, but rises to the higher Sistema Central in Castile, and ends in the S at the Sierra Morena. The Sierra Nevada range in Andalusia in the S contains Mulhacén, mainland Spain's highest peak at 3478 m (11 411 ft). The principal lowlands include the Ebro Valley in the NE, a plain around Valencia in the E, and Guadalquivir Valley in the S. The Balearic Islands in the Mediterranean comprise four main islands – Mallorca (Majorca), Menorca (Minorca), Ibiza and Formentera. The Canary Islands, off the coast of Morocco and the Western Sahara, comprise five large islands – Tenerife, Fuerteventura, Gran Canaria, Lanzarote and La Palma. Pico del Tiede in the Canaries is Spain's highest peak at 3716 m (12 192 ft). Ceuta and Melilla are enclaves on the N coast of Morocco. The SE has a Mediterranean climate with hot summers and mild winters. The dry interior is continental with warm summers and cold winters. The high Pyrenees have a cold Alpine climate, while the NW (Galicia) has a wet Atlantic climate with cool summers.

ECONOMIC ACTIVITY
Over 10% of the labour force is involved in agriculture. The principal crops include cereals, sugar beet, citrus fruit and grapes (for wine). Pastures for livestock occupy some 20% of the land. Manufacturing developed rapidly from the 1960s and Spain now has the largest economy outside the G7 nations. There are major motor-vehicle, textile, plastics, metallurgical, chemical and engineering industries. Foreign investors have been encouraged to promote new industry, but unemployment remains high. Banking and commerce are important, and tourism is a major foreign-currency earner. Over 30 000 000 foreign tourists a year visit Spain, mainly staying at beach resorts on the Mediterranean, Balearic Islands and the Canaries.

RECENT HISTORY
1898: Spanish-American War; Cuba, the Philippines, Guam and Puerto Rico lost. **1923–30:** Military dictatorship of Miguel Primo de Rivera. **1931:** Alfonso XIII abdicated; republic established. **1936–39:** Civil war; Nationalists – led by General Francisco Franco and supported by Germany and Italy – beat republicans. **1939–75:** Political expression restricted. **Since 1966:** Terrorist campaign by Basque separatists. **1975:** Death of Franco; mon-

archy restored under Juan Carlos. **1978:** Liberal constitution. **1981:** Attempted army coup. **1986:** Spain joined EC.

SRI LANKA

Before 1972 Sri Lanka was known as Ceylon. ***Area:*** 65 610 km² (25 332 sq mi). ***Population:*** 17 219 000 (1991 est.). ***Capitals:*** Colombo – administrative capital – 1 446 000 (city 615 000), (Sri Jayewardenepura) Kotte – part of the Colombo agglomeration; legislative capital – 109 000 (1987 est.). ***Languages:*** Sinhala (official; 72%), Tamil (official; 21%), English (official). ***Religions:*** Buddhist (69%), Hindu (15%). ***Government:*** Republic – multi-party system with executive presidency.

GEOGRAPHY
The central highlands rise to 2527 m (8292 ft). Most of the rest of the island consists of forested lowlands which in the N are flat and fertile. A tropical climate is modified by the monsoon.

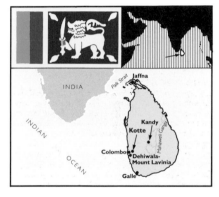

ECONOMIC ACTIVITY
About 50% of the labour force is involved in agriculture, growing rice for local consumption, and tea, rubber and coconuts for export. Major irrigation and hydroelectric projects are being constructed. Industries include food processing and textiles. Tourism is increasingly important.

RECENT HISTORY
1948: Independence after 150 years of British rule. **1958, 1961** and **since 1977:** Tamil-Sinhalese ethnic unrest. **1960–65** and **1970–77:** Ministry of Sirimavo Bandaranaike, the world's first woman PM. **1971:** Marxist rebellion. **Since 1979:** Separatist Tamil guerrillas active in N. **1987–89:** Indian peace-keeping forces in N.

SUDAN

Area: 2 505 813 km² (967 500 sq mi). ***Population:*** 29 129 000 (1991 est.). ***Capital:*** Khartoum 1 802 000 (city 476 000, Omdurman 526 000, Khartoum North 341 000; 1983 est.). ***Language:*** Arabic (over 50%; official). ***Religions:*** Sunni Islam (73%), animist (nearly 20%), Christian minority. ***Government:*** Republic – military government.

GEOGRAPHY
The Sahara Desert covers much of the N and W, but is crossed by the fertile Nile Valley. The southern plains are swampy. Highlands are confined to coastal hills and mountains on the Ugandan border. The S is equatorial, but the N is dry with some areas receiving negligible rainfall.

ECONOMIC ACTIVITY
Over 60% of the labour force is involved in agriculture, growing cotton for export and sorghum and millet for domestic consumption. Since the early 1980s Sudan has been severely affected by drought, civil war and famine.

RECENT HISTORY
1889: British intervention brought Sudan under

joint Egypto-British administration. **Since 1955:** Civil war between the Muslim N and the animist-Christian S. **1956:** Independence. **Since 1956:** Political instability; alternating civilian and military regimes. **Since 1989:** Islamic fundamentalist military government.

SURINAME

Area: 163 265 km² (63 037 sq mi). *Population:* 417 000 (1991 est). *Capital:* Paramaribo 246 000 (city 68 000; 1988 est). *Languages:* Dutch (official; 30%), Sranang Togo (Creole; 31%), Hindi (30%), Javanese (15%), Chinese, English (official), Spanish (official – designate). *Religions:* Hinduism (28%), Roman Catholic (22%), Sunni Islam (20%), Moravian (15%). *Government:* Republic – multi-party parliamentary system.

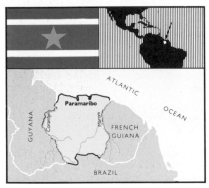

GEOGRAPHY
Suriname comprises a swampy coastal plain, a forested central plateau, and mountains in the S. The climate is tropical with heavy rainfall.

ECONOMIC ACTIVITY
The extraction and refining of bauxite is the mainstay of the economy. Other exports include shrimps, sugar and oranges.

RECENT HISTORY
1975: Independence from the Netherlands. **Since 1975:** Racial tension; several coups.

SWAZILAND

Area: 17 363 km² (6704 sq mi). *Population:* 798 000 (1991 est). *Capital:* Mbabane – administrative capital – 38 000, Lobamba – legislative capital – 6000 (1986 census). *Languages:* siSwati and English (both official). *Religions:* Animist (majority), various Christian Churches (18%). *Gov-

ernment: Kingdom – non-party restricted parliamentary system.

GEOGRAPHY
From the mountains of the W – which rise to 1869 m (6100 ft) – Swaziland descends in steps of savannah (veld) towards hill country in the E. The veld is subtropical; the highlands are temperate.

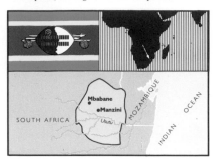

ECONOMIC ACTIVITY
The majority of Swazis are subsistence farmers. Cash crops include sugar cane (the main export).

RECENT HISTORY
1904: British protectorate proclaimed. **1968:** Independence. **1973:** Constitution suspended; royal power restored.

SWEDEN

Area: 449 964 km² (173 732 sq mi). *Population:* 8 586 000 (1990 census). *Capital and major cities:* Stockholm 1 471 000 (city 679 000), Göteborg (Gothenburg) 720 000 (city 432 000) (1990 census). *Languages:* Swedish (official), small Lappish minority. *Religion:* Evangelical Lutheran Church of Sweden (over 85%). *Government:* Kingdom – multi-party parliamentary system.

GEOGRAPHY
The mountains of Norrland – along the border with Norway and in the N of Sweden – cover two thirds of the country, rising at Kebnekaise to 2123 m (6965 ft). Svealand – in the centre – is characterized by a large number of lakes. In the S are the low Smaland Highlands and the fertile lowland of Skane. Sweden has long cold winters and warm summers, although the N is much more severe than the S, whereas Skane has a relatively mild winter.

ECONOMIC ACTIVITY
Sweden's high standard of living has been based upon its neutrality in the two World Wars, plentiful hydroelectric power and mineral riches. There are large reserves of uranium and iron ore – the latter provides the basis of domestic heavy industry and important exports to W Europe. Agriculture – like the bulk of the population – is concentrated in the S. The principal products include dairy produce, meat, barley, sugar beet and potatoes. Vast coniferous forests are the basis of the paper, board and furniture industries, and large exports of timber. Heavy industries include motor vehicles, aerospace and machinery.

RECENT HISTORY
1905: Union with Norway dissolved. **From 1932:** Sweden developed a comprehensive welfare state.

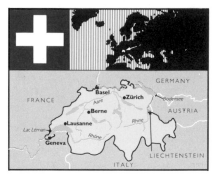

1986: Unresolved assassination of PM Olof Palme. **1990s:** Economic necessity obliged Sweden to dismantle aspects of the welfare system.

SWITZERLAND

Area: 41 293 km² (15 943 sq mi). *Population:* 6 820 000 (1991 est). *Capital and major cities:* Berne (Bern) 299 000 (city 134 000), Zürich 839 000 (city 343 000), Geneva (Genève) 389 000 (city 165 000) (1990 census). *Languages:* German (65% as a first language), French (18% as a first language), Italian (10% as a first language), Romansch (under 1%) – all official. *Religions:* Roman Catholic (48%), various Protestant Churches (44%). *Government:* Federal republic – multiparty parliamentary system.

GEOGRAPHY
The parallel ridges of the Jura Mountains lie in the NW on the French border. The S of the country is occupied by the Alps, which rise to Dufourspitze (Monte Rosa) at 4634 m (15 203 ft). Between the two mountain ranges is a central plateau that contains the greater part of Switzerland's population, agriculture and industry. Altitude and aspect modify Switzerland's temperate climate. Considerable differences in temperature and rainfall are experienced over relatively short distances.

ECONOMIC ACTIVITY
Nearly two centuries of neutrality have allowed Switzerland to build a reputation as a secure financial centre. Zürich is one of the world's leading banking and commercial cities. The country enjoys the highest standard of living in the world. Industry – in part based upon cheap hydroelectric power – includes engineering (from turbines to watches), textiles, food processing (including cheese and chocolate), pharmaceuticals and chemicals. Dairying, grapes (for wine) and fodder crops are important in the agricultural sector, and there is a significant timber industry. Tourism and the international organizations based in Switzerland are major foreign-currency earners. Foreign workers – in particular Italians – help alleviate the country's labour shortage.

RECENT HISTORY
1914–18 and **1939–45:** Neutrality in World Wars. **1920–39:** League of Nations based in Switzerland. **Since 1945:** Switzerland has avoided membership of any body that might compromise its neutrality (e.g. UN).

SYRIA

Area: 185 180 km² (71 498 sq mi) – including the Israeli-occupied Golan Heights. *Population:* 12 529 000 (1991 est). *Capital and major cities:* Damascus 1 361 000, Halab (formerly Aleppo) 1 308 000 (1989 est). *Languages:* Arabic (89%; official), Kurdish (6%), Armenian (3%). *Religion:* Islam (official; Sunni 90%, Shia and Druze minorities). *Government:* Republic – effectively single-party system with executive presidency.

GEOGRAPHY

Behind a well-watered coastal plain, mountains run from N to S, rising to Jabal ash Shaik (Mount Hermon) at 2814 m (9232 ft). Inland, much of the country is occupied by the Syrian Desert. The coast has a Mediterranean climate. The arid interior has hot summers and cool winters.

ECONOMIC ACTIVITY

Petroleum is the main export although Syria's petroleum reserves are small by Middle East standards. Agriculture involves 50% of the labour force, with farming concentrated in the coastal plain and irrigated land in the Euphrates Valley. Major crops include cotton, wheat and barley.

RECENT HISTORY

1917: During World War I, a combined British-Arab army took Turkish-ruled Syria. **1920–46:** French rule. **1946:** Independence. **1946–70:** Political instability; recurrent coups. **1948–49**, **1967** and **1973**: Wars with Israel. **1958–61:** Union with Egypt. **Since 1970:** Ba'athist leader Hafiz Assad in power; 1970–90 allied with USSR.

TAJIKISTAN

Area: 143 100 km² (55 300 sq mi). **Population:** 5 358 000 (1991 est). **Capital:** Dushanbe 604 000 (1989 census). **Languages:** Tajik (62%), Uzbek (24%), Russian (7%). **Religion:** Sunni Islam majority. **Government:** Republic – effectively single-party system with executive president.

GEOGRAPHY

The mountainous republic of Tajikistan lies within the Tien Shan range and part of the Pamirs. The highest point at 7495 m (24 590 ft) is Mount Garmo (formerly known as Pik Kommunizma). The only important lowland is the subtropical Fergana valley. High altitude and the country's position deep in the interior of Asia give most of Tajikistan a harsh continental climate.

ECONOMIC ACTIVITY

Cotton is the mainstay of the economy. Other agricultural interests include fruit, vegetables and raising cattle. Major natural resources include coal, natural gas, and iron ore. Industries include textiles and carpet-making. The economy remains centrally planned and largely state-owned.

RECENT HISTORY

1860–68: Annexation of Tajikistan by Tsarist Russia. **1920:** After the Russian Revolution, reconquest by Soviet Red Army. **1922–31:** Tajik revolts. **1991:** Independence upon dissolution of USSR. **Since 1992:** Civil war between former Communists and Islamic fundamentalists.

TANZANIA

Area: 945 087 km² (364 900 sq mi). **Population:** 25 096 000 (1991 est). **Capital and major cities:** Dodoma 204 000, Dar es Salaam 1 361 000 (1988 census). **Languages:** English, Swahili (90%; 9% as a first language) – both official. **Religions:** Animist (40%), Sunni Islam (33%), Roman Catholic (20%). **Government:** Republic – to adopt multi-party system with an executive presidency.

GEOGRAPHY

Zanzibar comprises three small islands. The mainland – formerly Tanganyika – comprises savannah plateaux divided by rift valleys and a N–S mountain chain rising to Kilimanjaro at 5894 m (19 340 ft), the highest point in Africa. The climate is tropical, although the mountains are cooler.

ECONOMIC ACTIVITY

Subsistence farming involves over 70% of the labour force. Cash crops include coffee and cotton. Mineral resources include diamonds and gold.

RECENT HISTORY

1884–1919: German rule on mainland (Tanganyika). **1890–63:** British protectorate over Zanzibar. **1919–61:** Tanganyika under British rule. **1961:** Tanganyika independent. **1963:** Zanzibar independent; sultan deposed in left-wing coup. **1964:** Tanganyika and Zanzibar united to form Tanzania. **1965–92:** Single-party state; Julius Nyerere president until 1985. **1992:** Return to multi-party rule conceded.

THAILAND

Before 1939 Thailand was known as Siam. **Area:** 513 115 km² (198 115 sq mi). **Population:** 57 150 000 (1990 est). **Capital:** Bangkok 5 876 000 (1990 census). **Language:** Thai (official). **Religions:** Buddhism (95%), Sunni Islam (4%). **Government:** Kingdom – multi-party parliamentary system.

GEOGRAPHY

Central Thailand is a densely populated fertile plain. The mountainous N rises to 2595 m (8514 ft). The infertile Khorat Plateau occupies the NE, while the mountainous Isthmus of Kra joins southern Thailand to Malaysia. The climate is subtropical with heavy monsoon rains from June to October, a cool season from October to March and a hot season from March to June.

ECONOMIC ACTIVITY

Two thirds of the labour force is involved in

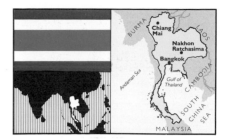

agriculture, mainly growing rice (a major export), tapioca and rubber. Manufacturing – based on cheap labour – is expanding and includes textiles, clothes, electrical and electronic engineering. Thailand has achieved high economic growth rates since the early 1980s. Tourism is a major foreign-currency earner.

RECENT HISTORY

1932: Bloodless coup; constitutional monarchy established. **Since 1932:** Recurrent military interventions in government. **1941–45:** During World War II Thailand was forced into an alliance with Japan. **Since 1945:** Closely allied with the USA. **1992:** Constitutional rule restored.

TOGO

Area: 56 785 km² (21 925 sq mi). **Population:** 3 531 000 (1990 est). **Capital:** Lomé 366 000 (1983 est). **Languages:** French, Ewe (47%), Kabre (22%) – all official. **Religions:** Animist (50%), Roman Catholic (26%), Sunni Islam (15%). **Government:** Republic – limited multi-party system with executive presidency.

GEOGRAPHY

Inland from a narrow coastal plain is a series of plateaux rising in the N to the Chaine du Togo. The climate is hot and humid, although the N is drier.

ECONOMIC ACTIVITY

The majority of the labour force is involved in subsistence farming, with yams and millet as the principal crops. Phosphates are the main export.

RECENT HISTORY

1884: German colony of Togoland established. **1914:** Togoland taken by Franco-British forces. **1919:** Togoland divided between France and Britain (British Togoland became part of Ghana). **1960:** French Togoland gained independence as Togo. **Since 1960:** Great political instability; several coups. **1979–91:** One-party state. **1991:** Multi-party system restored.

TONGA

Area: 748 km² (289 sq mi). **Population:** 97 000 (1991 est). **Capital:** Nuku'alofa 28 900 (1986).

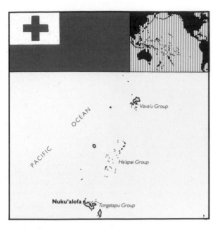

Languages: Tongan, English. **Religions:** Methodist (43%; official). **Government:** Kingdom – non-party limited parliamentary system.

GEOGRAPHY
The 172 Tongan islands – 36 of which are inhabited – comprise a low limestone chain in the E and a higher volcanic chain in the W. The climate is warm with heavy rainfall.

ECONOMIC ACTIVITY
Agriculture involves most Tongans with yams, cassava and taro being grown as subsistence crops. Coconut products are the main exports.

RECENT HISTORY
1900–70: British protectorate. **1970:** Independence restored. **Since 1987:** Pressure for constitutional reform.

TRINIDAD AND TOBAGO

Area: 5130 km² (1981 sq mi). **Population:** 1 234 000 (1990 census). **Capital:** Port of Spain 51 000 (1990 census). **Languages:** English (official), Hindi (25%). **Religions:** Roman Catholic (34%), Hinduism (25%), Anglican (15%). **Government:** Republic – multi-party parliamentary system.

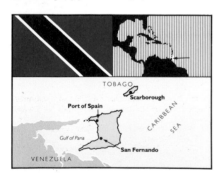

GEOGRAPHY
Trinidad is generally undulating, although the N rises to 940 m (3085 ft). Tobago is more mountainous. The climate is humid and tropical, with a dry season from January to May.

ECONOMIC ACTIVITY
Petroleum and petrochemicals are the mainstay of the economy. Trinidad also has important reserves of natural gas and asphalt. Tourism is a major foreign-currency earner.

RECENT HISTORY
1899: Unification of British colonies of Trinidad and Tobago. **1962:** Independence. **1970 and 1990:** Abortive uprisings.

TUNISIA

Area: 163 610 km² (63 170 sq mi). **Population:** 8 293 000 (1991 est). **Capital:** Tunis 1 395 000 (city 597 000; 1984 census). **Language:** Arabic (official). **Religion:** Sunni Islam (official; 99%). **Government:** Republic – multi-party system with executive presidency.

GEOGRAPHY
The Northern Tell and the High Tell mountains rise to 1544 m (5066 ft). Wide plateaux cover central Tunisia. The Sahara Desert lies S of a zone of shallow salt lakes. The N has a Mediterranean climate; the S is hot and dry.

ECONOMIC ACTIVITY
Phosphates and petroleum are the mainstay of the economy. The main crops are wheat, barley and vegetables, plus olives and citrus fruit for export. Tourism is a major foreign-currency earner.

RECENT HISTORY
1881–1942: French rule in Tunisia. **1942–43:** German occupation during World War II. **1943–1956:** French rule restored. **1956:** Independence. **1957:** Monarchy abolished. **1957–88:** Presidency of Habib Bourguiba. **Since 1988:** Multi-party politics have been permitted.

TURKEY

Area: 779 452 km² (300 948 sq mi). **Population:** 58 376 000 (1991 est). **Capital and major cities:** Ankara 2 560 000, Istanbul 6 620 000, Izmir 1 757 000 (all including suburbs; 1990 census). **Languages:** Turkish (official); Kurdish (20%). **Religions:** Sunni Islam (67%), Shia Islam (30%). **Government:** Republic – multi-party parliamentary system with executive presidency.

GEOGRAPHY
Turkey W of the Dardenelles – 5% of the total area – is part of Europe. Asiatic Turkey consists of the central Anatolian Plateau and its basins, bordered to the N by the Pontic Mountains, to the S by the Taurus Mountains, and to the E by high ranges rising to Ağridaği (Mount Ararat) at 5185 m

(17 011 ft). The coastal regions have a Mediterranean climate. The interior is continental with hot, dry summers and cold, snowy winters.

ECONOMIC ACTIVITY
Agriculture involves one half of the labour force. Major crops include wheat, rice, tobacco, and cotton. Both tobacco and cotton have given rise to important processing industries, and textiles are Turkey's main export. Manufacturing – in particular the chemical and steel industries – has grown rapidly. Unemployment is severe. Money sent back by the large number of Turks working in Western Europe is a major source of foreign currency. Tourism is increasingly important.

RECENT HISTORY
1912–13: Balkan Wars; Turkey virtually expelled from Europe. **1914–18:** Alliance with Germany in World War I ended in defeat and the loss of all non-Turkish areas. **1921–23:** War with Greece which claimed much of Anatolia. **1922:** Sultanate abolished. **1922–38:** Presidency of Mustafa Kemal (later known as Atatürk); Turkey transformed into a secular Westernized state. **1952:** Turkey joined Western alliance. **1960–61:** Military government following coup. **1961–80:** Constitutional rule restored. **1974:** Turkey invaded N Cyprus, where a Turkish administration was established (1975). **1980–83:** Military government following coup. **Since 1983:** Constitutional rule restored; unrest among Turkey's ethnic Kurds has intensified.

TURKMENISTAN

Area: 488 100 km² (188 500 sq mi). **Population:** 3 714 000 (1991 est). **Capital:** Ashkabad 411 000 (1990 est). **Languages:** Turkmen (72%), Russian (9%), Uzbek (9%). **Religions:** Sunni Islam majority. **Government:** Republic – restricted multi-party system with executive presidency.

GEOGRAPHY
The sandy Kara-Kum Desert occupies the centre of the republic, over 90% of which is desert. The Kopet Dag mountains form the border with Iran. A continental climate is characterized by hot summers, freezing winters and very low precipitation.

ECONOMY
Turkmenistan is rich in oil and natural gas. Industries include engineering, metal processing and textiles. Collective farms grow cotton under irrigation and raise sheep, camels and horses. The economy remains largely state-owned and centrally planned.

RECENT HISTORY
1881: Russian conquest completed. **1916:** Major revolt against Russia. **1919:** Turkmenistan recaptured by Soviet Red Army. **1991:** Independence upon the dissolution of the USSR.

TUVALU

Area: 26 km² (10 sq mi). **Population:** 9300 (1991

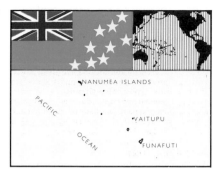

est). *Capital:* Fongafale on Funafuti atoll 2800 (1985). *Languages:* Tuvaluan and English. *Religion:* Protestant Church of Tuvalu (97%). *Government:* Dominion – non-party parliamentary system.

GEOGRAPHY
Tuvalu comprises nine small islands whose highest point is only 6 m (20 ft) above sea level. Tuvalu experiences high temperatures and heavy rainfall.

ECONOMIC ACTIVITY
Subsistence farming – based on coconuts, pigs and poultry – involves most of the labour force. The only export is copra from coconuts.

RECENT HISTORY
1892: The islands became the British Ellice Islands colony. **1978:** Independence.

UGANDA

Area: 241 139 km² (93 104 sq mi). *Population:* 16 538 000 (1991 census). *Capital:* Kampala 773 000 (1991 census). *Languages:* English and Swahili (both official), Luganda. *Religions:* Roman Catholic (45%), various Protestant Churches (17%), animist (32%). *Government:* Republic – military government.

GEOGRAPHY
Most of Uganda is a plateau. This ends in the W at the Great Rift Valley and the Ruwenzori Mountains, rising to Ngaliema at 5118 m (16 763 ft). Lake Victoria covers SE Uganda. The tropical climate is moderated by altitude.

ECONOMIC ACTIVITY
Agriculture involves over 75% of the labour force; coffee accounts for 90% of Uganda's exports. Subsistence crops include plantains, cassava and sweet potatoes.

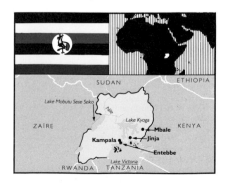

RECENT HISTORY
1884: British protectorate of Uganda established. **1962:** Independence. **1966:** Buganda monarchy suppressed. **1971–79:** Dictatorship of Idi Amin; expulsion of Asian population. **1979:** Army coup, supported by Tanzanian troops. **1979–85:** Widespread instability ended by army coup.

UKRAINE

Area: 603 700 km² (233 100 sq mi). *Population:* 51 944 000 (1991 est). *Capital and major cities:* Kiev (Kyiv) 2 587 000, Kharkov (Kharkiv) 1 611 000, Dnepropetrovsk (Dnipropetrovske) 1 179 000 (1989 census). *Languages:* Ukrainian (73%), Russian (22%). *Religions:* Ukrainian Uniat (Roman Catholic), Ukrainian and Russian Orthodox. *Government:* Republic – multi-party system with executive presidency.

GEOGRAPHY
Most of Ukraine – after Russia, the largest country in Europe – comprises plains (steppes), interrupted by low plateaux and basins. The N includes part of the Pripet Marshes. Central Ukraine comprises the Dnepr Lowland and the Dnepr Plateau. The most diverse scenery is in the W where an extensive lowland extends into Hungary and the Carpathian Mountains rise to 2061 m (6762 ft) at Mount Hoverla. The Crimean Peninsula – which has a Mediterranean climate – consists of parallel mountain ridges and fertile valleys. Most of Ukraine has a temperate climate, with heavy snowfall in the N and the Carpathians.

ECONOMIC ACTIVITY
Ukraine was known as the bread basket of the USSR. Large collectivized farms on the steppes grow cereals, fodder crops and vegetables. Potatoes and flax are important in the N; fruit farming is widespread, particularly in the Crimea. Large deposits of iron ore and the vast Donets coalfield are the base of Ukraine's iron and steel industry. Other major industries include consumer goods, heavy engineering (railway locomotives, shipbuilding, generators), food processing, and chemicals. The first steps in privatization have been taken but inflation is rampant and the economy has declined seriously.

RECENT HISTORY
1918: Independence declared in W; Ukrainian Soviet government established in E. **1919–21:** Civil war – Soviet Red Army intervened. **1922:** Ukraine became a Union Republic of the USSR. **From 1928:** Increased Russification. **1941–45:** German occupation during World War II. **1945–54:** Ukraine enlarged by the addition of areas from Poland, Romania, Czechoslovakia, and Russia (Crimea). **1986:** Nuclear accident at Chernobyl; Ukrainian nationalism spurred by perceived Soviet indifference. **1991:** Independence upon dissolution of the USSR. **Since 1991:** Tension with Russia over the status of Crimea and the Black Sea fleet.

UNITED ARAB EMIRATES

Area: 77 700 km² (30 000 sq mi). *Population:* 1 945 000 (1991 est). *Capital:* Abu Dhabi 243 000 (1985 census). *Language:* Arabic (official). *Religion:* Sunni Islam (official). *Government:* Federation of seven absolute monarchies.

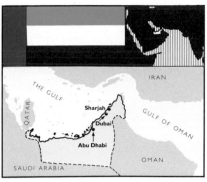

GEOGRAPHY
The country is mainly a low-lying desert. Summer temperatures may exceed 40 °C (104 °F); winter temperatures are milder. Rainfall is negligible.

ECONOMIC ACTIVITY
Large reserves of petroleum and natural gas give a high standard of living. Diversification – dry docks, fertilizer factories, commercial banking, and an entrepôt trade – has been encouraged.

RECENT HISTORY
Late 19th century: Treaties ('truces') signed with local rulers brought the Trucial States under British protection. **1958:** Discovery of oil. **1971:** UK withdrew; Trucial States formed the United Arab Emirates.

UNITED KINGDOM

Area: 244 103 km² (94 249 sq mi). *Population:* 57 533 000 (1991 est). *Capital and major cities:* London 7 797 000 (London Urban Area – Greater London 6 794 000), Birmingham 2 324 000 (West Midlands Urban Area; city 992 800), Manchester 2 310 000 (Greater Manchester Urban Area; city 446 700), Glasgow 1 650 000 (Central Clydeside Urban Area; city 689 200), Leeds-Bradford 1 547 000 (West Yorkshire Urban Area – Leeds 712 200, Bradford 468 800), Newcastle-upon-Tyne 762 000 (Tyneside Urban Area; city 277 800), Liverpool 659 000 (Urban Area; city 462 900), Sheffield 649 000 (Urban Area; city 525 800), Nottingham 615 000 (Urban Area; city 274 900), Bristol 530 000 (Urban Area; city 374 300), Edinburgh 523 000 (Urban Area; city 434 500) (1990 est). *Languages:* English; Welsh and Gaelic minorities. *Religions:* Anglican (55% nominal; 4% practising), Roman Catholic (9%), Presbyterian (3%, including Church of Scotland). *Government:* Kingdom – multi-party parliamentary system.

COUNTRIES OF THE UK
(with areas, populations in 1990 and capitals)
England – 130 441 km² (50 363 sq mi), 47 837 300, London.
Northern Ireland – 14 120 km² (5452 sq mi), 1 589 400, Belfast.
Scotland – 78 775 km² (30 415 sq mi), 5 102 400, Edinburgh.
Wales – 20 768 km² (8019 sq mi), 2 881 400, Cardiff.

CROWN DEPENDENCIES
– associated with but not part of the UK (with areas, populations in 1988 and capitals)
Guernsey and Dependencies (Alderney and Sark) – 75 km² (29 sq mi), 57 000, St Peter Port.
Isle of Man – 572 km² (221 sq mi), 64 300, Douglas.
Jersey – 116 km² (45 sq mi), 80 200, St Helier.

DEPENDENCIES
(with areas, populations in 1989–91 and capitals)
Anguilla – 96 km² (35 sq mi), 6900, The Valley.
Bermuda – 54 km² (21 sq mi), 60 000, Hamilton.
British Antarctic Territory – 1 810 000 km² (700 000 sq mi), uninhabited.
British Indian Ocean Territory – 60 km² (23 sq mi), no civilian population.

UK joined EC. **1979–90:** Restructuring of domestic economy and welfare state under the Conservative premiership of Margaret Thatcher. **1982:** Falklands War.

UNITED STATES OF AMERICA

Area: 9 372 614 km² (3 618 770 sq mi). *Population:* 252 177 000 (1991 est). *Capital and major cities:* Washington D.C. 3 924 000 (city 598 000), New York 18 087 000 (city 7 323 000, Newark 275 000), Los Angeles 14 532 000 (city 3 485 000, Long Beach 429 000, Anaheim 266 000), Chicago 8 066 000 (city 2 784 000), San Francisco 6 253 000 (city 724 000, San Jose 782 000), Philadelphia 5 899 000 (city 1 586 000), Detroit 4 665 000 (city 1 028 000), Boston 4 172 000 (city 574 000), Dallas 3 885 000 (city 1 007 000, Fort Worth 478 000), Houston 3 711 000 (city 1 631 000), Miami 3 193 000 (city 359 000) (1990 census). *Languages:* English (official), Spanish (6%, as a first language). *Religions:* Roman Catholic (23%), Baptist (10%), Methodist (5%), Lutheran (3%). *Government* Federal republic – multi-party system with executive presidency.

STATES

(with areas, populations in 1991 and capitals)
Alabama – 133 915 km² (51 705 sq mi), 4 089 000, Montgomery.
Alaska – 1 530 693 km² (591 004 sq mi), 570 000, Juneau.
Arizona – 295 259 km² (114 000 sq mi), 3 750 000, Phoenix.
Arkansas – 137 754 km² (53 187 sq mi), 2 372 000, Little Rock.
California – 411 047 km² (158 706 sq mi), 30 380 000, Sacramento.
Colorado – 269 594 km² (104 091 sq mi), 3 377 000, Denver.
Connecticut – 12 997 km² (5018 sq mi), 3 291 000, Hartford.
Delaware – 5294 km² (2045 sq mi), 680 000, Dover.
Florida – 151 939 km² (58 664 sq mi), 13 277 000, Tallahassee.
Georgia – 152 576 km² (58 910 sq mi), 6 623 000, Atlanta.
Hawaii – 16 760 km² (6471 sq mi), 1 135 000, Honolulu.
Idaho – 216 430 km² (83 564 sq mi), 1 039 000, Boise.
Illinois – 149 885 km² (57 871 sq mi), 11 543 000, Springfield.
Indiana – 94 309 km² (36 413 sq mi), 5 610 000, Indianapolis.
Iowa – 145 752 km² (56 275 sq mi), 2 795 000, Des Moines.
Kansas – 213 096 km² (82 277 sq mi), 2 495 000, Topeka.
Kentucky – 104 659 km² (40 410 sq mi), 3 713 000, Frankfort.
Louisiana – 123 677 km² (47 752 sq mi), 4 252 000, Baton Rouge.
Maine – 86 156 km² (33 265 sq mi), 1 235 000, Augusta.
Maryland – 27 091 km² (10 460 sq mi), 4 860 000, Annapolis.
Massachusetts – 21 455 km² (8284 sq mi), 5 996 000, Boston.
Michigan – 251 493 km² (97 102 sq mi), 9 368 000, Lansing.
Minnesota – 224 329 km² (86 614 sq mi), 4 432 000, St Paul.
Mississippi – 123 514 km² (47 689 sq mi), 2 592 000, Jackson.
Missouri – 180 514 km² (69 697 sq mi), 5 158 000, Jefferson City.
Montana – 380 847 km² (147 046 sq mi), 808 000, Helena.
Nebraska – 200 349 km² (77 355 sq mi), 1 593 000, Lincoln.
Nevada – 286 352 km² (110 561 sq mi), 1 284 000, Carson City.
New Hampshire – 24 032 km² (9279 sq mi), 1 105 000, Concord.

British Virgin Islands – 153 km² (59 sq mi), 16 600, Road Town.
Cayman Islands – 259 km² (100 sq mi), 25 500, George Town.
Falkland Islands – 12 170 km² (4698 sq mi), 2100, Port Stanley.
Gibraltar – 6.5 km² (2.5 sq mi), 31 000, Gibraltar.
Hong Kong – 1045 km² (403 sq mi), 5 674 000, Victoria.
Montserrat – 98 km² (38 sq mi), 12 400, Plymouth.
Pitcairn Islands – 48 km² (18.5 sq mi), 52, Adamstown.
St Helena and Dependencies (Ascension and Tristan da Cunha) – 419 km² (162 sq mi), 7100, Jamestown.
South Georgia and South Sandwich Islands – 4091 km² (1580 sq mi), no permanent population.
Turks and Caicos Islands – 430 km² (166 sq mi), 12 400, Cockburn Town on Grand Turk.

GEOGRAPHY
The UK comprises the island of Great Britain, the NE part of Ireland plus over 4000 other islands. Lowland Britain occupies the S, E and centre of England. In the E, low-lying Fenland is largely reclaimed marshland. The flat landscape of East Anglia is covered by glacial soils. The NW coastal plain of Lancashire and Cheshire is the only other major lowland in England. In the SW, Devon and Cornwall contain granitic uplands, including Dartmoor and Exmoor. The limestone Pennines form a moorland backbone running through N England. The Lake District (Cumbria) is a mountainous dome rising to Scafell Pike, the highest point in England at 978 m (3210 ft). Wales is a highland block, formed by a series of plateaux above which rise the Brecon Beacons in the S, and Snowdonia in the N, where Snowdon reaches 1085 m (3560 ft). In Scotland, the Highlands in the N and the Southern Uplands are separated by the rift valley of the Central Lowlands, where the majority of Scotland's population, agriculture and industry are to be found. The Highlands are divided by the Great Glen in which lies Loch Ness. Although Ben Nevis is the highest point at 1392 m (4406 ft), the most prominent range of the Highlands is the Cairngorm Mountains. To the W of Scotland are the many islands of the Inner and Outer Hebrides,

while to the N are the Orkney and Shetland Islands. Northern Ireland includes several hilly areas, including the Sperrin Mountains in the NW and the Mourne Mountains in the SE. Lough Neagh – at the centre of Northern Ireland – is the UK's largest lake. The temperate climate of the UK is warmed by the North Atlantic Drift. There is considerable local variety, particularly in rainfall.

ECONOMIC ACTIVITY
Nearly one quarter of the British labour force is involved in manufacturing. The principal industries include iron and steel, motor vehicles, electronics and electrical engineering, textiles and clothing, and consumer goods. British industry relies heavily upon imports of raw materials. The country is self-sufficient in petroleum (from the North Sea) and has important reserves of natural gas. The coal industry is declining as seams become uneconomic. As Britain is a major trading nation, London is one of the world's leading banking, financial and insurance centres, and the 'invisible earnings' from these services make an important contribution to exports. Tourism is another major foreign-currency earner. Agriculture involves about 2% of the labour force and is principally concerned with raising sheep and cattle. Economic problems have included repeated crises of confidence in the value of the pound, credit squeezes and high (regional) rates of unemployment. Since 1980 most major nationalized industries have been privatized.

RECENT HISTORY
By **1900:** Britain's economic dominance was challenged by the USA and Germany. **1908–16:** Reforming Liberal government of Herbert Asquith. **1914–18:** First World War. **1916:** Easter Rising in Ireland. **1922:** Partition of Ireland. **1931:** Statute of Westminster – independence of the 'old' dominions. **1939–45:** Britain – led by PM Sir Winston Churchill – played a major role in the defeat of the Axis powers. **1945–51:** Labour government of Clement Attlee established the 'welfare state'; dissolution of British Empire began, starting with the independence of India in 1947. **1956:** Franco-British intervention in Suez. **Since 1972:** Resurgence of terrorism and unrest in N Ireland; British troops stationed in N Ireland to keep order. **1973:**

New Jersey – 20 168 km² (7787 sq mi), 7 760 000, Trenton.

New Mexico – 314 924 km² (121 593 sq mi), 1 548 000, Santa Fe.

New York – 136 583 km² (52 735 sq mi), 18 058 000, Albany.

North Carolina – 136 412 km² (52 669 sq mi), 6 737 000, Rayleigh.

North Dakota – 183 117 km² (70 702 sq mi), 635 000, Bismarck.

Ohio – 115 998 km² (44 787 sq mi), 10 939 000, Columbus.

Oklahoma – 181 185 km² (69 956 sq mi), 3 175 000, Oklahoma City.

Oregon – 251 418 km² (97 073 sq mi), 2 922 000, Salem.

Pennsylvania – 119 251 km² (46 043 sq mi), 11 961 000, Harrisburg.

Rhode Island – 3139 km² (1212 sq mi), 1 004 000, Providence.

South Carolina – 80 582 km² (31 113 sq mi), 3 560 000, Columbia.

South Dakota – 199 730 km² (77 116 sq mi), 703 000, Pierre.

Tennessee – 109 152 km² (42 144 sq mi), 4 953 000, Nashville.

Texas – 691 027 km² (266 807 sq mi), 17 349 000, Austin.

Utah – 219 887 km² (84 899 sq mi), 1 770 000, Salt Lake City.

Vermont – 24 900 km² (9614 sq mi), 567 000, Montpelier.

Virginia – 105 586 km² (40 767 sq mi), 6 286 000, Richmond.

Washington – 176 479 km² (68 139 sq mi), 5 018 000, Olympia.

West Virginia – 62 758 km² (24 323 sq mi), 1 801 000, Charleston.

Wisconsin – 171 496 km² (66 215 sq mi), 4 955 000, Madison.

Wyoming – 253 324 km² (97 809 sq mi), 460 000, Cheyenne.

District of Columbia – 179 km² (69 sq mi), 598 000, Washington.

US TERRITORIES

(External Territories unless otherwise indicated; with areas, populations in 1990 and capitals) *North Mariana Islands* (Commonwealth Territory) – 471 km² (184 sq mi), 43 300, Chalan Kanoa on Saipan.

Puerto Rico (Commonwealth Territory) – 9104 km² (3515 sq mi), 3 522 000, San Juan.

Palau (also known as Belau; UN Trust Territory) – 497 km² (192 sq mi), 15 100, Koror.

American Samoa – 197 km² (96 sq mi), 47 000, Pago Pago.

Guam – 541 km² (209 sq mi), 133 000, Agaña.

Howland, Baker and Jarvis Islands – 5 km² (2 sq mi), uninhabited.

Johnston Atoll – 1.3 km² (0.5 sq mi), no permanent population.

Kingman Reef – 0.03 km² (0.01 sq mi), uninhabited.

Midway Islands – 5 km² (2 sq mi), no permanent population.

United States Virgin Islands – 352 km² (136 sq mi), 102 000, Charlotte Amalie.

Wake Island – 8 km² (3 sq mi), no permanent population.

GEOGRAPHY

The Atlantic coastal plain stretches along the entire E coast, including the lowland peninsula of Florida, and along the coast of the Gulf of Mexico, where it reaches up to 800 km (500 mi) inland. W of the plain rises the Blue Ridge escarpment, the most easterly part of the forested Appalachian Mountains, which stretch for some 2400 km (1500 mi) and reach 2037 m (6684 ft). The largest physical region of the USA is a vast interior plain drained by the Mississippi-Missouri and its tributaries. This lowland stretches from the Great Lakes in the N to the coastal plain in the S, and from the Rocky Mountains in the W to the Appalachians in the E. The Central Lowlands – the eastern part of the lowland – comprise the Cotton Belt in the S and the Corn (maize) Belt in the N. The Great Plains – the drier western part of the lowland – begin some 480 km (300 mi) W of the Mississippi. The W of the USA is the country's highest region and includes the Rocky Mountains in the E and the Cascades, the Sierra Nevada and the Coastal Ranges in the W. The mountains continue N into Alaska, where Mount McKinley – the highest peak in the USA – reaches 6194 m (20 320 ft). Within the mountains are deserts – including the Mojave and the Arizona Deserts – and the large Intermontane Plateau containing the Great Basin, an area of internal drainage around the Great Salt Lake. The 20 islands of Hawaii are volcanic in origin and contain active volcanoes. There are great regional differences in climate. The mountains behind the Pacific NW coast are the wettest region of the USA. Coastal California has a warm Mediterranean climate. Desert or semidesert conditions prevail in mountain basins. The continental Great Plains receive 250–750 mm (10–30 in) of rain a year, while the Central Lowlands to the E are generally wetter. Extremes of temperature are experienced in the N of the continental interior. The E is mainly temperate. The Appalachians and the E coastal plain are humid, with temperatures rising in the S where Florida is subtropical. Coastal Alaska has a cold maritime climate while the N and interior is polar. Hawaii has a Pacific climate with high temperatures and little seasonal variation.

ECONOMIC ACTIVITY

The USA's position as the world's leading economic power is threatened by Japan. The USA is self-sufficient in most products apart from petroleum, chemicals, certain metals and manufactured machinery, and newsprint. Agriculture is heavily mechanized and produces large surpluses for export. The main crops include maize, wheat, soyabeans, sugar cane, barley, cotton, potatoes and a wide variety of fruit (including citrus fruit in Florida and California). More than 25% of the USA is pastureland, and cattle and sheep are important in the Great Plains. Forests cover over 30% of the country and are the basis of a major timber industry. The USA has great natural resources, including coal (mainly in the Appalachians), iron ore, petroleum and natural gas (mainly in Texas, Alaska and California), copper and bauxite, and major rivers suitable for hydroelectric power plants. The industrial base is diverse including iron and steel, motor vehicles, electrical and electronic engineering, food processing, chemicals, cement, aluminium, aerospace industries, telecommunications, textiles and clothing, and consumer goods. Tourism is a major foreign-currency earner. Service industries involve over 75% of the labour force. Finance, insurance and banking are important, and Wall Street (New York) is one the world's major stock exchanges. US economic policy exerts an influence throughout the world, thus a revival of pressure for trade protectionism in the late 1980s and early 1990s caused international concern.

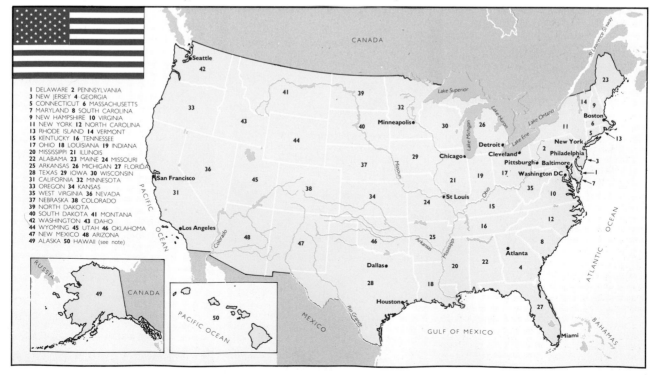

RECENT HISTORY

1880–1900: USA emerged as an industrial giant; large-scale immigration, in particular from E and Central Europe. **1898:** Spanish-American War; USA gained Philippines, Puerto Rico and Guam. **1917–18:** US participation in World War I; President Woodrow Wilson's idealistic 14 point peace plan compromised in the post-war settlement. **1918–41:** USA retreated into isolationism and protectionism in trade. **1919–33:** Prohibition increased smuggling and activities of criminal gangs. **1929:** Start of the Depression; collapse of the stock market. **1933–39:** Federal investment and intervention through the New Deal programme of President Franklin Roosevelt. **1941:** Japanese attack on Pearl Harbor brought USA into World War II. **After 1945:** USA committed to world role as a superpower. **1947–51:** Marshall Plan; US assistance to rebuild Europe. **Late 1940s–1991:** USA confronted USSR's perceived global threat in the Cold War. **1950–53:** US involvement in the Korean War (1950–53) against Chinese and North Korean forces. **From 1950s:** Civil rights movement – led by Martin Luther King – campaigned for full political rights for Blacks. **1954:** US intervention in Guatemala. **1958 and 1983–85:** US intervention in Lebanon. **1961:** US support for unsuccessful invasion of Cuba by exiles. **1963:** Assassination of President John F. Kennedy. **1964–73:** Vietnam War; US forces attempted to hold back Communist takeover of Indochina; growing disenchantment with the war forced US withdrawal. **1965:** US intervention in Dominican Republic. **1968 and 1989:** US intervention in Panama. **1968:** Assassination of Martin Luther King. **1983:** US intervention in Grenada. **1981–89:** Monetarist policies of President Ronald Reagan. **1990–91:** US led the coalition against Saddam Hussein's Iraq. **Since 1989–91:** Questions raised about USA's future world role after the collapse of Communism.

URUGUAY

Area: 176 215 km² (68 037 sq mi). *Population:* 3 112 000 (1991 est). *Capital:* Montevideo 1 312 000 (including suburbs; 1985 census). *Language:* Spanish (official). *Religion:* Roman Catholic (58%). *Government:* Republic – multi-party system with executive presidency.

GEOGRAPHY

Uruguay consists mainly of low plains and plateaux. Hills in the SE rise to over 500 m (1640 ft). The climate is temperate with warm summers and mild winters. Rainfall averages around 900 mm (35 in).

ECONOMIC ACTIVITY

Pastureland – for sheep and beef cattle – covers about 80% of the land. Meat, wool and hides are the leading exports. Despite a lack of natural resources, Uruguay has a high standard of living.

RECENT HISTORY

1903–07 and 1911–15: Presidencies of José Battle; Uruguay became a democracy and an advanced welfare state. **Late 1960s:** Period of social and political turmoil; urban guerrillas active. **1973–85:**

Military junta in power. **1985:** Constitutional multi-party rule restored.

UZBEKISTAN

Area: 447 400 km² (172 700 sq mi). *Population:* 20 708 000 (1991 est). *Capital:* Tashkent 2 079 000 (1989 census). *Languages:* Uzbek (71%), Russian (8%). *Religion:* Sunni Islam majority. *Government:* Republic – restricted multi-party system with executive presidency.

GEOGRAPHY

W Uzbekistan is flat and mainly desert. The mountainous E includes ridges of the Tien Shan and part of the Fergana valley. A warm continental climate is characterized by hot summers and low rainfall. Only the mountains receive over 500 mm (20 in) of rain a year.

ECONOMIC ACTIVITY

Uzbekistan is one the world's leading producers of cotton, but the extraction of irrigation from the Amu Darya and its tributaries has contributed to the gradual shrinkage of the Aral Sea. There are large reserves of natural gas and major machine and heavy engineering industries. The economy is still mainly state-owned and centrally planned.

RECENT HISTORY

1868–73: Russian conquest of area completed. **1918–22:** Revolt against Soviet rule. **1924:** Uzbekistan created when the USSR reorganized the boundaries of Soviet Central Asia. **1991:** Independence when the USSR was dissolved.

VANUATU

Area: 12 189 km² (4706 sq mi). *Population:* 150 000 (1991 est). *Capital:* Port-Vila 19 300 (1989 census). *Languages:* English (official; 60%), French (official; 40%), Bislama (national; 82%), 130 local dialects. *Religions:* Presbyterian (33%), Anglican (30%). *Government:* Republic – multi-party parliamentary system.

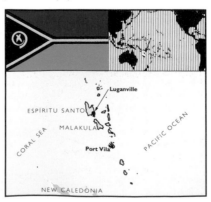

GEOGRAPHY

Vanuatu comprises over 75 islands, some of which are mountainous and include active volcanoes. A tropical climate is moderated by SE trade winds.

ECONOMIC ACTIVITY

Subsistence farming occupies the majority of the labour force. The main exports include copra, fish and cocoa. Tourism is increasingly important.

RECENT HISTORY

1906–80: UK and France ruled the New Hebrides as a condominium. **1980:** Independence as Vanuatu.

VATICAN CITY

Also known as the Holy See. *Area:* 0.44 km² (0.17 sq mi). *Population:* 750 (1989 est). *Languages:* Italian and Latin (both official). *Religion:* The Vatican is the headquarters of the Roman Catholic Church. *Government:* The Pope is head of state – temporal administration is by a papal-appointed commission.

GEOGRAPHY

The state consists of the Vatican City, a walled enclave in Rome, plus a number of churches in Rome (including the cathedral of St John Lateran) and the papal villa at Castelgandolfo.

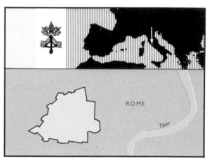

RECENT HISTORY

1870: Rome and Lazio – the last of the Papal States – lost when Italian forces entered Rome. **1870–1929:** No pope emerged from the Vatican as a protest against the loss of the papacy's temporal power. **1929:** Lateran Treaties; Italy recognized the Vatican City as an independent state.

VENEZUELA

Area: 912 050 km² (352 144 sq mi). *Population:* 20 226 000 (1991 est). *Capital:* Caracas 3 346 000

(including suburbs; 1990 est). *Language:* Spanish (official; 98%). *Religion:* Roman Catholic (nearly

92%). *Government:* Republic – multi-party system with executive presidency.

GEOGRAPHY
Mountains in the N – which include part of the Andes – rise to Pico Bolivar at 5007 m (16 423 ft). Central Venezuela comprises low-lying grassland plains (the Llanos). The Guiana Highlands in the SE include many high steep-sided plateaux. The tropical coast is arid. The cooler mountains and the tropical Llanos are wet, although the latter has a dry season from December to March.

ECONOMIC ACTIVITY
Petroleum and natural gas account for over 80% of export earnings. Agriculture is mainly concerned with raising beef cattle, and growing sugar cane and coffee for export; bananas, maize and rice are grown as subsistence crops.

RECENT HISTORY
1909–35: Dictatorship of Juan Vicente Gómez. **1935–58:** Military juntas. **Since 1958:** Constitutional multi-party rule restored.

VIETNAM

Area: 329 566 km^2 (127 246 sq mi). *Population:* 67 589 000 (1991 est). *Capital and major cities:* Hanoi 3 057 000 (city 1 089 000), Ho Chi Minh City (formerly Saigon) 3 934 000 (city 3 169 000) (1989 census). *Language:* Vietnamese (official; 84%). *Religion:* Buddhist (55%). *Government:* Republic – single-party (Communist) state.

GEOGRAPHY
Plateaux, hill country and chains of mountains in Annam (central Vietnam) lie between the Mekong River delta in the S and the Red River (Hongha) delta in the N. Vietnam has a hot humid climate, although winters are cool in the N. Heavy rainfall comes mainly during the monsoon season from April to October.

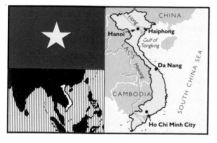

ECONOMIC ACTIVITY
Over 75% of the labour force is involved in agriculture, mainly cultivating rice for domestic use and rubber, tea and coffee for export. Natural resources include coal, phosphates and tin, which are the basis of industries in the N. The wars in Vietnam, involvement in Cambodia and the loss of skilled workers through emigration have all had a serious effect on the economy. Vietnam received aid from the USSR up to the end of the 1980s but remains underdeveloped. Attempts have been made to encourage Western investment since 1989–90.

RECENT HISTORY
1887: French Union of Indochina formed. **1930s:** Revolts against French rule. **1940–45:** Gradual Japanese occupation of Vietnam. **1946–54:** Nationalist forces – led by Ho Chi Minh – conducted a war against French colonial forces. **1954:** Partition of Vietnam into a Communist state in the N and a pro-Western state in the S. **1964–73:** American involvement in the Vietnam War; N and Communist guerrillas tried to takeover the S. **1975:** Communist takeover of the S; reunification. **Since 1975:** Large numbers of refugees – the 'Boat People' – have fled. **1979:** Border war with China. **1979–89:** Occupation of Cambodia by Vietnamese forces.

WESTERN SAHARA (see MOROCCO)

WESTERN SAMOA

Area: 2831 km^2 (1093 sq mi). *Population:* 160 000 (1991 census). *Capital:* Apia 33 000 (1991 census). *Languages:* English and Samoan (official). *Religion:* Congregational (47%). *Government:* State – multi-party parliamentary system; current head of state is analogous to a monarch.

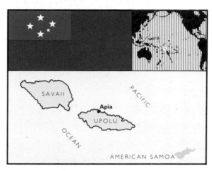

GEOGRAPHY
The country consists of seven small islands and two larger and higher volcanic islands. The climate is tropical with high temperatures and very heavy rainfall.

ECONOMIC ACTIVITY
The majority of Samoans are involved in subsistence agriculture. Copra (from coconuts), cocoa and bananas are the main exports.

RECENT HISTORY
1899–1914: German rule. **1914–62:** New Zealand administration. **1962:** Independence. **Since 1962:** Many Samoans have emigrated to New Zealand.

YEMEN

Area: 531 870 km^2 (205 360 sq mi). *Population:* 11 843 000 (1990 est). *Capital:* Sana'a 427 000 (1986 est). *Language:* Arabic (official). *Religions:* Sunni Islam (54%), Shia Islam (46%). *Government:* Republic – transitional government.

GEOGRAPHY
The Yemen Highlands rise from a narrow coastal plain to 3760 m (12 336 ft) at Jebel Hadhar. An arid plateau in the E extends into the Arabian Desert. Most of the highlands are temperate; the rest of the country is hot and dry.

ECONOMIC ACTIVITY
Cereal crops, coffee and citrus fruit are grown under irrigation in the fertile highlands. In the S,

subsistence farming and fishing occupy the majority of the labour force. Money sent back by Yemenis working in Saudi Arabia is an important source of revenue.

RECENT HISTORY
1911: Ottoman Turks finally expelled from the N. **1962:** Monarchy overthrown in N Yemen. **1963–67:** Rebellion against British rule in the S (Aden). **1963–70:** Civil war in N Yemen between republicans and monarchists. **1967:** Independence of Aden – as S Yemen – after over 120 years of British rule. **1967–90:** Marxist government in S Yemen. **1990:** Unification of the two Yemens.

YUGOSLAVIA

Area: 102 173 km^2 (39 449 sq mi). *Population:* 10 407 000 (1991 census). *Capital:* Belgrade (Beograd) 1 470 000 (1991 census). *Languages:* Serbo-Croat (including Montenegrin; 80%), Albanian (13%). *Religions:* Orthodox (over 75%), Sunni Islam (over 12%). *Government:* Federal republic – restricted multi-party system; executive power concentrated at republican rather than federal level.

REPUBLICS
(with areas, populations in 1991 and capitals)
Montenegro – 13 812 km^2 (5333 sq mi), 615 000, Podgorica (formerly Titograd).
Serbia – 88 361 km^2 (34 116 sq mi), 9 791 000, Belgrade.
Macedonia – see below.

GEOGRAPHY
Ridges of mountains occupy the S and centre of the country. The N (Vojvodina) is occupied by plains drained by the rivers Danube and Tisa. Since the secession of four republics, the Yugoslav coastline is confined to a short stretch on the Adriatic in Montenegro. Coastal Montenegro has a Mediterranean climate; the rest of Yugoslavia has a moderate continental climate.

ECONOMIC ACTIVITY
Agriculture involves over 25% of the labour force. Most of the land is privately owned. Major crops include maize, wheat, sugar beet, potatoes, citrus fruit and fodder crops for sheep. Industry – which is mainly concentrated around Belgrade – includes food processing, textiles, metallurgy and consumer goods. The economy was severely damaged by civil war (1991–2), rampant inflation and an international embargo on trade with Serbia. Money sent home by Yugoslavs working abroad remains an important source of foreign currency.

RECENT HISTORY
1912–13: Balkan Wars; Serbia acquired Macedonia. **1914–18:** World War I; Serbia and Montenegro overrun by (Habsburg) Austro-Hungarian Empire. **1918:** South Slav kingdom formed by merger of Serbia and Montenegro with Bosnia, Croatia and the Slovene lands formerly under Habsburg rule. **1929:** Name of Yugoslavia adopted. **1941:** Yugosla-

via attacked and dismembered by Nazi Germany. **1941–45:** Yugoslavs fought the Nazis and each other; Communist-led partisans of Josip Broz Tito emerged victorious. **1945:** Yugoslavia re-formed on Soviet lines. **1945–80:** Tito president. **1948:** Yugoslavia expelled from Soviet bloc. **After 1980:** Rise of local nationalism; Serbia suppressed Albanian nationalists in Kosovo province. **1990:** Free elections. **1991:** Slovenia and Croatia seceded; Serb-dominated Yugoslav federal forces conducted (unsuccessful) short campaign against Slovenia but occupied one third of Croatia. **1992:** Bosnia-Herzegovina and Macedonia declared independence; Serbian intervention in Bosnian civil war; international sanctions against Serbia and Montenegro.

MACEDONIA
(Former Yugoslav Republic of)
Macedonia effectively seceded Yugoslavia in 1992 but – owing to Greek opposition to the use of the name Macedonia – it has been unable to obtain general international recognition. *Area:* 25 713 km² (9928 sq mi). *Population:* 2 034 000 (1991 census). *Capital:* Skopje 563 000 (1991 census).

ZAIRE

Area: 2 344 885 km² (905 365 sq mi). *Population:* 34 964 000 (1991 est). *Capital:* Kinshasa 3 741 000 (1991 est). *Languages:* French (official), Kiswahili, Tshiluba, Kikongo and Lingala – all national. *Religions:* Roman Catholic (48%), various Protestant Churches (28%), Kimbanguists (17%). *Government:* Republic – restricted multi-party system with executive presidency.

GEOGRAPHY
Over 60% of the country comprises a basin of tropical rain forest, drained by the River Zaïre (Congo) and its tributaries. Plateaux and mountains surrounding the basin include the Ruwenzori Massif in the E, rising to Mount Ngaliema at 5109 m (16 763 ft). Zaïre has a humid, tropical climate

with little seasonal variation, although the N is drier from December to February.
ECONOMIC ACTIVITY
Over 65% of the labour force is involved in agriculture. Although subsistence farming predominates, coffee, tea and palm products are exported. Minerals are the mainstay of the economy, with copper, cobalt, zinc and diamonds accounting for about 60% of Zaïre's exports. Zaïre has one of the lowest standards of living in Africa.
RECENT HISTORY
1908: Congo Free State – the personal possession of King Leopold II of the Belgians – became the colony of the Belgian Congo. **1960:** Independence; collapse of administration; civil wars; Katanga province attempted to secede; UN intervention. **1965:** Colonel Mobutu Sese Seko took over. **1967–91:** One-party state. **1971:** Congolese Republic renamed Zaïre. **1991:** Multi-party politics permitted. **1991–93:** Increasing unrest and opposition to Mobutu.

ZAMBIA

Area: 752 614 km² (290 586 sq mi). *Population:* 7 818 000 (1991 est). *Capital:* Lusaka 870 000 (1988 est). *Languages:* English (official), Bemba (34%), Tonga (16%). *Religions:* Various Protestant Churches (50%), animist (25%) Roman Catholic (20%). *Government:* Republic – multi-party system with executive presidency.

GEOGRAPHY
Zambia comprises plateaux some 1000 to 1500 m (3300 to 5000 ft) high, above which rise the Muchinga Mountains. The tropical climate has a wet season from November to April.
ECONOMIC ACTIVITY
Zambia's economy depends upon the mining and processing of copper, lead, zinc and cobalt. Agriculture is underdeveloped and many basic foodstuffs have to be imported. Maize and cassava are the main crops.

RECENT HISTORY
1890s: Area brought under the control of the British South Africa Company. **1924–53:** British colony of Northern Rhodesia. **1953–64:** Part of the white-dominated Central African Federation. **1964:** Independence as Zambia. **1973–90:** One-party state. **Since 1990:** Multi-party system restored; 1991 elections – first democratic change of government in English-speaking Black Africa.

ZIMBABWE

Area: 390 759 km² (150 873 sq mi). *Population:* 9 619 000 (1991 est). *Capital:* Harare 863 000 (1989 est). *Languages:* English (official), Chishona, Sindebele. *Religions:* Animist (42%), Anglican (30%), Roman Catholic (15%). *Government:* Republic – multi-party system with executive presidency.

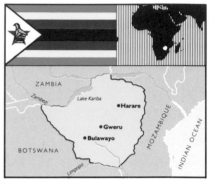

GEOGRAPHY
Central Zimbabwe comprises the ridge of the Highveld, rising to between 1200 and 1500 m (about 4000 to 5000 ft). The Highveld is bounded on the SW and NE by the Middle Veld and the Lowveld plateaux. The climate is tropical in the lowlands and subtropical at altitude.
ECONOMIC ACTIVITY
Agriculture involves over 65% of the labour force. Tobacco, sugar cane, cotton, wheat and maize are exported as well as being the basis of processing industries. Natural resources include coal, gold, asbestos and nickel.
RECENT HISTORY
1890s: Area occupied by the British South Africa Company; white settlement began. **1923–53:** British colony of Southern Rhodesia. **1953–64:** Part of the white-dominated Central African Federation. **1965–79:** White minority rule after unilateral declaration of independence. **1970s:** Increasingly effective African guerrilla campaign. **1980:** Majority rule – under Robert Mugabe – following brief reimposition of British rule. **Since 1987:** Virtual one-party state.

INDEX

Notes:
1. Illustrations and maps are indicated by *italicized* numbers; there are also illustrations and maps on some of the pages that indicate textual references.
2. Where there are several page references for an entry, the major reference is shown in **bold** numbers, except where it is already italicized to show an illustration.
3. Sub-entries are in alphabetical order.
4. The Countries of the World section (pp. 378–424) has not been indexed in detail. Facts on recent history, geography, government and economy can be obtained by looking in this section.
5. Prefixes to Arabic names, such as el-, al- and ibn-, are ignored for purposes of alphabetization.

A
Aalto, Alvar **326**
Abbasid dynasty 242
  arts 308
Abbey Theatre, Dublin 375
Abelard, Peter 304
aberrations, optical 24, 25
ABM agreement 281
Aborigines/Aboriginal culture 237
  puberty rites 159
Abraham 294, 300
absolute magnitude 5
absolute monarchy
  Henry VIII 254
  Louis XIV 256
absolute zero 18
absolutism 166
absorption
  digestive system **138–139**
  waves 20
Abstract Expressionism **324**
Abstraction (art) **323**
abyssal plains 76, 77
Abyssinia/Abyssinians 267, 392
  Italy and 267, 273
Académie française 362
Académie Royale de Danse 346
acceleration 14
  angular 16
  centripetal *15*
accumulators 28
Achaemenid Empire, official religion of 229, 286
achondroplasia 152
achromatic lens 24
acid rain 40, 130, 186
  major causes 43, 188
acids 35
  manufacture of 201
  reactions of 40
  weak and strong 41
acoustics **22–23**
acromegaly 143
Act of Union 255
ACTH 143
actin 137
acting, film 328
actinium *37*
Action painting **324**
Actium, battle of 232
Adam, Robert **326**
Adams, John **339**, 343
Adams, John Couch 9
adaptive radiation 85
addition 54
  inverse operation *see* subtraction
adipose tissue 139
Adorno, Theodor **305**
adrenal glands 143
adrenocorticotrophic hormone *see* ACTH
advanced gas-cooled reactors 189
aerials (antenna) 206, 207
aerodynes 222
aerostats 222
Aeschylus 356
Aesop 359
Aestheticism 372
affective disorders 150
Afghanistan **379**
  British ousted from 266–267
  invasion of India 236
  Soviet invasion of 281
Africa
  animals
    elephant 117
    hoofed mammals 116, 117
    hunting dog *114*, 115
  art **309**
  deserts 72, *185*
  ecosystems 128, 129
  history

Byzantine reconquest 241
  Christianity in 299
  colonial empires in 267
  conquest by Arabs 241
  decolonization 278–279
  Non-aligned movement 279
  Portuguese exploration and Empire 244, **253**
  prehistoric to colonial 226, **237**
  oil industry 195
  religions 284, 285, *284*
  weather systems 79
  see also specific countries
Agamemnon, King 230
age roles **158**
Aegean Sea, ancient civilizations of 230–231
agglutinative languages 348
Agincourt, battle of 245
aging **135**
  and learning ability 163
Agricultural Revolution 132
agricultural waste (and eutrophication) 131
agriculturalists **132–133**
  early American 238
  temple-cities 239
agriculture *see* farming
ahimsa 288–289
aid
  postwar European 280
  to the Third World **184**
AIDS 135, **155**
ailerons 222
air
  early medical beliefs 156
  in respiration 140
  light speed through 24
  pollution **186**, *187*
  principal constituents 61
  transmission of infections 154
  velocity of sound in 22
aircraft **222–223**
  altimeters 210
  jet engines **193**
  manufacture using synthetic polymers 47
  sonic booms 23
  World War I 269
  World War II 274
aircraft carriers 217
air forces (World War II) 274
airships 222
  lifting gases 42
  World War I 269
Akbar 236
Akkadian Empire 228
  language 228
  religions 286
  writing 350
Alamein, battle of 275
alanine 46
Albania **379**
  Communist government 280
Albee, Edward **375**
Alberti, Leon Battista **326**
Albertus Magnus 48
Alcaeus 356
alchemy **34**, *49*
alcohol **35**
  diseases from 153
  industrial *47*, 201
alcoholism 151
aldehydes 47
aldosterone 143
Aldrin, Edwin 'Buzz' 12
aleatory music 339
Alexander Severus 233
Alexander the Great 229, **231**
  and India 236
  influence on art 307
Alexander VI, Pope *250*
Alexius I, Emperor 244

Alfred the Great 243, 352
algae 82, **90**
  blue-green 83, 90, 111
    food manufacture 127
    nitrogen fixation 43
  reproduction 89
algebra **54–55**
  Boolean 51
  establishing geometrical proofs by 50
  fundamental theorem of 55
Algeria **379**
  independence 279
ALGOL 212
Ali, Mirza Husain 285
Ali (caliph) 242
alkaloids, manufacture of 201
alkenes 47
Allen, Woody 329
Allied Powers
  postwar confrontations 280
  World War I 268, 269
  World War II 274
alligators 103
allotropes *38*, 39
alloy steel 198
alloying *45*
  replacement by synthetic polymers 47
alluvial fans 69, 73
alluvial mining 196–197
alpaca 117
alpha (α) particles 31, 33
alphabet **350–351**
  first *228*
  use in algebra 54
alpine ecosystems 129
Alps (Europe)
  formation of 68, 69
    glaciers/glacial development 71, 226
  snowline 70
Alsace-Lorraine 269
Altaic languages 348
altarpieces
  early Baroque 315
  early Netherlandish 313
Altdorfer, Albrecht 313
alternating current 28–29
alternation of generations 89, 94
alternators 29, 220
altimeters 210
altostratus clouds 79, *79*
aluminium *37*, 196
  abundance and uses 197
  corrosive properties 45
  extraction of 44
Alvardo 252
alveoli 140, *141*
American War of Independence 166, 182, 257, 260–261
Americas
  animals 110, **122–123**
  discovery of 247, *247*
  history
    early modern humans 227
    pre-Columbian **238–239**
    Spanish colonization **252–253**
  native Indians 239, 252
  religions 284, 285
  United States sphere of influence 280–281
  see also Latin America; Meso-America; North America; South America
americium 33, *37*
Amerindian languages 348
amides 47
amines 47
amino acids 82, 138
  characteristics of natural acids 46–47
  in plants 88
  storage of 139

ammonia 39
  chemistry of 43
  fertilizers 34
  manufacture of 201
ammonium 88
Amnesty International 182
amniotic fluid 135
amoebic dysentery 154
Amorites (ancient people) 228
ampere (amp) 27
Ampère, André Marie 27, **49**
amphibians 102
  hibernation 125
amplifiers 29, **207**
  repeaters 208
amplitude 20, *21*
  varying 21
amplitude modulation (AM) 207
Anabaptists 299
anaemia 140
anaesthesia 157
analogue computer 211
analytic philosophy 303
analytical Cubism 322–323
anarchism 169
Anatolia, ancient 228
anatomy
  amphibians 102
  birds 106
  fishes 100
  insects 98
  marine mammals 120
  prehensile hands and feet 122
  reptiles **103**
  study of 156
    Renaissance interest in *312*
Anaximander of Miletus 48, 304
ancien régime 262
Andean Pact 180
Andes Mountains
  formation of 68, 69
  societies in 238–239
andesite 66
Andorra **379**
Angelico, Fra 312
angina 153
angiosperms 91, **92–93**
  reproduction 89
Anglicanism 299
see also England, Church of
Anglo-Saxons **241**
  art 310
  literature 358
  religions 287
  Viking invasion of kingdoms 243
Angola **379–380**
  independence 279
  Portuguese control 267
'angry young men' 375
animals
  behaviour **124–125**
  dependence on plants 88
  desert 73
  domesticated 132, **133**
  ecological niche 126
  ecosystems 128–129
  function of water 130
  importance of plants to 93
  primitive **94–95**
  ultrasonic technique 210
anion 38
Anne, Queen 255
annelid (segmented) worms 95
annuals (plants) 93
anode 28, 44, 45
Anschluss 273
Anselm 304
Antarctica 72
  hole in the ozone layer 187
  ice sheet 70
anteaters 111
antelopes 117
anthers 92

Anthony, Susan B. 183
Anti-Comintern Pact 273
anti-depressant drugs 151
anti-psycotic drugs 151
anti-slavery movement 182
antibiotics 154, 157
antibodies 142
    and autoimmune disease 153
    and infectious diseases 154
    transportation of 141
anticlericalism 245
anticyclones 79
antidiuretic hormone 143
antigens 142
Antigua and Barbuda 380
antilogarithms 55
antimony 37
    properties 44
antineutrinos 2, 31
antisemitism 272
antisepsis 157
Antisthenes 304
antlers 117
Antoninus Pius 233
ants 98
    organization 99, 125
anxiety neurosis 150
apartheid system 161
    and human rights 182
Apelles 306
apes 123
Apollinaire, Guillaume 372
Apollo programme 12
apparent magnitude 4
appeasement 273
applied mathematics 50
Apuleius 357, 364
aquifer 74
Aquinas, St Thomas 182, 304
Arab League 180
Arab–Israeli Wars 282–283
Arabian Desert 72
Arabs
    and Palestine 282, 283
    Arab Empire 236, 237, 241, 242
arachnids 97
Arafat, Yasser 283
Aral Sea, salinity 75
Aramaeans (ancient people) 228
Archaeopteryx 107
arches 214
Archilochus 356
Archimedes of Syracuse 17, 48, 50
Archimedes' principle 17
archipelagos, formation of 77
architecture 326–327
    ancient Near East 228
    Gothic style 214, 248
    Indian 308
    Renaissance 312
    Roman Empire 233
Arctic 72
Arctic Ocean, extent of sea ice in 70
Arden, John 375
Argentina 380
argon 37
Ariosto, Lodovico 360
Aristarchus of Samos 10, 48
Aristophanes 356
Aristotle 48, 83, 156, 302, 304, 304, 356, 362
arithmetic
    closed systems 54
    establishing geometrical proofs by 50
    laws of 54
    natural numbers and 54
    octal and hexadecimal 55
Arkwright, Richard 200
armadillos 111
armaments see weapons
armature (electric motor) 29
Armenia 180, 380
    ancient 231
    Byzantine conquest 241
    Christianity in 299
arms control 181
Armstrong, Louis 344
Armstrong, Neil 12, 12
aromatic compounds 47
aromatic hydrocarbons 186
Arp, Jean (Hans) 324
Arrest, Heinrich d' 9
arsenic 37
    properties 44
art (visual) 306–322
    ancient Chinese 234

Dutch school 316
    Greek 306–307, 306
    Ice Age 227
    medieval 310–311
    modern 322–325
    Mogul 236
    Netherlandish and German 313
    19th-century 318–321
    non-Western 308–309
    Renaissance 312–314
    Roman 306, 307, 307
    17th- and 18th-centuries 315–317
    see also mosaics; sculpture; specific movements
Art Nouveau see Jugendstil
Artaud, Antonin 374
arteries 141
    disease of 153
arthropods 96
    and infectious diseases 154
    insects 98
Arthur, King, and the Round Table 358–359
artificial insemination 133
artillery 224
artiodactyls 116
Aryans 236
asbestosis 153
ascorbic acid 139
asepsis 157
Ashanti 267
Ashkanazi Jews 295
Ashoka, King 236, 290
Ashton, Frederick 347
Asia
    ecosystems 129
    history
        decolonization 279
        Non-aligned movement 279
        part of Chinese empire 234
        Portuguese Empire in 253
        prehistory 226–227
    religions 284, 285, 299
    see also Southeast Asia; specific countries
Asia Minor, ancient 231
    Turkish conquest 241
asphalt 194
aspirin 35
Asquith, Herbert Henry 169
assault rifles 225
asses 116, 133
Association of South East Asian Nations (ASEAN) 180
associative law (arithmetic) 54
Assyrians/Assyrian Empire 228–229
    religions 286
astatine 37
asteroids 7
asthenosphere 61
    magma from 63
astrolabe 11
astronomers, early 10–11
astronomy 10–11
    astronomical distances 2
    detection of electromagnetic radiation 210
Atacama Desert 72
Atatürk, Kemal 269
Athapascan Indians 238
Athenian Empire 230–231
atheroma 153
atherosclerosis 135
Atlantic Ocean (oceanic ridge) 77
atmosphere, Earth 61
    air movement in see weather
    changes in gas concentrations 42
    chaos theory and 51
    function in biosphere 126
    gases 42–43
    importance of plants 93
    ozone in 187
    photosynthesis and 42
    plants and the 88
    pollution from fossil fuels 188
    see also 'greenhouse' effect and specific planets
atmospheric pressure 17
atom bomb 181
atomic number 36
atoms 30–31
    and thermal energy 18
    carbon 46–47
    changes in chemical bonding 38–39
    chemical classification and 35
    electrically neutral 36
    in compounds 34–35

in elements 34
    in magnetic resonance imaging 210
    in small molecules 42, 42–43
    magnetic fields 26
    number in a mole 41
    number in chemical reactions 41
    strength of metals and 45
    structure 30
        and chemical processes 34
    see also atom bombs; quantum mechanics
atonality 331
ATP (adenosine triphosphate) 139
atrium 140
Attenborough, Richard 329
Auden, W.H. 373
auditory ossicles 108, 144, 145
Augustine of Hippo, St 304
Augustus Caesar 232–233, 357, 363, 287
Aurangzeb 236
auricle 144, 145
aurochs 117
aurorae 7
Austen, Jane 368, 369
Australasia
    history
        early modern humans 227
        prehistoric to colonial 237
    mammals 109
    religions 284, 285
    tropical rain forests 186
Australia 380–381
    animals 94–124
        mammalian evolution 108, 110
        behaviour of 124
        deserts 72
        ecosystems 128, 129
        farming 132
    australopithecine 226
Austria 257, 381
    Expressionist art of 322
    history
        German unification 265
        Napoleonic Wars 263
        German occupation of 273
        revolts against 265
        War of Succession 257
    music (classical) 334, 336
Austro-Hungarian Empire 268
    break-up of 264, 265
    postwar settlement 269
authoritarianism, Fascism and 272
autogyros 223
autoimmune disease 153
automatic writing 324
autonomic muscle 137
autonomic nervous system 147
autotrophs 127
Avars 241
Averroës 48, 304
Avery, Oswald T. 49, 86
aviation, milestones in 223
    see also aircraft; airships; balloons
Avicenna (Ibn Sinna) 48, 156, 304
axioms 50
axis bone 137
Axis Powers 273, 274
axon 146
ayatollahs 300
Ayckbourn, Alan 375
aye-aye 122
Ayer, Alfred J. 305
ayre 332
Azerbaijan 180, 381
Aztec Empire 239
    overthrow of 252

B
B cells 142, 154
B-2 stealth bomber 223
B-lymphocytes 142
baboons 123
Babylonians/Babylonian Empire 228
    medical profession 156
    religions 286
    writing 350
Bach, Carl Philipp Emanuel 333
Bach, Johann Sebastian 333
    instruments 334
Bacon, Francis (artist) 325
Bacon, Francis (philosopher) 48, 304
Bacon, Roger 48
bacteria 82, 82, 83
    acid rain pollution and 186

and aquatic oxygen sypply 130
    and digestion 139
    and disease 154–155, 157
    and energy production 190
    genetic engineering 87
    immune system and 142
    in the food chain 127
    nitrogen fixation 43, 82
    production 88
bacteriostats 154
Bactria, kingdom of 231
badgers 115
badlands 73
Baekeland, Leo 199
Baha'ism 285
Bahamas 381–382
Bahrain 382
Baird, John Logie 206
Bakelite 199
balance 144–145
balance of payments 176
    equilibrium 174
Balanchine, George 347
Baldung, Hans 313
baleen 121
Balfour, Arthur 282
'Balfour Declaration' 282
Balkan Wars 265
Balkans
    nationalism in 265
    Slav settlement 241
    World War II 274, 275
ball-and-socket joint 136, 137
Balla, Giacomo 323
ballet
    classical 346–347
    modern 338
    17th-century 342
Ballets Russes 338
ballista 224
balloons 222
Balzac, Honoré de 368
Bandaranaike, Sirimavo 183
Bangladesh 382
banks/banking 170
    electronic funds transfer 209
    foundation of Bank of England 255
    medieval Italian 247
banteng 117
Bantu 237
    languages 348
baobab trees 92, 128
Baptism (christening) 159, 297
bar mitzvah 159
Barbados 382
Barbarian kingdoms 240
Barbizon School (art) 319
barium 37
barium sulphate 210
barley 132
barnacles 97
Barnard, Christiaan 157
Baroque
    architecture 327
    art 315
    music 333
barrier beach 77
Bartas, Guillaume Du 358
Bartolommeo, Fra 314
Bartók, Béla 338–339
baryon 31
basalt 60, 66
bases, chemical 35
    reactions of 40
    weak and strong 41
BASIC 212
basic oxygen furnace 198
Basie, Count 345
basking shark 101
basset horn 341
basso continuo 333
bassoon 340
bats 112
    echolocation 23, 210
    hearing 23
batteries 28
    'energy inefficency' 186
Baudelaire, Charles 372
'Bay of Pigs' invasion 281
Bayer, Johann 11
beaked whales 120
beaks 106, 107
beans see pulses

Beardsley, Aubrey **321**
bears **115**
Beatles **345**
Beauchamp, Charles Louis **346**
Beaumarchais, Pierre-Augustin Caron de **363**
Beaumont, Francis **361**
Beauvoir, Simone de 183, **305**
beavers **118**, 119
Beckett, Samuel **374–375**, **376**
Beckmann, Max **325**
'Beer-Hall Putsch' 272
bees 98, 99
    organization 99, 125, *124*
Beethoven, Ludwig van 331, **334**, 335, **336**, 340, **343**
beetles 98
behaviour
    animals **124–125**
    brain centre for 147
    instinctive **147**
Beiderbecke, Bix **345**
bel 22
Belarus 180, **382**
Belgium **382–383**
    colonial empire *266*
        decolonization 279
    industrialization 259
    voting 167
    World War II 274
Belisarius 241
Belize **383**
Bell, Alexander Graham 22, 208
Bellay, Joachim du **360**
Bellini, Giovanni **314**
Bellow, Saul **377**
Bembo, Pietro **360**
Benedict of Nursia, St 249
Benin **383**
Bennett, Alan **375**
Bentham, Jeremy 302, **304**
Benz, Karl 219
benzene 201
Berbers 244
Berg, Alban **338**, 339, **343**
Bergman, Ingmar **329**, *328*
Bergson, Henri **305**
Berio, Luciano **339**, 343
Berkeley, Busby **328**
Berkeley, George **304**
berkelium **37**
Berlin, Irving **344**
Berlin, Sir Isaiah **305**
Berlin airlift 280
Berlin Wall 280, 281
Berliner, Emile 207
Berlioz, Hector **336**, 340
Bernini, Gianlorenzo **315**
Bernstein, Leonard **344**
Berry, Chuck **345**
Berryman, John **373**
Bertolucci, Bernardo **329**
beryllium **37**
Bessemer process 198
beta (β) decay 31
Beuys, Joseph **325**
Béjart, Maurice **347**
Bhagavadgita 288
Bhutan **383**
Bible
    Christian **297**
        original language 228
        translations 249, 250
    Jewish 294, 297
biennials (plants) 93
'big bang' 2
big crunch 3
'Big Three' 269
bilharzia (schistosomiasis) **155**
Bill of Rights 182, 261
bills of exchange, commercial 171
binary stars **4**
binary system (numbers) 55
binocular vision 107, 122
biochemistry, development of 157
'biogas' 190
biogeochemical cycles 127, *127*
bioluminescence 101
biomass 127, **190**
    tropical rainforests 128, *128*
biosphere **126–127**
biotin **139**
birds **106–107**
    hearing and navigation 23
    territory, mating and social organization **124–125**

birds of prey 106
    sight 107
birth (human) **134–135**
    asepsis during 157
    customs during 159
Birtwhistle, Harrison 343
Bismarck, Otto von 265
bismuth **37**
    atomic number 36
bison 31, 129
bits (computer) 211, 212
    digital recording 207
bivalves 95
Bizet, Georges **343**
Black Death **245**
Black Forest 186
black holes **5**
    and quasars 4
Black music 344–345
Black rights 261
'Blackshirts' 272
Blake, William **367**
Blasis, Carlo **346**
blast furnace 198, *198*
Blaue Reiter, der 322
blastocyst 134
bleaching powder 201
Blitzkrieg 225, 274
blood **140–141**
    autonomic system and 147
    disorders of 152
    genetic engineering and 201
    humours theory 156
    purification *see* excretion
    transmission of infections 154
    transportation of nutrients 139
'Bloody Sunday' (Russian) 270
'blow-back' 225
blubber 120
blue shift 2
blue whale 120, 121
blues music **344–345**
Blücher, von 263
Boccaccio, Giovanni **359**, 364
Boccioni, Umberto **325**
bodhisattvas 291
body mutilation 159
Boer Wars 267
Boers 237
Boethius **304**, **357**
bogs, development of **131**
Bohemia
    religious revolt 245, 250, 251
Bohr, Niels 30, **49**
    atomic model 30, *30*
Bohras 301
boiling-water reactors 189
Boleyn, Anne 254
Bolivia **383–384**
Bologna
    academy of art 315
    University 248
Bolsheviks/Bolshevik revolution **270–271**
bombs, volcanic 65, *65*
Bond, Edward **375**
bonding
    carbon 46
    chemical 34
    conductivity of metals and 45
bone marrow 136
    blood cell production 142
bones **136**
    as tools 227
    birds 106
    diseases 135
    excess Growth Hormone and 143
    greenstick fractures 136
    in the ear 144–145
    X-ray imaging of 210
Bonnard, Pierre **320**
bony fish 100
book illustration, non-Western 308
Book of Changes 292
Book of the Dead 286
books
    'Index' of banned 251
    first printed 202
    medieval translations 248
    see also illuminated manuscripts
Boole, George 50
Boolean algebra **51**
Borges, Jorge Luis **377**
boron **37**
boroughs 247

Borromini, Francesco **326**
Bosch, Hieronymus 313, 324
Bosnia-Herzegovina **384**
bosons 31
'Boston Tea Party' 260
Botswana **384**
Botticelli, Sandro *312*, **313**
bottlenose dolphins *121*
Boucher, François **317**
Boudin, Eugène **319**
Boulez, Pierre **339**
bourgeoisie 160
Bournonville, August **346**
Boutros Ghali, Boutros 178
Bouts, Dierick **313**
bovids **117**
bow and arrows 227
Boxer Rebellion 235, 267
Boyle, Richard, Earl of Berlington **326**
Boyle, Robert **49**
Boyne, Battle of the 255
'Boys' Companies' 361
Brahe, Tycho **10**, **49**
brahman priests 288
Brahms, Johannes **337**
braided channels 75
brain **146–147**
    and learning 149
    and muscle movement 137
    and smell 145
    and vision 144
    computer architecture and 213
    development 134
    hemispheres of **149**
    hypothalamus 143
    pain receptors 145
    sensory nerve endings and 145
    whales 121
brainstem **146**
brakes
    car *221*
    hydraulic **16**, 17
Bramante, Donato **326**
Brancusi, Constantin **323**
Braque, Georges **322–323**
Braun, Werner von 12, 193
Brazil **384**
    exports to Europe 257
    independence 267
    Portuguese colonization 252, 253
Brazza, Savorgnan de 267
breathing *see* respiration
Brecht, Bertolt **374**
breech-loading weapons **224**
Brenton, Howard **375**
Bresson, Robert **329**
bridge construction **215**
bristleworms 95
Britain *see* United Kingdom
British East India Company 236, 257, **266**
    'Boston Tea Party' and 260
'British English' 353
Britten, Benjamin **339**, 343
brittle stars **94**
Broadway musicals **344**
Broglie, Louis Victor de 32
bromine **37**, 39
    chemical reactions 41
bronchioles 140
Brontë, Charlotte, Emily and Anne **369**, *370*
bronze, discovery of 44
Bronze Age 226, **227**
    in India and Southeast Asia 236
    metal extraction 196
bronzeworking
    Benin art 309
    in India 236
    International Gothic 311
    prehistoric 227
    Renaissance 312
    Shang dynasty 234
Bronzino, Agnolo **314**
Brooke, Rupert **373**
Brouwer, Adriaen **316**
Brown, Ford Madox **320**
Bruckner, Anton **337**
Brücke, die 322
Bruegel, Pieter, the Elder **313**
Brunei **384**
Brunel, Isambard Kingdom 217
Brunelleschi, Filippo **312**, **326**
bryophytes 90
buboes 245
bubonic plague 241, *245*

buckminsterfullerene 39, 46
Buddha 236
Buddhism 285, 288, **290–291**
    art 308
    expansion of 236
        in Chinese Empire 234
        in Japan 235, **293**
budget surplus/deficit 175
building societies 170
building techniques **214–215**
bulbs (plants) 93
Bulgaria **384–385**
    Communist government 280
    education in 163
    postwar settlement 269
    World War I 268
bulk carriers 216
bullfrog, American *102*
Buñuel, Luis **328**
buoyancy 17
    water and 130
Buran spacecraft 13
bureaucracy 167
    and resource allocation 170
    development in France 256
Burkina Faso **385**
Burma
    annexation by British 266
    decolonization 278
    World War II 274, 275
    see also Myanmar
Burne-Jones, Sir Edward **321**
Burns, Robert **367**
Burundi **385**
Bushmen 237
butane (in natural gas) 195
butterflies 98, 99
    defence 125
'butterfly effect' 51
buttes 73, *73*
Byrd, William **332**
Byron, Lord **367**
byte (computer) 211
Byzantine Empire 233, 240, **241**
    architecture **326**
    art **310**
    dam-building 215
    history
        conquest by Ottoman Turks 242
        Crusades and 244
        re-establishment of 241
        reconquest of the West 241
    literature 357

C
C (computer language) 212
cabinet government 167
cables
    optical **209**
    telegraph 208
Cabot, John **247**
cacti 128
CAD (Computer-aided Design) 213
cadmium **37**
caecilian, South American *102*
Caesar Octavian 232
caesium **37**
Cage, John **339**
calcium **37**, 138
    electrically neutral atom 36
calculus 51, 52, 58
    differential 58
Calderon, Pedro **361**
calendars **3**
    Meso-American 239
California
    central valley 60
    climate and ecosystems 129
    Death Valley 69
    San Andreas Fault 63, 64
californium **37**
Caligula 233
caliphs 242
calligraphy, non-Western 308
Callimachus **357**
calotype 204
Calvin, John **251**
Calvinism **251**, 299
Camargo, La **346**
Cambio, Arnolto di **310**
cambium 89
Cambodia 179, **385**
    independence 281
    Khmer Empire 236
    see also Indochina

Cambrai, battle of 269
Cambridge University 248
Cambyses 229
camel hair 200
camels 116–117, 133
camera obscura 204
cameras 204
  miniature 204–205
  modern 205
  television 206–207
Cameroon 385–386
  German control 267
Camões, Luis de 360
camouflage, animals 125
  insects 99
Camp David peace talks 283
Campaign for Nuclear Disarmament 181
Camus, Albert 374, 376
Canada 386
  history
    colonization 257
    independence 279
    War of 1812 261
    separatism in 161
Canaletto, Antonio 317
canals 215, 258, 259
cancer 152
  causes 186
  of the lungs 153
  X-ray treatment 210
Canova, Antonio 317
cantata, Baroque 333
cantilever bridge 215, 215
Cantor, Georg 50
canyons, formation of 69, 73, 73
Cape of Good Hope 253
Cape Verde 386
capillaries 141
  in the skin 145
capital (economics) 171
  and balance of payments 176
capital formation 171
capital goods 174
capital punishment 164, 165
capital stock 171
capitalism 259
  and the Cold War 280–281
Capra, Frank 329
capybara 118, 119
carapace 103
Caravaggio, Michelangelo Merisi da 315
caravel 217
carbohydrates 138
  plants and 88
carbon 37
  and biogeochemical cycles 127
  chemical bonding 39
  chemistry of 46–47
  in plants and animals 127
  in steel 198
  properties 34
  source of 88
  tetrahedral atom and chirality 46–47
carbon black 202
carbon dioxide
  and global warming 187
  chemistry of 42
  emission of 187, 188
  in respiration 140, 141
  increases in atmosphere 42
  on Venus 8
  plants and 88, 93
  removing from steel 198
carbon-14 31
carbon monoxide
  chemistry of 42, 43
  pollution from 186
  removing from steel 198
Carbonari 264
carboxylic acids 47
carburettor 220
cardiac muscle 137
carding 200
cargo shipping 216, 246, 246
  World War II 274
Caribbean Community 180
Caribbean Islands, the Cold War in 280–281
CARICOM 180
Carné, Marcel 329
carnivores 114–115
  finding food 125
  in the food chain 127
  plants 93, 93
Carnot, Sadi 19

Carolingian Empire 240
Carothers, Wallace 199
carpels, flower 92, 92
carpets, Islamic 308
Carra, Carlo 323
Carracci, Ludovico, Agostino and Annibale 315
carrack 217
carrier waves 206
cars 219–221
  bulk carriers for 216
  how they work 220, 221
  pollution from 186
Carter, Elliott 339
Cartesian coordinates 58
Carthage 228
  wars with Rome 232
cartilaginous fishes 100
Cartwright, Edmund 200, 258
Cassatt, Mary 320
cassava 132
cast iron 198
caste system 160, 288
Castelvetro, Lodovico 362
Castiglione, Baldassare 249
Castle, Irene and Vernon 347
Castner-Kellner process 201
Castor (star) 4
castrati 342
Castro, Fidel 281
Catalonia (revolt against Castile) 253
catalyst 41
catalytic converters 186, 219
catalytic cracking 195
cataract (eye) 144
caterpillars 99
Cathar (Albigensian) Church 244, 245
Catherine II, the Great 257
Catherine of Aragon 254
cathode 28
cathode-ray tube 206, 207
Catholic Church see Roman Catholic Church
cation 38, 44
cats 114
  marsupial 110
  sabre-toothed 108
cattle 117, 133
Catullus 357
Cauchy, Baron Augustin-Louis 50
caustic soda 201
cauterization 156
caves 75
cavies (guinea pigs) 119
Cavour, Camillo di 264
Caxton, William 202, 249, 353
CD-ROMs 211
cebid monkeys 123
Cellini, Benvenuto 314
cello 340
cells, artificial
  electric 28
  photoelectric 206
  'photovoltaic' 190
  solar 29
cells, living 82–83
  during reproduction 134
  function of water 130
  mineral salts and 138
  proteins and 138
  blood 140
    diseases of 152
    immune system 142
    nerve 146, 146
    phagocytic 142
    plant 88, 89, 92
    retinal 144
    skin 145
    viruses and 154
    xylem and phloem 90
  see also endocrine system and nervous system
celluloid 199
cellulose 88, 91
Celtic languages 352
Celtic religion 286, 287
Centaurus A 4
Central African Republic 386-387
Central America
  development of farming 132
  hoofed mammals 116
Central American Common Market 180
central nervous system 146
Central Powers 268–269

centripetal acceleration 14, 15
cephalopods 95
ceramics
  ancient Greek 306, 307
  industrialization and 259
  non-Western 308, 309
cerebellum 146
cerebral cortex 146
  divisions of 147
  in higher mammals 109
cerebrum 146
Ceres (asteroid) 7
cerium 37
Cervantes, Miguel de 364
cestodes 95
Ceylon see Sri Lanka
Cézanne, Paul 321, 322
CFCs
  alternatives to 187
  effect on atmosphere 42, 43, 187
  in refrigeration 193
Chabrol, Claud 329
Chad 387
  famine relief 179
Chagall, Marc 325
chain reaction, nuclear 188
Chalcolithic Age 227
Challenger space shuttle 13
Chambers, Sir William 326
chamois 117
change 58–59
chansons 332
chaos
  of a system see entropy
  theory of 51
Chaplin, Charlie 329
charcoal 198
Chardin, Jean-Baptiste-Siméon 317
Charlemagne 240
Charles Edward Stuart, Prince 255
Charles I, King 255
Charles II, King 255, 363
Charles IV, Emperor 240
Charles V, Emperor 240–241, 252, 252, 253
  and the Reformation 250–251
Charles VI, King 245
Charlotte Dundas (ship) 217
Charon (satellite) 9
Charter of Paris 180, 281
Chateaubriand, François-René de 366–367
Chaucer, Geoffrey 353, 358, 359
Chekhov, Anton 374
cheetahs, hunting technique of 125
Cheka 271
chelicerates, evolution 96
  see also arachnids
chemical industry 201
  development of 259
  raw materials 195
  use of natural gas 195
chemical reactions 40–41
chemical sedimentary rock 66
chemicals 201
  as plant defences 99
  diseases from 153
  insect senses and 99
  pollution by toxic 186
  use in medicine 156
chemistry 34–35
  chemical bonds 38–39
  organic 46–47
  use of chaos theory 51
chemotherapy 157
Chernobyl nuclear accident 187, 189
chevrotain (mouse deer) 117
chickenpox (varicella) 155
childbirth see birth
children/childhood
  education 162–163, 162, 163
  fractured bones 136
  growth in 135
  perception of the world 148
  rites of passage 159
  see also family; puberty
Chile 387
  United States covert operations 281
chimpanzee 123
China 387–388
  art 308–309
  customs 158, 159
  education in 162, 163
  German influence 267
  human rights in 182
  history

ancient ships 217
Cold War 280
  pro-democracy demonstrations 277
  to the colonial age 234–235
  20th century 161, 275, 276–277
  and Vietnam 281
  voyages of discovery 247, 247
  World War II 275
invention of printing 202
religions 292–293
trade 247, 267
UN membership 178
China, Republic of (Taiwan) 388
'Council of Five Hundred' 231
Chinese Communist Party 276–277
Chinese language 349, 350
Chinese Nationalists 276
chirality 46–47
Chirico, Giorgio de 324
chitin 91, 96
chivalry 249
chlorides 35
chlorine 37
  chemical bonding 34
  chemical reactions 41
chlorine gas 187
chlorofluorocarbons see CFCs
chlorophylls 88
cholera 155
Chomsky, Noam 213, 354, 355
Chopin, Frédéric 337
chords, musical 331
choreography
  classical ballet 346
  modern dance 347
Christianity 284–285, 296–297, 298–299
  and art 310–311, 312, 314
  and education 162, 163
  and government 166
  history
    ancient 233
    in Britain 241
    Crusades 244
    expansion 235, 237, 241, 244, 288
    medieval 240, 242, 245, 248, 249
    in Middle East 282
  and human rights 182
  and music 330, 332, 335
  and literature 359
  see also Bible, Orthodox Church, Protestantism, Roman Catholic Church
Christian Democracy 169
chromatic scale 331
chromatography 35
chromium 37
  abundance and uses 197
chromosomes 86, 134
  abnormal 152
  sex 87
chromosphere 6
Churchill, Caryl 375
Churchill, Winston 274–275, 280
chyme 139
Cicero 162, 249
ciliary body 144
Cimabue 310
cinder-cone volcanoes 65
cinema 328–329
circles 53, 53
circuit, electric 28
  connecting 28
circulation/circulatory system 140–141
  development of 134
  discovery of 156
  disorders 135
  muscles 137
  problems after menopause 135
  viscosity and turbulence in 17
circulation, non-flowering plants 90
cirques 69, 71
cirrostratus clouds 79
cirrus clouds 79
cities
  ancient Greek 230, 231
  ceremonial 238, 239
  Chinese 234, 235
citric acid 201
city-states 230, 231
  Greek, official religion of 287
  Rome as 232
civets 114
civil rights 182
civil law 165

civil liberties 182
civil rights 182
civil service/civil servants 167
civil wars
    American 261
    ancient Roman 232
    Chinese 276–277, 276
    English 254–255
    French 256
    Lebanon 283
    Russian 271
civilization, development of
    in the Americas 238–239
    in Africa, Australasia and Oceania 237
    ancient Chinese 234
    beginnings of 228
    in India and Southeast Asia 236
Clair, René 329
clarinet 340–341, 341
class struggle 168
class system 160–161
'classical liberalism' 169
Classical revival see Neoclassicism
Classicism
    in art 315–317
    in literature 362–363
    in music 334, 342–343
classifications
    algae 90
    birds 106
    chemical compounds 35
    class systems 160–161
    climate 80
    earthquakes 64
    faults and folds 67
    fishes 100
    flowering plants 93
    green plants 89
    hoofed mammals 116
    insects 98, 98
    languages 348–349
    mammals 109
    plants 90, 91
clastic sedimentary rock 66
Claudius 233
clavichord 340
claws
    anteaters 111
    birds 106–107
    cats 114
    moles 113
    sloths 111
Cleisthenes 230
Clemençeau, Georges 269
clerks 248
climate 80–81
    and ecosystems 128
    and vegetation 80, 81
    continental 81
    controls on 80–81
    desert 72
    latent heat and 19, 19
    maritime 81
    ocean currents and 77
    prehistoric 226
climatic effects 80
clipper ships 217
Clive, Robert 257
clones/cloning 133
    B cell 142
closed lakes 74, 75
cloth see textiles
clouds 79
club mosses 9, 90
clutch, car 220, 221
Cnut, King 243
coal 188, 195, 196
    origins 90
    types 196
coal mining
    Industrial Revolution and 258–259
cobalt 37
COBOL 212
coccyx 84
cochlea 144, 145
Cocteau, Jean 329
coelacanth 100
coelenterates 94
coevolution 85
    insects and plants 99
coinage 44, 229
coitus 134
Colbert, Jean Baptiste 256

cold, common 155
Cold War, the 280–281
    Chinese involvement 277, 281
    end of 180, 281
    United Nations and 179
Coleman, Ornette 345
Coleridge, Samuel Taylor 366, 367
collage 323
    Dadaist use of 324
collective bargaining 171
collectivization
    Chinese 277
    Soviet 271
colleges 163
collodion 204
Colombia 388
colon 139, 139
colonialism
    effect of nationalism on 278
    Middle Eastern 282
    see also decolonization; imperialism;
        specific countries
Colorado River 74
    Grand Canyon 75
colour
    as animal defence 125
    in cinema 328
    insect use of 99
    of light 2
    printing methods 203
    stars 5
    water 131
colour charge see quarks
colour photography 205
colour vision 144
cols 69
Columbia space shuttle 13
Columbus, Christopher 247
combustion 41
comets 7
'coming of age' 159
command economies 170
commerce see trade
commercial banks 170
    Third World loans 184
Commerson's dolphin 121
Committee of Public Safety 262
commodities, see also trade
    Third World 184–185
common law 164
    human rights in 182
common market 177
Commonwealth of Independent States 180
Commonwealth of Nations 180, 279
communes 159
    medieval 247
communication
    animal 124
    from the unconscious 151
communications
    computers and 211
    effect on industrialization 259
    radio, television and hi-fi 206–207
    telecommunications 208–209
    ionosphere and 61
    satellites 13
Communism/Communist Party 167
    and the Cold War 280–281
    in China 276–277
    in Germany 272
    in Indochina 281
    threat in Italy 272
    United States witch-hunts 280
    World War I 269
    see also Marxism-Leninism
community service 165
commutative law (arithmetic) 54
Comoros 388
compact cassette 207
compact discs 207
companies 247
    infrastructure 177
    monopolies/oligopolies 173
    multinational 176
compasses 26
    magnetic 27
competition, economic 170
complex numbers 55
composers see music
compound eyes 99
compounds
    aromatic 47
    chemical 34–35, 38–39, 38

ionic 40
    relative molecular mass 41
    water and 130
    organic 35
compression 20
    engine 192, 220
    wave theory 20
compression-ignition engines 193
Compsognathus 104
computer graphics 212, 212, 213
computer programs 211
computerized axial tomography 210
computers 211–213
    artificial intelligence 213, 355
    Boolean algebra and 51
    language comprehension 149
    oil exploration with 194
    printing by 202, 203
    spacecraft simulations 13
    transmission of data 209
    visual perception 149
    weapons systems 225
Comsats 13
Comte, Auguste 305
concentration camps 273
Conceptual art 325
concertante style 333
concerto 335
    Baroque 333
    development of 333
condoms 135, 154
conduction 18
conductivity 40–41, 45
conductors, electric 29
condyloid joint 137, 137
cone 53, 53
Confederation of the Rhine 263
confederations, Indian 239
Conference on Security and Cooperation in
    Europe 180
'confessional' poetry 373
Confucianism 235, 285, 292
Confucius 234, 292
    philosophy of teaching 162
Congo 388–389
Congress of Berlin 265
Congress of Europe 179
Congress of Vienna 263, 264
Congreve, William 363
conic sections 52, 52
conies see pikas
conifers 90, 91, 129
conquistadores 252
Conrad, Joseph 370–371
conservation of energy, law of 18, 19
Conservatism 169
Constable, John 318
Constantine 233
Constantinople 240, 241
    Crusaders capture 244
    Ecumenical Patriarch of 299
    sack of 241
    sieges of 241, 242
    Viking assault on 243
    World War I assault on 269
constitutional monarchy 167
construction 214–215
constructive interference 21
Constructivism 323
consubstantiation 297
consuls/consulships 232
consumers
    environmental awareness 187
    in food chain 127
    and macroeconomics 174
    and microeconomics 172, 173
container ships 216
contamination 154
    nuclear 187
continental crust 60
continental drift 62–63
continental margins 76, 77
continental rise 76, 77
continental shelf 76, 77
continental slope 76, 77
contraception methods 135
contract, law of 165
convection 18
convergent evolution 85
converging lens 24, 24
Cooke, William 208
Cooper, James Fenimore 371
copepods 97

Copernicus, Nikolaus (Nicholas) 10, 48
Copland, Aaron 339
copper 37
    abundance and uses 197
    discovery of 44
    mining 196
copperplate gravure 203
Coppola, Francis Ford 329
Coptic Church 299
cor anglais 340, 341
corals 77, 90, 94
cordite 224
core, Earth's 60, 61
Corelli, Arcangelo 333
corms (plants) 93
corn see maize
cornea 144
Corneille, Pierre 362
cornet (instrument) 341
Cornwallis, Admiral 260–261
corona 7
Corot, Camille 319
Correggio, Antonio 314
corries 69, 71
corrosion, metal 45
    use of synthetic polymers 47
Cortez 252
Cortona, Pietro da 315
cosine 52
cosmic waves 27
cosmic year 4
cosmology 2–3
Costa Rica 389
cotton 132, 200
cotton industry
    destruction of Indian 266
    textile production 258
couloirs 69
coulomb 26
Coulomb, Charles Augustin 26, 49
Coulomb's law 26
Council of Europe 179
Council of Trent 251
Counter-Reformation 250, 251
    effect on art 314
    literature 360
counterpoint 331, 333
'country and western' music 345
Couperin, François ('Le Grand') 333
couple 16
Courbet, Gustav 319, 319
courtly love 358
courtship/courtship displays
    animals 107, 124
covalent bonds/bonding 38–39, 46
Coward, Noel 363, 375
Cowell, Henry 339
coyote 115
Côte d'Ivoire 389
crabeater seal 121
crabs 97
crafts (association) 247
Cranach, Lucas 313
Cranko, John 347
craters, volcanic 65
    lakes in 75
creativity 148–149
cremation 159
Crete
    ancient 230
    Byzantine recovery 241
    German invasion of 274
cretinism 143
crevasses 71
Crécy, battle of 245
Crick, Francis 49, 86
crime/criminal behaviour 164
    criminal law 165
Crimean War 265
Cro-Magnon man 227
Croatia 389
    revolt against Austria 264
Croce, Benedetto 305
crocodiles 103
Crompton, Samuel 200
Cromwell, Oliver 255
Cromwell, Thomas 254
crops 93, 132
    as energy source 190
    four-field rotation 132
    monitoring diseases 13
crossbow 224

cruise missiles 225
Crusades/Crusaders **244**
  conquests 242
  Fourth 241, 244
crust, Earth's **60**, *61*
  rock formation in 66, 67
crustaceans **97**
  evolution 96
Crystal Palace, London 214
crystallization 35
crystals 38, 39
Cuba **389**
  Communist government 281
  revolution 161
  United States control 261
Cuban Missile Crisis 281
Cubism/Cubists 321, **322–323**
  influence on poetry 372, *373*
Cukor, George **329**
cults 284, 285
  ancient religious 286, 287
Cultural Revolution **277**
cumulonimbus clouds 79, *79*
cumulus clouds 79, *79*
cuneiform writing 228, 350, *350*
Cunningham, Merce **347**
curium *37*
currency
  electronic funds transfer 209
  exchange controls 177
  exchange rates **174**, 175
  quantity theory of money 175
  regulation of supply 175
  see also coinage
currents
  electric 28–29
  ocean (effect on climate) 70, 81, *80*
customs union 177
  Zollverein 265
Cuvier, Baron Georges 84
Cuyp, Aelbert **316**
cwms 69, 71
cyanobacteria 83, 90
  food manufacture 127
  lichen and 91
cyanocobalamin **139**
cycads 91
cyclic theory 3
cyclones 79
Cygnus X-1 (X-ray source) 5
cylinder **53**, *53*
cylinder press 203
Cyprus 179, **389–390**
  Byzantine recovery 241
  social divisions 161
Cyrus the Great 229
cystic fibrosis 152
Czech Republic **390**
Czechoslovakia
  Communist government in 280
  creation of 269
  German occupation of 273
  opera 343
  revolt against Austria 264
  Soviet invasion 280
  see also Czech Republic and Slovakia

D
D-Day 275
da capo aria 342
da Gama, Vasco **247**
Dada/Dadaism **323–324**
  influence on music 338
Daguerre, Louis 204
daguerreotype 204
daimyos 235
dairy products 132, 133
Dali, Salvador **324**
Dall's porpoise *121*
Dalton, John 30, **49**
damask 200
dam construction **215**
dance **346–347**
  early music for 332
  honeybees **124**
  in films 328
Danelaw 243
Dante Alighieri **359**
'Danzig Corridor' 269
Daoism (Taoism) 285, **292**
Darius I, King 229, 306
'Dark Ages' 248, 249
  architecture during 326

Darwin, Charles **49**
  evolutionary theory 84
dasyurid marsupials 110
data transmission **209**
database 212
Daubigny, Charles-François **320**
Daumier, Honoré **319**
David, Jacques-Louis **317**
David, King 228
Davidson, Donald **305**
Davies, Peter Maxwell **339**, 343
Davis, Miles **345**
Davy, Sir Humphrey 35
day 3
De Kooning, Willem **325**
De Mille, Cecil B. **329**
De Stijl **323**
death-feigning 125
death, customs 159
'Death Row' 165
debentures 171
debt, Third World **184**
Debussy, Claude **338**, *338,* **343**
decalomania 324
decapods **97**
decibel 22
decimal place-value system 55
Declaration of Independence 260
Declaration of the Rights of Man 182, 262
decolonization 267 **278–279**
decomposer organisms 127
  fungal 91
deer **117**
defence/defence behaviour
  animals 104, 113, 100, **125**
  nuclear weapons 181
  plants 99
  warships 217
  weaponry 224
Defoe, Daniel **364**, 368
deformation
  elastic 17, *16*
  metal 45, *45*
Degas, Edgar **320**
degaussing 217
Delacroix, Eugène **319**
Delaunay, Robert **325**
Delian League 231
delict, law of 165
delirium 151
Delius, Frederick **339**
Delsarte, François **347**
deltas, river 75, *74*
delusions 150
demand *see* supply and demand
dementia 151
demilitarized zone 269, 273
democracy 166
  ancient Athenian 231
  Chinese movement for 277
  Fascism and 272
  in Soviet satellite states 281
  modern 167
Democritus of Abdera 48, **304**
demonstrations
  anti-nuclear *181*
  Chinese pro-democracy 277
Demosthenes **356**
dendrites 146, *146*
Deng Xiaoping 277
Denmark **390**
  and Schleswig-Holstein 265
  colonial empire *266*
  early expansion/colonization 243
  World War II 274
deoxyribonucleic acid *see* DNA
depression (disorder) 150
depression (economic) 272–273
depression (weather) 79
depressive neurosis 151
Derain, André 321, **322**
Derby, Abraham 198
derivatives 59
dermis 145
Derrida, Jacques 303, **305**
Descartes, René 49, **50**, 303, **304**
desertification 72
deserts **72–73**
  ecosystems **128**
  precipitation 81
desktop publishing 212
desmans 113
Desprès, Josquin **332**

destructive interference 21
determinism, in literature 369
'detribalization' 278
deuterium 189
deuterium oxide 189
Dewey, John **305**
dharma 288, 290
dhole 115
diabetes 143, 152
Diaghilev, Serge **346–347**
dialect 355, *355*
dialectical materialism 168
'Diamond' Buddhism 291
diamonds 34, 39, 46
  mining 197
  stylus 207
diaphragm
  contraceptive 135
  muscle 140, *140*
Dias, Bartolomeu **247**
Dickens, Charles 368, **370**
Dickinson, Emily **371**
dicotyledons 93
dictators/dictatorships
  ancient Roman 232
  revolutionary France 262
  see also Hitler, Adolf; Mussolini, Benito; Napoleon I;
dictionaries 353
Diderot, Denis **365**
Dien Bien Phu, battle of 281
Diesel, Rudolf 193
diesel engines 193
  car 219
  locomotives 218
  ship 217
diet **138–139**
  amino acids in 138
  diseases from **153**
  fishes 101
  non-infectious diseases and **153**
dietary fibre 138
differential, car 220
differentiation 59
diffraction **21**
digestion and absorption **138–139**
  autonomic system and 147
digestive system
  birds 107
  human 137
  X-ray imaging of 210
digital computer 211
dimensions, Newton's theory of 14
dinosaurs **104**, *108*
Diocletian 233
diodes 29
diorite 66
dip-slip fault 67
diphtheria **155**
dipole 61
direct current 28–29
dirigibles *see* airships
disaccharides 138
discontinuities 60, *61*
discourse analysis 355
Discovery space shuttle 13
disease resistance, genetic engineering and 133
diseases and disorders
  of the aged 135
  and mental illness 151
  bacterial 82
  chemical study of 157
  eliminating in Third World 185
  from hormone imbalances 143
  from vitamin deficiency 138
  infectious **154–155**, 156
  localization of 157
  non-infectious **152–153**
  protist 82
  smoking and **153**
  viral 82
  see also infections; specific diseases and disorders
disorder of a system *see* entropy
dispersion, light 24
displacement 14, *15*
Disraeli, Benjamin 370
distance, measuring astronomical 2
distillation 35
  fractional 195
  hydrocarbons 201
distortion, visual 148

distribution
  carnivores 114
  fishes 101
distributive law (arithmetic) 54
'divine right of kings' 166, 256
division (arithmetic) **54–55**
divisionism (painting) 320
divorce 158–159
Djibouti **390**
DNA 83, **86**
  and enantiomers 47
  and natural selection 85
  bird classification by 106
  genetic engineering and 87, 201
  in viruses 82
  replication and cell division **86–87**
documentary films 329
dodecaphony music 331, 338
dogs **114–115**
dolphins 120–121, *121*
  echolocation 210
  hearing 23
Domenichino **315**
domes 326
Dominica **390**
Dominican Republic **390–391**
Domitian 233
Donatello **312**
Dongen, Kees van **325**
Donizetti, Gaetano **343**
Donne, John **360**
Doppler, C.J. 23
Doppler effect 2, **23**
Dostoevski, Fyodor **368–369**
double bass 340
'double pain' 145
Dowland, John **332**, **360**
Down's syndrome 152
drag 222
dragonflies 98–99
dragons *292*
Drake, Edwin 194
drama
  actresses 363
  modern **374–375**
  mystery and morality plays **359**
  Renaissance **360–361**
  unity rules 362
Dravidians 236
  languages 348
Dreadnought (ship) 217
dreams
  interpreting 151
  Surrealists and 324
Dreiser, Theodore **369**
drift mining *196*
drilling, oil and gas **194–195**
dromedary 116–117
drugs
  for infectious diseases 154
  manufacture of 201
  movement around the body 141
  opium trade 267
  pain-killing 145
  synthetic 201
  therapy for mental illness 151
  see also antibiotics
drumlins 71
drums (musical instruments) 341
dry-plate process 204
Dryden, John **363**
'dry ice' 42
Duccio di Boninsegna **311**
Duchamp, Marcel **324**
duck-billed platypus 109
Dufay, Guillaume **332**
Dufy, Raoul **325**
dugong **120**
duikers 117
Duma 270
Duncan, Isadora **347**
Dunkirk 274
duodenum **139**
Duras, Marguerite **377**
Dutch East Indies
  decolonization in 278
  Japanese invasion of 274
Dutch Republic
  English support for 254
  revolt against Spain 251, 253
Dürer, Albrecht **313**
Dvořák, Antonin **337**
dwarfism *see* achondroplasia

dyes, synthetic 201
Dylan, Bob **345**
dynamo 29, *29*
dysentery **155**
dyslexia 149
dysprosium *37*

E
Eakins, Thomas **320**
ear
  acoustics **22–23**
    hearing 22–23
  eardrum 144, *145*
    vibration rate 23
Earth 7, **8**, *9*, **60–61**, *61*
  beginnings of life on **82–83**
  circumnavigation of 247
  crust, composition of 36
  geothermal heat 191
  magnetic field 26, 27
  Newton's third law and 15
  principal source of energy *see* Sun
  rotation 10, 11
    and atmosphere 78
    and the seasons 80
    Ptolemaic system 10
  time systems **3**
  total water 42
Earth-resources satellites 13
earthquakes and earthquake zones **64**
  plate tectonics and 63
earthworms 95
East African Rift 63
East Franks 240
East India Company 257
East Indies, Dutch seizure of 257
East Pacific Rise 77
Eastern Empire *see* Byzantine Empire
Eastman, George 204
echidnas 109
echinoderms **94**, **95**
echolocation
  bats **112**
  mammals 23
  whales 120
ecology, chaos theory and 51
Economic and Social Council (UN) 178
Economic Community of West African
  States 180
economic imperialism 279
economic liberalism 173
economic systems **170–171**
economics/economy **170–171**
  and class 160–161
  Chinese 277
  effect of oil price rises 195
  effect on colonial territories 278
  growth in 174
  Japanese 235, 273
  liberal philosophy 169
  main European groupings *178*
  medieval and Renaissance **246–247**
  17th century 255, 256
  Soviet post-revolutionary problems **271**
  use of chaos theory 51
ecosystems **126**
  aquatic **130–131**
  biotic and abiotic components 126
  energy input 127
  main 81
  productivity **126**
  terrestrial **128–129**
Ecuador **391**
ecumenicalism 299
Edict of Nantes 251
  revocation of 256
Edison, Thomas 207, 328
education **162–163**
  around the world **163**
    British India 266
    Chinese 277
    colonial territories 278
  computer programs for 213
  government investment in 171
  vocational training 171
  women's access to 183
Edward III, King 245
Edward the Confessor, King 243
Edward VI, King 254
eels
  migration of 125
EFTA 177
Egypt 228, **391**

British control 267
  conquest by Arabs 241, 242
  Italian invasion of 274
  medieval monasticism 248
  Suez Canal crisis 279
  wars with Israel **282–283**
Egypt, ancient **229**
  architecture **326**
  disposal of the dead 159
  marriage customs 158
  medicine 156
  periods and dynasties **229**, 231
  religions **286**
  ships 217
  writing 350, *351*
Ehrlich, Paul **157**
eightfold way (nuclear particles) 31
Einstein, Albert 32, 33, **49**
einsteinium *37*
Eisenhower, General Dwight D. 275
Eisenstein, Sergei **328**
El Greco **314**
El Salvador **391**
Elamites (ancient people) 228
elastic modulus 17
elasticity **17**, *16*
  and sound 22
  and waves 20
elections 166, 167
electoral college 167
electric car 220
electric current **27**
  in telecommunications 208
electric fields **26**
  in nuclear accelerators 31
  of light waves 24
electric force 26
electric telegraph 208
electric-arc furnaces 198
electrical field, fishes and 101
electrical induction 29
electricity generation **188–189**, **190–191**,
  192
  development of 259
electricity **28–29**
  and magnetic field 61
  and thunder and lightning 79
  conduction by metal 45
  railway conversion to 218
  transmission of **188**
  see also electromagnetism; nerves
electrocardiograph 157
electrochemical reactions/series 44
electroconvulsive therapy 151
electrodes 28, 29
electroencephalograph 157
electrolysis 35, 41
  chemical extraction by 201
  metal extraction by 44
electrolyte solutions 40
electromagnetic fields **27**
electromagnetic force 15, 27, 30
electromagnetic induction 27
electromagnetic radiation 32–33
  absorption of 20
  see also X-rays
electromagnetic spectrum 20, **27**
  in photography 205
  see also optics
electromagnetic waves *see* radio waves
electromagnetism 15, **26–27**
  Maxwell's theory 27
  special relativity and 32
electron emission **29**
  see also photoelectric effect
electron microscopes 210
electron-transfer reactions **40–41**
electronic funds transfer 209
electronic mail 209
electrons 2, 36
  and heat conduction 45
  and static electric charges 26
  flow in electric current 27, 28
  formation of cations 44
  measuring with 210
  movement around an atom 30
  transfer reactions 38–39
  see also positrons
electroplating 41
electrovalent bond 38
electroweak force 31
elementary education 162–163

elements **34**, **36**
  artificial 44
  chemical symbols 34
  Earth 60
  Greek theory of 156
  groups and blocks **36**
  in sea water 76
  metals **44–45**
  number of compounds from 35
  Periodic Table 36, **37**
  plant uptake of 88
  unstable 36
  see also macroelements; microelements;
    specific elements
elephantiasis 154
elephants **117**
  hearing 23
elevators, aircraft 222
Elgar, Edward **339**
Eliot, George 369, **370**
Eliot, T.S. **373**, *375*
Elizabeth I, Queen 254, 360
Ellington, Duke **345**
ellipse 52
elliptical galaxies 4
embryo
  comparison of *84*
  development of human **134**, *135*
  plants 91
Emerson, Ralph Waldo **371**
emotions **147**
Empedocles of Acragas **156**, **304**
Empedocles of Agrigentum **48**
emperors
  ancient Roman 232, 233
  Chinese 234
  French 263
  Holy Roman 240–241, 253
  Japanese 235
emphysema 153
empiricism 303
employment
  macroeconimic policy 174
  regional policy 172
  Third World 185
  see also labour force
emulsion, film
  for black and white 204
  for colour 205
  infrared sensitive 210
enantiomers 46
endocrine system **143**
endoscopy 25
energy **18–19**
  atomic 30
  birds 107
  electrical potential energy 26
  electrons and levels of 36
  ionic bonding 38
  in a light bulb 29
  in chemical reactions 40
  in friction *see* kinetic energy
  in light 32
  in the biosphere **126–127**
  in the future **191**
  flying insects 99
  intensity of 20
  levels in nuclear accelerator 31
  plants **88–89**
  relativity theories and 33
  resources of 126, 127, 190
  transporting 216
  types of 18
  see also solar energy
  wave motion and 20
'energy inefficiency' 186
energy sources **188–189**
  coal 196
  food 138, 139
  gas 195
  nuclear 188, 189
  oil 194, 195
  solar 190
Engels, Friedrich 168
engines **192–193**
  aircraft **223**
  car 219, 220, *221*
  nitrogen oxides emission 43
  ships 217
  see also steam engines
England 254
  early music 332
  medieval, literature of 359

medieval population of London 247
  novels **364–365**
    Renaissance 360–361
  drama 361, 363
  see also United Kingdom
England, Church of
  early music 332
  establishment of 254
  see also Anglicanism
English Channel telegraph cable 208
English language 348–349, **352–353**
  sounds in 354
English Reformation 254
Ennius 357
Ensor, James **325**
entropy **19**
environment
  animal response to 124
  aquatic **130**
  Green politics and 169
  plant growth and development and **89**
  threats to **186–187**
environmental pollution *see* pollution
enzymes
  active sited 47
  in digestion 138–139
  manufacture of 201
Ephedra 91
Epic Theatre **374**
epicentre (earthquake) 64
Epicurus/epicurean 302, **304**
epidermis 145, *145*
epiphytes 93
  ferns 90
epistemology **303**
epistolary novels 364
Epstein, Jacob **325**
Equal Pay Act 183
equations 54
  kinematic **14**
equator, water temperature at 131
Equatorial Guinea **391**
equilibrium 16–17, *16*, 20
  of chemical reaction 41
  of temperature 19
equinoxes 80
Erasmus, Desiderius 249, **304**
Eratosthenes of Cyrene **10**, 48
erbium *37*
Eric the Red 243
Ericcson, John 217
Eriksson, Leif 243
Eritrea 267, **392**
ERM (Exchange Rate Mechanism) 174
Ernst, Max **324**
erosion
  and cave formation 75
  and sedimentary rock 66
  by rivers 75
  coastline **77**
  glacial 70, 71, *71*
  of volcanoes **68–69**
  wind 73, *73*
Eschenbach, Wolfram von **358**
Eskimo *see* Inuit
esparto grass 132
Esslin, Martin **374**
estates system **160**
  and political terms 168
  'Third World' 184
Estes, Richard **325**
Estonia **391–392**
estuaries, effect of longshore drift on 77
ethane (in natural gas) 195
ethanethiol **35**
Ethelred II, King 243
ethics **302**
Ethiopia **392**
  Christianity 237, *298*, 299
  effect of drought 185
ethylene 201
  polymerization of 199
Etna (volcano), Sicily 65
Etruscans
  art 307
  religious influence 287
eucalyptus trees 92
Eucharist (Holy Communion) *296*, 297
Euclid **50**, 52
Euclidean geometry 52
eukaryote cell 82, 83
Euler, Leonhard **50**, *54*
Euphrates River 228, 326

Eurasia
  prehistory 226, 227
EURATOM 179
Euripides **356**
Europe, Western
  economics
    development of 247
    main economic groupings *178*
  ecosystems 128–129
  history
    ancient 226–227
    Cold War in 280, 281
    Colonialism 257–258, 266–267
    Communism 270, 271, 272, 273
    Crusades 244–245
    Decolonization 278
    Fascism 272–273, 274–275
    France under Louis XIV 256–257
    French Revolution/Revolutionary
      Wars 262, 264
    Middle Ages 246–249
    Nationalism in 264–265
    Normans 243–244
    prehistory 226–227
    Renaissance 246–249
    Reformation 250
    Vikings 243–244
    World War I 268–269
    World War II 274–275
  social stratifications 160–161
  religions
    Christian Church in **298**
    criticism of the Church **245**
    Islam and 242
    pre-Christian 284, 285
  see also specific countries
Europe, Eastern
  Communist governments 280
  Cold War in 280–281
  see also specific countries
European Atomic Energy Authority 179
European Coal and Steel Community 179
European Commission (EC) 179
European Community **179–180**
  economics of 171
  ERM 174
  laws 164
European Convention for the Protection of
  Human Rights 179, *182*
European Court of Justice (EC) 179
European Economic Area 180
European Free Trade Association 180
European Parliament (EC) 179
europium *37*
Eutelsat II
eutrophication 131
Evangelical Revival 299
Everest, Mount 69
evolution **84–85**
  and brain structures 149
  arthropods **96**
  mammals **108**
  stellar **5**
  see also coevolution
Ewe language 354
exaltone **35**
exchange controls 177
exchange rates **174**, **175**
excise duties 175
excretion **139**, 141
  autonomic system and 147
  function of water 130
  hormone regulation of 143
  reptiles 103
execution, public *164*
executive (government) 166
exercise, respiration, circulation and **141**
exoskeleton **96**
  insects 98
exosphere 61
expenditure *see* income and expenditure
expert systems (computer) 213
expiration 140
exploration
  minerals and metals 197
  oil and gas **194–195**
  space **12–13**
  Spanish and Portuguese 252–253
  types of ships used 216, 217
  voyages of discovery **247**
Explorer I satellite 12
explosives 43
exports/exporters 176, 177, 179, 184–185
exposure meters 205

Expressionism/Expressionists
  in art 321, **322**
  in drama 374, 375
  in music 338
extended family 159
external auditory canal 144, *145*
extinctions
  bovids 117
  horse species 116
  prehistoric animals **104**, 108, 227
extrusive rock 66
Exxon Valdez 186
Eyck, Jan and Hubert van **313**
eye (human) 137, **144**
eye, insect 99
eye (of storm) 79

F

fabliau 359
Fabriano, Gentile da **311**
facsimile transmission (fax) 209
factories
  development of machinery 258
  Industrial Revolution and 258
  state-subsidized 256
factory farming 133
fairy (brine) shrimps **97**
faith 284
fallopian tubes 134, *134*
family **158–159**
  animals 125
  effect of mental illness on 151
  see also parents
family therapy 151
famine and hunger
  14th-century Europe 245
  in India 266
  Soviet 271
  Third World **185**
famine relief *179*
Far East
  development of farming 132
  exports to Europe 257
  see also specific countries
Faraday, Michael 27, **49**, 259
farming **132–133**
  Amazon region 238
  ancient Near East 228, 229
  arable 132–133
  chemistry and 34
  development 227, 234, 235, 236, 237,
    238
  effect of supply and demand 172–173, *173*
  importance of nitrogen fixation 88
  medieval system 246
  pollution damage 186
  Soviet collectivization 271
  support systems 185
  Third World 185
  'wind' 190, *190*
  see also horticulture
fasces 272
Fasci di Combattimento 272
Fascism **169**, *169*, **272–273**
  influence on poetry 373
Fassbinder, Rainer Werner **329**
fast breeder reactor 189, *189*
Fatimid dynasty 242, 301
fats, dietary **138**
  diseases from 153
  enzymes and 139
  hormone control of 143
fatty acids 138, 139
Faulkner, William **377**
fault-block mountains **68**, *69*
faults (rock) **67**
Fauré, Gabriel **338**
Fauvism/fauves **322**
Fawcett, Millicent Garrett 183
feathers **106**, 107
federal government 167
feedback 213
Feigenbaum's number 51
Fellini, Federico **329**
Ferdinand and Isabella 244, 252
  American empire **252–253**
Ferdinand II, Emperor 251
fermentation 201
  alcoholic 35
fermions 31
fermium *37*
ferns 89, **90**

ferries, roll-on/roll-off 216
fertilization
  amphibians 102
  fishes 101
  function of water in 130
  human **134**
  plants 89
    flowering 92–93
    non-flowering 91
fertilizers 132
  artificial 133, 201
    sources 43
  chemistry and 34
  pollution from 186
festivals, religious
  Chinese 292–293
  Christian **297**
  Indian **289**
  Japanese 292–293
  Jewish **295**
feudalism/feudal system **246**
  Japanese 235
Feuerbach, Ludwig **305**
fibre optics **25**
fibres
  natural 199
    sources 200
  synthetic 34, 47, 199, 200
Fichte, Johann Gottlieb **304**, **366**
fictions, visual 148, *148*
fiefs 246
Fielding, Henry **365**, 368
'fight, flight or fright' 147
Fiji **392**
  British control 267
Filippo Lippi, Fra **312**
film, photographic **205**
  formats 205
  panchromatic 205
  processing techniques 204
    Polaroid 205
finance
  balance of payments 176
  for Third World loans 184
  institutions and markets **170**
  medieval 247
  monetary policy **175**
  securities 171
  see also capital; currency
Finland **392**
Finnbogadottir, Vigdis 183
fire
  Parsi funeral customs 159
  prehistoric use of 226
firearms
  automatic **224–225**, *225*
  breech-loaded **224**, *224*
  early 224
firn/firnline 70
First Continental Congress 260
fiscal policy **175**
Fischer, Emil **157**
fishes **100–101**
  acid rain pollution 186
  defence behaviour **100**
  jawless 83
fission, nuclear 188
Fitzgerald, F. Scott **377**
Five-Year Plans, Soviet 271
fjords 71
flaps, aircraft 222
flash floods 69, 73
flash coloration 125
flat-bed press 203
flatworms **95**
Flaubert, Gustave **68**
flax 200
Fleming, Sir Alexander **157**
Fletcher, John **361**
flexible pavements 214
flies 98, 99
flight
  birds **106**, 107
  insects **99**
  principle of **222**
  see also aircraft
flintlock musket 224
Flodden, battle of 254
flood plains 75
floppy disk 211
Florida 160
'floating batteries' 217

fluids
  at rest **17**
  forces affecting **16–17**
  see also water
fluorine *37*, 38
  and the Periodic Table 36
  chemical reactions 41
    bonding 34
flute 340
fly ash 188
flying foxes *see* fruit bats
flying squirrels 118
focal length 24
focus (earthquake) 64
fold mountains **68**, *69*
folds (rock) **67**
folic acid **139**
folk dances 346
folk music 337, 344
  modern composers and 338–339
  Romantic composers and 337
Food and Agriculture Organization (FAO)
  178
food chain
  beginning of 127
  importance of plants 93
  pollution of 186, 187
food poisoning **155**
food/feeding **138–139**
  animals **125**
    whales 120, 121
  bats **112**, *112*
  birds 106
  edentates 111
  function of water 130
  insectivores 113
  plants and
    fodder crops 132
    importance of plants 93
    production of 88
  reptiles **105**
  rodents 118
  Russian shortages 270
  sense of taste and 145
  supply
    population growth and 185
    Third World 185
  transmission of infections 154
force **14–15**
  affecting solids and fluids **16–17**, *16*
  in chemical bonding 38–39
Ford, Henry 219
Ford, John **329**, **361**
Ford Motors 176
forebrain **146**
  limbic system *147*
forests
  destruction of rain forest 186
  development after Ice Age 227
  ecosystems **128–129**
  pollution of temperate forests 186
  precipitation 81
Forman, Milos **329**
formula, chemical 34
Forster, E.M. **377**
fortepiano 340
fortifications, medieval and Renaissance
  248
FORTRAN 212
Fosse, Bob **329**
fossil fuels
  by-products 188
  oxide emissions 43
  pollution from 188
  principal constituent 46
fossils/fossil record 84, 85
  bacteria 82
  continental drift and 62
  first human 226
  flowering plants 92
foundations (buildings) 214
Four Noble Truths **291**
four-stroke engines **192**
fovea 144
Fowles, John **377**
Fox Talbot, William 204
foxes 115
Fracastoro, Girolamo **156**
fractal geometry 51
Fragonard, Jean-Honoré **317**
frame of reference (physics) 15, 33

France **392–393**
    Alsace-Lorraine 265, 268, 269
    and American independence 260
    and Balkan nationalism 265
    and German unification 265
    and Gulf War 283
    and NATO 180
    and opening up of China 267
    and the Thirty Years War 251
    architectural styles 327
    ballet 346
    cinema 328, 329
    civil war in 256
    colonial empire 257, *266*
        decolonization 278, **279**
        extent of 267
        loss of American 260
        loss of colonies 257
        Middle Eastern mandates 282
    drama
        Classical **362–363**, *362*
        modern 374
    economic aid for Russia 270
    education 163
    energy sources
        nuclear programme 189
        tidal power station *191*
    government, electoral system 167
        Estates General 168
        estates system 160, 184
        human rights legislation 182
    Louis XIV's rule in **255**
        women's suffrage *183*
    industrialization 259
    in eastern Africa 237
    literature: medieval 358
        novels **365**, **368**
        Renaissance 360
        Romantics **366–367**
        Symbolists **372**
    music
        Baroque 333
        classical period 334
        opera 342
    the arts 256, 310
    'sister republics' 263
    Normandy 243
    prehistoric man 227, *227*
    religion, revival of 366
        Wars of Religion 251
    TGV service 218
    war with England *see* Hundred Years War
    World War I 268–269
        postwar settlement **269**
    World War II
        'appeasement' **273**
        liberation of 275
        surrender 274
    see also Franco-Prussian War; French
        Revolution; Napoleonic Wars
Francesca, Piero della **312**
Franciscana *121*
francium *37*
Franco-Prussian War 265
Franks 240
    Viking control of lands 243
Franz Ferdinand, Archduke 265, 268
Frasch process (mining) 197
fraternities 247
Frederick II, Emperor 244
Frederick the Great 257
Free Democratic Party 169
'free' market economy 171
free trade **177**
freemen **246**
'free verse' 373
Frege, Gottlob 51, 57, *303,* **305**
freight trains 218
French East India Company 257
French language 348
French Revolution **262**
    justification for 182
    national debt 262
    political ideologies 168
Freon-12 193
frequency, wave 20, *21*
    musical notes 330
frequency modulation 207
frescoes 307, 311, *311,* 312–313, 314, *314,*
    317
Freud, Sigmund **151**
friction **17**, 18
Friedan, Betty 183
Friedman, Milton 175

Friedrich, Caspar David 318
Friel, Brian **375**
Friendship 7 12
frigates 217
Frith, William Powell **319**
Froebel, Friedrich 162–163
frogs **102**
'Frondes' 256
Frost, Robert **373**
frottage 324
fruit bats 112
fruits, development of 93
Fry, Roger 321
fuel system, car **220**, *221*
fuels 190, 192–193, 194, 258
Fujiwara dynasty 235
Fujiyama (volcano) 65
functions **58–59**
    trigonometrical 52
funeral customs 159
    prehistoric burials 227
fungi **91**
    acid rain pollution and 186
    diseases from **154–155**
    immune system and 142
    in the food chain 127
further education **163**
fuse 28
Fuseli, Henry 318
fusion, nuclear **189**
fusional languages 348
Fust, Johann 202
Futurism **323**

G
gabbro 60, 66
Gabo, Naum **323**
Gabon **393**
Gaboon viper *105*
Gabrieli, Andrea and Giovanni **332**
gadolonium *37*
Gagarin, Yuri 12
Gainsborough, Thomas **317**
Gaius Gracchus 232
Gaius Marius 232
galagos (bushbabies) 122
galaxies **2, 3, 4,** 6
Galen of Pergamum (Galenus, Claudius)
    156
Galileo Galilei **11**, **49**
    and Jupiter's satellites 9
    study of motion 14
Galle, Johann 9
galleons 217
galley 217
galliard 332
gallium *37*
gallium arsenide 29
galvanization 45
Gambia **393**
gametes 87, 89
gametophytes 90–91
    reproduction 89
gamma (λ) decay 31
gamma rays 27
Gandhi, Mahatma 289
Ganges valley kingdoms 236
gangster movies 328
Garibaldi, Giuseppe 264, *265*
Garrett Anderson, Elizabeth 183
gas engines *see* jet engines
gases
    chemistry of **42–43**
    'greenhouse' 42
        and global warming 187
    kinetic theory of **19**
    poison gas 269
    properties 34
    see also natural gas; noble gases
Gaskell, Elizabeth **370**
'gasohol' 190
gastrointestinal tract 138–139
    diseases of 153
gastropods 95
Gaudi, Antonio **326**
Gaudier-Brzeska, Henri **325**
Gauguin, Paul **321**, 322
gaur 117
Gauss, Carl Friedrich **50**
Gautama, Prince 290
Gautier, Théophile 336
gavial 103
gearbox, car **220**, *221*
gelatin 132, 204
Gemara 294

gemstones 197
General Agreement on Tariffs and Trade
    (GATT) 177, 178
General Assembly (UN) 178
General Problem Solver program 213
general relativity 32, **33**
generators, electrical 188
    AC, DC **28–29,** *29*
    dynamo 27
genes **86, 87**
Genesis 345
genetic diseases 152
genetic engineering 87
    in arable farming 133
    in manufacturing 201
genetics **86–87**
    animal behaviour and 124
Geneva Accords and Conventions 182, 281
Genghis Khan 235
Gennep, Arnold van 159
genre painting **316**, 317
geological cycle 66, 67
geological time chart *66*
geometry **52–53**
    fractal 51
    proofs 52
        establishing 50
George I, King 255
George III, King 260
Georgia **393**
geothermal power **191**
German Confederation 265
German Empire 265
German measles (rubella) **155**
germanium 29, *37*
    properties 44
    semiconductor 45
Germany **394**
    cinema 328
    colonial empire *266,* 267
    languages 352
    peoples 240
    education in 163
    drama (Expressionism and Epic Theatre)
        374
    art 310, **313,** *322*
    French control of 263
    government 167, 169
    industrialization 258, 259
    law system 165
    literature: American adaptations 371
        Classicism in 363
        medieval sagas 358
        Naturalism in 369
        Romantics **366**
    opera **342–343**
    popular uprisings 264
    postwar settlement 269
    prehistoric man 226
    Reformation 250–251
    reunification 281
    totalitarianism in **272–273**
    unification of **265**
    World War I 268–269
    World War II 273, **274–275**
Germany, East (Communist government)
    280
Gershwin, George **344**
Gestapo (*Geheime Staatspolizei*) 273
gestation period 109
Gesualdo, Carlo **332**
Gettysburg, Battle of *260,* 261
Géricault, Théodore *318,* **319**
Ghana **394**
    British control 267
    kingdom of 237
Ghiberti, Lorenzo 311, **312**
Giacometti, Alberto **325**
Giambologna **314**
giant panda 115
giant spider crab 97
Gibbon, Edward 233
gibbons 123
Gide, André **377**
Gilbert, W.S. **344**
Gilbert, William **48–49**
Gilbert and George **325**
Gillespie, Dizzie **345**
gills **100–101,** 102
ginkgos 91
Giorgione **314**
Giotto di Bondone **310–311**
giraffes **116–117**

gizzard 107
glacial periods *see* Ice Ages
glaciers
    and landscape **71**
    erosion by 69
    formation of 70
    prehistoric development 226
glands **143,** 145, 147
glandular fever **155**
Glass, Philip **339**
glass, ancient Roman 307
glaucoma 144
Glenn, John 12
gliders 222
global warming 128, **187**
glockenspiel 341
Glorious Revolution **255,** 256
glucagon 143
Gluck, Christoph Willibald von **342–343**
glucose 139
glue 132
Gnetum 91
goats 117, **133**
    Angora 200
Gobi Desert 72, 128
god/gods
    ancient religions **286–287**
    Christian **296**
    Indian **288–289**
    Jewish, nature of **294**
    of Mount Olympus **287**
    religious classification by 285
Godard, Jean-Luc **329**
Goddard, Robert 12
Godwinson, Harold 243
Goebbels, Josef 272
Goes, Hugo van der **313**
Goethe, Johann Wolfgang von 336, **366**
Gogh, Vincent van **321**, *322*
Gogol, Nikolai **368**
Golan Heights 179, **398**
gold *37*
    abundance and uses 197
    early African trade 237
    uses 197, 227, 306
    mining **196–197**
    Portuguese colonies 253
    Spanish colonies **252–253**
golden mean 302
golden moles **113**
Golden Temple of Amritsar 289
Golding, William **377**
Goldsmith, Oliver 363
gonadotrophins 143
Goncharova, Natalia **323**
Gondwanaland 62
gonorrhoea **155**
Goodman, Benny **345**
goods trains 259, *258*
Goodyear, Charles 199
gorals 117
Gorbachov, Mikhail 281
Gordonstoun school 162
gorillas 123, *123*
Gorki, Maxim **369**
Gossaert, Jan **313**
Gothic Revival
    architecture 327
    novels 367
Gothic style
    art **310–311**
    architecture **327**
Goths, sack of Rome 240
government **166–167**
    and education 162, 163
    and environmental pollution 187
    Chinese concepts 234
    economics 171, **172, 174–175**
    Japanese systems 235
    pre-revolutionary France 262
    principle of 182
    regulatory bodies 173
    Renaissance idea of 249
    social capital 171
    industrialization policies 259
    postwar Communist 280
Goya y Lucientes, Francisco **318–319**
graben 67, *67*
Graham, Martha **347**
grain transportation 216
grammar, English 352, 353
    study of 354
gramophone records 207

Granada, Emirate of 244, 252
Grand Alliance 274
granite 60, 66
Grant, General Ulysses S. 261
graphite 46
    as nuclear moderator 188
graphs **58–59**
Grass, Günther **377**
grassland ecosystems temperate **128, 129**
Graves disease 143
gravimetric surveys 194, 197
gravitational acceleration 14
gravitational constant 15
gravitational force 30
gravity/gravitation **15**, 26
    and end of the universe 3
    and energy 18
    and formation of galaxies 3
    and ice movement 71
    and tides 76
    centre of *16*, 17
        aircraft 222
    comets and 7
    general relativity and 33
    measuring Earth's 60
    Solar System 7
gravure printing *202*, 203
Gray, Thomas **363**
Great Dark Spot 9
Great Northern War 257
Great Red Spot 9
Great Salt Lake, Utah 74
Great Schism 245
Great Wall of China 234, *234*
Great Western (ship) 217
'Greater Syria' 282
Greco-Roman Christianity **298**
Greece, ancient **230–231**
    and the Indus Valley 236
    Archaic Period **230–231**
    architecture **326**, *326*
    art **306–307**
    Athenian democracy 166
    Bronze and Iron ages 227
    Classical Period **230–231**
    education 162
    Hellenistic Age **231**
    legal system 164
    language, influence of 353
    literature **356–357**, 362
        rediscovery of 249
    medicine **156**
    Neolithic sites 227
    preservation of culture of 241
    religions **287**
    science 48
    ships 217
    writing 351, *351*
Greece, modern **394–395**
    German invasion of 274
    Italian invasion of 274
    nationalism in 265
'Green' politics 169, 187
Greene, Graham **377**
greenhouse effect 42, 128, 187
    on Venus 8
Greenland, Viking discovery of 243
Greenland Ice Sheet 70, 71
'Green Revolution' *133*
Greenwich Mean Time (GMT) 3
Greenwich Meridian 3
Greer, Germaine 183
Gregorian calendar 3
Gregorian chant 330
Gregory XIII, Pope 3
Grenada **395**
grey whales 121
grey wolf 115
Grieg, Edvard **337**
Grierson, John **329**
Griffith, D.W. **328**
Grimm, Jacob and Wilhelm Carl 348
Grimmelshausen, J.J.C. von **364**
Gris, Juan **325**
Gropius, Walter **326**
Gross Domestic Product (GDP) 175
Gross National Product (GNP) **175**
Grosz, George **324**
ground squirrels 118–119
groundwater 74
group therapy 151
growth hormone (GH) **143**, 201
Grünewald **313**, 324
Guam, United States control of 267

guanaco 117, 129
guano 112
Guardi, Gianantonio and Francesco **317**
Guatemala **395**
guilds 247
Guimard, Hector **326**
Guinea **395**
    independence 279
guinea pigs *see* cavies
Guinea-Bissau **395**
    independence 279
Gulf of Mexico, tidal range 77
Gulf War **283**
gunpowder 224
Guomindang (Kuomintang) 276
gurdwara 289
guru 288
Guru Granth Sahib 289
Gustavus Adolphus, King 251
Gutenberg, Johannes 202, 249
Gutenberg discontinuity 60, *61*
Guyana **395**
gymnosperms 89, 91, 92
gyrostabilization 99

H
Habeas Corpus Act 182
Haber, Fritz 201
Habermas, Jurgen **305**
habitats
    bats 112
    bovids 117
    fishes 101
    flowering plants 92
    insect **98**
    scent marking 115
Habsburg Empire
    and the Reformation 251
    Holy Roman Emperors 240–241
    Spanish 252
Hadrian, Emperor 233
hadrons 31
haemoglobin 140
hafnium 37
Hahn, Kurt 162
Hahn, Otto 181
hailstones 79
hair follicles 145
Haiti **395–396**
half-life 31
halftone process 203
Haller, Albrecht von **157**
Halley, Edmund 7
Halley's Comet 7
hallucinations 150
halogens 36
    chemical reactions 41
'halons' 43
Hals, Franz **316**
Hamilton, Alexander 261
Hamilton, Richard **325**
Hammarskjöld, Dag 178
Hammerstein, Oscar **344**
Hammurabi of Babylon 228
Han dynasty 234
    art 308
hand axe 226
Handel, George Frideric **333, 342**
    instruments 334
hangovers 35
Hannibal 232
Hanoverian dynasty 255
Hansa cog 217
Hanseatic League 217
Happenings 324–325
Harappan civilization 236
    arts 308
hard disk 211
Hardouin-Mansart, Jules **326**
Hardrada, Harold 243
hardware 211
Hardy, Thomas **370, 373**
Hare, David **375**
Hare Krishna movement 285
harems, animal 124
hares **119**
Hargreaves, James 200
Harijans 160
harmonics 23
harmony, musical 331
harp 341
harpsichord 332, 333, 340
Hart, Lorenz **344**
Harvey, William 140, **156**

Hassidic Jews 295
Hastings, battle of 243
Hattusilis III, King 228
Hausmann, Raoul **324**
Hawaii
    formation of 68, 77
    United States control 267
    volcano 65
Hawksmoor, Nicholas **326**
Hawthorne, Nathaniel **371**
Haydn, Franz Joseph **334–335**, 340
headaches 35
Heaney, Seamus **373**
hearing **144–145**
    birds 107
    insects 99
    mammals 108
    threshold of 22
hearsay (law) 165
heart **140**, 141, 147
    development 134
    diseases 138, 152, 153, 157
Heartfield, John **324**
heat **18–19**
    absorption by oceans 130
    conduction by metal 45
    generating 28
    latent **19**
    missile guidance by 225
    thermally isolated system and 19
    transfer of **18**
'heavy water' 189
Heckel, Erich **322**, *324*
hedgehogs 113
Hegel, Georg Wilhelm Friedrich 169, 303, **305, 366**
Hegelianism 303
Heian period, art 309
Heidegger, Martin 303, **305**
Heidelberg University 248
Heine, Heinrich 336, **366**
Heisenberg, Werner Karl 32
Heisenberg Uncertainty Principle 15
helicopters **223**
    on ships 216, 217
helium 6, 31, 37
    and fusion reaction in stars 5
    and the Periodic Table 36
    formation in 'big bang' 2
    properties 34
Hellenic kingdoms **231**
    Roman conquests 232
helots 230
hematite 198
Hemingway, Ernest **376–377**
hemispheres
hemp (fibre) 200
Hendrix, Jimi **345**
Henry, Joseph 27, **49**
Henry I, King (Germany) 240
Henry the Navigator, Prince 244, **247**
Henry V, King 245
Henry VII, King 254
Henry VIII, King 254
Henze, Hans Werner **339**, 343
hepatitis 155
    alcoholic 153
Hepworth, Barbara **325**
Heraclitus of Ephesus **304**
Heraclius, Emperor 241
Herald of Free Enterprise (ferry) 216
Herbert, George **360**
Herbert, Victor **344**
herbivores 116–117
    ecosystems 128, 129
    finding food 125
    in the food chain 127
    marine mammals 120
    migration and hibernation 125
herbs 93
Herder, Johann Gottfried **366**
heredity 151, **152**
heresy/heretics 245
    crusades against 244
    Inquisition and 251
Herodotus **356**
herpes virus 155
Herschel, Sir William 9
Hertz, Heinrich Rudolf 20, 27, **49**
hertz (measurement) 20
Hertzsprung, Ejnar 5
Hertzsprung-Russell diagram **5**, *4*
Herzog, Werner **329**
Hesiod **356**
heterotrophs 127

Hevea brasiliensis 199
hi-fi **206–207**
Hi-Tech architecture 327
hibernation 112, 119, **125**
hides and skins 132
hieroglyphics 350, *351*
    Meso-American 239
High-Speed Train 218
higher education **163**
Hijra 300
Hilbert, David **50**
Hildesheim Treasure 307
Himalaya mountains, formation of 68, *68*, 69
Himmler, Heinrich 273
Hindenburg, President von 272
Hinduism 285, **288**
    and caste system 160
    art 308
    expansion of culture **236**
    gods and goddesses **289**
hinge joint 136, *137*
Hipparchus of Nicea **48**
Hippocrates of Cos **156**
Hippocratic Oath 156
hippopotamuses **116**
Hiroshima 181, 275
Hitchcock, Alfred **329**
Hitler, Adolf **272–273**
    and the USSR 271
    suicide 275
Hittites/Hittite Empire **228**
    religions 286
HIV I virus 87
HMS *Rattler* 217
Ho Chi Minh 281
Hobbema, Meindert **316**
Hobbes, Thomas 166, **304**
Hockney, David **325**
Hohenstaufen dynasty 240
Hokusai, Katsushika 309, *308*
Holbein, Hans, the Younger **313**
Holiday, Billie **344**
Holly, Buddy **345**
holmium 37
holograms 25, *25*
Holst, Gustav **339**
Holy Roman Empire **240–241**
    official religion 248
'holy war' 242
Homer, Winslow **320**
Homer 287, **356**, 363
Homo erectus 226, 237
Homo sapiens neanderthalensis 226
Homo sapiens sapiens 227
    African development 237
homologous structures *84*
Honduras **396**
honeybees 99, **124**, *124*
Hong Kong 420
    British enlargement of 267
    Japanese invasion of 274
    reversion to Chinese control 277
Hongwu 235
Honthorst, Gerard van **316**
Hooch, Pieter de **316**
Hooke, Robert 17, **49**
Hooke's law 17
Hopkins, Sir Frederick Gowland **157**
hoplite warfare 230
Horace **357**, 363
hormones 134, 135, 141, **143**
horns, animals 117
horns, instruments 341
hornworts 90
'horses **116**, *133*
horsetails 90, *90*
horst 67, *67*
Horta, (Baron) Victor **326**
horticulture, prehistoric 237
hospitals, foundation of 156, 248
Hotol project 13
households, income and expenditure 174
hovercraft 216
hoverflies, defence 125
Hölderlin, Friedrich **366**
Huascarán (volcano), Peru 68
Hubble, Edwin 2, 23
    galaxy classification 4
Hubble's law 2, 3
Huggins, Sir William 2
Hughes, Ted **373**
Hugo, Victor **367**
Huguenots 251

human capital 171
human beings
  language aquisition **355**
  macroelements in 127
  population growth (and hunger) 185
  prehistory **226–227**
  threats to the environment 72, **73** 128, 129, 186–187
human organism **134–156**
  brain and nervous system **146–147**
  diseases
    infectious **154–155**
      non-infectious **152–153**
  food, diet and digestion **138–139**
  glands and hormones **143**
  immune system **142**
  learning, creativity and intelligence **148–149**
  mental disorders **150–151**
  movement **136–137**
  regulation of internal environment **143**
  reproduction and development 87, **134–135**
  respiration and circulation **140–141**
  senses **144–145**
human rights 182
  Council of Europe and 179
human sacrifice *238, 239*
human voice, transmitting 208–209
humanism/humanists 284
  and the Renaissance **249**
  revival of classical literature and art 312
  work on the Bible 249, 251
Humboldt, Wilhelm von 348
Humboldt Current, effect on climate 77
Hume, David **304**
humours, Greek theory of 156
humpback whales 121
Hundred Years War **245**
  Henry VIII and 254
Hungary 396
  Austrian reconquest of 257
  Communist government 280
  revolt against Austria 264
  Soviet invasion 280
hunger *see* famine and hunger
Hunt, William Holman **319**
Hunter, John **157**
hunter-gatherers
  Aborigines 237
  early Americans 238
  North American Indian 239
hunting, extinctions and 227
Huntington's chorea 152
hurricanes 79
Hus, John 245
Hussein, King 283
Hussein, President Saddam 283
Husserl, Edmund 303, **305**
Hussites 244, 245, 250
Huston, John **329**
Hutton, James **49**
Huxley, Aldous **377**
Huxley, T.H. 84
Huygens, Christiaan 21
Huygens' principle 21
Hyatt, John Wesley 199
hydrides 35
hydrocarbons 46, 47, 186, 194, 201
hydrochloric acid 40
hydroelectric power 191
hydrofoil 216
hydrogen 6, *37*
  atom of 30
  bonds **39**
  chemical reactions 41
  chemistry of **42**
  formation in 'big bang' 2
  in plants and animals 127
  in the Periodic Table 36
  liquid 193
hydrogen bomb 181
hydrological cycle **75**, *126*
hydrostatics **17**
hydroxides 40
hyenas **114**
Hyksos 229
hyperbola 52
hypermetropia 144
hypocentre (earthquake) 64
hypothalamus **143**, 146
hysteria 151

I
ibex 117
Ibsen, Henrik **374**
ice **70–71**
  chemistry of 42
  erosion by *69*
Ice Ages **70**
  last 226, 227, 237, 238
  mammals 108
  glacial erosion during 69
icebergs of *70*, 71
ice caps **70**
ice floes 71
Iceland **396**
  formation of 77
  geothermal heat 191
  Viking colonization 243
ice sheets **70**
ice shelf 70
iconography, Christian 310
ideal gas law *18, 19*
idealists 302
Ife art 309
igneous rock 66
ignition system, car 220, *221*
Ikeda Daisaku 293
illuminated manuscripts 310, 311
illusions, optical **148**
image intensifiers 210
imaginary numbers **55**
imam 300
Imamis 301
immune system **142**, 153
immunization 154
  invention of 157
  mass 185
imperialism, European **267**, 278
imports 177, 179, 185
Impressionism **320**
imprisonment 165
Inca Empire *239*, 252
incest 158
income and expenditure **174**, 175
  see also economics; prices and incomes policies
income tax 175
India **396–397**
  art **308**, *309*
  development of farming 133
  education in 162
  history
    colonial wars 257
    independence 279
    Neolithic to Colonial **236**
    the British in **266–267**
  mountain formation 68
  religions of **288–289**
    Christianity in 299
  social divisions **160**, 161
  weather systems 79
  women's suffrage 183
Indian Mutiny 266
Indian Women's Association 183
Indians, North American **239**
  ancestors 238
  reservation settlement 261
indicators, chemical 40
indium *37*
Indo-Chinese languages 348
Indo-European languages 348, *349*
Indochina
  decolonization 278, 279, 281
  French control 267
Indonesia **397**
  Dutch control 267
  independence 279
  see also Dutch East Indies
indri 122
Indus Valley civilization 236
industrial diseases 153
Industrial Revolution, the **258–259**
  chemistry and 34
  effects of **259**
  iron production 198
  mechanization of textile industry 200
  outside Britain **259**
industrialization
  Chinese 277
  Indian 266
  Japanese 235
  Russian 270
  Soviet Five-Year Plans 271
industry
  chemical plants 34
  environmental pollution 186–187

major powers
  Britain **258–259**
  United States 261
microeconomic policy 172
  and distribution of 173
steam power for 192
Third World development 184
inertia 15
inertial frame (physics) 33
INF Treaty 281
inflammation 141
inflation 174, 175
  Black Death and 245
  Russian 270
inflectional languages 348, 352–353, 354
influenza 155
infrared: photography 205
  radiation: missile guidance by 225
    use in imaging devices 210
  waves 27
infrasonics 23
inhabited scroll 310
inheritance, genetic *87*, *87*
injunction (law) 165
inks, printing **202**
inner city renewal 172, *172*
Inquisition 251
insectivores **113**
insects **98–99**
  defence 125
  evolution 96
  organization 125
inselbergs 73
inspiration (breathing) 140, *141*
instantaneous velocity 14, *15*
instinct, animal 124
instruments, astronomical **11**, 13
instruments, musical **340–341**
  brass **339**
  characteristics of notes *23*
  classical symphony 334
  early 332
insulator 29
insulin 87, 143
  manufacturing 201
insurance/insurance companies 170
  agricultural 185
integers 54
integrals **59**
integrated circuits 29
  in computers 211
intelligence **148–149**
  artificial **213**, 355
  mammals 109
Intelsat 209
intercostal muscles 140
interest rates 175
  effect in Third World 184
interference *21*, 32
interferon 154
intermedii 342
internal-combustion engines 192–193
International Atomic Energy Agency 178
International Bank for Reconstruction and Development 178
International Court of Justice (UN) 178, 179
International Gothic **311**
International Modernist architecture 327
International Monetary Fund (IMF) 178
  Third World loans 184
'interplanetary space' 61
Intifada 283
intrusive rock 66
Inuit 238
investment
  balance of payments and 176
  by businesses 174
  trust companies 170
invisible, seeing the **210**
involuntary muscle **137**
'involuntary nervous system' 147
iodine *37*
  chemical reactions 41
Ionesco, Eugene **374**
ionosphere 61
  effect on radio waves 206
ions/ionic compounds **38**, *38*, 40
  bonding **38**
Iran **397**
  ancient *see* Persians/Persian Empire
  invasion of India 236
  Iraqi invasion of 283
  Neolithic culture 227
  Shah of 283

Iraq 179, **397**
  ancient *see* Mesopotamia
  and Iran 283
  British mandate 282
  Shanidar cave 227
  war with Israel 282
  World War I campaign 269
Ireland **397–398**
  English control of 254, 255
  modern drama **375**
  modern poetry **373**
iridium *37*
iris (eye) 144
Irish Nationalist Movement 373
iron *37*, *138*, *196*, **198**
  abundance and uses 197
  corrosive properties 45
  discovery of 44
  metal extraction 196
  production 198, **258–259**
  ships built of **217**
Iron Age 226, **227**
  in Black Africa 237
  in India and Southeast Asia 236
Iron Curtain 280
ironclads 217
ironworking
  Zhou dynasty 234
  prehistoric West African 237
irrational numbers **55**
irregular galaxies 4
irrigation 185
Irving, Washington **371**
Islam 282, 284–285, **300–301**
  and Arab national 278
  and the Lebanon 283
  architecture **326**
  art **308**
  Christian conquests **242**
  early science 48
  history
    control of education 163
    early caliphates **24**
    loss of Spain 241, 242, **244**, 252
    rise of **242**
  in Black Africa 237
  in India **236**
  marriage customs 158
  religious leaders **300**
  sects **301**
    problems between 283
  see also Muslims
Islamic fundamentalist revival 283
islands
  effect of global warming 187
  formation of **77**
  mud 75, *74*
Ismailis 301
isobars 78
isolating languages 348
isotopes **30–31**
  of hydrogen 189
  of uranium 188
Israel **398**
  buffer zone with Lebanon 283
  history
    ancient kingdom 228
    creation of **282**
    from 1948 *283*
    Neolithic culture 227
    twelve tribes 294
Issigonis, Sir Alexander 219
Istanbul 242
Italy **398**
  architecture **327**
  art **310–311**, *312–314*
  cinema **329**
  colonial empire *266*
    conquest of Abyssinia 273
    extent of 267
    Middle Eastern 282
  culture (medieval and Renaissance) 248
  government 167, 169
  history
    Byzantine reconquest 241
    city-states 248
    French control 263
    Lombards 241
    Norman conquests 241, 243
    Ostrogoths 240
    revolution in 264
    unification of **264–265**
  literature
    medieval 359
    nationalist 367

Naturalism in 369
novellas 364
Renaissance 360
nuclear programme 189
opera 343
totalitarianism in **272**
volcanoes 65
women's suffrage 183
World War I 268
postwar settlement and 269
World War II
Allied invasion of 275
territorial gains 274
iteration 51
IUD (intra-uterine device) 135
Ives, Charles **339**
Ivory Coast see Côte d'Ivoire

J
jackal 115
Jackson, Andrew 261
Jacob 294
Jacobites 255
Jacquard, Joseph-Marie 200
Jainism 285, **288–289**
Jamaica **398–399**
James, Henry **370–371**
James, William **305**
James Francis Edward Stuart, Prince 255
James I, King 254, 361
James II, King 255
Janácek, Leos **343**
Jansenists 256
Jansky, Karl 11
Janssen, Zacharias 25
Japan **399**
art 309, *309*
colonial empire *266*, 278
estate system 160
government 169
history to the 20th century **235**
industrialization 259
military expansion
in the Pacific 274
invasion of China 273, **276**
religions **292–293**
Shinkansen (bullet train) 218, *218*
totalitarianism in 273
women's suffrage 183
World War II 274
surrender 275
Jarrow marchers *171*
jatis 160
Jawlensky, Alexei **325**
jazz **344–345**
Jazz Age 347, 377
Jefferson, Thomas 260, 261
jellyfish 94
Jenner, Edward **157**
Jerusalem, capture of
Babylonian 229
recaptured by Muslims 242
Crusades for releae of 244
Temple 295, *294*
Jesuits (Society of Jesus) 251
Jesus 298, 300
teachings of **296**
jet engines **193**
in rockets 225
jewellery, Bronze Age 227
Jews see Judaism/Jews
Jiang Jie Shi (Chiang Kai-shek) 276
jihad 242
Jin nomads 235
Joan of Arc 245
Johansson, Christian **346**
Johns, Jasper **325**
Johnson, Andrew 261
Johnson, President Lyndon 281
Johnson, Samuel 353
joints **136–137**
arthritis in 153
Jones, Inigo **326**, 361
Jones, Sir William 348
Jonson, Ben **361**
Joplin, Scott **344**
Jordaens, Jacob **315**
Jordan **399**
PLO and 283
war with Israel 28
Joule, James 18, 19, **49**
joule (J) 18, 19, 26
Joyce, James 365, **376**
Judah 228
Judaism/Jews 282, 284–285, **294–295**, 298
exodus 228

modern forms 295
persecution (Nazi) 273
ritual and worship 159, **294–295**
tolerance of 242, 262
traditions and sects 295
see also antisemitism; Zionists
Judd, Donald **325**
judges/judiciary 164, 165, 166
Jugendstil **321**
Julian calendar 3
Julian the Apostate 233
Julius Caesar 232, 287, 357
Jung, Carl Gustav **151**
Jupiter (planet) 7, **9**
jury/jury system 164–165
justice 164
justices of the peace 165
Justinian, Emperor 241
jute (fibre) 132, 200
Jutland, battle of 269
Juvenal **357**, 363

K
Kafka, Franz **376**
Kaiser, Georg **374**
Kalahari Desert 72
Kalf, Willem **316**
Kamakura period, art of 309
Kandinsky, Wassily **322**, 323
kangaroos **110**
Kant, Immanuel 302, **304**, 366
'Kapp Putsch' 272
karma 288, 290
Kassites (ancient people) 228
Kazakhstan 180, **399–400**
Kazan, Elia **329**
Keats, John **367**
kelvin/kelvin scale 18
Kent, William **326**
Kenya 267, **400**
Kepler, Johannes **10–11**, 49
keratin 106, 116, 145, *145*
Kerenski, Aleksandr Fyodorovich 270
Kern, Jerome **344**
ketones 47
kettledrums 341
Kevlar 47
'keynote' musical 331
Keynes, John Maynard 175
keys, musical 331, 335
Khannar (ship) 216
Khmer Rouge 281
Khojas 301
Khomeini, Ayatollah 283, 377
kibbutzes 159
kidneys
functions 141
nephron 139, *138*
transplants 157
Kiefer, Anselm **325**
Kierkegaard, Soren **305**
Kilimanjaro glaciers 70
killer whale *121*
kilogram (kg) 15
kinematic equations **14**
Kinetic art **325**
kinetic energy 17, 18
kinetic frictional force
kinetics, theory of gases **19**
'Kingdom of Italy' 264–265
'King's Men' 361
kinship system 158, 159
Kirchner, Ernst Ludwig **322**
Kiribati **400**
Kitab Akdas 285
'kitchen sink' drama 375
Kitti's hog-nosed bat 112
kiwi 107
Klee, Paul **323**
Kleist, Heinrich von **366**
Klien, Christian Felix **50**
Klimt, Gustav **321**, 322
'knight service' 246
knitting 200
knives, prehistoric 226
Knossos, palace of 230
knowledge, class system and 161
Knox, John 251
koalas **110**, 125
Koch, Robert **157**
Kodiak bear *115*
Kokoschka, Oskar **322**
Kongfuzi see Confucius
Korea 234, 235, 267
Korea, Democratic People's Republic of **400**

Korea, Republic of 178, **400**
Korean War 277, **280**
Krakatau (volcano), Indonesia 68
krill 97, 121
Krüger flaps 222
krypton 37
Ku Klux Klan *182*
Kublai Khan 235, 247
Kubrick, Stanley **329**
kulaks 271
Kurosawa, Akira **329**
Kuwait 179, **400–401**, 283
Kyd, Thomas **361**
Kylian, Jiri **347**
Kyrgyzstan 180, **401**

L
Laban, Rudolp **347**
'Labanotation' 347
labour camps, Soviet 271
labour/labour force **171**
Black Death and 245
effects on distribution of 173
estates system and 160
industrialization and 258, 259
women in 183
Labour Party 168
Labrador Current, effect on climate *80*, 81
Laclos, Choderlos de **365**
Laennec, René Théophile Hyacinthe **157**
Laforgue, Jules **373**
lagomorphs **119**
lagoons 77
Laika 12
'Lake Poets' 367
lakes 74, **75**
'aging' process 131
evolution to bogs **131**
Lamarck, Jean-Baptiste **49**
evolutionary theory 84
Lamartine, Alphonse de **36**
laminar flow 17
Lancaster, House of 254
Land, Edwin 205
land bridge, Asian–Alaskan 238
Lander, Harold **347**
landholding
communal system 270
medieval system 246
landmasses, and global warming 187
Landsat programme and satellites 13, 210
landscape
desert 72, **73**
effect on atmosphere 78
glaciers and 71
rivers and 74, **75**
landscape painting
Classicism 316
dutch school 316
Renaissance 313
Rococo 317
Romantic **318**
Venetian 314
Lang, Fritz **328**
language/languages
acquisition of **354**
ancient Near East 228
artificial intelligence and 213
brain centre for 147
Church use of 298
computer 212
French influence on English 243
how language works **354–355**
study of *see* linguistics
world **348–349**
lantanum 37
Lao Zi 292
Laos 281, **401**
see also Indochina
Larkin, Philip **373**
Las Navas de Tolosa, battle of 244
lasers **25**
in compact disc recorder 207
in computers 203, 212
in telecommunications 209
weapons systems 13, 225
Lassus, Roland de **332**
Lateran Treaty 272
latex 199
Latin America
Christianity in 299
Cold War in **280–281**
oil industry 195
Latin American Integration Association 180
Latin Empire 241

Latin language 348
influecne on English language 353
Roman literature **357**
latitude 70, 80
Latvia **401**
Laud, Archbishop 255
laughing gas 35
Laurasia *62*
lava/lava flows 65
see also basalt
Lavoisier, Antoine **49**
law **164–165**, 248
government and 166
human rights 182
introduction of legal system 229
Japanese system 235
sources of **164–165**
see also 'natural law'
laws, physical
of constant composition 41
of gravitation 15
of arithmetic **54**
of motion 11, **15**
planetary 10–11
uniformly accelerated 14
reflection and refraction 21
laws, religious
Islamic **301**
of Judaism 294
Lawrence, D.H. **373**, 376
Lawrence, T.E. 269
Lawrence, Thomas **317**
lawrecium 37
Le Corbusier **326**
Le Vau, Louis **326**
Le Verrier, Urbain 9
Le Witt, Sol **325**
lead 37
abundance and uses 197
pollution from 186
League of Arab States 180
League of Nations **273**
'mandates' 269, 278, 282
Lean, David **329**
leap year 3
learnability **149**
learning **148–149**
animal 124
medieval recovery and spread of 248
least weasel 115
leather 132
Lebanon 179, **283**, **401**
Israeli invasion and war 282, 283
social divisions 161
lebensraum 272
Leblanc, Nicolas 201
Lee, Robert E. 261
leeches 95
Leeuwenhoek, Anton van **157**
Left, the (politics) **168–169**
Léger, Fernand 325
legislature 16, 167
Leibniz, Gottfried Wilhelm von *302*, **304**
calculus 58
leks 107
lemmings 119
lemurs **122**
'Lend-Lease' 274
Lenin, Vladimir Ilyich 168, **270–271**
Leningrad, siege of 25
Lenoir, Étienne 192
lens/lenses **24**
camera 204, *204*
eye 144
light speed through 24
microscope 25
properties 24
Leonardo da Vinci 48, **312**, 313
Leoncavallo, Ruggiero **343**
Leopardi, Giacomo **367**
Leopold, King 267
Lepanto, Battle of 242, 253
leprosy **155**
leptons 31
Les Six **338**
Lesotho **401–402**
Lessing, Gotthold Ephraim **363**
letterpress printing 202–203
letters (post) 208
Leucippus **48**
Lewis, Wyndham **323**
Leyte Gulf, battle of 275
Lévi-Strauss, Claude **305**
libel 165
Liberalism **169**
and nationalism 264

development of 259
Fascism and 272
see also economic liberalism
'liberation theology' 299
Liberia **402**
Libertarians 169
'liberty, equality, fraternity' 168
Libya **402**
Italian control 267
lichens 90, **91**
see also litmus
Lichtenstein, Roy **325**, *324*
Lie, Trigve 178
Liebermann, Max **320**
Liechtenstein **402**
Lieder 366
life
beginnings of **82–83**
energy for **126–127**
simple forms **82**
source of 130
life cycles
amphibians **102**
birds **107**
coelenterates 94
fishes **101**
reptiles **103–105**
seaweeds 90
lift, aircraft 222, 223
Ligeti, György **339**
light: dual nature theory 32
fibre optics and 25
generating 28, 29
polarized: insects and 99
principal source of *see* solar system
rays 24
reaction with nitrogen dioxide 43
speed of 2, 33, 206
variations in 24
transmission of 25
waves/wavelength 24, **27**, 32
light years 2
calculating magnitude with 5
light-water reactors 189
lightning *26*, 79
lignin 88, 92
Limbourg Brothers **311**
limbs 84, 134
limestone 66, 67, 75
use in steel production 198
limonene 47
Lincoln, Abraham 261
line intaglio 203
linear motion 14
linguistics **354**
and cognitive science **355**
Linnaeus, Carl **49**
classification system 83
Linotype machine 202
Linz-Donawitz (L-D) process 198
lions, hunting technique 125
Lippershey, Hans 11
Lister, Joseph **157**
Liszt, Franz **337**
literature
classical **356–357**
revival of classical 312
Classicism in **362–363**
the Augustan Age **363**
Indian epics 288
medieval 248, **358–359**
vernacular 249
Norse 287
Realism in **368–371**
Renaissance 248, **360–361**
Romanticism in **366–367**
influence on music **336**
Surrealist 324
see also novels
lithium *37*
lithography **202–203**
screening and colour reproduction **203**
lithosphere 61
plate tectonics and 63
Lithuania **402**
litmus 40
liver
and nutrients 139
diseases of 153
hormone control of 143
liverworts 89, 90
livestock farming **132–133**
threat to ecosystems 128, 129
Livy **357**

lizards 103
defence 125
llama 117
Lloyd George, David 169, 269
loan capital 171
loans 171
agricultural 185
and the national debt 255, 256
for Russian industrialization 259
interest rates 175
see also debt
local government 167
Lochner, Steven **313**
Locke, John 166, 169, 303, **304**
lockjaw (tetanus) **155**
logarithms **55**
logic 51, **57**
Logic Theorem program 213
logographic writing **350**
'Lollards' 245, 250
Lombards 241
long-playing records 207
longbow 224
longitude *see* Greenwich Meridian
longitudinal oscillation 20
'Long March' 276
longship 217
longshore drift 77
longsightedness *see* hypermetropia
longwall mining 196
looms, powered 258
'Lord Chamberlain's Men' 361
'Lord Protector' 25
Lorenz, Edward N. 51
Lorenzetti, Ambrogio and Pietro **311**
lorises 122
Lorraine, Claude **317**
Lorris, Guillaume de **358**
Losey, Joseph **329**
Lotus Sutra 293
loudness 22,
of musical notes 23
loudspeakers **207**
Louis the Pious 240
Louis XIII, King 256
Louis XIV, King 255, **256**, *346*
Louis XV, King 256
Louis XVI, King 256, 262
Louis XVIII, King 263
Louisiana 257, 260
Louvois, Marquis de 256
Lowell, Robert **373**
Lower Palaeolithic Age **226**
lower primates **122**
Loyola, Ignatius 251
Lubitch, Ernst **329**
Lucius Sulla 232
'lucrative sciences' 248
Lucretius **357**
'Luddites' 258
Lully, Jean-Baptiste **333**, **342**
Luna 3 8
lunar eclipse 10
lungs
birds 107
fishes **100–101**
human **140–141**, 142, 153
lute 332
lutetium *37*
Luther, Martin **250–251**
Lutheran Church 250–251, 299
early music 332, 333
Lutoslawski, Witold **339**
Lutyens, Sir Edwin **326**
Luxembourg **402–403**
lycopods 90
lymph 142
lymph nodes 142
lymphocytes 142
lysozyme 142

M
Mabuse **313**
macaques 123
MacArthur, General Douglas 275
MacDiarmid, Hugh **373**
Macedonia 231
former Yugoslav republic 424
Machiavelli, Niccolò 166, 249, **304**
machine guns **224–225**
machine tools, development of 259
Macke, August **322**
'mackerel sky' 79

'mackintosh' 199
Mackintosh, Charles 199
Mackintosh, Charles Rennie **326**
Macmillan, Harold 279
Macmillan, Kenneth **347**
MacNeice, Louis **373**
macroeconomics 170, **174–175**
macroelements 127
macrophages/microphages 141, 142
Madagascar **403**
French control 267
Maderna, Carlo **326**
madrigal 332
Maecenas 357
Maeterlinck, Maurice 338
Mafia, demonstration against *165*
Magdalha, kingdom of 236
Magellan, Ferdinand **247**
'Magic Realism' 377
magistrates 165
Maglev trains 218
magma
chamber 64, 65, 66
plate tectonics and 63
source of 61
Magna Carta 182
magnesium *37*, 197
abundance and uses 197
oxidation of 38, **40–41**
use in galvanization 45
magnesium chloride extraction 197
magnet 26
magnetic disks 211
magnetic resonance imaging 210
magnetic surveys 194, 196
magnetic tape 207
magnetism/magnetic field 26
Earth's 60, **61**
continental drift and 63
interaction with solar wind 7
fishes and 101
iron ore and 197
Maglev trains 218
of light waves 24
recording with 207
telecommunications and 208
see also degaussing
magnetite 198
magnitude
earthquakes 64
Moon 4
stars **4–5**
magnox reactor 188
Magritte, René **324**
Magyars 240
Mahabharata 288
Mahayana Buddhism **291**
Mahler, Gustav **337**
maidenhair tree 91
Maimonides **304**
mainframe computers 212
maize **132**, 238
Makarova, Natalia **347**
Makiguchi Tsunesaburo 293
malaria 154, **155**
Malawi **403**
Malaysia **403**
British control 267
Japanese invasion of 274
Maldives, The **403**
Malevich, Kasimir **325**
Mali **403–404**
kingdom of 237
Mallarmé, Stéphane 338, **372**
Malle, Louis **329**
malnutrition 185
Malory, Thomas **359**
Malta **404**
World War II 274
Malthus, Thomas 185
Mamet, David **375**
Mamluks
defeat of Crusaders 244
recapture of Jerusalem 242
mammals **108–109**
aquatic *85*, **120–121**
edentate 111
hibernation 125
hoofed **116–117**
prehistoric 227
smallest 112, 113
territory, mating and social organization **124–125**
mammoth, woolly *108*
manatees **120**

Manchu dynasty, overthrow of 276
Manchuria
and Chinese empire 235
Chinese Nationalist takeover 276
Japanese occupation 235, 273, 276
Russian influence 267
mandrills 123
Manet, Edouard **320**, 323
mangabeys 123
manganese *37*
in steel 198
Mangzi 292
mania 150
manic-depressive psychosis 151
manioc 238
Mann, Thomas **377**
Mannerism
architecture **327**
art **314**, 316
Mantegna, Andrea 306, **313**
mantle, Earth's 60, *61*
Mao Zedong 168, **276**, *277*
Maoris 237
maps/mapping 210
Marathon, battle of 231
Marattia (fern) 90
marble 67
Marc, Franz **322**
Marcel, Gabriel **305**
Marconi, Guglielmo 206
Marcus Aurelius 233
Marcuse, Herbert **305**
'mare's-tails' 79
Marie Antoinette 262
marimba 341
Mariner 10 spacecraft 8
Marinetti, Filippo 323
Marivaux, Pierre **365**
Mark Antony (Marcus Antonius) 232, 357
market economies 170
market mechanism **173**
markets 172
colonial 258
common 177
financial **170**
medieval **246–247**
Marlowe, Christopher **361**
marmosets 122–123
marmots 119
Maronites 299
Marquet 321
Marquez, Gabriel Garcia **377**
marriage **158–159**
Mars (planet) 7, **8–9**
space missions to 13
Marshall Islands **404**
Marshall Plan 180, 280
marsupials 109, **110**
evolution of 108
Martel, Charles 240
martens 115
Martial 357
Martin, John **320**
Martini, Simone **311**
Marvell, Andrew **360**
Marx, Karl 160–161, 168, **305**, 366
society and resources theory 185
Marxism **168**
Fascism and 272
influence on poetry 372–373
theory 160–161
Marxism-Leninism 168, 284
and education *163*
and law 164
Mary I, Queen 254, 255
and the Counter-Reformation 251
Mary Queen of Scots 254
Masaccio **312**
Mascagni, Pietro **343**
masques 361
mass (physics) 15
centre of 17
measure of *see* mole
mutual force of attraction between *see* gravitation
relativity theories and 33
mass production
cars **219**
steel 258
masses (church service) 332, 335
Masson, André **325**
Massys, Quentin **313**
mastaba 326
mathematicians, eminent **50**

mathematics **50–51**
  computers and 211
  functions, graphs and change **58–59**
  geometry and trigonometry **52–53**
  Meso-American 239
mating, animal **124–125**
Matisse, Henri 321, **322**
matter, atomic theory of **30–31**
Matterhorn (mountain) 69
Mauchaut, Guillaume de **332**
Mauna Loa (volcano) 65, 68
Mauritania **404**
Mauritius **404**
Maurya, Chandragupta 236
Maurya civilization 236, 308
Maxwell, James Clerk 27, **49**
Maya Empire 239
  overthrow of 252
mayflies 98–99
Mazarin, Cardinal 256
Mazzini, Giuseppe 264
McAdam, John 214, 259
McCarthy, Senator Joseph 280
measles **155**
measurement/measuring 210
meat and meat products 132–133
mechanics 14
  Newton and, laws of 33
    theory 14
    of waves 20
  see also quantum mechanics
medical schools 156, 157
  foundation of 248
medicine 34, 210, *156–157*
Medievalism, in art 319
Mediterranean
  ancient Greek settlement 230
  ecosystems 129
  tidal range 77
megaliths *227*
megaparsec 2
Mehmed II, Sultan 242
meiosis 83, 87
Meistersingers **360**
Melanesia, settlement of 237
melody 330
meltwater, sediment deposition by 71
Melville, Herman **371**
Members of Parliament 167
Memling, Hans **313**
memory cells 142
men
  hormones and development 143
  reproduction **134, 143**
Menander **357**
Mendel, Gregor **49**, 86
mendelevium *37*
Mendeleyev, Dmitri **49**
Mendelssohn, Felix **337**
meningitis **155**
menopause **135**
Mensheviks 270
menstruation 134, 135
mental disorders **150–151**
menthol crystal *39*
Menzel, Adolph von **319–320**
mercantilism 257
merchant banks 170
Mercosur 180
mercury (element) *37*
  abundance and uses 197
  properties 44
Mercury (planet) 7, **8**, *9*
Merenptah, pharaoh 228
meristems 89
Merleau-Ponty, Maurice **305**
mesas 73
'Mersey Sound' 345
Meso-America: early agriculturalists **238**
  warrior states 239
Mesolithic Age 226, **227**
meson 31
Mesopotamia 228
  architecture 326
  conquest by Arabs 241, 242
  modern *see* Iraq
  religions 286
  writing 350
mesosphere 61
Messiaen, Olivier **339**, 343
Messina, Antonello da **314**
metabolism
  birds 107
  human **143**
  insects 99
  mammals 108

metal ores
  mining **196–197**
  transporting 216
metalloids 44
metals **44–45**
  alkali 36
    properties 44
  as electricity conductors 28–29
  discovery and extraction **44–45**
  extraction by reduction 41
  occurrence 44, 197
  oxides 40
  Periodic Table 37, *44*
  properties 44, **45**
  purification of 41
  reactivity series **44**
  uses 197
  velocity of sound through 22
  see also Bronze Age; Iron Age
metalwork, non-Western 308, 309
metamorphism/metamorphosis
  insects 98, **99**
  musical 337
  rocks **66–67**
metaphysics **302**
  poetry 360
meteors/meteorites/meteoroids 7, *7*
methane *43*, 194
  extraction of 190
  in natural gas 195
Meun, Jean de **358**
Mexico **404–405**
  Spanish colonization 252
  temple-cities 239
  US defeat of 261
mice 119
  marsupial 110
Michelangelo Buonarotti **313–314**, 360
Mickiewicz, Adam **367**
microcomputers **211**, 212
microeconomics 170, **172–173**
microelements 127
Micronesia **405**
  settlement of 237
microorganisms
  acid rain pollution and 186
  biotechnology and 201
  carbon monoxide utilization 43
  diseases from **154–155**, 156
  immune system and 142
microphones 207
  telephone 208
microscopes 25, *25*
  invention of 156–157
  photography through 205
  see also electron microscopes
microwaves 27
  from the 'big bang' 2–3
  transmitting with 209
Mid-Atlantic Ridge 77
Middle Ages
  culture **248–249**
  economy and society **246–247**
  musical instruments 332
  ships 217
middle class 161
  and development of liberalism 259
  demands for liberal government 264
Middle East, the **282–283**
  decolonization 278
  development of farming 132
  oil industry 195
  rise of Islam 241
  terrestrial ecosystems 128
Middle English language **352–353**
Middle Kingdom *see* China
Middle Palaeolithic Age **226–227**
Middle Stone Age 226
Middleton, Thomas **361**
Midway, battle of 275
migration, animals 112, **125**, 129
Milhaud, Darius **338**
military government 167
milk 108
Milky Way 4, *5*
Mill, John Stuart 302, **305**
Millais, John Everett **319**
Miller, Arthur 375, *375*
Miller, Glenn **345**
millet, domestication of 234
Millet, Jean-François **319**
Milton, John **358**
mimicry 99, 125

minerals
  and salinity 130
  dietary **138**
    hormone control of 143
  exploration by satellite 13
  in sedimentary rock 66
  mining **196–197**
  plant uptake and transport **88**, *89*
Ming dynasty 235
  ceramics 308
Mini Minor 219
miniature painting 308, *309*
minicomputers 212
Minimalism
  art **325**
  music 338, **339**
mining **196–197**
  environmental pollution 186
  Industrial Revolution 258
  steam power for 192, 258
    locomotive 218
ministers, religious 297
mink 115
Minoan civilization 230
minuet and trio **335**
Mir space station 12–13
Miró, Joan **324**
mirrors **24–25**
  telescope 25
Mishna 294
missiles 217, 225
  Cuban crisis 281
missions/missionaries **298**
  in Portuguese colonies 253
  in Spanish colonies 252
  Jesuits 251
Mississippi delta 75
mistletoe 93
Mitannians (ancient people) 228
mites **97**
Mithraism 287
mitosis 87
mixtures, chemical **35**
  separating 35
Model T Ford 219
modelling, mathematical 50
modem 209
Modernism/Modernists
  music 338
  novels **376**
  poetry **372–373**
Modified Mercalli Scale 65
Modigliani, Amedeo **325**
modulation 206, **207**
  music 331
  pulse-code 209
Mogul dynasty 236
mohair 200
Mohenjo-Daro 236
Mohorovicic discontinuity (Moho) 60, *61*
Moldova 180, **405**
mole (measurement) **41**
mole rats 119
molecules **34**
  and thermal energy 18
  and viscosity 17
  giant **39**
  in compounds 34–35
  in entropy 19
  intermolecular forces **39**
  Ideal gas law and 19
  organic
    chirality and recognition of 46
    designing synthetic **47**
    plant sources 88
  small **42–43**
moles **113**
  marsupial 110
Molière **362–363**
molluscs **95**
molybdenum *37*
  in steel 198
moment of force 16
momentum 15
Monaco **405**
monarchy: limitations on power 182
  see also absolute monarchy; parliamentary
monarchy
Monarco, Lorenzo **311**
monasteries 248, **249**
  dissolution in England 254
Mondrian, Piet **323**
Monet, Claude **320**
monetarism 175
money *see* coinage; currency

money market 170
Mongolia **405**
  Chinese rule 235
Mongols: invasion of China 235
  Islam and 242
monkeys **122–123**
Monmouth, Geoffrey of **358**
monocotyledons 93
monogamy 158
  animal 124
monomers 47
monophonic music 332
Monophysitism 298, 299
monopolies **173**
monosaccharides 138
monotheistic religions 285
monotremes 109
Monotype machine 202
Monroe, James 261
Monroe Doctrine 261
monsoons 79
Monte Cassino, battle of 275
Montenegro 179
  see also Yugoslavia
Montesquieu 166, 167
Montessori, Maria **162–163**
Monteverdi, Claudio **332–333**, **342**
Montgomery, General Bernard 275
Montreal Convention 187
monuments, prehistoric 227
mood disorders 150
Moon, the **8**
  and tides 76
  magnitude 4
  men on 12, *12*, 13
  phases *8*
moonrats (gymnures) 113
moons of Uranus 9
Moore, George Edward **305**
Moore, Henry **325**
moraines 71, *71*
morality plays **359**
Moreau, Gustave **321**
Morgagni, Giovanni Battista 157
Morgan, Thomas Hunt **49**
Moriscoes 242
Morisot, Berthe **320**
Morocco **405–406**
morphology, linguistic 348, 354
Morse code 206, 208
mortgages 171
Morton, William Thomas Green **157**
mosaics
  Byzantine *241*, 310, 326
  Roman 307
Moses 294, 300
mosque building 326
mosses 89, 90
motets **332**
Motherwell, Robert **325**
moths 98, 99
motion **14–15**
  circular **14–15**
  laws of 11
    Newton's **15**
  wave **20–21**
motor neurones 147
motor racing, first race 219
motors, electric 29
Motorwagen 219
moulting 96, 98
Mount St Helens 68
mountains/mountain ranges **68–69**
  alpine ecosystems **129**
  building processes 69
  erosion of **69**
  ocean-floor 63
  plate tectonics and 63
mouse (computer) 212
mouse deer 117
mouse lemurs 122
movable type 202
movement
  human **136–137**, 147
  kangaroos 110
movie camera **205**
Mozambique **406**
  independence 279
  Portuguese control 253, 267
Mozart, Wolfgang Amadeus **334–335**,
  336, 340, 341, 363
mucous membrane 145
Muhammad 242, 300
  see also Qur'an
Muhammad, Mirza Ali 285

Muir, Edwin 373
mules 133
mullah 300
multimedia 213
multiple stars 4
multiplexing 209
multiplication 54
mummification 159
mumps 155
Munch, Edvard 322
Murdoch, Iris 377
Murnau, Friedrich 329
Murray, James 353
muscles 134, 136, 137
    and respiration 140
    birds 106
    eye 144
    hormone control of 143
    insect 99
    nervous system and 147
    see also heart
music
    classical period 334–335
    structures 334, 335
    components of 330–331
    early 332–333
    'Mannheim School' of composers 334
    modern 338–339
    new music 339
    origins of 330
    popular 20th-century 344–345
    Romanticism in 336–337
    tonality 331
        'progressive' 339
    Viennese School
        First 334
        Second 338
musical comedy 344
musical films 328–329
music dramas 337
musk deer 117
Muslim law 164
Muslims see Arabs; Islam
Musorgsky, Modest 337
Musset, Alfred de 367
Mussolini, Benito 272
    overthrow of 275
mustelids 115
mutation, mutagenesis 85, 86
mutiny
    Indian 266
    Soviet navy 271
Mutsuhito, Emperor 235
mutualism 125
'mutually assured destruction' 181
Myanmar 406
mycelium 91
Mycenaean civilization 230
    shaft graves 227
myopia 144
myosin 137
myriapods 96
mystery plays 359
myxomatosis 119

N
Nabokov, Vladimir 377, 377
Nagasaki 181, 275
Namib Desert 72
Namibia 406
Nanak (guru) 289
Napoleon I 262, 336
Napoleonic Code 164
Napoleonic Wars 263
narwhal 121
nasal mucosa 145
Nash, John 326
Nash, Paul 325
Nasser, Gamal Abdel 282
National Socialist German Workers' Party see
    Nazis
Nationalism 169, 262–265
    and decolonization 278
    Arab 282–283
    Chinese empire 235
    Eastern European 265
    Fascism and 272
    influences on the arts
        drama 375
        literature 367
        music 337
        poetry 373
    Middle Eastern 282

nationalization
    of Suez Canal 279, 282
    post-revolutionary Soviet 271
NATO 280
natural cycle, nitrogen in 43
natural gas 194, 195
    processing 195
    transporting 195, 216, 216
natural law theories 182
natural numbers 54
natural selection, 83, 84–85
Naturalism
    in art 320
    in drama 374
    in literature 369
'nature versus nature' debate 183
Nauru 406
Navarino Bay, battle of 265
navies
    British 255
    deployment in Gulf War 283
    Napoleonic Wars 263
    Soviet (mutiny) 271
    Spanish see Spanish Armada
    United States (Pearl Harbor) 274
    World War I 269
    see also warships
navigation
    birds 23
    by insects 99
    radar for 210
Navigation Acts 257
Nazis 272–273, 272, 273
Ndebele revolt 267
Neanderthal man 226–227
neap tides 76
Near East
    ancient 228–229
        ancient religions 286
        architecture 326
        importance of flooding 228, 229
    modern see specific countries
    prehistory 226
        Neolithic development 227
Nebuchadnezzar 229
nebulae 4
negative/positive process see calotype
Negroes 237
Neill, A.S. 162
Nelson, Horatio 263
nematodes 95
Neo-Babylonians 228–229
Neo-Expressionism 325
neo-imperialism 279
Neoclassicism
    in architecture 327
    in art 317
    in literature 362–363, 366
neodymium 37
Neoimpressionism 320
Neolithic Age 226, 227
neon 37, 38
    in the Periodic Table 36
    intermolecular forces 39
Neoplatonist philosophy 313
Neorealist cinema 329
Nepal 406–407
    war against the British 266
Neptune (planet) 7, 9, 9
neptunium 37
Nero 233
nerves
    and hearing 144
        and touch 145
    in the peripheral nervous system 147
    in the skin 145
    on the tongue 145
    transmission of signals 146
    see also neurology
nervous system 146–147
    development 134
    thyroid hormone and 143
Nestorianism 298, 299
Netherlands, The 407
    Anglo-Dutch Wars 257
    colonial empire 266, 267
        capture of Portuguese colonies 257
        decolonization 279
        in eastern Africa 237
    establishment of 263
    Renaissance art 313
    social divisions 161
    trade with Japan 235
    World War II 274
    see also Dutch Republic

netsuke 309
Neumann, Balthasar 326
neural computing 213
neurology 157
neurones 147
    afferent and efferent 147
neurosis 150–151
neutrinos/antineutrinos 2, 31
neutron star 5
neutrons 2, 30
    in nuclear fission 188
'New Deal' 175
New Economic Policy, Soviet 271
New Guinea: German control 267
    prehistoric to colonial 237
New Model Army 255
'New Right' 169, 173
New Stone Age 226
New Wave films 329
New York 260
New Zealand 407
    independence 279
    law system 165
    prehistoric to colonial 237
    women's suffrage 183
    World War I 269
Newcomen, Thomas 192, 258
Newman, Barnett 325
newspaper production 203
Newton, Sir Isaac 11, 14, 16, 32, 49, 50
    calculus 58
    laws
        applied to gases 19
        first law 16
        of gravitation 15
        of mechanics 33
        of motion 15
        on stress 17
    newton (measurement) 15, 26
    newton metre 16, 18
    newts 102
    névé 70
    niacin see nicotinic acid
Nicaragua 407
niches, ecological 126
Nichiren 292, 293
Nichiren Buddhism 291
Nicholas II, Tsar 270, 271
Nicholson, Ben 325
nickel 37
    abundance and uses 197
    in steel 198
nicotinic acid 139
nidicolous birds 107
nidifugous birds 107
Nielson, Carl 339
Niepce, Nicéphore 204
Nietzsche, Friedrich Wilhelm 305
    influence on poetry 372–373
Niger 407–408
Nigeria 408
    art 309
    British control 267
Nightingale, Florence 157
'Night of the Long Knives' 273
Nile River 74, 326
    delta 75
    valley 229
        development of farming 133, 237
Nilo-Saharans 237
nimbostratus clouds 79
Nimitz, Admiral Chester 275
Ninevah 229
niobium 37
nitrates, plant uptake and transport 88, 89
nitric oxide 43
nitrogen 37, 42, 43
    and biogeochemical cycles 127, 127
    chemistry of 43
        bonding 34, 39
    cycle 88
    dioxide 43
        pollution from 186
    fixation 88
    in fertilizers 34
    in plants and animals 127
    oxides of 43, 186
        emission of 188
    source of 88
nitrous oxide 43
Nixon, President Richard 281
nobelium 37
noble gases 36, 42
    chemical bonding 38–39

'Nok culture' 309
Nolde, Emile 322
Non-aggression Pact 271, 273, 274
Non-aligned Movement 180
non-metals 37
Nono, Luigi 339
'Norman' architecture see Romanesque
Normans 243
    influence on English language 352–353
    invasions 243
'Norsemen' see Vikings
North Africa
    Vandals in 240
    World War II 274, 275
    see also specific countries
North America
    British colonization 257, 260
    Christianity in 299
    discovery of 247
    early agriculture 238
    ecosystems 128, 129
    English language 353
    exports to Europe 257
    French colonization 257
    Ice Age 70
    mountain formation 68
    post-Revolutionary, see United States
    Viking settlement 217, 243
    see also Canada; Indians, North American;
        United States
North American Free Trade Agreement 180
North Atlantic Drift, effect on climate 77,
    80, 81
North Atlantic Treaty Organization 180
north pole 26
Northern Ireland, social divisions in 161
'Northern Renaissance' 313
Norway 408
    acid rain pollution 186
    early expansion/colonization 243
    World War II 274
notes, musical 330
    characteristics 23
    names 331
    time values 330–331
Nouveau Roman 377
Novalis 366
novella 364
novels
    development of 364–365
    first-person narrative 364
    Gothic 367
    influence on vocabulary 353
    modern 376–377
        continuities 376–377
    of sentiment 364
    Realist 368–369
    Romantic 366–367
    serialization of 369
Noverre, Jean Georges 346
Nubia 237
nuclear accelerators 31
nuclear bombs 275
nuclear energy 188–189
nuclear family 159
nuclear forces 15, 30
nuclear fusion 6
nuclear particles/antiparticles 31
nuclear power 195
    fission and fusion 31
        in stars 4, 5
    pollution from 187
    submarines 217
nuclear reactions see nuclear power
nuclear reactors 31, 188–189
nuclear weapons 181, 225
    agreements on limitations 281
    Chinese research 277
    first Soviet 280
    type of energy 31
nucleic acids 47
nucleons 30
nucleus 30
    force of 26
    structure 30–31
    upper limit of protons 36
nuée ardente 65
null set 57
number systems 54–55
    binary 211
nunataks 70
Nuremberg Laws 273
Nureyev, Rudolph 347

nursing/nurses, development of modern 157
   social status 161
nutrients, circulation and 141
   cycling 127
   in freshwater ecosystems 131
   storage and use of **139**
nutrition 157
   plants **88**
   see also diet and food
Nyasaland 267
nylon 199
nymphs 98

O

O'Casey, Sean **375**
O'Neill, Eugene **375**
oasis 73
oats **132**
obesity 153
oboe 340, *341*
obsessive-compulsive disorder 150
occupational status system 160, **161**
ocean liners 216, 217
ocean-floor spreading 63
Oceania
   decolonization 279
   prehistoric to colonial **237**
   religions 284, 285
   World War II 274, 275
oceanic crust 60
oceanic ridges 63, 64, 68, 76, 77
oceans **76–77**
   absorption of energy 127
   absorption of ultraviolet 130
   average depth 130
   currents **77**
      and desert formation 72
      effect on climate *80*, 81
   ecosystems 131
   formation of 82
   salinity of 130
   trenches 76, 77
   velocity of sound in 22
Ockeghem, Johannes **332**
octave 331
Odo Nobunaga 235
Oedipus complex 151
Oersted, Hans Chhristian 27, 208
oesophagus 138, *139*
oestrogen 135
Offenbach, Jacques **344**
Office of Fair Trading 173
offset litho 203
ohm (measurement) 28
Ohm, Georg Simon 28
Ohm's law 28
oil **188, 194–195**
   crude 194
   products 199, 201
   tankers 216
   water pollution 186
oil print 202
okapi *116*, 117
old age *see* aging
Old English language **352**
'Old Pretender' 255
Old Stone Age 226
olfactory nerve 145
oligarchies 231, 232
oligopoly 173
Oman **408**
ombudsman 167
omnivores, finding food 125
Oort Cloud 7
Op art **325**
OPEC 180, 195
open market operation 175
open-hearth process 198
opencast (open-pit) mining 196
opera **342–343**
   Baroque 333
   classical 336
   early 332
   from Beethoven to Wagner **343**
   from Handel to Mozart **342–343**
   modern 338, 339
      Savoy Operas 344
      20th-century **343**
   Neapolitan School 342
   'rock operas' 345
   Romantic 337
   sources 358
opera seria **342–343**
operetta 344

Opium Wars 235, 267
opossums 110, 125
optics **24–25**, 144
   Doppler effect 23
   optical cable **209**
   see also fibre optics
orang-utan 123
oratorio **333**
orbits 3, 13
orchids 93
ore *see* metal ores
Oresme, Nicole d' **48**
organ (musical instrument) 340
organic chemistry **46–47**
   chemicals 201
organic sedimentary rock 66
organisms 82, 83
Organization for Economic Cooperation and
   Development 180
Organization of African Unity 180
Organization of American States 180
Organization of Petroleum Exporting
   Countries *see* OPEC
organizations, international **178–180**
Orman Quine, Willard van **305**
ornithopods 104
orogeny 68, *69*
Orthodox Christianity **298–299**
   creation of 241
Orton, Joe **375**
Orwell, George **377**
Osborne, John **375**
oscillation 20
Oshima, Nagisa **329**
osmium 37
osteoarthritis 153
osteoporosis 135
ostracism 231
Ostrogoths 240
otter shrews 113
otters 115
Otto, Nikolaus August 192
Otto cycle 192
Otto I, King 240
Ottoman Empire
   conquest of Constantinople 241
   defeat by Spanish 253
   defeat of Crusaders 244
   expansion of **242**
   in the Middle East 282
   loss of territories 265
   Napoleonic Wars 263
   World War I 268, 269
      postwar settlement 269
Ottonian dynasty 240
outlet glaciers 71
outwash plains 69
ova **134**
ovarian follicles 134
ovaries **143**
   flower 92
   human 134
overdrafts 171
overland flow 74
Ovid **357**
Owen, Robert 168
Owen, Wilfred **373**
oxbow lake 75
Oxford University 248
oxidation **40–41**
   in plants 89
   of metals 45
oxidation state 44
oxides 35, 44
   of nitrogen **43**
oxidizing agents 35
oxygen 37, **42–43**
   atmosphere and 126
   bonding 34, **38–39**
   in aquatic ecosystems 130
   in plants and animals 127
   in respiration 140, 141
   in the atmosphere 83
   liquid 193
   plant by-product 88
oxytocin 134, 143
ozone 61, 186
   chemistry of **42–43**
      pollution of 127, 186, **187**
      protection from solar radiation 61,
      126–127

P

Pacific Ocean
   and mountain formation 68
   oceanic ridge 77
   subduction zones 63
      and earthquakes 65
   volcanoes under 65, 69
   see also Oceania
pack ice 71
Paganini, Niccolò *337*
pain stimuli and receptors 145
Pakistan **408–409**
   independence 279
Palaeolithic Age **226–227**
   records from 350
Palestine/Palestinians 282, **283**
   ancient 228
   Crusades in 244
   World War I campaign 269
Palestine Liberation Organization 180, 283
Palestrina, Giovanni **332**
Palladianism **327**
Palladio, Andrea 306, **326**, 327
palladium 37
Palmer, Samuel **320**
pampas 129
Panama **409**
Panama Canal 215, 267
pancreas **143**
   cancer of 153
pandas, feeding habits 125
Pangaea 62
Pankhurst, Christabel 183
Pankhurst, Emmeline 183
'Pan-Slavism' 265
Papal States 264, 265
paper
   manufacture 132
   printing **202**
papillae 145
Papua New Guinea **409**
parabola 52
Paracelsus, Philippus Aureolus **48, 156**
paradoxes **57**
Paraguay **409**
parallax 2
parallel evolution **85**
parallelogram 53
paranoiac-critical activity 324
parasites/parasitism
   animals 107, **125**
   diseases from **154–155**
   fungal 91
   plants 93
parathyroid glands **143**
parathyroid hormone 143
parents *see* family
Paré, Ambroise **156**
Paricutín (volcano) 65
Paris 247, 248
Paris Peace Conference 269
Parker, Charlie 'Bird' *344*, 345
parliament
   British **254–255**, 260
   Russian 270
parliamentary government 166–167
parliamentary monarchy 254, **255**
Parmenides of Elea **304**
Parmigianino 314
parsec 2
Parsis/Parsiism 286, **289**
   funeral customs 159
Parsons, Charles 192
parts of speech 355
PASCAL (computer language) 212
pascal (Pa) 17
Pascal, Blaise **304**
Pasolini, Pier Paolo **329**
Passchendaele, battle of *268*, 269
passenger transport 259
   shipping **216**
Pasternak, Boris **377**
Pasteur, Louis 157
pastoral poetry 360
Patenir, Joachim *313*
Pathet Lao 281
pathogens 154
patricians 232
pavan 332
Paxton, Sir Joseph **326**
PCB pollution 186–187
Pearl Harbor, attack on 274
peas *see* pulses
peasants 246
   ancient Roman 232
   effects of the Black Death 245

   Indian 266
   Japanese 235
   revolt of Chinese 235
   Russian 270, 271
   kulaks 271
Peasants' Revolt 245, 250
peccaries **116**
Pechstein, Max **322**
Peckinpah, Sam **329**
Peirce, Charles S. **305**
Peisistratos 230
Peloponnesian League 230
Peloponnesian War 231
Penderecki, Krzysztof **339**
Peninsular War 263
Pennsylvania 260
'Penny Black' 208
pension funds 170
Pentacostalism 299
pentaprism 204, *204*
People's Liberation Army 277
Pepin the Short 240
peppered moth 85
peptides, manufacture of 201
perception 144
   mental illness and 150
percussion firing weapons 224
perennials (plants) 93
Perez de Cuellar, Javier 178
Performance art **324–325**
perfumes, synthetic 35
Pergamon, kingdom of 231
Pericles 231
peridotite 60
periodic oscillation 20
Periodic Table 36, **37**
   metals *37*, 44
   non-metals 37
   reactive series 44
peripheral nervous system 146, **147**
perissodactyls 116
Perón, Isabel 183
Persepolis, fall of 229
Persians/Persian Empire **228–229**
   ancient religion **286–287**
   and the Indus Valley 236
   collapse of 242
   defeat of 231
   invasions of Greece 231
   siege of Constantinople 241
personality 149, 150
perspective 312, 313
Peru **409–410**
   Spanish colonization 252
pesticides, pollution from **187**
pests, imbalance of 186
Peter I, Tsar, the Great 257
Petipa, Maurice **346**
Petit, Roland **347**
Petrarch **360**
petrol engines **192–193**
petrol/petroleum
   petrochemicals production chain 177
   producing 195
   pollution and 186
Petronius **357**, 364
Pettit-Smith, Francis 217
Pevsner, Antoine **323**
pharaohs 228, 229
   and religion 286
phenol 201
phenomenology 303
pheromones 99
Phidias 307
Philip II, King 231, 253
   and the Counter-Reformation 251
   invasion of England 253, 254, *255*
Philip VI, King 245
Philippine Sea, battle of the 275
Philippines, The **410**
   independence 279
   United States control 261, 267
   World War II 274, 275
Philistines 228
philology/philologists 348, 366
philosophers 181, **304–305**
   Romantic 366
philosophy **302–305**
   challenge to religion 287
   idealist thinking 366
   rediscovery of classical 248, 249
   Renaissance interest in 313
   theories **303**, 304–305
      natural law 182
Philostratus 306

phloem 90
phobias 150-151
Phoenicians 217, 228
phonetics 354
'Phoney War' 274
phonograph 207
phonology 348, 354
phosphorus 37, 138
  chemical bonding 34
  in plants and animals 127
Photo-Realism 325
photoelectric effect 29, 32
photography 204–205
  see also photomontage
photogravure 202–203
photomicrography 205
photomontage 324
photons 2, 30, 31, 32
  in gamma decay 31
  in lasers 25
photosphere 6
photosynthesis 88, 93
  and atmospheric gases 42
  and the food chain 127
  atmosphere and 126
  boreal forest 129
  in algae 90
  in bacteria 82, 83
  in corals 94
  in protists 82
photovoltaic effect 29
physics 14
  atoms and subatomic particles 30–31
  electricity in action 28–29
  electromagnetism 26–27
  optics 24–25
  quantum theory and relativity 32–33
  wave phenomena 20
physiology
  amphibians 102
  birds 107
  development of 156–157
  reptiles 103
  use of chaos theory 51
piano 340, 341
Picabia, Francis 324
picaresque novel 364, 365
Picasso, Pablo 322–323
piccolo 340
pidgin languages 348
Pietism 299
pigs 116, 133
pikas (conies) 119
pillow lava 65
Pindar 356
Pink Floyd 345
Pinter, Harold 375
pipelines, oil and gas 195
Pirandello, Luigi 374
Pisanello, Antonio 311
Pisano, Giovanni 310
Pisano, Nicola 310
Piscator, Erwin 374
Pissarro, Camille 320, 321
pitch, musical notes 23
pituitary gland 143
pivotal joint 137
Pizarro 239, 252
PKS 2000–330 4
placenta/placentals 109, 134, 135, 143
plague 155
plainsong 330, 332
Planck, Max 32, 49
plane figures 53
plane joint 137
planetary nebula 5
planets 7, 8–9
  laws of motion 110–11
  see also specific planets
planning programs 213
plants 88–89
  and the biosphere 126
  cloning 133
  ecological niche 126
  ecosystems 128–129
  edible 132
  flowering 92–93
  function of water 130
  insects and 99
  non-flowering 90–91
  pests 99
  pollution damage 186
  result of decomposition 127
  spore-bearing 90–91

vascular 90
  see also pollination
plasma 140
  cells 142
plastic flow 16
plastics 47, 199
  raw materials 195
  use in art 323
plate tectonics 62–63, 66, 67
  and earthquakes 64
  and island formation 77
  and mountain formation 68
platelets 140
platen press 203
Plath, Sylvia 373
platinum 37
  abundance and uses 197
  and rate of chemical ractions 41
Plato 249, 302, 303, 304, 356
Plautus 357, 363
plebeians 232
Pliny the Elder 48
Plisetskaya, Maya 347
Plotinus 304
plural society 161
Plutarch 357
Pluto (planet) 7, 9
plutonium 37
plutonium-239 31
pneumonia 155
Poe, Edgar Allen 371
poetry
  American 371
  Anglo-Saxon 358
  modern 372–373
  Neoclassical 363
  Renaissance 360
  Romantic 367
    music and 337
Poincaré, Jules Henri 51
pointillism 320
Poitiers, Battle of 245
Pol Pot 281
Poland 410
  Communist government 280
  conflict with Russia 271
  creation of 269
  nationalist literature 367
  partition of 257, 271
  Russian domination 263
  World War II 273, 274, 275
Polanski, Roman 329
polar bear 115
Polaroid camera and film 105
polecats 115
poliomyelitis 155
polis 230
politics/political power
  ancient Roman 232, 233
  and decolonization 278–279
  and education 162
  and oil 195
  Athenian 231
  ideologies 168–169
  Neolithic development 227
  non-aligned movement 279
  rights 182
  Russian literature and 368–369
Polo, Marco 247
polonium 37
polyandry 158
polychlorinated biphenyls see PCBs
Polycrates 306
polygamy/polygany 158
polygyny: animal 124
polygons/polyhedra 53
polymers/polymerization 199
  properties 47
  raw materials 195
  synthetic 47
polyphony 332
polypropylene 199

polysaccharides 138
  and enantiomers 47
  enzymes and 139
polystyrene 199
polysynthetic languages 348
polytechnics 163
polytheistic religions 285
polythene/polyurethanes 199
Pompey (Gnaeus Pompeius) 232
pond skaters 99
Pontormo, Jacopo 314
Pop art 325
Pope, Alexander 363
popes/papacy
  Reformation and 250
  see also specific popes
Popper, Sir Karl 305
popular songs 344
population
  Black Death and 245, 246
  Chinese empire 234, 235
  decline in Spanish colonies 252
  medieval European 246
  Third World 185
porcelain, discovery of 308
porcupines 119
porpoises 120, 121
Porter, Cole 344
portrait painting
  British artists 317
  Dutch school 316
  Early Baroque 315
  Venetian court 314
Portugal 410
  and the Napoleonic Wars 263
  colonial empire 252–253, 257, 266, 267
    decolonization 279
    Africa, exploration of 244
    in eastern Africa 237
    in India 236
  part of the Spanish Empire 253
  Reconquista 245
  Renaissance literature 360
  voyages of discovery 247, 247, 252
positrons 2, 31
post-and-lintel building 214
Post-Impressionism 320–321
Post-Modernism
  architecture 327
  innovation in novels 377
postal system 208, 229
postwar settlement 269
  Fascism and 169
  rise of Fascism and 272
potassium 37, 138
  chlorides and oxides 36, 38
potatoes 132, 238
potential energy 18
potholes 75
pottery see ceramics
pottos 122
'pouched mammals' see marsupials
Poulenc, Francis 338
poultry 133
Pound, Ezra 373
Poussin, Nicolas 315–317
power
  car engine 220
  electric 28
  medieval supply 246
  air pollution 186
  filtration systems 188
  nuclear 188–189
  tidal 191
pragmatics 355
Prague University 248
prairie 129
prairie dogs 118
praseodymium 37
Praxiteles 326
Pre-Raphaelite Brotherhood 319
precedent (law) 164
precipitation 79
  and climate classification 80
  and desert classifications 72
  and ecosystem types 81, 128–129
  effect of landscape on 81
  erosion by 69
precipitation, chemical 40
precipitator, electrostatic 188
predators/predation 119, 125
preening 106
pregnancy
  customs during 159
  ultrasound scanning 210

Preminger, Otto 329
presbyopia 144
presidential government 166
Presley, Elvis 345
pressure 17
  atmospheric 78–79
    and desert formation 72
    and rock formation 66, 67
pressure gradient 78
pressurized-water reactors 189
Prévost, Antoine-François (l'Abbé) 365
price system 172–173
prices and incomes policies 175
Priestley, Joseph 49, 199
priests 238, 297
primary education 162–163
primary productivity 127
primates 122–123
Prime Minister 166–167
  first British 255
'primeval broth' 82
principal quantum number 36
printing 202–203, 202
  development of the novel and 369
  effect on early medicine 156
  influence on English language 353
  medieval introduction of 248, 249
  presses 202, 203
printmaking
  Renaissance 313
  wood-block 308, 309, 322, 324
prisms 24, 53
  use in photography 204
prisoners of war 182
prisons 165
private enterprise 170, 171
privatization 171
probation (law) 165
problem solving 213
proboscis monkey 123
procyonids 115
producers/production/products 172
  and trade 177
  chemical 40
  command economies and 170
  intermediate 177
  mass production 219
  microeconomic policies 172
  primary and secondary 127
  raw material chain 177
  17th/18th-century European 257
  Third World 184
  see also commodities; companies
progesterone 134
programme music 336–337
projector, film 205
prokaryote cell 82, 82
Prokofiev, Sergey 339
prolactin 143
promethium 37
pronghorns 116–117, 129
propaganda 271, 272
propagation of waves 20
propane 195
propellers
  aircraft 223
  screw 217
proportional representation 167
proportionality, constant of 17
propulsion
  aircraft 223
  car transmission 220
protactinium 37
Protagoras of Abdera 162, 304
protectionism 177
proteins 138
  and enantiomers 47
  components 82
  enzymes and 139
  in voluntary muscle 137
  manufacture of 201
  sources of 88
  synthesis of 86
Protestantism 250–251, 299
  in Britain 254, 255
  in France 256, 262
protists 82, 83, 90
protons 2, 27, 30
  donators and acceptors 40
  number in atomic nucleus 36
protoplasm, properties of 130
protostars 4, 5
protozoans 82
  diseases from 154
  Radularia 83

Proudhon, Pierre-Joseph 169
Proust, Marcel **376**
Proxima Centauri 4
Prussia 157
   and German unification 265
   invasion of France 263
psychoanalysis **151**
   influence on poetry 372–373
psychosis 150
psychotherapy 151
pterosaur *104*
PTFE (polytetrafluoroethylene) 199
Ptolemy (Claudius Ptolemaeus) **10**,**48**, 229
puberty **135**
puberty rites 159
public health, improvements in 157
Puccini, Giacomo **343**
Puerto Rico, United States control of 261,
   267
Pugin, Augustus Welby Northmore **326**
pulmonary artery 141
pulmonary circulation 140
pulses **132**
pumps/pumping
   human *see* heart
   oil wells 194
   sulphur mining method 197
Punic Wars 232
punishment **165**
Punjab war 266
pupil (eye) 144
Purcell, Henry **333**, **342**
Pure Land Buddhism 291, 292
pure mathematics 50
pure writing 376
Puritans (Massachusetts Bay colony) 260
Pushkin, Alexander **367**, 368
PVC (polyvinyl chloride) 199
Pygmies 237
pygmy chimpanzee 123
pygmy white-toothed shrew 113
pyramids (mathematical) **53**
pyramids
   Egyptian 229
   pre-Columbian 239
   stepped 326
pyridoxine **139**
pyroclasts 65
Pyrrho of Elis **304**
Pythagoras **48**, **50**
   theorem 52, 55

Q
Qatar **410–411**
Qin dynasty 234
   art 308
Qing dynasty 235
   ceramics 309
quadrant (instrument) 11
quadrilaterals **53**
quagga 116
quanta/quantum mechanics **32–33**
quantum theory 15, **32–33**
   and light 24
Quarayaq Glacier 71
quarks 31
quartz 39
quartzite 67
quasars 4
quillworts 90
Quintilian 162
quotas 177
   Third World and 184
Qur'an **300**, *301*
   law based on 164
   teaching of 163
   use in art 308

R
rabbits **119**
Rabelais, François **358**
rabies 157
raccoons **115**
Racine, Jean **362**
racism, Fascism and 272
radar **210**
   missile guidance by *225*
   undetectable aircraft *223*
Radcliffe, Ann **367**
radiation 31
   cosmic background **2–3**
   from galaxies 4
   measuring with 210

radiation sickness 152–153
radio **206–207**
   cellular 209
   sources in galaxies 4
radio astronomy *11*
radio waves 27
   carrier waves 207, 209
   ionosphere and 61
   use in communications 206–207
radioactive decay 36
radioactivity **31**
   of elements 36, 44
radiotherapy, use of X-rays 210
radium *37*
radon *37*
Raeburn, Henry **317**
ragged school *162*
ragtime 344
railways **218**
   development of *258*, 259, 266
rain forest *see* forests
rain shadow 72, 81
rainbows *24*
rainfall *see* precipitation
Rakhmaninov, Sergey **339**
Ramayana 288
Rambert, Marie **347**
Rameau, Jean-Philippe **333**, **342**
Ramsay, Allan **317**
Ramses II, pharaoh 228
Random Access Memory (RAM) 211
Raphael **314**
rarefaction 20
Rasputin, Grigori Efimovich 270
rational numbers 54–55
rationalists 303
rats **119**
Rauschenberg, Robert **325**
Ravel, Maurice **338**
Ray, John 83
Ray, Man **324**
Ray, Satyajit **329**
Rayonists 323
Razes (al-Rhazi) **156**
reactants, chemical 40
reaction equilibria 41
reactivity 44, 46
Read-Only Memory (ROM) 211
reading, medieval spread of 249
'ready-mades' 324
real numbers 55
Realism/Realists
   in art **319–320**
   in drama 374, 375
   in literature 364, **368–371**
rebellions *see* revolts/rebellions
receiver
   radio and television 206
   telephone 208
recording (sound) **207**
rectangle 53
rectifier 29
Red Army 271
Red Cross *179*
   and human rights 182
red giant (star) 5
'Red Guards' 277
red panda 115
'Red Scare' 280
Red Sea, salinity 130
red shift 2, 23
red supergiants (stars) *5*
Redon, Odilon **321**
redox process 41
reducing agents 35
reduction, chemical **40–41**
Reed, Carol **329**
referenda 167
reflection **20–21**
   properties of mirrors 25
   total internal **24**
   in fibre optics 25
Reformation, the **250–251**, 299
   impact on Netherlandish and German art
      313
   in England 254, 353
refraction **20–21**, *21*
refractive index 21
refrigeration **193**
'reggae' music 345
Reich, Steve **339**
Reign of Terror 262
relative chronology 226
relativity **32–33**

religions
   ancient **286–287**
   and social divisions 160, 161
   beliefs and practices **284**
   modern primal 284, **285**
   what is it? **284–285**
   see also priests; temples/temple-cities;
      specific religions
Religion, Wars of 251, 253
   Thirty Years War 251
Rembrandt van Rijn **316**, *316*, 323
Renaissance
   architecture **327**
   art **312–314**
   Classical model 356, 362
   culture **248–249**
   economy and society **246–247**
   English language during 353
   humanism during 249
   literature **360–361**
   music **332–333**
'Renaissance man' 249
Reni, Guido **315**
Renoir, Jean **329**
Renoir, Pierre Auguste **320**
reproduction 127
   birds 107
   coelenterates 94
   fishes 101
   flowering plants **92–93**
   fungal 91
   hormones and **143**
   insects **98**
   human **134–135**
   marsupials 109
   plants 88, **89**, 90, 93
   primates 122
   protists 82
   reptiles 103–105
   wild pigs 116
   see also artificial insemination
reptiles **103–105**
   aquatic and flying **104**
   defence 125
   hibernation 125
   synapsids 108
research and development (R & D) 171
resistance, electric **28**
Resnais, Alain **329**
resources, allocation of *see* microeconomics
respiration **140–141**
   autonomic system and 147
   birds 107
   muscles 137
   oxygen and 43
   plants **88–89**
Restoration drama **363**
retina 144
retinol **139**
retrosynthetic analysis 47
revolts/rebellions/revolutions
   against Napoleon 263
   American **260**
   causes 161
   Chinese 235, 276, 280
   colonial African 267
   European 245, **264**
   French **262**
   Indian 266
   Ireland 254
   Palestinian 283
   popular **245**
   religious 251
   Russian **270–271**
   Tibetan 277
   Turkish 269
Revolutionary War **263**
Reynolds, Joshua **317**
rheas 129
rhenium *37*
rheumatoid arthritis **153**
rhinoceroses *108*, **116**
rhizomes 93
Rhodesia, British control of 267
rhodium *37*
rhyolite 66
rhythm
   in poetry 373
   musical 330
'rhythm and blues' 345
riboflavin **139**
ribonucleic acid *see* RNA
ribosomes 86

rice **132**
   ancient Chinese/Japanese farming 234,
      235
Richard I, King ('the Lionheart') 244
Richard II, King 245
Richard III, King 254
Richardson, Samuel **364**, *365*, 368
Richelieu, Cardinal 256
Richter, Charles 64
Richter magnitude 64
rifles, **224**, **225**
Right, the (politics) **169**
right whales 121
rigid pavements 214
Riley, Terry **339**
Rilke, Rainer Maria **372**
Rimbaud, Arthur **372**, *372*
Rimsky-Korsakov, Nikolay **338**
Risorgimento **264–265**
rites of passage **159**
   Jewish **294**
river dolphins 120, 121
rivers **74–75**
   and sedimentary rock 66
   desert 73
   drainage network 75
   meanders *74*, 75
   perennial **74–75**
   pollution of 186–187
   seasonal **74–75**
   see also specific rivers
RNA and enantiomers 47
   in viruses 82
road building **214**
   industrialization and 259
Robbe-Grillet, Alain **377**
Robbins, Jerome **347**
robots/robotics 213
Robespierre, Maximilien 262
rock cycle 66, 67
rock music **345**
rockets/rocketry
   as weapons 193, 225
   engines **192–193**
   launch vehicle sizes *13*
   pioneers of **12**
   Saturn V 12
rocks **66–67**
   continental drift and 62
   crustal 60
   desert weathering 73
   determining magnetic north from 63
   effect on earthquakes 65
   glacial erosion 71
   impermeable 74
   mantle 60
   permeable/porous 74
   and oil reserves 194
Rocky Mountains, formation of 68, 69
Rococo
   architecture **327**
   art 315, **317**
rodents **118–119**
Rodgers, Richard **344**
Rodin, Auguste **320**
Roeg, Nicholas **329**
Roehm, Ernst 273
Rogers, Richard **326**
rognon 71
Rohe, Ludwig Mies van der **326**
Rohmer, Eric **329**
rolling friction 17
Rolling Stones **345**
Rollo 243
Roman Catholic Church **299**
   and divorce 158
   control of education 163
   Counter-Reformation **251**
   death customs 159
   in France 256, 262
   music 330
   the Reformation and 250
   treaty with Fascists 272
Roman Empire **233**
   in Britain 241
   literature 357
   sack of Rome 240
   successors of **240–241**
   see also Rome, ancient
Roman law 164, 165
Roman Republic **232**
Romance language 353
romances, medieval **358–359**
Romanesque style

architecture 310, 326–327
art 310
Romania 411
  Communist government 280
Romano, Giulio 314
Romanticism
  in art 318, 319
  in ballet 346
  in literature 366–367
  in music 334, 336–337, 343
Rome, ancient 232–233
  architecture 326
  art 306, 307, 306, 310
  bridge construction 215
  education 162
  invasion of Celtic Europe 227
  legal system 164
  literature 249, 357, 362
  number system 55
  religions 287
  republican system 166
  road building 214
  spread of Christianity 298
  writing 351
Rome-Berlin Axis 273
Rommel, General Erwin 274
Romulus 232
Romulus Augustulus 233
rondo 335
Ronsard, Pierre de 360
Röntgen, Wilhelm Konrad 49, 157, 210
room-and-pillar mining 196
Roosevelt, President 274, 280
roots
  numbers 55
  plant 92
rope manufacture 132
rorquals 121
Rosa, Salvator 317
Ross Ice Shelf 70
Rossellini, Roberto 329
Rossetti, Dante Gabriel 319, 321
Rossini, Gioacchino 343, 363
rotary press 203
rotation 16
Rothko, Mark 325
rotors, helicopter 223
Rouault, George 321, 325
Rousseau, Jean-Jacques 166, 304, 366
Rousseau, Théodore 320
route-finding programs 213
rubber 199
rubbish
  energy from 190
rubella 155
Rubens, Peter Paul 306, 315
rubidium 37
rubies, mining 197
rudder
  aircraft 222
  ship 217
Ruggles, Carl 339
Ruisdael, Jacob van 316
ruminants/rumination 116
Rushdie, Salman 377
Russell, Bertrand 50, 51, 57, 303, 305
Russell, Henry Norris 5
Russell, Ken 329
Russell's paradox 56
Russia 180, 411–412
  Alaska purchased from 261
  and Balkans nationalism 265
  and the Napoleonic Wars 263
  colonial empire 266
  divorce in 158
  expansion 257
  industrialization 259
  literature 367, 368–369
  modern music 339
  oil industry 195
  post-revolutionary see Union of Soviet
    Socialist Republics
  Viking colonization 243
  World War I 268, 269, 270, 271
Russian Revolutions 270–271
Russo-Japanese War 235, 267, 270
rusting, oxygen and 42-43
ruthenium 37
Rutherford, Ernest 30, 49
Ruwenzori Mountains glaciers 70
Rwanda 412
rye 132
Ryle, Gilbert 305

S
Sachs, Hans 360
sacraments 296–297
sacro-iliac joint 137
saddle joint 136, 137
Sadowa, battle of 265
Safavid dynasty, arts 308
sagas 358
Sahara Desert 72
sail, the age of 217
sailfish 101
Saint Christopher and Nevis 412
Saint Lucia 412
Saint Vincent and the Grenadines 412
Saint-Simon, Claude 168
Saladin 242, 244
salamanders 102
Salamis, battle of 231
Salian dynasty 240
salicylic acid 35
salinity 130
  lakes 75
  sea water 76
Sallé, Marie 346
salmon migration 125
Salmonella 82
Salon des Refusés 320
salts 35
  common see sodium chloride
  excretion of 143
SALT agreement 281
Salyut 1 12
SAM missiles 225
samarium 37
samsara 288, 290
samurai 235
San (Bushmen), art 309
San Marino 412–413
sand bar 77
sand dunes 72, 73
sandblasting 73
sandstone 66, 67
Sao Tomé e Príncipe 413
sap 88
sapphires 197, 207
Sappho 356
saprotrophs 91
Sardinia, kingdom of 264
Sargon of Akkad 228
Sarto, Andrea del 314
Sartre, Jean-Paul 376
Sassanid Empire see Persian Empire
Sassoon, Siegfried 373
satellites (of the planets) 9
satellites (artificial) 12, 13
  surveying with 197, 210
  telecommunications 207, 209
Satie, Erik 338
satin 200
satraps 231
Satre, Jean-Paul 305
Saturn (planet) 7, 9
Saudi Arabia 413
Saul, King 228
sauropods 104
Saussure, Ferdinand de 354, 355
savannah 128
Savery, Thomas 192, 258
savings and loan societies 170
saxophone 341
scalar quantity 14
scales, musical 330
  Baroque music 333
Scandinavia
  ancient religions 287
  formation of mountains 68, 69
  Ice Age 70
  medieval sagas 358
  modern music 339
scandium 37
scanning electron microscope 210
Scarlatti, Alessandro 333, 342
Scarlatti, Domenico 333
scarlet fever 155
scarring, ritual 159
scavenger organisms 130
scent glands 115
scents 35
Schelling, F.W.J. von 366
Schiele, Egon 322
Schiller, Friedrich 366
schistosomiasis 155
schizophrenia 150, 151
Schleicher, August 348

Schleiffen Plan 268
Schlesinger, John 329
Schleswig-Holstein 265
Schmidt-Rotluff, Karl 322
Schoenberg, Arnold 331, 338
Schongauer, Martin 313
schools
  development of 246
  direct funding 167
  medieval and Renaissance 248
  types of 163, 164
schooner, five-masted 217
Schopenhauer, Arthur 305
Schrödinger, Erwin 30, 32
Schubert, Franz 334, 335, 336
Schumann, Robert 336
Schütz, Heinrich 333
Schwitters, Kurt 324
science/sciences 248
  history of 48–49, 256
'Scientific Revolution' 48
sclera 144
scorpions 97, 97
Scotland 254–255, 245
  Calvinism in 251
  education in 163
  Viking settlement 243
Scott, Sir George Gilbert 326
Scott, Sir Walter 367
scroll painting 309
sculpture
  African 309, 322
  ancient Greek 306, 307
  ancient Roman 307
  Constructivist 323
  Gothic 310, 311
  Indian 308
  living 325
  Renaissance 312–314
  wind 69
scurvy 138
sea 70–71, 76, 77
  effect of global warming 187
  mammals in 120–121
  pollution of 186–187
sea, lunar 8
sea anemones 94
sea cows 120
sea cucumbers 94
sea lilies 94
sea otters 115
sea slug 94
sea stars 94
sea urchins 94
sea-mounts 65, 69, 76, 77
seals 120, 121
'Sea Peoples' 228, 229
Search for Extra-Terrestrial Intelligence
  (SETI) 11
seasons 80, 81
seaweeds 90
sebaceous glands 145
Secession (art) 321
second 3
secret societies, Italian 264
secularism 285
Security Council (UN) 178, 179
sediment
  deposition by rivers 74, 75
  effect on earthquakes 65
sedimentary rock 66
  and oil reserves 194
seeds 88, 91
seismic waves 60
  energy transfer by 20
  from earthquakes 64
  see also surveys/surveying
selenium 37
Seleucid empire 231
'self-feeders' 127
self-government 278
Selim I, Sultan 242
Seljuk Turks 241, 242
semantics 355
semen 134
semi-submersible ships 216
semicircular canals 145
semiconductors 29
seminiferous tubules 134
Semitic-Hamitic languages/script 348,
  350–351
Senate 232
Seneca 357

Seneca Falls Convention 183
Senefelder, Aloys 203
Senegal 413
Sennet, Mark 328
senses/sense organs (human) 144–145, 147
  birds 107
  fishes 101
  insect 99
  moles 113
  primates 122
sensibility, cult of (literary) 364–365
separation of powers 166
separatism 161
Sephardic Jews 295
Septimus Severus 233
seracs 71
Serbia 179
  World War I 268
  nationalism in 265
  see also Yugoslavia
serfs/serfdom 246
  ancient Greek 230
  ancient Rome 233
  Black Death and 245
  Russian 270
serows 117
serpent stars 94
sets 56–57
  counting 54
Seurat, Georges 320
Seven Years War 257, 260
'Seven Weeks' War' 265
sewage/sanitation
  and eutrophication 131
  as energy source 190
  improvements in 157
  water pollution 130, 186
Sex Pistols 345
sex
  chromosomes 87
  development of 83
sexual behaviour 159
sexual development 151
sexual intercourse 134
  transmission of infections 154
Seychelles 413
Seymour, Jane 254
shaikhs 300
Shakespeare, William 360, 361, 367
  language 353
shamans 292–293
Shang dynasty 234
  art 308
share capital 171
shareholders 170
Sharia 301
Shaw, George Bernard 375
Shawn, Ted 347
sheep 117, 133
Shelley, Mary Wollstonecraft 367
Shelley, Percy Bysshe 367
Shepard, Sam 375
Sheridan, Richard 363
Sherman, General William T. 261
Shi Huangdi 234
shield volcano 65
Shiite Muslims 242, 283, 301
shingles (herpes zoster) 155
Shinto 285, 292, 293
ships/shipping 216–217
  development of 192, 217, 246, 247
  Industrial Revolution and 258
  oil tankers 195
  during World War I 269
  during World War II 274
Shnittke, Alfred 339
shogun 235
Sholokhov, Mikhail 377
Shona revolt 267
shortsightedness see myopia
Shostakovich, Dmitri 339
shrews 113
SI units of time 3
siamang 123
Sibelius, Jean 339
Sica, Vittorio de 329
Sicily
  Allied invasion of 275
  Byzantine reconquest 241
  volcano 65
Sickert, Walter 320
sickle-cell disease 152
sidereal time 3

Sidney, Sir Philip **360**
Sierra Leone **413**
sifakas 122, *122*
sight
  animal communication by 124
  human **144**
  insects 99
  primates/lower primates 122
Signac, Paul **320**, 322
Sihanouk, Prince 281
Sikhism 285
Sikhs *288*, **289**
silent films **328**
Silesia 257
silicon 29, *37*
  integrated circuits 211
  solar cells 190
silk 200
  spiders 97
silver *37*
  abundance and uses 197
  mining 196
  nitrate precipitation reaction 40
  Spanish colonies **252–253**
Silver Jubilee (train) 218
silverfish 98
Simpson, Sir James Young **157**
Sind war 266
sine 52
sinfonia 333
Singapore **414**
  British control 267
  Japanese invasion of 274
Singh, Gobind 289
singing/song
  animals 107, 121
  see also music; opera
single-lens reflex camera **204**, 205
single-parent families 159
singspiel 342, 344
Sino-Japanese War 235
sirenians 120
Sirius (ship) 217
Sirius (star) apparent magnitude 5
Sisley, Alfred **320**
Six-Day War 282
skeletal muscle 137
skeleton 134, **136–137**
  armadillos 111
  birds 106
  growth hormone and 143
  sloths 111
Skelton, John **359**
skin **145**
  amphibians 102
  defence against microorganism 142
  muscles 137
  reptiles 103
'skin-breathing' 102
Skryabin, Alexander **339**
skunks 115
Skylab space station 13
skyscrapers 215
slag 198
slate 67
slats, aircraft 222
slaves/slavery
  American 260, 261
  ancient Greek 230, 231
  ancient Rome 232
  Middle Ages **246**
  Portuguese Empire 253
  trade 237, 257
Slavs 241
Slipher, Vesto 2
sloops 217
slope/shaft mining *196*
sloths **111**
Slovakia **414**
Slovenia **414**
slums 259
Sluter, Claus **311**
Sluys, battle of 245
smell **145**
  animal communication by 124
  birds 107
  chirality and sense of 47
smelting 44, **198**, 258
Smetana, Bedrich **337**
Smith, Adam 169, **173**
Smith, Bessie **344**
smog 43, 186
smooth muscle 137
snakes 103, **105**, 125

Snell, Willebrord 21
Snell's Law 21, 22
Snider, Anton 62
snow/snowline 70, 71
Soane, Sir John **326**
social capital 171
social contract **166**
social democracy **168**
Social Democratic Party 168
  Russian 270
Social Revolutionaries 270
social status 161
social stratification and divisions **160–161**
  ancient Greek 230
  ancient Roman 232
  animals **124–125**
  'feudal system' 246
  Hindu system 288
  novels and 369, 370
  Pre-revolutionary France 262
  slaves, serfs and freemen **246**
Socialism **168**
  failure of planned economies 170
  Fascism and 272
  in drama 375
  socialist law 164
'Socialist Realism' 369
society
  development of
    Bronze Age 227
    in China 234
    Indian and Southeast Asian 236
    the Americas 238–239
  effect of industrialization 259
  in literature 368–369, 370–371
  medieval and Renaissance **246–247**
  primal 284, 285
  see also social stratification
Socrates 302, **304**
soda (sodium carbonate) 201
sodium *37*, 38, 138
  chloride 34–35
  and oxides 36
    and salinity 130
    mining methods 197
    precipitation reaction 40
    production of 40
  fluoride 38
software (computer) 211, **212–213**
soil
  acid rain pollution 186
  and the biosphere 126
  nutrients in 127
  protozoans in 82
Soka Gakkai 293
solar cells/collectors 29, 190
solar day 3
solar eclipse 10
Solar energy 6, **190**
  and ozone 187
  plant use of 88–89
solar flares/prominences 6–7
solar mass 4
solar nebula 7
solar radiation **27**
  and the biosphere 126–127
  ozone and 43
Solar System 6, **7**
  background radiation 2–3
solenodons **113**
solids **16–17**, **53**
Solomon, King 228
Solomon Islands **414**
Solon 230
solstices 80
solution, chemical 35
Solzhenitsyn, Alexander **377**
Somalia **414**
  control by Italy and Britain 267
  Italian invasion of 274
Somme, battle of the 269
sonar **210**
sonata 333, **335**, 336
sonata-rondo 335
Sondheim, Stephen **344**
Song dynasty 235
  ceramics 308–309
sonic booms **23**
sonnet 360
Sophocles **356**
'soul music' 345

sound
  in language **354**
  measuring with 210
  in motion pictures 328
  recording 207
  refraction of **22**
  transmitting 206, 207
  velocity of **22**
sound waves 20–21, **22**
  ear and 144
  energy transfer by 20
  recording 207
  sonic booms 23
South Africa 179, **414–415**
  apartheid 161, 182
  British control 267
  diamond mining 197
  ecosystems 129
  gold mines 196
  independence 279
South America
  dances from 347
  deserts 72
  ecosystems 128, 129
  mammalian evolution 108, 109, 116, 117
  mountain formation 68
  Spanish Empire **252–253**
south pole 26
South West Africa, German control of 267
Southeast Asia
  development *236*, 278
  rubber production 199
  tropical rain forests *186*
Southern Rhodesia 179
Southey, Robert 367
Soviets 270
space, relativity theories and 33
space exploration **12–13**
  special relativity theory and 33
space-time 33
spaceplane 13
Spain **415**
  Abbasids in 242
  and the Thirty Years War 251
  colonial empire **252–253**, 257, *266*
    decolonization 279
    loss of 260, 267
    Louis XIV and 256
  government 169
  Inquisition 251
  literature
    medieval 358
      picaresque novels 364
      Renaissance 360–361
  Reconquista 241, 242, **244**, 252
  separatism in 161
  Visigoths 240
  voyages of discovery 252
  war against Napoleon 263
  War of Succession 253, 256
Spanish Armada 253, 254, *255*
Spanish Sahara, independence of 279
Sparta/Spartans 230–231, *230*
'Spartacist' revolutionaries 272
spears/spear heads 226
special relativity 32, **33**
spectrum 24
  'big bang' 2
  Doppler effect and 23
  electromagnetic 24, **27**
  see also rainbows
speech 147
  computer recognition 213
  synthetic 355
speed 14
  cars 219
speleotherms 75
spelling, standards of 353
Spencer, Edmund **360**
Spencer, Herbert **305**
Spender, Stephen **373**
sperm **134**
sperm whales 120, 121
spermatogenesis 135
spermatophytes 91
spermiceti wax 121
sphere **53**
spherical geometry 52
spice trade 253, 257
spicules 6
spiders **97**, *97*
Spielberg, Steven **329**
spinning 200, 258

Spinoza, Benedict de **304**
spiracles 98
spiral galaxies 4
spleen 142
'split mind' 150
spoilers, aircraft 222
sponges 83, **94**
spore-bearing plants **90–91**
sporophytes 89, 90–91
spreading, wave 20
spreadsheet 212–213
spring tides 76
springs 74
  elasticity and plastic flow *16*, 17
springtails 98
Sputnik 12
spy satellites 13
square *53*, 53
squid, giant *95*
squirrels **118–119**
Sri Lanka **415**
  Hindu expansionism and 236
SS (*Schutzstaffel*) 273
St Andrews University 248
St Augustine 241
St Bartholomew's Day Massacre 251
St Denis, Ruth 347
stability, aircraft **222**
Stahl, Georg **49**
stainless steel 198
  corrosive properties 45
stalactites/stalagmites 75
Stalin, Josef 274, 271, 280
Stalingrad, siege of 275
'Stamboul' 241
Stamford Bridge, battle of 243
Stamitz, Johann and Karl **334**
stamp duty 260
standing stones 227
Stanton, Elizabeth Cady 183
star-nosed mole 113
starch 138
  plant manufacture of 88
starfish **94**
stars 2, **4–5**
  Doppler effect and 23
  early chart 11
  power source 31
'star time' *see* sidereal time
starvation 185
'Star Wars' 13, 181
state, economic systems and the 170, 171
static electric charges **26**
statics **16**
  friction 17
statute law 164
Stäel, Nicolas de **325**
'state-serfs' 230
stealth technology 47
steam engines **192**, *193*
  and the Industrial Revolution 258
  heat exchange 18
  locomotives 218
  turbines 217
steam ships 192, **217**
steel **198**
  steel production 34, **198**
  Industrial Revolution and **258–259**
steelworks *45*
Steen, Jan **316**
steering, car *221*
Steinbeck, John **377**
Stendhal **368**
Stephenson, George 218, 259
steppes 129
stereo **207**
stereoscopic vision 144
stereotyping 203
sterilization 135
Sternberg, Josef von **329**
Sterne, Laurence **365**
steroid hormones 143
stethoscope, invention of 157
Stevens, Wallace **373**
still life painting, Dutch school **316**
stinks **35**
stoat 115
stock exchange *170*
stock market 170
Stockhausen, Karlheinz 343
stocks and shares 170, 171
Stockton & Darlington Railway 218, 259
stoichiometry **41**

Stolypin, Petr Arkadievich 270
stomach 139, *139*
stomata 88
Stone Age 226
  in Australasia and Oceania **237**
Stoppard, Tom **375**
storms
  on the planets 9
  tropical 79
'stormtroops' 269
strain 17
Strassburg, Gottfried von **358**
strastosphere 61
Strategic Arms Limitation Talks (SALT) 181
stratocumulus clouds 79, *79*
stratosphere 187
  ozone in 43
  refraction of sound 22
Strauss, Johann **344**
Strauss, Richard **337**, 340, **343**
Stravinsky, Igor **338**, 340
stream of consciousness 375, 376
streams 69, 74
stress 17
  and hormone release 143
strike-slip fault 67, *67*
Strindberg, August **374**
string quartet 335, 336, 339
strip mining *196*
striped muscle 137
stroboscopy 205
Stromboli (volcano), Italy 65
strontium 37
Strowger switch **208**
'structured query language' 212
Stuart kings **254–255**
Stuart Mill, John 183
Sturm und Drang 366
subatomic particles **30–31**
  measurement of mass 33
  special relativity and 32
subduction zones 62, 63
  earthquakes along 64
submachine guns 225
submarines 217
  U-boats 269, 274
subscription concerts 334
subsets **56**
subtraction 54
sucrose 138
Sudan **415–416**
  British control of 267
Sudetenland 273
Suez Canal 215, 282
Suez Crisis 279, 282
suffragettes *see* women's movement
Sufism 300
sugars, plant manufacture of 88
suite (music) **333**
Suleiman the Magnificent 242
Sullivan, Arthur **344**
Sullivan, Louis **326**
sulphates, plant uptake and transport of **88**, *89*
sulphides 44
sulphonamides 157
sulphur 37
  chemical bonding 34, *38*, 39
  crystals *38*
  dioxide 43
    pollution from 186, 188
  in plants and animals 127
  in rubber manufacture 199
  mining method 197
  oxides of 43
  properties 34
  trioxide 43
sulphuric acid 40, 43, 201
Sultanate of Delhi 236
Sumatra (kingdom of Shrivijaya) 236
Sumerian Empire 228
  writing 350
Summerhill school 162
Sun, the 4, **6–7**
  and rock cycle 66
  and tides 76
  effect of heat on atmosphere 78
  power source 31, 126, 191
Sun Zhong Shan (Sun Yat-sen) 276
sunlight
  colours in 24
  energy from *see* solar energy
  penetration through water 130–131
Sunni Muslims 283, 301

'sun-and-planet' gear 192
sunspots 6
supercomputers 212
superconductivity 28
supernova 5
superphosphates 201
superposition principle 21
superstructure/substructure 214
Suppiluliumas I, King 228
supply and demand 172, 173
  and inflation 175
  effect on unemployment 174
Suprematists **323**
Supreme Court Anti-Trust Division 173
surgery/surgeons, development of 156, 157
Suriname **416**
Surrealism **324**
Surtsey (volcano) 69
surveillance, by satellite 13
surveys/surveying
  infrared imaging for 210
  for oil and gas 194
  seismic 22, 194, 197
    measuring the Earth 60, 61
'survival of the fittest' 85
suspension, car *221*
suspension bridge 215
Sutherland, Graham **325**
Swaziland **416**
sweat glands (and pores) 145
Sweden **416**
  acid rain pollution 186
  and the Thirty Years War 251
  Baltic empire 257
  early expansion/colonization 243
  energy sources 189, 190
  law system 165
sweet potatoes **132**
Swift, Jonathan **364**
swim bladder 100–101
'swing' music 345
Switzerland **416**
  and the United Nations 178
  Calvinism in 251
  political participation 167
syllabic writing **350**
symbiosis 91
  algae 90
  animals **125**
Symbolism/Symbolists **321**
  influence on music 338
  literature 369, 372
  modern drama 375
symphonic poem 337
symphonies
  classical **334–335**
  earliest forerunner of 333
  Romantic 336
symphony orchestra **340–341**, 334
synagogues 295
synapse 146
syncopation 333
Synge, J.M. **375**
synovial fluid 136
syntax 348
synthesizers, music 23
Synthetic Cubism 323
syphilis **155**
Syria **416–417**
  ancient 228, 241, 242
  Crusades/Crusader states 242, 244
  medieval monasticism 248
  wars with Israel **282–283**
Syrian Church 299
syrinx 107
systemic circulation 140

T

3-D vision 144
T-cells 142
Tacitus **357**
tahrs 117
taiga **129**
tailplane, aircraft 222
Taiping movement 235
Taiwan
  and the UN 178
  Japanese annexation 267
  Japanese control 235
  Nationalist government established 277
  see also China, Republic of
Tajikistan 180, **417**

takins 117
Tallis, Thomas **332**
Talmud 294
tamarins 122–123
Tamerlane (Timor) 242
Tang dynasty 235
  art 308
Tanganyika, German control of 267
tangent 52
tankers, oil 195
tanks/tank warfare **225**
  first deployment 269
  World War II 274
tantalum 37
Tantric Buddhism 291
Tanzania **417**
tape recorders 207
tapestries 311, 314
tapeworms 95, **155**
tapirs 116, *117*
tariffs 177, 184
Tarkovsky, Andrei **329**
tarmacadam 214
tarnishing, metal 45
tarpan 116
tarsiers 122
Tasmanian devil 110
Tasmanian wolf (thylacine) 110
Tasso, Torquato **360**
taste 145
  animal communication by 124
  snakes and lizards 103
taste buds 145
taxation 174, 175
  ancient Rome 233
  Japanese system 235
  of the American colonies 260
  revolts against 254
  revolutionary France 262
  17th-century England 255
  tariffs 177
taxonomy 83
Tchaikovsky, Pyotr Ilyich **337**
teachers 162
tear gas 35
technetium 37, 44
technology **188–224**
  and education 163
  research and development 171
  space 12–13
teeth
  carnivores 114
  elephant 117
  lagomorphs 119
  mammals 109
  rodents 118, *118*
  whales 120, 121
  wild pigs 116
Teflon 199
telecommunications **208–209**
  fibre optics and 25
telegraph, electric 259
telegraphone 207
telegraphy **208**
Telemann, Georg Philipp **333**
teleosts 100
telephones **208–209**
telescopes **25**
  in space 11
  optical **11**
television **206–207**
  effect on cinema 329
  satellite broadcasting 209
  viewdata 209
telex systems 209
Telstar satellite 209
temperate forests *see* forests
temperature **18**
  and rate of chemical reactions 41
  as measure of energy 18
  'big bang' 2, 3, *3*
  deserts 72
  for aluminium oxide reduction 44
  for nuclear fusion 189
  in metamorphism 67
  measuring 18
  nuclear reactor 188
  of ideal gas 19
  stars 5
  Sun 6
  see also heat; superconductivity
temperature, atmospheric **78–79**, 80, 81

  and atmospheric layers 61
  end of the Ice Age and 227
  increases from global warming 187
temperature, body
  amphibians **102**
  birds 107
  fishes 101
  mammals 108, 141, 145, 147
  reptiles 103
temperature, water
  as pollutant 186
  of aquatic ecosystems 130, 131
  of terrestrial ecosystems 128–129
tempered steel 198
Temple Mound culture 238
temples/temple-cities
  ancient Greek *287*, 326
  ancient Roman 326
  early American 238–239
  Hindu 288
  Indian 308
  Sikh 289
Tennyson, Alfred, Lord 367
tenrecs 113
Teotihuacán 239
tephra 65
terbium 37
Terborch, Gerard **316**
Terbrugghen, Hendrick **316**
Terence **357**, 363
terminal moraines 69
termites 99
  social organization 125, *125*
territory, animals **124–125**
testes **143**
testosterone 135
Tet Offensive 281
tetanus **155**
textiles **200**
  Industrial Revolution and **258**, *259*
  non-Western 308, 309
  raw materials 132
TGV trains 218
Thackeray, William Makepeace **370**
Thailand **417**
thalamus 146
thalassaemia 152
Thales of Miletus **10**, **48**, **304**
thallium 37
Thames Barrier, London *215*
Tharp, Twyla **347**
Theatre of the Absurd **374–375**, 376
theatres, purpose-built 361
theme and variations **335**
Themistocles 231
Theocritus **357**
Theodore of Samos 306
Theodosius I 233
theology 284
theorems 52
Theraveda Buddhism **290–291**
thermal energy 18
thermionic emission 29
thermodynamics 18, **19**
thermonuclear bomb 181
thermoplastic 199
thermosets 199
thermosphere 61
theropods 104
thiamin **139**
thiols 47
Third World **184–185**
  Cuban influence 281
  decolonization 278–279
  energy sources 190
  United Nations and 179
'Thirty tyrants' 231
Thirty Years War **251**, 253
Thirty-Nine Articles 254
Thomarists 299
Thomas, Dylan **373**
Thomas, R.S. **373**
Thompson, Benjamin (Count Rumford) **49**
Thompson, J.J. 30
Thomson, William, Lord Kelvin 18, **49**
thoracic cavity 140
Thoreau, Henry David **371**
thorium 36, *37*
thought, brain centre for 147
threadworms **155**
threat display 125
'Three Age System' **226**
throat sac 123
thrush **155**

thrust 222
Thucydides **356**
thulium *37*
thunder 79
thymus gland 142
thyroid gland **143**
thyroid hormone (TH) 143, 153
thyrotoxicosis 153
thyroxine 143
Tiberius Caesar 232, 233
Tibet, Chinese rule of 235, 277
ticks **97**
tidal waves *see* tsunami
tides **76–77**
  energy from 191, *191*
Tiepolo, Giambattista **317**
Tiglathpileser III, King 229
Tigris River 228, 327
timber *see* wood/timber
timbre 23
time
  relative 33, *33*
  systems **3**
timpani 341
tin *37*
  abundance and uses 197
  semiconductor properties 45
Tintoretto, Jacopo **314**
Tippett, Michael **339**, 343
Titan (satellite) 9
titanium *37*
  corrosive properties 45
  extraction of 44
Titian **314**
toads **102**
toadstools 91
tobacco 132
  plantations 260
Toda Josei 293
toes, ungulate 116
Togo **417**
Togoland, German control of 267
Tojo, General Hideki 273
Tokugawa Ieyasu 235
Tokugawa shogunate 235
Toller, Ernst **374**
Tolstoy, Leo **369**
Toltecs *238*, **239**
toluene 201
Tombaugh, Clyde 9
Tonga **417–418**
tongue 145
tools, prehistoric 226, 227
Torah 294
torque 16
tort, law of 165
tortoises 103
total internal reflection **24**, 25
totalitarianism **272–273**
totals **59**
touch **145**
  animal communication by 124
Toulouse-Lautrec, Henri **320**
'towers of silence' 159, 289
towns, development of 246–247
Toyatomi Hideyoshi 235
trachea 140, *140*
tracheophytes 90
trade **176–177**
  ancient Greek 230
  Black Africa 237
  Britain's dominance 258
  Continental System 263
  European overseas 257
    early trade with India 236
    Portuguese Empire 253
    17th-century French 256
    Spanish colonies **252–253**
  Iron Age 227
  medieval 247, *246*
  microeconomics of 172–173
  opening up of China 235
  opening up of Japan 235
  opium 267
  the law and 165
  Third World **184–185**
trade 'triangle' 257
trade associations, medieval 247
trade unions 171, 259
trade winds 77
tragi-comedy 361
Trajan 233
tranquillizers 151
Transcendental Meditation 285

Transcendentalism 371
transform faults 63, *63*, 64
transformation geometry 52
transformer *29*
transistor 29
Transjordan, British mandate of 282
translocation 88
transmigration 288
transmission, car **220**, *221*
transmitter, radio 206
transpiration 88
transplant surgery 157
transport
  effect on industrialization *258*, 259
  road development and 214
  railway 218
  shipping 216, *216*
  steam power for 192
  see also aircraft, cars
transubstantiation 297
transverse oscillation 20
trapezium 53
travelling wave 20
Treasury bills 171
Treaties
  Brétigny 245
  Lausanne 269
  Paris 179
  Rapallo 271
  Rome 179
  Sèvres 269
  St Germain 269
  Tordesillas 252
  Trianon 269
  Versailles 269, 273
tree ferns 90
trees, cross-section of **88**
trematodes 95
trench warfare **268–269**
Trevithick, Richard 192
triangles 53, *52*
triangulation **52**
tribunes 232
tributaries 75
triglicerides 138, 139
trigonometry **52–53**
Trinidad and Tobago **418**
trio (music) **335**
triode 29
tritium 189
Triton (satellite) 9
Trollope, Anthony **370**
trombones 341
tropical year 3
tropics, pressure systems in 79
troposphere 61
Trotsky, Leon 271
troubadours 332, 359
Troyes, Chrétien de **358**
Truffaut, François **329**
Truman, President Harry 275, 280
Truman Doctrine 280
trumpet 341
trunk (elephant) 117
truss (girder) bridge 215
Trusteeship Council (UN) 178
truth-functions 57
Tsiolkovsky, Konstantin 12
tsunami 64
tuatara 103
tuba 341
tuberculosis **155**, 157
tubers 93
Tudor dynasty **254**
Tughluq, Muhammed bin 236
tundra **129**
tungsten *37*, 197
Tunisia **418**
turbellarians 95
turbines 188, 191, *191*, 192
Turbinia (yacht) 192
turbofan engines 193, 223
turbojet engines 193, 223
turboprop engines 193, 223
turbulence **17**
Turgenev, Ivan **368**
Turing, Alan 213
Turkestan, Chinese rule of 235
Turkey **418**
  ancient 227, 228
  language 348
  nationalist revolt 269
  postwar settlement 269
Turkmenistan 180, **418**

Turner, Joseph Mallord William **318**, *319*
turtles 103
tusks
  elephants 117
  narwhals 121
  wild pigs 116
Tuvalu **418–419**
Twain, Mark **371**
Twelvers 300, 301
twill weaves 200
twin-lens reflex camera 205
twins, similarities in intelligence in 149
two-stroke engines 193
tympanic membrane 144, *145*
  vibration rate 23
tympanum, architectural 310
typesetting **202**
typhoid/typhus **155**
typhoons 79
typological linguistics 348
tyrants 230, 231
tyres, manufacture of 199

U

U Thant 178
U-boats 269, 274
Uccello, Paolo **312**
Uganda **419**
  British control 267
UHF waves 206
Ukiyo-e prints 309, *308*
Ukraine 180, **419**
Ulanova, Galina **347**
ultrasonics/ultrasound 23
  scanning 22, 157, **210**
ultraviolet radiation, ozone and 43, 61, 126–127, 130, 187
ultraviolet waves **27**
Umayyad dynasty 242
uncertainty principle **32**
underground mining 196, *196*
unemployment 171, *175*
  factors affecting 174
  Keynesian doctrine on 175
UNESCO 178
ungulates **116–117**
'Uniate' Churches 299
UNICEF 178
Unification Church (Moonies) 285
Union of Soviet Socialist Republics
  Chernobyl 189
  cinema 328
  and Cuban Crisis 281
  education in 163
  establishment of 271
  government 167
  history
    the Cold War 280–281
    Russian Revolution 270–271
    totalitarianism in 272–273
    and Vietnam 277
    World War I 268–269
    World War II 274–275
  human rights in 182
  literature 377
  modern music **339**
  nuclear weapons 181
  revolution 161
  space programme 12–13
  UN membership 178, 179
  see also Commonwealth of Independent States
unit trusts 170
unitary government 167
United Arab Emirates **419**
United Kingdom **419–420**
  architectural styles 327
  history
    Anglo-Saxon kingdoms **241**
    colonial empire 236, 237, 257, 260–261, 266–267, 282
    decolonization 278, **279**
    Glorious Revolution **255**
    Gulf War 283
    and industrial revolution 258
    Napoleonic Wars 263
    Norman conquest 243
    Reformation **254**
    rise of **254–255**
    Roman invasion of 233
    the Stuarts and the Civil War **254–255**
    Viking colonization/kingdoms 243

war with France *see* Hundred Years War
    World War I 268–269
    World War II 273, **274–275**
    see also Commonwealth of Nations
  divorce in 158
  drama, modern **375**
  education in 163
  foundation of universities 248
  government **167**
    human rights legislation 182
    political parties 169
    regulatory bodies 173
    parliamentary monarchy 254, **255**
  law system 164, 165
  literature
    Romantic movement **367**
    social and regional novels **370**
    19th-century novels **369**
    poetry, modern **373**
    towards the modern novel **370–371**
  local government 167
  marriage customs 159
  music **339**, 345
  nuclear programme 188–189
  spread of English language 353, *352*
  Neolithic sites 227
  nuclear energy 188–189
  railway 218
  UN membership 178
  women's suffrage 183
  see also Northern Ireland; Scotland
United Nations (UN) **178–179**
  and Gulf War 283
  and Palestine 282
  and Suez Crisis 282
  Korean War 277, 280
  peacekeeping role 179, *180*, 281
  Resolution 242 282
  Secretary General 178, 179
United Nations High Commissioner for Refugees 178
United States of America **420–422**
  cinema 328–329
  constitution 169
  dance 347
  divorce in 158
  drama, modern **375**, *375*
  education in 162, 163
  government 166, *166*, 167, 173
  history
    aid to postwar Europe 280
    American Revolution **260**
    and Arab-Israeli wars 282
    and Gulf War 283
    and Korea 280
    and Suez Crisis 279, 282
    Articles of Confederation 261
    birth of **260–261**
    Civil War **261**, *260*
    Cold War **280–281**
    colonial empire 261, *266*, 267
    industrialization 258, 259
    Reconstruction **261**
    relations with China 277, 281
    slavery issue 237, *261*
    war in Vietnam **281**, *281*
    World War I 269
    World War II **274–275**
  Gothic Revival in 327
  human rights legislation 182
  importance of railways 259
  law system 164, 165
  literature
    modern novels 370, **376–377**
    Naturalism in 369
    19th-century **371**
    poetry, modern **373**
  mining methods 196
  music **339**, 344–345
  nuclear weapons 181
  oil industry 194
  Organization of American States 180
  railway 218
  social divisions 161
  space programme 12–13
  Strategic Defense Initiative 13, 181
  UN membership 178
  women's suffrage 183
Universal Declaration of Human Rights 182
universal set **56–57**
Universal Time 3

universe, the **2–3**
  entropy of 19
  predicting the future of 15
  velocity of expansion 23
universities 163
  first to admit women 183
  medicine taught at 156
  medieval and Renaissance **248**
unnilennium 36, *37*
unnilhexium *37*
unniloctium *37*
unnilpentium *37*
unnilquadium *37*
unnilseptium *37*
'untouchables' 160
Upper Palaeolithic Age **227**
upwarped mountains **68**, *69*
Ur, Third Dynasty of 228
Ural Mountains, formation of 68, 69
uranium 36, *37*
  abundance and uses 197
  enrichment of 188
uranium-235 (U-235) 188
uranium-238 31
Uranus (planet) 7, **9**
Urban II, Pope 244
urea 139
Uruguay **422**
USS *Nautilus* (submarine) 217
Utamaro, Kitagawa **309**
uterus 134, *134*, 135, 137
utilitarians 302
Uzbekistan 180, **422**

V
V-1 rockets 225
V-2 rockets 12, 193
vaccines, immune system and 142
Vail, Alfred 208
Valéry, Paul **373**
valleys
  glacial 71
  rift 63
Valois, Ninette de **347**
valves
  car engine 220
  heart 140
  veins 141
vampire bat 112
Van Allen Zones 7
van der Waals forces 39
Van Dyck, Antony **315**
vanadium *37*
Vanburgh, Sir John **326**
Vandals 240
vanishing points 312
Vanuatu **422**
vapour-compression cycle 193
Vaquita *121*
Varèse, Edgard **339**
variable stars **4**
varicella **155**
Vasarély, Victor **325**
vasectomy 135
VAT (value-added tax) 175
Vatican City **422**
vector quantity 14
vectors 154
Veda religion 286
Vedas 288
Vega, Lope de **360**
vegetation
  and ecosystem productivity 126
  climate and **81**
  desert 72, 73
  erosion by 69
  precipitation and 81
  world chart *81*
  see also biomass
veins 141
Velasquez, Diego **315**, 323
veld 129
velocity 14, *15*
  of stars 23
vena cava 141
Venezuela **422–423**
Venice
  and the Crusades 241, 244
  Austrian control 263
  early music 332
  painting 314
venom/poison
  coelenterates 94
  fishes 100

myriapods 96
snakes **105**
ventricle 140
Venus (planet) 4, 7, **8**, *9*
Venus flytrap 93
Verdi, Giuseppe **343**
Verdun, battle of 268–269
Verga, Giovanni **369**
Verlaine, Paul *372*, *372*
Vermeer, Jan **316**, *316*
Verner, Karl 348
Veronese **314**
vertebrates, first 83
Vesalius, Andreas **156**, *156*
Vesuvius (volcano), Italy 65, 68
VHS waves 206
vibraphone 341
vibration
  animal communication by 124
  ear and 144, 145
Vicksburg, fall of 261
Victor Emmanuel III, King 272
Victoria, Luis de **332**
Victrex PEEK 47
vicuña 117, 200
video **207**
Vidor, King **329**
Vienna, sieges of 242
Vienna Secession 321
Viet Cong 281
Viet Minh 281
Vietnam **423**
  independence 281
  part of Chinese empire 234
Vietnam War 277, **281**, *281*
viewdata 209
Vigny, Alfred de **367**
Vikings **243**
  East Franks and 240
  influence on English language 352
  religions 287
  ships 217
villeins 246
vinegar 201
Vinland 243
vinyl chloride 201
violins 340
Viollet-le-Duc, Eugène-Emmanuel **326**
viols/violas 340
Virgil **357**, 360, 363
virginal 332
Virginia 260
Virginia opossum 110
viruses **82**
  diseases from **154–155**
  immune system and 142
Visconti, Luchino **329**
viscosity **17**, 18
Visigoths 240
  sack of Rome 233
vision **144**
  birds 107
  optical illusions **148**, *148*
  perception 149
  recording 206–207
  robotics and 213
Visual Basic 212
visual impairment **144**
vitamins **138**, **139**
  and regulation of internal environment
    143
  discovery of 157
Vitruvius 306, **326**
Vivaldi, Antonio **333**
viverrids 114
VKK (reusable spacecraft) 13
Vlaminck, Maurice de 321, **322**
vocabulary, English 353
volcanic lakes 75
volcanoes/volcanism **64–65**
  and island formation 77
  emissions 43
  hot-spot activity 77
  mountain formation by **68**, *69*
  plate tectonics and 63
  Thera eruption 230
Volta, Count Allesandro 26, **49**
Voltaire **365**
volts 26
voluntary muscle **137**, *136*
Vorticists **323**
Vostok I 12
vote/voting 167, 183, 261

Voyager 2 8, 9
Vuillard, Edouard **320**
vulcanization 199

W
Wace **358**
wadis 73
Wagner, Richard 331, **336–337**, 338, **343**,
  345, 358
Wajda, Andrzej **329**
Waldheim, Kurt 178
Waldsterben (tree death) 186
Wales 254 *see also* United Kingdom
wallabies 110
Wallace, Alfred Russel 84
Walpole, Horace **367**
Walpole, Sir Robert 255
walrus **120**
'War Communism' 271
War of 1812 261
War of the Austrian Succession 257
'war of the comedians'
  (Guerre des Bouffons) 342
War of the Spanish Succession 253, 256
warfare **224–225**
  ancient Greek 230
  medieval and Renaissance **248**, *248*
Warhol, Andy **325**
warning coloration 125
'Warring States' 234
Wars of the Roses 254
wars
  ancient Greek 230
  ancient Roman 232
  Anglo-Dutch 257
  Anglo-Indian 266
  Chinese 235
  colonial 257, 267, 279
    North American 257, 260
  Euro-Chinese 267
  human rights during 182
  Middle Eastern 282–283
  Napoleonic **263**
  nationalist 265
  Revolutionary **263**, 270–271
  Russo-Japanese 235, 267, 270
  Sino-Japanese 235, 273, **276**
  world wars 268–269, 274–275
  see also civil wars; revolts/rebellions/
    revolutions; specific wars
Warsaw Pact 180, 280
warships **216–217**
  anti-ship missile *225*
wart hogs 116
Washington, George 260–261
wasps 98, **99**, 125
waste, contamination from toxic 186, 187
water
  and desert landscapes 73
  boiling/melting point 39, 42
  chemistry of 34, 39, **42**, *42*
  early medical beliefs 156
  effect on climate 80–81
  electrolyte solutions 40
  energy from *see* hydroelectric power
  erosion by **69**
  formation of 41
  in nuclear reactors 189
  in the body 138, 141, 143
  insects and 98
  percentage in oceans 76
  in plants **88**, *89*, 90
  pollution damage of 186
  production of 40
  properties and functions 130
  purification 126
  reaction with potassium 40, 41
  to ice or water vapour 19, 35
  waves 20, *20*
  see also clouds; ecosystems, aquatic;
    hydrological cycle
water boatmen 99
water buffalo 117, **133**
water ferns 90
water frame 200, 258
water mills 246
water pollution **186–187**
water power, energy from **190–191**
watersheds 75
water vapour 42
  and solar radiation 126
Watson, James **49**, 86
Watt, James 28, 192, 258

Watteau, Antoine **317**
watts 28
Waugh, Evelyn **377**
wave theory **20–21**
wave-particle duality 32
wavelength 20, *21*
  factors affecting 77
  use in radar 210
waves **20**
  electromagnetic **27**
  water **77**, *76*, 91
weapons/weaponry **224–225**
  advance warning systems 210
  animals 124
  anti-tank 225
  atomic *see* nuclear weapons
  in satellites 13
  influence mines 216
  in Japan 235
  nuclear 275, **181**
  prehistoric 226, 227
  US–USSR agreements on limitation 281
  warships 216–217, *225*
  World War I 268, 269
  see also tanks; specific types
weasels **115**
weather **78–79**
  and atmospheric pressure 17
  effect of global warming 187
  see also climate
weather forecasting
  chaos theory and 51
  radar and 210
  satellites for 13
weaving 200
Weber, Carl Maria von **343**
Weber, Max 160, 161, 167
Webern, Anton **338**
Webster, John **361**
Wedgwood, Josiah 259
Weelkes, Thomas **332**
Wegener, Alfred 62
weight 15
Weill, Kurt **374**
Weimar Republic, collapse of 272
Weine, Robert **328**
Weir, Peter **329**
Welles, Orson **329**
Wellington, Duke of 263
Wells, Horace **157**
Welwitschia 91
Wenders, Wim **329**
Wesker, Arnold **375**
Wessex 243
West Indies 257, 279
westerlies (winds) 77
western films 328
Western Front 268
Western Sahara *see* Morocco
Western Samoa **423**
wet-plate process (photography) 204
Weyden, Rogier van der **313**
whale shark 101
whales **120–121**
  echolocation 210
  hearing 23
wheat **132**
Wheatstone, Sir Charles 208
wheel, invention of 228
whipstock 194
whisk ferns 90
Whistler, James McNeill **320**
White, Patrick **377**
white dwarf (star) 5, *5*
'White man's burden' 279
white whales 120, 121
Whitehead, Alfred North **305**
Whitman, Walt **371**, *371*
Whittle, Frank 193
Who, The **345**
whole numbers 54
whooping cough **155**
Wilbye, John **332**
wild ass 116
wild boar 116
Wilde, Oscar 363, **375**
Wilder, Billy **329**
Wilhelm I, Kaiser 265
Wilkenson, Ellen *171*
Wilkins, Maurice 49
William, Duke ('the conquerer') 243
William, King 255
William of Ockham 48

Williams, Ralph Vaughan **339**
Williams, Tennessee **375**
Wilson, Woodrow 269
wind
    and ocean currents 77
    and waves 77
    direction 78, 79
    energy from **190–191**
    erosion by (mountains) **69**
    sand dune formation 73
    see also monsoons
windmills 190–191, 246
wings 98, 106
Wittgenstein, Ludwig 303, **305**
Witz, Konrad **313**
wolf 115
Wolfe, General James 257
Wollstonecraft, Mary 183
Wolsey, Cardinal Thomas 254
wombat 110
women
    and Islam **301**
    hormones and pregnancy 143
    in the labour force 171
    menopause 135
    reproduction *134*, **143**
    social discrimination against 161
women's movement **183**
Women's Social and Political Union 183
wood/timber (as building material) 214, 215
wool 132, 200
    textile production 258
Woolf, Virginia **376**
word processing 212
Wordsworth, William 366, **367**

workers (labour force) 171, 173
working class 161
    education for 162
    in literature 369
    Russian (Soviet) 270, 271
    women 183
    see also labour
World Bank 178
World Health Organization 178
World War I **268–269**
    causes 265
    influence on poetry 373
World War II **274–275**, *275*
    aircraft development 223
    end of 181
    events leading up to **273**
    nationalist feelings after **278–279**
    nuclear weapons and 181
worms **95**, 154, 155
Wren, Sir Christopher **326**
Wright, Frank Lloyd **326**
writing **350–351**
    ancient Chinese 234, 235
    Cretan Linear A 230, 350
    earliest 228, **350**
    early materials 202
    Greek Linear B 230, 287, 350, 356, 287
Wycherley, William **363**
Wyclif, John 245
Wyler, William **329**

X
x-particles 27
X-30 project 13
X-rays **27**, **210**
    detecting black holes 5

photography 205
    use in medicine 157
Xenakis, Iannis **339**
xenon *37*
Xerxes, King 229, 231
xylem 90
xylophone 341

Y
yak 117
Yalta Conference 280
Yangtze River (Chang Jiang) 234, 235
yardangs 73
yarn *see* textiles
year 3
yeasts 91
Yeats, W.B. **373**, **375**
Yellow River (Hwang He) 234, 235
Yemen **423**
yoga 290
Yom Kippur War 282–283
Yorimoto Minamoto 235
York, House of 254
Yorktown, siege of 261
Yoruba language 348
Young, Lester **345**
Young, Thomas 21
Young Italy movement 264
'Young Pretender' 255
Ypres, battle of 269
ytterbium *37*
yttrium *37*
Yuan dynasty 235
Yucatán temple-cities 239, *238*
Yugoslavia 179, **423–424**
    creation of 269
    German invasion of 274

Z
Zaidis 301
Zaïre **424**
Zambia **424**
Zarathustra 286
zebras 116
Zen Buddhism 291, 292
Zeno of Citium **304**
Zeno of Elea **304**
Zeppelins 269
zero net force 16
Zeuxis 306
Zheng He **247**
Zhou dynasty 234
    art 308
Zhuang Zi 292
Zhukov, Marshal Georgi 275
Zimbabwe **424**
    kingdom of 237
Zimmermann, Bern-Alois 343
zinc *37*, 138
    abundance and uses 197
    corrosive properties 45
Zinneman, Fred **329**
Zionists 282
zirconium *37*
Zizka, John 245
Zola, Émile **369**
Zollverein 265
Zoroastrianism **286–287**, 289
Zulu 267
Zwingli, Ulrich 251
Zworykin, Vladimir 206
zygote 87, 134
    plants 91

We are grateful to the following for permission to reproduce the paintings listed.

page 322: 'Harmony in Red' (1908-1909), © Succession H. Matisse/DACS 1993.

page 323: 'Man with a Pipe' (1916) by Pablo Picasso, © DACS 1993.

page 324 (bottom right): 'The Melody Haunts My Reverie' (1965), © Roy Lichtenstein/DACS 1993.

page 325: 'Enchanted Wood' (1947) by Jackson Pollock, © 1993 Pollock-Krasner Foundations/ARS N.Y.